Professional Microsoft SQL Server Analysis Services 20

Continues

Professional

Microsoft® SQL Server®
Analysis Services 2008 with MDX

Professional
Microsoft® SQL Server®
Analysis Services 2008 with MDX

Sivakumar Harinath
Matt Carroll
Sethu Meenakshisundaram
Robert Zare
Denny Guang-Yeu Lee

WILEY

Wiley Publishing, Inc.

Professional Microsoft® SQL Server® Analysis Services 2008 with MDX

Published by
Wiley Publishing, Inc.
10475 Crosspoint Boulevard
Indianapolis, IN 46256
www.wiley.com

I dedicate this book in the grandest possible manner to my dear wife, Shreepriya,
who has been fully supportive and patient with me for all the late nights I worked on this book.
It is also dedicated to my twins, Praveen and Divya, who have seen me work long hours on this book.
I dedicate this book in memory of my father, Harinath Govindarajalu, who passed away in 1999 and
who I am sure would have been proud of this great achievement, and to my mother, Sundar Bai,
and my sister, Geetha Harinath. Finally, I dedicate this book in memory of my uncle, Jayakrishnan Govindarajalu,
who passed away in 2007 and who was very proud of me co-authoring the first edition of this book,
and was eagerly looking forward to seeing this book.

—Siva Harinath

Thanks to my wife, Wendy, for her love and patience. Love and hope to Lawrence,
Loralei, and Joshua.

—Matt Carroll

To my Parents, Uncle & Aunt, Guru(s), and the Lord Almighty for molding
me into who I am today.

—Sethu Meenakshisundaram

To the patience and love from Isabella and Hua-Ping.

—Denny Lee

About the Authors

Sivakumar Harinath was born in Chennai, India. Siva has a Ph.D. in Computer Science from the University of Illinois at Chicago. His thesis title was "Data Management Support for Distributed Data Mining of Large Datasets over High Speed Wide Area Networks." Siva has worked for Newgen Software Technologies (P) Ltd., IBM Toronto Labs, Canada; National Center for Data Mining, University of Illinois at Chicago; and has been at Microsoft since February of 2002. Siva started as a Software Design Engineer in Test (SDET) in the Analysis Services Performance Team and currently is a Senior Test Lead in the Analysis Services team. Siva's other interests include high-performance computing, distributed systems, and high-speed networking. Siva is married to Shreepriya and has twins, Praveen and Divya. His personal interests include travel, games, and sports (in particular carrom, chess, racquet ball, and board games). You can reach Siva at Sivakumar.harinath@microsoft.com.

Matt Carroll is currently a Senior Development Lead on the SQL Server Integration Services team at Microsoft. Prior to this, he spent 10 years working on the SQL Server Analysis Services team as a developer and then development lead. He's presented on Analysis Services at VSLive and compiled and edited the whitepaper "OLAP Design Best Practices for Analysis Services 2005."

Sethu Meenakshisundaram has more than 20 years of Enterprise System Software Development experience. Sethu spent a good portion of his career at Sybase Inc. in architecture, development, and management building world class OLTP and OLAP Database Systems. Sethu was instrumental in developing and leading highly complex clustered systems of Adaptive Server Enterprise. Early in the '90s, Sethu developed a version of Sybase Adaptive Server running on the Windows platform. Most recently he was an Architect in the SQL Server BI team driving technology and partner strategy. Prior to Microsoft, Sethu managed all of Server development as Senior Director at Sybase including building teams in the U.S., India, and China. He is currently a Vice President in charge of Technology Strategy at SAP Labs, USA.

Rob Zare is a program manager on the SQL Server development team. He's worked on the product since shortly before the first service pack of SQL Server 2000. During that time, he's focused primarily on Analysis Services, though for the next major release of SQL Server he'll be focused on Integration Services. He is the co-author of *Fast Track to MDX* and regularly speaks at major technical conferences around the world.

Denny Lee is a Senior Program Manager based out of Redmond, WA in the SQLCAT Best Practices Team. He has more than 12 years experience as a developer and consultant implementing software solutions to complex OLTP and data warehousing problems. His industry experience includes accounting, human resources, automotive, retail, web analytics, telecommunications, and healthcare. He had helped create the first OLAP Services reporting application in production at Microsoft and is a co-author of "SQL Server 2000 Data Warehousing with Analysis Services" and "Transforming Healthcare through Information [Ed. Joan Ash] (2008)". In addition to contributing to the SQLCAT Blog, SQL Server Best Practices, and SQLCAT.com, you can also review Denny's Space (http://denster.spaces.live.com). Denny specializes in developing solutions for Enterprise Data Warehousing, Analysis Services, and Data Mining; he also has focuses in the areas of Privacy and Healthcare.

Credits

Contributors
Akshai Mirchandani
Wayne Robertson
Leah Etienne
Grant Paisley

Executive Editor
Robert Elliott

Development Editor
Kelly Talbot

Technical Editor
Ron Pihlgren
Prashant Dhingra

Production Editor
Daniel Scribner

Copy Editor
Kim Cofer

Editorial Manager
Mary Beth Wakefield

Production Manager
Tim Tate

Vice President and Executive Group Publisher
Richard Swadley

Vice President and Executive Publisher
Barry Pruett

Associate Publisher
Jim Minatel

Project Coordinator, Cover
Lynsey Stanford

Proofreader
Nancy Carrasco

Indexer
Ron Strauss

Acknowledgments

Wow!!! It has been an amazing 15 months from when we decided to partner in writing this book. The first edition of this book started when Siva jokingly mentioned to his wife the idea of writing a book on SQL Server Analysis Services 2005. She took it seriously and motivated him to start working on the idea in October 2003. Because the first edition was well received, Siva identified co-authors for the new edition. All the co-authors of this book were part of the SQL Server team when they started writing this book. As always, there are so many people who deserve mentioning that we are afraid we will miss someone. If you are among those missed, please accept our humblest apologies. We first need to thank the managers of each co-author and Kamal Hathi, Product Unit Manager of the Analysis Services team for permission to moonlight. Siva specifically thanks his manager Lon Fisher for his constant encouragement and support to help Analysis Services customers. We thank our editors, Bob Elliott and Kelly Talbot, who supported us right from the beginning but also prodded us along, which was necessary to make sure the book was published on time.

We would like to thank our technical reviewers, Ron Pihlgren and Prashant Dhingra, who graciously offered us their assistance and significantly helped in improving the content and samples in the book. We thank Akshai Mirchandani, Wayne Robertson, Leah Etienne, and Grant Paisley for their contributions in the book for Chapters 5, 6, 14, 17, and 18. We thank all our colleagues in the Analysis Services product team (including Developers, Program Managers, and Testers) who helped us in accomplishing the immense feat of writing the book on a development product. To the Analysis Services team, special thanks go to Akshai Mirchandani, T. K. Anand, Cristian Petculescu, Bogdan Crivat, Dana Cristofor, Marius Dumitru, Andrew Garbuzov, Bo Simmons, and Richard Tkachuk from the SQL Server Customer Advisory team for patiently answering our questions or providing feedback to enhance the content of the book.

Most importantly, we owe our deepest thanks to our wonderful families. Without their support and sacrifice, this book would have become one of those many projects that begins and never finishes. Our families were the ones who truly took the brunt of it and sacrificed shared leisure time, all in support of our literary pursuit. We especially want to thank them for their patience with us, and the grace it took to not kill us during some of the longer work binges.

Contents

Contents

Contents

Contents

Contents

Part III: Advanced Administration and Performance Optimization

Chapter 13: Programmatic and Advanced Administration   441

Chapter 14: Designing for Performance   457

Contents

Part IV: Integration with Microsoft Products

Contents

Part V: Scenarios

Contents

Contents

Introduction

Analysis Services 2005 was a significant leap from Analysis Services 2000 in building your multidimensional databases right from the concept of building your cubes in Business Intelligence Development Studio to the concept of the Unified Dimensional Model with attribute and user hierarchies. The first edition of this book, *Professional SQL Server Analysis Services 2005 with MDX*, was aimed at novice to advanced users and was very well received by the readers. Analysis Services 2005 is a large and complex product that needed a lot of fine-tuning to get the best performance.

Analysis Services 2008 added enhancements to the Analysis Services 2005 tools that make it easy to use and build your databases right for efficient performance to significant enhancements on the server to provide improved performance. Hence, we decided to write this book to provide insight into the enhancements in Analysis Services 2008 and help you understand how to utilize them effectively for your business needs. If you have read the first edition of the book, you will find several chapters' titles to be the same. Because Analysis Services 2008 is an incremental release, we have made enhancements to each chapter appropriately. We have enhanced the performance chapters and added a few additional scenarios that we believe will help you to understand and build multidimensional databases efficiently. This book still is targeted at novice to advanced users. If you are not familiar with SQL Server Analysis Services 2005, we highly recommend you go through the chapters in sequence to understand and use Analysis Services 2008 effectively to build, process, and deploy top-of-the-line business intelligence applications.

We are not shy about admitting to the apparent complexity of the product when faced with the user interface, which happens to be embedded in the Microsoft Visual Studio shell. This is great for you, especially if you are already familiar with the Visual Studio development environment. With this book, we want to show that not only will you overcome any possible initial shock regarding the user interface, but you will come to see it as your friend. It turns out there are many wizards to accomplish common tasks, or you can design the analytic infrastructure from the ground up — it is up to you.

This formidable yet user-friendly interface will empower you to implement business analytics of a caliber formerly reserved for academicians writing up government grant proposals or Ph.D. dissertations. More importantly, this power to turn data into information, and we mean real, usable, business-related decision-making information, can impact the bottom line of your company in terms of dollars earned and dollars saved. And that is what data warehousing, ultimately, is all about. Put another way, the purpose of all this data warehousing is simple; it is about generating actionable information from the data stores created by a company's sales, inventory, and other data sources. In sum, it is all about decision support.

Who This Book Is For

What was the impetus for you to pick up this book? Perhaps you are passionate about extracting information from reams of raw data; or perhaps you have some very specific challenges on the job right now that you think might be amenable to a business analysis–based solution; or perhaps you have used Analysis Services 2005 and want to learn about Analysis Services 2008. Then, there is always the lure of fame and fortune. Please be aware that attaining expert status in data warehousing can lead to lucrative consulting and salaried opportunities. However, it won't likely make you as rich as becoming a purveyor of nothing-down real estate courses. If your desire is to leave the infomercial career path to others and get really serious about data warehousing in general and business intelligence in particular, you have just the book in your hands to start or continue on your path to subject mastery.

The obvious question now is what are the prerequisites for reading and understanding the content of this book? You certainly do not have to already know the intricacies of data warehousing, you will learn that here as you go. If you have only the foggiest notion of what a relational database is; well, this book is going to challenge you at best and bury you at worst. If you are not intimidated by what you just read, this book is for you. If you have worked on data warehouses using non-Microsoft products and want to learn how Microsoft can do it better, this book is for you. If you are a database administrator, MIS Professional, or application developer interested in exploiting the power of business intelligence, this book is definitely for you!

What This Book Covers

Analysis Services 2008 is the premier multidimensional database product from Microsoft. This is the most recent of four releases from Microsoft to date. In this release, the tools and server provided have been designed for use as an enterprise-class Business Intelligence Server and we think Microsoft has been successful. Analysis Services 2008 extends on top of Analysis Services 2005 and provides you with powerful tools to design, build, test, and deploy your multidimensional databases. By integrating the tools within Visual Studio you really get the feel of building a Business Intelligence (BI) project. Similar to any application you build within VS, you build your BI projects and deploy them to an Analysis Services instance. Due to the product design that is integrated with the Visual Studio shell and enhanced features you definitely have to know how to create cubes, dimensions, and many other objects, maintain them, and support your BI users. Similar to its well-liked predecessors, Analysis Services 2008 supports the MDX language, by which you can query data. MDX is for querying multidimensional databases much like SQL is for querying relational databases. The MDX language is a component of the OLE DB for OLAP specification and is supported by other BI vendors. Microsoft's Analysis Services 2008 provides certain extensions to the MDX supported by Analysis Services 2005 that help you to achieve best performance from your multidimensional databases.

This book walks you through the entire product and the important features of the product with the help of step-by-step instructions on building multidimensional databases. Within each chapter you will not only learn how to use the features, but also learn more about the features at a user level and what happens behind the scenes to make things work. We believe this will provide you with additional insight into how features really work and hence provide insight into how they are best exploited. It will also enhance your ability to debug problems that you might not have been able to otherwise. This behind-the-scenes view is often surfaced through exposure of XML for Analysis (XMLA), created by the product based on user interface settings. It works like this: Analysis Services 2008 uses the XMLA specification to communicate between client and server, and the Analysis Services 2008 tools communicate to the server using XMLA. Once you have designed your multidimensional database using the tools, you need to send the definition to the server. At that time the tools use XMLA to send the definitions. You will learn these definitions so that you have the ability to design a custom application that interacts with an Analysis Services instance.

MDX is the language used for data retrieval from Analysis Services. You will get an introduction to the MDX language with basic concepts and the various MDX functions in this book. When you are browsing data using Analysis Services tools, those tools send appropriate MDX to the instance of Analysis Services that contains the target data. By learning the MDX sent to the server for the various desired operations, you will begin to understand the intricacies of MDX and thereby improve your own MDX coding skills by extension. Finally, you will learn to optimize your MDX queries to get the best performance from your Analysis Services.

One of the key value-adds found in this book, which we think is worth the price of admission by itself, is that through the chapters you will begin to understand what design trade-offs are involved in BI application development. Further, the book will help you to do better BI design for your company in the face of those trade-off decisions — especially with the help of a few scenarios — and there are many scenarios discussed in this book. The scenarios are geared toward some of the common business problems that are currently faced by existing Analysis Services customers. Although there is no pretension that this book will teach you business per se, it is a book on BI and we did take the liberty of explaining certain business concepts that you are sure to run into eventually. For example, the often misunderstood concept of depreciation is explained in some detail. Again, this aspect of the book is shallow, but we hope what pure business concepts are covered will provide you with a more informed basis from which to work. If you know the concepts already, well, why not read about the ideas again? There might be some new information in there for you.

Finally, this book covers integration of Analysis Services with other SQL Server 2008 components: Data Mining, Integrations Services and Reporting Services, as well as Microsoft Office products. These chapters will help you go beyond just a passing level of understanding of Analysis Services 2008; it is really integration of these disparate components that ship in the box with SQL Server that allow you to build start to finish BI solutions that are scalable, maintainable, have good performance characteristics, and highlight the right information. Do not skip the chapters that do not at first seem crucial to understanding Analysis Services 2008 itself; it is the whole picture that brings the real value. Get that whole picture for stellar success and return on your investment of time and energy.

How This Book Is Structured

The authors of books in the Wrox Professional series attempt to make each chapter as stand-alone as possible. This book is no exception. However, owing to the sophistication of the subject matter and the manner in which certain concepts are necessarily tied to others has somewhat undermined this most noble intention. In fact, unless you are a seasoned data warehousing professional, or otherwise have experience with earlier versions of Analysis Services, it is advised you take a serial approach to reading chapters. Work through the first seven chapters in order because they will collectively provide you with some architectural context, a good first look at the product, as well as how to effectively design your cubes, an introduction to MDX, and an introduction to managing your Analysis Services server. Just to remind you, in the simplest terms, MDX is to Analysis Services what SQL is to SQL Server. Ok, that was just too simple an analogy; but let's not get ahead of ourselves! As for the actual layout of the book, we have divided the book into roughly four major sections.

In Part I we introduce the basic concepts and then get you kick-started using Analysis Services with most of the common operations that you need to design your databases. You will become familiarized with the product if you aren't already, and hopefully it will provide you some sense of achievement, which will certainly help motivate you to go beyond the simple stuff and move to the advanced.

Part II contains chapters that prepare you for the more advanced topics concerning the creation of multidimensional databases such as multiple measure groups, Business Intelligence wizards, Key Performance Indicators, and Actions. You will learn about the calculation model in Analysis Services 2008 and enhance your dimensions and cube designs using Business Intelligence Development Studio. Further, you will learn more about extending MDX via external functions, as well as how to effectively do data writeback in your cube.

In Part III of the book, you will learn how to administer your Analysis Services programmatically as well as designing and optimizing your cube for best performance.

In Part IV, we cover the integration of Analysis Services with other SQL Server 2008 components and Microsoft Office products that help you build solutions and provide the best support possible to your administrators and BI users. This is also the section where you will discover Data Mining and how Data Mining along with Microsoft Office 2007 makes it easy to use and effective to perform analysis on data.

Finally in Part V, we provide various scenarios from securing your data, to budgeting, to analyzing Web traffic analysis. These scenarios will help you to understand and model similar business requirements.

Together, these five sections, that is to say, this book, will provide you a full-blown BI learning experience. Because BI and BI applications constitute such an incredibly complex and massive field of endeavor, no one book can possibly cover it all. In terms of BI though the eyes of SQL Server Analysis Services 2008, we hope this book has got it covered!

We also encourage you to download and take a look at Appendix A; it is the complete MDX Reference. We thank Microsoft for providing the content for Appendix A. In the first edition of the book, Appendix A was included along with the book. Due to the Analysis Services 2008 features we have covered in this book and the additional scenarios, we have made Appendix A available for download so that the book doesn't become too large. You can find it on this book's page on www.wrox.com.

What You Need to Use This Book

You need a computer running some version of the Windows operating system, like Windows Vista Professional, for example, and a copy of SQL Server 2008 installed on that system. In addition you also need the SQL Server 2008 Business Intelligence samples that can be downloaded from www.codeplex.com. Please see the appropriate documentation from Microsoft for the hardware requirements needed to support the particular version of Windows you own.

Conventions

To help you get the most from the text and keep track of what's happening, we've used a number of conventions throughout the book.

> **Boxes like this one hold important, not-to-be forgotten information that is directly relevant to the surrounding text.**

Tips, hints, tricks, and asides to the current discussion are offset and placed in italics like this.

As for styles in the text:

- ❏ We *highlight* new terms and important words when we introduce them.
- ❏ We show keyboard strokes like this: Ctrl+A.
- ❏ We show URLs and code within the text like so: persistence.properties.
- ❏ We present code in two different ways:

```
In code examples we highlight new and important code with a gray background.
```

```
The gray highlighting is not used for code that's less important in the present
context, or has been shown before.
```

Source Code

As you work through the examples in this book, you may choose either to type in all the code manually or to use the source code files that accompany the book. All of the source code used in this book is available for download at www.wrox.com. Once at the site, simply locate the book's title (either by using the Search box or by using one of the title lists) and click the Download Code link on the book's detail page to obtain all the source code for the book.

You'll also want to have the databases from the SQL2008.AdventureWorks_OLTP_DB_v2008.zip and SQL2008. AdventureWorks_DW_BI_v2008.zip files installed. These databases are not installed with SQL Server 2008 by default. The AdventureWorks DW files (along with the other SQL Server database files) can be downloaded from `www.wrox.com/go/SQLServer2008RTMDataSets`. Download and install the SQL Server 2008 Adventure Works DW 2008 sample database for your machine's architecture. For example, if you have an x64 machine, the sample database to install is: SQL2008.AdventureWorks_DW_ BI_v2008.x64.msi.

> *Because many books have similar titles, you may find it easiest to search by ISBN; for this book the ISBN is 978-0-470-24798-3.*

Once you download the code, just decompress it with your favorite compression tool. Alternatively, you can go to the main Wrox code download page at `www.wrox.com/dynamic/books/download .aspx` to see the code available for this book and all other Wrox books.

Errata

We make every effort to ensure that there are no errors in the text or in the code. However, no one is perfect, and mistakes do occur. If you find an error in one of our books, like a spelling mistake or faulty piece of code, we would be very grateful for your feedback. By sending in errata you may save another reader hours of frustration and at the same time you will be helping us provide even higher quality information.

To find the errata page for this book, go to `www.wrox.com` and locate the title using the Search box or one of the title lists. Then, on the book details page, click the Book Errata link. On this page you can view all errata that has been submitted for this book and posted by Wrox editors. A complete book list including links to each book's errata is also available at `www.wrox.com/misc-pages/booklist.shtml`.

If you don't spot "your" error on the Book Errata page, go to `www.wrox.com/contact/techsupport.shtml` and complete the form there to send us the error you have found. We'll check the information and, if appropriate, post a message to the book's errata page and fix the problem in subsequent editions of the book.

p2p.wrox.com

For author and peer discussion, join the P2P forums at `p2p.wrox.com`. The forums are a Web-based system for you to post messages relating to Wrox books and related technologies and interact with other readers and technology users. The forums offer a subscription feature to e-mail you topics of interest of your choosing when new posts are made to the forums. Wrox authors, editors, other industry experts, and your fellow readers are present on these forums.

At `http://p2p.wrox.com` you will find a number of different forums that will help you not only as you read this book, but also as you develop your own applications. To join the forums, just follow these steps:

1. Go to `p2p.wrox.com` and click the Register link.

2. Read the terms of use and click Agree.

3. Complete the required information to join as well as any optional information you wish to provide and click Submit.

4. You will receive an e-mail with information describing how to verify your account and complete the joining process.

You can read messages in the forums without joining P2P but in order to post your own messages, you must join.

Once you join, you can post new messages and respond to messages other users post. You can read messages at any time on the Web. If you would like to have new messages from a particular forum e-mailed to you, click the Subscribe to this Forum icon by the forum name in the forum listing.

For more information about how to use the Wrox P2P, be sure to read the P2P FAQs for answers to questions about how the forum software works as well as many common questions specific to P2P and Wrox books. To read the FAQs, click the FAQ link on any P2P page.

Part I

Introduction

1

Introduction to Data Warehousing and SQL Server 2008 Analysis Services

Business intelligence (BI) helps enterprises to gain insight from historical data and formulate strategic initiatives for the future. The historical data are stored as an electronic repository, which is called a data warehouse. A data warehouse is a system of records (a business intelligence gathering system) that takes data from a company's operational databases and other data sources and transforms it into a structure conducive to business analysis. Business calculations are often performed on the organized data to further its usefulness for making business decisions. Finally, the data is made available to the end user for querying, reporting, and analysis. A data warehouse system that is cleansed, is organized, and has optimized storage of historical records gives the business an intelligence gathering system to understand the business dynamics. Business analysis can be done in reactive mode or predictive mode. Reactive mode business analysis (also known as business analytics) is a function where information workers, business analysts, and other business users investigate the system of records and identify patterns and trends, and make business decisions to improve their business processes. Predictive mode analysis (also known as predictive analytics or data mining) is done using mathematical models to predict future trends on the system of records. The general approach to storing business data in a dimensional model and providing quick answers by slicing and dicing the business data is known as On Line Analytical Processing (OLAP). OLAP systems are architected in different ways. The most common types are MOLAP (Multidimensional OLAP), ROLAP (Relational OLAP), and HOLAP (Hybrid OLAP). SQL Server 2008 is a business intelligence platform that provides a scalable infrastructure with server (Analysis Services and Reporting Services) and tools (Integration Services and Reporting Services) to extract, transform, load, build, query, and report data warehouse solutions. Now that you have the big picture of data warehousing, take a look at what you learn in this chapter.

In this chapter you learn what data warehousing really is and how it relates to business intelligence. This information comes wrapped in a whole load of new concepts, and you get a look at the best known approaches to warehousing with the introduction of those concepts. We explain data warehousing in several different ways and we are sure you will understand it. You will finally see how SQL Server 2008 Analysis Services (SSAS 2008) puts it all together in terms of architecture — at both client and server levels.

A Closer Look at Data Warehousing

Data warehousing has existed since the beginning of computers and information systems. Initially, concepts of data warehousing were referred to as Decision Support Systems (DSS). In the book *Building the Data Warehouse*, Bill Inmon described the data warehouse as "a *subject oriented, integrated, non-volatile,* and *time variant* collection of data in support of management's decisions." According to Inmon, the subject orientation of a data warehouse differs from the operational orientation seen in *OnLine Transaction Processing* (OLTP) systems; so a subject seen in a data warehouse might relate to customers, whereas an operation in an OLTP system might relate to a specific application like sales processing and all that goes with it.

The word *integrated* means that throughout the enterprise, data points should be defined consistently or there should be some integration methodology to force consistency at the data warehouse level. One example would be how to represent the entity Microsoft. If Microsoft were represented in different databases as MSFT, MS, Microsoft, and MSoft, it would be difficult to meaningfully merge these in a data warehouse. The best-case solution is to have all databases in the enterprise refer to Microsoft as, say, MSFT, thereby making the merger of this data seamless. A less desirable, but equally workable, solution is to force all the variants into one during the process of moving data from the operational system to the data warehouse.

A data warehouse is referred to as non-volatile because it differs from operational systems, which are often transactional in nature and updated regularly. The data warehouse is generally loaded at some preset interval, which may be measured in weeks or even months. This is not to say it is never measured in days; but even if updates do occur daily, that is still a sparse schedule compared to the constant changes being made to transactional systems.

The final element in this definition regards time variance, which is a sophisticated way of saying how far back the stored data in the system reaches. In the case of operational systems, the time period is quite short, perhaps days, weeks, or months. In the case of the warehouse, it is quite long — typically on the order of years. This last item might strike you as fairly self-evident because you would have a hard time analyzing business trends if your data didn't date back further than two months. So, there you have it, the classic definition that no good book on data warehousing should be without.

OLAP systems are architected in different ways depending on how the data warehouse is built. A classic OLAP or MOLAP system's data warehouse is built using a multidimensional store that is optimized for performance and uses dimensional models. Alternatively, the data warehouse is built using the Relational Tables in the operational databases using a specialized schema design that is optimized for storage. Hybrid OLAP is an architecture that provides performance and optimized storage. There is more to come in this chapter on the differences between relational and multidimensional databases.

Data warehousing is the process by which data created in an operational database is transformed and stored and provides a context so as to facilitate the extraction of business-relevant information from the source data. An operational or transactional database, like a point-of-sale (POS) database, is transaction-based and typically normalized to reduce the amount of redundant data storage generated. The result makes for fast updates, but this speed of update capability is offset by a reduction in speed of information retrieval at query time. For speed of information retrieval, especially for the purpose of business analytics, a multidimensional database is called for. A multidimensional database is highly denormalized and therefore has rows of data that may be redundant. This makes for very fast query responses because relatively few joins are involved. And fast responses are what you want while doing business intelligence work. Figure 1-1 shows information extracted from transactional databases and consolidated into multidimensional databases, then stored in data marts or data warehouses. Data marts can be thought of as mini–data warehouses and quite often act as part of a larger warehouse. Data marts are subject-oriented data stores for well-manicured (cleaned) data. Examples include a sales data mart, an inventory data mart, or basically any subject rooted at the departmental level. A data warehouse, on the other hand, functions at the enterprise level and typically handles data across the entire organization. The data warehouse designer will be able to see a consolidated view of all the objects in a data warehouse in the form of an entity relationship diagram as shown in Figure 1-2. The appropriate level of access might be provided to the end users based on the levels of access they are able to see and query from the data warehouse. Even though your data warehouse might contain information about all the departments in your organization, the finance department might only be able to see the objects relevant to finance and any other related objects for which they have access.

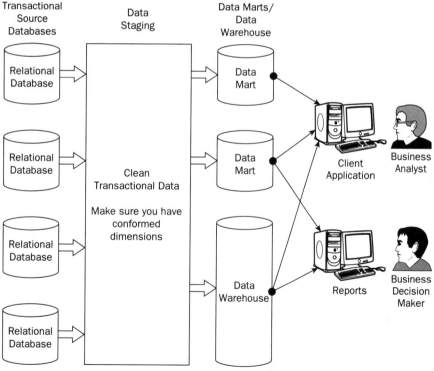

Figure 1-1

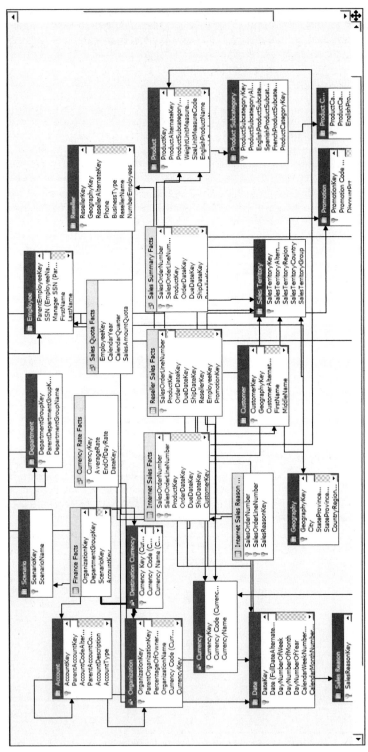

Figure 1-2

Key Elements of a Data Warehouse

Learning the elements of a data warehouse or data mart is, in part, about building a new vocabulary; the vocabulary associated with data warehousing can be less than intuitive, but once you get it, it all makes sense. The challenge, of course, is to understand it in the first place. Two kinds of tables form a data warehouse: fact tables and dimension tables.

Figure 1-3 shows a fact and a dimension table and the relationship between them. A fact table typically contains the business fact data such as sales amount, sales quantity, the number of customers, and the foreign keys to dimension tables. A *foreign key* is a field in a relational table that matches the primary key column of another table. Foreign keys provide a level of indirection between tables that enable you to cross-reference them. One important use of foreign keys is to maintain referential integrity (data integrity) within your database. Dimension tables contain detailed information relevant to specific attributes of the fact data, such as details of the product, customer attributes, store information, and so on. In Figure 1-3, the dimension table Product contains the information Product SKU and Product Name. The following sections go into more detail about fact and dimension tables.

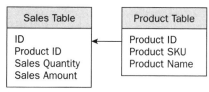

Figure 1-3

Fact Tables

With the end goal of extracting crucial business insights from your data, you will have to structure your data initially in such a way as to facilitate later numeric manipulation. Leaving the data embedded in some normalized database will never do! Your business data, often called detail data or fact data, goes in a de-normalized table called the fact table. Don't let the term "facts" throw you; it literally refers to the facts. In business, the facts are things such as number of products sold and amount received for products sold. Yet another way to describe this type of data is to call them *measures*. Calling the data measures versus detail data is not an important point. What is important is that this type of data is often numeric (though it could be of type string) and the values are quite often subject to aggregation (pre-calculating rollups of data over hierarchies, which subsequently yield improved query results). A fact table often contains columns like the ones shown in the following table:

Product ID	Date ID	State ID	Number of Cases	Sales Amount
1	07/01/2008	6	3244	$ 90,842
1	07/01/2008	33	6439	$184,000
1	07/01/2008	42	4784	$ 98,399
1	08/01/2008	31	6784	$176,384
1	08/01/2008	6	2097	$ 59,136
1	08/01/2008	33	7326	$ 8,635
1	08/01/2008	42	4925	$100,962

Product ID	Date ID	State ID	Number of Cases	Sales Amount
1	09/01/2008	31	8548	$176,384
1	09/01/2008	6	945	$ 26,649
1	09/01/2008	33	8635	$246,961
1	09/01/2008	42	4935	$101,165
1	10/01/2008	31	9284	$257,631
1	10/01/2008	33	9754	$278,965
1	10/01/2008	42	4987	$102,733
...	...	...	...	...

This table shows the sales of different varieties of beer between the months of July and October 2008 in four different states. The product ID, date ID, and state IDs together form the primary key of the fact table. The number of cases of beer sold and the sales amount are facts. The product ID, date ID, and state ID are foreign keys that join to the products, date, and state tables. In this table the state IDs 6, 31, 33, and 42 refer to the states MA, CA, OR, and WA, respectively, and represent the order in which these states joined the United States. Building the fact table is an important step toward building your data warehouse.

Dimension Tables

The fact table typically holds quantitative data; for example, transaction data that shows number of units sold per sale and amount charged to the customer for the unit sold. To provide reference to higher-level rollups based on things like time, a complementary table can be added that provides linkage to those higher levels through the magic of the join (how you link one table to another). In the case of time, the fact table might only show the date on which some number of cases of beer was sold; to do business analysis at the monthly, quarterly, or yearly level, a time dimension is required. The following table shows what a beer products dimension table would minimally contain. The product ID is the primary key in this table. The product ID of the fact table shown previously is a foreign key that joins to the product ID in the following table:

Product ID	Product SKU	Product Name
1	SBF767	SuperMicro Ale
2	SBH543	SuperMicro Lager
3	SBZ136	SuperMicro Pilsner
4	SBK345	SuperMicro Hefeweizen
...	...	...

For illustrative purposes, assume that you have a dimension table for time that contains monthly, quarterly, and yearly values. There must be a unique key for each value; these unique key values are called *primary keys*. Meanwhile, back in the fact table you have a column of keys with values mapping to the primary keys in the dimension table. These keys in the fact table are called *foreign keys*. For now it is enough if you get the idea that dimension tables connect to fact tables and this connectivity provides you with the ability to extend the usefulness of your low-level facts resident in the fact table.

A multidimensional database is created from fact and dimension tables to form objects called dimensions and cubes. Dimensions are objects that are created mostly from dimension tables. Some examples of dimensions are time, geography, and employee, which would typically contain additional information about those objects by which users can analyze the fact data. The cube is an object that contains fact data as well as dimensions so that data analysis can be performed by slicing or dicing dimensions. For example, you could view the sales information for the year 2005 in the state of Washington. Each of those slices of information is a dimension.

Dimensions

To make sense of a cube, which is at the heart of business analysis and discussed in the next section, you must first understand the nature of dimensions. We say that OLAP is based on multidimensional databases because it quite literally is. You do business analysis by observing the relationships between dimensions like Time, Sales, Products, Customers, Employees, Geography, and Accounts. Dimensions are most often made up of several hierarchies. Hierarchies are logical entities by which a business user might want to analyze fact data. Each hierarchy can have one or more levels. A hierarchy in the geography dimension, for example, might have the following levels: Country, State, County, and City.

A hierarchy like the one in the geography dimension would provide a completely balanced hierarchy for the United States. *Completely balanced hierarchy* means that all leaf (end) nodes for cities would be an equal distance from the top level. Some hierarchies in dimensions can have an unbalanced distribution of leaf nodes relative to the top level. Such hierarchies are called *unbalanced hierarchies*. An organization chart is an obvious example of an unbalanced hierarchy. There are different depths to the chain of supervisor to employee; that is, the leaf nodes are different distances from the top-level node. For example, a general manager might have unit managers and an administrative assistant. A unit manager might have additional direct reports such as a dev and a test manager, whereas the administrative assistant would not have any direct reports. Some hierarchies are typically balanced but are missing a unique characteristic of some members in a level. Such hierarchies are called *ragged hierarchies*. An example of a ragged hierarchy is a geography hierarchy that contains the levels Country, State, and City. Within the Country USA you have State Washington and City Seattle. If you were to add the Country Greece and City Athens to this hierarchy, you would add them to the Country and City levels. However, there are no states in the Country Greece and hence member Athens is directly related to the Country Greece. A hierarchy in which the members descend to members in the lowest level with different paths is referred to as a ragged hierarchy. Figure 1-4 shows an example of a Time dimension with the hierarchy Time. In this example, Year, Quarter, Month, and Date are the levels of the hierarchy. The values 2005 and 2006 are members of the Year level. When a particular level is expanded (indicated by a minus sign in the figure) you can see the members of the next level in the hierarchy chain.

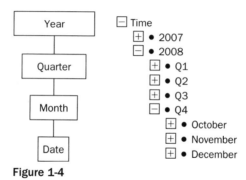

Figure 1-4

To sum up, a dimension is a hierarchical structure that has levels that may or may not be balanced. It has a subject matter of interest and is used as the basis for detailed business analysis.

Cubes

The *cube* is a multidimensional data structure from which you can query for business information. You build cubes out of your fact data and the dimensions. A cube can contain fact data from one or more fact tables and often contains a few dimensions. Any given cube usually has a dominant subject under analysis associated with it. For example, you might build a Sales cube with which you analyze sales by region, or a Call Processing cube with which you analyze length of call by problem category reported. These cubes are what you will be making available to your users for analysis.

Figure 1-5 shows a Beer Sales cube that was created from the fact table data shown previously. Consider the front face of the cube that shows numbers. This cube has three dimensions: Time, Product Line, and State where the product was sold. Each block of the cube is called a *cell* and is uniquely identified by a member in each dimension. For example, analyze the bottom-left corner cell that has the values 4,784 and $98,399. The values indicate the number of sales and the sales amount. This cell refers to the sales of Beer type Ale in the state of Washington (WA) for July 2008. This is represented as [WA, Ale, Jul '08]. Notice that some cells do not have any value; this is because no facts are available for those cells in the fact table.

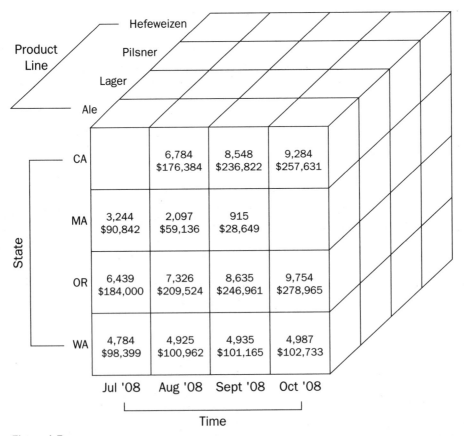

Figure 1-5

The whole point of making these cubes involves reducing the query response time for the information worker to extract knowledge from the data. To make that happen, cubes typically contain pre-calculated summary data called *aggregations*. Querying existing aggregated data is close to instantaneous compared to doing cold (no cache) queries with no pre-calculated summaries in place. This is really at the heart of business intelligence, the ability to query data with possibly gigabytes or terabytes of pre-summarized data behind it and yet get an instant response from the server. It is quite the thrill when you realize you have accomplished this feat!

You learned about how cubes provide the infrastructure for storing multidimensional data. Well, it doesn't just store multidimensional data from fact tables; it also stores something called *aggregations* of that data. A typical aggregation would be the summing of values up a hierarchy of a dimension. An example would be summing of sales figures up from stores level, to district level, to regional level; when querying for those numbers, you would get an instant response because the calculations would have already been done when the aggregations were formed. The fact data does not necessarily need to be aggregated as sum of the specific fact data. You can have other ways of aggregating the data such as counting the number of products sold. Again, this count would typically roll up through the hierarchy of a dimension.

The Star Schema

The entity relationship diagram representation of a relational database shows you a different animal altogether as compared to the OLAP (multidimensional) database. It is so different in fact, that there is a name for the types of schemas used to build OLAP databases: the star schema and the snowflake schema. The latter is largely a variation on the first. The main point of difference is the complexity of the schema; the OLTP schema tends to be dramatically more complex than the OLAP schema. Now that you know the infrastructure that goes into forming fact tables, dimension tables, and cubes, the concept of a star schema should offer little resistance. That is because when you configure a fact table with foreign key relationships to one or more of a dimension table's primary keys, as shown in Figure 1-6, you have a star schema. Looks a little like a star, right?

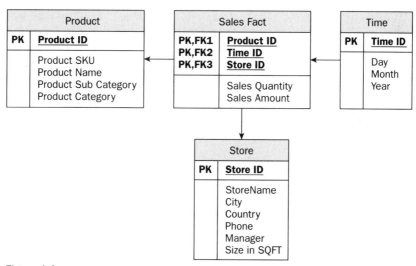

Figure 1-6

The star schema provides you with an illustration of the relationships between business entities in a clear and easy-to-understand fashion. Further, it enables number crunching of the measures in the fact table to progress at amazing speeds.

The Snowflake Schema

If you think the star schema is nifty, and it is, there is an extension of the concept called the snowflake schema. The snowflake schema is useful when one of your dimension tables starts looking as detailed as the fact table it is connected to. With the snowflake, a level is forked off from one of the dimension tables, so it is separated by one or more tables from the fact table. In Figure 1-7 the Product dimension has yielded a Product Category level. The Product Sub Category level is hence one table removed from the Sales Fact table. In turn, the Product Sub Category level yields a final level called the Product Category — which has two tables of separation between it and the Sales Fact table. These levels, which can be used to form a hierarchy in the dimension, do not make for faster processing or query response times, but they can keep a schema sensible.

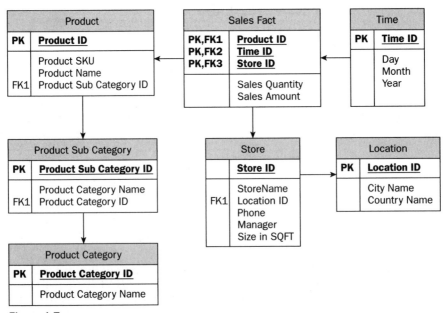

Figure 1-7

You have so far learned the fundamental elements of a data warehouse. The biggest challenge is to understand these well, and design and implement your data warehouse to cater to your end users. There are two main design techniques for implementing data warehouses: the Inmon approach and the Kimball approach.

Inmon Versus Kimball — Different Approaches

In data warehousing there are two commonly acknowledged approaches to building a decision support infrastructure, and both can be implemented using the tools available in SQL Server Analysis Services (SSAS) 2008. It is worth understanding these two approaches and the often-cited difference of views that result. These views are expressed most overtly in two seminal works: *The Data Warehouse Lifecycle Toolkit* by Ralph Kimball, Laura Reeves, Margy Ross, and Warren Thornthwaite, and *Corporate Information Factory* by Bill Inmon, Claudia Imhoff, and Ryan Sousa.

Kimball identified early on the problem of the stovepipe. A stovepipe is what you get when several independent systems in the enterprise go about identifying and storing data in different ways. Trying to connect these systems or use their data in a warehouse results in something resembling a Rube-Goldberg device. To address this problem, Kimball advocates the use of conformed dimensions. *Conformed* refers to the idea that dimensions of interest — sales, for example — should have the same attributes and rollups (covered in the "Cubes" section earlier in this chapter) in one data mart as another. Or at least one should be a subset of the other. In this way, a warehouse can be formed from data marts. The real gist of Kimball's approach is that the data warehouse contains dimensional databases for ease of analysis and that the user queries the warehouse directly.

The Inmon approach has the warehouse laid out in third normal form (not dimensional) and the users query data marts, not the warehouse. In this approach the data marts are dimensional in nature. However, they may or may not have conformed dimensions in the sense Kimball talks about.

Happily it is not necessary to become a card-carrying member of either school of thought in order to do work in this field. In fact, this book is not strictly aligned to either approach. What you will find as you work through this book is that by using the product in the ways in which it was meant to be used and are shown here, certain best practices and effective methodologies will naturally emerge.

Business Intelligence Is Data Analysis

Having designed a data warehouse, the next step is to understand and make business decisions from your data warehouse. Business intelligence is nothing more than analyzing your data and making actionable decisions. An example of business analytics is shown through the analysis of results from a product placed on sale at a discounted price, as commonly seen in any retail store. If a product is put on sale for a special discounted price, there is an expected outcome: increased sales volume. This is often the case, but whether or not it worked in the company's favor isn't obvious. That is where business analytics come into play. We can use SSAS 2008 to find out if the net effect of the special sale was to sell more product units. Suppose you are selling organic honey from genetically unaltered bees; you put the 8-ounce jars on special — two for one — and leave the 10- and 12-ounce jars at regular price. At the end of the special you can calculate the *lift* provided by the special sale — the difference in total sales between a week of sales with no special versus a week of sales with the special. How is it you could sell more 8-ounce jars on special that week, yet realize no lift? It's simple — the customers stopped buying your 10- and 12-ounce jars in favor of the two-for-one deal; and you didn't attract enough new business to cover the difference for a net increase in sales.

You can surface that information using SSAS 2008 by creating a Sales cube that has three dimensions: Product, Promotion, and Time. For the sake of simplicity, assume you have only three product sizes for the organic honey (8-ounce, 10-ounce, and 12-ounce) and two promotion states ("no promotion" and a "two-for-one promotion for the 8-ounce jars"). Further, assume the Time dimension contains different levels for Year, Month, Week, and Day. The cube itself contains two measures, "count of products sold" and the "sales amount." By analyzing the sales results each week across the three product sizes you could easily find out that there was an increase in the count of 8-ounce jars of honey sold, but perhaps the total sales across all sizes did not increase due to the promotion. By slicing on the Promotion dimension you would be able to confirm that there was a promotion during the week that caused an increase in the number of 8-ounce jars sold. When looking at the comparison of total sales for that week (promotion week) to the earlier (non-promotion) weeks, lift or lack of lift is seen quite clearly. Business analytics are often easier described than implemented, however.

Microsoft Business Intelligence Capabilities

Different types of organizations face different challenges. Whether you work in a large or a small company, business intelligence (BI) is critical to provide the business insight you need to help everyone in every department of your organization succeed. To help you address specific BI needs, you typically need to perform various operations or tasks on your data. Figure 1-8 provides you with a list of various tasks typically performed for business intelligence in an organization and how SQL Server 2008 helps in various parts of business intelligence. You can have a single tool helping you with multiple BI tasks or multiple tools being used for each BI task. Your organization may only be utilizing some tasks for your BI needs. Now let's look at each operation in detail and how Microsoft SQL Server 2008 products help you in performing these operations.

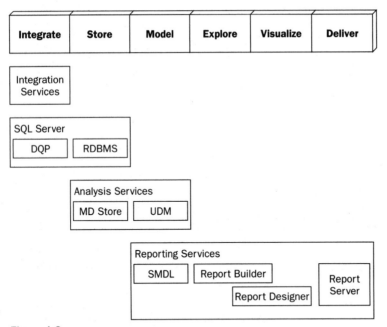

Figure 1-8

Integrating Data

Typically, organizations have data available from different backend systems. In order to build a data warehouse, you typically integrate all the data into a staging database. SQL Server Integration Services (SSIS) helps you in integrating data from backend systems to a single system. SSIS helps you in extracting data, cleaning the data, and then loading it to a single system. If you have multiple SQL Server relational databases, you can integrate the data for your data warehouse using distributed queries.

Storing Data

Your organization's data grows over time. Hence you do need to store the data for efficient access. You can store the data in multiple ways, from simple text files to an efficient database management system. SQL Server 2008 provides you with the ability to store your data in a relational database engine or the multidimensional database engine (SQL Server Analysis Services).

The Model

Once your organization's data has been stored, you need to create a model to analyze the data. You can create models on the data stored in an Analysis Services database or the relational database system. Databases created in Analysis Services conform to the Unified Dimensional Model (UDM). You learn more about UDM later in this chapter and throughout this book. In order to analyze the data from your relational database system, SQL Server Reporting Services provides you with a way to model the data using the Semantic Model Definition Language (SMDL). SMDL then helps you to analyze and report the data to satisfy your business needs.

Exploring Data

Once you have a model and the underlying data, you need to explore the data to interpret and get the intelligence from the data that will help you to meet your business needs. SQL Server Reporting Services helps you to explore the data from your models via two ways: ad-hoc analysis using Report Builder and through a structured format using Report Designer. Report Builder and Report Designer help you to easily explore the data using the models without the need of learning the query language to query your database engines. You learn more about Report Builder and Report Designer and how to explore data from Analysis Services in Chapter 20.

Visualizing

Once you explore the data, you typically build reports that can be delivered to end users who can interpret the data and make intelligent business decisions to enhance your organization. Report Designer helps you to visualize the data as efficient reports that can then be deployed on to your Reporting Services server.

Deliver

Once you build your report on top of the data, you need a way for users to retrieve the reports easily. The Reporting Services server helps users to view the reports with appropriate authentication. In addition, Reporting Services allows you to deliver the reports at needed intervals to the appropriate users in your organization.

Microsoft SQL Server 2008 provides a platform to perform various business intelligence tasks to access, integrate, and manage data for your organization and help in building an efficient data warehouse. In addition, SQL Server 2008 offers a robust, scalable, and enterprise-ready data warehouse platform. With Microsoft SQL Server 2008, you can bring together and manage all your data assets to help ensure that the critical information you put in decision-makers' hands is high-quality, complete, and timely, which can help them make better decisions. In addition to SQL Server 2008, which forms the core of the business intelligence platform, Microsoft offers additional products that form a fully integrated set of BI technologies to help make building, managing, and using BI for your organization less complicated and more economical. The result is that you and your organization can have the advantage of a complete set of BI capabilities. Figure 1-9 shows Microsoft business intelligence products. You can see that SQL Server Analysis Services is the core business intelligence platform from Microsoft.

The majority of the consumers use Microsoft Office Excel as a core BI client for their organization. Due to this, there is very tight integration between SQL Server Analysis Services and Excel 2007 so you can analyze the data from your multidimensional databases effectively via pivot tables in Excel. You can use Excel 2007 to retrieve and view calculations that define your organization's performance from SQL Server Analysis Services such as Key Performance Indicators. This helps end users to easily interpret and understand how your organization is performing and make appropriate decisions.

In addition to Excel 2007, SharePoint Server 2007 and Performance Point 2007 form the suite of products from Microsoft that help in business intelligence for your organization.

Performance Point 2007 helps in analysis, forecasting, input from multiple people and departments, and the combination of multiple related reports. It offers an integrated performance management application that delivers a robust infrastructure to support your business planning. Built on the Microsoft BI platform, Office Performance Point Server 2007 can help your people continuously interact and contribute throughout the process of business planning, budgeting, and forecasting. With Office Performance Point Server 2007, you can manage consolidation and provide monitoring tools such as scorecards and analysis tools that can help your organization track its changing performance — all through the familiar and easy-to-use Microsoft Office system environment.

Microsoft Office SharePoint Server 2007 offers an integrated suite of server capabilities that can help organizations connect people, processes, and information. With Office SharePoint Server 2007, decision-makers can easily access all their BI information, including scorecards, reports, and Office Excel spreadsheets. Office SharePoint Server 2007 also offers collaboration and powerful built-in search and content management features. When you deliver Microsoft BI through Office SharePoint Server 2007, you have one central location from which you can provide business intelligence capabilities to every employee and quickly connect your people to the information they need.

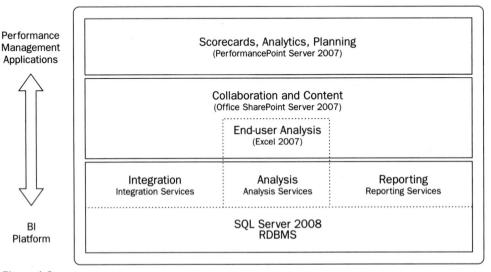

Figure 1-9

SQL Server Analysis Services 2008

SQL Server 2008 is the Microsoft business intelligence platform. Analysis Services 2008 is the multidimensional database engine. In addition to Analysis Services, SQL Server 2008 contains other services such as Integration Services (tools and engine to Extract, Transform, and Load) and Reporting Services, among other things. Integration Services, Analysis Services, and Reporting Services together form the core of the business intelligence platform with SQL Server as the backend. Analysis Services not only provides you with the ability to build dimensions and cubes for data analysis but also supports several data mining algorithms, which can provide business insight into your data that are not intuitive. Next you learn about the overall architecture of Analysis Services 2008 followed by the concept of the Unified Dimensional Model (UDM), which helps you to have a unified view of your entire data warehouse.

SSAS 2008 is a scalable, reliable, and secure enterprise class multidimensional database server. The architecture of Analysis Services allows it to provide scalability in terms of scale-out and scale-up features and in terms of very large database capabilities. Several instances of Analysis Services can be integrated together to provide an efficient scale-out solution. Similarly, Analysis Services is also 64-bit enabled and scales-up on a large-scale system. On the other hand, the service has been architected with efficient algorithms to handle large dimensions and cubes on a single instance. Analysis Services provides a rich set of tools for creating multidimensional databases, efficient and easy manageability, as well as profiling capabilities.

The *Business Intelligence Development Studio* (BIDS) integrated within Visual Studio 2008 is the development tool shipped with SQL Server 2008 used for creating and updating cubes, dimensions, and Data Mining models. The *SQL Server Management Studio* (SSMS) provides an integrated environment for managing SQL Server, Analysis Services, Integration Services, and Reporting Services. SQL Server Profiler in the SQL Server 2008 release supports profiling SSAS 2008, which helps in analyzing the types of commands and queries sent from different users or clients to SSAS 2008. You learn more about BIDS and SSMS in Chapter 2 with the help of a tutorial. You learn about profiling an instance of SSAS 2008 using SQL Server Profiler in Chapter 15. In addition to the above-mentioned tools, SSAS 2008 provides two more tools: the Migration Wizard and the Deployment Wizard. The Migration Wizard helps in migrating SQL Server 2000 Analysis Services databases to SQL Server 2008 Analysis Services. The Deployment Wizard helps in deploying the database files created using BIDS to SSAS 2008.

The SSMS provides efficient, enterprise-class manageability features for Analysis Services. Key aspects of an enterprise class service are availability and reliability. SSAS 2008 supports fail-over clustering on Windows clusters through an easy setup scheme, and fail-over clustering certainly helps provide high availability. In addition, SSAS 2008 has the capability of efficiently recovering from failures. You can set up fine-grain security so that you can provide administrative access to an entire service or administrative access to specific databases, process permissions to specific databases, and read-only access to metadata and data. In addition to this, certain features are turned off by default so that the service is protected from hacker attacks.

Analysis Services 2008 natively supports XML for Analysis (XMLA) specification defined by the XMLA Advisory Council. What this means is that the communication interface to Analysis Services from a client is XML. This facilitates ease of interoperability between different clients and Analysis Services. The architecture of Analysis Services 2008 includes various modes of communication to the service as shown in Figure 1-10. Analysis Services 2008 provides three main client connectivity components to communicate to the server. The Analysis Management Objects (AMO) is a new object model that helps you manage Analysis Services and the databases resident on it. The OLE DB 10.0 is the client connectivity component used to interact with Analysis Services instances for queries that conform to the OLE DB standard. The ADOMD.Net is .NET object model support for querying data from Analysis Services. In addition to the three main client connectivity components, two other components are provided by Analysis Services 2008. They are DSO 10.0 (Decision Support Object) and HTTP connectivity through a data pump. DSO 8.0 is the extension of the management object of Analysis Server 2000 so that legacy applications can interact with migrated Analysis Server 2000 databases on Analysis Server 2005. The data pump is a component that is set up with *IIS* (Internet Information System) to provide connection to Analysis Services 2008 over *HTTP* (Hypertext Transfer Protocol).

Even though XMLA helps in interoperability between different clients to Analysis Server, it comes with a cost on performance. If the responses from the server are large, transmission of XML data across the wire may take a long time depending on the type of network connection. Typically slow wide area networks might suffer from performance due to large XML responses. To combat this, SSAS 2008 supports the options for compression and binary XML so that the XML responses from the server could be reduced. These are optional features supported by SSAS 2008 that can be enabled or disabled on the server.

Analysis Services 2008 stores metadata information of databases in the form of XML. Analysis Services provides you with the option of storing the data or aggregated data efficiently in an optimized multidimensional format on an Analysis Services instance or storing them in the relational database as a relational format. Based on where the data and/or aggregated fact data is stored, you can classify the storage types as MOLAP (Multidimensional OLAP), ROLAP (Relational OLAP), or HOLAP (Hybrid OLAP).

MOLAP is the storage mode in which the data and aggregated data are both stored in proprietary format on the Analysis Services instance. This is the default and recommended storage mode for Analysis Services databases because you get better query performance as compared to the other storage types. The key advantages of this storage mode is fast data retrieval while analyzing sections of data and therefore provides good query performance and the ability to handle complex calculations. Two potential disadvantages of MOLAP mode are storage needed for large databases and the inability to see new data entering your data warehouse.

ROLAP is the storage mode in which the data is left in the relational database. Aggregated or summary data is also stored in the relational database. Queries against the Analysis Services are appropriately changed to queries to the relational database to retrieve the right section of data requested. The key advantage of this mode is that the ability to handle large cubes is limited by the relational backend only. The most important disadvantage of the ROLAP storage mode is slow query performance. You will encounter slower query performance in ROLAP mode due to the fact that each query to the Analysis Services is translated into one or more queries to the relational backend.

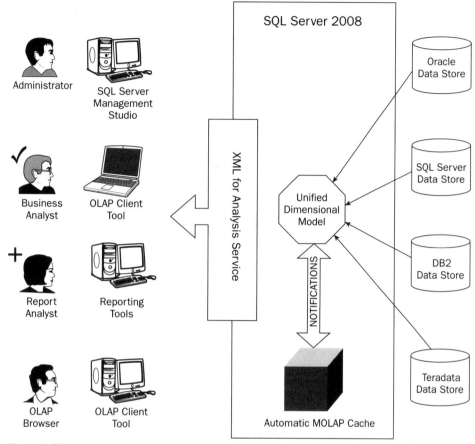

Figure 1-10

The HOLAP storage mode combines the best of MOLAP and ROLAP modes. The data in the relational database is not touched while the aggregated or summary data is stored on the Analysis Services instance in an optimized format. If the queries to Analysis Services request aggregated data, they are retrieved from the summary data stored on the Analysis Services instance and they would be faster than data being retrieved from the relational backend. If the queries request detailed data, appropriate queries are sent to the relational backend and these queries can take a long time based on the relational backend.

If you choose the data and/or aggregated data to be stored in the optimized MOLAP format, you get better query performance than the ROLAP format, where data is being retrieved from the relational database. The MOLAP format helps Analysis Services to retrieve the data efficiently and thereby improves the query performance.

Based on your requirements and maintainability costs you need to choose the storage mode that is appropriate for your business. SSAS 2008 supports all three storage modes.

The Unified Dimensional Model

Central to the architecture is the concept of the Unified Dimensional Model (UDM) which, by the way, is unique to this release of the product. UDM, as the name suggests, provides you with a way to encapsulate access to multiple heterogeneous data sources into a single model. In fact, with the UDM, you will be buffered from the difficulties previously presented by multiple data sources. Those difficulties were often associated with cross-data-source calculations and queries — so, do not be daunted by projects with lots of disparate data sources. The UDM can handle it! The UDM itself is more than a multiple data-source cube on steroids; it actually defines the relational schema upon which your cubes and dimensions are built. Think of the UDM as providing you with the best of the OLAP and relational worlds. UDM provides you with the rich metadata needed for analyzing and exploring data along with the functionality like the complex calculations and aggregations of the OLAP world. It supports complex schemas, and is capable of supporting ad-hoc queries that are needed for reporting in the relational world. Unlike the traditional OLAP world that allows you to define a single fact table within a cube, the UDM allows you to have multiple fact tables. The UDM is your friend and helps you have a single model that will support all your business needs. Figure 1-11 shows a UDM within SQL Server Analysis Services 2008 that retrieves data from heterogeneous data sources and serves various types of clients.

Key elements of the UDM are as follows:

- ❑ **Heterogeneous data access support:** UDM helps you to integrate and encapsulate data from heterogeneous data sources. It helps you combine various schemas into a single unified model that gives end users the capability of sending queries to a single model.

- ❑ **Real-time data access with high performance:** The UDM provides end users with real-time data access. The UDM creates a MOLAP cache of the underlying data. Whenever there are changes in the underlying relational database, a new MOLAP cache is built. When users query the model, it provides the results from the MOLAP cache. During the time the cache is being built, results are retrieved from the relational database. UDM helps in providing real-time data access with the speed of an OLAP database due to the MOLAP cache. This feature is called proactive caching. You learn more about proactive caching in Chapter 21.

- ❑ **Rich metadata, ease of use for exploration, and navigation of data:** UDM provides a consolidated view of the underlying data sources with the richness of metadata provided by the OLAP world. Due to rich metadata supported by OLAP, end users are able to exploit this metadata to navigate and explore data in support of making business decisions. UDM also provides you with the ability to view specific sections of the unified model based on your business analysis needs.

- ❑ **Rich analytics support:** In addition to the rich metadata support, the UDM provides you with the ability to specify complex calculations to be applied to the underlying data; in this way you can embed business logic. You can specify the complex calculations by a script-based calculation model using the language called MDX (MultiDimensional eXpressions). UDM provides rich analytics such as Key Performance Indicators and Actions that help in understanding your business with ease and automatically take appropriate actions based on changes in data.

- ❑ **Model for Reporting and Analysis:** The UDM provides the best functionality for relating to both relational and OLAP worlds. UDM provides you with the capability of not only querying the aggregated data that are typically used for analysis, but also has the ability to provide for detailed reporting up to the transaction level across multiple heterogeneous data sources.

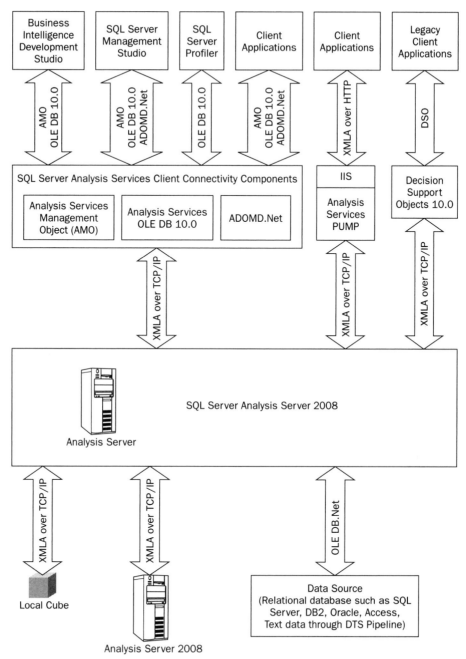

Figure 1-11

Another handy aspect of using the UDM is the storage of foreign language translations for both data and metadata. This is handled seamlessly by the UDM such that a connecting user gets the metadata and data of interest customized to his or her locale. Of course, somebody has to enter those translations into the UDM in the first place; it is not actually a foreign language translation system.

Summary

Reading this chapter may have felt like the linguistic equivalent of drinking from a fire hose; it is good you hung in there because now you have a foundation from which to build as you work through the rest of the book. Now you know data warehousing is all about structuring data for decision support. The data is consumed by the business analyst and business decision-maker and can be analyzed through OLAP and Data Mining techniques.

OLAP is a multidimensional database format that is a world apart in form and function when compared to an OLTP relational database system. You saw how OLAP uses a structure called a cube, which in turn relies on fact tables (which are populated with data called facts) and dimension tables. These dimension tables can be configured around one or more fact tables to create a star schema. If a dimension table is deconstructed to point to a chain of sub-dimension tables, the schema is called a snowflake schema.

By choosing SQL Server 2008 you have chosen a business intelligence platform with great features with reliability, availability, and scalability. The SQL Server business intelligence platform is the fastest growing with highest market share product in the market. The rest of this book illustrates the power of SQL Server Analysis Services 2008, which is the core part of the BI platform from Microsoft.

In the unlikely event that you didn't read the Introduction, mention was made that you should read at least the first three chapters serially before attempting to tackle the rest of the book. So, please do not skip Chapter 2, an introduction to Analysis Services, and Chapter 3, an introduction to the technology behind the most famous acronym in business analytics, MDX.

2

First Look at Analysis Services 2008

In Chapter 1 you learned general data warehousing concepts, including some key elements that go into successful data warehouse projects, the different approaches taken to build data warehouses, and how the data warehouses are subsequently mined for information. This chapter introduces you to SQL Server Analysis Services 2008 and related tools. These are the tools, resident in two different environments, which you'll need to develop and manage Analysis Services databases. This chapter also covers some of the differences between Analysis Services 2008, Analysis Services 2005, and Analysis Services 2000.

You will familiarize yourself with the Analysis Services development environment by working through a tutorial based on a sample relational database for SQL Server Analysis Services 2008 called *Adventure Works DW 2008*, which you can download from www.codeplex.com. This tutorial covers many basic Analysis Services concepts by taking you through the process of building and browsing a cube. The tutorial shows you how to use the tools and also provides you insight into what the product is doing behind the scenes.

In the management environment, you learn the basic operations associated with managing Analysis Services 2008. Further, you learn about the constituent objects that make up an Analysis Services 2008 database and what actions can be taken against them in the management environment. Finally, you are introduced to using the MDX Query Editor to query cube data.

> *MDX, which stands for MultiDimensional eXpressions, is the query language used to retrieve data from multidimensional databases.*

By the end of this chapter you will be familiar with the key components that constitute the Analysis Services Tools, the process of building Analysis Services databases, and how to use MDX to retrieve data from Analysis Services databases. So, snap on your seatbelt and let's get started!

Differences between Analysis Services 2000, Analysis Services 2005, and Analysis Services 2008

Analysis Services 2005 was not just an evolutionary step up from Analysis Services 2000, but a quantum leap forward in functionality, scalability, and manageability. Analysis Services 2008 builds on the Analysis Services 2005 architecture and enhances its functionality to make it easy and efficient for Analysis Services database developers and administrators to do their jobs. Some of the key enhancements include improvements in cube and dimension wizards to help build your multi-dimensional database to perform more effectively; added guidance in the Analysis Services Tools for improving design; query performance enhancements in the Analysis Services engine; and Analysis Services features such as a read-only database that help in scalability. You learn more about these key enhancements in Analysis Services 2008 throughout the book. Relational databases provide a flexible, well-known model for storing data optimized for rapid incremental updates. They also provide the end user with access to data that can be easily condensed into information-rich reports. OLAP databases, on the other hand, are typically used because of their high-end performance and rich analytic and exploration capabilities. Analysis Services 2008 merges the capabilities of the relational and OLAP worlds, providing a unified view of data to the end user. This unified model is called the *Unified Dimensional Model* (UDM). In sum, Analysis Services 2008 is a powerful, enterprise-class product that you can use to build large-scale OLAP databases and implement strategic business analysis applications against those databases. You learn more about the UDM and the advanced analytic capabilities of Analysis Services 2008 in Chapters 6, 9, 21, 22, 23, 24, and 25. This chapter gives you hands-on experience with both the development and management environments.

Development, Administrative, and Client Tools

If you have used Analysis Services 2000, you have used the Analysis Manager. The Analysis Manager was implemented as a *Microsoft Management Console* (MMC) snap-in. It served as both the development environment and the management environment for Analysis Services 2000. This tool had limited functionality but did allow you to browse Analysis Services data. A sample application called *MDX Sample* was also shipped in the product and provided the capability of building and sending queries to Analysis Services databases and viewing the results.

Analysis Services 2005 and Analysis Services 2008 have separate environments for development and management. The development environment is called *Business Intelligence Development Studio* (BIDS) and is integrated with Microsoft Visual Studio. Similar to building a Visual Basic or C++ project, you can build a Business Intelligence project. The management environment is called *SQL Server Management Studio* (SSMS). SSMS is a complete, integrated management environment for several services (including SQL Server itself, Analysis Services, Reporting Services, Integration Services, and SQL Server Compact Edition). SSMS was built to provide ease of use and manageability for database administrators in one single environment. The capability of analyzing and retrieving data from Analysis Services 2008 is integrated into both BIDS and SMSS. You can browse source data from both of these environments as well. In SSMS you are provided with a query builder for writing queries to retrieve data from Analysis Services. The query builder replaces the MDX Sample application that came with Analysis Services 2000. In addition, the query builder provides IntelliSense support for the MDX language including auto completion and syntax coloring.

If you have used Microsoft SQL Server 2000, you might also be familiar with the SQL Server Profiler. In the SQL Server 2005 release, the capability of tracing, or profiling, Analysis Services queries was added. The SQL Server 2008 SQL Server Profiler also supports Analysis Services profiling. Analysis Services

Profile information can be utilized to analyze and improve performance. You learn more about the SQL Server Profiler in Chapter 15.

Analysis Services Version Differences

Analysis Services 2000 provided a rich feature set that helped in building solid data warehouses. The features combined with the MDX query language provided customers with rich analytic capabilities. As with any software package, though, Analysis Services 2000 had limitations. Some of the limitations of Analysis Services 2000 were:

❑ Even though Analysis Services 2000 had a rich feature set, modeling certain scenarios either resulted in significant performance degradation or simply could not be accomplished.

❑ There were size limitations on various database objects such as dimensions, levels, and measures.

❑ Analysis Services 2000 loaded all databases at startup. If there were a large number of databases and/or very large databases, starting the server could take a long time.

❑ Analysis Services 2000 was implemented using a thick client model that helped in achieving very good query performance but did not scale very well in 3-tier applications (for example, Web scenarios).

❑ The metadata of the databases was either stored in an Access or SQL Server relational database. Maintenance of data and metadata had to be done carefully.

❑ The backup format used by Analysis Services limited the file size to 2GB.

Analysis Services 2008 and Analysis Services 2005, in addition to providing the best of the relational and OLAP worlds, overcame most of the limitations of Analysis Services 2000. The following are some of the improvements implemented:

❑ The thin client architecture improves scalability of 2-tier and 3-tier applications.

❑ XML/A (XML for Analysis) was implemented as the native protocol for communication with the server.

❑ Several new OLAP and Data Mining features were added to facilitate easy and optimal design of data warehouses.

❑ Most of the size limits of objects have been greatly increased; or for all practical purposes, eliminated.

❑ Better manageability, scalability, extensibility, fine-grain security, and higher reliability are provided by supporting fail-over clustering.

❑ Native support of Common Language Runtime (CLR) stored procedures with appropriate security permissions is included.

❑ Metadata information is represented as XML and resides in Analysis Services along with the data. This allows for easier maintainability and control.

❑ Analysis Services 2008 uses a different backup format (you learn about backup in Chapters 7 and 13) than the one used in Analysis Services 2000. The 2GB backup file limit from Analysis Services 2000 has been eliminated. The backup format used in Analysis Services 2005 is compatible with Analysis Services 2008. Analysis Services 2008 significantly enhances the scalability of Analysis Services 2005 backups for databases larger than 20GB.

Analysis Services 2008 builds on top of Analysis Services 2005 and provides the following additional benefits:

❑ Analysis Services 2008 enhances your design experience in BIDS by making it easy and efficient to design your databases right from the beginning. BIDS provides informative warnings based on Analysis Services best practices that will help you make optimal choices when designing your Analysis Services databases. You see this in Chapters 5, 6, and 9.

❑ Analysis Services 2008 provides several trace events and performance counters that help you monitor and understand query performance bottlenecks. Several performance enhancements are built into the server that will automatically improve query performance significantly in certain scenarios (which you learn more about in Chapter 15) compared to Analysis Services 2005.

❑ Analysis Services 2008 has much improved database backup performance as compared to Analysis Services 2005. You will notice the improved backup performance in databases that are larger than 20GB. You learn more about backup in Chapter 7.

❑ Analysis Services 2008 provides you with dynamic management views (DMVs) of all current users and activities that will help you manage your Analysis Services instance efficiently. These help you in understanding operations within Analysis Services with such things as number of queries and memory consumption. You learn about DMVs in Chapter 13.

❑ Analysis Services 2008 provides you with shared scalable databases (also called read-only databases) that enable enterprise scale-out scenarios that can handle concurrent requests of several hundreds or thousands of users. You learn about read-only databases and shared scalable databases in Chapters 7 and 15, respectively.

Two fundamental changes in Analysis Services 2005 that are still applicable in Analysis Services 2008 are the thin client architecture and support for the native XML/A (XML for Analysis) protocol for communication between client and server.

Overall, Analysis Services 2008 provides you with a great combination of functionality and ease of use that enables you to analyze your data and make strategic business decisions. You will see these capabilities emerge step-by-step as you advance through this book.

Upgrading to Analysis Services 2008

You can upgrade to Analysis Services 2008 from Analysis Services 2000 or Analysis Services 2005. If you currently do not have a requirement of upgrading your previous Analysis Services instances to Analysis Services 2008 or if you are a first time user of Analysis Services you can jump to the next section. The Analysis Services upgrade process in general is not a seamless process and not without its share of gotchas. This is especially true when much of the product has been redesigned, such as you are faced with going from Analysis Services 2000 to Analysis Services 2008. Fortunately, Analysis Services 2008 provides a tool called Upgrade Advisor to prepare you to upgrade databases from Analysis Services 2000 and Analysis Services 2005 to Analysis Services 2008. Upgrade Advisor is available as a redistributable package with SQL Server 2008. You need to install Upgrade Advisor from the <processor architecture>\redist\Upgrade Advisor folder on your CD/DVD. Install the Upgrade Advisor on your machine. When you run Upgrade Advisor on your existing Analysis Services 2000 or 2005 instance, Upgrade Advisor informs you whether or not your database(s) will be upgraded successfully without any known issues. Errors and warnings are provided by Upgrade Advisor in cases where upgrade of some of the objects/definitions is not feasible or when there are potential changes in the names of dimensions or cubes during the upgrade process due to the Analysis Services 2008 architecture. Once you have reviewed all the information from Upgrade Advisor, you are ready to start the upgrade. Follow these steps to use Upgrade Advisor for analyzing the effects of upgrading your Analysis Services 2000 or 2005 instance to Analysis Services 2008:

1. Choose Start ⇨ All Programs ⇨ SQL Server 2008 ⇨ SQL Server 2008 Upgrade Advisor on your machine. The welcome screen appears, as shown in Figure 2-1. Click the Launch Upgrade Analyzer Analysis Wizard link at the bottom of the page.

Figure 2-1

2. You will now see the Welcome to Upgrade Advisor for Microsoft SQL Server 2008 page. Click the Next button.

3. In the SQL Server Components selection page, shown in Figure 2-2, enter the name of a machine that contains the Analysis Services 2000 or 2005 instance you want to upgrade. In this illustration, an Analysis Services 2000 server name is specified. If you click the Detect button, Upgrade Advisor will populate the SQL Server Components page with the services running on the server whose name you provided. You can also manually select which services you want Upgrade Wizard to analyze. Select the Analysis Services component as shown in Figure 2-2 and click Next.

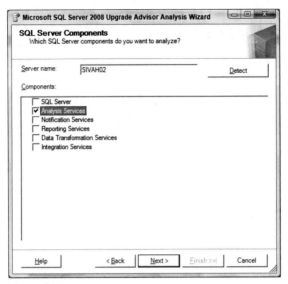

Figure 2-2

4. In the Analysis Services Parameters page, as shown in Figure 2-3, you can select the Analysis Services instance name. Analysis Services only supports Windows Authentication. Analysis Services 2000 only supports a single instance on one machine, whereas Analysis Services 2005 supports multiple instances. Select the instance name and click Next.

Figure 2-3

5. In the Confirm Upgrade Advisor Settings page, as shown in Figure 2-4, you can review your selections. If your selections are not correct, go back to the previous page and make the appropriate changes. Click the Run button for upgrade analysis.

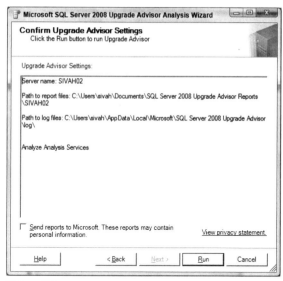

Figure 2-4

In the next screen you see the Upgrade Advisor analyzing the databases on your Analysis Services instance. You should be aware that the Upgrade Advisor needs the DSO component to connect to your Analysis Services instance. Hence, you need to make sure you install the backward compatibility MSI (SQLServer2005_BC.msi) available with the SQL Server 2008 setup. At the end of the analysis you see the errors and warnings reported by the Upgrade Advisor, as shown in Figure 2-5.

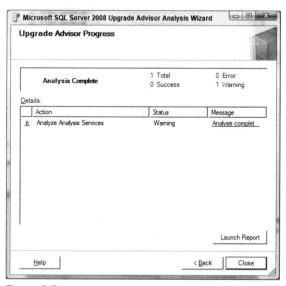

Figure 2-5

6. Click the Launch Report button to see the detailed report of the analysis and the actions you need to take for a smooth migration of your databases, as shown in Figure 2-6.

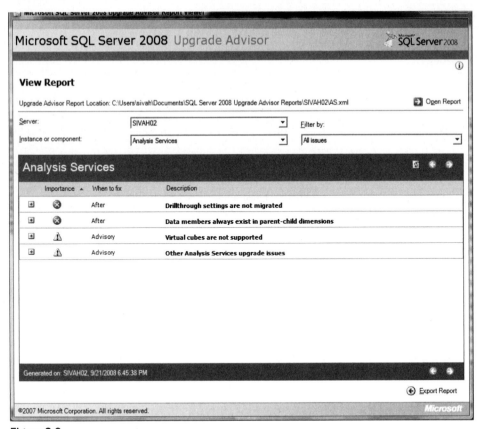

Figure 2-6

We strongly recommend that you run the Upgrade Advisor utility, analyze all the errors and warnings reported, and take the appropriate actions. In certain cases, you might have to perform some operations on your existing Analysis Services database. For example, if you have a writeback partition in your Analysis Services 2000 database that contains data, the recommended approach is to convert the writeback partition to a MOLAP partition, upgrade the database to Analysis Services 2008, reprocess the partition, and then re-create a new writeback partition. Similarly, you might have to perform several steps either before or after the upgrade on your Analysis Services database to ensure your existing applications will work correctly. Similar to the example shown for analyzing your Analysis Services 2000 database, you need to utilize the Upgrade Advisor to analyze the Analysis Services 2005 database. Because Analysis Services 2008 builds upon Analysis Services 2005 architecture, you may not see a significant number of errors or warnings reported by the Upgrade Advisor for an Analysis Services 2005 database. Even so, you still should test your applications on your Analysis Services 2008 database before proceeding with the upgrade process.

Once you have analyzed the Upgrade Advisor report on your Analysis Services 2000 or Analysis Services 2005 databases you are ready for upgrade. Install the product and select the option to upgrade your Analysis Services 2000 or 2005 databases. Analysis Services 2008 only upgrades the metadata of your Analysis Services 2000 databases, but it upgrades both metadata and data for your Analysis Services 2005 databases. Hence, when you upgrade your Analysis Services 2000 databases you will need your corresponding relational data source available so that source data can be repopulated into your cubes. You need to process the databases that have been upgraded from Analysis Services 2000. Once this is completed, all your cubes and dimensions will be available for querying. If warnings in Upgrade Advisor indicate that names of dimensions or hierarchies will be changed, your applications might also have to be updated accordingly. Please plan to spend time to verify that all your applications are working for your customers after the upgrade process. We have an additional experienced-based recommendation — perform the entire upgrade process on a test machine. In this way, you can verify if your existing applications are working as expected using the Analysis Services 2008 instance. Finally, with confidence, you can perform the upgrade on your production machine. The upgrade process from an Analysis Services 2005 instance to Analysis Services 2008 should be relatively simple. The Upgrade Advisor will report warnings for the issues that affect the upgrade of your Analysis Services 2005 databases that you need to be aware of and handle appropriately.

If you do not have a test machine for upgrading your Analysis Services 2000 instance, you should install Analysis Services 2008 as a named instance and then run the Analysis Services Migration Wizard to migrate your databases from an Analysis Services 2000 server to an Analysis Services 2008 instance. For testing the upgrade process for your Analysis Services 2005 databases, we recommend that you install Analysis Services 2008 as a named instance. You then need to back up your Analysis Services 2005 databases and restore them on your Analysis Services 2008 instance. You then need to test the databases. Once you have confirmed that your applications work against your Analysis Services 2008 instance as expected, you can upgrade your Analysis Services 2005 instance to Analysis Services 2008 using SQL Server 2008 setup's upgrade path. Analysis Services 2008 provides you with an integrated environment to manage all SQL Server 2008 products using SQL Server Management Studio (SSMS). SSMS is the newer version of the famous Query Analyzer, which is available in SQL Server 2000.

Because Analysis Services 2008 builds upon the Analysis Services 2005 architecture, the upgrade process from Analysis Services 2005 to Analysis Services 2008 should be fairly smooth. However, the upgrade process from Analysis Services 2000 to Analysis Services 2008 is bit more involved. Hence, we are including step-by-step instructions. In general we recommend you re-design your Analysis Services 2000 databases in Analysis Services 2008. However, if you do need to upgrade, the tutorial in this section will be helpful to you. If you do not have Analysis Services 2000 databases to upgrade, you can skip the rest of this section.

Using the following tutorial you learn to upgrade from Analysis Services 2000 to Analysis Services 2008. In the following short tutorial, we will reference FoodMart2000 as a sample database and you can use your own databases where appropriate. To migrate your Analysis Services 2000 databases to an Analysis Services 2008 instance, follow these steps:

1. Launch SQL Server Management Studio, which comes with Analysis Services 2008, by choosing Start ➪ All Programs ➪ Microsoft SQL Server2008 ➪ SQL Server Management Studio. Connect to the Analysis Services 2008 instance using SQL Server Management Studio's Object Explorer. Right-click the server name and select Migrate Database as shown in Figure 2-7. This takes you to the welcome screen of the wizard. If someone else had used this wizard and disabled the welcome page you might not see the welcome page. If you are in the welcome page, click the Next button to proceed to step 2.

Figure 2-7

2. In the Specify Source and Destination page, the wizard pre-populates the name of your Analysis Services 2008 instance. Enter the machine name of your Analysis Services 2000 server as shown in Figure 2-8 and click Next.

Figure 2-8

3. In the Select Databases to Migrate page you will see the list of databases in your Analysis Services 2000 instance itemized and pre-selected for migration as shown in Figure 2-9. A column on the right side provides you with the names of the Destination Databases in your Analysis Services 2008 instance. You have the option of selecting all the databases or just a few databases from your Analysis Services 2000 instance to migrate. Deselect all the databases and select the FoodMart 2000 database; this is the sample database that is shipped with Analysis Services 2000.

Figure 2-9

4. The Migration Wizard now validates the selected databases and contained objects for migration. As the Migration Wizard does this, it provides a report including warnings for objects that will be changed during the migration process, as shown in Figure 2-10. You can save the logs to a file for future reference. Once you have analyzed the entire report, click Next to deploy the migrated database to your Analysis Services 2008 instance.

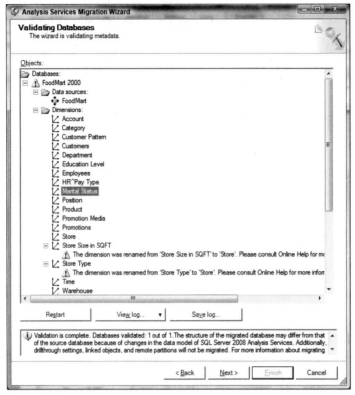

Figure 2-10

5. The Migration Wizard now sends the metadata of the migrated database to the Analysis Services 2008 instance. The new database with migrated objects is created on your Analysis Services 2008 instance and the Migration Wizard reports the status of the migration. Once the migration process is complete, click the Next button.

6. In the completion page, the Migration Wizard shows the new databases that have been migrated in a tree view. Click Finish to complete the migration.

You should be aware that the Migration Wizard will only migrate databases from Analysis Services 2000. In addition, the wizard only migrates the metadata of an Analysis Services 2000 database and not the data. Hence the migrated cubes and dimensions are not accessible for querying until you reprocess them. Process all the databases that have been migrated, and test your applications against the migrated databases on your Analysis Services 2008 instance. You need to direct your applications to the new Analysis Services 2008 instance name. Once you have verified that all applications are working as expected, you can uninstall Analysis Services 2000 and then rename your Analysis Services 2008 named instance to the default instance using the instance rename utility, ASInstanceRename.exe, which you can find in the \Program Files\Microsoft SQL Server\100\Tools\Binn\VSShell\Common7\IDE directory.

Using Business Intelligence Development Studio

Business Intelligence Development Studio (BIDS) is the development environment for designing your Analysis Services databases. To start Business Intelligence Development Studio, click the Windows Start button and go to All Programs ⇨ Microsoft SQL Server 2008 ⇨ SQL Server Business Intelligence Development Studio. If you're familiar with Visual Studio, you might be thinking that BIDS looks a lot like the Visual Studio environment. You're right; in Analysis Services 2008, you create Analysis Services projects in an environment that is Visual Studio. Working in Visual Studio offers many benefits, such as easy access to source control and support for multiple projects within the same Visual Studio solution (a solution within Visual Studio is a collection of projects such as an Analysis Services project, a C# project, an Integration Services project, or a Reporting Services project).

Creating a Project in the Business Intelligence Development Studio

To design your Analysis Services database you need to create a project using BIDS. Typically you will design your database within BIDS, make appropriate changes, and finally send the database to your Analysis Services instance. Each Analysis Services project within BIDS becomes a database on the Analysis Services instance when all the definitions within the project are sent to the server. You can also use BIDS to directly connect to an Analysis Services database and make changes to the database.

Follow these steps to create a new project. To start BIDS, click the Start button and go to All Programs ⇨ Microsoft SQL Server 2008 ⇨ SQL Server Business Intelligence Development Studio. In BIDS, select File ⇨ New ⇨ Project. You will see the Business Intelligence Projects templates as shown in Figure 2-11. Click the Analysis Services Project template. Type **AnalysisServices2008Tutorial** as the project name and select the directory in which you want to create this project. Click OK to create the project.

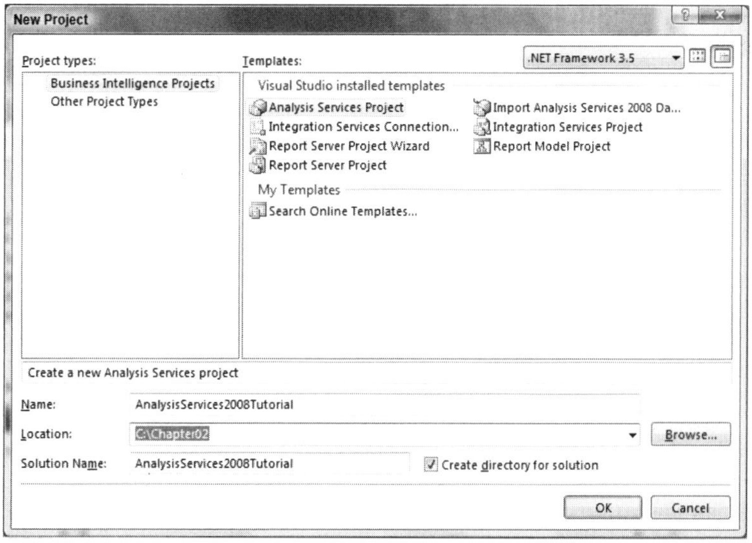

Figure 2-11

You are now in an Analysis Services project, as shown in Figure 2-12.

When you create a Business Intelligence project, it is created inside a solution with the same name. (A Visual Studio solution is a container for one or more projects.) When you create a new project with a solution open in Visual Studio, you have the option of adding the project to the existing solution or creating a new one. BIDS contains several panes; of most concern here are the Solution Explorer, Properties, and Output panes.

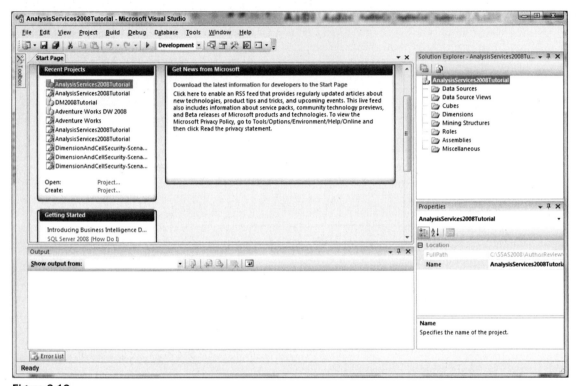

Figure 2-12

The Solution Explorer Pane

The Solution Explorer in Figure 2-12 shows eight folders:

❏ **Data Sources:** Your data warehouse is likely made up of disparate data sources such as Microsoft SQL Server, Oracle, DB2, Teradata, and so forth. Analysis Services 2008 can easily deal with retrieving relational data from various relational databases. Data source objects contain details of a connection to a data source, which include server name, catalog or database name, and login credentials. You establish connections to relational servers by creating a data source for each one.

❏ **Data Source Views:** When working with a large operational data store you don't always want to see all the tables in the database. With Data Source Views (DSVs), you can limit the number of visible tables by including only the tables that are relevant to your analysis. DSVs allow you to create a logical data model upon which you build your Unified Dimensional Model. A DSV can contain tables from one or more data sources, and one of these data sources is called a primary data source. Data sources and DSVs are discussed in Chapter 4.

❑ **Cubes:** Cubes are the foundation for analysis. A collection of *measure groups* (discussed later in this chapter) and a collection of dimensions form a cube. Each measure group is composed of a set of *measures*. Cubes can have more than three dimensions; they are mathematical constructs and not necessarily the three-dimensional objects their name suggests. You learn more about cubes later in this chapter and throughout the book.

❑ **Dimensions:** Dimensions are the categories by which you slice your data to view specific quantities of interest. Each dimension contains one or more *hierarchies*. Two types of hierarchies exist: attribute hierarchies and user hierarchies. In this book, attribute hierarchies are referred to as attributes, and user or multilevel hierarchies are referred to as hierarchies. Attributes correspond to columns in a dimension table, and hierarchies are formed by grouping several related attributes. For example, most cubes have a Time dimension. A Time dimension typically contains the attributes Year, Month, Date, and Day and a hierarchy for Year-Month-Date. Sales cubes often contain Geography dimensions, Customer dimensions, and Product dimensions. You learn about dimensions in Chapter 5.

❑ **Mining Structures:** Data mining (covered in Chapter 16) is the process of analyzing raw data using algorithms that help discover interesting patterns not typically found by ad-hoc analysis. Mining Structures are objects that hold information about a data set. A collection of mining models form a mining structure. Each mining model is built using a specific data mining algorithm and can be used for analyzing patterns in existing data or predicting new data values. Knowing these patterns can help companies make their business processes more powerful. For example, the book recommendation feature on Amazon.com relies on data mining.

❑ **Roles:** Roles are objects in a database that are used to control access permissions to the database objects (read, write, read/write, process). If you want to provide only read access to a set of users you could create a single role that has read access and add all the users in that set to this role. There can be multiple roles within a database. If a user is a member of several roles, the user inherits the permissions of those roles. If there is a conflict in permissions, Analysis Services grants the most liberal access to the user. You learn more about roles in Chapters 7 and 22.

❑ **Assemblies:** Assemblies are user-defined functions that can be created using a .NET language such as Visual Basic.NET, Visual C# .NET, or through languages such as Microsoft Visual Basic or Microsoft C++ that can produce Component Object Model (COM) binaries. These are typically used for custom operations that are needed for specific business logic and are executed on the server for efficiency and performance. Assemblies can be added at the server instance level or within a specific database. The scope of an assembly is limited to the object to which the assembly has been added. For example, if an assembly is added to the server, that assembly can be accessed within every database on the server. On the other hand, if an assembly has been added within a specific database, it can only be accessed within the context of that database. In BIDS you can only add .NET assembly references. You learn more about assemblies in Chapter 11.

❑ **Miscellaneous:** This object is used for adding any miscellaneous objects (design or meeting notes, queries, temporary deleted objects, and so on) that are relevant to the database project. These objects are stored in the project and are not sent to the Analysis Services instance.

The Properties Pane

If you click an object in the Solution Explorer, the properties for that object appear in the Properties pane. Items that cannot be edited are grayed out. If you click a particular property, the description of that property appears in the Description pane at the bottom of the Properties pane.

The Output Pane

The Output pane (seen later in this chapter) is used to report warnings and errors during builds. When a project is deployed to the server, progress reporting and error messages are displayed in this pane.

Creating an Analysis Services Database Using Business Intelligence Development Studio

You are now ready to create a cube. The cube you create in this chapter is based on the relational database Adventure Works DW 2008 that is available at http://www.codeplex.com as part of Microsoft SQL Server 2008 sample databases. Many versions of Adventure Works are available on CodePlex. Download and install the SQL Server 2008 Adventure Works DW 2008 sample database for your machine's architecture. For example, if you have an x64 machine, the sample database to install is SQL2008.AdventureWorks_DW_BI_v2008.x64.msi.

Adventure Works DW 2008 contains the sales information of a fictional bicycle company. Figure 2-13 shows the structure of the data warehouse you will build in this chapter, which consists of two fact tables and eight dimension tables. FactInternetSales and FactResellerSales are fact tables. They each contain several measures and foreign keys related to their dimension tables. Both fact tables contain three dimension keys, ShipDateKey, OrderDateKey, and DueDateKey, which are joined to the dimension table DimDate. The FactInternetSales and the FactResellerSales fact tables join to the other appropriate dimension tables by a single key as shown in Figure 2-13. The ParentEmployeeKey in the Employee table is joined with EmployeeKey in the same table, which is modeled as a parent-child hierarchy. You learn about parent-child hierarchies in Chapter 5.

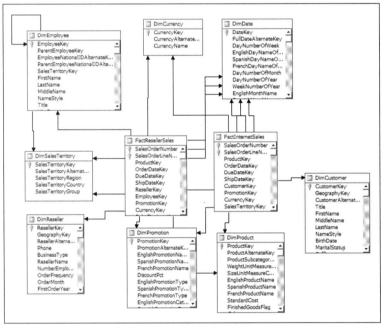

Figure 2-13

Creating a Data Source

Cubes and dimensions of an Analysis Services database must retrieve their data values from tables in a relational data store. This data store, typically part of a data warehouse, must be defined as a data source. An OLE DB data provider or .NET data provider is used to retrieve the data from the data source. OLE DB and .NET data providers are industry standard technologies for retrieving data from relational databases. If your relational database provider does not provide a specific OLE DB data provider or a .NET data provider, you can use the generic Microsoft OLE DB provider to retrieve data. In this chapter you will be using a SQL Server database and hence you can use the Native OLE DB provider for SQL Server also called as the SQL Server Native Client. If you need to use the .NET data provider, you would select SqlClient Data provider.

To create a data source, follow these steps:

1. Select the Data Sources folder in the Solution Explorer.

2. Right-click the Data Sources folder and click New Data Source, as shown in Figure 2-14.

Figure 2-14

This launches the Data Source Wizard. This wizard is self-explanatory and you can easily create a data source by making the appropriate selection on each page of the wizard. The first page of the wizard is the welcome page that provides additional information about a data source. Click Next to continue.

3. You're now in the connection definition page of the Data Source Wizard, as shown in Figure 2-15. In this page, you will provide the connection information about the relational data source that contains the "Adventure Works DW 2008" database. Click the New button under Data Connection Properties to specify the connection details. The Connection Manager dialog box launches.

Figure 2-15

4. On the page shown in Figure 2-16, specify the connection properties of the SQL Server containing the Adventure Works DW 2008 database. The provider used to connect to any relational database by default is the Native OLE DB\SQL Native Client 10.0 provider. If that provider is not selected, click the Provider drop-down and select SQL Server Native Client 10.0. If you have installed the SQL Server 2008 database engine and the Adventure Works DW 2008 sample database on the same machine, type **localhost** or the machine name in the Server name field as shown in Figure 2-16. If you have restored the sample Adventure Works DW 2008 database on a different SQL Server machine, type that machine name instead. You can choose either Windows Authentication or SQL Server Authentication for connecting to the relational data source. Select Use Windows Authentication. If you choose SQL Server Authentication, you need to specify a SQL Server login name and password. Make sure you check the Save My Password option. Due to security restrictions in Analysis Services 2008, if you do not select this option you will be prompted to key in the password each time you send the definitions of your database to the Analysis Services instance. From the drop-down list box under Select or Enter a Database Name, select AdventureWorksDW2008. You have now provided all the details needed for establishing a connection to the relational data in Adventure Works DW 2008. Click OK.

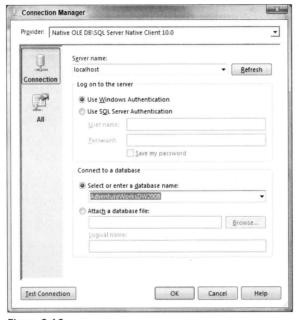

Figure 2-16

5. The connection properties you provided in the connection dialog are now shown in the "Select how to define the connection" page of the Data Source Wizard, as shown in Figure 2-17. Click the Next button.

Figure 2-17

6. In the Impersonation Information page you need to specify the impersonation details that Analysis Services will use to connect to the relational data source. There are four options as shown in Figure 2-18. You can provide a domain username and password to impersonate or select the Analysis Service instance's service account for connection. The option Use the credentials of the current user is primarily used for data mining where you retrieve data from the relational server for prediction. If you use the Inherit option, Analysis Services uses the impersonation information specified for the database. Select the Use the service account option and click Next.

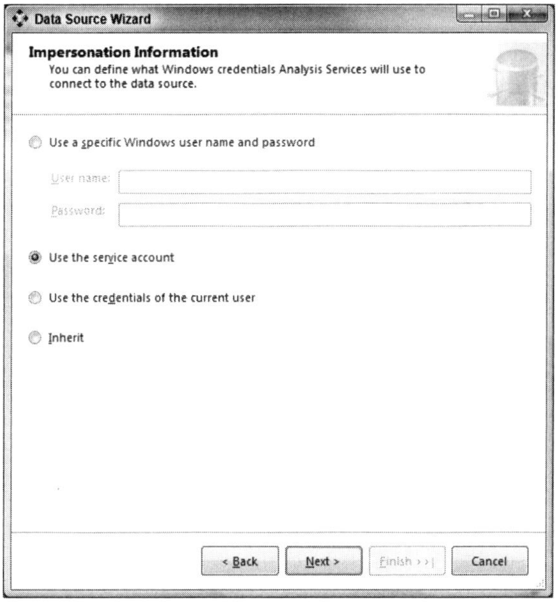

Figure 2-18

7. On the final page, the Data Source Wizard chooses the relational database name you have selected as the name for the data source object you are creating. You can choose the default name specified or specify a new name here. Specify the name Adventure Works DW as shown in Figure 2-19. The connection string to be used for connecting to the relational data source is shown under Preview. Click Finish.

Figure 2-19

Super! You have successfully created a data source.

Creating a Data Source View (DSV)

The Adventure Works DW database contains 25 tables. The cube you build in this chapter uses 10 tables. Data Source Views give you a logical view of the tables that will be used within your OLAP database. A Data Source View can contain tables and views from one or more data sources. Although you could accomplish the same functionality by creating views in the relational server, Data Source Views provide additional functionality, flexibility, and manageability, especially when you do not have privileges to create views on the relational backend.

To create a Data Source View, follow these steps:

1. Select the Data Source Views folder in the Solution Explorer.

2. Right-click Data Source Views and select New Data Source View, as shown in Figure 2-20.

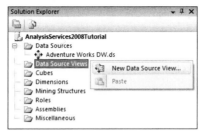

Figure 2-20

This launches the Data Source View Wizard. Similar to the Data Source wizard, this wizard allows you to create a Data Source View just by choosing an appropriate selection on each page of the wizard. Click the Next button to go to the next page of the wizard.

3. The second page of the DSV Wizard (see Figure 2-21) shows the list of data source objects from which you might want to create a view. The New Data Source button allows you to launch the Data Source Wizard so that you can create new data source objects from the wizard. You have already created a data source for the Adventure Works DW 2008 database that you will use for this example. Select this data source and click Next.

Figure 2-21

4. When you click the Next button, the DSV Wizard connects to the Adventure Works DW 2008 relational database using the connection string contained in the data source object. The wizard then retrieves all the tables, views, and relationships from the relational database and shows them in the third page. You can now select the tables and views that are needed for the Analysis

Services database you are creating. For this tutorial, navigate through the Available Objects list and select the FactInternetSales and FactResellerSales tables. Click the > button so that the tables move to the Included Objects list. Select the two tables in the Included objects list. When you select these tables you will notice that the Add Related Tables button is enabled. This button allows you to add all the tables and views that have relationships with the selected tables in the Included objects list. Click the Add Related Tables button. You will notice that all the related dimension tables mentioned earlier as well as the FactInternetSalesReason table are added to the Included objects list. In this tutorial you will not be using the FactInternetSalesReason table, so you should remove this table. Select the FactInternetSalesReason table in the Included Objects list and click the < button to remove it from the Included Objects. You have now selected all the tables needed to build the cube in this tutorial. Your Included Objects list of tables should match what's shown in Figure 2-22.

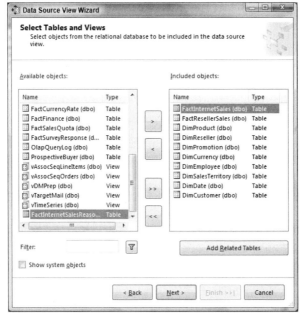

Figure 2-22

5. Click the Next button and you are at the final page of the DSV Wizard! Similar to the final page of the Data Source Wizard, you can specify your own name for the DSV object or use the default name. Specify the "Adventure Works DW" for the DSV Name in the wizard and click Finish.

You have now successfully created the DSV that will be used in this chapter. The DSV object is shown in the Solution Explorer and a new designer page is created in the main area of the BIDS as shown in Figure 2-23. This is the Data Source View editor. The Data Source View editor contains three main areas: Diagram Organizer, the Tables view, and the Diagram view. The Diagram view shows a graphical representation of the tables and their relationships. Each table is shown with its columns with an indication of the key attribute. The connecting lines show the relationships between tables. If you double-click a connecting line you will find the columns of each table that are used to form the join that defines the relationship. You can make changes to the Data Source View by adding, deleting, or modifying tables and views in the DSV Designer. In addition, you can establish new relationships between tables. You learn more about the DSV Designer in Chapter 4.

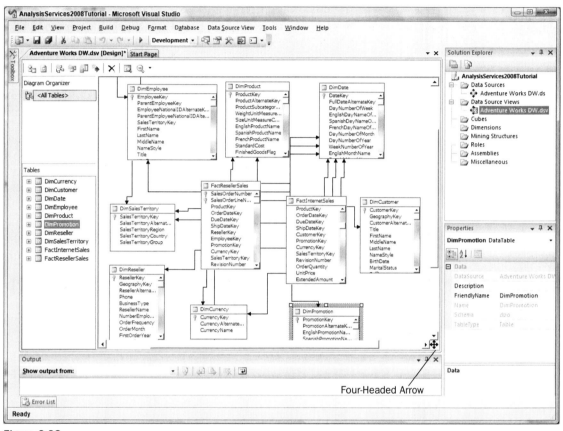

Figure 2-23

The number of tables you can see in the Diagram view depends on the resolution on your machine. In this view, you can zoom in to see a specific table enlarged or zoom out to see all the tables within the Diagram view. To use the zoom feature, you can right-click anywhere within the Diagram view, select Zoom, and set the zoom percentage you want. Alternatively, you can select View ⇨ Zoom and then select the zoom percentage. Select a zoom percentage of 150%. Figure 2-24 shows a zoomed-in Diagram view so that you can see the FactResellerSales table clearly.

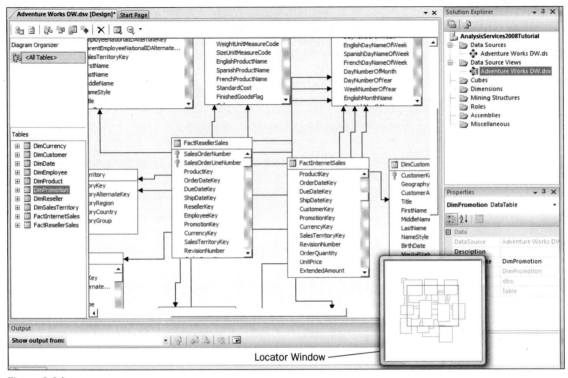

Figure 2-24

The Diagram view in the DSV arranges the tables to best fit within the view. Sometimes the number of tables in the DSV can be quite large. In such circumstances, navigating to the tables in the Diagram view can be difficult. For easier navigation you can use the Locator window (see Figure 2-24). The Locator window shows the full DSV diagram as a thumbnail. You can open it by performing a left mouse click on the 4-headed arrow in the lower-right corner of the diagram, as highlighted in Figure 2-23. The Locator window remains open while the mouse button is held down. This allows you to navigate through the visible area in the Diagram view by moving the mouse.

You have now learned the basic operations used within a Data Source View. Next, you move on to creating a cube using the Cube Wizard.

Creating a Cube Using the Cube Wizard

In Analysis Services 2008 you can build cubes via three approaches — top-down, bottom-up, or an empty cube. The traditional way of building cubes is bottom-up from existing relational databases. In the bottom-up approach, you need a Data Source View from which a cube can be built. Cubes within a project can be built from a single DSV or from multiple DSVs. In the top-down approach, you create the cube and then generate the relational schema based on the cube design. In Analysis Services 2008 you also have the option to first create an empty cube and then add objects to it.

A cube in Analysis Services 2008 consists of one or more measure groups from a fact table (typically you will have one measure group per fact table) and one or more dimensions (such as Product and Time) from the dimension tables. Measure groups consist of one or more measures (for example, sales, cost, count of objects sold). When you build a cube, you need to specify the fact and dimension tables you want to use. Each cube must contain at least one fact table, which determines the contents of the cube. The facts stored in the fact table are mapped as measures in a cube. Typically, measures from the same fact table are grouped together to form an object called a measure group. If a cube is built from multiple fact tables, the cube typically contains multiple measure groups. Before building the cube, the dimensions need to be created from the dimension tables. The Cube Wizard packages all the steps involved in creating a cube into a simple sequential process:

1. Launch the Cube Wizard by right-clicking the Cube folder in the Solution Explorer and selecting New Cube.

2. Click the Next button in the welcome page.

3. You are now asked to select the method to create the cube. Choose the default value (Use existing tables) and click Next (see Figure 2-25).

Figure 2-25

4. In the Select Measure Group Tables page, select the Data Source View Adventure Works DW2008 as shown in Figure 2-26.

Figure 2-26

5.   The Suggest button helps you identify the measure group tables. If you click the Suggest button, the Cube Wizard will analyze the relationships between the tables in the Data Source View and select the potential measure group tables. For this example, select Fact Internet Sales and Fact Reseller Sales as measure groups as shown in Figure 2-27 and click Next.

Figure 2-27

6. The Select Measures page allows you to select specific columns from the measure group tables as measures as shown in Figure 2-28. By default all the columns in the selected measure group tables except the key column are shown as measures and selected. Choose the default selection shown by the wizard and click Next.

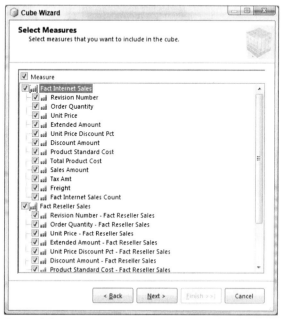

Figure 2-28

7. In the Select New Dimensions page, the Cube Wizard shows you the potential dimensions along with their attributes. The Cube Wizard by default will include the key attribute in each dimension, which is highlighted in this page as shown in Figure 2-29. Deselect the Fact Internet Sales and Fact Reseller Sales dimensions as shown in Figure 2-29 and click Next.

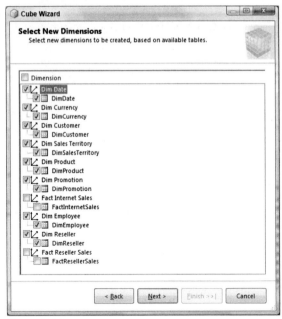

Figure 2-29

8. In the Final page of the Cube Wizard, provide the cube name Adventure Works DW as shown in Figure 2-30 and click Finish.

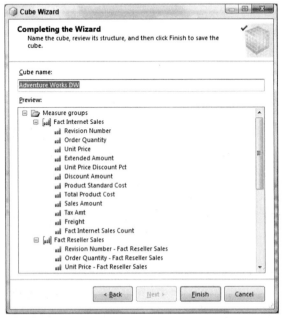

Figure 2-30

9. After the wizard completes you will notice that the Adventure Works DW cube and Dim Date, Dim Currency, Dim Customer, Dim Sales Territory, Dim Product, Dim Promotion, Dim Employee, and Dim Reseller dimensions are created in the Solution Explorer as shown in Figure 2-31.

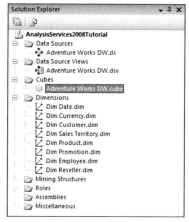

Figure 2-31

The Adventure Works DW cube is automatically opened in the Cube Editor, as shown in Figure 2-32.

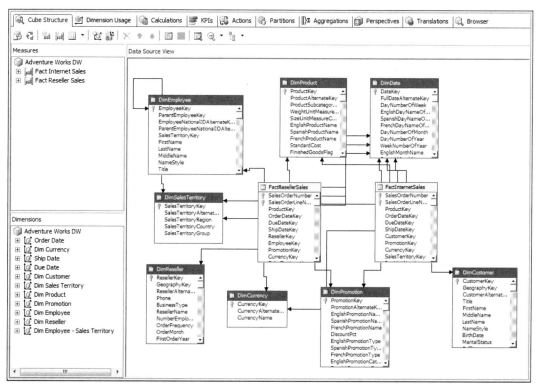

Figure 2-32

The Cube Editor has several panes that allow you to perform various operations on a cube object. The default pane upon completion of the Cube Wizard is the Cube Structure pane. Other panes of the Cube Editor are Dimension Usage, Calculation, KPIs, Actions, Partitions, Aggregations, Perspectives, Translations, and Browser. In this chapter you will become familiar with basic operations in the Cube Structure and the Browser panes. You learn more about the Cube Editor in Chapters 6 and 9.

The Cube Structure pane is divided into three windows: Measures, Dimensions, and the Data Source View. If you need to add or modify measure groups or measures you will do that in the Measures window. The Dimensions window is used to add or modify the dimensions relevant to the current cube. The Data Source View shows all the fact and dimension tables used in the cube with appropriate colors (yellow for fact tables and blue for dimension tables). Actions such as zoom in, zoom out, navigation, finding tables, and different diagram layouts of the tables are available in the DSV of the Cube Editor.

If you right-click within the Measures, Dimensions, or Data Source View windows you will be able to see the various actions that can be accomplished within each window. The actions within the Measures, Dimensions, or DSV windows of a Cube Editor can also be accomplished by clicking the appropriate buttons (see Figure 2-32) in the Cube Editor toolbar.

You have now successfully created a cube using Business Intelligence Development Studio. The Cube Wizard has only added the most essential attributes to the dimensions created. This is a change from Analysis Services 2005 to make sure the cube designer includes only the necessary attributes. The default dimensions created by the Cube Wizard need to be refined further in order to analyze the data in the cube. Because this is the first cube you are creating and we wanted to have very simple instructions, the following steps include most of the attributes from the dimensions. In reality when you create a cube based on your needs, you would usually include only the dimension attributes that are required. Continue with the following steps to refine the dimensions created by the Cube Wizard so that you can perform a simple analysis.

10. Double-click the Dim Date dimension (Dim Date.dim object) in the Solution Explorer.

11. You will now be in the Dimension Editor with the Dim Date dimension loaded. The Dimension Editor contains three panes: Attributes, Hierarchies, and Data Source View as shown in Figure 2-33. Select all the columns in the DimDate table in the Data Source View except the key column Date Key.

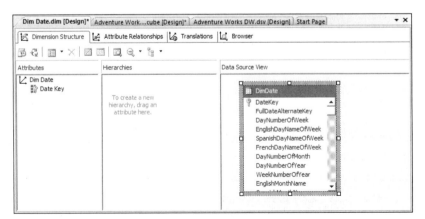

Figure 2-33

12. Drag and drop the selected columns to the Attributes pane. This action creates an attribute hierarchy for each of the columns in the DimDate table.

13. Rename the key attribute from Date Key to Dim Date.

14. Drag and drop Fiscal Quarter from the Attributes pane to the Hierarchies pane. This creates a new hierarchy called Hierarchy.

15. Drag and drop Month Number of Year onto the Hierarchies pane below the Fiscal Quarter. This creates a second level in the Hierarchy hierarchy.

16. Drag and drop the key attribute Dim Date onto the Hierarchies pane below the Month Number of Year.

17. Right-click the Hierarchy hierarchy and select Rename. Rename the hierarchy to Fiscal Quarter – Month Number Of Year. The Dimension Editor with the Dim Date dimension should appear as shown in Figure 2-34.

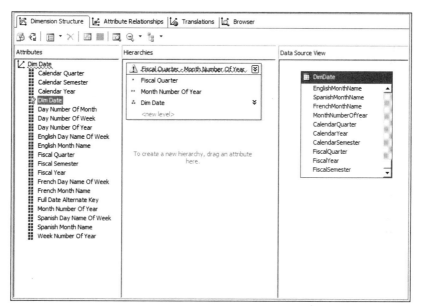

Figure 2-34

18. Double-click the Dim Currency dimension (Dim Currency.dim object) in the Solution Explorer.

19. Drag and drop Currency Alternate Key to the Attributes pane.

20. Rename the key attribute from Currency Key to Dim Currency.

21. Double-click the Dim Customer dimension (Dim Customer.dim object) in the Solution Explorer.

22. Rename the key attribute from Customer Key to Dim Customer.

23. Drag and drop all the columns except Customer Key from the DimCustomer table in the Data Source View pane to the Attributes pane.

24. Double-click the DimSalesTerritory dimension (Dim Sales Territory.dim object) in the Solution Explorer.

25. Drag and drop all the columns from the DimSalesTerritory table in the Data Source View pane except the key attribute SalesTerritoryKey to the Attributes pane.

26. Rename the key attribute from Sales Territory Key to Dim Sales Territory.

27. Double-click the Dim Product dimension (Dim Product.dim object) in the Solution Explorer.

28. Rename the key attribute from Product Key to Dim Product.

29. Drag and drop all the columns of the DimProduct table except ProductKey and LargePhoto from the Data Source View pane to the Attributes pane.

30. Double-click the Dim Promotion dimension (Dim Promotion.dim object) in the Solution Explorer.

31. Rename the key attribute from Promotion Key to Dim Promotion.

32. Drag and drop all the columns of the DimPromotion table except PromotionKey from the Data Source View pane to the Attributes pane.

33. Drag and drop English Promotion Category from the Attributes pane to the Hierarchies pane. This creates a new Hierarchy.

34. Drag and drop the attribute Discount Pct from the Attributes pane to the Hierarchies pane below English Promotion Category. This creates a new level in the Hierarchy hierarchy.

35. Drag and drop the key attribute Dim Promotion from the Attributes pane to the Hierarchies pane below the Discount Pct level.

36. Rename the hierarchy to English Promotion Category – Discount Pct. The Dimension Editor with the Dim Promotion dimension should look like Figure 2-35.

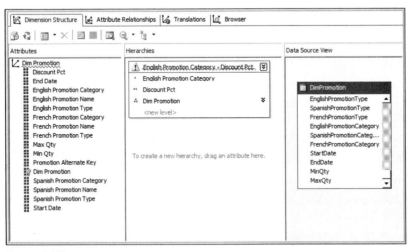

Figure 2-35

37. Double-click the Dim Reseller dimension (Dim Reseller.dim) in the Solution Explorer.

38. Rename the key attribute from Reseller Key to Dim Reseller.

39. Drag and drop all the columns of the DimReseller table except ResellerKey from the Data Source View pane to the Attributes pane.

40. Drag and drop the Annual Revenue attribute from the Attributes pane to the Hierarchies pane. A new hierarchy with the name Hierarchy is created.

41. Drag and drop Number Employees from the Attributes pane to the Hierarchies pane under Annual Revenue. This creates a new level called Number Employees.

42. Drag and drop the Dim Reseller attribute from the Attributes pane to the Hierarchies pane under Number Employees.

43. Rename the hierarchy Hierarchy to Annual Revenue – Number of Employees. Your Dim Reseller Dimension Editor should look like Figure 2-36.

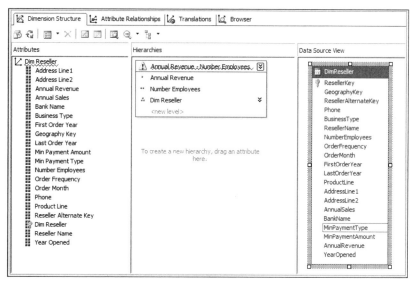

Figure 2-36

44. Double-click the Dim Employee dimension (Dim Employee.dim) in the Solution Explorer. This opens up the Dimension Editor with the Employee dimension loaded.

45. Notice that this dimension has three attributes created by the Cube Wizard compared to the single attribute created for all the other dimensions you opened. This is due to the fact that the Cube Wizard detected a parent-child relationship within the Dim Employee dimension. You learn more about parent-child dimensions in Chapter 5.

46. Drag and drop all the columns in the DimEmployee table except the three attributes that have already been created by the Cube Wizard from the Data Source View pane to the Attributes pane.

47. Rename the key attribute from Employee Key to Dim Employee.

48. Drag and drop Department Name from the Attribute pane to the Hierarchies pane. This creates a new hierarchy called Hierarchy with a single level.

49. Drag and drop the Title attribute from the Attributes pane to the Hierarchies pane below Department Name.

50. Drag and drop the Dim Employee attribute from the Attributes pane to the Hierarchies pane below Title.

51. Rename the hierarchy to Department Name – Title.

You have successfully created a cube using Business Intelligence Development Studio and refined the dimensions in order to do simple analysis. You might have noticed warning symbols in the Dimension Editor for the dimensions where you created hierarchies. You learn more about these warnings, the creation of dimensions, attributes, hierarchies, and attribute relationships in Chapters 5 and 9. All you have done, though, is create the structure of the cube. There has not been any interaction with the Analysis Services instance at this point. This method of creating the cube structure without any interaction with the Analysis Services instance is referred to as project mode. Using BIDS you can also create these objects directly on the Analysis Services instance. That method of creating objects on the Server is called online mode, which is discussed in Chapter 7. Now you need to send the schema definitions of the newly created cube to the Analysis Services instance. This process is called *deployment*.

Deploying and Browsing a Cube

To deploy the database to the Analysis Server, right-click the project name and select Deploy, as shown in Figure 2-37. You can also deploy the project to the server from the main menu in BIDS by selecting Debug ⇨ Start or just by pressing the F5 function key on your keyboard.

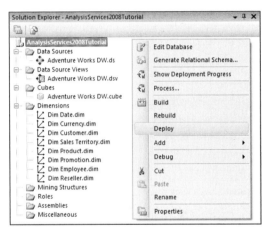

Figure 2-37

When you deploy an Analysis Service project, BIDS first builds the project you have created and checks for preliminary warnings and errors such as invalid definitions. If there are no errors with respect to project definitions, BIDS packages all the objects and definitions you have created in the project and sends them to the Analysis Services instance. By default these definitions are sent to the Analysis Services instance on the same machine (localhost). A database with the name of the project is created and all the objects defined in the project are created within this database. When deploying, BIDS not only sends all the schema definitions of the objects you have created, but also sends a command to process the database.

If you want to deploy your project to a different machine that is running Analysis Services 2008, you need to right-click the project and select Properties. This brings up the Properties Pages dialog in which you can specify the Analysis Services instance to deploy the project to. This page is shown in Figure 2-38. Change the Server property to the appropriate machine and follow the steps to deploy the project.

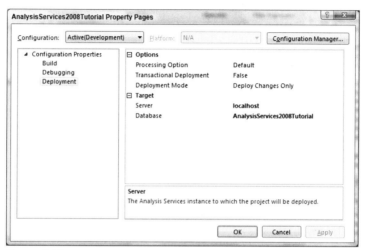

Figure 2-38

After you deploy the project you will see a Deployment Progress window at the location of the Properties window. The Output pane in BIDS shows the operations that occur after selecting Deploy — building the project, deploying the definitions, and the process command that is sent to the server. BIDS retrieves the objects being processed by the Analysis Services instance and shows the details (the object being processed; the relational query sent to the relational database to process that object including the start and end time; and errors, if any) in the Deployment Progress window. Once the deployment is completed, appropriate status will be shown in the Deployment Progress window as well as in the Output pane. If there were errors reported from the server these will be presented to you in the Output pane. You can use the Deployment Progress window to identify which object caused the error. BIDS waits for results from the server. If the deployment succeeded (successful deployment of schema and processing of all the objects), that information is shown as "Deploy: 1 succeeded, 0 failed, 0 skipped". You will also notice the message "Deployment Completed Successfully" in the Deployment Progress window. If there are any errors reported from Analysis Services, deployment will fail and you will be prompted with a dialog box. The errors returned from the service will be shown in the Output pane. In your current project, deployment will succeed as shown in Figure 2-39 and you will be able to browse the cube.

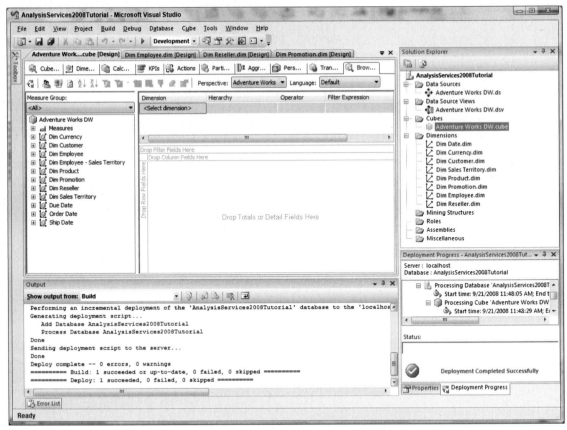

Figure 2-39

To browser your successfully deployed cube, use the following steps:

1. Double-click the Adventure Works DW cube to open the Cube Editor.

2. Switch to the Browser pane. The Browser pane has three main windows, as shown in Figure 2-40. The left window shows the available measures and dimensions. This is called the Measure Group window. You can expand the tree nodes to see the measure groups, measures, dimensions, and hierarchies. On the right side, you have two windows split horizontally. The top pane is referred to as the Filter window because you can specify filter conditions to use while browsing the cube. The bottom pane hosts the Office Web Components (OWC) pivot table control, which is used for analyzing results. You can drag and drop measures and dimensions from the Measure Group pane to the OWC to analyze data.

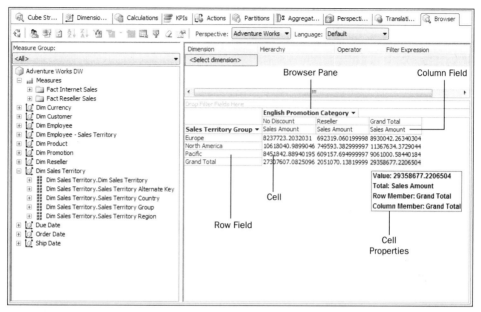

Figure 2-40

Drag and drop the "English Promotion Category" hierarchy of the "Dim Promotion" dimension and the "Sales Territory Group" hierarchy of the "Dim Sales Territory" dimension on to the Column and Row fields, respectively, of the OWC as shown in Figure 2-40.

3. Drag and drop the Sales Amount measure from the Fact Internet Sales measure group to the Data area. You can similarly drag and drop multiple measures within the data area. You will now see the measure values that correspond to the intersection of the different values of the two hierarchies English Promotion Category and Sales Territory Group. As shown in Figure 2-40 you will notice "Grand Total" generated for each dimension along the Row and Column axes. The Grand Total values are retrieved by OWC by sending appropriate MDX queries to the server. Each measure value corresponding to the intersection of the dimension values is referred to as a cell. If you hover over each cell you will see a window that shows the properties of that cell. In Figure 2-40 you can see the basic cell properties for the cell at the intersection of English Promotion Category = Reseller and Sales Territory Group = North America shown in a tooltip.

Using SQL Server Management Studio

SQL Server Management Studio (SSMS) is ground zero for administering the Analysis Services servers resident on your network. Not only that, you can also administer instances of SQL Server, Reporting Services, Integration Services, and SQL Server Compact Edition from within SSMS. In this book you learn how to administer and manage Analysis Servers. This chapter specifically discusses the Analysis Services objects shown in the Object Explorer. Administering Analysis Services is discussed in more detail in Chapters 7 and 13.

The first step in the process of working with objects in the Object Explorer is connecting to the servers you wish to manage. In fact, as soon as you start Management Studio, you get a dialog prompting you to connect to one of the server types as shown in Figure 2-41. Create a connection to the Analysis Services through your login.

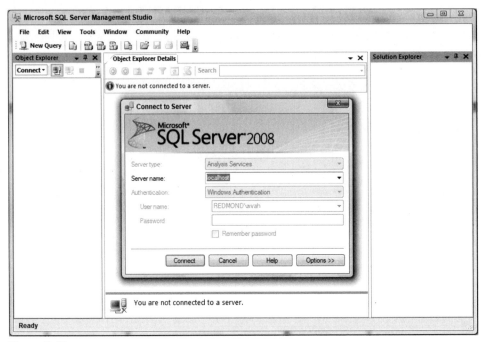

Figure 2-41

SSMS provides you with a way to register your servers so that you do not have to specify the login credentials each time you need to connect. Click the View menu and select Registered Servers. You will see a window called Registered Servers in SSMS as shown in Figure 2-42. In the Registered Servers pane, click the toolbar icon second from left; this enables you to register an Analysis Services instance. Now, right-click the Local Server Groups folder and select New Server Registration. In the resulting New Server Registration dialog (see Figure 2-43) you need to specify the name of the Analysis Services instances you wish to connect to and optionally specify connection parameters such as time out and enabling encryption. If the server instance you wish to connect to is a named instance, enter its name in the Server name field, otherwise, type in **localhost**, which means you want to register the default instance of Analysis Services on your machine. Once you have filled in the Server name field, you can test the connection by clicking the Test button at the bottom of the dialog. If the connection does not succeed, you need to make sure Analysis Services is running and that your authentication scheme is correct. Once the connection is working, click Save.

Figure 2-42

Figure 2-43

The Object Explorer Pane

When you connect to an Analysis Services instance, you see it in the Object Explorer pane (see Figure 2-44). This section reviews the various objects in Analysis Services. Open the Databases folder to see the AnalysisServices2008Tutorial database and expand each object type folder. You should be looking at a list of the seven major object types (Data Sources, Data Source Views, Cubes, Dimensions, Mining Structures, Roles, and Assemblies) as shown in Figure 2-44.

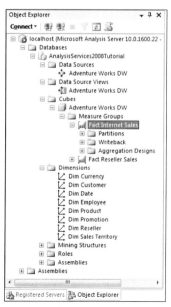

Figure 2-44

The following list describes each of the objects:

❏ **Databases:** Database objects are where your deployed Analysis Services projects are listed; note that these objects could have been created in On-line mode or Project mode.

❏ **Data Sources:** The Data Sources folder will, at minimum, contain a single object pointing to a data source like SQL Server 2008 if you have cubes or dimensions or mining models. Behind the scenes, these objects store connection information to a relational data source, which can be for a .NET provider or an OLE DB provider. In either case, you can establish a connection to a data source. In Figure 2-44, you can see the data source called "Adventure Works DW." Most databases will have multiple data sources.

❏ **Data Source Views:** A Data Source View object refers to a subset of the data identified by its parent data source object. The reason this object type exists is because, in the enterprise environment, a data source might contain thousands of tables, though here you're interested in working with only a small subset of those tables. Using a DSV object, you can restrict the number of tables shown in a given view. This makes working on even the largest database a manageable task. On the other hand, you might want to create a DSV to contain not only all tables in one database, but a portion of tables from a second database. Indeed, you can have a DSV that uses more than one data source for an optimal development environment.

❏ **Cubes:** You have already looked at the details of cubes in BIDS; they are the lingua franca of Business Intelligence. Well, cubes can also be viewed in the Object Explorer pane. Further, four sections under the Cubes object provide information about how the cube is physically stored and whether or not it will allow you to write data back to the cube:

   ❏ **Measure Groups:** Measure groups are comprised of one or more columns of a fact table which, in turn, are comprised of the data to be aggregated and analyzed. Measure groups combine multiple logical measures under a single entity.

   ❏ **Partitions:** Partitioning is a way of distributing data to achieve efficient management as well as improved query performance. You typically partition fact data if you have a large fact table. In this way you can make the queries run faster. This works because scanning partitions in parallel is faster than scanning serially. There is a maintenance benefit as well; when you do incremental updates (process only data changed since the last update) it is more efficient for the system to update only those partitions that have changed. A typical partitioning strategy adopted is partitioning the data based on a time dimension. A variation of the partitioning strategy is to also have different storage modes for some partitions. In this way, a single fact table might have only up to five years of the most recent data in a few MOLAP partitions and is therefore subject to queries, whereas the older, less often accessed data can lie fallow in a ROLAP partition. If you right-click the Partitions folder in the FactInternetSales measure group, you will see a number of administrative tasks associated with partitions that can be dealt with directly in SSMS.

   ❏ **Writeback:** Writeback provides the flexibility to perform a "what if" analysis of data or to perform a specific update to a measure such as budget when your budget for next year gets changed. The Writeback folder is empty in AnalysisServices2008Tutorial because it has not been enabled. By default writeback is not turned on. To see what options are available, right-click the Writeback object.

   ❏ **Aggregation Designs:** Aggregation designs help in pre-aggregating fact data for various dimension members and storing them on disk. Aggregation designs are created using the Aggregation Designer or Usage Based Optimization wizards. You learn about the benefits of aggregations and how to design them in Chapters 9, 14, and 15. Once aggregations are designed for a cube, you can see the aggregation designs of a partition in this folder. You can assign aggregation designs to a partition or edit existing aggregation designs using SSMS. Right-click the Aggregation Designs folder or specific aggregation designs to see the various options.

❑ **Dimensions:** Dimensions are what cubes are made of, and you can see what dimensions are available for use in a given project by looking at the contents of this folder. Note that you can browse, process, and delete dimensions from here with a right-click of the mouse.

❑ **Mining Structures:** Data mining requires a certain amount of infrastructure to make the algorithms work. Mining structures are objects that contain one or more mining models. The mining models themselves contain properties like column content type, your data mining algorithm of choice, and predictable columns. You create mining models based on a mining structure. You learn about data mining in Chapter 16.

❑ **Roles:** Roles are objects that define a database-specific set of permissions. These objects can be for individual users or groups of users. Three types of permissions can be set for a role: Administrator level or Full control, Process Database level, and Read Database Metadata level. Roles are discussed with the help of a scenario in Chapter 22.

❑ **Assemblies:** You learned earlier in this chapter that assemblies are actually stored procedures (created with .NET or COM-based programming languages) used on the server side for custom operations. The assembly support in Analysis Services 2005 is continued in Analysis Services 2008. If you are familiar with Analysis Services 2000 and UDFs (user-defined functions), note that assemblies can do anything UDFs can do and more. Also note that COM UDFs in Analysis Services 2000 are also supported in Analysis Services 2008 for backward compatibility. The scope of these assemblies is database-specific; that is, an assembly can only operate on the Analysis Services database for which it is run.

❑ **Server Assemblies:** If you want to operate on multiple databases in Analysis Services, you have to create this type of object, the server assembly. Server assemblies are virtually the same as assemblies, except their scope is increased; they work across databases in Analysis Services.

Querying Using the MDX Query Editor

Just to recap, MDX is a language that allows you to query multidimensional databases similar to the way SQL is used to query relational databases. MDX is used to extract information from Analysis Services cubes or dimensions. Whereas SQL returns results along two axes — rows and columns — MDX returns data along multiple axes. You learn about MDX in depth in Chapters 3 and 10. For now, let's look at a simple MDX query to learn how to execute it and view its results.

The syntax of a typical MDX query is as follows:

```
SELECT [<axis_specification>
    [, <axis_specification>...]]
  FROM [<cube_specification>]
  [WHERE [<slicer_specification>]]
```

The MDX SELECT clause is where you specify the data you need to retrieve across each axis. The FROM clause is used to specify the cube from which you retrieve the data. The optional WHERE clause is used to slice a small section of data from which you need results.

In Analysis Services 2000, an MDX Sample application was included that could be used to send queries to cubes and retrieve results. In Analysis Services 2005 and 2008, query editors are integrated right into SSMS for sending queries to SQL Server and Analysis Services instances. These query editors have

IntelliSense (dynamic function name completion) capabilities built in. When MDX queries are saved from SSMS they are saved with the extension .mdx. You can open the MDX query editor in SSMS by selecting File ⇨ New ⇨ Analysis Services MDX Query as shown in Figure 2-45 or by clicking the MDX query button as shown in Figure 2-46.

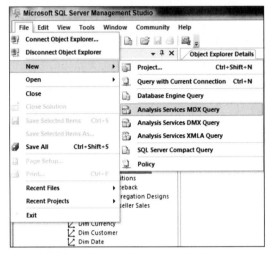

Figure 2-45

Figure 2-46

You will be prompted to connect to your Analysis Services instance. After you establish a connection, you can select the name of the database you wish to use from the Database Selection drop-down box shown in Figure 2-47. Select the AnalysisServices2008Tutorial database that you created in this chapter. In this database you created a single cube called Adventure Works DW, which is shown in the Cube drop-down box. The Query Editor is composed of two window panes, the Metadata pane on the left and the Query pane on the right. In the Query pane, you can make use of the IntelliSense feature by pressing Ctrl and Spacebar after typing in a few characters of an MDX keyword.

Now you can type the following query in the Query pane:

```
SELECT [Measures].members on COLUMNS
FROM [Adventure Works DW]
```

Database Selection drop-down   Cube Selection drop-down   MDX Query Construction pane

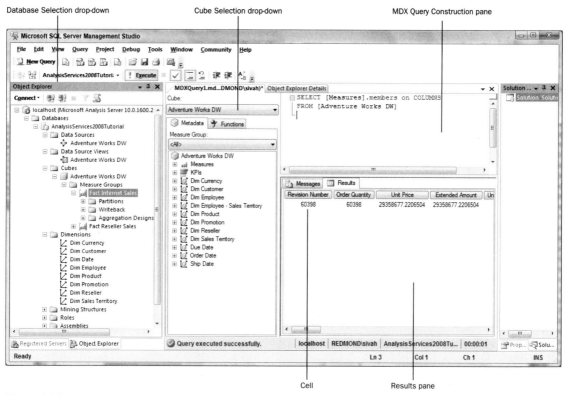

                                                                   Cell   Results pane

Figure 2-47

You can now execute the query by pressing the Ctrl+E key combination or clicking the Execute button. On execution, the query construction pane splits in two, and the results from the server are shown in the bottom half. All MDX queries cited in this book can be executed using this method. Congratulations, you just ran your first MDX query! You can see the results of the MDX query in the Results pane where you can see the members on axes and the corresponding cell values as shown in Figure 2-47.

Summary

In this chapter you were introduced to Analysis Services 2008 and learned how it overcomes the limitations of its predecessors, Analysis Services 2000 and Analysis Services 2005. In addition to trumping these limitations, Analysis Services 2008 provides a rich suite of tools for development and management of Analysis Services databases, which were first introduced as part of Analysis Services 2005.

You were also introduced to Business Intelligence Development Studio, which is core to designing Analysis Services cubes and dimensions. You successfully created a cube using the Cube Wizard. In the course of building that cube, you learned about data sources, Data Source Views, dimensions, and the wizards used to create these objects. You successfully deployed the cube to Analysis Services and then browsed it within Business Intelligence Development Studio.

In the second part of this chapter you learned about the integrated management environment of SQL Server 2008, SQL Server Management Studio, which is used to manage SQL Server and Analysis Services. You were familiarized with the various objects within an Analysis Services database by browsing them in the Object Explorer.

Finally, you learned that MDX does not require a Ph.D. in nuclear physics to use. The MDX Query Editor can be used easily to execute an MDX query, in this case, against the cube you built. Finally, you were able to view query results. In the next chapter you learn the basics of MDX, which will form the foundation of your deeper understanding of Analysis Services 2008.

3

Introduction to MDX

In Chapter 2 you ran a simple MDX query to retrieve data from Analysis Services 2008. Building on that, in this chapter you learn the fundamental concepts underlying MDX and how you can manipulate and query multidimensional objects within Analysis Services. This chapter forms the basis for many of the subsequent chapters in this book. In fact, in several places in this chapter and throughout the book you see how each interaction between the client tools and the Analysis Services instance results in the generation of MDX. You not only see the MDX that is generated, but you also glean some insight as to what the MDX does.

SQL Server 2008 provides a sample Analysis Services project that demonstrates the majority of the features provided by Analysis Services 2008. In this chapter you use the sample Analysis Services project available from www.codeplex.com to learn MDX. The illustrations are limited to three dimensions to help you understand the concepts. You can extend these concepts, if you want, to view data across additional dimensions. In this chapter you learn the basic concepts regarding cells, members, tuples, and sets. In addition, you learn how to create MDX expressions and MDX queries for data analysis.

What Is MDX?

Just as SQL (Structured Query Language) is a query language used to retrieve data from relational databases, MDX (Multi-Dimensional eXpressions) is a query language used to retrieve data from multidimensional databases. More specifically, MDX is used for querying multidimensional data from Analysis Services and supports two distinct modes. When used in an expression, MDX can define and manipulate multidimensional objects and data to calculate values. As a query language, it is used to retrieve data from Analysis Services databases. MDX was originally designed by Microsoft and introduced in SQL Server Analysis Services 7.0 in 1998.

MDX is not a proprietary language; it is a standards-based query language used to retrieve data from OLAP databases. MDX is part of the OLE DB for OLAP specification sponsored by Microsoft. Many other OLAP providers support MDX, including Microstrategy's Intelligence Server, Hyperion's Essbase Server, and SAS's Enterprise BI Server. There are those who wish to extend the standard for additional functionality, and MDX extensions have indeed been developed by individual vendors. MDX extensions provide functionality not specified by the standard, but the constituent parts of any extension are expected to be consistent with the MDX standard. Analysis Services 2008 does provide several extensions to the standard MDX defined by the OLE DB for OLAP specification. In this book you learn about the form of MDX supported by Analysis Services 2008.

When one refers to MDX they might be referring either to the MDX query language or to MDX expressions. Even though the MDX query language has similar syntax as that of SQL, it is significantly different. Nonetheless, we will use SQL to teach you some MDX. Before you get into the details of MDX query language and MDX expressions, you need to learn some fundamental concepts.

Fundamental Concepts

A multidimensional database is typically referred to as a cube. The cube is the foundation of a multidimensional database, and each cube typically contains more than two dimensions. The Adventure Works cube in the sample database contains 21 dimensions. The SQL Server 2008 product samples need to be downloaded from `http://www.codeplex.com/MSFTDBProdSamples`. Find and download the SQL2008.AdventureWorks_DW_BI_v2008<architecture>.msi and install it on your machine where the architecture is x86, x64, or ia64. This package contains the sample relational database AdventureWorksDW2008 and the Analysis Services project AdventureWorks. You need to specify the SQL Server 2008 relational database instance to install the sample. Using Business Intelligence Development Studio (BIDS), open the sample Adventure Works project from Program Files\Microsoft SQL Server\100\ Tools\Samples\AdventureWorks 2008 Analysis Services Project\Enterprise. Deploy the project to your Analysis Services instance. If your SQL Server 2008 relational server and/or Analysis Services instance are named instances, you need to make changes to the data source and the Analysis Services target server as mentioned in Chapter 2. If you open the Adventure Works cube in BIDS you can see the measures and dimensions that make up the cube in the Cube Structure tab as shown in Figure 3-1.

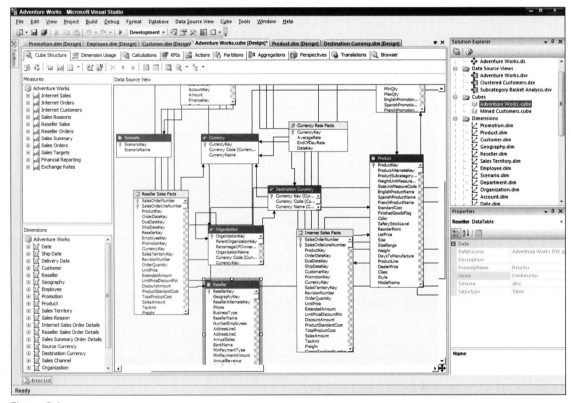

Figure 3-1

The *Measures* object within a cube is a special cube dimension that is a collection of measures. Measures are quantitative entities that are used for analysis. You can see the measures in the sample project in Figure 3-1. Each measure is part of an entity called a measure group. *Measure groups* are collections of related measures and each measure can only be part of a single measure group. Often you will want to have one measure group for each fact table in your data warehouse. Measure groups are primarily used for navigational purposes by design tools or client tools in order to have better readability or ease of use for end users. Measure groups are never used in MDX queries when querying measures. However, they can be used in certain MDX functions which, by the way, you see in this chapter and in Chapter 10. By default, Analysis Services generates a measure group for each fact table, so you don't have to worry about changing the measure group's design. If you want to, of course, you can.

In Figure 3-1 you can see the dimensions that are part of the Adventure Works cube. Each dimension has one or more hierarchies and each hierarchy contains one or more levels. You learn more about dimensions, hierarchies, and levels in Chapters 5 and 8. To demonstrate the fundamental concepts of MDX, we will use three of the dimensions: Product, Customer, and Date. We will use the hierarchies Calendar, Product Line, and Country from the dimensions Date, Product, and Customer, respectively, to illustrate fundamental concepts in MDX. Figure 3-2 shows a section of the Adventure Works cube using the three hierarchies: Calendar, Product Line, and Country. The Calendar hierarchy of the Date dimension contains five levels: Calendar Year, Calendar Semester, Calendar Quarter, Month, and Date. The Product Line and Country are attribute hierarchies and have two levels: the All level and the Product Line or Country level, respectively. For illustration purposes, Figure 3-2 does not contain all the members or levels of the Calendar, Product Line, and Country hierarchies and hence Figure 3-2 does not reflect the actual data in the sample cube.

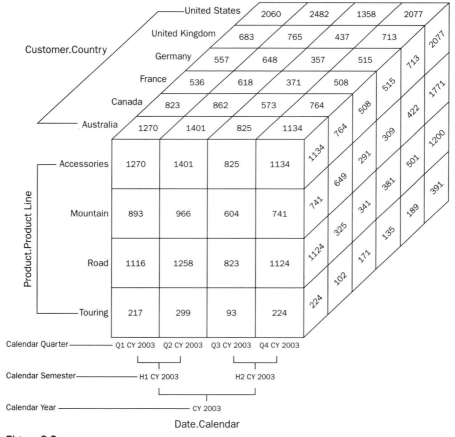

Figure 3-2

Members

Each hierarchy of a dimension contains one or more items that are referred to as *members*. Each member corresponds to one or more occurrences of that value in the underlying dimension table. Figure 3-3 shows the members of the Calendar hierarchy in the Date dimension. In the Calendar hierarchy, the items CY 2003, H1 CY 2003, H2 CY 2003, Q1 CY 2003, Q2 CY 2003, and Q3 CY 2003 and Q4 CY 2004 are the members. You can see that the items at each level together form the collection of the members of the hierarchy. You can also query the members of a specific level. For example, Q1 CY 2003, Q2 CY 2003, Q3 CY 2003, and Q3 CY 2004 are members of the Calendar Quarter level for the calendar year CY 2003.

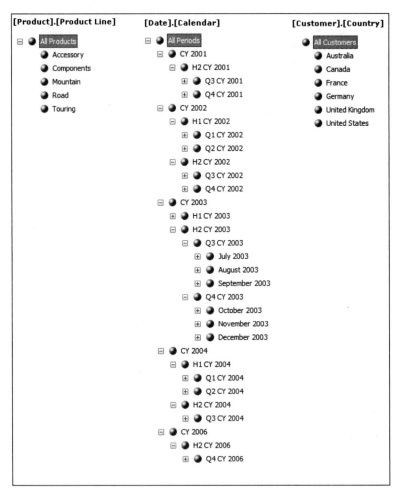

Figure 3-3

In MDX, each member of a hierarchy is represented by a unique name. The unique name is used to identify a specific member. The unique name for a member is dependent upon the dimension properties such as MemberUniqueNameStyle and HierarchyUniqueNameStyle. The algorithm determining the unique name of a member is not discussed in this book. You can access members of a dimension using the name path (using the name of the member) or the key path (using the key of the member). Using the default properties in BIDS to create your cubes and dimensions, you can access a member in a dimension with its dimension name, hierarchy name, and level name. For example, member Q1 CY 2004 in the Calendar hierarchy is represented as

```
[Date].[Calendar].[Calendar Quarter].[Q1 CY 2004]
```

The brackets are used to enclose the names of the dimension, hierarchy, levels, and members. It is not necessary that these names be enclosed within the square brackets every time, but whenever you have a name that contains a space, has a number in it, or is an MDX keyword, brackets must be used. In the preceding expression the dimension name Date is an MDX keyword and hence must be enclosed within brackets.

The following three representations are also valid for the member Q1 CY 2004:

```
[Date].[Calendar].[Q1 CY 2004]                              (1)
[Date].[Calendar].[CY 2004].[H1 CY 2004].[Q1 CY 2004]       (2)
[Date].[Calendar].[Calendar Quarter].&[2004]&[1]            (3)
```

In the first representation the member is represented in the format Dimension.Hierarchy.Member name. You can use this format as long as there are no two members with the same name. For example, if quarter 1 in each year is called Q1, you cannot use the preceding format; you would need to qualify using the level name in the MDX expression. If you do use the preceding format it will always retrieve Q1 for the first year in the hierarchy. In the second format, you can see the navigational path for the member clearly because you see all the members in the path. So far, the formats you have seen for accessing members all use the names of the members. The final format uses the key path where the keys of the members in a path are represented as &[membername]. When you use the key path, the members are always preceded with the ampersand (&) symbol.

Another example is the Australia member of the Country hierarchy in the Customer dimension, which would be specified as:

```
[Customer].[Country].Australia
```

Notice that there are no square brackets in the expression for the member Australia. This is because Australia is one word and no numbers are involved. In general, you can use the following format for accessing a member:

```
[DimensionName].[HierarchyName].[LevelName].[MemberName]
```

This format is predominantly used in this chapter as well as the rest of the book. If you are developing client tools we recommend you retrieve the unique name of the members directly from Analysis Services and use that in the MDX queries generated from the client tool instead of hard-coding the unique name in the client tool.

Cells

In Figure 3-2 you can see three faces of the cube. The front face has been divided into 16 small squares, and each square holds a number. Assume the number within each square is the measure "Internet Sales Amount" of the AdventureWorksDW cube. If you view the remaining visible faces of the cube you will realize that each square you analyzed in the front face of the cube is actually a small cube itself. The top-right-corner square of the front face contains the value 1134; you will notice that the same number is represented on the other sides as well. This smaller cube is referred to as a *cell*.

A cell is an entity from which you can retrieve data that is pertinent to an intersection of the dimension members. The number of cells within a cube depends on the number of hierarchies within each dimension and the number of members in each hierarchy. As you can imagine, cells hold the data values of all measures in a cube. If the data value for a measure within a cell is not available, the corresponding measure value is Null.

If you are familiar with three-dimensional coordinate geometry, you are aware of the three axes X, Y, and Z. Each point in the three-dimensional coordinate space is represented by an X, Y, and Z coordinate value. Similarly, each cell within a cube is represented by dimension members. In the illustration shown in Figure 3-4, you can see the three dimensions: Product, Customer, and Date. Assume that each of these dimensions has exactly one hierarchy as is shown in Figure 3-4, namely, Product Line, Country, and Calendar. From Figure 3-4 you can see that Product Line has four members, Calendar has four members (considering only quarters), and Country has six members. Therefore the number of cells is equal to 4*4*6 = 96 cells.

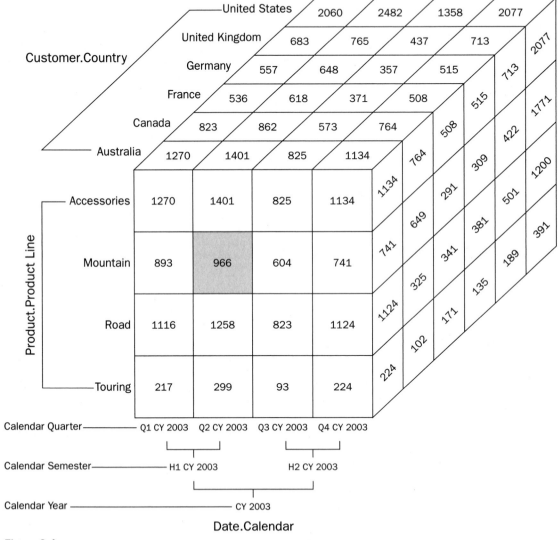

Figure 3-4

Now that you have learned what a cell is, you need to understand how to retrieve data from it. Assume you want to retrieve the data shown by the shaded area in the cube. The Sales amount value in this cell is 966. This cell is located at the intersection of Product=Mountain, Date=Quarter2, and Customer=Australia. To retrieve data from the cube you need to send an MDX query to Analysis Services. The query needs to retrieve the "Internet Sales Amount" from the Cube based on the conditions that uniquely identify the cell that contains the value 966. That MDX query is:

```
SELECT Measures.[Internet Sales Amount] ON COLUMNS
FROM [Adventure Works]
WHERE ( [Date].[Calendar].[Calendar Quarter].&[2003]&[2],
    [Product].[Product Line].[Mountain],
    [Customer].[Country].[Australia] )
```

You can see from this query that you are selecting the Measures.[Internet Sales Amount] value from the Adventure Works cube based on a specific condition mentioned in the WHERE clause of the MDX query. That condition uniquely identifies the cell. All you have done in the condition is list the members (which you learned about in the previous section) that uniquely identify the cell, separated by commas. An MDX expression like this that uniquely identifies a cell is called a tuple.

Tuples

As you saw in the previous section, a *tuple* uniquely identifies a cell or a section of a cube. A tuple is represented by one member from each dimension, separated by a comma, and is enclosed within parentheses. A tuple does not necessarily have to explicitly contain members from all the dimensions in the cube. Some examples of tuples based on the Adventure Works cube are:

1. ([Customer].[Country].[Australia])
2. ([Date].[Calendar].[2004].[H1 CY 2004].[Q1 CY 2004], [Customer].[Country].[Australia])
3. ([Date].[Calendar].[2004].[H1 CY 2004].[Q1 CY 2004], [Product].[Product Line].[Mountain], [Customer].[Country].[Australia])

In the preceding examples, tuples 1 and 2 do not contain members from all the dimensions in the cube. Therefore they represent sections of the cube. A section of the cube represented by a tuple is called a *slice* because you are slicing the cube to form a section (slice) based on certain dimension members.

When you refer to the tuple ([Customer].[Country].[Australia]) you actually refer to the sixteen cells that correspond to the country Australia in the example shown in Figure 3-4. Therefore when you retrieve the data held by the cells pointed to by this tuple you are actually retrieving the Internet Sales Amount of all the customers in Australia. The Internet Sales Amount value for the tuple [Customer].[Country].[Australia] is an aggregate of the cells encompassed in the front face of the cube. The MDX query to retrieve data represented by this tuple is:

```
SELECT Measures.[Internet Sales Amount] ON COLUMNS
FROM [Adventure Works]
WHERE ([Customer].[Country].[Australia])
```

The result of this query is $9,061,000.58.

The order of the members used to represent a tuple does not matter. What this means is that the following tuples:

1. ([Date].[Calendar].[2005].[H1 CY 2004].[Q1 CY 2004], [Product].[Product Line].[Mountain], [Customer].[Country].[Australia])

2. ([Product].[Product Line].[Mountain], [Customer].[Country].[Australia], ([Date].[Calendar].[2005].[H1 CY 2004].[Q1 CY 2004])

3. ([Customer].[Country].[Australia], [Date].[Calendar].[2005].[H1CY 2005].[Q1CY 2005], [Product].[Product Line].[Mountain])

are equivalent and uniquely identify just one cell. Because a tuple uniquely identifies a cell, it cannot contain more than one member from each dimension.

A tuple represented by a single member is called a *simple tuple* and does not have to be enclosed within parentheses. ([Customer].[Country].[Australia]) is a simple tuple and can be referred to as [Customer].[Country].[Australia] or simply Customer.Country.Australia. When there is more than one dimension in a tuple, it needs to be enclosed in parentheses. A collection of tuples forms a new object called a set. Sets are frequently used in MDX queries and expressions.

Sets

An MDX *set* is a collection of tuples that are defined using the exact same set of dimensions, both in type and number. In the context of Analysis Services 2008, a set of dimensions will actually be a set of hierarchies in your MDX expressions or queries. Hence we refer to hierarchies in this section and throughout the book. A set is specified within curly brace characters ({ and }). Set members are separated by commas. The following examples illustrate sets:

❑ **Example 1:** The tuples (Customer.Country.Australia) and (Customer.Country.Canada) are resolved to the exact same hierarchy Customer.Country. A collection of these two tuples is a valid set and is specified as:

```
{(Customer.Country.Australia), (Customer.Country.Canada)}
```

❑ **Example 2:** The tuples (Customer.Country.Australia, [Product].[Product Line].[Mountain]) and (Customer.Country.Canada, [Date].[Calendar].[2004].[H1 CY 2004].[Q1 CY 2004]) cannot be combined to form a set. Even though they are formed by two hierarchies, the dimensions used to resolve the tuple are different. Both tuples have the Customer.Country hierarchy dimension but the second hierarchies are different.

❑ **Example 3:** Each of the following tuples has the three dimensions Date, Product, and Customer:

```
1.   ([Date].[Calendar].[2004].[H1 CY 2004].[Q1 CY 2004], [Product].
         [Product Line].[Mountain], [Customer].[Country].[Australia]),
2.   ([Product].[Product Line].[Mountain], [Customer].[Country].[Australia],
         ([Date].[Calendar].[2002].[H1 CY 2002].[Q1 CY 2002])
3.   ([Customer].[Country].[Australia], [Date].[Calendar].[2003].
         [H1 CY 2003].[Q1 CY 2003], [Product].[Product Line].[Mountain] )
```

The members in the Date.Calendar hierarchy of the three preceding tuples are different and therefore these tuples refer to different cells. As per the definition of a set, a collection of these tuples is a valid set and is shown here:

```
{ ([Date].[Calendar].[2004].[H1 CY 2004].[Q1 CY 2004], [Product].[Product
Line].[Mountain], [Customer].[Country].[Australia]), ([Product].[Product
Line].[Mountain], [Customer].[Country].[Australia],
```

```
([Date].[Calendar].[2002].[H1 CY 2002].[Q1 CY
2002]),([Customer].[Country].[Australia], [Date].[Calendar].[2003].[H1 CY
2003].[Q1 CY 2003], [Product].[Product Line].[Mountain] )}
```

A set can contain zero, one, or more tuples. A set with zero tuples is referred to as an empty set. An empty set is represented as:

```
{   }
```

A set can contain duplicate tuples. An example of such a set is:

```
{Customer.Country.Australia, Customer.Country.Canada,
        Customer.Country.Australia}
```

This set contains two instances of the tuple Customer.Country.Australia. Because a member of a dimension by itself forms a tuple, it can be used as such in MDX queries. Similarly, if there is a tuple that is specified by only one hierarchy, you do not need the parentheses to specify it as a set. When there is a single tuple specified in a query you do not need curly braces to indicate it should be treated as a set. When the query is executed, the tuple is implicitly converted to a set.

Now that you have learned the key concepts that will help you understand MDX better, the following section dives right into MDX query syntax and the operators used in an MDX query or an MDX expression.

MDX Queries

Chapter 2 introduced you to the MDX SELECT statement. The syntax for an MDX query is as follows:

```
[WITH <formula_expression> [, <formula_expression> ...]]
SELECT [<axis_expression>, [<axis_expression>...]]
FROM [<cube_expression>]
[WHERE [slicer_expression]]
```

You might be wondering whether the SELECT, FROM, and WHERE clauses are the same as those in Structured Query Language (SQL). Even though they look identical to those in SQL, the MDX language is different and supports more complex operations. You learn about some of these operations in this chapter and throughout the book.

The keywords WITH, SELECT, FROM, and WHERE along with the expressions following them are referred to as a *clauses*. In the preceding MDX query template, anything specified within square brackets means it is optional; that is, that section of the query is not mandatory in an MDX query.

You can see that the WITH and WHERE clauses are optional because they are enclosed within square brackets. Therefore, you might be thinking that the simplest possible MDX query should be the following:

```
SELECT
FROM [Adventure Works]
```

Super! You are absolutely correct. This MDX query returns a single value. Which value, you might ask? Recall that fact data is stored in a special dimension called Measures. When you send the preceding query to the Analysis Services instance, you get the value of the default member from the Measures dimension which, for the Adventure Works cube, is Reseller Sales Amount from the Reseller Sales measure group. The result of this query is the aggregated value of all the cells in the cube for this measure for the default values of each cube dimension.

The WITH clause is typically used for custom calculations and operations, and you learn about this later in this chapter. First, though, let's take a look at the SELECT, FROM, and WHERE clauses.

The SELECT Statement and Axis Specification

The MDX SELECT statement is used to retrieve a subset of the multidimensional data in an OLAP cube. In SQL, the SELECT statement allows you to specify which columns will be included in the row data you retrieve, which is viewed as two-dimensional data. If you consider a two-dimensional coordinate system, you have the X and Y axes. The Y axis is used for the COLUMNS and the X axis is used for ROWS. In MDX, the SELECT statement is specified in a way that allows retrieving data with more than just two dimensions. Indeed, MDX provides you with the capability of retrieving data on one, two, or many axes.

The syntax of the SELECT statement is:

```
SELECT [<axis_expression>, [<axis_expression>...]]
```

The axis_expressions specified after the SELECT refer to the dimension data you are interested in retrieving. These dimensions are referred to as axis dimensions because the data from these dimensions are projected onto the corresponding axes. The syntax for axis_expression is:

```
<axis_expression> := <set> ON (axis | AXIS(axis number) | axis number)
```

Axis dimensions are used to retrieve multidimensional result sets. The set, a collection of tuples, is defined to form an axis dimension. MDX provides you with the capability of specifying up to 128 axes in the SELECT statement. The first five axes have aliases. They are COLUMNS, ROWS, PAGES, SECTIONS, and CHAPTERS. Axes can also be specified as a number, which allows you to specify more than five dimensions in your SELECT statement. Take the following example:

```
SELECT    Measures.[Internet Sales Amount] ON COLUMNS,
          [Customer].[Country].MEMBERS ON ROWS,
          [Product].[Product Line].MEMBERS ON PAGES
FROM [Adventure Works]
```

Three axes are specified in the SELECT statement. Data from dimensions Measures, Customers, and Product are mapped on to the three axes to form the axis dimensions. This statement could equivalently be written as:

```
SELECT    Measures.[Internet Sales Amount] ON 0,
          [Customer].[Country].MEMBERS ON 1,
          [Product].[Product Line].MEMBERS ON 2
FROM [Adventure Works]
```

Axis Dimensions

The axis dimensions are what you build when you define a SELECT statement. A SELECT statement specifies a set for each dimension; COLUMNS, ROWS, and additional axes — if you have them. Unlike the slicer dimension (described later in this chapter), axis dimensions retrieve and retain data for multiple members, not just single members. Please note that when we refer to axis dimension, this actually corresponds to a hierarchy for Analysis Services 2008 because you include hierarchies in the MDX statement.

> **No Shortcuts!** In MDX you cannot create a workable query that omits lower axes. If you want to specify a PAGES axis, you must also specify COLUMNS and ROWS.

The FROM Clause and Cube Specification

The FROM clause in an MDX query determines the cube from which you retrieve and analyze data. It's similar to the FROM clause in a SQL query where you specify a table name. The FROM clause is a necessity for any MDX query. The syntax of the FROM clause is:

```
FROM <cube_expression>
```

The cube_expression denotes the name of a cube or a subsection of a cube from which you want to retrieve data. In SQL's FROM clause you can specify more than one table, but in an MDX FROM clause you can define just one cube name. The cube specified in the FROM clause is called the *cube context* and the query is executed within this cube context. That is, every part of axis_expressions are retrieved from the cube context specified in the FROM clause:

```
SELECT [Measures].[Internet Sales Amount] ON COLUMNS
FROM [Adventure Works]
```

This is a valid MDX query that retrieves data from the [Internet Sales Amount] measure on the X-axis. The measure data is retrieved from the cube context [Adventure Works]. Even though the FROM clause restricts you to working with only one cube or section of a cube, you can retrieve data from other cubes using the MDX LookupCube function. When there are two ore more cubes having common dimension members, the LookupCube function retrieves measures outside the current cube's context using the common dimension members.

The WHERE Clause and Slicer Specification

In pretty much any relational database work that you do, you issue queries that return only portions of the total data available in a given table, set of joined tables, and/or joined databases. This is accomplished using SQL statements that specify what data you do and do not want returned as a result of running your query. Here is an example of an unrestricted SQL query on a table named Product that contains sales information for products:

```
SELECT *
FROM    Product
```

Assume the preceding query results in five columns being retrieved with the following four rows:

Product ID	Product Line	Color	Weight	Sales
1	Accessories	Silver	5.00	200.00
2	Mountain	Grey	40.35	1000.00
3	Road	Silver	50.23	2500.00
4	Touring	Red	45.11	2000.00

The * represents "all," meaning that query will dump the entire contents of the table. If you want to know only the Color and Product Line for each row, you can restrict the query so that it returns just the information you want. The following simple example demonstrates a query constructed to return just two columns from the table:

```
SELECT ProductLine, Color
FROM Product
```

This query returns the following:

Product Line	Color
Accessories	Silver
Mountain	Grey
Road	Silver
Touring	Red

The concept of crafting queries to return only the data you need maps directly to MDX from SQL. In fact, they share a conditional statement that adds a whole new level of power to restricting queries to return only desired data. It is called the *WHERE* clause. After taking a look at the SQL WHERE clause you will see how the concept is similar to its use in MDX. Here is a SQL query that uses WHERE to restrict the returned rows to those products whose color is silver:

```
SELECT ProductLine, Sales
FROM Product
WHERE Color = 'Silver'
```

This query returns the following:

Product Line	Sales
Accessories	200.00
Road	2500.00

The same concept applies to MDX. The MDX SELECT statement is used to identify the dimensions and members a query will return and the WHERE statement limits the result set by some criteria. The preceding SQL example restricts the returned data to records where Color = 'Silver'. Note that in MDX members are the elements that make up a dimension's hierarchy. The Product table, when modeled as a cube, will contain two measures, Sales and Weight, and a Product dimension with the hierarchies ProductID, ProductLine, and Color. In this example the Product table is used as a fact as well as a dimension table. An MDX query against the cube that produces the same results as that of the SQL query is:

```
SELECT Measures.[Sales] ON COLUMNS,
   [Product].[Product Line].MEMBERS on ROWS
FROM  [ProductsCube]
WHERE ([Product].[Color].[Silver])
```

The two columns selected in SQL are now on the axes COLUMNS and ROWS. The condition in the SQL WHERE clause, which is a string comparison, is transformed to an MDX WHERE clause, which refers to a slice on the cube that contains products that have silver color. As you can see, even though the SQL and MDX queries look similar, their semantics are quite different.

The Slicer Dimension

The *slicer dimension* is what you build when you define the WHERE statement. It is a filter that removes unwanted dimensions and members. As mentioned earlier in this chapter, in the context of Analysis Services 2008, the dimensions will actually be hierarchies in Analysis Services 2008. What makes things interesting is that the slicer dimension includes any axis in the cube including those that are not explicitly included in any of the queried axes. The default members of hierarchies not included in the query axes are used in the slicer axis. Regardless of how it gets its data, the slicer dimension will only accept MDX expressions (described later in this chapter) that evaluate to a single set. When there are tuples specified for the slicer axis, MDX will evaluate those tuples as a set and the results of the tuples are aggregated based on the measures included in the query and the aggregation function of that specific measure.

The WITH Clause and Calculated Members

Often business needs involve calculations that must be formulated within the scope of a specific query. The MDX WITH clause provides you with the ability to create such calculations and use them within the context of the query. In addition, you can also retrieve data from outside the context of the current cube using the LookupCube MDX function.

Typical calculations that are created using the WITH clause are named sets and calculated members. In addition to these, the WITH clause provides you with functionality to define cell calculations, load a cube into an Analysis Server cache for improving query performance, alter the contents of cells by calling functions in external libraries, and additional advanced capabilities such as solve order and pass order. You learn about named sets, calculated members, and calculated measures in this chapter. Chapter 10 covers the rest.

The syntax of the WITH clause is:

```
[WITH <formula_expression> [, <formula_expression> ...]]
```

You can specify several calculations in one WITH clause. The formula_expression will vary depending upon the type of calculations. Calculations are separated by commas.

Named Sets

As you learned earlier, a set is a collection of tuples. A set expression, even though simple, can often be quite lengthy and this might make the query appear to be complex and unreadable. MDX provides you with the capability of dynamically defining sets with a specific name so that the name can be used within the query. Think of it as an alias for the collection of tuples in the set. This is called a *named set*. A named set is nothing but an alias for an MDX set expression that can be used anywhere within the query as an alternative to specifying the actual set expression.

Consider the case where you have customers in various countries. Suppose you want to retrieve the Sales information for customers in Europe. Your MDX query would look like this:

```
SELECT Measures.[Internet Sales Amount] ON COLUMNS,
{[Customer].[Country].[Country].&[France],
[Customer].[Country].[Country].&[Germany],
[Customer].[Country].[Country].&[United Kingdom]} ON ROWS
FROM [Adventure Works]
```

This query is not too lengthy, but you can imagine a query that would contain a lot of members and functions being applied to this specific set several times within the query. Instead of specifying the complete set every time it's used in the query, you can create a named set and then use it in the query as follows:

```
WITH SET [EUROPE] AS '{[Customer].[Country].[Country].&[France],
[Customer].[Country].[Country].&[Germany],[Customer].[Country].[Country].
        &[United Kingdom]}'

SELECT Measures.[Internet Sales Amount] ON COLUMNS,
[EUROPE] ON ROWS
FROM [Adventure Works]
```

The formula_expression for the WITH clause with a named set is

```
Formula_expression :=  [DYNAMIC] SET <set_alias_name> AS [']<set>[']
```

The set_alias_name can be any alias name and is typically enclosed within square brackets. Note the keywords SET and AS that are used in this expression to specify a named set. The keyword DYNAMIC is optional. The actual set of tuples does not have to be enclosed within single quotes. The single quotes are still available for backward compatibility with Analysis Services 2000.

You can create named sets within an MDX query using the WITH clause shown in this section. You can also create them within a session using the CREATE SET option. Additionally, you can create them globally in MDX scripts using CREATE statements. Sets can be evaluated statically or dynamically at query execution time. Hence the keyword DYNAMIC is typically used within MDX scripts to be evaluated at the query execution time. Chapter 10 shows how to create a DYNAMIC set.

Calculated Members

Calculated members are calculations specified by MDX expressions. They are resolved as a result of MDX expression evaluation rather than just by the retrieval of the original fact data. A typical example of a calculated member is the calculation of year-to-date sales of products. Let's say the fact data only contains sales information of products for each month and you need to calculate the year-to-date sales. You can do this with an MDX expression using the WITH clause.

The formula_expression of the WITH clause for calculated members is:

```
Formula_expression := MEMBER <MemberName> AS [']<MDX_Expression>['],
               [ , SOLVE_ORDER = <integer>]
               [ , <CellProperty> = <PropertyExpression>]
```

MDX uses the keywords MEMBER and AS in the WITH clause for creating calculated members. The MemberName should be a fully qualified member name that includes the dimension, hierarchy, and level under which the specific calculated member needs to be created. The MDX_Expression should return a value that calculates the value of the member. The SOLVE_ORDER, which is an optional parameter, should be a positive integer value if specified. It determines the order in which the members are evaluated when multiple calculated members are defined. The CellProperty is also optional and is used to specify cell properties for the calculated member such as the text formatting of the cell contents including the background color.

All the measures in a cube are stored in a special dimension called Measures. Calculated members can also be created on the measures dimension. In fact, most of the calculated members that are used for business are created on the measures dimension. Calculated members on the measures dimension are referred to as calculated measures. The following are examples of calculated member statements:

❑   **Example 1:**

```
WITH MEMBER MEASURES.[Profit] AS [Measures].[Internet Sales Amount]-
[Measures].[Internet Standard Product Cost]
SELECT measures.profit ON COLUMNS,
  [Customer].[Country].MEMBERS ON ROWS
FROM [Adventure Works]
```

In Example 1 a calculated member, Profit, has been defined as the difference of the measures [Internet Sales Amount] and [Internet Standard Product Cost]. When the query is executed, the Profit value will be calculated for every country based on the MDX expression.

❑ **Example 2:**

```
WITH
SET [Product Order] AS 'Order([Product].[Product Line].MEMBERS,
   [Internet Sales Amount], BDESC)'
MEMBER [Measures].[Product Rank] AS 'Rank([Product].[Product Line].CURRENTMEMBER,
   [Product Order])'
 SELECT {[Product Rank], [Sales Amount]} ON COLUMNS,
 [Product Order] ON ROWS
 from [Adventure Works]
```

Example 2 includes creation of a named set and a calculated member within the scope of the query. The query orders the Products based on the Internet Sales Amount and returns the sales amount of each product along with the rank. The named set [Product Order] is created so that the members within this set are ordered based on the Sales. This is done by using an MDX function called Order (you can learn more about Order in Appendix A, available online on this book's page at www.wrox.com). To retrieve the rank of each product, a calculated member, [Product Rank], is created using the MDX function Rank.

The result of the preceding query on the Adventure Works cube from the Adventure Works DW 2008 sample database is:

Product	Rank	Sales Amount
All Products	1	$109,809,274.20
Road	2	$48,262,055.15
Mountain	3	$42,456,731.56
Touring	4	$16,010,837.10
Accessory	5	$2,539,401.59
Components	6	$540,248.80

❑ **Example 3:**

```
WITH MEMBER Measures.[Cumulative Sales] AS 'Sum(
  YTD(),[Internet Sales Amount])'

SELECT {Measures.[Internet Sales Amount],Measures.[Cumulative Sales]} ON 0,
  [Date].[Calendar].[Calendar Semester].MEMBERS ON 1
FROM [Adventure Works]
```

In Example 3 a calculated member is created so that you can analyze the [Internet Sales Amount] of each half year along with the cumulative sales for the whole year. For this, two MDX functions are used: Sum and YTD. The YTD MDX function is called without any parameters so that the default Time member at that level is used in the calculation. The Sum function is used to aggregate the sales amount for that specific level. The result of the preceding query on the sample Analysis Services database is shown in the following table. You can see that the Cumulative Sales corresponding for the members H2 CY 2002, H2 CY 2003, and H2 CY 2004 show the sum of Internet Sales Amount for that member and the previous half year.

	Internet Sales Amount	Cumulative Sales
H2 CY 2001	$3,266,373.66	$3,266,373.66
H1 CY 2002	$3,805,710.59	$3,805,710.59
H2 CY 2002	$2,724,632.94	$6,530,343.53
H1 CY 2003	$3,037,501.36	$3,037,501.36
H2 CY 2003	$6,753,558.94	$9,791,060.30
H1 CY 2004	$9,720,059.11	$9,720,059.11
H2 CY 2004	$50,840.63	$9,770,899.74
H2 CY 2006	(null)	(null)

❑   **Example 4:**

```
WITH MEMBER [Date].[Calendar].[%Change] AS
   100* (([Date].[Calendar].[Calendar Quarter].[Q2 CY 2002] -
   [Date].[Calendar].[Calendar Quarter].[Q1 CY 2002])/
   [Date].[Calendar].[Calendar Quarter].[Q2 CY 2002])

SELECT {[Date].[Calendar].[Calendar Quarter].[Q1 CY 2002],
   [Date].[Calendar].[Calendar Quarter].[Q2 CY 2002],
   [Date].[Calendar].[%Change]} ON COLUMNS,
   Measures.[Internet Sales Amount] ON ROWS
FROM [Adventure Works]
```

This query shows an example of a calculated member defined in the Date dimension to return a quarter-over-quarter comparison of the sales amount. In this example, quarter 1 and quarter 2 of the year 2002 are used. The result of this query is:

	Q1 CY 2002	Q2 CY 2002	%Change
Internet Sales Amount	$1,791,698.45	$2,014,012.13	11.0383486486941

MDX Expressions

MDX expressions are partial MDX statements that evaluate to a value. They are typically used in calculations or in defining values for objects such as default members and default measures, or for defining security expressions to allow or deny access. MDX expressions typically take a member, a tuple, or a set as a parameter and return a value. If the result of the MDX expression evaluation is no value, a Null value is returned. Following are some examples of MDX expressions:

❑   **Example 1**

```
Customer.[Customer Geography].DEFAULTMEMBER
```

This example returns the default member specified for the Customer Geography hierarchy of the Customer dimension.

❑ **Example 2**

```
(Customer.[Customer Geography].CURRENTMEMBER, Measures.[Sales Amount]) -
(Customer.[Customer Geography].Australia, Measures.[Sales Amount)
```

This MDX expression is used to compare the sales to customers of different countries with sales of customers in Australia.

Such an expression is typically used in a calculated measure. Complex MDX expressions can include various operators in the MDX language along with the combination of the functions available in MDX. One such example is shown in Example 3.

❑ **Example 3**

```
COUNT(INTERSECT( DESCENDANTS( IIF( HIERARCHIZE(EXISTS[Employee].
        [Employee].MEMBERS,
STRTOMEMBER("[Employee].[login].[login].&["+USERNAME+"]")),
        POST).ITEM(0).ITEM(0).PARENT.DATAMEMBER is
HIERARCHIZE(EXISTS([Employee].[Employee].MEMBERS,
        STRTOMEMBER("[Employee].[login].[login].&["+USERNAME+"]")),
        POST).ITEM(0).ITEM(0),
HIERARCHIZE(EXISTS([Employee].[Employee].MEMBERS,
        STRTOMEMBER("[Employee].[login].[login].&["+username+"]")),
        POST).ITEM(0).ITEM(0).PARENT,
HIERARCHIZE(EXISTS([Employee].[Employee].MEMBERS,
STRTOMEMBER("[Employee].[login].[login].&["+USERNAME+"]")),
        POST).ITEM(0).ITEM(0))
).ITEM(0) , Employee.Employee.CURRENTMEMBER)) > 0
```

This example is an MDX cell security expression used to allow employees to see Sales information made by them or by the employees reporting to them and not other employees. This MDX expression uses several MDX functions (you learn some of these in the next section). You can see that this is not a simple MDX expression. The preceding MDX expression returns a value "True" or "False" based on the employee that is logged in. Analysis Services allows appropriate cells to be accessed by the employee based on the evaluation. This example is analyzed in more detail in Chapter 22.

MDX has progressed extensively since its birth and you can pretty quickly end up with a complex MDX query or MDX expression like the one shown in Example 3. There can be multiple people working on implementing a solution and hence it is good to have some kind of documentation for your queries or expressions. Similar to other programming languages, MDX supports commenting within queries and MDX expressions. At this time there are three different ways to comment your MDX. They are:

```
// (two forward slashes) comment goes here
-- (two hyphens) comment goes here
/* comment goes here */ (slash-asterisk pairs)
```

We highly recommend that you add comments to your MDX expressions and queries so that you can look back at a later point in time and interpret or understand what you were implementing with a specific MDX expression or query.

Operators

The MDX language, similar to other query languages such as SQL or other general-purpose programming languages, has several operators. An operator is a function that is used to perform a specific action, takes arguments, and returns a result. MDX has several types of operators including arithmetic operators, logical operators, and special MDX operators.

Arithmetic Operators

Regular arithmetic operators such as +, −, *, and / are available in MDX. Just as with other programming languages, these operators can be applied on two numbers. The + and − operators can also be used as unary operators on numbers. Unary operators, as the name indicates, are used with a single operand (single number) in MDX expressions such as + 100 or −100.

Set Operators

The +, −, and * operators, in addition to being arithmetic operators, are also used to perform operations on the MDX sets. The + operator returns the union of two sets, the − operator returns the difference of two sets, and the * operator returns the cross product of two sets. The cross product of two sets results in all possible combinations of the tuples in each set and helps in retrieving data in a matrix format. For example, if you have two sets, {Male, Female} and {2003, 2004, 2005}, the cross product, represented as {Male, Female} * {2003, 2004, 2005}, is {(Male,2003), (Male,2004), (Male,2005),(Female,2003),(Female,2004), (Female,2005)}. The following examples show MDX expressions that use the set operators:

❑ **Example 1:** The result of the MDX expression

```
{[Customer].[Country].[Australia]} + {[Customer].[Country].[Canada]}
```

is the union of the two sets as shown here:

```
{[Customer].[Country].[Australia], [Customer].[Country].[Canada]}
```

❑ **Example 2:** The result of the MDX expression

```
{[Customer].[Country].[Australia],[Customer].[Country].[Canada]}*
{[Product].[Product Line].[Mountain],[Product].[Product Line].[Road]}
```

is the cross product of the sets as shown here:

```
{([Customer].[Country].[Australia],[Product].[Product Line].[Mountain])
([Customer].[Country].[Australia],[Product].[Product Line].[Road])
([Customer].[Country].[Canada],[Product].[Product Line].[Mountain])
([Customer].[Country].[Canada],[Product].[Product Line].[Road])}
```

Comparison Operators

MDX supports the comparison operators <, <=, >, >=, =, and <>. These operators take two MDX expressions as arguments and return TRUE or FALSE based on the result of comparing the values of each expression.

Example:

The following MDX expression uses the greater than comparison operator, >:

```
Count (Customer.[Country].members) > 3
```

In this example Count is an MDX function that is used to count the number of members in Country hierarchy of the Customer dimension. Because there are more than three members, the result of the MDX expression is TRUE.

Logical Operators

The logical operators that are part of MDX are AND, OR, XOR, NOT, and IS, which are used for logical conjunction, logical disjunction, logical exclusion, logical negation, and comparison, respectively. These operators take two MDX expressions as arguments and return TRUE or FALSE based on the logical operation. Logical operators are typically used in MDX expressions for cell and dimension security, which you learn about in Chapter 22.

Special MDX Operators — Curly Braces, Commas, and Colons

The curly braces, represented by the characters { and }, are used to enclose a tuple or a set of tuples to form an MDX set. Whenever you have a set with a single tuple, the curly brace is optional because Analysis Services implicitly converts a single tuple to a set when needed. When there is more than one tuple to be represented as a set or when there is an empty set, you need to use the curly braces.

You have already seen the comma character used in several earlier examples. The comma character is used to form a tuple that contains more than one member. By doing this you are creating a slice of data on the cube. In addition, the comma character is used to separate multiple tuples specified to define a set. In the set {(Male,2003), (Male,2004), (Male,2005),(Female,2003),(Female,2004),(Female,2005)} the comma character is not only used to form tuples but also to form the set of tuples.

The colon character is used to define a range of members within a set. It is used between two non-consecutive members in a set to indicate inclusion of all the members between them, based on the set ordering (key-based or name-based). For example, if you have the following set:

```
{[Customer].[Country].[Australia], [Customer].[Country].[Canada],
[Customer].[Country].[France], [Customer].[Country].[Germany],
[Customer].[Country].[United Kingdom], [Customer].[Country].[United States]}
```

the following MDX expression

```
{[Customer].[Country].[Canada] : [Customer].[Country].[United Kingdom]}
```

results in the following set:

```
{[Customer].[Country].[Canada], [Customer].[Country].[France],
[Customer].[Country].[Germany], [Customer].[Country].[United Kingdom]}
```

MDX Functions

MDX functions can be used in MDX expressions or in MDX queries. MDX forms the bedrock of Analysis Services 2008. BIDS builds MDX expressions that typically include MDX functions to retrieve data from the Analysis Services database based upon your actions like browsing dimensions or cubes. MDX functions help address some of the common operations that are needed in your MDX expressions or queries including ordering tuples in a set, counting the number of members in a dimension, and string manipulation required to transform user input into corresponding MDX objects.

This section splits the MDX functions into various categories and provides some basic examples. The best way to learn MDX functions is to understand their use in business scenarios so that you can apply the right MDX function in appropriate situations. In this book, you will often see the MDX that the product generates. Paying attention to and experimenting with such MDX is critical to your transition from basic understanding of Analysis Services 2008 to complete mastery — and, though it is a profound challenge, mastery is attainable. You can do it. Again, when you slice a dimension in any cube-viewing software, like Office Web Components, it is MDX that is generated and executed to retrieve the results. Also, when you create a report based on a cube (UDM) using Excel (as you see in Chapter 17) or using Reporting Services (Chapter 20), it is MDX that is created behind the scenes to capture the contents with which to populate the report. Almost all these MDX queries or expressions generated by BIDS or by client tools use MDX functions; some of which you learn about in detail as you work through this book.

In Chapter 11 you learn about the stored procedure support in Analysis Services 2008 and how you can write your custom functions that can be called within your MDX expressions or queries. For example, the following MDX query contains a custom function `MyStoredProc` that takes two arguments and returns an MDX object:

```
SELECT MyStoredProc (arg1, arg2) ON COLUMNS FROM CorporateCube
```

What we expect will get you even more excited about Chapter 11 is that the .NET assemblies that implement stored procedures can themselves contain MDX expressions within them due to an object model that exposes MDX objects! It should be obvious if you are experienced with Analysis Services that the new version opens up whole new approaches to problem solving in the Business Intelligence space. Because MDX functions are so central to successful use of Analysis Services 2008, it is best if you jump right in and learn some of them now. Putting those functions together to accomplish more meaningful tasks will come later in the book. For now, please snap on your seatbelt; it's time to learn about MDX functions.

MDX Function Categories

MDX functions are used to programmatically operate on multidimensional databases. From traversing dimension hierarchies to calculating numeric functions over fact data, there is plenty of surface area to explore. In this section, the MDX functions have been categorized in a specific way to help you understand them efficiently. You also see some details on select functions of interest, where interest level is defined by the probability you will use a given function in your future BI development work. You can see all of the MDX functions in detail in Appendix A (available online at www.wrox.com). We have categorized the MDX functions into several categories very similar to the product documentations of MDX functions. MDX functions can be called in several ways:

❑   .Function (read *dot* function)

Example: Dimension.Name returns the name of the object being referenced (could be a hierarchy or level/member expression). Perhaps this reminds you of the dot operator in VB.NET or C# programming — that's fine. It's roughly the same idea.

```
WITH MEMBER measures.LocationName AS [Customer].[Country].CurrentMember.Name
SELECT measures.LocationName ON COLUMNS,
Customer.Country.members on ROWS
FROM [Adventure Works]
```

❑   Function

Example: `Username` is used to acquire the username of the logged-in user. It returns a string in the following format: domain-name\user-name. Most often this is used in dimension or cell security related MDX expressions. The following is an example of how `username` can be used in an MDX expression:

```
WITH MEMBER Measures.User AS USERNAME
SELECT Measures.User ON 0 FROM [Adventure Works]
```

❏ Function ( )

> **Example:** The function `CalculationCurrentPass ( )` requires parentheses, but takes no arguments. You can find more on `CalculationCurrentPass ( )` in Appendix A (available online at `www.wrox.com`).

❏ Function (arguments)

> **Example:** OpeningPeriod ([Level_Expression [, Member_Expression]]) is an MDX function that takes an argument that can specify both level_expression with member_expression or just the member_expression itself. This function is most often used with Time dimensions, but will work with other dimension types. It returns the first member at the level of the member_ expression. For example, the following returns the first member of the Day level of the April member of the default time dimension:

```
OpeningPeriod (Day, [April])
```

Set Functions

Set functions, as the category name suggests, operate on sets. They take sets as arguments and often return a set. Some of the widely used set functions are `Crossjoin` and `Filter`, which we are quite sure you will be using in your MDX queries. Hence these two functions are discussed here with examples.

`Crossjoin` returns all possible combinations of sets as specified by the arguments to the `Crossjoin` function. If there are N sets specified in the `Crossjoin` function, this will result in a combination of all the possible members within that set on a single axis. You see this in the following example:

```
Crossjoin ( Set_Expression [ ,Set_Expression ...] )

SELECT Measures.[Internet Sales Amount] ON COLUMNS,
CROSSJOIN( {Product.[Product Line].[Product Line].MEMBERS},
{[Customer].[Country].MEMBERS}) on ROWS
FROM [Adventure Works]
```

This query produces the cross product of each member in the Product dimension with each member of the Customer dimension along the sales amount measure. The following are the first few rows of results from executing this query:

		Sales Amount
Accessory	All Customers	$604,053.30
Accessory	Australia	$127,128.61
Accessory	Canada	$82,736.07
Accessory	France	$55,001.21
Accessory	Germany	$54,382.29
Accessory	United Kingdom	$67,636.33
Accessory	United States	$217,168.79
Components	All Customers	(null)
. . .	. . .	. . .

Sometimes the result of the combination of the members of the set results in values being null. For example, assume that there is one product that is sold only in Australia. The sales amount for this product in other countries is going to be Null. Obviously you are not interested in the empty results. It does not help in any business decision. Instead of retrieving all the results and then checking for null values, there is a way to restrict these on the server side of Analysis Services. In addition to this, Analysis Services optimizes the query so that only the appropriate result is retrieved and sent. For this, you use the NonEmptyCrossjoin function or the NonEmpty function. The syntax for these two functions are:

```
NonEmptyCrossjoin(
        Set_Expression [ ,Set_Expression ...][ ,Crossjoin_Set_Count ] )

NonEmpty(Set_Expression [ ,FilterSet_Expression])
```

To remove empty cells in these query results using Crossjoin you can use one of the following queries, which use the NonEmptyCrossjoin and NonEmpty functions. When using the NonEmptyCrossjoin function, you need to apply the filter condition on [Internet Sales Amount] and then retrieve the crossjoin of members from the first two sets. This is due to the fact that the default measure for the Adventure Works cube is not [Internet Sales Amount] and hence, if the measure is not included as a parameter in the function, NonEmptyCrossjoin will use the default measure. When using the NonEmpty function, you first do the crossjoin and then filter out the tuples that have null values for the Internet Sales amount as shown in the second query in the following code. The NonEmpty MDX function was first introduced in Analysis Services 2005.

```
SELECT Measures.[Internet Sales Amount] ON COLUMNS,
NONEMPTYCROSSJOIN( {Product.[Product Line].[Product Line].MEMBERS},
{[Customer].[Country].MEMBERS},Measures.[Internet Sales Amount],2 )  ON ROWS
FROM [Adventure Works]
SELECT Measures.[Internet Sales Amount] ON COLUMNS,
NONEMPTY(CROSSJOIN ( {Product.[Product Line].[Product Line].MEMBERS},
{[Customer].[Country].MEMBERS}),Measures.[Internet Sales Amount]) ON ROWS
FROM [Adventure Works]
```

Most users and client tools interacting with Analysis Services use the NonEmptyCrossjoin function extensively. You see more examples of this function in later chapters of this book.

Another MDX function that is quite useful is the Filter function. The Filter function helps restrict the query results based on one or more conditions. The Filter function takes two arguments: a set expression and a logical expression. The logical expression is applied on each item of the set and returns a set of items that satisfy the logical condition. The function arguments for the Filter function are:

```
Filter( Set_Expression , { Logical_Expression | [ CAPTION | KEY | NAME ]
        =String_Expression } )
```

The result of the example query shown for the Crossjoin function results in 35 cells. If you are only interested in the products for which the sales amount is greater than a specific value and are still interested in finding out amounts by countries, you can use the Filter function as shown here:

```
SELECT Measures.[Internet Sales Amount] ON COLUMNS,
FILTER(CROSSJOIN( {Product.[Product Line].[Product Line].MEMBERS},
{[Customer].[Country].MEMBERS}),[Internet Sales Amount] >2000000) on ROWS
FROM [Adventure Works]
```

This query filters out all the products for which the sales amount is less than 2,000,000 and returns only the products that have the sales amount greater than 2,000,000. The result of execution of this query is as follows:

		Sales Amount
Mountain	All Customers	$10,251,183.52
Mountain	Australia	$2,906,994.45
Mountain	United States	$3,547,956.78
Road	All Customers	$14,624,108.58
Road	Australia	$5,029,120.41
Road	United States	$4,322,438.41
Touring	All Customers	$3,879,331.82

Member Functions

Member functions are used for operations on the members such as retrieving the current member, ancestor, parent, children, sibling, next member, and so on. All the member functions return a member. One of the most widely used member functions is called ParallelPeriod. The ParallelPeriod function helps you to retrieve a member in the Time dimension based on a given member and certain conditions. The function definition for ParallelPeriod is:

```
ParallelPeriod( [ Level_Expression [ ,Numeric_Expression [ , Member_Expression ] ] ] )
```

Figure 3-5 shows an illustration of ParallelPeriod function. ParallelPeriod is a function that returns a member from a Time dimension (you learn about time dimensions in Chapter 5) relative to a given member for a specific time period. For example, ParallelPeriod([Quarter], 1, [April]) is [January]. You might be wondering how this result came about. The following steps describe the execution of the ParallelPeriod function and how Analysis Services arrives at the result:

1. The ParallelPeriod function can only be used in conjunction with time dimensions. For the illustration shown in Figure 3-5, assume you have a time dimension with a Calendar hierarchy that contains the levels Year, Semester, Quarter, and Month.

2. The ParallelPeriod function first finds the ancestor member of last argument, April, in the specified level, Quarter, which is the first argument. It identifies that the ancestor of April at the specified level is Quarter2.

3. The sibling of [Quarter2] is then evaluated based on the numeric expression. A positive number indicates that the sibling of interest exists as a predecessor to the current member in the collection of members at that level. A negative number indicates that the sibling of interest is a successor of the current member. In this example, the sibling of interest is [Quarter1] because the numeric expression is 1.

4. Next, the member at the same position as that of member [April] is identified in [Quarter1], which is January.

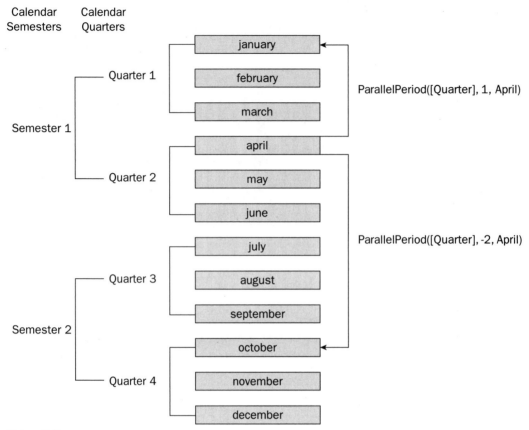

Figure 3-5

The `ParallelPeriod` function is used to compare measure values relative to various time periods. Typically a customer would be interested in comparing Sales between Quarters or over Years, and this function really comes in handy when you want to make relative comparisons. Most of the client tools interacting with Analysis Services use this function.

Numeric Functions

Numeric functions come in very handy when you are defining the parameters for an MDX query or creating any calculated measure. Note that there are plenty of statistical functions in this group, including standard deviation, sample variance, and correlation. The most common of the numeric functions is a simple one called `Count` along with its close cousin, `DistinctCount`. The `Count` function is used to count the number of items in the collection of a specific object like a Dimension, a Tuple, a Set, or a Level. The `DistinctCount` function, on the other hand, takes a Set_Expression as an argument and returns a number that indicates the number of distinct items in the Set_Expression, not the total count of all items. Here are the function definitions for each:

```
Count ( Dimension | Tuples | Set| Level)
DistinctCount ( Set_Expression )
```

Please take a look at the following query:

```
WITH MEMBER Measures.CustomerCount AS DistinctCount(
Exists([Customer].[Customer].MEMBERS,[Product].[Product Line].Mountain,
"Internet Sales"))
SELECT Measures.CustomerCount ON COLUMNS
FROM [Adventure Works]
```

The `DistinctCount` function counts the number of distinct members in the Customer dimension who have purchased products in the Mountain product line. If a customer has purchased multiple products from the specified product line, the `DistinctCount` function will count the customer just once. The MDX function `Exists` is used to filter customers who have only purchased product line Mountain through the Internet. You learn more about the `Exists` function in Chapter 10. The result of the `Exists` function is the set of Internet customers who have purchased products from the Mountain product line. The result of the preceding query is 9590.

Dimension Functions, Level Functions, and Hierarchy Functions

Functions in these groups are typically used for navigation and manipulation. Here is an example of just such a function, the "Level" function from the Level group:

```
SELECT [Date].[Calendar].[Calendar Quarter].[Q1 CY 2004].LEVEL ON COLUMNS
FROM [Adventure Works]
```

This query results in a list of all the quarters displayed in the results. The reason is because [Date] .[Calendar].[Calendar Quarter].[Q1 CY 2004].LEVEL evaluates to [Date].[Calendar Year].[Calendar Semster].[Calender Quarter]. From this, you get the list of all quarters for all calendar years.

String Manipulation Functions

To extract the names of sets, tuples, and members in the form of a string, you can use functions like MemberToStr (<Member_Expression>) and to do the inverse, take a string and create a member expression, you can use StrToMember (<String>). Consider the following case, in which there is a client application that displays sales information for all countries. When a user selects a specific country, you need to extract the sales information for the specific country from Analysis Services. Because the countries are represented as strings in the client application, you need to translate this string to a corresponding member, and then you can retrieve the data. String manipulation functions are useful when accepting parameters from users and transforming them to corresponding MDX objects. However there is a significant performance cost involved when using string manipulation functions. Hence we recommend you use these functions only if necessary.

```
SELECT STRTOMEMBER ('[Customer].[Country].[Australia]' ) ON COLUMNS
FROM [Adventure Works]
```

Other Functions

Four other function categories exist: `Subcube` and `Array` both have one function each. The final two categories are logical functions, which allow you to do Boolean evaluations on multidimensional objects, and tuple functions that you can use to access tuples. In addition, Analysis Services 2005 and 2008 have introduced a few new MDX functions. You have seen some of them in this chapter such as `NonEmpty` and `Exists`. You learn more about these in Chapter 10 and Appendix A (available online at www.wrox.com).

Summary

Congratulations, you have made it through the first three chapters! Ostensibly, you should now feel free to take on the rest of the chapters in no particular order. But you got this far, so why not go immediately to Chapter 4 and jump right in? Now you know the fundamental elements of MDX — cells, members, tuples, and sets. Further, you learned that MDX has two forms: queries and expressions.

You saw that MDX queries, which are used to retrieve data from Analysis Services databases, retain a superficial resemblance to SQL, but that the resemblance breaks down the more you drill down on the details. MDX expressions, on the other hand, are simple yet powerful constructs that are partial statements — by themselves they do not return results like queries. The expressions are what enable you to define and manipulate multidimensional objects and data through calculations, like specifying a default member's contents, for example.

To solidify your basic understanding of MDX, you learned the common query statements, WITH, SELECT, FROM, and WHERE, as well as the MDX operators like addition, subtraction, multiplication, division, and rollup, and the logical operators AND and OR. These details are crucial to effective use of the language. You got a good look at the eleven MDX function categories, saw the four forms MDX functions can take, and even saw detailed examples of some commonly used functions like Filter, ParallelPeriod, MemberToStr, and StrToMember. You learn more advanced MDX concepts and functions in Chapters 8, 9, 10, 11, and 12. All the MDX functions supported in Analysis Services 2008 are provided with examples in Appendix A, available online at www.wrox.com. Coming up next in Chapter 4 are the details of creating a data source, a Data Source View, and how to deal with multiple data source views in a single project.

Working with Data Sources and Data Source Views

You have completed the first three chapters of the book where you learned the concepts of data warehousing, worked hands on with SQL Server Analysis Services (SSAS) 2008 tools, and finally learned the basics of the MDX language and used it to retrieve data from Analysis Services. The next three chapters of the book guide you in the use of the product to design dimensions and cubes. The traditional approach of designing your dimensions and cubes is based upon an existing single-source data set. In the real world, you will be working with multiple relational data sources when you develop business intelligence applications. In this chapter you learn what Data Sources are and how they feed into the creation of Data Source Views (DSVs). These DSVs provide you a consolidated, single-source view on just the data of interest across one or more Data Sources you define. The Data Sources and DSVs form the foundation for subsequent construction of both dimensions and cubes. Note that more than one data source per project is supported as are multiple DSVs per project. You learn how this infrastructure plays out in this chapter.

Data Sources

In order to retrieve data from a source you need information about the source such as the name of the source, the method used to retrieve the data, security permissions needed to retrieve the data, and so on. All this information is encapsulated into an object called a *Data Source* in SSAS 2008. An Analysis Services database contains a collection of Data Sources, which stores all the data sources used to build dimensions and cubes within that database. Analysis Services will be able to retrieve source data from data sources via the native OLE DB interface or the managed .NET provider interface.

In the simplest case you will have one data source that contains one fact table with some number of dimensions linked to it by joins; that data source is populated by data from an OLTP database and is called an *Operational Data Store* (ODS). Figure 4-1 shows a graphical representation of this data source usage. The ODS is a single entity storing data from various sources so that it can serve as a single source of data for your data warehouse.

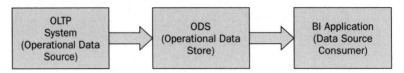

Data Source path commonly used prior to introduction of the UDM; data is first transformed to a more usable format and stored in the ODS.

Figure 4-1

A variant on the data source usage, which is enabled by the UDM first introduced in Analysis Services 2005, is the ability to take data directly from the OLTP system as input to the BI application. This is shown in Figure 4-2.

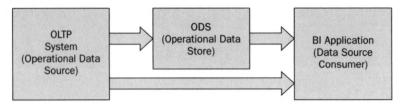

Data Sources enabled with UDM; data is transformed to a more usable format and stored in the ODS and data can be easily obtained from different data sources without going through the ODS.

Figure 4-2

Prior to the introduction of the Analysis Services UDM, certain limitations were associated with the use of data sources. Pre-UDM versions of Analysis Services only supported one fact table per cube. Therefore, only one data source could be used for specifying the fact table of a cube. You could still specify multiple data sources within Analysis Services in those earlier versions because dimensions referenced did not have to be in the same data source as the fact table but the fact table data had to come from a single data source. A workaround addressing the single fact table constraint was to create a SQL view on the multiple fact tables to create what appeared to Analysis Services as a single fact table. A more common and straightforward solution adopted by many users was to have multiple cubes based on disparate data sources and combine them into a single cube that was called a *virtual cube.*

With the UDM, Analysis Services now natively supports the capability of specifying multiple fact tables within a single cube. Each of these fact tables can be from a different data source. Analysis Services 2008 provides you with the capability of creating what are essentially virtual cubes; this is accomplished using linked objects (discussed in Chapter 9). Because Analysis Services 2008 provides you with the capability of creating cubes from various data sources, you need to be extremely careful about how you model your cube — that is, you must specify the right relationships (primary key and foreign key mappings) between tables from various data sources. In this way you can make sure your cube is designed to provide you the results you want.

Using the pre-UDM data source method is like carving on a bar of soap with a butter knife: You could create a statue, but it might not win any awards for beauty. Conversely, the kind of power and flexibility in Analysis Services 2008 puts you in a position similar to that of carving a bar of soap with a razor blade. Carving with a razor blade, you can make a gorgeous and intricate statue, but if you're not careful, you could cut the heck out of your fingers. So, be careful and craft some beautiful dimensional schemas! To do so, keep your schemas as simple as possible relative to the flexibility requirements imposed by the application specification you're working with.

Data Sources Supported by Analysis Services

Strictly speaking, Analysis Services 2008 supports all data sources that expose a connectivity interface through OLE DB or a .NET Managed Provider. This is because Analysis Services 2008 uses those interfaces to retrieve the schema (tables, relationships, columns within tables, and data types) information it needs to work with those data sources. If the data source is a relational database, then by default it uses the standard SQL to query the database. Analysis Services uses a cartridge mechanism that allows it to use the appropriate SQL language and extensions to talk to different relational database systems.

Analysis Services 2008 officially supports specific relational data sources. The major relational data sources for Analysis Services databases include Microsoft SQL Server, IBM's DB2, Teradata, Oracle, Sybase, and Informix. Figure 4-3 shows various data sources supported by Analysis Services 2008 on one of the machines that has SQL Server 2008 installed. For a specific data source you need to install the client components of the data provider so that the OLE DB provider and/or .NET provider for that specific data source is available on your machine. These client components should not only be supported on your development machine where you use the Business Intelligence Development Studio (BIDS) to design your database, but also on the server machine where an Analysis Services instance will be running. For relational databases DB2 and Oracle it is recommended you use the Microsoft's OLE DB data provider for Oracle or DB2 instead of the OLE DB providers provided those databases. Please make sure appropriate connectivity components from Oracle and IBM's DB2 are installed on your machine in addition to the OLE DB providers from Microsoft.

Figure 4-3

In Chapter 2 you used the Data Source Wizard to create a data source that included impersonation information. We will use the AnalysisServices2008Tutorial project created in Chapter 2 for the illustrations and examples in this chapter. In addition to providing impersonation information you can optionally specify additional connection properties such as query time out for connection, isolation level, and maximum number of connections in the Connection Manager dialog as shown in Figure 4-4 at the time of creation of the data source. Alternatively you can define additional connection properties after the creation of the data source by double-clicking the created data source and using the Data Source Designer dialog as shown in Figure 4-5. The isolation level property has two modes: Read Committed and Snapshot. By default Read Committed is used for all the data sources. The Snapshot isolation mode, which is supported by the relational data sources SQL Server and Oracle, is used to ensure that the data read by SSAS 2008 is consistent across multiple queries sent over a single connection. What this means is that if the data on the relational data source keeps changing and if multiple queries are sent by SSAS 2008 to that relational data source, all the queries will be seeing the same data seen by the first query. Any changes to the data between the first query and Nth query sent over a specific connection will not be included in the results of the first through Nth query. All the specified connection properties will be stored and applied whenever a connection is established to that specific data source. The Data Source Wizard also allows you to create data sources based on an existing data source connection already created so that a single connection can be shared by Analysis Services for multiple databases. The wizard also allows you to establish connections to objects within the current Analysis Services project, such as establishing an OLE DB connection to the cube being created in the project. Such a connection is typically useful while creating mining models (discussed in Chapter 16) from cubes.

Figure 4-4

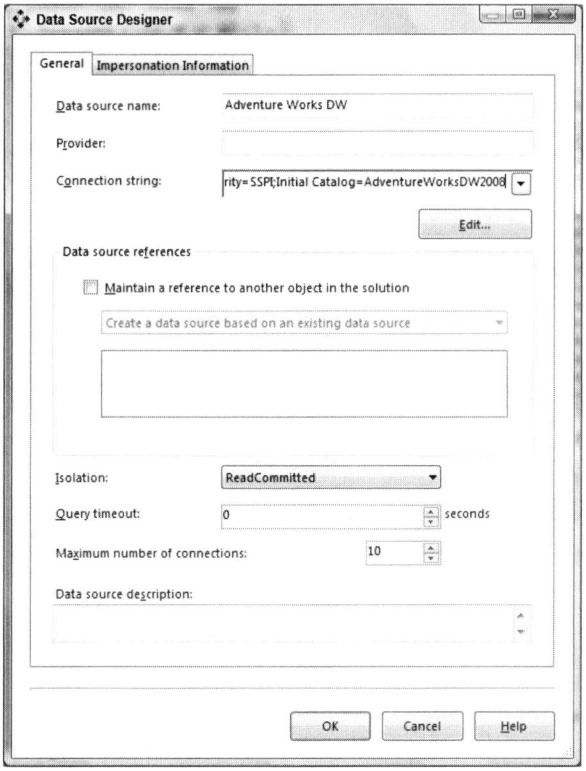

Figure 4-5

The Impersonation Information dialog in the Data Source Wizard has four options to choose from as shown in Figure 4-6. You briefly learned about these options in Chapter 2. At development time, BIDS uses the current user's credentials to connect to the relational backend and retrieve data. However, after the Analysis Services project is deployed, Analysis Services needs credentials to connect to and retrieve data. You specify the impersonation information so that Analysis Services can use the right credentials to make that connection. The following lists more details on the four options and when each option is likely to be used:

❑ **Use a specific Windows user name and password:** You typically would choose this option when the SSAS instance service startup account does not have permissions to access the relational backend. When you select this option you need to specify a Windows username and password that SSAS will use to connect to the relational backend. Due to security reasons the username and password are encrypted and stored. Only the encrypted password is sent to the SSAS instance when the project is deployed.

❑ **Use the service account:** This is the option typically selected by most users. You need to make sure the service startup account of the SSAS instance has access to the relational backend.

❑ **Use the credentials of the current user:** This option is typically selected for data mining. This option can be used for out-of-line bindings, DMX OPENQUERY statements, local cubes, and mining models. Do not select this option when you are connecting to a relational backend for processing, ROLAP queries, remote partitions, linked objects, and synchronization from target to source.

❑ **Inherit:** This option instructs Analysis Services to use the impersonation information specified for the database connection. This option used to be called "Default" in SQL Server 2005 edition.

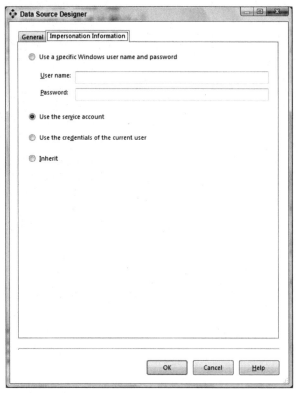

Figure 4-6

.NET versus OLE DB Data Providers

There are two types of data providers that most data sources support. OLE DB defines a set of COM interfaces that let you access data from data sources. There is also a .NET managed code interface similar to OLE DB. Providers implementing that interface are called .NET providers. SSAS 2008 has the ability to use OLE DB or .NET providers to access data from data sources ranging from flat files to large-scale databases such as SQL Server, Oracle, Teradata, DB2, Sybase, and Informix. SSAS retrieves data from the data sources using the chosen provider's (OLE DB or .NET) interfaces for processing of Analysis Services objects. If any of the Analysis Services objects are defined as ROLAP, the provider is also used to retrieve data at query time. Updating the data in the UDM is called writeback. Analysis Services also uses the provider interfaces to update the source data during writeback (you learn about writeback in Chapter 12).

.NET Providers

Microsoft has created the .NET Framework and programming languages that use the framework to run in the Common Language Runtime (CLR) environment. The relationship between the Microsoft languages and the CLR are analogous to that of Java the language and the Java Runtime (the virtual machine). The .NET Framework itself is a huge class library that exposes tons of functionality and does so in the context of managed code. The term *managed* refers to the fact that memory is managed by the CLR and not the coder. You can write your own managed provider for your data source, or you can leverage .NET providers that use the .NET Framework. With the installation of SQL Server 2008 you will have .NET providers to access data from Microsoft SQL Server and Oracle as shown in Figure 4-3. If your relational data source has a .NET provider, you can install it and use that provider. In the Connection Manager page of the Data Source Wizard, you can choose the .NET provider to connect to your data source.

OLE DB Data Providers

OLE DB is an industry standard that defines a set of COM (Component Object Model) interfaces that allow clients to access data from various data stores. The OLE DB standard was created for client applications to have a uniform interface from which to access data. Such data can come from a wide variety of data sources such as Microsoft Access, Microsoft Project, and various database management systems.

Microsoft provides a set of OLE DB data providers to access data from several widely used data sources. These OLE DB providers are delivered together in a package called MDAC (Microsoft Data Access Components). Even though the interfaces exposed by the providers are common, each provider is different in the sense they have specific optimizations relevant to the specific back-end data source. OLE DB providers, being implementations of the OLE DB COM interfaces, are written in unmanaged code.

The Microsoft OLE DB provider for SQL Server has been the primary way of connecting to a Microsoft SQL Server prior to the release of SQL Server 2005. From the SQL Server 2005 release, this OLE DB provider has been repackaged and named SQL Server Native Client. SQL Server Native Client provides easy manageability of upgrades to the OLE DB provider. The SQL Server 2008 release provides version 10 of SQL Server Native Client and is used in the data source connection string as shown in Figure 4-5. SSAS 2008 provides the capability of connecting to any data source that provides an OLE DB interface, including the Analysis Services OLE DB provider.

The Trade-Offs

Versions of Analysis Services prior to Analysis Services 2005 supported connecting to data sources through OLE DB providers only. SSAS 2008 and SSAS 2005 have much tighter integration with the .NET Framework and support connections via both OLE DB and .NET data providers. If you deployed the .NET Framework across your entire organization, we recommend you use the .NET providers to access data from relational data sources. You might encounter a small amount of performance degradation using the .NET provider; however, the uniformity, maintainability, inherent connection pooling capabilities, and security provided by .NET data providers are worth taking the small hit on performance. If you are really concerned about the fastest possible performance, we recommend you use OLE DB providers for your data access.

Data Source Views

Data Source Views (DSVs) enable you to create a logical view of only the tables involved in your data warehouse design. In this way, system tables and other tables not pertinent to your efforts are excluded from the virtual workspace. In other words, you don't have to look at what you're never going to use directly anyway. DSVs are a powerful tool. In fact, you have the power to create DSVs that contain tables from multiple data sources, which you learn about later in this chapter. You need to create a DSV in your Analysis Services database because cubes and dimensions are created from a DSV rather than directly from the data source object. The DSV Wizard retrieves the schema information including relationships so that joins between tables are stored in the DSV. These relationships help the Cube and Dimension Wizards identify fact and dimension tables as well as hierarchies. If the right relationships do not exist in the data source, we recommend you create them within the DSV. Defining the relationships between the tables in the DSV helps you to get a better overview of your data warehouse. Taking the time to create a DSV ultimately pays for itself in terms of speeding up the design of your data warehouse.

Back in Chapter 2 you used the DSV Wizard to create a view on the Sales fact tables in Adventure Works DW. The DSV Wizard is a great way to get a jump-start on DSV creation. Then, once the DSV is created, you can perform operations on it such as adding or removing tables, specifying primary keys, and establishing relationships. These operations are accomplished within the DSV Designer. You learn more about the DSV Wizard and the DSV Designer and the operations within them in the following sections.

DSV Wizard

In Chapter 2, the DSV Wizard helped you create a DSV by going through a few dialogs. You need a data source to create a DSV. If you had not created a data source object in your database, the DSV Wizard allows you to create new data sources from the DSV Wizard's Select a Data Source page by clicking the New Data Source button. In addition, the DSV Wizard also allows you to restrict specific schemas as well as filter certain tables, which helps you to work with only the tables you need to create your DSV.

DSV Designer

The DSV Designer contains three panes, as shown in Figure 4-7. The center pane contains a graphical view of all the tables in the DSV and their primary keys. The relationships between tables are represented by lines with an arrow at the end. The top-left pane is called the *Diagram Organizer*, which is helpful in creating and saving concise views within large DSVs. When a DSV contains more than 20 tables it is difficult to visualize the complete DSV in the graphical view pane. When there are a large number of tables you will likely perform operations only on a subset of these tables at any given time. The Diagram Organizer is a handy way to create several diagrams that include just such subsets of relevant tables. Note that operations done on the tables within this diagram are reflected real-time in the entire DSV. By default you get one diagram that is called All Tables and contains the entire DSV.

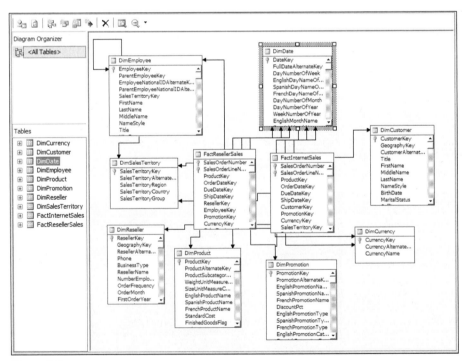

Figure 4-7

Figure 4-7 shows part of the default diagram All Tables that is created at the completion of the DSV Wizard. The lower-left pane of the DSV Designer is called Tables and is used to show the tree view of all the tables of the DSV along with their relationships to other tables. Figure 4-8 shows the Tables pane with detailed information of the DimCurrency table; you can see the primary key of the DimCurrency table, CurrencyKey, which is distinguished by a key icon. In addition, there is a folder that indicates all the relationships between the DimCurrency table and other tables in the DSV. If you expand the Relationships folder (as shown in Figure 4-8) you will see that the DimCurrency table joins to the FactInternetSales and FactResellerSales tables through the CurrencyKey — where the join column is specified within parentheses.

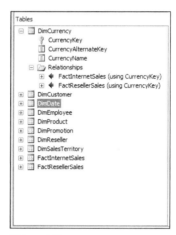

Figure 4-8

Adding/Removing Tables in a DSV

It is most common to initially create DSVs using the DSV Wizard. Also common is the desire to modify what the wizard generates to maximize the usefulness of the view. What the wizard generates is usually good, but subject to improvements. The DSV Designer provides you with the capability to easily modify the DSV. To modify the existing tables, right-click the diagram view pane and select Add/Remove Tables, as shown in Figure 4-9.

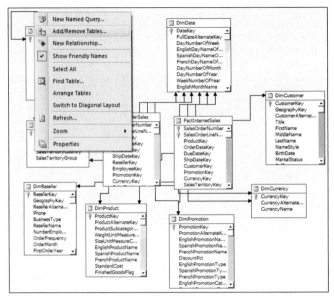

Figure 4-9

This invokes the Add/Remove Tables dialog shown in Figure 4-10. Using this dialog you can add additional tables to the DSV by moving tables from the Available objects list to the Included objects list or remove existing tables by moving them from the Included objects list to the Available objects list. You can also remove a table from the DSV in the DSV Designer in the graphical view pane or the table view pane using the following steps:

1. Select the table to be deleted.

2. Right-click the table and click Delete Table from DSV.

3. Click OK in the confirmation dialog that appears.

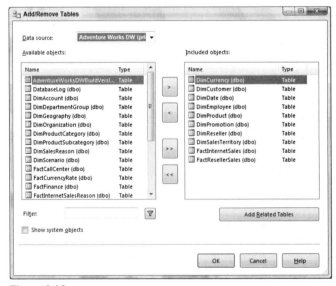

Figure 4-10

Specifying Primary Keys and Relationships in the DSV

It is likely that you will encounter underlying databases without the primary key to foreign key relationships that you will need in place for preparation of data for analysis — that is, for building dimensions and cubes. The DSV Wizard extracts the primary keys and the relationships specified in the underlying relational database to form primary keys and the relationships represented in the DSV. But perhaps some of the OLTP systems you use do not have the primary keys and relationships specified in the relevant tables — or when you design your data warehouse you might want to change these to suit your data warehouse design. The DSV Designer provides you with the functionality to specify primary keys for the tables that do not have them already, and in this way you can effectively modify or add new relationships between the tables in the DSV.

To specify the primary key(s) for a table, you need to do the following in the DSV Designer:

1. Select the column in the table that you want to specify as a primary key. If there is more than one column that forms the primary key, you can select multiple columns by holding down the Ctrl key while selecting. If the tables have auto-increment setup for the key column in the database, you will not be able to change the primary key(s) of the tables.

2. Right-click and select Set Logical Primary Key. When there is a relationship between two tables, Table1 and Table2, you typically have columns A in Table1 and B in Table2 that are involved in the join. Typically, column B is the primary key in Table2. Column A is referred to as the foreign key. An example would be a Sales fact table that has a Product ID as a column that joins with the Product ID column in the Products dimension table. In order to specify relationships between tables in the DSV, you use the following steps:

3. Select column A in Table1 that is involved in the join to Table2.

4. With column A selected, drag and drop it to column B in Table2. This forms a relationship between Table1 and Table2. A line will be created between these two tables with an arrow pointing toward Table2. If you double-click this line you will see details on the relationship — the tables involved in the relationship and the columns used for the join. Figure 4-11 shows the relationship between the FactResellersSales and DimReseller tables. You can modify the relationship using this Edit Relationship dialog by either changing the columns involved in the join or by adding additional columns that are involved in the join.

You can also create a new relationship by right-clicking a table and selecting New Relationship. You will be asked to specify the relationship in the Create Relationship dialog, which is similar to the Edit Relationship dialog shown in Figure 4-11. You need to choose the columns in the source and destination tables that are involved in the join.

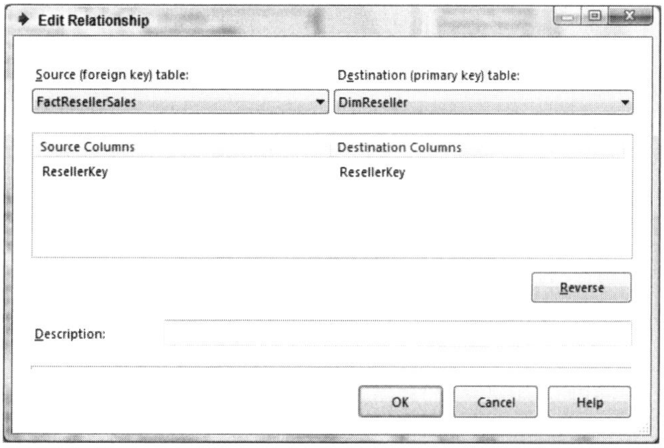

Figure 4-11

> All graphical operations such as drag-and-drop and specifying primary keys that are accomplished in the diagram view can also be accomplished in the table view.

Customizing Your Tables in the DSV

While modeling your data warehouse you will often want to select a few columns from tables, or restrict the fact table rows based on some specific criteria. Or you might want to merge columns from several tables into a single table. All these operations can be done by creating views in the relational database. SSAS 2008 provides the functionality of performing all these particular operations within the DSV using a *Named Query*. You can invoke the Named Query editor by right-clicking a table and selecting Replace Table ⇨ With New Named Query, as shown in Figure 4-12. If you want to add a specific table twice in your DSV or add some columns of a new table, you can launch the query designer by right-clicking the DSV Designer and selecting With New Named Query.

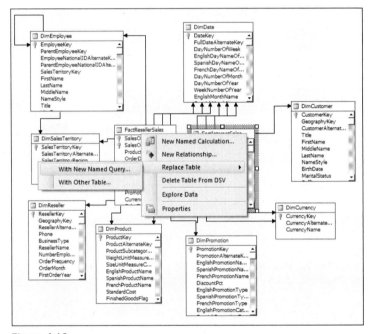

Figure 4-12

Named Queries are created using a query designer that helps you build custom queries to create a view. The Create Named Query designer dialog is shown in Figure 4-13. The Named Query editor in the designer is Visual Studio's Visual Database Tools query (VDT) editor. This shows the tight integration SQL Server 2008 has with Visual Studio 2008. In this dialog you can add tables from the data source, select specific columns from the tables, and apply restrictions or filters using the graphical interface. A SQL query is created based on your selections and is displayed in the SQL pane in the editor. If you're a SQL wizard, you can forego filling out the dialog elements and enter or paste a valid SQL query directly into the SQL pane. We recommend that you then execute the query to make sure the query is correct. The results from the underlying relational database will then be visible in a new pane beneath the SQL pane. Click OK once you have formed and validated your query. The table is now replaced with results from the Named Query you have specified in the DSV.

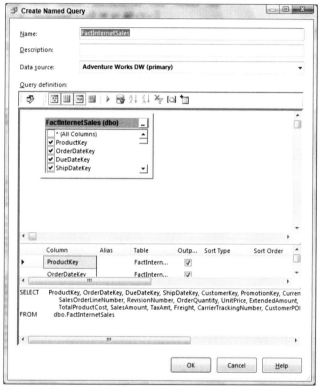

Figure 4-13

In certain instances you might want to create a new column in the table. An example of this would be to create the Full Name of an Employee from the first name, middle initial, and last name. One way to accomplish this task would be to replace the table with a named query and write the appropriate SQL to create this additional column. However, SSAS 2008 provides a simpler way to do the same operation. Right-click the Employee table and select New Named Calculation as shown in Figure 4-14. This action invokes the Create Named Calculation dialog shown in Figure 4-15. To add a column called Full Name to the Employee table you just need to combine the first name, middle name, and last name. You can type the expression for this in the Expression pane as shown in Figure 4-15 and then click the OK button.

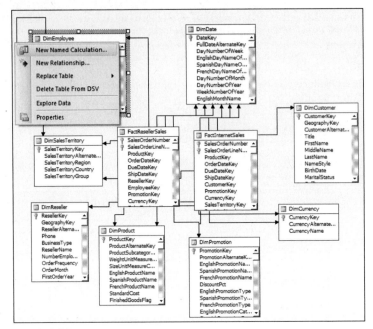

Figure 4-14

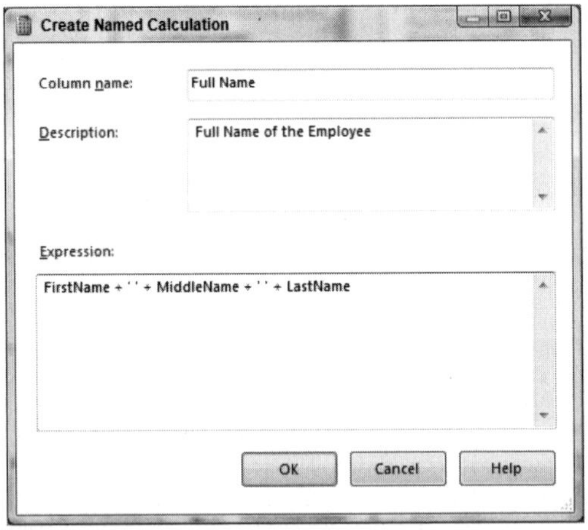

Figure 4-15

A new column is added to the Employee table as shown in Figure 4-16. The data type of this calculated column will be determined based on the data types of the actual columns involved in the calculation or data used within the expression. If the expression results in a number, the data type for this column will be an integer. In the preceding example the data type of this column is a string.

The DSV maintains the calculated column of a table as a computed column in the metadata; it does not write it out to the underlying tables. When you want to view the data of this table (which you see later in this chapter), the expression must be added to the SQL query so that you can see the data of this computed column.

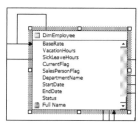

Figure 4-16

Data Source Views in Depth

Data warehouse designs consist of several fact tables and all the associated dimension tables. Small data warehouses are usually comprised of 10 to 20 tables, whereas larger data warehouses can have more than a hundred tables. Even though you have a large number of tables in your data warehouse, you will likely work with a small subset of those tables; each of which has relationships between them. For example, assume you have sales, inventory, and human resources (HR) data to analyze and the HR data is not strongly related to the sales and inventory data but there is a desired linkage. Then you might create two cubes, one for Sales and Inventory information and another one for HR. It is quite possible the Sales, Inventory, and HR information could be stored in a single data source — in the ODS or OLTP system.

Employee information (HR) could be related to the sales and inventory information within the company so far as there is a link between a given sales event and the employee who made the sale. You might want to slice the sales data by a specific employee, but to do so you must access information that is a part of a separate cube only accessible to the HR department (for security reasons). You can get around this problem by making a single DSV containing all the tables that store sales, inventory, and HR information of a company. From that DSV, both cubes can be formulated and permissions set such that only members of the HR group can drill down on personal employee data.

Having a lot of tables in the DSV definitely makes the navigation and usability a bit complex. When you are working on HR data you will only want to see the tables related to this alone. For easy manageability you will need customizable views within your DSV that show only certain tables. SSAS 2008 provides you with the capability of having several views within the DSV that each contains a subset of the DSV's tables. These views are called diagrams. By default you get a diagram called <All Tables> when you complete the DSV Wizard. You can create additional diagrams and select the tables that you want to include within them. Next, you learn how to create a new diagram and include only the tables you need.

To create a new diagram, you need to do the following:

1. Right-click the Diagram Organizer pane and select New Diagram, as shown in Figure 4-17.

Figure 4-17

2. Name the new diagram "Internet Sales."

3. You now have an empty diagram view. Right-click the diagram view and select Show Tables (see Figure 4-18). You are presented with a dialog where you can choose the table(s) you want to include in this diagram.

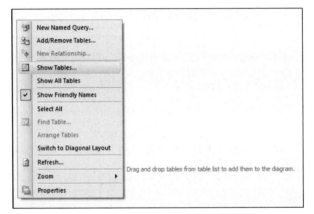

Figure 4-18

4. Select all the tables that are part of the InternetSales fact table and click OK.

This gives you a diagram view of Internet Sales that contains the Internet Sales fact table and the related dimension tables as shown in Figure 4-19. Alternatively you can add the FactInternetSales table to the diagram, right-click it, and select Show Related Tables to achieve the same result. This Internet Sales diagram has seven of the ten tables in the DSV. This makes it much easier to understand the relationship between these tables only.

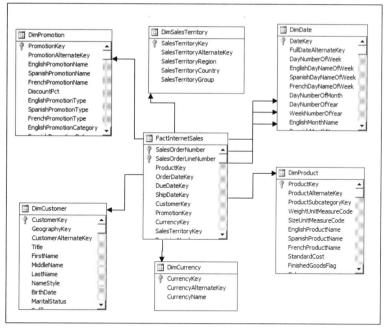

Figure 4-19

If you do not want a specific table in your diagram view you can right-click the table and select Hide. Instead of steps 3 and 4 in the preceding list you can add tables to the diagram view by dragging and dropping them from the Table pane to the Diagram pane. Create another diagram called Reseller Sales and add the FactResellerSales table and related tables.

Data Source View Properties

Each object created within BIDS has certain properties. Within the DSV you can view the properties of the objects in the DSV such as tables, views, columns, and relationships. Properties of these objects are shown in the Properties window within BIDS, as shown in Figure 4-20.

Figure 4-20 shows the properties of a column in a table, calculated column, a table, and a relationship. For the regular columns in a table you have the properties AllowNull, Data Type, Description, Friendly Name, Length, and Name. The properties of a column are populated by retrieving the corresponding property from the data source. The data type of this column is retrieved from the data source. Based on the properties defined in the data source, the properties AllowNull, Data Type, Length, Name, and Friendly Name are populated. The Length property is applicable only for the string data type. For all other data types the Length property has a value of –1. You cannot change certain properties; they are not editable in the Properties window and are grayed out. You can change the Friendly Name and provide a description to each column. Often columns of a table in the relational database might not have user-friendly names. User-friendly means the name of the column should indicate clearly or intuitively the data stored in the column. Friendly Name is a property that can be changed so that this friendly name is shown in the DSV for an easier understanding of the model. You can also provide an optional Description to each column if needed. The DSV Designer provides you with the option of switching between the original column names and the friendly names. You can right-click in the DSV diagram view and toggle between the friendly name and the original column name by selecting the Show Friendly Name option.

109

Figure 4-20

Named columns created in the DSV do not have a Friendly Name property because you will define the name to this column and we expect you to provide a name that is intuitive and understandable. Instead, named columns have the Expression property because each named column is created from a SQL expression. You can change this expression only in the Named Column dialog and not in the Properties window.

Tables have the properties Data Source, Description, FriendlyName, Name, Schema, and Table Type. The Data Source indicates the name of the data source of the Table. The Table Type shows whether the object in the underlying data source is a table or a view. Similar to the columns, tables also have the option to specify a friendly name.

Relationships between tables are provided with a name that includes the tables that participate in the relationship. Similar to named columns, named queries do not have a Friendly Name property. They have a property called Query Definition that shows the query used to specify the named query object.

Different Layouts in DSVs

The DSV Designer provides you with two layout types to view the tables in the DSV. When you create a DSV the default layout type is rectangular layout. In the default layout, the lines representing the relationships between tables are composed of horizontal and vertical lines, and the lines emerge from any of the sides of the table. The second layout type offered by the DSV Designer is called diagonal layout. In diagonal layout, the tables are arranged in a way such that the lines showing the relationships between tables are originating at the end points of the table, so that these lines appear to be along the diagonal of the tables — hence the name "diagonal layout." You can switch between rectangular layout and diagonal layout in the DSV by right-clicking in the DSV Designer and selecting the layout type of your choice. Figures 4-21 and 4-22 show rectangular and diagonal layout, respectively, of the Internet Sales diagram.

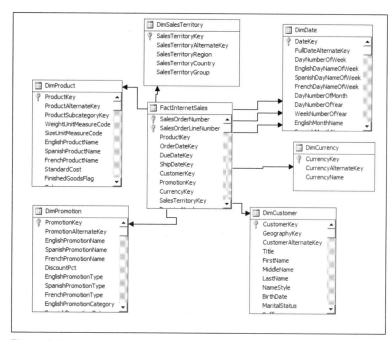

Figure 4-21

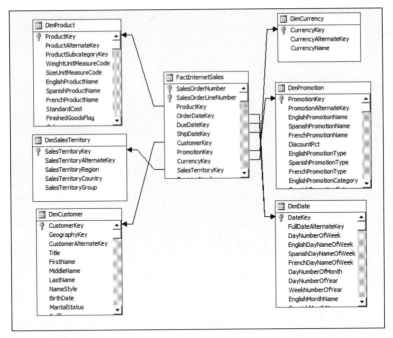

Figure 4-22

Validating Your DSV and Initial Data Analysis

The relationships specified in the DSV will be used in creating your dimensions and cubes. Therefore, validating your DSV is crucial to your data warehouse design. The DSV Designer provides a first level of validation when you specify relationships. If the data types of column(s) involved in the relationship do not match, the DSV will not allow you to establish the relationship. This forces you to make sure you cast the data types of the column(s) involved in the relationships appropriately. You might need another level of validation by looking at the data within each table. You can do this by issuing queries to the tables in the relational data source. The DSV provides a way of looking at sample data for validation. A few validations you can do within the DSV by looking at sample data are as follows:

1. Looking at the fact table data helps you in making sure this table contains fact data, the primary key has been specified correctly, and appropriate relationships needed for dimensions are established.

2. Analyzing a dimension table's sample data ensures that you have all the relationships established between the fact and dimension tables and any relationships within each table are established correctly. For example, if you have an Employee table that contains an employee and his manager, you might want to establish a relationship so that your model can take advantage of this.

In addition, a sample of data from the tables in the DSV helps you in identifying the measures of the cube as well as the hierarchies of each dimension. Analyzing sample data in the DSV also helps you identify dimensions that can be created from the fact table data. The analysis of sample data within the DSV is even more important when creating Data Mining models. You learn more about analyzing the data with respect to Data Mining in Chapter 16.

To see a sample of the data specified by your DSV, right-click a table in the DSV Designer and select Explore Data. You can now see rows from the underlying table presented within the Explore <tablename> Table window as shown in Figure 4-23. The data presented is only a subset of the underlying table data. By default the first 5,000 rows are retrieved and shown within this window. You can change the number of rows retrieved by clicking the Sampling Options button. Clicking the Sampling Options button launches the Data Exploration Options dialog where you can change the sampling method, sample count, and number of states per chart, which is used for displaying data in the chart format. Once you have changed the sample count value you can click the Resample Data button to retrieve data based on the new settings. The Explore Table window has four tabs: Table, Pivot Table, Chart, and Pivot Chart. The Table tab shows the raw sampled data from the data source as rows and columns with column headings.

Resample Data

Sampling Options

Explore FactInternetSales Table / Adventure Works DW.dsv [Design]*

Table | Pivot Table | Chart | Pivot Chart

ProductKey	OrderDateKey	DueDateKey	ShipDateKey	CustomerKey	PromotionKey	CurrencyKey	SalesTerritoryKey
310	20010701	20010713	20010708	21768	1	19	6
346	20010701	20010713	20010708	28389	1	39	7
346	20010701	20010713	20010708	25863	1	100	1
336	20010701	20010713	20010708	14501	1	100	4
346	20010701	20010713	20010708	11003	1	6	9
311	20010702	20010714	20010709	27645	1	100	4
310	20010702	20010714	20010709	16624	1	6	9
351	20010702	20010714	20010709	11005	1	6	9
344	20010702	20010714	20010709	11011	1	6	9
312	20010703	20010715	20010710	27621	1	100	4
312	20010703	20010715	20010710	27616	1	100	4
330	20010703	20010715	20010710	20042	1	98	10
313	20010703	20010715	20010710	16351	1	6	9
314	20010703	20010715	20010710	16517	1	6	9
314	20010704	20010716	20010711	27606	1	100	1
311	20010704	20010716	20010711	13513	1	29	8
310	20010705	20010717	20010712	27601	1	100	4
311	20010705	20010717	20010712	13591	1	98	10
314	20010705	20010717	20010712	16483	1	6	9
311	20010705	20010717	20010712	16529	1	6	9
336	20010705	20010717	20010712	25249	1	6	9
311	20010706	20010718	20010713	27668	1	100	1
312	20010706	20010718	20010713	27612	1	100	4
311	20010706	20010718	20010713	13264	1	29	8

Figure 4-23

When you click the Pivot Table tab you get an additional window called PivotTable Field List that shows all the columns of the table, as shown in Figure 4-24. You can drag and drop these columns inside the pivot table in the row, column, details, or filter areas. The values in the row and column provide you with an intersection point for which the detailed data is shown. For example, you can drag and drop CustomerKey, SalesTerritoryKey, and Sales Amount to the row, column, and detail data areas, respectively. The pivot table now shows you the sales amount of each product by each customer. The pivot table actually allows you to view multidimensional data from a single table. You learn more about pivot tables in Chapter 17.

Analysis Services analyzes the sample data, identifies the most important columns within the table, and provides you distributions in the Chart tab. The Pivot Chart tab provides you functionality similar to the Pivot Table tab but in a chart view. The Chart and Pivot Chart tabs are typically used to do an initial analysis of the data so that appropriate columns can be used to create good Data Mining models.

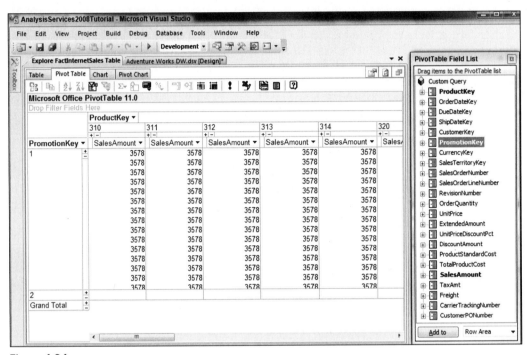

Figure 4-24

Multiple Data Sources within a DSV

Data warehouses usually consist of data from several data sources. Some examples of data sources are SQL Server, Oracle, DB2, and Teradata. Traditionally, the OLTP data is transferred from the operational data store to the data warehouse — the staging area that combines data from disparate data sources. This is not only time intensive in terms of design, maintainability, and storage but also in terms of other considerations such as replication of data and ensuring data is in sync with the source. SSAS 2008 helps you avoid this and gives you a better return on your investment.

The DSV Designer provides you with the capability of adding tables from multiple data sources, which you can then use to build your cubes and dimensions. You first need to define the data sources that include the tables that are part of your data warehouse design using the Data Source Wizard. Once this has been accomplished, you create a DSV and include tables from one of the data sources. This data source is called the primary data source and needs to be a SQL Server. You can then add tables in the DSV Designer by right-clicking in the diagram view and choosing Add/Remove Tables. You need to have a data source defined in your Analysis Services project to be able to add tables from it to the DSV. The Add/Remove Tables dialog allows you to choose a data source as shown in Figure 4-25 so that you can add its tables to the DSV. To illustrate the selection of tables from a second data source, as shown in

Figure 4-25, we have created a second data source in the AnalysisServices2008Tutorial project from the SQL Server Master database. You should be aware that there might be performance implications to retrieving data from secondary data sources because all the queries are routed through the primary data source.

Once you have added the tables from multiple data sources to your DSV, you can start creating your cubes and dimensions as if these came from a single data source. The limitation that the primary data source needs to be a SQL Server is due to the fact that Analysis Services instance uses a SQL Server–specific feature called OPENROWSET to retrieve data from other data sources.

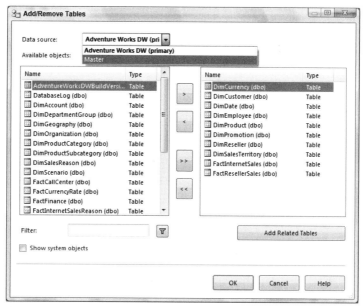

Figure 4-25

Summary

You now have the skills to deal with the challenges real-world data warehouses will throw at you in terms of multiple data sources. You learned about OLE DB and managed data providers that are used by SSAS 2008 to retrieve data from data sources and the trade-offs of using one versus another. Indeed, you learned to tame the disparate data source beast by using multiple data sources. Then you learned to consolidate the tables and relationships of interest in Data Source Views (DSVs), and finally, to refine the tables and relationships in the DSVs so you only have to deal with what's relevant.

Note that when key changes are made in the DSV that is where the changes stay — in the DSV. The changes are not written out to the underlying tables as you might expect. This is a good thing. To see why, take a look at the alternative to using the DSV capability. The alternative method is to create a view in SQL with real relationship transforms in the underlying tables. It's not that we strongly oppose this method, but if your data spans multiple databases, you may have to create linked servers and that can become time-consuming. SSAS 2008 provides an easy way to specify these cross-database relationships within a DSV without the overhead of having to use linked servers. However, when multiple data sources are included in a single DSV the primary data source should support the ability to send queries and retrieve results from other servers. You can incur performance degradation due to this method; however, you do have the flexibility of not having to manage the data on multiple servers to create your data warehouse.

You're doing great! In fact, you're now ready to tackle core business intelligence constructs like dimension design (Chapter 5) and cube design (Chapter 6). If you already know these topics from working with earlier versions of SQL Server Analysis Services, we recommend working through the chapters anyway. There have been some important changes to the Cube and Dimension Wizards in Analysis Services 2008.

5

Dimension Design

Prior to the advent of cable, when you brought home a new television, the first order of business was to manually tune in one of the few existing local channels. To accomplish this you manipulated the dials, rabbit-ear antennae positioning, and other controls to eventually obtain an optimal picture, audio, and vertical hold configuration. The process of designing a data warehouse using Analysis Services 2008 is similar to that. Analysis Services 2008 provides you with various wizards that help you build the initial framework, just like the rotary tuner on the television got you close to the desired channel. With the basic infrastructure in place, some fine-tuning can optimize the initial framework to your needs. In fact, you saw this approach in the previous chapter when you learned about creating data sources and DSVs. Likewise, here you learn how to create dimensions using the Dimension Wizard and then use the Dimension Designer to fine-tune the dimension based on your business needs.

Cubes are made up of dimensions and measures, where the measures are aggregated along each dimension. Without an understanding of dimensions and how measures are aggregated along them, you can't create and exploit the power of cubes, so let's jump right into learning about building and viewing dimensions. Once the dimensions are created, they need to be added to the cube and the right relationship type between the fact data and dimension needs to be defined. Analysis Services 2008 supports six relationship types (no relationship, regular, fact, referenced, many-to-many, and data mining). You learn about relationship types in this chapter and Chapters 8 and 16. In addition, you learn about the attributes and hierarchies that form an integral part of dimensions. You learn how to model the Time dimension and Parent-Child dimensions, which are different from regular dimensions and are found in many data warehouses. Finally, you learn how to process and browse dimensions.

Working with the Dimension Wizard

Dimensions help you define the structure of your cube so as to facilitate effective data analysis. Specifically, dimensions provide you with the capability of slicing data within a cube, and these dimensions can be built from one or more dimension tables. As you learned in Chapter 1, your data warehouse can be designed as a star or snowflake schema. In a star schema, dimensions are created from single tables that are joined to a fact table. In a snowflake schema, two or more joined dimension tables are used to create dimensions where one of the tables is joined to the fact table. You create both of these dimension types in this chapter.

You also learned in Chapters 1, 2, and 3 that each dimension contains objects called hierarchies. In Analysis Services 2008 you have two types of hierarchies to contend with: the attribute hierarchy, which corresponds to a single column in a relational table, and multilevel hierarchies, which are derived from two or more attribute hierarchies where each attribute is a level in the multilevel hierarchy. A typical example of an attribute hierarchy would be Zip Code in a Dim Geography dimension, and a typical example for a multilevel hierarchy would be Country-State-City-Zip Code also in a Geography dimension. In everyday discussions of multilevel hierarchies, most people leave off the "multilevel" and just call them "hierarchies."

For the exercises in this chapter, you use the project you designed in Chapter 2. If you don't happen to have the project handy, you can download it from www.wrox.com. Regardless of whether you download, you will still need to add the Geography Dimension (dbo.DimGeography) to the DSV. To add this dimension to your DSV, follow these steps:

1. Double-click the DSV named "AdventureWorksDW.dsv" in Solution Explorer.

2. Click the Add/Remove Objects toolbar button (the top-left button in the DSV Designer toolbar) as shown in Figure 5-1.

Figure 5-1

3. In the Available objects list, select DimGeography and click the > (right arrow) button as shown in Figure 5-2. This will move the Geography dimension into the Included objects list in the Add/Remove Tables dialog. Click OK to continue.

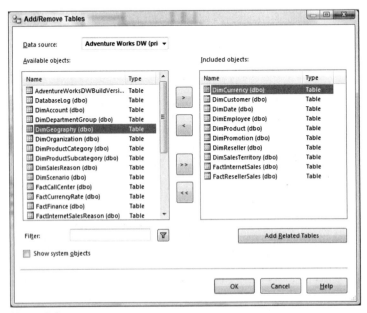

Figure 5-2

4. All tables in the DSV should have the logical primary key set in order to allow Analysis Services to determine the key attribute columns if the table is used in a dimension or the foreign key columns in the case of fact tables. Review the DimGeography table in the DSV designer to make sure the DimGeography column has been set as the primary key as shown in Figure 5-3.

If the primary key column is not retrieved for a table, you can right-click the key column in the table and select Set Logical Primary Key as shown in Figure 5-3. If the primary key for the table has already been set, the option to Set Logical Primary Key will be disabled.

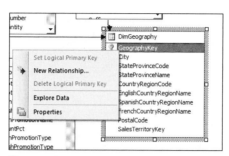

Figure 5-3

Now you are ready to explore use of the Dimension Wizard in Analysis Services 2008. Continue to follow these steps to create a Geography dimension.

5. Launch the Dimension Wizard by right-clicking Dimensions in the Solution Explorer and selecting New Dimension as shown in Figure 5-4. If the welcome screen of the Dimension Wizard opens up, click Next.

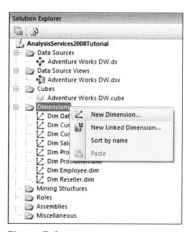

Figure 5-4

6. In the Select Creation Method screen, shown in Figure 5-5, you will see four options:

- ❏ Use an existing table
- ❏ Generate a time table in the data source
- ❏ Generate a time table on the server
- ❏ Generate a non-time table in the data source

Using an existing table in the data source allows for the creation of a standard dimension, which can later be modified to become any sophisticated dimension type. This makes for a great generic starting point.

A Time dimension, on the other hand, is a unique type of dimension typically created from a table that contains time information such as year, semester, quarter, month, week, and date. A Time dimension is unique because its members are fixed (a year always has 12 months in it) and typical business analyses are performed over time. Due to the uniqueness of the Time dimensions and how they are used in business analysis, there are special MDX functions that can be used with time dimensions. Furthermore, aggregation of data on a Time dimension does not have to be a garden variety additive aggregation like sum or count.

Most business decision makers want to analyze their data across a Time dimension to understand, for example, the month with maximum sales for a quarter or some other time period. Analysis Services provides you a distinct way to aggregate measure data across a Time dimension. This is done with semi-additive measures. You learn more about semi-additive measures in Chapters 6 and 9. In a Time dimension, some standard hierarchies are commonly used, such as fiscal year and calendar year, both of which can be built automatically. The Time dimension can be built using either a table from the data source or without any associated tables in the data source. To create a table to serve as the source of your Time dimension, you choose the second option on the Creation Method screen. To create an Analysis Server–based Time dimension you would select the third option. You learn more about server Time dimensions in Chapter 8.

In addition to Time, Analysis Services 2008 is also aware of several other common dimension types used in Business Intelligence applications such as Account, Customer, Employee, and Currency, and can create the necessary tables in the data source to support these dimension types. In this chapter we're concerned with creating dimensions from a data source.

In the Select Creation Method dialog, select "Use an existing table" and click Next.

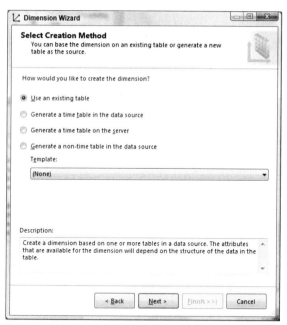

Figure 5-5

7. In the Specify Source Information page (shown in Figure 5-6), you need to select the DSV for creating the dimension, select the main table from which the dimension is to be designed, specify the key columns for the dimension, and optionally specify a name column for the dimension key value. By default, the first DSV in your project is selected. Because the current project has only one DSV (the Adventure WorksDW DSV), it is selected.

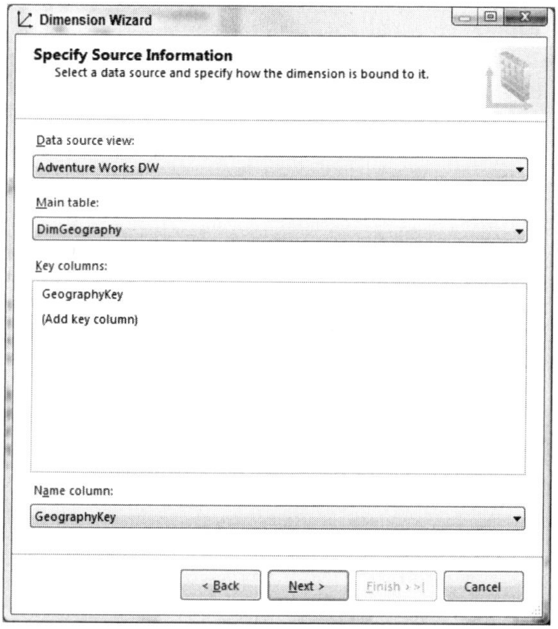

Figure 5-6

In the Main Table listbox on the screen, you need to select the main table from which the dimension is to be designed. If a dimension is to be created from a star schema, the dimension is created from the single pertinent table. A snowflake schema dimension actually contains several tables, one of which is the primary table of the dimension. This primary table is chosen as the main table in the Main Table selection of the Dimension Wizard.

Select the DimGeography table from the Main table drop-down list as shown in Figure 5-6.

After selecting the Main Table for the dimension, the Key Columns list and the Name Column combo box will automatically be set to the logical primary key of the selected table. If no logical primary key is set, you will need to specify the key columns yourself. If the logical key for the main dimension table is a collection of columns, you must select a single column for the Name Column before proceeding. You have already defined a logical primary key column for the DimGeography table in the DSV.

Click the Next button to proceed to the next step in the Dimension Wizard.

8. The Dimension Wizard now analyzes the DSV to detect any outward-facing relationships from the DimGeography table. An outward-facing relationship is a relationship between the DimGeography table and another table, such that a column in the DimGeography table is a foreign key related to another table. The Select Related Tables screen (see Figure 5-7) shows that the wizard detected an outward relationship between the DimGeography table and the DimSalesTerritory table. In this example you will be modeling the DimGeography table as a star schema table instead of snowflake schema. Deselect the DimSalesTerritory table and click Next.

Figure 5-7

9. The Select Dimension Attributes screen of the Dimension Wizard (see Figure 5-8) displays the columns of the main table that have been selected for the dimension you're creating. Each selected column on this screen results in an equivalent attribute being created in the new dimension. Even though you are building just a dimension here, that dimension is going to be part of a cube, which is described by the Unified Dimensional Model (UDM). The UDM combines the best of the relational and OLAP worlds. One important aspect of the relational model is the ability to query each column for reporting purposes. The columns selected from the relational table are transformed to attributes of a dimension that can then be used for querying from the UDM. You can control which of the attributes are available for browsing and querying by checking or un-checking the Enable Browsing option for each attribute. In addition, you can set the Attribute Type property to allow Analysis Services to provide special functionality based on the attribute's type and/or Analysis Services client tools to utilize this property to provide appropriate navigational paths. By default the wizard assigns the column name as the attribute name. You can change the attribute name for each selected attribute in this page.

   In the Select Dimension Attributes screen, select all the attributes of the DimGeography table (all the attributes in the screen), leave their Attribute Type as Regular, allow them to be browsed as shown in Figure 5-8, and click Next.

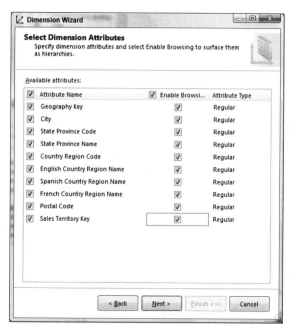

Figure 5-8

10. The final screen of the Dimension Wizard shows the attributes that will be created for the dimension based on your choices in the wizard (see Figure 5-9). Click the Finish button.

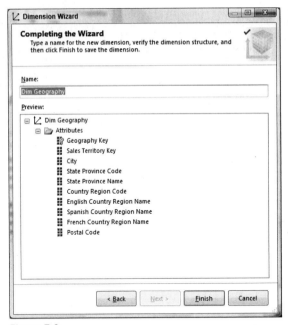

Figure 5-9

The wizard has created the dimension object Dim Geography and opened it up in the Dimension Designer. Congratulations!!! You have successfully created your first dimension using the Dimension Wizard. Next, you learn how to use the Dimension Designer to enhance the dimension to fit your business needs.

Working with the Dimension Designer

The Dimension Designer, shown in Figure 5-10, is an important tool that helps you to refine the dimension created by the Dimension Wizard. You can define the properties such as unary operators, custom roll-ups, and so forth, which help you to define how data should be aggregated for cells referred to by members of hierarchies in the dimension. The Dimension Designer itself is composed of four pages, which can be accessed from the tabs at the top of the designer: Dimension Structure, Attribute Relationships, Translations, and Browser. The first of these pages, Dimension Structure, contains three panes: Attributes, Hierarchies, and Data Source View. In addition to that you have the toolbar, which contains several buttons that help you to enhance the dimension. The Attributes pane shows all the attributes, the Hierarchies pane shows all the hierarchies along with their levels, and the Data Source View pane shows the tables that are used in the dimension. If you hover over each toolbar button you will see a tooltip that describes the functionality of that button. Some of the buttons are the same as the ones you saw in the DSV Designer and are used for operations within the Dimension Designer's Data Source View pane. The functionality of some of the other buttons is discussed later in this chapter and in Chapter 8.

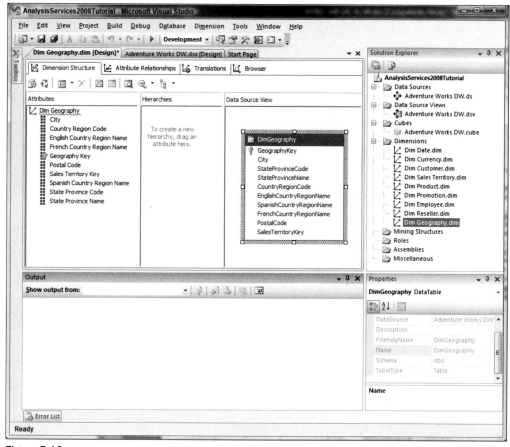

Figure 5-10

Attributes

Attributes are hierarchies that have only two levels: the leaf level, which contains one member for each distinct attribute value, and the All level, which contains the aggregated value of all the leaf level members. The All level is optional. Each attribute directly corresponds to a table's column in the DSV. The Attributes pane in the Dimension Designer shows all the attribute hierarchies of the dimension. The default view of all the attributes within the Attributes pane window is a Tree view as shown in Figure 5-11. Two additional views are supported in the Dimension Designer: List view and Grid view. These views show the attributes and associated properties in different ways.

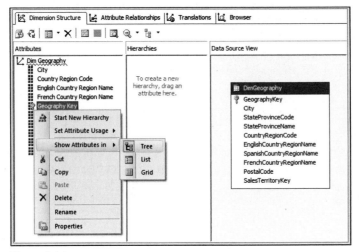

Figure 5-11

The List view repositions the Attributes pane below the Hierarchies pane and shows only the attributes of the dimension in a flat list (it doesn't show the dimension name as a parent node). This view is useful when your dimension has a lot of multilevel hierarchies. Because you get a wider area for the Hierarchies pane, you get a visually optimized view for this kind of dimension.

The Grid view is laid out similarly to the List view but includes additional columns that allow you to easily edit some of the important dimension properties right in the Attributes pane. When you're working with more than one attribute, editing these properties in the Attributes pane is less cumbersome than having to select each attribute and then switching over to the Properties window to change the attribute's value. (All the properties shown in the Grid view are also present in the Properties window.)

You can toggle between the different views by right-clicking in the Attributes pane and selecting the view type you desire, as shown in Figure 5-11. Just choose the view that best suits you to visualize and design your dimension easily.

Figure 5-12 shows the List view and Grid view of the attributes shown in Figure 5-11.

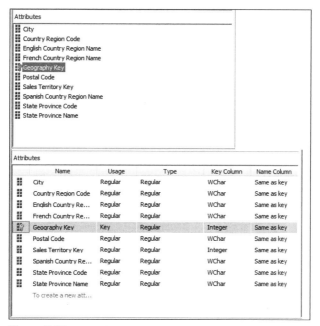

Figure 5-12

Attribute Relationships

Attribute relationships can be defined when attributes within the same dimension have a one-to-many relationship with each other. For example, if you have the attributes Country, State, and City, you have one-to-many relationships between country and state, as well as between state and city. Each dimension has to have at least one attribute that is defined as the key attribute. By definition, the key attribute has a one-to-many relationship with every attribute in the dimension. The Dimension Wizard automatically establishes relationships, such that all attributes of the dimension are related to key attributes.

If you are aware of one-to-many relationships between attributes, we highly recommend that you specify these relationships in the Dimension Designer with attribute relationships. Specifying the attribute relationship helps improve query performance as well as changing the aggregation design for multilevel hierarchies so as to include the attributes that are part of a hierarchy. Because the Dim Geography dimension contains one-to-many relationships, you need to specify attribute relationships to get query performance improvements. You learn more about the benefits of attribute relationships in Chapter 14.

If you are familiar with Analysis Services 2005, you will notice that attributes in the Tree view no longer expand to show attribute relationships for the attributes in the tree. Analysis Services 2008 has added a separate page in the Dimension Designer to make definition of attribute relationships easier for the user. To view and edit the attribute relationships in Analysis Services 2008, you use the Dimension Designer's Attribute Relationships page shown in Figure 5-13. The Attribute Relationships page contains three panes. The top pane graphically shows attribute relationships, the Attributes pane on the lower left shows the list of attributes in the dimension, and the Attribute Relationships pane in the lower right shows the list of defined relationships. The attributes shown in the top pane below the Geography Key attribute are all the attributes of the dimension that have one-to-many relationships with the key attribute. All these attributes are also referred to as member property attributes or related attributes.

Because the attribute relationship is defined for each member in the Geography Key attribute, you can retrieve its properties from the related attributes using member property MDX functions.

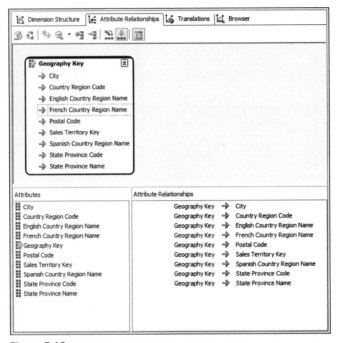

Figure 5-13

You can create new or modify existing attribute relationships using various methods within each of these panes. Follow these steps to update the Geography dimension's attribute relationships:

1. In the visualization (top) pane, modifying attribute relationships is accomplished by dragging and dropping member property attributes onto the attribute to which they are related.

For example, if a State-Province Name has a one-to-many relationship with City, you would create the relationship by dragging the City attribute onto the State-Province Name attribute as follows: In the Attribute Relationships page's visualization pane, select the City attribute and drag and drop it onto the State-Province Name attribute. This creates a new attribute relationship node as shown in Figure 5-14. Note the change in the Attribute Relationships pane to reflect the newly defined relationship. In the visualization pane, editing and deleting attribute relationships is accomplished by right-clicking a relationship's line and selecting the desired action from the context menu.

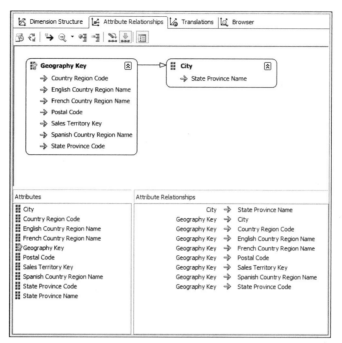

Figure 5-14

2. To define a new relationship using the Attributes pane, you right-click the attribute that makes up the many side of the one-to-many relationship and select New Attribute Relationship. This will launch the Create Attribute Relationship dialog. The Source Attribute is the attribute corresponding to the "many" side of the relationship, and the Related Attribute is the attribute corresponding to the "one" side. You can also set the relationship type in this dialog to either Flexible (default) or Rigid. By default, Analysis Services tools define all the relationships to be flexible. A relationship is flexible if the value can change over time. A relationship is rigid if the relationship does not change over time. For example, the birth date of a customer is fixed and hence the relationship between a customer's key/name and the birth date attribute would be defined as rigid. However, the relationship between a customer and his city is flexible because the customer can move from one city to another. You can't delete or alter existing relationships from the Attributes pane. You have a one-to-many relationship between English Country Region Name and State-Province Name. To specify that the attribute English Country Region Name has a one-to-many relationship or is a member property of State-Province Name, perform the following steps in the Attribute Relationships tab of the Dimension Designer.

3. Right-click the State-Province Name attribute (source attribute) in the Attributes pane of the Attribute Relationships page and select New Attribute Relationship from the context menu.

4. In the Create Attribute Relationship dialog select the English Country Region Name as the Related Attribute (see Figure 5-15).

5. Click OK to create the relationship.

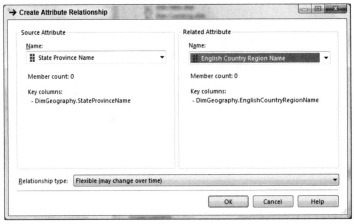

Figure 5-15

Your Attribute Relationships display should be similar to that shown in Figure 5-16.

Establishing attribute relationships is important for two reasons: It can improve processing performance (as you learn in Chapter 14), and it affects calculations that are aggregated across these attributes. You can view and modify the cardinality of the attribute relationships you establish using the Cardinality property in the Properties window. Click the relationship in the visualization pane or in the Attribute Relationships pane to bring up its properties. By default the Cardinality is set to many. If you know that the relationship between the attributes is one-to-one you can change the cardinality to one. For example, the cardinality between a customer's ID and social security number is one-to-one, however the cardinality between the English Country Region Name attribute and the State-Province Name attribute is one-to-many.

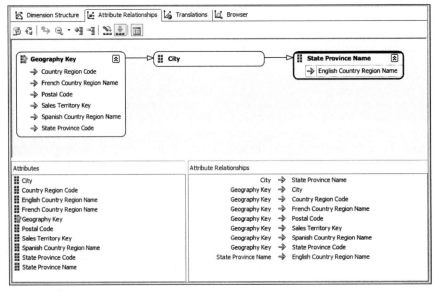

Figure 5-16

To define a new relationship using the Attribute Relationships pane you must first select an attribute from either the visualization or Attributes pane and then right-click in the Attribute Relationships pane in the area not occupied by existing attribute relationships. This can be a bit cumbersome. We recommend you use the visualization pane or the Attributes pane for creating new attribute relationships. Editing and deleting existing relationships in the Attribute Relationships pane, however, is as simple as right-clicking the relationship and choosing the desired action from the context menu as shown in Figure 5-17. Editing a relationship launches the Relationship Editor dialog, whose functionality and layout is identical to the Create Attribute Relationships dialog shown in Figure 5-15; only the title is different.

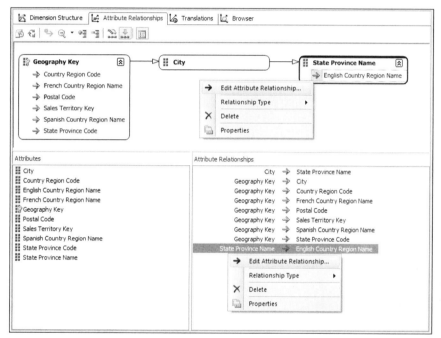

Figure 5-17

Use the Attribute Relationships pane to edit the existing relationships for the French and Spanish Country Region Name attributes using the following steps:

6. Click the Geography Key to French Country Region Name relationship in the Attribute Relationships pane.

7. Right-click and select Edit Attribute Relationship.

8. In the Edit Attribute Relationship dialog select the English Country Region Name as the Source Attribute (see Figure 5-18).

9. Click OK to save the change to the relationship.

10. In the Properties window, change the Cardinality property corresponding to the relationship between English Country Region Name and French Country Region Name from Many to One.

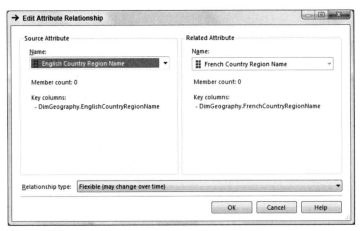

Figure 5-18

Repeat the previous five steps for the Spanish Country Region Name attribute relationship.

You have now used three different methods for working with attribute relationships. Often in business analysis when you are analyzing a specific member of a dimension, you need to see the properties of the dimension member to understand it better. In such circumstances, instead of traversing the complete hierarchy you can retrieve the member by querying the member properties. This once again is a performance improvement from the end user's perspective. A wide variety of client tools support the ability to retrieve member properties of a specific member when needed by the data analyst. You can add additional attributes by dragging and dropping a column from the DSV to the Attributes pane or delete an existing attribute by right-clicking that attribute and selecting Delete.

Hierarchies and Levels

Hierarchies (also called multilevel hierarchies) are created from attributes of a dimension. Each multilevel hierarchy contains one or more levels, and each level is an attribute hierarchy itself. Based on the attributes of the Geography dimension you created, the logical multilevel hierarchy to create would be Country-State-City-Postal Code. You can create this hierarchy using the following steps:

1. Switch to the Dimension Structure tab of the Geography dimension and drag and drop the attribute English Country Region Name from the Attributes pane to the Hierarchies pane. This creates a multilevel hierarchy called Hierarchy with one level: English Country Region Name. This level actually corresponds to a country. To make this name more user friendly, rename the English Country Region Name to "Country" by right-clicking the attribute within the multilevel hierarchy and selecting Rename.

2. Drag and drop State-Province Name from the Attributes pane to the Hierarchies pane such that the State-Province Name attribute is below Country in the multilevel hierarchy. Rename State-Province Name to "State-Province" by right-clicking the attribute and selecting Rename.

3. Drag and drop City and Postal Code attributes to the multilevel hierarchy in that order so that you now have a four-level hierarchy Country-State-City-Postal Code.

4. The default name of the hierarchy you have created is "Hierarchy." Rename it to "Geography" by right-clicking its name and selecting Rename (see Figure 5-19). You can also rename hierarchy and level names in the Hierarchies pane by selecting the item and changing the value of its Name property in the Properties pane.

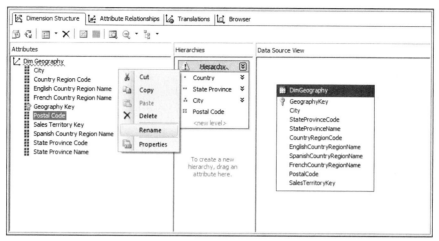

Figure 5-19

You have now created a multilevel hierarchy called Geography that has four levels, as shown in Figure 5-20. You can click the arrows to expand the attribute in each level to see all the member properties. You can create additional hierarchies in the Hierarchies pane.

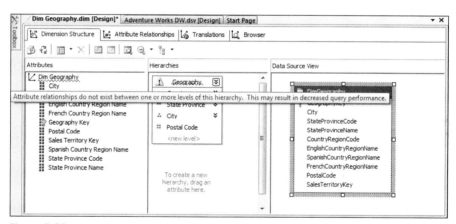

Figure 5-20

Notice the warning icon next to the Geography hierarchy name and squiggly line under the name of the hierarchy. If you place your mouse over this icon or the hierarchy name, you will see a tooltip message indicating that attribute relationships do not exist between one or more levels of the hierarchy and could result in decreased performance as shown in Figure 5-20.

The current hierarchy design is what is called an unnatural hierarchy. An unnatural hierarchy exists when knowing the attribute value of one level of the hierarchy is not sufficient to know who its parent is in the next level up the hierarchy. Another example of an unnatural hierarchy would be a Customer Gender-Age hierarchy, where Gender is the top level of the dimension and Age is the second level. Knowing that a customer is 37 years old does not give any indication of their gender.

Conversely, in a natural hierarchy, knowing the value of an attribute at one level clearly indicates who its parent is on the next level of the hierarchy. An example of a natural hierarchy would be a Product Department hierarchy with Category and Sub-Category levels. By knowing that a product is in the Mountain Bike Sub-Category, we would know that it belongs to the Bike Category. This relationship between attribute values is defined through attribute relationships. In order for a hierarchy to be considered natural, attribute relationships must exist from the bottom level of the hierarchy all the way to the top. Analysis Services 2008 will only materialize hierarchies that are considered natural. Use the following steps to refine the current Geography hierarchy so that it is natural:

5.   Switch back to the Attribute Relationships page. The page should look similar to Figure 5-21.

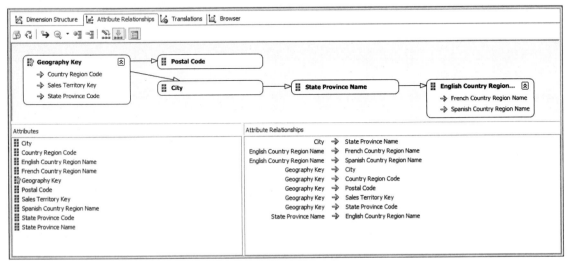

Figure 5-21

6.   There is no relationship between Postal Code and City. In the visualization pane drag and drop the Postal Code attribute to the City attribute.

An attribute relationship between the Postal Code attribute and the City attribute is created as shown in Figure 5-22. Notice that the visualization of the attribute relationships extends beyond the visualization pane. (Depending on the resolution of your monitor, you might be able to view the all the attribute relationships.) You can zoom in or zoom out using the Zoom item in the context menu of the visualization pane to adjust the size of the content of the visualization pane to see all the attribute relationships. Sometimes the attribute relationships view can be quite large depending on the number of attributes and the relationships you have established. You can easily navigate to the area of the visualization pane you're interested in by clicking the "+" symbol at the far right of the horizontal scrollbar and using the locator window (as shown in Figure 5-23).

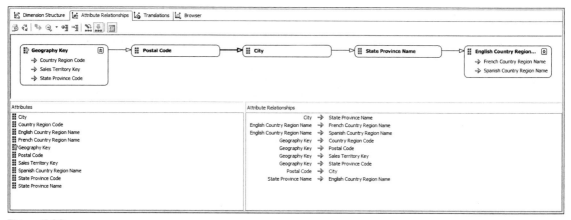

Figure 5-22

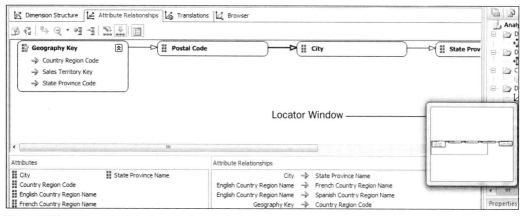

Figure 5-23

7. Switch back to the Dimension Structure tab, verify the warning is gone, and save the dimension as shown in Figure 5-24.

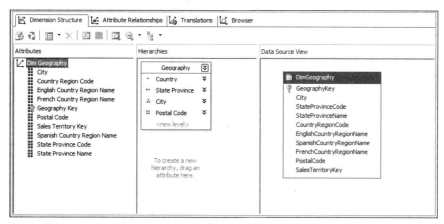

Figure 5-24

Browsing the Dimension

After successfully creating the Dim Geography dimension, you definitely would like to see the results of what you have created and find out how you can see the members of the dimension. So far, the dimension has been designed but not deployed to the server. Indeed, there has been no interaction with the instance of Analysis Services yet. To see the members of the dimension, Analysis Services needs to receive the details of the dimension (the attributes, member properties, and the multilevel hierarchies you have created). The Analysis Services 2008 tools communicate to the instance of Analysis Services via XMLA (XML for Analysis).

XMLA is an industry-standard, Simple Object Access Protocol (SOAP)–based XML Application Programming Interface (API) that is designed for OLAP and Data Mining. The XMLA specification defines two functions, Execute and Discover, which are used to send actions to and retrieve data from the host instance. The Execute and Discover functions take several parameters that define the actions the instance of Analysis Services will perform. One of the parameters of the Execute function is the command sent to an instance of Analysis Services. Note that in addition to supporting the functionality defined in the XMLA specification, Analysis Services supports extensions to the standard. Following is a sample Execute request sent to an instance of Analysis Services using XMLA. The Execute request is a modified version of the one in XMLA specification available at `http://www.xmla.org`.

```
<Execute xmlns="urn:schemas-microsoft-com:xml-analysis"
SOAP-ENV:encodingStyle="http://schemas.xmlsoap.org/soap/encoding/">
<Command>
<Statement> select [Measures].members on Columns from Adventure
Works</Statement>
</Command>
<Properties>
<PropertyList>
<DataSourceInfo> Provider=SQL Server 2008;Data Source=local; </DataSourceInfo>
<Catalog>AnalysisServices2008Tutorial</Catalog>
<Format>Multidimensional</Format>
<AxisFormat>ClusterFormat</AxisFormat>
</PropertyList>
</Properties>
</Execute>
</SOAP-ENV:Body>
</SOAP-ENV:Envelope>
```

In the preceding XMLA, a request is sent to execute an MDX query that is specified within the command Statement on the catalog AnalysisServices2008Tutorial. The XML request shown results in the query being executed on the server side and the results returned to the client via XMLA.

Several different commands are used to communicate to Analysis Server 2008. Some of the common ones are Create, Alter, Process, and Statement. These commands are used to change the structure of objects referenced in the command. Each object in Analysis Services 2008 has a well-defined set of properties. The definition of the objects is accomplished by commands referred to as Data Definition Language (DDL) commands in this book. Other commands work with data that has already been defined. Those commands are referred to as Data Manipulation Language (DML) commands. You learn some of the DML and DDL commands used in Analysis Services 2008 in various chapters of the book through examples. For in-depth understanding of DML and DDL commands, we recommend you read the Analysis Services 2008 documentation.

You might recall that you deployed the AnalysisServices2008Tutorial project in Chapter 2. When you deploy a project, the BIDS packages all the design change information in the project into a single XMLA request and sends it to the server. In this case, you want to see the contents of the dimension you have created. Therefore you need to deploy the project to an instance of Analysis Services. When you deploy the entire project using BIDS to Analysis Services, several XMLA requests are sent by BIDS. They are:

1. Request a list of the databases from Analysis Services to determine if the current project already exists on the instance. The project name you specified while creating the object will be used as the database name. Based on the deployment settings in your project, BIDS either sends the entire definition of all the objects or only the changes you have made since the last deploy. BIDS will send either a Create or Alter command based upon whether the database already exists on the Analysis Services instance. We have not included the Create/Alter XMLA request in the following code because it is quite large. You can use the SQL Server Profiler to analyze the XMLA request (you learn to use SQL Server Profiler in Chapter 15).

2. BIDS then sends an XMLA request to process the objects on the instance of Analysis Services. Following is the request that would be sent to the server to process the dimension Dim Geography:

```
<Batch xmlns="http://schemas.microsoft.com/analysisservices/2003/engine">
  <Parallel>
    <Process xmlns:xsd="http://www.w3.org/2001/XMLSchema"
xmlns:xsi="http://www.w3.org/2001/XMLSchema-instance"
xmlns:ddl2="http://schemas.microsoft.com/analysisservices/2003/engine/2"
xmlns:ddl2_2="http://schemas.microsoft.com/analysisservices/2003/engine/2/2"
xmlns:ddl100_100="http://schemas.microsoft.com/analysisservices/2008/engine/100/100">
      <Object>
        <DatabaseID>AnalysisServices2008Tutorial</DatabaseID>
        <DimensionID>Dim Geography</DimensionID>
      </Object>
      <Type>ProcessDefault</Type>
      <WriteBackTableCreation>UseExisting</WriteBackTableCreation>
    </Process>
  </Parallel>
</Batch>
```

BIDS performs certain validations to make sure your dimension design is correct. If there are errors, BIDS will show those errors using red squiggly lines. In addition to that, a set of error handling properties in the Analysis Services instance helps in validating errors in your dimension design when data is being processed. BIDS sends the default error handling information to the Analysis Services instance for the server to raise any referential integrity errors as part of the deployment process. The default error handling mode in BIDS has been changed in SQL Server 2008 to make sure the developer is aware of all the warnings and errors by default. Follow these steps to deploy your Analysis Services2008Tutorial project:

1. Deploy the AnalysisServices2008Tutorial project to your Analysis Services 2008 instance by either hitting the F5 key or right-clicking the project in the Solution Explorer window and selecting Deploy. BIDS deploys the project to the Analysis Services 2008 instance. You will get a dialog indicating that you have deployment errors as shown in Figure 5-25.

Figure 5-25

2. Click the No button in the deployment errors dialog shown in Figure 5-25.

BIDS will now report all the warnings as well as errors identified by BIDS and from the Analysis Services instance using the Errors tab as shown in Figure 5-26.

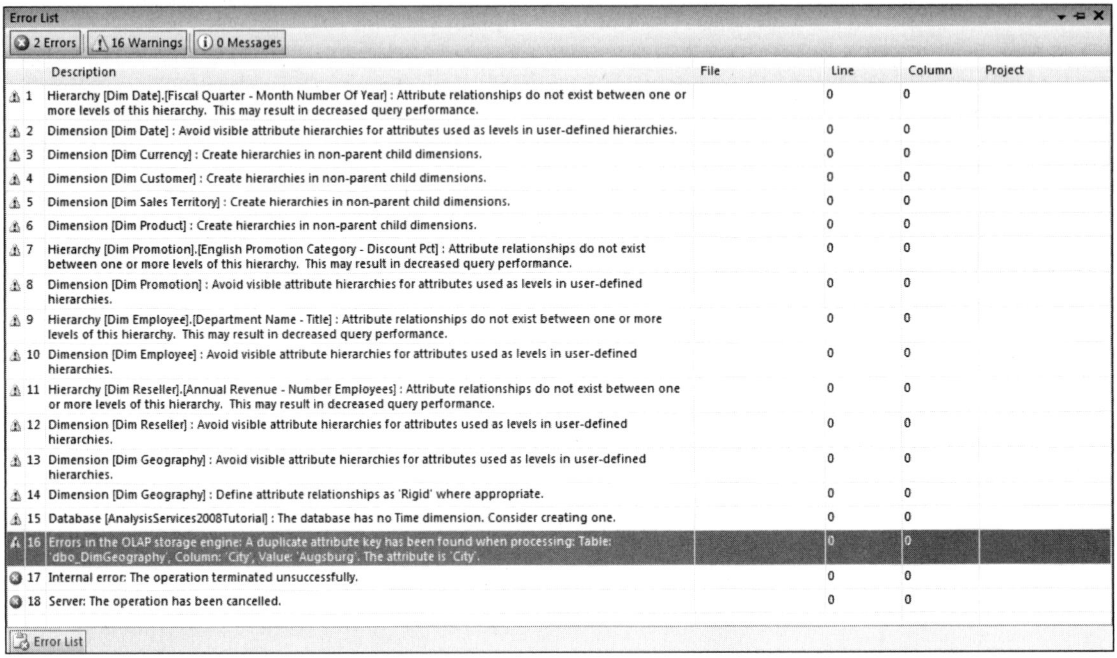

Figure 5-26

BIDS in Analysis Services 2008 has added a new feature by which you can see warnings identified by BIDS in addition to the errors that were shown in previous versions of Analysis Services. The first 15 warnings shown in Figure 5-26 are an example of this new feature in action. Some of the warnings detected by BIDS might be the result of valid design decisions you made for your Analysis Services database. Hence BIDS supports a warning infrastructure by which you can disable warnings for specific objects or even disable specific warnings from reappearing in future deployments. When you right-click one of the first 15 warnings, you can see an option to Dismiss the warning. Note, however, that you cannot dismiss a warning reported by the Analysis Services instance or any error. If you click the sixteenth warning, you can see that the warning cannot be dismissed. This is the first warning reported by the Analysis Services instance followed by two errors that fail the deployment of your AnalysisServices2008Tutorial project. You learn more about the warning feature in Chapter 9.

The Analysis Services instance warning (warning 16 shown in Figure 5-26) indicates that there was an issue while processing the City attribute and duplicate attribute keys were identified. This warning indicates that there are several cities with the same name. This warning is, in fact, an error raised by the Analysis Services instance. The reason why this error is raised is because you have defined and guaranteed a one-to-many attribute relationship between the City attribute and the State-Province Name attribute. The Analysis Services instance identifies that there are several different Cities with the same name and is unable to decide which State-Province name has the relationship to a specific City. If you query the City column in the DimGeography table, you will see that City names are not unique. For example, London, Paris, and Berlin all appear in excess of a dozen times in the DimGeography table of the AdventureWorksDW database. Hence the Analysis Services instance raises the error with the text

"Errors in OLAP Storage Engine." Due to this error, the Analysis Services instance fails the processing of the City attribute and subsequently the Dim Geography dimension and the deployment fails.

To correct this issue, you need to make sure each City is unique. You can do this by creating a surrogate key for the City that makes each city unique and use that key as the key column for the City attribute. Alternatively you can use composite keys to uniquely identify a City attribute. In the following steps, you use a collection of columns to define the keys for several attributes of the Dim Geography dimension. To uniquely identify a City, you need to know the State-Province Name to which it belongs. Therefore, the key collection for the City attribute should be City and State-Province Code. Follow these steps to make the City attribute have unique members:

1. Open the Dim Geography dimension in the Dimension Designer and click the City attribute in the Attributes pane.

2. In the Properties pane, locate the KeyColumns property and click the ellipses (as shown in Figure 5-27) to open the Key Columns selection dialog.

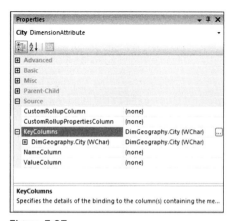

Figure 5-27

3. In the Key Columns selection dialog, add the StateProvince Code to the list of columns and click OK as shown in Figure 5-28.

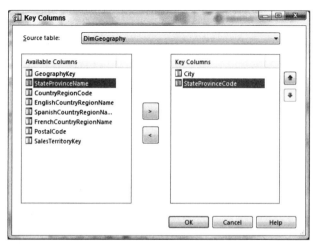

Figure 5-28

By default, the Dimension Wizard uses the column name as the key column for the attribute. The Analysis Services instance automatically infers the same column to be the name column (the column that is used to display the member names for the attribute). Whenever you define a composite key, you need to define a name column for the attribute because BIDS and the Analysis Services instance do not know which of the composite key columns should be used as the name column for the attribute.

4. In the NameColumn property for the City attribute, click the ellipses to open the Name Column selection dialog (shown in Figure 5-29) and select City as the source for the name of the City attribute.

Figure 5-29

The DimGeography table in the data source also contains duplicate PostalCodes. As you just did for the City attribute, you need to make the PostalCode attribute members unique.

5. Select the PostalCode attribute in the Dimension Designer's Attributes pane.

6. In the Properties pane, locate the KeyColumns property and click the ellipses to open the Key Columns selection dialog.

7. Change the KeyColumns for the PostalCode attribute to include the StateProvinceCode, City, and PostalCode columns from the data source. Click OK.

8. Change the NameColumn property by clicking the ellipses next to the NameColumn property in the Properties window.

9. In the Name Column dialog, set the NameColumn property to PostalCode. Click OK.

10. Deploy the AnalysisServices2008Tutorial database to the Analysis Services instance.

The AnalysisServices2008Tutorial database now successfully deploys. Now that you have successfully deployed the database, you can browse the data for the Dim Geography structure by switching to the Browser tab of the Dimension Designer as shown in Figure 5-30. To display the data in the browser, BIDS obtains schema information through several Discover requests to retrieve information such as the hierarchies and levels available for the dimension. Finally, an MDX query is sent to the server by BIDS to retrieve dimension data. The MDX query is:

```
SELECT HEAD( [Dim Geography].[Geography].LEVELS(0).MEMBERS, 1000 ) on 0
FROM [$Dim Geography]
```

Figure 5-30

Because you have some familiarity with MDX by now you might have deciphered most of the query. This query uses the HEAD function to request the first 1,000 members from Level 0 of the hierarchy Geography in dimension [Dim Geography]. In the FROM clause you see [$ Dim Geography]. Though you have not created any cube in your data warehouse project yet, you know that the FROM clause should contain a cube name, so how does this MDX query work? When a dimension is created, the server internally stores the values of the dimension as a cube. This means that *every dimension is internally represented as a cube* with a single dimension that holds all the attribute values. The dimension you have created is part of the Analysis Services database AnalysisServices2008Tutorial and is called a database dimension. Because each database dimension is a one-dimensional cube, they can be queried using MDX using the special character $ before the dimension name. This is exactly what you see in the query, [$Dim Geography].

The hierarchy first shown in the hierarchy browser is the most recently created multilevel hierarchy (in this case, Geography). You can choose to browse any of the multilevel hierarchies or attribute hierarchies by selecting one from the drop-down list labeled Hierarchy. This list contains the multilevel hierarchies followed by the attribute hierarchies. Each attribute hierarchy and multilevel hierarchy within a dimension has a level called the All level. In Figure 5-30 you can see the All level for the hierarchy Geography. The All level is the topmost level of most hierarchies (the All level can be removed in certain hierarchies) and you can change the name of the All level by changing the property of the hierarchy. It makes sense to call the level "All" because it encompasses all of the sub-levels in the hierarchy. If a hierarchy does not contain the All level, the members of the topmost level would be displayed as the first level in the Dimension Designer's Browser page.

Assume you want to change the All level of the Geography hierarchy to "All Countries." The following steps show how to do this:

1. Go to the Dimension Structure view of the Dimension Designer.

2. Click the Geography hierarchy in the Hierarchies pane.

3. The Properties window now shows all the properties of this hierarchy. The first property is AllMemberName and it displays no value. Add a value by typing **All Countries** in the text entry box to the right of AllMemberName as shown in Figure 5-31.

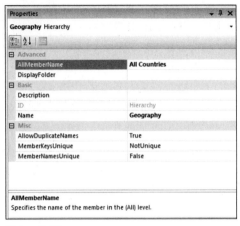

Figure 5-31

4. Deploy the project once again.

5. After successful deployment, BIDS switches from the Dimension Structure page to the Browser page. If your Deployment "Processing Option" has been set to "Do Not Process," you will see a warning in the Dimension Browser pane asking you if you need to process the dimension. If you see this message, click the Process link to launch the Process dialog. Click OK to process the Dim Geography dimension and click the Reconnect button in the Dimension Designer Browser toolbar to view your All member name changes. If your Deployment mode processing has been set to Full or Default, the Dim Geography dimension would be processed along with the deployment and you will see a message in the Dimension Browser to click Reconnect in order to see the latest changes. Click the Reconnect link.

You can now see that the All level of the Geography hierarchy has changed to All Countries, as shown in Figure 5-32. You can also see in the figure that the All Countries level has been expanded to show all members in the next level.

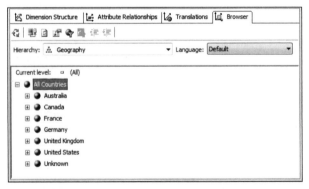

Figure 5-32

When you expand the All Countries level, the following MDX query is sent to the Analysis Services instance to retrieve the members in the next level:

```
WITH MEMBER [Measures].[-DimBrowseLevelKey 0-] AS
'[Dim Geography].[Geography].currentmember.properties("key0", TYPED)'

SELECT { [Measures].[-DimBrowseLevelKey 0-] } ON 0,
HEAD( [Dim Geography].[Geography].[All Countries].Children, 1000) ON 1
FROM [$Dim Geography]
CELL PROPERTIES VALUE
```

The goal of the MDX query is to retrieve all the members that are children of the All Countries level. Similar to the MDX query that was sent to retrieve members in level 0, this query only retrieves the first 1,000 children of All Countries level. This is accomplished by use of the HEAD function as seen in the MDX query. This query includes a calculated measure called Measures.[-DimBrowseLevelKey 0-], which is selected in the MDX query. The calculated measure expression in this query retrieves the key of the current member by using the MDX function *Properties*. The MDX function Properties returns a string value based on the parameters passed to it. The Properties function returns the value of the member property that is specified as the first argument to the expression. In this query the value requested is the Key of the current member.

Other parameters that can be passed to the Properties function are NAME, ID, and CAPTION, or the name of a member property or related attribute. The properties NAME, ID, KEY, and CAPTION are called *intrinsic member properties* because all attributes and hierarchies will have these properties. The second argument passed to the Properties function is optional and the only value that can be passed is TYPED. If the Properties function is called without the second parameter, the function returns the string representation of the property. If the second argument TYPED is passed to the Properties function, the function returns the data type of the property (data type that was defined in the data source) requested. For example, if the first argument is Key and if the Key of this attribute is of type integer, the Properties function returns integer values. Typically the second parameter TYPED is useful if you want to filter the results based on a member property. For example, if the key of the Geography hierarchy is an integer and if you want to see only the children of member United States, you can use the FILTER function along with the calculated measure that has been created using the parameter TYPED.

The result of the preceding MDX query is shown in the following table. The Dimension Browser retrieves this information and shows the names of the members in the hierarchical format shown in Figure 5-32.

	-DIMBROWSEKEY 0-
Australia	Australia
Canada	Canada
France	France
Germany	Germany
United Kingdom	United Kingdom
United States	United States
Unknown	Unknown

When you defined an attribute relationship between the State-Province Name and City attribute earlier in the chapter, you implicitly set member properties for those attributes. Now you can see these member properties in the Dimension Designer Browser. To do that you can either click the Member Properties button in the Dimension Designer Browser toolbar (highlighted in Figure 5-33) or choose Member Properties from the Dimension menu. A dialog appears that has all the attributes of the dimension that participate in attribute relationships. Select the attributes English Country Region Name, State-Province, and City and click OK. The member properties you have selected are now shown in the Dimension Browser as shown in Figure 5-33.

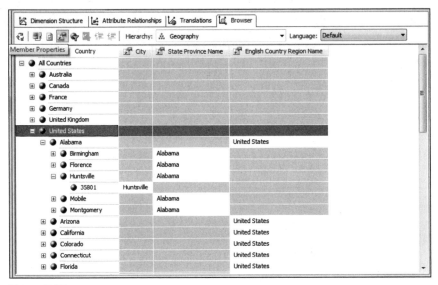

Figure 5-33

Expand the members of United States to see the member properties of the States and Cities under United States. The member properties of a member are also retrieved with the help of an MDX query. For example, when you want to see all the cities in Alabama, the following MDX query is sent to the server:

```
WITH MEMBER [Measures].[-DimBrowseLevelKey 0-] AS
'[Dim Geography].[Geography].currentmember.properties("key0", TYPED)'
MEMBER [Measures].[-DimBrowseLevelKey 1-] AS
'[Dim Geography].[Geography].currentmember.properties("key1", TYPED)'
MEMBER [Measures].[-DimBrowseProp State Province Name-] AS
'[Dim Geography].[Geography].currentmember.properties("State Province Name", TYPED)'

SELECT { [Measures].[-DimBrowseLevelKey 0-], [Measures].[-DimBrowseLevelKey 1-],
[Measures].[-DimBrowseProp State Province Name-] } ON 0,
HEAD( [Dim Geography].[Geography].[State-Province].&[Alabama].Children, 1000) ON 1
FROM [$Dim Geography]
CELL PROPERTIES VALUE
```

Similar to the MDX query you analyzed earlier to retrieve all the members of the All level, this query retrieves all the Alabama City members. The City attribute's member property State-Province Name is retrieved (along with the values that make up the City attribute's composite key, City, and State-Province

Code) with the same query as calculated members using the WITH MEMBER clause as seen in the preceding query.

Sorting Members of a Level

Members of a level are the members of the attribute that defines that level. For example, the members of the level Country in the Geography hierarchy are actually the members of the attribute English Country Region Name. The member name that is shown in the Dimension Designer Browser is the text associated with the Name of the Country. It is not uncommon for dimension tables to have one column for the descriptive name and one column that is the key column of the table. You can use the descriptive name column to display the name of the attribute and the key column to sort the members in that attribute. The attributes' properties help you sort members of a level.

Each attribute in a dimension has two properties: KeyColumns and NameColumn. The KeyColumns property is used to specify the columns that are used for sorting the members, and the NameColumn is used for the descriptive name of the member. By default, the Dimension Wizard and the Dimension Designer set the KeyColumns attribute when an attribute is added to the dimension. They do not set the NameColumn property. If the NameColumn property is empty, Analysis Services will return the KeyColumns value for the descriptive names in response to client requests.

Figure 5-34 shows these properties for the attribute English Country Region Name (Country Level in the Geography multilevel hierarchy). The data type of the attribute is also shown in the KeyColumns property. Country is of data type WChar, which means the members are strings. Therefore, when you view the members in the Dimension Browser the members are sorted by the names. The Dim Geography dimension table has the column Country Region Code. You can define the sort order of the countries based on the Country Region Code instead of their names by changing the KeyColumns and NameColumn properties appropriately. The following exercise demonstrates how you can change the order of the countries based on the order of Country Region Code (AU, CA, DE, FR, GB, and US) instead of the country names.

Figure 5-34

1. Click English Country Region Name in the Attributes pane; then in the Properties pane, click the NameColumn property value ellipses. This opens an Object Binding dialog showing all the columns in the Dim Geography table. Select the column EnglishCountryRegionName and click OK.

2. Click the KeyColumns property value (the ellipsis button). This action launches the Key Columns dialog. Remove the column EnglishCountryRegionName from the collection. In the list of available columns, select CountryRegionCode and add it to the Key Columns list. The Key Columns selection dialog should look like Figure 5-35. Click the OK button.

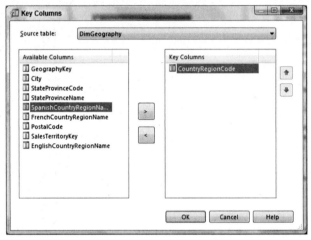

Figure 5-35

3. Click the Advanced Properties for the attribute EnglishCountryRegionName. Make sure the value of the property OrderBy is Key as shown in Figure 5-34. This instructs the server to order this attribute using the Key attribute (CountryRegionCode), which you specified in step 2.

4. Deploy the project to the Analysis Services instance.

Deploying the project to the Analysis Services instance results in sending the new changes defined in steps 1 through 3 followed by processing the dimension. BIDS will switch to the Broswer tab. (If it doesn't, switch to the Browser tab and click the Reconnect option to retrieve the latest dimension data.) In the Dimension Browser select the Geography hierarchy. The order of the countries has now changed based on the order of Country Region Code (AU, CA, DE, FR, GB, and US followed by the Unknown members) instead of the country names you viewed in Figure 5-32. The new order of countries is shown in Figure 5-36.

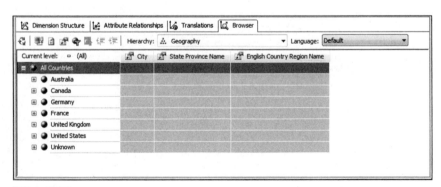

Figure 5-36

Optimizing Attributes

During the design of a dimension you might want to include certain attributes in the dimension, but not want to make the attribute hierarchies available to end users for querying. Two attribute properties allow you to manipulate visibility of attributes to end users. One property, AttributeHierarchyEnabled, allows you to disable the attribute. By setting this property to False you are disabling the attribute in the dimension; you cannot include this attribute in any level of a multilevel hierarchy. This attribute can only be defined as a member property (related attribute) to another attribute. Members of this attribute cannot be retrieved by an MDX query, but you can retrieve the value as a member property of another attribute. If you disable an attribute you might see improvements in processing performance depending on the number of members in the attribute. You need to be sure that there will be no future need to slice and dice on this attribute.

Another property called AttributeHierarchyVisible is useful for setting an attribute hierarchy to invisible for browsing; but even with this set, the attribute can be used as a level within a hierarchy and it can be used for querying. If you set this property to False, you will not see this attribute in the Dimension Browser. The properties AttributeHierarchyEnabled and AttributeHierarchyVisible are part of the Advanced group in the Properties window, as shown in Figure 5-37.

Figure 5-37

> If you want to create a dimension that contains only multilevel hierarchies and no attributes, you can mark the AttributeHierarchyVisible property to False for all the attributes. When you go to the Dimension Browser you will only see the multilevel hierarchies. Even though you have disabled the attribute for browsing, you will still be able to query the attribute using MDX.

Defining Translations in Dimensions

If your data warehouse is to be used globally, you want to show the hierarchies, levels, and members in different languages so that customers in those countries can read the cube in their own language. Analysis Services 2008 provides you with a feature called Translations (not a super-imaginative name but a name that is intuitive) that helps you create and view dimension members in various languages. The benefit of this feature is that you do not have to build a new cube in every language. For the translation feature to be used, you need to only have a column in the relational data source that will have the translated names for the members of a specific attribute in the dimension.

For example, the Dim Geography table has two columns, Spanish Country Region Name and French Country Region Name, which contain the translated names of the countries that are members of the attribute English Country Region Name. The following steps describe how to create a new translation:

1. Switch to the Translations page in the Dimension Designer.

2. Click the New Translation toolbar button shown in Figure 5-38 or choose New Translation from the Dimension menu to create a new translation and choose a language. The Select Language dialog now pops up.

Figure 5-38

3. Select the language French (France) and click OK.

4. A new column with the title French (France) is added as shown in Figure 5-39. Select the cell from the column French (France) in the English Country Region Name row. Then click the button that appears on the right side of the cell. You now see the Attribute Data Translation dialog.

5. Select the French Country Region Name column in the Translation Columns tree view as shown in Figure 5-40 and click OK.

6. Repeat steps 2 through 5 for the language Spanish (Spain).

You have now created two translations in French and Spanish languages. In addition to specifying the columns for member names, you can also change the metadata information of each level. For example, if you want to change the level Country in the Geography hierarchy in the French and Spanish languages, you can do that by entering the names in the row that show the Country level. Type **Pays** and **Pais** as shown in Figure 5-39 for French and Spanish translations, respectively. You have defined translations for the Country attribute in two languages making use of the columns in the relational data source. To see how this metadata information is shown in the Dimension Browser, first deploy the project to your Analysis Services instance.

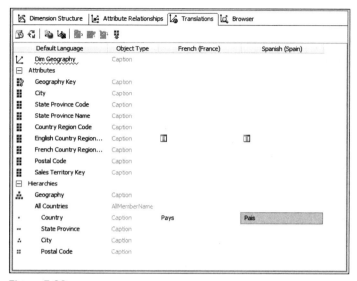

Figure 5-39

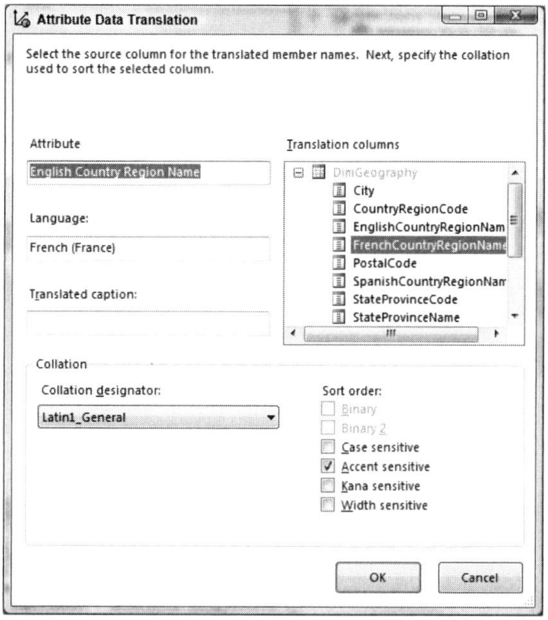

Figure 5-40

Next, to see the effect of the translations you have created, select language French (France) from within the Dimension Browser as shown in Figure 5-41. Select the Geography hierarchy and expand the All level. Now you can see all the members in French. If you click any of the countries, the metadata shown for the level is "Pays" (French for country) as shown in Figure 5-39. There is a negligible amount of overhead associated with viewing dimension hierarchies, levels, and members in different languages from your UDM.

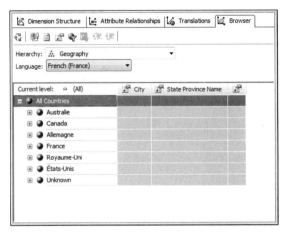

Figure 5-41

Creating a Snowflake Dimension

A snowflake dimension is a dimension that is created using a set of dimension tables. A snowflake dimension normally suggests that the tables in the data source have been normalized. Normalization is the process by which tables of a relational database are designed to remove redundancy and are optimized for frequent updates. Most database design books, including *The Data Warehouse Toolkit* by Ralph Kimball (Wiley, 1996) and *An Introduction to Database Systems* by C. J. Date (Addison Wesley, 2003), talk about the normalization process in detail.

The columns from different tables of a snowflake dimension often result in levels of a hierarchy in the dimension. The best way to understand a snowflake dimension is to create one yourself. To create one you're going to need two additional tables added to your DSV. Here is how to add the two tables:

1. Open the AdventureWorksDW DSV and click the Add/Remove Tables button (top-left button in the DSV).

2. Click DimProductCategory, then Control-Click DimProductSubcategory, then click the right arrow > to move the two tables from the source to the DSV and click OK.

The DSV Designer identifies the relationships defined in the relational backend and shows the relationships between the DimProduct, DimProductSubCategory, and DimProductCategory tables within the DSV Designer graphical design pane. Now that you have the necessary tables in the DSV and the relationships and logical primary keys defined, you can create a snowflake Product dimension. You can either delete the existing Product dimension in the AnalysisServices2008Tutorial project and create a snowflake dimension using the Dimension Wizard or refine the existing Product dimension and make it a snowflake dimension. In this illustration you will be refining the existing Product dimension and making it a snowflake dimension. Follow these steps to create a snowflake dimension called Dim Product:

1. Double-click the Dim Product dimension in the Solution Explorer to open the Dimension Designer for the Dim Product dimension.

2. Within the Data Source View pane of the Dimension Designer, right-click and select Show Tables as shown in Figure 5-42.

Figure 5-42

3.   In the Show Tables dialog select the DimProductSubCategory and DimProductCategory tables
      as shown in Figure 5-43 and click OK.

Figure 5-43

You will now see the DimProductCategory and DimProductSubCategory tables added to the Data Source View pane of the Dimension Designer as shown in Figure 5-44. Notice that the new tables added to the pane have a lighter colored caption bar. This indicates that none of the columns in the tables are included as attributes within the dimension.

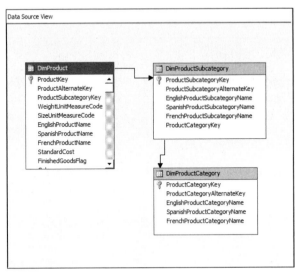

Figure 5-44

4. Drag and drop the column ProductCategoryKey from the DimProductSubCategory table in the DSV pane to the Attributes pane.

5. Launch the Name Column dialog for the ProductCategoryKey attribute by clicking the ellipsis next to the Name Column property in the Properties window.

6. Select EnglishProductCategoryName from the DimProductCategory table as the Name Column and click OK.

7. Select the attribute ProductSubCategoryKey from the Attributes pane.

8. Launch the Name Column dialog for the ProductSubCategoryKey attribute by clicking the ellipsis next to the Name Column property in the Properties window.

9. Select EnglishProductSubCategoryName from the DimProductSubCategory table as the Name Column and click OK.

10. Launch the Name Column dialog for Dim Product (the key attribute) by clicking the ellipsis next to the Name Column property in the Properties window.

11. Select English Product Name as the Name Column and click OK.

12. Create a Product Categories multilevel hierarchy with levels ProductCategoryKey, ProductSubCategoryKey, and Dim Product by dragging and dropping the attributes to the Hierarchies pane and naming the hierarchy as Product Categories.

13. Rename the level ProductCategoryKey to ProductCategory.

14. Rename the level ProductSubCategoryKey to ProductSubCategory.

15. Rename the level Dim Product to Product Name.

16. Change the EnglishProductName attribute to Product Name.

17. Figure 5-45 shows the Dimension Designer after all the refinements to the Product dimension.

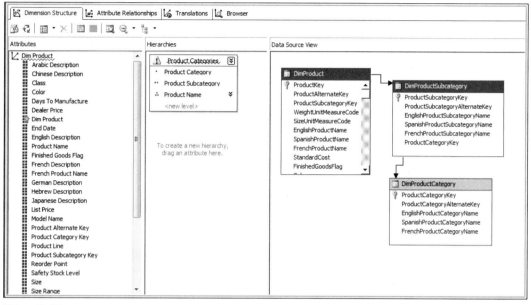

Figure 5-45

You have now successfully created a snowflake Dim Product dimension. You can perform most of the same operations in a snowflake dimension as you can in a star schema dimension, including adding attributes, creating hierarchies, and defining member properties. We recommend you deploy the AnalysisServices2008Tutorial project and browse the snowflake dimension Dim Product.

Creating a Time Dimension

Almost every data warehouse will have a Time dimension. The Time dimension can be comprised of the levels Year, Semester, Quarter, Month, Week, Date, Hour, Minute, and Seconds. Most data warehouses contain the levels Year, Quarter, Month, and Date. The Time dimension helps in analyzing business data across similar time periods; for example, determining how the current revenues or profit of a company compare to those of the previous year or previous quarter.

Even though it appears that the Time dimension has regular time periods, irregularities often exist. The number of days in a month varies across months, and the number of days in a year changes each leap year. In addition to that, a company can have its own fiscal year, which might not be identical to the calendar year. Even though there are minor differences in the levels, the Time dimension is often viewed as having regular time intervals. Several MDX functions help in solving typical business problems related to analyzing data across time periods. ParallelPeriod is one such function, which you learned about in Chapter 3. Time dimensions are treated specially by Analysis Services and certain measures are aggregated across the Time dimension uniquely and are called semi-additive measures. You learn more about semi-additive measures in Chapters 6 and 9.

The AnalysisServices2008Tutorial project has a Dim Date dimension that was created by the Cube Wizard in Chapter 2. Even though the dimension has been created from the Dim Date table, it does not have certain properties set that would allow Analysis Services to see it as the source for a Time dimension. In the following exercise you first delete the Dim Date dimension and then create a Time dimension. Follow these steps to create a Time dimension on the Dim Date table of the AdventureWorksDW2008 database:

1. In the Solution Explorer right-click the Dim Date dimension and select Delete.

2. In the Delete Objects and Files dialog, Analysis Services requests you to confirm the deletion of corresponding Cube dimensions (you learn about Cube dimensions in Chapter 9). Select OK to delete the Dim Date dimension.

3. Launch the Dimension Wizard by right-clicking Dimensions in the Solution Explorer and selecting New Dimension. When the welcome screen of the Dimension Wizard opens up, click Next.

4. In the Select Creation Method page of the wizard, select the "Use an existing table" option and click Next.

5. In the Specify Source Information page, select DimDate as the main table from which the dimension is to be designed and click Next.

6. In the Select Dimension Attributes page, in addition to the Date Key attribute, enable the checkboxes for the following attributes: Calendar Year, Calendar Semester, Calendar Quarter, English Month Name, and Day Number Of Month.

7. Set the Attribute Type for the "Calendar Year" attribute to Date ⇨ Calendar ⇨ Year as shown in Figure 5-46.

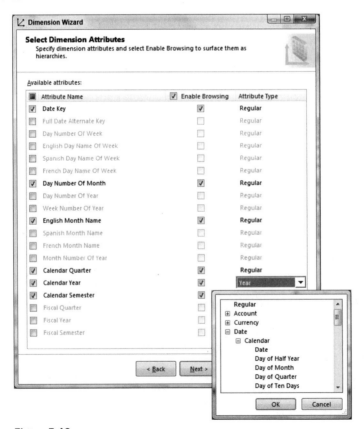

Figure 5-46

8. Set the Attribute Type for the remaining enabled attributes so they match those shown in Figure 5-47 and click Next to continue.

Figure 5-47

9. Set the name of the dimension to "Dim Date" and click Finish to close the Dimension Wizard. You have now successfully created a Time dimension using the Dimension Wizard.

10. Create a multilevel hierarchy Calendar Date with the levels Calendar Year, Calendar Semester, Calendar Quarter, Month (rename English Month Name), and Day (rename Day Number Of Month).

11. Save the project and deploy it to the Analysis Services instance.

12. Switch to the Browser pane of the Dim Date dimension.

Figure 5-48 shows the Calendar Date hierarchy that you created. Notice that the order of months within a quarter is not the default calendar order. For example, the order of months of CY Q1 of year 2002 is February, January, and March. To change the order, change the KeyColumns, NameColumn, and SortOrder appropriately and redeploy the project. We recommend that you define the necessary attribute relationships and attribute key values as defined by your business needs.

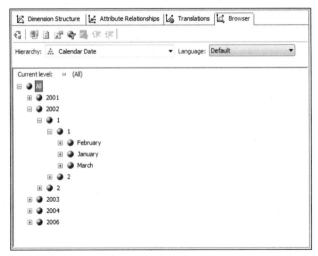

Figure 5-48

You have now successfully created a Time dimension. If you review the properties of the Dim Date dimension you will see the property "Type" set to Time which indicates to Analysis Services that the Dim Date dimension is a Time dimension. If you review the basic properties of each attribute in the Dim Date dimension, you will notice that the property Type has values such as Quarters, HalfYears, Years, DayOfMonth, and Months. You can use the Properties pane to set the right property type for the chosen attribute. Setting the right property type is important because a client application could use this property to apply the MDX functions for a Time dimension.

Creating a Parent-Child Hierarchy

In the real world you come across relationships such as that between managers and their direct reports. This relationship is similar to the relationship between a parent and child in that a parent can have several children and a parent can also be a child, because parents also have parents. In the data warehousing world such relationships are modeled as a Parent-Child dimension and in Analysis Services 2008 this type of relationship is modeled as a hierarchy called a Parent-Child hierarchy. The key difference between this relationship and any other hierarchy with several levels is how this relationship is represented in the data source. Well, that and certain other properties that are unique to the Parent-Child design. Both of these are discussed in this section.

When you created the Geography dimension, you might have noticed that there were separate columns for Country, State, and City in the relational table. Similarly, the manager and direct report can be modeled by two columns, ManagerName and EmployeeName, where the EmployeeName column is used for the direct report. If there are five direct reports for a manager, there will be five rows in the relational table. The interesting part of the Manager-DirectReport relationship is that the manager is also an employee and is a direct report to another manager. This is unlike the columns City, State, and Country in the Dim Geography table.

It is probably rare at your company, but employees can sometimes have new managers due to reorganizations. The fact that an employee's manager can change at any time is very interesting when you want to look at facts such as sales generated under a specific manager, which is the sum of sales generated by the manager's direct reports. A dimension modeling such a behavior is called a slowly changing dimension because the manager of an employee changes over time. You can learn slowly changing dimensions and different variations in detail in the book *The Microsoft Data Warehouse Toolkit: With SQL Server 2005 and the Microsoft Business Intelligence Toolset* by Joy Mundy et al. (Wiley, 2006).

The DimEmployee table in AdventureWorksDW has a Parent-Child relationship because it has a join from ParentEmployeeKey to the EmployeeKey. You have already created a DimEmployee dimension in the AnalysisServices2008Tutorial project in Chapter 2 using the Cube Wizard. In the following exercise you refine the existing Dim Employee dimension and learn how to create a dimension with a Parent-Child hierarchy using the Dimension Wizard. Note that you will actually be refining, not creating, the Dim Employee dimension in the illustration.

1. Launch the Dimension Wizard by right-clicking Dimensions in the Solution Explorer and selecting New Dimension. If the welcome screen of the Dimension Wizard opens up, click Next.

2. Make sure the "Use an existing table" option is selected and click Next.

3. In the Specify Source Information page, select DimEmployee as the main table from which the dimension is to be designed and click Next.

4. On the Select Related Tables screen, uncheck the DimSalesTerritory table and click Next.

   In the Select Dimensions Attributes dialog, the Dimension Wizard has detected three columns of the DimEmployee table to be included as attributes. The Dimension Wizard will select columns if they are either the primary key of the table or a foreign key of the table or another table in the DSV. Figure 5-49 shows two of the attributes. The attributes suggested by the Dimension Wizard in this example are the key attribute Employee Key, the parent-child attribute Parent Employee Key, and the Sales Territory Key, which is a foreign key column to the DimSalesTerritory table.

5. Select all the columns of the DimEmployee table as attributes and click Next.

6. Notice in the preview pane of the Completing the Wizard dialog that the Parent Employee Key attribute has a unique icon (see Figure 5-50) indicating that Analysis Services detected a parent-child relationship in the DimEmployee table. The wizard was able to identify the parent-child relationship due to the join within the same table in the DSV.

7. Click the Cancel button because you will not be creating another DimEmployee dimension.

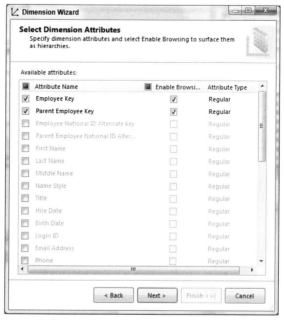

Figure 5-49

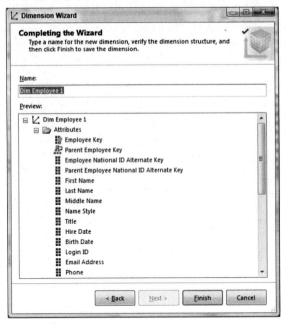

Figure 5-50

By default the Dimension Wizard defines the properties for the attribute modeling the Parent-Child hierarchy at the completion of the Dimension Wizard or the Cube Wizard.

8. Double-click the DimEmployee dimension in the Solution Explorer to open the Dimension Designer.

9. See the properties of the Parent Employee Key attribute that indicate that this attribute defines a Parent-Child hierarchy as shown in Figure 5-51.

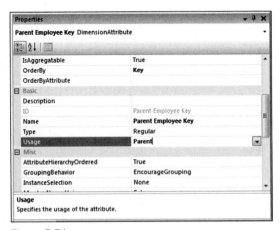

Figure 5-51

Notice that the hierarchy doesn't appear in the Hierarchies pane of the Dimension Designer. That's because the Parent-Child hierarchy is actually a special type of attribute hierarchy that can contain multiple levels, unlike the other attributes. The Parent-Child hierarchy that the wizard created is on the attribute ParentEmployeeKey. The Usage property for this attribute is set to Parent, which indicates that this attribute is a Parent-Child hierarchy. If you browse the Parent-Child hierarchy of the DimEmployee dimension, you will notice that you see the IDs of parent and employee as a multilevel hierarchy as seen in Figure 5-52.

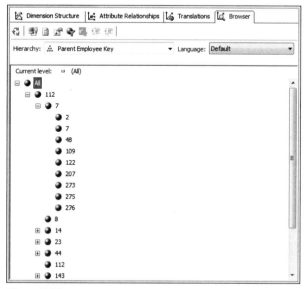

Figure 5-52

Typically, you would want to see the names of the employees rather than their IDs. You learned earlier that you can use the named column to specify the name that is shown in the browser and use the key column for ordering. Because the Parent-Child hierarchy retrieves all the information from the Key attribute, which is the DimEmployee attribute in this example, you need to modify the named column of the DimEmployee attribute rather than the named column of the Parent-Child hierarchy attribute.

10. Change the NameColumn property of the Key attribute Dim Employee to LastName and deploy the project to your Analysis Services instance.

When you browse the Parent-Child hierarchy, you will see the members of the hierarchy showing the last names of the employees, as shown in Figure 5-53.

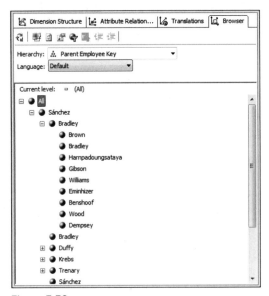

Figure 5-53

Summary

Using the Dimension Wizard and other wizards in BIDS is only the starting point for designing objects in Analysis Services 2008. For optimal results, you will need to fine-tune what those wizards produce. At the beginning of each episode of the television serial *The Outer Limits* the viewers were exhorted to not adjust their television set. Just the opposite is true with Analysis Services 2008, because you do need to refine your objects created by the Dimension and Cube Wizards. A couple of examples are using the Properties window to assign descriptive names to an attribute that might otherwise harbor some obscure name coming from a source database and defining attribute relationships to optimize dimension performance. More profoundly, you can use the Dimension Designer to create translations for the attributes and hierarchies of a dimension into another language.

In addition to learning about dimensions, you learned the necessity of deploying your dimension to the instance of Analysis Services where the dimension is processed by retrieving the data from the data source. Processing is essential to enable the user to browse a dimension. The communication between BIDS and an instance of Analysis Services is accomplished through a SOAP-based XML API called XMLA (XML for Analysis), which is an industry standard. Even more interesting is that dimensions stored in Analysis Services are represented internally as cubes — one-dimensional cubes; and, what a coincidence, cubes are the topic of Chapter 6.

6

Cube Design

In Chapter 5 you learned to create dimensions using the Dimension Wizard and to refine and enhance dimensions using the Dimension Designer. Dimensions eventually need to be part of your cube for you to analyze data across various dimension members. In previous chapters, you read about the Unified Dimensional Model (UDM). Now, prepare yourself for significantly more detail because all the fact and dimension tables you see when you're looking at a DSV in the Cube Designer comprise the UDM. Yes, the UDM is more than a multiple data-source cube on steroids, but to make it as clear as possible, think of the UDM as a cube for now. In this chapter you learn how to create cubes using the Cube Wizard and enhance the cube using the Cube Designer. You learn to add calculations to your cube that facilitate effective data analysis followed by analyzing the cube data itself in the Cube Designer.

The Unified Dimensional Model

To generate profits for a business, key strategic decisions need to be made based on likely factors such as having the right business model, targeting the right consumer group, pricing the product correctly, and marketing through optimal channels. To make the right decisions and achieve targeted growth you need to analyze data. The data can be past sales, expected sales, or even information from competitors. The phrase "Knowledge is power" is very fitting here because in the world of business, analyzing and comparing current sales against the expected sales helps executives make decisions directly aligned with the goals of the company. Such sales information is typically stored in a distributed fashion and must be collected from various sources. Executives making the business decisions typically do not have the capability to access the raw sales data spread across various locations and subsequently optimize it for their use. The decision-makers typically rely on the data that has already been aggregated into a form that is easy to understand and that facilitates the decision-making process. Presenting aggregated data to the decision-makers quickly is a key challenge for business intelligence providers. Analysis Services 2008 enables you to design a model that bridges the gap between the raw data and the information content that can be used for making business decisions. This model is called the Unified Dimensional Model (UDM).

The UDM is central to your Analysis Services database architecture. UDM is your friend because it helps you narrow the gap between end users and the data they need. Analysis Services provides you with features that help you design a model that will serve the needs of end users. UDM, as the name suggests, provides you with a way to bring data from multiple heterogeneous sources into a single model. The UDM buffers you from the difficulties of managing the integration of various data sources so you can build your model easily. It provides you with the best of the OLAP and relational worlds, exposing rich data and metadata for exploration and analysis.

Figure 6-1 shows the architecture of the Unified Dimensional Model that is implemented in Analysis Services 2008. As shown in the figure, the UDM helps you to integrate data from various data sources such as Oracle, SQL Server, DB2, Teradata, and flat files into a single model that merges the underlying schemas into a single schema. The end users do not necessarily have to view the entire schema of the UDM. Instead, they can view sections of the UDM relevant to their needs through the functionality provided by Analysis Services 2008 called *perspectives*.

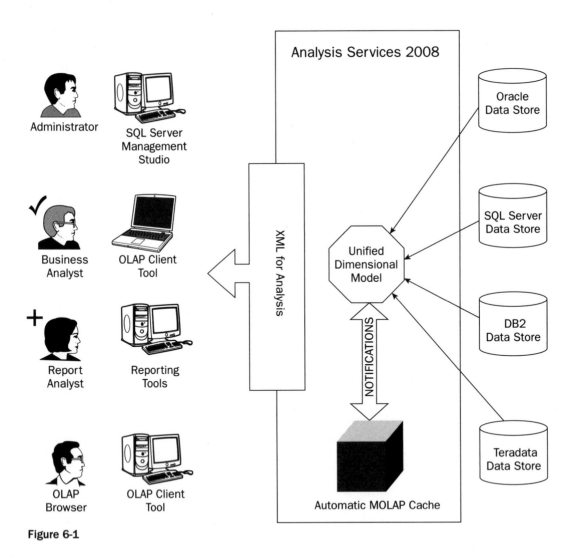

Figure 6-1

In the OLAP world, data analyzed by end users is often historical data that might be a few days, months, or even years old. However, the responses to the OLAP queries are typically returned within a few seconds. In the relational world the end users have instant access to the raw data but the responses to queries can take much longer, on the order of minutes. As mentioned earlier, the UDM merges the best of both the OLAP and relational worlds and provides the end users with real-time data with the query performance of the OLAP world. The UDM is able to provide the query performance of the OLAP world with the help of a feature in Analysis Services 2008 that creates a cache of the relational data source that also aggregates the data into an Analysis Services instance. During the time the cache is being built, the UDM retrieves the data directly from the data sources. As soon as the cache is available, the results are retrieved from the cache in response to relevant queries. Whenever there is a change in the underlying data source, the UDM receives a notification and appropriate updates are made to the cache based on the settings defined for cache updates.

The UDM also provides rich, high-end analytic support through which complex business calculations can be exploited. Such complex calculations can be extremely difficult to formulate in the relational world at the data-source level. Even if such calculations are defined on the relational data source, responses from OLAP-style queries against the relational data source might be really slow compared to responses from Analysis Services.

UDM natively interfaces to end-user clients through the XML for Analysis (XMLA) standard, which allows client tools to retrieve data from Analysis Services. Client tools such as Office Web Components (OWC) and Excel pivot tables allow the end users to create ad-hoc queries for data analysis. In addition, the UDM supports rich analytic features such as Key Performance Indicators (KPIs), Actions, and Translations that help surface the status of your business at any given time so that appropriate actions can be taken.

The UDM provides an efficient interface for detail-level reporting through dimension attributes that are common in the relational world. In addition to that, the UDM is easily understandable by a relational user. The ability to transform the UDM results into views that are helpful to end users and the ability to perform ad-hoc queries on data from high-level aggregations data to detail-level items make the UDM a powerful construct indeed. The UDM also allows you to design the model in the end user's language, which is needed in a global market.

Creating a Cube Using the Cube Wizard

Cubes are the principal objects of an OLAP database that help in data analysis. Cubes are multidimensional structures that are primarily composed of dimensions and facts. The data from a fact table that is stored within the cube for analysis are called *measures*. In Analysis Services 2008 you can store data from multiple fact tables within the same cube. In Chapter 2 you became familiar with the Cube Wizard and in this chapter you see more details of the Cube Wizard followed by refinements to your cube in the Cube Designer.

Similar to the Dimension Wizard you used in Chapter 5, the Cube Wizard facilitates creation of cube objects from the DSV. For this exercise, you continue with the AnalysisServices2008Tutorial project you created in Chapter 5, which contained the dimensions [Dim Geography], [Dim Employee], and

[Dim Date]. To start with a clean slate, please delete the existing cube Adventure Works DW if it is still there from Chapter 2. To completely understand the functionality of the Cube Wizard, follow these steps to build a new cube:

1. Open the AnalysisServices2008Tutorial project from Chapter 5. If the Adventure Works DW cube exists, delete the cube by right-clicking it in the Solution Explorer and selecting Delete.

2. Right-click the Cubes folder and select New Cube, as shown in Figure 6-2. Click Next on the introduction page to proceed.

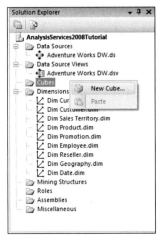

Figure 6-2

3. In the Select Creation Method page you have the option to build a cube from existing tables, create an empty cube, or create a cube based on a template and generate new tables in the data source. In this tutorial you build the cube from the existing tables in the Adventure Works DW data source. Click Next to proceed to the next step in the Cube Wizard.

4. The next page of the Cube Wizard is the Measure Group Tables selection page. If you have multiple DSVs, you need to select the DSV upon which you are creating the cube. In the current project you only have the Adventure Works DW DSV. You now must select one or more tables that will serve as fact tables for your Measure Group. The Suggest button on this screen can be used to have the Cube Wizard scan the DSV to detect the fact tables in the DSV and detect fact tables. Click the Suggest button to have the Cube Wizard automatically select potential Measure Group tables.

    The Cube Wizard now scans the DSV to detect the fact and dimension tables in the DSV, automatically selects the candidate tables, and updates the list as shown in Figure 6-3. Any table that has an outgoing relationship is identified as a candidate fact table, whereas a table that has an incoming relationship is detected as a dimension table.

Figure 6-3

5. You have the option to select or deselect a table as a fact or dimension table. The wizard has identified the FactInternetSales, FactResellerSales, and DimReseller tables as measure group tables. The DimReseller table was detected as a measure group table because there is an outgoing relationship from it. However, it will not be used as a measure group table in this example. Deselect the DimReseller table from being a fact table and click Next.

6. On the Select Measures page, the Cube Wizard shows all the columns from the fact tables that it detects as potential measures of the cube as shown in Figure 6-4. The Cube Wizard does not select the primary and foreign keys in a table as measures. There is a one-to-one mapping between a column in the fact table and a measure in the cube. The Cube Wizard groups measures from a fact table under an object called a *measure group*. Therefore, by default, there will be one measure group for each fact table included in the cube. In the DSV you are using there are two fact tables, and therefore two measure groups named Fact Internet Sales and Fact Reseller Sales are created. You can select or deselect the measures you want to be part of the cube in this page. Use the default selection and click Next.

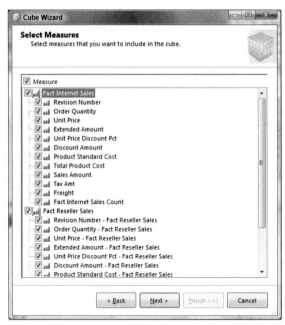

Figure 6-4

7. In the Select Existing Dimensions page (Figure 6-5), the Cube Wizard displays a list of all existing dimensions defined in the project. Accept the selection of all the dimensions and click Next.

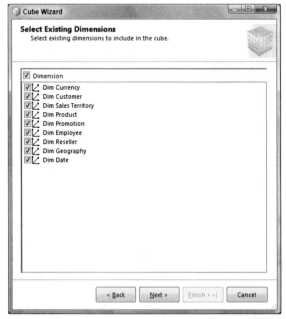

Figure 6-5

8. The Cube Wizard asks you to select any new dimensions to be created from existing tables in the data source that are not already used for dimensions in the project as shown in Figure 6-6. You can deselect dimensions that are not needed for your cube on this page. This illustration will use the Fact tables only as measure groups and not for dimensions. Deselect the Fact Reseller Sales and Fact Internet Sales dimensions on this page and click Next.

Figure 6-6

9. In the final page of the Cube Wizard (shown in Figure 6-7) you can specify the name of the cube to be created and review the measure groups, measures, dimensions, attributes, and hierarchies. Use the default name Adventure Works DW suggested by the Cube Wizard and click Finish.

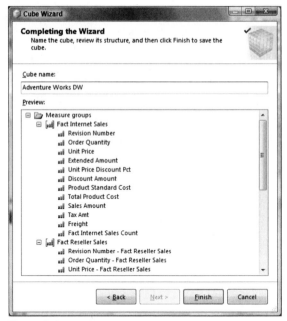

Figure 6-7

The Cube Wizard creates the cube after you click the Finish button. The created Adventure Works DW cube is opened within the Cube Designer as shown in Figure 6-8. The Cube Designer contains several pages that help perform specific operations that will refine the initial cube created by the Cube Wizard. The default page is the Cube Structure page as shown in Figure 6-8. In the Cube Structure page you can see three panes that show the Measures, Dimensions, and the Data Source View. The Data Source View contains all the tables that are part of the cube. Operations such as adding or deleting tables in the DSV and zooming in or out with the DSV Designer are possible within the cube Data Source View pane. The Dimensions pane shows the dimensions that are part of the current cube and the Measures pane shows the cube's measure groups and measures. You can add or delete measures and dimensions in the Cube Structure view. The dimensions within the cube shown in the Dimensions pane are called cube dimensions. You can have multiple instances of the shared dimensions of the database within a cube. For example, the fact tables FactInternetSales, and FactResellerSales have a relationship with the Dim Date dimension through Order Date, Ship Date, and Due Date. Hence you can see three cube dimensions Ship Date, Due Date, and Order Date in the Dimensions pane, which refer to the Dim Date dimension. A dimension such as Dim Date, which plays the role of three cube dimensions, is called a role playing dimension. You learn more about role playing dimensions in Chapters 8 and 9. Within the Dimensions pane you can see the Hierarchies and Attributes of each dimension under separate folders when you expand each dimension.

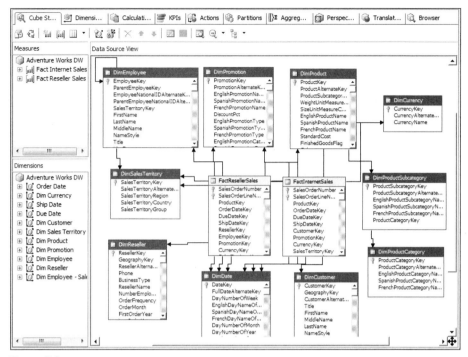

Figure 6-8

So far you have created an Analysis Services database containing the Adventure Works DW cube. You have to deploy the project to the Analysis Services instance so that you can analyze the data within the cube. You can deploy the project to the server in one of the following ways:

1. Select Debug ⇨ Start Debugging from the menu.

2. Right-click the database AnalysisServices2008Tutorial in the Solution Explorer and select Deploy.

3. Right-click the Adventure Works DW cube and choose Process — from which you will first be prompted to deploy the project, followed by Process dialog to process the cube.

4. Use the shortcut key F5 to deploy and process.

When you deploy the project to the Analysis Services instance, BIDS sends an XMLA request containing object definitions to the instance of the Analysis Services server selected in the project. By default the Analysis Services project is deployed to the default instance of Analysis Services on your machine. The object definitions are of the cubes and dimensions you created. If you have installed Analysis Services 2008 as a named instance, you need to change the deployment server name. Then BIDS sends another request to process the objects within the database.

Browsing Cubes

Now that you deployed the cube to an Analysis Services instance, switch the BIDS Cube Designer view to the Browser page. In the Browser page you will see three panes: a Measure Group pane, a Filter pane, and a Data pane along with a toolbar as shown in Figure 6-9.

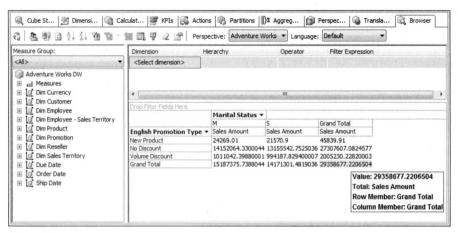

Figure 6-9

The Measure Group pane, at the left-side of the Cube Browser, shows the measure groups (includes measures) and the dimensions that are related to each measure group (includes attributes and hierarchies) of the cube. The Data pane, at the bottom right, uses the Office Web Components (OWC) control used for analyzing multidimensional data. You can drag and drop hierarchies on the rows and/ or columns and measures in the data area to analyze the data. Indeed, you can have multiple hierarchies in the row and column areas. The OWC also has a filter area (above the column area) that can be used to filter the data being analyzed. You can slice the data you want to analyze based on specific members of a hierarchy.

The top-right pane also allows you to filter your multidimensional data for analysis, but it has additional filtering options above those provided by the OWC control. Whereas the filter area in OWC allows you to select or deselect members of a hierarchy, the Filter pane allows you to perform comparison operations like equal, not equal, contains, in, not in, begins with, range operations, and any MDX expression. With the help of the filter functionality in the Filter pane and OWC, you will be able to analyze your multidimensional data.

Suppose you want to analyze the Internet sales of products based on the promotions offered to customers and the marital status of those customers. First you would need to drag and drop [Dim Promotion].[English Promotion Type] from the Measure Group pane to the OWC rows area. You will learn the MDX statements that are generated by the OWC in this section. SQL Server Profiler in SQL Server 2008 has the ability to trace the MDX statements that are sent to Analysis Services instances. For more information on how to obtain traces please refer to the section on using SQL Server Profiler in Chapter 15.

The first statement sent from OWC to Analysis Service instance is:

```
DROP VISUAL TOTALS for [Adventure Works DW]
```

When you drag and drop members of a hierarchy on a row (or column), or a measure in the fields area, OWC creates a row (or column) called Grand Total, which will automatically provide totals of the measure value for that hierarchy. By default the OWC in the Cube Browser shows you the totals of visible members of the hierarchy in the OWC. This is called Visual Totals because the total is calculated only for the members that are visible in the Browser. You have the option of disabling Visual Totals in the OWC. To do so, right-click OWC, select Commands and Options, click the Report tab, and select the "All Items (including hidden items)" option for the "Calculate totals based on" section. When the OWC calculates totals based on visual items only, it uses Visual Totals. The preceding MDX statement, DROP VISUAL TOTALS for [Adventure Works DW], removes references to visual totals from cells and clears the memory cache for visual totals thereby ensuring that values for current members selected will be accurate. The full syntax for the Drop Visual Totals statement is shown in the following code snippet. You can optionally specify the MDX set upon which the visual totals will be dropped. If the MDX set expression is not specified, visual totals are dropped for the entire cube.

```
DROP VISUAL TOTALS FOR <cube name> [ON '<MDX set expression>']
```

The second statement sent to the Analysis Services server by OWC is:

```
CREATE SESSION
   SET [Adventure Works DW].[ {7868741D-072F-458A-8A8D-EA3FED4A3FA7}
        Pivot0Axis1Set0] AS
   '
    {
      { [Dim Promotion].[English Promotion Type].[All] },
      AddCalculatedMembers([Dim Promotion].[English Promotion Type].[English
            Promotion Type].MEMBERS)
    }
   '
```

This statement creates a set called {7868741D-072F-458A-8A8D-EA3FED4A3FA7}Pivot0Axis1Set0, which contains the members of the hierarchy [Dim Promotion].[English Promotion Type]. Because OWC creates the queries in an automated manner, it dynamically creates a session name that includes a descriptive name (Pivot0Axis1Set0) and the session ID. The Analysis Services instance allows you to create sets and other MDX objects within a specific scope. You can create objects within the scope of the database or within the scope of your connection. In the preceding statement OWC creates the set within the scope of the current session and the set will be available only for this specific session.

Finally, OWC sends the following query to retrieve and show the members of the hierarchy [Dim Promotion].[English Promotion Type]:

```
SELECT
   NON EMPTY [{7868741D-072F-458A-8A8D-EA3FED4A3FA7}
        Pivot0Axis1Set0]
   DIMENSION PROPERTIES MEMBER_NAME, PARENT_UNIQUE_NAME ON COLUMNS
   FROM [Adventure Works DW]
CELL PROPERTIES VALUE, FORMATTED_VALUE, FORE_COLOR, BACK_COLOR
```

Next, drag and drop [Dim Customer].[Marital Status] from the Measure Group pane to the OWC columns area. OWC now sends a series of MDX statements followed by an MDX query to retrieve the members on rows and columns. The following code shows the sequence of MDX statements sent by the OWC to the Analysis Services instance. First the OWC drops visual totals followed by creating two sets for the members of the hierarchies selected on rows and columns of the OWC. OWC then queries the members from the created sets and finally drops the earlier set Pivot0Axis1Set0 because OWC has created new sets for members on rows and columns of the OWC.

```
Drop visual totals for [Adventure Works DW]
CREATE SESSION
   SET [Adventure Works DW].[{7868741D-072F-458A-8A8D-EA3FED4A3FA7}
        Pivot1Axis0Set0] AS
   '
    {
      { [Dim Customer].[Marital Status].[All] },
      AddCalculatedMembers([Dim Customer].[ Marital Status].[ Marital
            Status].MEMBERS)
    }
```

(continued)

171

(continued)

```
   '
   SET [Adventure Works DW].[{7868741D-072F-458A-8A8D-EA3FED4A3FA7}
       Pivot1Axis1Set0] AS
   '
   {
     { [Dim Promotion].[English Promotion Type].[All] },
     AddCalculatedMembers([Dim Promotion].[English Promotion Type].[English
         Promotion Type].MEMBERS)
   }
   '
SELECT
  NON EMPTY [{7868741D-072F-458A-8A8D-EA3FED4A3FA7}Pivot1Axis0Set0]
  DIMENSION PROPERTIES MEMBER_NAME, PARENT_UNIQUE_NAME ON COLUMNS,
  NON EMPTY [{7868741D-072F-458A-8A8D-EA3FED4A3FA7}Pivot1Axis1Set0]
  DIMENSION PROPERTIES MEMBER_NAME, PARENT_UNIQUE_NAME ON ROWS
  FROM [Adventure Works DW]
CELL PROPERTIES VALUE, FORMATTED_VALUE, FORE_COLOR, BACK_COLOR

DROP SET [Adventure Works DW].[{7868741D-072F-458A-8A8D-
      EA3FED4A3FA7}Pivot0Axis1Set0]
```

Finally, drag and drop the measure [Sales Amount] from the Fact Internet Sales measure group to the Drop Totals or Detail Fields Here area of the OWC pane. The OWC once again generates statements to drop existing sets and create new sets for members on rows and columns. These sets are used in the query to retrieve the measure data along with the properties of the cells. The cell properties returned by the instance of Analysis Services are used by the OWC to display values. From the query you can see that the properties of formatted values, foreground colors, and background colors are being retrieved by the OWC. The OWC uses the formatted value to display the cell values. The statements and query sent to Analysis Services by the OWC are shown here:

```
Drop visual totals for [Adventure Works DW]

CREATE SESSION
  SET [Adventure Works DW].[{7868741D-072F-458A-8A8D-EA3FED4A3FA7}
      Pivot2Axis0Set0] AS
  '
  {
    { [Dim Customer].[Marital Status].[All] },
    AddCalculatedMembers([Dim Customer].[ Marital Status].[ Marital
        Status].MEMBERS)
  }
  '
  SET [Adventure Works DW].[{7868741D-072F-458A-8A8D-EA3FED4A3FA7}
      Pivot2Axis1Set0] AS
  '
  {
    { [Dim Promotion].[English Promotion Type].[All] },
    AddCalculatedMembers([Dim Promotion].[English Promotion Type].[English
        Promotion Type].MEMBERS)
  }
```

172

```
SELECT
  NON EMPTY [{7868741D-072F-458A-8A8D-EA3FED4A3FA7}Pivot2Axis0Set0]
  DIMENSION PROPERTIES MEMBER_NAME, PARENT_UNIQUE_NAME ON COLUMNS,
  NON EMPTY [{7868741D-072F-458A-8A8D-EA3FED4A3FA7}Pivot2Axis1Set0]
  DIMENSION PROPERTIES MEMBER_NAME, PARENT_UNIQUE_NAME ON ROWS,
  {
    [Measures].[Sales Amount]
  }
  ON PAGES
  FROM [Adventure Works DW]
CELL PROPERTIES VALUE, FORMATTED_VALUE, FORE_COLOR, BACK_COLOR

DROP SET [Adventure Works DW].[{7868741D-072F-458A-8A8D-
      EA3FED4A3FA7}Pivot1Axis0Set0]

DROP SET [Adventure Works DW].[{7868741D-072F-458A-8A8D-
      EA3FED4A3FA7}Pivot1Axis1Set0]
```

If you hover over a particular cell you can see the cell values without formatting, along with the row and column member values that correspond to that cell as shown in Figure 6-9.

Cube Dimensions

The Cube Wizard helps you create your cube object from the DSV by creating appropriate dimension objects. The wizard detects the relationships between dimension tables and fact tables in the DSV, creates appropriate dimensions if needed, and establishes appropriate relationships between the dimensions and measure groups within the cube. As mentioned in the previous section, a cube contains an instance of the database dimension referred to as cube dimension. There can be multiple instances of a database dimension within a cube. There exists a relationship between the cube dimension and the measure groups within the cube. In this section you learn about various types of relationships between the cube dimensions and the measure groups within, as well as refine the Adventure Works DW cube created by Cube Wizard by adding a new dimension.

The Cube Wizard establishes relationships between the measure groups and cube dimensions based on its analysis of relationships in the DSV. You might have to refine these relationships based on your business needs. You can change these relationships in the Dimension Usage tab of the cube editor. If you switch to the Dimension Usage tab you will see the dimensions, measure groups of the cube, and the relationships between them, as shown in Figure 6-10.

The cube dimensions and measure groups are represented in a matrix format as rows and columns, respectively, where the relationship between them corresponds to the intersection cell. The intersection cell shows the dimension type along with the attribute that is used in the relationship to join.

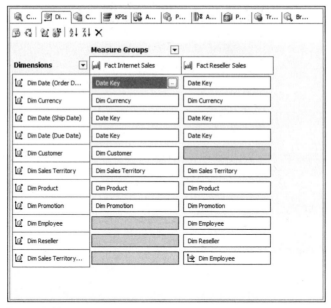

Figure 6-10

Relationship Types

Six different types of relationships can exist between a dimension and a measure group: No Relationship, Regular, Fact, Referenced, Many-to-Many, and Data Mining. In Figure 6-10 you see three of the six relationship types: No Relationship, Referenced, and Regular. Cells corresponding to a specific dimension and measure group can have an attribute specified that indicates that the dimension type is Regular. Further, such attributes can be used in the join condition between the dimension and the measure group. Often this attribute is the key attribute of the dimension and is called the *granularity attribute*. The granularity attribute can be an attribute that is above the key attribute of the dimension. When you browse a dimension along with measures of a measure group where the dimension and measure group have a regular relationship, Analysis Services aggregates the data appropriately. If you have your granularity attribute above the key attribute of your dimension, it is critical that you define appropriate attribute relationships in your dimension to make sure the data that is getting aggregated is accurate. The relationship between Dim Customer and Fact Internet Sales measure group is a regular relationship. The granularity attribute is shown in the cell intersecting the dimension and measure group as shown in Figure 6-10.

Cells that are shaded gray indicate there is no relationship between the dimension and measure group. Whenever there is no relationship between a dimension and measure group, the measure group property IgnoreUnrelatedDimension controls the results of queries involving any hierarchy of that dimension and any measure from the measure group. The measure values will either be null (IgnoreUnrelatedDimension=False) or the same value for each member of the dimension (IgnoreUnrelatedDimension=True). For example, there is no relationship between the dimension [Dim Employee] and the [Fact Internet Sales] measure group. If you browse the Gender hierarchy of [Dim Employee] and the measure [Sales Amount], you see that the measure values for each member of Gender hierarchy are the same value as the Grand Total as shown in Figure 6-11. This is because the IgnoreUnrelatedDimension value is set to True by the Cube Wizard as a default. You learn more about properties of measure groups and measures later in this chapter.

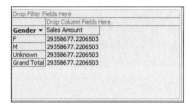

Figure 6-11

When a table is used as both a fact and dimension table, it constitutes a unique relationship between the dimension and measure group called the *fact* relationship. The relationship is similar to that of the regular dimension, but specifying it as a fact dimension helps improve query performance for a certain class of MDX queries. You learn more about fact dimensions in Chapter 9.

Typically there is a one-to-many relationship between a fact and a dimension member for regular relationships. When you have a one-to-one relationship between a fact and a dimension member, you typically have a fact relationship. When there is a many-to-many relationship between a fact and a dimension member, the dimension member has a one-to-many relationship with various facts and a single fact is associated with multiple dimension members. The definition for a many-to-many relationship can be well understood via an example. Assume you have a fact table (for sales of books) that is related to a dimension table containing author information. There is another fact table that contains authors' salary information, which is related to the Authors dimension table as well as the geographical information of the publisher who is paying the authors. In this example you have a one-to-many relationship between authors and books. The salary fact data is related to the publisher's geographical information and the authors. If you want to analyze the book sales based on the geographical information of the publisher, the Geography dimension of publishers acts as a many-to-many relationship with the fact Book Sales. You learn about the usage of fact and many-to-many relationships in Chapter 9.

Data Mining dimensions are another item type in the list of relationships; these are used to establish linkage between a cube and a dimension created from a Data Mining model. You learn more about this in Chapters 9 and 16.

When a dimension is related to the fact data through another dimension, you define this indirect relationship between the measure group and the dimension as a *reference relationship*. In Figure 6-10 the Dim Sales Territory (Dim Employee – Sales Territory) dimension is related to the Fact Reseller Sales measure group through the Employee dimension. The icon at the intersection of the dimension and measure group indicates this reference relationship. You might also recall that you added the Dim Geography dimension in the Select Existing Dimensions page of the Cube Wizard. However, the Cube Wizard was not smart enough to figure out there is a relationship between the Fact tables and the Dim Geography dimension table through other dimension tables. Hence the Cube Wizard did not add the Dim Geography dimension as a cube dimension. Because the relationship between the Dim Geography dimension and the measure groups in the Adventure Works DW cube is through another dimension, you can say that there is an indirect relationship between the Dim Geography dimension and the measure groups.

Follow these steps to add the Dim Geography dimension to the cube and establish the reference relationship:

1. To add the Dim Geography database dimension to the cube, right-click in the Dimension pane of the Dimension Usage tab and select Add Cube Dimension, as shown in Figure 6-12.

2. A dialog showing all the shared dimensions within the project launches, as shown in Figure 6-13. Select the Dim Geography dimension and click OK.

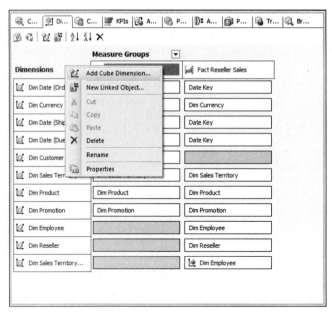

Figure 6-12

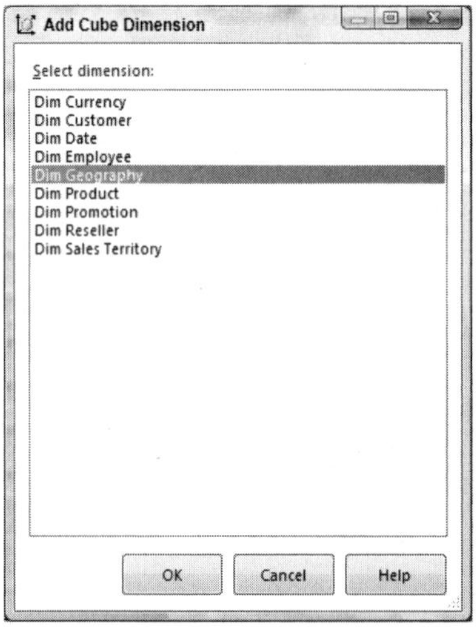

Figure 6-13

The cube editor is unable to identify a relationship through an attribute between the existing measure groups and the Geography dimension and as a result leaves the relationship definition up to you. There exists an indirect relationship between the [Dim Geography] dimension and [Fact Internet Sales] measure group through the [Dim Customer] dimension. There is an indirect relationship between the [Dim Geography] dimension and the Fact Reseller measure group through the [Dim Reseller] dimension. You need to define these reference relationships.

3. To define the relationship between [Dim Geography] and the [Fact Internet Sales] measure group, select the corresponding cell in the matrix and you will see an ellipsis in that cell. Click the ellipsis (". . .").

4. This opens the Define Relationship dialog shown in Figure 6-14. Select Referenced from the Select relationship type drop-down list box. The [Dim Geography] dimension forms an indirect or reference relationship with the [Fact Internet Sales] measure group through the [Dim Customer] dimension. You define the intermediate dimension through the Intermediate Dimension field in the wizard. Once you have defined the intermediate dimension, you need to select the attributes that are involved in the join of the relationship. The "Reference dimension attribute" is the attribute in the reference dimension that is used in the join between the intermediate dimension ([Dim Customer]) and the reference dimension ([Dim Geography]). The "Intermediate dimension attribute" is the attribute of the intermediate dimension that is involved in the join between the reference dimension and the intermediate dimension. Define the Intermediate dimension as [Dim Customer], Reference dimension attribute as [Geography Key], and Intermediate dimension attribute as [Geography Key] as shown in Figure 6-14 and click OK. In Figure 6-14 you see a checkbox with the text Materialize. This checkbox is enabled by default in SQL Server Analysis Services 2008. By enabling this checkbox you are ensuring Analysis Services will build appropriate indexes to get improved query performance while querying fact data along with reference dimension hierarchies.

5. Similar to step 4, establish a referenced relationship between the [Dim Geography] dimension and the [Fact Reseller Sales] measure group through the [Dim Reseller] dimension. Once you have completed specifying the relationship between [Dim Geography] and the two measure groups of the cube, your Dimension Usage tab will resemble Figure 6-15.

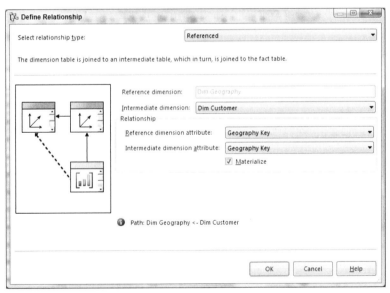

Figure 6-14

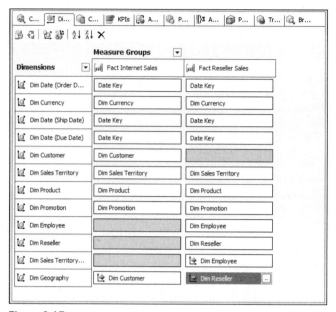

Figure 6-15

The reference relationship between a dimension and a measure group is indicated by an arrow pointing to the intermediate dimension as shown in Figure 6-15. This graphical view of the reference relationship helps you identify the type of relationship between a dimension and measure group when you are looking at the Dimension Usage tab of the cube editor. Similar graphical representations are available for fact, many-to-many, and Data Mining dimensions, and you learn about these relationships later in Chapters 9 and 16.

Browsing Reference Dimensions

Having added the [Dim Geography] dimension as the reference dimension to the cube, assume you want to analyze the Reseller Sales based on different business types in various countries. To do so you need redeploy and process the cube with the changes. Then go to the Cube Browser and drag and drop the [English Country Region Name] hierarchy from the [Dim Geography] dimension to the rows, the [Business Type] hierarchy of the [Dim Reseller] dimension to the columns, and the measure [Sales Amount – Fact Reseller Sales] of the [Fact Reseller Sales] measure group to the details area. You can now analyze the Sales data based on the business type in each country, as shown in Figure 6-16. Based on this sales knowledge, the costs associated with the products, and your business goals, you can strategically promote the business type yielding the maximum profit for your company. Reference dimensions help you to analyze fact data even though they are not directly related to the facts.

English Country Region Name ▾	Business Type ▾			
	Specialty Bike Shop	Value Added Reseller	Warehouse	Grand Total
	Sales Amount - Fact Reseller Sales	Sales Amount - Fact Reseller Sales	Sales Amount - Fact Reseller Sales	Sales Amount - Fact Reseller Sal
Australia	327171.5382	799552.060499998	467611.778	1594335.3767
Canada	1216909.29569999	4855218.34759999	8305797.95319992	14377925.5965001
Germany	164090.0319	625523.421499999	1194374.5839	1983988.03729999
France	418643.6974	948247.751599999	3240646.48599999	4607537.93499999
United Kingdom	330178.3808	1793112.8225	2155717.6233	4279008.82659999
United States	4299173.23570002	25945862.9237999	23362765.0507001	53607801.2102
Grand Total	6756166.17970001	34967517.3274999	38726913.4751	80450596.9822983

Figure 6-16

178

The OWC sends the following statements and queries to retrieve data for analyzing the reseller sales fact of various business types across various countries of the resellers. The OWC creates sets for the members on the columns and rows of OWC and then queries the facts added to the detail data along with the sets.

```
Drop visual totals for [Adventure Works DW]

CREATE SESSION
  SET [Adventure Works DW].[{76D2D6C7-D50B-4C12-8DBF-DA53595646F5}
      Pivot24Axis0Set0] AS

  '
    {
      { [Dim Reseller].[Business Type].[All] },
      AddCalculatedMembers([Dim Reseller].[Business Type].[Business
        Type].MEMBERS)
    }
  '
  SET [Adventure Works DW].[{76D2D6C7-D50B-4C12-8DBF-DA53595646F5}
      Pivot24Axis1Set0] AS

  '
    {
      { [Dim Geography].[English Country Region Name].[All] },
      AddCalculatedMembers([Dim Geography].[English Country Region Name].
        [English Country Region Name].MEMBERS)
    }
  '


SELECT
  NON EMPTY [{76D2D6C7-D50B-4C12-8DBF-DA53595646F5}Pivot24Axis0Set0]
  DIMENSION PROPERTIES MEMBER_NAME, PARENT_UNIQUE_NAME ON COLUMNS,
  NON EMPTY [{76D2D6C7-D50B-4C12-8DBF-DA53595646F5}Pivot24Axis1Set0]
  DIMENSION PROPERTIES MEMBER_NAME, PARENT_UNIQUE_NAME ON ROWS,
  {
    [Measures].[Sales Amount - Fact Reseller Sales]
  }
  ON PAGES
  FROM [Adventure Works DW]
CELL PROPERTIES VALUE, FORMATTED_VALUE, FORE_COLOR, BACK_COLOR


DROP SET [Adventure Works DW].[{76D2D6C7-D50B-4C12-8DBF-
    DA53595646F5}Pivot23Axis0Set0]

DROP SET [Adventure Works DW].[{76D2D6C7-D50B-4C12-8DBF-
    DA53595646F5}Pivot23Axis1Set0]
```

The OWC provides you with the option of slicing the data you are analyzing. Therefore OWC creates the MDX statements to create sets within the specified session. It then queries the multidimensional data on three different axes and displays them on the Rows, Columns, and Fields area. Because the query used by the OWC control retrieves data on three-dimensional axes, you cannot execute the same query in SQL Server Management Studio (SSMS). SSMS will only be able to display two-dimensional results. Therefore if you need to see the exact same results in SSMS, you need an MDX query that will retrieve results in a two-dimensional format. The MDX query generated by OWC can be re-written using the CrossJoin function or the cross join operator (*) so that the results can be retrieved on two axes. The simplified MDX query that will return the same results as the OWC is:

```
SELECT
{
        [Measures].[Sales Amount - Fact Reseller Sales]
}
ON COLUMNS,
NON EMPTY {[Dim Reseller].[Business Type].members  *
[Dim Geography].[English Country Region Name].members}
DIMENSION PROPERTIES MEMBER_NAME ON ROWS
FROM [Adventure Works DW]
CELL PROPERTIES VALUE, FORMATTED_VALUE, FORE_COLOR, BACK_COLOR
```

So far you have learned about cube dimensions, how to add them to a cube, how to define relationships, and then how to query data along with the dimensions. Cube dimensions and their attributes and hierarchies contain several properties. Some properties such as AttributeHierarchyEnabled, AttributeHierarchyVisible, and the AttributeHierarchyOptimizedState reflect the state of the cube dimension hierarchies or attributes in the shared dimension by default. You can override these properties so that appropriate settings are applied for the cube dimensions within the cube. The properties AggregationUsage for attributes and AllMemberAggregationUsage for cube dimensions control the behavior of aggregations designed on the cube. You learn more about these properties in Chapters 9 and 14.

Measures and Measure Groups

You learned about editing cube dimensions and establishing the right relationships between dimensions and measure groups in a cube. Similarly, you can add or delete measures and measure groups in a cube. Measures are the focus point for data analysis and therefore they are the core objects of a cube. Measures are columns from the fact table that contain meaningful information for data analysis. Usually measures are of type numeric and can be aggregated or summarized along hierarchies of a dimension. You can specify the type of aggregation to be applied for each measure. The most widely used aggregate functions are Sum, Count, and Distinct Count. A collection of measures forms an object called a measure group, and a collection of measure groups forms the dimension called *Measures* in the cube. "Measures" is a keyword in Analysis Services that refers to a special dimension that only contains the fact data.

If you click the Cube Structure tab in the cube editor you will see the Measures pane on the top-left corner. Click the cube named Adventure Works DW within the Measures pane to see the associated properties in the Properties window located on the bottom-right corner of the BIDS. Figure 6-17 shows the Measures and Properties panes. The Measures pane shows the cube name and the measure groups within the cube. You can see the two measure groups Fact Reseller Sales and Fact Internet Sales that correspond to the two fact tables. Fact table columns that become measures of the cube are contained within the corresponding measure group. There is typically a one-to-one relationship between a fact table and measure group in the cube.

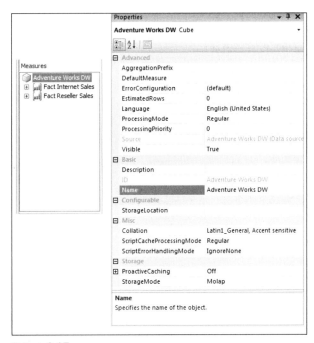

Figure 6-17

In your source data, if you had partitioned your fact data into multiple fact tables across a specific dimension, it needs to be handled differently when designing the cube. For example, if you have Fact Internet Sales data stored in separate fact tables for each quarter (fact data has been partitioned into multiple fact tables across the Time dimension), then with respect to the cube all these are considered a single fact table because they have the same schema. You typically partition your relational fact data into multiple fact tables due to design or scalability considerations, but when you want to analyze the data you will be looking to aggregate the data appropriately across various dimensions, especially the Time dimension. You can either merge the data from all the fact tables within the DSV with a named query or you can utilize the partitioning feature in Analysis Services so that Analysis Services aggregates the data correctly during browsing. You learn more about partitions in Chapters 7 and 14.

You can see several properties of the cube in Figure 6-17. The most important property is DefaultMeasure. As the name indicates, this property is used to define the measure used by default whenever queries are sent to the cube. The reason why the default measure is important is that whenever your MDX query does not explicitly contain a member from the measures dimension, the default measure is returned. In addition to that, the default measure is used whenever restrictions are applied in the query with the WHERE clause, and based on the default measure your results can be different. If you select the DefaultMeasure property you can see a drop-down list box that shows all the measures of the cube. You can choose the measure you want to define as the default measure of the cube. If the default measure is not specified, the first measure of the first measure group of the cube (as seen in the Measures pane) will be the default measure of the cube.

The next most important property is the StorageMode property. This defines whether your fact data will be stored in Analysis Services, your relational data source, or both. The StorageMode property has three options: Multidimensional OLAP (MOLAP), Relational OLAP (ROLAP), and Hybrid OLAP (HOLAP). The default value is MOLAP, which means that when the cube is processed, Analysis Services reads the relational data and stores it in a proprietary format for fast retrieval. You learn more about the defining storage modes in Chapter 9. In Analysis Services 2008, you have the option to instruct the Analysis

Services instance to automatically update cube and dimension objects if there was a change in the relational data. The ProactiveCaching property lets you specify the frequency of the update of the cube data based on changes in the relational data. You learn about the benefits of proactive caching with the help of a complete scenario in Chapter 21. The ErrorConfiguration property helps in handling the various errors that can occur while processing the fact data and defining what actions should be taken under such error circumstances such as ignoring the error, converting to a specific value, or stopping processing when errors are encountered. One of the main features of an OLAP database is the ability to create aggregations that facilitate fast query response times. The AggregationPrefix property is used to prefix the name of the aggregations that are created for the cube. The remaining properties are self-explanatory and you can find detailed information for each property in Analysis Services 2008 product documentation.

If you click one of the measure groups, you will see the properties associated with that measure group. Most of the properties at the cube level are also applicable to the measure group. If you specify a value for a property at the cube level as well as the measure group level for a common property, the value specified at the measure group level will be honored by the Analysis Services instance. Expand the measure group Fact Internet Sales and select the measure Sales Amount. The Properties pane now shows the properties of the measure, as shown in Figure 6-18. Next, you learn the important properties of a measure in detail.

The AggregateFunction property defines how the measure value is to be aggregated from one level to another level of a hierarchy in a dimension. For example, assume the Product dimension contains a hierarchy called Products that contains two levels, Model Name and Product Name. Each model contains one or more products. If you want the sales amount of a specific product to be aggregated to the model, you need to specify the aggregate function to be Sum. Whenever you browse the cube along the Products hierarchy, you will see that the sales of each product are aggregated to the corresponding model. However, sometimes you might not want the measure value to be aggregated while browsing a hierarchy. Therefore, Analysis Services 2008 provides you with several aggregate functions. Aggregation functions supported in the properties can also be done using MDX scripts. (You learn about MDX scripts in Chapter 9.) However, we recommended that you use the built-in aggregation functions supported in the Properties window to get optimal performance from your Analysis Services instance.

Figure 6-18

Other than the Sum aggregate function, the most commonly used aggregate functions are Count and Distinct Count. The Count aggregate function, as the name indicates, is used whenever you want to count each occurrence of the measure value rather than add the measure values. For example, if you want to find the number of transactions in a day or number of customers in a day, you would use a Count aggregate function on a fact table column that indicates the customers who came to the store on a specific day. The Distinct Count aggregate function, on the other hand, can be used to identify the unique number of occurrences of a specific measure. For example, a customer can buy a specific product every month. If you want to find the unique number of customers who purchase a specific product, you use the Distinct Count aggregate function. You will see examples of Count and Distinct Count aggregate functions in this section. The None aggregate function is used when you do not want to aggregate the values of a specific measure across a dimension. An example of where the None aggregate function would be used is for the price of a specific product or discount provided on a unit product.

When you build and browse a cube you will see all the measures occurring under the dimension called [Measures] in the Measure Groups pane of the Cube Browser. If you want to organize the related measures in a logical structure that is more meaningful for users, you use the property called DisplayFolder. You can specify a measure to be part of one or more display folders by editing the DisplayFolder property. If you enter a name in the DisplayFolder property, that specific measure will become part of the newly entered display folder. You can make a specific measure part of multiple display folders by specifying the display folders separated by a semicolon. When display folders are specified, while browsing the cube you will see the display folders under the appropriate measure group name in the metadata pane of the Browser. Therefore you cannot have measures from different measure groups under a single display folder.

In some business applications you only allow access to the aggregated results of a measure. For such applications you need a way to aggregate the results of a measure but do not want to show the base measure. You can aggregate the results of a measure by specifying a measure called the calculated measure (you learn more about calculations a little later in this chapter) and hide the base measure. The measure property Visible allows you to hide the base measure from viewing for such applications.

The FormatString property allows you to show the measure value in a format of your choice. If you select the FormatString property you will see the various format options available. The MeasureExpression property is used for specifying the expression that evaluates the value for the measure. For example, if you have Sales information you might want to ensure the Sales information is presented in the local currency based on the currency conversion rates. In such a case you will define an appropriate expression for the MeasureExpression property for the measure Sales. You learn about the MeasureExpression property in Chapter 9.

The easiest way to see the effect of some of the properties mentioned is to try them yourself in your own project. Specify two display folders named DisplayFolder1 and DisplayFolder2 for the measure Sales Amount. Because the measure Sales Amount is a currency data type, you can select the currency format. Select the $#,##0.00;($#,##0.00) format from the FormatString property drop-down list. The Properties window for the measure Sales Amount should resemble the Figure 6-19.

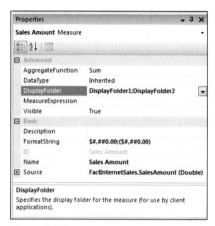

Figure 6-19

You learned examples of where the aggregate functions Count and Distinct Count can be useful. In your Adventure Works DW cube, if you want to count the number of customers and distinct customers who have bought specific products, you need to use these aggregate functions. Customer Key identifies the customer who has bought a specific product in the fact table. Therefore, in order to see the counts of customers you need to create two new measures using the fact table column Customer Key. To create the two new measures follow these steps:

1. Right-click the measure group Fact Internet Sales and select New Measure.

2. In the New Measure dialog, select the checkbox "Show all columns."

3. Select the column Customer Key and click OK. A measure called Customer Key is now created.

4. In the Measures pane, change the name for this measure from [Customer Key] to [Distinct Customers] by right-clicking the measure and selecting Rename.

5. Change the aggregate function for this measure to be Distinct Count.

At this point you will notice that a blue squiggly line shows up under the Distinct Customers measure. Analysis Services 2008 has built-in checks for many of the best practices for dimension and cube design. These best practices are implemented as warnings in the Analysis Management Objects (AMO) API. BIDS surfaces these AMO warnings through warning icons and blue squiggly lines for objects that don't meet these design best practices. To discover the rules that generate these warnings, you simply have to move the mouse over the blue squiggly lines or warning icon to see a tooltip with the best practice design rule. In this case the rule suggests that distinct count measures be broken out into separate measure groups (see Figure 6-20).

The reason for this warning is that distinct count measures are semi-additive and require storing records at a finer level of detail than measures utilizing other aggregate functions. For a distinct count of customers to be accessible, the individual customer IDs must be available. Therefore, Analysis Services must use the Customer Key attribute for any and all aggregations. Consider the following example. If you are interested in the total Sales (sum) for a product in a given year, it is not necessary to retain the individual customer IDs that purchased the product within the desired year. The Analysis Services engine should be able to pre-aggregate data at the Product ID and Year attribute levels as part of the normal processing of the cube. However, if there is a requirement that you know the distinct number of customers who purchased the product within the year, you must retain the customer keys throughout any aggregated data.

If the product in question was purchased by 50,000 customers over the year, the aggregate goes from one row of data per product per year to 50,000 rows per product for the year. Separating Distinct Count measures into different measure groups allows maximum pre-aggregation of other additive measures with minimal storage and on-the-fly aggregation requirements.

If you drag and drop the Customer Key column into the Measures pane to create a new measure, you will notice that the Cube Designer automatically creates a new measure group and adds the measure based on the assumption that you are probably defining a distinct count aggregation function. For this illustration we will ignore this best practice warning and move on to the next steps.

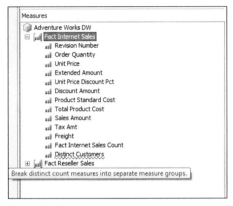

Figure 6-20

1. Right-click the Fact Internet Sales measure group and select New Measure.

2. In the New Measure dialog select the checkbox "Show all columns."

3. Select the column [Customer Key] and click OK. A measure called [Customer Key] is now created.

4. In the Measures pane, change the name for this measure from [Customer Key] to Total Customers by right-clicking the measure and selecting Rename.

5. In the Properties window change the AggregateFunction property for the [Total Customers] measure from Sum to Count.

6. The Unit Price of a product is the same value. Therefore this value should not be aggregated. In order to see the same value for a specific product you need to choose the aggregate function FirstNonEmpty.

7. Create a user hierarchy called Products in the Dim Product dimension with two levels, Model Name and English Product Name, where Model Name is the parent level of English Product Name. Rename the level English Product Name as Product Name.

8. Deploy the project to the Analysis Services instance.

9. Once the deployment is complete, switch to the Cube Browser tab. Click the Reconnect link to get the updated metadata and data from the Analysis Services instance. When you expand the [Fact Internet Sales] folder under the Measures node, you will see two folders called DisplayFolder1 and DisplayFolder2 that contain the measure [Sales Amount] as shown in Figure 6-21.

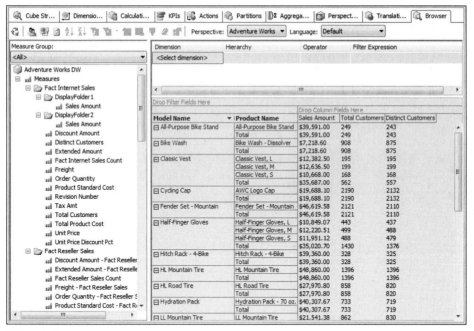

Figure 6-21

10. Clear any data in your OWC browser by right-clicking within the OWC area and selecting Clear Results or by dragging and dropping each measure or hierarchy from rows/columns to outside of the OWC area.

11. Drag and drop the measures [Sales Amount], [Total Customers], and [Distinct Customers] for the [Fact Internet Sales] measure group to the data area of the OWC.

12. Then drag and drop the hierarchy Products from the Dim Product dimension to the rows and expand the member Classic Vest.

You can now see that the values for the measures are aggregated for the hierarchy Products that contains two levels, Model Name and Product Name, based on the aggregate function chosen. Choosing the aggregate functions Count and Distinct Count will not only count the values for the members of a hierarchy, but will also aggregate the counts to the next level. Notice that the values of [Sales Amount] are formatted based on the format string you specified earlier.

You should be able to add the measure [Unit Price] in the same browser and see the results of the FirstNonEmpty aggregate function. However we believe there is a bug in the product that causes the values for [Sales Amount] and [Total Customers] to be cleared in the Cube Browser. We recommend you clear the fields [Sales Amount] and [Total Customers] from the data area and drag and drop [Unit Price]. You can see that the Unit Price is aggregated from the members in the Product Name level to Model Name level based on the FirstNonEmpty aggregate function. You see the Total value for the measure Unit Price for the Classic Vest model as 63.5. The Unit Price value shown for the Mountain-100 model name is the Unit Price Mountain-100 Silver 42, one of the members of the Mountain-100. In the example shown in Figure 6-21, all the products under the model name Classic Vest have the same unit price. If you expand the Model Name member Mountain-100 you will see that the Products under the model Mountain-100 have different values.

You have now successfully enhanced the cube created by the Cube Wizard by adding cube dimensions and measures to the cube. In the process you have also learned about the properties of cube dimensions, measures, and measure groups. Most often businesses need complex logic to analyze the relational data. Analysis Services 2008 provides you with the ability to embed the complex calculations required for solving business problems in several ways. The most basic operation that every business will need is creating simple arithmetic operations on the base measures or dimension members. Objects created via such operations are called calculated members.

Calculated Members

The term *calculated member* refers to the creation of any MDX object through a calculation. The calculated member can be part of the Measures dimension where a simple MDX expression such as addition or subtraction of two or more base measures results in a new measure. Such calculated members on the Measures dimension are referred to as *calculated measures*. You can also create calculated members on other dimensions by specifying an MDX expression. These members are simply referred to as calculated members. To create a calculated member, click the Calculations tab of the cube editor. This takes you to the Calculations view, as shown in Figure 6-22. The Calculations view contains three window panes: Script Organizer, Calculation Tools, and Script.

The Script Organizer window pane shows the names of the calculation objects of the cube. Various types of calculations can be created in the Calculations view such as calculated members and calculated measures. You can apply a name to a subset of dimension members. This is referred to as a *named set*. In addition to calculated members and named sets, you can define a script containing complex MDX expressions to perform complex business logic calculations. If you right-click within the Script Organizer you can see the selections to create a calculated member, named set, or a script command. These operations can also be performed by clicking the buttons in the toolbar as indicated in Figure 6-22. You create calculated measures in this chapter. The creation of script commands and named sets are detailed in Chapters 9 and 10.

The Calculation Tools pane contains three pages: Metadata, Functions, and Templates. The Metadata view is identical to the Measure Groups pane you have become familiar with in the Cube Designer's Browser page. It shows the measures and dimensions of the current cube. The Functions view shows all the MDX functions along with a template of the arguments needed for each function. In the Templates view you can see templates for some common calculations used in certain applications such as budgeting and financial.

The Script window pane shows the details of calculation scripts. The default view of the Script window is called the Form View. It can also be toggled to a different view called the Script View. In the Form View, the Script Organizer pane will be visible and you can see the calculations of each object in the Script window pane. If the Script window is switched to the Script View (using the appropriate button as shown in Figure 6-22), all the calculations are shown as a single script and the Script Organizer pane becomes invisible. You can toggle between the two views by clicking the icons shown in Figure 6-22 or by selecting the option through the menu item Cube ⇨ Show Calculations In, which contains options for Script or Form views.

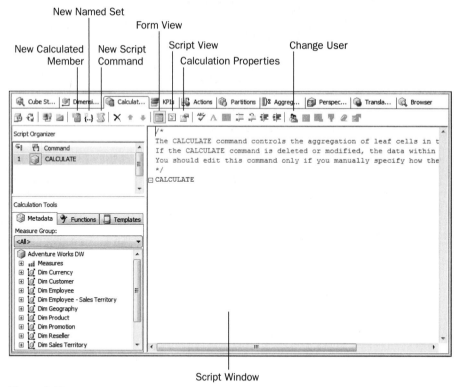

Figure 6-22

All commands and selections available in Analysis Services 2008 are accessible via keyboard controls. You can switch between the three panes of the Script tab of the Cube Designer using the F6 function key or by making the appropriate selection via menu items.

Calculated Measures

Calculated measures are the most common type of calculated members created in a cube. In your project you have the measures Sales and Product Cost in the two measure groups, Fact Internet Sales and Fact Reseller Sales. An important question to ask about any business concerns profits gained. Profits gained is the difference between total sales and cost of goods sold. In the Adventure Works DW cube you have Sales through the Internet as well as through resellers. Therefore you need to add these two sales amounts to calculate the total sales of products. Similarly, you need to calculate the total product cost by adding the costs of products sold through the Internet and resellers. Two calculated measures must be formed to perform these operations. Once you have created these two calculations, you can calculate the profit. Follow these steps to create the calculated measure for profit:

1. Right-click in the Script Organizer pane and select New Calculated Member, as shown in Figure 6-23. An object called Calculated Member is created. The Script window now shows several text boxes for you to specify the name of the calculation, the MDX expression for the calculated member, and other properties for the calculated member.

Figure 6-23

2. Specify the name of the calculated member as [Total Sales Amount] in the Script window. In the Expression text box you need to type the MDX expression that will calculate the Total Sales Amount. As mentioned earlier, the Total Sales Amount is the sum of sales from the sales amounts in the Fact Internet Sales and Fact Reseller Sales measure groups. Drag and drop these measures from the Metadata window and add the MDX operator "+" between these measures as shown in Figure 6-24.

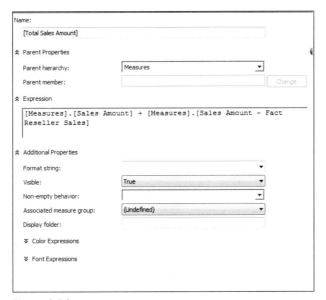

Figure 6-24

3. For cost of goods sold, create a new calculated member called [Total Product Costs] using a method similar to the one described in step 2 but with appropriate Product Cost measures from the two measure groups.

4. Create a calculated member called [Profit]. The MDX expression to evaluate Profit is the difference of the calculated measures you have created in steps 2 and 3. Enter the MDX expression [Measures].[Total Sales Amount] – [Measures].[Total Product Costs] in the Expression text box as shown in Figure 6-25. Since Measures is a special dimension, we do not necessarily have to precede the measure name with [Measures].

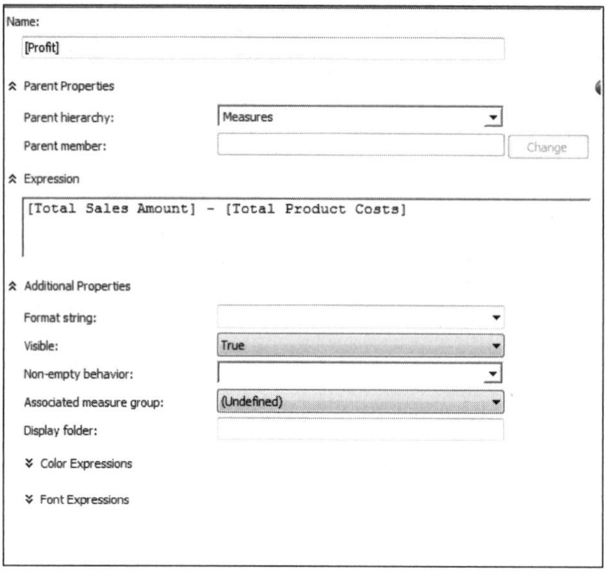

Figure 6-25

5. You have the option of specifying certain additional properties for the calculated measures you have created based on an MDX expression. By default all the calculated measures created are visible. You can specify color, font, and format strings for the calculated measures based on certain conditions. For example, if you want to highlight the profit in red if the amount is less than one million dollars and in green if it is greater than or equal to one million, you can do so by specifying the appropriate background color for the calculated member.

6. Enter the following MDX expression for the Color Expressions ⇨ Back color: in the Script Window.

```
iif ( [Measures].[Profit] < 1000000,    255 /*Red*/,
      65280 /*Green*/)
```

This MDX expression uses the IIF function. This function takes three arguments. The first argument is an expression that should evaluate to true or false. The return value of the IIF function is either the second or the third argument passed to the function. If the result of the expression is true, the IIF function returns the second argument; if the expression is false, it returns the third argument. The first argument passed to the IIF function is to see if the profit is less than one million. The second and third arguments passed to the function are the values for the colors red and green. The values for the colors can be selected by clicking the color icon next to the background color text box.

To see the effect of the calculations you have created:

7. Go to the Cube Browser tab.

8. Deploy the AnalysisServices2008Tutorial project to your Analysis Services instance.

9. As soon as the deployment is complete, switch to the Cube Browser tab and click the Reconnect button to get the updated metadata and data from the Analysis Services instance.

10. Expand the Measures folder to see the newly created calculated measures as shown in Figure 6-26.

11. Drag and drop the measure Profit to the OWC detail area, hierarchy English Country Region name of the Dim Geography dimension on rows, and hierarchy Style of the Dim Product dimension on columns.

You will see the background color for the cells are either red or green based on the Profit value as shown in Figure 6-26.

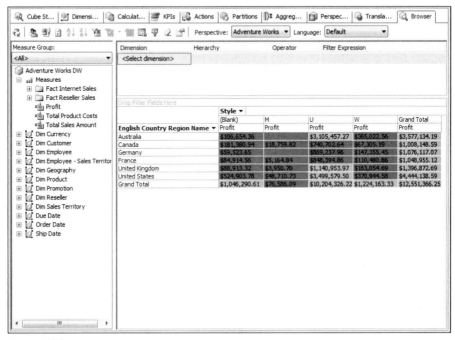

Figure 6-26

Querying Calculated Measures

You can query the calculated measures similar to other measures in the cube by referencing them by name. For example, if you want to query the calculated member Profit based on Model Name, you execute the following query:

```
SELECT [Measures].[Profit] on COLUMNS,
[Dim Product].[Model Name].MEMBERS on ROWS
FROM [Adventure Works DW]
```

If you want to retrieve all the measures in the cube instead of specifying each measure, you use [Measures].MEMBERS. However, calculated members are not returned in your query result when you specify [Measures].MEMBERS. You need to execute the following MDX query to retrieve the base measures along with the calculated members:

```
SELECT [Measures].ALLMEMBERS on COLUMNS,
[Dim Product].[Model Name].MEMBERS on ROWS
FROM [Adventure Works DW]
```

You have learned to enhance the Adventure Works DW cube by creating calculated measures and learned to set certain properties for the calculated measures via MDX expressions. The NonEmptyBehavior property for calculated measures is discussed in Chapter 15.

Creating Perspectives

Analysis Services 2008 provides you with the option of creating a cube that combines many fact tables. Each cube dimension can contain several attributes and hierarchies. Even though the cube might contain all the relevant data for business analysis combined into a single object, the users of the cube might only be interested in sections of the cube. For example, you can have a cube that contains sales and budget information of a company. The Sales department is only interested in viewing sales-relevant data, whereas the users involved in budgeting or forecasting next year's revenue are only interested in budget-relevant sections of the cube. Typically, users do not like to see too much extra information. In order to accommodate this, Analysis Services 2008 provides you with the option of creating a view of a cube that only contains a subset of its objects, called a *perspective*.

In the Adventure Works DW cube you have two fact tables, FactInternetSales and FactResellerSales. To understand the behavior of perspectives, create a perspective for Internet Sales and a perspective for Reseller Sales. The following steps show you how to create new perspectives:

1. Click the Perspectives tab in the Cube Designer. You will see a column on the left showing the measures, dimensions, and calculated members as shown in Figure 6-27.

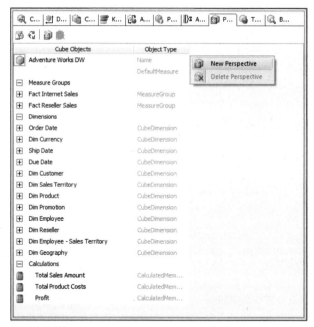

Figure 6-27

2. Right-click in the window pane and select New Perspective as shown in Figure 6-27. You can also create a new perspective by clicking the New Perspective button in the toolbar. A new column with the name Perspective is created. You have a checkbox next to each object in the cube and these are selected by default. Rename the perspective Internet Sales. Deselect the Fact Reseller Sales measure group and the dimensions Dim Employee and Dim Reseller.

3. Create another perspective called Reseller Sales. Deselect the Fact Internet Sales measure group and the Dim Customer dimension.

Your Perspective window will now look similar to Figure 6-28. Now deploy the project. BIDS sends the definitions for the new perspectives to the server. Perspectives are not new cubes on the server, but only a view of an existing cube object. Keep in mind that perspectives are represented as different cubes with the cube names represented as the perspective name when a client queries for the cube in a database.

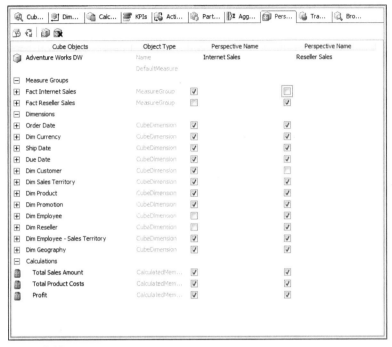

Figure 6-28

In Chapter 5 you learned to specify translations to attributes in a dimension. Similarly, you can create translations for the cube. You see the effect of perspectives along with translations after learning how to create translations for a cube.

Creating Translations

Translations facilitate the display of data and metadata in a regional language. Unlike translations for dimensions, where a column from the relational table is specified as containing the translation for members of an attribute hierarchy, cube translations are specified for the cube's metadata objects.

To create a new translation for the Adventure Works DW cube, do the following:

1.   Click the Translations tab in the Cube Editor. Similar to the Perspective view, the left column shows the names of all the metadata objects in the default language. There is another column that indicates the object type, which indicates Caption because defining translations for a cube is only providing translated names for the metadata object names.

2.   Right-click in the Translation window pane and select New Translation. You can also create a new translation using the New Translation button in the toolbar. In the Select Language dialog, select French (France) as the language and click OK. You now have a new column where you

can provide the translations of each object (measure, display folders, dimension name, attribute names). Specify the translations in French as shown in Figure 6-29. (If you don't know French you can enter the translations in a language of your choice.) You can define translations for each metadata object in the cube such as measure names, measure group names, dimension names, perspective names, as well as calculated member names.

3. Deploy the project to your Analysis Services instance.

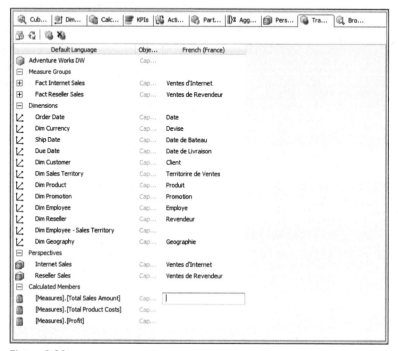

Figure 6-29

Browsing Perspectives and Translations

You have successfully created perspectives and translations for the Adventure Works DW cube. To see the effect, you need to be in the Browser tab of the Cube Designer. In the Browser, if you click the Perspective drop-down list box you will see three perspectives: Adventure Works DW (the default perspective that contains all cube objects), Internet Sales, and Reseller Sales. Select the Internet Sales perspective. If you expand the measures in the Measure Group window you will notice that all the measures relevant to the reseller are now not visible. Drag and drop the Sales Amount, English Product Name hierarchy in the Dim Product dimension, and the English Education hierarchy of the Dim Customer dimension to the OWC browser. You will see the sales amount data along with product names and education of customers as shown in Figure 6-30.

To see the translated names in French you need to select the language French (France) in the Cube Browser. As soon as you select the French (France) language you will notice that all the metadata and data members for the hierarchies in the OWC automatically change to values in French for those objects where translations have been defined, as shown in Figure 6-31. Thus you have created translated values in French for a French client who wants to analyze the same values, but who would be able to understand and interpret the results better in French than English. Each language has a corresponding id called the locale id. When you select a specific language in the Browser, BIDS connects to the server with the corresponding locale id for the language. Analysis Services automatically provides you with the metadata and data corresponding to the locale id whenever queries are sent to the server on the same connection.

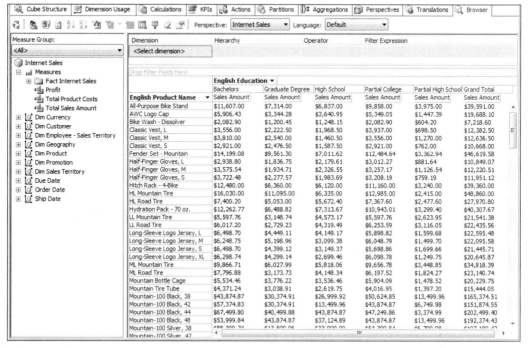

Figure 6-30

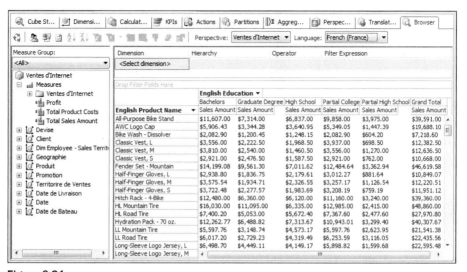

Figure 6-31

Instead of creating new cubes for various users and clients understanding different languages and the overhead of maintaining the cubes in each language, Analysis Services 2008 provides you with the functionality through the perspectives and translations features.

Summary

You traversed the Cube Wizard for a second time in this book, but also at a different level of granularity and hopefully with more understanding of what was going on. You learned how to create calculated members and set properties concerning the display of those members; for example, different color foregrounds and backgrounds. And finally, you learned how to create and browse perspectives and translations. In the real world of business, you will have additional enhancement requirements to meet after running the Cube Wizard. These requirements may include creating calculated members on dimensions, creating cube scripts containing complex MDX expressions to meet your business needs, and adding Key Performance Indicators (KPIs), which will graphically represent the state of your business in real time. The Cube Designer contains additional tabs for KPIs and Actions. These features help enhance your cubes for business analysis. In addition to that, the Cube Designer helps in partitioning fact data, and defining aggregations, which in turn help you achieve improved performance while querying your UDM. These are covered in Chapter 9, with additional coverage in other chapters as well. In the next chapter you learn how to manage your Analysis Services databases using the SQL Server Management Studio.

7

Administering Analysis Services

Administration is an important task on any server product. As an administrator of SQL Server Analysis Services (SSAS) you need to make sure Analysis Services is secure, reliable, and provides efficient access to the end users. You can administer AnalysisServices in two ways: through the SQL Server 2008 Tool set — SQL Server Management Studio (SSMS) and Business Intelligence Development Studio (BIDS) — or programmatically using an object model called AMO (Analysis Management Objects). You can accomplish tasks like processing objects, providing access to Analysis Services objects in databases, and synchronization of databases between Analysis Services instances using SSMS. You can use BIDS to connect to a specific OLAP database to perform design changes and accomplish follow-on tasks such as processing and providing access to users. SSMS and BIDS both use AMO behind the scenes to accomplish all management tasks. The AMO object model itself is installed and registered into the GAC (Global Assembly Cache) when the product is installed. The AMO .NET assembly, by the way, is Microsoft.AnalysisSevices.dll.

In this chapter you learn about key administrative tasks and how to accomplish those tasks using SSMS and BIDS. In Chapter 13 you learn about administering SSAS programmatically using AMO.

Administration Using SQL Server 2008 Tools

Let's just jump in and get our feet wet, shall we? In Chapter 2 you used SSMS to view the objects found in an Analysis Services 2008 database. We'll start here on a similar footing:

1. Launch SSMS from All Programs ⇨ Microsoft SQL Server 2008 ⇨ SQL Server Management Studio.

2. Using Object Explorer, connect to the Analysis Services instance.

3. Open the Databases folder.

You will see a tree view of those databases you have saved on the server to date, as shown in Figure 7-1. One of those databases should be titled AnalysisServices2008Tutorial — you should take a moment to review the tree nodes and what they contain because you will be learning the administrative tasks associated with those objects.

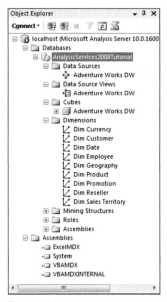

Figure 7-1

Managing Analysis Servers

SSMS, the integrated management environment for SQL Server 2008 products, provides you the flexibility of managing several Analysis Services instances. In this chapter we use the word "server" to denote an instance of Analysis Services, and "servers" to denote one or more. If you have a set of production servers that are being used by customers and a set of test servers that are being used for development and testing purposes, you typically want to manage them differently. The most logical thing is to group these servers. Using the Register Servers window of SQL Server Management Studio, you can group a set of Analysis Services servers to form a Server group as shown in Figure 7-2. You can register Analysis Services servers and organize them into groups using the New Server Group and New Server Registration dialogs that can be launched by right-clicking the Local Server Groups folder under the Analysis Services folder in the Registered Servers window of SSMS.

Some of the common tasks of starting, stopping, restarting, and configuring Analysis Services servers can also be accomplished from the Registered Servers window. You can right-click the specific Analysis Services instance and choose the appropriate operation. In addition, you can switch to the Object Explorer window of the connected SSAS instance, or launch the MDX query editor or SQL Server Configuration Manager dialog from this window.

Figure 7-2

Once you are connected to an Analysis Services server in the Object Explorer window, you can accomplish various administrative tasks on that server, such as creating new databases, providing permissions, processing objects, and moving databases from test servers to production servers. First and foremost for the Analysis Server admin is providing access permissions to the users who will be administering the server. The following steps show how to add a user as an administrator of an Analysis Services server by making them part of the object called Server Role:

1. In the Object Explorer window right-click the Analysis Services instance and select Properties. You will now see the Analysis Services Properties dialog.

2. Click Security in the page as shown in Figure 7-3.

3. Click the Add button to add a user to the Analysis Services administrators group. You can add domain users, local machine users, or groups as part of the administrator group for Analysis Services. If your user is a local user you can specify <machinename>\username or just the username to add the user to this server administrator group.

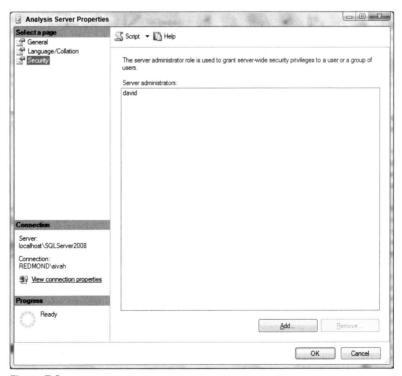

Figure 7-3

Another important management task is to set appropriate Analysis Server properties so that Analysis Services performs optimally. You can do this using the Analysis Server Properties dialog shown in Figure 7-4. Analysis Services needs to be restarted for certain properties to take effect. This is indicated by a "yes" in the Restart column for those properties in the Analysis Services Properties dialog. Some of the most important properties involve control of parallelism for processing and querying and changing the read buffer size for faster query response time. Equally important are the maximum amount of memory used by the Analysis Services processes, the maximum number of connections to the server, and the ability to turn certain features on or off. You learn some of these properties in this chapter and others in Chapter 14. The properties dialog has a checkbox that enables you to view and modify the advanced properties of the Analysis Services server. Adding users to the Server role or Database role and setting properties are considered part of securing your Analysis Services server. You learn more about managing security at the end of this chapter.

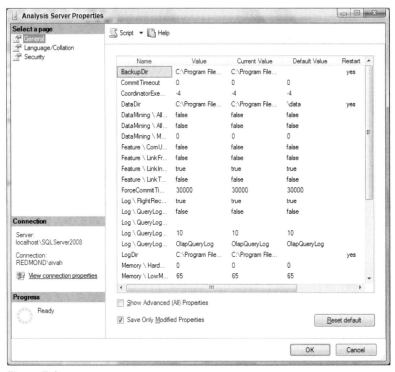

Figure 7-4

Managing Analysis Services Objects

Several management tasks can be performed on Analysis Services objects. Some of the most important tasks are processing cubes and dimensions, providing access permissions to various objects within a database, managing the partitions of a cube based on usage, and adding assemblies to databases. Even though the SQL Server Management Studio provides a great interface to manage Analysis Services 2008 and abstracts all the internal details, it is beneficial to understand the underlying operations that take place when you perform the management operations. Knowledge of these server internals gives you an edge in better understanding its operation and helps you more effectively manage the server when unforeseen problems occur.

All communications to Analysis Services is through XML for Analysis (XMLA). The management tasks executed through SSMS use the management object model AMO (Analysis Management Objects), which in turn sends XMLA Execute commands to the Analysis Services instance. You will see some of the commands sent to the Analysis Services server when performing management tasks in this chapter.

Database Creation

SQL Server Analysis Services 2008 allows a server administrator to create databases and assign database administrative permissions to a user. The following steps show how to do this:

1. In the SSMS Object Explorer, right-click the Databases folder and select New Database as shown in Figure 7-5.

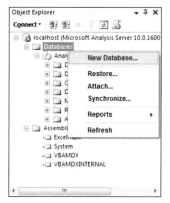

Figure 7-5

2. Enter a new database name called DBATest as shown in Figure 7-6 and click OK. SSMS sends an XMLA command to SSAS to create the new database called DBATest. SSMS then refreshes the Databases folder by retrieving the list of Databases from SSAS. You should see the DBATest database as shown in Figure 7-7. If you are an administrator of SSAS, your account is a member of the Analysis Services server administrator role as seen in Figure 7-3. If you want to provide a user with database administrator privileges and not Analysis Services server-wide privileges, you need to provide appropriate permissions at the database level. Follow the next steps to provide database administrator permissions for a user.

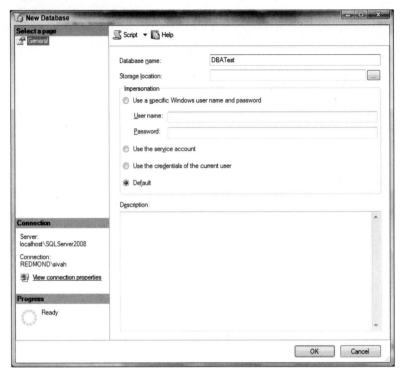

Figure 7-6

Figure 7-7

3. Expand the folder DBATest. You will see the various folders under DBATest.

4. Right-click the folder Roles and select "New Role" as shown in Figure 7-7.

5. In the Create Role dialog, check the "Full control (Administrator)" checkbox (shown in Figure 7-8) to provide full database administrator privileges.

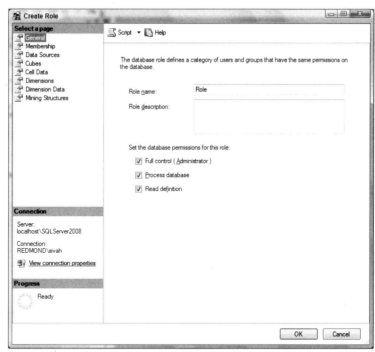

Figure 7-8

6. Select the Membership page in the dialog as shown in Figure 7-9.

Figure 7-9

7. Click the Add button on the Membership page to bring up the Select Users or Groups dialog.

8. Enter the user or users for whom you want to provide database permissions as shown in Figure 7-10 and click OK. You should now see the user you specified in the list of users who will have database permissions listed in the Create Role dialog.

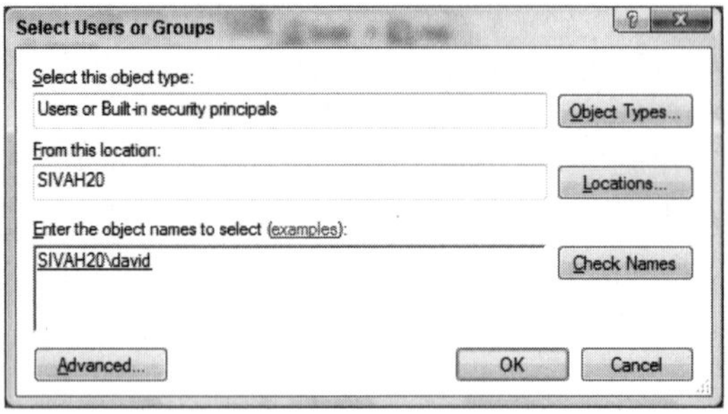

Figure 7-10

9. Click OK in the Create Role dialog.

You have successfully created a database called DBATest and provided full database permissions to a specific user. The user listed under the role Role will have full permissions to modify any of the objects that are part of the database DBATest including deleting the database. This user does not have permissions to perform any database operations outside of the DBATest database unless the same user is part of the Analysis Server administrator role. To create data sources, Data Source Views, cubes, dimensions, and mining models we recommend creating/modifying the objects in the DBATest using the online mode in Business Intelligence Development Studio (BIDS). You learn to work with SSAS databases using the online mode of BIDS later in this chapter.

Processing Analysis Services Database Objects

One of the important jobs of an Analysis Services DBA (database administrator) is to process the objects (such as Cubes, Dimensions, and Mining Models) in an Analysis Services database. Analysis Services 2008 provides fine-grain control to the Analysis Services DBA to process the objects within an Analysis Services database using the Process dialog. You can launch the Process dialog by right-clicking the object folders such as Cubes, Dimensions, and Mining Structures — this works just as well on individual objects or groups of objects too. Based on the location from which the Process dialog is launched, the options for processing the object or group of objects will vary. In addition to this you can select an object and launch the Process dialog. To process the database AnalysisServices2008Tutorial, do the following:

1. Right-click the database AnalysisServices2008Tutorial and select Process as shown in Figure 7-11.

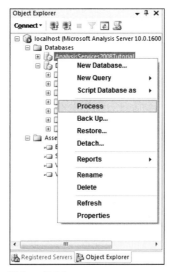

Figure 7-11

You will see the Process dialog as shown in Figure 7-12. This dialog shows the name of the object to be processed along with the type of object. Several processing options are available for each object. The default option for the database object is Process Full. As the name implies, the Process Full option allows you to process the selected object completely even if the object had been processed earlier. It will clear any data that was processed earlier.

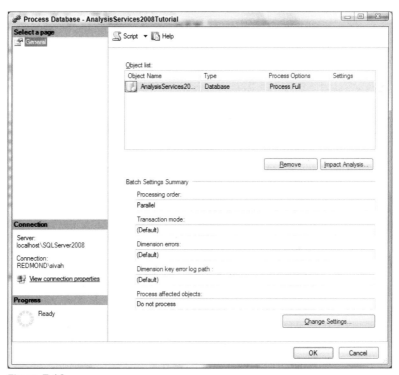

Figure 7-12

2. When you click the OK button the Process dialog sends an XMLA command to the Analysis Services instance to process the selected object. If you click on the Script button shown in Figure 7-12 and then select Script Action to New Query Window, you can see the Process XMLA command to be sent to the Analysis Services instance. You will see the following script command:

```
<Batch xmlns="http://schemas.microsoft.com/analysisservices/2003/engine">
  <Parallel>
    <Process xmlns:xsd="http://www.w3.org/2001/XMLSchema"
        xmlns:xsi="http://www.w3.org/2001/XMLSchema-instance"
        xmlns:ddl2="http://schemas.microsoft.com/analysisservices/
        2003/engine/2" xmlns:ddl2_2="http://schemas.microsoft.com/
        analysisservices/2003/engine/2/2" xmlns:ddl100_100="http://
        schemas.microsoft.com/analysisservices/2008/engine/100/100">
      <Object>
        <DatabaseID>AnalysisServices2008Tutorial</DatabaseID>
      </Object>
      <Type>ProcessFull</Type>
      <WriteBackTableCreation>UseExisting</WriteBackTableCreation>
    </Process>
  </Parallel>
</Batch>
```

3. Click OK in this dialog to process the AnalysisServices2008Tutorial database. When you click OK the Process dialog uses AMO to send the Process command to the Analysis Services instance.

The Process XMLA script contains several commands that are interpreted by Analysis Services. Because the medium of communication to Analysis Services is an XMLA request, the script is embedded within SOAP Envelope tags. This script can be executed from the XMLA editor within SQL Server Management Studio. SSMS adds the appropriate SOAP envelope tags to send the script to Analysis Services. The commands in the script are Batch, Parallel, and Process. The Process command is part of a set of commands that manipulate the data in Analysis Services. These commands that change the data in Analysis Services databases are called the DML (data manipulation language). The Batch command allows multiple commands to be executed within a single statement. The Parallel command allows you to instruct the Analysis Services instance to execute all the commands within the command in parallel. The Process command is used to process an Analysis Services object and needs several properties such as DatabaseID, Process Type, and processing options (not shown in the above XMLA script) such as parallelism for processing objects, and actions to be taken during dimension key errors that can be changed using the Change Settings button in the Process dialog . You learn the processing options provided by the Process dialog in this chapter.

As mentioned earlier, when you click OK in the Process dialog, a Process command with appropriate options is sent to the Analysis Services instance. This command requests the server to process the database. When processing the objects within a database, the server needs to read data from the data source, which is done by issuing queries to it. You will now see the Process Progress dialog that shows details of each processing operation on the server. As you can see from Figure 7-13, the operations on each object within the database that is being processed are reported along with the timing information and whether the operation succeeded or failed. You can also see the query sent to the relational data source to retrieve the data. The detailed information returned from Analysis Services is very helpful if you need to investigate any issues in processing including the performance of processing an object.

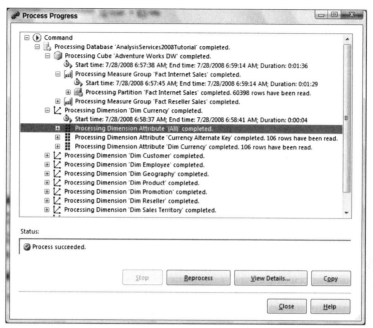

Figure 7-13

Once all the objects have been processed you will see the results of the processing command. If all the objects were successfully processed, you will see Process succeeded in the status as shown in Figure 7-13. If there were errors during processing, the status bar will show an appropriate message. The operations that resulted in an error are shown in red in the tree view of the Process Progress dialog. You can drill down into the details of the processing to understand the reasons for failure.

Several operations take place in the preceding processing command. All the objects within the database are processed in parallel based on the settings of the Analysis Services instance. If there are dependencies, the dependent objects are processed first. For example, the dimensions that are part of a cube need to be processed before the cube can be processed. Analysis Services processes all the objects of the database under a single transaction. What this means is that if one of the objects failed during processing, the remaining objects will not be processed and the effects of any previous operations will be rolled back. For example, if all the dimensions of a cube were successfully processed and if there were errors while processing the cube, the processing of the dimension objects will be rolled back. Once all the objects have been successfully processed, the server commits the transaction, which means that the objects are marked as processed and are available for querying.

Assume an Analysis Services object has been processed and is being queried by users. At the time users are querying the object, you can initiate processing on the same object. Because a version of the object is currently being queried, Analysis Services stores the uncommitted processed object in a temporary file. At the time of commit, the server first ensures that the user is not using the objects, removes the previous version of the processed objects, and then marks the temporary files as primary. You see this in detail in the following section.

Processing a Cube

An Analysis Services database can contain several cubes and dimensions. You have the flexibility to control the processing of individual cubes and dimensions by launching the Process dialog from appropriate cube or dimension objects. There are several processing options for processing a cube, as shown in Figure 7-14. All of the same processing options available for partitions and measure groups are available for the cube because a cube is a collection of measure groups, which in turn is a collection of partitions.

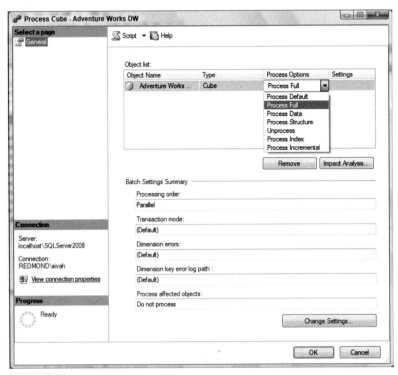

Figure 7-14

When a cube is created you will typically do a full process (*Process Full* in the Process dialog) of it so that you can browse the cube. Usually the cube structure will not change after the initial design is completed. In this case, you will be processing in order to get additional fact data that you would want to add to the cube. For example, you might have a Sales cube that you have created and you might be getting sales fact data from each store every month. Processing the entire cube whenever new data comes in will take a considerable amount of time, causing end users to have to wait for a long period to see the most up-to-date data. Analysis Services 2008 provides you with an option to process only the new fact data instead of the entire cube. This is called incremental processing. In order to add new fact data to the cube you can add a new partition to the cube and process that partition. Alternately, you can use the *Process Incremental* option in the Process dialog and specify the query that provides the new fact data that needs to be processed. Process Incremental is a common management task for data warehouses. If you specify the *Process Default* option in the Process dialog, the server checks for all the objects that have not been processed and only processes those objects. If the cube data has been processed and if aggregations and indexes are not processed, then those are processed.

When you choose the *Process Full* option for processing a cube, the server performs three internal operations. If the storage mode for the cube is MOLAP, the server first reads the data from the relational data and stores it in a compact format. If there were aggregations defined for the cube, the server will build those aggregations during this processing. Finally, the server creates indexes for the data that helps speed access to data during querying. Even if there were no aggregations specified for the cube, the server still creates the indexes. The *Process Data* option actually is the first step of the Process Full option where the server reads data from relational data sources and stores it in proprietary format. The second and third steps of processing aggregations and indexes can be separately accomplished by the *Process Index* option. You might be wondering why you have the Process Data and Process Index options when the Process Full and Process Default options actually accomplish the same task. These options provide the administrator with a fine grain of control. These are especially important when you have limited time to access the relational data source and want to optimize the processing on your machine. Having multiple processing operations running in parallel can require more system resources. Specifically on a 32-bit (X86 machines) system, a large cube that fails on Process Full may be able to be successfully processed by sending Process Data and Process Index commands one after another. In such instances, we recommend you first get the data from your relational backend into SSAS using the Process Data option. Once you have all the data in the Analysis Services instance, you can then create your aggregations and indexes, which do not need access to the relational data source.

If you choose the *Process Structure* option, the server processes all the cube's dimensions and the cube definitions so that the cube's structure is processed without any processing of the data. The server will not process the partitions or measure groups of the cube, therefore you cannot see any of the fact data; however, you can browse the cube because the cube definitions are processed. You can retrieve metadata information about the cube (measure names, measure groups, dimensions, KPIs, actions, and so on) after processing the cube's structure. However, you will not be able to query the cube data. For a cube that has been processed with Process Structure, you can see the cube in the SQL Server Management Studio MDX query editor when you select the drop-down list for the cube. If your cube contains linked measure groups and if they have been processed successfully, processing the cube with the Process Structure option will allow you to query the measures in linked measure groups. Often when you design your UDM you will want to make sure your design is correct and your customers are able to see the right measures and dimensions. Process Structure is helpful in validating your design. As soon as the data for the cube is available the cube can be processed with the Process Default option so that end users can query the data from the cube.

You can clear the data in the cube using the *Unprocess* option. The processing options provided in the Process dialog are different than the process types that are specified in the process command sent to Analysis Services. The following table shows how the various processing options map to the process types sent to Analysis Services:

Process Options in Process Dialog	Process Type in Process Command
Process Full	ProcessFull
Process Default	ProcessDefault
Process Data	ProcessData
Process Structure	ProcessStructure
Unprocess	ProcessClear
Process Index	ProcessIndexes
Process Incremental	ProcessAdd
Process Script Cache	ProcessScriptCache

The processed data of a cube are stored in a hierarchical directory structure that is equivalent to the structure you see in the Object Explorer. Figure 7-15 shows the directory structure of the processed data of the AnalysisServices2008Tutorial database in Analysis Services 2008. The directory also shows the files within a partition. The metadata information about the cubes and dimensions are stored as XML files, and the data is stored in a proprietary format. Every time an object is processed, a new version number is appended to the object. For example, the files shown in Figure 7-15 are under a specific partition directory. The file info.<versionnumber>.xml is used to store the metadata information about the partition. Similar metadata files are stored within the directories of each object, cube, dimension, and measure group. We recommend you browse through each object folder to see the metadata information. The fact data is stored in the file with extension .data. The key to an OLAP database is the fast access to data. You learned about a cell, which was represented by a tuple. A tuple is the intersection of various dimension members. For fast data access, Analysis Services builds indexes to access data across multiple dimensions. The index files in Analysis Services have the extension "map". In Figure 7-15 you can see the .map files that have the format <version>.<Dimension>.<Hierarchy>.fact.map. There is an associated header file for each map file. Analysis Services stores the data as blocks called segments for fast access. The associated header file contains offsets to the various segments for fast access during queries.

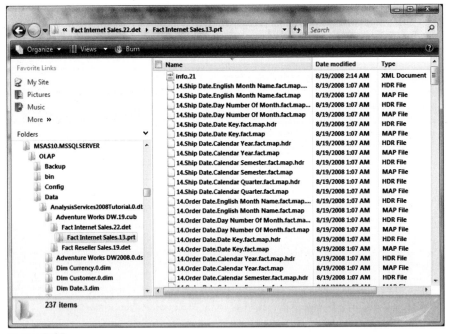

Figure 7-15

The processing dialog provides you the flexibility of processing objects in parallel or within the same transaction. If errors are encountered during processing, you can set options to handle these errors. You can configure the parallelism and error options by selecting the Change Settings button in the Process dialog. You will see the Change Settings dialog as shown in Figure 7-16, which enables you to configure certain processing options and error settings during processing. Setting the parallelism option is as simple as selecting the appropriate option in the Processing Order section of the dialog. By default all the objects are processed in parallel and within the same transaction. If you do want failure of one object to impact other objects, you should process the objects under different transactions by choosing the sequential option.

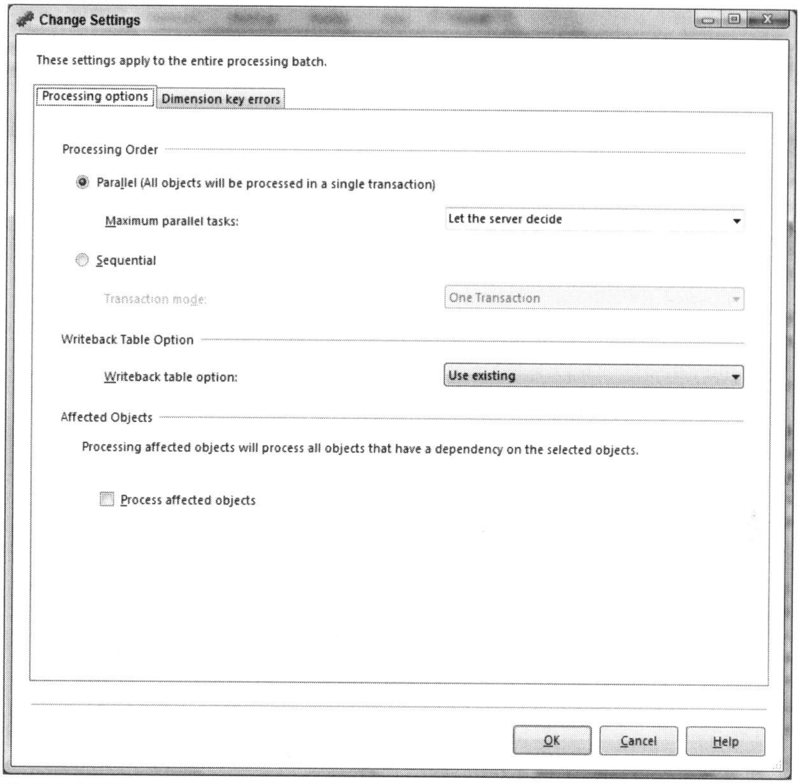

Figure 7-16

You might encounter errors while processing your Analysis Services objects due to incorrect design or referential integrity problems in the relational data source. For example, if you have a fact record that contains a dimension id that is not available in the dimension table, you will see a "Key not found" error while processing the cube. By default, when an error is encountered during processing, the processing operation fails. You can change the settings in the processing dialog to take appropriate action other than failing the processing operation. The Dimension Key Errors page of the Change Settings dialog shown in Figure 7-17 allows changing the error configuration settings for all the objects selected for processing. Whenever you encounter key errors you can either convert the values to unknown or discard the erroneous records. You can run into key errors while processing facts or dimensions. If you encounter a key error while processing a cube, that means Analysis Services was unable to find a corresponding key in the dimension. You can assign the fact value to a member called the Unknown Member for that specific dimension. You can encounter key errors while processing a snowflake dimension when an attribute defined as a foreign key does not exist in the foreign table or when there are duplicate entries. The two most common types of key errors that you might encounter during dimension processing are key not found and duplicate key errors.

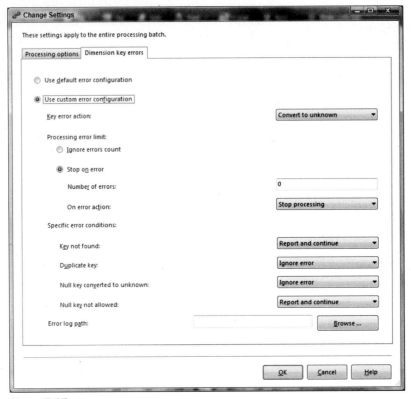

Figure 7-17

Processing a Dimension

You can process dimensions independent of the cubes they are a part of. After the initial processing of a dimension, you might process the dimensions on a periodic basis if additional records are added in the dimension table or there were changes to columns of an existing row. An example of additions to a dimension is new products being added to the products dimension. You would want this information to be reflected in the dimensions so that you can see the sales information for the new products. Another example of changes in dimension is when an employee moves from one city to another city; the attributes of the employee will need to change. Therefore the Process dialog provides you with various options for processing the dimension, as shown in Figure 7-18.

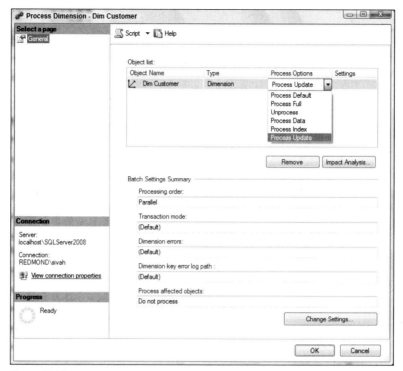

Figure 7-18

While processing a dimension, Analysis Services reads data from the dimensions tables. When a dimension is processed, each attribute of the dimension is processed separately. Based on the parallelism specified on Analysis Services, these attributes can be processed in parallel. Each dimension contains an attribute called the All attribute. This is not exposed to the user but used internally by Analysis Services. You can see the files associated with this attribute as <version>.(All).<extension> in Figure 7-19. When each attribute is processed, several files are created. Similar to fact data, dimension data is stored in a proprietary format. Each attribute of a dimension has a key column and a named column. These directly map into two different files with the extensions kstore and sstore, which refer to key store and string store, respectively. In addition, there are additional files that get created for each attribute of the dimension, which help in fast access to name, key, and levels of attributes and hierarchies. Files with the extension .map are created when indexes are processed for each attribute and help in fast retrieval of related attributes of the dimension for a dimension member.

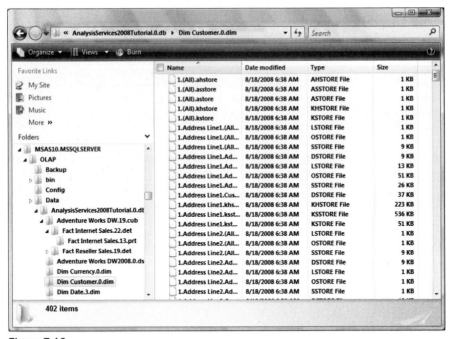

Figure 7-19

The amount of time it takes to process a dimension depends on the number of attributes and hierarchies in the dimension as well as the number of members in each hierarchy. When a processing command is sent to the Analysis Services instance, the server reads the data from the relational data source and updates the dimension. When a dimension is processed, each attribute of the dimension is processed separately. Some attributes can be processed in parallel, whereas some cannot. The order of processing of various attributes is dependent on the relationships between the attributes in the dimensions and resources available on the machine. The relationships between attributes are defined at the dimension design time using the Attribute Relationships tab of the dimension designer, which you learned about in Chapter 5. For example, say you have a Customer dimension that contains the attributes Customer Name, SSN, City, State, and Country. Assume SSN is the Key attribute for this dimension and by default all attributes within the dimension are related to the key attribute. In addition, assume additional attribute relationships have been established. They are Country ⇨ State, State ⇨ City, City ⇨ Customer Name, State ⇨ Customer Name, and Country ⇨ Customer Name. Based on the preceding relationships, the order of processing of the attributes in the Customer dimension is Country, State, City, Customer Name, and SSN. This is because Analysis Services needs to have information about Country in order to establish the member property relationship while processing the State, Customer Name, or SSN. The key attribute is always the last attribute processed within a dimension.

When the Process Default option is chosen for processing, the dimension's data or indexes are processed if they have not been processed or are out-of-date. If the Process Full option is chosen, the entire dimension is re-processed. When the Process Full option is used, dimension data and indexes that have been processed initially will be dropped and data is retrieved from the data source. The dimension processing time depends on the dimension size (number of dimension members as well as number of attributes and hierarchies in the dimension) and your machine resources.

Similar to incremental processing of the cubes you can incrementally process dimensions using the *Process Update* option. The *Process Update* option in the Process dialog maps to the *ProcessUpdate* process type in the process command, which is applied only to dimensions. Some dimensions such as Employees or Customers or Products can potentially contain a large number of members. Additional members may have been added to these dimensions or some attributes of these dimension members might have changed. Often a full processing of any dimension is not only unnecessary but cannot be afforded due to business needs. Under these circumstances incremental processing of the dimension or an update of the attributes of the dimension should be sufficient. When you choose the *Process Update* option for the dimension, the server scans all the dimensions in the dimension table. If there were changes to the dimension's properties, such as caption or description, they are updated. If new members are added to the dimension table, these members are added to the existing dimension using incremental processing. The attributes of each dimension member will also be updated. The key of each dimension member is assumed to be the same, but expect some attributes to be updated. The most important attribute that is updated is the member property for each member. When you have a parent-child hierarchy in a dimension and if the parent attribute has been changed, that information is updated during the Process Update processing option.

The Process Data option for dimensions is used to process the dimension data. The indexes will not be processed when the Process Data option is used. The Process Index option is used to create indexes for attributes in the dimensions. If the ProcessMode dimension property is set to LazyAggregations, Analysis Services builds indexes for new attributes of the dimension as a lazy operation in the background thread. If you want to rebuild these indexes immediately you can do so by choosing the Process Index option. The Unprocess option is used to clear the data within the dimension.

Managing Partitions

Partitions enable you to distribute fact data within Analysis Services and aggregate data so that the resources on a machine can be efficiently utilized. When there are multiple partitions on the same server, you will reap the benefits of partitions because Analysis Services reads/writes data in parallel across multiple partitions. Fact data on the data source can be stored as several fact tables — Sales_Fact_2002, Sales_Fact_2003, and so on — or as a single large fact table called Sales Fact. You can create multiple partitions within a measure group; one for each fact table in the data source or by splitting data from a single large fact table through several queries. Partitions also allow you to split the data across two or more machines running Analysis Services, which are called Remote partitions. As an administrator you might be thinking what the size of each partition should be to achieve the best results. Microsoft recommends each partition to be 3–5GB or 20 million records. You learn more about optimizing partitions in Chapter 14.

A sales cube's partitions usually contain data spread across time, that is, a new partition might be created for every month or a quarter. As an administrator you would create a new partition from SQL Server Management Studio and process it so that it is available for users. To create a new partition, perform the following steps in BIDS:

1. Open the AnalysisServices2008Tutorial project you have used in previous chapters.

2. Change the FactInternetSales table to a named query so that there is a where condition DueDateKey<20020101. In case you don't recall how this is done, we've included the steps here:

   a. Open Adventure Works DW.dsv under the Data Source Views folder.

   b. Right-click the FactInternetSales table in diagram view and select Replace Table ⇨ With New Named Query menu item.

   c. In the Create Named Query dialog, in the DueDateKey Filter text entry box, enter <20020101. Your change will automatically be reflected in the query window as shown in Figure 7-20. Click OK to continue.

Figure 7-20

3. In the DSV, right-click in the diagram view and select Add/Remove Tables from the context menu.

4. Add the FactInternetSales table to "Included objects:" list and click OK.

5. In the diagram view, replace the FactInternetSales table with a named query.

6. In the named query, set Filter to DueDateKey >=20020101.

7. Rename the named query as FactInternetSalesNew.

8. Deploy the AnalysisServices2008Tutorial project to your Analysis Services instance.

9. Connect to the AnalysisServices2008Tutorial database using SSMS.

10. Navigate to the measure group FactInternetSales.

11. Right-click the Partitions folder and select New Partition as shown in Figure 7-21.

Figure 7-21

12. Click Next on the welcome screen of the Partition Wizard.

13. Choose the named query FactInternetSalesNew to create a new partition as shown in Figure 7-22 and click Next. Select the checkbox "Specify a query to restrict rows". As suggested by the warning in the Restrict Rows page (Figure 7-23) you may need to specify a restriction on the query to filter appropriate data for a partition. In this example FactInternetSalesNew already has the appropriate query restriction.

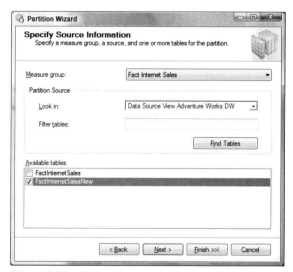

Figure 7-22

Figure 7-23

14. Click the Next button.

15. One way Analysis Services provides scalability is by use of remote partitions, where the partitions reside in two or more Analysis Services instances. On the Processing and Storage Locations page, as shown in Figure 7-24, you can specify where to store the partition. You can specify the remote Analysis Services instance on this page, but the data source to the remote Analysis Services instance should have been defined in this database. You can also change the storage location where you want the data for the partition to reside on any of the Analysis Services instances. Choose the default options as shown in Figure 7-24 and click Next.

Figure 7-24

16. In the final page of the Partition Wizard, select Design aggregations later, Process Now as shown in Figure 7-25 and click Finish.

17. In the Process Partition dialog, click OK to process the FactInternetSalesNew partition.

Figure 7-25

The partition will be processed and you can browse the cube data. The number of partitions for a specific cube typically increases over time. Users might not be browsing historical data with the same granularity as that of the recent data. For example, you might be more interested in comparing Sales data for the current month to that of the previous month rather than data from five years ago. However, you might want to compare year-over-year data for several years. By merging the partition data you can see some benefits during query performance. You learn about the considerations you should take into account to merge partitions in Chapter 14.

There are two main requirements to merge partitions: The partitions should be of the same storage type, and they need to be on the same Analysis Services instance. Therefore if you have remote partitions, they can be merged together only if they are on the same Analysis Services instance. To merge partitions, do the following:

1. Launch the Merge Partition dialog by right-clicking the Partitions folder under the Fact Internet Sales measure group.

2. In the Merge Partition dialog shown in Figure 7-26, select the Target partition that will contain the merged data and the list of partitions to merge data and click OK.

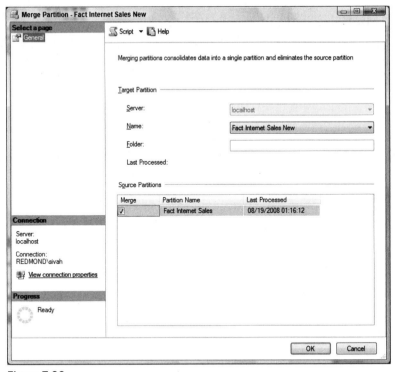

Figure 7-26

All the data from the source partitions will merge into the target partition, and the source partitions are deleted due to this operation. SSMS sends the following command to Analysis Services to merge the partitions:

```xml
<MergePartitions xmlns="http://schemas.microsoft.com/analysisservices/
        2003/engine">
  <Sources>
    <Source>
      <DatabaseID>AnalysisServices2008Tutorial</DatabaseID>
      <CubeID>Adventure Works DW</CubeID>
      <MeasureGroupID>Fact Internet Sales</MeasureGroupID>
      <PartitionID>Fact Internet Sales</PartitionID>
    </Source>
  </Sources>
  <Target>
    <DatabaseID>AnalysisServices2008Tutorial</DatabaseID>
    <CubeID>Adventure Works DW</CubeID>
    <MeasureGroupID>Fact Internet Sales</MeasureGroupID>
    <PartitionID>Fact Internet Sales New</PartitionID>
  </Target>
</MergePartitions>
```

Managing Assemblies

Assemblies, also called stored procedures, help you in performing specific tasks on the Analysis Services database or across the server. For example, Analysis Services has four assemblies installed that provide you with the functionality of calling Excel or VBA functions within your MDX queries. The System Assembly is used for operations such as Backup or Restore in retrieving information such as folders containing Analysis Services backup files, as well as supporting data mining algorithm requests. Analysis Services 2008 supports two types of assemblies: COM user-defined functions (UDFs) and .NET assemblies. COM UDFs are primarily supported for backwards compatibility with Analysis Services 2000. You learn about .NET and COM assemblies and how to build and deploy them in Chapter 11. In this section you learn about managing assemblies on your Analysis Services instance.

Assemblies can be added only by Analysis Services administrators. You need to make sure your instance of Analysis Services is safe and secure irrespective of the operations done by the stored procedures. Security is always a concern, and you do not want any assemblies to bring down the server. Because hackers try to hack servers, most software products now are built to be secure by default. The administrator needs to enable certain components and options to make them available to users. By default, Analysis Services does not allow execution of stored procedures. The administrator first needs to enable the server property Feature\ComUdfEnabled to true (value of 1 in the Analysis Services config file) for enabling COM UDFs. This is accomplished using the Analysis Server Properties dialog.

The key to managing assemblies is to understand the nature of the assembly and setting appropriate properties while adding assemblies to your Analysis Services server. Figure 7-27 shows the dialog used to add assemblies to the server or to a specific database. This dialog can be launched by right-clicking the Assemblies folder under a specific database and choosing New Assembly.

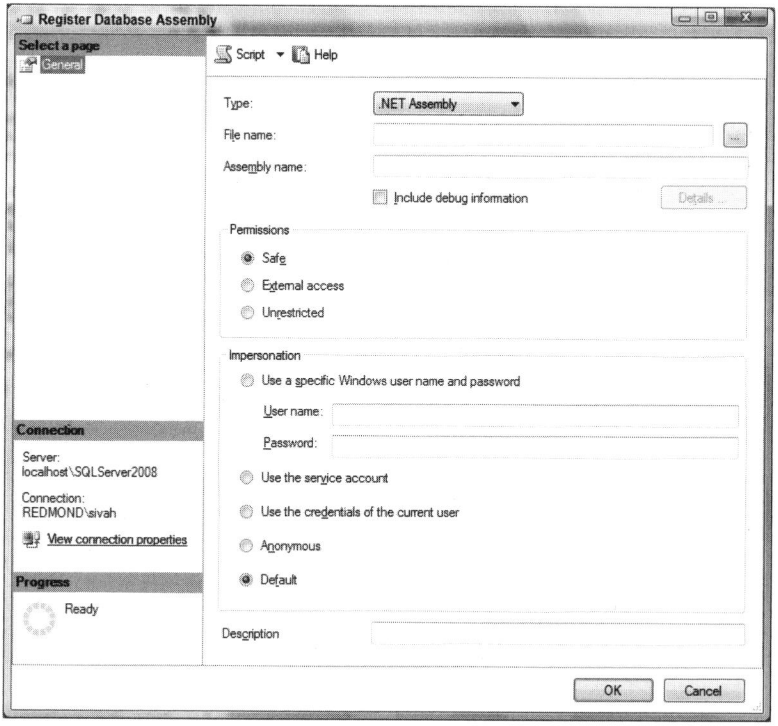

Figure 7-27

Analysis Services supports two types of assemblies: COM and .NET CLR assemblies. Once you specify the type and name of the assemblies in the Register Assembly dialog, you need to specify the security information for these assemblies. Two parameters control the security of these stored procedures: Impersonation and Permissions. Permissions allow you to define the scope of access for the assembly, such as accessing the file system, accessing the network, and accessing unmanaged code. There are three different values for permissions. They are:

❑ **Safe:** The most secure of the three permissions. When the Safe permission set is specified for an assembly, it means that the assembly is intended only for computation and the assembly cannot access any protected resource. It guarantees protection against information leaks and elevation attacks by malicious code.

❑ **External access:** This permission value allows access to external resources by the assembly without compromising reliability, but does not offer any specific security guarantees. You can use this if you as the DBA trust the programmer's ability to write good code and if there is a need to access external resources such as data from an external file.

❑ **Unrestricted:** This set value is primarily intended for people who have a very good understanding of programming on servers and need access to all resources. This permission set does not guarantee any code security or reliability. Unrestricted access should only be allowed to assemblies that have been written by users who absolutely need access to external resources and have a very good understanding of all security issues, such as denial of service attacks and information leakage, and are able to handle all these within the stored procedures. We recommend you use this option only when it is absolutely essential and you have full confidence in the programming abilities of the developer who has developed the assembly.

All COM DLLs will have the Permissions parameter set to Unrestricted. The Impersonation parameter allows you to specify the account under which the stored procedure will be executed. There are five different values for Impersonation:

❑ **Default:** The Default value allows you to execute the stored procedure under a secure mode with the minimum privileges. If the assembly is of type COM the default value is "Use the credentials of the current user." For a .NET assembly, the default value depends on the permission set defined. If the permission set is Safe, the Impersonation mode will be Impersonate Service Account, but if the permission set is External Access or Unrestricted, the Impersonation mode will be Impersonate Current User.

❑ **Anonymous:** If you want the stored procedure to be executed as an anonymous user, you need to select Impersonate Anonymous. You will have limited access when the stored procedure is executed under this setting.

❑ **Use the credentials of the current user:** This impersonation mode is typically used when you want the stored procedure to be executed with the user's credentials. This is a safe option to select. If the stored procedure accesses external resources and the current user executing the stored procedure does not have permissions, execution of the stored procedure will not cause any ill effects. A use of this impersonation mode is to define dynamic data security where the current user's credential is needed to access external resources.

❑ **Use the service account:** If you choose to use the service account, whenever the stored procedure is executed it will be executed under the credentials of service startup account for Analysis Services. An example of a stored procedure that would need this impersonation mode is an AMO stored procedure that does management operations on the server.

❑ **Use a specific Windows username and password:** If your business needs a stored procedure to always be executed in the context of a specific user, you need to choose this option. You need to specify a Windows account name and password for this impersonation mode. A typical example where you might use this option is when you access an external data source or web service to retrieve data with this account and utilize that value within the stored procedure for computation. If you choose this option, you will need to make sure you update the password on the account when there is a password change.

We recommend that COM assemblies use the credentials of the current user impersonation, whereas for .NET CLR assemblies you should use the appropriate impersonation mode based on your customer scenario. As an administrator of Analysis Services, you need to choose the impersonation and permission setting that suits your business needs and does not compromise the security of your Analysis Services instance.

When you register an assembly with a specific Analysis Services database or for the server using the Register Assembly dialog, AMO will be used to set up the correct properties. This, in turn, sends a Create command to the Analysis Services instance as shown here:

```
<Create AllowOverwrite="true" xmlns="http://schemas.microsoft.com/
      analysisservices/2003/engine">
  <ParentObject>
    <DatabaseID>AnalysisServices2008Tutorial</DatabaseID>
  </ParentObject>
  <ObjectDefinition>
    <Assembly xmlns:xsd="http://www.w3.org/2001/XMLSchema"
        xmlns:xsi="http://www.w3.org/2001/XMLSchema-instance"
        xmlns:ddl2="http://schemas.microsoft.com/analysisservices/2003/
        engine/2" xmlns:ddl2_2="http://schemas.microsoft.com/analysisservices/
        2003/engine/2/2" xmlns:ddl100_100="http://schemas.microsoft.com/
        analysisservices/2008/engine/100/100" xsi:type="ClrAssembly">
      <ID>AmoSproc</ID>
      <Name>AmoSproc</Name>
      <Description />
      <ImpersonationInfo>
        <ImpersonationMode>Default</ImpersonationMode>
      </ImpersonationInfo>
      <Files>
        <File>
          <Name>AmoSproc.dll</Name>
          <Type>Main</Type>
          <Data>
            <Block>------------Content about the stored procedure------
                </Block>
            <Block>------------Content about the stored procedure------
                </Block>
            <Block>------------Content about the stored procedure------
                </Block>
            <Block>------------Content about the stored procedure------
                </Block>
          </Data>
        </File>
      </Files>
      <PermissionSet>Safe</PermissionSet>
    </Assembly>
  </ObjectDefinition>
</Create>
```

The information within the BLOCK tag is a large amount of text content, which for illustration purposes has been restricted to a single line. This text within the BLOCK tag is the assembly to be registered that will be stored within the Analysis Services instance. When queries use functions within the assembly, Analysis Services loads the assembly within the same process and executes the CLR assembly with appropriate parameter passing. The results from the assembly are appropriately passed back to Analysis Services for further evaluation of a query.

Backup and Restore

Backup is an operation that is part of every individual's life. If you have an important document, you make a photocopy as a backup. Similarly, backup is an extremely critical operation for any data warehouse. There are several reasons why you should periodically back up your Analysis Services database. One reason is for disaster recovery; another is for auditing purposes. Irrespective of purpose, it is always a good idea to back up your database on a periodic basis. You can back up databases on your Analysis Services instance through SSMS. Follow these steps to back up the AnalysisServices2008Tutorial database:

1. Connect to the Analysis Services instance using SSMS.

2. Navigate to the database AnalysisServices2008Tutorial in the Object Explorer window.

3. Right-click the database and select Back Up.

   You will see the Backup dialog shown in Figure 7-28. By default the dialog chooses the database name as the backup name. By default the backup file will be created in the Backup folder of your Analysis Services installation. If you want the backup to be stored in a location on a different drive or directory, you first need to change the Analysis Services server property AllowedBrowsingFolder by adding the appropriate directory. You can then choose the folder by clicking Browse in the Backup Database dialog.

   You have the option to encrypt the database and specify a password. You'll need that password to restore the database. If you have remote partitions in the database, you have the option of specifying the backup location for each remote partition. Backup of these partitions is done on respective Analysis Services instances on that machine.

4. Disable the option to Encrypt the backup file.

5. Select the option "Allow file overwrite" to overwrite any existing backup files with the same name.

6. Choose the default backup file name and click OK.

The following command is sent to the Analysis Services instance by SSMS to back up the database AnalysisServices2008Tutorial:

```
<Backup xmlns="http://schemas.microsoft.com/analysisservices/2003/engine">
  <Object>
    <DatabaseID>AnalysisServices2008Tutorial</DatabaseID>
  </Object>
  <File>AnalysisServices2008Tutorial.abf</File>
  <AllowOverwrite>true</AllowOverwrite>
</Backup>
```

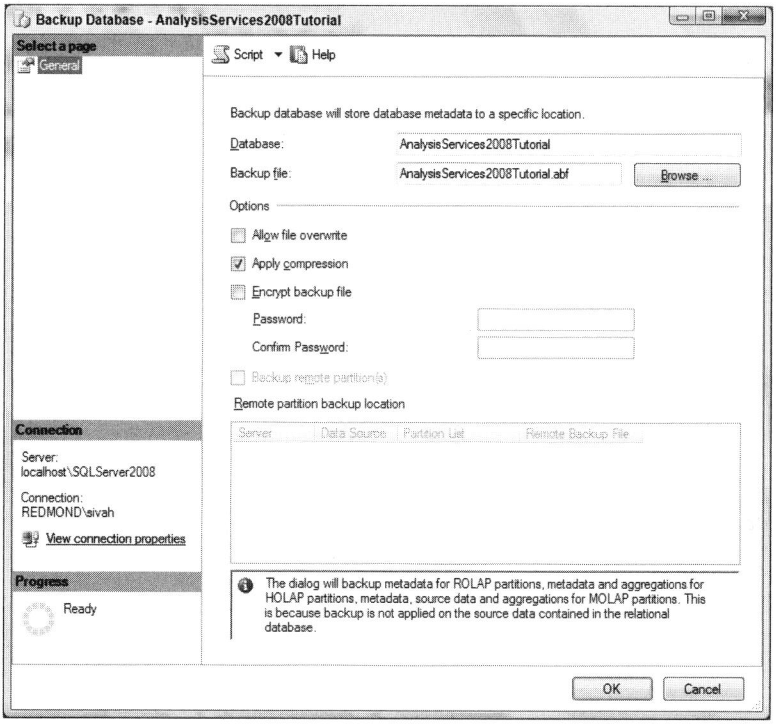

Figure 7-28

If you have specified a password, an Analysis Services 2008 backup file with the extension .abf will be created in the Backup folder. Backing up Analysis Services 2005 databases of sizes greater than 10GB used to take a long time. Analysis Services 2008 has made specific enhancements to backup performance intended to result in shorter backup times for databases of any size. Analysis Services 2008 also allows you to back up multiple databases at the same time. Through the SQL Server Management Studio you can launch the backup command from multiple databases and run backups in parallel. Alternatively, you can create a DDL that will execute backup of multiple databases within the same command.

Whenever you want to restore an Analysis Services database for which you have a backup, you can do so using the Restore Database dialog. Follow these steps to restore the AnalysisServices2008Tutorial backup:

1. In SSMS Object Explorer, right-click the AnalysisServices2008Tutorial and select Delete.

2. In the Delete Objects dialog shown in Figure 7-29, click OK.

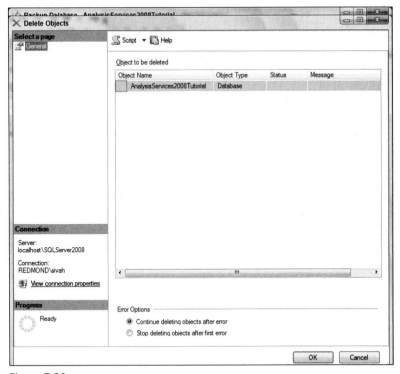

Figure 7-29

3. In the SSMS Object Explorer, right-click the Databases folder as shown in Figure 7-30 and select Restore.

Figure 7-30

4. In the Restore Database dialog (see Figure 7-31) click the Browse button next to Backup File.

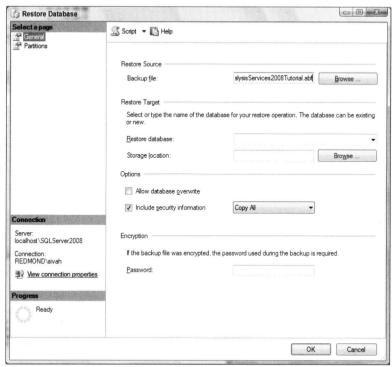

Figure 7-31

5. In the Locate Database Files dialog, navigate to the Backup folder and select the AnalysisServices2008Tutorial.abf file as shown in Figure 7-32 and click OK.

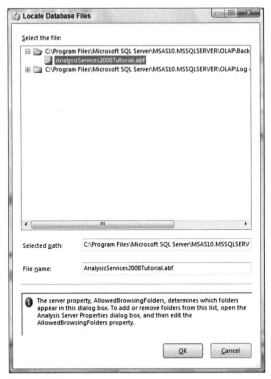

Figure 7-32

6. Type **AnalysisServices2008Tutorial** in the combo box next to Restore Database and click OK.

SSMS now sends the following XMLA command to restore the database on your Analysis Services instance:

```
<Restore xmlns="http://schemas.microsoft.com/analysisservices/2003/engine">
    <File>C:\Program Files\Microsoft SQL Server\MSAS10.MSSQLSERVER\OLAP\Backup\
        AnalysisServices2008Tutorial.abf</File>
    <DatabaseName>AnalysisServices2008Tutorial</DatabaseName>
</Restore>
```

If you refresh the list of databases on your Analysis Services instance, you should now see the AnalysisServices2008Tutorial database in the SSMS Object Explorer. If a database with the same name and ID exists on your Analysis Services instance, you can restore the newer database by clicking the Allow Database Overwrite checkbox in the Restore dialog.

Once the database has been restored you can query the database. You can take a backup of a database from your test servers and restore it on your production server. In such a circumstance you might choose to skip the security information if the security defined on production servers is different from those on your test servers. In such a circumstance you would need to ensure you secure the database by defining the right security on production servers. In a circumstance where the backup was taken on your production server and you are restoring the database on an upgraded production machine we do expect users to restore the database with the security information.

Detach and Attach

Analysis Services provides you the functionality to detach and attach a complete database from an Analysis Services instance. These detach and attach commands differ from backup and restore commands. The attach operation allows you to mark a specific database read-only, and the database's data files do not have to be stored in the default Data folder path of your Analysis Services instance. The read-only feature allows you to have a shared scalable architecture of Analysis Services for situations where you have a need to scale out the server to multiple users who are querying a specific Analysis Services database.

Follow these steps to detach the AnalysisServices2008Tutorial database:

1. In SSMS right-click the AnalysisServices2008Tutorial database and select Detach as shown in Figure 7-33.

Figure 7-33

2. In the Detach Database dialog shown in Figure 7-34, click OK.

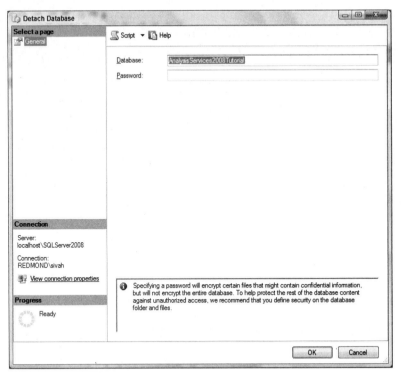

Figure 7-34

SSMS sends the following XMLA command to the Analysis Services instance:

```
<Detach xmlns="http://schemas.microsoft.com/analysisservices/2003/engine">
   <Object>
      <DatabaseID>AnalysisServices2008Tutorial</DatabaseID>
   </Object>
</Detach>
```

After receiving the detach command, Analysis Services first takes a write lock on the database to be detached. Taking a write lock means all existing DDL operations must complete before the detach command is started. The Analysis Services instance creates a detach log file that contains the version information, the key used for encrypting the database (if specified), and a few additional pieces of information about the database with the name AnalysisServices2008Tutorial.detach_log. This log file is created within the database folder as shown in Figure 7-35. Analysis Services then commits and deletes the database. The entire database folder is now independent and can be copied and attached to another Analysis Services instance.

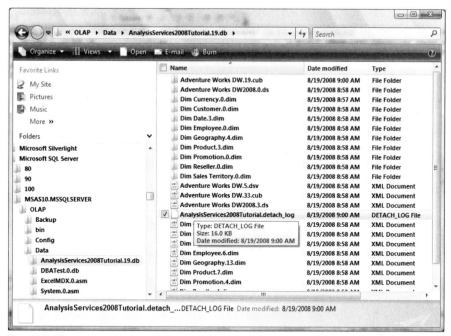

Figure 7-35

You can now attach the detached database to your Analysis Services instance. Follow these steps to attach the database in read-only mode:

1. Move the AnalysisServices2008Tutorial database folder that was detached from its original location under %Program Files%\Microsoft SQL Server\MSAS10.SQLServer\OLAP\ Data to %Program Files%\Microsoft SQL Server\MSAS10.SQLServer\OLAP.

2. If prompted by the operating system to provide administrative privileges to move the folder, provide the permissions.

3. In the SSMS Object Explorer, right-click the Databases folder and select Attach as shown in Figure 7-36.

Figure 7-36

4. In the Attach Database dialog, specify the full path of the AnalysisServices2008Tutorial database as shown in Figure 7-37.

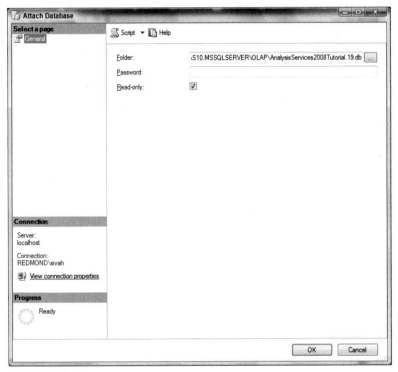

Figure 7-37

5. Enable the checkbox next to Read-only and click OK.

6. Refresh the Databases folder in the SSMS Object Explorer.

You will now see that the AnalysisServices2008Tutorial database has been attached to the Analysis Services instance. Because you attached the database as read-only, you will notice that this database has been marked in gray in the SSMS Object Explorer as shown in Figure 7-38. You can also confirm that the database is read-only by right-clicking the database and selecting Properties. You will see the Read-Write Mode property set to ReadOnly in the Database Properties dialog. The read-only database feature in Analysis Services helps in having a shared scalable database architecture where you can have a single database folder on a Storage Area Network (SAN) attached to multiple Analysis Services instances. You learn how this is helpful in query performance in Chapter 15.

Figure 7-38

Synchronization

Synchronization sounds like a sophisticated, highly technical area of endeavor, but actually, it couldn't be simpler; consider synchronization as just replication for Analysis Services 2008 databases. The name actually is suitable because it allows you to "synchronize" the Analysis Services database resident on one Analysis Services instance to the same database on another Analysis Services instance. Typically we expect Analysis Services DBAs to test the designed Analysis Services database in a test environment before they move them to their production servers. The DBAs often have to back up their database on test servers and restore them on production servers. However, through the synchronization feature in Analysis Services 2008 one can move well-tested databases from test servers to production servers with ease.

If you have an Analysis Services instance actively supporting a population of users, you want to be able to update the database they're querying against without taking the system down to do so. Using the Synchronize Database Wizard, you can accomplish the database update seamlessly. The wizard will copy both data and metadata from your development and test machine (staging server) to the production server and automatically switch users to the newly copied data and metadata based on conditions defined on production server. To try this out, you need to have two instances of Analysis Services installed on another machine, or have a second instance of Analysis Services installed on your current machine. We recommend you install another instance called SS2008 on the same machine. Follow these steps to synchronize a database from the default instance to the new named instance SS2008:

1. Launch SSMS and connect to your default instance (localhost) and named instance (localhost\ SS2008) of Analysis Services as shown in Figure 7-39.

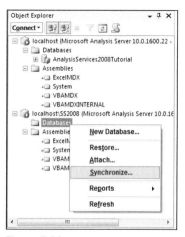

Figure 7-39

2. Right-click the Databases folder of the named instance and select Synchronize as shown in Figure 7-39.

3. If you see the welcome screen click Next.

4. In the Select Database to Synchronize page of the Synchronize Database Wizard, type the default instance **localhost** as the Source server and select the Source database AnalysisServices2008Tutorial as shown in Figure 7-40 and click Next. In the Specify Locations for Local Partitions page you can change locations of the partitions during synchronizations if the destination server allows it. In Figure 7-41 you can see that all the partitions of AnalysisServices2008Tutorial will be restored in the default location.

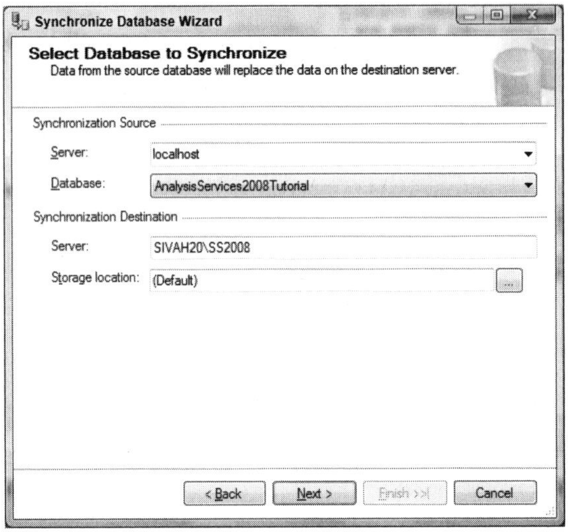

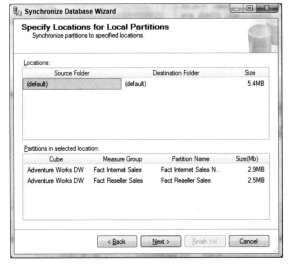

Figure 7-40

Figure 7-41

5. Click Next in the Specify Locations for Local Partitions page. On the Synchronization Options page you can specify the level of security information to copy when you synchronize as shown in Figure 7-42. You can choose to copy all the roles and members, skip the membership information for the roles, or skip all the security information. Analysis Services 2008 has been designed to provide these options because customers might choose to synchronize databases from test servers to production servers. While synchronizing databases from test to production servers you can choose to keep all roles if the security permissions in the test environment are identical to the ones in the production environment. If the security permissions have been defined in such a way that they can be utilized in the production environment but the users in the production environment are different, you can use the Ignore all option. If you choose the Ignore all option you will need to define membership after synchronization.

6. Select the Skip membership option as shown in Figure 7-42 and click Next. In the Select Synchronization Method page you can choose to start the synchronization process immediately or script the command to a file and later send the command to the destination server using SSMS or through other programs.

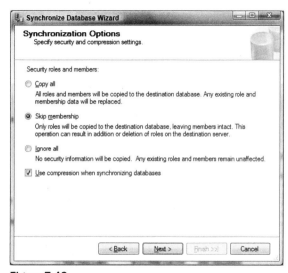

Figure 7-42

7. Select the Synchronize now method as shown in Figure 7-43 and click Next.

Figure 7-43

8. Review the synchronization options you have selected in the Completing the Wizard page and click Finish.

    SSMS sends the following XMLA command to the Analysis Services SS2008 instance to synchronize the AnalysisServices2008Tutorial database from the SQLServer2008 instance:

```
<Synchronize xmlns:xsi="http://www.w3.org/2001/XMLSchema-instance"
      xmlns:xsd="http://www.w3.org/2001/XMLSchema"
      xmlns="http://schemas.microsoft.com/analysisservices/2003/engine">
  <Source>
    <ConnectionString>Provider=MSOLAP.4;Data Source=localhost\SQLServer2008;
      ConnectTo=10.0;Integrated Security=SSPI;
      Initial Catalog=AnalysisServices2008Tutorial</ConnectionString>
    <Object>
      <DatabaseID>AnalysisServices2008Tutorial</DatabaseID>
    </Object>
  </Source>
  <SynchronizeSecurity>SkipMembership</SynchronizeSecurity>
  <ApplyCompression>true</ApplyCompression>
</Synchronize>

<PropertyList xmlns="urn:schemas-microsoft-com:xml-analysis">
      <LocaleIdentifier>1033</LocaleIdentifier>
      </PropertyList>
```

You should be aware that the destination server contacts the source server for synchronization using the credentials of the service startup account and not the user who initiated the synchronize operation from SSMS. You do need to make sure the service startup account of the destination server has credentials to access the databases on the source server. The source server creates a backup of the objects that have changed in the source server, compresses them, and then sends them to the destination server. On the destination server these objects are first restored under a temporary name. If there are active queries being executed against the database on the destination server, the server waits for those queries to complete and then updates the objects. On the source server, the objects are locked during synchronization. Until the time the objects are sent to the destination server you cannot perform operations, such as processing, or other actions that will modify the objects.

9.   You will see the progress of the synchronization operation in the Database Synchronization Progress dialog as shown in Figure 7-44. You will see the progress percentage of the synchronization shown on this page, which gets updated periodically. After the synchronization completes, you will see the message in the page as shown in Figure 7-44. Click Close.

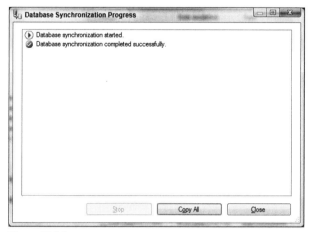

Figure 7-44

You can use the synchronization wizard periodically to synchronize the database from source server to destination server. We typically expect the source server to be your test environment and the destination server to be the production environment. Synchronization is a pull model operation where the destination server pulls data from the source server. If a version of the database exists on the destination server, the source server only sends the data. Typically on the destination server you might have established new membership or security permissions. If you choose appropriate options to skip membership or ignore roles during synchronization, security permissions on the destination servers will not be changed.

There is an important security requirement you must implement to complete a successful synchronization. The destination server's service startup account must have access to the databases on the source server that are expected to be synchronized.

Managing Security

As an administrator, managing security is the most critical operation for the Analysis Services database. The phrase "managing security" can mean several things: managing the roles of Analysis Services databases, using the Analysis Services security features dimension and cell security, enabling and disabling features in Analysis Services, and setting up Analysis Services with appropriate firewall protection. The latter will ensure your Analysis Services instance can appropriately communicate via Internet and intranet.

Server and Database Roles

Roles are of vital importance to securing databases on your Analysis Services instance. You will deal with two kinds of roles when using the product: the server role and database roles. The server role is required for use by a login that performs administrative functions through the user interface (SSMS) or programmatically using AMO. The database roles are defined on an as-needed basis. You can provide read/write permissions to users for all objects in the database or as fine grain as certain cells in a cube. You learned about the server role and how to specify membership earlier in this chapter. In Chapters 9 and 22 you learn to define read/write access for dimensions and cubes in a database.

The Create Role dialog, accessed by right-clicking the Roles folder under a database node in Object Explorer, has the ability to provide full database access to a user as seen earlier in this chapter. In addition, Roles objects in a database help the DBA define fine-grain access to various database objects. The pages in the Create Role dialog are identical to the Role designer, which you learn more about in Chapter 22. Please see Chapter 9 for more details on granting dimension and cube access to Analysis Services users. Chapter 22 provides extensive coverage of database role management through a scenario that shows how to restrict access to specific dimension members (dimension security) or cells in a cube (cell security).

To recap briefly, you as the database administrator can add roles to a specific database, add members to a role, and provide read, write, or read/write access to a role. In addition, you can specify the cell security and dimension security for this role using MDX expressions to limit access to specific cell data or dimension members. When a user is part of multiple roles, Analysis Services provides you access to data in a least restrictive manner. If a user has been restricted access to members of a dimension in one role and has been provided access to the same members in another role, the user will be able to access the members.

Enabling or Disabling Features

Managing database roles is one aspect of securing data in Analysis Services. You can add users to the server role so that you can have several administrators for your Analysis Services instance. Administrators can define appropriate levels of access to databases and objects within a database. However, there is another level of protection that Analysis Services 2008 provides. You can disable features that are not used by your users. One of the most common ways to protect your server from security attacks is to reduce your attack surface by running your server or application with minimum functionality. For example, you can turn off unused services of an operating system that listens for requests from users by default. As and when features are needed, they can be enabled by an administrator. Similarly, Analysis Services allows you to enable or disable certain features to prevent security attacks, thereby making your Analysis Services installation more secure. The following is the list of server properties that can be used to enable or disable certain features or services of your Analysis Services instance:

- ❑ Feature\ManagedCodeEnabled
- ❑ Feature\LinkInsideInstanceEnabled
- ❑ Feature\LinkToOtherInstanceEnabled
- ❑ Feature\LinkFromOtherInstanceEnabled
- ❑ Feature\COMUDFEnabled
- ❑ Feature\ConnStringEncryptionEnabled
- ❑ Datamining\AllowAdhocOpenRowSetQueries
- ❑ Security\RequireClientAuthentication

The properties LinkInsideInstanceEnabled, LinkToOtherInstanceEnabled, and LinkFromOtherInstanceEnabled enable or disable linked objects (measure groups and dimensions) within the same instance and between instances of Analysis Services. The properties ManagedCodeEnabled and COMUDFEnabled allow/disallow loading assemblies to Analysis Services. You can allow or deny ad-hoc open row set data mining queries using the property Datamining\ AllowAdhocOpenRowSetQueries. The server property Security\RequireClientAuthentication allows or denies anonymous connections to Analysis Services. You can force clients to connect using encryption using the ConnStringEncryptionEnabled property. You can change these properties using the properties dialog for an Analysis Services instance.

Online Mode

As an administrator, you need to ensure that databases and their objects are kept up to date. Otherwise, your end users will query out-of-date information. After creating an OLAP database in SSMS you can use the Create Role dialog to create roles and provide permissions to specific users that allow them to be database administrators. To reduce confusion, deployed Analysis Services projects should be named the same as the database created by the server administrator. Once the database is created, the server or the database administrator can perform administrative operations using SSMS such as adding new roles, adding assemblies, or processing objects periodically. There might be certain design changes that you will have to make to the database based on additional requirements from the end users. In such a circumstance you would not be able to make the changes in the original project and deploy that project to the Analysis Services instance because the new objects added to the database will likely be deleted. Analysis Services 2008 provides you two ways to make additional changes. You can connect to the Analysis Services database on the server directly through BIDS and then make the changes in a mode called "online mode." The second option is to import the database into your Analysis Services instance using the Import Analysis Services 2008 Database project (one of the Business Intelligence Project templates that can be used from BIDS), make changes to the database in project mode, and then re-deploy the project to the Analysis Services instance. We recommend the former because you can not only make changes directly on the server, which updates the objects immediately, but you can also perform processing tasks on objects. Instead of designing your Analysis Services database in project mode and then deploying it to the Analysis Services instance you can design the entire database by connecting to the database in online mode. Follow these steps to connect to an Analysis Services database in online mode using BIDS:

1. Launch BIDS from All Programs ⇨ Microsoft SQL Server 2008 ⇨ SQL Server Business Intelligence Development Studio.

2. To open an Analysis Services database in online mode select File ⇨ Open ⇨ Analysis Services Database as shown in Figure 7-45. In the Connect To Database dialog you have the choice of opening an existing database or creating a new database on the Analysis Services instance. You need to be a server administrator to create a database on the Analysis Services instance.

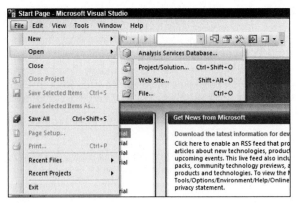

Figure 7-45

3. Type the Analysis Services instance name and select a database to open in online mode as shown in Figure 7-46 and click OK.

Figure 7-46

BIDS connects to the Analysis Services instance and retrieves all the database objects. You will see all the objects of the database in the Solution Explorer similar to the project mode as shown in Figure 7-47. Notice that with the database connected in online mode the Analysis Services instance name is indicated next to the database name in the Solution Explorer. All the operations that you were able to perform on the objects within a database in the project mode can be performed in the online mode. You do not have the deployment option for the database. Instead, you save all your changes directly to the server. We recommend that you explore making changes or adding new objects in the online mode and then saving the changes directly on the Analysis Services instance.

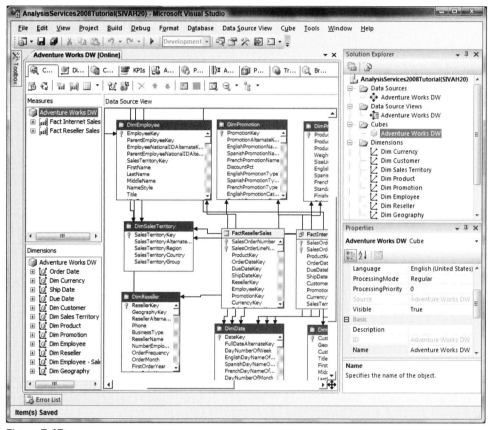

Figure 7-47

Summary

In this chapter you learned to administer SQL Server Analysis Services 2008 using SSMS. You learned the various management operations that can be accomplished on the Analysis Services databases. If you're a database administrator experienced with administering Analysis Services 2000, this chapter may have been largely about getting used to the new management console SSMS. If you have been a database administrator with Analysis Services 2005, you will notice the most important administration feature is being able to detach and attach databases. You have seen that SSMS provides the ability to manage your Analysis Services instances effectively. In addition to learning the various management operations from SSMS, you also learned what XMLA commands are sent by SSMS to the Analysis Services instance, and you have a better understanding of the interactions between SSMS and an Analysis Services instance.

In this chapter you learned that for each administrative task there is a way to execute it through the user interface using SSMS or BIDS. You learn to perform Analysis Services management operations programmatically using the AMO (Analysis Services Management Object) object model in Chapter 13.

You learned how useful backup and restore can be for auditing purposes — specifically by providing snapshots in time of cubes to auditors and analysts. And how security is configured for administrative versus user access to the server; this by using server and database roles, respectively. Finally, in this chapter you were exposed to properties. In the next chapter you learn some of the advanced topics in creating dimensions.

Part II
Advanced Topics

8

Advanced Dimension Design

In this look at advanced dimension design, you learn to aggregate data up to the parent member through custom rollup (aggregate) operations, and you learn about the effects of various dimension and hierarchy properties. For example, you would normally expect data to be aggregated along a dimension from a child to its parent. If you have a hierarchy such as Time, then sales per month will be rolled up to calculate first the sales of a quarter, and sales of a quarter will be rolled up to calculate the sales of a year. Even though this is the most common way a user would expect the data to be aggregated, there are dimensions in which the data does not get rolled up by a simple sum. You also learn about the Business Intelligence Wizard, which helps you to enhance cubes and dimensions with the logic and structure needed to solve common business problems. Finally, you are introduced to dimension writeback, which is a way to enable changes to the dimension structure, typically to facilitate "what if" analysis.

Consider first the details you already learned regarding dimension design back in Chapter 5; you learned that dimensions are made up of hierarchies, which in turn consist of tiers called levels. The two types of hierarchies, attribute and multilevel, were described, as well as two specific types of dimension constructs: Time and Parent-Child dimensions. The material in this chapter builds on the initial baseline that has been established to this point. Consequently, this is a good time to refer back to Chapter 5 if you're not feeling completely comfortable with the material covered there.

If you don't get the in-depth details of this chapter just from reading the narrative descriptions, don't worry; the concepts are demonstrated through examples as well. This area is a classic example of "It seems profoundly difficult until you get it, but once you get it, it is so simple as to seem obvious." If you already know the aforementioned concepts or otherwise understand them after reading this paragraph, read the chapter anyway; it goes far beyond the basics.

Please note that most of the examples in this chapter make use of the project created in Chapter 6, and a few of them use the "official" Adventure Works DW 2008 sample project that can be downloaded from SQL2008.AdventureWorks DW BI_v2008.<architecture>.msi available at http://www.codeplex.com/MSFTDBProdSamples. The project being used will be explicitly mentioned preceding each example.

> If you came to this chapter looking for information on calculated members or Data Mining dimensions (both being perfectly reasonable to expect here), they are not covered here. For information on calculated members, please see Chapter 3, and for Data Mining dimensions, please see Chapter 16.

Custom Rollups

The name "custom rollup" is very much self describing. Custom refers to the "user-defined" nature of a rollup or aggregate formula, such that a measure value for a member is not a simple sum of values of its children as you move up a hierarchy. Rollup describes how those calculations typically start at the leaf or lower-level node and aggregate (roll) up toward the root. There are several ways in which you can apply a custom rollup to a hierarchy: by using the attribute property CustomRollupColumn, using unary operators (used for parent-child hierarchies), and by using MDX scripts to specify custom rollup for members in a level. Note that unary operators can be used on non–parent-child hierarchies too, though this is not a very common application in practice.

A business scenario will help you better understand the need for and concept of the custom rollup. Perhaps you are familiar with the word *depreciation*. Technically, the definition of depreciation is "mapping an asset's expense over time to benefits gained through use of those assets." It simply means that the value of an asset decreases over time. There are two types of depreciation you should be familiar with and understand. They are called straight-line and accelerated. Typically, businesses keep two (sometimes more) sets of accounting books, which, by the way, is completely legal. One set of books is for the IRS and one set is for investors. The books for the IRS often use accelerated depreciation because this provides optimal tax benefits (less taxable income is initially reported), and the books for investors use straight-line depreciation because this yields higher net earnings per share for that quarter or year and a more favorable ROE (Return on Equity), which is the net income divided by the shareholder's equity.

Accelerated depreciation on a delivery van, illustrated in Figure 8-1, can be thought of as "front loaded" depreciation; the percentages associated with each year indicate the percentage of total value depreciated or "written off" for that year. The fact that 40% is depreciated the first year and 10% the last year speaks to the notion that the depreciation is front loaded. There is no cash involved in recognizing depreciation, yet there is a reduction in asset value and an expense is logged; hence it is called a non-cash expense. The company can write off more of the van's value earlier on its taxes. That means less taxable income for the company in the earlier years and that is a good thing.

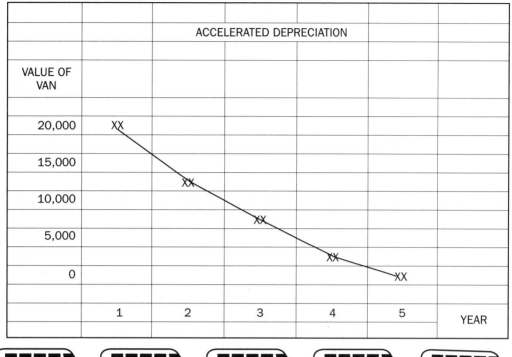

Figure 8-1

Straight-line depreciation on the same delivery van, illustrated in Figure 8-2, again happens over time until the van is essentially worthless with no salvage value (in this case after five hard-driving years). Notice that the rate at which the van falls apart is the same, regardless of how depreciation is logged on the financial records. In this case, the non-cash expense is logged in equal amounts over the life of the asset at 20% per year. The effect this method has is that an investor sees an asset retaining value for a longer period. That is a good thing because value ultimately relates to stock price.

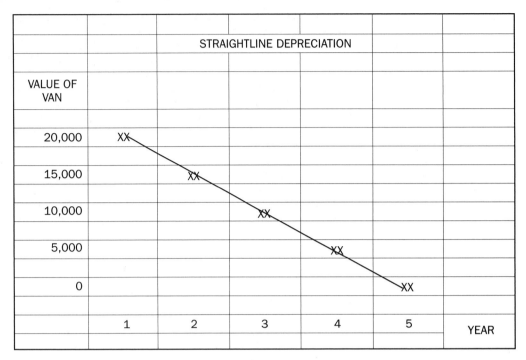

		STRAIGHTLINE DEPRECIATION				

Figure 8-2

Having learned about depreciation you can understand the need for custom rollup of member values in a hierarchy to their parent — it all depends on the type of depreciation being logged and therefore will be custom, by definition. In order to calculate the net profit of your company, you would typically add up the sales revenue, any increase in asset values, and subtract the expenditures (Cost of Goods Sold) and depreciation values appropriately. You might be wondering if these are just measure values, what is so complex about them? Why not just write an appropriate calculated measure? That would be a reasonable question to ask. And if it is just measures you're dealing with, you don't have a problem.

By definition, depreciation indicates that values change over time. So, your calculations that reflect the value of physical assets (like delivery vans) should be adjusted for appropriate percentage changes based on the Time dimension you are querying. Similarly, there might be other dimensions or measure groups that calculations might depend on. For example, say you have a Budget measure group and a Sales measure group in your cube. Your budget for next year might depend on the sales of the previous year and you need to use appropriate MDX expressions to arrive at the budget amount. You can create such custom calculations using MDX scripts with appropriate SCOPE statements, but it will be quite a lengthy script, especially if the calculations are different for each member in a dimension. Also, verifying that your calculations are giving the correct values will be time-consuming. To help better solve these types of problems, Analysis Services allows you to specify the calculations through MDX expressions as a property of the hierarchy.

Take the following example: If there is an Account dimension that indicates the types of accounts of your company, such as asset, liability, income, and expenditure, and you have a measure called Amount, the rollup of the values to the parent member is not a simple sum. In such a case, you need to specify a custom rollup, typically per account type. If the hierarchy is a parent-child hierarchy, Analysis Services allows you to perform a custom rollup using a feature called unary operators. Unary operators allow specification of basic aggregate functions: add, subtract, multiply, multiply by a specified factor, divide, and a special case for a no-op good measure. However, if the value of a member is not derived from its children or you have a user hierarchy where you have to rollup the values to the parent using a complex operation or custom formula, you would then likely specify the custom rollup using a property called CustomRollupColumn for an attribute hierarchy.

The CustomRollupColumn property of an attribute should be set to a column in the relational table that will contain the custom rollup calculation — which is an MDX expression. For example, in the Account dimension in the Adventure Works DW 2008 sample project, the value for Account Average Unit is calculated from the Accounts Net Sales and Units, which are members in the Account dimension under different parents. To specify the custom formula for a member, the column in the relational table should contain an MDX expression that evaluates the value for the member. You need to specify an MDX expression for each member that a custom formula needs to be applied to. For the sake of clarity, it likely would have been better to name this property CustomFormula instead of CustomRollup. At any rate, follow these steps to understand the behavior of a custom rollup by using the sample Adventure Works DW 2008 relational database:

1. Open the AnalysisServices2008Tutorial project you completed in Chapter 6. This project can be downloaded from the book's accompanying web site and can be found in the Chapter 6 files.

2. Select the Adventure Works DW cube from the Solution Explorer, right-click, and select Delete.

3. Open the Adventure Works DW DSV. Right-click in the DSV designer and select Add/Remove Tables. Add all the dimension and fact tables in the Adventure Works DW data source except AdventureWorksBuildVersion, DatabaseLog, ProspectiveBuyer, and the views as shown in Figure 8-3.

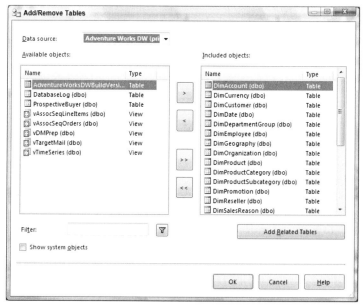

Figure 8-3

4. Create the dimensions Dim Account, Dim Department Group, Dim Organization, Dim Sales Reason, and Dim Scenario using the existing table path of the Dimension Wizard and selecting the tables Dim Account, Dim Department Group, Dim Organization, Dim Sales Reason, and Dim Scenario, respectively. While creating these dimensions, do not include any related tables detected by the Dimension Wizard, but instead select all the columns in the tables as attributes of the dimension and choose the default dimension names suggested by the Dimension Wizard. After you have created all the dimensions, right-click the Dimensions folder in Solution Explorer and select Sort by Name.

You should finally end up with dimensions as shown in Figure 8-4. In this example for illustration and quick understanding, we have requested you to select all the columns in the tables as attributes. When you design your dimensions, we highly recommend you only choose the right set of columns as attributes, and the ones that you want to slice or dice should only be enabled for browsing. Choosing the right attributes for your dimension helps you to design your dimension right from the start and thereby helps in optimal dimension and cube design. The Dimension Wizard will automatically detect parent-child relationships for dimensions DimAccount, DimDepartmentGroup, and DimOrganization and will create appropriate parent-child hierarchies.

Figure 8-4

5. Create a new cube using the Cube Wizard. In the Select Measure Group Tables page, select all tables beginning with the word Fact as measure group tables as shown in Figure 8-5. Accept the defaults in the Select Measures and Select Existing Dimensions pages of the wizard. In the Select New Dimensions page, uncheck any potential dimension whose name starts with "Fact." Click Finish in the Completing the Wizard page.

You will now have the Adventure Works DW cube created. The Cube Wizard detects the relationship between the fact and dimension tables based on relationships in the DSV and creates appropriate dimension usage. If you do need to change the relationships you can do so on the Dimension Usage tab within the cube editor. If you look at the relationships in the Dimension Usage tab you will notice that there are multiple instances of certain dimensions. For example, you will see four instances of the DimDate dimension: Dim Date, Dime Date (Due Date), Dim Date (Order Date), and Dim Date (Ship Date). Instead of creating four database dimensions and using them within the cube, Analysis Services 2008 is smart enough to create multiple cube dimensions from a single database dimension, when needed. Typically, when you have multiple relationships between a fact table and dimension table, the optimal way to model them is with a single database dimension, and multiple cube dimensions. We refer to these types of cube dimensions as *role playing* dimensions. Now that the cube is created, deploy the project.

Figure 8-5

6. Double-click the Dim Account dimension in Solution Explorer. Notice the attribute hierarchies of the Dim Account dimension within the Dimension Designer. If you switch to the Dimension Browser and browse the parent-child hierarchy, you will see the account numbers. To view the Account names while browsing the parent-child hierarchy you need to specify the NameColumn property for the key attribute, which you learned about in Chapter 5. Select the key attribute Account Key and specify the relational column AccountDescription as the NameColumn property for the key attribute and then deploy the changes to the Analysis Services instance. If you go to the Dimension Browser you will see the names of the accounts.

In the properties for an attribute you will see a property called CustomRollupColumn, as shown in Figure 8-6. This property needs to be set to the relational column that has the MDX expression for the custom rollup formula. The MDX expression specified in this property gets evaluated on the cells when the value's corresponding members of the hierarchy are being retrieved in the query.

Figure 8-6

7. The sample AdventureWorksDW2008 relational database provides a column with custom rollups for the Account dimension. Right-click the DimAccount table in the DSV of the dimension DimAccount and select Explore Data.

You will see the data in the relational table as shown in Figure 8-7. The relational column CustomMembers contains the MDX expression for custom rollup. In the AdventureWorksDW2008 relational database, there is an MDX expression defined for an Account, which has AccountKey = 98 as shown in Figure 8-7. There are no children for the Account with AccountKey = 98 (Account Name is "Average Unit Price") and there are no corresponding fact rows in the fact table FactFinance. Therefore, if you browse the current Adventure Works DW cube in the Cube Browser, you will see a null value for the Average Unit Price account. The MDX expression in the relational table for Average Unit Price account is:

```
[Account].[Accounts].[Account Level 04].&[50]/[Account].[Accounts].
        [Account Level 02].&[97]
```

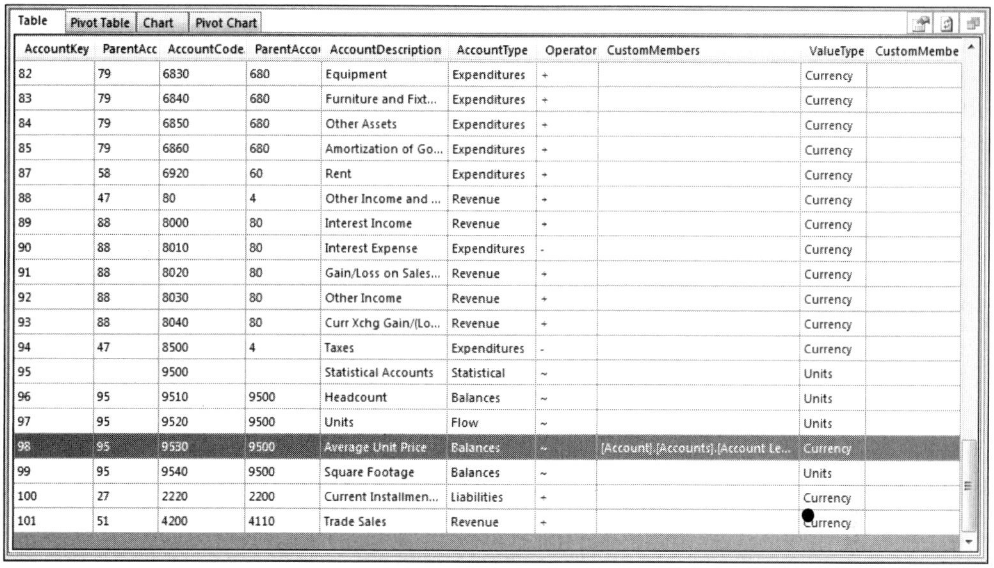

AccountKey	ParentAcc	AccountCode	ParentAcco	AccountDescription	AccountType	Operator	CustomMembers	ValueType	CustomMembe
82	79	6830	680	Equipment	Expenditures	+		Currency	
83	79	6840	680	Furniture and Fixt...	Expenditures	+		Currency	
84	79	6850	680	Other Assets	Expenditures	+		Currency	
85	79	6860	680	Amortization of Go...	Expenditures	+		Currency	
87	58	6920	60	Rent	Expenditures	+		Currency	
88	47	80	4	Other Income and ...	Revenue	+		Currency	
89	88	8000	80	Interest Income	Revenue	+		Currency	
90	88	8010	80	Interest Expense	Expenditures	-		Currency	
91	88	8020	80	Gain/Loss on Sales...	Revenue	+		Currency	
92	88	8030	80	Other Income	Revenue	+		Currency	
93	88	8040	80	Curr Xchg Gain/(Lo...	Revenue	+		Currency	
94	47	8500	4	Taxes	Expenditures	-		Currency	
95		9500		Statistical Accounts	Statistical	~		Units	
96	95	9510	9500	Headcount	Balances	~		Units	
97	95	9520	9500	Units	Flow	~		Units	
98	95	9530	9500	Average Unit Price	Balances	~	[Account].[Accounts].[Account Le...	Currency	
99	95	9540	9500	Square Footage	Balances	~		Units	
100	27	2220	2200	Current Installmen...	Liabilities	+		Currency	
101	51	4200	4110	Trade Sales	Revenue	+		Currency	

Figure 8-7

When evaluated this MDX expression will provide the amount for Account Average Unit Price from Accounts Net Sales and Units. Accounts Net Sales and Units are not children of the Average Unit Price account and hence the custom formula mentioned earlier calculates the value for Average Unit Price Account. In the preceding expression you see that the dimension and hierarchy names specified are Account and Accounts, respectively. Notice the members specified in the MDX expression for custom rollup include the level names Account Level 04 and Account Level 02. By default, the level names for parent-child hierarchies have the names "Level xx." Hence you also need to make sure you specify the appropriate property to have the level names as shown in the MDX expression. Therefore you need to change the name of the dimension and the parent-child hierarchy in your database.

8. In the Solution Explorer, right-click the dimension name Dim Account.dim and click Rename. Enter the name "Account.dim." When asked if the object name needs to be changed, click Yes. Open the Account dimension in the Dimension Designer. Right-click the parent-child hierarchy Parent Account Key and rename it Accounts. You now need to specify the level names for the parent-child hierarchy. Enter the value "Account Level *;" for the Accounts parent-child hierarchy property NamingTemplate and set the IsAggregatable property to False. You learn more about these properties later in this chapter. Don't think you have completed all the renaming yet. You have currently renamed the dimension and hierarchy. When an MDX expression within a cube is calculated, the dimension name addressed with the cube is the cube dimension and not the database dimension that you just renamed. Hence you also need to rename the cube dimension name for dimension Account. Open the Adventure Works DW cube. Click the Cube Structure tab; right-click the Dim Account dimension in the Dimensions pane and select Rename. Enter the name "Account." You have successfully made changes to your cube to define the custom rollup formula for the Accounts hierarchy.

9. Select the property CustomRollupColumn for the Accounts hierarchy in the Account dimension. Click the button at the right of the value column (with the "..." caption) in the Properties window to bring up the Custom Rollup Column dialog. In the Custom Rollup Column dialog

select the CustomMembers column in the Dim Account table as the column for the CustomRollupColumn property as shown in Figure 8-8 and click the OK button.

You have successfully specified a custom formula for members of the Accounts hierarchy. In addition to specifying a custom formula using CustomRollupColumn, you can also specify the CustomRollupPropertiesColumn property to apply custom properties on the cell value. The CustomRollupPropertiesColumn property also takes a column in the relational table as input and that column should contain an MDX expression specifying the cell properties such as background color and foreground color. The sample relational database does not contain values for CustomRollupPropertiesColumn and hence we leave the exercise of exploring those properties to you.

Figure 8-8

Deploy the project to the Analysis Services instance. To make sure the CustomRollupColumn MDX expression is correctly evaluated for the Average Unit Price account attribute, go to the Cube Browser and browse the Accounts dimension and the measure Amount from the Fact Finance measure group. You will see the value for Average Unit Price is now calculated using the MDX expression as shown in Figure 8-9. Using a calculator you can easily verify that the value for Average Unit Price is equal to the value of Net Sales divided by the Units.

Figure 8-9

You have now successfully learned to apply a custom formula to members of a hierarchy. In this example, a parent-child hierarchy was used to help you understand the CustomRollupColumn property;

however, the custom rollup is not limited to parent-child hierarchies and can be used on any hierarchy. As mentioned, Analysis Services provides a way to specify a custom formula for a level within a hierarchy. You can specify such a formula in your MDX script or specify the custom formula for the members in a relational column and use the CustomRollupColumn property for that hierarchy. If an attribute hierarchy is part of multiple user hierarchies and you need to apply different custom rollup behaviors based on the hierarchy, you need to apply these custom formulas in the MDX script. Analysis Services 2008 provides another way to aggregate data for members in parent-child hierarchies using a property called *UnaryOperatorColumn*. The next section provides further details.

Enhancements to Parent-Child Hierarchies

The parent-child hierarchy structure is a particularly intuitive and quite common technique to model various business entities, and for this reason it is very important to master the modeling techniques related to it. In this section, the concepts discussed in the previous section are extended. Several important properties are supported by Analysis Services 2008 for parent-child hierarchies. One of those important properties is the UnaryOperatorColumn property.

Unary Operators

Unary operators are used for custom rollup of members to their parent where the rollup operation is a unary operation. A unary operator, as the name suggests, is an operator that takes a single argument — the member — and rolls up the value of the member to its parent. As with the custom rollup column, you need to have the unary operators specified as a column in the relational table, and this column must be set or mapped as a property for the parent-child hierarchy. Unary operators can be applied also to non parent-child hierarchies, but this is not a common scenario so it will not be covered here. The following table shows the various unary operators supported by Analysis Services and a description of their behaviors:

Unary Operator	Description
+	The value of the member is added to the aggregate value of the preceding sibling members. This is the default operator used if no unary operator column is specified.
-	The value of the member is subtracted from the aggregate value of the preceding sibling members.
*	The value of the member is multiplied by the aggregate value of the preceding sibling members.
/	The value of the member is divided by the aggregate value of the preceding sibling members.
~	The value of the member is ignored.
N	The value is multiplied by N and added to the aggregate values. N can be any numeric value (typically N is between 0 and 1).
	An empty unary operator is equivalent to "+".

A business scenario commonly used to demonstrate the usefulness of rollups using unary operators is the case where Net Income equals Sales minus Cost of Goods Sold. As for the calculation of tax at different rates depending on tax bracket, that will come a little later because calculating those values will require custom rollups, and for now the topic of discussion is the unary operator. In this example, Sales figures will be added, hence the "+" operator is used, and for Cost of Goods Sold, which is subtracted, the "-" operator is used. Were depreciation included in the following example, given that it is a non-cash expense, you might choose to ignore it in the hierarchy by using the tilde (~) unary operator. Follow these steps to set up unary operators for the parent-child hierarchies in the Account and Organization dimensions:

1. Open the Account dimension and click the Accounts hierarchy. In the Properties window you will see the properties associated with parent-child hierarchies under a section called Parent-Child, as shown in Figure 8-10. You'll first do a bit of housekeeping so that the dimension is a bit more user-friendly to browse. Locate the MembersWithData property and set its value to NonLeafDataHidden.

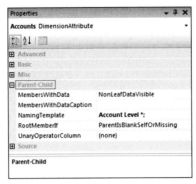

Figure 8-10

2. Select the Unary Operator Column property and click the button at the right of the value column (with the ". . ." caption) in the Properties window to bring up the Unary Operator Column dialog box. In the Unary Operator Column dialog box, select Operator as the Source column, as shown in Figure 8-11. Click the OK button and deploy the changes to your Analysis Services instance.

Figure 8-11

If you explore the data for DimAccount table in the DSV Designer, you can see the unary operators associated for each account as shown earlier in Figure 8-7. Note that there are "~" operators indicating "ignore this," which is required for members that are calculations in and of themselves. Because the Operator column is an attribute hierarchy in the Account dimension, it becomes a member property of the key attribute. All member properties of the key attribute are automatically inherited by the parent attribute, the parent-child hierarchy. Therefore you can view the unary operators associated with each account in the Dimension Browser while browsing the Accounts parent-child hierarchy by including the member property Unary Operator using the Member Property icon as shown in Figure 8-12.

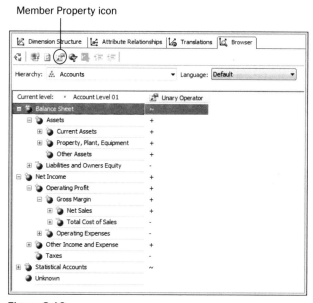

Figure 8-12

3. The next step is to ensure that you have set the unary operators correctly and the rollup to parent occurs as desired. For verification, edit the Adventure Works DW cube and click the Browser tab. Drag and drop the Amount measure and the parent-child hierarchy Accounts from the Measure Group pane to the data and row areas, respectively, and then expand the levels Net Income ➪ Operating Profit ➪ Gross Margin. Before specifying the unary operator, Analysis Services aggregates the values for Net Sales and Total Cost of Sales as a sum to calculate the value for Gross Margin. Because a unary operator has been specified, you should see the value for Gross Margin is the difference of Net Sales and Total Cost of Sales, as shown in Figure 8-13.

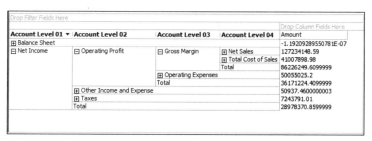

Figure 8-13

Analysis Services has a unary operator that is referred to as N in the unary operator table. N is a numerical value that is used as a weighting factor so that the value of the member is multiplied by the value N and then aggregated to the parent. For example, a company might calculate overhead costs for utilities like electricity at the level of an entire factory. Electricity consumption is not evenly distributed across the organizations within the factory, though; the manufacturing floor might be sucking up power at a rate completely disproportionate to the administrative section. This disparity is something that should be accounted for when doing internal costing analysis. One way managerial accountants address the problem is to calculate the overhead at the departmental level and at the factory level. The amount of electricity consumed can be weighted by some predetermined amount such that cost assignments are rolled up to the correct parents. For example, the manufacturing department could be assigned a ratio of 1 to 9 for factory level overhead versus department level overhead. That is, 10% of the electricity used by manufacturing facilities is assigned to factory overhead, and the other 90% is assigned as a department-specific cost.

In some organizations, even though a group is reporting to a parent (higher-level group), the measure value of the sub-group might be rolled up as a fraction of the total measure value to the parent. This is because parent groups only own a part of the organization. If you know the percentage of ownership for various organizations as a measure, you can specify CustomRollupColumn with an appropriate MDX expression. However, with the unary operator N, you can simply specify the rollup using numerical values.

The AdventureWorksDW2008 relational database provides an example of the unary operator N for the Organization dimension, where the percentage of ownership is specified in a column in the Dim Organization table. Follow these steps to enhance the Dim Organization dimension created by the Dimension Wizard so that the dimension is modeled to match the actual business results:

1. Open the Dim Organization dimension. Specify the NameColumn property for the key attribute as OrganizationName.

2. Rename the Parent Organization Key parent-child hierarchy to Organizations. Select the Unary Operator Column property and click the button at the right of the value column (with the "..." caption) in the Properties window to bring up the Unary Operator Column dialog. In the Unary Operator Column dialog, select the PercentageOfOwnership column and click OK.

At this point, you have specified the weighted average for the Organization's parent-child hierarchy. You might immediately want to see the results by deploying the changes. However, if you do deploy as such, you might see odd results because of the way calculations are applied in the cube. This is because when Analysis Services retrieves data for measures across a specific hierarchy, it takes the default members of other hierarchies while doing this evaluation. For most hierarchies the All member is the default. In the Account dimension the IsAggregatable property is set to false because aggregating the data for the top-level members in the Account dimension does not make business sense. In such circumstances, Analysis Services uses the default member of the hierarchy. If a default member is not specified, Analysis Services retrieves the first member of the hierarchy. The first member of the Accounts hierarchy is Balance Sheet and the unary operator for Balance Sheet, ~ (tilde), will result in non-intuitive results. In order for you to see meaningful results, you need to make sure you choose the right default.

3. For the Accounts hierarchy in the Account dimension, click the DefaultMember property. In the Set Default Member dialog, select the "Choose a member to be the default:" option, select Net Income, and click the OK button. The Net Income member has a unary operator of +, which will result in meaningful data being seen while browsing the Amount measure for other dimensions. Now, deploy the changes to the Analysis Services instance. This percentage of ownership will be applied for the measures being queried.

4. If you browse the Organization dimension along with the measure Amount you will notice appropriate rollups based on the weighted unary operator. Figure 8-14 shows the amount for various organizations, and you can see that the amount from the French and German organizations is only partially aggregated to the European Operations organization.

Figure 8-14

When multiple calculations are specified for a cell, Analysis Services 2008 uses a specific order to evaluate calculations. Due to the order of calculations, cell values might not always be intuitive and you can sometimes see unexpected results. We highly recommend you know your cube design well, know Analysis Services' calculation precedence (order of calculations), and verify the results. Several calculations can be applied to a measure: semi-additive calculation, unary operator, and custom rollup. You learn more about semi-additive measures briefly in this chapter and in detail in Chapter 9. When Analysis Services is evaluating the measure value for a member, it initially calculates the regular aggregate of the measure value. This aggregate can be Sum, Count, or any of the built-in semi-additive functions (to be discussed later). If a unary operator is specified, the unary operator rollup is applied for the member across that specific dimension and the value of the measure is overwritten. Finally, if a custom rollup is specified for the member, the value resulting from the custom rollup MDX expression is evaluated as the final result. The evaluation of a cell value is done across each dimension, and if dimensions have custom rollups and unary operators, then all the unary operators are applied, followed by custom rollups based on the order of the dimensions within the cube. As you might expect, you can modify the order of the dimensions by dragging and dropping dimensions to the desired position in the cube editor's dimension list.

Specifying Names of Levels in a Parent-Child Hierarchy

When you create multilevel hierarchies, various attribute hierarchies form the levels of those hierarchies. For example, in a Geography hierarchy you may have Country, State, City, and Zip Code as levels, and when you browse the dimension you can see the names of the levels as the names of the attribute hierarchies. Parent-child hierarchies are different in this respect from user hierarchies. While creating regular hierarchies, you can see the various levels in the dimension editor, but for parent-child hierarchies you cannot visually see the number of levels unless you process and browse the hierarchy. The levels within a parent-child hierarchy are embedded within the self-referential relationships. However, Analysis Services allows you to define custom names for each level of the parent-child hierarchy. By default, Analysis Services 2008 provides basic names for the levels — Level 01, Level 02, and so on. Level N is based on the depth of the parent-child hierarchy.

If you want custom names to be specified for each level, Analysis Services provides a property for just that. For example, if you have an org-structure parent-child hierarchy, you can name the levels CEO, Presidents, Vice Presidents, General Managers, Product Unit Managers, Managers, Leads, and Individual Contributors. If you want to specify common prefix, use the parent-child property called NamingTemplate. If you click the selection for NamingTemplate, you will launch the Level Naming Template dialog, as shown in Figure 8-15. In this dialog you can specify the name for each level in the parent-child hierarchy. If you want a constant prefix name followed by the level number, such as Employee Level 1, Employee Level 2, and so on, you just need to specify Employee Level * as shown in Figure 8-15 and Analysis Services will automatically append the level number at the end of each level. Edit the Dim Employee dimension, select the Parent Employee Key hierarchy, and click the value for the NamingTemplate property. In the Level Naming Template dialog specify the level names as Employee

Level * as shown in Figure 8-15. Change the name of the parent-child hierarchy to Employees. Add a new calculated column called Full Name in the DimEmployee table within the DSV, which is the sum of FirstName, a space, and LastName. Make the Full Name relational column as the NameColumn for the key attribute of the Dim Employee dimension. Deploy the changes to the Analysis Services instance. When you browse the Employees hierarchy you will see the new level names as shown in Figure 8-16. When you click a member, you will see the level name shown next to the Current Level.

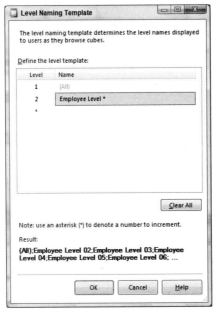

Figure 8-15

Figure 8-16

In Figure 8-16 you can see that the member David Bradley also reports to David Bradley. This is because each parent member is also included as its child, so that the value for that parent member is an aggregate of all its children and its own value. By way of example, if you have a Sales organization of employees and each manager manages a few sales employees in a region in addition to being in charge of certain sales, the total sales by the manager is a sum of all the direct reports plus the manager's own sales. That is why you sometimes see a member reporting to him- or herself while browsing a parent-child hierarchy. If you know that the non-leaf members (as with managers in an employee organization) do not have fact data associated with them and are just an aggregate of the children, Analysis Services provides a property by which you can disable a member being a child of itself. This property is called MemberWithData and setting the value to NonLeafDataHidden, as shown in Figure 8-17, allows you to disable a member being shown as reporting to itself.

You have now learned several enhancements to parent-child hierarchies. The properties for parent-child hierarchies provided by Analysis Services help you model requirements for different business scenarios. In the next section you look at other properties of attributes and dimensions that help you enhance dimensions.

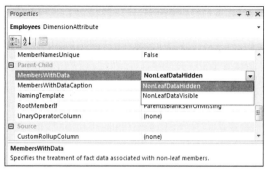

Figure 8-17

Using Properties to Customize Dimensions

Analysis Services provides several properties for use with hierarchies and dimensions. If every property were explained with illustrations and examples, this chapter would be quite large, so in this section you learn about the properties that are most important with respect to optimal design or more likely to be used in fulfillment of common business requirements.

Ordering Dimension Members

In Chapter 5 you learned to order dimension members of a hierarchy based on key or named columns specified for the attribute. Based on that, Analysis Services sorted the members in the hierarchy and you were able to see the order while browsing the dimension. In certain business scenarios, you might have a need to sort the members based on a specific value or based on some other condition. Analysis Services provides properties to sort members of a hierarchy in a variety of ways other than by the attribute's key or name columns.

Specifically, you have the option to sort members of a given attribute based upon members of another, related attribute. The related bit is important here. In order for this technique to be used, you must define the ordering attribute as a related attribute (also known as member property) of the attribute to be ordered. For example, if you have an Employees parent-child hierarchy and if you have the age of the employees defined as an attribute, you can set the appropriate properties to the key attribute of the dimension to achieve a sorting of employees in the parent-child hierarchy based on age. You need to set the property OrderByAttribute to age and then set the property OrderBy to either AttributeKey or AttributeName depending on your requirements, and then deploy the changes to the Analysis Services instance. These properties are shown in Figure 8-18. You can see the changes take effect by viewing the members in the Dimension Browser.

Figure 8-18

The All Member, Default Member, and Unknown Member

Each hierarchy within a dimension has a member that is called the *default member*. When a query is sent to Analysis Services, Analysis Services uses the default member for all the hierarchies that are not included in the query in order to evaluate the results for the query. If a default member is not specified, Analysis Services uses the first non-calculated member in the hierarchy based on the default ordering for the hierarchy. If the property IsAggregatable is set to True, that means that the values of members of the hierarchy can be aggregated to form a single member. This single member is, by default, called the "All" member and is most commonly the default member for the hierarchy. You can change the name of the All member for the attribute hierarchies within the dimension by changing the dimension property AttributeAllMemberName, as shown in Figure 8-19. To select the Properties window for the dimension, you can click the dimension name in the Attributes pane in the dimension editor or anywhere in the Hierarchies pane. If you deploy the project after changing the value for the AttributeAllMemberName property as shown in Figure 8-19, you will see that the All member for the Dim Employee dimension now shows up as "All Employees" in the Dimension Browser. For multilevel hierarchies the property to set the name of the (All) member is AllMemberName.

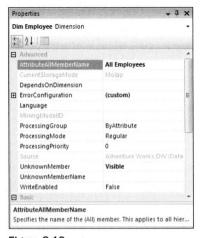

Figure 8-19

To change the default member for a hierarchy, you set the property DefaultMember to the correct member in the hierarchy. Click the ellipsis next to the DefaultMember property for the Employees hierarchy and you will see the Set Default Member dialog shown in Figure 8-20. You have three options for specifying the default member: using the system default member, selecting the member by browsing the hierarchy, or specifying an MDX expression to arrive at the default member. For the last option you can paste the MDX expression that evaluates the default member for the hierarchy or use the dialog to build the MDX expression that will evaluate the default member. Once the default member has been set for a specific hierarchy, Analysis Services uses that default member in query evaluation. You can send the following MDX query to ensure the default member you have set in the property is being used by Analysis Services:

```
SELECT [Dim Employee].[Employees].DefaultMember ON 0
FROM [Adventure Works DW]
```

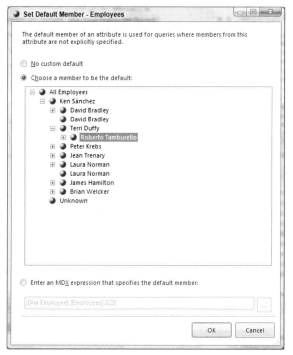

Figure 8-20

The UnknownMember is another property for each dimension in your database. If there are referential integrity issues in your relational database, then during partition processing Analysis Services will raise appropriate errors. If you have set specific processing options to ignore errors, but include the fact data corresponding to errors in the cube, Analysis Services allocates the fact data to a member called the Unknown member in the dimensions for which it is unable to find members due to referential integrity issues. You have the option of allowing the Unknown member to be visible or hidden, using the dimension property UnknownMember. When the UnknownMember is set to be visible, the member name is set to UnknownMember and will be included in the results of the MDX queries that contain the hierarchy. Similar to the All member name, Analysis Services gives you the option of changing the name of the Unknown member to a more meaningful name corresponding to that specific dimension. Note that the name you choose will be used across the entire dimension (that is, you cannot set per-attribute unknown member names), so make sure to pick a sufficiently general name.

Error Configurations for Processing

One of the challenges in designing a data warehouse is creating a perfect schema without any referential integrity issues. However, this is often not possible and a significant amount of the time spent in designing a data warehouse is typically spent in data cleansing. Analysis Services, by default, will stop processing dimensions whenever it encounters specific referential integrity issues. Some data warehouse designers might want to ignore the referential integrity issues by ignoring the records causing errors and include corresponding fact data to the Unknown member of dimensions so that they can see the results of their cube design. Analysis Services gives you fine-grain control for various referential integrity issues that can happen during processing. The dimension property ErrorConfiguration allows you that control for dimension processing. If you click the ErrorConfiguration property and select Custom, you will see all the settings that allow you fine-grain control as well as the default values as shown in Figure 8-21.

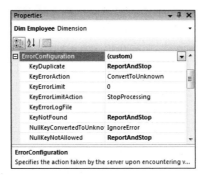

Figure 8-21

The possible errors Analysis Services can encounter while processing a dimension are related to key attributes of the dimension. Typically, when you have a snowflake dimension you can encounter dimension key errors while processing, whenever Analysis Services is unable to find corresponding keys in the dimension tables involved in the snowflake schema. The main errors that Analysis Services encounters are duplicate key errors (multiple occurrences of the key attribute in the dimension table), key not found error (unable to find a key in the dimension table in the snowflake schema), and null keys being encountered when you do not expect null keys to be present. You can set properties to stop processing after a specific number of errors have been reached, continue processing by reporting the errors, or ignore all errors. We leave it to you as an exercise to set various error configurations while building your data warehouses.

Storage Mode

Analysis Services supports two storage modes for dimensions. Your dimensions can be configured to be MOLAP or ROLAP dimensions. If a dimension is configured as MOLAP, Analysis Services reads all the dimension data from the relational data sources at the time of processing and stores the data in a compressed format. Due to the proprietary, patented format, Analysis Services is able to retrieve dimension data efficiently, resulting in fast query response times. When the storage mode is set to ROLAP, Analysis Services retrieves all data from the relational data source, in effect translating and redirecting at run time. At the time of processing, all appropriate metadata information is logged. Thereafter, each query involving retrieval of data from a ROLAP dimension results in the aforementioned translation from MDX to a SQL variant, followed by a redirection of the query to the underlying relational data source. Next, Analysis Services performs necessary calculations (aggregate computation, calculated members, and so on) prior to providing the results of the query to the client. Typically, ROLAP storage mode is chosen only when there are a large number of members in a dimension (on the order of hundreds of millions of members). You need to evaluate the trade-off between query performance, which will be significantly slower, versus storage or business requirement and set the correct storage mode for your dimensions. Disks have become quite cheap these days and we almost universally recommend setting the storage mode for dimensions to MOLAP. However, in certain business scenarios where you have the dimension data constantly changing and you need real-time data, you might want to set the storage mode to ROLAP. Even in cases where your customers need real-time data, you might be able to set the property called Proactive Caching that helps in providing real-time data. For more details on real-time data, see Chapter 21. Figure 8-22 shows the dimension property for storage mode.

Figure 8-22

Grouping Members

Some of the hierarchies might have continuous data, and typically you might not be interested in viewing each and every member. An example of such a hierarchy is the salary of customers. Typically one would be interested in customers within a specific salary range rather than querying for customers with a specific salary. In such circumstances, Analysis Services allows you to model your hierarchy so that the members of the hierarchy are ranges rather than individual values. Analysis Services provides two properties to control this behavior so that you can group a set of members to a single group. These properties are DiscretizationBucketCount and DiscretizationMethod.

Follow these steps to understand the behavior:

1. Open the Dim Customer dimension in the Dimension Designer.

2. The Yearly Income attribute hierarchy of the Dim Customer dimension has the annual income amount for each customer. In order to group these values into a few members, you need to set the properties DiscretizationBucketCount and DiscretizationMethod. Set the DiscretizationBucketCount to 10 and the DiscretizationMethod to Automatic, as shown in Figure 8-23. The DiscretizationBucketCount instructs Analysis Services to generate N members in the hierarchy. The DiscretizationMethod specifies the way in which you want the customer salaries to be grouped. The Automatic setting instructs Analysis Services to find the most efficient way of grouping the values after analyzing all the values. Deploy the changes to your Analysis Services instance.

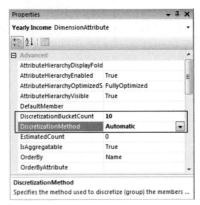

Figure 8-23

You will see the various buckets generated by Analysis Services in the Dimension Browser, as shown in Figure 8-24.

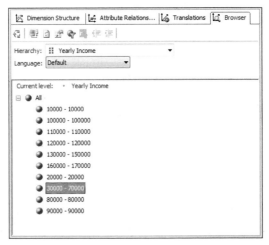

Figure 8-24

You have learned most of the commonly used properties that will help you in enhancing your dimensions and hierarchies for your business. In the next section you add intelligence to your dimensions by means of the Business Intelligence Wizard. This wizard can help you model common business logic within your dimensions and cubes without you having to write any code.

Dimension Intelligence Using the Business Intelligence Wizard

The Business Intelligence Wizard contains multiple features, but we will focus on three of the more commonly applicable ones in this chapter: Account Intelligence, Time Intelligence, and Dimension Intelligence. Analysis Services 2008 natively supports the Account dimension type in the engine. In this way, Analysis Services is able to aggregate data for members in Account dimensions based on account names. The Time Intelligence feature creates calculations for common business questions, such as year-over-year or quarter-over-quarter revenue. Analysis Services 2008 enables support for these calculations natively so that all client and custom tools can take advantage of these calculations. The Dimension Intelligence feature allows you to map your dimension to commonly used dimension types, so that client tools can discover and present them to customers in a way that is easily interpreted.

Account Intelligence

In Chapter 6 you learned about measures and aggregation functions that are specified for measures such as Sum, Count, and Distinct Count. Analysis Services 2008 supports calculations specifically for the Account dimension type so that an appropriate aggregation function is applied based on account names. In fact, there is a special type of aggregation function called ByAccount. Based on the type of account, Analysis Services can apply the right aggregation function. The Account Intelligence Wizard allows you to qualify a dimension as an Account dimension and then map the dimension to well known account types. Based on these mappings the wizard informs you of the type of aggregation function that will be applied for the account. If your Account uses a specific account type and aggregation function, you will be able to specify that at the database level. Follow these steps to map the Account dimension as a dimension of type Account and specify necessary attributes so that appropriate aggregation functions are applied:

1. Double-click the Account.dim dimension in the AnalysisServices2008Tutorial you have been working with to open it in the Dimension Designer.

2. Launch the Dimension Intelligence Wizard from the menu item Dimension ⇨ Add Business Intelligence or by clicking the first icon in the Dimension Designer. If you see the Welcome screen, click the Next button.

3. In the Choose Enhancement page select Define account intelligence as shown in Figure 8-25 and click Next.

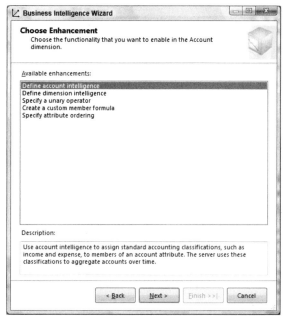

Figure 8-25

4. In the Configure Dimension Attributes page, shown in Figure 8-26, you need to define the mapping between the attributes in the current dimension named Account to the standard attributes of the Account dimension. Map the Chart of Accounts to the parent-child hierarchy Accounts; Account Name to the key attribute Account Key that contains the name of the Accounts; Account Number to the Account Code Alternate Key (Account Code Alternate Key uniquely identifies a member in the account); and the Account Type to the attribute Account Type and click Next.

Figure 8-26

The Account Type identifies the type of an account member and is used by Analysis Services to use the appropriate aggregation function for measures that have the AggregationFunction property set to ByAccount.

5. In the Define Account Intelligence page (Figure 8-27), the account types from the source table are mapped to the built-in account types in Analysis Services. If the name of account types in the source table do not directly map to the built-in account types you would need to map them correctly in this page. In this example all the account types are mapped correctly. Click Next.

Figure 8-27

6. The final page of the Business Intelligence Wizard shows the various account types along with the aggregation functions associated with accounts (Figure 8-28). Please review the aggregation functions and click Finish.

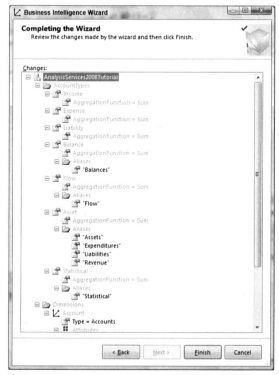

Figure 8-28

You have now successfully enhanced your Account dimension. If you look at the properties for the Account dimension you will see that the Type property is set to Accounts. The aggregation functions for various account types are pre-defined in Analysis Services. However, Analysis Services allows you the flexibility to add additional account types as well as to make changes to the AggregationFunction for the account types to suit your business needs. To make modifications, right-click the project name AnalysisServices2008Tutorial in the Solution Explorer and select Edit Database. You will see a new designer where you could make changes at the database level as shown in Figure 8-29.

Figure 8-29

As mentioned earlier the enhancement made to the Account dimension will only be applicable for measures that have their aggregation function defined as ByAccount. Open the Adventure Works DW cube. In the Cube Structure pane select the measure Amount in the Fact Finance measure group and set the Aggregation Function for this measure to ByAccount as shown in Figure 8-30. Deploy your changes to the Analysis Services instance.

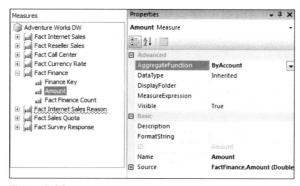

Figure 8-30

In the Cube Browser browse the measure Amount along with the Account dimension members, and notice that the right aggregation functions are used to aggregate the measure values based on the account type. However, you will notice that the member Statistical Accounts is not visible in the OWC browser. This is because accounts of type Statistical should have the value rolled up based on the aggregation function Sum; however, all the children of member Statistical Accounts have unary operator column set to ~, which means those values are not rolled up to the parent. To view the Statistical Accounts member and its children you need to define a value for members. Switch to the Calculations tab in the Cube Designer. Right-click the Script Organizer pane and select New Script Command. In the script command window enter the following statement to set the Amount for the Account member Statistical Account to be NA. Save the changes, switch to the Browser tab, and deploy the changes to your Analysis Services instance.

```
( [Account].[Accounts].&[95], [Measures].[Amount] ) = "NA"
```

If you reconnect to the Analysis Services instance in the Cube Browser, you will the Statistical Account member and its children as shown in Figure 8-31. You can see the Amount for Statistical Accounts is set to NA even though the aggregation function is Sum. This is because Analysis Services applies Unary operator evaluation on a cell after the regular rollup across the dimension (in this specific case ByAccount aggregation).

Account Level 01 ▼	Account Level 02	Account Level 03	Amount
⊟ Balance Sheet	⊟ Assets	⊞ Current Assets	450129760.81875
		⊞ Property, Plant, Equipment	37316656.2825
		⊞ Other Assets	5547024.02125
		Total	492993441.1225
	⊟ Liabilities and Owners Equity	⊞ Liabilities	178075963.27
		⊞ Owners Equity	314917477.8525
		Total	492993441.1225
	Total		0
⊟ Net Income	⊟ Operating Profit	⊞ Gross Margin	76095995.83375
		⊞ Operating Expenses	44021633.75125
		Total	32074362.0825
	⊟ Other Income and Expense	⊞ Interest Income	127449.25375
		⊞ Interest Expense	195772.35
		⊞ Gain/Loss on Sales of Asset	-156310.55
		⊞ Other Income	102483.76
		⊞ Curr Xchg Gain/(Loss)	176236.875
		Total	54086.9887499999
	⊞ Taxes		6295587.4925
	Total		25832861.57875
⊟ Statistical Accounts	⊞ Headcount		6205.875
	⊞ Units		174977.75
	⊞ Average Unit Price		640.008519997543
	⊞ Square Footage		10809187.5
	Total		NA

Figure 8-31

Because the aggregation functions specific to an Account Type are done natively with Analysis Services rather than in calculations in scripts, you should expect better query performance.

Time Intelligence

Certain calculations are frequently used in business such as calculating Year to Date and Year over Year Growth for measures such as Sales. These calculations are related to Time dimensions and can be created within the scope of the query or session as necessary. Analysis Services 2008 provides a wizard to enhance your cube to add such calculations. The Time Intelligence enhancement is a cube enhancement, because calculations such as Year to Date and Year over Year Growth are all calculated in the context of measures. Because this enhancement adds appropriate calculations to the cube as well as attributes to the Time dimension, we've decided to include it in this chapter. Follow these steps to define Time Intelligence enhancement:

1. Open the Adventure Works DW cube and switch to the Cube Structure page.

2. Launch the Business Intelligence Wizard from the menu Cube ⇨ Add Business Intelligence or by clicking the Add Business Intelligence icon (first icon in the Cube Structure tab). If you see the Welcome screen, press Next.

3. In the Choose Enhancement page select Define time intelligence as shown in Figure 8-32 and click Next.

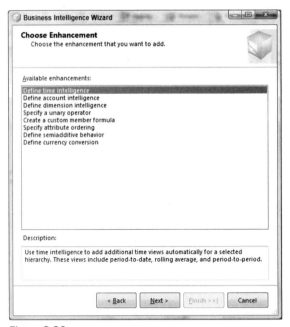

Figure 8-32

4. In the Choose Target Hierarchy and Calculations page you need to select which time calculations to use as well as the hierarchy in the Time dimension that will use those calculations. In the drop-down list box for "Use the following hierarchy to analyze time calculations:" you will see the four Time dimensions: Dim Date, Order Date, Ship Date, and Due Date. All these cube dimensions are role-playing dimensions of the database dimension Dim Date. Select the multilevel hierarchy Calendar Date in the cube dimension Order Date as shown in Figure 8-33. Select the calculations Year to Date, Year Over Year Growth, and Year Over Year Growth % and click Next.

5. In the Define Scope of Calculations page you need to select the measures for which you need the time calculations to be applied. Select the measure Sales Amount as shown in Figure 8-34. Click Next.

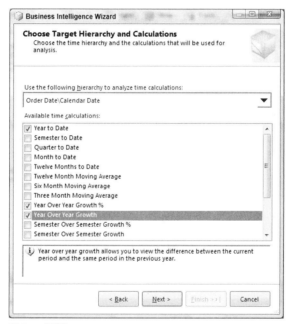

Figure 8-33

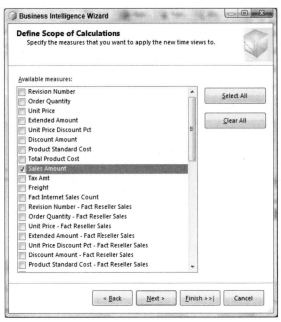

Figure 8-34

6. The final page of the wizard shows the changes to the database Time dimension Dim Date as well as the calculations as shown in Figure 8-35. You can see that the wizard adds a calculated column to the dbo_DimDate table in the DSV and adds that column as an attribute in the Dim Date dimension in addition to the calculations that will be added to the cube's script. Click the Finish button.

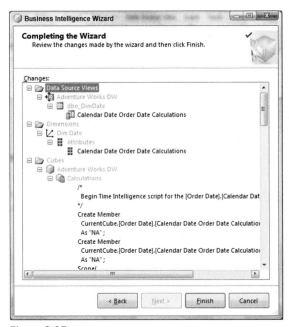

Figure 8-35

Switch to the Calculations tab of the cube and explore the calculations created by the Business Intelligence Wizard. Also look at the Named Calculation added to the DimDate table in the DSV. These will help you to understand the calculations you need to create if you didn't have the Time Intelligence enhancement. The Business Intelligence Wizard makes it easy for data warehouse designers to add the enhancements related to Time dimensions without defining and verifying the calculations by hand, which can take a considerable amount of time.

You have successfully enhanced your cube and Time dimension to analyze growth of the Sales Amount measure. To use the calculations for analysis, deploy the enhancements to your Analysis Services instance and switch to the Cube Browser. Drag and drop the measure [Sales Amount] to the data area, [Order Date].[Calendar Date hierarchy] –date.Fiscal on Rows and, [Order Date].[Calendar Date Order Date Calculations] on Columns. You will be able to see the Year to Date, Year over Year Growth, and Year over Year Growth % as shown in Figure 8-36.

Calendar Year ▼	Calendar Date Order Date Calculations ▼			
	Current Order Date	Year to Date	Year Over Year Growth %	Year Over Year Growth
	Sales Amount	Sales Amount	Sales Amount	Sales Amount
⊞ 2001	3266373.65660002	3266373.65660002		
⊞ 2002	6530343.52639994	6530343.52639994	99.93%	3263969.86979992
⊞ 2003	9791060.29770386	9791060.29770386	49.93%	3260716.77130393
⊞ 2004	9770899.74000424	9770899.74000424	-0.21%	-20160.5576996282
⊞ 2006			-100.00%	-9770899.74000424
Grand Total	29358677.2207081	NA	NA	NA

Figure 8-36

Dimension Intelligence

Analysis Services provides you a way to map your dimensions to standard dimension types such as Customer, Organization, and Currency. These mappings can help client tools that might have customized views of presenting such dimension types to end users. To map your dimensions to standard dimension types, follow these steps:

1. Open the Dim Organization dimension in the Dimension Designer.

2. Launch the Business Intelligence Wizard by clicking the Add Business Intelligence icon or from the menu Dimension ⇨ Add Business Intelligence. If you see the Welcome screen, click Next.

3. In the Choose Enhancement page select Define dimension intelligence (as shown in Figure 8-37) and click Next.

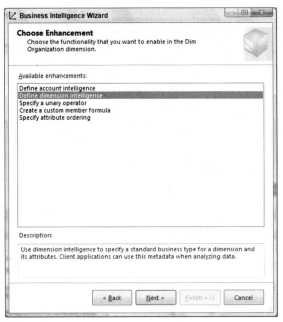

Figure 8-37

4. In the Define Dimension Intelligence page select the Dimension type as Organization as shown in Figure 8-38 and enable the Attribute Types Company and Ownership Percentage and how they map to corresponding attributes in the Dim Organization dimension and click Next.

Figure 8-38

5. The final page of the wizard shows the definitions specified in the previous page. It shows that Dim Organization is of standard dimension type Organization. This dimension contains several companies, which are represented by the attribute Organizations and the PercentOwnership is determined by the attribute Percentage Of Ownership (see Figure 8-39). Click Finish.

Figure 8-39

You have successfully defined dimension intelligence for the Dim Organization dimension. You can see that the property Type for the dimension and the attributes selected in the Dimension Intelligence enhancement have been set appropriately. We recommend you apply the Dimension Intelligence enhancement to the remaining dimensions. You will be able to view the effect of these only through client tools that utilize the dimension property Type.

Server Time Dimension

In certain data warehouses you might not have a special table for Time. However, the fact table might contain Date as a column. Analysis Services 2008 provides you the functionality of creating a Time dimension with appropriate hierarchies based on a time range. You can configure the range based on the beginning and end dates found in your fact tables. This range-based Time dimension is created in Analysis Services and is called a Server Time dimension. Once a Server Time dimension is created you can add it to the cube and specify appropriate granularity. Follow these steps to create a Server Time dimension:

1. Right-click the Dimensions folder in the Solution Explorer and select New Dimension to launch the Dimension Wizard.

2. Select the option to "Generate a time table on the server," as shown in Figure 8-40 and click Next.

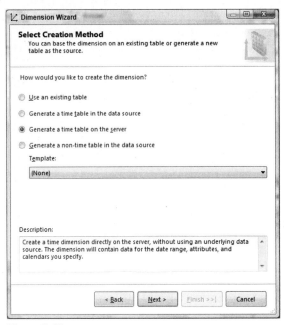

Figure 8-40

3. In the Define Time Periods page select the date ranges as shown in Figure 8-41 and the Time periods Year, Quarter, Month, Week, and Date and click Next.

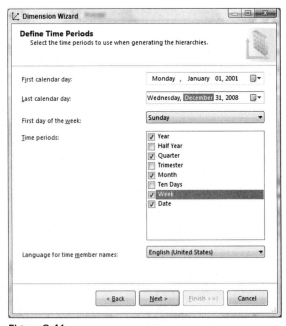

Figure 8-41

4. In the Select Calendars page select Fiscal Calendar as shown in Figure 8-42 and click Next.

Figure 8-42

5. In the final page of the wizard enter the name of the dimension as ServerTimeDimension as shown in Figure 8-43 and click Finish.

Figure 8-43

The ServerTimeDimension is now created and you can see its hierarchies and attributes in the Dimension Designer as shown in Figure 8-44. Because this dimension is created from Analysis Services instead of the DSV you will see a pane called Time Periods that lists all the periods that are available for selection. You can add additional Time Periods as attributes in the dimension. Date is the key attribute of this dimension and cannot be deleted. In fact, you'll very likely need this attribute in order to define relationships to your fact tables.

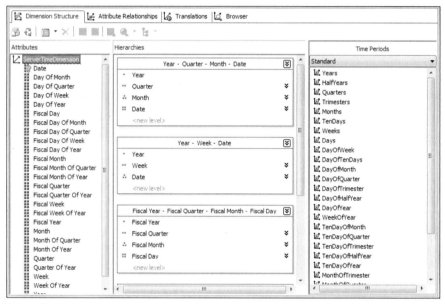

Figure 8-44

Deploy the changes to the Analysis Services instance. You can now browse the hierarchies in ServerTimeDimension as shown in Figure 8-45. The formats used for members of various levels cannot be changed, which is something to consider when opting to use this feature. You will need to add this dimension to your cubes and then manually define the relationship between it and your measure groups. Server Time dimensions are especially useful when your data source does not already contain a Time dimension and you do not have write access to the underlying data source. If you do have write access and find yourself needing to create a Time dimension, the "Generate a time table in the data source" option is far more favorable because you can subsequently customize the dimension via named calculations.

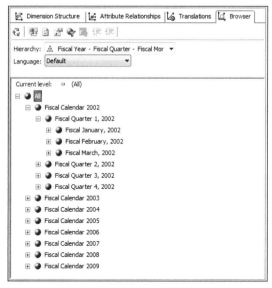

Figure 8-45

Dimension Writeback

Dimension writeback is another enhancement to dimensions and is available through the Dimension Intelligence Wizard. This is an important though rarely used feature that allows you to create or modify members in your dimension without having to go to your relational data source. Once you enable your dimension for writeback, Analysis Services provides you the functionality to add or modify members through the Dimension Browser pane. Some business scenarios where dimension writeback can be used are:

❑   When employees of an organization move from one location to another and their reporting structure in the organization and attributes of employee such as address and phone number change.

❑   When an employee's status changes due to marriage or childbirth and these changes need to be updated in the dimension.

❑   When you have an Account dimension and new types of accounts are being introduced and you need to add members to the dimension.

When you writeback data through the dimension, Analysis Services propagates the change in the data to the relational data source and does an incremental process of the dimension, such that affected members are processed. During this time, the dimension and cube will be available for querying by other users. To understand dimension writeback we will use the official Adventure Works 2008 sample Analysis Services project. Because we will make changes to the sample project, we recommend you make a copy of the sample project. The following steps show how to enable writeback on the Employee dimension and will also help you understand dimension writeback behavior by having you perform writeback operations on certain employees:

1.   Open the Employee dimension of the Adventure Works 2008 sample Analysis Services project in the Dimension Designer and look at the Properties pane.

2.   Set the dimension property WriteEnabled to True as shown in Figure 8-46.

3. If you build your project, you will see three errors in the Employee dimension that state the discretization method for the attributes Sick Leave Hours, Vacation Hours, and Base Rate needs to be set to None. Change the discretization method for the attributes Sick Leave Hours, Vacation Hours, and Base Rate to None.

> Enabling dimension writeback has several restrictions. In order to make the Employee dimension fully write-enabled, you need to make a few additional changes. You learn more about the restrictions needed to enable a dimension for writeback in Chapter 12.

4. Change the property AttributeHierarchyEnabled to False for the attributes Start Date, End Date, Hire Date, Salaried Flag, Sales Person Flag, and Pay Frequency.

5. Change the NameColumn property of Gender from GenderDesc to the column Gender.

6. Save and deploy the changes to your Analysis Services instance.

Figure 8-46

7. After deployment succeeds, BIDS should automatically switch the view from the Dimension Structure pane to the Dimension Browser pane. If not, switch to the Dimension Browser pane. Click the Member Properties icon and select the member properties Birth Date, Gender, Status, Phone, and Title, which are related to the Employees dimension.

8. Assume the employee John Wood got a new phone and you need to update his phone number. Click the Writeback toolbar button or from the top menus select Dimension ⇨ Writeback to enter writeback mode. Double-click the member property Phone for John Wood. The Marital Status field for John is now editable, as shown in Figure 8-47.

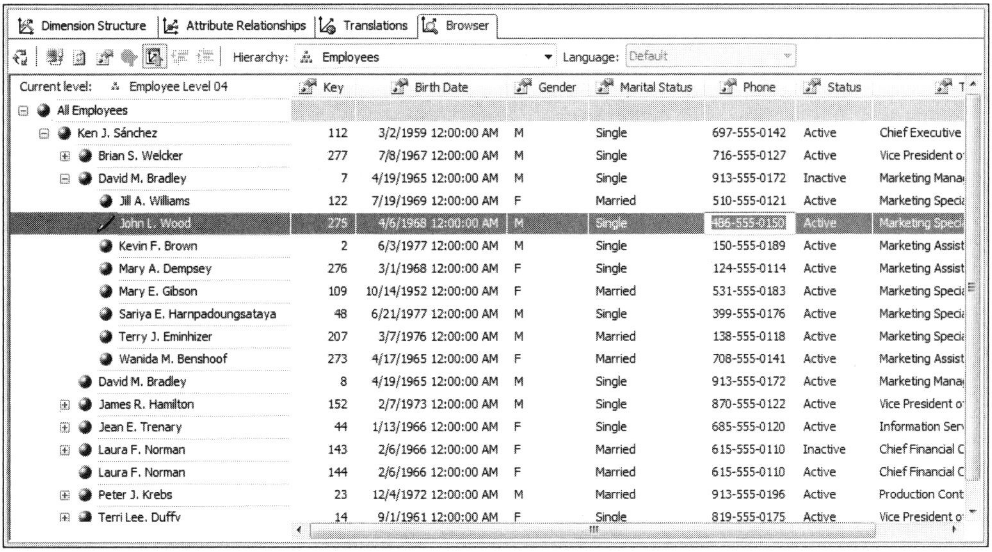

Figure 8-47

9. Change the Phone value to 486-555-0151 and then move the cursor to a different row.

At this time BIDS sends the following dimension writeback request to the Analysis Services instance. You can see that an Update statement for the cube dimension $Employee is sent to the Analysis Services instance. Note the key attribute is critical for Analysis Server to make the appropriate update. If the operation was successful, you will be able to make other operations. If there are errors, you should get feedback from the Analysis Services with the appropriate error messages. Once a dimension member is updated via writeback, Analysis Services will process the dimension and related objects.

In the following example you see an error that the writeback operation failed. If you analyze the operations on the Analysis Services instance using SQL Server Profiler (you learn about SQL Server Profiler and debugging operations on your Analysis Services in Chapter 15), you will see that the processing of the dimension Employee completes successfully, but while processing the related objects you get a failure that causes the writeback to fail. This example is just to help you understand how to enable a dimension for writeback and use the Dimension Browser to perform dimension writeback.

```
<Update xsi:type="Update" xmlns:xsd="http://www.w3.org/2001/XMLSchema"
xmlns:xsi="http://www.w3.org/2001/XMLSchema-instance"
xmlns:ddl2="http://schemas.microsoft.com/analysisservices/2003/engine/2"
xmlns:ddl2_2="http://schemas.microsoft.com/analysisservices/2003/engine/2/2"
xmlns:ddl100_100="http://schemas.microsoft.com/analysisservices/2008/engine/100/100"
xmlns="http://schemas.microsoft.com/analysisservices/2003/engine">
  <Object>
    <Database>Adventure Works DW 2008</Database>
    <Cube>$Employee</Cube>
    <Dimension>Employee</Dimension>
  </Object>
  <Attributes>
    <Attribute>
      <AttributeName>Phone</AttributeName>
      <Keys>
```

(continued)

(continued)

```
            <Key xsi:type="xsd:string">486-555-0151</Key>
          </Keys>
      </Attribute>
    </Attributes>
    <Where>
      <Attribute>
        <AttributeName>Employee</AttributeName>
        <Keys>
          <Key xsi:type="xsd:int">275</Key>
        </Keys>
      </Attribute>
    </Where>
  </Update>
```

You have successfully learned to enable a dimension for writeback in the Employee dimension. You can perform additional operations such as creating new members, moving a member along with descendants, and deleting members through dimension writeback. These are operations that update the members or properties of members on dimensions, and you learn these operations with examples in detail in Chapter 12. You should be aware that you cannot change the values of the existing key attributes in the dimension because the key attribute is used by the Analysis Services instance to perform the writeback operation.

Summary

You have experienced more chapter flashbacks than usual here, but that merely suggests certain loose ends are getting tied together and certain mental connections are being reinforced. In this chapter you learned about custom rollups using the common business concept of depreciation, which addresses the nature of value change over time. Any type of change over time is a recurrent theme in business intelligence, and this chapter discussed use of the Time Intelligence enhancement, which can be used on cubes with a Time dimension to provide views by time period. Similarly, the Account Intelligence enhancement was explored; it maps known business entities like Income, Expense, Asset, and Liability to the dimensions in your cube so that appropriate rollup can be done for accounts natively in Analysis Services.

The Account Intelligence enhancement also allows you to add additional accounts and change aggregation functions for specific accounts based on your business requirements. The Server Time dimension helps you to define range-based Time dimensions quickly when there is no time table in your data source. The Dimension Wizard also provides you with the ability to create the standard dimension types such as Customers, Organizations, Time, Currency, and so on, along with appropriate attributes and hierarchies, and generates appropriate schemas in your data source, which is not discussed in this chapter. You would need to populate these tables with appropriate data before processing the dimensions. We leave it you to explore this option from the Dimension Wizard by selecting the option to "Generate a non-time table in the data source." Finally, dimension writeback was discussed and you learned how data can be written back to the original relational table, and that an incremental process is kicked off so that related members in the dimension are processed along with the corresponding cube. Speaking of cubes, that is what the next chapter is about. Now that you have learned about dimension enhancement, it is time to move on to advanced cube design!

9

Advanced Cube Design

You landed the job! You got the coveted "Cube Enhancement Analyst" position, which coincidentally requires you to read this chapter before starting. But are you even qualified to read this chapter? The answer is yes if you meet the following criteria: You learned about creating and browsing a cube in Chapter 6, and in Chapter 8 you learned about enhancing dimensions by using special dimension properties and by adding business intelligence — oh, and some understanding of MDX, which you learned in Chapter 3, wouldn't hurt either. Please review those topics if you are not confident in your understanding of them. Indeed, this chapter builds on what you have learned already, focusing on enhancements to your cube in support of specific business requirements. The focus here is on working with measures in your cube by modifying properties to change how measures appear in cubes and how values are aggregated. There is also a focus on using enhanced dimension relationships. You also work with Actions and Key Performance Indicators (KPIs), features that add functionality that help end users view and interpret data efficiently. To implement many of the techniques described in this chapter, you use advanced MDX. In some cases, you can use the Business Intelligence Wizard to simplify the addition of complex MDX. Once you have the design techniques mastered, attention is turned to techniques for managing scalability through partitioning, assigning storage modes, and building aggregations.

If this book were the movie *The Matrix*, now is the time when Morpheus would hold out a red pill in one hand and a blue pill in the other, and say, "You put the book down and take the blue pill — the story ends, you wake up in your bed and believe whatever you want to believe. You take the red pill — and I show you how to build powerful cubes." To be honest, this chapter might not be as dramatic as all that, but it will bring together many of those gnarly concepts you have learned so you can fine-tune the process of turning data into information (the essential theme of this book). At the risk of belaboring the point, this chapter really is central, not just in the sense it is near the middle of the book, but in the sense it will help you understand some of the more important features in Analysis Services 2008. In this chapter, you use the AnalysisServices2008Tutorial project you have been enhancing in previous chapters as well as the Enterprise version of the Adventure Works 2008 Analysis Services project included with Microsoft SQL Server 2008 (via Codeplex.com) to understand how to apply advanced design techniques to cubes. So, gear up and get ready for a deep dive into the core of Analysis Services.

Measure Groups and Measures

In Chapter 6, you learned about measure groups and measures within a cube. To recap, a cube can contain one or more measure groups and each measure group can contain one or more measures. You also learned about the various aggregation functions for each measure, and reviewed some MDX examples of how measure values are rolled up while browsing the cube. In this section, you learn how to use an MDX function to simplify querying measure groups and how to group measures within a measure group to help users navigate them more easily. You also learn how to use properties to control how measure values are aggregated when unrelated to dimensions in the same query or when performing currency conversions. Lastly, you learn how to reuse measure groups in multiple cubes.

With Analysis Services 2008 it is quite possible to end up with a cube containing several measure groups. If you open the Adventure Works cube in the Enterprise version of the Adventure Works DW 2008 sample project, you will have measures as shown in Figure 9-1.

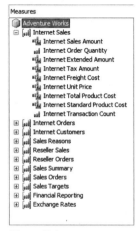

Figure 9-1

If you expand each measure group, you can see that most measure groups contain multiple measures. For example, the Internet Sales measure group has 9 measures and the Reseller Sales measure group has 11. Often, business analysis questions are targeted at measures within a single measure group rather than all the measures within a cube. One way to write an MDX query targeting a specific measure group is to include each measure one by one. For instance, if you want all visible regular measures (that is, no calculated measures and no measures with the Visible property set to False) within the Internet Sales measure group, your MDX query could look like this:

```
SELECT
{[Measures].[Internet Sales Amount],
 [Measures].[Internet Order Quantity],
 [Measures].[Internet Extended Amount],
 [Measures].[Internet Tax Amount],
 [Measures].[Internet Freight Cost],
 [Measures].[Internet Total Product Cost],
 [Measures].[Internet Standard Product Cost]
} ON COLUMNS
FROM [Adventure Works]
```

It is time-consuming to form an MDX query that includes each measure of the measure group within the query because you need to drag and drop each measure individually or type the name of each measure into the query. Fortunately, an MDX function called MeasureGroupMeasures is provided to retrieve all the measures within a measure group. The following query shows how to use this function to return the same results as the preceding query:

```
SELECT MeasureGroupMeasures("Internet Sales") ON 0
FROM [Adventure Works]
```

Lots of measures in a single measure group can also be overwhelming for end users. Another feature can be used to create logical groupings of measures within each measure group so users can locate measures more easily while browsing a cube. Simply assign the same value to the DisplayFolder property of each measure (in the same measure group) that you want to group together.

Not only do you need to consider measure groups and how measures appear in a cube, but also consider how they interact with dimensions. For example, when you have multiple measure groups within a single cube, you will find that certain dimensions do not have relationships with certain measure groups. Recall from Chapter 6 that relationships between dimensions and measure groups are defined on the Dimension Usage tab of the Cube Designer. If you look at Dimension Usage in the Adventure Works cube of the Enterprise version of the Adventure Works DW 2008 Analysis Services sample project, you see there is no relationship between the Internet Sales measure group and the Reseller dimension. A query that includes a measure from the Internet Sales measure group and members from the Reseller dimension, as shown in the following code, returns the same value for each Reseller member — the value for the All member:

```
SELECT {[Measures].[Internet Extended Amount]} ON 0,
[Reseller].[Reseller Type].MEMBERS ON 1
FROM [Adventure Works]
```

If users find this result confusing, you can override this default behavior by changing the value of the IgnoreUnrelatedDimensions property for the measure group, as shown in Figure 9-2.

If the IgnoreUnrelatedDimensions property is set to False, a query that includes a measure with a dimension having no relationship to it will return null values. If, for example, you change the IgnoreUnrelatedDimensions property of the Internet Sales measure group to False and then deploy the project, the preceding MDX query returns null cell values for each member of the Reseller dimension except the All Resellers member.

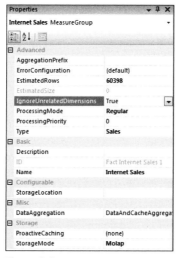

Figure 9-2

IgnoreUnrelatedDimensions is a property that modifies the functionality of the ValidMeasure MDX function. The ValidMeasure function returns a cell value corresponding to the All member for a dimension that does not have a relationship with the current measure. In other words, the dimension is not represented by a foreign key column in the fact table containing the current measure.

To continue the previous example, with the IgnoreUnrelatedDimensions property for the Internet Sales measure group set to False, you can execute the following MDX query to see that the cell values for all the members in the Reseller Type hierarchy have the same value for measure x, whereas the real measure Internet Extended Amount has null values:

```
WITH MEMBER measures.x AS ValidMeasure(([Measures].[Internet Extended Amount],
[Reseller].[Reseller Type]))
SELECT { measures.x,[Measures].[Internet Extended Amount]} ON 0,
[Reseller].[Reseller Type].MEMBERS ON 1
FROM [Adventure Works]
```

Another important measure property to know about is MeasureExpression. On the Cube Structure tab of the Cube Designer, click the Internet Sales Amount measure in the Internet Sales measure group to see its properties, as shown in Figure 9-3. A valid value for MeasureExpression is an MDX expression that typically includes the product (multiplication operator) or ratio (division operator) of two measures (or constant). This type of expression is used for currency conversions or when aggregating values with many-to-many dimensions, which are both discussed later in this chapter. When you specify a measure expression, Analysis Services 2008 evaluates the expression for each dimension member first and then aggregates the values across the dimension.

Measures used in the MDX expression can be from the same measure group or from different measure groups. In Figure 9-3, for example, the MeasureExpression divides Internet Sales Amount, from the Internet Sales measure group, by Average Rate, from the Exchange Rates measure group. The Exchange Rates measure group contains the Average Rate and End of Day Rate to be used for currency conversions.

Figure 9-3

If you look at the Dimension Usage tab of the Cube Designer, you can see both measure groups, Internet Sales and Exchange Rates, have a direct relationship with the Date dimension. You can also see that dimension Destination Currency is directly related to the Exchange Rate measure group, but has a many-to-many relationship with the Internet Sales measure group. These relationships are required when you store transaction data, such as sales amounts, in the fact table using the local currency, but need the ability to summarize that data in reports using a different currency. For instance, you have sales recorded in the fact table in Mexican pesos, but you need to report sales in Euros.

Because exchange rates vary over time, you might choose to average the exchange rate at the day or month level (depending on your business situation) to calculate the total sales in a specific currency. In the Adventure Works cube, the Average Rate measure is stored in the fact table at the day level. Because it's defined as a semi-additive measure, which you learn more about later in this chapter, its value is determined by calculating the average of the children of the current member of the Time dimension. That is, if the current member is a month member, the average rate is calculated by averaging the Average Rate measure for all days in that month.

You can best see the effect of Average Rate on Internet Sales Amount by browsing the cube. Place Destination Currency on rows, and add the measures Average Rate and Internet Sales Amount as shown in Figure 9-4.

In Figure 9-4 you can see the U.S. dollar is the base currency because it has an Average Rate of 1. Please note that the Internet Sales Amount for the other currencies is not derived from the division of Internet Sales Amount shown in U.S. dollars by the destination currency's Average Rate. The MeasureExpression defined for Internet Sales Amount causes Analysis Services to calculate a value for each individual transaction, dividing Internet Sales Amount in U.S. dollars by the Average Rate for that day, and then aggregating the calculated values to show the Internet Sales Amount in the desired currency. (You learn later in this chapter how the individual transactions were converted to U.S. dollars before the MeasureExpression is applied.)

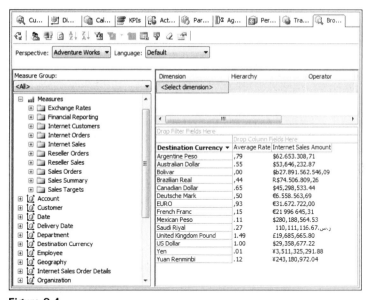

Figure 9-4

Once you have a measure group and its measures designed just right, you can add that measure group into another cube. With Analysis Services 2008, you can use the Linked Object Wizard to add a measure group from another cube in the same database, a cube on the same server, or a cube in any other Analysis Services instance. You can launch the wizard from either the Cube Structure tab, as shown in Figure 9-5, or use the New Linked Object icon in the Cube Structure or Dimension Usage tabs of the cube editor.

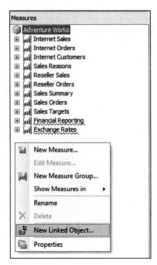

Figure 9-5

Using the wizard, you can define a data source for the Analysis Services database containing the measure group you want to include in your current cube, and then select the desired measure group from the list of available objects. The Linked Measure Group Wizard is self-explanatory and we leave it to you to add a linked measure group.

Take a look at the Mined Customers cube in the Adventure Works DW sample project to see how all measure groups in a cube can be linked measure groups, as shown in Figure 9-6. Linked measure groups are identified by a linking chain icon.

After adding a linked measure group, you still need to define the right relationships between the dimensions in the cube and the linked measure group. By using a linked measure group, you have access to data in the source cube without the maintenance overhead of multiple separate measure groups for the same data.

Figure 9-6

> You can have a cube where all the real measures are hidden. All the measures exposed to the end users are calculated measures. Some Analysis Services customers design their cubes this way to model specific business requirements.

Adding and Enhancing Dimensions

Dimensions are an integral part of a cube. In this section, you learn about specific properties that affect a dimension's behavior within a cube as well as special types of relationships that can be defined between a dimension and a measure group. These features allow you to address special business requirements and thereby enhance overall analytical capabilities.

When you create a dimension within an Analysis Services 2008 database, you are actually creating a *database dimension*, which can be shared across multiple cubes within the same database or used multiple times within a single cube. Each instance of a database dimension within a cube is called a *cube dimension*. Right-click within the Dimensions pane of the Cube Structure page as shown in Figure 9-7 to add a new cube dimension.

Figure 9-7

For each cube dimension, you can selectively exclude certain hierarchies or attributes by modifying properties. In the Dimensions pane on the Cube Structure tab, select the hierarchy or the attribute to be hidden and then change the applicable property in the Properties window to False. If you want to hide a hierarchy, use the Visible property. To hide an attribute, use the AttributeHierarchyVisible property.

Another important property of a cube dimension is AllMemberAggregationUsage. This property is associated with the cube dimension object itself. Changing the value of this property affects how Analysis Services builds aggregations to improve query performance. You learn more about cube dimension properties for hierarchies and attributes in Chapter 14.

Most changes to database dimensions, such as the addition or deletion of attributes or hierarchies as well as changes to most properties, are automatically reflected in the corresponding cube dimensions. However, certain changes, such as renaming a database dimension, will not result in a similar change to the cube dimension. In such circumstances you could either delete the existing cube dimension and then re-add the database dimension within the cube, or simply rename the cube dimension.

As soon as you add a cube dimension, Analysis Services attempts to detect relationships based on the DSV and to create appropriate relationships between the newly added dimension and the existing measure groups in the cube. You should switch to the Dimension Usage tab of the Cube Designer to verify that relationships between dimensions and measure groups were detected correctly.

The most common type of relationship between a dimension and a measure group is a regular relationship, but several other types could be defined: referenced, fact, many-to-many, data mining, and no relationship. You reviewed regular and referenced relationships in depth in Chapter 6. In this chapter, you learned how to use the IgnoreUnrelatedDimensions property to determine whether you see values or nulls when there is no relationship between a measure group and a dimension. The following sections discuss the remaining three relationship types.

Fact Dimensions

A fact relationship is a relationship that exists between a dimension and a measure group that are both based on the same relational table. In the Adventure Works 2008 Analysis Services sample project, the Internet Sales Order Details dimension and the Internet Sales measure group retrieve data from the FactInternetSales relational table. Fact dimensions are typically created to support detail-level reporting or scenarios in which the database does not have a well-structured star or snowflake schema but instead contains all information in a single table. Figure 9-8 shows the fact relationship defined between the measure group Internet Sales and the dimension Internet Sales Order Details.

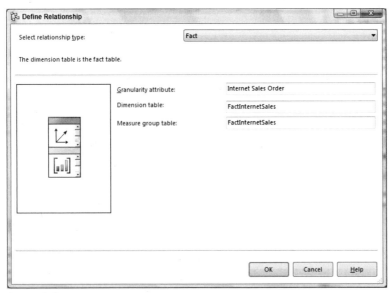

Figure 9-8

To define a fact relationship, switch to the Dimension Usage tab, and click the cell that intersects the measure group and the dimension. When you select the Fact relationship type, the Define Relationship dialog automatically assigns the key attribute of the dimension as the granularity attribute. You can define a fact relationship only when the dimension and measure group are based on the same table; a validation in the Define Relationship dialog enforces this requirement. Otherwise, a fact relationship is very similar to a regular relationship. For example, browsing the dimension with this measure group, whether in a Cube Browser or with your own custom MDX, will look similar to browsing data in a regular relationship. If that's the case why do we need a fact relationship type? Two reasons:

1. Specific optimizations are done by Analysis Services during Drillthrough (a command to get detailed data from your cube which is discussed later in this chapter) when a fact relationship is defined between a measure group and a ROLAP dimension.

2. Certain client tools can present data from this relationship in a way that makes it easier for users to interpret the data during analysis.

Many-to-Many Dimensions

Analysis Services 2008 includes support for a relationship type called many-to-many. You were introduced to many-to-many dimensions during the discussion of measure expressions. You can recognize a many-to-many relationship when a single fact row is associated with multiple members in the dimension table. Figure 9-9 shows an example of a many-to-many relationship that exists in the Adventure Works DW 2008 Analysis Services sample database.

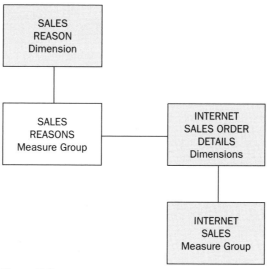

Figure 9-9

As you learned in the previous section, the Internet Sales measure group is related to the Internet Sales Order Details dimension through a fact relationship. Figure 9-9 adds new relationships — the Sales Reasons measure group is related to the Sales Reason dimension through a regular relationship and to the Internet Sales Order Details dimension through a regular relationship. In other words, each line item in a sales order (in the Internet Sales measure group as a single fact row) can have one or more sales reasons (in the Sales Reason dimension). An *intermediate dimension*, Internet Sales Order Details, joins the two measure groups, one of which is an *intermediate fact table*. This intermediate fact table, Sales Reasons (the measure group) joins the intermediate dimension to the many-to-many dimension, Sales Reason (the dimension). When Analysis Services aggregates the values for each many-to-many dimension member, it aggregates the values in the measure group based on the set of distinct regular dimension members related to the current many-to-many dimension member. As a result, data is aggregated to each level exactly once. For example, consider a sales order that has two different sales reasons A and B. If you request Internet Sales measure values for that sales order by Sales Reason — specifically members A, B, and All — you will see that the measure values are aggregated to the "All" member exactly once because there is only one distinct sales order related to the All member. Similarly, there is only one distinct sales order related to A and to B, so all three members will display the same values in this example.

Many-to-many relationships are common in data warehouses, and now, you have the ability to model and analyze the data from many-to-many dimensions. You can use a many-to-many relationship to perform currency conversion as you saw previously in this chapter when learning about measure expressions. Many-to-many relationships can be modeled for any schema that contains at least one common dimension between the regular measure group and the intermediate measure group. If there are multiple common dimensions between the measure groups, Analysis Services aggregates values for each distinct combination of members in those dimensions related to the current many-to-many dimension member.

On the Dimension Usage tab, click the cell that intersects the measure group and the dimension for which you want to define a many-to-many relationship. In the Adventure Works sample cube, take a look at the many-to-many relationship between the Sales Reason dimension and the Internet Sales measure group. You can see the relationship requires the intermediate measure group Sales Reasons, as shown in Figure 9-10.

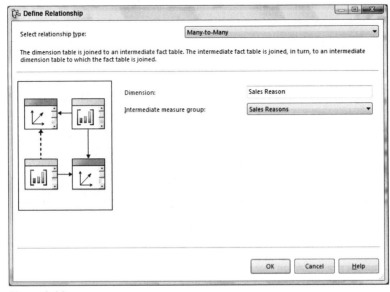

Figure 9-10

With this relationship defined, you can browse the many-to-many dimension Sales Reason along with the Internet Sales measure group, as shown in Figure 9-11.

Reason Type ▾	Sales Reason	Internet Sales Amount	Internet Order Quantity
⊟ Marketing	Television Advertisement	$27,475.82	730
	Total	$27,475.82	730
⊟ Other	Manufacturer	$5,998,122.10	1,818
	Other	$248,483.34	3,653
	Price	$10,975,842.56	47,733
	Quality	$5,549,896.77	1,551
	Review	$1,694,881.98	1,640
	Total	$18,678,948.02	51,314
⊟ Promotion	On Promotion	$6,361,828.95	7,390
	Total	$6,361,828.95	7,390
Grand Total		$29,358,677.22	60,398

Figure 9-11

The sum of the Internet Order Quantity values for the various sales reasons grouped with Sales Reason Type Other is 56,395, which is greater than the Total shown for Other, which is 51,314. Because a many-to-many relationship is defined between the Internet Sales measure group, which includes Internet Order Quantity, and the Sales Reason dimension, the aggregated measure values correctly use the distinct members to avoid double-counting

Data Mining Dimensions

The technical definition of data mining is the process of automatic or semi-automatic discovery of hidden patterns in large data sets. Several data mining algorithms are available to discover different kinds of patterns. Some data mining algorithms predict future values based on the patterns detected in historical values. For example, you can first classify customers of a retail store as Platinum, Gold, Silver, and Bronze based on selected attributes, such as income, number of children, and so on. You can then use data mining to automatically classify new store customers based on the patterns discovered in existing customer data. Additionally, a retail store could decide to boost sales by providing coupons to targeted customers based on the buying patterns of existing customers. Analysis Services 2008 supports several data mining algorithms, which you learn about in detail in Chapter 16.

In Analysis Services 2008, the UDM is tightly integrated with data mining features. You can, for example, create a data mining model not only from a relational data source, but also from an existing cube. When a data mining model is created from a cube, you can also create a data mining dimension from the mining model. You can then add this new dimension to a new cube in order to perform analysis of cube data according to the data mining classification.

Figure 9-12 shows the relationship definition for a data mining relationship. The target dimension, Clustered Customers, is a dimension that was derived from a data mining model. The source dimension, Customers, is the dimension from which the data mining model was originally created.

If you open the Mined Customers cube in the Adventure Works 2008 Analysis Services sample project and switch to the Dimension Usage tab, you can see the data mining relationship defined between the Cluster Customers dimension and Internet Sales measure group. Open the Cube Browser to view the breakdown of Internet sales based on the Clustered Customers dimension as shown in Figure 9-13. This dimension represents the data mining model's classification of all members in the Customers dimension into 10 different clusters. To see the characteristics of each cluster, you need to review the mining model. By combining data mining results with cube data, you can make specific business decisions. For example, using the sales information shown in Figure 9-13 in combination with the characteristics of clusters defined by the data mining model, you could decide to boost sales by developing promotions or other incentives for a specific set of customers.

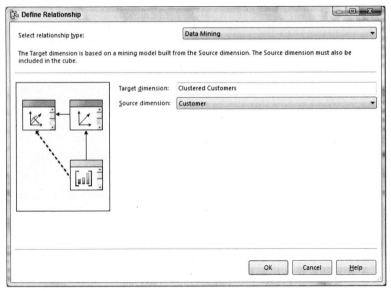

Figure 9-12

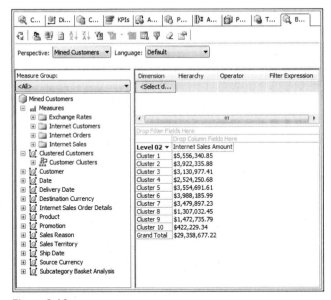

Figure 9-13

Role-Playing Dimensions

A role-playing dimension is a database dimension that acts as multiple dimensions within a cube. Instead of requiring the creation of two database dimensions that serve different purposes but depend on the same data source table, a single database dimension can be used to create separate cube dimensions. For example, if you have a geography dimension as a database dimension, you can add it to a cube as Customer Geography and Employee Geography cube dimensions. Similarly, you can have one Time dimension called Date, and then you can add Ship Date and Received Date as cube dimensions. In these examples, Geography and Date dimensions are role-playing dimensions because they can play different roles within the same cube.

Figure 9-14 shows how the Date dimension is used as a role-playing dimension in the Adventure Works cube of the Adventure Works DW 2008 Analysis Services sample project. The Date dimension plays the role of three date dimensions: Date, Ship Date, and Delivery Date. When a dimension plays multiple roles in a single measure group, the fact table for the measure group contains one foreign key column for each role, each of which must have a relationship to a single dimension table defined in the DSV.

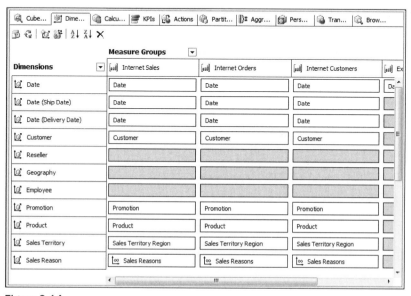

Figure 9-14

Adding Calculations to Your Cube

In Chapter 3, you learned about the calculation model in Analysis Services 2008 and the concept of MDX scripts. In Chapter 6, you learned how to use the Calculations tab in the Cube Designer for creating calculated members and named sets. In this section, you learn how to review and test cell calculations.

You use the Calculations tab in the Cube Designer to define all calculations, which then become part of the MDX script of your cube. In this section, you continue using the Adventure Works DW 2008 Analysis Services sample project to explore the functionality available in the Calculations tab.

The following steps show how to review the definitions of some of the calculations defined in the Adventure Works sample cube and how to verify the results as the calculations are applied to the specific cells:

1. Open the Adventure Works DW 2008 Analysis Services sample project and, if you haven't done so already, deploy the project to the Analysis Services instance on your machine. If you have a default Analysis Services instance, you can deploy the project without changing the project properties. However, if you have installed named instances of Analysis Services and SQL Server you must change the project's deployment properties to target the right instance of Analysis Services and you must also change the relational data source in the project to point to your SQL Server instance.

2. Open the Adventure Works cube and click the Calculations tab. You will see all the calculated members, named sets, and calculations specified within the MDX script as shown in Figure 9-15. The first command selected in the Script Organizer, which is also the first command in the MDX script, is the Calculate statement. The Calculate statement is automatically added to each cube created by the Cube Wizard. The Calculate statement can be anywhere within the MDX script, but it must be included, so be careful not to delete it. You can also add comments to the MDX script to make it easier to understand the purpose of the calculations by inserting your comments between the /* and */ characters as shown in Figure 9-15. All comments within the MDX script are detected by the Cube Designer and converted to a green font color for easier reading.

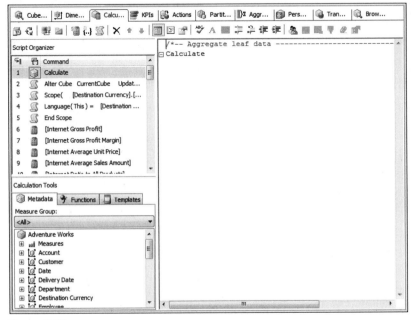

Figure 9-15

3. The Calculations tab has two views: the Form View and the Script View. Figure 9-15 shows the Form View in which you can select a command listed in the Script Organizer pane to see its definition independently. Figure 9-16 shows the Script View, which displays when you click the Script View button in the Calculations toolbar. In Script View, you can see all the commands together in the script pane.

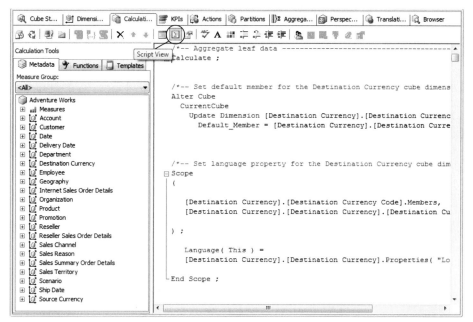

Figure 9-16

4. Click the Form View icon on the Calculations toolbar, scroll through the Script Organizer pane, and click the second Scope statement. As you can see in Figure 9-17, when you select an item in the Script Organizer, the corresponding script displays on the right side. This Scope command restricts the cube space to Sales Amount Quota for Fiscal Quarters in Fiscal Year 2005.

5. Click the statement that appears below the Scope statement in the Script Organizer to see the following assignment statement, which allocates the Sales Amount Quota for the Fiscal Year 2005 based on 135 percent of the Sales Amount Quota in the Fiscal Year 2004:

```
This = ParallelPeriod
        (
            [Date].[Fiscal].[Fiscal Year], 1,
            [Date].[Fiscal].CurrentMember
        ) * 1.35
```

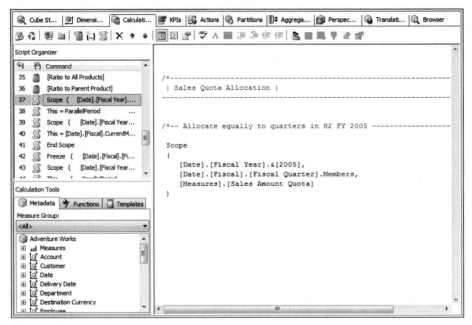

Figure 9-17

6. As you add statements and commands to the MDX script, you should test the script to ensure the affected cells or members get the correct values. One way to test an MDX expression is to use it in a query and evaluate the results. This approach can become time-consuming, especially when you have complex expressions. A better alternative is to use the debugging capabilities of the Analysis Services Cube Designer, in which you can quickly validate results. Because a cube's MDX script is just a sequence of MDX statements, you can evaluate each statement separately by using the Cube Designer's debugging feature. Debugging your MDX script is similar to debugging application code. You can set breakpoints to evaluate a sequence of MDX statements that precede the statement specified as a breakpoint. To try the debugging capabilities, click the Script View icon in the Calculations toolbar, scroll through the list of MDX statements to locate the second Scope statement in the MDX script, and set a breakpoint as shown in Figure 9-18. Set the break point by clicking in the margin to the left of the Scope statement. The breakpoint appears as a solid red circle as shown in Figure 9-18. Once you have set the breakpoint, you see the statement being highlighted in red.

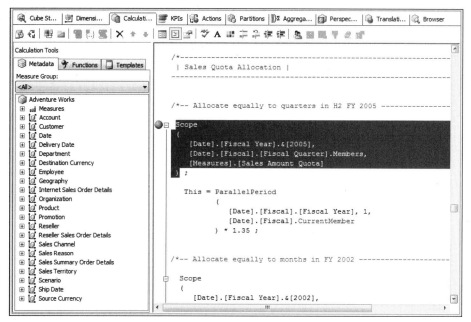

Figure 9-18

7. To start debugging mode, press the F10 function key from the Calculations tab in the cube editor. After deploying the database, the Cube Designer switches to debugging mode, which divides the script pane into two sections, as shown in Figure 9-19. Standard Visual Studio environment debugging windows, such as Autos, Locals, and Breakpoints, among others, might also automatically open when debugging starts. Close these windows to allocate more screen space to the script pane. The top half of the script pane now contains the MDX script with the breakpoint statement highlighted in yellow. The bottom half now includes an Office Web Components Pivot Table control loaded as well as several sub-panes labeled MDX1, MDX2, MDX3, and MDX4. The Pivot Table is useful for browsing the dimensions and measures as you execute the statements. The MDX panes 1 through 4 can be used to execute regular MDX queries during the debugging session.

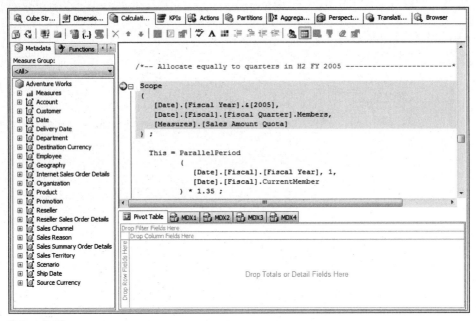

Figure 9-19

8.   The debugger stopped execution of the MDX script at the statement with the breakpoint. You can monitor the effect of the subsequent statements by placing the Fiscal hierarchy of the Date dimension and the Sales Amount Quota measure in the Pivot Table, as shown in Figure 9-20. Expand the Fiscal Years 2004 and 2005 to see the Fiscal Semesters.

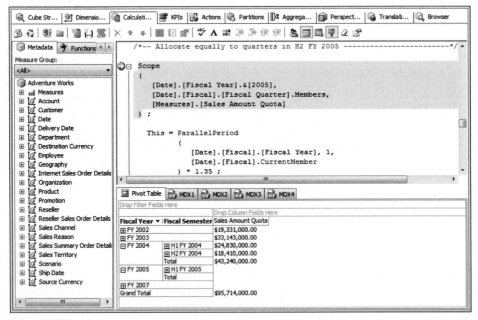

Figure 9-20

9. The next statement, which is the assignment MDX expression to specify the Sales Amount Quota for the Fiscal Year 2005, is now ready for execution. Press F10 to step through the Scope statement. The assignment statement is now highlighted with a yellow background, shown in Figure 9-21, but has not yet been executed.

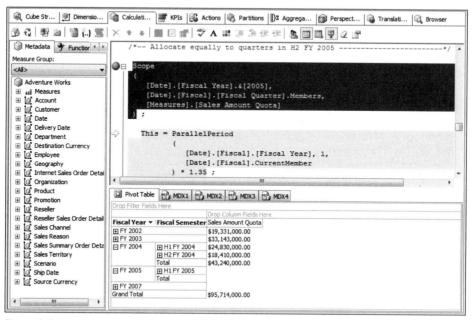

Figure 9-21

10. Execute the assignment statement by pressing the F10 key, which executes one statement at a time. As soon as the assignment statement is executed, the Sales Amount Quota value for the year 2005 changed from empty to 18,539,550.00. The cells corresponding to Fiscal Year 2005 and the Grand Total are both affected by the assignment statement and are the highlighted cells, as shown in Figure 9-22. You can use the fifth icon from the right in the Calculations tab, Highlight Changed Cells, to toggle the behavior to highlight cells.

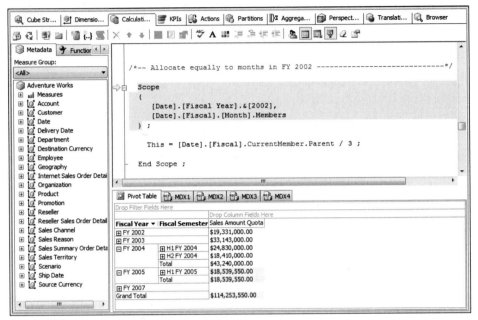

Figure 9-22

You have now successfully tested the MDX script calculations you learned about in Chapter 3. You can also use the MDX1 through MDX4 panes for additional debugging. For example, before stepping into the statement that assigns values to the quarters of year 2005 you can send the following MDX query to query the current values for 2005 quarters:

```
SELECT [Measures].[Sales Amount Quota] ON 0,
[Date].[Fiscal].[Fiscal Quarter].MEMBERS ON 1
FROM [Adventure Works]
```

Just click one of the MDX tabs as shown in Figure 9-23, type the MDX query, and click the Execute MDX button. The Execute MDX button is the button containing the green arrow. The MDX query executes in the current context of debugging, retrieving the cells specified by the query and displaying the results in the MDX pane.

Execute MDX

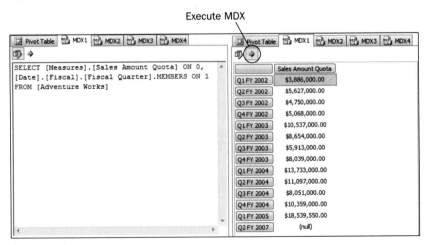

Figure 9-23

If you currently have one of the MDX panes open during execution of the MDX script, the results of the executed statements are immediately reflected in the results. Figure 9-24 shows the results of the MDX query before and after the execution of the MDX script to assign a sales quota for the year 2005.

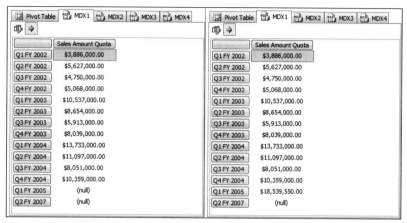

Figure 9-24

The debugger also allows you to simulate a different user during execution. Click the Change User icon (sixth icon from the right on the Calculations toolbar) to change to a different user or a role when you need to verify the results of an MDX script with appropriate security for your end users. Obviously, you don't want users to view data that they aren't supposed to see.

Now that you have learned how to use and debug calculations in Analysis Services, you're ready to learn about two other important types of cube enhancements, KPIs and Actions.

Key Performance Indicators (KPIs)

Key Performance Indicators, most often called KPIs, may also be referred to as Key Success Indicators (KSIs). Regardless of what you call them, they can help your organization define and measure quantitative progress toward organizational goals. Business users often manage organizational performance using KPIs. Many business application vendors now provide performance management tools (namely dashboard applications) that collect KPI data from source systems and present KPI results graphically to end business users. Microsoft Office Excel 2007 and Microsoft Office PerformancePoint Server 2007 are examples of applications that can leverage the KPI capabilities of Analysis Services 2008.

Analysis Services provides a framework for categorizing the KPI MDX expressions for use with the business data stored in cubes. Each KPI uses a predefined set of data roles — actual, goal, trend, status, and weight — to which MDX expressions are assigned. Only the metadata for the KPIs is stored by an Analysis Services instance, whereas a set of MDX functions is available that allows applications to easily retrieve KPI values from cubes using this metadata.

The Cube Designer provided in Business Intelligence Development Studio (BIDS) also lets cube developers easily create and test KPIs. You learn how to do this in the following section. Figure 9-25 shows the KPIs in the Adventure Works cube using the KPI browser in the Cube Designer. You can get to the KPI browser by clicking the KPI tab in the Cube Designer and then clicking the KPI browser icon (second button in the toolbar in the KPI tab).

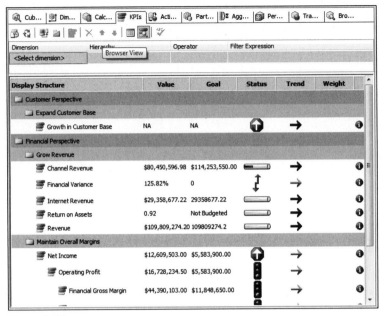

Figure 9-25

KPI Creation

Consider the following scenario: The Adventure Works sales management team wants to monitor the sales revenue for the fiscal year. Sales revenue for prior fiscal years is available in the Adventure Works cube. The management team has identified the goal of 15 percent growth for sales revenue year over year. If current sales revenue is over 95 percent of the goal, sales revenue performance is satisfactory. If, however, the sales revenue is within 85 percent to 95 percent of the goal, management must be alerted. If the sales revenue drops under 85 percent of the goal, management must take immediate action to change the trend. These alerts and calls to action are commonly associated with the use of KPIs. The management team is interested in the trends associated with sales revenue; if the sales revenue is 20 percent higher than expected, the sales revenue status is great news and should be surfaced as well — it's not all doom and gloom.

Use the following steps to design the KPIs for the sales management team:

1. Open the Enterprise version of the Adventure Works 2008 Analysis Services sample project.

2. Double-click the Adventure Works cube in the Solution Explorer to open the Cube Designer.

3. Click the KPIs tab to open the KPI editor.

4. Click the New KPI button in the KPI toolbar to open a template for a new KPI. As you can see in Figure 9-26, there are several properties to fill in.

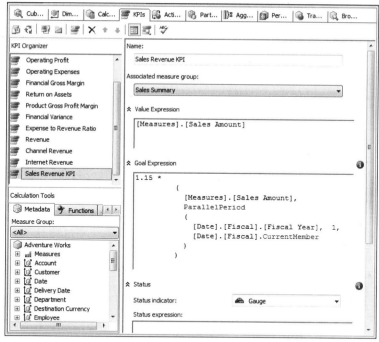

Figure 9-26

5. Type **Sales Revenue KPI** in the Name text box and then choose Sales Summary in the drop-down box for Associated Measure Group. The revenue measure is Sales Amount, which is included in the Sales Summary measure group.

6. Type the following MDX expression in the Value Expression text box as shown in Figure 9-26:

```
[Measures].[Sales Amount]
```

When managers browse the KPI, the value of Sales Amount value will be retrieved from the cube.

7. Now you need to translate the sales revenue goal to increase 15 percent over last year's revenue into an MDX expression. Put another way, this year's sales revenue goal is 1.15 times last year's sales revenue. Use the ParallelPeriod function to get the previous year's time members for each current year time member. Type the MDX expression, shown here, in the Goal Expression text box as shown in Figure 9-26:

```
1.15 *
(
   [Measures].[Sales Amount],
   ParallelPeriod
   (
     [Date].[Fiscal].[Fiscal Year],  1,
     [Date].[Fiscal].CurrentMember
   )
)
```

8. In the Status section of the KPI template, you can choose a graphical indicator for the status of the KPI to display in the KPI browser. You can see several of the available indicators in Figure 9-27. For your own KPI applications, you must programmatically associate the KPI status with your own graphical indicator. For now, select the Traffic Light indicator. The MDX expression that you define for status must return a value between –1 and 1. The KPI browser displays a red traffic light when the status is –1 and a green traffic light when the status is 1. When the status is 0, a yellow traffic light displays.

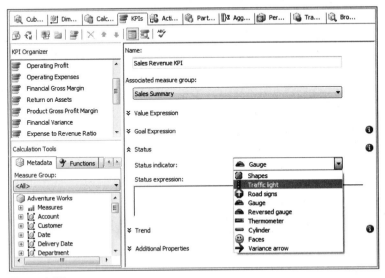

Figure 9-27

9. Type the following expression in the Status Expression text box:

```
CASE
    WHEN KpiValue("Sales Revenue KPI")/KpiGoal("Sales Revenue KPI")>=.95
        THEN 1
    WHEN KpiValue("Sales Revenue KPI")/KpiGoal("Sales Revenue KPI")<.95
        AND
            KpiValue("Sales Revenue KPI")/KpiGoal("Sales Revenue KPI")>=.85
        THEN 0
        ELSE -1
END
```

This expression uses the Case MDX statement available for use with Analysis Services. In addition, you now have a set of MDX functions to use with KPI metric values. In the preceding MDX expression, the KpiValue function retrieves the value of Sales Revenue KPI, and the KpiGoal function retrieves the goal value of Sales Revenue KPI. More precisely, the KpiValue function is a member function that returns a calculated measure from the Measures dimension. By using these KPI functions, you can avoid a lot of typing if your value or goal expression is complex. This Status expression will return one of three discrete values: 1 if revenue exceeds 95 percent of goal, 0 if revenue is between 85 percent and 95 percent of goal, and –1 if revenue is below 85 percent of goal.

10. Choose the default indicator (Standard Arrow) for Trend indicator. Type the following MDX expression in the Trend Expression text box. This expression compares current KPI values with last year's values from the same time period to calculate the trend of the KPI:

```
CASE
    WHEN (
          KpiValue( "Sales Revenue KPI" ) -
          (
            KpiValue ( "Sales Revenue KPI" ),
            ParallelPeriod
            (
              [Date].[Fiscal].[Fiscal Year],
              1,
              [Date].[Fiscal].CurrentMember
            )
          )) /
          (
            KpiValue ( "Sales Revenue KPI" ),
            ParallelPeriod
            (
              [Date].[Fiscal].[Fiscal Year],
              1,
              [Date].[Fiscal].CurrentMember
            )
          )
          <=-.02
    THEN -1
    WHEN ( KpiValue( "Sales Revenue KPI" ) -
          (
            KpiValue ( "Sales Revenue KPI" ),
            ParallelPeriod
            (
              [Date].[Fiscal].[Fiscal Year],
              1,
              [Date].[Fiscal].CurrentMember
            )
          )) /
          (
            KpiValue ( "Sales Revenue KPI" ),
            ParallelPeriod
            (
              [Date].[Fiscal].[Fiscal Year],
              1,
              [Date].[Fiscal].CurrentMember
            )
          ) >.02
    THEN 1
    ELSE 0
END
```

11. Expand the Additional Properties section at the bottom of the KPI template to type a name in the Display Folder combo box for a new folder, or to pick an existing display folder. The KPI browser will show all KPIs in a folder separate from other measures and dimensions, but you can further group related KPIs into folders and subfolders. A subfolder is created when the folder names are separated by a backslash, "\". In the Display Folder combo box, type **SampleKPI\RevenueFolder** as shown in Figure 9-28.

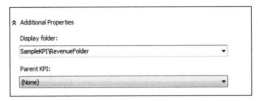

Figure 9-28

You can also choose to set Parent KPI so that the KPI browser displays KPIs hierarchically. Using the Parent KPI setting is for display purposes only and doesn't actually create a physical relationship between parent and child KPIs. You could, however, design a Parent KPI that uses values from child KPIs via KPI functions; there is even a Weight expression to adjust the value of a Parent KPI. The Display Folder setting is ignored if you select a Parent KPI because the KPI will display inside its parent's folder. To complete your KPI, leave the Parent KPI as (None).

Congratulations, you just created your first KPI! Deploy the project to an instance of Analysis Services so you can view the KPI values. To deploy, select the Build menu item and then select Deploy Adventure Works DW 2008. Like MDX scripts, KPI definitions are only metadata, so changing and saving the KPI definitions will only update the metadata store. A cube reprocess is not required, allowing you to use a KPI right after deploying it to the Analysis Services instance.

To view the KPI, follow these steps:

1. In the Cube Designer, click the Browser View button in the KPI toolbar, as shown in Figure 9-29.

Figure 9-29

Your new KPI is at the bottom of the view window and should look like Figure 9-30

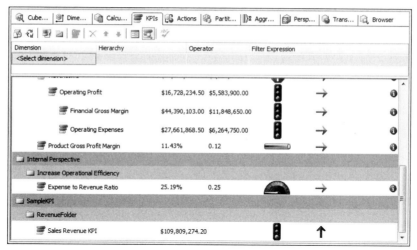

Figure 9-30

2. The KPI browser supports the standard slicer window at the top of the browser. You can select specific members to narrow down the analysis to areas of interest. For example, suppose you are interested in the sales revenue KPI for August 2003. In the slicer window, select the Date dimension, Fiscal hierarchy, and August 2003 (found in semester H1 FY 2004 and quarter Q1 FY 2004) as shown in Figure 9-31.

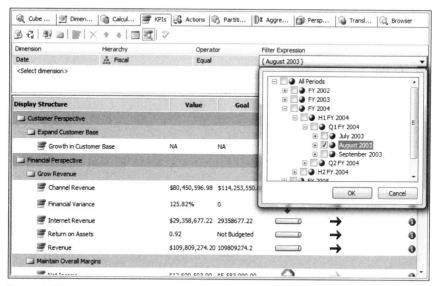

Figure 9-31

You will notice the KPI values have changed as shown in Figure 9-32, as have the Goals — August beats the goal!

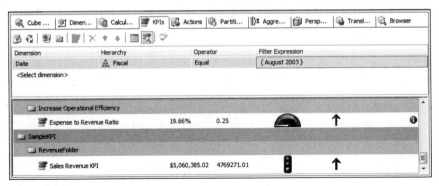

Figure 9-32

KPIs in Depth

Every Analysis Services cube can have an associated collection of KPIs, and each KPI has five properties as its set of metadata. These properties are MDX expressions that return numeric values from a cube as described in the following table.

KPI-Specific Properties	Description
Value	An MDX expression that returns the actual value of the KPI. It is mandatory for a KPI.
Goal	An MDX expression that returns the goal of the KPI.
Status	An MDX expression that returns the status of the KPI. To best represent the value graphically, this expression should return a value between –1 and 1. Client applications use the status value to display a graphic indicator of the KPI trend.
Trend	An MDX expression that returns the trend of the KPI over time. As with Status, the Trend expression should return a value between –1 and 1. Client applications use the trend value to display a graphic indicator of the KPI trend direction.
Weight	An MDX expression that returns the weight of the KPI. If a KPI has a parent KPI, you can define weights to control the contribution of this KPI to its parent.

Analysis Services creates hidden calculated members on the Measures dimension for each KPI metric (value, goal, status, trend, and weight). However, if a KPI expression directly references a measure, Analysis Services uses the measure directly instead of creating a new calculated measure. You can query the calculated measure used for KPIs in an MDX expression, even though it's hidden.

To see how this works, open SSMS and connect to Analysis Services. Click the Analysis Services MDX Query icon in the toolbar to open a new MDX query window. Make sure you're connected to the Adventure Works DW 2008 database in the Available Databases list box, type the following query in the MDX query window, and click the Execute button:

```
SELECT {Measures.[Sales Revenue KPI Goal] } ON 0,
[Date].[Fiscal].[Fiscal Quarter].MEMBERS ON 1
FROM [Adventure Works]
```

Figure 9-33 shows the results of executing the query.

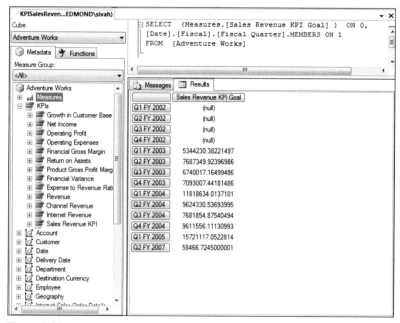

Figure 9-33

Using ADOMD.NET to Query KPIs

The Analysis Services instance hosting the database cubes also maintains the KPI definition metadata. As you learned in the previous section, you can access KPI values directly by using KPI functions. Client applications can also access this KPI metadata information and retrieve values programmatically through an Analysis Services client-side component: ADOMD.NET.

ADOMD.NET provides support for KPIs. It includes a KPI class that contains a method called Kpi.Properties("KPI_XXX"), which is used to retrieve the properties of each KPI. This method returns a string of unique measures for the developer to use in the construction of MDX queries that retrieve the KPI values. The following code example demonstrates how to access a KPI using ADOMD.NET and how to construct a parameterized MDX query. Because KPI metrics are just calculated measures, you execute a KPI query with ADOMD.NET the same way you execute regular MDX queries.

```csharp
using System;
using System.Collections.Generic;
using System.Text;
using Microsoft.AnalysisServices.AdomdClient;

namespace QueryKPIs
{
    class Program
    {
        static void Main(string[] args)
        {
            string connectionString =
                "Provider = MSOLAP;" +
                "Data Source=localhost;" +
                "Initial Catalog=Adventure Works DW 2008";
            AdomdConnection acCon = new AdomdConnection(connectionString);
            try
            {
                acCon.Open();
                CubeDef cubeObject = acCon.Cubes["Adventure Works"];
                string commandText =
                    "SELECT { strtomember(@Value), strtomember(@Goal), " +
                    "strtomember(@Status), strtomember(@Trend) } " +
                    "ON COLUMNS FROM [" + cubeObject.Name + "]";
                AdomdCommand command = new AdomdCommand(commandText,
                        acCon);
                foreach (Microsoft.AnalysisServices.AdomdClient.Kpi kpi in
                        cubeObject.Kpis)
                {
                    command.Parameters.Clear();

                    command.Parameters.Add(new AdomdParameter("Value",
                        kpi.Properties["KPI_VALUE"].Value));
                    command.Parameters.Add(new AdomdParameter("Goal",
                        kpi.Properties["KPI_GOAL"].Value));
                    command.Parameters.Add(new AdomdParameter("Status",
                        kpi.Properties["KPI_STATUS"].Value));
                    command.Parameters.Add(new AdomdParameter("Trend",
                        kpi.Properties["KPI_TREND"].Value));
                    CellSet cellset = command.ExecuteCellSet();

                    Console.WriteLine("KPI Name:" + kpi.Name);
                    Console.WriteLine("Value:" +
                        cellset.Cells[0].FormattedValue);
                    Console.WriteLine("Goal:" +
                        cellset.Cells[1].FormattedValue);
                    Console.WriteLine("Status:" +
                        cellset.Cells[2].FormattedValue);
                    Console.WriteLine("Trend:" +
                        cellset.Cells[3].FormattedValue);
                }

            }
```

```
                finally
                {
                    acCon.Close();
                }
            }
        }
    }
```

Note that this example uses a parameterized MDX query and the StrToMember function to avoid MDX injection. The developer of a client-side application needs to be cautious with user input; a simple string concatenation would allow a malicious user to input and run harmful code. You can create a new C# program called QueryKPI, copy the preceding code, add the Microsoft.AnalysisServices.AdomdClient DLL as a reference, and run the program. We recommend you explore the .NET Adomd client object model by writing client programs that use it.

Drillthrough

Drill down is the process of navigating from a summary level to more detailed levels across a cube dimension. Drillthrough is a completely different animal. Drillthrough retrieves fact data corresponding to a cell or some specified range of cells. Often the lowest level of detail in a cube is still comprised of aggregated values, but users occasionally have a need to see the associated row-level data from the fact table. In Analysis Services 2008, even if you use the MOLAP storage mode (discussed later in this chapter), you can still use Drillthrough. You can modify a server configuration advanced property, OLAP\Query\DefaultDRILLTHROUGHMaxRows, to control the default size of the returned dataset.

By default, Drillthrough returns the granularity attribute of each dimension and all measures. If you want your Drillthrough action to behave like Drillthrough in Analysis Services 2000, you can create a ROLAP dimension from the fact table that contains the measures to return. And just how do you define Drillthrough? You could create an application that performs Drillthrough programmatically using the SQL query supported by Analysis Services 2008. Excel 2007 is an application that creates Drillthrough commands to Analysis Services when you double-click a cell in a pivot table (you learn about analyzing a cube using pivot tables in Excel 2007 in Chapter 17). Another option is to create a Drillthrough action. The following section describes the available action types, including how to create a Drillthrough action.

For some insight on how Drillthrough actually works in Analysis Services 2008, it is informative to contrast it to the implementation of Drillthrough in Analysis Services 2000. Analysis Services 2000 fetched all requested measures directly from the relational data source, which is potentially a slow process. Analysis Services 2008 retrieves the requested measures from the MOLAP database directly and therefore runs much faster. Indeed, the system is self-contained and requires no connection to SQL Server. As mentioned, Drillthrough can be defined as an Action (to be seen in the next section) and can drill-through on cells that have the Drillthrough action defined. You learn to define Drillthrough and understand its behavior in the next section.

Actions

Actions are predefined metadata components stored on the server that send commands to client applications to perform certain operations based on a selection by the user in the Cube Browser. For example, the user could select dimension members, levels, a set, specific cube cells, and so on. An action command usually includes a command string, such as a URL, and the suggested command behavior, such as opening a web browser for the URL. MDX expressions are often built into commands to include the context of the user selection in the action. If a user initiates an action by selecting a product, for example, an MDX expression could be used to generate a URL for a catalog page describing the selected product.

Action Types

Analysis Services 2008 supports seven action types. These action types empower client applications with more analytical capabilities than traditional OLAP analysis drill up, drill down, and pivot activities. For example, if a sales manager is analyzing sales for cities in Washington State, the ability to click a city member to view an MSN city map would be helpful. Similarly, if your implementation includes Reporting Services, you could link a report that analyzes sales reasons by product category to the product category members by adding an action to the cube. When the sales manager clicks a product category, the action passes the selected product category as a parameter to the report, which then displays in a web browser. If a sales number for a specific region appears to be surprisingly high or low, the sales manager could use a Drillthrough action to retrieve all detailed transactions contributing to the value. The seven action types supported in Analysis Services are listed in the following table along with the information on what can be done by a client when such an action type is returned.

Action Type	Description
CommandLine	Returns a command that can be run under a command prompt.
HTML	Returns an HTML script that can be rendered using an HTML browser.
URL	Returns a URL that can be launched using a browser. Report Action (to be seen later) uses this Action type.
Statement	Returns a statement that can be run as an OLE DB command.
Rowset	Returns a rowset to a client application.
Proprietary	Performs an operation by using an interface other than those listed in this table. The client application retrieving this action type should know how to use this proprietary action type.
Dataset	Returns a data set to a client application.

Action Target Types

Each action is tied to a target type. Target types refer to a specific object or objects, inside the cube. If a user clicks an object that has been defined as a target for an action, the action will be enabled in the client application for that specific object. For example, if you define a URL action to be associated with attribute members of the geography.city attribute, that action will be available when the user selects any member of the city attribute. When you define an action, you must specify the type of objects that will be targets of the action. Analysis Services 2008 supports the following action target types:

Target Type	Description
Attribute Members	The only valid selection is a single attribute hierarchy. The target of the action will be all members of an attribute wherever they appear (that is, it will apply to multilevel hierarchies as well).
Cells	All Cells is the only selection available. If you choose Cells as a target type, type an expression in Condition to restrict the cells with which the action is associated.
Cube	CURRENTCUBE is the only selection available. The action is associated with the current cube.
Dimension Members	You need to select a single dimension. The action will be associated with all members of the dimension.
Hierarchy	You need to select a single hierarchy. The action will be associated with the hierarchy object only. Attribute hierarchies appear in the list only if their AttributeHierarchyEnabled and AttributeHierarchyVisible properties are set to True.
Hierarchy Members	You need to select a single hierarchy. The action will be associated with all members of the selected hierarchy. Attribute hierarchies appear in the list only if their AttributeHierarchyEnabled and AttributeHierarchyVisible properties are set to True.
Level	You need to select a single level. The action will be associated with the level object only.
Level members	You need to select a single level. The action will be associated with all members of the selected level.

URL Action

In these next sections you learn to create a few types of actions, starting with a URL action. The URL action is probably one of the actions we expect customers to use widely. Follow these steps to create a URL action:

1. Using BIDS, open the Adventure Works 2008 Analysis Services sample project and double-click the Adventure Works cube in the Solution Explorer to open the Cube Designer. Click the Action tab to open the actions editor, as shown in Figure 9-34.

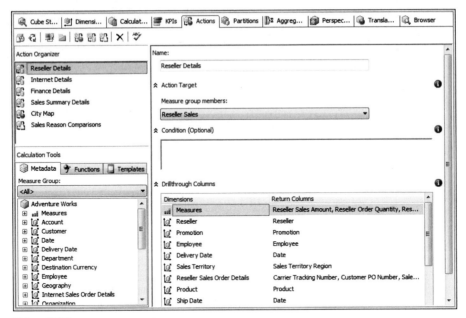

Figure 9-34

2.   Click the New Action button in the Actions toolbar. Type a name for the new action: **My City Map.** Open the Target type list box (by clicking the down arrow) to see the available action target types, and then choose Attribute Members, as shown in Figure 9-35.

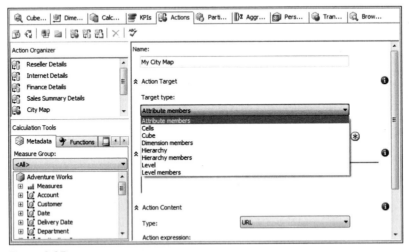

Figure 9-35

3. In the Target Object drill-down box, pick Geography.City as the attribute target (shown in Figure 9-36) and click the OK button.

4. Leave the Action Condition text box blank. If you want to enable the action only under certain conditions, you can enter an MDX expression that returns a Boolean value. Because you always want the My City Map action to be enabled, you don't need an Action Condition expression here.

Figure 9-36

5. In the Action Content section of the editor, keep the default action type, URL. In the Action Expression text box, type the following MDX expression:

```
// URL for linking to MSN Maps
"http://maps.msn.com/home.aspx?plce1=" +

// Retreive the name of the current city
[Geography].[City].CurrentMember.Name + "," +

// Append state-province name
[Geography].[State-Province].CurrentMember.Name + "," +

// Append country name
[Geography].[Country].CurrentMember.Name +

// Append region parameter
"&regn1=" +
// Determine correct region parameter value
Case
    When [Geography].[Country].CurrentMember Is
        [Geography].[Country].&[Australia]
    Then "3"
    When [Geography].[Country].CurrentMember Is
        [Geography].[Country].&[Canada]
        Or
        [Geography].[Country].CurrentMember Is
        [Geography].[Country].&[United States]
    Then "0"
    Else "1"
End
```

This MDX expression returns a string URL used by the client application to open MSN Map for the user-selected City. The user's selection is passed into the MDX expression as:

```
[Geography].[City].CurrentMember
```

If the user selects a different city and launches the action, the MDX expression is re-evaluated and returns a different URL.

6. Scroll down to the section Additional Properties, and expand the section to review the available properties. There are three options for the property Invocation shown in the following table along with their meaning. Because you want the action to be triggered by the user, leave the default Invocation value Interactive. You can also leave the application and description fields blank, because they are informational properties.

The following table describes the possible values for the Invocation property:

Method	Description
Interactive	The action is triggered by user interaction.
Batch	The action runs as a batch operation.
On Open	The action runs when a user opens the cube.

7. In the Caption text box, type the following MDX expression:

```
[Geography].[City].CurrentMember.Member_Caption + " City Map ..."
```

The specified caption is displayed to end users to indicate an action is available. The user clicks the caption to initiate the action. The "Caption Is MDX" property controls how the server evaluates the contents of the caption. If you leave this property value as false, the server treats the caption as a static string.

8. Change the Caption Is MDX value to True. The server evaluates the MDX expression in the Caption text box to construct the caption, which in this case will result in different city names included in the caption as different cities are selected in the browser.

Now that you've created a My City Map action, deploy the project to save the action to the server. Just as with KPI definition, an action definition is metadata stored on the server with the cube. Adding or changing the action won't impact the cube data and doesn't require a reprocess. When the project deploys, you can verify the newly created action right away.

Browse URL Action in the Cube Browser

Many standard OLAP client applications, such as pivot tables in Office Web Components and the BIDS Cube Browser, support actions out-of-the-box. In this section, you learn to invoke the action My City Map from the Cube Browser.

1. In the Cube Designer, click the Browser tab to open the Cube Browser for the Adventure Works cube.

2. In the metadata pane on the left, open the Geography dimension. Then, open the Geography hierarchy and drag the City level from metadata window to Rows in the data window on the right side, as shown in Figure 9-37.

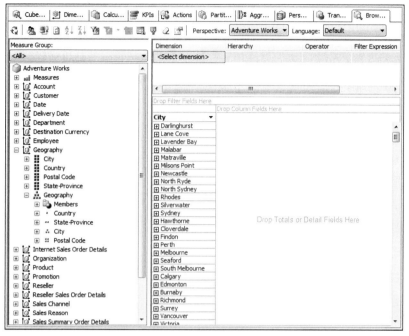

Figure 9-37

3. Right-click any city in the data window. Notice actions listed on the pop-up menu. The corresponding city map action captioned as <CityName> City Map is one of the actions listed. Figure 9-38 show the action for the city Newcastle.

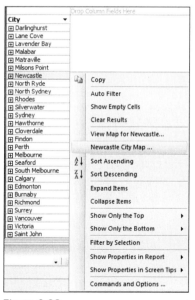

Figure 9-38

4. Click Newcastle City Map. BIDS will invoke a web browser and construct a URL from the predefined MDX expression. The result of the action is shown in Figure 9-39.

Figure 9-39

Report Actions

Report actions are similar to URL actions, except a Report action has additional properties to build the report server access to a URL for you. These properties are described in the following table:

Property	Description
ReportServer	The name of the Report Server
Path	The path exposed by the Report Server
ReportParameters	Extra parameters for the report
ReportFormatParameters	Extra parameters for the report format

When a Report action is invoked, Analysis Services generates a URL string similar to the string here:

```
http://ReportServer/Path&ReportParameter1Name=ReportParameter1Value&
ReportParameter2Name=ReportParameter2Value.......&
ReportFormatParameter1Name=ReportFormatParameter1Value&
ReportFormatParameter2Name=ReportFormatParameter2Value ...
```

To review a Report action, follow these steps:

1. With the Adventure Works 2008 Analysis Services sample project still open in BIDS, click the Actions tab of the Cube Designer and then click Sales Reason Comparisons Report in the Action Organizer. Let's take a look at the properties of this Report action (see Figure 9-40). The optional parameter values are MDX expressions that provide the action with the context of the user selection.

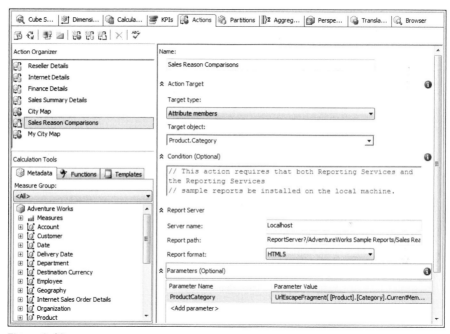

Figure 9-40

2. As with a URL action, you can invoke a Report action from the Cube Browser. Click the Clear Results button in the toolbar to start a new query. The Sales Reason Comparisons action's targets are members of the Product.Category hierarchy. Drag and drop the Product.Product Categories hierarchy from the metadata pane to OWC's columns. Right-click the member Bikes to see the action's caption on the pop-up menu as shown in Figure 9-41.

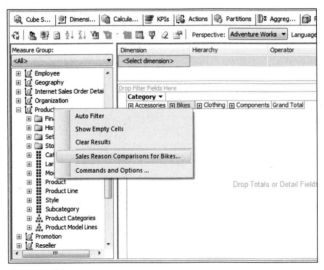

Figure 9-41

3.   Click Sales Reason Comparisons for Accessories. A browser window will open. If Reporting Services is installed, you will see a message "The item '/AdventureWorks Sample Reports/ Sales Reason Comparisons' cannot be found"; in other words, rsItemNotFound. This is because the report is fictitious. If this was a valid report, it would display the sales reasons for the Bike category.

Drillthrough Action

OLAP is all about aggregating data and serving aggregated data to end users quickly. Users want to analyze data hierarchically by drilling up and drilling down, which may require aggregated data from millions of daily transaction rows. Sometimes it is very useful for users to be able to retrieve the transaction rows that have been aggregated into a particular cell. Access to such details often helps business users understand any abnormal business activities (such as extremely large or small numbers) and investigate root causes. Drillthrough provides this access to details by enabling users to fetch fact table rows that contribute to an aggregated value of a cube cell.

Drillthrough is an MDX command in Analysis Services 2008. However, Analysis Services 2008 also supports an action type called Drillthrough. A Drillthrough action's target is always one or more cube cells associated with a specific measure group. In other words, cells with measures in the target measure group will display the available Drillthrough actions on the pop-up menu. Drillthrough actions return the related fact table rows in a tabular rowset. As the action developer, you specify which columns the action returns. The columns returned from a rowset Drillthrough action are not limited to the actual fact table columns. Any dimension attributes linked to the selected measure group target can be included. Many-to-many dimensions and referenced dimensions are also supported, so attributes from these special dimensions are available for Drillthrough return columns as well.

In Analysis Services 2000, you explicitly had to set the Enable drill-through flag in the Drillthrough options dialog for each cube. This flag to allow Drillthrough is deprecated in Analysis Services 2005 onwards. Cube designers in Analysis Services 2008 can allow or deny Drillthrough by defining a security role on each cube. Only an Analysis Services administrator can perform Drillthrough against any cube without explicit permissions. If a user does not have Drillthrough rights on a specific cube, the Drillthrough will not execute and an error message will be displayed.

In addition, the cubes and partitions properties DRILLTHROUGHFilter, DRILLTHROUGHFrom, and DRILLTHROUGHJoin in Analysis Services 2000 are no longer valid in Analysis Services 2005/2008. The same functionality can now be achieved using Data Source View. Follow these steps to understand an existing Drillthrough action in the Adventure Works DW 2008 sample database and enhance it:

1. With the AdventureWorks DW 2008 Analysis Services sample project still open in BIDS, click the Actions tab.

2. Click Finance Details in the Action Organizer, as shown in Figure 9-42.

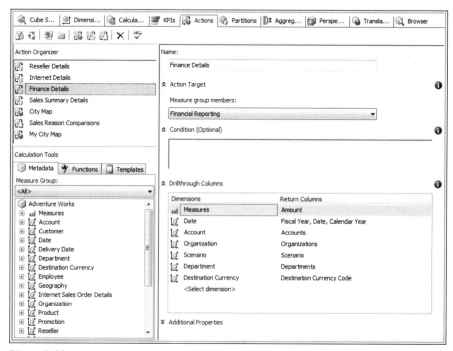

Figure 9-42

You can see the action target is the Financial Reporting measure group. The Drillthrough columns to be returned by the action are Amount, Fiscal Year, Date, and Calendar Year from the Date dimension, Accounts from the Account dimension, and so on.

3. Suppose the business user also wants Account Type and Account Number to be included as additional Drillthrough columns. Click the Accounts dimension attribute in the column labeled Return Columns to open the drop-down box. All available attributes for the Account dimension are listed here. Choose Account Type and Account Number as shown in Figure 9-43. Click OK.

4. In the Additional Properties section, the Maximum Rows setting is very useful for the designer to limit the maximum number of rows that can be returned for a Drillthrough action. This is important because a cell, especially a top-level cell, could be aggregated from millions of fact table rows. Setting the maximum rows value is always a good practice to protect your server from accidental or malicious operations, which will consume huge server resources. If the property is not set, the default max Drillthrough row count from server property Olap\Query\ DefaultDRILLTHROUGHMaxRows is used. The default value of the setting is 10000. In the Maximum Rows text box, type in **5000** as shown in Figure 9-44. Deploy the project to save the action to the server.

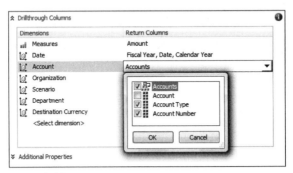

Figure 9-43

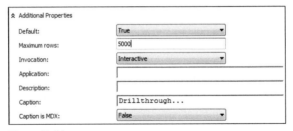

Figure 9-44

5. You can now view the Drillthrough results in the Cube Browser. Click the Browser tab to open the Cube Browser. Because the action for Finance details is on the measure group Financial Reporting, you need to drag and drop Measure.Amount in the Financial Reporting folder to the OWC's Detail Fields area. Right-click the cell and you will see Drillthrough as a menu item on the pop-up menu, as shown in Figure 9-45, indicating you can invoke the Drillthrough action for the cell. Before you actually invoke the action, you should limit your Drillthrough to a much narrower data region to prevent the action from returning all fact tables rows if no maximum row count limit is specified.

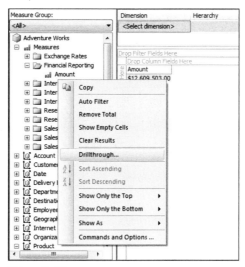

Figure 9-45

6. Drag and drop the Account dimension on rows, and drag and drop the Date.Fiscal hierarchy (in the Fiscal folder) on columns. Then set the slicers at the top of the Cube Browser for customers in the city Redmond (in USA and Washington) and the Research and Development department, as shown in Figure 9-46.

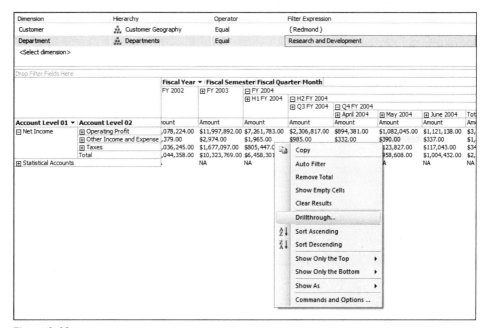

Figure 9-46

7. Suppose you are interested in Other Income and Expense from May 2004. Expand Net Income on rows, and on columns expand FY 2004, H2 FY 2004, and Q4 FY 2004. Right-click the cell intersection of May 2004 and Other Income and Expense, and then choose Drillthrough, as shown in Figure 9-46. A new window opens to display the fact table rows that aggregate to the cell value, as shown in Figure 9-47. Note that the newly added account type and account number is returned.

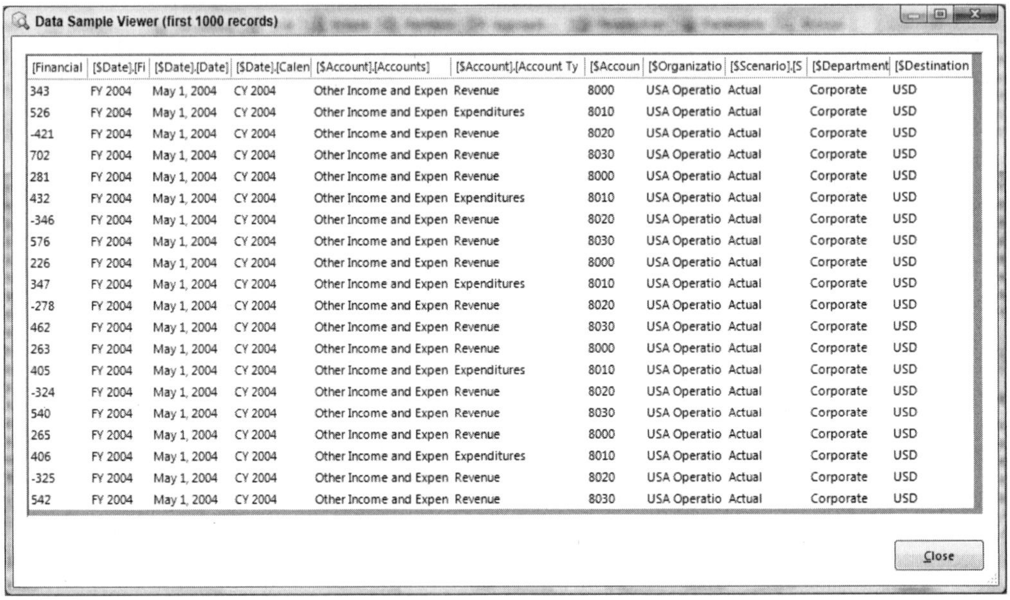

[Financial	[$Date].[Fi	[$Date].[Date]	[$Date].[Calen	[$Account].[Accounts]	[$Account].[Account Ty	[$Accoun	[$Organizatio	[$Scenario].[S	[$Department	[$Destination
343	FY 2004	May 1, 2004	CY 2004	Other Income and Expen	Revenue	8000	USA Operatio	Actual	Corporate	USD
526	FY 2004	May 1, 2004	CY 2004	Other Income and Expen	Expenditures	8010	USA Operatio	Actual	Corporate	USD
-421	FY 2004	May 1, 2004	CY 2004	Other Income and Expen	Revenue	8020	USA Operatio	Actual	Corporate	USD
702	FY 2004	May 1, 2004	CY 2004	Other Income and Expen	Revenue	8030	USA Operatio	Actual	Corporate	USD
281	FY 2004	May 1, 2004	CY 2004	Other Income and Expen	Revenue	8000	USA Operatio	Actual	Corporate	USD
432	FY 2004	May 1, 2004	CY 2004	Other Income and Expen	Expenditures	8010	USA Operatio	Actual	Corporate	USD
-346	FY 2004	May 1, 2004	CY 2004	Other Income and Expen	Revenue	8020	USA Operatio	Actual	Corporate	USD
576	FY 2004	May 1, 2004	CY 2004	Other Income and Expen	Revenue	8030	USA Operatio	Actual	Corporate	USD
226	FY 2004	May 1, 2004	CY 2004	Other Income and Expen	Revenue	8000	USA Operatio	Actual	Corporate	USD
347	FY 2004	May 1, 2004	CY 2004	Other Income and Expen	Expenditures	8010	USA Operatio	Actual	Corporate	USD
-278	FY 2004	May 1, 2004	CY 2004	Other Income and Expen	Revenue	8020	USA Operatio	Actual	Corporate	USD
462	FY 2004	May 1, 2004	CY 2004	Other Income and Expen	Revenue	8030	USA Operatio	Actual	Corporate	USD
263	FY 2004	May 1, 2004	CY 2004	Other Income and Expen	Revenue	8000	USA Operatio	Actual	Corporate	USD
405	FY 2004	May 1, 2004	CY 2004	Other Income and Expen	Expenditures	8010	USA Operatio	Actual	Corporate	USD
-324	FY 2004	May 1, 2004	CY 2004	Other Income and Expen	Revenue	8020	USA Operatio	Actual	Corporate	USD
540	FY 2004	May 1, 2004	CY 2004	Other Income and Expen	Revenue	8030	USA Operatio	Actual	Corporate	USD
265	FY 2004	May 1, 2004	CY 2004	Other Income and Expen	Revenue	8000	USA Operatio	Actual	Corporate	USD
406	FY 2004	May 1, 2004	CY 2004	Other Income and Expen	Expenditures	8010	USA Operatio	Actual	Corporate	USD
-325	FY 2004	May 1, 2004	CY 2004	Other Income and Expen	Revenue	8020	USA Operatio	Actual	Corporate	USD
542	FY 2004	May 1, 2004	CY 2004	Other Income and Expen	Revenue	8030	USA Operatio	Actual	Corporate	USD

Figure 9-47

Under the hood, client applications, including the Cube Browser, use a schema rowset to get the proper Drillthrough query for a specific action. Then the client application sends the Drillthrough query to the server, which returns a rowset with the detailed fact table rows. Following is the query sent by the Cube Browser to get the previous Drillthrough results. The Cube Browser sends the Drillthrough statement to retrieve the first 1000 rows. The Cube Browser first sets a restriction to the cell coordinate corresponding to the value $390.00 and then issues the Drillthrough statement. The `SELECT` clause of the Drillthrough query is therefore specific to the cell that was selected when activating Drillthrough.

```
DRILLTHROUGH  SELECT  ([Date].[Fiscal].[Month].&[2004]&[5],
[Measures].[Amount],[Account].[Accounts].&[88])  ON 0
FROM [Adventure Works]
RETURN
[Financial Reporting].[Amount],
[$Date].[Fiscal Year],
[$Date].[Date],[$Date].[Calendar Year],
[$Account].[Accounts],
[$Account].[Account Type],
[$Account].[Account Number],
[$Organization].[Organizations],
[$Scenario].[Scenario],
[$Department].[Departments],
[$Destination Currency].[Destination Currency Code]
```

Adding Intelligence to the Cube

Similar to adding intelligence to dimensions (which you learned about in Chapter 8), you can add intelligence to the cube. Figure 9-48 shows the various enhancements that can be done to a cube using the Business Intelligence Wizard. You have learned most of these enhancements in earlier chapters. In this chapter you learn the enhancements used to define and understand semi-additive behavior as well as defining currency conversion whenever fact data needs to be converted to appropriate local currency.

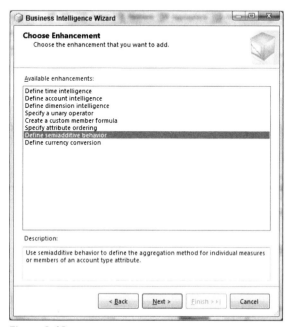

Figure 9-48

Semi-Additive Measures

Semi-additive measures are measures whose data is not aggregated as a sum or a count over the various levels of a hierarchy. The semi-additive aggregate functions for measures are ByAccount, AverageOfChildren, FirstChild, LastChild, FirstNonEmpty, LastNonEmpty, and None. For example, assume you have a Time hierarchy and the measure Sales Value to be rolled up as an average of the sales of its children. Assume the levels in the Time hierarchy are Year, Half Year, Quarter, Month, and Date. If you have a member Quarter 1 of the year 2004 whose children are months July, August, and September, then the value for Quarter 1 will be the average of the sales values for the three months.

Using the Business Intelligence Wizard you can change the behavior of the Aggregation Function of various measures in the cube. Launch the Business Intelligence Wizard, select "Define semi-additive behavior" in the Choose Enhancement page and click Next. In the Define Semiadditive Behavior page (shown in Figure 9-49) you have three options. The default option is the detection of a dimension of type account, which contains semi-additive members. You learned in Chapter 8 to define semi-additive behavior for various Account types. If this selection is made, the Business Intelligence Wizard sets the aggregate function to ByAccount for all the measures of the measure group that have relationships defined with a dimension of type account. In the sample Adventure Works DW 2008 database there is only one measure, Amount, that has the ByAccount aggregate function. The first option turns off all the semi-additive behavior for all the measures that have the Aggregate Function property set to a semi-additive behavior. When this option is selected any measure that has a semi-additive aggregation function will be set to the Sum aggregate function. The last option "Define semiaddtive behavior for individual measures" allows you to change the Aggregation Function for each measure. Once you make the selection in the Define Semiadditive Behavior page click Next. The final page of the Business Intelligence Wizard shows the new Aggregate Function for the measures that will be affected. You can review the changes to be applied to the measures and click Finish. BIDS then changes the Aggregate Function property for the measures.

Figure 9-49

You can verify the Aggregate Function property of the measures that are expected to be changed by the selections in the semi-additive behavior enhancement through the Business Intelligence Wizard. You learned the semi-additive behavior of the ByAccount aggregate function in Chapter 8. To see the results of LastNonEmpty and AverageOfChildrence semi-additive aggregate functions, deploy the sample Adventure Works DW 2008 database and browse the measures in the Exchange Rate in the Cube Browser along with the Date.Fiscal hierarchy and DestinationCurrency.DestinationCurrency hierarchy as shown in Figure 9-50. Select the members Australian Dollar and Euro in the Destination Currency hierarchy. You can see the value for the members in the Date.Fiscal hierarchy are calculated based on the aggregate functions LastNonEmpty (for End of Day Rate measure) and AverageOfChildren (for AverageRate measure) applied to their children.

Drop Filter Fields Here				Destination Currency ▼			
				Australian Dollar		EURO	
Fiscal Year ▼	Fiscal Semester	Fiscal Quarter	Month	Average Rate	End of Day Rate	Average Rate	End of Day Rate
⊟ FY 2002	⊟ H1 FY 2002	⊟ Q1 FY 2002	⊞ July 2001	.64	.63	1,02	1,00
			⊞ August 2001	.65	.67	1,02	1,01
			⊞ September 2001	.65	.63	,99	,99
			Total	.64	.63	1,01	,99
		⊞ Q2 FY 2002		.60	.57	,95	,91
		Total		.62	.57	,98	,91
	⊟ H2 FY 2002	⊞ Q3 FY 2002		.59	.58	,93	,90
		⊞ Q4 FY 2002		.55	.52	,87	,86
		Total		.57	.52	,90	,86
	Total			.60	.52	,94	,86
⊟ FY 2003	⊟ H1 FY 2003	⊞ Q1 FY 2003		.54	.54	,91	,93
		⊞ Q2 FY 2003		.51	.52	,90	,88
		Total		.53	.52	,90	,88
	⊟ H2 FY 2003	⊞ Q3 FY 2003		.52	.52	,86	,90
		⊞ Q4 FY 2003		.51	.52	,91	,89
		Total		.51	.52	,89	,89
	Total			.52	.52	,90	,89
⊞ FY 2004				.54	.56	,93	1,01
⊞ FY 2005				.55	.55	,99	,97
Grand Total				.55	.55	,93	,97

Figure 9-50

Currency Conversion

If your organization does business in more than one country, you might need to deal with converting currencies between countries. Analysts and managers may want to analyze transactions in the currency used for the transaction (also known as the local currency), while corporate management may want to convert all transactions to a single currency to get a complete view of all transactions globally. This scenario can be thought of as a many-to-one currency conversion. Or you might load data in the data warehouse in one currency, but need to report financial results in different currencies. This scenario describes a one-to-many currency conversion. Yet another possibility is a combination of these two scenarios in which transaction data is in the local currency and needs to be reported in more than one different currency — a many-to-many currency conversion. Fortunately, Analysis Services 2008 provides a wizard to make it easy for you to add currency conversions to a cube for any of the three scenarios just described.

Before you can use the wizard, however, you need to build a currency dimension and an exchange rate measure group in your cube. These database objects are already in the Adventure Works cube that you've been using throughout this chapter, which gives you an opportunity to take a look at the proper structure before you have to build your own.

To review database objects used for currency conversion, follow these steps:

1. Using BIDS, open the Adventure Works cube in the Enterprise version of the Adventure Works DW 2008 sample project. Double-click the Adventure Works cube in the Solution Explorer to open the Cube Designer.

2. Click the Exchange Rates Measure Group in the Measures pane, then take a look at the Type property for the measure group, shown in Figure 9-51. You must set the Type property value to ExchangeRate so that Analysis Services can correctly specify this measure group in the currency conversion calculations added to the MDX script when you use the wizard. The Exchange Rates measure group is based on a fact table that contains daily average and end of day exchange rates by day and by currency.

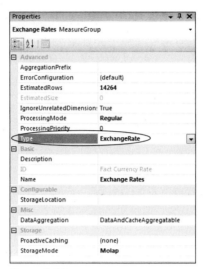

Figure 9-51

3. Open the Exchange Rates measure group; click the Average Rate measure, and look at its AggregateFunction property. As you learned earlier in this chapter, Average Rate is a semi-additive measure that cannot be summed to get value for the month, quarter, or year level. Instead the aggregate function AverageOfChildren is used.

4. Now double-click the Source Currency dimension in the Solution Explorer. In the Properties window, you can see the Type property for this dimension is set to Currency. Click the Source Currency attribute in the Attributes pane. You can see its Type property is CurrencySource. Lastly, click the Source Currency Code attribute and verify its Type property is CurrencyIsoCode. You can make sure you get the property settings right by selecting Currency as the Dimension Type when using the Dimension Wizard to create the dimension. The wizard will prompt you for the column in your table containing the currency's ISO code and for the key attribute. Alternatively you can change the properties after the dimension is created.

5. Now you're ready to start the Business Intelligence Wizard. The wizard will create a second currency dimension, one used for reporting the converted currencies, for you as well as updating the MDX script with calculations that ensure the currency conversion is correctly applied to affected measures. Right-click the Adventure Works cube in the Solution Explorer, click Add Business Intelligence, click Next, click Define Currency Conversion, and then click Next.

6. In the Set Currency Conversion Options page, the wizard looks for measure groups of type ExchangeRate and pre-selects that measure group. If such a measure group does not exist, it selects the first measure group. Click Exchange Rates in the "Select the measure group that contains exchange rates" list. In the "Specify the pivot currency" list box, click USD, and then click OK. Lastly, click the n USD per 1 ARS radio button, as shown in Figure 9-52. The

FactCurrencyRate table, on which the Exchange Rate measure group is based, has rates to convert one unit of local currency (such as one Australian dollar) into a standard currency (US dollars in this case), which is called the pivot currency. If the table contained rates to convert 1 unit of the pivot currency into the local currency, you would select the N ARS Per 1 USD radio button. The drop-down list contains a predefined list of currencies to help you make the right selection. Click Next to continue.

Figure 9-52

7. In the Select Members page (see Figure 9-53), select the checkboxes next to Internet Sales Amount and Reseller Sales Amount. This page of the wizard identifies the members that will be converted. Another approach to currency conversion involves converting specific members in an attribute hierarchy of an Account dimension, such as certain expense accounts, or certain account types, such as all revenue accounts. You can select the measure from the measure group selected in the previous page of the dialog that is to be used for currency conversion. The Average Rate measure is selected by default. These options are useful when your cube is dedicated to financial data for balance sheets and profit and loss statements.

Figure 9-53

8. Click Next to view the next page of the wizard, as shown in Figure 9-54. Here you describe your conversion scenario for the wizard. Your selection here determines what information you must supply on subsequent pages of the wizard. The selections are self explanatory. Choose the Many-to-many selection and click Next.

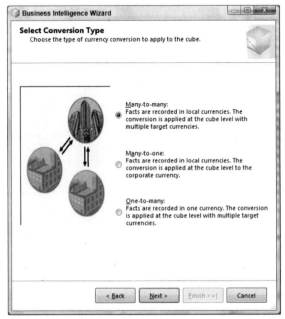

Figure 9-54

9. In the Define Local Currency Reference page (Figure 9-55), you define the location of the column that contains the currency key. After you specify whether it's in a fact table (which it is in the Adventure Works DW 2008 sample database) or in a dimension table, you select the attribute with which a currency is associated. If a currency attribute is in the fact table, it is likely to be a dimension key that is related to a dimension table. Otherwise, the attribute is a column in a dimension table that typically corresponds to geography, such as business divisions that are located in separate countries.

In this example, the Destination Currency is automatically selected because the currency conversion definition is already in the Adventure Works cube. If you were to start completely from scratch, you would choose the Source Currency dimension's key attribute on this page.

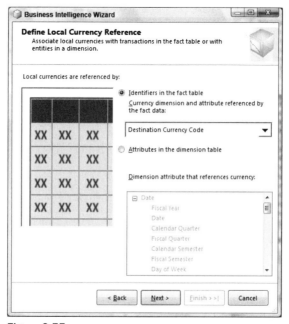

Figure 9-55

10. Click Next again, and then click the box to the left of Reporting Currencies to select all of the available items as shown in Figure 9-56. On this page, you identify the currencies to include in the reporting currency (called Destination Currency in the Adventure Works cube). The Business Intelligence Wizard builds a new dimension according to your selections here. If you forget to select a currency that exists in the exchange rate fact table, cube processing will fail — be careful!

Figure 9-56

11. Click Next, and then click Cancel on the final page of the wizard. Because the Destination Currency and currency conversion calculations are already in the cube, the wizard doesn't need to do anything. But if you are adding this capability to your own cube, there's still more to explore to better understand what the wizard would do if you started the process with only a Source Currency dimension and an Exchange Rates fact table.

12. Double-click the Adventure Works Data Source View in the Solution Explorer. In the Tables pane, right-click DestinationCurrency, and then click Edit Named Query. A query similar to the following query would be created by the Business Intelligence Wizard when creating a reporting currency. The WHERE clause of this query would detail currencies selected on the Specify Reporting Currencies page of the wizard (see Figure 9-56) if you picked some, but not all, available currencies. Notice that the main foundation for the named query is the DimCurrency table, which is also used for the Source Currency dimension in the Adventure Works DW 2008 database.

```
SELECT      CurrencyKey, CurrencyAlternateKey, CurrencyName,
            CASE WHEN CurrencyAlternateKey = 'ARS' THEN '11274' WHEN
                 CurrencyAlternateKey = 'AUD' THEN '3081' WHEN
                 CurrencyAlternateKey = 'DEM' THEN '1031' WHEN
                 CurrencyAlternateKey = 'GBP' THEN '2057' WHEN
                 CurrencyAlternateKey = 'MXN' THEN '2058' WHEN
                 CurrencyAlternateKey = 'CAD' THEN '4105' WHEN
                 CurrencyAlternateKey = 'SAR' THEN '1025' WHEN
                 CurrencyAlternateKey = 'EUR' THEN '2067' WHEN
                 CurrencyAlternateKey = 'FRF' THEN '1036' WHEN
```

```
                          CurrencyAlternateKey = 'BRL' THEN '1046' WHEN
                          CurrencyAlternateKey = 'JPY' THEN '1041' WHEN
                          CurrencyAlternateKey = 'CNY' THEN '2052' WHEN
                          CurrencyAlternateKey = 'VEB' THEN '16394' WHEN
                          CurrencyAlternateKey = 'USD' THEN '1033' END AS LCID
FROM            dbo.DimCurrency
WHERE           (CurrencyKey IN
                 (SELECT DISTINCT CurrencyKey
                     FROM    dbo.FactCurrencyRate))
```

13. Switch to the Cube Designer, click the Dimension Usage tab, and locate the relationships between the Exchange Rate measure group and other dimensions. Only the Date and Destination Currency dimensions have a regular relationship with Exchange Rate. Recall that you learned about many-to-many relationships earlier in this chapter. In the current example, Internet Sales has sales amounts in many local currencies, which need to be converted — by way of Exchange Rates — to multiple destination currencies. Accordingly, Internet Sales has a regular relationship with Source Currency (representing the local currency) and a many-to-many relationship with Destination Currency with Exchange Rate as the intermediate measure group.

Working with Partitions

When building business intelligence solutions at the enterprise level, it is common to work with terabytes of source (also known as fact or detail) data. Even if you are working with just a few hundred gigabytes, you will find the use of partitions to be critical to your success.

By adding partitions to your overall cube design strategy, you can manage how and where cube data is physically stored, how a cube is processed as well as the time required for processing, and how efficiently Analysis Services 2008 can retrieve data in response to user queries. One key benefit of partitioning is the distribution of data over and across one or more hard disk drives and the ability of Analysis Services to process or query the partitions in parallel using multiple processors or cores that helps in processing and query performance. And in the case of remote partitions, the data can be spread over various machines. Partitions can even be processed in parallel on the remote machines. In this section, you first learn how to set up a local partition. Then, in the section that follows, you learn how to set up a remote partition configuration — which, by the way, is not the simplest procedure.

In order to work with partitions, you first need administrator privileges on both the local and remote instances of Analysis Services you intend to use. Administrator privileges are granted to member groups or users assigned to the Analysis Services server role. Being a member of the server role is analogous to being a member of the OLAP Administrator's group in Analysis Services 2000. To join the Server role first open SSMS and connect to each Analysis Services instance you plan to use. For each instance, you need to perform the following steps:

1. Right-click the instance name and select Properties. In the Analysis Server Properties dialog, shown in Figure 9-57, click the Security tab in the top-left pane. Then, click the Add button.

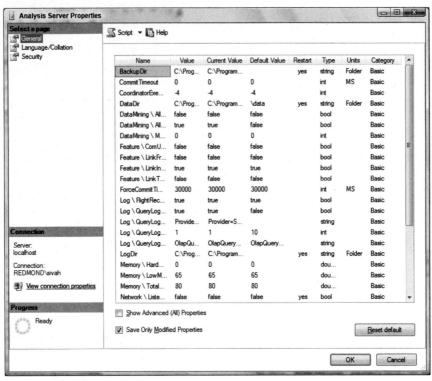

Figure 9-57

2. Next you need to enter your fully articulated username in the "Enter the object names to select" text box. In Figure 9-58, you can see how domain\username (enter a valid Windows account) was entered. To validate your entry, just click the Check Names button. Finally, click OK to close all dialogs. You now have server-wide administrator rights. Be sure to repeat these steps on the local and the remote servers.

Figure 9-58

Building a Local Partition

An important thing to know about partitions is that one partition per measure group in a cube is created behind the scenes to accommodate the storage of data and metadata of your cube — so without any action on your part, beyond the creation of the measure groups, you already have partitions on your computer. When you explicitly create a local partition, you add it to the group of existing partitions for a measure group. So, why should you take extra steps to add partitions? Well, by using partitions, you can spread data across multiple hard disk drives on a single computer. Because very large partitions slow down cube-related activities, dividing one large partition into multiple smaller partitions can improve processing and query times.

In the following exercise, your goal is to replace the single Internet Sales partition for 2004 into two partitions of equal size. This will require you to change the parameters on the existing partition to make room for the new partition; otherwise, Internet sales for 2004 would be double-counted because both partitions would contain the same data. Double-counting, by the way, is something you must be very alert for because it will result in incorrect results.

To create a local partition, follow these steps:

1. Using BIDS, open the Adventure Works DW 2008 sample database. Double-click the Adventure Works cube name in the Solution Explorer to open the Cube Designer.

2. Click the Partitions tab. Your screen should look similar to Figure 9-59.

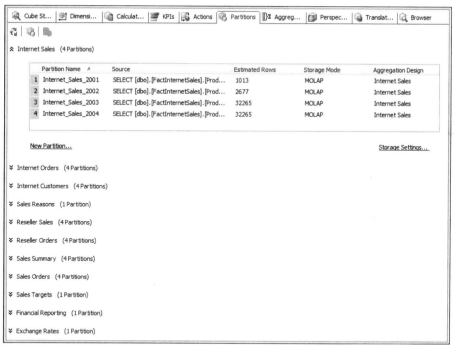

Figure 9-59

3. If necessary, expand the Internet Sales section by clicking the arrows to the left of Internet Sales. Click the Source box for Internet_Sales_2004, and then click the button with two dots appearing in the box to open the Partition Source dialog.

4. Because you need to use a very similar filter query when you create the second Internet Sales 2004 partition, highlight the query and copy it to the clipboard or Notepad. You will modify the query to change the partition such that it contains only data with OrderDateKeys between 20040101 and 20040531 (inclusive) as shown in Figure 9-60, and click OK.

Figure 9-60

5. Next, click the Partition Name "Internet_Sales_2004" and change it to "Internet_Sales_2004a."

6. Click the New Partition link to launch the Partition Wizard.

7. In the Partition Wizard, under Available Tables select the checkbox next to FactInternetSales and then click Next.

8. You should see the wizard page as shown in Figure 9-61. Click the Specify a Query to Restrict Rows checkbox. Delete the default query that shows up in the query window and paste in the query you previously saved. Edit the WHERE clause to limit partition data to rows with OrderDateKey = '20040601' AND OrderDateKey <= '20041231' as shown in Figure 9-61.

Figure 9-61

9. Click Finish (you're storing your partition to the default location). In the Name box, type **Internet_Sales_2004b**, click the Design aggregations later radio button, and then click Finish.

Naturally, you would want to design aggregations for your new partition, and deploy and process it. Designing aggregations for partitions is an important part of data warehouse design. You learn more about aggregation design later in this chapter and in Chapter 14. In this case, you have learned how to use the Partition Wizard for creating a new partition without duplicating data in the process. Again, data duplication must be guarded against because it leads directly to wrong results. The next section takes on the formidable and useful remote partition.

Building a Remote Partition

The basic architecture of the remote partition keeps data definitions (metadata) in the cube on the master (or parent) machine and off-loads the measure or detail data to the remote partitions on subordinate machines. In terms of administration tasks related to remote partitions, the host machine containing the cube metadata acts as the point of control for all related remote partitions.

To implement a remote partition in the most meaningful way, you need two computers. Earlier in this chapter, you followed steps to make sure the permissions were set to work with the local and remote computers with appropriate credentials. In addition, you must have the firewall settings on the master computer (the host box) and subordinate box configured to accept outside connections for Analysis Services. The computer storing the remote partition on it is called the Subordinate (Target) computer. In the tutorial that follows, we are using two instances on one machine (localhost and localhost\SS2008) to demonstrate remote partitions; in this case, firewall settings are not necessary. If you are going for a two machine configuration, of course, you will need to set the firewalls appropriately. Before working with the subordinate computer, you set the stage for successful inter-server interactions by starting your work on the Master computer.

1. In BIDS, open the Adventure Works DW 2008 Analysis Services sample project.

2. Right-click the project name, Adventure Works DW 2008, in the Solution Explorer and click Properties to access the Property Pages, as shown in Figure 9-62. Select the third item down below Configuration Properties in the pane on the left (Deployment). Make your settings consistent with those shown in the figure; be sure the correct name is listed for the Master Server which, if you're not using a named instance, should be localhost. Click OK.

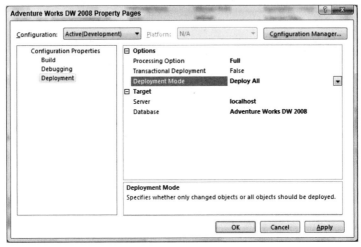

Figure 9-62

3. In the Solution Explorer, right-click the Adventure Works DW 2008 database icon and select Deploy to deploy and process the project.

4. Now it's time to work on the target, or subordinate, machine (or instance). Open a new instance of BIDS, and then create a new Analysis Services project called Target.

5. Right-click the Data Sources folder in the Solution Explorer and select New Data Source. In the Data Source Wizard dialog, click the New button to open the Connection Manager dialog.

6. First, change the Provider to Native OLE DB\Microsoft OLE DB Provider for Analysis Services 10.0. In the Connection Manager dialog, there is a Server or File Name text box, into which you type the name of your master Analysis Services instance. If you are using the default instance on the Master machine, type the machine name (or **localhost**). Set the authentication properties in Log on to the Server consistent with your own configuration. Finally, click the down arrow for Initial Catalog and select Adventure Works DW 2008 (the dialog should look like Figure 9-63) and click OK.

Figure 9-63

7. In the Data Source Wizard, click Next. Set the Impersonation Information at this time to verify correct security settings. If you are unsure what to use, try Inherit. Click Next.

8. You need to provide a new name on this page; we suggest "ASDB_AdvWorksDW" and then click Finish to dismiss the dialog.

9. Just to be clear, you're still on the subordinate machine or instance. Right-click the project name in the Solution Explorer and choose Edit Database. Now, in the Properties window change the MasterDataSourceID property from empty to **ASDB_AdvWorksDW** as shown in Figure 9-64.

Figure 9-64

10. Right-click the database name in the Solution Explorer and choose Properties. Click Configuration Properties and then click Deployment. Finally, click Server and set the name to the subordinate instance of Analysis Services as shown in Figure 9-65. Click OK to close the dialog.

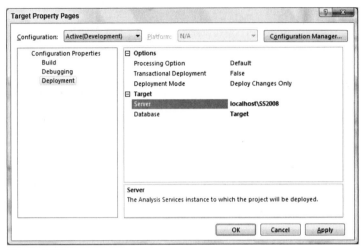

Figure 9-65

11. Deploy the project to move the metadata to the Analysis Services instance (localhost\SS2008).

12. For both localhost and localhost\SS2008 do the following in SSMS:

    a. Connect to the service.

    b. Right-click the instance name and select Properties.

    c. Change the Value (first column) of both Feature\LinkToOtherInstanceEnabled and Feature\LinkFromOtherInstanceEnabled to True.

    d. Click OK to close the Analysis Server Properties dialog.

    e. To make the server property changes take effect, you need to restart the instance of Analysis Services; just right-click the instance name in the SSMS Object Explorer and click Stop. When asked to run in administrator mode click Continue. Click Yes when asked to verify you want to stop the service. Right-click the instances in the SSMS Object Explorer and click Start to restart the instance.

13. In BIDS, create a second data source in the Adventure Works DW 2008 project to connect to the subordinate (target) instance of Analysis Services, and specifically at the target project (named Target here). Use the Native OLE DB\ Microsoft OLE DB Provider for Analysis Services 10.0 (see Figure 9-66).

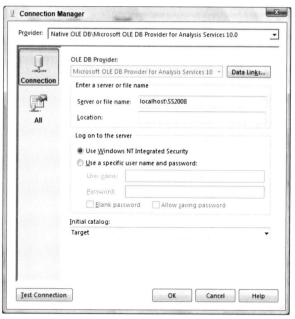

Figure 9-66

14. Click OK to close the Connection Manager dialog. Select the created data source for the Target database; then click Next. On the Impersonation Information page, select Inherit and click Next. Accept the default name provided by the Data Source Wizard and click Finish.

15. It is nearly time to create the remote partition; but first you need to make room for one by deleting an existing partition. Let's sacrifice one of the Fact Internet Sales partitions by opening the Adventure Works cube and clicking the Partitions tab; then click the double down arrows next to Fact Internet Sales to open the section for the Internet Sales measure group. To delete the Internet_Sales_2001 partition, right-click the partition and click Delete as shown in Figure 9-67.

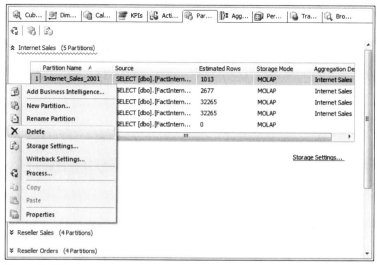

Figure 9-67

16. To build the remote partition, click the New Partition link. On the second page, click the checkbox next to Internet Sales Facts under Available Tables, and then click Next.

17. On the Restrict Rows page of the wizard; enable "Specify a query to restrict rows."

The Partition Wizard creates a relational select query up to the WHERE clause. At the end of the WHERE clause, type in **OrderDateKey<='20011231'** as shown in Figure 9-68 and click Next.

Figure 9-68

18. In the Processing and Storage Locations page, select the option "Remote Analysis Services Data Source," select the data source Target as shown in Figure 9-69, and click Next.

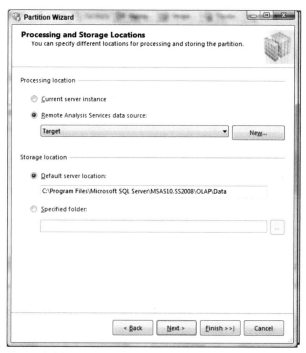

Figure 9-69

19. Select the Design aggregations later radio button, name the partition **Internet_Sales_2001** as shown in Figure 9-70, and click Finish.

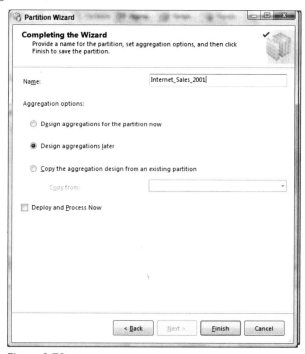

Figure 9-70

20.   Open the Internet Sales Order Details dimension and change the storage mode from ROLAP to MOLAP in the Properties window.

> **Important Security Information for Remote Partitions: We have chosen the Impersonation mode to be "Inherit" for the Data Sources within the master and subordinate databases (instances). By choosing Inherit, at the time of processing, Analysis Services instances use the service's start-up account while connecting to Analysis Services 10.0 databases. If your server start-up account for both instances is a Windows domain (user) account, you would have appropriate permissions to access the databases (so long as that start-up account has admin permissions). However, if both instances were installed with server start-up accounts as "Local System," you might encounter an access permissions error when the master database is trying to connect to the subordinate. This is because connections to named instances of Analysis Services are routed via SQL Browser and by default the server start-up account for SQL Browser is "Network Service." If your installation has the SQL Browser server start-up account as "Network Service" and the Analysis Services instances server start-up account is "Local System," please change the server start-up account of SQL Browser and the two Analysis Services instances to a Windows domain account using SQL Server Configuration Manager. The Configuration Manager can be launched from Start\All programs\Microsoft SQL Server 2008\ Configuration Tools\SQL Server Configuration Manager.**

21.   Finally, to populate the partition on the remote machine change the deployment properties by right-clicking the Adventure Works DW 2008 project name and selecting Properties. Select Deployment in the Property page and change Processing Option to "Do not process" and Deployment mode to Deploy All. Right-click the cube Adventure Works in the Solution Explorer and select Process. If asked to deploy the project, select No. In the Process dialog click Run. After processing is complete, you will be able to query data from the remote partitions.

Once the Adventure Works DW 2008 database has been processed, you can see the remote partitions quite clearly after processing as shown in Figure 9-71. And if it doesn't work for you the first time (you get errors back from your Analysis Services instance), don't worry, there are a lot of steps and therefore lots of opportunities to get things messed up. Most likely though, there are security errors; be sure to verify you have all the correct Firewall settings and Impersonation settings. Impersonation settings are changed in a secondary tab in the Data Source Wizard.

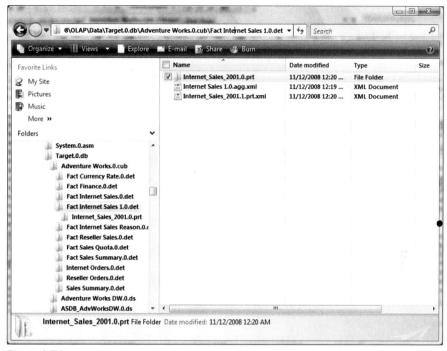

Figure 9-71

Storage Modes and Storage Settings

In Analysis Services, the storage and processing schemes are linked through the setting of caching options. Caching is a way to increase query response time by keeping the data used most often on a local disk. Where you store partition data is just one part of the storage picture; the mode in which you store it is the other. The storage modes used with Analysis Services solutions include MOLAP (Multidimensional OLAP), ROLAP (Relational OLAP), and HOLAP (Hybrid OLAP). These storage types were discussed in some detail way back in Chapter 1, so this section contains only a brief review. The main difference between these storage modes concerns where the data and (or) aggregated fact data is stored. MOLAP is the traditional storage mode for OLAP servers and involves keeping both data and aggregations on the server. This results in fast query response times, but it is not as scalable as other solutions. ROLAP is the storage mode in which the data is left in the relational database. Aggregated or summary data is also stored in the relational database. The key advantage here is that ROLAP will scale as well as your relational hardware/software will support, but will typically result in slower queries. The HOLAP storage mode theoretically combines the best features of MOLAP and ROLAP, but is not recommended in practice because the difference in query performance between queries that involve aggregations and those that require queries to the source data is so great that users will typically find this disconcerting. In HOLAP, the data in the relational database is not touched while the aggregated or summary data is stored on the Analysis Server in a proprietary format; queries that can be resolved in the Analysis Server are, and those that cannot are redirected to the relational backend.

MOLAP is generally the preferred mode due to the performance gains and efficiency in its use of storage space. If you need to analyze real-time data, ROLAP is probably more appropriate. ROLAP is also a better option when you have a very large data warehouse and you do not want to duplicate the data.

Each partition can have its own storage mode, which you specify on the Partitions tab of the Cube Designer in BIDS. Just click the Storage Settings link as shown in Figure 9-72.

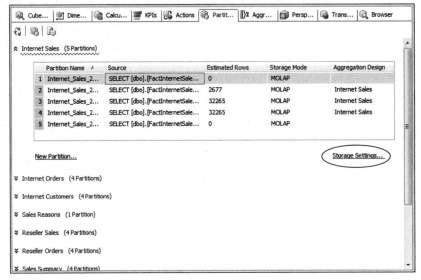

Figure 9-72

When you click Storage Settings, the dialog displays the Proactive Caching configuration screen from the Partition Wizard (see Figure 9-73). Proactive Caching is a mechanism that gives you control over the latency associated with moving data to MOLAP and reprocessing data too. You learn more about Proactive Caching options suited for various real-world scenarios in Chapter 22.

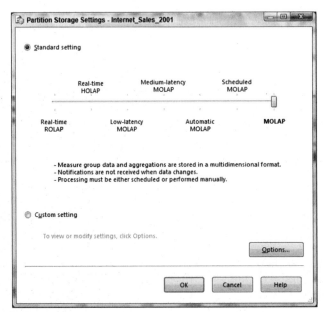

Figure 9-73

Building Aggregations

Aggregations are what makes querying OLAP systems fast. An aggregation is nothing more than a pre-calculated summary of a specific subset of partition data. Note that many partitions may share the same aggregation design or blueprint, but the actual aggregations that are pre-computed and written to disk are specific to a given a partition. The collection of all aggregations, typically in the tens up to low hundreds, is what we mean when we refer to the aggregation strategy or aggregation level for a given partition or set of partitions.

In Analysis Services 2008, a new tab has been added within the Cube Designer specifically for aggregations, as shown in Figure 9-74. The aggregation designer has two views: a standard view (Figure 9-74) that displays measure groups and aggregation designs and an advanced view (Figure 9-75) that shows the individual aggregations of a given aggregation design, in a given measure group.

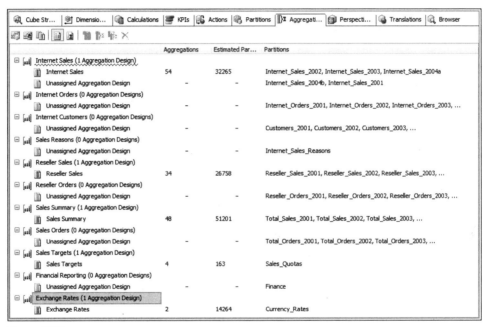

Figure 9-74

Advanced View

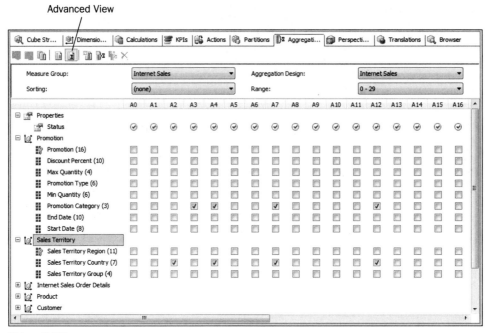

Figure 9-75

Aggregation designs are essentially blueprints for aggregations within a measure group and are intended to be shared among multiple partitions. The concept of aggregation designs, though first introduced in Analysis Services 2005, was not something that the user interface displayed explicitly until now. One of the motivations for exposing aggregation designs in the Analysis Services 2008 user interface was to avoid the bad practice of creating too many aggregation designs! In practice, you may have a need for multiple aggregation designs to differentiate highly queried partitions from those that are less often queried, but it would be very rare to need more than three.

The standard view is what most people should use most of the time. This view enables launching the aggregation wizards, changing a partition's aggregation design, assigning aggregation designs to additional partitions, and getting an overall picture of how the aggregations look within a cube. The advanced view of the aggregation designer allows for viewing, editing, and creating both aggregation designs and aggregations by hand. This view should only be used when you need either particular attributes included in one or more aggregations or particular aggregations defined when the wizards are not enabling this. In the advanced view, if you create aggregations that may not be beneficial with respect to query performance due to redundant attributes in a dimension, you will see a warning provided by the designer as shown in Figure 9-76. The designer warns you to look further into your aggregation design and make sure this is essential.

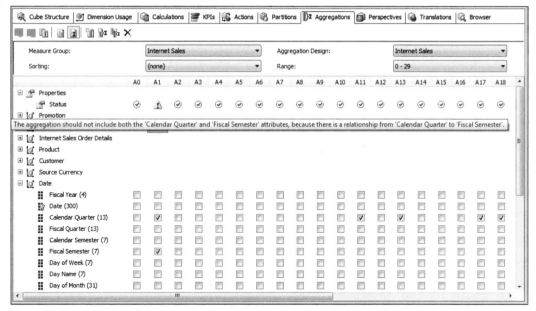

Figure 9-76

To start the Aggregation Design Wizard, click Design Aggregations in the standard view of the Aggregations tab. This wizard helps you to create aggregations for each partition, using statistical analysis of the metadata combined with custom heuristics to improve overall query performance independent of usage data. You learn Aggregation design and benefits in detail in Chapter 14. Follow these steps to understand the Aggregation Design Wizard outcome:

1. Select the Internet Sales measure group and start the Aggregation Design Wizard using the first icon in the standard view of the Aggregations tab in the Cube Designer.

2. In the Select Partitions to Modify page, select all the partitions and click Next.

3. Select the defaults in "Review Aggregation Usage" page and select Next.

4. In the Specify Object Counts page, click the Count button to get the counts for attribute members and click Next. These counts are used by an algorithm to create the optimal aggregation design.

5. In the Set Aggregation Options page, you can specify various options to design aggregations for the chosen partitions. Click the Performance gain reaches 30 percent option and click Start.

6. The performance benefits gained are graphically compared to the storage space required to store the aggregations, as shown in Figure 9-77, where you can see that the Performance Gain is set to 30 percent. A good starting target should be around 25 percent to 30 percent, but you learn about the Usage-Based Optimization wizard in Chapter 14 for fine-tuning performance gains even further using actual usage data. Click Cancel in the Aggregation Design Wizard.

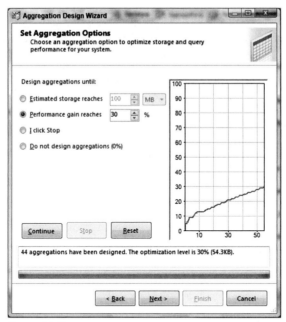

Figure 9-77

You can validate that the aggregations were defined by the wizard by expanding the relevant measure group in the Aggregations tab, locating the row corresponding to the aggregation design, and clicking the button in the cell corresponding to the Partitions column or reviewing the Aggregation Design column for each partition in the Partitions tab, as shown in Figure 9-72. You do need to deploy the aggregations created by the wizard to your Analysis Services instance to make sure the aggregations are processed and available for querying. To validate that the aggregations defined by the wizard are useful, you need to trace the query execution using SQL Server Profiler, which you learn how to do in Chapter 15.

The Aggregation Design Process

You can design aggregations in three ways:

❑ **Use the Aggregation Design Wizard:** This wizard uses built-in heuristics combined with statistical techniques to determine candidate aggregations based on database metadata. It's important to note that no usage information is required here. The only requirement is that you can successfully deploy (not process) the database to a server.

❑ **Use the Usage-Based Optimization (UBO) Wizard:** As the name implies, this wizard takes the queries recorded in the query log as the primary input and reconciles these with database metadata in order to generate candidate aggregations.

❑ **Manually design aggregations using the Advanced View of the Aggregation Designer:** This is an inherently risky and error-prone option that should only be used by very advanced users. As the name implies, this method requires you to work at the level of individual aggregations and make decisions regarding which attributes will be included.

All three methods are of course valid, but there are recommendations around how and when to use each method. Generally speaking, the safest and best starting point in the absence of usage data is to run the Aggregation Design Wizard, selecting an optimization level of between 20 and 30 percent. This will provide you with a baseline set of aggregations while you build your query log. Another option is to populate the query log yourself if you are confident that you have a representative query set. In this case, you would skip the Aggregation Design Wizard and go straight to the Usage-Based Optimization (UBO) Wizard. For reasons discussed in the UBO section in this chapter , the recommendation when running the Analysis Services 2008 UBO Wizard is to use a 100 percent optimization level. Lastly, very advanced users with detailed knowledge of query patterns, attribute and fact sizes, and a good feeling for sparseness levels, can manually design the initial set of aggregations.

When using the Aggregation Design Wizard, you can leverage a new feature in SSAS 2008, the Aggregation Usage screen (see Figure 9-78), to lower or raise the importance level of cube dimension attributes. This is not a new property — what's new is displaying this is in a single location rather than needing to cycle through each cube attribute in the Structure tab prior to running the wizard. The effect of this property is to control the way in which the aggregation design algorithm considers the attribute (raise or lower importance), or, optionally, to exclude the attribute altogether. We cover how the algorithm deals with attributes and what the various settings mean shortly, but the key initial takeaway is that you should view the functionality of this screen as a way to both reduce the search space of the algorithm and give certain attributes increased weighting.

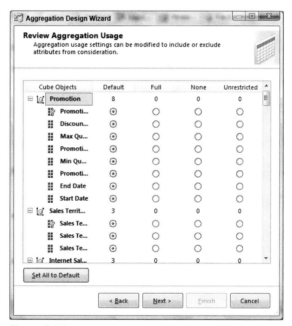

Figure 9-78

By default, all cube attributes have their aggregation usage property value set to Default, as you might expect. Before modifying this property, it's important to understand what each of the respective values mean:

❑ **Full:** Every aggregation for the cube must include this attribute or a related attribute that is lower in the attribute chain. For example, you have a date dimension with the following chain of related attributes: Date, Month, and Quarter. If you specify the Aggregation Usage for Quarter to be Full, Analysis Services may create an aggregation that includes Month as opposed to Quarter, given that Month is related to Quarter and can be used to derive Quarter totals.

❑ **None:** No aggregation for the cube may include this attribute. This is a good value to set when you know the attribute in question is unlikely to be queried by end users.

❑ **Unrestricted:** No restrictions are placed on the aggregation designer. However, the attribute must still be evaluated to determine whether it is a valuable aggregation candidate. This is a good middle ground between Default and Full, and it should generally be used when application of the default rule does not result in a commonly queried attribute to be considered.

❑ **Default:** The designer applies a default rule based on the type of attribute and dimension.

What follows is the set of rules that determine how the value Default is interpreted by the wizards. In general, the wizard is highly conservative about which attributes are considered for aggregation when the aggregation usage is set to default.

❑ **Default Constraint 1 — Unrestricted for the Granularity and All Attributes:** For the dimension attribute that is the measure group granularity attribute and the All attribute, apply **Unrestricted**. The granularity attribute is the same as the dimension's key attribute as long as the measure group joins to a dimension using the primary key attribute.

❑ **Default Constraint 2 — None for Special Dimension Types:** For all attributes (except All) in many-to-many, non-materialized reference dimensions, linked, and data mining dimensions, use **None**. The wizard will simply remove these dimension types from the UI. The designer, in turn, will do the same.

❑ **Default Constraint 3 — Unrestricted for Natural Hierarchies:** For all user hierarchies, apply a special scanning process to identify the attributes in natural hierarchies. As you might recall, a natural hierarchy is a user hierarchy where all attributes participating in the hierarchy contain attribute relationships at every level of the hierarchy. To identify the natural hierarchies, Analysis Services scans each user hierarchy, starting at the top level and then moving down through the hierarchy to the bottom level. For each level, it checks whether the attribute of the current level is linked to the attribute of the next level via a direct or indirect attribute relationship. For every attribute that passes the natural hierarchy test, apply **Unrestricted**, except for nonaggregatable attributes, which are set to **Full**.

❑ **Default Constraint 4 — None For Everything Else:** For all other dimension attributes, apply **None**.

Now that you know what the various values of the Aggregation Usage mean, you can correctly modify the setting in order to obtain better quality aggregations when designing aggregations using the Aggregation Design Wizard. Note that this property does not apply (it's ignored) when running the Usage-Based Optimization Wizard. The Aggregation Usage screen will only display dimensions that are eligible to participate in the aggregation usage process. Changes made in this screen will overwrite the cube attribute's Aggregation Usage property. When an attribute is going to be considered, the text of the name will be bolded; this applies to Default, Unrestricted, and Full settings. Additionally, the first time the Full value is selected, a pop-up message appears warning that this value should be used very sparingly. You may ask why the UI goes to such lengths to call-out this scenario. The reason for this is that if a large (high cardinality) attribute is selected and/or multiple attributes have their values set to Full, every single potential aggregation may be thrown out due to excessive size. What would result in such cases is fewer or even no aggregations being designed because the wizard will automatically discard any aggregations that are greater than 30 percent of the size of the partition tables. Aggregation design is also discussed in Chapter 14 because it is critical to optimal cube design to get the best query performance.

Usage-Based Optimization

The UBO wizard can be launched using the second icon in the Aggregations tab of the Cube Designer in BIDS. There are several key enhancements to the Usage-Based Optimization (UBO) Wizard in SSAS 2008. An often lamented omission for SSAS 2005 was the ability to append the results of a UBO pass to an existing set of aggregations (aggregation design). This capability is now available in SSAS 2008 via an option on the Finish page of the wizard that allows the choice of either creating a new aggregation design or appending new aggregations to an existing aggregation design (see Figure 9-79). The UI will automatically strip out any duplicates when doing the merge, but logically equivalent aggregations (those that essentially cover the same or very similar cube space) will not be detected. In practice, this means that you must be careful not to over-aggregate via this option. So, how do you know when you've over-aggregated? Having several hundred aggregations or more is a good initial indication. Another indication, which is more common in practice, has to do with the inability to process your data in the allotted window of time. Remember, aggregations must be computed in memory and subsequently written to disk during processing, so it's important to validate the impact on processing as well as query performance.

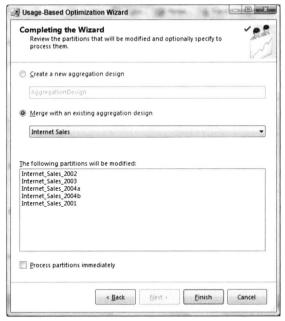

Figure 9-79

The next big change made to UBO for 2008 is a modification of the algorithm itself. The new algorithm focuses exclusively on the cube space as described by the query log. The net effect of this change is to produce more effective aggregations in less time. In internal product team testing, we've seen great improvements along three key dimensions of performance: time to converge (which is the time it takes to design aggregations in the UI), time to process, and query performance.

The algorithm changes have necessitated a few UI tweaks, which we'll now cover. First off, all attributes now need to be counted, and the UI will accordingly enforce this. Secondly, 100 percent optimization is the recommend setting for optimization level, and the defaults in the UI have been modified accordingly. This setting will ensure that all possible aggregations are considered and typically lead to a better end result. If time and/or space considerations dictate the need for fewer aggregations, you can always edit the aggregation design in the new aggregation editor and delete any aggregations you find to be less useful.

Designing aggregations using UBO is discussed in the context of designing high-performing cubes in Chapter 14.

Defining Security

Now that you know how to create and enhance a cube to meet your business needs, you also need to know how to provide the right level of access to end users. Many people consider security to be a management task that should be assigned to the administrators. However, your solution might require Analysis Services to perform fine-grain security checks, which can adversely impact calculations. Hence, the cube developer should be actively involved in defining and testing security to verify that users see the right data and experience good query performance.

Analysis Services provides you with fine-grain security settings to control access to metadata and data. You can also grant permissions to certain users who need the ability to process a database, but who do not need full control of the database. You can choose to secure data at the cube level, the dimension level, or even the cell level. Because security is an important topic for you to understand, especially with regard to dimension and cell security, Chapter 22 provides a complete example of a security definition. In this section, you learn the basic steps involved in granting write access permissions to a cube and its dimensions. The following steps will help you better understand how access permissions can be applied to your cubes and dimensions:

1. Right-click the Roles folder in the Solution Explorer of the sample Adventure Works DW 2008 project and choose New Role. BIDS will create a new role called Role. and open the Role designer as shown in Figure 9-80.

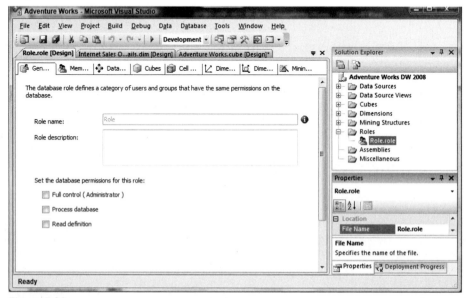

Figure 9-80

2. In the General tab, you can give members you assign to this role full control of the database, or you can limit their activities to processing the database or simply reading the database definitions. Selecting Full Control automatically grants full access including write permissions to change the objects within the current database. The Process Database option grants access to the users so that they can read the metadata about database objects and process the objects. Users who have Process Database control will not be able to make changes to dimensions and cubes or even data within these. Read Definition allows the users to read metadata of the objects within the database, however it does not give you access to the data. Select the option that is best-suited for your users and provide some description for the current role in the Role description box.

3. Click the Membership tab. In the Membership tab, you can add the list of users for whom you want the specific access you have selected. Analysis Services accepts all domain users or machine users in this dialog. Analysis Services verifies that the user entered is a valid user and then stores the ID of the user within the database. Add a local machine user or a domain user in your company to the membership list and then click the Data Sources tab.

4. Figure 9-81 shows the Data Sources tab, which you use to restrict users from accessing the cube's data sources. By default, access to data sources is set to None. Typically, access to data sources might be needed in data mining scenarios in which you might query the relational source data for prediction. Enabling the Read Definition option allows the users to retrieve information such as database name, tables, views, and so on of the data source.

Figure 9-81

5. The Cubes tab is shown in Figure 9-82. Here you have the option to grant access to specific cubes. By default, users have no access to any cube in a database to ensure that developers or administrators do not accidentally provide cube access to users who are not supposed to have access. You have the option of providing read access only or read/write access to each cube in the database. You can also see there is the option of Local Cube/Drillthrough Access. These options allow you to specifically grant users the ability to create local cubes or drill through to more detailed data. In addition, you can limit access to Drillthrough only or to Drillthrough and Local Cube. Local cubes are typically created from Excel so that small versions of cubes can be shared with other users. Local cubes (also called offline cubes) are covered in Chapter 17. The Process option allows you to grant users the ability to process selected cubes. Select Read/Write access to the Adventure Works cube, and then click the Dimensions tab.

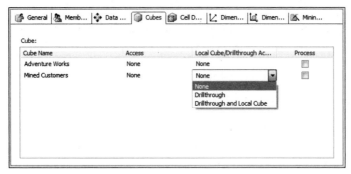

Figure 9-82

6. In the Dimensions tab, you have the option to control which database dimensions or cube dimensions a user can access if they've already been granted access to the cube. Figure 9-83 shows how you can define security for the database dimensions or the cube dimensions of the Adventure Works cube. If you select the All database dimensions option, you will see all the dimensions listed with three columns in which you specify the type of access, Read Definition access, and Process capabilities. The Process column is used to provide process permission to specific dimensions. By default, Read access is applied to all the dimensions, but you can change the access type to Read/Write for any dimension. If you allow the Read/Write option, the users have the ability to alter the dimension structure or data. The Read Definition access allows users to query for certain properties of the dimension such as count of hierarchies, members, and levels in the dimension.

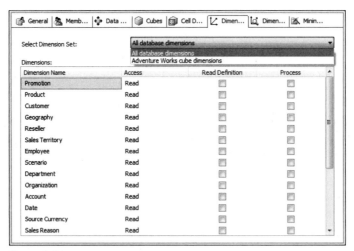

Figure 9-83

If you select the cube dimensions option, you will see two columns called Inherit and Access for each of the dimensions, as shown in Figure 9-84. By default, the Inherit column is selected, meaning that all the permissions specified for the database dimension are inherited by the cube dimension. You do have the option of overriding the database dimension access permissions. For example, you might provide Read access to all the database dimensions, Inherit for all the cube dimensions, and then Read/Write permissions on a specific dimension so that you allow certain users to writeback data to the dimension or alter dimension structure. To override the database dimension permission access, you need to deselect the Inherit option and then select the Read/Write option from the Access column.

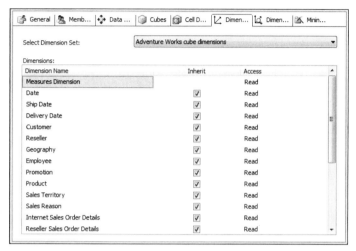

Figure 9-84

As you can see, the role of designer lets you easily specify the right access permissions to the dimensions and cubes within an Analysis Services database. If you have provided access only to the Adventure Works cube, but not to the Mined Customers cube, then when you connect to Analysis Services through SQL Server Management Studio as one of the users listed in the role's membership, you will not see the Mined Customers cube. On the other hand, if you assign a user to two roles, with one role granting access to the Adventure Works cube and the other role granting access to the Mined Customers cube, the user will see both cubes because role permissions are additive. In BIDS, you can test the effect of security, including membership in multiple roles, by browsing the cube under a specific role or a user. If you try to browse a cube for which the current user or role has not been granted permissions, you will get an error message that says you do not have access to the cube.

In this section, you have learned how to define access permissions (read or write permissions) for cubes and dimensions. This ensures correct access restriction to a specific cube or a dimension as a whole to certain users querying the database. Some business scenarios call for restricted access to just a part of the dimension or cube. For example, if I am a sales manager in a chain of retail stores, I might only be given access to view sales information specific to my store. Defining the right security for dimension and cell data is best learned through a scenario; expect to find out more about restricting data access to users in Chapter 22. As for mining models, the Mining Structures tab allows you to define security for mining models, which we will not be covering in this book.

AMO Warnings

AMO (Analysis Services Management Object) Warnings is the name given to a set of best practices built into the Analysis Services object model and exposed by the design tools. There's a lot of history behind this feature. When working on the 2005 release of SQL Server Analysis Services, we introduced the notion of real-time designer validations of errors. These validations were surfaced via red squiggly lines under the offending object. The validations proved to be a real benefit to cube designers because they allowed for a very tight temporal correlation between an action and the result of that action. Practically speaking, it's much easier to correct errors as they happen, while the action that triggered the error is still fresh in your mind, rather than doing it infrequently (such as on build or deploy) and then having to remember what you were thinking when you made the change that caused the error and to parse through potentially many such errors.

All of this formed the backdrop of the AMO Warnings feature. After the release of the SSAS 2005, it became clear that the product was very complex, with a very open-ended and sometimes overly optimistic set of tools, and dispersed best practices (blogs, forums, whitepapers, and so on) that were not immediately obvious to the average user. To this end, work was done to pull together the most important best design practices (you learn the best practices in Chapter 14) and place this information in the product via warnings, which unlike errors would not prevent deployment and could therefore be dismissed and/or ignored. The goal was to provide a path of success through the product that was built-in (and thus minimize the need to search blogs, forums, whitepapers, and so on), obvious, efficient (real/design time rather than after deployment), and unobtrusive (no pop-ups or anything else that might result in blockage of workflow).

The mechanism for exposing the warnings is via blue squiggly lines that, like their red counterparts, surface tooltips on hover. On build, any warnings will be displayed in the error list. More than 50 such warnings are in the product. Over time, expect this list to grow and change in response to customer and community feedback.

Design Experience

If you open the AnalysisServices2008Tutorial project provided online for Chapter 9 and open the Dim Date Dimension you will see two warnings as shown in Figure 9-85. Like errors, most of the OLAP designers now check (on every change, otherwise periodically) with AMO to validate the structure of the object in question. In fact, the existing VALIDATE method was simply extended in SSAS 2008 to enable receiving warning information as well.

As mentioned, hovering over a given warning will surface the textual description (see Figure 9-85). Additionally, each AMO warning has a dedicated help topic that can be queried when more information is needed about the warning in question.

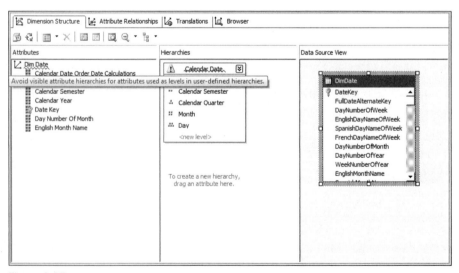

Figure 9-85

Dismissing Warnings

Figure 9-86 shows the integration with the Error List window as well as the Dismiss Warning dialog. The Error List window will show the list of AMO warnings when you build your Analysis Services project. You can right-click a specific warning and click Dismiss to remove warning from future project builds. Each warning can be individually dismissed via the Dismiss Warning dialog, which is invoked from the Error List. Additionally, a comment can be specified, which is especially useful if you are working in a team environment. It's important to note that you are only dismissing a single instance of a single warning via this dialog. For example, there is a warning about not setting the Unknown Member property of a dimension to None. This warning is then shown for each and every dimension that violates the best practice. Using the Dismiss Warning dialog, you are able to handle each dimension on a case-by-case basis. To dismiss a given warning globally (in other words, turn it off), you need to deselect the warning in the database editor (more on this in the next section).

Where do dismissed warnings go? This information is not lost. Dismissed warnings, whether individual or global, are recorded as database annotations and displayed in the database editor. One of the main benefits of this approach is that the information is not user-specific and can be viewed by anyone who opens the project. As you learn in a moment, dismissed warnings can also be re-enabled.

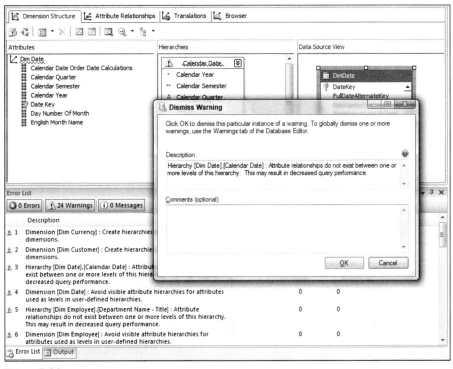

Figure 9-86

Warnings Designer

Figure 9-87 shows the Warnings tab, which is a new addition to the Database Designer for SSAS 2008. You can access this editor by right-clicking the Analysis Services project name and selecting Edit Database. The designer consists of two grids: The top grid contains the available warning rules. The lower grid contains any individually dismissed warnings.

Warning rules are grouped by area:

❑ Cube Design

❑ Data Source Design

❑ Database Design

❑ Dimension Design

❑ Partition and Aggregation Design

Warning rules also have a notion of importance, with three such levels: High, Medium, and Low. Warnings rules can be turned off using the top grid. As with the Dismiss Warning dialog, a comment may optionally be specified for the benefit of teammates or even if only to jog your memory down the line.

Individually dismissed warnings are displayed in the lower grid. There is also a button to re-enable warnings should you find that you've changed your mind. Generally speaking, it's strongly recommended to heed the high importance warnings. Medium importance warnings vary (in reality there's a spectrum here), but those should be carefully considered as well. The low importance warnings are obviously less important and less of an issue to dismiss.

Figure 9-87

Summary

Okay Neo, crawl up out of the rabbit hole; you have reached the conclusion of this chapter. And what a profound trip that was! This chapter has hopefully provided you with amazing new tools for your BI repertoire. In fact, consider yourself admitted to the knowledgeable inner-circle of BI professionals because you know that you can add measure groups from any accessible cube to your own cube without the use of views in SQL Server. This one change encapsulates a lot of power, and you are going to have fun discovering that power. Similarly, with remote partitions there is that compelling scalability factor that kicks in; it's great! The Cube Wizard also provides you with the ability to create cubes without a data source through templates similar to the Dimension Wizard, which was not discussed in this chapter. The Cube Wizard has two templates to choose from. Once the cube has been created you would need to populate the tables with appropriate data before processing the cube. We leave it to you to explore this option from the Cube Wizard by selecting the build method "build a cube without a data source."

You've also learned about partition and aggregation design, including the enhancements made to the wizards, as well as the new UBO algorithm and dedicated aggregation designer. These new aggregation tools in Analysis Services 2008 will enable better initial aggregation designs, better usage-driven aggregations, and the ability to gain insight and even modify individual aggregations. AMO Warnings are another new feature in Analysis Services 2008 and represent the first time that best practices in design have been natively integrated into the object model and design environment. With the inclusion of these best practices, even novice cube builders can build optimized, well-performing databases!

Much of this chapter was dedicated to cube enhancements, which fall directly to the bottom line of providing business information; using actions and KPIs both will enhance any digital dashboard you might create. In fact, when you start building custom front ends for consumption of your business intelligence applications, like the now ubiquitous dashboards, which reflect current business operations; there are cases where you will have to write your own application for filtering based on real-time data. Indeed, some complex and custom operations cannot even be defined in a cube. For such operations, Analysis Services provides support for the writing of custom code that interacts with Analysis Services data. There is more on the programmatic approach in the next chapter.

10

Advanced Topics in MDX

This chapter follows up on and extends what you learned back in Chapter 3: the basic concepts of the MDX language and how to write MDX queries. You also learned about the MDX operators and functions that are supported by the MDX language; including calculated member and named sets creation. If you are thinking, "that was several chapters ago, I already forgot everything!" you might want to go back and review the material before continuing here. In Analysis Services 2008, the majority of calculations are defined in a dedicated location, called the MDX script. (Technically, there can be multiple scripts per cube, though the UI only surfaces one.)

MDX scripts can contain complex calculations on multidimensional data and consist of various types of MDX statements and commands, each separated by semicolons. CALCULATE, SCOPE, IF-THEN-ELSE, and CASE are just a few of the MDX statements that can be used within an MDX script. MDX scripts are meant to be structured in a way that the flow of the statements is simple and readable. The scripting language itself is based on a procedural programming model and although it may sound complex, it is actually simpler to use than certain predecessor technologies. This is due to simplification of syntax. You can actually step through statements in MDX scripts and see results formulated in real-time, which is a real boon to the debugging process, as you saw in Chapter 9.

Of particular importance for successful MDX Script usage is an understanding and mastery of the various ways calculation order can be specified. In this chapter, you learn more about that functionality — specifically, about how calculations are implemented and evaluated in Analysis Services 2008 MDX scripts. Additionally, this chapter provides you with examples of MDX queries that can be written to solve common business problems. These examples are created for use with the sample Adventure Works DW project updated for Analysis Services 2008. For details on the process of debugging calculations, refer back to Chapter 9, which covered this and other advanced topics related to cubes. Some of the MDX queries you will need to write to solve business problems necessitate the use of cube space restriction, empty cell removal, and parameterized queries — all concepts covered in this chapter.

Calculation Fundamentals

At the core of the Analysis Services engine is the ability to model various complex business problems using calculations. In older versions of Analysis Services, calculations were based on dimensions such that each dimension typically contained one or more multilevel hierarchies. Starting with Analysis Services 2005, the calculation model changed due to the introduction of a new multidimensional approach that combined the traditional OLAP and relational worlds. That combination leveraged the Unified Dimensional Model through attribute hierarchies (which are entities within a dimension). Attributes and relationships between attributes form the basis of the new calculation model. Hierarchies (attribute or multilevel) are the way of navigating the dimensional space. Attribute hierarchies typically have two levels, the optional "All" level and another level that contains all the members of the attribute. Hence, cells in the cube space can be accessed directly through the attribute hierarchies or multilevel hierarchies. Though most of the calculation definitions for a cube are defined within the MDX Script, some calculations are specified as properties of dimension attributes. Even while defining security for various hierarchies within a dimension, you specify the security restrictions through the attribute hierarchies of the dimension. Hence, attributes form the fundamental building blocks for all calculations in Analysis Services 2008.

MDX Scripts

As previously mentioned, MDX Scripts contain a set of MDX Statements separated by semicolons. MDX Scripts typically contain the calculations that need to be applied to a cube including creation of calculated members, named sets, and calculations for the cells in Analysis Services 2008 cubes. The cube is populated based on the calculations defined in the cube. Users of the cube can have different security permissions defined for dimensions and cubes within a database (you learn about securing data in Chapters 9 and 22). Therefore, when a user connects to a cube, Analysis Services evaluates the security permissions for the user. After the security permissions are evaluated, the user gets assigned a cube context. Calculations applied to a user's cube context are based on their security permissions. The data populated within the cube for the user is based on the security permissions of that user. If a cube context with that specific set of permissions already exists, the user is automatically assigned to that cube context.

You use MDX Scripts to write your business calculations. All calculations are a sequence of statements that are self contained, similar to a procedural language. Analysis Services allows multiple people to collaborate and develop the UDM for a company. Even if more than one user is defining the calculations for the UDM, the calculation can be included in a single MDX script with appropriate comments, which can reduce potential errors. No more quarrels with your co-worker about who made the mistake and why the cube is not working. Analysis Services 2008 tools help you debug MDX scripts interactively, more like debugging a program, to identify any semantic errors in calculations defined in the script. Syntactic errors are automatically flagged by Analysis Services when the cube is deployed to the Analysis Services instance. The real value of the MDX script is to define calculations that assign values to cells in the cube space based upon potentially complex business logic. Analysis Services, with the help of the SCOPE statement, helps you narrow down the cube space to which the calculation needs to be applied. For complex conditions that cannot be covered using the SCOPE statement, use the CASE statement. An example of an assignment is to allocate your sales quota for next year based on the sales of the current year. You see more about this later in this chapter.

When you have a large script with several calculations, there might be instances where you will want the calculations to be applied in a different order than that dictated by the MDX script. Some calculations are specified as properties of dimension attributes, such as custom rollup column and unary operator column (which are shown in Chapter 8). Calculations applied to a cell not only depend on the calculations in MDX scripts but also how the calculations' custom rollups and unary operators change the cell value. Analysis Services 2008 applies calculations to cube cells based on a set of precedence rules.

The CALCULATE Statement

When you create a cube using the Cube Wizard within the Business Intelligence Development Studio, a default MDX script is created for you. You can see the script definitions in the Calculations tabs of the Cube Designer as shown in Chapter 6 and again in Chapter 9. The CALCULATE statement is added to the script by the Cube Wizard. This statement indicates that the Analysis Services instance is to aggregate the data from the lowest level of attributes and hierarchies to higher levels. Aggregation of data to various levels of a hierarchy is illustrated in Figures 10-1 through 10-3. Assume you have a cube that has three dimensions: Geography, Products, and Time, with hierarchies Customer Geography, ProductLine, and Date, respectively. For illustration purposes assume Customer Geography and ProductLine are single-level hierarchies and Date is a multilevel hierarchy with levels Quarter, Semester, and Year.

When a user accesses the cube, the fact data first gets loaded into the cube as shown in Figure 10-1, which represents data for a specific year. Depending on the storage type (ROLAP, MOLAP, or HOLAP) the fact data would be retrieved from the relational data source or from local Analysis Services storage. This is referred to as PASS 0 within Analysis Services. Consider PASS as an analogy of doing a first visit of all the cells within the cube. Once the fact data has been loaded into the cube, Analysis Services applies calculations for the cells based on the calculations specified in the MDX scripts or dimension attributes. Assume this cube has the default MDX script with a CALCULATE command. After loading the fact data, Analysis Services executes the MDX script. When the CALCULATE statement is encountered, the fact data aggregated for appropriate levels of the dimension hierarchies is made accessible to end users. Because the Product.Product Line and Customer.Country hierarchies have only one level, there is no need to aggregate the data. The Date hierarchy has the levels Semester and Year for which the data needs to be aggregated from the Quarter level. When the CALCULATE statement is encountered a new PASS, PASS 1, is created where aggregated data can be seen for various levels. Analysis Services aggregates the data for the Semester level from the Quarter level as shown in Figure 10-2 and then to the Year level as shown in Figure 10-3. You will be able to query the aggregated data.

> Note the difference in visualization of Figures 10-2 and 10-3. Think of the X-axis as Year and how the data gets aggregated. Figure 10-3 has Year in focus and how the data is aggregated. For example, the corresponding layer to Product Line and Geography and Quarter 1 cell can still be seen from the top as 1270, and from the side it is hidden.

If the CALCULATE statement is not specified in the MDX script, you will not be able to query the aggregated data for Semester and Year. If you attempt such a query you will get null values for those levels. If you are missing a CALCULATE statement in the MDX script, you can retrieve the fact data for aggregated levels only when you include all hierarchies of all dimensions in your query. For example, if you have the following query for the cube illustrated in Figure 10-1:

```
SELECT [Measures].[Internet Sales Amount] ON COLUMNS,
[Product].[Product Line].MEMBERS ON ROWS
FROM [Adventure Works]
```

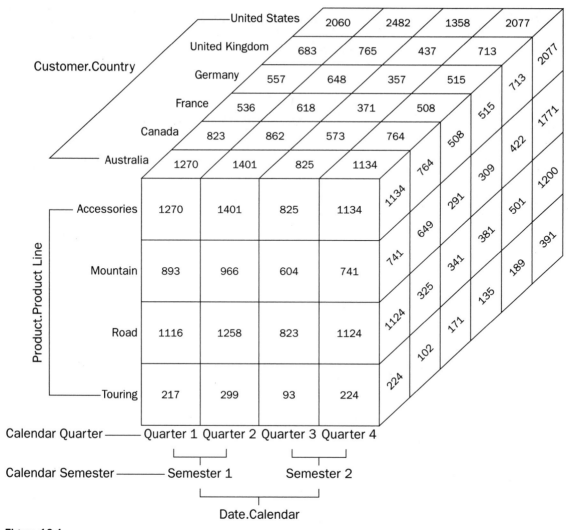

Figure 10-1

you will only see null values. If you wanted to retrieve the fact data, you would need to send the following MDX query to Analysis Services. This MDX queries each hierarchy in each dimension to retrieve the fact data.

```
SELECT [Measures].[Internet Sales Amount] ON COLUMNS,
[Product].[Product Line].MEMBERS *
[Customer].[Country].MEMBERS *
[Date].[Quarter].MEMBERS *
[Date].[Semester].MEMBERS *
[Date].[Year].MEMBERS *
[Date].[Date].MEMBERS
ON ROWS
FROM [Adventure Works]
```

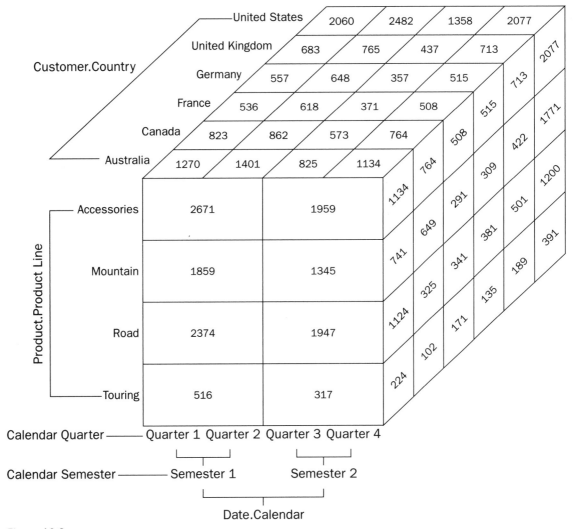

Figure 10-2

If a cube does not have an MDX script defined, a default MDX script with a CALCULATE statement is used by Analysis Services. It is not expected that users will have MDX scripts without the CALCULATE statement other than by mistake. If you do not have any calculations defined in MDX scripts and your queries return null values for various hierarchies, we recommend you check if the CALCULATE statement is included in the MDX script.

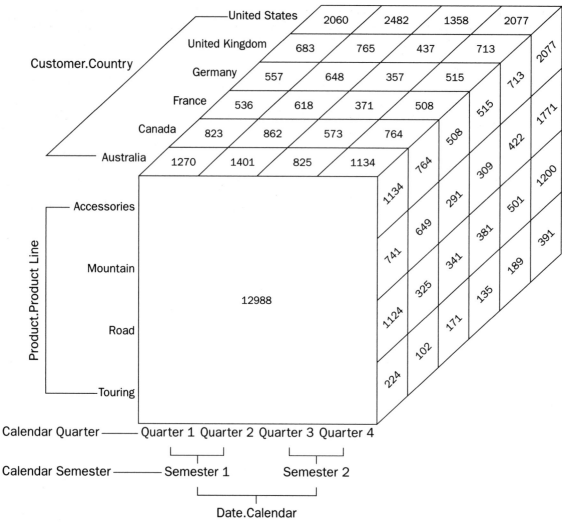

Figure 10-3

Named Sets

In Chapter 3 you learned that you can create named sets within your MDX queries and access them. Following is the example of named sets created within an MDX query:

```
WITH SET [Europe] AS { [Customer].[Country].[Country].&[France],
    [Customer].[Country].[Country].&[Germany],
    [Customer].[Country].[Country].&[United Kingdom] }
SELECT [Measures].[Internet Sales Amount] ON COLUMNS,
[Europe] ON ROWS
FROM [Adventure Works]
```

When the named sets are created within an MDX query they can only be accessed within the scope of the query. Other queries within the same session or other users in different sessions cannot access these named sets in their queries. Some of the named sets might be useful for several users, and it would be better to create them so that they can be shared across several queries or even several users. Analysis Services provides ways of defining named sets within a specific session where you can send multiple queries, or in a cube's MDX script where they can be accessed by multiple users. This is done using the CREATE statement. In both cases you create sets as shown here:

```
CREATE SET [Adventure Works].[Europe]
AS '{ [Customer].[Country].[Country].&[France],
   [Customer].[Country].[Country].&[Germany],
   [Customer].[Country].[Country].&[United Kingdom] }';
```

Instead of the WITH clause that you used in the MDX query for set creation, the CREATE statement allows you to create a set within the scope of a session or the entire cube. When you define sets using the CREATE command, you need to specify the cube name as a prefix as shown in the CREATE statement in the preceding code. You do not specify the name of the dimension when you specify the set. This is because a set can contain tuples that are formed by multiple hierarchies that are from one or more dimensions. Hence, irrespective of whether or not all the tuples in a set are from a single hierarchy, the created set is not considered to be part of any single dimension.

Once the set has been created using the CREATE SET command, it can be accessed in any query. If the named set was created within a session, it would be valid only within that specific session and could not be used by users in other sessions. If named sets are to be used by several users, we recommend you create them in the cube scope by defining them in the MDX script. Named sets can be in one of three scopes when an MDX query is being executed:

❑   They can be within the query scope where they are defined with the WITH clause in MDX.

❑   They can be within the session scope where they can be created within a specific session using the CREATE SET statement you just learned.

❑   They can be scoped as global and defined within an MDX script using the CREATE SET statement.

Analysis Services checks for resolving members or sets in an MDX query within query, session, and global scopes in that order. Analysis Services 2008 adds the very useful ability to define dynamically evaluated sets. Before speaking further about dynamic sets, it makes sense to discuss static sets a little bit. We'll use the following CREATE SET statement to illustrate our point. The following statement is meant to be added to your MDX script and will be of a global scope:

```
CREATE SET CURRENTCUBE.[Static Top 10 Customers]
   AS TopCount
     (
        [Customer].[Customer].[Customer].MEMBERS,
        10,
        [Measures].[Internet Sales Amount]
     ) ;
```

Prior to Analysis Services 2008, a set would be evaluated once in whatever context it was created. Imagine this example defined in a query scope using WITH SET rather than CREATE SET. Evaluating the top ten customers once in the context of a query is just fine because the query will set the dimensional context and use it once. Defining the set in the scope of a session or at the cube level (to be used across all future client sessions) is clearly problematic for this type of data-bound set. The set will be evaluated when the client connects or in the current session context so any subsequent filters (say by product or time period) will not result in the set membership being updated and will effectively return bad data.

Dynamic sets in Analysis Services 2008 solve this issue by allowing sets to be defined as dynamic. In practice, this means that the set will not be static and will be evaluated in the context of every query that directly or indirectly references them and with respect to the WHERE clause and/or SUB-SELECTS.

Here is the preceding set, defined to be dynamic:

```
CREATE DYNAMIC SET CURRENTCUBE.[ Dynamic Top 10 Customers]
  AS TopCount
    (
      [Customer].[Customer].[Customer].MEMBERS,
      10,
      [Measures].[Internet Sales Amount]
    ) ;
```

A final addition to named sets in Analysis Services 2008 is the capability to specify, in MDX, the following two properties:

❑   CAPTION

❑   DISPLAY_FOLDER

The CAPTION property is primarily for scenarios involving session scoped calculations where greater flexibility in naming (for example, when defining reports) may be desired and as such is not exposed in the user interface. The DISPLAY_FOLDER property allows for defining a customizable folder structure in which to display metadata. A hierarchical organization may be specified by separating display folders by backslashes (\). The DISPLAY_FOLDER property was possible to define in Analysis Services 2005 but only existed as an XML property, not in the MDX language. By moving this property into the MDX language, the MDX Script becomes more complete and descriptive, and client applications can leverage this to provide richer end-user experiences, especially around personalization.

Named sets are really convenient and useful for querying because the MDX queries using them are easy to read and allow multiple users to access them. However, you should be aware that there is a memory cost associated with holding them in Analysis Services. If you need to create a large number of named sets that are quite large in terms of number of tuples, exercise caution. We recommend you drop any named sets whenever they are not used. Just as there is a CREATE SET statement, there is a statement to delete named sets or calculated members as well. The DROP SET statement does the job of deleting sets and calculated members. The syntax for the DROP SET statement is simple:

```
DROP SET <setname>
```

Calculated Members

Similar to named sets, you learned that calculated members can be created using the WITH clause within a query. Following is the query used in Chapter 3 for creating a calculated member:

```
WITH MEMBER [Measures].[Profit] AS '( [Measures].[Internet Sales Amount] -
  [Measures].[Total Product Cost] )'
SELECT [Measures].[Profit] ON COLUMNS,
[Customer].[Country].MEMBERS ON ROWS
FROM [Adventure Works]
```

As with named sets, calculated members can also be created using the CREATE statement as follows as session calculated members:

```
CREATE MEMBER [Adventure Works].[Measures].[Profit] AS
  '([Measures].[Internet Sales Amount] - [Measures].[Total Product Cost])';
```

When you create a calculated member in the MDX script you use the CURRENTCUBE keyword instead of the cube name as shown here:

```
CREATE MEMBER CURRENTCUBE.[Measures].[Profit] AS
  '([Measures].[Internet Sales Amount] - [Measures].[Total Product Cost])';
```

For creating a calculated member you use CREATE MEMBER followed by the member name. While creating named sets you did not specify which dimension the named set belonged to. However, when creating calculated members you do specify the cube and dimension name. Notice that all measures within a cube are always within a special dimension called Measures. Hence, in the preceding CREATE statement, the cube name and the dimension Measures are specified. The calculated members that are most often created by users are calculated measures, that is, calculated members on the Measures dimension. For convenience, Analysis Services 2008 assumes that a calculated member will be in the Measures dimension if it is not explicitly prefixed with Measures. Hence the following statement is valid syntax in your cube's MDX script:

```
CREATE MEMBER [Profit]
AS '( [Measures].[Internet Sales Amount] - [Measures].[Total Product Cost] )';
```

Once the calculated members have been created, you can use them as shown in the following query. The query scope, session scope, and global scope seen for named sets also apply to calculated members.

```
SELECT [Measures].[Profit] ON COLUMNS,
       [Customer].[Country].MEMBERS ON ROWS
FROM [Adventure Works]
```

Similar to named sets, calculated members can also be dropped using the DROP MEMBER statement. The syntax for DROP MEMBER is:

```
DROP MEMBER <member name>
```

Typically, client tools, interacting with Analysis Services that create MDX queries dynamically based on user actions on the front end, create and drop calculated members within sessions. One example is the OWC Pivot table control, which is used in the Cube Browser. You will see some of the MDX queries that are sent to the Analysis Services instance by client tools in Chapter 17, with detailed explanations of what these MDX queries mean.

Analysis Services 2008 provides another way to define calculated members at global scope within MDX scripts. This involves declaring a member first without any definition and later defining the expression. The following MDX statements demonstrate this new definition method for calculated members. The following statements will evaluate to the same results as that of the previous CREATE MEMBER statement. If the dimension name is not specified it is assumed the calculated member is part of the Measures dimension. They are semantically the same but it is a matter of convenience if, say, you want to create a calculated measure and are not sure about the actual expression. You can define the calculated member, use it in statements, and finally create the actual expression in the MDX script.

```
CREATE MEMBER [Profit] AS NULL;

[Measures].[Profit] = [Measures].[Sales Amount] - [Measures].
      [Total Product Cost];
```

Analysis Services 2008 further extends the calculated member syntax by enabling the definition of three properties:

- ❑ CAPTION
- ❑ DISPLAY_FOLDER
- ❑ ASSOCIATED_MEASURE_GROUP

ASSOCIATED_MEASURE_GROUP is a direct reference to an existing measure group and is used to visually group calculated measures with the appropriate physical measures. The ASSOCIATED_ MEASURE_GROUP property was available in Analysis Services 2005, but like DISPLAY_FOLDER only existed as an XML property, not in the MDX language. The CAPTION property simply controls the displayed name, as you have likely guessed. Changing the caption is most useful for session scoped calculations, and for this reason it's not exposed in the development tools.

Named sets and calculated members are the basic objects created within MDX scripts most likely to be exploited by users of the cube. You can specify properties such as format string, font, color, and background color for the calculated members as discussed in Chapter 6. Next, you see some of the additional statements that are used within MDX scripts and how they help you define your business calculations.

Cube Space and Autoexists

The cube space (cells) in an Analysis Services cube can be calculated as the product of the member count of each attribute from each dimension. As you can imagine, this space can be quite large even for a small cube that contains less than ten dimensions, with each dimension containing around ten attributes. Often the cells that have data are quite sparse compared to the entire cube space. When we refer to the data in the cube space we do not just refer to the data in the fact table. You can apply calculations through MDX expressions to various cells in your cube space. Most of these calculations are defined within MDX scripts.

Before you learn to specify cell calculations, you need to have a better understanding of the cube space that comprises all the cells in a cube. Some cells in the cube space retrieve data through calculations or are aggregated up across dimensions based on your business definitions within the cube. For example, consider the budget of your company for next year or the sales quota for next year, which are typically calculated based on profit or sales of the current year. This data is not available in the fact table but is likely based on a calculation of the data in the fact table. Similarly, you can have cell values for which data is aggregated from fact data due to the cube modeling scheme.

Assume you have a sales cube with a Time dimension containing a Time hierarchy with levels Year, Quarter, Month, and Date. In this case, the fact table contains data for each day. Analysis Services would aggregate the data for cells corresponding to month, quarter, and year. We refer to the cube space that is accessible to the users and which can be manipulated through calculations, as the real cube space. Certain cells in the cube space can be accessed through MDX queries but are actually not part of the real cube space. For example, assume a Customer dimension that has attributes Name, Gender, and Marital Status. There is a customer named Aaron Flores who is Male in the Adventure Works DW2008 sample database. The cell corresponding to Customer.Customer.[Aaron Flores] and Customer.Gender.Female does not exist in the cube space:

```
SELECT [Customer].[Customer].[Aaron Flores] ON 0,
[Customer].[Gender].&[F] ON 1
FROM [Adventure Works]
```

You can request the cell corresponding to this coordinate with the preceding MDX query and you will get a null value. You might want to see multiple attributes of a dimension on a specific axis. If you do a cross-join of multiple attributes you will get the entire cross product of all the members of the attributes involved in the cross-join. However, if you do a cross-join of attributes within the same dimension, Analysis Services eliminates the cells corresponding to attributes members that do not exist with one another in the cube space. This specific behavior is called AUTO EXISTS, which can be interpreted as an EXISTS function automatically being applied to attributes within the same dimension. The EXISTS MDX function, which you learn about later in this chapter, takes two sets and returns members of one set that exist with one or more tuples of one or more other sets. For example, if you query Internet Sales Amount along with customers across states and countries, your MDX query will be:

```
SELECT [Measures].[Internet Sales Amount] ON COLUMNS,
[Customer].[Country].[Country].MEMBERS *
[Customer].[State-Province].[State-Province].MEMBERS
ON ROWS
FROM [Adventure Works]
```

The results of this MDX query will only have the states that are within a specific country instead of a regular cross-join of the members of both hierarchies. Alberta, which is a state in Canada, does not exist in Australia and hence you do not have a tuple containing Australia and Alberta in your result.

The SCOPE Statement

If you want to perform certain operations within the scope of the entire cube, you will typically have the calculations defined within MDX scripts. CREATE and DROP SUBCUBE statements, which you learn about later in this chapter, are statements that can be used to restrict the cube space within the session scope at query time. You cannot use the CREATE SUBCUBE statement within MDX scripts. However, Analysis Services provides another statement called SCOPE. The SCOPE statement restricts the cube space so that all MDX statements and expressions specified within the SCOPE statement are evaluated exactly once against the restricted cube space. Named Sets in the MDX script are not affected by the SCOPE statement. The syntax of the SCOPE statement is:

```
SCOPE <SubCubeExpression>
 <MDX Statement>
 <MDX Statement> ...
END SCOPE
```

You can have one or more MDX statements within the SCOPE statement and you can have nested SCOPE statements. Nested SCOPE statements can often be simplified as a single SCOPE statement as long as all the MDX statements are within the innermost SCOPE statement. MDX statements expressed within SCOPE statements are really cell calculations, which you learn about in the next section. An example of SCOPE statement is:

```
SCOPE
  (
     [Date].[Fiscal Year].&[2002],
     [Date].[Fiscal].[Month].MEMBERS,
     [Measures].[Sales Amount Quota]
  ) ;

        THIS = [Date].[Fiscal].CurrentMember.Parent / 3 ;

END SCOPE ;
```

In this example the SCOPE statement restricts the cube space to the Year 2002, all the members of the Month under the Fiscal hierarchy of the Date dimension, and the measure Sales Amount Quota. The default members of the hierarchies not specified in the subcube expression become part of the subcube. The MDX expression specified within the SCOPE statement uses the keyword "THIS" to refer to the current subcube. In the preceding example, the MDX expression will take the Sales Amount Quota measure and iterate through all the members in Fiscal hierarchy of the Date dimension and replace existing measure values with one-third the value of the parent of the current member. This MDX expression is referred to as an assignment because the cells referenced within the subcube (using "THIS") are assigned values based on the MDX expression. In this specific example, the Fiscal hierarchy level Month has Sales Amount Quota allocated based on the Quarter level. A nested SCOPE statement can re-scope a hierarchy that was already scoped by an earlier SCOPE statement. For example, if you have a SCOPE statement to create a subcube for Fiscal Year 2002 and a nested scope to create a subcube for Fiscal Year 2003, then the Fiscal Year hierarchy is re-scoped to subcube of 2003.

Cell Calculations and Assignments

Now you have learned about the cube space and were introduced to calculations affecting cell values. In this section you learn about cell calculations in depth. MDX provides several ways to specify calculations, such as calculated members, calculated measures, custom rollups (which were discussed in Chapter 8), and unary operators (also discussed in Chapter 8). Using these features to affect a group of cell values or even a single cell value is not easy. Analysis Services allows you to create or apply calculations to cell values, which can help you in scenarios such as budgeting. The root of cell calculations lies in a feature first introduced in Analysis Services 2000, called (appropriately enough) Calculated Cells. You next spend some time learning about Calculated Cells because this is a great background for better understanding the current syntax and implementation.

Analysis Services 2000 introduced the statement CREATE CELL CALCULATION, which, similar to calculated members and named sets, can be specified at a query, session, or cube scope. The syntax for the CREATE CELL CALCULATION statement is:

```
CREATE CELL CALCULATION  <CubeName>.<formula name>
FOR <SetExpression> AS <MDX Expression>, <cell property list>
CONDITION = <Logical Expression>
```

In the preceding syntax, the <formula name> is an identifier for the cell calculation statement. The Set expression resolves to a set of tuples for which the cell values will be changed based on the MDX expression. The cell property list is an optional set of properties for the cell such as DISABLED, DESCRIPTION, CALCULATION_PASS_NUMBER, and CALCULATION_PASS_DEPTH, which can be applied to the cells being evaluated separated by commas. These properties help in the application of specific properties to certain cells so that the calculations are evaluated in the right order. Further, correct use of cell properties can help client tools identify these cells uniquely so that they can be represented appropriately to the end users.

An example of the CREATE CELL CALCULATION statement for the Adventure Works DW sample database can be applied to the task of making the [Sales Amount Quota] for the Fiscal Year 2005 set twice the value of the [Sales Amount] in the Fiscal Year 2004 set:

```
CREATE CELL CALCULATION [Adventure Works].[SalesQuota2005]
FOR '( [Date].[Fiscal Year].&[2005],
      [Date].[Fiscal].[Month].MEMBERS,
      [Measures].[Sales Amount Quota] )'

AS '(ParallelPeriod( [Date].[Fiscal].[Fiscal Year],
      1,
      [Date].[Fiscal].CurrentMember),
      [Measures].[Sales Amount] ) * 2 '
```

Here the set expression returns tuples for which the cell values need to be updated — in this case the months of Fiscal Year 2005. The MDX expression evaluates to the Sales Amount values of Fiscal Year 2004, which is then multiplied by 2. You can verify the results of the the cell calculation via the following MDX query:

```
SELECT {[Measures].[Sales Amount Quota],[Measures].[Sales Amount]} ON 0,
DESCENDANTS( { [Date].[Fiscal].[Fiscal Year].&[2004],
      [Date].[Fiscal].[Fiscal Year].&[2005] },
```

```
      3,
   SELF ) ON 1
FROM [Adventure Works]
```

You can see that the [Sales Amount Quota] for the months July and August 2004 (which are months in fiscal year 2005) are exactly twice the Sales Amount for the months July and August of 2003 (the corresponding months for the fiscal year 2004). The particular variant of the Descendants function (there are others) used in the preceding MDX query is used to retrieve the months of the fiscal years 2004 and 2005. The second parameter indicates the level in the hierarchy from which members need to be retrieved and the last parameter indicates whether to retrieve members only from the current level or from other levels before or after the current level. For further details on the Descendants function, please refer to Appendix A, which is available for download from this book's web site at www.wrox.com.

For the session scope and global scope you can follow the [Sales Amount Quota] example mentioned above. For global scope you need to define the cell calculation statements within MDX scripts. If you want to use this within the query scope, you need to use the CREATE CELL CALCULATION statement with the WITH clause, like this:

```
WITH CELL CALCULATION [SalesQuota2005]
FOR '( [Date].[Fiscal Year].&[2005],
    [Date].[Fiscal].[Month].MEMBERS,
    [Measures].[Sales Amount Quota] )'
AS '( ParallelPeriod( [Date].[Fiscal].[Fiscal Year], 1,
    [Date].[Fiscal].CurrentMember), [Measures].[Sales Amount] ) * 2`
SELECT { [Measures].[Sales Amount Quota],
    [Measures].[Sales Amount] } ON 0,
DESCENDANTS( { [Date].[Fiscal].[Fiscal Year].&[2004],
    [Date].[Fiscal].[Fiscal Year].&[2005] }, 3, SELF ) ON 1
FROM [Adventure Works]
```

This example can be re-written with a condition clause as shown in the next code snippet, which will result in exactly the same behavior. In the following MDX statement the condition checks for the Current Member of the Fiscal Year hierarchy and only applies the calculation to the cells if the condition is satisfied. Even though both these cell calculation statements result in the same behavior, we recommend you use the first flavor because the condition gets evaluated for each and every cell. Analysis Services restricts the cube space in the preceding example due to the selection of Fiscal Year 2005, which would give better performance if the number of cells to be updated is large.

```
CREATE CELL CALCULATION [Adventure Works].[SalesQuota2005]
FOR '([Date].[Fiscal].[Month].MEMBERS,[Measures].[Sales Amount Quota]
    )'
AS '(ParallelPeriod( [Date].[Fiscal].[Fiscal Year],
1,[Date].[Fiscal].CurrentMember),[Measures].[Sales Amount])*2 ',
CONDITION = '[Date].[Fiscal Year].CurrentMember IS
[Date].[Fiscal Year].&[2005]'
```

Cell calculations not only help you evaluate specific cell values, but also avoid the addition of members in the cube space. The properties CALCULATION_PASS_NUMBER and CALCULATION_PASS_DEPTH provide the functionality to specify complex recursive calculations such as goal-seeking equations. The CALCULATION_PASS_NUMBER specifies the PASS number at which the calculation is to be performed.

Analysis Services 2008 supports the CREATE CELL CALCULATION syntax for backward-compatibility reasons. However, assignment statements are the recommended method for defining global cell calculations in Analysis Services 2008. This syntax allows you to model complex business logic through the SCOPE statement, the CASE statement, and MDX functions such as Root and Leaves. You must be familiar with the SCOPE statement along with assignments using the "THIS" keyword from the previous section. Each assignment statement in MDX Scripts results in a new PASS value. The cell calculation example with SCOPE is as follows:

```
SCOPE([Date].[Fiscal Year].&[2005],
    [Date].[Fiscal].[Month].MEMBERS,
    [Measures].[Sales Amount Quota]);
THIS = (ParallelPeriod( [Date].[Fiscal].[Fiscal Year],
1,[Date].[Fiscal].CurrentMember),[Measures].[Sales Amount])*2;
END SCOPE;
```

The preceding cell calculation is simple in the sense that it does not require special conditions. It is referred to as a simple assignment because the cell value for the current coordinate indicated by "THIS" is assigned a value, which is evaluated from the MDX expression on the right-hand side. If you have a complex expression with several conditions to apply to the cell calculation, a simple assignment will not be sufficient. You can use the IF statement to check for conditions before applying the cell calculation. For example, if you want the Sales Amount Quota to be two times the previous year's Sales Amount just for the first quarter, your calculation using the IF statement will be:

```
SCOPE( [Date].[Fiscal Year].&[2004],
    [Date].[Fiscal].[Month].MEMBERS,
    [Measures].[Sales Amount Quota] );

    THIS = ( ParallelPeriod( [Date].[Fiscal].[Fiscal Year], 1,
        [Date].[Fiscal].CurrentMember ),
        [Measures].[Sales Amount] ) * 1.3;
    IF ( [Date].[Fiscal].CurrentMember.Parent IS
        [Date].[Fiscal].[Fiscal Quarter].&[2004]&[1] )
    THEN THIS = ( ParallelPeriod( [Date].[Fiscal].[Fiscal Year], 1,
        [Date].[Fiscal].CurrentMember ),
        [Measures].[Sales Amount] ) * 2.0
    END IF;

END SCOPE;
```

The syntax of the IF statement is:

```
IF <conditional_expression> THEN <assignment_expression> END IF;
```

As you can you see, the statement is pretty straightforward. In fact it is quite easy to debug statements in MDX scripts with the help of the MDX debugger within the Cube Designer (you learned how to debug MDX scripts in Chapter 9). The assignment_expression is a valid MDX assignment statement. Examples of assignment_expression include MDX expressions assigned to a subcube or calculation properties applied to a subcube. END IF indicates the end of the IF statement. In the preceding example, you first assign values to all the cells corresponding to the subcube to be 1.3 times the value of the Sales amount in the previous year. Then you use the conditional IF statement to update the first quarter's cell values to be two times the Sales Amount.

You can get into more complex expressions that may require multiple IF statements, which can lead to updating cells multiple times. The cube space is large, and applying cell calculations on a large cube space can lead to performance degradation. Hence, Analysis Services provides the CASE statement to perform assignments.

The syntax for the CASE statement is:

```
CASE <value_expression>
WHEN <value_expression> THEN <statement>
ELSE  <statement>
END;
```

Here an MDX statement is assigned one of the values specified by the CASE statement. Assume for the Fiscal Year 2004 you need to specify the Sales Amount Quota based on some condition, such as: The Sales Quota for the first quarter must be 1.3 times the previous year's sales amount; for the second quarter, the quota is 2 times the previous year's sales amount; and for the third and fourth quarters, the quota is 1.75 times the previous year's sales amount. You can specify this condition easily using the CASE statement as follows:

```
SCOPE ( [Date].[Fiscal Year].&[2004],
    [Date].[Fiscal].[Month].MEMBERS,
    [Measures].[Sales Amount Quota] );


    THIS = CASE


    WHEN ( [Date].[Fiscal].CurrentMember.Parent IS
        [Date].[Fiscal].[Fiscal Quarter].&[2004]&[1] )
    THEN ( ParallelPeriod( [Date].[Fiscal].[Fiscal Year], 1,
        [Date].[Fiscal].CurrentMember ),
        [Measures].[Sales Amount] ) * 1.3


    WHEN ( [Date].[Fiscal].CurrentMember.Parent IS
        [Date].[Fiscal].[Fiscal Quarter].&[2004]&[2] )
    THEN ( ParallelPeriod( [Date].[Fiscal].[Fiscal Year], 1,
        [Date].[Fiscal].CurrentMember ),
        [Measures].[Sales Amount] ) * 2.0


    ELSE ( ParallelPeriod( [Date].[Fiscal].[Fiscal Year], 1,
        [Date].[Fiscal].CurrentMember ),
        [Measures].[Sales Amount] ) * 1.75


    END;


END SCOPE;
```

The preceding CASE statement applies the correct calculations based on the Quarter the month belongs to. The MDX CASE statement is similar to the switch statement in languages such as C/C++ or C#. Based on the conditional expression provided after the WHEN, the statement is assigned to the expression on the left-hand side ("THIS" in the preceding code sample). You can have multiple WHEN-THEN's within the CASE expression as shown in the preceding example.

In all the previous examples you have seen SCOPE-END SCOPE being used. Use SCOPE when you have multiple calculations that need to be applied within the SCOPE. However, if it is a single MDX expression, you can write the cell calculation by direct assignment to the subcube as shown here:

```
( [Date].[Fiscal Year].&[2005],
    [Date].[Fiscal].[Month].MEMBERS,
    [Measures].[Sales Amount Quota] ) =
( ParallelPeriod( [Date].[Fiscal].[Fiscal Year], 1,
    [Date].[Fiscal].CurrentMember ),
    [Measures].[Sales Amount] ) * 2;
```

So far, you have learned about cell calculations using assignments in Analysis Services 2008, which is recommended over the CREATE CELL CALCULATION syntax. You also learned about the IF statement and how to use the CASE expression to apply cell calculations based on business conditions. There are two additional MDX functions that help you write cell calculations with ease. These functions are Root and Leaves, which are great if you want to apply cell calculation to the leaf-level members or the root of a hierarchy. These functions appropriately position a coordinate so that the cell calculations can be applied to that coordinate. Following are some examples that use the Root and Leaves MDX functions:

```
CREATE MEMBER CURRENTCUBE.[Measures].[Ratio To All Products] AS
    [Measures].[Sales Amount] /
        ( Root( [Product] ), [Measures].[Sales Amount] ),
    FORMAT_STRING = "Percent",
    NON_EMPTY_BEHAVIOR = [Sales Amount];

SCOPE( Leaves( [Date] ), [Measures].[Sales Amount Quota] );
    THIS = THIS * 1.2;
END SCOPE;
```

In the first part of the example, you see a calculated measure that computes the contribution of Sales of a product as a portion of total product sales. This is accomplished through use of Root(Product), which will provide the sales information for all the products. Root(Product) is often used to calculate ratios of a measure for a single member against all the members in the dimension. In the second part of the example, the Sales Amount Quota is being applied to Leaf members of the Date dimension so that the Sales Amount Quota is increased by 20%. The Leaves MDX function would help in budgeting and financial calculations where you want the calculations applied only to the leaf-level members and then rolled up to the members at other levels. The Leaves MDX function (like the Root function) takes a dimension as its argument and returns the leaf-level members of the dimension that exist with the granularity attribute of the dimension.

Recursion

Recursive calculations can be quite common in MDX. Recursive calculation occurs when a calculated member references itself for calculations. For example, if you want to calculate the cumulative sales over time, you can apply an MDX expression that calculates the Sales of current time member and the cumulative sales for previous time member. This leads to recursion because the cumulative sales of the previous time member needs to be evaluated with the same MDX expression for the previous time member. In Analysis Services 2008, infinite recursions due to single expression are avoided by the use of a PASS value. Consider the following MDX statements in your MDX script:

```
SCOPE ([Date].[Fiscal Year].&[2004]);
    [Sales Amount Quota] = [Sales Amount Quota] * 1.2;
END SCOPE;
```

The evaluation of [Sales Amount Quota] would result in infinite recursion had the equivalent logic been defined in Analysis Services 2000. Analysis Services 2008 (as well as the previous version, 2005) is able to automatically handle these types of scenarios by virtue of internally assigning a value from the previous calculation pass.

The Freeze Statement

The Freeze statement is used in circumstances where you might want to change the cell value that was used in an MDX expression to determine results for another cell value without changing the cell value from an earlier calculation. The syntax for the Freeze statement is:

```
Freeze <subcube expression>
```

This Freeze statement is only used within MDX Scripts. It is easier to understand the Freeze statement with an example. Assume the following MDX statements, where A, B, and C are MDX expressions:

```
A=B;
B=C;
```

Due to recursion the final value for A will be equal to the value of C. However, if you want to ensure that the value of A is pinned to the value assigned by MDX expression B, you would introduce a Freeze statement between the two assignments as shown here:

```
A=B;
Freeze(A);
B=C;
```

You can use the Freeze statement when you perform budget allocations. An example of the Freeze statement is used in the sample Adventure Works DW 2008 Analysis Services sample project:

```
Freeze
(
   [Date].[Fiscal].[Fiscal Quarter].MEMBERS,
   [Measures].[Sales Amount Quota]
) ;
```

In the MDX statements that follow the Freeze statement, a weighting factor is calculated and inserted into the cells corresponding to months. We recommend you open the Adventure Works DW 2008 sample project and review the calculations after the Freeze statement shown in the preceding example. The purpose of the Freeze statement in the preceding example is to avoid incorrectly re-aggregating values at the quarter level once this weighting factor is inserted.

Restricting Cube Space/Slicing Cube Data

A typical cube contains several dimensions and each dimension can have several hundred or even thousands of members. For example, if you have a sales cube that contains products, the products dimension would likely have hundreds of products, if not thousands. During analysis, you would typically want to slice the data or drill down into specific sections of the cube to glean insights hidden in the data. Client tools help you to slice, dice, and drill down in cubes. These client tools dynamically generate MDX to restrict the cube space and generate queries. In this section, we refer to restricting the cube space in the context of MDX scripts or restricting the data being returned to the client when users slice and dice the data. Several ways exist to restrict the cube space when analyzing data and this section discusses using MDX to do this and appropriately retrieve the sections of the data you care about.

Using the SCOPE Statement

You already learned some techniques to restrict the searchable cube space, the use of which would depend on the context of your problem and what you are trying to accomplish. To refresh your memory, the SCOPE statement within MDX Scripts is used to restrict the cube space to form a subcube, which is a part of the cube projected along the dimensions specified within the SCOPE statement. The SCOPE statement is often used for cell calculations where the assignment statement typically is used with the "THIS" function to restrict the assignment to the specified subcube. An example to recap what you learned in the previous section is:

```
SCOPE( [Date].[Fiscal Year].&[2005],
    [Date].[Fiscal].[Month].MEMBERS,
    [Measures].[Sales Amount Quota]);


THIS = ( ParallelPeriod( [Date].[Fiscal].[Fiscal Year], 1,
    [Date].[Fiscal].CurrentMember ),
    [Measures].[Sales Amount] ) * 2;

END SCOPE;
```

Using CREATE and DROP SUBCUBE

By default, all cells in the cube space are in scope. For obvious reasons, you will typically want to restrict your analysis to specific slices or sections of the cube. For example, if you are analyzing the sales information for the year 2005, you might want to reduce your search space to just the year 2005. There are several ways to restrict your cube space in Analysis Services 2008. If you are querying the cube, you can restrict the cube space with the CREATE SUBCUBE statement, which then restricts the cube space for subsequent queries.

Assume you are analyzing the Internet Sales information in the Adventure Works DW2008 database for various quarters. You use the following MDX query:

```
SELECT [Measures].[Internet Sales Amount] ON 0,
[Date].[Fiscal].[Fiscal Quarter].MEMBERS ON 1
FROM [Adventure Works]
```

If you want to restrict your cube space and only analyze the Internet sales data for the fiscal year 2004, one way to do so is to use the CREATE SUBCUBE statement. The syntax of the statement is:

```
CREATE SUBCUBE <SubCubeName> AS <SELECT Statement>
```

where the SELECT statement is an MDX SELECT clause that returns the results for the restricted cube space based on specific criteria.

The following MDX statements restrict the cube space to year 2004 using the CREATE SUBCUBE statement and then querying the Internet sales for all the quarters in that year:

```
CREATE SUBCUBE [Adventure Works] AS
SELECT { [Date].[Fiscal].[Fiscal Year].&[2004] } ON 0
FROM [Adventure Works]

SELECT [Measures].[Internet Sales Amount] ON 0,
[Date].[Fiscal].[Fiscal Quarter].MEMBERS ON 1
FROM [Adventure Works]

DROP SUBCUBE [Adventure Works]
```

Note that if the All member of a hierarchy is included in the subcube, all the members of that specific hierarchy are included in the subcube. Subsequent queries to the Adventure Works cube will evaluate to the restricted cube space corresponding to the year 2004. The query selecting Fiscal Quarters provides the results shown in the following table. If you did not create the subcube, you will see quarters for all the Fiscal Years in the cube.

Fiscal Quarter	Internet Sales Amount
Q1 FY 2004	$2,744,340.48
Q2 FY 2004	$4,009,218.46
Q3 FY 2004	$4,283,629.96
Q4 FY 2004	$5,436,429.15

Once you have completed your analysis on the restricted cube space you can revert back to the original cube space by dropping the subcube using the DROP SUBCUBE statement followed by the name of the subcube you just created. The CREATE SUBCUBE statement is typically used within the scope of a query session where you want to perform analysis on a subset of the total cube space. At query time you can reduce the cube space using the CREATE SUBCUBE statement then query within the context of the subcube created.

Using EXISTS

As mentioned earlier, the cube space in Analysis Services 2008 is typically quite large and sparse due to having an attribute-based model. Remember AUTOEXISTS? That's where querying the cross-join of attributes within the same dimension results in reducing the cross-join set so that only members that exist with one another are returned. Well, EXISTS is a function that allows you to explicitly do the same operation of returning a set of members that exists with one or more tuples of one or more sets. The EXISTS function can take two or three arguments. The syntax of the EXISTS function is:

```
EXISTS( Set, <FilterSet>, [MeasureGroupName])
```

The first two arguments are Sets that get evaluated to identify the members that exist with each other. The third optional parameter is the Measure group name so EXISTS can be applied across the measure group. EXISTS identifies all the members in the first set that exist with the members in the FilterSet and returns those members as results. The following is an example of EXISTS where you analyze the sales of all customers who have four cars. In this example we use restricting cube space loosely to restrict the members in the Customer hierarchy. You can achieve similar results using a FILTER or NONEMPTYCROSSJOIN function, which you explore later in this chapter.

```
WITH SET [HomeOwnerCustomer] AS
Exists( [Customer].[Customer].[Customer].MEMBERS,
    [Customer].[Number Of Cars Owned].&[4] )
SELECT [Measures].[Internet Sales Amount] ON 0,
[HomeOwnerCustomer] ON 1
FROM [Adventure Works]
```

Out of 18,000 customers in the customer dimension, the query returns 1,262 customers.

An example of using EXISTS with the measure group name follows:

```
WITH SET [HomeOwnerCustomer] AS
Exists( [Customer].[Customer].[Customer].MEMBERS,
    [Product].[Product Categories].[Category].&[1],
    "Internet Sales" )
SELECT [Measures].[Internet Sales Amount] ON 0,
[HomeOwnerCustomer] ON 1
FROM [Adventure Works]
```

This example identifies the customers who have bought products of category 1, which is Bikes. The measure group name [Internet Sales] is specified so that EXISTS uses the measure group to determine the set of customers who have bought bikes.

Using EXISTING

By now, you are quite familiar with the WHERE clause in the MDX SELECT statement. The WHERE clause only changes the default members of the dimensions for the current subcube and does not restrict the cube space. It does not change the default for the outer query and gets a lower precedence as compared to the calculations specified within the query scope. For example, look at the following MDX query:

```
WITH MEMBER [Measures].[X] AS
COUNT ( [Customer].[Customer Geography].[State-Province].MEMBERS)
SELECT [Measures].[X] ON 0
FROM [Adventure Works]
WHERE ( [Customer].[Customer Geography].[Country].&[United States] )
```

The query returns a value of 71. You know that there are 50 states within the United States and the count of customers' states should be <= 50. You get the value 71 because calculations are done at a scope larger than the one defined by the WHERE clause. In order to restrict the cube space so that calculations are done within the scope of the conditions specified in the WHERE clause, you can use several methods. One way to accomplish this is using the keyword EXISTING, by which you force the calculations to be done on a subcube under consideration by the query rather than the entire cube. Following is an MDX query using EXISTING:

```
WITH MEMBER [Measures].[X] AS
COUNT ( EXISTING [Customer].[Customer Geography].[State-Province].MEMBERS)
SELECT [Measures].[X] ON 0
FROM [Adventure Works]
WHERE ( [Customer].[Customer Geography].[Country].&[United States] )
```

The EXISTING keyword forces sets to be evaluated in the current context. One can argue that the current context is defined due to the WHERE clause, which does not actually restrict the cube space. As mentioned earlier we are using the term "restricting cube space" loosely just to show examples of how you can restrict the data in a cube to retrieve the results you are looking for. The result for the preceding MDX query is 36.

Using Subselect

MDX queries can contain a clause called subselect, which allows you to restrict your query to a subcube instead of the entire cube. The syntax of the subselect clause along with SELECT is:

```
 [WITH <formula_expression> [, <formula_expression> ...]]
SELECT [<axis_expression>, <axis_expression>...]]

FROM [<cube_expression> | (<sub_select_statement>)]
[WHERE <expression>]
[[CELL] PROPERTIES <cellprop> [, <cellprop> ...]]

<sub_select_statement> =
SELECT [<axis_expression> [, <axis_expression> ...]]
FROM [<cube_expression> | (< sub_select_statement >)]
[WHERE <expression>]
```

The cube_expression in the MDX SELECT statement can now be replaced by another SELECT statement called the sub_select_statement, which queries a part of the cube. You can have nested subselect statements up to any level. The subselect clause in the SELECT statement restricts the cube space to the specified dimension members in the subselect clause. Outer queries will therefore be able to see only the dimension members that are specified in the inner subselect clauses. Look at the following MDX query that uses subselect syntax:

```
SELECT NON EMPTY { [Measures].[Internet Sales Amount] } ON COLUMNS,
NON EMPTY { ([Customer].[Customer Geography].[Country].ALLMEMBERS ) }
DIMENSION PROPERTIES MEMBER_CAPTION, MEMBER_UNIQUE_NAME ON ROWS
FROM (
```

```
    SELECT ( { [Date].[Fiscal].[Fiscal Year].&[2004],
             [Date].[Fiscal].[Fiscal Year].&[2005]
           }
         )
    ON COLUMNS
    FROM (
         SELECT ( { [Product].[Product Categories].[Subcategory].&[26],
                  [Product].[Product Categories].[Subcategory].&[27] } )
         ON COLUMNS
         FROM [Adventure Works]
         )
      )
    WHERE ( [Product].[Product Categories].CurrentMember,
          [Date].[Fiscal].CurrentMember
         )
    CELL PROPERTIES VALUE, BACK_COLOR, FORE_COLOR, FORMATTED_VALUE
```

The query contains two subselect clauses. The innermost clause returns a subcube that only contains Products whose SubCategory ids are 26 or 27. Assume that this subcube is named subcube A. The second subselect uses subcube A and returns another subcube with the restriction of Fiscal Years 2004 and 2005. Finally, the outermost SELECT statement retrieves the Internet Sales for Customers in various countries. Here subselect clauses restrict the cube space to certain members on Product and Date dimensions and thereby the outermost SELECT statement queries data from a subcube rather than the entire cube space. If you execute the preceding query in SSMS, you will see the results shown in the following table. You can rewrite most queries using subselect clauses with the WHERE clause in Analysis Services 2008, which accept sets as valid MDX expressions. There are instances where subselects and WHERE clauses can return different results. More information is provided in the book *MDX Solutions: With SQL Server Analysis Services 2005 and Hyperion Essbase, Second Edition* by George Spofford, et, al. (Wiley Publishing, Inc., 2006). Analysis Services 2008 supports including calculated members within subselects. Analysis Services 2008 only uses subselect syntax for queries built through the designer that creates reports. You learn more about creating reports on Analysis Services UDMs in Chapter 20.

Country	Internet Sales Amount
Australia	$16,335.00
Canada	$12,168.00
France	$ 6,021.00
Germany	$ 6,060.00
United Kingdom	$ 7,932.00
United States	$30,435.00

Removing Empty Cells

The total number of cells in a cube consists of the uniquely identifiable space within the cube. It is the product of the number of members in each attribute of each dimension. This is referred to as the cube space. As you can imagine, the entire cube space can be quite large. Of the entire cube space, the cells that constitute the product of attribute hierarchies of each dimension can potentially have fact data. However, in a typical cube most of these cells will not have fact data. For example, take a simple cube that contains the dimensions: product, time, and store. Assume the fact table contains IDs for the dimensions: product, time, and the sales amount. The product dimension table typically contains columns pertaining to the dimension, such as product name, product category, product weight, product color, and discount. The store dimension table would contain information about the store such as city, state, country, and number of employees. The time dimension might contain day, month, and year. As the owner of existing stores you might be interested in looking at the sales of various products in stores across various time periods every week, month, or quarter to make a decision on what product lines to enhance to grow your business. The store manager may be interested in identifying the sales of the products along with discounts so that he can stock products that sell the most while having discounts to maximize the profit of the store. Hence, the types of questions that might be requested from your UDM might be different based on the user.

Because the cube space is typically quite large, a vast majority of the cells might be nulls, meaning no data is associated with those cells. If your queries include attributes from the same dimension such as sales of products that have 10% discount, Analysis Services automatically returns the sale of products that have exactly 10% discount. As you learned earlier in this chapter, Analysis Services uses AUTO EXISTS and eliminates all members in the products hierarchy that do not exist with the 10% discount member in the discount hierarchy. Hence the results you get will not contain null values. However, if you query for data across dimensions, you can end up with several cells that are nulls. Often you are not interested in the cells with null values and you do not want to retrieve them in the result set to begin with. Analysis Services provides several functions and keywords that help you in eliminating null values in your result set.

Assume you want to analyze the Internet Sales amount across various countries for various products. Every product might not be sold in every country and so you can end up with certain country-product combinations that do not have any sales. To eliminate the null values you can use the keyword NON EMPTY on the axis or the MDX functions NONEMPTYCROSSJOIN, NONEMPTY, and FILTER. These are the basic ways of removing empty cells from the result set.

The operator NON EMPTY is used on an axis to remove the members that result in empty (null) cell values. When NON EMPTY is applied, cells with null values are eliminated in the context of members on other axes. You can see this in the following query:

```
SELECT [Measures].[Internet Sales Amount] ON 0,
NON EMPTY [Customer].[Customer Geography].[Country].MEMBERS *
[Product].[Product Categories].MEMBERS ON 1
FROM [Adventure Works]
```

You can also use the FILTER function as shown in the following query with the condition to eliminate null values for Internet Sales Amount:

```
SELECT [Measures].[Internet Sales Amount] ON 0,
FILTER ( [Customer].[Customer Geography].[Country].MEMBERS *
[Product].[Product Categories].MEMBERS,
[Measures].[Internet Sales Amount] ) ON 1
FROM [Adventure Works]
```

The following two queries use the NONEMPTYCROSSJOIN and NONEMPTY functions, which have similar arguments of taking a set and a filter set and eliminating cells that contain nulls. If you use the NONEMPTYCROSSJOIN function, you can specify the sets that need to be crossjoined, and in the final result you can specify the sets that need to be included in the result set. In this example, two sets are specified:

```
SELECT [Measures].[Internet Sales Amount] ON 0,
NonEmptyCrossJoin( [Customer].[Customer Geography].[Country].MEMBERS,
    [Product].[Product Categories].MEMBERS,
    [Measures].[Internet Sales Amount], 2 ) ON 1
FROM [Adventure Works]
```

If you use the NONEMPTY function, the set passed as an argument needs to be a crossjoin of the sets involved as shown in the following query:

```
SELECT [Measures].[Internet Sales Amount] ON 0,
NonEmpty( [Customer].[Customer Geography].[Country].MEMBERS *
    [Product].[Product Categories].MEMBERS,
    [Measures].[Internet Sales Amount] ) ON 1
FROM [Adventure Works]
```

When the NONEMPTY function is used, the members in the set are filtered based on the argument passed (Measures.[Internet Sales Amount] in the preceding example).

To sum up, there are several ways of removing the nulls in your result set so that you can analyze results that are meaningful. You can choose one of the preceding examples to eliminate null cell values. However, you should be aware that the NONEMPTYCROSSJOIN function is being deprecated because there are certain limitations while using this function with calculated members.

Filtering Members on Axes

Filtering members on axes is a common requirement. The filtering process can be extremely simple or require an advanced MDX expression. The FILTER function is one of the most common ways of filtering sets and projecting onto axes. You saw some examples of the FILTER function in Chapter 3. To refresh, assume you want to look at the gross profit of all the products whose Sales have been greater than $50,000. You can use a simple FILTER condition in your MDX query as shown in the following example:

```
SELECT { [Measures].[Gross Profit] } ON 0,
Filter( [Product].[Product Categories].[Subcategory].MEMBERS,
    [Sales Amount] > 50000 ) ON 1
FROM [Adventure Works]
```

You have already learned that you can eliminate empty cells in a variety of ways. Assume you have a large crossjoin on one of the axes and you want to apply complex filter conditions. In such a case the filter condition needs to evaluate over all the cells being represented by the crossjoin, and it might be quite a performance hit. It is more efficient to eliminate cells that have null values and then apply the filter condition on the resulting set. Analysis Services provides a clause called the HAVING clause, which allows you to do this. The syntax for the HAVING clause is:

```
SELECT <axis_specification> ON 0,
NON EMPTY <axis_specification> HAVING <filter condition> ON 1
FROM <cube identifier>
```

The following MDX query uses the HAVING clause to analyze the gross profit of all the products that have sales amounts greater than $100,000 for a product in any city:

```
SELECT { [Measures].[Gross Profit] } ON 0,
NON EMPTY [Product].[Product Categories].[Product] *
    [Customer].[Customer Geography].[City]
    HAVING [Sales Amount] > 100000 ON 1
FROM [Adventure Works]
```

Ranking and Sorting

Ranking and Sorting are pretty common features in most business analyses. MDX provides several MDX functions such as TopCount, BottomCount, TopPercent, BottomPercent, and Rank that help you stack rank information for better business decisions. You saw an example of Rank in Chapter 3. This section uses the Adventure Works DW2008 sample database to show a few examples of some common business questions in the retail industry that business analysts might be looking at.

Example 1

If you want to get an overview of the various products sold across various countries and through Internet sales, the following MDX query will provide you the results. You can set a Sales Quota for subsequent years to improve revenue on specific countries or specific products to have an overall impact for the company.

```
SELECT [Customer].[Customer Geography].[Country] ON 0,
[Product].[Category].MEMBERS ON 1
FROM [Adventure Works]
WHERE ( [Measures].[Internet Sales Amount] )
```

Example 2

In the case of companies that manufacture and sell products, it is desirable to take a look at how various products are performing on a periodic basis. If you are looking for the top N product categories or subcategories based on the sales in all the countries, the following queries will provide you the answer. Based on the results you can invest more in marketing campaigns and other initiatives to further boost the sales and revenue for the company.

```
SELECT [Measures].[Internet Sales Amount] ON COLUMNS,
TopCount( [Product].[Product Categories].[Category].MEMBERS, 3,
    [Measures].[Internet Sales Amount] ) ON ROWS
FROM [Adventure Works]
```

```
SELECT [Measures].[Internet Sales Amount] ON COLUMNS,
TopCount( [Product].[Product Categories].[Subcategory].MEMBERS, 10,
    [Measures].[Internet Sales Amount] ) ON ROWS
FROM [Adventure Works]
```

Example 3

If you want to drill down further on the top 10 product categories within the United States, you can use the following query. Based on this information you can improve sales on products that are doing well or try to boost sales on the remaining products after some market research on why they are not doing well.

```
SELECT [Measures].[Internet Sales Amount] ON COLUMNS,
TopCount( [Product].[Product Categories].[Subcategory].MEMBERS, 10,
    [Measures].[Internet Sales Amount] ) ON ROWS
FROM [Adventure Works]
WHERE ( [Customer].[Customer Geography].[Country].&[United States] )
```

Example 4

If you want to see growth figures for the top 5 products in the last 4 quarters, you can use the following MDX query. This query provides you with the trend information that allows you to see if the top 5 products have been consistently increasing in sales. If you see that some products do not show a positive trend, you do need to drill down further for details and take appropriate action.

```
WITH SET [Top5Products] AS
    'TopCount( [Product].[Product Categories].[Subcategory].MEMBERS, 5,
    [Measures].[Internet Sales Amount] )'
SET [CurrentQuarter] AS
    'Tail( Filter( [Date].[Fiscal].[Fiscal Quarter].MEMBERS,
    Not IsEmpty( [Date].[Fiscal].CurrentMember) ), 1)'
SET [Previous4Quarters] AS
    '[CurrentQuarter].Item(0).Item(0).Lag(4) :
    [CurrentQuarter].Item(0).Item(0).Lag(1)'
MEMBER [Measures].[Growth] AS

    ((( [Date].[Fiscal].CurrentMember,
    [Measures].[Internet Sales Amount] ) -
    ( [Date].[Fiscal].CurrentMember.PrevMember,
    [Measures].[Internet Sales Amount] )) /
    ( [Date].[Fiscal].CurrentMember.PrevMember,
    [Measures].[Internet Sales Amount] ))

    , FORMAT_STRING='Percent'

SELECT [Top5Products] ON COLUMNS,
[Previous4Quarters] ON ROWS
FROM [Adventure Works]
WHERE [Growth]
```

Example 5

To maximize your business you might discontinue products that are not providing your best sales. Assume you want to analyze your products to see the bottom 10% in terms of Internet sales. You can send the following MDX queries from SSMS:

```
//Total number of products contributing towards internet sales - 159 products

SELECT { [Measures].[Internet Sales Amount] } ON COLUMNS,
NON EMPTY [Product].[Product Categories].[Product].MEMBERS ON ROWS
FROM [Adventure Works]

//Bottom 10% (Sales) of the products sold through the internet - 95 products
SELECT { [Measures].[Internet Sales Amount] } ON COLUMNS,
NON EMPTY BottomPercent(
    [Product].[Product Categories].[Product].MEMBERS, 10,
    [Measures].[Internet Sales Amount] ) ON ROWS
FROM [Adventure Works]
```

You can see that there are 159 products that contribute toward Internet sales and out of these, 95 products contribute to the bottom 10% of the overall sales. Now you can further drill down at each product and identify the cost of selling them over the Internet and see if it really makes sense to keep selling these products.

Parameterize Your Queries

Parameterized queries in MDX, as the name suggests, help in passing parameters to a query where the values for the parameters are substituted before query execution. Why are parameterized queries important? You might have heard about attacks on web sites where users hack the sites by entering their own SQL and, as a result, see data they should not see or change the data in relational databases. This is because applications that are used to get input from users use the raw input string to form SQL queries. Often such applications run the queries under administrative privileges. Knowing this, hackers can enter inputs that are SQL constructs that are executed along with the full SQL query. This is called *SQL injection* because hackers inject their own SQL queries within the overall query. Similar threats exist for MDX as well. One of the main reasons why such attacks are possible is because user input is not validated.

Analysis Services overcomes the MDX injection by allowing parameters to be passed along with queries. Analysis Services validates these parameters, replaces the parameters in the query with the values, and then executes the query. The parameters to a query are represented within the query prefixed with the @ symbol. The following is a parameterized query. In this query the Number of children of a customer is the parameter.

```
SELECT NON EMPTY { [Measures].[Internet Sales Amount] } ON COLUMNS,
NON EMPTY { ([Customer].[Customer Geography].[Country].ALLMEMBERS ) }
    DIMENSION PROPERTIES MEMBER_CAPTION, MEMBER_UNIQUE_NAME ON ROWS
FROM (
    SELECT ( StrToSet( @CustomerTotalChildren, CONSTRAINED) ) ON COLUMNS
    FROM (
        SELECT ( { [Date].[Fiscal].[Fiscal Year].&[2004],
            [Date].[Fiscal].[Fiscal Year].&[2005] } ) ON COLUMNS
        FROM (
            SELECT ( { [Product].[Product Categories].[Subcategory].&[26],
                [Product].[Product Categories].[Subcategory].&[27] }
                ) ON COLUMNS
            FROM [Adventure Works])
        )
    )
    WHERE ( [Product].[Product Categories].CurrentMember,
        [Date].[Fiscal].CurrentMember,
        IIF( StrToSet( @CustomerTotalChildren, CONSTRAINED).Count = 1,
            StrToSet( @CustomerTotalChildren, CONSTRAINED),
            [Customer].[Total Children].currentmember )
    )
CELL PROPERTIES VALUE, BACK_COLOR, FORE_COLOR, FORMATTED_VALUE,
    FORMAT_STRING, FONT_NAME, FONT_SIZE, FONT_FLAGS
```

Your client application would send the preceding query along with the list of parameters and values. When you execute the query you will get the results similar to executing regular queries. The following is an XMLA script that shows how the parameters are sent to Analysis Services. You have a name and value pair specified for each parameter in the query under the Parameters section of the XMLA script for query execution.

```
<Envelope xmlns="http://schemas.xmlsoap.org/soap/envelope/">
  <Body>
    <Execute xmlns="urn:schemas-microsoft-com:xml-analysis">
      <Command>
        <Statement>
select [Measures].members on 0,
```

```
            Filter(Customer.[Customer Geography].Country.members,
                   Customer.[Customer Geography].CurrentMember.Name =
                   @CountryName) on 1
    from [Adventure Works]
    </Statement>
          </Command>
          <Properties />
          <Parameters>
            <Parameter>
              <Name>CountryName</Name>
              <Value>'United Kingdom'</Value>
            </Parameter>
          </Parameters>
        </Execute>
      </Body>
    </Envelope>
```

You see an example of parameterized queries using the client object model ADOMD.NET in Chapter 9.

MDX Functions

Analysis Services 2008 uses several MDX functions to facilitate data extraction from the UDM. The following table covers some of the MDX functions in Analysis Services 2008 and gives a brief description about their behavior for quick reference. Detailed information about these functions is provided in Appendix A (available online at www.wrox.com). We recommend you learn more about the MDX functions used in MDX scripts with scenarios in *MDX Solutions: With SQL Server Analysis Services 2005 and Hyperion Essbase, Second Edition* by George Spofford et al. (Wiley, 2006).

MDX Function	Description
Iif(<Condition>, <Then Expression> [Hint [Eager ∣ Strict]], <Else expression> [hint [Eager ∣ Strict]])	Two query hints have been added as optional parameters to this function for 2008. The Hint Eager hint instructs Analysis Services to evaluate the expression for both branches of the expression. Conversely, Hint Strict instructs Analysis Services to only identify the cube space corresponding to each branch of the expression and only evaluate a given branch where needed. These hints are useful in a minority of cases where the Analysis Services engine does not automatically select the best option.
MeasureGroupMeasures (<Measure Group Name>)	This function retrieves all the measures within a specific measure group. Because the UDM can contain several measure groups, this function helps by making the query more specific.
EXISTS (<set>,<filterset>) EXISTS(<set>,<filterset>, <measuregroup name>)	This function is used to determine if tuples in the set exist with the tuples in the filter set. If yes, those tuples are returned. When the measure group argument is used, the measure group is used to determine the EXISTS operation.

(continued)

(continued)

MDX Function	Description
KPI Functions – KPICURRENTTIMEMEMBER («String Expression») KPIGOAL(«String Expression») KPISTATUS(«String Expression») KPITREND(«String Expression») KPIVALUE(«String Expression») KPIWEIGHT(«String Expression»)	KPI functions help in retrieving the values for the KPI, which help in displaying the status of KPI through KPI graphic icons. Some of these functions return normalized values between –1 and 1. All the KPI functions except KPICurrentTimeMember take the KPI name as an argument and return values that can be matched with the corresponding graphic. These functions are helpful for client-side programming where you retrieve the value and show the corresponding icon that visually represents the status. Analysis Services internally treats these as just calculations. KPICurrentTimeMember retrieves the time member corresponding to the KPI, which can be different from the default member on the Time dimension.
UnOrder(<set>)	MDX usually returns an order set in the results. Often this ordering takes additional overhead on the server. The UnOrder function instructs Analysis Services to return results without ordering. This often helps in improving performance on large results sets, which are typically crossjoins of several hierarchies.
Error(<Error message>) Error	This helps in throwing user-defined errors in cases where certain operations are not possible.
Root (Dimension) Leaves(Dimension)	Root and Leaves functions are used in scripts for appropriately positioning the coordinate on a dimension for allocations or assignments.

Summary

You have learned about calculation fundamentals in Analysis Services 2008, and the use of MDX scripts to apply global scope calculations. MDX scripting includes creating calculated members, named sets, and assignments. Kind of makes you want to specialize in MDX, doesn't it? This is great stuff! This chapter does not provide an in-depth view of the Analysis Services calculations and various overwrite semantics of calculations due to the relationship between attributes simply because those subjects are too vast to cover here. This chapter is meant to serve as an introduction to the Analysis Services 2008 calculation model with some examples of solving common problems. Several sections in this chapter cover the sort of MDX used to answer common business questions. MDX is like an ocean. Even when you think you have mastered it you might end up finding there are things you have not learned. Typically you will learn a lot of MDX as and when you implement customer solutions. If you want to dive fully into MDX and understand the concepts discussed in the chapter in detail including the calculation precedence rules, we highly recommend you read *MDX Solutions: With SQL Server Analysis Services 2005 and Hyperion Essbase, Second Edition* by George Spofford et al. (Wiley, 2006).

Having learned some of the fundamental calculation concepts, you are now ready for a deeper understanding of the dimensions and cubes discussed in subsequent chapters. Don't think you are done learning about MDX with this chapter. You learn additional MDX in subsequent chapters through illustrations and examples wherever applicable. Your journey through the Analysis Services landscape will become even more interesting and exciting as you work your way through the book.

Extending MDX Using External Functions

The MDX language supports an extensive set of functions for business analysis. In addition, Analysis Services exposes certain VBA (Visual Basic for Applications) and Excel functions as built-in external functions, which can be accessed through MDX. These functions already supported in Analysis Services should meet most of your design and query requirements. However, you may sometimes have a need for custom operations. Analysis Services provides an extensible architecture by which you can add your own custom functions to Analysis Services and access them through MDX. These external functions are referred to as *user-defined functions* (UDFs).

UDFs offer the power of the programming language of your choice seamlessly integrated into Analysis Services. This allows you to extend the MDX language to support any business needs not covered out-of-the-box such as accessing external data or computing complex calculations. As an example, you could write a function to retrieve live stock data for calculations in MDX queries or expressions. By building a UDF to collect and pass along relevant data, your MDX query can reflect such up-to-date information.

Three types of external functions are described and demonstrated in this chapter: built-in UDFs, .NET-based UDFs (commonly referred to as stored procedures), and COM-based UDFs. Built-in UDFs are VBA and Excel functions that are exposed automatically in Analysis Services. .NET UDFs can be written using any .NET language like VB.NET, C#, or even C++/CLI. COM UDFs are created using any language that supports creating COM components, such as C/C++ or VB6.

In this chapter you learn how to use built-in UDFs and see examples of .NET UDF creation in C#. In addition to learning how to use and write UDFs, you'll see how they can be deployed, debugged, and secured.

Built-In UDFs

The MDX language does not support certain common utility functions like performing operations on strings, such as trimming or getting the first substring match, or date operation functions. Such functions are available in the SQL language, and they might be quite useful in MDX queries. Because Visual Basic for Applications (VBA) and Excel contain a rich set of such functions, they are readily available as a COM DLL. Analysis Services 2008 takes advantage of this and exposes certain Excel and VBA functions out-of-the-box.

The VBA functions provided with Analysis Services 2008 come from Microsoft Office. Because Microsoft Office is currently only a 32-bit application but Analysis Services is also available on 64-bit platforms, the Analysis Services team has implemented 64-bit versions of VBA functions. Important functions that can impact performance are implemented natively in a 64-bit COM assembly, while the remaining supported VBA functions are implemented in a .NET assembly.

Calling a user-defined function in MDX is similar to calling a function in most programming languages. You make the call with the function name followed by an opening parenthesis, with each argument in the correct order separated by commas, and finally a closing parenthesis. For example, if you want to get today's date, you can use the VBA function `Now()`. The following MDX query will retrieve today's date:

```
WITH MEMBER Measures.[Today's Date] AS 'Now()'
SELECT Measures.[Today's Date] ON 0
FROM [Adventure Works DW]
```

In the preceding example the value returned by the VBA function `Now()` is stored as a calculated measure and then retrieved using the MDX query.

But what if you want to manipulate MDX objects with COM UDFs? MDX provides some conversion functions to help work with COM UDFs. These MDX functions can convert MDX types to strings so that COM UDFs can work with them and then convert strings back to MDX types so the results can be integrated back into the MDX. The following MDX query will retrieve profit for the current month:

```
WITH MEMBER [Order Date].[English Month Name].[CurrentMonth] AS
        StrToMember("[Order Date].[English Month Name].&[" + Format(Now(),
        "MMMM") + "]")
SELECT {[Measures].[Profit]} ON 0
FROM [Adventure Works DW]
WHERE ([Order Date].[English Month Name].[CurrentMonth])
```

In this example, a calculated member is defined referring to the Order Date dimension member corresponding to today's month. This is done by using the VBA `Format()` function to transform the results of the VBA `Now()` function into the same format as the member names in the `[Order Date].[English Month Name]` hierarchy. The MDX `StrToMember()` function then translates this date string into a reference to the actual `[Order Date].[English Month Name]` hierarchy member. This member is then used as a filter to get the orders for the current month in past years.

Interacting with Server Objects in COM

The MDX language provides functions that are helpful in translating MDX objects to external data structures such as strings or arrays or from external structures to MDX objects. The MDX conversion functions most useful in working with built-in UDFs are:

Conversion Function	Purpose
MemberToStr	Converts an MDX Member into a string.
TupleToStr	Converts an MDX Tuple into a string.
SetToStr	Converts an MDX Set into a string.
StrToMember	Converts a string back to an MDX Member.
StrToSet	Converts a string back to an MDX Set.
StrToTuple	Converts a string back to an MDX Tuple.
SetToArray	Converts an MDX Set into an array of strings.

The functions that VBA and Excel provide will likely help you meet your business application requirements. However, each business need is unique and your business might require special computing that cannot be solved using the MDX, VBA, or Excel functions. Perhaps you need to base some of your calculations on an external data source that is dynamically changing. In such circumstances you can write a custom .NET assembly and add this to Analysis Services as shown in the next section.

.NET User-Defined Functions (Stored Procedures)

If you have been programming on the Microsoft platform, you are probably familiar with the .NET Framework and the .NET languages. .NET is Microsoft's framework and strategy to connect people, business, systems, and devices. Several programming languages help in building applications using the framework, which helps in seamless integration with other applications. Analysis Services 2008 couples tightly with UDFs based on .NET languages. In addition to the tight integration, the .NET Framework provides leverage through use of its security model. The model is provided by the framework and gives an additional type of security, code access security, on .NET assemblies added to Analysis Services. In this book we refer to UDFs built using .NET languages as stored procedures and the DLLs they are contained in as .NET assemblies. This section describes how to create, add, query, and debug stored procedures in Analysis Services 2008.

Creating Stored Procedures

.NET stored procedures are the easiest way to extend MDX. You can create .NET stored procedures using any .NET language, such as C# or VB.NET. These stored procedures can be used to perform complex computations catered toward your business applications. A few examples of stored procedures are performing custom business computations that involve business logic based on certain conditions, accessing external resources such as stock price of the company from a web service to perform calculations, and accessing external resources such as data from a SQL Server to apply permissions on Analysis Services. Chapter 22 shows an example of applying permissions in Analysis Services by means of a stored procedure that retrieves data from an external service.

Analysis Services 2008 exposes MDX objects such as cubes, dimensions, sets, and tuples via an object model called ADOMD Server. This server-side object model used in stored procedures is very similar to the client-side ADOMD.NET object model used in client applications that query the server. However, certain differences exist between these two object models based on the kinds of applications they support. In addition to providing an object model for interacting with MDX queries in stored procedures, Analysis Services 2008 allows you to perform management operations via stored procedures using Analysis Management Objects, which you learn about in some detail in Chapter 13. Later in this section you see examples of stored procedures using the ADOMD server and AMO object models.

The Adventure Works DW cube you created in the previous chapters contains the calculated measure Profit. Assume you want to see a cumulative sum of the profits based on the ship date along with the net profit for each year. To perform a cumulative sum, you can write a function that takes three arguments of the dimension, the measure value, and the location up to which the cumulative sum has to be performed. Open Visual Studio 2008 and create a C# class library application called PartialSumSproc. Enter the following code and compile the class library:

```csharp
using System;
using System.Collections.Generic;
using System.Text;

namespace PartialSumSproc
{
  public class PartialSumSproc
  {
    public static double PartialSum(double [] Val, string [] Member,
      string stopMember)
    {
      double PartialSum = 0;
      int l = 0; //Lower bound value of the array
      int u = Val.Length; //upper bound value of the array.

      for(int i=1;i<u;i++)
      {
        //add tuple into the return set
        PartialSum = PartialSum + Val[i];

        //if the unique name of both tuple is same then break and return

        if (string.Compare(Member[i], stopMember) == 0)
          break;
      }

      //return the set back to server
      return PartialSum;
    }
  }
}
```

The .NET assembly needs to be added to the database and you can use the function PartialSum in your queries. (Steps for adding stored procedures are described later in this chapter.)

ADOMD Server Stored Procedure

A key advantage of .NET stored procedures is the ability to use the ADOMD Server object model, which is exposed by Analysis Services. ADOMD Server allows you to interact with server objects inside of your stored procedure. This allows you to create stored procedures that integrate better with the server and the MDX queries calling them.

The following is C# code that uses the ADOMD Server object model. This stored procedure contains a function called CustomFilter that filters a set of tuples based on a sampling percentage. This stored procedure is useful when you want a sample of customers for whom you want to do a marketing study. For example, you identify that there are one million customers who are extremely important for your business. You assume they are highly valued customers based on the purchases they make. Now you want to do a marketing study of a sample of such customers or send surveys to a subset of these customers to expand your line of business. How would you go about getting the sample of customers? You can retrieve all the customers, pick the top N percentage of customers, and perform a sampling operation on the server side using a stored procedure. The following stored procedure shows how this is done. The stored procedure's CustomFilter function takes an MDX Set and a sampling percentage as inputs and returns an MDX Set as an output. The `CustomFilter` function is simple in the sense that it takes every Nth member based on the sampling percentage from the Set and adds them to a new Set.

```csharp
using System;
using System.Collections.Generic;
using System.Text;
using AdomdServer = Microsoft.AnalysisServices.AdomdServer;

namespace AdomdSproc
{
  public class AdomdSproc
  {
    public static AdomdServer.Set CustomFilter(AdomdServer.Set mdxSet,
                        int samplingPercentage)
    {
      AdomdServer.SetBuilder sampleSet = new
          Microsoft.AnalysisServices.AdomdServer.SetBuilder();

      int iTupleCount = mdxSet.Tuples.Count;
      int iTupleSample = iTupleCount * samplingPercentage/100;

      for (int i = 0; i < iTupleCount; i++)
      {
        if (i % (samplingPercentage) == 0)
        {
          sampleSet.Add(mdxSet.Tuples[i]);
        }
      }
      return sampleSet.ToSet();
    }

    public int TupleCount(AdomdServer.Set mdxSet)
    {
      return mdxSet.Tuples.Count;
    }
  }
}
```

This code is just an example of how to create a stored procedure that uses the ADOMD Server object model. Using the server object model, you can manipulate tuples and sets, evaluate MDX expressions, and convert MDX types, all within the context of an MDX query. Some of the commonly used classes that set ADOMD Server apart from ADOMD Client are listed in the following table:

Class	Description
TupleBuilder	Provides an easy way to build tuples from members.
SetBuilder	Provides an easy way to build sets from tuples.
Expression	Provides the ability to evaluate MDX expressions.
MDXValue	Provides conversion to and from various MDX types.
Context	Provides information about the context in which a stored procedure is running.

To create an ADOMD stored procedure you need to include the assembly msmgdsrv.dll inside your C# class library references. You can find msmgdsrv.dll in the Analysis Services bin directory (Program Files\ Microsoft SQL Server\MSAS10.MSSQLSERVER\OLAP\bin).

The AMO Stored Procedure

Analysis Management Objects (AMO) is the object model used to create and manage Analysis Services databases and their contents. With it you can build, update, and administer OLAP cubes and Data Mining models. You learn more about AMO in Chapter 13.

By using AMO in Analysis Services 2008 stored procedures, you can make administrative tasks as simple as calling MDX. You can easily author stored procedures to create new database partitions or database backups and then invoke these stored procedures through MDX. AMO stored procedures also allow you to query information about the management structure of an Analysis Services database and create queries and build reports that help monitor the state and health of your Analysis Services databases.

The following code is an AMO stored procedure in C# that returns a list of partitions in the current database along with basic information about those partitions such as the current state, the time of last processing, estimated size, and storage mode. The list of partitions is returned as a table, which makes it easy to work with and include in reports. The stored procedure connects to the Analysis Server instance, locates the current database, and iterates through the cubes and measure groups to find all of the partitions in that database.

```csharp
#region Using directives

using System;
using System.Data;
using Microsoft.AnalysisServices.AdomdServer;
using AMO = Microsoft.AnalysisServices;

#endregion

namespace AmoSproc
{
  public class AmoSproc
  {
    [SafeToPrepareAttribute(true)]
    public static DataTable ListPartitions()
    {
      DataTable partitionsTable = new DataTable("Partitions");
      partitionsTable.Columns.Add("ParentDatabase",      typeof(string));
      partitionsTable.Columns.Add("ParentCube",          typeof(string));
      partitionsTable.Columns.Add("ParentMeasureGroup",  typeof(string));
      partitionsTable.Columns.Add("Name",                typeof(string));
      partitionsTable.Columns.Add("State",               typeof(string));
      partitionsTable.Columns.Add("LastProcessed",       typeof(DateTime));
      partitionsTable.Columns.Add("EstimatedRows",       typeof(long));
      partitionsTable.Columns.Add("EstimatedSize",       typeof(long));
      partitionsTable.Columns.Add("StorageMode",         typeof(string));
      partitionsTable.Columns.Add("Type",                typeof(string));

      if (!Context.ExecuteForPrepare)
      {
        AMO.Server server = new AMO.Server();
        using (server)  // Ensures Dispose is called to disconnect if necessary
```

```
        {
            server.Connect("*"); // * connects to the instance running this sproc
            string currentDatabaseName = Context.CurrentDatabaseName;
            AMO.Database currentDatabase = server.Databases.
                FindByName(currentDatabaseName);
            foreach (AMO.Cube cube in currentDatabase.Cubes)
            {
                foreach (AMO.MeasureGroup measureGroup in cube.MeasureGroups)
                {
                    foreach (AMO.Partition partition in measureGroup.Partitions)
                    {
                        partitionsTable.Rows.Add(
                            currentDatabase.Name,
                            cube.Name,
                            measureGroup.Name,
                            partition.Name,
                            partition.State.ToString(),
                            partition.LastProcessed,
                            partition.EstimatedRows,
                            partition.EstimatedSize,
                            partition.StorageMode.ToString(),
                            partition.Type.ToString()
                        );
                        Context.CheckCancelled();  // Allows this sproc to be cancelled
                    }
                }
            }
        }

    return partitionsTable;
    }
}
}
```

You may have noticed that the using directive for Microsoft.AnalysisServices has been aliased to AMO. This is done because some objects such as Server and Database exist in both AMO and ADOMD Server. To avoid confusion we explicitly prefix the AMO objects.

The SafeToPrepareAttribute on the stored procedure is used to tell the Analysis Services server that the stored procedure can be prepared to get the structure of the results without the cost of getting any of the data. To prepare the stored procedure, the server calls it with Context.ExecuteForPrepare set to true. When Context.ExecuteForPrepare is true, the table structure should be returned without any data. The SafeToPrepareAttribute and the Context.ExecuteForPrepare flag are only useful for stored procedures that return DataTables.

The Context.CurrentDatabaseName method is used to get the name of the current database in which the stored procedure is running. The Context object is very useful for understanding information about the context in which a stored procedure is being used. The Context.CheckCancelled method is called to allow the user to cancel the stored procedure in case there are many cubes with many partitions. If the MDX query that invokes this stored procedure is canceled, then Context .CheckCancelled will throw an appropriate exception.

To create this stored procedure, first create a new C# project for a class library using Visual Studio, and include the assembly msgdsrv.dll in the references as with the previous sample. Then add the .NET assembly Analysis Management Objects (Microsoft.AnalysisServices.dll) to the references as shown in

Figure 11-1. Add the preceding code to your project and compile the project. Congratulations! You just created an AMO stored procedure. You can write similar functions within the same stored procedure that can perform various management operations on your server.

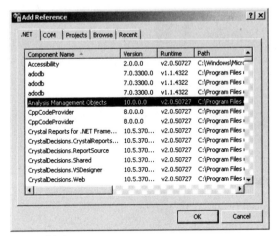

Figure 11-1

Static versus Non-Static Functions

Analysis Services 2008 supports using static (shared in VB.NET) as well as non-static (instance) functions. If a function is not defined as static then each time the function is called, Analysis Services needs to create a new instance of its parent class. This creation of class instances can be expensive and is done every time the function is called — even within the same query. In contrast, when a static function is called, no instance of the parent class needs to be created. If you must preserve state, you can access static variables from within your static function to avoid this problem. We recommend avoiding using non-static functions from MDX.

Code Access Security

It's clear that keeping your system secure means controlling the permissions users have. However, in an age of shared components and interactive web sites, this is not enough. You need to control the permissions code has. If a malicious user can get you to run his code, then it will do what the malicious user wants but under your user credentials. Imagine running a program that acts like a fancy calculator but secretly sends your account information over the Internet. Code access security was introduced with the .NET Framework to help protect against this by limiting the ability of code that is not fully trusted to perform dangerous actions or access protected resources. The fancy calculator can crunch numbers, but because the source of the code is not trusted, it does not have access to your account information or the Internet. Analysis Services 2008 uses three levels of code access security to help protect against malicious or poorly coded .NET stored procedures. These three levels of code access security are described in the next section on adding stored procedures.

Adding Stored Procedures

Once you have created the stored procedures you can add them as server-scoped assemblies or database-scoped assemblies. You need to use SQL Server Management Studio to add the stored procedures. The following steps show how to add a stored procedure:

1. Connect to your database using SQL Server Management Studio.

2. Navigate to your database, right-click the Assemblies folder, and select New Assembly.

3. You will now be in the register assembly dialog. Leave the type of the assembly as .NET assembly and specify the assembly file as shown in Figure 11-2.

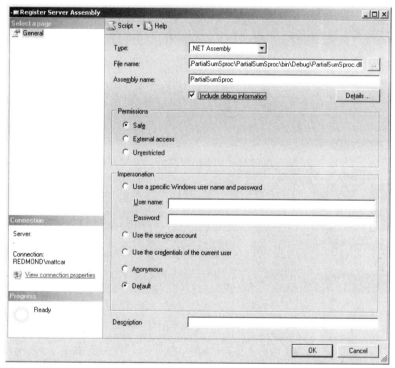

Figure 11-2

4. Select the option to include debug information so that you can debug the assembly within the Analysis Server in case you run into problems. If you click the Details button, you will see all the functions that are part of the assembly as shown in Figure 11-3. This is because .NET assemblies are compiled to an intermediate language and, using reflection, Analysis Services Tools are able to retrieve the functions available in the assembly. During runtime this code is compiled into machine language and then executed by the .NET Framework.

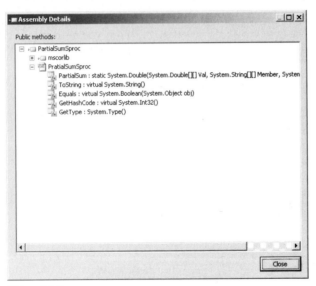

Figure 11-3

5. Select a permission set option for the assemblies you are adding. Analysis Services leverages permission sets from the .NET Framework to provide code access security on the assemblies being added to Analysis Services. You can select three different permission set options:

    a. **Safe:** The Safe permission set forces the assembly to only perform computation operations. Whenever a stored procedure marked with the Safe permission set tries to access external resources, the .NET Framework restricts the permission and throws an exception.

    b. **External Access:** The External Access permission set is intended to allow managed code to access external resources from the server. Because this permission allows stored procedures to access normally protected external resources such as the network, the registry, and full access to the file system, it should only be used with code from trusted sources.

    c. **Unrestricted:** If an assembly has been marked with the Unrestricted permission set, it can perform any operations on the server or on any external resources. The Unrestricted permission set should be used with caution and only for operations that need it. You should only use Unrestricted with code from trusted sources.

    Only database administrators can add assemblies to Analysis Server.

    The PartialSumSproc and AdomdSproc stored procedures only perform computation, hence the Safe permission set is sufficient.

6. Next, you need to specify the impersonation of the assembly. Don't let the verbiage throw you; it just means you need to indicate what credentials Analysis Services will execute this assembly under. Analysis Services 2008 provides five options for impersonation modes:

    a. **Use a Specific username and password:** This option should be used whenever you have an assembly that has to be executed only under certain account credentials because that specific account has access to an external source that is used within the stored procedure. This is typically used whenever you want to read some data from a web service or from a relational data source or any other external resource.

b. **Use the service account:** Whenever you have operations that need to be performed under the credentials of the Analysis Services instance, you need to specify this operation. An example of a stored procedure that would need this is an AMO stored procedure that does management operations on the server.

c. **Use the credentials of the current user:** This option is recommended when you want the stored procedure to be executed under the credentials of the user accessing it. This setting can help protect data from being accessed by the stored procedure when the user running the procedure does not have permissions to that data.

d. **Run the assembly under an anonymous account:** This is the least-privileged account and will not have any access to any data. Typically, stored procedures that are computation-intensive can be specified with this option.

e. **Default:** When the default option is chosen it is actually translated to one of the previous four options based on the selected permission set. If the permission set is Safe, selecting the default option for impersonation will set the impersonation mode to Impersonate Service Account. If the permission set is Unrestricted or External Access, selecting the default impersonation mode results in the impersonation mode being set as Impersonate Current User.

Select the default option and click OK.

7. Following steps 2 through 6, add the AMO stored procedure ListPartitions but select the permission as Unrestricted. You learn why Unrestricted permission is used for ListPartitions in the next section.

You have successfully created stored procedures and added them to the database. Next, you see examples of using them in queries.

Querying Stored Procedures

You can use the PartialSumSproc assembly's `PartialSum` function to calculate the cumulative profit as shown in Figure 11-4.

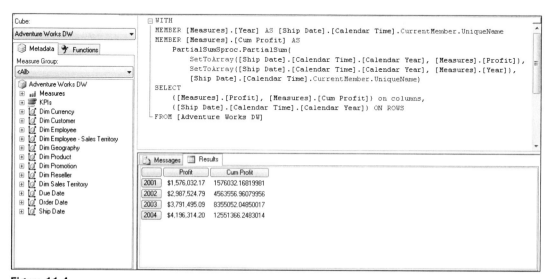

Figure 11-4

Now that you have added the ADOMD stored procedure, you'll want to see how to use it. Assume you want to see all the cities that contributed to a profit of $1000 or more; you would use the following MDX query:

```
SELECT measures.profit ON 0,
FILTER([Dim Geography].[City].[City].MEMBERS, measures.profit > 1000) ON 1
FROM [Adventure Works DW]
```

The query results in all cities that have a profit greater than $1000. If you want to do a marketing campaign in only 10 percent of those cities, you can use the CustomFilter function in addition to the MDX FILTER function as follows:

```
SELECT measures.profit ON 0,
AdomdSproc.CustomFilter(
FILTER([Dim Geography].[City].[City].MEMBERS, measures.profit > 1000),
10)
ON 1
FROM [Adventure Works DW]
```

As you can see, your stored procedure takes the results of an MDX function because the MDX FILTER function returns an MDX set. That set is the parameter taken by your stored procedure. Vice versa, your stored procedure also has the capability of taking in MDX objects as parameters and returning MDX objects. Stored procedures are powerful features in Analysis Services 2008.

You have seen how stored procedures can be used within MDX queries. Another way of invoking stored procedures being executed in Analysis Services 2008 is via the CALL statement. You have added the AMO stored procedure assembly to your database. You can use the CALL statement to execute stored procedures outside of the context of a normal MDX query. To get a listing of the partitions in your current database you can send the following MDX statement:

```
CALL AmoSproc.ListPartitions()
```

This simple query can also be used as the source for a SQL Server Reporting Services report.

You have added the AMO stored procedure with Unrestricted permission set access. Now see what happens if you change the permission set to External Access. You can change the permission set of an assembly by selecting the properties of the assembly and then changing the appropriate permission set.

Executing the preceding CALL statement to list partitions now results in the following error message:

```
Execution of the managed stored procedure ListPartitions failed with the
following error: Exception has been thrown by the target of an invocation.
That assembly does not allow partially trusted callers..
```

As mentioned earlier, when you specify the external access permission set, the .NET Framework only allows assemblies to have external access. In this case your assembly AmoSproc uses an assembly Microsoft.AnalysisServices that is not fully trusted by the .NET Framework and does not have the full privilege of performing any operation in the specified permission set. Therefore, the .NET Framework raises the error and does not execute the assembly. If you are a DBA and you restrict access to assemblies that you do not fully trust, your Analysis Server will be well secured and reliable.

Debugging Stored Procedures

Whenever you write code there are bound to be instances or conditions under which your stored procedure might not operate in accord with expectations. You can obviously test your stored procedure external to Analysis Services in conditions where you do not use the object models of Analysis Services. If you are using the ADOMD Server object model, debugging the stored procedure external to Analysis Services is difficult, especially in the conditions where differences between client and server models exist. For example, the server ADOMD has an object called MDXExpression that helps you to evaluate MDX expressions within your stored procedure. This is not available in the client object model, so you will need a different method for debugging your stored procedure. The new method is not that complicated and is similar to debugging any program, but you need to debug within Analysis Services. Assume you want to debug your ADOMD stored procedure example in this chapter because you are not getting expected results. The following steps show how to debug it:

1. Execute the MDX query that uses the stored procedure.

2. Launch Visual Studio and attach it to your Analysis Server instance. You can attach the debugger to Analysis Services by selecting Tools ⇨ Attach to Process. (The location of Visual Studio menus may vary depending on your settings. If this menu item is not available, you can right-click on the menu bar and use the Customize command to add it.) In the Attach to Process window, check the box to show processes from all users, search for the process msmdsrv.exe, and select the process. Select the Managed option for the Attach to field as shown in Figure 11-5 and click Attach.

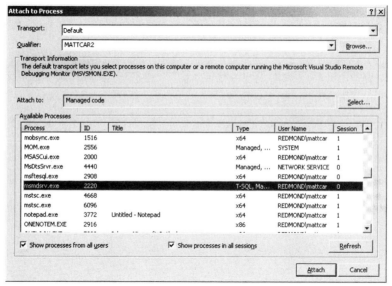

Figure 11-5

3. Now you need to make sure you load all the symbol information of your stored procedure. For this, select Debug ⇨ Window ⇨ Modules in Visual Studio. (Again, the presence of this menu item depends on your settings, so if it's missing use Customize to add it.) You will now see the modules window that shows all the DLLs loaded by the Analysis Services executable msmdsrv.exe. Search for the DLL AdoMdServerExample.DLL, right-click, and select Load Symbols. In the Find Symbol dialog, point to the folder that contains the symbol information for the AdoMdServerExample.DLL (that is, the file AdoMDServerExample.pdb).

4. In Visual Studio select File ⇨ Open and select the source file for ADOMD stored procedure example, which is AdomdSproc.cs.

5. Select break points at certain lines within the `CustomFilter` function.

6.   Execute the MDX query once again. You will now hit the break point within Visual Studio as shown in Figure 11-6.

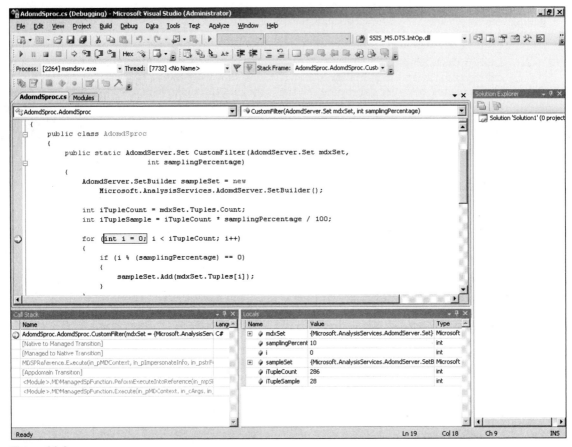

Figure 11-6

7.   You can see all the local variables and you will be able to perform all the debugging operations that are feasible within Visual Studio. If your function calls other functions within the same stored procedures or other stored procedures, you can debug those similar to debugging any of your programs.

8.   Once you have identified your problem and made changes to the code and built a new version of the binary, add the new version of the binary to Analysis Services by deleting the older version and adding the new version using the Register Database Assembly dialog.

Analysis Services 2008 Plug-Ins

Analysis Services 2008 provides a new advanced feature that allows .NET stored procedures to respond to a limited set of server events. By marking a .NET stored procedure's class with the PlugInAttribute, you can run code every time a session is opened or closed or when a cube is first accessed within a session. (A session is the context of a connection. Usually, each connection has its own session, but it is possible for connections to share a session.) The following plug-in stored procedure writes a custom event to the trace log recording the cube name, username, and date whenever a cube is first accessed in a session:

```
#region Using directives

using System;
using Microsoft.AnalysisServices.AdomdServer;
using AMO = Microsoft.AnalysisServices;

#endregion

namespace PlugIn
{
  [PlugInAttribute]
  public class PlugIn
  {
    public PlugIn()
    {
      Context.Server.SessionOpened += new EventHandler( Server_SessionOpened
                 );
    }

    void Server_SessionOpened( object sender, EventArgs e )
    {
      Context.CurrentConnection.CubeOpened += new EventHandler(
            CurrentConnection_CubeOpened );
    }

    void CurrentConnection_CubeOpened( object sender, EventArgs e )
    {
      Context.TraceEvent( ( int )AMO.TraceEventSubclass.Other, 0,
          String.Format( "Cube '{0}' opened by user '{1}' on {2}.",
          Context.CurrentCube.Name, Context.CurrentConnection.User.Name,
          DateTime.Now.ToShortDateString() ) );
    }
  }
}
```

The presence of the PlugInAttribute on the class tells the Analysis Services server to call the constructor of this class on startup. The class constructor then registers for the SessionOpened event. In the SessionOpened event, it then registers for the CubeOpened event for that session. Finally, on CubeOpened the stored procedure uses the Context.TraceEvent method, which is also new to Analysis Services 2008 to send a custom trace message. Add this assembly to your Analysis Services 2008 server being sure to use an unrestricted permission set. Restart the server service, and you can then use SQL Server Profiler to watch for this custom trace event when a cube is first accessed on a connection.

COM User-Defined Functions

COM is Microsoft's architecture for building software from binary components that expose functionality with a well-defined interface. Analysis Services understands COM components and has the ability to use COM DLLs so that functions within the DLL can be accessed through MDX. To create a new function that will perform a customized operation for your business, we recommend you use .NET stored procedures. However, if you already have a COM DLL that provides the functionality you need, you can still use it in Analysis Services 2008. This section helps you use existing COM UDFs in Analysis Services 2008.

Adding a COM UDF to an Analysis Services Database

To use a COM UDF in MDX queries, you must add it to an Analysis Services database. You do this the same way as with .NET stored procedures by using SQL Server Management Studio and simply setting the Type of the assembly to COM DLL. As with .NET UDFs, you can add a COM UDF to Analysis Services at the scope of the Analysis Services instance or at the scope of an existing database. If your UDF is added at the server scope, it can be shared across multiple databases similar to the Excel and VBA DLLs that default to server-level scope.

All COM assemblies added to Analysis Services have unrestricted permissions, which means they can access files or network services in addition to any computation. Code access security is only available for .NET assemblies. As a result, you should only add COM assemblies that come from a source you trust.

Disambiguating between Functions

COM UDFs can be used in MDX queries in very much the same way as built-in UDFs. However, you can add multiple COM UDFs that contain the same function names to a database or Analysis Services instance. If you have more than one function with the same name within Analysis Services, any query using the function name will result in an error. This is due to the inability to resolve to the correct function name. In such a circumstance, you can explicitly specify the fully qualified name of the function by prepending it with the classID of the library. The classID of a function looks like this: `PackageName.ClassName`. If you have created your UDF using a Visual Basic project that contains a package name called `COMExample` and a class name `COMExampleClass`, you need to access the function as `COMExample!_COMExampleClass.Function`.

COM UDFs versus .NET Stored Procedures

.NET stored procedures have the big advantage that you get better integration with the Analysis Services server via ADOMD Server and AMO. You also get the added protection of code access security and the easier development of .NET languages with .NET stored procedures.

Analysis Services supports COM UDF primarily for backward compatibility because there might be several existing applications using it in production. If you are migrating your Analysis Services 2000 databases containing COM UDFs to Analysis Services 2008 using the migration wizard and need existing applications to utilize UDFs, we recommend using the COM UDFs. If you are very passionate about COM UDFs, you can develop your UDFs as COM libraries. However, COM UDF support is being deprecated in Analysis Services 2008, which means that the support for COM UDFs might not be available in future versions.

Even if you have VB6 COM UDFs in your Analysis Services implementation, you might be able to port these to .NET using VB.NET. We highly recommend that you use .NET languages for UDFs. Analysis Services 2008 has been architected to leverage the .NET Framework and provides developers with the best aspects of .NET languages, such as the memory management and garbage collection technology provided by .NET languages coupled with code access security settings for the assemblies provided by Analysis Services 2008. If you are already familiar with .NET languages, that is great. If not, seriously consider ramping up and learning at least one .NET language. That ramp-up time will be time well spent. We don't recommend that you attempt to learn a new programming paradigm under some tight development schedule. If you have code access security considerations associated with your business application, then use .NET assemblies. Note that if you will want to perform custom operations on your multidimensional data on your Analysis Services instance using the ADOMD Server object model, you will have to use the .NET languages to implement your stored procedures.

Summary

Did the impending sense of programming power make you dizzy while reading? You no doubt experienced a thrill akin to a roller coaster ride while reading this chapter. Think about it. There is a way to do basically whatever you want programmatically as long as you are capable of coding it up in concert with all the power of SQL Server Analysis Services 2008. Consider what you learned in the three sections of this chapter. In the first section you learned about the built-in UDFs that provide the power of VBA and Excel functions in MDX. In the second section you learned how to create stored procedures using the ADOMD Server and AMO object models. Finally, you learned how to use an existing COM UDF in MDX queries. You also learned under what circumstances COM UDF is preferred over a .NET UDF. With the help of the UDFs you can now perform any custom operations that you need in your multidimensional database. You have so far learned to design and refine your databases. In the next chapter you learn the intricacies of updating underlying UDM data on dimensions as well as cells.

Data Writeback

In previous chapters you saw how metadata constituting OLAP databases (the UDM) can be manipulated using the Analysis Services 2008 development environment. You learned that the metadata changes are propagated to the Analysis Services instance through Create or Alter statements. You've also learned that Analysis Services reads data from relational sources during processing. You learn more about how processing is used to update cubes and dimensions with the latest data in the relational source in Chapter 13.

However, what if you want to update data in your cube or in a dimension it contains without going directly to the relational source? For example, change of marital status for an employee, where marital status is an attribute within the Employee dimension, or perhaps an update for the next fiscal year's budget based on the current year's revenue where budget is a measure within your cube. Analysis Services 2008 provides you with the ability to directly update dimension as well as cube data. Data updates within your UDM are referred to as a writeback because you are writing data back into an existing UDM. Updating members within your dimension is referred to as dimension writeback and updating the measure values within your cube is called cell writeback. By the way, don't let the three letter acronym throw you off; a UDM is another way of referring to a cube.

Dimension writeback enables a user to add, update, or delete dimension members while working with a cube. For example, when a new employee joins the company, the user can update the Employee dimension by adding a new member. Likewise, when an employee changes departments or leaves the company altogether, the user can update or delete relevant dimension members. When you update dimension members, Analysis Services automatically updates the corresponding tables in the data source, processes the dimension, and then cascades changes to affected cubes. In Analysis Services 2008, the operations Delete, Add, Move, and Update on dimension members are supported through BIDS, and through XMLA statements.

Cell writeback enables a user to change the values referred to by tuples in a cube. In a typical user scenario, a company's budget for next year is allocated based on market conditions and other factors. Analysis Services supports in-session writeback (what-if), which enables the user to change cell values directly in memory, and check resulting effects such as aggregate results and calculated values. The user can then choose to commit or discard (abort transaction) the changes. If the changes are committed, other users will be able to see those changes. You learn to use writeback to change dimension and cube data in this chapter through examples with the help of the sample Adventure Works DW2008 relational database.

With the exception of some performance enhancements to cell writeback discussed later, both dimension and cell writeback behave and are used the same in both Analysis Services 2005 and Analysis Services 2008.

Dimension Writeback

Dimension data requires an update under several circumstances. If an organization is selling products, then adding new products to the catalog may end up on the "to do" list and hence the changes need to be reflected in the product dimension. You might come up with new promotions for a holiday season line to increase your sales and hence need to update data in your promotions dimension. One of the most common scenarios is changing data for employees. As new employees join the organization their information needs to be added to the appropriate dimension. Or existing employees' information might have to be updated due to a change in properties of the employees.

Analysis Services 2008 allows you to change the dimension data directly through the Dimension Browser in the BIDS as well as SSMS. You can manually create dimension members for small dimensions within the Dimension Browser. It is very helpful to users during the development phase of your UDM so that you can make appropriate modifications to your dimension data. To update the dimension data in your UDM, Analysis Services updates the data in the underlying relational table and then does an incremental process to update the data in the UDM. You should be aware that using BIDS for updating dimension data can reduce performance. This is because Analysis Services sends relational queries for each member update separately to update the dimension data in the relational database followed by the incremental process. If your scenario is to do bulk operations such as moving an entire organization from one geographical location to another and you need to update all the dimension members, you are better off updating the relational database through bulk update and then processing the dimension.

The dimension writeback supported by the Dimension Browser in BIDS or SSMS can be helpful under specific circumstances. This would be helpful during modeling and adding new members to see the dimension structure. Most often the relational database that stores the dimension data might not be accessible to the person who is involved in maintenance of your cubes and dimensions. The Analysis Services administrator might have granted permissions to a specific account that can access the relational backend that is part of the server role of Analysis Services or specified as part of the database data source impersonation, as seen in Chapter 7. Under such circumstances, as an administrator of the Analysis Services database, you can update the dimension data through the dimension writeback supported by Analysis Services tools. We recommend the use of dimension data update through the Dimension Browser whenever you have limited data to update or the frequency of updates is quite low (once a month, for example). Not everyone accessing the UDM can perform updates on dimensions. Only users who are part of a role that has explicit write permissions and process permissions specified for dimensions can do dimension writeback.

To update the dimension data, the dimension first needs to be write-enabled, which means the users with write permissions on the dimension can update data. You learned the basics of dimension writeback in Chapter 8, and in this chapter you learn dimension writeback through a user scenario. You learn how to add, delete, and update dimension members using the dimension writeback technique.

Dimension Writeback Prerequisites

Before you start implementing the scenario, you should understand that certain prerequisites must be addressed before you can write data to a dimension. These prerequisites are as follows:

1. The dimension property WriteEnable needs to be set to True. This can be done in BIDS.

2. The dimension to be write-enabled must be derived from a single table, which means all dimension attributes' key and name columns have to come from the same table. A snowflake dimension cannot be write-enabled.

3. If a dimension has been created from a named query, that dimension cannot be write-enabled. Dimension writeback works by updating the data in backend relational database tables. Dimensions based on named queries (or backend relational database views, for that matter) do not correspond directly to tables in the backend relational database. In sum, Analysis Services does not support write-enabling dimensions that have been created from named queries or views in a relational database.

4. Analysis Services should have write permissions for the tables while impersonating the account specified in the data source and the dimension table cannot have an auto increment key column while adding new rows.

In addition to the preceding prerequisites, which are required by the Analysis Services service, you should also be aware of two requirements for performing dimension writeback through the Analysis Services Dimension Browser:

1. If attributes within the dimension have different name and key columns defined, you cannot writeback to the dimension. The only exception is for the attributes that have Usage set to Key and Parent.

2. All dimension attributes need to have Discretization Method specified to None. This is because if an attribute has been discretized into a specific bucket, you cannot write the discretized value back to the relational data.

These two limitations are only due to the design of the Dimension Browser. If you write your own tool to update dimension data, you can send appropriate DDL commands to Insert, Update, or Delete dimension members.

Enabling Dimension Writeback

Now that you know the requirements of dimension writeback in Analysis Services, you can try dimension writeback on a database to understand the behavior better. Follow these steps to perform dimension writeback operations:

1. Create a UDM from a subset of the relational AdventureWorks DW2008 data. Execute the following SQL script against the relational database to create the subset of data needed for this scenario. The following SQL script (CreateWriteBackExampleTables.sql in the Chapter 12 folder that can be downloaded from this book's accompanying web site) creates three tables, WB_Employee, WB_Period, and WB_Fact, and retrieves a subset of the data from the DimEmployee, DimTime, and FactSalesQuota tables of the Adventure Works relational sample database. You are now ready to create an UDM on top of these three tables. Note that you should ignore any "cannot drop the table" messages if you get them.

```
USE [AdventureWorksDW2008]
GO
DROP TABLE [WB_Employee]
GO
DROP TABLE [WB_Period]
GO
DROP TABLE [WB_Fact]
GO

CREATE TABLE [dbo].[WB_Employee](
  [EmployeeKey] [int] NOT NULL,
  [ParentEmployeeKey] [int] NULL,
  [FullName] [nvarchar](101) COLLATE SQL_Latin1_General_CP1_CI_AS NOT NULL,
```

(continued)

(continued)

```
    [DepartmentName] [nvarchar](50) COLLATE SQL_Latin1_General_CP1_CI_AS NULL
) ON [PRIMARY]
GO


SELECT DISTINCT [CalendarQuarter]+[CalendarYear]*10 as QuarterKey,
    CAST([CalendarYear] AS VARCHAR(10) )+' Q'+
    CAST(CalendarQuarter AS VARCHAR(10)) AS QuarterName
    , [CalendarYear]
INTO WB_Period
FROM [AdventureWorksDW2008].[dbo].[DimDate]


GO

INSERT INTO [WB_Employee]
SELECT [EmployeeKey]
    , [ParentEmployeeKey]
    , [LastName]+','+ [FirstName] AS FullName
    , [DepartmentName]
FROM [AdventureWorksDW2008].[dbo].[DimEmployee]
GO

SELECT [EmployeeKey]
    , [CalendarYear]*10 +[CalendarQuarter] AS Quarterkey
    , [SalesAmountQuota] AS BudgetExpenseAmount
INTO WB_Fact
FROM [AdventureWorksDW2008].[dbo].[FactSalesQuota]
GO


INSERT INTO WB_Fact
SELECT 275, quarterkey, budgetexpenseamount
FROM dbo.WB_Fact
GO
```

2. Create a new Analysis Services project using BIDS and name it WriteBackExample.

3. Create a data source to the Adventure Works DW2008 sample database. Make sure you set the Impersonation mode for the data source to Inherit in the Data Source Wizard.

4. Create a DSV and include the tables WB_Fact, WB_Period, and WB_Employee from the Adventure Works DW2008 data source. Make sure the primary keys for all the tables are marked appropriately and establish the relationships between the tables in the DSV as shown in Figure 12-1. Note that to get the parent-child relationship, just drag and drop ParentEmployeeKey onto EmployeeKey.

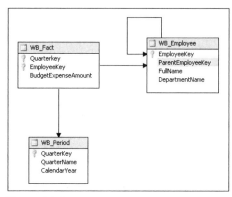

Figure 12-1

5. Launch the Dimension Wizard and select "Use an existing table" and click Next. Use WB_Employee as the main table, set the Name Column to Full Name and click Next. Rename the Employee Key attribute to Employee, the Parent Employee Key attribute to Manager, and make sure all three available attributes are checked for inclusion in the dimension. Click Next and then Finish to create the new WB Employee dimension.

6. Launch the Dimension Wizard and again select "Use an existing table" and click Next. This time use WB_Period as the main table, QuarterKey as the key column, QuarterName as the name column, and click Next. Rename the Quarter Key attribute to Quarter and check the Calendar Year attribute for inclusion. Click Next and then Finish to create the new WB Period dimension.

7. Launch the Cube Wizard, use WB_Fact as the measure group table, and then select the defaults on the remaining pages to create the cube. The wizard will use the two newly created dimensions: WB_Employee and WB_Period.

8. To write-enable the WB Employee dimension, edit the dimension and then click the WB Employee dimension node in the attributes tree of the Dimension Designer. Then in the Properties panel change the property WriteEnabled to True, as shown in Figure 12-2.

Figure 12-2

417

9. Select the Employee attribute in the attributes tree of the Dimension Designer. In the Properties panel set the AttributeHierarchyVisible property to True. This is necessary for the Dimension Browser in BIDS and SSMS to be able to identify and display member properties associated with employees.

10. Deploy the Analysis Services project to your Analysis Services instance.

Adding a Member to a Dimension

In this scenario, a new employee named "Smith, James" who just joined the Adventure Works Company needs to be added as a member to the Employee dimension. James will report to "Bradley, David" in the Marketing department. You can add a member to the Employee dimension through the key attribute or the parent attribute of the Employee dimension because the Employee dimension contains a parent-child hierarchy. You need to enter the values for all the properties for the dimension member to be added. Because you need to add a member under "Bradley, David," it is most convenient to use the Parent attribute of the Employee dimension, which is the parent-child hierarchy. Follow these steps to add "Smith, James" to the Employee dimension:

1. Open the Employee dimension and switch to the Browser tab.

2. In the Hierarchy drop-down box, choose the Manager hierarchy.

3. Click the member properties icon in the Dimension Browser as shown in Figure 12-3. Select the (Show All) checkbox to select all the member properties and click OK.

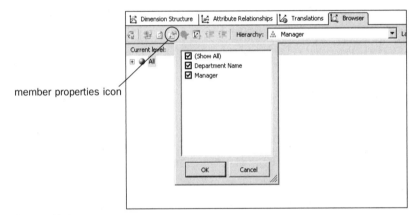

Figure 12-3

4. Click the Writeback icon (shown in Figure 12-4) to enter writeback mode in the dimension. You will now see a new column called Key added to the Browser view, as shown in Figure 12-4. This column shows the Id of the employee. The ID of the employee is the value in the key attribute hierarchy (Employee) in the dimension. If you browse the Employee attribute hierarchy you will see these values for the members of the attribute.

5. In the Dimension Browser you can see two David Bradleys (Figure 12-4), which indicates David Bradley is a manager as well as an employee. In the tree view showing the employees, right-click the first "Bradley, David" and choose Create Child from the pop-up menu as shown in Figure 12-5. Notice that you can also create James Smith as a sibling member by selecting one of the employees reporting to David Bradley.

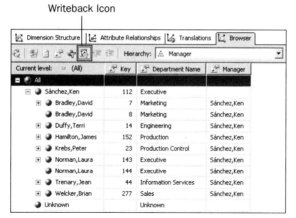

Writeback Icon

Figure 12-4

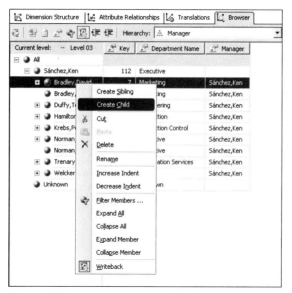

Figure 12-5

6. You will now see a new row being created under "Bradley, David" with the Manager field already pre-populated with "Bradley, David." The cursor is located in the column where all the members are shown so that you can enter the name of the new employee. Enter the name "Smith, James." Enter the value 300 for the member key and Marketing as the Department Name as shown in Figure 12-6.

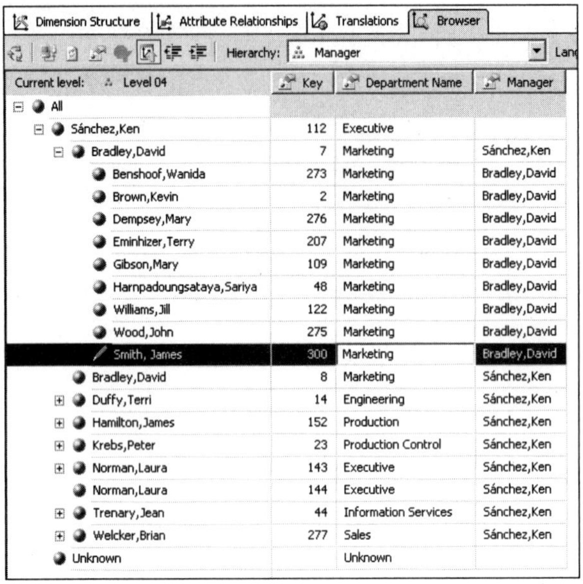

Figure 12-6

This parent-child hierarchy has a member property called Manager, which is a column in the Dimension Browser. That column is read only because when you input a new member under a certain manager, the existing parent is populated into the Manager column automatically. Note that if you want to undo changes to a new member that was created, click the ESC key. Otherwise, after you have entered all necessary values, move the cursor to a different member to add the new member to the dimension. BIDS sends the values for the new member "Smith, James" to the Analysis Services instance. The DDL sent by BIDS to Analysis Services for the dimension writeback is shown here. The Insert command does the writeback of the new member's values in the dimension.

```
<Insert xsi:type="Insert" xmlns:xsd="http://www.w3.org/2001/XMLSchema"
        xmlns:xsi="http://www.w3.org/2001/XMLSchema-instance"
        xmlns:ddl2="http://schemas.microsoft.com/analysisservices/2003/
        engine/2" xmlns:ddl2_2="http://schemas.microsoft.com/analysisservices/
        2003/engine/2/2" xmlns:ddl100_100="http://schemas.microsoft.com/
        analysisservices/2008/engine/100/100" xmlns="http://
        schemas.microsoft.com/analysisservices/2003/engine">
  <Object>
    <Database>WriteBackExample</Database>
    <Cube>$WB Employee</Cube>
    <Dimension>WB Employee</Dimension>
  </Object>
  <Attributes>
    <Attribute>
      <AttributeName>Employee</AttributeName>
      <Name>Smith, James</Name>
      <Keys>
        <Key xsi:type="xsd:int">300</Key>
      </Keys>
    </Attribute>
```

```
      <Attribute>
        <AttributeName>Manager</AttributeName>
        <Keys>
          <Key xsi:type="xsd:int">7</Key>
        </Keys>
      </Attribute>
      <Attribute>
        <AttributeName>Department Name</AttributeName>
        <Keys>
          <Key xsi:type="xsd:string">Marketing</Key>
        </Keys>
      </Attribute>
    </Attributes>
  </Insert>
```

The DDL has two sections, Object and Attributes. The Object section is where the object is defined and where the cube and dimension names are specified. You already learned that each database dimension is considered a cube of a single dimension within that Analysis Services database. Hence the new member is being created in the database dimension rather than the cube dimension. Therefore, you see the name $WB Employee being used to refer to the WB Employee database dimension. The newly added dimension member and its properties are specified as part of the Attributes section. Whenever dimension data is being updated, the corresponding data gets updated in the relational database and then Analysis Services does an incremental update of that dimension. Analysis Services, after receiving the command to add the new members, creates a corresponding SQL statement to update the data in the relational table WB_Employee. If there are some constraints set on this table, such as FullName cannot be null, the corresponding SQL update will fail and this will get propagated back to the Dimension Browser and shown to the user. If the relational update statement succeeds, the Analysis Services instance automatically does an incremental update of the dimension so that the newly added dimension gets added to the database dimension, and thereby can be accessed by all the cubes that use the dimension. Once the incremental update is successful, Analysis Services sends a response back to the Dimension Browser and you can proceed with additional operations.

If you query the relational table WB_Employee, you will see that a new row has been added to the relational table with the values you had entered as shown in the following table:

Key	Parentkey	FullName	Department
300	7	Smith, James	Marketing

You have now successfully added a new member to the Employee dimension using the dimension writeback functionality supported through BIDS. Next, you learn about modifying member properties of existing members.

Modifying Data of Members in a Dimension

Assume that James Smith worked for a year in the Marketing department and wanted to move to a different department for his career growth. He interviewed with the Engineering group and secured a new position. This data needs to be reflected in the Employee dimension. Assume James' new manager is Gail Erickson. Updating James' information in the Employee dimension so that he has moved to a different organization needs to be done as a two-step process. You need to update the reporting structure for James so that Erickson becomes his manager and then you need to update his new department information. Now let's go ahead and update James' information.

As mentioned in the previous section, the Dimension Browser does not allow you to edit the parent attribute (Manager column in this example) when you add a new member. Similarly, you cannot update or edit the Manager column directly. Therefore the BIDS provides the functionality of dragging and dropping James' information under Erickson so that his manager's name gets updated. Select the record for James in the Dimension Browser view with writeback enabled and then drag and drop James under "Erickson, Gail." The drag-and-drop operation can also be accomplished by cut-and-paste options available in the Dimension Browser. To do so, select James' record, right-click, and select Cut to remove the link from James' current manager. Then select "Erickson, Gail," right-click, and select Paste so that James is moved under "Erickson, Gail."

You will see that James has now moved under "Erickson, Gail" and his manager information has been automatically updated as shown in Figure 12-7. However, other attributes of James do not get updated automatically. This is because Analysis Services does not know what attributes of a child are to be inherited from the parent. For example, you might have an attribute join date instead of department. James' join date and Erickson's join date need not be the same and hence join date for James should not be updated automatically. Even for something like Department Name, you can have a business scenario where your manager might be a person from a different department but the work you are doing might still be the same. For example, you might have two departments coming under a general manager. Hence BIDS does not automatically update the member properties of a member when the member is moved from one parent to another. Appropriate values need to be updated by the end user.

Current level: ⁘ Level 06	Key	Department Name	Manager
⊟ ● All			
⊟ ● Sánchez,Ken	112	Executive	
⊟ ● Bradley,David	7	Marketing	Sánchez,Ken
● Benshoof,Wanida	273	Marketing	Bradley,David
● Brown,Kevin	2	Marketing	Bradley,David
● Dempsey,Mary	276	Marketing	Bradley,David
● Eminhizer,Terry	207	Marketing	Bradley,David
● Gibson,Mary	109	Marketing	Bradley,David
● Harnpadoungsataya,Sariya	48	Marketing	Bradley,David
● Williams,Jill	122	Marketing	Bradley,David
● Wood,John	275	Marketing	Bradley,David
● Bradley,David	8	Marketing	Sánchez,Ken
⊟ ● Duffy,Terri	14	Engineering	Sánchez,Ken
⊟ ● Tamburello,Roberto	3	Engineering	Duffy,Terri
⊞ ● Cracium,Ovidiu	267	Tool Design	Tamburello,Roberto
⊟ ● Erickson,Gail	11	Engineering	Tamburello,Roberto
● Smith, James	300	Marketing	Erickson,Gail
● Goldberg,Jossef	13	Engineering	Tamburello,Roberto

Figure 12-7

BIDS sends the following update DDL to the Analysis Services instance server:

```
<Update xsi:type="Update" xmlns:xsd="http://www.w3.org/2001/XMLSchema"
        xmlns:xsi="http://www.w3.org/2001/XMLSchema-instance"
        xmlns:ddl2="http://schemas.microsoft.com/analysisservices/2003/
        engine/2" xmlns:ddl2_2="http://schemas.microsoft.com/analysisservices
        /2003/engine/2/2" xmlns:ddl100_100="http://schemas.microsoft.com/
        analysisservices/2008/engine/100/100" xmlns="http://
        schemas.microsoft.com/analysisservices/2003/engine">
  <Object>
    <Database>WriteBackExample</Database>
    <Cube>$WB Employee</Cube>
    <Dimension>WB Employee</Dimension>
  </Object>
```

```
  <Attributes>
    <Attribute>
      <AttributeName>Manager</AttributeName>
      <Keys>
        <Key xsi:type="xsd:int">11</Key>
      </Keys>
    </Attribute>
  </Attributes>
  <Where>
    <Attribute>
      <AttributeName>Employee</AttributeName>
      <Keys>
        <Key xsi:type="xsd:int">300</Key>
      </Keys>
    </Attribute>
  </Where>
  <MoveWithDescendants>true</MoveWithDescendants>
</Update>
```

Similar to adding a new member, Analysis Services updates James' information in the relational database through appropriate relational update queries as shown in the following SQL query followed by an incremental process of the dimension. The update queries sent to the relational database can be seen if you monitor the trace (with progress events enabled) coming back from Analysis Services. You learn to trace events on Analysis Services instances using SQL Server Profiler in Chapter 15. Analysis Services creates parameterized relational queries (the ? symbol indicates a parameter) to avoid SQL injection (a type of security vulnerability). The queries generated will depend on the relational backend and Analysis Services' use of an appropriate cartridge (information that tells Analysis Services how to form the relational queries for this database provider) for that specific relational database.

```
UPDATE [dbo].[WB_Employee]
    SET [dbo].[WB_Employee].[ParentEmployeeKey]=  ?
    WHERE
    (
    (
      [dbo].[WB_Employee].[EmployeeKey]  =  ?
    )
    )
```

To correctly update James' department to Engineering, you need to click James' record and then click a second time. James' record is now enabled for updates. Then click the Department Name column and change the department value from Marketing to Engineering. To complete the writeback, move the cursor to a different member. The record in the dimension table will be changed as shown in the following table:

Key ParentKey	Key	FullName	Department
300	11	Smith, James	Engineering

In the DDL that was sent to the Analysis Services instance when you moved Smith, you can see a tag MoveWithDescendants set to true as shown in the following code. This tag informs Analysis Services to move all the descendants of the current member to the new parent. This is an example of a business scenario where an entire organization or division moves under a new manager.

```
<MoveWithDescendants>true</MoveWithDescendants>
```

Another common scenario is when a manager moves to a different department and all his or her direct reports automatically report to the second line manager until a new manager is identified. In such a circumstance, the MoveWithDescendants tag should be set appropriately to achieve the behavior. The Dimension Browser does not allow this functionality; however, you can create your own DDL and send it directly to the Analysis Services instance to achieve this behavior.

The BIDS Dimension Browser also facilitates moving members from one parent to another parent. All you have to do is to select multiple members by holding down the Ctrl key, and move the members to the new parent by using drag-and-drop or cut-and-paste operations. This would be helpful in circumstances where you have a re-org in your organizations.

Deleting Dimension Data

One scenario that eventually happens in all companies is an employee leaves the company. The human resources department often deletes the employee record from the main database so that payroll and benefits are terminated for the ex-employee. Analysis Services provides you support to delete members in a dimension from the Dimension Browser. Assume John Wood leaves the company and you need to delete the member corresponding to him in the Employee dimension. To delete the member from the dimension, select the record for "Wood, John" and click the Delete button. The Delete Members dialog is launched, as shown in Figure 12-8. This dialog prompts to either delete all the descendants reporting to John Wood or make them report to John Wood's manager. If an entire group of employees under John Wood are leaving the company to start a new business or getting laid off, you would choose the Delete their descendants option. A more common scenario is the second choice, which is Promote their descendants. Click OK after making the selection.

Figure 12-8

The BIDS Dimension Browser sends the drop statement to the Analysis Services instance as shown in the following code. Analysis Services sends a relational command to delete the member from the relational table and then does an incremental process of the dimension.

```
<Drop xsi:type="Drop" xmlns:xsd="http://www.w3.org/2001/XMLSchema"
        xmlns:xsi="http://www.w3.org/2001/XMLSchema-instance"
        xmlns:ddl2="http://schemas.microsoft.com/analysisservices/2003/
        engine/2" xmlns:ddl2_2="http://schemas.microsoft.com/analysisservices/
        2003/engine/2/2" xmlns:ddl100_100="http://schemas.microsoft.com/
        analysisservices/2008/engine/100/100" xmlns="http://
        schemas.microsoft.com/analysisservices/2003/engine">
  <Object>
    <Database>WriteBackExample</Database>
    <Cube>$WB Employee</Cube>
    <Dimension>WB Employee</Dimension>
  </Object>
  <Where>
    <Attribute>
      <AttributeName>Employee</AttributeName>
      <Keys>
        <Key xsi:type="xsd:int">275</Key>
      </Keys>
    </Attribute>
  </Where>
</Drop>
```

If the dimension member had fact data in a fact table associated with him or her, the fact data will not be available for querying. Even though the data is processed inside the cube while querying, Analysis Services will not be able to identify the associated member and hence not return results for this member. You can send the following query to the Analysis Services instance before and after deletion of the member John Wood to see the difference between the returned result sets:

```
select measures.members on columns,
{[WB Employee].[Manager].&[7],
[WB Employee].[Manager].&[7].children } on rows
from [Adventure Works DW2008]
```

Be aware that Analysis Services automatically deletes dimension entries from a dimension table, but does not automatically delete the corresponding fact table entry from the fact table. The fact table entries for the deleted "Wood, John" (key 275) are still in the fact table. Before you remove the dimension member, you need to make sure that the dimension member doesn't have any data in the fact table. The fact data does exist within the UDM; it is just being restricted by Analysis Services. It is being restricted because the corresponding dimension member was deleted. Such fact data is referred to as orphan fact data. Because the dimension data corresponding to John Wood has been deleted and the fact data is still available, if you do a full process of the database you will see processing errors because Analysis Services by default checks for referential integrity. You can change the error configuration settings on the cube to handle the rows (delete or associate it with Unknown member of the dimension) associated with John Wood or you can delete the entries corresponding to John Wood using the following SQL statement and then reprocess the entire database:

```
delete from WB_Fact
where employeekey = 275
```

Now that you have successfully learned to update dimension data, the following section discusses the need to update cell values in your cube. This is a common scenario for a lot of business organizations and we hope you will find the next section extremely useful.

Cell Writeback

The ability to create "hypothetical" what-if scenarios is central to business intelligence because it enables the executive to explore contingencies associated with the financial landscape. In this way, the executive can seek out the profit maximizing potential of the firm while minimizing risk and generally mitigating threats. Because these concepts are so much better explained by way of example, here are two specific examples to help you understand what is meant by what-if scenarios.

In the first example, a company president is considering her options in terms of resource allocation for the coming fiscal year. Her BI team has astutely developed a UDM that calculates key business drivers for the company. Because the user can writeback new values into those seed measures, new configurations of company resource allocation can be tried and the results assessed. The key business metrics will be recalculated due to new values entered into the system. The sorts of questions that can be "asked" of the system through the use of these simulations depend on how many measures are designed to act as seed values. Typical questions include, "What if we increase our advertising budget for the next fiscal year?," "What if we charge more (or less) for our product?," and "What if we take on more debt to expand production facilities and therefore enhance manufacturing capacity?" Keep in mind that not just any question could be asked of the system. Only those questions that have the required measures available for use as seed values and underlying calculations or KPIs in support of cascading correct changes will provide meaningful results.

The second example considers the needs of a bank. The vice-president is considering strategies for the coming year regarding appropriate risk distribution for commercial loan application acceptance. The bank has good metrics from which to base calculations on successful loan repayments versus defaults and those metrics have been entered into the relevant cubes. If banks are anything like most bureaucratic organizations, they likely have regulations that mandate certain minimum distributions of loans to different risk categories. For example, in the interest of economic development and creating new active bank customers in the future, a certain percentage of high-risk loans should be accepted. The vice-president is most likely looking to give loans so as to maximize income from loans for the bank. With a fund of $500 million from which to make loans, the president can consider the manipulation of multiple seed values like interest rates and risk acceptance percentages. In the end, some optimal state will emerge, such as allocating $100 million to low risk, $250 million for moderate risk, and $150 million to high risk businesses.

In financial applications (corporate plan, budget, and forecast systems), most of the time the UDM is applied as a data gathering and analysis business model to gather data input from all departments, and perform many what-if analyses for future business decisions. Once the analysts make a final decision, the data values need to be updated in the cube for appropriate actions to be taken. For example, the budget for a department might get allocated based on the current year's revenue and that department would have to plan the next fiscal year's financial plans based on the allocated budget. If the executives have made a forecast of achieving specific revenue for the next year, other business decisions need to be propagated to the people in the corporate food chain appropriately. For example, if the sales target for the organization was to have 500 million dollars (10% growth over the current year), the business goals or commitments for the individual sales employees need to be appropriately set to reach the organization goal.

In this section you learn how to effectively use Analysis Services to provide what-if scenarios to top executives and to update the cube data so that it can be appropriately propagated to the entire organization. Updating the data in an Analysis Services cube is referred to as cell writeback because you are updating the cell values in the cube space.

You are aware that a cube contains one or more measure groups. When a cube is write-enabled, it means that one or more measure groups in the cube are enabled for writeback of data. Each measure group contains one or more partitions. The data from the relational data source is read and stored within partitions by Analysis Services. To writeback cell data within the cube, you need to have a new partition called the writeback partition for each measure group you want to enable for writeback of data. Any data (measure values) that gets updated in the cube space will be entered into this writeback partition. Similar to a regular partition, the writeback partition points to a table in a relational data source. However, unlike regular partitions, Analysis Services will populate the rows of this table based on writeback operations performed on the cube. This data can reside within the same relational data source used by the cube or in a different relational database.

Cell Writeback Prerequisites

The prerequisites for enabling writeback to a measure group are simpler than those for enabling dimension writeback. You can write-enable a cube for updating data only when all the measures in the measure group have an aggregation function as Sum. Even if one of the measures has an aggregation function as Count, Distinct Count, or any of the semi-additive aggregation functions, the measure group cannot be enabled for writeback. Hence, whenever you want to enable a cube for cell writeback, you need to move any measures that have an aggregation function other than Sum to be in a separate measure group.

Enabling Cell Writeback

You will use the cube created in the previous section to learn about updating data within the cube. Consider the scenario where you need to allocate the budget amount for the group lead by Amy Alberts. Amy has three employees reporting to her and the budget needs to be distributed to her reports based on certain business factors. You will consider examples of various ways in which allocation of data can be accomplished with the cube's data. Analysis Services 2008 does not provide a front-end interface to update cube data unlike updating dimension data through the Dimension Browser. However, you can build your own application once you know what MDX statements to send to Analysis Services. Hence the examples you see in this section are primarily MDX statements, which you need to execute through SQL Server Management Studio to help you understand how to update the cube data.

The following steps show how to make modifications to the cube so that you can use the database for understanding data allocation and update of cube data:

1. Execute the SQL queries in CreateWriteBackExampleTables.sql (in the Chapter 12 folder that can be downloaded from the accompanying web site) again to ensure you have all the dimension members.

2. Open the dimension WB Period in the Analysis Services cube used in the previous section. Create a user hierarchy named Period that has two levels, Calendar Year and Quarter, as shown in Figure 12-9.

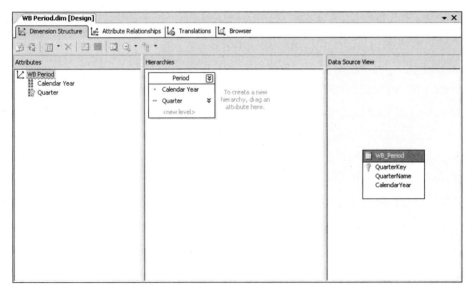

Figure 12-9

3. Open the Adventure Works DW2008 cube in the WriteBackExample database and delete the measure WB Fact Count that was created by the Cube Wizard.

4. Deploy the changes to your Analysis Services instance. If you receive processing errors, you may need to force the server to perform a full process during deployment. You can do this by right-clicking the WriteBackExample database in the Solution Explorer, selecting the Properties menu item, setting the Processing Option on the Deployment page to Full, and then re-deploying.

5. Send the following MDX query to the cube:

```
select {[WB Employee].[Manager].&[290],
[WB Employee].[Manager].&[290].children} on 1 ,
[WB Period].[Period].&[2004].children on 0
from [Adventure Works DW2008]
```

The results of this MDX query are shown in the following table. The cell values show the Budget Expense amount for various quarters for employees reporting to Amy Alberts. Notice that the values for 2004 Q3 are not available.

Name	2004 Q1	2004 Q2	2004 Q3
Alberts, Amy	2072000	2865000	(null)
Alberts, Amy	116000	1000	(null)
Pak, Jae	883000	1329000	(null)
Valdez, Rachel	366000	627000	(null)
Varkey Chudukatil, Ranjit	707000	908000	(null)

6. To enable updating data within the cube, connect to the database you have deployed. You can either use BIDS or SQL Server Management Studio. Within BIDS, click the Partitions tab of the Adventure Works DW2008 cube. Select the partition WB Fact, right-click, and select Writeback Settings as shown in Figure 12-10. Or in SQL Server Management Studio, connect to the Analysis Services database, navigate to the measure group, right-click the measure group, and select Writeback Options ⇨ Enable Writeback.

7. You will now be presented with the Enable Writeback dialog shown in Figure 12-11. When data is being written back to the cells of a cube, Analysis Services stores appropriate information in a relational database table. You learn about this information later in this chapter. For now assume it is stored in a table. Because Analysis Services needs to store some information in a relational table, you need to specify a data source that points to a database where Analysis Services has write permissions. In the Enable Writeback dialog you need to specify the data source and the name of the table to store the cell writeback data. By default, Analysis Services chooses the existing data source that is used by the partition with the writeback table named as WriteTable _<PartitionName>. If you do not want the writeback table within the same database as that of your relational backend, you can specify a new data source in the Enable Writeback dialog by clicking New. Once you have specified the writeback table information, click the OK button. Once you click OK, the Partition editor automatically creates a partition for the Writeback_WB Fact table. You can see a new partition called Writeback_WB Fact added to the measure group WB Fact in the partition list.

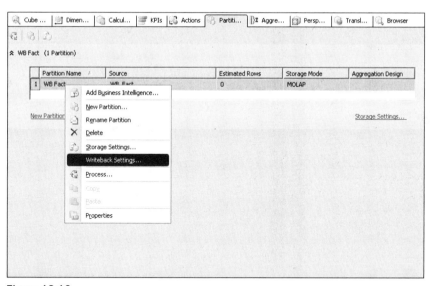

Figure 12-10

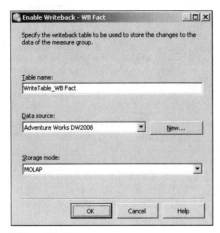

Figure 12-11

8. Deploy the entire project to the Analysis Services instance. The writeback partition metadata gets updated for the WriteBackExample database. BIDS then sends a process command to process the database. At the time of processing the writeback partition, Analysis Services checks if the writeback table exists in the specified data source. If not, the Analysis Services instance creates the writeback table by sending the following CREATE SQL statement. You do have the option of forcibly creating the writeback table at the time of each process of the measure group in the DDL, but by default Analysis Services creates the table only if it does not exist in the database.

```
CREATE TABLE [WriteTable_WB Fact] (
  [BudgetExpenseAmount_0] float,
  [EmployeeKey_1] int,
  [QuarterKey_2] int,
  [MS_AUDIT_TIME_3]    datetime,
  [MS_AUDIT_USER_4]    nvarchar(255)
)
```

Once the writeback table has been created, the cube has been enabled for writeback. You can now update the budget values for 2004 Q3. You have the option to writeback to a single cell or multiple cells depending on where you write the data. You learn the various options in the next few sections.

One interesting thing to note is you can still do what-if analysis on a cube, even if the cube is not enabled for writeback. The changed measure cannot be committed back to the server if the cube doesn't have a writeback partition. However, you can still do a "begin transaction," update cell values, and send MDX queries to view the results of the measure (cell value) change, and then simply "rollback transaction" when finished.

Update a Single Cell Value

The update statement is used to update the cell values in the cube. The syntax of the update statement is as follows:

```
UPDATE CUBE <CubeName>
SET <Tuple Expression> = Numeric or String value
[ALLOCATION TYPE clause]
```

The update cube syntax is pretty straightforward: You specify the coordinates in the cube to update and the new values. The allocation type clause is an optional clause by which you can specify the nature of the allocation. You see examples of various allocation types later in this chapter.

One of the scenarios is to update a single cell value in the cube. For example, you need to allocate a budget of $1000 for Jae Pak. Follow these instructions to update the cell value corresponding to Jae Pak:

1. Open SSMS and create two new MDX query windows.

2. Select the database WriteBackExample and the Adventure Works DW2008 cube.

3. In step 5 of the previous section you saw the budget value for 2004 Q3 for employee Jae Pak was null. Send the following update statement to update the budget value for employee Jae Pak:

```
UPDATE CUBE [Adventure Works DW2008]
SET ( [WB Employee].[Manager].&[291]
, [WB Period].[Period].&[20043]) = 1000
//Updating the budget for employee Jae Pak for Quarter 3 of year 2004
```

In the update statement, the coordinate pointed to by the tuple ([WB Employee].[Manager].&[291],[WB Period].[Period].&[20043]) refers to the budget value for Jae Pak. The statement updates the cell value to 1000.

4. In the same query window, send the following query to the cube and you will see that the budget value for Jae Pak is now 1000:

```
SELECT {
[WB Employee].[Manager].&[291] } ON 1 ,
[WB Period].[Period].&[20043] ON 0
FROM
[Adventure Works DW2008]
```

5. Send the same query in the second MDX query editor window. You will see the original value null rather than the new value 1000. The update statement and the value only take effect for the first MDX window, which holds one connection (or session). Other connections (or sessions) are not affected by the updated value. This is because Analysis Services saves and shares the new cell value only if you request it to make these changes permanently in the cube. In order to do that you need to send the commit statement to the server as shown in the following step.

6. In the first query window, send the following query to the server:

```
COMMIT
```

COMMIT is a short form for the COMMIT TRANSACTION statement. By default, when you start executing new queries within SQL Server Management Studio, an implicit statement called BEGIN TRANSACTION is executed. Due to the changes, cell values will get updated only after you call the COMMIT TRANSACTION or just the COMMIT statement. When the COMMIT statement is executed, Analysis Services gets the new value to be written, subtracts the original cell value for that tuple, and then writes back the difference in the partition that has been set up for writeback. Because the original cell value was null and the new value is 1000, you should see 1000 in the writeback partition.

7. Open a SQL query window and send the following query to the relational table in the Adventure Works DW2008 database. You will see that there is a new entry in the relational table that has a BudgetExpenseAmount_0 value of 1000.

```
select * from [WriteTable_WB Fact]
```

8. If you go to the second MDX query window and query the cell value for Jae Pak, you will see the new value 1000.

Analysis Services allows you to send multiple updates within a transaction so that you have the ability to roll back or commit the entire transaction that does an update to the cube.

9. After the update statement, send the first MDX query in the same query window:

```
SELECT {[WB Employee].[Manager].&[290],
[WB Employee].[Manager].&[290].children
} on 1 ,
[WB Period].[Period].&[2004].children on 0
FROM [Adventure Works DW2008]
```

You will see the results shown in the following table. Notice that "Alberts, Amy," parent member of "Pak, Jae," got the 1000 aggregated. Analysis Services takes care of calculations and aggregations of the data written back to the cells automatically.

Name	2004 Q1	2004 Q2	2004 Q3
Alberts, Amy	2072000	2865000	1000
Alberts, Amy	116000	1000	(null)
Pak, Jae	883000	1329000	1000
Valdez, Rachel	366000	627000	(null)
Varkey Chudukatil, Ranjit	707000	908000	(null)

10. Switch to the first MDX window, and send the following query to update the same cell to 800. If you are executing the following statements in SQL Server Management Studio, execute them as separate statements by selecting the statement and then pressing the execute button or Ctrl+E to execute. Begin Transaction should first be highlighted and executed, followed by the update statement and then the commit transaction statement.

```
BEGIN TRANSACTION

UPDATE CUBE [Adventure Works DW2008]
SET ( [WB Employee].[Manager].&[291]
, [WB Period].[Period].&[20043]) = 800

COMMIT TRANSACTION
```

11. If you send a query to retrieve the data for Jae Pak for Quarter 3 of 2004 in both MDX query windows, you will see the exact same value of 800.

Analysis Services uses the writeback partition to implement cell writeback. When you send the update cell query, the cell data value is held in memory for that specific session and transaction. When a user sends the commit statement, the change in cell value is written to the writeback table by Analysis Services. If the writeback partition is ROLAP, other connections or users will pick up the data change immediately without reprocessing the cube. If the writeback partition is MOLAP, Analysis Services will incrementally process the partition from the cache to ensure all other connections and users pick up the change immediately. MOLAP writeback partitions are new to Analysis Services 2008.

Now open a SQL query window and connect to the Adventure Works DW2008 relational database and send the SQL query to retrieve all the rows in the Writeback table. You will see results similar to those shown in the following table.

Budget Expense Amount_0	EmployeeKey_1	QuarterKey_2	MS_AUDIT_TIME_3	MS_AUDIT_USER_4
1000	291	20043	42:31.0	Sivah04\sivah
−200	291	20043	45:40.0	Sivah04\sivah

In the table you will see two rows being entered for the measure value. Recall that the first value of 1000 was the first update statement you executed. When you executed the second update statement, you updated the cell value to 800. The difference of −200 is therefore entered for the same tuple within the writeback table. When a new query comes in, the aggregated data of 1000 −200 + the cell value based on all other partitions within the cube is seen by the user. Note Analysis Services logs the time and the user who did the update to the cell. Consider this as a tracking mechanism for you to trace the writeback operations. If you notice serious discrepancies in your data, due to the logging of user and time when the update was done, users cannot deny what they did and this might come in handy if you are audited.

Update Non-Leaf Cell Value Using Allocation

The previous example demonstrated how to update budget data for Jae Pak who is a leaf member in the dimension and does not have any reports under him. A leaf-level cell in Analysis Services means all dimension members of that cell are on the granularity level; for example, member "Pak, Jae" doesn't have children and you choose to write to Q4. If you have another dimension, you would have to include a member from that dimension for the granularity attribute. However, in many cases, a user might want to input a number at a higher-level granularity and allocate down to the leaf-level members via different rules. For instance, a user can input an entire year's budget and allocate to each quarter by last year's sales. In this section, you allocate the budget for each employee reporting to Amy Alberts using the value allocated to Amy Alberts. Analysis Services provides several ways to allocate/update values for non-leaf level cells. Because the actual data being allocated cannot be held directly in a non-leaf cell within Analysis Services, the data needs to be propagated to the leaf-level cells. The most obvious and easiest way to allocate in this way is to allocate the value equally to all the leaf-level cells.

Equal Allocation

Consider the scenario where Amy Alberts is allocated $1,000 and this needs to be propagated to her and all her direct reports, because she also needs to budget for the work she does. As seen with the update statement syntax you have an optional allocation clause. To allocate this value equally to her direct reports, you need to specify the keyword USE_EQUAL_ALLOCATION. Before you execute the following update statement, send an update statement to set the budget value for Jae Pak to 0. The following MDX query will update the budget value for Amy Alberts by equally allocating the value to her direct reports:

```
UPDATE CUBE [Adventure Works DW2008]
SET (
[WB Employee].[Manager].&[290]
, [WB Period].[Period].&[20043]) = 1000
USE_EQUAL_ALLOCATION
```

After executing this update statement, if you send the following query you will see that each of the employees reporting to Amy Alberts will get a value of 250, as shown in the following table.

```
SELECT {[WB Employee].[Manager].&[290],
[WB Employee].[Manager].&[290].children
} on 1 ,
[WB Period].[Period].&[2004].children on 0
FROM [Adventure Works DW2008]
```

Name	2004 Q1	2004 Q2	2004 Q3
Alberts, Amy	2072000	2865000	1000
Alberts, Amy	116000	1000	250
Pak, Jae	883000	1329000	250
Valdez, Rachel	366000	627000	250
Varkey Chudukatil, Ranjit	707000	908000	250

If you did not specify the allocation clause to be USE_EQUAL_ALLOCATION, Analysis Services assumes that the data allocated needs to be equally distributed to all the children. Therefore, the following update statement will also result in the same results as shown in the previous table:

```
UPDATE CUBE [Adventure Works DW2008]
SET (
[WB Employee].[Manager].&[290]
, [WB Period].[Period].&[20043]) = 1000
```

Now that you have learned how to update data to a non-leaf member, next you learn the remaining allocation options provided by Analysis Services.

Weighted Allocation

In a more complex scenario, allocation of budgets depends on the size of the organization or the revenue generated by the person (or group) in the previous year. A common form of allocation in the real-world is to allocate values based on rates calculated by using the last period's budget rate plus some percentage increase to determine this period's value, or to just use last year's sales to allocate this year's budget. Analysis Services provides a way to write back data to leaf levels using various proportions, and hence such an allocation is called a weighted allocation.

Consider a case such that Amy Alberts gets $1,000 as a budget and she wants to allocate it to her direct reports and herself based on the ratio calculated from the previous quarter. Now, how do you go about forming an update statement that will accomplish this scenario? Let's first break it down and build the MDX.

First, you know the update statement to allocate to Amy Alberts is:

```
UPDATE CUBE [Adventure Works DW2008]
SET (
[WB Employee].[Manager].&[290]
, [WB Period].[Period].&[20043]) = 1000
```

Next, you need to add the allocation clause. For weighted or ratio allocation you need to use the keyword USE_WEIGHTED_ALLOCATION BY, which gets added at the end of the preceding statement. Following the USE_WEIGHTED_ALLOCATION BY you need to specify a ratio or weight that will derive the rate based on the previous quarter. The following MDX expression calculates the ratio of budget for the previous quarter for the employees reporting to Amy Alberts:

```
([WB Period].[Period].[20042], [WB Employee].[Manager].currentmember)/
([WB Employee].[Manager].&[290],[WB Period].[Period].[20042])
```

The first part of the MDX expression takes the current member in the context of the query, which will be one of the direct reports of Amy Alberts and their budget value in the second quarter of 2004. The second part of the MDX query provides the budget value for Amy Alberts for the second quarter of 2004. Because the value for Amy Alberts is the aggregated value of all her reports, you get a ratio of each employee's budget as compared to the overall budget allocated to Amy Alberts in the second quarter of 2004.

Combining all the sections of the MDX you have seen, you will have the following MDX query to allocate the budget to Amy Albert's team based on a ratio of the previous quarter:

```
update cube [Adventure Works DW2008]
set (
[WB Employee].[Manager].&[290]
, [WB Period].[Period].&[20043]) = 1000 use_weighted_allocation by
([WB Period].[Period].&[20042], [WB Employee].[Manager].currentmember)/
([WB Employee].[Manager].&[290],[WB Period].[Period].&[20042])
```

If you execute the MDX query to retrieve the budget amount for all the children of Amy Alberts for various quarters of 2004 after executing the update statement, you should see the results shown in the following table.

Name	2004 Q1	2004 Q2	2004 Q3
Alberts, Amy	2072000	2865000	1000
Alberts, Amy	116000	1000	0.34904014
Pak, Jae	883000	1329000	463.8743455
Valdez, Rachel	366000	627000	218.8481675
Varkey Chudukatil, Ranjit	707000	908000	316.9284468

Incremental Allocation

The third scenario is where a cell has an existing value and you want to update that value and have the incremental change allocated down. This allocation of the incremental change can be done based on either equal or weighted allocation. Consider an organization that receives funding from multiple sources and these funds need to be allocated to subdivisions one by one. Further, you do not want to overwrite the previous data. Before you learn about incremental allocation, please delete the Writeback table in the relational data source and reprocess the WriteBackExample database.

Let's say Amy Alberts obtained funding in the amount of $1,000 for Jae Pak in support of the project he is working on. Amy allocates this budget directly to Jae for quarter 3 of 2004. Send the following update statement to allocate the budget to Jae.

```
UPDATE CUBE [Adventure Works DW2008]
SET (
[WB Employee].[Manager].&[291]
, [WB Period].[Period].&[20043]) = 1000
```

Now assume Amy gets funding in the amount of $1,000 for the entire group and she wants to allocate this equally to all her direct reports. She obviously does not want to overwrite the existing budget value allocated for Jae already. Analysis Services provides a way to allocate this new budget amount to the leaf-level cells either through equal or through weighted allocation. The allocation clause keyword that needs to be used is USE_EQUAL_INCREMENT or USE_WEIGHTED_INCREMENT along with the weight as seen in the weighted allocation example.

Consider the scenario where Amy wants to allocate the amount equally. The MDX query to do this allocation is:

```
update cube [Adventure Works DW2008]
set (
[WB Employee].[Manager].&[290]
, [WB Period].[Period].&[20043]) = 2000 use_equal_increment
```

Send the following MDX query to see if the allocation with increment worked correctly:

```
select {[WB Employee].[Manager].&[290],
[WB Employee].[Manager].&[290].children
} on 1 ,
[WB Period].[Period].&[2004].children on 0
from
[Adventure Works DW2008]
```

You will see the results shown in the following table whereby Jae Pak's budget for 2004 Q3 is now $1,250 and the budget for remaining employees is $250 each. Note the total budget allocated for Amy and her direct reports is $2,000, which is the sum of the budget of all employees reporting to her.

Name	2004 Q1	2004 Q2	2004 Q3
Alberts, Amy	2072000	2865000	2000
Alberts, Amy	116000	1000	250
Pak, Jae	883000	1329000	1250
Valdez, Rachel	366000	627000	250
Varkey Chudukatil, Ranjit	707000	908000	250

Similarly, you can use the USE_WEIGHTED_INCREMENT option to writeback to the cell corresponding to Amy Alberts and see that the budget gets distributed based on weights and also gets added to existing budget amounts.

Cautions

There are some things you should be aware of while updating cell values using the update statement. Assume you have a reasonably sized cube with several dimensions that each contain several attributes. Due to multidimensionality, every cell is referred to by a co-ordinate for every attribute hierarchy in every dimension. If you do an allocation using the update statement that includes only a few dimensions' granularity attributes, Analysis Services will try to equally distribute the value allocated to a cell in the cube to all the leaf-level cells (across all the hierarchies in each dimension). Hence if you do an update on a cell that is referred to by the topmost-level on certain dimensions, the update to leaf levels can be quite expensive because Analysis Services needs to equally distribute the value across all members of all dimensions. This can happen easily because the default member for hierarchies not included in an update statement is usually a top-level member such as an All member. Such an update of several non-leaf members can result in a huge number of rows being entered into the writeback table. Hence whenever possible please make sure you do the writeback to the appropriate level intended. We are just warning you about data expansion.

To understand the data expansion problem better, consider the following example of updating Amy Alberts' budget for the year 2003, which is referred to by the tuple ([WB Employee].[Manager].&[290], [WB Period].[Period].&[2003]). This will update all the leaf-level members, which is the product of all the members reporting to Amy Alberts and all the quarters in 2003. This update results in changes to 16 cells at the leaf level. Imagine dimensions that have hundreds or even thousands of members. As with a Product dimension, a simple mistake of updating at the topmost level will cascade out with millions of leaf-level cells being updated — and you will see millions of rows in the writeback table. To mitigate this problem you need to identify meaningful leaf-level cells and then writeback to just those specific cells.

What's New in Analysis Services 2008?

As mentioned previously, MOLAP storage mode for writeback partitions was added in Analysis Services 2008. When a cell update is committed to a writeback partition in MOLAP mode, Analysis Services performs the following steps:

1. Begin SQL Transaction
2. Update SQL
3. Incremental process from cache
4. Commit Lock
   a. Commit SQL Transaction
   b. Commit incremental process
5. End Commit Lock

These steps ensure that the MOLAP writeback partition stays up-to-date and is consistent with the data written back to the relational writeback table. MOLAP writeback partitions can be significantly faster for querying than ROLAP writeback partitions. However, because of the extra steps that occur during writeback, ROLAP writeback partitions can perform writeback operations faster. Given that most cubes read data much more often than it is written back, MOLAP is generally the best choice and is the default.

Also in Analysis Services 2008, the new Update Isolation Level connection string property was added as an optimization hint when doing multiple updates within a single update cube statement. When set to 1, this property guarantees to the server that no cells will be affected by more than one SET statement within the same update cube statement. This should be used with caution because incorrect data can result if it is misused. Generally your best bet is to stick with one SET statement per update statement as shown in the preceding examples, and then you won't need to worry about this connection string property.

Summary

In this chapter you worked with simple examples that demonstrated dimension writeback and cell writeback. You learned how to enable a dimension for writeback and then how to add, edit, and delete members of that dimension. You learned how those dimension writeback operations result in changes directly to the relational table that is behind the dimension.

You learned how to update a cube's cell data using the cell writeback feature of Analysis Services 2008. You also learned that the changes are propagated back to the cube only when you issue a commit statement. Therefore, you can perform many what-if scenarios by doing allocations followed by queries and discover the influence of potential allocations on the financial status of the company. Typically we expect calculations to be defined in MDX scripts that make use of the measure values such as budget, which will reflect the overall profit or key performance indicators of the company. If the updates you have done do not yield the expected results, you can roll back the incomplete transaction thereby preventing the entire update operation to be propagated to the writeback table. You also learned to be cautious of data explosion in cell writeback and about the new performance enhancements for cell writeback in Analysis Services 2008.

So far in this book you have learned to design dimensions and cubes, extend MDX using stored procedures, and finally to writeback data in dimensions and cubes. These abilities are all targeted toward data warehouse designers and developers. As with any server product, administrators are required to provide high availability of the servers and maintain a secure environment. In the next chapter you learn to perform administrative tasks on Analysis Services instances through SSMS as well as through custom code using the management object model Analysis Management Objects (AMO).

Part III
Advanced Administration and Performance Optimization

Programmatic and Advanced Administration

Chapter 7 showed you how to administer Analysis Services 2008 using SQL Server Management Studio (SSMS). In Analysis Services 2005 and 2008 you also have the option of automating administrative processes using XMLA commands or using AMO, which in turn communicates with the server using XMLA. AMO provides a well-defined, extremely helpful object model that extracts execute and discover XMLA commands that need to be sent to the server. Almost all the user interfaces you saw in SQL Server Management Studio use the AMO object model while communicating to the server. In this chapter, you learn to manage Analysis Services using AMO. You learn about using XMLA commands and SQL Server Integration Services (SSIS) to automate some of the management tasks in Chapter 19. You don't have to type in the long code snippets that follow; they are available for download on the book's web site.

Analysis Management Objects (AMO)

As mentioned, AMO is an object model that can be used for programmatic administration of an Analysis Services instance. AMO is the replacement for DSO (Decision Support Objects), which shipped in Analysis Services 2000. It is installed and registered into the GAC (Global Assembly Cache) when Analysis Services is installed. The GAC itself is part of the .NET infrastructure where all commonly used .NET assemblies are registered. Now then, the best way to actually learn AMO is to jump in and use it! In this section you learn a few sample AMO applications that will perform some of the administrative operations you learned to do using SSMS in Chapter 7. With the help of AMO, you can automate almost all your administrative tasks.

Processing Analysis Services Databases

As you learned in Chapter 7, processing is one of the most important operations for an administrator. Usually administrators want to automate this process using scripts or programs. In this section, you learn to build an AMO-based console application that takes four command-line parameters: server name, target type (cube or dimension), processing type (full, incremental, update, or unprocess), and finally, the object's name (to be processed). Before building this console app, please read the following source code in advance and don't worry if you don't get it right away; you will soon learn the purpose of all but the most self-explanatory lines of code. The following code is a sample to kick-start you into learning AMO with some of the processing options for processing dimension or cube objects within a database:

```
#region Using directives
using System;
using System.Collections.Generic;
using System.Text;
using AMO = Microsoft.AnalysisServices;
#endregion

namespace AnalysisServicesProcess
{
  public enum ASObjectType
  {
    Database,
    Cube,
    Dimension,
    MiningStructure
  }

  public class ProcessASObjects
  {
    public static void Main(string[] args)
    {
      try
      {
        if (args.Length != 5)
        {
          throw new Exception(@"Usage: ProcessASObjects <serverName>
              <ObjectType = 'Cube'|'Dimension'> <ProcessType =
              'ProcessDefault'|'ProcessFull'|'ProcessAdd'|'ProcessUpdate'|
              'ProcessClear'> <databaseName> <objectName>");
        }
        string serverName = args[0];
        ASObjectType objectType = (ASObjectType)Enum.Parse
              (typeof(ASObjectType), args[1], true);
        AMO.ProcessType processType = (AMO.ProcessType)Enum.Parse
              (typeof(AMO.ProcessType), args[2], true);
        string databaseName = args[3];
        string objectName = args[4];

        using (AMO.Server server = new AMO.Server())
        {
          server.Connect(serverName);
          AMO.Database database = server.Databases.GetByName( databaseName );
          AMO.IProcessable processableObject;
          switch (objectType)
          {
            case ASObjectType.Database:
              processableObject = database;  // objectName is not needed
              break;
```

```
              case ASObjectType.Cube:
                processableObject = database.Cubes.GetByName(objectName);
                break;
              case ASObjectType.Dimension:
                processableObject = database.Dimensions.GetByName(objectName);
                break;
              case ASObjectType.MiningStructure:
                processableObject = database.MiningStructures.GetByName
                (objectName);
                break;
              default:
                throw new Exception("Unrecognized ASObjectType encountered: " +
                objectType.ToString());
          }
          processableObject.Process(processType);
        }

        Console.WriteLine("Process completed.");
      }
      catch (Exception ex)
      {
        Console.WriteLine(ex.GetType().ToString());
        Console.WriteLine(ex.Message);
      }
    }
  }
}
```

To create an AMO-based console application for Analysis Server administration, open Visual Studio 2008 and select New Project under the File menu. In the New Project dialog, select project type Visual C# and use the Console Application template. Name your project AnalysisServicesProcess and be sure the Create Directory For Solution checkbox is checked. Finally, click OK to continue. The next step involves adding a reference to the AMO assembly to your project. You do this by right-clicking References in the Solution Explorer and selecting Add Reference. In the Add Reference dialog, scroll down to find Analysis Management Objects (Microsoft.AnalysisServices.DLL) and double-click it. This causes Microsoft.AnalysisServices to be added to your list References.

To accomplish the tasks required in this program, you will need the following directives; please add any you don't already have listed:

```
using System;
using System.Collections.Generic;
using System.Text;
using AMO = Microsoft.AnalysisServices;
```

Next, create a class called ProcessASObjects within the AnalysisServicesProcess namespace. For more information on namespaces or classes, please see Microsoft's C# online documentation.

```
namespace AnalysisServicesProcess
{
  class ProcessASObjects
  {
    // the rest of the code in this application will go here...
  }
}
```

First, add an enum definition for the ASObjectType. This enum will be used to know what type of Analysis Services object is to be processed.

```
public enum ASObjectType
{
  Database,
  Cube,
  Dimension,
  MiningStructure
}
```

Then add the main method of the program. This static method is called by the CLR with the command-line parameters passed in using the args array. In this method you add basic exception handling that will report errors on the console. Use the try-catch syntax to do this and then write the exception type followed by the error message to the console. Because AMO will report errors it encounters by throwing exceptions, this is a simple and easy way to manage errors for this small application.

```
public static void Main(string[] args)
{
  try
  {
    // code for processing will go here...
  }
  catch (Exception ex)
  {
    Console.WriteLine(ex.GetType().ToString());
    Console.WriteLine(ex.Message);
  }
}
```

Then add the code for processing the command-line parameters. First, check if the wrong number of parameters is used. If the number of command-line parameters does not equal 5, throw an exception with parameter usage information. The previously added exception handling code will ensure this usage information is shown to the user on the command line. Next convert the command-line arguments from the strings passed in to the program into forms you need. For serverName, databaseName, and objectName you just need these strings so you'll use them as is. However, for objectType and processType you need enumeration values. To get these you'll use the CLR's Enum.Parse method, which will convert the string to the appropriate enumeration value and will throw an exception if no conversion can be made.

```
if (args.Length != 5)
  {
    throw new Exception("Usage: ProcessASObjects <serverName> <ObjectType =
            'Cube'|'Dimension'> <ProcessType = 'ProcessDefault'|
            'ProcessFull'|'ProcessAdd'|'ProcessUpdate'|'ProcessClear'>
            <databaseName> <objectName>");
  }
  string serverName = args[0];
  ASObjectType objectType = (ASObjectType)Enum.Parse(typeof(ASObjectType),
            args[1], true);
  AMO.ProcessType processType = (AMO.ProcessType)Enum.Parse
            (typeof(AMO.ProcessType), args[2], true);
  string databaseName = args[3];
  string objectName = args[4];
```

Now that you've got your input parameters cleaned-up, it's time to actually process. The first thing you need to do here is to connect to the Analysis Services server. To do this you can simply create a new AMO.Server object and use the Connect method with the serverName passed in to you. When using connections, it is important that you remember to close your connection to the server when you are done with it. You can do this by calling the Disconnect method on the server when you are done. However, if an exception occurs along the way, you'll still want to make sure your connection was closed. The easiest and safest way to do this is put the sever object in a C# using statement. This ensures that whatever happens, Dispose is called on the server object when execution leaves the using block. Dispose on the server object will ensure that the connection is closed if it was opened. If there is any problem connecting or processing, AMO will throw an exception, the using block ensures the connection is closed if necessary, and your try-catch will report the error nicely on the command line.

```
using (AMO.Server server = new AMO.Server())
{
  server.Connect(serverName);

  // processing code will go here...
}
```

You have a connection so now you need to get the appropriate Analysis Services object. To do this you must find the object using the name of the database that contains it and name and type of the object itself. First, you get the database by using AMO's GetByName method on the collection of databases on the server:

```
AMO.Database database = server.Databases.GetByName( databaseName );
```

GetByName looks for an object in a collection and will throw a descriptive exception if the object is not found. You could also use FindByName, which will return null if the object is not found, but you want the exception to be thrown because you have code that handles that already. AMO Objects can also be located in collections by using the indexer and passing in either the position or the ID of the object you are looking for. (IDs are very much like names in AMO, except they don't change when the object is renamed and are not displayed to end users.)

Now you can get the object to be processed by using a switch statement on the objectType and using FindByName in the appropriate collection. Then in the switch statement you could call the Process method for each type of object this program can handle. AMO makes this easier by providing an IProcessable interface, which any object that can be processed can be cast to. This allows you to simply store a reference to the object as an instance of IProcessable and then you can use the same code to process all types of processable objects.

```
AMO.IProcessable processableObject;
switch (objectType)
{
  case ASObjectType.Database:
    processableObject = database;  // objectName is not needed
    break;
  case ASObjectType.Cube:
    processableObject = database.Cubes.GetByName(objectName);
    break;
  case ASObjectType.Dimension:
    processableObject = database.Dimensions.GetByName(objectName);
    break;
  case ASObjectType.MiningStructure:
    processableObject = database.MiningStructures.GetByName(objectName);
    break;
  default:
    throw new Exception("Unrecognized ASObjectType encountered: " +
            objectType.ToString());
}
processableObject.Process(processType);
```

To complete the program all you need to do now is report success when processing has completed:

```
Console.WriteLine("Process completed.");
```

Once you have mastered the AMO and basic programming concepts shown in this section, you will find it easy to extend the code to take on other administrative tasks like tracing server events, designing aggregations, and writing custom AMO programs for your management tasks.

Back-Up and Restore

To convince you that it really is not difficult to extend the concepts demonstrated in the preceding processing program and to complete other console apps for administrative purposes, please read through these source code samples covering back-up and restore capabilities.

Here is a simple program for backing up Analysis Services databases from the command line:

```
using System;
using System.Collections.Generic;
using System.Text;
using AMO = Microsoft.AnalysisServices;

namespace ASBackup
{
  class Program
  {
    static void Main(string[] args)
    {
      try
      {
        if (args.Length != 2)
        {
          Console.WriteLine("Usage: ASBackup <servername> <databasename>");
          return;
        }
        using (AMO.Server myServer = new AMO.Server())
        {
          myServer.Connect(args[0]);
          AMO.Database database = myServer.Databases.GetByName(args[1]);
          database.Backup(args[1] + ".abf", true); //Backup the database with
                                                   //the provided file name
        }
      }
      catch (Exception e)
      {
        Console.WriteLine("Exception occurred:" + e.Message);
      }

    } // end Main
  } // end class
} // end namespace
```

Here is a simple program for restoring Analysis Services database backups from the command line:

```
using System;
using System.Collections.Generic;
using System.Text;
using AMO = Microsoft.AnalysisServices;

namespace ASRestore
{
  class Program
  {
    static void Main(string[] args)
    {
      try
      {
        if (args.Length != 2)
        {
          Console.WriteLine("Usage: ASRestore <servername> <backupfilename>");
          return;
        }
        using (AMO.Server myServer = new AMO.Server())
        {
          myServer.Connect(args[0]);
          myServer.Restore(args[1]);
        }
      } //end try
      catch (Exception e)
      {
        Console.WriteLine("Exception occurred:" + e.Message);
      }
    } // end Main
  } // end class
} // end namespace
```

As you can see from the preceding code segments, it really is quite simple—create an AMO server object, and connect to the Analysis Services instance. Depending on the operation (backup or restore) call the appropriate method to perform the operation using AMO. The more you experiment with AMO programming, the more interesting and useful solutions you will generate. So come up with some solutions yourself and code them up!

Adding Assemblies to Analysis Services

You can create your own application in AMO to register assemblies in an Analysis Services database. You just need to get the full path of the assembly, set the right permission and impersonation mode, and then register the assembly. The following is sample code of a console application that registers the assembly to a specific database in an Analysis Services instance:

```
using System;
using System.IO;
using AMO = Microsoft.AnalysisServices;

namespace RegisterAssembly
{
  class RegisterAssembly
  {
```

(continued)

(continued)

```
[STAThread]
static void Main(string[] args)
{
  try
  {
    if (args.Length != 5)
    {
      throw new Exception(@"Usage: RegisterAssembly <server>
          <assemblyPath>
          <database> <PermissionSet = 'Safe'|'ExternalAccess'|
          'Unrestricted'> <ImpersonationMode = 'Default'|
          'ImpersonateAccount'|'ImpersonateAnonymous'|
          'ImpersonateCurrentUser'|'ImpersonateServiceAccount'> ");
    }
    string serverName = args[0];
    string assemblyPath = args[1];
    string databaseName = args[2];
    AMO.PermissionSet permisionSet = (AMO.PermissionSet)Enum.Parse
          (typeof(AMO.PermissionSet), args[3], true);
    AMO.ImpersonationMode impersonationMode = (AMO.ImpersonationMode)
          Enum.Parse(typeof(AMO.ImpersonationMode), args[4], true);

    //Connect to the Analysis Services instance
    using (AMO.Server server = new AMO.Server())
    {
      server.Connect(serverName);

      //get the assembly name
      FileInfo fileInfo = new FileInfo(assemblyPath);
      string assemblyName = fileInfo.Name.Replace(fileInfo.Extension, "");
      assemblyName = assemblyName.Replace("AMO", "");
      AMO.ClrAssembly amoAssembly = new AMO.ClrAssembly(assemblyName,
          assemblyName);
      amoAssembly.LoadFiles(fileInfo.FullName, true);

      amoAssembly.ImpersonationInfo = new Microsoft.AnalysisServices.
          ImpersonationInfo(impersonationMode);
      amoAssembly.PermissionSet = permisionSet;

      //add assembly to database
      AMO.Database db = server.Databases.GetByName(databaseName);
      db.Assemblies.Add(amoAssembly);

      amoAssembly.Update(); //Sends the DDL to the Server
    }
    Console.WriteLine("Assembly registered.");
  }
  catch (Exception e)
  {
    Console.WriteLine(e.Message);
  }
}
}
}
```

In previous examples, the Process method, the Backup method, and the Restore method would cause AMO to send the appropriate XMLA commands to the server to perform these management operations. However, in this latest example, you are actually modifying the definition of an Analysis Services database. To tell AMO to send the change in the definition of the database to the server, you must use the Update method:

```
amoAssembly.Update(); //Sends the DDL to the Server
```

The Update method exists on AMO object types that Analysis Services considers important enough to allow updating on their own. These updatable objects are called major objects and derive from the MajorObject base class in AMO. Databases, Cubes, Dimensions, Mining Models, and in this case assemblies are a few examples of MajorObjects. For more details on how to use the Update method, see MajorObject.Update in SQL Server Books Online.

The AMO code samples provided in this section are primarily to help you start using AMO for the various management tasks. The samples provided in this chapter have been tested for appropriate operations. However, these are still code samples and if you need to write your own AMO programs for management operations we expect you to write robust code for your production environment with appropriate error handling. AMO contains several classes that help you perform more than just management operations. You can design an entire database programmatically and deploy the entire database to an Analysis Services instance. http://www.CodePlex.com is a good resource for finding more programming samples using AMO as well as other Microsoft technologies.

Synchronization is one of the administrative task operations to move databases from test environments to production environments. However, AMO does not have methods to perform the synchronize operation. AMO allows you to send XMLA scripts to the Analysis Services instances. You can take the script that can be generated from the Synchronization Wizard and send the script using AMO to perform management operations for synchronization. We leave it to you to explore the AMO object model and write the code for synchronization.

PowerShell and Analysis Services

PowerShell is a very powerful command-line shell and scripting language that is ideal for automating many administrative tasks. It is an extensible environment with built-in support for easily manipulating managed objects. If you've spent any significant amount of time working with batch files, you'll find PowerShell worth looking into.

Analysis Services 2008 does not ship with a PowerShell provider. However, that does not prevent you from taking advantage of the built-in capabilities of PowerShell to manipulate .NET objects from the command line. To begin using AMO with PowerShell, you'll first need to load the Microsoft. AnalysisServices.DLL assembly. Open a PowerShell window and run the following command to do this:

```
PS C:\Windows\System32> [reflection.assembly]::loadfile("C:\Program Files\
            Microsoft SQL Server\100\SDK\Assemblies\
            Microsoft.AnalysisServices.DLL")
```

Then you can connect to the server by creating an AMO server object in a variable, which you'll call $asserver, and using the AMO Connect method:

```
PS C:\Windows\System32> $asserver = new-object -typename
            Microsoft.AnalysisServices.Server
PS C:\Windows\System32> $asserver.Connect("localhost")
```

You can now view and modify the contents of the server using AMO just as you would in another language. So if you had a role named "Role" in the "AnalysisServices2008Tutorial," you could add a new member to that role by typing the following lines into the PowerShell prompt:

```
PS C:\Windows\System32> $db = $asserver.Databases.GetByName
             ("AnalysisServices2008Tutorial")
PS C:\Windows\System32> $role = $db.Roles.GetByName("Role");
PS C:\Windows\System32> $roleMember = new-object -typename
             Microsoft.AnalysisServices.RoleMember
             -argumentlist "domain\name"
PS C:\Windows\System32> $role.Members.Add($roleMember)
PS C:\Windows\System32> $role.Update()
```

In addition, you can take advantage of PowerShell's object piping capabilities to do many things. For example, the following line will pass the databases in the server to a filter that removes all but those databases where the State property equals "Unprocessed" and then passes those databases to a foreach that will process them all:

```
PS C:\Windows\System32> $asserver.Databases | where-object { $_.State -eq
             "Unprocessed" } | foreach-object {$_.Process()}
```

PowerShell also allows you to create scripts and functions, which can be parameterized and re-used to make management of Analysis Services from the command line even easier. To learn more about PowerShell, you can find and download the PowerShell install on http://www.Microsoft.com and find documentation on http://msdn.Microsoft.com.

Resource and Activity Monitoring

Analysis Services 2008 has added new schema rowsets and extended some existing schema rowsets to help better enable monitoring of server usage and resources. As with relational SQL Server, schema rowsets provide information about the contents and state of the server and its databases. Analysis Services 2005 has schema rowsets that provide information about the content of the server, but have limited information about the state of the server. However, the new and improved schema rowsets in Analysis Services 2008 tell much more about the state of the server. These schema rowsets can show you the connections on a machine, the objects those connections use, the memory those objects consume, locks held by sessions, and other valuable information for understanding how your server is performing and diagnosing issues.

In addition to adding and extending the set of schema rowsets, Analysis Services 2008 has made it much simpler to query schema rowsets. In Analysis Services 2005 you needed a special tool such as the OLE DB rowset viewer or you needed to be comfortable writing and sending XMLA Discover queries in order to get back schema rowsets. In Analysis Services 2008, these schema rowsets have been exposed as Dynamic Management Views (DMVs). DMVs allow you to write simple SQL statements to query schema rowsets. To try this, open SQL Server Management Studio and connect to an Analysis Services database. Then open a new MDX query window and try the following examples.

This query will show you all the tables in the current database including the schema rowsets:

```
SELECT * FROM $SYSTEM.DBSCHEMA_TABLES
```

As you can see, there's quite a list and it includes tables representing actual objects in the database as well as schema rowsets. To just see the names of schema rowset tables, use the following query:

```
SELECT TABLE_NAME FROM $SYSTEM.DBSCHEMA_TABLES WHERE TABLE_TYPE = 'SCHEMA'
```

Now you can see there is a nice list of useful schema rowsets to choose from. To use any of these tables, just add the $SYSTEM schema prefix to the table name and query away. So to see the list of connections, try the following query:

```
SELECT * FROM $SYSTEM.DISCOVER_CONNECTIONS
```

If you want to learn more about the columns in a schema rowset, you can use the DBSCHEMA_COLUMNS rowset. This can be useful when there are many long column names or you want to know the data type of a column. To learn about the columns available in the DISCOVER_COMMANDS rowset, try the following query:

```
SELECT * FROM $SYSTEM.DBSCHEMA_COLUMNS WHERE TABLE_NAME = 'DISCOVER_COMMANDS'
```

Now you can build a more interesting query such as the following query that shows commands ordered by the amount of CPU time they've consumed:

```
SELECT * FROM $SYSTEM.DISCOVER_COMMANDS ORDER BY COMMAND_CPU_TIME_MS DESC
```

Another interesting query would be to look for commands that have taken longer than 1 second (1000 milliseconds) to be completed:

```
SELECT * FROM $SYSTEM.DISCOVER_COMMANDS WHERE COMMAND_ELAPSED_TIME_MS > 1000
```

If your server is performing well and isn't handling any difficult commands, this query probably came back with no results. That's a good thing.

Note that the SQL accepted for querying schema rowsets is fairly simple and does not include support for many SQL capabilities including joins. The lack of joins means that if you want to follow an investigation through several schema rowsets, you'll just have to write separate queries and use simple WHERE restrictions. For example, to see the commands belonging to a connection, first query connections, then query sessions restricting based on a connection ID, and then query commands restricting based on a session ID.

Some schema rowsets cannot be queried using SQL: DSCHEMA_ACTIONS and DISCOVER_XML_METADATA. These schema rowsets do not show up in the DBSCHEMA_TABLES and are not of much interest in the context of server monitoring and troubleshooting.

Though there are some limitations to the SQL syntax supported for schema rowset queries, these limitations are relatively minor and the ability to use SQL to query information about the state of the server is a great step forward in Analysis Services 2008. This ability to see into the state and activity of the server adds a new degree of transparency into the management of Analysis Services. If you are facing potential performance concerns or just want to better understand how your server is operating, using SQL to query these rowsets is a very valuable tool to have on your belt.

HTTP Connectivity to Analysis Services

You expect customers would want to expose the data from Analysis Services to the end users through web applications. Analysis Services 2000 supported data access from the web through a component called DATA PUMP. Analysis Services 2005 and 2008 use a similar architecture to support data access for web applications. The PUMP component needs to be loaded within Internet Information Server (IIS) as an ISAPI DLL. To provide web access to data from Analysis Services you need to configure your IIS appropriately. You need to set up virtual directories, copy appropriate DLLs provided by Analysis Services, and set up appropriate permission on IIS so that users can access data from Analysis Services. The PUMP does not necessarily have to be set up on the same machine as Analysis Services. Using Analysis Services 2008 you can configure several data PUMPs to be directing queries to various Analysis Services instances. Each PUMP has a configuration file where the server name and certain other properties are configured. To access Analysis Services data over the web a user would connect to IIS using HTTP. IIS in turn directs the request to the Analysis Services instance over TCP/IP with appropriate credentials set up on IIS. The architecture of the connection to Analysis Services over HTTP is shown in Figure 13-1.

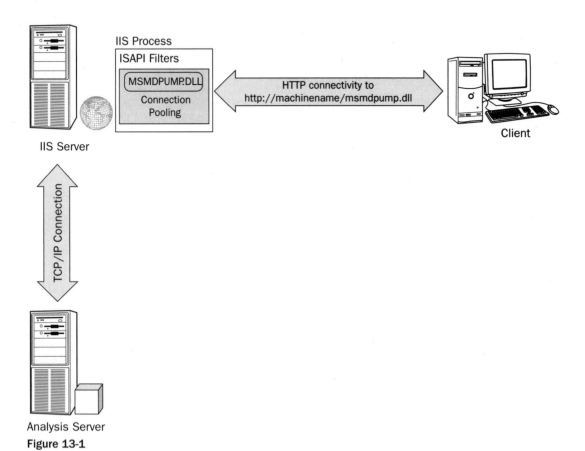

Figure 13-1

You can configure security on IIS to use an anonymous connection to Analysis Services, perform username and password authentication on IIS, or perform Windows authentication. The steps for setting up HTTP connectivity using data PUMP includes configuring your IIS by creating virtual directories and configuring the PUMP and security for the users. Microsoft has published a white paper called "Configuring HTTP Access to SQL Server 2005 Analysis Services on Microsoft Windows XP," Published: July 27, 2005. We recommend you go to http://www.microsoft.com and search for the paper with the provided title.

Analysis Services and Fail-Over Clustering

Both Analysis Services 2008 and 2005 provide fail-over clustering out-of-the-box. By that we mean SQL Server 2005 and 2008 setup supports installing Analysis Services on a Windows clustered environment. You first need to have Microsoft Cluster Services (MSCS) set up to form a cluster of two or more nodes. We recommend you look at Windows product documentation to set up and configure MSCS. You need to have a shared disk with sufficient disk space that can hold the Analysis Services data files. After setting up a cluster, you can then use Microsoft SQL Server setup to install Analysis Services with fail-over capability. In the SQL Server 2005 setup you need to provide a virtual server name with an IP (Internet Protocol) address and the shared data folder for the Analysis Services data. The virtual server name will be the name of the Analysis Services server. SQL Server 2005 setup installs Analysis Services 2005 binaries on all the nodes of the cluster and the data folder is set up on the shared disk with appropriate permissions. In SQL Server 2008 setup you will need to install Analysis Services on each of the cluster nodes and then use the Cluster UI to create the failover virtual instance based on one of the standalone instances.

Although the setup of clustering has changed between Analysis Services 2005 and 2008, the behavior of the cluster is the same. Figure 13-2 shows the overall architecture of the Analysis Services fail-over cluster. Users of Analysis Services will only be aware of the virtual server name. At a given time only one of the physical machines will service users' requests and have access to the shared disk containing Analysis Services data. When one of the nodes in the cluster fails due to network or power problems, MSCS makes the second node as the primary and provides control to the shared disk. MSCS identifies failure in the primary node through the heart beat, which is typically a connection through a second network card between the machines involved in the cluster. The second node gains control of the Analysis Services data, and all future user requests are directed to the second node. Existing users originally connected to the first node would have to re-establish their connections. To make sure you are isolated from disk problems, it is recommended that the shared disk is a RAID (Redundant Array of Independent or Inexpensive) Disks to provide fault tolerance. Due to fail-over clustering support you have higher availability of Analysis Services for your users whenever there are hardware problems.

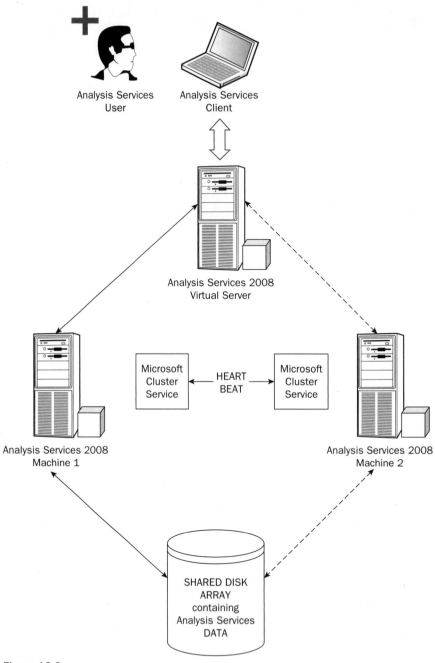

Figure 13-2

Summary

If you have never created programs to dynamically administer a server, perhaps you found this to be one of the most exciting chapters yet! It is great how you can apply the power and flexibility of programming with direct access to server-side functionality. You've seen how to use the Analysis Management Objects (AMO) object model to perform management tasks as well as to update the definition of Analysis Services databases. AMO provides you the power to program custom UIs and gain full access to the capabilities of the server. More important, AMO allows you to automate common tasks, such as processing, adding new users, or even the management of partitions. You've seen how .NET languages such as C# can be used to work with AMO, as well as how PowerShell can be used to work more interactively or to script AMO.

You've also learned how to perform some advanced administration tasks not available directly through the SQL Server Management Studio user interface. You've learned to monitor the resources and activities of a server using schema rowsets. You've seen how Analysis Services 2008 has extended the schema rowset support to provide much more transparency into the status of the server and how these rowsets can now be easily queried using SQL. You've learned how Analysis Services can be configured to support connections over HTTP and also how a fail-over cluster can be used to provide improved reliability without any visible difference to the end user.

The next chapter discusses performance optimization, where you will find several interesting ways to tweak properties to achieve maximal processing and query throughput.

14

Designing for Performance

As any good English dictionary will tell you, performance has several possible meanings. In computer science, performance most often refers to the functioning efficiency of software and can relate to both speed and scalability. There are established standards and benchmarks to measure and compare the performance of products and services. Why care about performance? Well, consider your job performance; assuming you are an employee, your job review and, therefore, salary raise and bonus, will hinge on how well you do your job. To get the best work out of you, your manager needs to know what your interests are, what motivates you, and then assign appropriate tasks to get the maximum performance from you. Your manager will be rewarding you for your performance — usually in the currency you like most, cash.

It follows that if you are a data warehouse designer using Analysis Services you need to know how to get the best performance from the system so as to satisfy the customers. Just like your boss can push certain buttons to motivate you, Analysis Services provides various parameters that can be set to achieve maximum performance. As for server products such as Analysis Services, one can attribute performance results to how well server properties are tuned in the context of speed and scalability requirements.

Various factors influence the performance of an application. SQL Server's performance depends not only on the system (processors, memory, and disk speed) but also on the operating system's configuration and the properties of the application that can be fine-tuned to get the best performance. The graph shown in Figure 14-1 is a typical server scalability graph. The query throughput lines show the server throughput (queries served per minute) as more users are using the system concurrently for two different hardware configurations. For Hardware 1, up to about 50 users, the server throughput increases linearly. That means the server has sufficient resources to support 50 concurrent users. Then after about 50 users, the throughput starts to flatten out. In the 50-to-100 user range, the server doesn't have enough resources (CPU or memory or disk) to serve requests of all concurrent users. In this circumstance, some user requests would be queued in the system request queue to keep the system from slowing down all the user requests. At about 100 users, the system is running at maximum capacity. The curve flattens off at high loads because internally, the server executes only a few queries concurrently, and queues the rest. This is so that with many outstanding queries, new users can still get reasonable response time while connecting to the server and executing non-query commands.

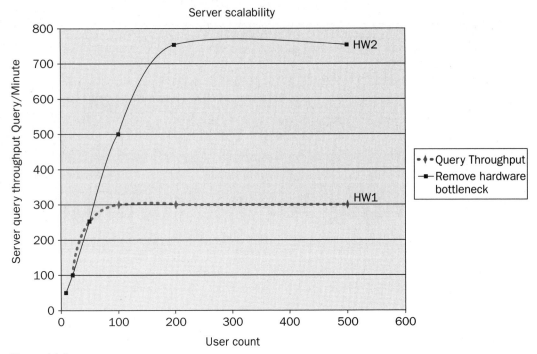

Figure 14-1

From the perspective of a user, when a server is under an extreme load with many outstanding queries, some of the execution time is spent waiting in the queue, and some time is spent actually working on the query. You might compare it to waiting in line for food in a crowded baseball stadium. When the load is high, the wait time can easily exceed the time to actually do the business. Hardware 2 has better resources (CPUs, memory, network) as compared to Hardware 1. Hence if you run the server on Hardware 2 you obviously get a better throughput because the saturation to maximum users occurs at about 200 users.

If you have a well architected server, Figure 14-2 shows the average query response under load. The average response time starts to increase, and eventually the average response time will increase linearly. If your system only needs to support 10 to 50 members, you don't have to do anything. But if your system needs to support 100+ users, you need to identify the system bottlenecks. Typically servers will expose performance monitoring counters to expose internal values. You can use the task manager and performance counters to identify bottlenecks; whether the system is CPU-bound (such that the Server CPU is pegged at 100%) or memory-bound (memory usage is constantly maxed out) or disk-bound (reads or writes to disk). By removing the system hardware bottleneck and adding more CPU or memory to the server, you should be able to get performance improvements and support more concurrent users as shown in Figure 14-2 for Hardware 2.

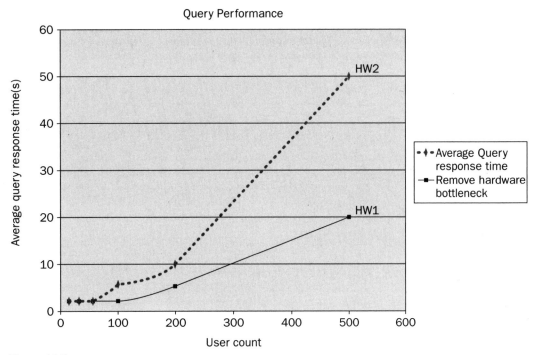

Figure 14-2

Assume HW1 is obtained by adding more CPU and/or memory to HW2. Note that although we expect to see the general shape of the curves described in the figures, the limits will be different for your hardware, your cube design, the queries your users execute, and the frequency with which queries are executed. With respect to Analysis Services, in a typical query scenario, CPU, memory, and disk read speed can all be potential bottlenecks for your system. In a cube or dimension processing scenario, CPU, memory, disk writing speed, and network speed between the relational source and Analysis Services can all be candidate areas for system optimization work.

For Analysis Services performance we refer to three main areas — database design and processing, querying, and configuring Analysis Services (setting properties). The first involves design optimization to facilitate the optimized processing of dimensions and cubes. The second relates to optimization to speed up MDX queries or Analysis Services configuration properties of features, which you learn about in Chapter 15. The third involves fine-tuning Analysis Services or appropriate hardware acquisition based on requirements. Does performance imply both scalability and optimization of Analysis Services? Depending on whom you ask, one or both are true. The bottom line is that you need best query performance with regard to your OLAP cubes. That is true regardless of size, and however you can get it that doesn't involve the violation of federal or state laws is fine. In the next section you learn some of the design techniques that can help in improving your Analysis Services performance.

Optimizing UDM Design

You learned to create the UDM and refine it in Chapters 4 through 12. The data modeling completed during UDM creation has a significant impact on both query performance and processing performance, so it is not something to be rushed through. Even before starting to build your UDM, you must understand the business requirements of the system under assembly as much as possible. You need to have clarity regarding the goal of the system, and that, in turn, feeds directly into creating the analysis requirements, and what potential queries the system needs to support. That understanding will also provide insight into what dimension attributes the user won't be interested in analyzing. Based on your design requirements, certain attributes do not have to be included in your UDM design or can be fine-tuned to with dimension properties for optimal UDM design.

Every dimension, and attribute in a dimension, will demand processing time for your UDM. In addition, because adding unnecessary dimensions and attributes will increase the cube space, it can slow the query performance too. You should use the business requirements to drive your design; just be sure to avoid unnecessary dimensions and keep your system compact and performant. In this section you learn various techniques to optimize your dimension and cube using the dimension or attribute properties as well as best practices for designing your cube so that you can get the best performance from your UDM. For modeling your UDM you start with modeling your dimension. The next section helps you to fine-tune the dimensions for your UDM design.

Fine-Tuning Your Dimensions

In Analysis Services 2005 and 2008, dimensions can contain several hierarchies. When you create your dimension using the wizard in Analysis Services 2005, you will often find that all the columns in the relational tables are added as attribute hierarchies in support of relational and OLAP querying. You can easily end up with a dimension that can have hundreds of attributes. In most business scenarios, the attributes within a dimension are not used in many queries. Only a subset of the attributes might be heavily used.

Including unnecessary attributes and hierarchies in your UDM causes a performance hit in some cases. Therefore, the wizards have been updated in Analysis Services 2008 to address this, and you have to be more specific about which attributes you want to include in the dimensional model. The design tools also allow you to better visualize the relationships between the attributes that you need and thus help you build a better dimensional model.

In this section you learn various techniques that guide you regarding how to design the right dimension suited to your business needs and get the optimal performance acceptable for your business.

Choosing the Right Key Attribute

Each dimension needs to have a key attribute. The key attribute helps in identifying each dimension member uniquely and in most cases is used as the granularity attribute when the dimension is added to be part of a cube. The relational dimensional tables will typically have a column defined as the primary key, and that is automatically inferred as the key attribute by the Dimension Wizard. In certain relational databases, the relationships between the fact and dimension tables using the primary and foreign keys might not be defined, and hence the DSV Wizard is unable to automatically infer the relationship and show this in the DSV. In such cases you would need to define the relationships between the tables in your DSV. Choosing the key attribute can actually impact processing and query performance. If you know that you have two columns in the dimension table that each uniquely identifies a row in the table and if they are of different data types, such as integer and string, try to choose the column that is an integer. Key attributes that are of integer data types occupy less storage and are faster to retrieve than those of type string, because the number of bytes used to store string types are typically larger than that for integer data types. In addition, if you have a choice of choosing a single column as a key attribute as compared to choosing multiple columns in the table, choose the single column as the key column. If you are already aware of these techniques and have designed your database accordingly, it's great. Some might think that all they need is just more disks — we consider that disk space is quite cheap to buy and disks are much faster than before — and some might think a few bytes might not make a big difference. However, imagine your dimension has millions of members — no matter how much disk space you have, accessing each member during queries takes time.

The fastest processing time of fact-table partitions occurs when the fact table has integer foreign keys for the dimension, and the dimension contains the integer key as an attribute (perhaps hidden). This allows the SQL query sent by Analysis Services during processing to be efficient in terms of query performance. We are aware of several international major customers with large data warehouses using composite keys with long strings. Each of these companies had a data warehouse before they started using Analysis Services and they consider a change prohibitively expensive. Their design works, and their business benefits from using Analysis Services. But their time window for processing fact-table partitions would be much smaller if they had used integer keys.

To summarize, we recommend you always consider integer attributes to be chosen as key attributes, having single columns as the key attribute instead of composite keys, and having only the necessary attributes added to your dimension design.

Avoiding Unnecessary Attributes

Because Analysis Services supports attributes hierarchies, you can create many attributes that allow the users to analyze their data along those attributes. However, if you create too many attributes that are never used in customer queries, it will waste system data storage slowing both processing and query performance. We recommend you look at each dimension in detail and eliminate attributes that will never be queried by users. Although your dimension tables might contain several columns, it is usually not necessary to convert every single column in the dimension tables to attribute hierarchies in the dimension. You can see an example in the sample Adventure Works DW 2008 project's Customer dimension. Figure 14-3 shows the Customer dimension, where you can see the list of columns in the DSV and compare it against the list of attribute hierarchies included within the dimension.

You can see that the Customer relational table contains several columns. However, the Customer dimension includes only a subset of those columns that are essential for data analysis as attribute hierarchies. For example, the column Title in the Customer table is not used in data analysis and hence it is not included as an attribute in the Customer dimension.

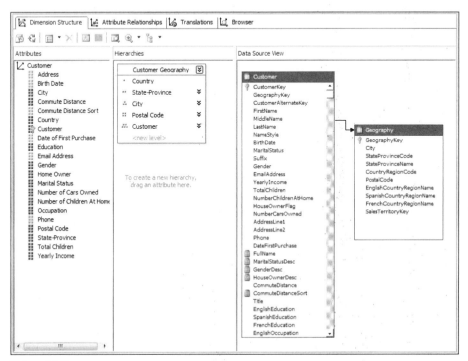

Figure 14-3

Turning Off Optimization for Rarely Used Attributes

Although some attributes in a dimension are used for data analysis, they might be needed only on rare occasions. For example, you might be querying an employee's zip code or phone number infrequently for analysis. By default, Analysis Services creates indexes for each attribute, assuming the attribute hierarchy will be used often in queries. By turning off attributes' optimization via their AttributeHierarchyOptimizedState, you will save processing time and resources by not creating indexes for such attributes. A query involving any NotOptimized attribute will be slower; however, because it is rarely used, it won't hurt most of your users' query performance. Most often you will have certain attributes that are used as member properties. We recommend you set the AttributeHierarchyOptimizedState for member property attributes as well as attributes that might be used infrequently during querying to be NotOptimized because those attributes are not involved in queries. The improvement for data storage and processing time would justify this choice.

The AttributeHierarchyOptimizedState is a property for each attribute. If you click an attribute you will see this property under the Advanced section in the Properties window. Figure 14-4 shows the AttributeHierarchyOptimizedState property. To turn off the property for an attribute in the dimension, change the value from FullyOptimized to NotOptimized.

Figure 14-4

Turning Off AttributeHierarchy for Member Properties

Some attributes are not relevant to data analysis per se, which means user queries will never pivot on those attributes. Still, it is useful to display and use those attributes as member properties. Consider the "birth date" attribute; although customer queries may never break down fact data by birth date, customer birth date might be displayed next to customer names in reports, perhaps as a sorting criteria for listing customers. You can turn off the AttributeHierarchyEnabled property for "birth date" to tell Analysis Services not to build an attribute hierarchy for this attribute, but keep it as a member property. This reduces the time and space needed for dimension processing.

It also has the benefit of reducing the cube space that the server has to work with. Internally, the server maintains cell coordinates that include all the browsable attributes in the cube. The size of these cell coordinates impacts the performance of calculations as well as the memory usage during query execution. By disabling attribute hierarchies, the size and complexity of cell coordinates is reduced, which will have a positive impact on query performance.

Figure 14-5 shows the AttributeHierarchyEnabled property for a dimension attribute. If this property is set to false for an attribute, you will not be able to browse the hierarchy. Rather, you can query the attribute members as member properties.

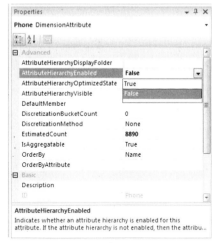

Figure 14-5

Defining Relationships between Attributes

If attributes within a dimension are related by a one-to-many relationship, we recommend you establish that relationship in the Dimension Designer. For example, in a geography dimension you will typically have Country, State, and City attributes and know that there is a one-to-many relationship between these attributes. Define these relationships in the Dimension Designer for improved processing and query performance. If you create user hierarchies within a dimension, and if the user hierarchies have multiple levels and there is a natural relationship between these attributes, we highly recommend you define these relationships. Often when user hierarchies are created, they will be used in queries, and defining the natural relationships helps significantly in query performance. The attribute relationship will help the server build efficient indexes, which will benefit query performance along the user hierarchies significantly. To really understand this issue, you first need to learn about natural and unnatural hierarchies.

All attributes within a dimension are related to the key attribute because the key attribute is unique, and by definition a key has a one-to-many relationship with all the attributes. As for the natural hierarchy, consider the multilevel hierarchy Full Name ⇨ Postal Code ⇨ City ⇨ State-Province ⇨ Country shown in Figure 14-6. A hierarchy is called a natural hierarchy if there is a one-to-many relationship between every pair of attributes that are from successive levels of a user hierarchy. In the example shown in Figure 14-6, you can see that the relationship between attributes of various levels has been established in the Dimension Designer, namely, the Customer attribute (called FullName in the multilevel hierarchy) has a relationship with Postal Code, Postal Code has an attribute relationship with City, City has an attribute relationship with State-Province, and State-Province has an attribute relationship with Country. Essentially, a chain of relationships from the bottom-level attribute to the top-level attribute is created. Such a hierarchy is called a natural hierarchy.

In a natural hierarchy, the attribute at a given level maintains a many-to-one relationship with an attribute directly above it. The many-to-one relationship is defined by the attribute relationship, as shown in Figure 14-6, and the server builds indexes for fast navigations. A natural hierarchy for which indexes are created during processing time is referred to as a materialized hierarchy. For the customer hierarchy example shown in Figure 14-6, indexes for State-Province to Country, City to State-Province, and so on are built and stored in the server. Analysis Services will utilize those indexes to accelerate query performance; it can easily find all states in the USA because the query can be directly resolved from the "State-Province to Country" index. Also, if the data cache or aggregated data that is stored in Analysis Services has data for State-Province, Analysis Services can use the same index to quickly get an aggregate value for Country.

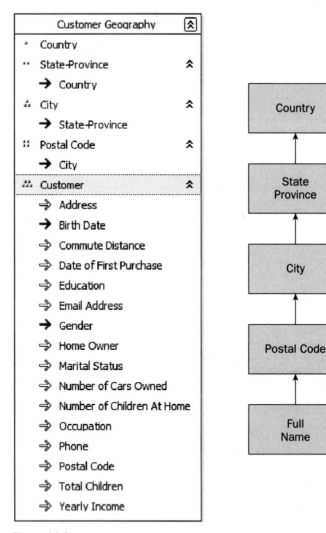

Figure 14-6

Defined relationships not only help during query performance but also during processing. Analysis Services processes the key attribute of the dimension after processing all the remaining attributes. If no relationships are defined, then at the time of processing the dimension the server needs to retrieve the keys for all the attributes while processing the key attribute. This increases the processing time of the key attribute and the dimensions. If you have defined the natural relationships between attributes, the cost of looking up the keys of the related attributes is distributed across the attributes in the dimension. This reduces the cost of key attribute processing, which otherwise has to look up the keys for fewer attributes, thereby reducing the overall dimension processing time. You will see significant differences in processing times for large dimensions that have hundreds of attributes. For some large dimensions (>10 million members and > 100 attributes) you might reach the physical processing limits of a 32-bit environment and might have to move to 64-bit servers. Establishing relationships (as discussed) combined with other dimension optimizations (also discussed) can facilitate processing for large dimensions on a 32-bit platform.

In the case of an unnatural hierarchy, only the key attribute has an attribute relationship to all other attributes, so the relationship resembles Figure 14-7. The system will only build indexes along attribute relationships, and build one-to-many indexes for Country to Customer, State-Province to Customer, City to Customer, and Zip Code to Customer. When you create a user hierarchy such as Customer ⇨ ZipCode ⇨ City ⇨ StateProvince ⇨ Country, no additional indexes get created.

Unnatural hierarchies need to be materialized (identifying navigation paths for members from one level to the next level and data corresponding to members in a level need to be aggregated from the members at the lowest level) during query time and will result in slow query performance. For example, to resolve a simple [USA]. Children MDX expression that requests for all the states of the country USA, the server must use the Country ⇨ Customer relationship to find all customers in the USA and then use the Customer ⇨ State Province relationship to find all states for those customers in the USA. If there are millions of customers in the USA, the query will traverse the millions of records, thereby resulting in slow performance. In addition, if the server has cached values or pre-calculated aggregations for "State-Province," the cache cannot be used to resolve a country query because there are no direct relationships between Country and State-Province.

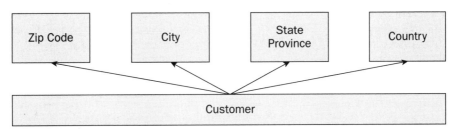

Figure 14-7

You should specify one-to-many relationships whenever possible. Not only will it help significantly for query performance, but it also will save storage space. For the Country to Customer index in the unnatural hierarchy example, every customer member in the USA will have an entry in the index. However, by moving the relationship to State-Province to Country, you will only need 50 entries for that index. In Analysis Services 2008, you can use the new Attribute Relationship tab in the dimension editor to visualize and manage the attribute relationships. To establish the attribute relationship as shown in Figure 14-8, you drag a relationship from each attribute to the related attribute. For example, you click State-Province and drag it to the Country attribute.

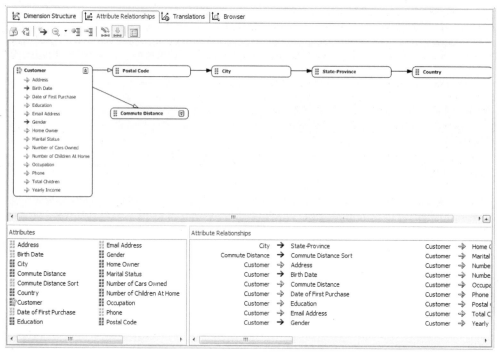

Figure 14-8

Fine-Tuning Your Cube

You have so far seen some of the design techniques for your UDM that will help you achieve improved dimension processing and query performance. Similarly, certain design optimizations within the cube can also help you in achieving better performance during processing or querying. This section discusses cube optimization design techniques.

Fact Table ⇨ Measure Groups or Partitions

When you run the Cube Wizard on a DSV containing multiple fact tables, the wizard creates a separate measure group for each fact table identified. However, such a UDM may or may not be the right design for your business analysis. For example, if you have two fact tables, salesfact2005 and salesfact2006, which have the sales information of your business for the years 2005 and 2006 (containing identical columns), the Cube Wizard will be creating two measure groups. However, for your purposes these should actually be modeled within the same measure group as two partitions so that appropriate data can be rolled up. If you are creating the cube using the Cube Wizard, select one of the fact tables in the Cube Wizard Table Selection page, and then the other fact table can be added as a partition to the measure group. If you select both tables by mistake and the Cube Wizard has already created two measure groups for the two fact tables, you can delete one of them from the Cube Designer and add that table as a partition in the Partitions tab. A way to think about this is a measure group contains the union of all partitions.

You can have fact data spread across multiple tables. For business reasons it might make sense to have all the fact data within the same measure group. Consider a measure group as an entity within your

466

UDM that represents a set of measures that are grouped logically for business reasons; or in Analysis Services terms, share the same dimensionality and granularity. Hence even if you have fact data spread across multiple tables and for business reasons, you actually need to combine the data; make sure you have them added within a single measure group. You can join the fact tables containing measures into a single view within the DSV and create a measure group from that, or you can add measures from either of the fact tables within a single measure group using the Cube Designer.

Optimizing Reference Dimensions

If your UDM contains reference dimensions, you need to be aware of making optimizations for the reference dimensions. If you are querying a reference dimension that is not optimized, you might not get the best query performance. Figure 14-9 shows the relationship definition for a reference dimension. You have a small checkbox called Materialize. You learned in Chapter 6 about reference dimensions and materializing them. To recap, materializing the reference dimensions ensures that the reference dimension keys are materialized into the partition fact records. Once you materialize the reference dimensions, Analysis Services views those reference dimensions as regular dimensions. This helps to improve the query performance. An unmaterialized reference dimension requires dynamic lookups at query time to join between the partition records and the reference dimension through the intermediate dimension.

Also, materializing a reference dimension is the only way to create a chain of two or more dimensions as reference dimensions that include intermediate reference dimensions.

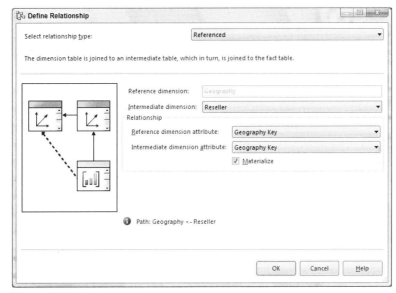

Figure 14-9

Many-to-Many Dimensions

One of the modeling features available in Analysis Services 2008 is called many-to-many dimensions. The "Sales Reason" dimension is used as a many-to-many dimension in the Adventure Works sample UDM. It expresses the notion that a single sale in the Internet Sales measure group may be caused by multiple Sales Reason members. When analyzing what the reasons are for a sale, you want each sale to be counted for each applicable reason. In fact, this means that a single record is added more than once to the result. In SQL terminology this can be thought of as being somewhat similar to a join between two fact tables based on the common dimension tables.

This feature is very powerful in terms of the modeling capabilities it provides to the designer of a UDM. However, it must be used with care due to the performance implications. Queries that involve a many-to-many dimension are apt to be much slower than regular queries. There is a significant price to be paid to query two measure groups and dynamically perform a join between them based on the shared dimensions. A general guideline to follow is to avoid many-to-many dimensions where the intermediate measure group contains more than one million records.

Some techniques exist for optimizing for many-to-many dimensions. For example, building good aggregations on the appropriate measure groups will help performance. A recent white paper published by Microsoft called "Analysis Services Many-to-Many Dimensions: Query Performance Optimization Techniques" describes this in more detail, as well as some advanced optimization techniques that may be adopted to help improve performance when many-to-many dimensions are necessary.

Partitions

Partitions store cube fact data in one of the storage modes — MOLAP, ROLAP, or HOLAP. By dividing the data in fact tables into multiple partitions you can take advantage of parallelism, which can reduce the processing time for the cube and get improved query performance. Assume you have fact data for various months since the year 2002, which is part of a specific measure group. The following table shows a partition scheme that uses time to partition the fact data. Partitions 1–3 include data for past years, and they do not change. Partition 4 includes data for past months in the year 2005, which also does not change. Only Partition 5, that contains current month data, changes daily.

Partition 1	Partition 2	Partition 3	Partition 4	Partition 5
2002	2003	2004	2005	CurrentMonth

Assume the fact data is in a single fact table called Yearly Sales, and you have a measure group within your UDM that has been created from this fact table. By default the Cube Wizard creates a single partition that points to the relational table Yearly Sales. By dividing the data into multiple partitions, all the partitions can be processed in parallel, which will utilize the processor and memory resources of your machine more efficiently. Analysis Services 2008 processes objects in parallel by default. If the server machine has more than one CPU and sufficient memory, parallel processing will reduce total process time as compared to a machine with a single CPU. Analysis Services analyzes each request and splits them into many smaller units when possible that can be processed in parallel to accomplish the tasks. It then schedules them to be executed on multiple threads. Hence, if you have multiple processors or cores on your machine, you will get the benefit of parallelism. During query time, if cubes contain several partitions, Analysis Services can scan those partitions in parallel, and queries can return results quickly because the server has multiple jobs running in parallel, each one scanning a partition. In addition to that, when you divide the data into multiple partitions based on a specific dimension member, Analysis Services 2008 by default retrieves data only from relevant partitions needed for the query if the cube is of storage type MOLAP. For example, if a query requests data for partition 2002, Analysis Services will only query the data from the partition containing 2002 data.

To create multiple partitions, you can create multiple tables in the relational database and then create the partitions. Alternatively, you can create named queries within your DSV that correspond to your desired partition strategy. Or you can simply define the SQL query for the partition when you create it.

The second benefit of creating partitions in an environment where most of the data does not change is that you only need to process the current partition, which has new data added or modified. You need to only process the currentMonth partition in the partition scheme to refresh the latest data changes within your UDM. The data volume to process is reduced and the process time will be significantly decreased compared to processing the entire UDM.

The third benefit of partitioning data is that you can set up different storage modes for each partition. In business scenarios where a certain amount of data is not changing and the data volume is huge, it is better to use MOLAP to increase query performance. In addition, if you need real-time access to your data for analysis, you can create a small partition with the current month's data and set the storage mode for that partition as ROLAP. Analysis Services retrieves the data from the appropriate partitions and provides you with the aggregated real-time data for your business analysis.

Yet another benefit of partitioning data is that you can create different aggregations (pre-calculated data cache for improved query performance) for maximum benefit. Creating aggregations for your UDM is covered in detail later in this chapter. You can design heavy aggregations for those partitions that are queried most (the current year data) to maximize query performance, and create fewer aggregations for old data that are queried less to save the server storage. Creating such aggregations not only saves storage space but also reduces processing times if the entire UDM is processed.

Finally, refreshing the data within a partition is much faster than refreshing the entire UDM. You do not have to apply incremental processing on all the partitions. You just have to do incremental processing on the partition whose data needs to be updated. During incremental processing of the current partition, a temporary partition is created and then merged into the existing partition, which could possibly result in data fragmentation. By refreshing the partition, the server will re-sort the data for optimized query performance.

Merging Partitions

If you have multiple partitions where data is used sparsely, merge the partitions so that data from each partition does not get aggregated every time a query is issued. Assume you have your measure group data partitioned by month for the year 2002. If every user's query is asking for the entire year's data, Analysis Services needs to retrieve the data from all the partitions and aggregate data within the server. Having too many partitions could hurt query performance because the server needs to scan those partitions and aggregate data from them. Instead you can merge the data from all the partitions to form a single partition. Queries referring to 2002 will henceforth touch a single partition. If you have aggregations created at the year level, your queries can be instantaneous.

A common scenario for many Analysis Services users is to partition by time, and have a weekly or monthly schedule of updating the cube. This typically involves merging the most recent partition into the year-to-date partition, and creating a new partition for the next period. Sometimes SSIS (SQL Server Integration Services, which you learn about in Chapter 19) is used to control the flow of operations. This is another scenario where data from existing partitions need to be merged.

Consider the example reviewed in the "Partitions" section, where data was partitioned by time. If you want to merge the partitions to a single partition because queries are infrequent, you can do so using SMSS by following these steps:

1. Deploy the sample Adventure Works DW 2008 enterprise project sample that is available from www.codeplex.com. The Adventure Works cube contains several measure groups. Connect to the Adventure Works DW database using SSMS.

2. Navigate through the cube and notice the four partitions under the Internet Sales measure group as shown in Figure 14-10.

3. Right-click the Internet_Sales_2003 partition and select Merge Partitions. Assume you want to merge the 2004 data into this partition.

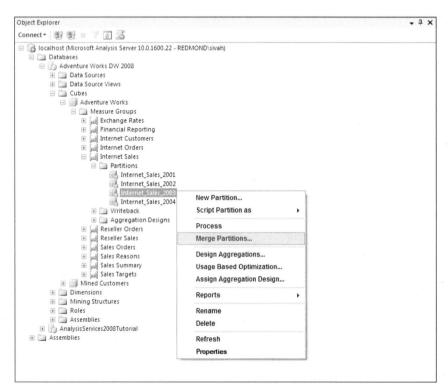

Figure 14-10

4. In the Merge Partition dialog, select Internet_Sales_2004, as shown in Figure 14-11, and click OK. You are done! You have now successfully merged 2004 partition data into the 2003 partition.

5. In the SSMS object browser, refresh the measure group object. The partition of Internet_Sales_2004 is gone because it was just merged to the Internet_Sales_2003 partition. You can see this in Figure 14-12. You can still query the data for 2004 and 2003 as before. The cube still contains the same data and all queries still return the same result.

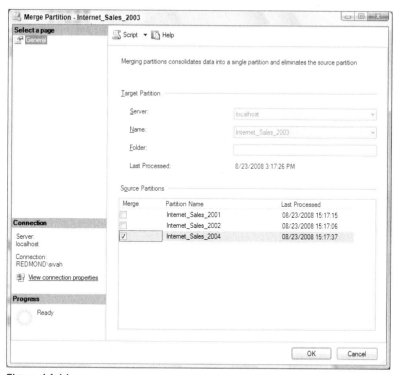

Figure 14-11

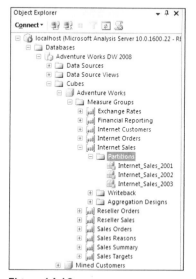

Figure 14-12

We expect your UDM to have several partitions for each of your measure groups, especially the ones that contain a large volume of fact data. We recommend you investigate the queries that are sent to your UDM and identify the requirements of your business users. One mechanism used to identify the queries sent to Analysis Services is SQL Server Profiler. You learn about profiling Analysis Services using SQL Server Profiler in Chapter 15. Most measure groups partitioned are data that map to time. This is the most logical and common scenario for most businesses. If after analyzing the queries you see that your user queries are targeted to specific partitions, and the remaining partitions are infrequently queried or queries to those partitions retrieve data at a higher grain, we recommend you merge such partitions.

Partition Slices

The partition slice is a simple MDX expression that defines what parts of the cube are present in a particular partition. For example, a partition slice could be:

```
{ [Date].[Calendar Year].&[2001], [Date].[Calendar Year].&[2002] }*
{ [Product].[Product Categories].[Category].&[1] }
```

In the preceding MDX expression the member referred to by the unique name [Product].[Product Categories].[Category].&[1] refers to the product category Bikes. Therefore the entire MDX expression would indicate that this partition only contains data for the years 2001 and 2002 and for the Product Category "Bikes."

What is the value of the partition slice? It allows the server to detect which partitions can be simply ignored for a query. If a query is querying the months January, February, and March in the year 2005, a partition with a slice defined on the years 2001 and 2002 doesn't even need to be scanned.

For MOLAP partitions, the server is able to automatically infer single-member attribute slices. For example, a partition with data for only the year 2001 would automatically have a slice for the Year attribute for the member 2001. However, if the partition has data for more than one member as in the preceding example, the server will not infer this slice and it should be set explicitly on the partition using the Slice property.

Partition Slices and ROLAP

The partition slice can be even more important when there are ROLAP partitions in the UDM. The server cannot even infer single-member slices on attributes for those partitions and it is required to send a SQL query for every ROLAP partition unless the DBA can help by specifying good partition slices.

Assume a large-scale UDM containing several partitions where all the partitions are ROLAP. In such a scenario, when a query comes in requesting data Analysis Services sends relational queries to each partition with appropriate conditions to retrieve the data. Analysis Services then aggregates the data retrieved from the different partitions and sends the results to the end user. However, generating the queries for each partition, establishing connection to the data source, and then retrieving results is an operation that takes a certain amount of time. If the Slice property is not specified, by default, Analysis Services assumes data can be contained in that partition for any MDX query.

A Partition Slice Example

Assume you have partitioned the data by time, five partitions for five years. Typically, most of the queries will involve only the current year. In this case there is no need to send five queries, of which four will return no data. By setting the slice property indicating that the 2001 partition contains data for year 2001, 2002 partition contains data for year 2002, and so on, you provide a hint to Analysis Services so that it can optimize the relational queries sent. The Slice property for a partition can be set in BIDS or SSMS. For example, if you need to set a specific partition's data for year 2004, you will provide the MDX expression for 2004 as [Date].[Calendar].[Calendar Year].&[2004]. By default the value for the slice property is set to null, which indicates to Analysis Services that this specific partition can contain data for all the queries. The following steps show how to set the slice property.

1. Open the Adventure Works 2008 sample project shipped with SQL Server 2008. Deploy the sample Adventure Works DW 2008 project and ensure the database is processed. Connect to the Adventure Works DW 2008 database using SSMS.

2. Navigate through the partitions of Internet Sales measure group. Change the storage mode for all the partitions to HOLAP using the Proactive Settings in the Properties dialog. The effect of the partition slice property can be seen even for MOLAP partitions, but the example is more visible for ROLAP partitions, as you can see the SQL queries being executed against the relational database. Because the Internet Sales measure group has aggregations defined, you change the storage mode from MOLAP to HOLAP. Process all the partitions of the Internet Sales measure group.

3. Right-click the Internet_Sales_2001 partition object and select Properties. Alternatively, you can double-click the partition, which will bring up the Properties page of the partitions as shown in Figure 14-13.

4. Click the ellipsis next to the Slice property. This launches the MDX editor, as shown in Figure 14-14.

5. Navigate through the Date dimension and select the member [Date].[Calendar] .[Calendar Year].&[2001]. When you double-click this member, the MDX expression corresponding to it appears in the text box. Click Check to verify the MDX syntax and then click OK.

6. Similar to step 5, specify the slice property for the remaining partitions Internet_Sales_2002, Internet_Sales_2003, and Internet_Sales_2004 with corresponding members in the Date dimension for the years 2002, 2003, and 2004.

7. If you use MOLAP partitions, you will need to re-process them after making these changes.

Figure 14-13

Figure 14-14

You have now successfully defined the slice for all the partitions in the Internet_Sales measure group of the Adventure Works cube. To verify that Analysis Services is able to utilize the slice information, you can send an MDX query that retrieves measures from the Internet_Sales measure group containing specific members from the [Date].[Calendar] hierarchy, such as year 2001. If you trace the queries sent to the SQL Server using SQL Server Profiler without setting the slice information, you will see that Analysis Services sends four queries to the relational server. After setting the slice information you can see that exactly one query is sent to the SQL Server.

An important factor to note is that Analysis Services does not validate your slice information for ROLAP partitions. Analysis Services just honors the slice property you have set, assuming you have the in-depth knowledge of your data. If you set an incorrect slice on a partition, you will get incorrect query results. For example, if you set the slice for partition Internet_Sales_2002 with a time member corresponding to 2001, a query requesting data for year 2002 will result in no data (assuming slice information is set for the remaining partitions correctly). The slice property is a directive to Analysis Services, and you need to be careful about setting the correct slice. Because Analysis Services is aware of the slice information for MOLAP partitions, if you set an incorrect slice for a specific partition and try to process the partition, the processing will result in errors. Each row being processed is validated against the slice, and processing will fail if it does not fit within the space defined for the partition.

Distinct Count Partitioning

Distinct count measure groups have some special behaviors that are worth mentioning from a performance standpoint. Each distinct count partition that is processed is ordered by the distinct count measure column. For example, the Internet Order Count measure in the Internet Orders measure group in Adventure Works 2008 is processed using a SQL query:

```
SELECT
   [dbo_FactInternetSales].[SalesOrderNumber] AS
   [dbo_FactInternetSalesSalesOrderNumber0_0],
   [dbo_FactInternetSales].[PromotionKey] AS
   [dbo_FactInternetSalesPromotionKey0_1],
   ...
FROM
   facttable AS [dbo_FactInternetSales]
ORDER BY
   [dbo_FactInternetSales].[SalesOrderNumber] ASC
```

As you can see, there is an ORDER BY clause in the SQL query that enforces that the fact records stored in the Analysis Services partition files are ordered by the values of the distinct count measure. This is very important for two reasons.

First, it impacts the cost of processing. The ORDER BY clause can make the SQL query take much longer to execute, and you may find it possible and valuable to build indexes in the relational database to optimize the SQL query performance.

Second, the partitioning strategy in Analysis Services is also impacted by this, albeit somewhat indirectly. For example, take a partitioning strategy where there are 12 partitions based on the Month attribute in the Date dimension. This is generally a reasonable approach for partitioning. However, when a query hits a distinct count measure group asking for the total across all months, the server has to scan all the partitions in a relatively inefficient manner. It has to synchronize the records scanned across all the partitions to match up the records that have the same measure value, such that all these records will be counted for the total value.

An alternative strategy is to partition based on the Distinct Count column value. In the case of the Internet Order Count measure group, this would be the "Sales Order Number" column. The benefit of this type of partitioning scheme is that the partitions now have distinct ranges for the distinct count measure values (no two partitions have data for the same measure value). The server detects this and is able to avoid the synchronization and can scan all the partitions in parallel. Essentially, it now knows that the same "Sales Order Number" can never be in any of the other partitions and so it can simply count the records in the current partition to determine the distinct count.

An extended variation of this is to partition by the distinct count measure and also by one or more dimensions. In this case, you get the benefit of avoiding partition scans for partitions that don't match the current slice in the query (for example, queries to the year 2004 don't need to scan partitions for years 2001, 2002, and 2003). You also get some benefit of better parallelism because the server will group partitions together for the synchronization that have overlapping distinct count ranges. Therefore the partitions that have disjointed ranges can be queried in parallel and will have reduced overhead.

For example, say that you define partitions like this:

```
P1: Year 2001 and       0 < Sales Order Number < 10000
P2: Year 2001 and   10000 < Sales Order Number < 20000
...
P10: Year 2001 and 90000 < Sales Order Number

P11: Year 2002 and       0 < Sales Order Number < 10000
...
```

Now all the partitions for each year can be scanned independently because their ranges are disjointed. If a query crosses years (for example, All Years), the partitions that have the same ranges will be grouped together but the groups can operate independently of each other, which improves performance.

In this section, you have learned various design techniques that can help you to optimize your UDM for better performance during processing and querying. In the next section you learn about other optimizations that will help you reduce processing time.

Optimizing for Processing

To understand how to improve UDM processing performance you first need to understand the processing operation of Analysis Services. Analysis Services 2008 supports ROLAP and MOLAP storage modes for dimensions and ROLAP, MOLAP, and HOLAP storage modes for partitions. Assume the data source is a relational database. Figure 14-15 shows the architecture of a regular processing operation when the storage mode for the dimensions and cubes is MOLAP. Analysis Services sends separate relational queries to the retrieve dimension and fact data. The relational data source executes the query and sends the records to Analysis Services. Analysis Services reads the records from the relational data source and stores it in a proprietary format for fast data access. During dimension processing Analysis Services sends separate queries to process each attribute of the dimension. Members from each attribute are stored and indexed by Key and Name for fast data access. The related properties to the attribute are also indexed. If an attribute has a related attribute defined, the related attribute needs to be processed first before the attribute itself. Analysis Services processes attributes in parallel based on resource availability, parallelism specified, and dependencies. The key attribute of the dimension is the last attribute processed because all the attributes are related to the key attribute. While processing the partitions Analysis Services reads fact data from the relational data source and stores it in proprietary format. Analysis Services then creates indexes to access the data efficiently. If aggregations are designed for the partitions, then aggregations are built followed by indexes.

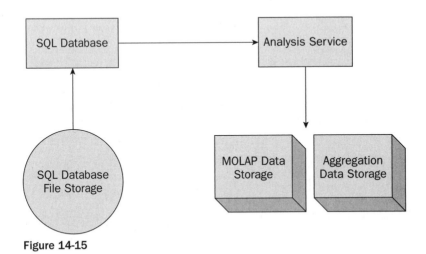

Figure 14-15

If the storage type is ROLAP, Analysis Services only needs to store the metadata in Analysis Services. There is no data transfer between the relational data source and the Analysis Services database, and there is no actual data storage on the Analysis Services side. Hence ROLAP processing is faster. Use of the ROLAP storage format does impose a performance penalty at query time; queries will be slower when compared to MOLAP. This is because at query time data needs to be retrieved from the data source, aggregated within Analysis Services, and then results returned to the end user.

When the storage type is HOLAP the source data resides in the data source while aggregations are calculated and stored on Analysis Services. HOLAP storage is typically used only when you primarily have space constraints on replicating the data on Analysis Services. HOLAP storage mode doesn't save much processing time as compared to MOLAP. Given the performance advantage of MOLAP data storage, we recommend using MOLAP storage for Analysis Services databases instead of HOLAP. For small and active partitions (current period data) where data cannot be allowed to be stale, we recommend use of ROLAP storage mode in combination with the Real-Time Proactive Caching feature to get the most recent data.

You can have users querying the cube when you initiate processing. Analysis Services uses locks inside transactions to ensure atomic changes and consistent views of data. The lock is referred to as database (DB) commit lock. Usually everything just works and one does not need to even know about the DB commit lock. However, for sophisticated usage scenarios, understanding this process can help explain system behavior that might otherwise seem anomalous. This can also help you to perform processing operations based on the load on the system.

During a query, the server takes a read DB commit lock. This ensures the database will not be deleted or modified during the query. During processing, a new version of the object (dimension, fact-table partition, and so on) is created. The original version on disk is not immediately overwritten though; a shadow copy is created. Once the new version has been successfully created, within the process transaction, a write DB commit lock is acquired. Then the new files automatically replace the old files, and the lock is released. The duration over which the lock is held is typically very small, perhaps less than 1 second. However, acquiring this lock requires waiting for current lock holders to relinquish their locks. Thus a long-running query can block the completion of a processing command.

The ForceCommitTimeout server property specifies the period of time a process command has to wait to acquire the DB commit lock. The default is 30000 milliseconds (30 seconds) and is specified in the configuration file \Program Files\Microsoft SQL Server\<MSSQL.x>\OLAP\Config\msmdsrv.ini. After the timeout, all transactions holding the lock will be forced to fail. For the English version of Analysis Services the error message returned is "The operation has been cancelled." There are other scenarios under which this message will also be returned, but this is one cause to keep in mind when troubleshooting. Typically the holder of the read lock will be one or more long-running queries, and for the system as a whole, forcing them to fail is probably the better choice.

Lock chains can result when long-running queries coexist with processing commands. While a process command is waiting for a long-running query, new queries must wait for the processing command to complete. Although the request for a new read lock is compatible with existing granted read locks, granting the new request could lead to starvation of the processing command, so locks are queued. The resulting behavior can appear to be a server hang, even though it is not. You can see this behavior if you try to connect to Analysis Services using SSMS when you have a long-running query along with a processing command that is waiting for the long-running query to complete. This is due to the fact that SSMS sets a default database that requires a read DB commit lock. Here is a list of events creating a lock chain:

```
1. Long-running query acquires and holds read DB commit lock.
2. Process command completes and waits to acquire write DB commit lock.
3. New query waits to acquire read DB commit lock.
```

Having learned the basic trade-offs in terms of processing time and query performance benefits for the various storage modes supported by Analysis Services, next you look at some of the techniques that help in optimizing processing.

Creating Partitions to Speed Up Processing

We expect Analysis Services to be installed on a multi-processor machine to take advantage of multiple processors and have better performance. When a fact table is partitioned into multiple partitions within a measure group, due to the inherent parallelism in Analysis Services, the partitions are processed in parallel. You can also specify the parallelism to be used by Analysis Services through the processing option as discussed in Chapter 7. Hence having multiple partitions reduces the processing time for the measure group as compared to a single partition.

As discussed in the design optimization section, creating partitions can significantly improve processing performance during the typical daily, weekly, or monthly updates. Most often the partition corresponding to the most recent time period needs to be updated. Because a small subset of the data (most recent partition) is processed you speed up the processing time for the entire measure group.

We recommend you create multiple partitions for the measure groups whenever you have large volumes of data. Based on the performance guide for *Microsoft SQL Server 2008 Analysis Services*, you should consider having partitions of sizes 3–5GB, or 20 million rows. Based on your business scenario, you might need to create partitions outside of that size profile.

Creating too many partitions can potentially hurt processing performance. Analysis Services processes objects in parallel based on your system resources. If all the partitions are processed in parallel they can be competing for resources. Furthermore, the relational data source can also slow down processing performance if Analysis Services sends requests to retrieve data for all the partitions. Analysis Services allows you to control the number of objects to be processed in parallel (described later in this chapter). Make sure you design the right number of partitions based on user queries and process with a certain degree of parallelism.

Choosing Small and Appropriate Data Types and Sizes

Choosing integers as keys for your tables helps improve processing and query performance. Using single integer keys (rather than strings or composite keys) results in faster processing time due to decreased size, decreased network usage, and the handling of keys internal to the relational data source, and Analysis Services can be done with simple native machine instructions. Analysis Services looks up the keys of dimension members while processing dimensions as well as cubes. The key lookup routines used by Analysis Services can run tens or hundreds of times faster for integer data types compared to other data types that are used as the key. In general, we recommend you set appropriate keys and or consider a design using integer surrogate keys in the relational data source in advance of building your UDM.

SQL Server and Analysis Services Installations

When you install SQL Server 2008, you can have SQL Server and Analysis Services installed on the same machine or a different machine. There are some trade-offs that you might want to consider for processing when you have UDMs retrieving data from the SQL Server. If you have both installations on the same machine, SQL Server and Analysis Services may compete for resources. You need to make sure you have sufficient processors and memory configurations on your system. Whenever your Analysis Services dimensions are large (millions of members) there will be an impact on processing speed. If SQL Server and Analysis Services are competing for memory, you might have significant paging of data to disk, which could slow down operations dramatically.

For 32-bit versions of Windows we recommend turning on the /3GB flag. By default each process running in Windows can access a maximum of 2GB. By turning on the /3GB flag, you allow the Analysis Services process to access up to 3GB of addressable space. This increases the accessible memory and facilitates large dimension processing and aggregation building. To enable the /3GB option, open your boot.ini file on your system drive and add the /3GB option as shown here, and then reboot the machine:

```
multi(0)disk(0)rdisk(0)partition(2)\WINNT="????" /3GB
```

In addition to turning on the /3GB option on a 32-bit machine, consider using a machine with a large amount of memory (for example, 8GB) whenever you have SQL Server and Analysis Services installations on the same machine and your UDMs have large dimensions (on the order of millions of members). The additional memory on the 32-bit machine can be accessed by SQL Server 2008 through Address Windowing Extensions (AWE). Hence adding the additional memory helps ensure that both servers have sufficient memory resources to provide good performance. Another option is to use SQL Server and Analysis Services on 64-bit machines with larger memory.

If you do install SQL Server and Analysis Services on separate machines, they do not compete for resources, but you need to make sure you have a good high-speed network connection between the servers, such as gigabit Ethernet. Having good network connectivity helps reduce the network transfer time for queries returning large volumes of data. To stay legal, we recommend you check your licensing agreement for installing SQL Server and Analysis Services on separate machines.

Optimizing a Relational Data Source

When you read fact table data in Analysis Services 2008, you send the fact table scan query without joining dimension tables during MOLAP partition processing. Analysis Services 2008 sends a table scan query similar to the following to get the fact data without the join:

```
SELECT [dbo_WB_Fact].[BudgetExpenseAmount] AS
[dbo_WB_FactBudgetExpenseAmount0_0], [dbo_WB_Fact].[EmployeeKey] AS
[dbo_WB_FactEmployeeKey0_1], [dbo_WB_Fact].[quarterkey] AS
[dbo_WB_Factquarterkey0_2]          FROM [dbo].[WB_Fact] AS [dbo_WB_Fact]
```

This query is a pure table scan query for the whole partition. It is unnecessary to put an index on the fact table because there are no joins involved with the dimension table.

However, if you do have ROLAP partitions set up, we recommend you have appropriate indexes created on your relational database so that queries sent to the relational data source at query time return results faster because those will involve joins to dimension tables. If you trace the operations of Analysis Services with the help of SQL Server Profiler, you can identify the queries sent to your relational server. We recommend that you set up efficient indexes for the queries targeted to your relational server for best performance when querying ROLAP partitions.

Dimension processing may also benefit from indexes in some cases. The queries generated by Analysis Services for each attribute look something like this:

```
SELECT DISTINCT
[dbo_DimProductCategory].[ProductCategoryKey] AS
      [dbo_DimProductCategoryProductCategoryKey0_0],
[dbo_DimProductCategory].[EnglishProductCategoryName] AS
        [dbo_DimProductCategoryEnglishProductCategoryName0_1],
[dbo_DimProductCategory].[SpanishProductCategoryName] AS
        [dbo_DimProductCategorySpanishProductCategoryName0_2],
[dbo_DimProductCategory].[FrenchProductCategoryName] AS
        [dbo_DimProductCategoryFrenchProductCategoryName0_3]
FROM [dbo].[DimProductCategory] AS [dbo_DimProductCategory]
```

For the key attribute, all the key columns of the related attributes will also be included in the list of columns. The DISTINCT clause can sometimes be an expensive operation for the relational database, and indexes on the dimension table may be worth considering. This is usually not an issue for typical dimensions and is worth considering only if it appears that a dimension is taking unusually long to process.

Avoiding Excessive Aggregation Design

Aggregation design is a way to define aggregated data that needs to be created during processing of partitions. You learn more about aggregations later in this chapter. If you have the right aggregations created, it will help in query performance. However, having excessive aggregations for partitions will increase the processing time of the partitions. Analysis Services may need additional temporary files during the process and need to write more data onto the disk for each partition. As a general rule of thumb we recommend you create aggregations to improve performance by 10–30 percent. If you do need additional query performance improvements, we recommend you use a usage-based aggregation design to create targeted aggregations based on the requests sent by the users accessing the cubes. You also have the choice of using different aggregations for each partition, which will help in removing unwanted aggregations for certain partitions and hence speed up cube processing time. Consider designing more aggregations on heavily queried partitions, and using fewer aggregations for partitions rarely used. This may seem like a fairly obvious guideline, but it does have a management overhead because creation and management of partitions will now need to take into consideration multiple candidate aggregation designs.

Using Incremental Processing When Appropriate

Often, data changes in the relational data source. These changes could be due to new rows being added to existing tables or updates on existing rows. If you have set up the storage mode for dimensions and partitions as ROLAP, you will be retrieving the data from the relational data source for queries sent by users. In situations where the result set has been cached on Analysis Services due to a previous query, Analysis Services will not be fetching data from the relational database by default. You can force Analysis Services to always fetch data from the relational data source by using ROLAP (see Chapter 22 for more details). However, if the storage mode for all your cubes and dimensions is MOLAP, Analysis Services serves queries only from the processed MOLAP data that resides on Analysis Services. Future updates to relational tables will not be available to end users unless you update the MOLAP data on Analysis Services.

You have several ways of updating the data on Analysis Services. You can do a full process of the corresponding dimensions and/or cubes that need to be refreshed due to changes in the corresponding relational tables. Several processing options are available to optimize your processing needs. Process Incremental and Process Add are options that help you process the dimensions and partitions so that they are updated with the new data on the relational data source as necessary. Not all the data in the partitions or dimensions gets updated during these operations; only data that changed since the last round of processing will be refreshed.

During an incremental process of partitions Analysis Services retrieves the new data from the relational data source and adds it to a temporary partition. Aggregations are then created for this new data, and finally the temporary partition is merged to the existing partition. As soon as the data is merged it is available for querying and you will see the new data reflected in user queries. Because Analysis Services only retrieves the new data added to relational tables, the incremental processing option for partitions helps you to process the partition quickly as compared to full process. However, if your partition is to be processed frequently due to data changes in the relational data source, we recommend you do a full process on that partition periodically (not often), because full processing will have a better layout of data on disk and result in some performance benefits similar to the defragment technique in file storage.

Dimensions can be incrementally processed using the ProcessIncremental or ProcessAdd options. ProcessIncremental retrieves the data from the relational data source, compares the data to existing dimension members on Analysis Services, and then makes updates to existing dimension members if there are any changes. If there are new members, they are added to the dimension and this does not affect the partitions. However, if the dimension members are updated such that the relationship between attributes has changed (an employee's marital status changed from single to married), then the aggregations for the corresponding partitions will be dropped. The cube will still be available for querying but it can impact the performance of the queries that were using the dropped aggregations. ProcessIncremental takes more time than full process of the same dimension because Analysis Services does the additional work of checking for updates for existing members; however, it provides you with the flexibility of having the dimension available for querying and the cube does not have to be reprocessed. This option allows you to add new dimension members that have been added in the relational data source to existing processed dimensions. We recommend using the ProcessAdd option for dimensions whenever you have new members being added to the corresponding dimension tables in the relational data source. ProcessAdd for dimensions is very useful in cases where new products are added to the products table on a periodic basis. You need to specify relational queries to the data source that will return the new rows that have been added since the last dimension update. The query to retrieve new data along with the data source and Data Source View elements is to be specified in the DDL along with the ProcessAdd called out of line binding. The following is an example of using DDL using ProcessAdd with out of line binding:

```
<Batch xmlns="http://schemas.microsoft.com/analysisservices/2003/engine">
 <Parallel>
  <Process xmlns="http://schemas.microsoft.com/analysisservices/2003/engine">
   <Object>
    <DatabaseID>Adventure Works DW 2008 </DatabaseID>
    <DimensionID>Dim Customer</DimensionID>
   </Object>
   <Type>ProcessAdd</Type>
   <DataSourceView>
    <ID>Adventure Works DW</ID>
    <Name>Adventure Works DW</Name>
    <DataSourceID>Adventure Works DW</DataSourceID>
    <Schema>
     <xs:schema id="Adventure_x0020_Works_x0020_DW 2008" xmlns=""
         xmlns:xs="http://www.w3.org/2001/XMLSchema" xmlns:msdata=
         "urn:schemas-microsoft-com:xml-msdata" xmlns:msprop="urn:schemas-
         microsoft-com:xml-msprop">
      <xs:element name="Adventure_x0020_Works_x0020_DW 2008"
         msdata:IsDataSet="true" msdata:UseCurrentLocale="true">
       <xs:complexType>
        <xs:choice minOccurs="0" maxOccurs="unbounded">
         <xs:element name="dbo_DimProduct" msprop:FriendlyName="DimProduct"
             msprop:DbSchemaName="dbo" msprop:DbTableName="DimProduct"
             msprop:QueryDefiniton ="SELECT
           * FROM DimProduct WHERE ProductKey &gt; 600"
             msprop:DbTableName="DimProduct"
             msprop:IsLogical="True"
             msprop:TableType="View">
          <xs:complexType>
```

(continued)

(continued)

```
            ... //Details of columns returned
        </xs:complexType>
      </xs:element>
    </xs:choice>
  </xs:complexType>
</xs:element>
</xs:schema>
</Schema>
</DataSourceView>
</Process>
</Parallel>
</Batch>
```

Parallelism during Processing

When compared to Analysis Services 2000, Analysis Services 2008 has improved processing behavior by using max parallelism to process independent components by default. If you have 16 partitions, all 16 partitions will be processed in parallel. Having too much parallelism can actually hurt performance through context switching and disk thrashing — happily, Analysis Services provides you with several options to control the amount of parallelism used for processing. Based on the complexity of the cube and the set of aggregations, we suggest you have two to three objects being processed per CPU.

You can control the amount of parallelism by changing certain server properties. For processing, the main server property impacting processing performance is CoordinatorExecutionMode. The server properties can be changed using the properties dialog from SQL Server Management Studio or in the config file msmdsrv.ini located in the %System Drive%\Program Files\Microsoft SQL Server \MSSQL.x\OLAP\Config folder. The CoordinatorExecutionMode server property sets the maximum parallelism allowed for a specific job, such as processing that needs to be executed on the server at a specific time. This property can have a positive or negative value. If the value is positive, the actual value is used and if the value is negative, it is multiplied by the number of processors and the absolute value of the result is used. For example, the default Analysis Services 2008 value is –4, which on a 4-processor machine indicates that the maximum parallelism to be used on the machine is 16 for each request. By setting this property you can avoid the server being overloaded with processing operations, perhaps to allow some resources for queries.

Another property, ThreadPool\Processing\MaxThreads, specifies the maximum number of threads in the processing thread pool. We recommend this not be used as a way to limit concurrency because internally the server often executes tasks by queuing other tasks and waiting for completion. The server is designed to be smart enough to know that more threads are needed to avoid deadlocking by exceeding MaxThreads.

When all the objects within a database are processed in parallel, Analysis Services sends queries to the data source for dimension as well as partition processing. Sometimes having too many connections and queries to the data source can increase processing time. You can limit the number of connections Analysis Services establishes with the data source. You can limit concurrent connections using the Data Source property "Maximum Number of Connections." This value can be altered from SQL Management Studio. See Figure 14-16.

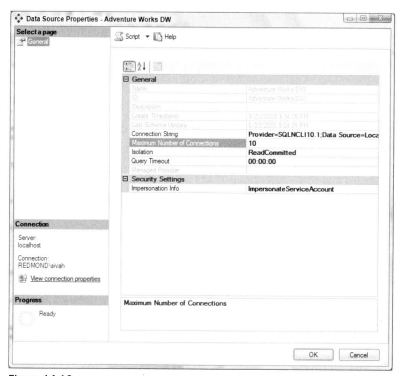

Figure 14-16

You can specify the amount of parallelism for a specific processing operation along with the processing command. Follow these steps to restrict the parallelism in the Processing dialog while processing a database:

1. Open the sample Adventure Works DW 2008 project and deploy it to the Analysis Services instance.

2. Open SSMS and connect to the Analysis Services instance.

3. Navigate to the Internet_Sales measure group for the Adventure Works cube in the Object Browser window.

4. Right-click the measure group and choose Process to open the Process dialog shown in Figure 14-17.

5. Click the Change Settings button to open the settings dialog.

6. The settings dialog shown in Figure 14-18 allows you specify the amount of parallelism while processing the current object. Select the value 8 as shown in the figure and click OK.

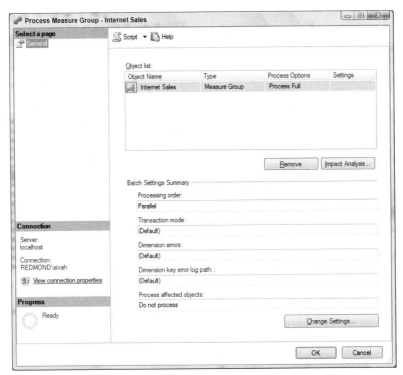

Figure 14-17

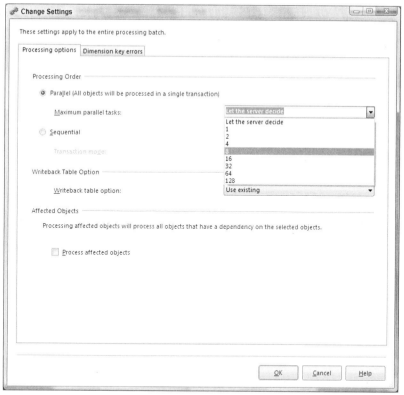

Figure 14-18

7. You learned in Chapter 7 that you can process the objects on an Analysis Services instance using the dialogs or through scripts. The Process dialog has the option to script the current settings to process the Internet_Sales measure group into XMLA. Click the Script to New Window button in the Process dialog shown in Figure 14-17. A processing script is now opened within SSMS as shown next. Note that you could also use SQL Server Profiler to view the process command received by the server.

```
<Batch xmlns="http://schemas.microsoft.com/analysisservices/2003/engine">
  <Parallel MaxParallel="8">
    <Process xmlns:xsd="http://www.w3.org/2001/XMLSchema"
        xmlns:xsi="http://www.w3.org/2001/XMLSchema-instance"
        xmlns:ddl2="http://schemas.microsoft.com/analysisservices/2003/
        engine/2" xmlns:ddl2_2="http://schemas.microsoft.com/analysisservices/
        2003/engine/2/2" xmlns:ddl100_100="http://schemas.microsoft.com/
        analysisservices/2008/engine/100/100">
      <Object>
        <DatabaseID>Adventure Works DW 2008</DatabaseID>
        <CubeID>Adventure Works</CubeID>
```

(continued)

(continued)

```
            <MeasureGroupID>Fact Internet Sales 1</MeasureGroupID>
        </Object>
        <Type>ProcessFull</Type>
        <WriteBackTableCreation>UseExisting</WriteBackTableCreation>
    </Process>
  </Parallel>
</Batch>
```

In the processing script you can see the option MaxParallel=8, which instructs the Analysis Services instance to process a maximum of 8 objects in parallel.

Identifying Resource Bottlenecks

Analysis Services processing and query performance requires well-configured hardware resources for best results. Processing performance requires sufficient memory, CPU speed, and good hard disk IO speed. These three play a significant role in getting the best performance. Analysis Services allows you to monitor resources used during operations of the server by way of perfmon counters. There are specific perfmon counters that show the memory utilization on the Analysis Services instance. You can monitor the server behavior during the processing operation via perfmon counters of the objects \\<machinename>\Processor, \\<machinename>\Memory, \\<machinename>\PhysicalDisk and specific counters provided by Analysis Services \\<machinename>\MSAS 2008: Processing, \\<machinename>\MSAS 2008: ProcIndexes, \\<machinename>\MSAS 2008: ProcAggregations, and \\<machinename>\ProcIndexes. After identifying the bottlenecks of the system, you can take appropriate action to relieve the server performance hot spots.

Some simple hardware additions, such as increasing server memory, adding more CPU, or using fast writing disks can potentially improve the system processing performance. As mentioned earlier, if you have memory over 3GB for a 32-bit machine, you might consider using the /3GB flag to allow Analysis Services to use memory over the 3GB limit as discussed earlier in this chapter. If memory is the main bottleneck we highly recommend you consider using 64-bit machines to increase the performance and capacity of your system, especially for cubes with large dimensions (10> million dimension members).

In certain cases where the number of partitions is in the order of hundreds, processing partitions in parallel on a 32-bit machine can result in partitions competing among themselves for memory resources. In such circumstances, processing can result in errors that say the system does not have sufficient memory. You can split the processing of the partitions by one of the following techniques:

1. Process fewer partitions at a time and stagger them to complete processing of all the partitions.

2. Use one of the techniques mentioned in the "Parallelism during Processing" section.

3. Instead of doing a full process of the partitions, which includes processing data, indexes, and aggregations, split the processing as Process Data first for all partitions followed by Process Indexes.

4. If you are running on 64-bit hardware and you have a lot of memory at your disposal, you could change the settings for the OLAP\Memory\LowMemoryLimit and TotalMemoryLimit. These settings default to 65 percent and 80 percent of available memory. On a machine with large amounts of available memory, you could increase these if other processes on the server do not need significant amounts of memory. This would allow Analysis Services to make use of more memory during processing and queries.

Designing Aggregations

The power of Analysis Services is its ability to provide fast query response time for decision makers who need to analyze data, draw conclusions, and make appropriate changes in business. As per The OLAP Report (http://www.olapreport.com), OLAP is defined as Fast Analysis of Shared Multidimensional Information (FASMI). The word fast means that system is able to deliver results to users within 5 seconds, with a very few complex queries that may take more than 20 seconds. We expect most of the business users to use business client tools that graphically represent that data from Analysis Services for easy interpretation and understanding. As an end user you would expect to see the data quickly (the OLAP Report cites users typically wait for only 30 seconds as per an independent study in the Netherlands) to analyze and make decisions. Some of the common operations the client tools offer are drill down, drill up, and compare data year over year. Users do not have the time to wait hours for a response. Hence the queries sent to Analysis Services need to return data within seconds, at most in minutes. The query performance is pivotal to a successful Business Intelligence project deployment. A system that has very good performance will bring great business value to your system and company.

Even though Analysis Services supports storage modes MOLAP, ROLAP, and HOLAP, you obtain the best performance when your UDM storage mode is MOLAP. When you choose MOLAP storage, Analysis Services 2008 will store the dimension data and fact data in its own efficient, compact, and multidimensional structure format. Fact data are compressed and the size is approximately 10–30 percent of the size in the relational database. In addition to its own efficient and compact data store, Analysis Services builds specialized dimension attribute indexes for efficient data retrieval. The data is stored specifically in a multidimensional structure to best serve MDX query needs. If you use the ROLAP or HOLAP storage modes, queries to Analysis Services might have to fetch data from the relational data source at query time. Retrieving data from the relational data sources will significantly slow your query performance because you incur relational query processing time — the time needed to fetch the data over the network and then finally aggregating the data within Analysis Services.

Analysis Services 2008 tries to achieve the best of the OLAP and relational worlds. OLAP queries typically request aggregated data. For example, if you have sales information for products each day, a typical OLAP query might be to get the aggregated sales for the month or quarter or year. In such circumstances, every day's sales data needs to be aggregated for the entire year. If the users are requesting aggregated data on a single dimension, you will be able to do a simple sum in the relational database. However, OLAP queries are typically multidimensional queries, which need aggregated data across multiple dimensions with complex business logic calculations applied to each dimension. To improve the query performance, Analysis Services allows you to specify the multidimensional intersections for which data needs to be pre-aggregated so that queries requesting such data will be served instantaneously. Assume you have a database with a dimension called Products having a multilevel hierarchy Product Category ⇨ Product Sub Category ⇨ Product Name, a Time dimension having the hierarchy Year ⇨ Quarter ⇨ Month ⇨ Date, and a Geography dimension having a hierarchy Country ⇨ State ⇨ County ⇨ City. Fact data is typically at the lowest levels — sales of a specific product on a specific date at a specific city. For analysis you would request aggregated data of Sales at a city for a month for various product categories. You can have pre-aggregated data for the cross product of various levels in each hierarchy such as Quarter, State, and Year. To create the pre-aggregated data you need to specify the dimensions for which Analysis Services needs to pre-calculate the data. The pre-calculated data along with definitions are referred to as aggregations.

Understanding Aggregations

Analysis Services 2008 allows you to build pre-calculated subtotals for each partition of your cubes, and store them in either an OLAP data store or relational database based on the storage modes chosen for the partitions. Because most OLAP queries typically request aggregated data at various levels of dimension hierarchies, storing pre-aggregated data will help in getting the results to end users quickly. When you query for data at higher levels of hierarchies (other than the granularity level, which is the level at which fact data is available), the server can directly fetch those aggregate numbers instead of bringing all related detailed fact data and aggregating them within the engine. In this section you learn to create aggregations for cubes using the Adventure Works sample database.

Using Adventure Works dimensions as an example, assume you have a measure group using the Date, Product, and Customer dimensions, and each dimension has hierarchies and levels as shown in the following table. Assume the granularity attribute for the dimensions Date, Products, and Customer are Date, Product Name, and Full Name, respectively. If you query the data for [Date].[2004].[Q3] and if there is no aggregated data stored in your OLAP database, the server needs to retrieve the lowest-level fact data for all dates in quarter Q3 of year 2004 for all products and all the customers in that State-Province. This can result in a large data scan on the OLAP fact data, followed by the server aggregating the data and returning the results to you.

Date Dimension		Products Dimension		Customer Dimension	
Year	4	Category	4	Country	6
Semester	8	SubCategory	37	State-Province	71
Quarter	16	Product Name	395	City	587
Month	48			Postal Code	646
Date	1461			Full Name	18484

Analysis Services 2008 provides wizards that help define the combinations of dimension hierarchies for which aggregated data needs to be created, either by analyzing the statistics of members at each level and/or based on the queries requested by users. Once the aggregations are defined you need to process the partitions so that Analysis Services creates the pre-aggregated data and stores them in the OLAP data store. In addition to the pre-aggregated data, Analysis Services also creates indexes to access the aggregated data, which speeds up data retrieval. Reviewing the preceding example, if the server has aggregations for levels Quarter, Subcategory, and State-Province of the user hierarchies in Date, Product, and Customer dimensions, respectively, then a query for Quarter Q3 of year 2004 can be fulfilled right away from the aggregation. In this case, a fact scan is not needed and you receive the results much more quickly because the amount of data that has to be scanned is significantly smaller. Furthermore, queries requesting data for the levels above Quarter, Subcategory, and State-Province will also benefit from the aggregation. For example, if you query for Year, Subcategory, and State-Province, the server only needs to get the data for Quarter from the existing aggregations and aggregate a much smaller data set than a huge fact table scan. Thus aggregations help in improving the query performance time of your MDX queries.

Storing aggregation values in the Analysis Services database is a typical trade-off of database size and performance. Aggregation values will take disk space, and it will benefit query performance for queries sent to the server. In addition to that, the time to build aggregations during processing can also play an important role in performance with respect to when the UDM is available. In the example discussed in the preceding paragraph, if you count the permutations of all levels in the three dimensions you will see there are 74 combinations (5*3*5 −1 [fact table] = 74) to build aggregations. You might immediately have the following questions:

❑   Do I need to build aggregations for all the combinations? Will that be useful?

❑   Can I build a subset of the aggregations?

❑   What parameters will affect the choice of Analysis Services for aggregation design?

❑   How much disk space will these aggregations take?

❑   What percentage of optimization will I get based on the aggregations designed?

The estimated dimension members count of all the hierarchies in a dimension is an important metric to calculate the cost of storage for aggregations. For example, aggregation (Month, Product Name, Postal Code) will potentially result in 12 million (48*395*646 = 12,248,160) cells to compute and store. However, not every cell will have data just as the fact data doesn't have all combinations for every dimension key. Because Analysis Services only stores data for coordinates that have fact values, the equation needs to be adjusted to consider the partition fact count. Analysis Services assumes the data is of uniform distribution, and uses an algorithm to calculate the estimated aggregation cells for a specific aggregation. Analysis Services by default selects attributes from cube dimensions to be considered for aggregation. Analysis Services estimates the aggregation size and the benefit due to the aggregation for various combinations of attributes. Based on the aggregation disk size or percentage of optimization chosen by the user, Analysis Services stops iteration of calculating the optimized aggregation designs as soon as one of the criteria is met.

For query benefits, the lower the aggregation design, the more useful the aggregation, because all higher-level queries can benefit from the aggregation. However, the lower the aggregation design, the bigger the size of the aggregation data store and the longer the aggregation build time will be. It does not make sense to have aggregated cells with a size very close to the fact size; it won't save any disk scan time because the server will read almost the same amount of data from the disk. Therefore, building too many aggregations actually will not benefit query performance and sometimes might actually hurt it. Analysis Services, however, allows you to create aggregations up to 100 percent. As previously mentioned, we recommend you have aggregations where the estimated size is between 10 and 30 percent of the fact table size.

Creating Aggregations

Analysis Services allows you to specify the percentage of aggregation of the disk space to be used for creating aggregations. Analysis Services uses a complex algorithm to estimate the best aggregations based on the number of fact table and dimension members that will provide you with the maximum benefit. The following steps show how to design aggregations for the Adventure Works sample Internet Sales partitions:

1.   Open the Adventure Works DW 2008 sample project in BIDS.

2.   Open the Adventure Works cube and switch to the Aggregations tab.

3.   Right-click the Internet Sales measure group and select Design Aggregations as shown in Figure 14-19.

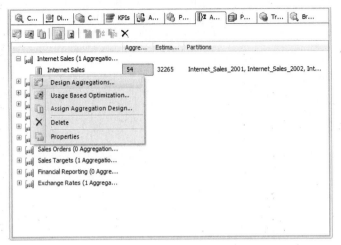

Figure 14-19

4. You will now be in the Aggregation Design Wizard as shown in Figure 14-20. Select the Internet_ Sales_2001 partition and click Next.

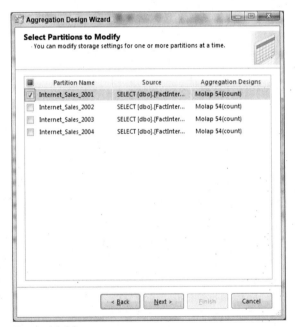

Figure 14-20

5. The Review Aggregation Usage page shown in Figure 14-21 allows you to control which attributes in each dimension should be considered for the aggregation design. Marking an attribute as Full means that all aggregations will include that attribute. Marking an attribute as None means that no aggregation will include that attribute. The setting of Unrestricted lets the server decide according to the heuristic-based algorithm. The setting of Default means that certain attributes default to None (such as attributes that do not participate in a user hierarchy), while others are Unrestricted.

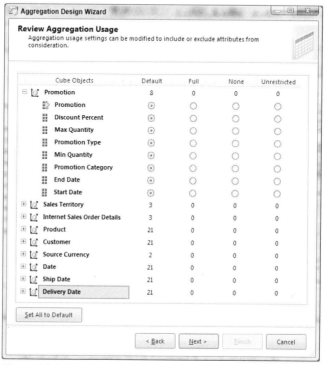

Figure 14-21

6. The Specify Object Counts page allows you to retrieve the count of dimension members relevant to the current partition and the count of fact table rows as shown in Figure 14-22. At the top of the grid is the fact table count; Estimated Count is the total number of fact table rows for all partitions in the current measure group. The Partition Count contains the count of fact table rows for the current partition. This page also allows you to override the values for the current partition. Click the Count button. Analysis Services retrieves the count of dimension members and the partition by sending queries to the relational database. Estimated Count is the count for the entire measure group and the Partition Count has the values for the current partition. If the values of the current partition will have different values in your production environment, you can enter the new counts in the Partition Count column. The count specified in the Object Counts page is used to calculate appropriate weights to design aggregations. Hence, make sure you provide the right counts. Otherwise you might end up with a suboptimal aggregation design.

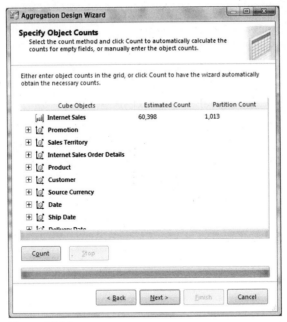

Figure 14-22

7. If you expand the Customer dimension, you will find that all the attributes being considered for aggregation design are shown along with the estimated count of members as shown in Figure 14-23. You should be aware that the attributes of the Customer dimension that are not considered for aggregation design are not shown in this wizard. For the Partition Count column, because the fact table only includes the granularity attribute (the customer key), that count is also available for Analysis Services to determine the aggregation design. You have the option to include or exclude attributes for consideration for aggregation design. By default, Analysis Services includes the key attributes for consideration during aggregation design. All the attributes that are levels of natural hierarchies are considered for aggregation design. If a user hierarchy is unnatural the topmost level is considered for aggregation design. The remaining levels of the unnatural hierarchy from the topmost level are included for consideration if there is a one-to-many relationship from that level to the next level. As soon as there is no relationship between successive levels, the remaining levels below that level of the unnatural hierarchy are not considered during aggregation design. Click the Next button.

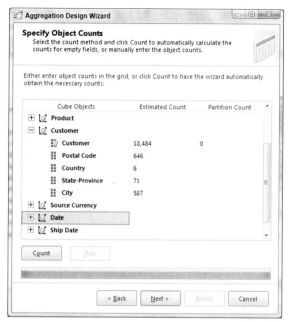

Figure 14-23

8. You are now in the Set Aggregation Options page, as shown in Figure 14-24. The engine gives you four possible options for how to design the aggregations:

❏ **Setting the storage limit for estimated aggregation data:** The system will look for the aggregation combinations whose total estimated size is within the user specified limit.

❏ **Performance gain setting:** You can choose a percentage of performance gain. The system will use the cost and performance gain algorithms to search for the best combinations that will fulfill the performance gain metric. The lower the percentage is, the fewer aggregations will be built and the fewer queries will be answered through pre-calculation. We recommend you begin with 30 percent aggregation performance gain for most cubes.

❏ **User click stop option:** The system will start to analyze the aggregation design and design aggregations. The server will stop searching for more aggregations when the user click-stops or the performance gain reaches 100 percent.

❏ **Do not design aggregations (0%):** The server will not design any aggregations for the current partition.

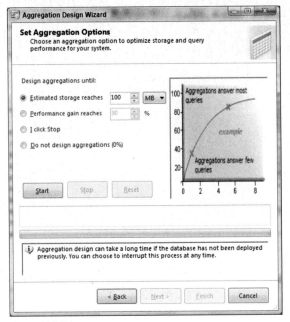

Figure 14-24

9. Choose the second option, Performance Gain Reaches, and set the number to 30 percent. Click the Start button to design the aggregation.

10. The server starts to analyze the aggregation design, and sends feedback on the aggregations being generated. The feedback is shown graphically in the Set Aggregation Options page as shown in Figure 14-25. The X-axis of the graph contains the amount of storage used and the Y-axis of the graph shows the percentage of performance gain. The status bar shows the number of aggregations that have been created during that time. Once the performance gain reaches the percentage you have specified (30%), the server stops designing further aggregations. You can see 27 aggregations have been created for 30 percent performance gain and the estimated storage is 30.6KB. Click the Next button.

11. In the final page of the aggregation wizard you have two choices to either deploy and process the partition or save the aggregation design and process later. Choose Save The Aggregations But Do Not Process Them and click the Finish button.

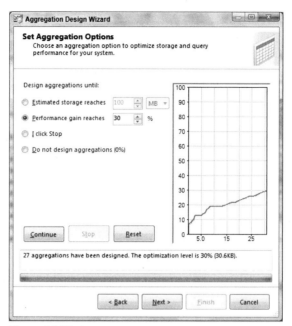

Figure 14-25

You have now successfully created aggregations for the partition Internet_Sales_2001 using the Aggregation Design Wizard. To find out what partition aggregations have been created for this partition, you can either deploy the project followed by scripting from SSMS or open the file Adventure Works.partitions in your current project's directory in an XML editor. If you look at the partition Internet_Sales_2001 you will find the following definition, which indicates that the partition has an aggregation design defined and the aggregation design used has the ID AggregationDesign:

```
<Partition>
 <ID>Internet_Sales_2001</ID>
 <Name>Internet_Sales_2001</Name>
 <CreatedTimestamp>0001-01-01T08:00:00Z</CreatedTimestamp>
 <LastSchemaUpdate>0001-01-01T08:00:00Z</LastSchemaUpdate>
 ........
 <EstimatedRows>1013</EstimatedRows>
 <AggregationDesignID>AggregationDesign</AggregationDesignID>
</Partition>
```

You can find the aggregation designed by the server in the AggregationDesign section for the measure group Internet Sales. Following is a section of the definition for the aggregation that has been designed. Each aggregation design can have one or more aggregations defined. The dimension section within Aggregations includes the estimated counts for dimension attributes. In the aggregation section, it lists the detailed aggregation design for each aggregation. The definitions for each aggregation contain the combination of the hierarchies that are to be included for aggregating the data. If a hierarchy has not been specified in the aggregation design, by default it is implied that the top-level member or the default member of that hierarchy is included.

```xml
    <AggregationDesigns>
     <AggregationDesign>
<ID>AggregationDesign</ID>
<Name>AggregationDesign</Name>
<CreatedTimestamp>2008-08-24T05:08:31Z</CreatedTimestamp>
<LastSchemaUpdate>2008-08-24T05:08:31Z</LastSchemaUpdate>

<EstimatedRows>1013</EstimatedRows>
<Dimensions>
......
 </Dimensions>

  <Aggregations>
          <Aggregation>
            <ID>Aggregation 0</ID>
            <Name>Aggregation 0</Name>
            <Dimensions>
              <Dimension>
                <CubeDimensionID>Dim Promotion</CubeDimensionID>
              </Dimension>
              <Dimension>
                <CubeDimensionID>Dim Sales Territory</CubeDimensionID>
              </Dimension>
              <Dimension>
                <CubeDimensionID>Internet Sales Order
                     Details</CubeDimensionID>
              </Dimension>
              <Dimension>
                <CubeDimensionID>Dim Product</CubeDimensionID>
                <Attributes>
                  <Attribute>
                    <AttributeID>Safety Stock Level</AttributeID>
                  </Attribute>
                </Attributes>
              </Dimension>
              <Dimension>
                <CubeDimensionID>Dim Customer</CubeDimensionID>
              </Dimension>
              <Dimension>
                <CubeDimensionID>Dim Currency</CubeDimensionID>
              </Dimension>
              <Dimension>
                <CubeDimensionID>Destination Currency</CubeDimensionID>
              </Dimension>
              <Dimension>
                <CubeDimensionID>Order Date Key - Dim Time</CubeDimensionID>
              </Dimension>
              <Dimension>
                <CubeDimensionID>Ship Date Key - Dim Time</CubeDimensionID>
              </Dimension>
              <Dimension>
                <CubeDimensionID>Due Date Key - Dim Time</CubeDimensionID>
              </Dimension>
              <Dimension>
```

```
                    <CubeDimensionID>Sales Reason</CubeDimensionID>
                </Dimension>
            </Dimensions>
        </Aggregation>
   ......
        </Aggregations>
    </AggregationDesigns>
</AggregationDesign>
```

Applying Aggregation Design

You have so far designed aggregations for a single partition. If all your partitions contain the same fact table data and characteristics in terms of dimension member distributions, you can design the same aggregations. You can select a group of partitions in the Business Intelligence Development Studio (BIDS) and then select Design Aggregations to design the same aggregation. Alternatively, Analysis Services 2008 allows you to apply an existing aggregation of a partition to other partitions in the same measure group. However, if you have some partitions that include fact records for an entire year and one partition holding current or last month's data, you may want to design separate aggregations to have the most optimal performance. To design the same aggregations for a group of partitions from BIDS, follow these steps:

1. Open the Adventure Works cube of the sample project in BIDS and switch to the Aggregations tab.

2. Right-click the Internet Sales measure group and choose Design Aggregations as shown in Figure 14-26 to bring up the design aggregation window.

3. Select all the partitions for which you want the same aggregation design to be applied in the Specify Partitions to Modify page. Go through the same steps to design aggregations for the first partition. The wizard will automatically copy the aggregation design to other partitions.

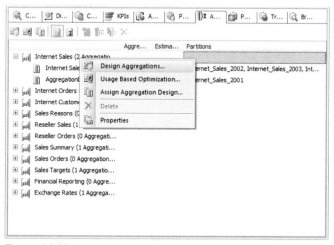

Figure 14-26

To assign an existing aggregation design to other partitions, perform the following steps:

4. Launch SSMS and connect to your Analysis Services instance.

5. Navigate to the Adventure Works cube in the Object Explorer.

6. In the Measure Groups folder, open the Internet Sales measure group, and open the Partitions folder.

7. Right-click the Internet_Sales_2001 partition, and select Assign Aggregation Design as shown in Figure 14-27.

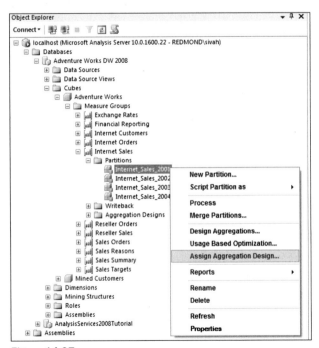

Figure 14-27

8. You will now see the Assign Aggregation Design Wizard. You can choose to assign any existing aggregation design to one or many partitions in this measure group. Select the partition for which you want to apply the same aggregation design as shown in Figure 14-28 and click OK.

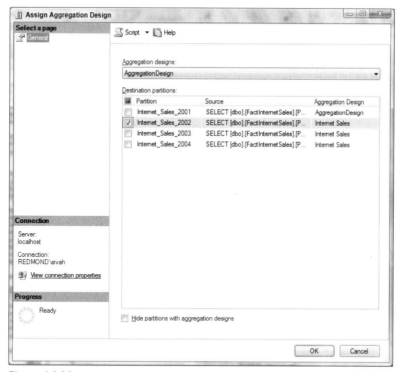

Figure 14-28

You can see each partition and which aggregation design (if any) is currently assigned to it. By selecting the available aggregation designs from the drop-down, you can assign a new aggregation design to one or more of the partitions. In this example we have shown how to apply aggregation design from SSMS. You can do the same steps outlined to applying aggregation design from the Aggregations tab of the Cube Designer in BIDS. You will need to process all the modified partitions using the ProcessIndexes option so that Analysis Services creates the aggregated data. You can later send a query that requests data for a specific level and analyze its performance. If aggregations have been built for the cells that have been requested, Analysis Services will serve the query from the aggregations. Based on the size of your cube and aggregations designed you can notice performance gain for queries touching the aggregations. Finally, you can use SQL Server Profiler to see if specific aggregations are getting hit (you see this in Chapter 15).

Usage-Based Aggregation Design

In addition to the Aggregation Design Wizard, Analysis Services supports aggregation design based on the user queries sent to Analysis Services. Designing aggregations based on user queries is called usage-based optimization because aggregations are designed based on users' requests and making sure performance gains are achieved for those specific queries. In order for Analysis Services to analyze the queries and design aggregations, the queries served by Analysis Services need to be logged at a specific location. Analysis Services provides a way to log the queries in a relational table with specific parameters. Because this aggregation design technique is dependent on the usage pattern, it is more likely that Analysis Services can create more useful aggregations to increase performance of future queries. To create the user-based aggregation design, you first need to enable Analysis Services to log the queries sent to the server. Follow these steps to enable query logging and design aggregations based on a set of queries:

1. Launch SSMS and connect to Analysis Services.

2. Right-click the Analysis Services instance connected and choose Properties. You will see the Analysis Server Properties window as shown in Figure 14-29.

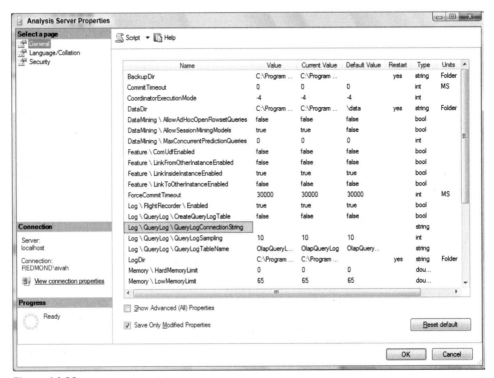

Figure 14-29

3. Set the Log\QueryLog\QueryLogConnectionString property so that it has a connection string pointing to a relational database where queries can be logged. To do so, click the ellipsis (...) to launch the connection string dialog.

4. You will see the Connection Manager dialog as shown in Figure 14-30, which you have used to specify data sources. Specify the connection details to your SQL Server that contains the sample relational database AdventureWorksDW2008. Click OK once you have specified the connection details.

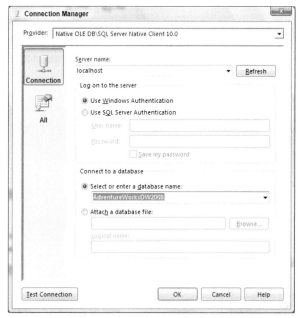

Figure 14-30

5. The connection string will be copied as the value for the server property Log\QueryLog\QueryLogConnectionString.

6. Define the server property Log\Query Log\QueryLogTableName with a table name OLAPQueryLog.

7. Make sure the server property Log\Query Log\CreateQueryLogTable is set to true so that the query log table can be created by Analysis Services.

8. By default, the server logs a query for every 10 queries executed. You can change Log\ QueryLog\QueryLogSampling. Change it to 1 to log every query into the query log table.

9. Click OK to save the server properties.

10. Restart Analysis Services so that the new properties are set for Analysis Services and the query log table can be created on the relational database.

11. Connect to SQL Server and open AdventureWorksDW; you will find that an OLAPQueryLog table has been created. The table definition is shown here:

```
CREATE TABLE [OlapQueryLog]
( [MSOLAP_Database]     nvarchar
  ( 255 )
  ,
  [MSOLAP_ObjectPath]     nvarchar
  ( 4000 )
  ,
  [MSOLAP_User]     nvarchar
  ( 255 )
  ,
```

```
[Dataset]     nvarchar
( 4000 )

,
[StartTime]    datetime    ,
[Duration]     bigint        )
```

12. In SQL Server Management Studio connect to your Analysis Services instance.

13. Right-click the Adventure Works cube and select Browse. Drag and drop measures into the data grid and drag and drop several dimensions. Perform some drill up and drill down to log some MDX queries into the query log.

14. Open a relational query window in SQL Server Management Studio and send the following query:

```
SELECT [MSOLAP_Database]
   , [MSOLAP_ObjectPath]
   , [MSOLAP_User]
   , [Dataset]
   , [StartTime]
   , [Duration]
FROM [AdventureWorksDW2008].[dbo].[OlapQueryLog]
```

You will find many records are logged in the OLAPQueryLog table. Analysis Services logs the username, time stamp, and the subcubes that are hit during the MDX query. The subcube definition is a sequence of 0s and 1s, which indicate which hierarchies are involved in the query.

15. In the Object Browser, right-click the Internet_Sales_2001 partition and choose Usage Based Optimization as shown in Figure 14-31.

16. You will see the Usage-Based Optimization Wizard. Click Next in the welcome screen. Choose Internet_Sales_2001 to modify aggregation settings as shown in Figure 14-32 and click Next.

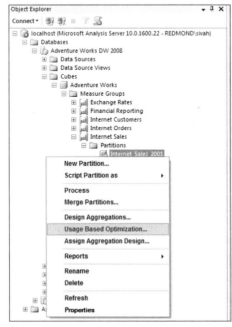

Figure 14-31

Chapter 14: Designing for Performance

Figure 14-32

17. In the Specify Query Criteria dialog, you can select the queries based on time, users, or frequency and request those queries to be used for aggregation design as shown in Figure 14-33. In addition to that, this dialog also provides statistics of the queries that have been logged. You can specify a beginning and ending date to get specific queries running in a certain time period, or choose specific queries for a particular user or users, or the user can choose the latest percentage of queries. We will select all the queries logged so far to design aggregations. Do not make any selection in the Specify Query Criteria dialog and click Next.

Figure 14-33

18. In the query list window (see Figure 14-34), Analysis Services provides information for all the queries requested by the users. Select all the queries and click Next.

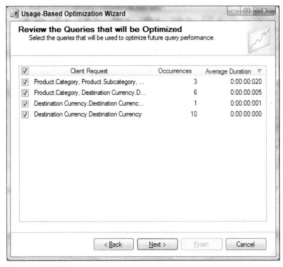

Figure 14-34

19. You will now see the Review Aggregation Usage dialog that you saw during aggregation design. Click Next.

20. In the Specify Object Counts dialog, you do not have to update object counts because you did this during aggregation design. Click the Next button to proceed to the Aggregations Options page.

21. In the set design aggregation options, choose 30 percent performance gain and click the Start button to request aggregations be designed based on the queries selected. At this moment, Analysis Services explores the various aggregations that would benefit in improving the performance gain for the selected queries. If a specific aggregation would benefit a specific query, that aggregation is allocated more weight so that that aggregation can be chosen from all possible aggregations. Analysis Services does a breadth-first search to explore the search space. Hence, if you have a cube that has a large dimensionality, sometimes you might explore aggregations at a very low level (closer to the key) due to the queries and performance optimization that you have chosen. We recommend you look at the aggregations that are getting created in the script and if you are really interested in a specific aggregation being created, you can specify a higher performance gain (>30%) that forces Analysis Services to expand the search space to deeper levels. Typically while designing aggregations based on query usage using the UBO, we recommend specifying 70–80 percent performance gain. Click the Next button after the aggregations have been designed.

22. In the Completing the Wizard dialog you can either create a new aggregation design or merge the created aggregations within existing aggregation designs. Select the option to create a new aggregation design and select the Process partitions immediately checkbox as shown in Figure 14-35 and click Finish. The new aggregations will be created and applied to the Internet_Sales_2001 partition.

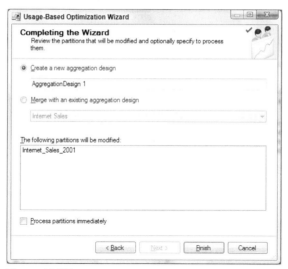

Figure 14-35

If you have existing aggregations at the start of design usage-based aggregation, Analysis Services doesn't take that existing aggregation design into consideration. You can design custom aggregations using the Aggregation Design tab (new in Analysis Services 2008) to visualize, create, and manage aggregation designs. This new user interface is explained later in this chapter in the "Managing Aggregation Designs" section. Alternatively you can design your own aggregations using a custom AMO program.

Aggregation Design Options

So far you have learned to design aggregations using the Aggregation Design Wizard and the Usage-Based Optimization Wizard. In both wizards you have seen that some of the dimension attributes are being considered by Analysis Services for aggregations and some are not. The Aggregation Design Wizard considers certain attributes when designing aggregations based on the design of the attributes (as part of natural hierarchies), as well as the properties of the dimensions and cube dimensions. In addition to that, the user can give hints to tell the aggregation designer to consider, include, or exclude hierarchies while designing aggregations.

Designing Efficient Aggregations Using Hints

The aggregation design algorithm uses the partition fact data count and dimension-level member count to estimate the cost of aggregation design. Having an accurate fact data count and dimension-level member count is crucial for Analysis Services to find the aggregation designs that would yield the best performance. The fact table row count and level member count are metrics that are counted once at design time, stored in the Analysis Services metadata, and never changed afterwards. Therefore, it is important for the user to update the member counts and fact table counts for changing dimensions, and increasing rows in fact tables. You can click the Count button in the Specify Object Counts window to get the newest counts for various objects.

Typically, partitions contain only a specific slice of the fact data. The member count for dimension attributes and the partition are by default the same. In the Aggregation Design Wizard it is a good practice for you to provide Analysis Services with the hint of accurate member count in the Partition

Count column. In the Adventure Works DW 2008 sample, partitions contain data for each year, so we recommend entering a value of 1 in the Fiscal Year column as shown in Figure 14-36. This helps Analysis Services use the value 1 instead of 4 (which is the total number of years that contain partition data) to calculate the cost of the aggregation while including the Fiscal Year attribute.

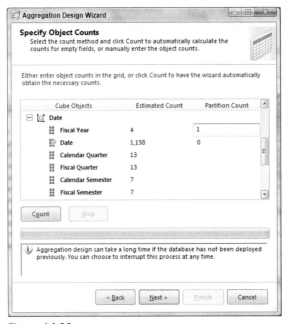

Figure 14-36

Relationships between Attributes

All the attributes within a dimension are related to the key attribute because there is a one-to-many relationship. When you establish a relationship between two attributes within a dimension, you can specify the type of relationship between these attributes. Two types of relationships are allowed in Analysis Services 2008, Rigid and Flexible, and they refer to the dimension attribute relationship changeability. Rigid relationships mean that there will be no change in the data value for this relationship. For example, if you have the relationship between City and State set to be rigid, it indicates that a specific city will always belong to only one state and the initial value will never change over time. Flexible relationships, however, mean that the values of the relationship can change over time. By default all the relationships between the attributes and the key attributes of the dimension are flexible. The relationship type determines how Analysis Services treats partition aggregation data when you choose to perform an incremental process of the partition. Assume a relationship between two attributes has been specified as rigid and the value changes for the attribute nonetheless. When an incremental process of the dimension is initiated, Analysis Services will present an error that the data has changed for an attribute whose relationship has been specified as rigid.

You can set the relationship type between attributes in BIDS by doing the following:

1. Open the sample Adventure Works DW 2008 Analysis Services project.

2. Open the Customer dimension by double-clicking that dimension in Solution Explorer.

3. In the Attribute Relationships pane, click one of the relationships to the key attribute Customer such as Phone.

4. Look at the Properties window for the Customer-Phone relationship and you will see a Relationship Type property as shown in Figure 14-37, which has the values Flexible and Rigid.

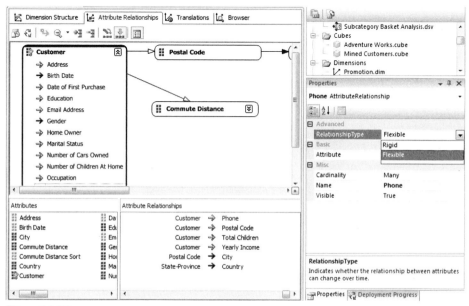

Figure 14-37

5. Click the relationship between the Country attribute and the State-Province attribute as shown in Figure 14-38. In the Properties window you will find that its relationship type is set as Rigid because a state's country won't change over time. On the other hand, click the customer address relationship and you will see it is set to Flexible because a customer's address can change over time.

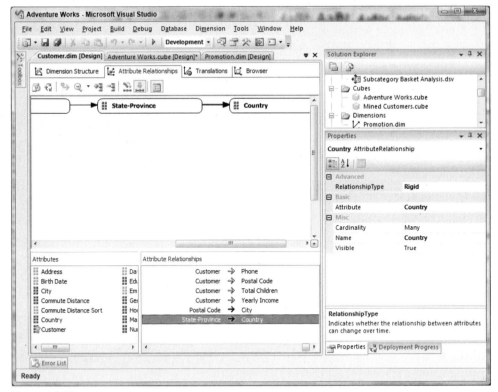

Figure 14-38

The aggregation design algorithm bases the aggregation being designed on the type of relationships between the attributes it's using, allowing you to classify aggregations as rigid or flexible. Rigid aggregations are aggregations that include attributes that have a rigid relationship with the granularity attribute. Attributes from the remaining dimensions either need to be the All level or the lowest level. The aggregation created in the previous section that included Customer.Country, and all other dimensions where the other dimensions included the top level, is an example of rigid aggregation. Flexible aggregations are aggregations that are built on one or more attributes with a flexible relationship with the granularity attribute. An example of a flexible aggregation is an aggregation that uses the Customer.Address attribute.

Rigid aggregations are updated when partitions are incrementally processed. If attributes that are part of rigid aggregations are incrementally processed, existing aggregations are not dropped. Analysis Services will keep the old aggregation data as such and create a temporary aggregation store for the newly coming data. Finally, Analysis Services merges the temporary aggregation store with the old aggregation data within a transaction. Old aggregation will still be available for query access when aggregations are being processed. The aggregated data only gets rebuilt when the user chooses to do ProcessFull on the partition or cube.

Flexible aggregations are fully rebuilt whenever a cube and partition is incrementally processed. When attributes that are part of a flexible aggregation are incrementally processed, Analysis Services drops all the flexible aggregations, because the old aggregation data is not valid anymore due to dimension member changes. After dropping the flexible aggregations, Analysis Services recalculates those dropped aggregations. If you choose the option to create aggregations lazily (ProcessingMode property of a dimension), flexible aggregations are re-calculated as a background task. Users will still be able to query without aggregations; however, you might see that the queries are slow. Once the aggregations are rebuilt, future queries will be fast.

Properties Controlling Attributes and Aggregation Design

In addition to the dimension member count and partition member count, Analysis Services allows you to fine-tune the aggregation design via a property called AllMemberAggregationUsage for cube dimensions and an AggregationUsage property for CubeDimensionAttributes. Various values of these properties hint the Aggregation Design Wizard to consider and include the attribute or dimension while designing aggregations. The following steps show you how to set the various values for these properties in BIDS:

1. Open the Adventure Works DW 2008 Analysis Services sample project.

2. Open the Adventure Works cube.

3. Click the cube dimension Customer in the Cube Designer. You can see the associated properties in the Properties pane, as shown in Figure 14-39.

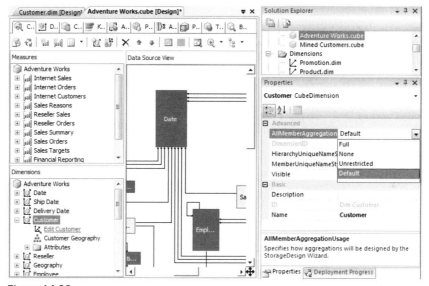

Figure 14-39

4. You will see the property AllMemberAggregationUsage. This property enables you to either include or exclude the "All Member" of the dimension while creating aggregations. Based on the value set for this property, the Aggregation Design Wizard will consider this dimension while performing the design task. There are four choices for the AllMemberAggregationUsage property:

❏ **Full:** Always include the All member while creating aggregations.

❏ **None:** Never include the All member while creating aggregations.

❑ **Unrestricted:** Let Analysis Services consider the dimension during aggregation design, and it can choose to build or not build aggregation for all members of the dimension.

❑ **Default:** Same as unrestricted.

If most of your users query the All member of this dimension, we recommend that you change the AllMemberAggregationUsage property to Full. This ensures that aggregations include the All member and that your user queries hit and benefit from the aggregations. If most of your users query this dimension at the detail level, we recommend you set it to None to avoid aggregation at the All level. If you are not sure about the All member usage, then leave it to Default (which also means Unrestricted). There is no need to create aggregations at the All level because most of the queries will not hit the aggregation.

Set AllMemberAggregationUsagePropoerty to Full or None if the user uses All aggregation or if the user uses detail.

5. Leave the setting for the customer dimension as Default, and expand the cube dimension Customer. Under the Attributes folder click the Country attribute as shown in Figure 14-40.

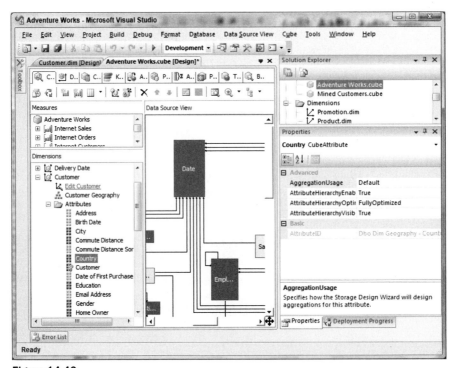

Figure 14-40

6. Click any of the cube dimension attributes. If you look at the Properties window, you will see the property AggregationUsage as shown in Figure 14-40. Similar to AllMemberAggregationUsage, the AggregationUsage property also has four possible values. They are Full, None, Unrestricted, and Default. These properties once again instruct the aggregation design algorithm to appropriately include or exclude a dimension attribute while designing aggregations. The meanings of the values are as follows:

❏ **Full:** Always include this attribute in any of the aggregation designs being considered while designing aggregations.

❏ **None:** Never include this attribute in any of the aggregation designs being considered while designing aggregations.

❏ **Unrestricted:** Analysis Services might consider this attribute during aggregation design as any other attribute.

❏ **Default:** Same as unrestricted.

If most of your users query the data by customer country, you can change the country attribute's AggregationUsage to Full. However, if you know your users rarely break down numbers for one attribute, you can turn it off by setting the property to None. You need to analyze your user's MDX queries using SQL Server Profiler and then set the appropriate values for these properties for various dimensions and attributes. If you have made an incorrect setting to the aggregation usage property and see that some queries for which you wanted aggregations to be created are not getting created, you need to review and update the properties and then run aggregation design or usage-based optimizations.

Yes, query performance can be improved by designing aggregations and fine-tuning. However, your users might be generating MDX queries that are not optimal. Next you see a few ways to optimize MDX queries.

Managing Aggregation Designs

The development environment in Analysis Services 2008 has added a new tab to the cube editor called Aggregations. This new viewer/editor allows you to better understand the aggregation designs in your cube and helps you to modify and apply them to partitions in a very powerful way.

Look at an example with Adventure Works DW. In Figure 14-41, you can see the Aggregations design tab, which shows a list of all the measure groups and a high-level summary of the aggregation designs that apply to each measure group. For example, you can see that the partition Internet Sales has two aggregation designs (called Internet Sales and AggregationDesign), which have 54 and 28 aggregations, respectively. The estimated partition size for the Internet_Sales_2001 partition is 1013 records. You can also see that the estimated partition size for the aggregation Internet Sales is 32265, which covers all the four partitions.

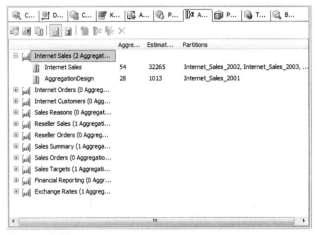

Figure 14-41

The other partitions shown under the AggregationDesign section have other aggregation designs assigned to them.

A common problem with Analysis Services 2005 was that old aggregation design objects remained in the UDM but ended up being unused and inaccessible. Old aggregation designs can now be deleted in this viewer or they can be revived by easily assigning aggregation designs to partitions via the Assign Aggregation Design button.

There are also convenient toolbar options for designing new aggregations using the Aggregation Design Wizard as well as the Usage-Based Aggregation Design Wizard.

One of the great features of this tab is visible when you switch to the Advanced view. In this view, you can select a measure group and aggregation and examine exactly which properties have granularity defined in each aggregation. Figure 14-42 shows what this looks like.

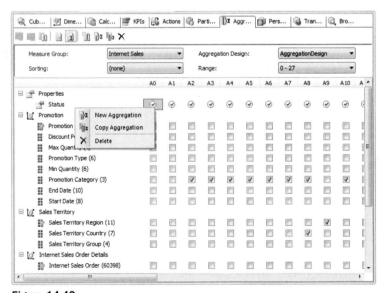

Figure 14-42

As you can see in the figure, each aggregation in the design shows up across the top (titled A0, A1, A2, and so on), and for each aggregation you can examine which dimension attributes have granularity by examining the checkboxes in the grid. This view lets you understand what your aggregation design looks like, and at the same time it lets you modify it by checking and unchecking the intersection of attribute and aggregation.

This view also lets you manually customize an aggregation design by adding and deleting aggregations. By right-clicking the Status for an aggregation, you can delete it or copy it to a new aggregation or just create an empty aggregation, which you can then customize as needed.

The new aggregation design viewer/editor is a very powerful tool. It provides a much greater understanding of the aggregations that have been designed, and it lets you customize them based on your knowledge of long-term query patterns and your partitioning strategy.

Scalability Optimizations

Scalability with respect to Analysis Services indicates how well Analysis Services handles parameter value increases for dimension sizes, number of dimensions, size of the cube, number of databases, and number of concurrent users — all of which affect server behavior. Analysis Services provides several scalability parameters, such as handling a large number of partitions or a dimension with a large number of members (>5 million). In this section you learn about optimizations relevant specifically to scalability of Analysis Services.

For Analysis Services 2008 you can control the number of queries executed concurrently with the advanced configuration property ThreadPool\Query\MaxThreads. The default value 10 works well for most scenarios, but on a machine with many processors it should be increased, or for scenarios combining short-running queries with long-running queries there may be benefits from decreasing the value.

Configuring Server Configuration Properties

Several configuration properties are provided by Analysis Services with which to fine-tune the server. The default values for these properties have been set for the most common scenarios. However, for specific requirements you might have to change these settings to achieve the best performance from Analysis Services. In general, Microsoft recommends you change configuration settings only when working with Microsoft product support. Documentation of all the supported server configuration properties has been released by Microsoft and can be found at Microsoft's TechNet at http://go.microsoft.com/fwlink/?LinkId=81895. Here we provide information on some of the configuration properties:

❑ **Memory\Total Memory Limit:** The value for this property is between 0 and 100 because it is a percentage of the available memory. On a 4GB memory machine if you have not enabled the /3GB switch the msmdsrv.exe process will have a maximum of 2GB available.

❑ **Memory\Low Memory Limit:** Analysis Services contains a cleaner thread, which reclaims memory from jobs that are idle or have lower priority. The cleaner thread constantly wakes up and reclaims memory based on the Low Memory Limit. The default value is 65 percent. As soon as the low memory limit crosses the 65 percent threshold, the cleaner thread requests existing jobs to shrink memory and starts to reclaim the memory. In certain instances while processing multiple partitions in parallel the cleaner thread might not be fast enough to wake up and reclaim memory. Due to this existing processing, jobs could fail. By lowering the Low Memory Limit you can make sure the cleaner thread starts to reclaim memory earlier and hence all the processing jobs will complete.

❑ **CoordinatorExecutionMode:** This property is used for parallelism of jobs and takes a negative or positive value. The value indicates the number of coordinator jobs that can be in parallel at a given point in time. If the value is negative, the number is multiplied by the number of processors on the machines. Having a high value can deteriorate performance because multiple threads are competing for resources. The default value is –4.

❑ **ThreadPool\Query:** This node contains several properties such as minimum and maximum number of threads to be allocated for a query and the priority for these threads. The MinThreads property indicates the minimum number of threads that will stay available for query execution and the MaxThreads property indicates the maximum number of threads that may be available to execute a query. This thread pool sometimes also executes other tasks that may be long-running (for example, Proactive Caching), and you may therefore find it necessary to increase this limit for a greater concurrency of queries.

❑ **ThreadPool\Processing:** Similar to ThreadPool\Query this node contains the same sub-properties. However, the properties are applicable for each processing operation as well as threads that are performing scans of storage engine data.

❑ **Query\DefaultDrillthroughMaxRows:** While performing drill-through on a specific cell the number of resulting rows can be quite large. This impacts the performance of drill-through. Most often users might look for a top 100 rows. While defining drill-through you can specify the number of rows to be returned. However, if that option is not specified in the drill-through statement, the value specified for this property is used to restrict the number of rows returned.

Scaling Out

If your cube contains a large number of partitions (thousands of partitions), queries retrieving data from all the partitions might be slow. This is because Analysis Services needs to read the data from all the partitions and then needs to aggregate the data. For efficient data reads you need to have high-speed disks optimized for reads. Keep in mind that the aggregation of the data from various partitions is a CPU-intensive operation; you can certainly increase the number of processors on the machine to reduce latency. Another alternative provided by Analysis Services is to make the partitions remote so that multiple Analysis Services are involved in reading data from various partitions. This scale out solution helps in distributing the read and data aggregation on multiple Analysis Services and thereby reduces the overall query time. You do have the master Analysis Services, which still needs to gather the data from various slave machines and then aggregate the final data to the end user. We recommend you perform cost benefit analysis where you calculate the total costs of all the Analysis Services machines and the benefit you would be getting from it — all before implementing a solution using remote partitions.

One of the new features in Analysis Services 2008 is the ability to attach and detach a Read-Only database. This lets you have several servers that share a common SAN (Storage Attached Network). The SAN hosts a read-only database that is attached to all the servers. A standard Windows Network Load Balancing (NLB) solution will then allow you to scale-out active users over the different servers. The advantage of this solution is that the data is maintained just once on the SAN, and a good SAN will provide good I/O performance that justifies having multiple servers sharing it as a resource. However, when the read-only database needs to be updated, the servers will have to be drained of their users before the database is detached, refreshed, and then attached again by the servers. You learn more about the read-only database and scale out strategy in terms of improving query performance in Chapter 15.

This type of solution can also be applied without using the Read-Only feature. However, it would require the databases to be distributed and managed manually.

Scaling Up

For large databases where the queries are data intensive or the load on the system is quite heavy with several users, you need to consider adding additional CPUs. Typically, commodity machines for servers are four processors. Based on your system load, consider increasing the number of processors. Your system might be bottlenecked by memory as well. Assuming you have a system with 4GB (maximum on a 32-bit machine), by default each process can access up to 2GB of memory. We recommend you change the boot.ini file to enable the /3GB option so that Analysis Services can utilize maximum memory on the system. If your database is large (dimensions having greater than 10 million members) and the user load on your system high, consider moving to a 64-bit system and adding additional processors and memory.

Handling Large Dimensions

Certain Analysis Services databases can contain very large dimensions. Analysis Services 2008 handles loading very large dimensions by loading parts of dimensions that are requested. For MOLAP dimensions you might reach the theoretical maximum of 32-bit systems. Based on our experience of working with certain customers with very large dimensions, we have identified that you might reach the 32-bit system limit if you have dimensions containing memory in the range of around 10 to 15 million members along with several hundred attributes in the dimensions. Typically, when you have customer or product dimensions along with various properties of the customer, you can encounter processing issues due to unavailability of system resources. You can certainly tweak certain server configuration properties to get the maximum from Analysis Services. However, we recommend you move to 64-bit systems if you have dimensions having more than 10 million members. Another suggestion is to have very large dimensions as ROLAP dimensions. Consider the alternatives mentioned in this section while handling large dimensions.

Summary

After reading this chapter, on hearing the very word *performance*, your head should swell with visions of highly performing, scalable systems, each optimized to fulfill its designated mission — never again will this word simply evoke images of entertainment provided by a theatrical group! To build a system that scales up and performs well, you have to consider high- and low-level issues. At the high level, aggregation design forms the foundation for an optimally performing OLAP system; take the time to analyze the requirements of the application to get this step right. Another high-level consideration is the type of storage you choose for your system, be it MOLAP, HOLAP, or ROLAP. At lower levels there are many ways to optimize design, like avoiding the use of unnecessary attributes that are never used in customer queries. They can waste precious system data storage and slow down both processing performance and query performance. You learned other lower-level issues, about natural and unnatural hierarchies, and about how you should specify one-to-many relationships whenever possible for better query performance and reduced system data space requirements. You even dove down deep into tuning the Analysis Services instance by changing certain server properties. Finally, you learned how aggregations can be created and how they help to achieve better query performance. We are confident you will exploit all the best practices provided in this chapter and design you OLAP databases optimally based on your business needs. In the next chapter you learn how an MDX query gets executed within the Analysis Services and how to analyze bottlenecks and optimize your MDX queries to achieve better query performance.

15

Analyzing and Optimizing Query Performance

The power of Analysis Services lies in its ability to provide fast query response time for decision makers who need to analyze data, draw conclusions, and make appropriate changes in their business. The OLAP Report defines OLAP as Fast Analysis of Shared Multidimensional Information (http://www.olapreport.com/fasmi.htm). The word "fast" in this context means that the system is able to deliver results to users in less than 5 seconds (with a few highly complex queries taking more than 20 seconds). We also expect that most business decision makers will use client tools that graphically represent the data from Analysis Services for easy interpretation and understanding. As an end user, you expect to see the data quickly in order to analyze and make decisions. Some common operations that OLAP client tools offer are drill down, drill up, and compare data year over year. Users do not have time to wait for hours to get a response. Hence, queries sent to Analysis Services need to return data within seconds, at most in minutes. Query performance is pivotal to a successful Business Intelligence project deployment. A system that has very good performance will bring great business value to your company. However, you should be aware there can be queries to Analysis Services that can take more than a few minutes. Typically such queries are issued via overnight reporting systems.

Analysis Services supports three storage modes: MOLAP, ROLAP, and HOLAP. You will usually obtain the best performance when your UDM storage mode is MOLAP. When you choose MOLAP storage, Analysis Services 2008 will store the dimension data and fact data in its own efficient, compact multidimensional structure format. Fact data is compressed and its size is approximately 10 to 30 percent of the size as when stored in a relational database. In addition to its own efficient and compact data store, Analysis Services builds specialized dimension attribute indices for efficient data retrieval. The data is stored specifically in a multidimensional structure to best serve MDX query needs. If you use the ROLAP or HOLAP storage modes, queries to Analysis Services might have to fetch data from the relational data source at query time. Retrieving data from the relational data sources will significantly slow your query performance because you incur relational query processing time, the time needed to fetch the data over the network, and finally the time it takes to aggregate the data within Analysis Services.

Analysis Services 2008 tries to achieve the best of the OLAP and relational worlds. OLAP queries typically request aggregated data. For example, you may store daily sales information for products. Typical OLAP queries will request aggregated sales by month, quarter, or year. In such circumstances, every day's sales data needs to be aggregated for the period requested by the query, for example the entire year. If users are requesting aggregated data on a single dimension, you will be able to do a simple sum in the relational database. However, OLAP queries are typically multidimensional and need aggregated data across multiple dimensions with complex business logic calculations applied to each dimension. To improve query performance, Analysis Services allows you to specify aggregations, which you learned about in Chapter 14. In addition to aggregations, you learned several design techniques in that chapter to optimize your UDM to get the best performance from your Analysis Services database. Having done your best UDM design to satisfy your business needs, you might still encounter performance issues at query time. In this chapter you learn about the various components of Analysis Services that work together to execute MDX queries. You also learn how to analyze Analysis Services query performance issues as well as techniques and best practices for improving query performance.

The Calculation Model

Before we start looking at the overall Analysis Services query execution architecture, let's recap what you learned about the calculation model of Analysis Services in previous chapters of this book. When using the MOLAP storage mode, the data that comprises the cube is retrieved from a relational database and stored in SSAS's proprietary format. The data will be aggregated by the SSAS engine based on the MDX query. SSAS provides a way to pre-calculate aggregated data. This helps speed the retrieval of query results for MDX queries that can be satisfied with these pre-calculated aggregations. Most of the calculations that apply specific business logic in the UDM are written in MDX scripts, objects within your Analysis Services 2008 database that provide a procedural way to define calculations. SSAS features such as unary operators and custom rollups also help in defining MDX calculations needed within your UDM. The cube editor in Business Intelligence Development Studio provides a way to debug the calculations defined in your MDX scripts. However, there is complex calculation logic within the SSAS engine that defines how the calculations are applied to a specific cell. Each cell within the cube is either a value from your relational database or a calculation, as illustrated in Figure 15-1.

	All	WA	Seattle	Redmond	CA	Los Angeles	San Francisco	San Diego
All	1237	475	176	299	762	148	149	465
Q1	367	110	44	66	257	53	32	172
Jan	148	55	12	43	93	10	-	83
Feb	164	32	32	-	132	25	32	75
Mar	55	23	-	23	32	18	-	14
Q2	360	17	65	113	182	28	65	89
Apr	55	23	23	-	32	9	23	-
May	135	73	19	54	62	19	19	24
Jun	170	82	23	59	88	-	23	65
Q3	235	122	11	111	113	11	17	85
Jul	24	12	-	12	12	-	-	12
Aug	42	34	-	34	8	-	-	8
Sep	169	76	11	65	93	11	17	65
Q4	275	65	56	9	210	56	35	119
Oct	133	24	21	3	109	21	-	88
Nov	100	23	23	-	77	23	23	31
Dec	42	18	12	6	24	12	12	-

Figure 15-1

Figure 15-1 shows cells with sales corresponding to various months in the year and cities in the states of Washington and California. The members of the axes and the cell values that are calculated from the relational backend are shown in one color. You can see that some cells have a dash (–), indicating that no value was available for that specific cell from the relational backend. The remaining cells contain aggregated data and are shown in a darker color. For example, cells corresponding to Seattle and the months April, May, and June were all retrieved from the relational backend table. However, the cell value for the Q2 quarter and Seattle is aggregated from the sales for Seattle for the months of April, May, and June.

You can have several MDX calculations defined for a specific cell. The value for a cell that contains multiple MDX calculations is the value of the last calculation that gets applied to the cell. Several types of calculations can be defined in your MDX scripts: calculated members, named sets, unary operators, custom rollups, assignments, and calculations in sessions or queries. You have learned about all these types of calculations in Chapters 3 through 10. The remainder of this section offers a quick review of calculations in Analysis Services before we look at the details of the MDX query execution architecture.

MDX Script

There are multiple ways calculations can be defined in Analysis Services 2008. Most are defined using the MDX Script, which is a centralized calculation store for the cube. Dimension calculations such as unary operators and custom rollups are a part of the dimension and can be defined using attribute properties. You can define these calculations via MDX script but we highly recommend using the support for defining them via dimension attribute properties to achieve better performance. Each cube in Analysis Services 2008 contains a single MDX Script. Business Intelligence Development Studio (BIDS) exposes the MDX Script object to editing and debugging via the Calculations tab (shown in Figure 15-2), as you learned in Chapters 6 and 9. MDX Script provides a procedural execution model and easier debugging of calculations, as seen in Chapter 6. The commands in the script are executed in the order they have been defined. You learned about the Pass Value (also called Pass Order) in Chapter 10, which refers to stages of calculations applied to the cube when there are multiple calculations such as custom rollup, unary operators, and assignment statements that are applied to the cells of a cube. In Analysis Services 2008, a new Pass Value is created for each MDX calculation defined in the MDX Script to avoid infinite recursion. The creation of a new PASS Value for each cell calculation also eliminates the need for Solve Order. (Solve Order is used to help in determining the order of calculations within a single Pass in SQL Server Analysis Services 2000, which is deprecated from SSAS 2005.)

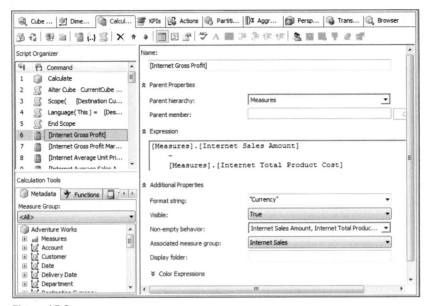

Figure 15-2

The single view of the calculations via the MDX Script simplifies the maintenance of your MDX calculations as well as debugging. As part of your UDM development, you can use source code control and check in various versions of your Analysis Services project. This helps you track the history of changes to your project and also aids in maintenance. Because the calculations are part of the Analysis Services project, you automatically get version control of the calculation changes.

We recommend you periodically check in the changes made to your Analysis Services project similar to what you would do for a C# or a C++ project.

The first and foremost command in an MDX script is the CALCULATE command. The CALCULATE command populates each cell in the cube along with aggregated data from the fact level data (also called leaf level data). Without the CALCULATE command the cube will only contain the fact level data. The syntax of the CALCULATE command is

```
CALCULATE   [<subcube>];
```

If the <subcube> argument is not specified, the current cube is used. The CALCULATE command is automatically added by the Cube Wizard when you create a cube in Business Intelligence Development Studio. BIDS typically adds the CALCULATE statement at the beginning of the MDX Script, resulting in the default aggregation behavior for the measures, which you see in previous versions of SQL Server Analysis Services. When Analysis Services evaluates the cells, it first loads the fact data into the cube's cell values. Then it does the default aggregation of the non-leaf cell values. Finally, the MDX calculations as defined by the Analysis Services rules are applied to determine the final values of the cells in the cube. The assignment calculations in the MDX Script are evaluated using the Pass Value, which gets incremented for each MDX Script assignment. Note that the CALCULATE statement does not have any effect on calculated members defined in the MDX Script.

Scope and Assignments

Analysis Services 2008 supports multiple ways to define cell calculations. Each cell can have one or more calculations defined for it. Unary operators, custom rollups, and Assignments are three ways you can define cell calculations while designing a cube. In addition, you can define calculations as part of sessions (session calculations) or queries (query calculations). Unary operators and custom rollups are defined as part of dimension creation using the dimensions' attribute properties, and Assignments are statements that define cell calculations and are defined in the MDX Script.

Assignments are typically enclosed within a Scope statement, which helps define calculations on a subcube. Following is the syntax for the Scope and Assignment statement (=) that you learned about in Chapter 10. You can have one or more assignments within each Scope statement. In addition, you can have nested scopes. Scopes by default inherit the parent scope, however you can override this. For example, you can have a parent scope of `Customers.USA`, which will scope to all customers in the country USA. You can have a nested scope of `Customers.Canada`, which will override the parent and change the scope to customers in Canada.

```
Scope(<subcube>);
    <subcube1 definition> = expression; [Example: this = 1000;]
    …
End Scope;
```

Analysis Services restricts the cube space as defined by the Scope statement. Then the assignment statement is evaluated for all the cells within the specified subcube1 definition. The term `this` is a special keyword that denotes the assignment to be evaluated on the default measure of the subcube defined within the Scope statement. You can have multiple assignment statements that overwrite a specific cell within the same Scope statement.

Dimension Attribute Calculations

You learned about the Custom Rollup and Unary Operators features in Analysis Services 2008 in Chapter 8. These features help define how to aggregate data to parent members or other members in the hierarchy. Analysis Services uses special rules while aggregating data when performing cell calculations in MDX scripts. In general, you can assume that the last cell calculation is the one that will be the final cell value. This behavior is referred to as "Latest Wins." In addition, there are instances where a calculation called as the closest calculation for the cell being aggregated will be the final value; this is called "Closest Wins." Richard Tkachuk, Program Manager from Microsoft, has written a white paper, "Introduction to MDX Scripting in Microsoft SQL Server 2005," that demonstrates examples of Latest Wins and Closest Wins (http://msdn.microsoft.com/en-us/library/ms345116.asp).

Session and Query Calculations

As you learned in Chapter 10, Analysis Services allows you to specify cell calculations in session, query, or global scopes. Following are the examples from Chapter 10 that show how a cell calculation is defined at query, session, or global scopes, respectively:

```
WITH CELL CALCULATION [SalesQuota2005]
FOR '( [Date].[Fiscal Year].&[2005],
    [Date].[Fiscal].[Month].MEMBERS,
    [Measures].[Sales Amount Quota] )'
AS '( PARALLELPERIOD( [Date].[Fiscal].[Fiscal Year], 1,
    [Date].[Fiscal].CurrentMember), [Measures].[Sales Amount] ) * 2'
SELECT { [Measures].[Sales Amount Quota],
```

(continued)

(continued)

```
        [Measures].[Sales Amount] } ON COLUMNS,
DESCENDANTS( { [Date].[Fiscal].[Fiscal Year].&[2004],
      [Date].[Fiscal].[Fiscal Year].&[2005] }, 3, SELF ) ON ROWS
FROM [Adventure Works]
```

```
CREATE CELL CALCULATION [Adventure Works].[SalesQuota2005]
FOR '([Date].[Fiscal].[Month].MEMBERS,[Measures].[Sales Amount Quota]
      )'
AS '(PARALLELPERIOD ( [Date].[Fiscal].[Fiscal Year],
1,[Date].[Fiscal].CurrentMember),[Measures].[Sales Amount])*2 ',
CONDITION = '[Date].[Fiscal Year].CurrentMember IS
[Date].[Fiscal Year].&[2005]'
```

```
SCOPE([Date].[Fiscal Year].&[2005],
      [Date].[Fiscal].[Month].MEMBERS,
      [Measures].[Sales Amount Quota]);

      THIS = (ParallelPeriod( [Date].[Fiscal].[Fiscal Year],
            1,[Date].[Fiscal].CurrentMember),[Measures].[Sales Amount])*2;

END SCOPE;
```

Having calculations at appropriate scopes is based on the requirements of your cube and the client tools used to interact with the cube. Analysis Services 2008 has specific optimizations that cache the results of calculations at each scope. When a query is being evaluated, Analysis Services 2008 first tries to retrieve the results from query scope. If this is not possible, it looks at session scope and finally at global scope. This is a specific optimization implemented in Analysis Services to help improve query performance, however some calculations may not be cached (such as calculations that include locale-related information).

Having reviewed the calculation model of Analysis Services, let's now look at the architecture and the steps involved when executing an MDX query.

Query Execution Architecture

Microsoft SQL Server Analysis Services 2008 consists of server and tools components that enable you to create databases and manage them. The server components are a set of binaries that comprise the Analysis Services service. BIDS, SQL Server Management Studio (SSMS), Profiler, and a few additional binaries constitute the tools components. The multidimensional databases are stored on the server, which is also referred to as the SSAS engine. SSAS clients communicate to the SSAS engine via XML for Analysis, a standardized application programming interface for online analytical processing (OLAP). The XMLA API has two main methods, Discover and Execute. Discover allows callers to request metadata and data from the databases. Execute lets callers send commands such as Create, Alter, and Process, which are used for creating/updating the multidimensional database or MultiDimensional Expressions (MDX) queries. MDX query results can be retrieved in multidimensional or tabular format by the client. The Create, Alter, Delete, and Process statements are part of the Data Definition Language (DDL). SSAS provides a set of object models that abstract XMLA and make it easy for developers to build applications that can communicate with the SSAS engine.

Analysis Services Engine Components

Figure 15-3 shows the Analysis Services query execution architecture. Five major components constitute the Analysis Services server: Infrastructure, Data Mining, Metadata Manager, Storage Engine, and Formula Engine. These are detailed in the following list.

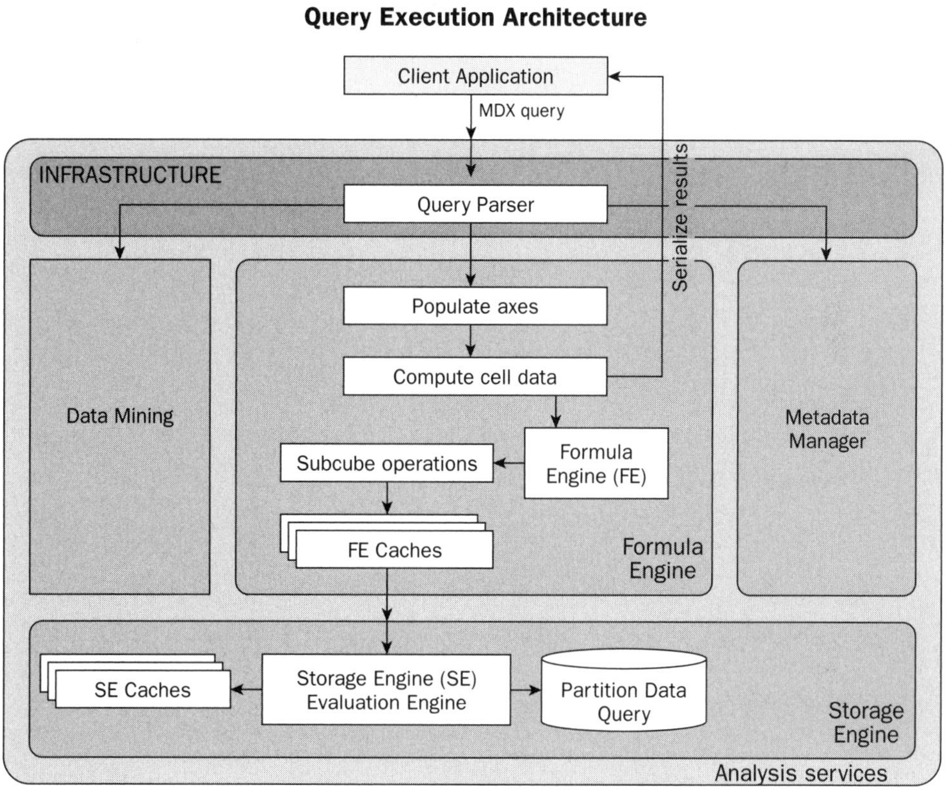

Query Execution Architecture

Figure 15-3

❏ **Infrastructure:** The Infrastructure handles operations such as accepting requests from clients, distributing the requests to the appropriate components, scheduling the jobs, and memory management. Parsing and validating the XMLA requests are also part of this component, as well as providing the support for retrieving data from external data sources. Consider this component as being the main interface for the client and also providing appropriate infrastructure to support the operation of the remaining components.

❏ **Metadata Manager:** The Metadata Manager handles the DDL statements that operate on the multidimensional database objects. DDL statements such as Create, Alter, Delete, and Process are directed from the infrastructure component to the Metadata Manager. This component also implements the transaction handling for all Analysis Services objects. When processing statements are issued, it coordinates with the storage engine or data mining component and the infrastructure to retrieve data from the relational data sources and store them in an optimized storage format within Analysis Services.

❑ **Data Mining:** The Data Mining component (you learn about data mining in Chapter 16) serves all Data Mining requests. It coordinates with the infrastructure and metadata manager at the time of processing data mining models. If there are OLAP mining models, the data mining component sends queries to the storage engine and formula engine components to retrieve appropriate data from the cube. This component handles Discover and DMX queries sent to the data mining models.

❑ **Storage Engine:** The Storage Engine is one of the core components of an OLAP database. It populates the multidimensional database with data from relational databases and optimally stores them on disk. It also optimizes the storage for dimension and cube data and builds relevant indices to aid in fast and efficient retrieval of the data from the disk. Typically you will see around a 10:1 compression ratio between the relational data and the OLAP data. The storage engine component provides internal interfaces to the formula engine component so that subcubes of data can be retrieved; these can then be used by the formula engine for efficient retrieval and aggregation of the data to satisfy MDX query requests.

❑ **Formula Engine:** The MDX Query Processor, also referred to as Formula Engine, determines the execution strategy for each MDX query. The Formula Engine can be considered the most important component with respect to MDX queries and calculations because the query evaluation and computation is done by this component. It translates each query into a sequence of requests to the Storage Engine to access the data, and computes the results of the query based on any calculations defined in the multidimensional database. It also implements caching for optimal query performance.

Stages of Query Execution

A query is sent from a client to the Analysis Services engine, as shown in Figure 15-3. The Analysis Services engine first parses the client request and routes it to the Data Mining Engine, the Formula Engine, or the Metadata Manager. Figure 15-3 shows the query execution architecture for serving Discover and MDX queries. There are several key steps in query evaluation: parsing the query, populating and serializing the axes, computing the cell data, and serializing the results back to the client. The following list provides more detail of each of the steps:

❑ **Parsing the query:** The MDX query is first analyzed by the query parser and then passed on to the Formula Engine. If there is a syntactical error in the query, the parser returns an appropriate error message to the client.

❑ **Populating the axes:** The Formula Engine evaluates the members of the axes of the MDX query. After this has been done, the details of the axes are populated.

❑ **Serializing the axes:** After the axes are evaluated and populated, Analysis Services sends details of the cube being queried back to the client, including the hierarchies and levels of the cube dimensions. Then the axes information, which includes the tuples and members that form the axes, are serialized. Some dimension properties of the members such as caption, unique name, and level name are sent to the client by default. If additional properties are requested in the MDX query, they will be included as well.

❑ **Evaluating the cell data:** After the axes data has been populated, the Analysis Services engine understands which cell coordinates need to be evaluated. The Formula Engine (FE) first tries to retrieve the results from the FE cache. If the query cannot be retrieved from the FE cache, appropriate internal queries are sent to the Storage Engine. The Storage Engine (SE) has its own cache. The SE determines if the query can be satisfied from the SE cache. If the query results are not available in the SE cache, results are retrieved from partition data on the disk, stored in the SE cache, and sent to the FE. The FE then performs the calculations needed to satisfy the query and is then ready to send the results back to the client.

❑ **Serializing the cells:** After the results are available, they are sent back to the client. The results are sent in the XMLA format.

Query Evaluation Modes

Now that you understand the various stages of MDX query evaluation, it's time to look at the two query evaluation modes in Analysis Services 2008: cell by cell mode and subspace computation.

Cell by Cell Mode

When an MDX query has been parsed, it is evaluated to see if the query can use the subspace computation mode. (The factors that determine whether the query can use the subspace computation mode are addressed in the next section.) If the query cannot be evaluated in the subspace computation mode, it is evaluated in the cell by cell mode.

Query evaluation can include several thousand or even millions of cells, and thus evaluating every cell, which happens in the cell by cell mode, is typically slower than the subspace computation mode. The following example, an MDX query against the sample Adventure Works DW 2008, will help you see how cell by cell mode works:

```
WITH MEMBER Measures.ContributionToParent AS
 ([Measures].[Internet Sales Amount]/
              ([Measures].[Internet Sales Amount],
              [Customer].[Customer Geography].CurrentMember.Parent)),
FORMAT_STRING="Percent"
SELECT {[Product].[Product Categories].[Category].MEMBERS} ON 1,
[Customer].[Customer Geography].[Country].MEMBERS ON 0
FROM [Adventure Works]
WHERE (Measures.ContributionToParent)
```

The preceding MDX query contains a calculated member that calculates the contribution of [Internet Sales Amount] from each country for each product. If you execute this query in the SSMS MDX query editor, you will see the results as shown in Figure 15-4.

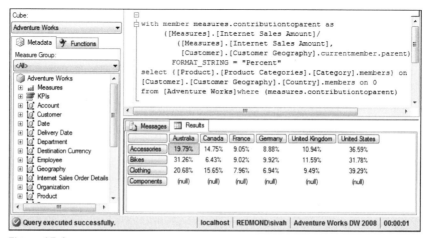

Figure 15-4

You can see that there are six countries and four products in the results. If you aggregate the percentage for each product across all countries you will get 100 percent. You can easily see that the United State's contribution for the company's [Internet Sales Amount] is the maximum for all the products. Once the axes information is populated, Analysis Services needs to calculate the values for 24 cells. The cell by cell mode in Analysis Services does this using the following steps:

1. Evaluate the measure [Internet Sales Amount] for a cell.

2. Evaluate the [Internet Sales Amount] for the member [Customer].[Customer Geography].[All Customers] for that cell.

3. Evaluate the measure ContributionToParent, which is the calculated member in the MDX query for that cell.

4. Repeat steps 1, 2, and 3 for each cell including cells that have null values.

Results of steps 1 and 2 for all the cells are shown in Figure 15-5.

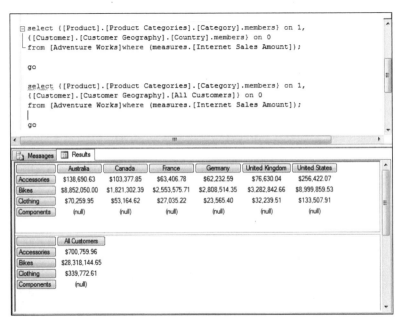

Figure 15-5

In this example you can see that the evaluation of step 2 needs to be done only once. In addition, the cells for which [Internet Sales Amount] is null don't have to be calculated because the calculated measure ContributionToParent for null values will be null. When there are millions of cells, evaluation of each and every cell can take a considerable amount of time. The next evaluation mode, subspace computation, helps optimize query evaluation.

Subspace Computation

The Analysis Services 2008 cube space is typically sparse. This means that only some of the cells in the dimensional space have values. The remaining cell values are null. The goal of the subspace computation query evaluation mode is to evaluate MDX expressions only when they need to be evaluated. For example, if a cell value is null, an MDX expression using that value will result in a null value and therefore doesn't have to be evaluated. Subspace computation can reduce cell evaluation time by orders of magnitude, depending on the sparseness of the cube. Some queries that run in minutes using cell by cell mode are evaluated within seconds using subspace computation mode. Subspace computation was first introduced in Analysis Services 2005 Service Pack 2 for a limited number of scenarios. In Analysis Services 2008, subspace computation mode has been enhanced to cover a wider scope of MDX evaluations and automatic query optimizations.

The subspace computation mode can be taken by Analysis Services only under specific conditions. Some of the important conditions where Analysis Services will use the subspace computation mode are given here:.

❑ Basic operations that involve arithmetic operators (*, /,+, –), and relational operators (<, >, <=, >=, =).

❑ Static references to members and tuples as well as constant scalars such as NULL.

❑ Scalar operations using functions IS, MemberValue, Properties, Name, IIF, IsNonEmpty, Case, IsLeaf, IsSiblings, CalculationPassValue, and member functions such as PrevMember, NextMember, Lag, Lead, FirstChild, LastChild, Ancestor, and so on.

❑ Basic Aggregate functions such as Sum, Min, Max, and Aggregate on static sets; as well as sets built using functions PeriodsToDate, YTD, QTD, MTD, Crossjoin, Cousin, Descendants, Children, Hierarchize, and Members.

❑ The CurrentMember function (only on the Measures dimension) and basic unary operators and semi-additive measures.

Some examples where subspace computation mode will not be chosen include named sets when used with Aggregate functions, dynamic operations (for example: [Date].[Fiscal].Lag([Measures].[Count])), and when encountering recursion.

As an example, consider the simple MDX query from the previous section. The MDX query is first analyzed to determine if it can be evaluated using subspace computation mode. Because the answer is yes, Analysis Services uses the following steps for evaluating the query:

1. Retrieve non-null values of the [Internet Sales Amount] measure for the query results space.

2. Retrieve the [Internet Sales Amount] for member [Customer].[Customer Geography] .[All Customers] once.

3. Evaluate the ContributionToParent measure for the non-null values retrieved.

Figure 15-6 provides a graphical illustration comparing the cell by cell and subspace computation modes. Assume the machine in the diagram is the Analysis Services engine. The figure on the left shows the cell by cell mode, where all the cells are evaluated. The figure on the right shows that the cells that have non-null values (highlighted by darker color) are first identified via storage engine requests and then evaluation is only done for those cells. Note that when Analysis Services serializes the results back to the client, it only includes the cell values that contain data. The remaining cell values are assumed to be null. This is shown in Figure 15-7 with an MDX query. This MDX query should return 24 cells with cell ordinals 0 to 23. However, this only returns 18 cell values because the cell values corresponding to the product member Components ([Product].[Product Categories].[Category].&[2]) are null. The client object models provided by Analysis Services 2008 interpret the results returned from the Analysis Services engine and populate the missing cells with null values for the client accessing the data.

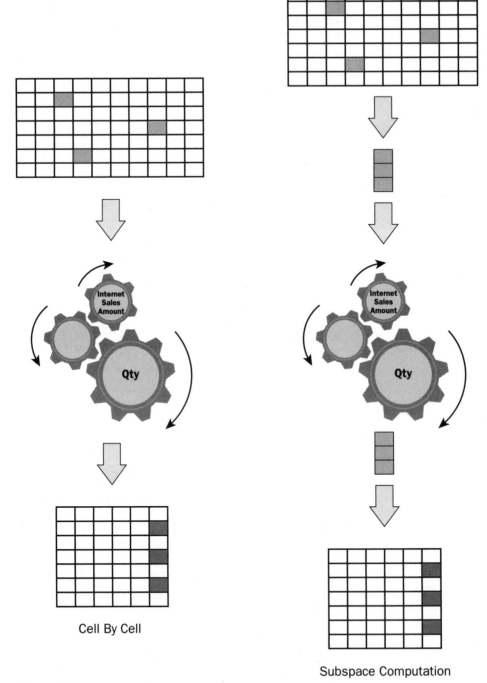

Cell By Cell

Subspace Computation

Figure 15-6

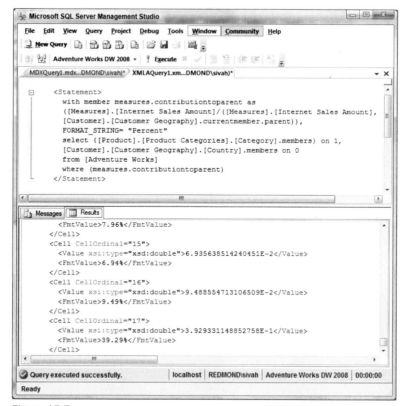

Figure 15-7

Analysis Services has two NON EMPTY code paths that would eliminate null cell values: Naïve NON EMPTY and Express NON EMPTY. The Naïve NON EMPTY code path was used in the cell by cell mode and the Express NON EMPTY path was used to identify the tuples that contained data. However, in Analysis Services 2005 Express NON EMPTY was restricted to measures that did not have calculations or where NON_EMPTY_BEHAVIOR (discussed later in this chapter) was specified. Analysis Services 2008 Express NON EMPTY has been enhanced to support measures with calculations (except for recursive or complex overlapping calculations). Now that you've learned more about the Analysis Services query execution architecture and query evaluation modes, let's look into analyzing performance bottlenecks and fine-tuning them.

Performance Analysis and Tuning Tools

Analysis Services 2008 includes significant enhancements targeted at getting the best query performance. Improvements include tools to help in designing cubes, subspace computation optimization, caching enhancements, and improved writeback query performance (you learn about this later in the chapter). You might still have queries that are not performing as expected, however, due to cube design or the way MDX has been written. To analyze and improve your query performance, you can use tools that will help you analyze the performance of your queries and then tune them to get the best performance from Analysis Services 2008.

SQL Server Profiler

SQL Server Profiler is a tool used to trace operations on the SQL Server and Analysis Services database engines. SQL Server Profiler is the primary performance analysis tool used to debug performance bottlenecks in SQL Server (including Analysis Services). The ability to trace Analysis Services operations through SQL Server Profiler was first introduced in SQL Server 2005.

Analysis Services exposes the commands sent to it as well as internal operations that occur within the server through what are called *events*. Some examples of these events are Command Begin, Command End, Query Begin, and Query End. Each event has properties associated with it such as start time, end time, and the user sending the query. These properties are shown as columns in the tool. SQL Server Profiler requests these events and their properties through trace commands to the server. Analysis Services periodically sends the events to the clients who have subscribed to a trace. SQL Server Profiler shows the events and event column values in a grid. Only Analysis Services administrators can trace Analysis Services events. To learn more about how to use the Profiler, follow these steps:

1. Make sure you are an administrator on the Analysis Services server you want to profile. You can connect to Analysis Services through SSMS and use the Analysis Services Server Properties dialog to add users as administrators of Analysis Services, as you learned in Chapter 7.

2. Launch SQL Server Profiler from the Start menu: All Programs ⇨ Microsoft SQL Server 2008 ⇨ Performance Tools ⇨ SQL Server Profiler.

3. The SQL Server Profiler application appears. Create a new trace by selecting File ⇨ New Trace.

4. In the Connect to Server dialog, shown in Figure 15-8, select Analysis Services as the Server type and enter the name of your Analysis Services instance. Click Connect.

Figure 15-8

5. In the Trace Properties dialog, enter the Trace name, for example "FirstTrace." SQL Server Profiler provides three trace templates with pre-selected events to trace. Select the Standard template as shown in Figure 15-9.

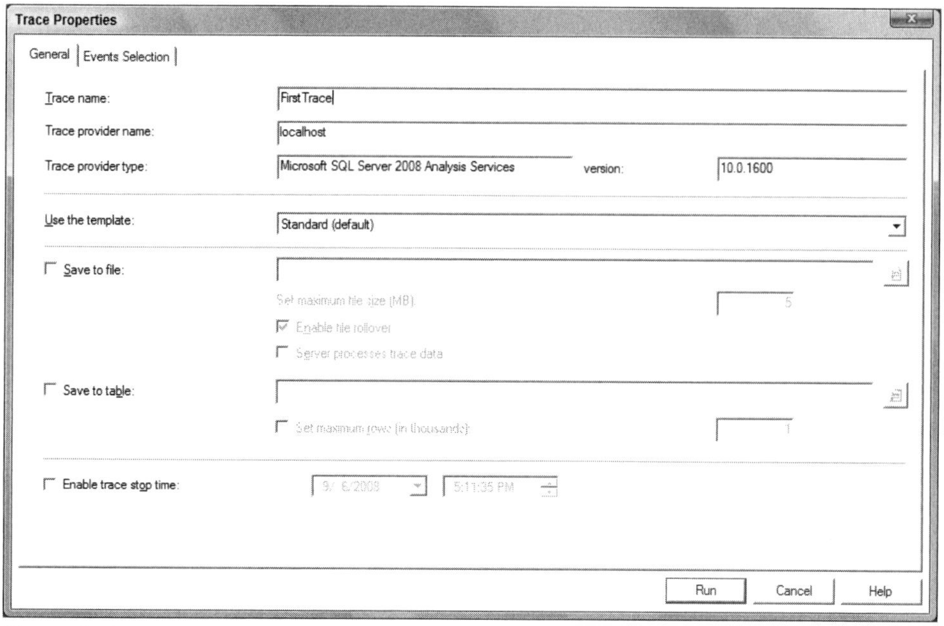

Figure 15-9

6. To see the events selected in the standard template, click the Events Selection tab. You will see the event columns that have been selected, as in Figure 15-10. This page only shows the events that have properties that have been selected. To see all the events and event properties supported by Analysis Services, check the Show All Events and Show All Columns checkboxes, respectively. Familiarize yourself with the various events and click Run.

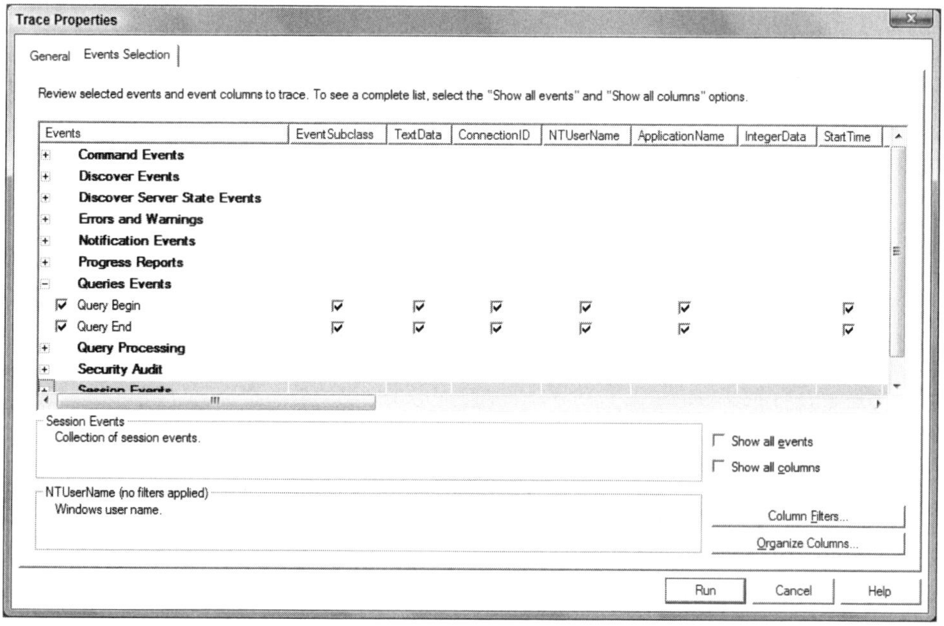

Figure 15-10

7. You will see the various event property columns within Profiler. To see processing operations events, open the Adventure Works DW sample project and deploy it to the Analysis Services instance. You will see the events that happen during processing, including the processing duration of each object, as shown in Figure 15-11. The SQL Server Profiler gives you useful information such as the time it takes to process each dimension, the partition processing time, and the overall processing time of the entire database.

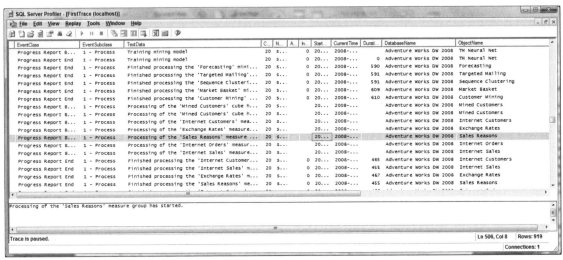

Figure 15-11

After the processing has completed for the Adventure Works cube, send the following MDX query using SQL Server Management Studio:

```
SELECT {[Measures].[Sales Amount],[Measures].[Gross Profit]} ON 0,
[Customer].[Customer Geography].MEMBERS ON 1
FROM [Adventure Works]
```

You can see the Query events in the SQL Server Profiler as shown in Figure 15-12. You can see the duration of each event in the Profiler trace (not shown in Figure 15-12). One piece of information that is interesting to notice is the subcubes accessed by this query and how long each subcube query took. The subcube events indicate the requests of the storage engine to retrieve data from disk. You can utilize this subcube information to build custom aggregations to optimize query performance.

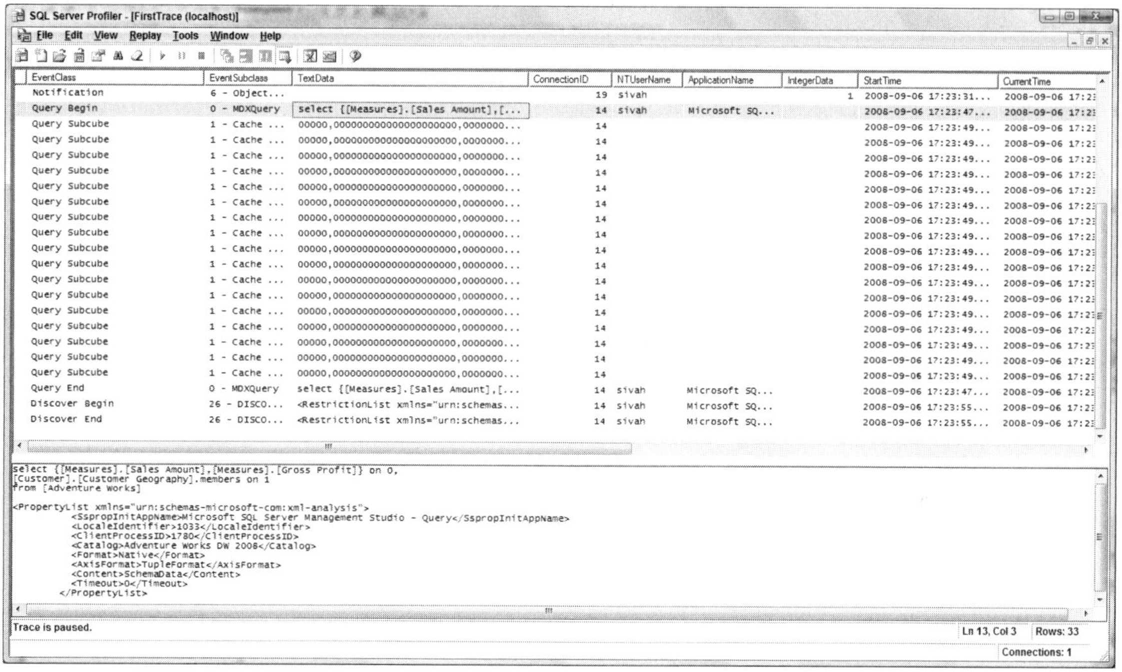

Figure 15-12

Assume you built aggregations using a usage-based optimization wizard. You would like to find out if the aggregations are being utilized. Analysis Services provides events that help you identify if the aggregations are hit. Create a new Trace and switch to the Events Selection tab. Check the box next to Show All Events. Expand the events under the Query Processing event group. You can see the events related to query processing that are provided by Analysis Services as shown in Figure 15-13.

If you select the events under Query Processing and monitor the trace events you will be able to obtain information such as if the Non Empty code path is being utilized, if the MDX script is being evaluated, if data is retrieved from Aggregations (Get Data From Aggregation event) or from the existing cache (Get Data From Cache event). These events help you identify more details about the queries sent by the users as well as their duration. You can later analyze the MDX queries, build usage-based optimization aggregations for long-running queries, enhance your aggregations using the new Aggregation Designer (which is discussed in Chapter 9), or try to optimize the long-running MDX queries (which is discussed later in this chapter). You do need to know a little bit about the internals of the server to fine-tune it. We believe the ability to trace Analysis Services activity through SQL Server Profiler will help with that, so try it out.

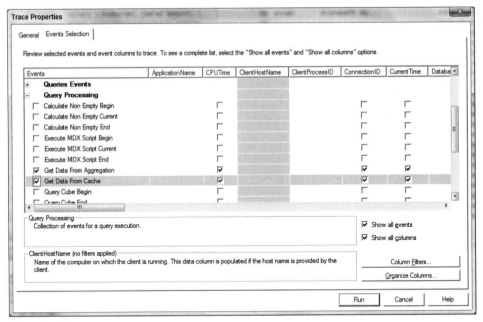

Figure 15-13

Performance Monitor

Analysis Services provides several performance monitoring counters that help you understand internal operations of your Analysis Services server, as well as help in debugging and troubleshooting performance issues. You need to be an administrator on the Analysis Services server to utilize PerfMon, a tool that lets you observe and analyze the Analysis Services 2008 performance counter values. The following steps walk you through working with Analysis Services performance counters:

1. Click Start and type **perfmon**, as shown in Figure 15-14, and select perfmon.exe from the Programs list.

Figure 15-14

2. You will see the Reliability and Performance Monitor application. Select the Performance Monitor page as shown in Figure 15-15.

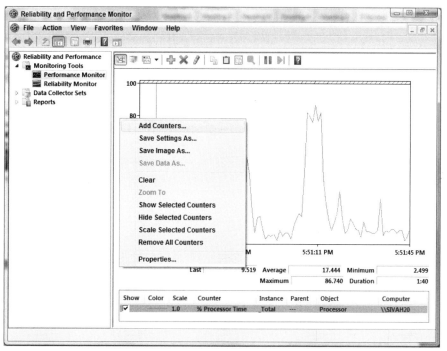

Figure 15-15

3. Right-click the page and select Add Counters. You will see the groups of Analysis Services performance counters as shown in Figure 15-16. You can expand a specific group to see the list of counters in that group.

4. Select the MSAS 2008:MDX category of performance counters and click Add to include these counters.

5. Click OK in the Add Counters dialog.

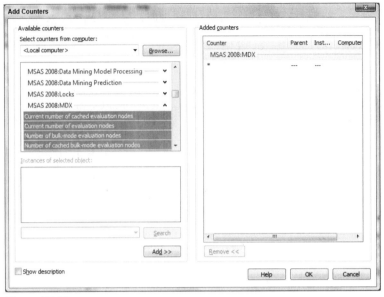

Figure 15-16

The MDX counters are added to the Performance Monitor page as shown in Figure 15-17. If you click a specific counter you can see the line view of that value over time. It is easier to understand and analyze the counters using their raw numbers.

6. Click the down arrow beside the Change Graph Type icon and select Report, as shown in Figure 15-17.

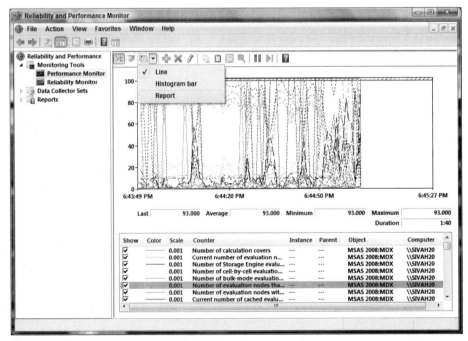

Figure 15-17

You will see the list of MDX counters along with their values in a report format as shown in Figure 15-18. If you execute MDX queries from SSMS or browse the cube using the Cube Browser in SSMS or BIDS, you should see these values getting updated. For example, you can see the "Number of bulk-mode evaluation nodes" (nodes during subspace computation evaluation) and "Number of cell-by-cell evaluation nodes" performance counters for a specific query to understand if the query is using the subspace computation or a cell by cell evaluation mode. This can help you to understand and optimize your MDX query. Similar to MDX performance counters, there are Analysis Services performance counters in other categories such as Processing, Aggregations, Connections, and so on. These counters are very valuable when you are troubleshooting specific problems and are not able to understand or resolve the problem using SQL Server Profiler traces. We recommend that you take a look at the various Analysis Services counter groups. In addition to the performance counters provided by Analysis Services, you can also look at other performance counters such as processors, memory, and disk I/O on your computer system to understand and troubleshoot relevant issues such as long-running queries, which are CPU intensive or memory/disk intensive.

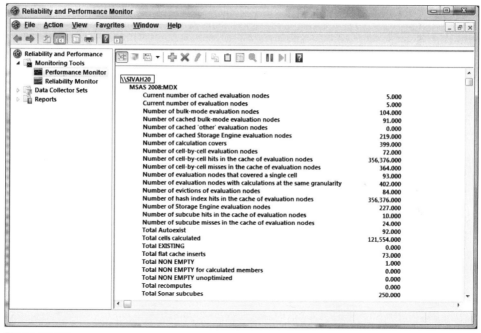

Figure 15-18

Task Manager

Most of you have used the Task Manager on your computer to look at the percentage of CPU time or memory consumed by a process. You can get the same information for Analysis Services using the Task Manager as shown in Figure 15-19. The process msmdsrv.exe is the Analysis Services 2008 process. If you have multiple instances of Analysis Services installed you will see multiple instances of msmdsrv. exe in Task Manager. You can also see the various instances of Analysis Services on your machine using the Services tab in Task Manager. The Task Manager gives you a quick way to understand if your Analysis Services server is CPU-intensive or its memory usage is growing when you have executed a long-running query.

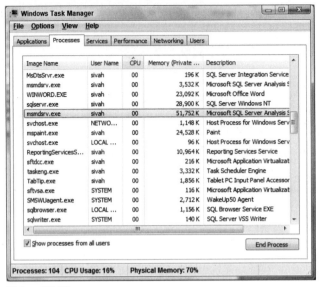

Figure 15-19

SQL Server Profiler, Performance Monitoring counters, and Task Manager help you analyze and troubleshoot issues with your Analysis Services. SQL Server Management Studio and Business Intelligence Development Studio are tools that help you tune your Analysis Services instance.

SQL Server Management Studio

You can use SSMS to execute your MDX queries and get the query execution time or look at the query results. You can also use it along with the Profiler to troubleshoot specific query issues. In addition, you can also use SSMS for debugging processing issues or tuning your Analysis Services server processing options. SSMS also helps you define aggregations to help speed up query performance. Other important uses of SSMS are changing your Analysis Services server properties, fine-tuning engine behavior, and restarting your Analysis Services service if needed.

Business Intelligence Development Studio

You can use BIDS to refine your cube and dimension design based on the troubleshooting you have done using other tools (discussed in Chapters 5, 6, 8, and 9). In addition, BIDS helps you build custom aggregations and make use of usage-based optimization, which helps you improve query performance.

Analyzing Query Performance Issues

Analysis Services 2008 has significant query optimization features. However, there are still factors that can affect query performance such as the complexity of the cube's design, aggregations, server configuration properties, hardware resources, and so on. Before you start analyzing query performance you need to understand where time is being spent during the overall execution. You already learned that there are two major components, Formula Engine (FE) and Storage Engine (SE), where the majority of the execution time is being spent. The time spent in the infrastructure component is negligible and hence we can arrive at the following equation:

```
MDX Query execution time = Formula Engine time + Storage Engine time
```

In the "SQL Server Profiler" section earlier in the chapter, you learned that query subcube events indicate requests to the SE. Hence the SE time is the duration of time spent for all the query subcube events. The overall query execution time for the query can be obtained from the SQL Server Profiler trace. The time spent by the query in the FE component is equal to the difference of total execution time minus the SE time. These relationships are expressed in the following equations:

```
Storage Engine time = Time needed to evaluate all query subcube events


Formula Engine time = Total query execution time - Storage Engine time
```

Assuming you want to analyze and optimize your query execution time, we recommend that you focus your efforts on the following recommendations:

❑   If the SE time is greater than 30 percent of the total execution time, look at optimizing it.

❑   If the FE time is greater than 30 percent of the total execution time, look at optimizing it.

❑   If both FE and SE times are greater than 30 percent of the total execution time, then look at optimizing both areas.

Understanding FE and SE Characteristics

The FE performs the evaluation of the results and sends the results back to the client. This component is mostly single-threaded and CPU-intensive because it might have to iterate over millions of cells to perform calculations. If you observe, using Task Manager, that Analysis Services is consuming 100 percent of one of the processors during a query evaluation, then you can assume that the time is being spent in the Formula Engine. The FE has very little disk utilization.

The SE retrieves data for subcubes from the SE cache or from disk when requested by the FE. Partition and dimension data is stored as segments that can be read in parallel. Hence the SE component is heavily multithreaded to maximize the hardware resources and perform I/O operations in parallel. The SE is CPU- and disk-intensive. Hence if you see all the processors of your machine utilized and heavy disk usage (using Task Manager or performance counters), you can be confident that the query is spending time in the SE component.

When analyzing query performance, one important thing you need to be aware of is predictability. Analysis Services caches data in the SE and FE components. In addition, you have caching done by the operating system for disk I/O and the multi-user environment that play a critical factor in query performance. Hence, executing the same MDX query a second time can result in improved performance due to caching in Analysis Services. The recommended approach is to investigate query performance in single-user mode. In addition, Analysis Services has the Clear Cache command that clears all the Analysis Services caches. This improves the predictability of query execution when you are investigating performance issues. The syntax for the Clear Cache statement is shown in the following code. You need to pass the database ID as input to the statement to clear the caches of a specific database.

```
<ClearCache xmlns="http://schemas.microsoft.com/analysisservices/2003/engine">
  <Object>
    <DatabaseID>MyDatabaseID</DatabaseID>
  </Object>
</ClearCache>
```

Operating system file caching can also impact query performance. To get repeatable results, you can shut down and restart the Analysis Services service or even the entire machine if needed. In most cases you should be able to get repeatable results using the Clear Cache statement.

Common Solutions for Slow Queries

MDX query execution time is the sum of time spent in the FE and SE components. The issues causing queries to be slow can be classified into three main categories: large SE requests, multiple SE requests, and FE-intensive queries.

Large Storage Engine Requests

As you learned earlier, query evaluation plans are decided by the FE. A large SE request translates to a subcube query that takes a really long time. This means the majority of the query execution time is being spent getting results for a single SE request. An SE request can take a very long time due to factors such as having a very large partition, no aggregations, or aggregations getting missed. You need to follow the best practices mentioned in Chapter 14 to design the right cube, including defining effective attribute relationships, adopting an effective partitioning scheme, and designing aggregations using Aggregation Designer or usage-based optimization. These will help resolve the issue of an MDX query being slow due to a large storage engine request.

Several Storage Engine Requests

If you see several subcube query events in the SQL Server Profiler when you execute an MDX query repeatedly, it means that the SE caches are being missed each time and hence the SE component has to retrieve data from the disk. Retrieving data from disk is an expensive operation compared to getting the data from the SE caches. The EventSubclass property of the Query Subcube Verbose event shows whether the query is retrieved from cache or non-cache data. If the query is retrieved from non-cache data, the data is being retrieved from disk. Analysis Services 2008 provides you a way to forcibly cache the data in SE component using the Create Cache statement. The syntax of the statement is

```
CREATE CACHE FOR <CubeName> AS <MDX Expression>
```

The Create Cache statement applies to a specific cube. This is extremely useful in cases where you are aware of long-running queries due to several storage engine requests. You can "warm up" the Analysis Services SE cache using this statement, which can help improve performance of MDX queries using this cache.

Formula Engine–Intensive Query

The FE component is single threaded. Hence, if an MDX query contains intensive calculations, it could spend a significant amount of its execution time in the FE component. You should be able to identify an FE-intensive query using Task Manager. Look for msmdsrv.exe pegging one CPU on your machine at 100 percent. One of the critical factors in getting the best performance from your MDX query is to make sure your query uses the subspace computation code path. Looking at MDX performance counters and SQL Server Profiler traces should help you identify if your queries are not using subspace computation. In addition, other MDX query optimization techniques can help you reduce the time spent in the FE component, which you learn about in the next section.

Figure 15-20 provides a summary of the three categories of problems that can contribute to slow MDX queries and what techniques to investigate to improve query performance.

Scenario	Large SE Request	Several SE Requests	FE Intensive Query	
Solution	Partitioning, aggregations	CREATE CACHE	Cell-by-cell → Subspace	Optimizations: NEB, Auto-exists, Scope, MemberValue ...

Figure 15-20

Query Optimization Techniques

As you learned earlier in this chapter, MDX query execution time can be impacted by several factors such as cube design, Analysis Services caching, and hardware. One of the important factors in getting the best MDX query execution time is the efficiency of your MDX. Using the right MDX query optimization technique is not simple and involves a deeper understanding of your cube and MDX. In this section you learn some of the important techniques that can help you optimize your MDX queries.

Using NON EMPTY on Axes

Most cubes are quite sparse. By sparse we mean that many of the cells in the cube space do not have a value associated with them. For example, in the Adventure Works DW 2008 sample Analysis Services database, if every coordinate of the Internet Sales measure group has data and assuming only the key attribute in each dimension, the total number of cells with data would be (Date) 1189 * Date (Ship Date) 1189 * Date (Delivery Date) 1189 * Customer (18485) * Promotion (17) * Product (398) * Sales Territory (12) * Sales Reason (11) * Source Currency (106) * Destination Currency (15) * Internet Sales Order Details (60,399), which is $2.66*10^{27}$ cells. This result increases when additional attributes are added from each dimension. Although most of the cells do not have any business meaning associated with them — for example, if delivery date is ahead of order date — they belong to cube space and can be queried by the users. Querying such cells results in a null value, which indicates that data is not available for that cell's coordinates.

The fact table rows represent the leaf-level cells for a cube. The fact table row count is much less than possible cube space. The Analysis Services engine has many optimizations for improving query performance by limiting the search space. The basic rule is that if a cube doesn't have calculations (such as calculated scripts, custom rollup, and custom members), the non-empty space of the cube is defined by fact table cells and their aggregations. Analysis Services allows users to write effective, optimized MDX queries to prevent empty cells from being returned. This is because those empty cells simply do not add value for business analysis. By limiting the search space, Analysis Services can find the results much more quickly.

Analysis Services 2008 supports many ways for users to eliminate cells containing null values in a query. The keyword NON EMPTY eliminates members along an axis whose cell values are null. The NON EMPTY keyword is used at the beginning of the axis statement in an MDX query as shown here:

```
SELECT Measures.Members on COLUMNS,
NON EMPTY Dimension.Hierarchy.Members on ROWS
From <CubeName>
```

The NON EMPTY keyword can be used on rows or columns (or any axis). In most cases, only results with non-empty cells are meaningful for end users. Hence, most Analysis Services 2008 client tools generate MDX queries with the NON EMPTY keyword. We recommend that you use the NON EMPTY keyword in your MDX cell set and row set queries whenever possible. Not only will it limit the size of the returned cell set, but additional optimizations are applied when you do this that will speed up your query execution time.

Following is an MDX query without the NON EMPTY keyword. Execute this query using SQL Server Management Studio against a deployed sample Adventure Works project.

```
SELECT [Customer].[Customer Geography].[Customer].members *
    Descendants([Product].[Product Categories].[Category].&[3],[Product].
    [Product Categories].[Product Name]) ON 1,
    {[Measures].[Internet Sales Amount]} ON 0
FROM [Adventure Works]
```

The query returns 18,485 cells. Now change the query to include the NON EMPTY keyword on both axes as shown here and execute the new query in SQL Server Management Studio:

```
SELECT NON EMPTY [Customer].[Customer Geography].[Customer].members *
    Descendants([Product].[Product Categories].[Category].&[3],[Product].
    [Product Categories].[Product Name]) ON 1,
    {[Measures].[Internet Sales Amount]} ON 0
FROM [Adventure Works]
```

This query, which includes the NON EMPTY keyword, returns just 6,853 cells, which is a reduced number of cells to evaluate. The execution time for the query with NON EMPTY is lower than that of the query without NON EMPTY. We recommend that you follow these steps to observe the performance:

1. Connect to the sample Adventure Works 2008 Analysis Services database.

2. Start SQL Server Profiler.

3. Create a New Trace with Query Begin and Query End events selected.

4. Send the Clear Cache statement.

5. Send the query without NON EMPTY.

6. Send the Clear Cache statement.

7. Send the MDX query with NON EMPTY.

8. Observe the Duration column to see the performance difference between the two queries.

You can see the performance difference in duration times between the two queries as shown in Figure 15-21. This example highlights the benefit of eliminating empty cells using NON EMPTY.

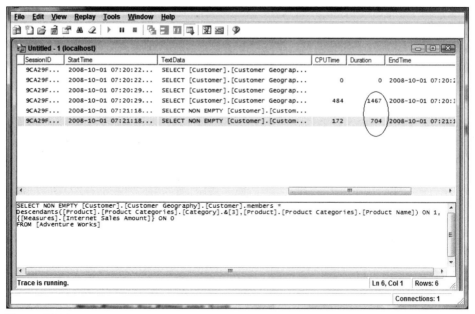

Figure 15-21

Using Non Empty for Filtering and Sorting

Many users apply filter conditions on a set or try to evaluate the top N members of a set based on certain conditions using the Filter and TopCount functions, respectively. In most cases, only non-empty members are needed in the results of the Filter and TopCount functions. You can improve the performance dramatically by first using NONEMPTY() to retrieve non-empty sets, followed by the Filter, Sort, or TopCount functions on the smaller set. In the Adventure Works sample, for example, if you want to get the top ten Customer/Product combinations to start a marketing campaign, your query will look like the following:

```
SELECT
TopCount([Customer].[Customer Geography].[Customer].members*
    [Product].[Product Categories].[Product].members, 10 ,
    [Measures].[Internet Sales Amount]) ON ROWS ,
    [Measures].[Internet Sales Amount] ON COLUMMNS
FROM [Adventure Works]
```

Notice this query contains a cross-join of customers and products (shown by the following expression). Whenever a cross-join is applied, the server sorts the result based on the order of the hierarchies.

```
([Customer].[Customer Geography].[Customer].members*[Product].
    [Product Categories].[Product].members)
```

The cross-join of the customer and product dimension results in 18484 * 397 = 7,338,148 cells. Analysis Services now evaluates the top 10 cells out of the seven million cells to return the results for the preceding query. This query took around 48 seconds on the machine we used to run the query and it consumed 1 CPU at 100 percent during the entire execution. Most of the cells of the cross-join were actually empty cells that need not have been part of the result of the cross-join. Not only did the server take the time in sorting these cells, but it also had to iterate through the seven million cells to determine the top 10. The following query uses the NonEmtpyCrossJoin function, which eliminates the empty cells:

```
SELECT
TopCount(NONEMPTYCROSSJOIN(
  [Customer].[Customer Geography].[Customer].members*
  [Product].[Product Categories].[Product].members,
  {[Measures].[Internet Sales Amount]},1),10,
  [Measures].[Internet Sales Amount]) ON ROWS ,
  [Measures].[Internet Sales Amount] ON COLUMNS
FROM [Adventure Works]
```

In this query, the NonEmptyCrossJoin function first eliminates all empty cells, and hence the TopCount function had a smaller set of cells to work on. The query took 3 seconds on the same machine used in the previous example because of the optimization provided by using the NonEmptyCrossJoin function. Only cells containing fact data were sorted and the top 10 values were returned. The performance improvement is dramatic (can be observed in SSMS or in the SQL Server Profiler duration column) and both queries returned the exact same results. The rule of thumb is that the fewer tuples or cells involved in calculations, the better the query performance. Because Analysis Services has an efficient algorithm to get non-empty sets, you should use NonEmpty whenever it is applicable and appropriate for your business requirements. You can use the NonEmptyCrossJoin function whenever you are aware that a real measure will be used by the server for Non-Empty evaluation, but use it with caution when you have calculated measures because certain optimization may not be available for all calculated measures. You can also use the HAVING clause, which eliminates cells with null values as shown in Chapter 10.

Using NON_EMPTY_BEHAVIOR for Calculations

The NON EMPTY keyword checks the fact data to determine empty cells. However, if cell values are the result of calculations, Non Empty can be slow. If you query for cells that involve evaluation of complex calculations, then the cells' emptiness (if the cell returns a null value) is not determined by fact data; each cell must be evaluated to return the correct results. Analysis Services provides you with a keyword called NON_EMPTY_BEHAVIOR to instruct the server to use an optimized algorithm to determine cells' emptiness. The following query returns the forecast sales by applying different rates:

```
WITH MEMBER [Measures].[ForecastSales] AS
'iif([Measures].[Internet Sales Amount] >500 ,
  [Measures].[Internet Sales Amount]*1.2,
  [Measures].[Internet Sales Amount]*1.2)'
SELECT NON EMPTY [Customer].[Customer Geography].[Customer].members*
  Descendants([Product].[Product Categories].[Category].&[3],[Product].
  [Product Categories].[Product]) ON 1 ,
NON EMPTY {[Measures].[ForecastSales]} ON 0
FROM [Adventure Works]
```

Even though this query uses NON EMPTY, MDX queries with calculations like this one can be slow. This is because the optimized code path is not applied on complex calculated members. In this query you have a calculated member that is multiplied by 1.2 and hence the server needs to evaluate the expression to identify if the corresponding cells are empty. In order to have Analysis Services apply NON EMPTY behavior to the calculated member, you can specify the NON_EMPTY_BEHAVIOR property, which ties the calculated measure to a real fact measure. The server will then use the optimized code path for the non-empty determination. Execute the following modified query that specifies NON_EMPTY_BEHAVIOR:

```
WITH MEMBER [Measures].[ForecastSales] AS
'iif([Measures].[Internet Sales Amount] >500 ,
    [Measures].[Internet Sales Amount]*1.2,
    [Measures].[Internet Sales Amount]*1.2)',
NON_EMPTY_BEHAVIOR = '[Measures].[Internet Sales Amount]'
SELECT NON EMPTY [Customer].[Customer Geography].[Customer].members*
    Descendants([Product].[Product Categories].[Category].&[3],[Product].
    [Product Categories].[Product]) ON 1 ,
NON EMPTY {[Measures].[ForecastSales]} ON 0
FROM [Adventure Works]
```

Here you have provided a hint to Analysis Services to use the [Internet Sales Amount] measure while evaluating the calculation. Such hints help reduce the query execution time because Analysis Services is able to determine if the calculation returns a null value using the base measure.

Using SCOPE versus IIF and CASE

You learned about the SCOPE, IIF, and CASE statements in Chapter 10. Using SCOPE helps improve query performance when evaluating cells compared to the IIF and CASE statements. When using SCOPE, calculations only get applied to the subcube, compared to other calculations, which get evaluated for the entire cube space. In addition, SCOPE statements are evaluated once statically, compared to IIF/CASE, which are evaluated dynamically. These two factors contribute to improving query performance when using SCOPE. The following code is an example of an MDX expression that is translated from IIF to SCOPE:

```
CREATE MEMBER Measures.[ Sales Amount] AS
   IIF([Destination Currency].CurrentMember IS Currency.USD,
   Measures.[Internet Sales Amount], Measures.[Internet Sales Amount] *
   Measures.AverageRate);

CREATE MEMBER Measures.[Sales Amount] AS Null;
SCOPE(Measures.[Sales], [Destination Currency].Members);
   THIS = Measures.[Internet Sales Amount]* Measures.AverageRate;
   SCOPE(Currency.USA);
      THIS = Measures.[Internet Sales Amount];
   END SCOPE;
END SCOPE;
```

Auto Exists versus Properties

When you include attributes and hierarchies within a dimension in a query, Analysis Services only returns the relevant members. For example, take the following MDX query:

```
SELECT [Measures].[Internet Sales Amount] ON 0,
   [Customer].[City].&[Seattle]&[WA] * [Customer].[State-Province].MEMBERS ON 1
FROM [Direct Sales]
```

This query only returns results for (Seattle, Washington) and (Seattle, All Customers). It does not return the complete cross product of Seattle and all the States in the Customer.[State-Province] hierarchy. As you learned in Chapter 10, this behavior is called *auto exists* and helps improve performance. Hence we recommend using Exists or CrossJoin functions instead of using the Properties function in your MDX expression. The following code is an example of how you can rewrite your MDX expressions that use the Properties function:

```
Filter(Customer.Members,
   Customer.CurrentMember.Properties("Gender") = "Male")

Exists(Customer.Members, Gender.[Male])
```

Member Value versus Properties

Analysis Services 2008 has an attribute member property called Value Column. When defined, this is helpful in retrieving the values in a typed format. For example, if you have the yearly income of a customer, you can retrieve its value as integer rather than as a string and then converting it using one of the VBA functions. Here is an example of how to use the MemberValue MDX function to retrieve the Value Column:

```
Create Set [Adventure Works].RichCustomers As
   Filter(Customer.Customer.Members,
   CInt(Customer.CustomerCurrentMember.Properties("Yearly Income"))
   > 100000);

Create Set RichCustomers As
   Filter(Customer.Customer.Members,
   Customer.Salary.MemberValue > 100000);
```

In this example, the first expression creates a set of customers whose Yearly Income is greater than 100000 using the Properties MDX function, which retrieves the member property. The return type for the MemberProperty function is a string and you need to use the CInt VBA function to convert this to an integer value before you compare it with 100000. Please note that the preceding example is provided for illustration purposes only. The actual data in the sample Adventure Works 2008 in the Yearly Income is a range represented as string. We recommend you try the preceding illustration on a large database with appropriate data to see the benefits. When you have a large number of customers, converting strings to integers becomes expensive. The second MDX expression uses the MemberValue MDX function to retrieve the value directly as an integer.

Move Simple Calculations to Data Source View

If there are very simple static calculations such as converting based on exchange rates, these calculations can be changed to calculated columns in the Data Source View (DSV). Analysis Services does these calculations at processing time and stores the values in the cube rather than calculating these expressions during query execution time. These simple calculations should be really fast in Analysis Services 2008 and you may not observe the performance hit. However, as a general best practice, we recommend that you move them to DSV.

Features versus MDX Scripts

Analysis Services 2008 provides features such as many-to-many dimensions, measure expressions, unary operators, custom rollup, and semi-additive measures. You have learned about these features and how and when to use them during the course of this book. Almost all of these features can be defined as MDX expressions in MDX script. We highly recommend that you design your cubes using built-in features rather than defining the equivalent functionality as MDX expressions in MDX Script. The built-in features will provide better performance for most scenarios. If you do find a specific feature causing query performance degradation, you can re-visit implementing the functionality in MDX scripts.

We have looked at some of the common problems the Analysis Services team has observed while investigating customer performance issues and how to solve them in this section. There are additional MDX optimizations that you can perform. We recommend that you look at the following resources for additional information on MDX optimizations:

- ❏ *MDX Solutions: With Microsoft SQL Server Analysis Services*, 2nd edition by George Spofford et al., (Wiley, 2006), www.wiley.com
- ❏ The SQL Customer Advisory Team, http://www.sqlcat.com
- ❏ Microsoft OLAP by Mosha Pashumansky, http://sqlblog.com/blogs/mosha
- ❏ Richard Tkachuk's Analysis Services Page, http://www.sqlserveranalysisservices.com

Scale Out with Read-Only Database

After performing all these query optimization techniques you might still find query performance degradation when multiple users are connected to your Analysis Services instance and actively querying the database. This is one of the problems Analysis Services customers face when the customer load on a specific database increases. You can try to use larger machines with more CPUs if memory or CPU is the bottleneck. You can also move to 64-bit machines if you are currently using 32-bit hardware. Of course, as you scale up, the cost of your machines will become higher. Analysis Services 2008 provides the new read-only database feature, which is discussed in Chapter 7. If your customer needs are only to improve query performance and your customers are only performing read-only queries (no updates, no writeback), you can use the read-only database feature and create a scale out strategy as shown in Figure 15-21 to improve query performance for this type of multi-user scenario.

We recommend that you have multiple Analysis Services 2008 servers configured to read from a single database on a shared SAN (Storage Area Network) to form Scalable Shared Databases that can be queried by multiple users. These servers need to be load balanced using a network load balancer as shown in Figure 15-22. You need a separate isolated machine for processing the database when there are data updates. Once the database has been processed you can detach the database and copy it to your SAN. You can then utilize XMLA scripts to attach the database to the Analysis Services query servers in read-only mode. All the query servers will have an identical copy of the database and be able to serve multiple users. This scale out strategy will help you improve query performance for this type of multiple user scenario.

Scalable Shared Databases

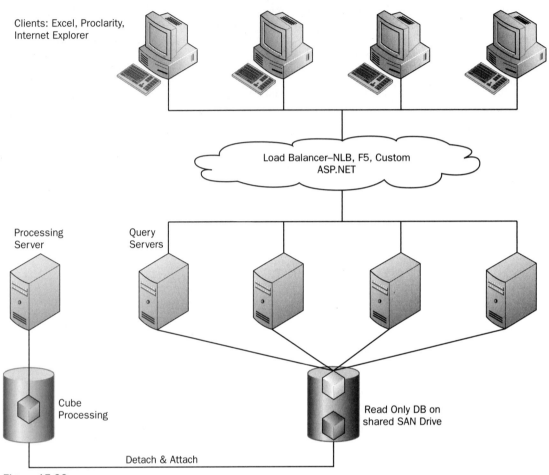

Clients: Excel, Proclarity,
Internet Explorer

Load Balancer–NLB, F5, Custom
ASP.NET

Processing
Server

Query
Servers

Cube
Processing

Read Only DB on
shared SAN Drive

Detach & Attach

Figure 15-22

Writeback Query Performance

As you learned in Chapter 12, with Analysis Services 2008 you can obtain improved writeback performance by enabling the MOLAP storage option when you enable writeback. When you perform cell writeback, Analysis Services writes data back to the relational table specified. In addition, the MOLAP partition associated with the writeback partition is reprocessed automatically. Because of this, all queries using the writeback partition will retrieve the data from the MOLAP storage rather than fetching the data from the relational table and then aggregating the data. Thus, using MOLAP storage for the writeback partition helps improve query performance. We recommend that you set MOLAP storage mode for the writeback partition when you enable the cube for cell writeback.

Summary

In this chapter you first learned about the calculation model in Analysis Services, followed by the query execution architecture of Analysis Services. You learned about the various tools that can be used to investigate the performance of Analysis Services. The SQL Server Profiler and perfmon counters in particular are very valuable tools that can help you investigate performance bottlenecks. You then learned about various classes of problems that can contribute to slow queries, along with recommendations on how to solve these problems. Finally, you learned about important query optimization techniques and best practices that can help you fine-tune your MDX queries. After reading Chapters 14 and 15, upon hearing the very word *performance*, your head should swell with visions of highly performing, scalable systems, each optimized to fulfill its designated mission!

Part IV

Integration with Microsoft Products

16

Data Mining

Not everyone is well versed in the area of data mining, so this chapter starts straight away with what data mining is and what it can be used for. So, without further ado, data mining is the process of applying algorithms to data sets with the goal of exposing patterns in the data that would not otherwise be noticed. The reason such patterns would not otherwise be noticed owes to the complexity and volume of data within which the patterns are embedded. Another, less academic, way to look at data mining is as a technology that can be used to answer questions like the following:

❑ When customers visit our corporate web site, what paths are they most likely to take when navigating through the site?

❑ When a $10 credit card transaction is processed at a gas station immediately followed by a $600 purchase on the same account from an electronics store in a different zip code, should a red flag be raised?

❑ For optimal sales revenue generation in a grocery store, which products should be placed in close proximity to one another?

❑ What additional products can we recommend to our online shoppers that will help increase our revenue?

To address these types of questions, and many others, you turn to data mining technology. In this chapter you learn about data mining and how it helps you answer questions by creating and using data mining models and applications. You will understand the data mining algorithms supported by SQL Server Analysis Services 2008 and how they can be used. In addition, you learn two data mining algorithms in depth. You learn to create data mining models in SSAS from relational data sources (relational mining models) as well as from OLAP cubes (OLAP mining models).

Data mining results depend on machine architecture. Therefore, there might be differences between the results you see shown in this chapter and those you see as you work through the samples. Don't be alarmed that you are not seeing the exact results as shown by the samples in this chapter.

The Data Mining Process

Wherever you look, people and businesses are collecting data, in some cases without even an obvious immediate purpose. Companies collect data for many reasons, including accounting, reporting, and marketing. Those companies with swelling data stores have executives with many more questions than answers; in this book you have seen how executives can use UDM-based analysis to find the answers they need. This is typically a process in which you know what you are looking for and can extract that information from your UDM. However, there might be additional information in your data that can help you make important business decisions that you are not aware of because you don't know what to look for. Data mining is the process of extracting interesting information from your data such as trends, clusters, and other patterns that can help you understand your data better. Data mining is accomplished through the use of statistical methods, as well as machine learning algorithms. The ultimate purpose of data mining is the discovery of subtle relationships between data items. It can also entail the creation of predictive models. When data mining is successfully applied, rules and patterns previously unknown and potentially useful emerge from heaps of data.

You don't need a vintage coal-mining helmet with a lamp to begin the data mining process (but if you feel more comfortable wearing one, you can likely find one on eBay). What really is required is a problem to solve with a very good understanding of the problem space; this isn't just an exploratory adventure. The main requirement is having the appropriate hardware to store the data to be analyzed and the analysis results. Then you need off-the-shelf data mining software or, if you are particularly knowledgeable, you can write your own software. In terms of hardware, you're going to need a machine for storing the data (typically relational databases that can store gigabytes or even terabytes of data) and a machine to develop and run your data mining application on. Though those are normally two different machines, these functions can all reside on a single machine. We discuss data mining software in terms of data mining algorithms, the infrastructure to use them, and data visualization tools for use in evaluating the results, such as the SQL Server 2008 Data Mining Add-Ins for Office 2007. Once you have the software and the required hardware, you need to have a good understanding of the data you are about to mine as well as the problem you are trying to solve. This is a critical prerequisite to have before you start using the software to perform data mining. You learn more about understanding the problem space and data in subsequent sections. Having the hardware and right software setup is a necessary precursor to the data mining process. If data miners had to go through a pre-flight checklist like pilots and co-pilots do, it might look something like this:

> **Data Miner 1:** "Ready to start pre-mine check."
>
> **Data Miner 2:** "Ok, data store on-line with verified access?"
>
> **Data Miner 1:** "Roger on the data store with access."
>
> **Data Miner 2:** "Software loaded and ready to run?"
>
> **Data Miner 1:** "Check."
>
> **Data Miner 2:** "Data visualization tools; loaded and ready to run?"
>
> **Data Miner 1:** "That's affirmative."
>
> **Data Miner 2:** "Then we're ready to start, call it in."
>
> **Data Miner 1:** "Sysadmin, sysadmin, this is miner 1, come in."
>
> *Static crackles over the communications equipment.*
>
> **Sysadmin:** "This is Sysadmin, go ahead miner 1."
>
> **Data Miner 1:** "Checklist complete, request clearance on server tango."
>
> **Sysadmin:** "Roger, miner 1, you are cleared for mining on tango. Over."

Once you have the hardware and software requirements satisfied you then get into the process of building a model or representation of your data, which helps you visualize and understand information in your data better. Over time, through systematic efforts and by trial and error, several methodologies and guidelines emerged. Figure 16-1 shows the typical process of data mining divided into five steps. First and foremost you need to understand the domain area and what your business needs. Once you understand the domain area you then need to understand the data. You might run some initial statistics on the data to understand it better. After understanding the data, you create mining models and train them with input data. You need to analyze the mining models and validate the results from the models. Once you have built mining models to suit your business needs, you deploy the models to your production system. Your end users can consume the results from the model directly from the model or through applications that utilize content from the model. You might have to go through this data mining lifecycle periodically to meet the changing needs of your business or data or both.

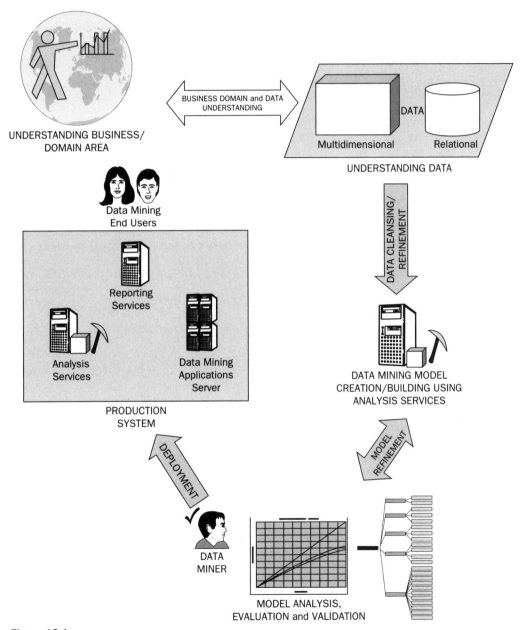

Figure 16-1

A great public resource on the data mining process (independent of specific data mining software products) is CRISP-DM (`http://www.crisp-dm.org`). CRISP-DM has a process guide that is available for free download. Yes, the process you see here maps roughly to the CRISP-DM process guide, but that would probably be true for any reasonable description of the data mining process.

Topic Area Understanding

In the preceding section we stated that, before a data miner begins to mine data, he or she first needs to understand the data and the problem space. Problem type and scope vary dramatically by subject area; from retail business, sales forecasts, and inventory management to logistics. Outside the realm of business there are data-mining-relevant science questions such as, "Some star has luminosity L, radiates brightly in the ultraviolet spectrum, and appears to have a small surface area. How hot is it likely to be?" If we have a reasonably sized database from which to train initially — more on what that means later — predictive data mining could uncover that the hotter the star, the shorter the wavelength peak in the star's spectrum and that the hottest stars peak in the ultraviolet area of the spectrum. You do need to have an idea about the topic or subject area and the problem you want to solve in order to identify non-intuitive relationships and patterns using data mining as a tool.

To accomplish the goal of your data mining project, you must understand what business you're in; moreover, what success means for your business in quantitative terms. By "understand the business" you have to sometimes ask hard questions like does your company sell sugar water with flavoring? Or does it really sell an imagined lifestyle of fun, action, and perpetual happiness through the marketing of sugar water? What metrics can be used to measure gradients of success? For example, volumes of sales, market share ownership, or customer feedback scores? You, as the person to mine your company's data or as a data mining consultant at a customer's site, need to know as much information as possible about the customer and what they are trying to achieve so that you can interpret the data mining results and make good recommendations. The bottom line is the company wants to improve profits. That can be accomplished by targeting the best sellers, adding value for customers (in the form of making suggestions based on customer usage patterns or detecting fraud against the customer's credit cards), and loss reduction (by identifying processes that drain the business of funds unnecessarily).

Data: Understand It, Configure It

First off, you must know how to collect data from disparate sources and then ensure the data description scheme (metadata) is integrated, consistent, and makes sense for all the data to be used. It is a good idea at this point, though not required, to explore the data by creating distributions, and running simple statistical tests. It is critical that the data be clean and free of type mismatches; otherwise the algorithms might not extract important information or, if they do, they might yield erroneous results. Other preparatory actions might be taken; for example, you might want to construct derived attributes, which are also called computed attributes or calculated columns. To verify the accuracy of the data mining algorithm's results, the source data is often divided into training and testing data. We recommend splitting your source data as follows: two-thirds for training purposes and the remaining one-third for testing and verification of results.

Understanding the data also involves understanding attributes of the data. For example, if you are looking at customer data, then name, gender, age, income, children, and so on, are possible attributes of the customer. You need to have a good understanding of the values of the attributes that will best represent attributes to the data mining model you are about to create. For example, gender of a customer can typically have values Male, Female, or Unknown. There are only three possible values for the gender attribute. If you look at income of the customer, though, the income can have a wide variance such as 0 to millions of dollars. These attributes need to be modeled appropriately for the chosen data mining algorithm to get the best results. The gender attribute would typically be modeled as a discrete attribute, which means fixed number of values, whereas the income would typically be modeled as continuous because there is a wide variation of the values for income. Understanding your data is critical.

Choose the Right Algorithm

Once you have a good understanding of your business and matching your needs to the data, you then need to choose the right data mining algorithm. A data mining algorithm is a technique or method by which data is analyzed and represented as patterns or rules, which are typically called data mining models. Choosing the right algorithm is not always easy. There might be several data mining algorithms that can solve your business problem. First, identify the algorithms that can solve your problem. The data mining model created by the algorithm is later analyzed to detect patterns or predict values for new data. Now, if you are aware of each data mining algorithm in depth, you can potentially pick the right one. If not, identify the algorithms that can potentially solve your problem and analyze results from each algorithm. Later in this chapter you learn about various algorithms supported by Analysis Services 2008 and what class of problems they are helpful in solving. Fine-tune the models of various algorithms and pick the most efficient one that provides you with the maximum satisfaction for your business needs. Several techniques can be used to compare the results of several mining models, such as lift versus profit chart (you learn about these later in this chapter). Once you have compared and identified the right model, you can use the specific algorithm for more detailed analysis.

Train, Analyze, and Predict

With the data mining algorithm in hand, you now need to choose the data set to identify and analyze interesting information for your business. Data mining is used not only to analyze existing data, but also to predict characteristics of new data. Typically the data set to be analyzed will be divided into two — a training set and a validation set — usually in the ratio 2:1. The training data set is fed as input to the data mining algorithm. The algorithm analyzes the data and creates an object called a data mining model, which represents characteristics of the data set to be analyzed. You need to identify the right training data set to best represent your data. You also need to consider training data size because that will directly impact training time. Training of a model is also referred to as *model building* or *processing of a model* in this book. Once you have determined the training data set, you train the model with the chosen algorithm. Once you have the trained model, you can analyze it and have a better understanding of the training data set and see if that provides you with useful information for your business.

Prediction is the process of predicting a value or values of a data set based on characteristics of the data set. For example, if you own a store and create a mining model of all your customers, you might classify them as Platinum, Gold, Silver, or Bronze membership based on several factors, such as salary, revenue they bring to your store, number of household members, and so on. Now, if a new member shops at your store you might be able to predict his or her membership based on salary, household members, and other factors. Once you have this information, you can send membership-relevant promotional coupons to the member to increase your sales. One of the new features in SQL Server 2008 is structured columns Drillthrough. This feature allows the addition of informational data such as email, address, and phone number into the mining structure that you do not want to consider when building the mining model, but do want to return when you query the data mining structure.

In addition to analyzing your data using a mining model, you can perform prediction for new data sets by simply providing the new data set as input to the model and retrieving the prediction results. To determine the accuracy of the model, you could use the validation data set, predict values for the validation set, and compare the actual values with the predicted values. Based on the number of accurate predictions, you will know how good the model is. If the model is not providing prediction results as per your expectations, you might be able to tweak it by changing properties of the data mining algorithm, choosing the right attributes as inputs, or choosing a different mining algorithm. You might have to periodically maintain the model based on additional information available to you — in this way, your model is trained well with the most up-to-date information and should yield optimal results.

Real-World Applications

Mapping theory to the real world is not always the most intuitive process imaginable. Several successful data mining applications have been deployed across various sectors. In this section you learn examples of real-world applications that use data mining technology. These applications will help you understand data mining and its use.

Fraud Detection

Have you ever received a call from your credit card company asking whether you made a specific credit card purchase? Do you know why you received the call? Chances are very good that it was due to an anomaly detected in your credit card usage as part of the company's fraud detection effort. Typically, customer usage patterns on credit cards are quite consistent. When a credit card is stolen, the usage pattern changes drastically. In spite of increasingly advanced theft protection schemes, credit card companies still lose a lot of money due to theft. Because credit card fraud is roughly 10 percent higher on the Internet than off, Visa introduced Cardholder Information Security Processing (CISP) in 2000 and MasterCard followed with its Site Data Protection Service (SDPS) in 2001. The CISP and SDPS only help in securing and validating the data and do not actually prevent the use of stolen credit cards. To detect anomalies and act immediately, credit card companies are now using data mining to detect unusual usage patterns of credit cards; and once such a pattern is detected, the customer is called to verify the legitimacy of certain purchases.

Increasing Profits in Retail

Now here is an example almost everyone can relate to. Have you shopped at Amazon (the online book seller) and seen a suggestion pop up that read something like this: "Customers who bought this book also bought the following" and then some list of pertinent books followed? Do you know how they do this? This is typically accomplished with the use of a data mining algorithm called "association rules." To boost sales, companies like Amazon use this algorithm to analyze the sales information of many customers. Based on your book buying behavior, Amazon uses the algorithm to predict what other books you would likely be interested in. From the list of books provided by the algorithm, they typically choose the top 5 books that have the highest likelihood of being purchased by the customer — then they suggest those books. Another example of where just such an algorithm is being used is in the area of DVD rentals. The Data Mining Add-In for Excel 2007 that you learn in Chapter 18 has a Table Analytics tool for Market Basket Analysis, which is an example of this type of application.

Data Mining in the NBA

As many of you sports fans know, NBA coaches need to analyze opponent teams and adopt appropriate strategies for winning future games. Typically, the coach will look for key players on the opposing team and appropriately match up his own players to counter the opposing team's strengths and expose their weaknesses. Relevant information can be gleaned from past games that have been analyzed and other sources. The NBA is fast paced, and coaches need to adapt based on current game situations. For this purpose, they need to analyze information every quarter and often in real time.

NBA coaching staffs collect information on players and points scored during a game and feed it into a data mining software application called Advanced Scout. With the help of this software, coaches are able to analyze patterns — when did the opponent score the most points, who was guarding the highest point scorer on the opposing team, where were the shots taken, and so on. With such information readily available, coaches can adapt to the situation and make decisions that will help their team to win.

Yes, but how was Advanced Scout helpful, you ask? When the Orlando Magic was devastated in the first two games of the 1997 season finals, which was against the second-seed Miami Heat, the team's fans began to hang their heads in shame. Advanced Scout showed the Orlando Magic coaches something that none of them had previously recognized. When Brian Shaw and Darrell Armstrong were in the game, something was sparked within their teammate Penny Hardaway — the Magic's leading scorer at that time. Armstrong was provided more play-time and hence Hardaway was far more effective. The Orlando Magic went on to win the next two games and nearly caused the upset of the year. Fans everywhere rallied around the team, and naysayers quickly replaced their doubts with season-ticket purchases for the following year.

Data Mining in Call Centers

Companies spend a lot of money on call center operations to meet customer needs. Customers use a toll-free number provided by the company and the company pays for each call based on the duration of the call. Typically, most calls target a few specific questions. For example, if the documentation for product setup was not sufficient, the call center might get calls with the same question or related questions on getting the product set up and configured properly.

Often the information obtained from customers is entered into the computer system for further analysis. With the help of Text Mining, the customers' questions can be analyzed and categorized. This type of analysis can identify a set of questions that are due to a specific problem. Companies can use this information to create a FAQ site where they can post answers on how to solve the specific problem. Making the FAQ available to provide answers to common problems helps the company and its customers have a faster turnaround, saving both time and money. In addition to this, the call center operators can be trained to use the information provided by Text Mining to easily nail down a solution to the problem posed by the customer. The duration of each call is reduced, thereby saving valuable cash for the company.

Data Mining Algorithms in SQL Server Analysis Services 2008

Analysis Services 2008 provides you with nine data mining algorithms that you can utilize to solve various business problems. These algorithms can be broadly classified into five categories based on the nature of the business problem they can be applied to. They are:

- ❑ Classification
- ❑ Regression
- ❑ Segmentation
- ❑ Sequence analysis
- ❑ Association

Classification data mining algorithms help solve business problems such as identifying the type of membership (Platinum, Gold, Silver, Bronze) a new customer should receive or whether the requested loan can be approved for a customer based on his or her attributes. Classification algorithms predict one or more discrete variables based on the attributes of the input data. Discrete variables are variables that contain a limited set of values. Some examples of discrete variables are gender, number of children in a house, and number of cars owned by a customer.

Regression algorithms are similar to classification algorithms; instead of predicting discrete attributes, however, they predict one or more continuous variables. Continuous variables are variables that can have many values. Examples of continuous variables are yearly income, age of a person, and commute distance to work. Algorithms belonging to the regression category should be provided with at least one input attribute that is of type continuous. For example, assume you want to predict the sale price of your house, a continuous value, and determine the profit you would make by selling the house. The price of the house would depend on several factors, such as square feet area (another continuous value), zip code, and house type (single family, condo, or town home), which are discrete variables. Hence regression algorithms are primarily suited for business problems where you have at least one continuous attribute as input and one or more attributes that are predictable.

Segmentation algorithms are probably the most widely used algorithms. Segmentation is the process of creating segments or groups of items based on the input attributes. Customer segmentation is one of the most common business applications, where stores and companies segment their customers based on the various input attributes. One of the most common uses of segmentation is to perform targeted mailing campaigns to those customers who are likely to make purchases. This reduces cost when compared with sending mail to all customers, thereby maximizing the profit for the company.

Sequence analysis algorithms analyze and group input data based on a certain sequence of operations. For example, if you want to analyze the navigation patterns of Internet users (sequence and order of pages visited by a user on the Internet) and group them based on their navigations, sequence analysis algorithms would be used. Based on the sequence of pages visited you can identify interests of people and provide appropriate information to the users as a service or show advertisements relevant to the users' preferences to increase sales of specific products. For example, if you navigate through pages of baby products on www.amazon.com, subsequent visits to Amazon pages might result in baby product–related advertisements. Similarly, sequence analysis is also used in genomic science to group a sequence of genes with similar sequences.

Association data mining algorithms help you to identify association in the data set. Typically these algorithms are used for performing market-basket analysis where association between various products purchased together are analyzed. Based on the analysis, associations between various products are identified and these help in the cross-selling of products together to boost sales. One famous data mining example highlights associations — customers buying diapers also bought beer, and the purchases occurred on Thursday/Friday. One of the reasons is that diapers often need replenishing and women request their husbands or significant others to buy them. Men often buy over the weekend, and hence these purchases were made together. Based on this association, supermarkets can have diapers and beer stocked adjacently, which helps boost the sales of beer.

The following sections give brief descriptions of the nine data mining algorithms supported in Analysis Services 2008. The description gives you an overview of the algorithm and scenarios where it can be utilized. We recommend you refer to SQL Server Analysis Services 2008 documentation for details such as algorithm properties, their values, and various content types supported by the algorithm for input and predictable columns. Following these descriptions you learn two data mining algorithms in detail by creating mining models using the Data Mining Wizard.

Microsoft Decision Trees

Microsoft Decision Trees is a classification algorithm that is used for predictive modeling and analysis. A classification algorithm is an algorithm that selects the best possible outcome for an input data from a set of possible outcomes. A data set called the *training data* that contains several attributes is provided as input to the algorithm. Usage of the attributes as either input or predictable are also provided to the algorithm. The classification algorithm analyzes the attributes of the input data and arrives at a distribution, which includes a combination of input attributes and their values that result in the value of the predictable column. Microsoft Decision Trees is helpful in predicting both discrete and continuous attributes. If the data type of the predictable attribute is continuous, the algorithm is called Microsoft Regression Trees and there are additional properties to control the behavior of the regression analysis.

Microsoft Naïve Bayes

Naïve Bayes is another classification algorithm available in Analysis Services 2008 that is used for predictive analysis. The Naïve Bayes algorithm calculates the value of the predictable attribute based on the probabilities of the input attribute in the training data set. Naïve Bayes helps you predict the outcome of the predictable attribute quickly because it assumes the input attribute is independent. Compared to the other data mining algorithms in Analysis Services 2008, Naïve Bayes is computationally less intense for model creation.

Microsoft Clustering

The Microsoft Clustering algorithm is a segmentation algorithm that helps in grouping the sample data set into segments based on characteristics of the data. The clustering algorithm helps identify relationships that exist within a specific data set. A typical example would be grouping store customers based on their characteristic purchasing patterns. Based on this information you can classify the importance of certain customers to your bottom-line. The Microsoft Clustering algorithm is unique because it is a scalable algorithm that is not constrained by the size of the data set. Unlike the Decision Trees or Naïve Bayes algorithm, the Microsoft Clustering algorithm does not require you to specify a predictable attribute for building the model.

Microsoft Sequence Clustering

As the name indicates, the Sequence Clustering algorithm groups sequences in the sample data. Similar to the clustering algorithm, the sequence clustering algorithm groups the data sets but based on the sequences instead of the attributes of the customers. An example of where Sequence Clustering would be used is to group the customers based on the navigation paths of the web site they have visited. Based on the sequence, the customer can be prompted to go to a web page that would be of interest.

Microsoft Association Rules

The Microsoft Association algorithm is an algorithm that typically identifies associations or relationships between products that are purchased. If you have shopped at Amazon.com you have likely noticed information "people who have purchased item one have also purchased item two." Identifying the association between products purchased is called market basket analysis. The algorithm analyzes products in a customer's shopping basket, and predicts other products the customer is likely to buy. That prediction is based on purchase co-occurrence of similar products by other customers. This algorithm is often used for cross-selling through product placement in the store.

Microsoft Neural Network

The Microsoft Neural Network algorithm is a classification algorithm similar to Microsoft Decision Trees. It calculates probabilities for each value of the predictable attribute, but it does so by creating internal classification and regression models that are iteratively improved based on the actual value. The algorithm has three layers (the input layer, an optional hidden layer, and an output layer) that are used to improve the prediction results. The actual value of a training case is compared to the predictable value and the error difference is fed back within the algorithm to improve the prediction results. Similar to the decision trees algorithm, the Neural Network algorithm is used for predicting discrete and continuous attributes. One of the main advantages of neural networks over the decision trees algorithm is that neural networks can handle complex as well as large amounts of training data much more efficiently.

Microsoft Time Series

The Microsoft Time Series algorithm is used in predictive analysis but is different from other predictive algorithms in Analysis Services 2008 because during prediction it does not take input columns to predict the predictable column value. Rather, it identifies trends in the input data and predicts future values based on those trends. A typical application of a time series algorithm is to predict the sales of a specific product based on the sales trend of the product in the past, along with the sales trend of a related product. Another example would be to predict stock prices of a company based on the stock price of another company.

Analysis Services 2008 Time Series algorithm is used for predicting continuous attributes. Analysis Services 2005 supported a Time Series algorithm called ARTxp (Auto Regression Trees with Cross Predict). In addition to that, SSAS 2008 supports the time series algorithm called ARIMA (Auto-Regressive Integrated Moving Average). Hence a time series analysis scenario can be modeled by using the previous ARTxp algorithm, the new ARIMA algorithm, or can be modeled by simultaneously creating both these algorithms. In the latter case, the future predictions are a blend of the values predicted by both algorithms. For the time series algorithms, the DMX language was extended with statements accepting prediction join syntax for time series that allow new data to be appended to the data used for training and to obtain future predictions using the new extended data. You can use this approach to split the training data into two groups, D1 and D2. You can first create a model using D1 and then use the join syntax in DMX to either append D2 or replace data in D1 to obtain future predictions.

Microsoft Linear Regression

Microsoft Linear Regression is a special case of the Microsoft Decision Trees algorithm where you set an algorithm property so that the algorithm will never create a split and thereby end up with a linear regression. The algorithm property MINIMUM_LEAF_CASES for the Microsoft Decision Tree will be set to a value greater than the number of input cases used to train the model. The linear regression algorithm will typically be used when you want to find the relationship between two continuous columns. The algorithm finds the equation of a line that best fits data representing the relationship between the input columns. The Microsoft Linear Regression algorithm only supports input columns that have certain content types. The content type typically used will be continuous. The algorithm does not support the content types discrete or discretized. For more details on the content types supported by the algorithm, please refer to product documentation.

Microsoft Logistic Regression

Microsoft Logistic Regression is a variation of the Microsoft Neural Networks algorithm where the hidden layer is not present. The simplest form of logistic regression is to predict a column that has two states. The input columns can contain many states and can be of different content types (discrete, continuous, discretized, and so on). You can certainly model such a predictable column using linear regression but the linear regression might not restrict the values to the minimum and maximum values of the column. Logistic Regression is able to restrict the output values for the predictable column to the minimum and maximum values with the help of an S-shaped curve instead of the linear line, which would have been created by a linear regression. In addition, logistic regression is able to predict columns of content type discrete or discretized and is able to take input columns that are content type discrete or discretized.

Working with Mining Models

SQL Server Analysis Services 2008 provides two types of mining models: the relational mining model and the OLAP mining model. Relational mining models are created directly from the relational data source and OLAP mining models are created from an existing cube or part of a cube. Use of the nine types of data mining algorithms is made within the context of the relational or OLAP mining models. In this chapter you learn both these models by creating mining models using a few algorithms and analyzing the results.

Relational Mining Model

The Adventure Works DW 2008 sample relational database has specific patterns that can be used to demonstrate the various algorithms available in Analysis Services 2008. In this section you learn how to create and analyze a decision tree model and a clustering model. Obviously, you need to create a new mining model to explore and analyze the information. When you build a mining model, Analysis Services 2008 retrieves data from the data source and stores it in a proprietary format. Building several mining models from the same data set will result in redundant data stored in Analysis Services 2008. In order to share data across several mining models, Analysis Services 2008 stores the information about the data that can be shared across several mining models in an object called a *mining structure*. Internally the information read from relational data sources is stored in a cube in order to efficiently retrieve the data during mining model creation. The mining structure stores data type of attributes, the corresponding column in the data source, and allows you to modify the certain data mining properties that are common across all of your mining models.

Have you received coupons in the mail? If you have a postal address, you have. Retail companies used to send coupons to all customers and even some people who weren't customers. That was expensive and of less than optimal efficiency. In order to minimize cost and maximize profit, companies now use data mining to select targets for coupon or other special postal distributions. Based on certain attributes, retail companies can classify customers into groups (for example; Gold, Silver, or Bronze membership). By doing this they clearly identify unique characteristics of the group. From there, targeted mailing to those groups can be made instead of mailing to every address on file. This practice saves marketing money for companies and results in a better probability of making sales.

The following steps show you how to solve the targeted mailing type problem by creating a relational mining model on top of the vTargetMail view in the AdventureWorksDW2008 relational database that is available as part of the SQL Server 2008 samples. To create a relational mining model, you first need a Data Source View containing the table(s) on top of which you want to build a mining model.

1. Create a new Analysis Services project named DM2008Tutorial.

2. Create a data source to the AdventureWorksDW2008 relational database.

3. Create a DSV called Adventure Works that includes the vTargetMail view from the Adventure Works DW2008 data source.

   vTargetMail is a view that retrieves information from several tables in the AdventureWorksDW2008 database. The vTargetMail view contains information about customers who buy bicycles. Based on the information in the view, you can identify potential customers who are likely to buy bicycles. The vTargetMail view has been specifically designed to contain patterns that can be identified by the data mining algorithms. As the name of the view indicates, vTargetMail is used to demonstrate the usefulness of the data mining where the customers can be categorized based on their attributes, and targeted mails with discounts or attractions can be sent only to customers who are likely to buy bicycles.

4. To create a relational mining model, right-click the Mining Structures folder in the Solution Explorer and select New Mining Structure as shown in Figure 16-2 to launch the Data Mining Wizard that helps you to create data mining structures and models.

Figure 16-2

5. The welcome page provides information about the Data Mining Wizard. Click the Next button.

You will now see the Select the Definition Method page as shown in Figure 16-3. This page allows you to create a mining model from a relational data source or from a cube.

6. Select the "From existing relational database or data warehouse" radio button and click Next.

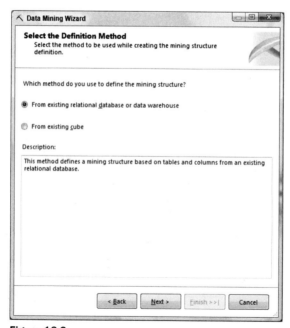

Figure 16-3

On the Create the Data Mining Structure page you can select the data mining technique to use for modeling. If you click the drop-down list box you can see all the available algorithms, as shown in Figure 16-4. Analysis Services also provides you the option of adding your own data mining technique. If you have added a custom data mining technique and exposed it you will see your data mining technique in this drop-down list box.

7. Select Microsoft Decision Trees and click Next.

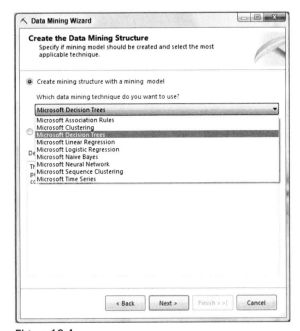

Figure 16-4

8. On the Select Data Source View page, select the DSV that contains vTargetMail (the DSV you created in step 3) and click Next.

The Specify Table Types page allows you to select the table(s) upon which you create a mining model. The Specify Table Types page, as shown in Figure 16-5, shows two selections: Case (the primary table) and Nested. Certain algorithms are used for problems such as market-basket analysis and the need to analyze data across multiple tables. In such cases you need to select certain table(s) as Nested tables. Typically there is a one-to-many relationship between the case and nested tables.

Figure 16-5

9. Select vTargetMail as a Case table and click Next.

On the Specify the Training Data page of the wizard you select the columns from the source table(s) that are to be used in the creation of mining models. In addition, you need to specify whether a specific column should be used as a key column, input column, or predictable column. If you specify a column as an input column, Analysis Services uses this column as an input to the mining model for determining patterns. If a specific column is marked as predictable, Analysis Services allows you to predict this column for a new data set based on the existing model if the input columns for the new data set are provided.

In the current data set you want to predict if a customer is a potential buyer of bikes. The column BikeBuyer determines if an existing customer bought bikes before. Therefore, you need to mark this column as a predictable column. Once you have marked this column as predictable, you need to identify the potential factors that can influence a customer who buys bikes. If you think certain factors can influence a customer to buy bikes we recommend you select those columns as input columns. The wizard provides you a way to recommend columns as input columns by analyzing a sample data set.

10. Select the BikeBuyer column as predictable by enabling the checkbox as shown in Figure 16-6.

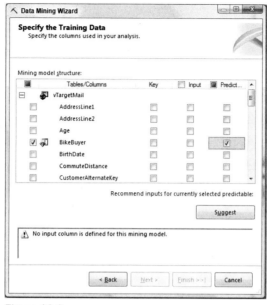

Figure 16-6

11. Click the Suggest button.

The wizard analyzes a sample of the data set and provides you with the list of columns that are related to the selected predictable attribute BikeBuyer, as shown in Figure 16-7. The score column indicates how close an attribute is related to the BikeBuyer column; a higher number indicates a stronger relationship. Stronger relationship can mean that a specific column can influence the chosen predictable column. Based on the score the wizard will auto select certain columns as input columns. You can deselect these attributes or select additional attributes that you think might influence a customer's decision on buying bikes.

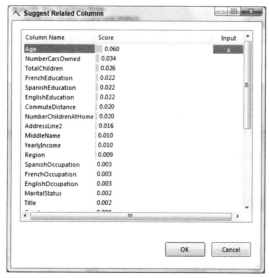

Figure 16-7

12. Click OK to continue.

13. The selections you made in the Suggest Related Columns page can now be seen in the Specify the Training Data page, as shown in Figure 16-8.

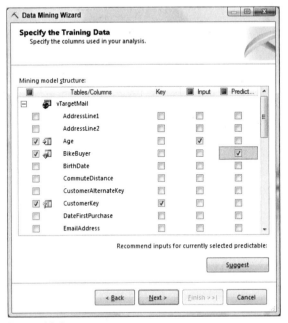

Figure 16-8

14. Select the columns Age, CommuteDistance, EnglishEducation, Gender, HouseOwnerFlag, MaritalStatus, NumberCarsOwned, NumberChildrenAtHome, Region, TotalChildren, and YearlyIncome as input columns and click Next.

The selected columns along with their content types and data types are shown in the Specify Columns' Content and Data Type page. The relational data type of a column is mapped to the corresponding data type used within Analysis Services 2008 by the Data Mining Wizard. As shown in Figure 16-9, the column Content Type indicates how each selected column will be used by Analysis Services when creating the mining model. You learn more about these content types when refining this model.

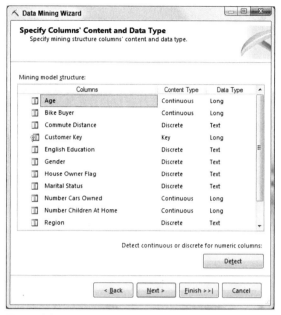

Figure 16-9

15. Make all of the Continuous content types Discrete except Yearly Income and click Next.

In SSAS 2008 the ability to specify some percentage of your data for testing the model is built into the product. The Create Testing Set page shown in Figure 16-10 allows you to specify the percentage of data to hold back and also the maximum number of cases in the testing data set. You can specify both options to restrict the testing data used for verifying model accuracy.

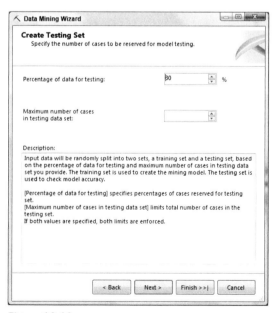

Figure 16-10

16. In the Create Testing Set page, accept the default value of 30 percent for "Percentage of data for testing" and click Next.

Because all mining models are contained within a mining structure, Analysis Services automatically creates a mining structure with the same name as the mining model. However, similar to the completion pages of dimension and cube wizards, you can specify a different name for the mining structure as well as the mining model in the completion page of the Data Mining Wizard. You also have the option to allow drill through while analyzing a mining model to understand the training data corresponding to a specific node.

17. Enable the Allow drill through option so that you have the ability to see additional details when you browse the mining model. Keep the default mining structure and model names and click Finish to create the mining model.

The mining structure object can be seen in the mining structure editor, as shown in Figure 16-11. The mining structure editor contains five views: Mining Structure, Mining Models, Mining Model Viewer, Mining Accuracy Chart, and Mining Model Prediction. By default you will be in the Mining Structure tab. The mining structure view contains two panes. The Data Source View pane shows the tables used by the mining structure and allows you to perform the operations available within a DSV. The pane on the left shows the columns of the mining structure in a tree view. You can delete existing columns or add columns to the mining structure by dragging and dropping them from the DSV. The properties of a column can be edited in the Properties pane when the column is selected.

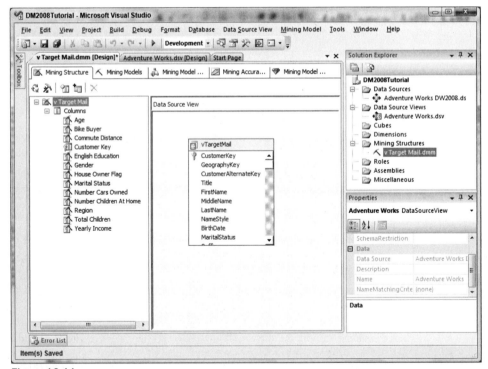

Figure 16-11

Figure 16-12 shows the Mining Models view. The Mining Models view shows the mining models in the current mining structure. You can have one or more mining models within each mining structure. The columns of the mining structure are by default inherited as columns of a mining model. Each column of a mining structure can be used for a specific purpose in a mining model. A column can be used as input to the mining model, used as a predictable column, used for both input and as a predictable column, or not be used by the mining model at all. These four usages are represented as Input, Predict Only, Predict, and Ignore, respectively, in the Mining Models view. These usages can be selected from the drop-down list box corresponding to a column in a mining model. You can add additional mining models within a mining structure by right-clicking in the Mining Models view and selecting New Mining Model. The Mining Structure Wizard detects the content type of the mining model columns based on a sample of the data.

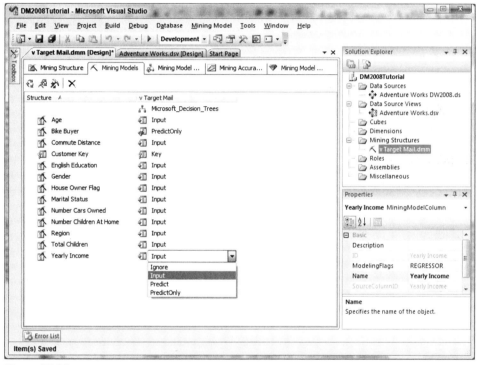

Figure 16-12

The mining structure editor is used to make refinements to the mining model created by the Data Mining Wizard. You will learn to make refinements in the mining structure editor by making a few refinements to the decision tree mining model you have created. You will make two refinements: Change the content type for column Age and the usage of the Bike Buyer column. Age is a unique attribute that can be viewed as discrete, because the value is recorded as an integer between 0 and 100. If you have ever participated in a market survey you know they generally ask your age within a specific range rather than your exact age. Almost no adult likes to admit his or her age publicly, especially in the later years, so if you find yourself extremely reticent to mention your age, be worried. Be very worried. In this example you model Age as a set of ranges rather than a discrete value. This content type is called Discretized. Discretized means that the values will be split across N number of ranges and any value of Age will be assigned the new value based on the range. The number of ranges is controlled by the property DiscretizationBucketCount. Based on the value set for the DiscretizationBucketCount property, Analysis Services 2008 will identify the right ranges based on the minimum and maximum values of Age.

18. In the Mining Models view, select Age in the Structure column. The properties for the Age column can be seen in the Properties window as shown in Figure 16-13.

19. Change the Content property from Discrete to Discretized and set the DiscretizationBucketCount property to 10.

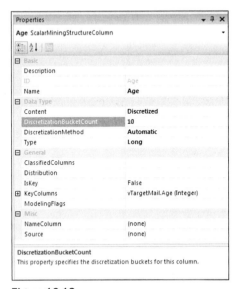

Figure 16-13

20. Change the usage of the Bike Buyer column to Predict.

The usage of the column Bike Buyer was initially set to Predict Only because this is what you selected in the wizard. The value Predict means that the Bike Buyer attribute will be used as an input as well as an output to the mining model. By choosing the Bike Buyer as an input column you are providing additional information to the mining model algorithm so that the model accurately represents the input data. You have now completed all the refinements to the decision tree mining model and it is ready to be deployed on your SSAS instance.

21. Hit the F5 button to deploy the mining model.

Business Intelligence Development Studio (BIDS) sends the definition of the entire project you created to the server along with a process request. Once the database is processed, BIDS switches the view to the Mining Model Viewer as shown in Figure 16-14. The decision trees algorithm identifies the factors influencing customers to buy bikes and splits customers based on those factors and stores it within the model. The Mining Model Viewer represents the contents of the mining model in the form of a tree view. The root of the tree starts with a single node that represents all the customers. Each node shows the percentage of customers (shown by the horizontal bar within the node) who have bought bikes based on the input set. Each node is split into multiple nodes based on the next most important factor that determines why a customer has bought a bike. The tree contains nodes at several levels from 1 to N based on the number of splits determined by the decision tree algorithm. Each node in the tree is associated with a specific level in the tree. The root node is at level 1, which is the topmost level. The depth of the tree is measured by the number of splits or levels of the tree. In the Mining Model Viewer you can select the depth of the tree to view using the Show Level slider above the tree view. Figure 16-14 shows nodes with horizontal bars that are shaded with two colors: red and blue. The Mining Legend window shows the legend for the colors in the horizontal bars of a node. If the Mining Legend window is not visible, right-click in the Mining Model Viewer and select Show Legend.

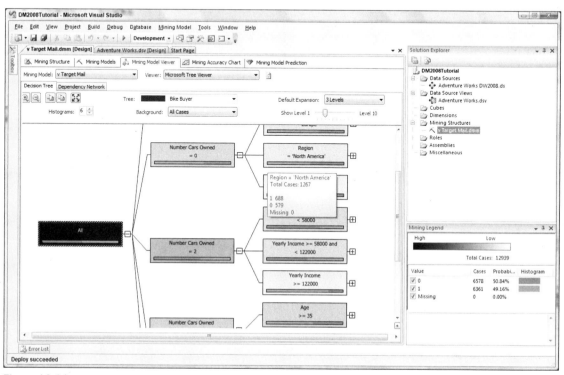

Figure 16-14

The Mining Legend window in Figure 16-14 shows that blue (Value=0) indicates customers who are not bike buyers, red (Value=1) indicates the customers who have bought bikes, and white indicates customers for whom the BikeBuyer value is missing. The split from a node at one level to nodes in the next level is based on a condition that is determined by an input column that influences the predictable attribute, which is shown within the node such as Region=North America.

In the sample that you are analyzing, the most important factor that determines a customer buying a bike is the number of cars owned by the customer. The root node is split into five nodes based on the values for the number of cars owned (zero to four); three of these nodes are shown in Figure 16-14. If you click the node with Number Cars Owned =2 you will see that 39.41 percent of such customers are likely to be bike buyers. The next most important influencing factor when the number of cars owned is 2 is the customer's Yearly Income. You can traverse the tree from each node to identify the conditions that are likely to affect customers' decisions to buy a bike. Based on the information available in the mining model, you can not only understand factors influencing the customers' decisions to buy bikes, but now you predict if a customer is a potential bike buyer based on his or her properties. Once you identify potential customers you can send targeted mails to customers who are potential buyers rather than all customers.

Once created, can your model predict accurately? If so, how accurate is it? How much trust can you place in the results of the model? To answer these questions the data mining editor has a view called the Mining Accuracy Chart, as shown in Figure 16-15. The Mining Accuracy Chart view contains four sub-views or sub-tabs that help you validate model accuracy. These are Input Selection, Lift Chart, Classification Matrix, and Cross Validation. The Input Selection view provides you with three panes.

The first pane allows you to select certain predictable attributes and specific values to use in Lift Chart comparison. In this example we only have the Bike Buyer column as predictable. You can choose a specific value 0 or 1 for Bike Buyer to analyze the accuracy for specific values if needed. The second pane allows you a way to specify an input data set to validate the mining model as shown in Figure 16-15. You can use the test cases in mining model or test cases in mining structure based on the data you have held back while creating the model. The third option allows you to specify an entirely new data set. If you select the third option you will see a button that allows you to map the columns from a new data set to the columns of the mining model. If you select a new data set to validate against, you can use the third pane to specify a filter condition using the Open Filter Editor button in the Filter pane. This editor allows you to specify conditions to restrict the data set or enter your own query to restrict the data set.

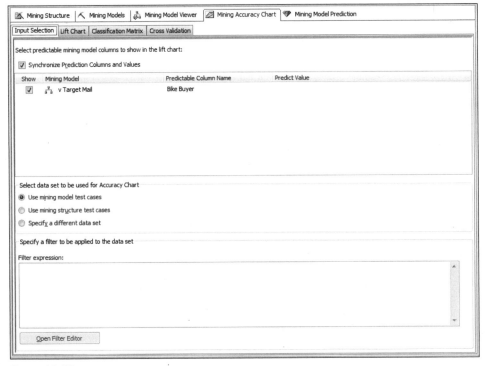

Figure 16-15

The mining model is used to predict the Bike Buyer value for each customer. If the predicted value is the same as the actual value in the validation data set you have chosen, the model has predicted the value correctly. If not, the model has inaccurately predicted the Bike Buyer value for the customer.

To analyze the accuracy of the mining model, do the following:

1. In the Mining Accuracy Chart view, select "Use mining model test cases."

Analysis Services knows the original data source that was selected and the input data set that was held back for validation. SSAS will now use the 30 percent of the data set that was held back to validate the accuracy of the mining model. Analysis Services 2008 provides two ways to analyze the validity of the model. One is to show the results graphically and the other is to show the actual numbers. To see the validity of the model graphically, select the Lift Chart page of the Mining Accuracy Chart view. You will see the graph as shown in Figure 16-16. The X-axis shows the percentage of data set used for prediction and the Y-axis shows the percentage of prediction correctness. You can see a legend window providing details on the two lines. If you created a perfect model that predicted all inputs correctly, the percentage correctness will always be 100 percent. This is represented by a blue line in the graph (the 45 degree line in Figure 16-16). In the current model the predictable attribute value can only have one of the two values: 0 or 1. Obviously you would want a model that predicts values very close to that of an ideal model. This graph gives you a visual way to easily compare the prediction correctness of the model as compared to the ideal model. The prediction correctness percentage of the model is shown with a red line. You can see from Figure 16-16 that the prediction correctness of the model does not match that of the ideal model but it is reasonably good because the prediction results are correct for 75 percent (population correct % for 100% of overall population) of the overall data set as shown in the Mining Legend.

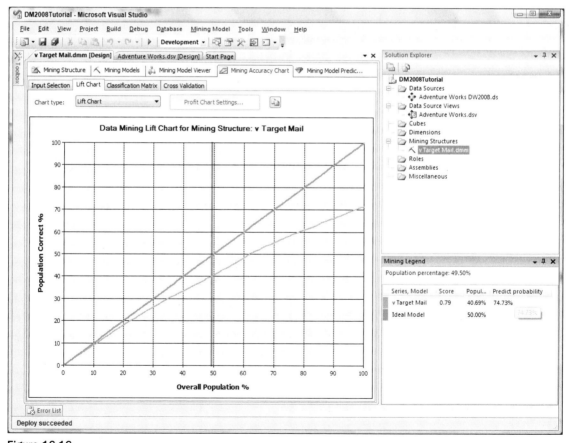

Figure 16-16

This is all well and good, but how is the lift chart calculated and visually represented? Analysis Services 2008 predicts the Bike Buyer attribute for every row in the input table. Each prediction also has a value called Predict Probability that provides a confidence value associated with the prediction. If you have a predict probability of 1.0, it means that the model believes the predicted value is always correct. If the predict probability for an input is 0.90, that means there is a 90 percent probability the predicted value is correct. After predicting the values for all the input rows, the results are ordered based on the predict probability. Then the predicted results are compared with the original values to calculate the prediction correctness percentage, and they are plotted on a graph. This can be seen in the graph in Figure 16-16 where the lines indicating the current model and ideal model are nearly identical up to 10 percent of the population. The Mining Legend shows the Score, Population Correct percentage, and Predict Probability values for a specific population selection. Figure 16-16 shows that the population percentage is 49.50 percent, which is indicated by a darker vertical line. You can select a different population percentage by clicking the mouse on a specific population. When 100 percent of the data set is considered, the decision tree mining model is able to predict correct values for 71 percent of the data set correctly. For an ideal model this prediction value is 100 percent. The score for a model helps you to compare multiple models within a mining structure. The value is between 0 and 1 and shows the effectiveness of one model versus another model. A higher score value means the model is more efficient.

Two types of charts are provided by the Mining Accuracy Chart viewer to help in analysis of the mining model. You have just seen the lift chart. The second chart is called the profit chart. The profit chart helps you analyze the potential profit your business would make based on four input parameters: number of samples, fixed cost incurred, cost per each row, and profit gained due to prediction. You will see the benefit of the profit chart only when there is a significant cost involved per sample.

2. Select the chart type Profit Chart in the drop-down list box.

3. In the Profit Chart Settings dialog, specify the Individual Cost as 11 to indicate the cost of mailing to a customer.

4. Leave the remaining values set to their defaults and click OK.

You will now see the profit chart as shown in Figure 16-17.

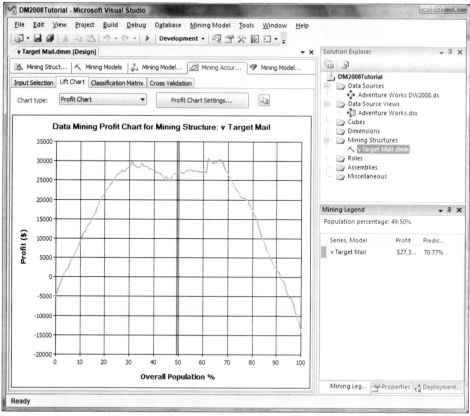

Figure 16-17

Analysis Services 2008 predicts the Bike Buyer value and calculates profit based on the profit chart settings you have provided. Similar to the lift chart, you can move the gray vertical line. The Mining Legend shows the Profit and Predict Probability values for the corresponding population percentage selected by the gray vertical line as shown in Figure 16-17. Similar to the lift chart, the predicted values are sorted based on prediction probability and then plotted on the graph. Therefore, the lower values of overall population percentage have higher prediction probability values. As you can see from the profit chart, the profit increases with increase in the sample size, reaches a maximum profit, and then drops down. If you send mail to the entire population, you are likely expected to incur a loss of about $14,000. You definitely want to get the maximum profit. The maximum profit you can obtain for the specified lift chart parameters is around $30,800 when you mail to about 62.38 percent of the population. To maximize your profit, you need to send mails only to customers who have a prediction probability greater than the prediction probability corresponding to the population percentage that has maximum profit. Thus the profit chart helps improve the profit of a business by saving the cost that would have been incurred for mailing to customers who are not potential buyers.

The third sub-view in the Mining Accuracy Chart view is called the Classification Matrix. The classification matrix of the decision tree model on vTargetMail is shown in Figure 16-18. The classification matrix shows the original and predicted values for the Predict attribute. In the decision tree model, the predictable values for Bike Buyer are 0 or 1. The matrix shows the actual and predicted values for all the specified input rows. As shown in Figure 16-18, the columns indicate the actual values and the rows indicate the predicted value. There are a total of 2,774 input rows that have the Bike Buyer value 0. Of these, the model predicted 2145 of them to be the correct value 0, whereas it predicted the remaining 629 rows incorrectly to value 1. Similarly, the model predicted 1856 of 2774 input rows correctly to have a value of 1. Please note the prediction values might be slightly difference based on your machine. This matrix provides you an overview of how good the predicted values are as compared to the actual values in a matrix format.

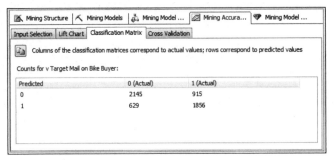

Figure 16-18

The last view in the Mining Accuracy Chart is the Cross Validation tab. Analysis Services 2008 provides you with the ability to validate the chosen mining models using cross validation methods. It does this by splitting the training data set into a specified number of folds. (Fold count is a value that you input in the Cross Validation tab as shown in Figure 16-19.) Folds are also called partitions. Once the data set is split into multiple partitions, Analysis Services creates a mining model for each partition. The training data set corresponding to a mining model for a specific partition is the data set from all the remaining partitions other than the current partition. Analysis Services then evaluates the accuracy of the model using the data set in the current partition. The result will be the quality of the model measured on a fold of the input data set as captured by the following measures: for discrete attributes, the number of false and true classifications, log score, lift, and root mean square error; for continuous attributes, root mean square error, mean absolute error, and log score; for clustering model, the case likelihood measure. The last page in the Mining Accuracy Chart view helps in using the cross validation feature and analyzing the effectiveness of model. Follow these steps to perform cross validation.

1. Switch to the Cross Validation page in the Mining Accuracy Chart view.

2. Set Fold Count to 4.

3. Set Max Cases to 3000.

4. Click the Get Results button.

You will now see the results of the cross validation as shown in Figure 16-19. This view allows you analyze the results of the cross validation done comparing the data set against the mining model. In Figure 16-19 for the decision tree model, you can see the first two tables indicating the accuracy of the overall model. The key factors to consider here are the average percentage of values where the mining model predicts accurately as well as the standard deviation. Ideally you want the Value column as close as possible to the partition size with a low standard deviation. Please be aware that the cross validation results for various mining model algorithms are different and need to be interpreted appropriately.

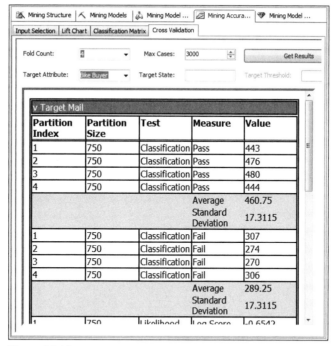

Figure 16-19

Having seen the accuracy of the model created by Analysis Services 2008, you can meaningfully start predicting the values using the model. The Mining Model Prediction view helps you perform predictions and save the results. Figure 16-20 shows the Mining Model Prediction view. Similar to the Mining Accuracy Chart view, you can specify the case table that contains the input data for which you want to perform prediction. Follow these steps to understand how to predict if new customers are bike buyers.

1. In the Select Input Table(s) section of the Mining Model Prediction view, click the Select Case Table button. In the Select Table dialog that appears, select the source table vTargetMail for which you will now predict the Bike Buyer value.

   You can select columns from the input table and certain data mining prediction functions or custom expressions on the predicted values to retrieve results such as the top 10 percent of the customers or the top 10 customers. The columns from the input table or applying certain data mining prediction functions can be selected in the lower half of the window pane as shown in Figure 16-20.

2. Select the CustomerKey, FirstName, LastName, and EmailAddress columns from the input table vTargetMail as shown in Figure 16-20.

3. Select the Bike Buyer predictable column from the mining model vTargetMail as shown in Figure 16-20.

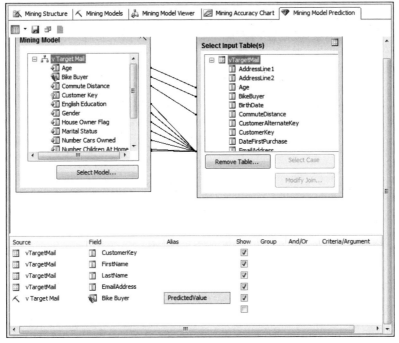

Figure 16-20

4. Click the "Switch to query result view" button (leftmost button on the Mining Model Prediction view toolbar) as shown in Figure 16-21 to see the prediction results.

You will see the results of the prediction as shown in Figure 16-21. You can specify constraints to the predicted value such as predicted value = 1 so that the results view only shows customers who are likely to buy bikes.

	FirstName	LastName	EmailAddress	PredictedValue
	Jon	Yang	jon24@adventure-works.com	1
	Eugene	Huang	eugene10@adventure-works.com	1
	Ruben	Torres	ruben35@adventure-works.com	0
11003	Christy	Zhu	christy12@adventure-works.com	0
11004	Elizabeth	Johnson	elizabeth5@adventure-works.com	0
11005	Julio	Ruiz	julio1@adventure-works.com	1
11006	Janet	Alvarez	janet9@adventure-works.com	1
11007	Marco	Mehta	marco14@adventure-works.com	0
11008	Rob	Verhoff	rob4@adventure-works.com	0
11009	Shannon	Carlson	shannon38@adventure-works.com	0
11010	Jacquelyn	Suarez	jacquelyn20@adventure-works.com	0
11011	Curtis	Lu	curtis9@adventure-works.com	0
11012	Lauren	Walker	lauren41@adventure-works.com	0
11013	Ian	Jenkins	ian47@adventure-works.com	0
11014	Sydney	Bennett	sydney23@adventure-works.com	0

Query execution completed with 18484 rows fetched

Figure 16-21

You were able to predict the Bike Buyer value for the input case table using the designer. The designer creates a query that retrieves the predicted data from SSAS. The query language used to retrieve predicted results from mining models is called DMX, which stands for Data Mining Extensions. The DMX language is specified in the OLEDB for Data Mining specification. The DMX language is similar to SQL and contains statements for data definition and data manipulation. The data definition language includes statements for model creation and the data manipulation language contains statements for training the model, which includes inserting data into the model and retrieving prediction results from it. Just as the SQL language has a SELECT statement to retrieve data from a relational database, DMX has a SELECT statement to retrieve data from mining models. The DMX SELECT statement has several variations based on the nature of the results being retrieved. For detailed information on the data definition language and data manipulation language of DMX, please refer to the Analysis Services 2008 documentation.

Click the drop-down arrow of the button that you used to switch between design and result view (shown in Figure 16-21) and select the Query option. You can see the following DMX query, which was generated to retrieve prediction results:

```
SELECT
  t.[CustomerKey],
  t.[FirstName],
  t.[LastName],
  t.[EmailAddress],
  ([v Target Mail].[Bike Buyer]) as [PredictedValue]
From
  [v Target Mail]
PREDICTION JOIN
  OPENQUERY([Adventure Works DW2008],
    'SELECT
      [CustomerKey],
      [FirstName],
      [LastName],
      [EmailAddress],
      [MaritalStatus],
      [Gender],
      [YearlyIncome],
      [TotalChildren],
      [NumberChildrenAtHome],
      [EnglishEducation],
      [HouseOwnerFlag],
      [NumberCarsOwned],
      [CommuteDistance],
      [Region],
      [Age],
      [BikeBuyer]
    FROM
      [dbo].[vTargetMail]
    ') AS t
  ON
  [v Target Mail].[Marital Status] = t.[MaritalStatus] AND
  [v Target Mail].[Gender] = t.[Gender] AND
  [v Target Mail].[Yearly Income] = t.[YearlyIncome] AND
  [v Target Mail].[Total Children] = t.[TotalChildren] AND
  [v Target Mail].[Number Children At Home] = t.[NumberChildrenAtHome] AND
  [v Target Mail].[English Education] = t.[EnglishEducation] AND
  [v Target Mail].[House Owner Flag] = t.[HouseOwnerFlag] AND
```

(continued)

(continued)

```
[v Target Mail].[Number Cars Owned] = t.[NumberCarsOwned] AND
[v Target Mail].[Commute Distance] = t.[CommuteDistance] AND
[v Target Mail].[Region] = t.[Region] AND
[v Target Mail].[Age] = t.[Age] AND
[v Target Mail].[Bike Buyer] = t.[BikeBuyer]
```

The preceding prediction query is one of the variations of the DMX SELECT query that has the following syntax:

```
SELECT [FLATTENED] [TOP <n>] <select expression list>
FROM <model> | <sub select> [NATURAL]
PREDICTION JOIN  <source data query>
[ON <join mapping list>]
[WHERE <condition expression>]
[ORDER BY <expression> [DESC|ASC]]
```

The input data for prediction is specified after the keywords PREDICTION JOIN. The <select expression list> contains the columns to be retrieved as part of the results and includes columns from the input/case table and the predicted columns, which are specified after the SELECT keyword. The mining model used for prediction is specified after the FROM keyword. The mapping of columns from input data set to the mining model attributes is specified in the ON clause as seen in the preceding prediction query. The prediction query retrieves four columns from the input table along with the predicted column for each input row. Similar to executing MDX queries from SQL Server Management Studio, you can execute the preceding DMX query. You have only seen a simple DMX query in this example. Analysis Services 2008 tools help you build DMX queries graphically, but if you are the kind of person who wants to write your DMX, this query will be a good start. You can learn more about DMX and writing prediction queries from the Analysis Services 2008 documentation and the book *Data Mining with Microsoft SQL Server 2008* by Jamie MacLennan, Zhao Hui Tang, and Bogdan Crivat.

You can create multiple mining models within the same mining structure and they can use either the same or a different mining algorithm. You would typically want to create a new mining model with the same algorithm if you want to see the accuracy of the existing mining model with a slight change in properties of the columns, such as disabling certain input columns or changing columns from PredictOnly to Predict. Alternatively, you can create a new mining model with a different mining algorithm and have the same attributes. A typical example would be to create a clustering or Naïve Bayes algorithm on a data set for which you have created a decision tree model. Next, you learn to create a clustering algorithm on the same data set and analyze the results. Follow these steps to create a new clustering algorithm:

1. Switch to the Mining Models view in the Mining Structure editor.

2. Right-click anywhere within the mining pane and select New Mining Model as shown in Figure 16-22.

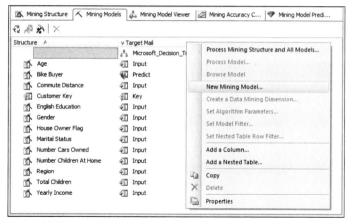

Figure 16-22

3.   Enter **Clustering** as the Model Name in the New Mining Model dialog as shown in Figure 16-23.

4.   Select Microsoft Clustering from the Algorithm Name drop-down list and click OK.

Figure 16-23

A new mining model is created with the name "Clustering" in the Mining Models view, as shown in Figure 16-24.

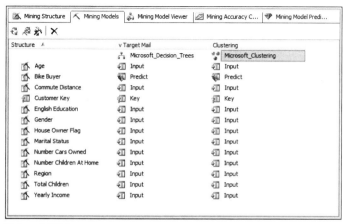

Figure 16-24

5. Deploy the project.

6. After deployment completes, switch to the Mining Model Viewer.

7. Click the Mining Model drop-down list and select Clustering, the name of the clustering mining model you have created (Figure 16-25).

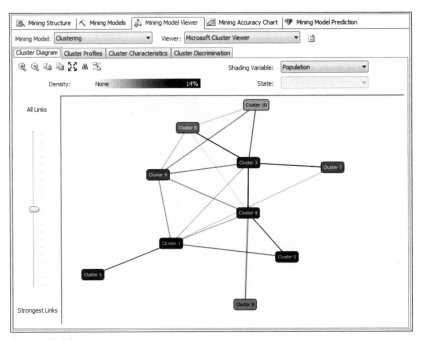

Figure 16-25

You will now see the clustering mining model represented as several nodes with lines between these nodes as shown in Figure 16-25. By default the clustering mining model groups the customer into ten different clusters. The number of clusters generated can be changed from a property for the cluster mining model. Each cluster is shown as a node in the cluster viewer. The shade of the node is dependent upon the shading variable column and a specific state of the column that is shown in the viewer. Darker shading on the node indicates that the cluster favors a specific input column and vice versa. If there is a relationship (that is, similarity) between two clusters, that is indicated by a line connecting the two nodes. Similar to the shade of the color node, if the relationship is stronger between two nodes, it is indicated via a darker line such as the relationship between clusters, Cluster 3 and Cluster 8. You can move the slider on the left of the cluster diagram from All Links to Strongest Links. As you do this you can see the weaker relationships between the clusters are not displayed. You can change the cluster name by right-clicking the cluster and selecting Rename. The cluster diagram helps you get an overall picture of the clusters, how the cluster is affected based on a specific column of the model that is used as the shading variable, as well as the relationships between clusters.

In Figure 16-25 the chosen column is Population. Population is the name that is used in the Mining Model Viewer for the entire data set used for training the mining model. You can select desired input columns of the mining model from the Shading Variable drop-down to see the effect of the column on the various clusters. When you choose a specific shading variable column you need to choose one of the states of the column to be used as the shading variable for the clusters.

For example, if you choose the shading variable as Age, then you have several options for the State such as missing value, < 35, >=86, and so on as shown in Figure 16-26. You can see that Cluster 5 has a darker shade indicating that cluster is predominantly populated with customers whose age is < 35. Overall the Cluster Diagram page provides you with the ability to analyze the various clusters, their characteristics, and relationships between clusters based on a specific column value, which enables you to get a quick grasp of the cluster's characteristics.

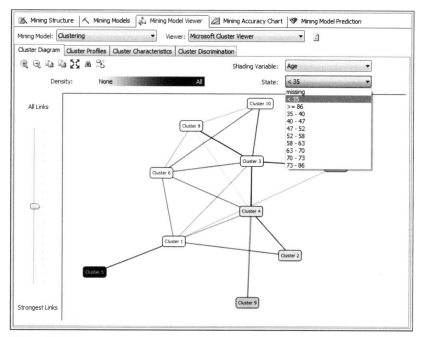

Figure 16-26

Once you have a good overview of the clusters from the Cluster Diagram view, the next step is to learn more about each cluster along with the distributions of various values for each column.

1. Click the Cluster Profiles tab to learn more details about each cluster and various values for each column.

The Cluster Profiles view shows the relationship between the mining columns of the model and the clusters in a matrix format as shown in Figure 16-27. The intersection cell of a specific column and a cluster shows a histogram bar of the various values of the column that are part of the cluster. The size of each bar reflects the number of items used to train the model. If you hover over the histogram you will be able to see the size of each bar as shown in Figure 16-27. The number of histogram bars shown is controlled by the value set for Histogram bars. The histogram bars are sorted based on the size and the first N bars (where N is the value set for Histogram bars) are shown. For example, for the Age attribute, there are eleven groups shown in the legend. Because the Histogram bars value is 4, the cluster viewer picks up the four most important buckets of the column Age and shows how this column contributes toward the profile of a specific cluster.

Part IV: Integration with Microsoft Products

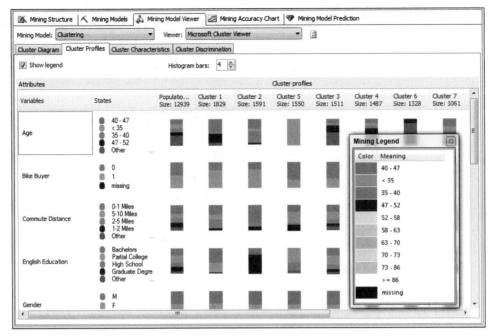

Figure 16-27

Each column has a histogram bar called "missing" for the input records that do not have any value specified for that column during training. Columns that have more states than the number of states shown in the view (number of states shown is controlled by the value set for Histogram bars) have a bucket called Other that shows the value for all the histogram states that are not shown explicitly.

2. Click the Cluster Characteristics tab to see the characteristics of a single cluster and how the various states of the input columns make up the cluster.

On this page, you see the cluster characteristics of the entire data set as shown in Figure 16-28. You can view the characteristics of a specific cluster by selecting the cluster name from the drop-down list for Cluster. The probability associated with a specific value for an input column such as Number Cars Owned = 0 is calculated based on the number of input records having that specific value. The Probability column shows the calculated probability for an input variable for the chosen cluster. If you hover over the bar in the Probability column you will see the corresponding probability value as shown in Figure 16-28.

586

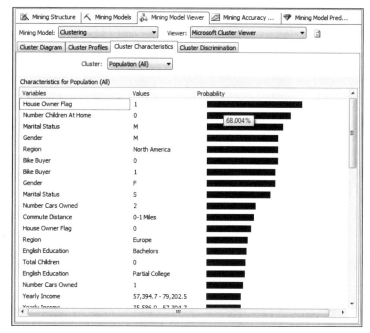

Figure 16-28

Once clusters are formed, one of the typical operations that one would want to do is compare the characteristics of two clusters in order to have a better understanding of each cluster; especially clusters that are related. The Mining Model Viewer provides a way to explore these differences between clusters.

3. Click the Cluster Discrimination tab.

   You will see the characteristics of Cluster 1 and the complement of Cluster 1. Using the cluster diagram you can see that the strongest relationship for the entire data set is between Cluster 3 and Cluster 8.

4. To compare the differences between these clusters select Clusters 3 and 8 from the drop-down list next to Cluster 1 and Cluster 2 as shown in Figure 16-29.

   Please note that the strongest clusters on your machine might be different. We recommend you review the cluster diagram and choose the strongest clusters for comparing differences.

   In the Cluster Characteristics page (Figure 16-28), you can see the characteristics of a single cluster. In the Cluster Discrimination page, you can see the states of an input column that favor one cluster over another. The states of the input columns indicate the differences between the two clusters and are ordered based on the importance of the difference the column contributes toward the clusters. The two columns on the right indicate which cluster the specific column value favors and the length indicates how strong the value influences the cluster as shown in Figure 16-29. For example, from the figure you can see that when customers own 4 cars, Cluster 3 is favored and when customers own 2 cars, Cluster 8 is favored. Similarly, you can review the other input columns' states to get a better understanding of the clusters' relationships.

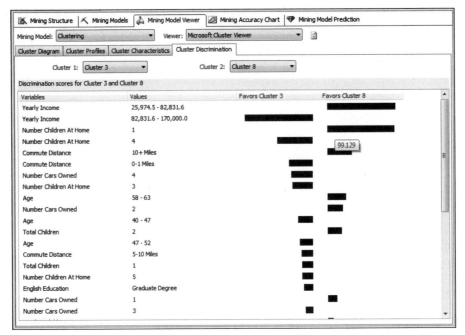

Figure 16-29

New mining models can also be created using the Data Mining Wizard. However, when you create a new mining model with the wizard, the wizard will automatically create a new mining structure and then create the mining model within this mining structure. Whenever you need to create multiple mining models for comparison we recommend you create the first model using the wizard and the remaining models within the same mining structure using the Mining Structure editor. The Data Mining Wizard is self-explanatory and you can explore the creation of other mining models such as Microsoft Sequence Clustering, Microsoft Regression Trees, Neural Networks, and Sequence clustering using the data sets available in the Adventure Works DW2008 sample relational database.

OLAP Mining Models

Certain types of business problems necessitate the use of aggregated data for analysis instead of individual input rows. For example, assume a customer buys several products from various stores. You might want to segment the customers not only by their individual attributes but also by the total amount they have spent in the stores. The mining model would require aggregated sales from the various purchases made by the customer, and include that amount as an input attribute to the clustering mining model. You can certainly add such a column to the customer table using a named query, but if the sales information table has billions of records, the aggregation of the relational data source will be slow. You should also consider maintainability of the mining model because you might want to process it on a periodic basis. There is a better solution than aggregating the data at the relational data source level. What better way to aggregate data than by creating a cube?

Because Analysis Services helps you create cubes as well as mining models, it provides a way of creating mining models from cubes. Such mining models are called OLAP mining models because the data source for the mining models is a cube and cubes contain OLAP data. Analysis Services 2008 also provides the functionality of creating new cubes that include content from the created mining model along with the original cube data, which provides you with the power and flexibility to analyze the cubes based on patterns discovered by the mining model. Such an analysis can help you understand your data better and make better business decisions. You create and analyze cubes containing mining model content in this section. Use the AnalysisServices2008Tutorial you created earlier to create OLAP mining models in this chapter. When you download the samples for this book you will find the AnalysisServices2008Tutorial project under the Chapter16 folder. To create an OLAP mining model, do the following:

1. Open the AnalysisServices2008Tutorial project.

2. Deploy the entire project to your Analysis Services instance.

3. In Solution Explorer, right-click the Mining Structures folder and select New Mining Structure to launch the Data Mining Wizard.

4. Click the Next button in the welcome screen.

5. In the Select the Definition Method page of the Data Mining Wizard, select the option "From existing cube" as shown in Figure 16-30 and click Next.

Figure 16-30

6. In the algorithm selection page, select the Microsoft Clustering algorithm as shown in Figure 16-31and click Next.

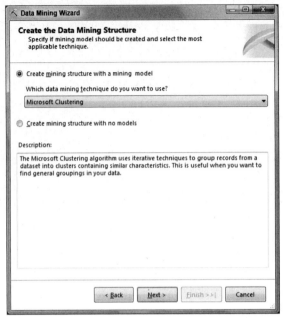

Figure 16-31

You will now be in the Select the Source Cube Dimension page as shown in Figure 16-32. This page lists the cube dimensions within the database upon which a mining model can be created. You need to select the cube dimension that will be used as the case table for creating the mining model.

7. Select the cube dimension Dim Customer from the Adventure Works DW cube and click Next.

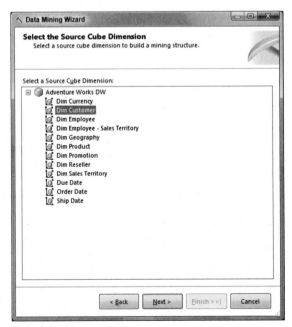

Figure 16-32

8. In the Select the Case Key page of the wizard select the Dim Customer attribute, the key of the Dim Customer dimension, to be the key for the mining structure as shown in Figure 16-33 and click Next.

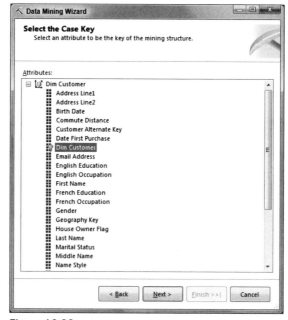

Figure 16-33

The Dim Customer attribute you selected in the Select the Case Key page will be used as the key for the mining model. On the Select Case Level Columns page you need to select all the attributes that will be part of the mining model. Attributes that will be used as input or predictable should be selected on this page.

9. Select the cube dimension attributes: Commute Distance, English Education, English Occupation, Gender, House Owner Flag, Marital Status, Number Cars Owned, Number Children At Home, Total Children, and Yearly Income. Also, select the facts Order Quantity and Sales Amount from the measure group Fact Internet Sales, as shown in Figure 16-34 and click Next.

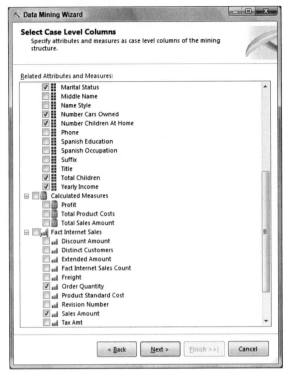

Figure 16-34

10. On the Specify Mining Model Column Usage page select the Sales Amount as predictable as shown in Figure 16-35 and click Next.

On the Specify Columns' Content and Data Type page, you can change the data type and content type for each attribute if needed. Both the content type and data type play an important role in the creation or training of the mining model.

11. Accept the defaults in the Specify Columns' Content and Data Type page and click Next.

You will now be in the Slice Source Cube page. This page allows you to slice the cube and build the mining model based only on a specific part of the cube. You can specify the constraints for slicing the cube on this page similar to specifying filter conditions in the Cube Browser. You have the option to filter on dimensions other than the Dim Customer dimension, such as specific dates for Order Date or specific categories or products.

12. Accept the default (no slicing on the cube) in the Slice Source Cube page as shown in Figure 16-36 by clicking Next.

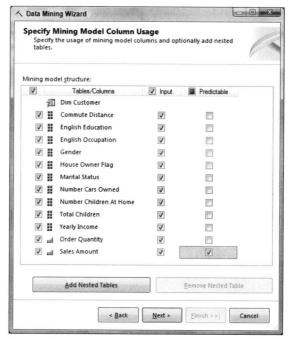

Figure 16-35

Figure 16-36

13. In the Create Testing Set page, select the defaults as shown in Figure 16-37 and click Next.

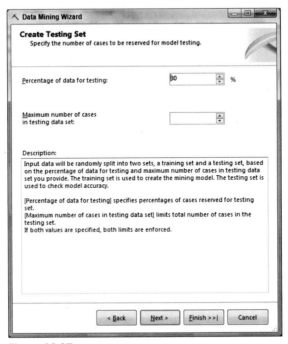

Figure 16-37

14. In the final page, specify the name for the mining structure as OLAPMiningStructure and for the mining model as **CustomerOLAPMiningModel** as shown in Figure 16-38.

15. Click the checkboxes for Create Mining model dimension, Create cube using mining model dimension, and Allow drill through as shown in Figure 16-38 and click Finish.

You can analyze the mining model separately using the Mining Model Viewer, but Analysis Services 2008 takes it one step further by allowing you to create a cube that will include the results of the mining model. In Analysis Services 2008 you can create a dimension from the results of the mining model and add this to the existing cube. The Mining Structure Wizard facilitates the creation of the new cube that will include the existing cube and results of the mining model.

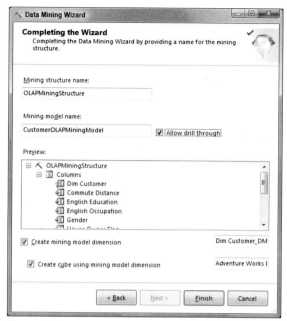

Figure 16-38

The OLAP mining model is created and you will now see it in the Mining Structure editor as shown in Figure 16-39. The input columns of the data mining structure are mapped to the corresponding cube dimension and measure group of the cube, which is indicated by the line connecting the Case Level Columns and Fact Internet Sales within the DSV pane of the Mining Structure editor. When the mining model is processed, the aggregated data of the measures will be used instead of the individual transactions.

16. Deploy the Analysis Services project to the SSAS instance.

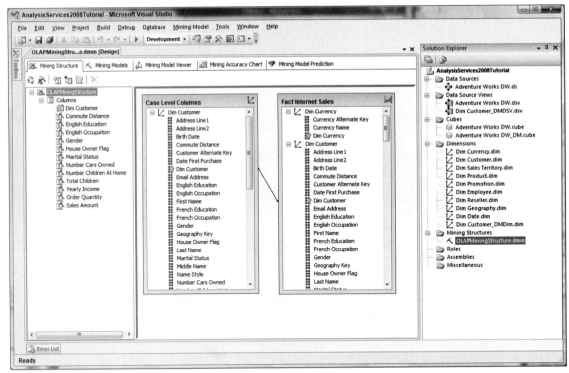

Figure 16-39

Once processing is complete, switch to the Mining Model Viewer where you can see the various clusters created based on the chosen attributes from the cube. Ten clusters are created by default. If you move the slider to strongest link, you will find the strongest relationship between clusters, Cluster 1 and Cluster 3 as shown in Figure 16-40. Similar to analyzing the relational mining model clusters, you can use the Cluster Profiles, Cluster Characteristics, and Cluster Discrimination tabs to learn more about the clusters created from the cube. We recommend you explore the OLAP cluster mining model.

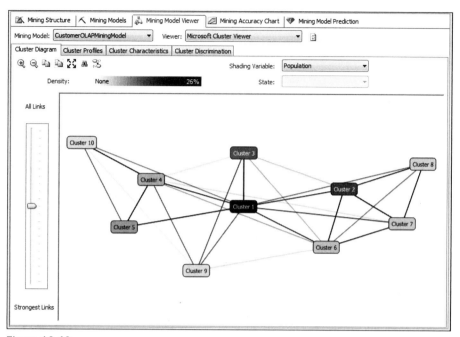

Figure 16-40

Analyzing the Cube with a Data Mining Dimension

When you created the OLAP mining model you selected creation of a data mining dimension and a cube in the Data Mining Wizard. To create a new dimension and cube you need a DSV. Hence a DSV that includes a query to the OLAP mining model to retrieve the data from the mining model was created by the wizard. You will see a DSV called Dim Customer_DMDSV created in the DSV folder in the Solution Explorer. Also, a dimension called [Dim Customer_DMDim] that includes attributes from the data mining model was created. Finally, a cube called [Adventure Works DW_DM] was created that includes all the cube dimensions and measure groups of the Adventure Works DW cube and also the newly created data mining dimension [Dim Customer_DMDim]. In Chapter 9 you learned about the data mining relationship between a dimension and a cube. The data mining relationship is defined between a dimension derived from a data mining model and a cube that contains it. The cube [Adventure Works DW_DM] that was created by the Data Mining Wizard includes a data mining dimension. If you open the Dimension Usage tab of the [Adventure Works DW_DM] cube you will see there is a data mining relationship as shown in Figure 16-41.

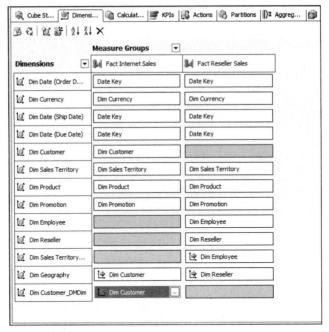

Figure 16-41

You can browse the [Adventure Works DW_DM] cube along with the data mining dimension to analyze the Internet sales you have obtained from various clusters as shown in Figure 16-42. How is this information useful? You can perform an analysis of the current sales with various clusters, and then perform a comparison of sales after the targeted mailing to analyze the sales and identify the effectiveness of the targeted mailing. Analysis Services thereby provides an integrated environment for creating mining models and cubes that help you with effective business analysis.

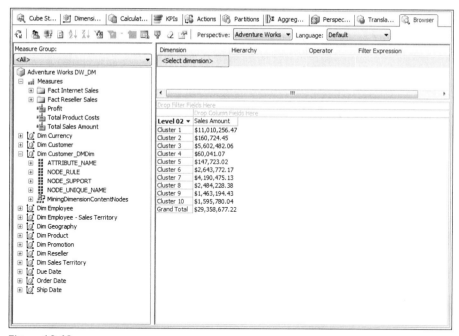

Figure 16-42

Summary

In this chapter you learned about data mining, what it is used for, and what specific algorithms are available for use in SSAS 2008. The most important answer is to the question, "How does it help your business?" If you are now a step or two closer to that answer, you're doing great.

After understanding the data mining algorithms supported by SSAS 2008, you drilled down on two, developing step-by-step Microsoft Decision Trees and Microsoft Clustering models using data from a relational data source. You also learned about OLAP mining models, where you essentially built a model on top of a cube. With the OLAP mining model you segmented the customers based on Internet Sales, and you were able to utilize the results of that mining model within a cube.

Aside from those off-the-shelf algorithms, SSAS 2008 provides a way to plug in your own data mining algorithm and/or data visualization capability (viewer). For details on this, please refer to the SSAS 2008 product documentation. In a nutshell, you utilize the plug-in architecture provided by SSAS 2008 and implement certain interfaces so that the server can utilize the results coming out of the algorithm you created. Once you have implemented your algorithm you can expose it using the SSAS server properties. For an in-depth understanding of data mining in Analysis Services 2008, we recommend you read *Data Mining with Microsoft SQL Server 2008*, by Jamie MacLennan, ZhaoHui Tang, and Bogdan Crivat.

SSAS aims at providing Business Intelligence for everyone. Aligned with this goal, SQL Server 2008 has data mining add-ins for Office 2007. In Chapter 18, you learn how to use these add-ins to analyze data in Microsoft Excel 2007 and how to present mining models using Microsoft Visio 2007.

In the next chapter you learn to analyze cube data from client tools other than the ones provided within the Analysis Services 2008. Microsoft Office products are tightly integrated with Analysis Services so you can use them to analyze data from cubes. Products like Microsoft Excel, Microsoft Excel Services, Microsoft Office web components, Microsoft Proclarity, and Microsoft Performance Point Server are tightly integrated with SQL Server Analysis Services. Excel and Proclarity are the two most widely used SSAS clients to analyze cube data in a way that is easy to interpret by users.

17

Analyzing Cubes Using Microsoft Office Components

We spent a good deal of time in this book exploring design and implementation options, but we haven't spent much time on the end-user experience — until now. In this chapter you learn about the many ways your aggregated data can be presented to the end user for analysis. You can slice the cube data, meaning that you will present the data so that it can be looked at across some axis, or you can dice the data, which means that you will drill down into the data by breaking it into smaller and smaller cubes.

In Chapter 1 you learned about the overall Business Intelligence stack from Microsoft. You learned that SQL Server Analysis Services (SSAS) is the business intelligence server that is the core of the business intelligence platform offering from Microsoft. As a developer the Business Intelligence Development Studio (BIDS) and SQL Server Management Studio (SSMS) help you to analyze the SSAS data, but these are not suitable tools for end users making decisions based on SSAS data.

However, various Microsoft Office products are available that leverage SSAS and present the SSAS data to end users in an effective way. One of the most widely used products to analyze data from SSAS is Microsoft Excel. Most of the customers use the pivot table functionality in Excel to analyze the data. You learn more about this in detail in this chapter. You also learn how to create offline cubes using Excel that you can share with your peers. ProClarity, a BI product recently acquired by Microsoft, is another tool that helps you effectively visualize SSAS data so that you can make appropriate business decisions. You learn more about this product in this chapter as well. Finally, you learn about Performance Point Server, an analysis and planning tool whose functionality is built on top of SSAS.

Analyzing Data in Excel 2007

Microsoft Office Excel 2007, also called Excel 12, has been redesigned to provide a better user experience. It has a new layout called the Ribbon that helps Excel users easily identify and use the various features. It can support up to 1,048,576 rows and 16,384 columns in a spread sheet, which is a significant enhancement when compared to previous versions of Excel. It also provides improved formatting and better visualization, such as Data bars, Color bars, and Icon sets, which help you to visualize and interpret data efficiently.

Excel 2007 also has a tighter integration with SSAS since the 2005 release. Several new features such as attributes, hierarchies, Key Performance Indicators, and folder structure for measures are visible to the end users via the pivot table. In this section you learn how to analyze SSAS 2008 data using a pivot table in Excel 2007.

Analyzing Data Using Pivot Tables

We are confident you have probably used Excel before. You might be familiar with the pivot table feature, especially considering that pivot tables date back to Excel Version 5. The pivot table feature is used to create reports for Excel users, which help them analyze data with ease. The pivot table feature can work on data stored in Excel or some other data source that can be accessed by Excel. The only requirement for using the pivot table with Analysis Services is that Excel should be able to connect to the Analysis Services instance. In such a case, Analysis Services becomes a data source for Excel. Because there is a tight integration between Excel and Analysis Services, Excel is well aware of the Analysis Services models and objects and can present them effectively to the end users. As you might expect, Excel provides a wizard you can use to create pivot tables. It has advanced features that can even help you create what it calculates to be the best resulting layout.

As for the capabilities of a pivot table, they are similar in nature to the Cube Browser seen in BIDS — you can drag and drop dimensions and measures to analyze the data. Not only can you arrange data to best surface the information contained in it, but also the pivot table technology will sum the appropriate columns for you automatically. It is quite common for people to construct pivot tables to some planned configuration that is suited to act as a foundation for building charts and graphs. Charting and graphing capability come with Excel off the shelf, so you don't need to buy any additional software to utilize a pivot table in this way.

> Why is it called a pivot table? Why not call it what it really is, a digital fulcrum for tabulated compilations? The name suggests the user can swivel or pivot on data that is tabular in nature. In the simplest possible terms, it is a way to display data so that it is very easy to arrange and view how different columns interact with each other.

Figure 17-1 shows a pivot table in Excel 2007 that retrieves data from SSAS 2008. You can see from the figure that the pivot table helps you to view multidimensional data in a two-dimensional nested tabular form. Normally, you will find that users only pivot on two or three dimensions at a time while engaged in data analysis. The reason for this is simple: If you add fourth and fifth dimensions to a pivot table, the results become too confusing to understand. The pivot table client component helps you visualize the interactions between dimensions, and if used properly will, in fact, facilitate insights about the nature of the results being analyzed.

Note that this book focuses on using Excel 2007 with Analysis Services 2008 and not on Excel 2007 itself. For more information on Excel 2007 and its new features such as the Ribbon, please refer to *Excel 2007 Bible* by John Walkenbach (Wiley, 2007).

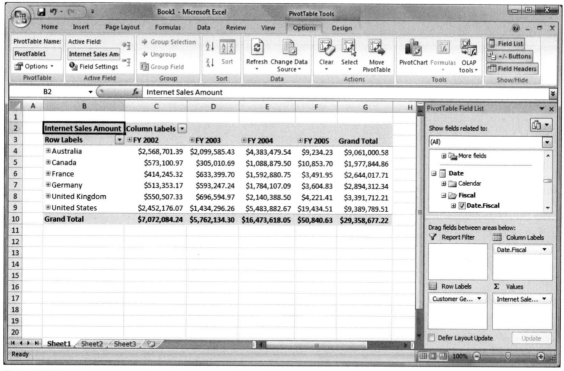

Figure 17-1

Creating a Pivot Table Using Analysis Services Data

To create a pivot table using Analysis Services data as the source to populate the table, perform the following steps:

1. Download the AdventureWorks 2008 Analysis Services sample project and the associated relational database from `http://www.codeplex.com/MSFTDBProdSamples/Release/ ProjectReleases.aspx?ReleaseId=16040`, Microsoft's open source project hosting web site. Note that for 2008 the Analysis Services project is installed as part of the AdventureWorks DW BI sample database.

2. Deploy the Adventure Works Analysis Services enterprise sample project to your Analysis Services 2008 instance.

3. Launch Excel 2007.

4. Click the Microsoft Office button, select New ⇨ Blank Workbook, and click Create.

5. Select the Data tab on the Excel Ribbon as shown in Figure 17-2. You will see the various groups where the commands related to Data are organized.

6. In the Get External Data group, select From Other Sources as shown in Figure 17-2.

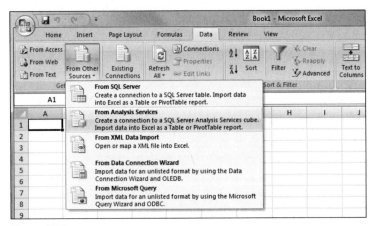

Figure 17-2

7. Select From Analysis Services. You should see the Data Connection Wizard dialog box shown in Figure 17-3.

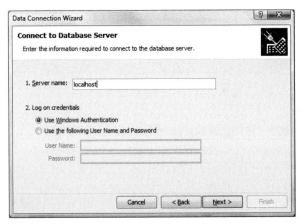

Figure 17-3

8. On the Connect to Database Server page, enter the Analysis Services instance name as shown in Figure 17-3 and click Next.

9. On the Select Database and Table page, you will see the list of available cubes and perspectives in the Adventure Works DW 2008 database. Select the Adventure Works DW 2008 sample database you deployed in step 2 and the Adventure Works cube (as shown in Figure 17-4) and click Next.

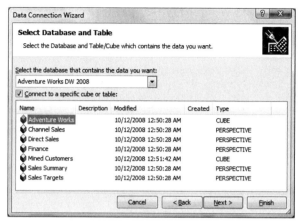

Figure 17-4

10. On the Save Data Connection File and Finish page, add a description for your data source connection as shown in Figure 17-5 and click Finish.

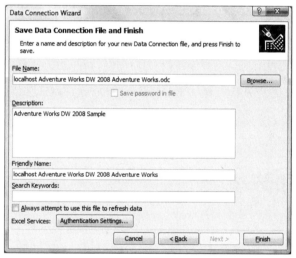

Figure 17-5

11. In the Import Data dialog, select a location for your pivot table in the active worksheet as shown in Figure 17-6 and click OK.

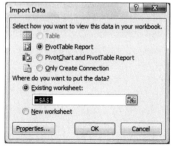

Figure 17-6

You should now see the pivot table along with the PivotTable Field List showing hierarchies and measures in your Excel worksheet as shown in Figure 17-7. There's a lot of information in the PivotTable Field List and it can feel like information overload. If you are familiar with pivot tables in Excel 2003, you'll notice that with Excel 2007 you'll no longer need to drag and drop fields to add them to the pivot table. The PivotTable Field List contains areas for adding items to the row, column, values, and report areas. To add a measure or a hierarchy to the pivot table you just need to check the box next to the field item.

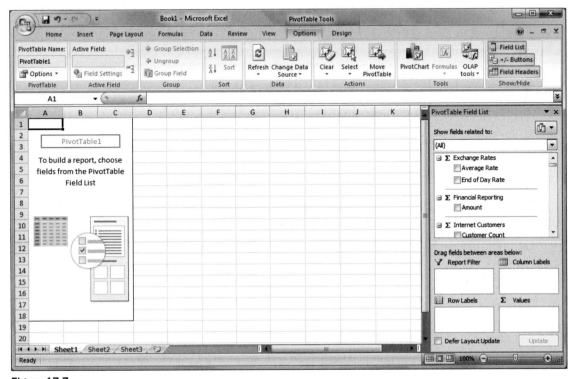

Figure 17-7

Updating SSAS Connection Information

If you have used Excel 2003, you know that it was not easy to add connection properties to SSAS. Excel 2007, unlike Excel 2003, provides a way to add additional connection string properties while connecting to SSAS. If you need to obtain or update connection information, perform the following steps:

1. Select the Data tab on the Ribbon.

2. In the Connections Group select Connections, shown in Figure 17-8, to open the Workbook Connections dialog.

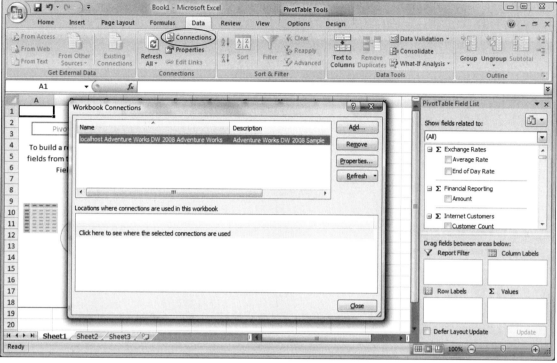

Figure 17-8

3. In the Workbook Connections dialog, select the connection you just created. For this example it is localhost Adventure Works DW 2008 Adventure Works.

4. Click the Properties button. You should see the dialog shown in Figure 17-9.

Figure 17-9

5. In the Connection Properties dialog, click the Definition tab to see the connection string used to connect to SSAS.

When you create a connection to an SSAS instance, an Office Data Connection (ODC) file is created to store all the information relevant to the connection. The file is by default saved at %*USERPROFILE*%\ My Data Sources\localhost Adventure Works DW 2008 Adventure Works.odc. You can see the location of the file in the "Connection File" text box. For this sample connection, Excel 2007 has generated the following connection string to connect to your SSAS 2008 instance:

```
Provider=MSOLAP.4;Integrated Security=SSPI;Persist Security Info=True;Initial
Catalog=Adventure Works DW 2008;Data Source=localhost;MDX
Compatibility=1;Safety Options=2;MDX Missing Member Mode=Error
```

You can edit the connection string and authentication settings in this dialog and click OK to save the settings.

Analyzing Data in Pivot Tables

Now that you have learned how to view or edit connection strings used with SSAS, next you learn about data analysis using a pivot table. In the PivotTable Field List you can see the various measures in the AdventureWorks cube listed under each measure group followed by the list of dimensions. The attributes and hierarchies in a dimension are organized under folders as defined in the cube. This can be seen in Figure 17-10. You can also see the KPIs in the cube listed under a separate folder.

Figure 17-10

You learned earlier that the list of all the measures and dimensions might be overwhelming. Excel 2007 allows you a way to restrict the measures and related dimensions based on the measure group. You can utilize the "Show fields related to" drop-down menu to select a specific measure group:

1. Select the drop-down list box below "Show fields related to" and select Internet Sales as shown in Figure 17-11. Excel 2007 sends a list of discover statements to retrieve the corresponding list of measure groups and dimensions to populate the PivotTable Field List.

2. Navigate the list of measures and click the checkbox next to the Internet Sales Amount measure in the Internet Sales measure group. You will now see the measure being added to the Values area in the PivotTable Field List and the value in the pivot table as shown in Figure 17-11. The selected measure is highlighted in bold as well as shown in Figure 17-11.

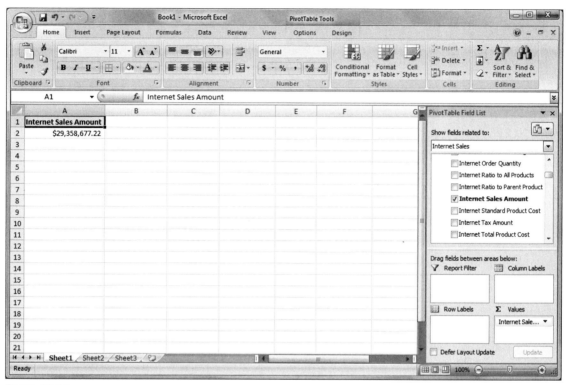

Figure 17-11

Excel 2007 sends the following MDX query to retrieve the Internet Sales Amount for the entire cube and shows the results in the pivot table:

```
SELECT  FROM [Adventure Works] WHERE ([Measures].[Internet Sales Amount]) CELL
PROPERTIES VALUE, FORMAT_STRING, LANGUAGE, BACK_COLOR, FORE_COLOR, FONT_FLAGS
```

If you send the query using the MDX query editor in SQL Server Management Studio (SSMS) you'll see the same result of $29,358,677.22. Now let's analyze the Internet Sales Amount for various customers and years.

3. Scroll down in the PivotTable Field List and click the checkbox next to the Customer ⇨ Customer Geography hierarchy. You will notice that the Customer Geography hierarchy is added to Row Labels and the customer countries along with the relevant sales amounts are shown in the pivot table.

4. Click the Date ⇨ Fiscal ⇨ Date.Fiscal hierarchy as shown in Figure 17-12. Excel 2007 sends the following MDX query to retrieve the data:

```
SELECT NON EMPTY Hierarchize( {DrilldownLevel(
                             {[Date].[Fiscal].[All Periods]})})
             DIMENSION PROPERTIES PARENT_UNIQUE_NAME ON COLUMNS,
      NON EMPTY Hierarchize( {DrilldownLevel(
                 {[Customer].[Customer Geography].[All Customers]})})
                 DIMENSION PROPERTIES PARENT_UNIQUE_NAME ON ROWS
FROM  [Adventure Works]
WHERE ([Measures].[Internet Sales Amount])
CELL PROPERTIES VALUE, FORMAT_STRING, LANGUAGE, BACK_COLOR,
                FORE_COLOR, FONT_FLAGS
```

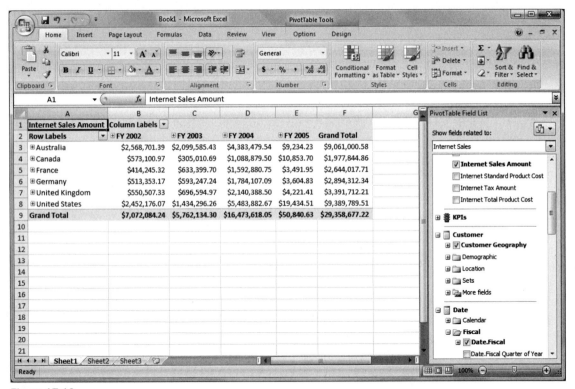

Figure 17-12

Excel 2007 understands the Time dimension that is specified in the cube and adds the hierarchy to the columns area. You will see the top level Date.Fiscal hierarchy members in the pivot table along with the [Internet Sales Amount] as shown in Figure 17-12. You can now see [Internet Sales Amount] data for various countries and various fiscal years. In one view you can see the sales trend for each country across various years and also a comparison of sales for a year across various countries. You will notice that you can see a + symbol next to each member. The + symbol helps you to drill down further to analyze data under a specific member. Before getting into drill down, take a look at the MDX query sent by Excel so you understand it. You can execute the MDX query in SSMS to retrieve the results. Figure 17-13 shows the MDX query results in SSMS.

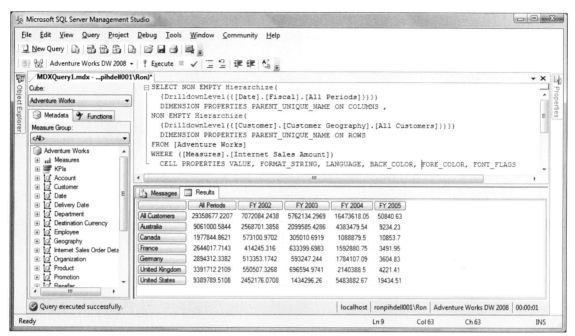

Figure 17-13

If you hover over a specific member or a cell you will notice the corresponding properties in tool tips. You can also view the dimension or cell properties returned back for each cell by double-clicking a member or a cell in SSMS. The results shown in SMSS are identical to the results you see in Figure 17-12, but the order in which the results are presented differs. The first row and first column of the results shown in SSMS are the final rows and columns you see in the pivot table, which correspond to the aggregated data corresponding to that specific member in the dimension based on the aggregation function specified for the measure. The members All Customers and All Periods shown in the table are actually the names of the All members specified in the respective dimensions.

Excel generates a two-dimensional MDX query that requests data on the axes columns and rows in this example. For the dimension added on the columns of the pivot table (Date.Fiscal), the following MDX expression is specified:

```
NON EMPTY Hierarchize({DrilldownLevel({[Date].[Fiscal].[All Periods]})})
    DIMENSION PROPERTIES PARENT_UNIQUE_NAME ON COLUMNS
```

Let's start with the innermost function and work our way out. When you add a specific hierarchy to the Pivot table, the member in the topmost level of that hierarchy is identified and used in the query. In the previous example, the All member in the Date.Fiscal hierarchy, All Periods, is used. The DrilldownLevel MDX function is a function that can take multiple parameters. The syntax of the DrilldownLevel function is as follows:

```
DrilldownLevel( <Set>, [ ,<Level> | ,,<Index> ] )
```

The first argument to the DrilldownLevel function is a Set. The second and third arguments are optional. The DrilldownLevel function returns the members of the specified Set (provided as the first argument) that are one level lower than the level of the members specified in the set. If the optional Level parameter is specified, the function returns members one level below the specified level. If the set contains tuples, the index is used to reference the dimension for which the drill down has to be applied.

611

In the query you are currently examining, the members at the Year level of the hierarchy Date.Fiscal is returned. You could have retrieved the members by specifying the MDX expression, but the DrilldownLevel function provides you with more options and is useful while drilling down to multiple levels, which is why Excel uses this function. We talk about drilling down to multiple levels later in this section. Now, let's review the next MDX function using the Customer Geography hierarchy as shown in the following:

```
NON EMPTY Hierarchize({DrilldownLevel({[Customer].[Customer Geography].[All
    Customers]})}) DIMENSION PROPERTIES PARENT_UNIQUE_NAME
```

The result of the DrilldownLevel function is a set of members and is passed as an argument to the Hierarchize function. Hierarchize is an MDX function used for sorting the members in a set. The syntax is as follows:

```
Hierarchize( <Set> [, POST] )
```

The Hierarchize function takes a Set and returns the members in the set after a sort. If the second parameter POST is not specified, the default sort ordering of the hierarchy is used to sort the members in the set. If the parameter POST is specified, the members are sorted based on the default ordering but the parent member will be at the end. This is illustrated by the following two MDX queries:

```
SELECT Hierarchize( {DrillDownLevel(
                    {[Customer].[Customer Geography].[Country]})}) ON 0,
       Measures.[Internet Sales Amount] ON 1
FROM   [Adventure Works]                 //MDX Query 1 -- Default sort ordering


SELECT Hierarchize( {DrillDownLevel(
            {[Customer].[Customer Geography].[Country]})}, POST) ON 0,
       Measures.[Internet Sales Amount] ON 1
FROM   [Adventure Works]                 //MDX Query 2 -- Sort based on POST
```

The first MDX query uses the default sort ordering of the hierarchy and returns the members in Country and State levels in the format {<Country Member 1>, <State members for Country Member 1>, <Country Member 2>, <State members for Country Member 2> ...}. However, the second query that specified POST sorts the results as {<State members for Country Member 1>, <Country Member 1>, <State members for Country Member 2>,<Country Member 2>, ...}. The Hierarchize MDX function does not eliminate duplicate members.

You have just learned about the one part of the MDX query and why these functions are used to retrieve the results. Now it is time to examine the next part of the MDX query.

The keyword NON EMPTY is used to ensure empty values are eliminated in the results. To refresh your memory, here is the MDX query that is generated by Excel:

```
SELECT  NON EMPTY Hierarchize({DrilldownLevel({[
                        Date].[Fiscal].[All Periods]})})
        DIMENSION PROPERTIES PARENT_UNIQUE_NAME ON COLUMNS ,
        NON EMPTY Hierarchize({DrilldownLevel({
            [Customer].[Customer Geography].[All Customers]})})
        DIMENSION PROPERTIES PARENT_UNIQUE_NAME ON ROWS
FROM    [Adventure Works]
WHERE   ([Measures].[Internet Sales Amount])
        CELL PROPERTIES VALUE, FORMAT_STRING, LANGUAGE,
        BACK_COLOR, FORE_COLOR, FONT_FLAGS
```

The members being retrieved for COLUMNS and the members retrieved for ROWS use the same approach to retrieve members. Member properties of dimension members can be retrieved using the Dimension Properties option on an axis. The MDX expression "Dimension Properties PARENT_UNIQUE_NAME" is used to retrieve the member property PARENT_UNIQUE_NAME, which, in turn, is returned for each member that can be used in subsequent MDX queries based on the user's actions in the pivot table. Finally, the WHERE clause is used for retrieving the right measure used in the pivot table and also for restricting the multidimensional coordinate space so that the right values are being sliced based on [Customer].[Customer Geography].[All Customers]. Excel appropriately displays the result from the query within the pivot table. Excel identifies the values for All members of each hierarchy and uses those values for subtotals along the row or column.

Filtering in Pivot Tables

You have so far successfully created a pivot table and have been able to analyze the Internet Sales data for customers in various countries for various fiscal years. Assume you want to analyze the data for the United States. Because you are interested in the [Internet Sales Amount] data for customers in the United States, you will need to filter out the data relating to customers from other countries. In this section you learn several ways to filter data you want in pivot tables.

PivotTable Field List

One of many ways to restrict the data is through the PivotTable Field List via the Customer Geography field:

1. Click the drop-down arrow next to the hierarchy Customer Geography or Country. You will see all the members of the Country level in Customer Geography hierarchy as shown in Figure 17-14. The boxes next to each member act as toggle switches. If a checkmark is within the box that means the specific member is selected. To select or deselect all members, Excel provides you with a checkbox called Select All.

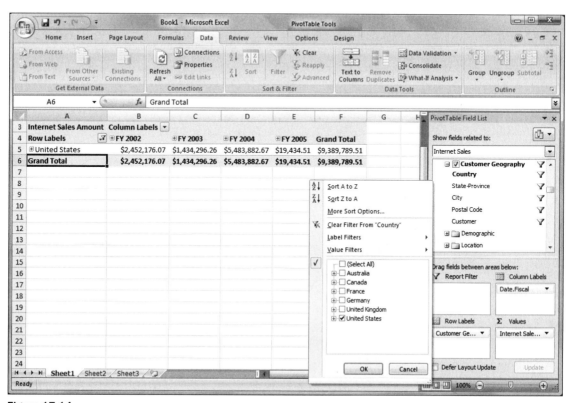

Figure 17-14

2. Click the box next to (Select All) to deselect all the members and then select the member United States, as shown in Figure 17-14.

3. Click OK.

You will now see the Sales data only for United States for various years. Excel sends the following MDX query to retrieve the data:

```
SELECT      NON EMPTY Hierarchize( {DrilldownLevel({
                     [Date].[Fiscal].[All Periods]})})
            DIMENSION PROPERTIES PARENT_UNIQUE_NAME ON COLUMNS ,
            NON EMPTY Hierarchize( {DrilldownLevel({
                     [Customer].[Customer Geography].[All Customers]})})
            DIMENSION PROPERTIES PARENT_UNIQUE_NAME ON ROWS
FROM (
            SELECT ( {
                  [Customer].[Customer Geography].[Country].&[United States]})
                                                      ON COLUMNS

            FROM    [Adventure Works])
            WHERE   ([Measures].[Internet Sales Amount]
       )
CELL        PROPERTIES VALUE, FORMAT_STRING, LANGUAGE, BACK_COLOR,
            FORE_COLOR, FONT_FLAGS
```

In the MDX query just shown, Excel 2007 uses the sub-select MDX construct, which was added in SSAS 2005, to restrict the data to the country United States. Excel 2007 will determine if the version of SSAS supports the sub-select MDX syntax using SSAS properties and will generate the right set of queries, including those that will allow you to filter the data by Label, Date, and Value. The following sub-select query restricts the cube space to the United States:

```
(
    SELECT ({[Customer].[Customer Geography].[Country].&[United States]})
                                                      ON COLUMNS

    FROM [Adventure Works]
)
```

The outer SELECT query will then retrieve the Internet Sales data for all the years only for United States.

The Report Filter

The Report Filter area in the PivotTable Field List also allows you to filter the data in the pivot table by hierarchies you add to the Report Filter area. Adding a hierarchy to the Report Filter allows you to create Excel reports that let the end user apply filters directly in the pivot table. Assume a scenario where you want to analyze the [Internet Sales Amount] of customers in the United States to see if the customer's level of education has an impact. You might want to filter using one or more Education types. The following steps show you how to do the analysis using Report Filters:

1. Drag and drop the Customer ➪ Demographic ➪ Education attribute to the Report Filter area. You will notice Education added to the pivot table along with the default member shown next to it as shown in Figure 17-15. By default the filter only allows a single member filter. You can enable multi-member selection in the filter in Excel. The following steps show how to analyze the Internet Sales of customers who have a degree.

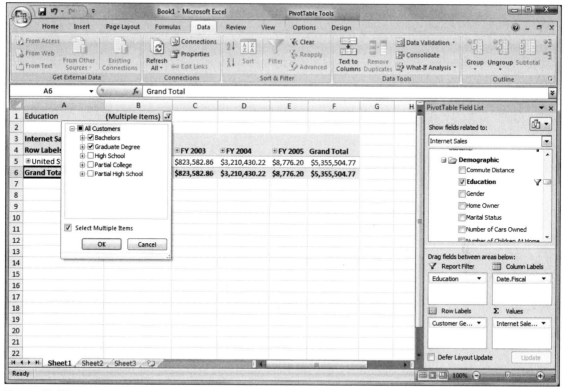

Figure 17-15

2. Drop down the list box next to the default member All Customers and select the box next to Select Multiple Items as shown in Figure 17-15.

3. Expand the + sign next to All Customers.

4. Deselect the check mark next to All Customers and then select the members Bachelors and Graduate Degree.

5. Click OK.

You will now see the [Internet Sales Amount] for the United States has dropped from its previous value because the filter you applied includes only customers who have a degree. Excel 2007 sends the following MDX query to retrieve the results shown in the pivot table:

```
SELECT   NON EMPTY Hierarchize({DrilldownLevel(
                         {[Date].[Fiscal].[All Periods]})})
         DIMENSION PROPERTIES PARENT_UNIQUE_NAME ON COLUMNS ,
         NON EMPTY Hierarchize({DrilldownLevel(
                 {[Customer].[Customer Geography].[All Customers]})})
         DIMENSION PROPERTIES PARENT_UNIQUE_NAME ON ROWS
FROM (
         SELECT ({[Customer].[Customer Geography].[Country].&[United States]})
             ON COLUMNS
         FROM (
             SELECT   ({[Customer].[Education].&[Bachelors],
```

(continued)

(continued)

```
                            [Customer].[Education].&[Graduate Degree]})
                      ON COLUMNS
               FROM [Adventure Works]
               )
      )
WHERE ([Measures].[Internet Sales Amount])
CELL PROPERTIES VALUE, FORMAT_STRING, LANGUAGE, BACK_COLOR, FORE_COLOR,
FONT_FLAGS
```

In the MDX query you can see the nested sub-select MDX statement used to filter the data being retrieved. First the filter is applied to the United States using the sub-select followed by another sub-select for members having bachelor's and graduate degrees. The inner most sub-select, which will retrieve all members with degrees, gets evaluated first, followed by the sub-select restricting the data to members of United States. The result of this sub-select is a slice of the cube based on the restriction called a sub-cube. Finally, the [Internet Sales Amount] is retrieved based on the members requested in the columns and rows axes on the outermost MDX query.

The Row Filter

The pivot table also provides another way to perform the analysis based on Education. Instead of using the Report Filter you can add the hierarchy to the Row and apply a filter there. To accomplish this go to the PivotTable Field List and drag the Education hierarchy from the Report Filter section to Row Labels underneath Customer Geography. You will see the Education hierarchy as a second level in the Row area as shown in Figure 17-16. You will notice that the filter condition you had applied to customers having a degree is still maintained.

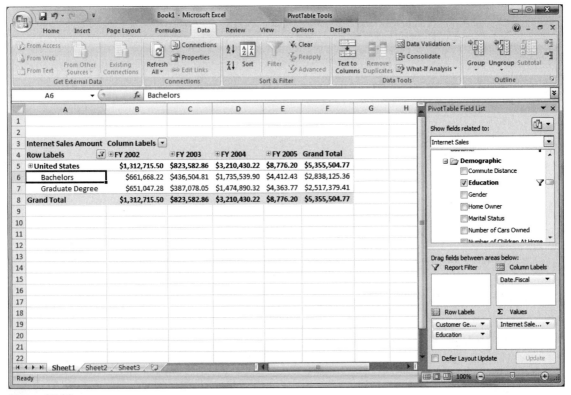

Figure 17-16

Excel sends the following MDX query to retrieve the results shown in the pivot table. Notice that the following query is different from the one used to retrieve the pivot table data when you had Education as a Report Filter. First you will notice that the nested sub-select statements used to restrict the cube data based on Customer Geography and Education have been combined into a single sub-select statement. Second, the axes data on ROWS for the outermost SELECT statement includes a crossjoin of members of the Customer Geography as well as members of the Education hierarchies.

```
SELECT    NON EMPTY Hierarchize({DrilldownLevel(
                       {[Date].[Fiscal].[All Periods]})})
          DIMENSION PROPERTIES PARENT_UNIQUE_NAME ON COLUMNS ,
          NON EMPTY CrossJoin( Hierarchize({DrilldownLevel(
                  {[Customer].[Customer Geography].[All Customers]})}),
              Hierarchize({DrilldownLevel(
                  {[Customer].[Education].[All Customers]})}))
          DIMENSION PROPERTIES PARENT_UNIQUE_NAME ON ROWS
FROM      (
          SELECT (
              {[Customer].[Customer Geography].[Country].&[United States]},
              {[Customer].[Education].&[Graduate Degree],
              [Customer].[Education].&[Bachelors]}) ON COLUMNS
          FROM [Adventure Works]
          )
WHERE ([Measures].[Internet Sales Amount])
CELL PROPERTIES VALUE, FORMAT_STRING, LANGUAGE, BACK_COLOR, FORE_COLOR,
FONT_FLAGS
```

Whenever there are multiple hierarchies in rows or columns, the pivot table creates an automatic grouping for each member in the hierarchy and creates a subtotal. In Figure 17-16 you can see a row showing the subtotal for each year. Because you wanted to analyze the data for Bachelors and Graduate degree customers, you need to restrict the visible members. You can change the filter selection from customers with degrees to customers with some sort of high school education by performing the following steps:

1. Select one of the members in the Education hierarchy such as Bachelors. Click the Filter icon next to Row Labels as shown in Figure 17-17.

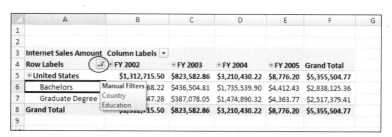

Figure 17-17

2. In the Select Field drop-down make sure Education is selected and then deselect Bachelors and Graduate Degree and select the High School and Partial High School members as shown in Figure 17-18.

3. Click OK.

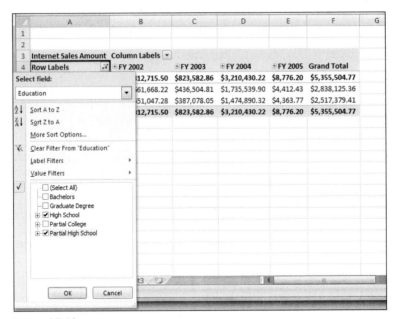

Figure 17-18

You will now see the [Internet Sales Amount] of Customers with only some form of High School education. Applying the filter to the Row area has the benefit of allowing you to see data for each member in a separate row. Similar to applying a filter in the Row Labels area you can also apply filters in the Column Labels area.

Drilling Down to Detailed Data

So far you have used the pivot table to analyze data using the axes rows, columns, and pages (Report Filter area); you have seen how to pivot on select members and view corresponding measure values. One of the key aspects of analyzing OLAP data is not only viewing the aggregated data, but also drilling down or up to view member details as needed. The following steps show how to drill down to detail data in pivot tables:

1. Update your pivot table so that Product Categories is added to the Report Filter section.

2. Remove the filter applied to the Education hierarchy by clicking the Row Labels filter and selecting all the members.

3. Drag and drop the Education hierarchy from the Row Labels area in the PivotTable Field List to the area where all the measures and hierarchies are shown. Your pivot table should now contain Date.Fiscal in the Column Labels, Customer.Geography in the Row Labels that is filtered for the United States, Product.Product Categories hierarchy in the Report Filter, and Internet Sales Amount in the Values field.

4. To drill down to details of the Internet Sales within the United States, double-click the United States member. You will now see that the level State-Province is shown in the row axis and you see all the states within United States that have sales data as shown in Figure 17-19. You can also drill down by clicking the + sign next to United States or by selecting the United States member and then clicking the Expand Entire Field icon in the Options tab on the Ribbon as shown in Figure 17-20.

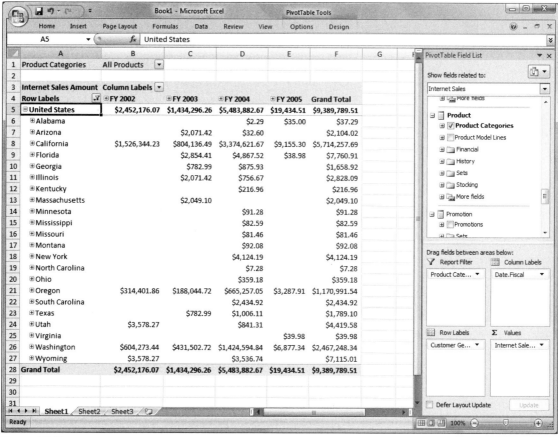

Figure 17-19

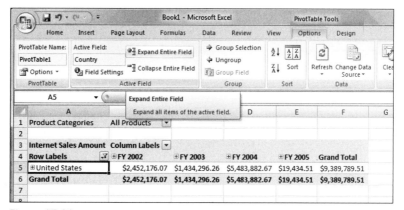

Figure 17-20

If you want to drill up from the current level you can once again double-click the member United States or click the member and then click the Collapse Entire Field icon on the Options tab on the Ribbon. You can choose certain members after the drill down in the pivot table.

5. In the PivotTable Field List select the drop-down list next to the Country or State-Province level and select the members Alabama, Arizona, and California, which are under United States. Alternatively, you can select one of the members in Row Labels and then use the Row Labels filter to select the three states. You can drill down on members on each axis.

6. On the column axis, drill down on Fiscal Year up to the Month level by double-clicking the first member FY 2002 for each level. Your pivot table will show the sales amount for three states within the United States for various fiscal years, with detailed data for the months in the first quarter of fiscal year 2002 as shown in Figure 17-21.

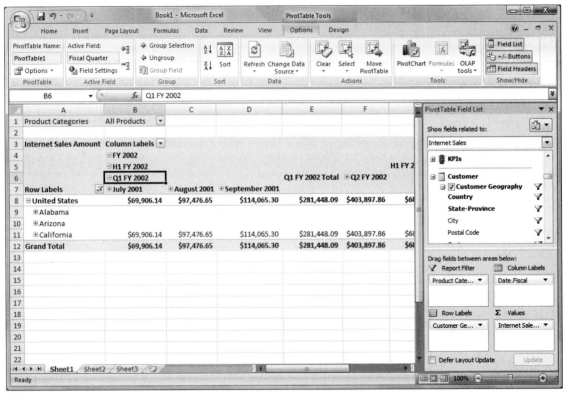

Figure 17-21

In order to understand the type of MDX query sent by Excel while drilling down to member details, we will use a simpler example where your pivot table contains the Customer Geographies on Row Label without any filter on Country or State-Province, Product Categories on Report Filter, and Date.Fiscal on

Column Label. We apply a drill down on the Column Label for the first member in Date.Fiscal, 2002. The following MDX query is sent by Excel 2007 to Analysis Services:

```
SELECT NON EMPTY Hierarchize( DrilldownMember({{DrilldownLevel(
                {[Date].[Fiscal].[All Periods]})}},
                {[Date].[Fiscal].[Fiscal Year].&[2002]}))
            DIMENSION PROPERTIES PARENT_UNIQUE_NAME,
        [Date].[Fiscal].[Fiscal Semester].[Fiscal Year] ON COLUMNS ,
    NON EMPTY Hierarchize( DrilldownLevel({
            [Customer].[Customer Geography].[All Customers]})})
            DIMENSION PROPERTIES PARENT_UNIQUE_NAME ON ROWS
FROM   [Adventure Works]
WHERE ([Product].[Product Categories].[All Products],
        [Measures].[Internet Sales Amount])
CELL PROPERTIES VALUE, FORMAT_STRING, LANGUAGE, BACK_COLOR, FORE_COLOR,
FONT_FLAGS
```

The MDX functions DrilldownMember and DrilldownLevel are used in the preceding MDX query. The function DrilldownMember takes two sets — Set1 and Set2 — as parameters and returns a set that contains the drill down of members in Set1 that are included in Set2. You can see that the innermost DrilldownMember is called with the sets DrillDownLevel({[Date].[Fiscal].[All Periods]}) and {[Date].[Fiscal].[Fiscal Year].&[2002]}. The first parameter is another MDX function that returns all the members in the Year level. [Date].[Fiscal].[Fiscal Year].&[2002] is one of the members in the first set and hence a drill down on this member will result in the members "H1 FY 2002" and "H2 FY 2002." Subsequent DrilldownMember functions drill down on the first half of fiscal year 2002 and the first quarter of fiscal year 2002 and Excel would generate a series of DrilldownLevel calls in the MDX query based on each level being drilled down. There is an optional third parameter for the DrilldownLevel MDX function, which takes the flag RECURSIVE. This prompts a recursive drill down on members in Set1 based on the members in Set2. You can understand the behavior of the RECURSIVE flag by looking at the results of the following MDX queries:

```
SELECT   DrilldownMember(
         {DrilldownLevel({[Date].[Fiscal].[All Periods]})},
         {[Date].[Fiscal].[Fiscal Year].&[2002],
         [Date].[Fiscal].[Fiscal Semester].&[2002]&[1],
         [Date].[Fiscal].[Fiscal Quarter].&[2002]&[1]}, RECURSIVE) ON 0
FROM     [Sales Summary]
WHERE    ([Measures].[Sales Amount], [Product].[Product Categories].[All])
SELECT   DrilldownMember(
         {DrilldownLevel({[Date].[Fiscal].[All Periods]})},
         {[Date].[Fiscal].[Fiscal Year].&[2002],
         [Date].[Fiscal].[Fiscal Semester].&[2002]&[1],
         [Date].[Fiscal].[Fiscal Quarter].&[2002]&[1]}) ON 0
FROM     [Sales Summary]
WHERE    ([Measures].[Sales Amount], [Product].[Product Categories].[All])
```

Execute these queries in SSMS to see the results of the queries. The first query returns all the months of the first quarter of fiscal year 2002, but the second query returns only the members in the semester level for the fiscal year 2002. You have now successfully learned to drill down to details in your pivot table report and we hope you learned more about DrilldownMember and DrilldownLevel MDX functions.

Analyzing Multiple Measures

So far you have been analyzing a single measure within your pivot table. Sometimes you might need to see more than one measure in your pivot table. For example, as an executive making financial decisions, you might need to analyze the Internet Sales along with the initial targets or to analyze the budgeted cost versus actual cost. In the Cube Browser within BIDS you were able to select multiple measures. However, within a pivot table you cannot have more than one measure in the Data or Values area. In this section, you learn how to analyze multiple measures within a pivot table.

As an extension to the pivot table you analyzed in the previous section assume you want to see the quantity ordered along with the sales amount in your pivot table. The following steps show you how to analyze the Internet Sales Amount along with Order Quantity:

1. Drill up to the fiscal year level on the Column Labels.

2. In the PivotTable Field List check the measure Internet Order Quantity. Notice that the measure gets added to the Values section in the PivotTable Field List and the Values label for the measure automatically gets added to the Column Labels section as shown in Figure 17-22.

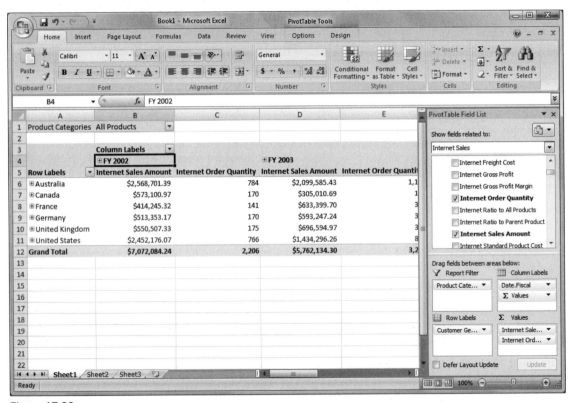

Figure 17-22

The pivot table now creates a new hierarchy called Values on the Columns axis, and adds the two measures [Internet Sales Amount] and [Internet Order Quantity] to the Values area. If you move the Values hierarchy to the Row area you will get the layout shown in Figure 17-23. You can see the subtotals for each measure in separate rows. The MDX query sent to SSAS to populate the data in the pivot table includes a crossjoin of the Customer Geography hierarchy and a Set with the two measures Internet Sales Amount and Internet Order Quantity on the Rows axis.

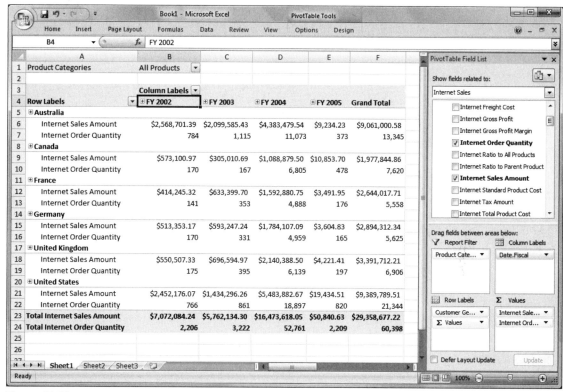

Figure 17-23

Custom Grouping

When you analyze the results within a pivot table you might want to group certain members and analyze the data for those specific members. For example, if you have sales data for all the countries you might want to analyze the sales based on continents. If continent is not a level in the hierarchy, you might have to modify the cube design and add this information. Instead the pivot table helps you to group members and provide a name. Perform the following steps to group the countries' level of the Customer Geography hierarchy into two groups, North America and Europe, within the pivot table:

1. Remove Internet Order Quantity from the Values list so Internet Sales Amount is the only value in the pivot table.

2. Hold down the Ctrl key and select the members United States and Canada.

3. Right-click and select Group as shown in Figure 17-24. You can also accomplish this by clicking the Group Selection button in the Group section of the Options tab in the Ribbon.

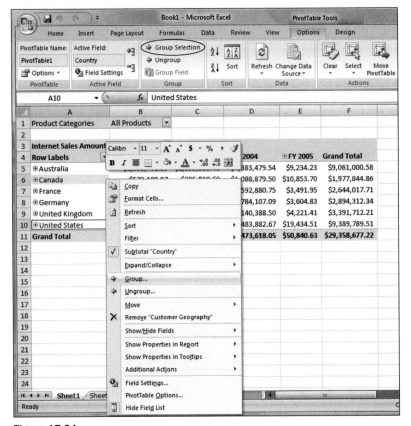

Figure 17-24

A new group will appear called Group 1. Under that group will be the members United States and Canada. Excel uses the session cube feature of SSAS to create an intermediate level to group. Following is the query sent by Excel to SSAS (reformatted and elided to show the important points):

```
CREATE SESSION CUBE [Adventure Works_XL_GROUPING2] FROM [Adventure Works]
( MEASURE [Adventure Works].[Internet Sales Amount],
  MEASURE [Adventure Works].[Internet Order Quantity],
  MEASURE [Adventure Works].[Internet Extended Amount],
  ...
  DIMENSION [Adventure Works].[Ship Date].[Month Name] HIDDEN,
  DIMENSION [Customer].[Customer Geography] NOT_RELATED_TO_FACTS
  FROM _XL_GROUPING7
  (
    LEVEL [(All)],
    LEVEL [Customer Geography1] GROUPING,
    LEVEL [Country],
    LEVEL [State-Province],
    LEVEL [City],
    LEVEL [Postal Code],
    LEVEL [Customer],
```

```
GROUP [Customer Geography1].[CountryXl_Grp_1]
(
    MEMBER [Customer].[Customer Geography].[Country].&[Canada],
    MEMBER [Customer].[Customer Geography].[Country].&[United States]
)
)
)
```

You can see that the create session cube statement is sent to SSAS where all the measures and dimensions are included and an intermediate level, [Customer Geography1], created on the Customer Geography hierarchy. That level includes Canada and United States as shown in the MEMBER lines in the code.

4. Select the cell containing the member Group1, and rename it to North America.

5. Create another group for France, Germany, and United Kingdom and name it Europe. When you are done the pivot table should look like Figure 17-25.

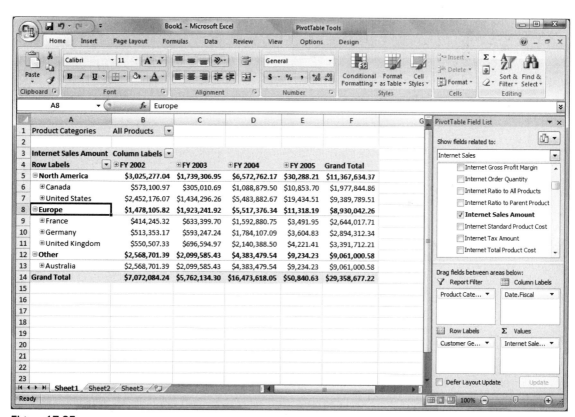

Figure 17-25

You have now successfully grouped members in the Customer Geography hierarchy without making design changes in the cube. As mentioned earlier, Excel uses the session cube feature of SSAS to create the intermediate levels. The intermediate levels will persist only in the context of the current session and will not be seen by other users. Totals are created for the new members North America and Europe, which allows the end user to drill down or drill up. If you click the drop-down list for Row Labels, you can see the new members created due to custom grouping along with the members in the Country level as shown in Figure 17-26. If you double-click a cell containing a group member, you will see that the double-click acts as a toggle switch to hide or show details in the next level. For example, if you double-click Europe, you will see the members France, Germany, and United Kingdom change from visible to hidden and vice versa. The groupings help you analyze the [Internet Sales Amount] for various continents across various fiscal years.

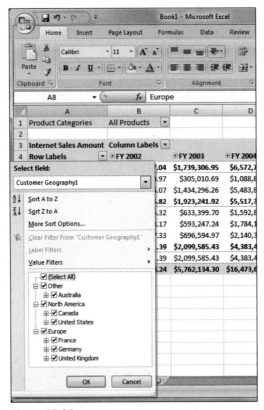

Figure 17-26

You can also create nested groups by grouping groups that have been created such as grouping Europe and North America into a Northern Hemisphere group. The Grouping feature in Excel provides you with the flexibility to do multiple levels of grouping, which is really useful when there are several members in a hierarchy and you want to perform data analysis by grouping the members into several groups. You can ungroup a group of members by right-clicking the group name and selecting Ungroup from the context menu or clicking the Ungroup icon on the Ribbon under the Options tab in a similar manner as the grouping that was shown in Figure 17-24.

It is important to know the limitations of grouping hierarchy members in Excel pivot tables. You cannot group members of a parent-child hierarchy and hierarchies of ROLAP dimensions using Excel pivot tables. Having learned to use various options in the pivot table for data analysis, you now learn to present the data effectively to end users in the following sections.

Organizing Attributes in the PivotTable Field List

You can edit the folder names that the attributes belong to in BIDS. You are going to change the folders for some customer attributes to help you organize information in a mailing list.

1. Launch Business Intelligence Development Studio.

2. Open the Adventure Works DW 2008 sample project.

3. In the Solution Explorer under Dimensions, double-click the Customer.dim dimension.

4. In the Attributes pane select Education.

5. Change the AttributeHierarchyDisplay property of the Education attribute in the Properties pane to Personal as shown in Figure 17-27.

6. Make the same change to the Gender and Marital Status attribute properties.

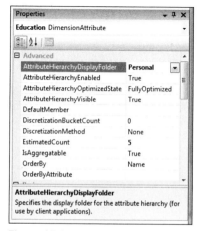

Figure 17-27

7. Deploy the Adventure Works DW 2008 project onto your Analysis Services instance.

When your project has finished deploying the server will have updated information that will organize and display the hierarchies in the folder that you specified. This way you can organize the attributes the way you want in the PivotTable Field List for your end users. Now use the following steps to see the updated information within Excel:

1. Switch to your Excel application.

2. In the Ribbon select the Data tab.

3. In the Connections group select Refresh All.

4. View the Customer dimension in the PivotTable Field List.

You'll notice that the Customer dimension in the PivotTable Field List has been updated with a new folder called Personal, which now contains the attributes Education, Gender, and Marital Status as shown in Figure 17-28.

Figure 17-28

Number Formatting

If you are familiar with Excel you might be aware that you can apply various kinds of formatting to a cell in Excel such as String, Number, and Currency. Excel requests the formatted value for the measures retrieved from Analysis Services cubes. It uses the formatted value to display the cell values. You will notice that the measure InternetSaleAmount is of type Currency in the Adventure Works DW 2008 sample database. That's why you see the InternetSalesAmount displayed as currency in the pivot table. If you change the formatting on the Analysis Services instance Excel will be able to display the new formatting. The following steps show how to change the formatting for the InternetSalesAmount from currency to three decimal places on your cube and see how this is displayed in Excel:

1. Open the Adventure Works cube in BIDS.

2. Select the InternetSalesAmount measure.

3. In the Properties window change the FormatString property from Currency to #,#.000 as shown in Figure 17-29.

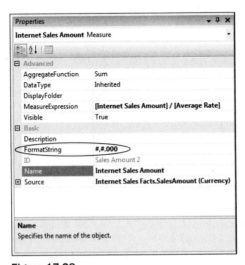

Figure 17-29

4. Deploy the project to your Analysis Services instance.

5. Switch to your Excel application with the pivot table connected to the AdventureWorks cube.

6. Select the Data tab in the Excel Ribbon.

7. In the Connections group select Refresh All. The [Internet Sales Amount] is now refreshed in the pivot table and you will see each cell value has three decimal places displayed as shown in Figure 17-30. Perform the following three steps to get back to the original cube state for the subsequent exercises.

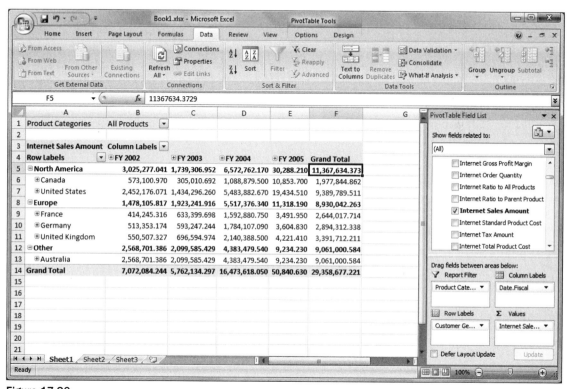

Figure 17-30

8. Switch back to BIDS.

9. Change the FormatString property of the [Internet Sales Amount] measure back to Currency.

10. Deploy the changes to your Analysis Services instance.

Highlighting Exceptions

Highlighting exceptions, which we also call bubbling up exceptions, provides a way to quickly read through the report and examine exceptions in the data. This is one technique that will help with faster data analysis, especially when you are looking at a pivot table with a large amount of data. SQL Server Analysis Services 2008 allows you to specify the background color for each cell value, which can be utilized by any Analysis Services client tool to highlight exceptions. You learned how to format the background color of cell values in Chapter 6. The following steps show you how to update the MDX script to specify background color for [Internet Sales Amount] based on its value and then view the results in Excel:

1. Switch to the BIDS that has the Adventure Works DW 2008 sample project open.

2. Double-click the AdventureWorks.cube file to open the AdventureWorks cube in the cube editor and select the Calculations tab.

3. In the Calculations tab click the icon to switch to Script View as shown in Figure 17-31.

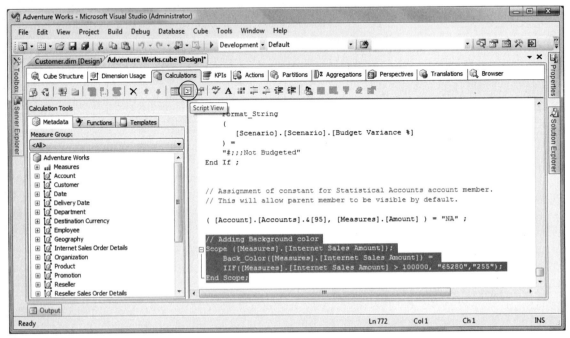

Figure 17-31

4. Scroll to the end of the MDX script and add the following MDX expression in the MDX script editor as shown in Figure 17-31:

```
//Adding background color
Scope ([Measures].[Internet Sales Amount]);
    Back_Color ( [Measures].[Internet Sales Amount] ) =
    IIF([Measures].[Internet Sales Amount]100000,"65280","255");
End Scope;
```

This MDX expression specifies the background color based on the cell value. If the cell value is greater than 100000, the background color assigned is green (65280), otherwise a red background color (255) is assigned to the cell.

5. Deploy the updated Adventure Works DW 2008 project to your Analysis Services instance.

6. Switch to the Excel application connected to the AdventureWorks cube and select the Data tab in the Excel Ribbon.

7. In the Connections group select Refresh All.

The pivot table will now be refreshed with the updated data from your Analysis Services instance that now contains the background cell values as shown in Figure 17-32. We recommend you drill down on the cells corresponding to the United States members. You will be able to see the background color applied to each state. In this example we have shown a simple illustration of the background color. Typically the MDX expressions in the cubes for the background will have appropriately highlighted the business objectives of your company. Having the background color highlight exceptions in the data helps you identify key areas to focus on to improve your business results. Perform steps 8 through 10 to get back to the original cube state for the subsequent exercises.

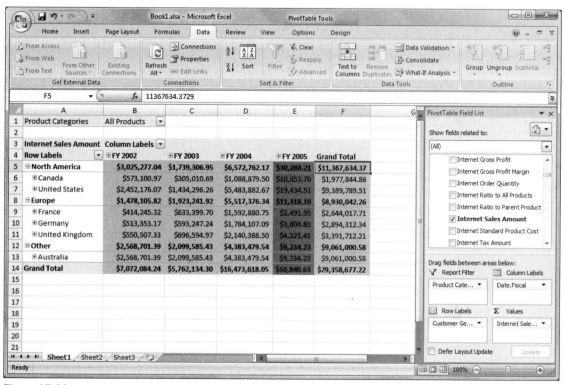

Figure 17-32

8. Switch back to BIDS.

9. Delete the MDX expression you added in this section for background color.

10. Deploy the Adventure Works DW 2008 project to your Analysis Services instance.

Viewing Member Properties

In Analysis Services 2008 the relationship between attributes within a dimension are defined using the Attribute Relationship page of the Dimension Designer. By default all the attributes are related to the key attribute of a dimension because there is a one-to-many relationship. Member properties are properties that define certain aspects of a member. For example, a customer's name, age, and salary are properties of the customer. The Attribute Relationship page of the Dimension Designer is also used to define member properties as you learned in Chapter 5. While analyzing the data in a pivot table you may want to see the properties of a member. Excel provides two ways to see member properties within pivot tables: using tool tips or adding the data to the pivot table. The following sections show you how to view member properties within Excel.

Tool Tips

Tool tips provide you with an easy way to view the properties of members you are analyzing in the pivot table as you hover the mouse arrow over a specific member. To use tool tips, follow these steps:

1. Remove all the fields from your pivot table. You can do this by clicking the arrow on the right side of each attribute in the field areas of the PivotTable Field List and selecting Remove Field from the context menu, dragging each item from the field areas to the fields section, or un-checking the appropriate boxes in the fields section of the PivotTable Field List.

2. In the PivotTable Field List filter drop-down ("Show fields related to"), select [Internet Customers] and then add the Customer Geography and Customer hierarchies to the Row Labels as shown in Figure 17-33.

3. Select the first Customer in North America, Aaron A. Allen, and hover the mouse over the member.

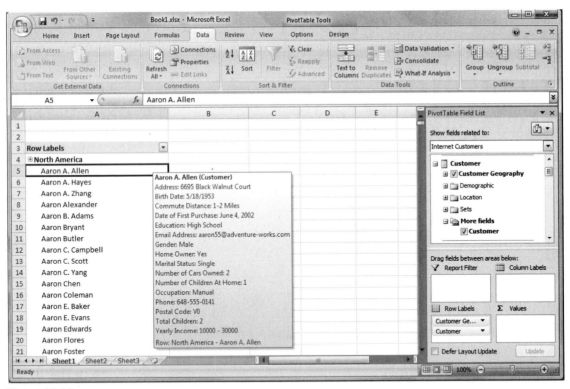

Figure 17-33

You will see the member properties of the Customer Aaron A. Allen as a tool tip as shown in Figure 17-33. Because the Customer hierarchy is the key attribute in the Customer dimension you will see all the properties of the member from the Customer hierarchy. As you perform your data analysis in the pivot table and want to get more information about a specific member, this tool tip feature really helps you understand the data better

The Pivot Table Report

As an alternative to viewing the tool tips, Excel provides you with a way to have the member properties added into your pivot table. To use the pivot table from the previous section to view a member property as part of the pivot table report, follow these steps:

1. Right-click one of the Customer members and in the context menu select Show Properties in Report ⇨ Education.

2. Add the Date.Fiscal hierarchy to the Column Labels.

3. Add the Customer Count to the Values.

4. Expand the North America member to show the Countries in North America.

You will now see the Education member property of each customer shown as a column in the pivot table as shown in Figure 17-34. Notice that the member property added into the pivot table report is a column that appears before the attributes part of the Column Labels. Including all the member properties would make the pivot table difficult to analyze so we recommend you choose the appropriate member properties to include in the pivot table reports so that the end user is able to easily utilize those properties for effective data analysis.

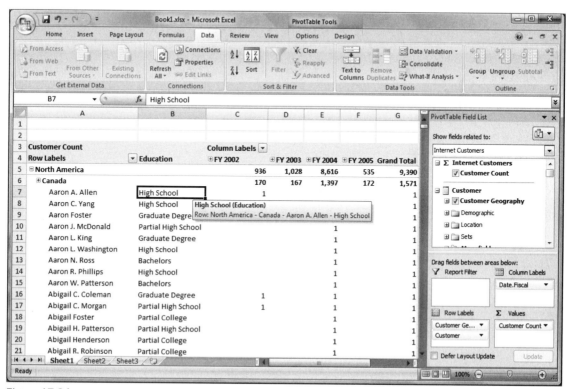

Figure 17-34

Sorting Data

You may have observed from the previous example that the list of members in a pivot table can be fairly long. To help you with further analysis, Excel 2007 provides you with new and simpler filtering and sorting options. In this section you learn how to sort in Excel 2007. Let's go back to analyzing Internet Sales by location:

1. Clear all the fields in the pivot table by removing the measures from values and hierarchies from Row Labels and Column Labels.

2. Select Internet Sales measure group as a filter in the PivotTable Field List.

3. Add the [Internet Sales Amount] to Values.

4. Add Customer Geography to the Row Labels.

5. Add Date.Fiscal to the Column Labels.

6. Drill down on the country France in the Customer Geography hierarchy as shown in Figure 17-35.

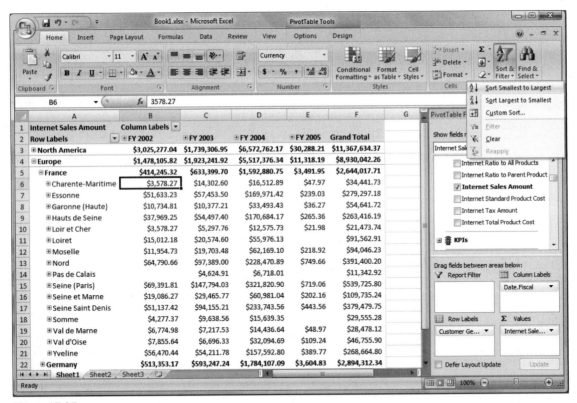

Figure 17-35

You will now see the [Internet Sales Amount] for the various provinces in France for various fiscal years. However it is not easy to identify the provinces with minimum and maximum internet sales for fiscal year FY02. Excel 2007 provides you with an easy way to sort the data in the pivot table that helps you easily identify the minimum and maximum InternetSalesAmounts.

7. Switch to the Home tab in the Excel Ribbon.

8. Select the [Internet Sales Amount] value for state Charente-Maritime and FY02.

9. Click the Sort & Filter icon in the Editing group as shown in Figure 17-35 and select Sort Smallest to Largest.

Excel sends the appropriate MDX query to retrieve the data from SSAS and sorts the members on the axes based on the column selected and cell values returned back. You will now notice the pivot table has been sorted based on the [Internet Sales Amount] values for FY02 as shown in Figure 17-36. From the pivot table shown in Figure 17-36 you can see that the province Pas de Calais didn't have any Internet sales and the province Seine (Paris) had the maximum Internet sales. You can also see the year-to-year trend in Internet sales easily from this pivot table view.

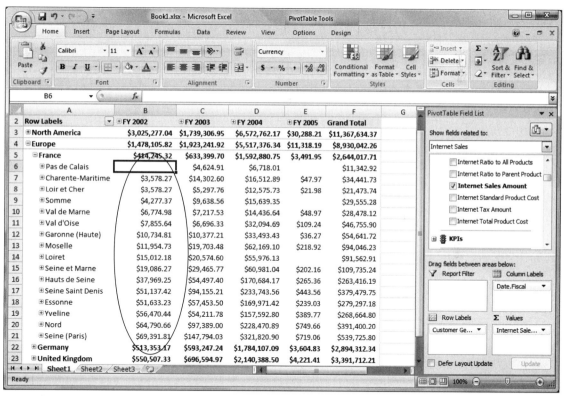

Figure 17-36

Filtering Data

In the previous section you learned about sorting the data in pivot tables. When your pivot table is large with several hundred or thousands of members on rows or columns, data analysis becomes challenging. Excel 2007 provides you with three common ways to filter data in a pivot table. The three ways of filtering are based on Labels, Values, or Top 10. Label filters are used to apply values such as the sales amount of the cities beginning with "Seine." Value filters help in filtering the data in the pivot table based on any of the measure values. For example, you might be analyzing the [Internet Sales Amount] data and can apply a value to filter the data showing the [Internet Tax Amount] that is greater than a specific amount or even within a specific range. One of the most common data analysis requests is for the Top 10 values. The Top 10 filter helps you to quickly narrow down the pivot table to the Top 10 items so that you can analyze the Top 10 values efficiently. The following steps show you how to apply each of these filters and how they affect the data in the pivot table:

1. Right-click any State-Province in the country France and in the context menu select Filter ⇨ Label Filters.

2. In the Label Filter dialog set the criteria to State-Province contains Seine as shown in Figure 17-37 and click OK.

Figure 17-37

Excel sends the following MDX query to retrieve the data based on the filter condition. The MDX expression (InStr(1,[Customer].[Customer Geography].CurrentMember.member_caption,"Seine")>0) helps filter the members in the Customer Geography hierarchy that contain "Seine" in their member caption. InStr, a Visual Basic for Applications (VBA) function used in this expression, returns a value greater than 0 only when it finds the substring "Seine" in the member caption. Excel then uses the sub-select MDX statement to filter the cube space to members in the Customer Geography hierarchy that contain the value "Seine" in their names. Because there are two groups created in the pivot table called Europe and North America, Excel has created a session cube with the name Adventure Works_XL_GROUPING0, which is the name you will see in the following MDX expression. Also note the hierarchy for Customer Geography has been changed to Customer Geography1 within this session because the new levels have been created in the Customer Geography hierarchy.

```
SELECT   NON EMPTY Hierarchize( {DrilldownLevel({
             [Date].[Fiscal].[All Periods]})})
         DIMENSION PROPERTIES PARENT_UNIQUE_NAME ON COLUMNS ,
         NON EMPTY Hierarchize(DrilldownMember({{
             DrilldownMember( {{DrilldownLevel({
             [Customer].[Customer Geography].[All Customers]})}}},
             {[Customer].[Customer Geography].[Customer Geography1].
             [GROUPMEMBER.[CountryX1_Grp_2]].[Customer]].[Customer Geography]].
             [All Customers]]]})}},
             {[Customer].[Customer Geography].[Country].&[France]}))
         DIMENSION PROPERTIES PARENT_UNIQUE_NAME,
         [Customer].[Customer Geography].[State-Province].[Country] ON ROWS
FROM     (SELECT
             Filter([Customer].[Customer Geography].[State-Province].Members,
             (InStr(1,
             [Customer].[Customer Geography].CurrentMember.member_caption,
             "Seine")0)) ON COLUMNS  FROM [Adventure Works_XL_GROUPING0]
         )
WHERE ([Measures].[Internet Sales Amount])
CELL PROPERTIES VALUE, FORMAT_STRING, LANGUAGE, BACK_COLOR, FORE_COLOR, FONT_FLAGS
```

The pivot table will now be filtered to State-Provinces containing the word Seine in them as shown in Figure 17-38.

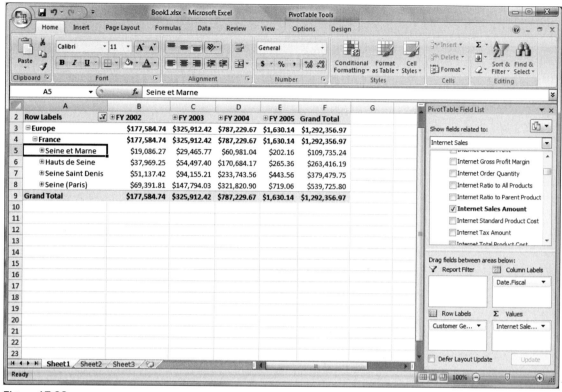

Figure 17-38

3. Clear the Label filtering by right-clicking one of the State-Province members in France and selecting Filter ⇨ Clear Filter State-Province in the context menu.

4. Filter the Column Labels to only show FY 2002 using the drop-down list next to it and selecting only FY 2002.

5. Right -click a member on Row Labels and select Filter ⇨ Value Filters.

6. In the Value Filter dialog, select the filter condition "is greater than" and have the value 600000 as shown in Figure 17-39.

Figure 17-39

You will now see the pivot table showing all the members in Customer Geography that have an [Internet Sales Amount] greater than $600,000 as shown in Figure 17-40.

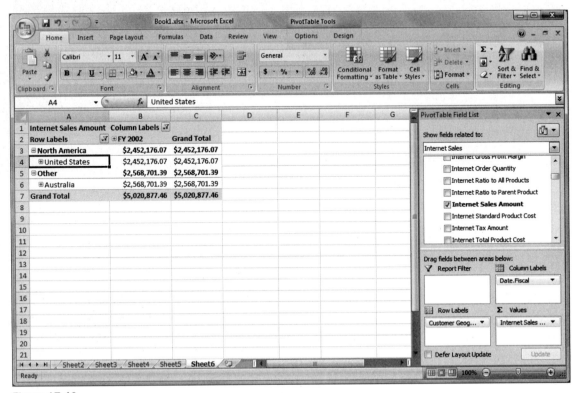

Figure 17-40

Excel sends the following query to retrieve the data from Analysis Services. In this query you can see the cube is initially filtered on Customer Geography members who have Internet Sales Amount greater than 600,000 using the sub-select MDX clause, and then the outer SELECT clause retrieves the data for the pivot table including the two groups created in this specific session.

```
SELECT    NON EMPTY Hierarchize( {DrilldownLevel({
          [Date].[Fiscal].[All Periods]})})
          DIMENSION PROPERTIES PARENT_UNIQUE_NAME ON COLUMNS ,
          NON EMPTY Hierarchize(DrilldownMember({{DrilldownLevel(
          {[Customer].[Customer Geography].[All Customers]})}},
          {[Customer].[Customer Geography].[Customer Geography1].
          [GROUPMEMBER.[CountryXl_Grp_1]].[Customer]].[Customer Geography]].
              [All Customers]]],
          [Customer].[Customer Geography].[Customer Geography1].
          [GROUPMEMBER.[CountryXl_Grp_2]].[Customer]].[Customer Geography]].
              [All Customers]]],
          [Customer].[Customer Geography].[Customer Geography1].
          [OTHERMEMBER.[Customer]].[Customer Geography]].[All Customers]]]}))
          DIMENSION PROPERTIES PARENT_UNIQUE_NAME ON ROWS
   FROM (
          SELECT Filter( Hierarchize(
```

```
                         [Customer].[Customer Geography].[Country].Members),
                         ([Measures].[Internet Sales Amount]>600000)) ON COLUMNS
             FROM (
                SELECT ( {[Date].[Fiscal].[Fiscal Year].&[2002]}) ON COLUMNS
                FROM [Adventure Works_XL_GROUPING0]
                   )
         )
WHERE ([Measures].[Internet Sales Amount])
CELL PROPERTIES VALUE, FORMAT_STRING, LANGUAGE, BACK_COLOR, FORE_COLOR,
FONT_FLAGS
```

7. Remove the Value filter criteria specified earlier by clicking the Sort & Filter icon in Home Ribbon and selecting Clear as shown in Figure 17-41.

Figure 17-41

8. Click the member Europe, right-click, and select Ungroup.

9. Click the member North America, right-click, and select Ungroup. Now let's see how the Top 10 filter helps in easier data analysis. Assume you need to analyze the Internet sales of all the states within the United States and you want to identify the top 10 states' Internet sales based on gross profit. Perform the following steps in the pivot table to achieve the desired results.

10. Drill down on the members of United States by clicking the + sign next to it.

11. Select one of the States within United States.

12. Right-click and select Filter ⇨ Top 10.

13. In the Top 10 Filter for the State-Province hierarchy, select the Internet Gross Profit measure as shown in Figure 17-42 and click OK.

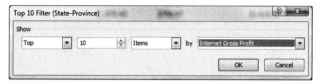

Figure 17-42

The number of states shown in the pivot table for United States now gets filtered from 22 to the top 10 states as shown in Figure 17-43.

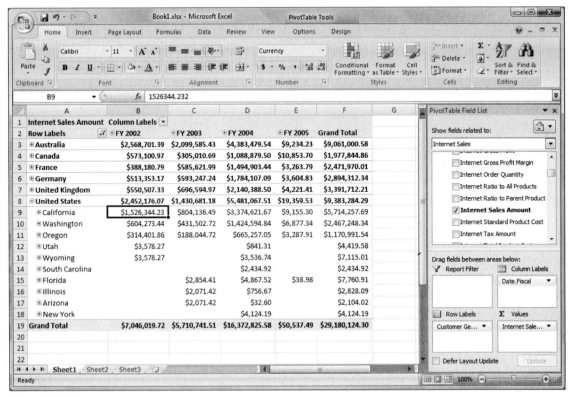

Figure 17-43

Excel sends the following MDX query to Analysis Services to apply the Top 10 filter on Internet Gross profit. You can see Excel creates a sub-select clause to filter the cube space. Initially it is a set containing all the countries. Then for each country the Filter condition is applied on the members at the State-Province level using the TopCount(Filter(Except(DrilldownLevel(....)))) MDX expression to filter the top 10 states. The MDX query generated also excludes states that do not have any sales using IsEmpty([Measures].[InternetGrossProfit]) MDX expression.

```
SELECT    NON EMPTY Hierarchize({DrilldownLevel({
              [Date].[Fiscal].[All Periods]})})
          DIMENSION PROPERTIES PARENT_UNIQUE_NAME ON COLUMNS ,
          NON EMPTY Hierarchize(DrilldownMember({{DrilldownLevel(
              {[Customer].[Customer Geography].[All Customers]})}},
              {[Customer].[Customer Geography].[Country].&[United States]}))
          DIMENSION PROPERTIES PARENT_UNIQUE_NAME,
          [Customer].[Customer Geography].[State-Province].[Country] ON ROWS
FROM      (
          SELECT Generate(Hierarchize(
              [Customer].[Customer Geography].[Country].Members) AS
                  [XL_Filter_Set_0],
              TopCount(Filter(Except(DrilldownLevel([XL_Filter_Set_0].Current
```

```
                        AS [XL_Filter_HelperSet_0], , 0), [XL_Filter_HelperSet_0]),
                    Not IsEmpty([Measures].[Internet Gross Profit])), 10,
                [Measures].[Internet Gross Profit])) ON COLUMNS
            FROM [Adventure Works]
            )
    WHERE ([Measures].[Internet Sales Amount])
    CELL PROPERTIES VALUE, FORMAT_STRING, LANGUAGE, BACK_COLOR,FORE_COLOR,
    FONT_FLAGS
```

In this section you have learned the various ways you can filter the data in a pivot table. You also learned about the MDX queries sent by Excel during these filter conditions and identified that Excel uses the sub-select MDX clause to filter the cube space based on the filter condition to achieve the final filter results.

Style and Design

Pivot tables are often created as reports that end users use for data analysis. That's why formatting the pivot table in an end-user consumable way is really critical. Excel 2007 provides you with preset styles to use on the pivot tables. These styles are shared between tables and other Excel objects. Follow these steps to make the existing pivot table an end-user oriented report:

1. Remove the filter condition in the previous section by right-clicking the Sort & Filter icon on the Data tab of the Ribbon and selecting Clear.

2. Make sure your pivot table shows all the countries and a drill down only on United States.

3. Switch to the Design tab in the Ribbon as shown in Figure 17-44.

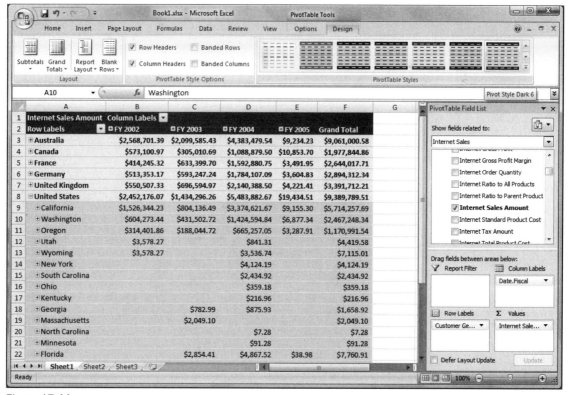

Figure 17-44

You will see various styles in the Design tab. If you hover over each of the styles you will see the style applied to your pivot table. This helps you to preview how a specific style will look on your pivot table report.

4. Choose the style shown in Figure 17-44 for your pivot table.

You can see that all the formatting in your pivot table is still available. Excel 2007 also allows you to create your own customized style. Please refer to Excel 2007 documentation to learn about creating custom styles.

Excel 2007 Conditional Formatting

Excel 2007 has a conditional formatting feature that allows you to analyze the data efficiently in your pivot table. In this section you learn how you can set up conditional formatting with a few clicks. For this example you will analyze the moutain bike product sales on various models delivered for various fiscal years so that you can determine which product models are performing well without reviewing in detail the actual numbers.

1. Clear the fields in your pivot table by removing the meausure in the Values area and the hierarchies in the Row Labels and Column Labels areas.

2. Select the Internet Ratio to All Products measure on Values.

3. Drag and drop Product Categories onto Row Labels.

4. Drag and drop Delivery Date.Fiscal Year onto Column Labels.

5. Drill down to Bikes ⇨ Mountain Bikes. Notice the number of bikes.

6. Select the cell range that contains the ratios of mountain bikes delivered.

7. On the Home tab of the Ribbon select the Conditional Formatting icon and select the first option, Green-Yellow-Red Color Scale, under Color Scales as shown in Figure 17-45.

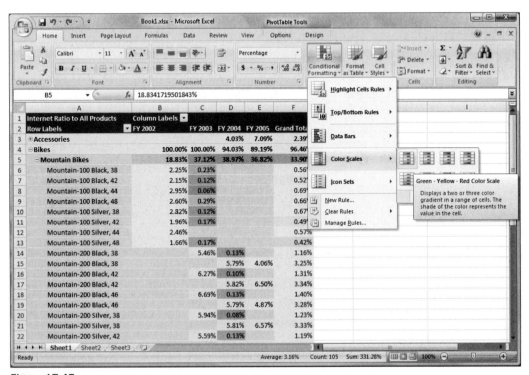

Figure 17-45

You will now see the various colors applied to the data area you have selected. Red indicates the cells that have the least contribution to the sales, and green indicates the models that have contributed to the maximum sales. This method clearly helps you to analyze the pivot table data better because it visually differentiates the data.

If you hover over the various color scales, you can preview them before selecting one.

Note that the percentage does not need to be 100 percent for it to be green. Excel calculates the range of values based on the selection the user made. You also have the option to apply the other conditional formatting options in Excel 2007 such as Data bars or Top/Bottom Rules or Icon Sets. You can use any combination of these conditional formats to make your pivot table reports most efficient for data analysis for your end users. We recommend you explore the various conditional formatting options in Excel 2007.

Perspectives and Translations

In Chapters 5 and 6 you learned about the Perspectives and Translations features supported by Analysis Services. Excel 2007 has knowledge of these features. In this section you learn how to use these features in pivot table reports.

Perspectives

Similar to views on relational databases, perspectives provide another layer for filtering data on the server. You can use perspectives as one of the ways to filter the data being viewed from your Analysis Services instance. The filter occurs on the Analysis Services server. There are several perspectives in the sample Adventure Works DW 2008 database. The following steps show you how to create a new pivot table based on a perspective:

1. On a new worksheet in the Excel workbook, select the Data Tab on the Ribbon and select From Other Sources ⇨ From Analysis Services.

2. In the Data Connection Wizard enter **localhost** for the server name and click Next.

3. Select the Adventure Works DW 2008 database in the Select Database and Table page of the wizard. You will see the cubes and perspectives in the Adventure Works DW 2008 database.

4. Select the Finance perspective and click Next.

5. Accept the default name for the data connection file and click Finish.

6. Click OK in the Import Data dialog.

7. From the PivotTable Field List, add the Amount measure to the Values area, the Departments hierarchy to the Row Labels area, and the Date.Fiscal hierarchy to the Column Labels area.

You will now see the pivot table created on the Finance perspective as shown in Figure 17-46. You can see that the measure groups and the dimensions shown in the field list are only the ones related to the Finance perspective. This is another way of filtering the amount of metadata and data to be shown to the end user in the pivot table. When using perspectives for filtering in a pivot table, all the filtering of data and metadata occurs on the Analysis Services instance.

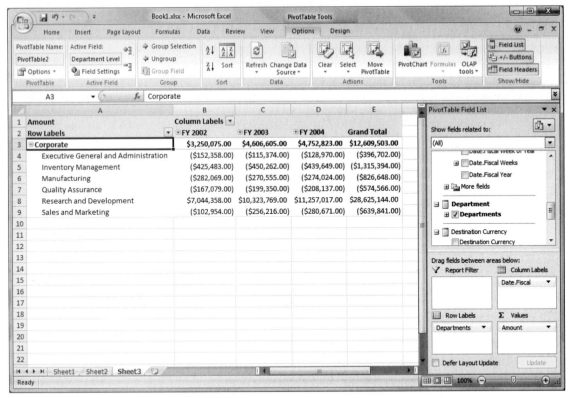

Figure 17-46

Translations

You learned about the Translations feature in SSAS in Chapters 5 and 6. When a client connects using a specific client locale such as Japanese, German, or French and if corresponding translations are defined in your UDM for data and metadata, SSAS sends the appropriate captions specified for the locale. This SSAS feature is extremely useful when you are designing a UDM for your organization where end users in various countries want to see the same data but with appropriate translated metadata. Normally an end user will have a localized version of Excel connecting to an SSAS instance and will see the localized information if the UDM has been designed with translations. The locale-specific information is transferred by Excel. In this section you learn how to verify that an end user using a non-English locale will see translated metadata from Excel.

Assume you have created a UDM for all users in your company with translations in French. You need to ensure that those using French Excel will see the translations. You can either install a French version of Excel to test this out, or using your English version of Excel, test this by changing the connection string used to connect to SSAS. You need to update the connection string properties to inform Analysis Server to use specific locales. The AdventureWorks DW 2008 Sample has localized names in the database for Spanish and French. The following steps show you how to see the French data in your pivot table:

1. Switch to a new sheet in Excel and select the Data tab.

2. Click Existing Connections and select the connection to the AdventureWorks cube in the Adventure Works DW 2008 database that you created earlier in this chapter, as shown in Figure 17-47, and click Open.

Figure 17-47

3. In the Import Data dialog, click the OK button.

4. Add the [Internet Sales Amount] to the Values area.

5. Add the Date.Fiscal hierarchy to the Column Labels.

6. Add Product.Product Categories to the Row Labels. You should now have a pivot table as shown in Figure 17-48.

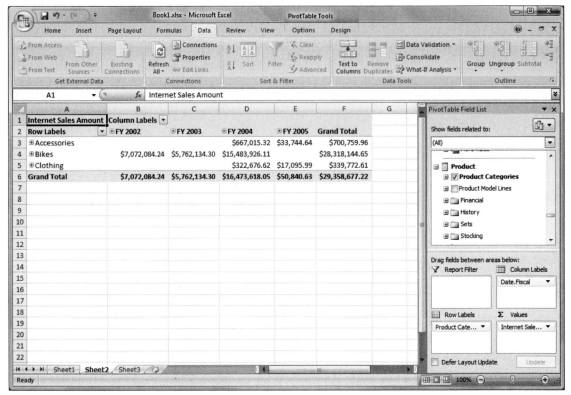

Figure 17-48

7. Click the Data tab in the Excel Ribbon. Then under the Connections group, click the Properties button.

8. In the Connection Properties dialog, switch to the Definition tab and add the text **LocaleIdentifier=1036** to the connection string as shown in Figure 17-49.

9. Click OK.

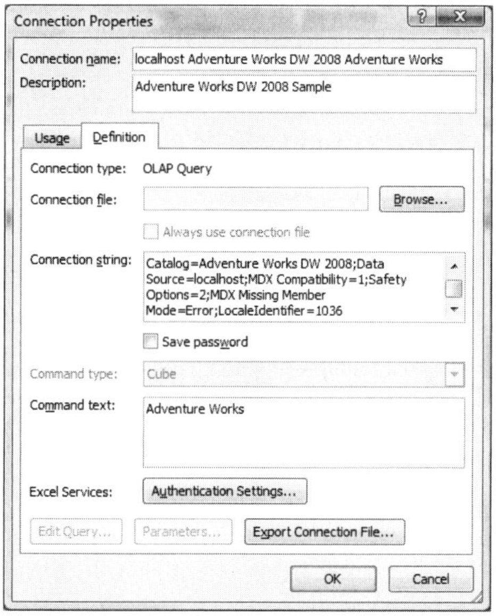

Figure 17-49

Excel modifies your entry of LocaleIdentifier=1036 in the connection string to ExtendedProperties="LocaleIdentifier=1036". You can the see the updated connection string as shown if you click the Properties icon in the Connection group.

```
Provider=MSOLAP.4;Integrated Security=SSPI;Persist Security Info=True;Initial
Catalog=Adventure Works DW 2008;Data Source=localhost;Extended
Properties="LocaleIdentifier=1036";MDX Compatibility=1;Safety
Options=2;MDX Missing Member Mode=Error
```

Excel sends a series of discovers to retrieve the metadata and data to be shown in the pivot table with the updated connection string. The MDX query to retrieve the data for the pivot table is the same but Excel sends the additional property of LocaleIdentifier=1036. Analysis Services understands the French client (LocaleIdentifier=1036) and sends the translated data and metadata. Now your pivot table is updated to show the members of the Product and Date hierarchies in French captions as shown in Figure 17-50. Note the actual Internet Sales Amount data values do not change. You have now successfully verified that your French users can connect to your UDM and view your translations successfully. If you are creating an Excel report that the clients are going to be using you would actually need to update the saved connection string with the LocaleIdentifier=1036 property. You can do this by changing the connection's properties in the Workbook Connections dialog. You open the dialog by clicking the Connections button on the Data tab of the Ribbon.

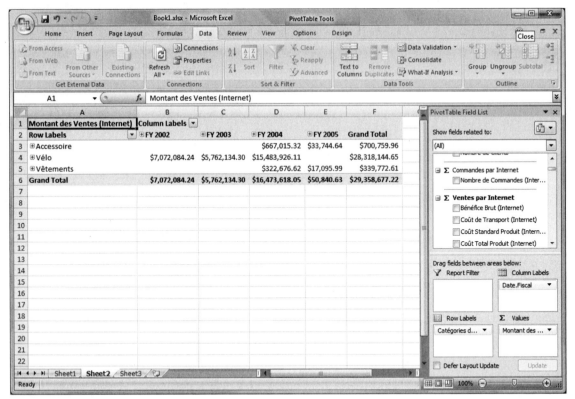

Figure 17-50

Key Performance Indicators

Key Performance Indicators (KPI's) are business measurements used to track trends and progress toward some predefined goal. You learned how to define and use KPIs in Chapter 9. Excel 2007 understands SSAS KPIs and is able to retrieve and show the appropriate KPI icons within Excel. In this section you learn how to analyze data from Adventure Works using KPIs. The following steps show you how to review KPIs in pivot tables:

1. Change the language used by the connection string from the pivot table in the previous section to English by removing the LocaleIdentifier=1036 string in the Connection Property dialog.

2. Clear all the fields from your pivot table by removing them from Values, Row Labels, and Column Labels.

3. Navigate the PivotTable Field List, and add Date.Fiscal to the Row Labels. Expand the KPIs folder, and then select the [Growth In Customer Base] KPI as shown in Figure 17-51.

4. Add the Date.Fiscal hierarchy to the Row Labels.

Figure 17-51

As shown in Figure 17-52 you will see the Growth in Customer Base KPI's value, goal, status, and trend for various fiscal years. From the pivot table you can analyze that for FY 2002 there was no growth in customers because there was no previous year to compare against. Hence, the status doesn't really matter in this case and the trend is flat. For FY 2003 growth was 46 percent compared with the previous fiscal year and the goal was 30 percent. Therefore the KPI status indicator is green and the trend indicator is up.

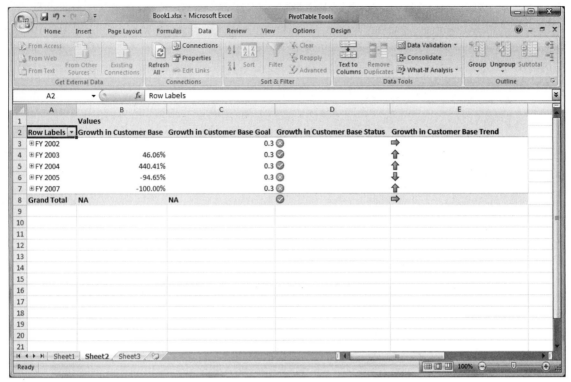

Figure 17-52

The definitions of the KPIs are in the cube. Excel retrieves the KPIs using the following MDX query:

```
SELECT      {[Measures].[Growth in Customer Base],
             [Measures].[Growth in Customer Base Goal],
             [Measures].[Growth in Customer Base Status],
             [Measures].[Growth in Customer Base Trend]}
            DIMENSION PROPERTIES PARENT_UNIQUE_NAME ON COLUMNS ,
            NON EMPTY Hierarchize({DrilldownLevel({
               [Date].[Fiscal].[All Periods]})})
            DIMENSION PROPERTIES PARENT_UNIQUE_NAME ON ROWS
FROM [Adventure Works]
CELL PROPERTIES VALUE, FORMAT_STRING, LANGUAGE, BACK_COLOR, FORE_COLOR,
FONT_FLAGS
```

If you execute the MDX query in SSMS, you will see the KPI values as numbers as shown in
Figure 17-53, which are the basis for the graphical information that is shown in Excel. Excel retrieves the
numerical information defined on the UDM for the KPIs and translates the values to appropriate KPI
graphics in the pivot table. The graphical KPI helps you understand the data more easily than actual
numbers. For example, green indicates the goal of 30 percent increase in customer base is being
accomplished for a specific year, and red indicates the goal is not being accomplished for that specific
year. Therefore having a KPI graphic within the pivot table report enhances the end-users' ability to
understand them easily and take appropriate business actions.

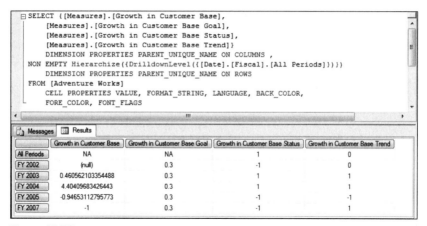

```
SELECT {[Measures].[Growth in Customer Base],
    [Measures].[Growth in Customer Base Goal],
    [Measures].[Growth in Customer Base Status],
    [Measures].[Growth in Customer Base Trend]}
DIMENSION PROPERTIES PARENT_UNIQUE_NAME ON COLUMNS ,
NON EMPTY Hierarchize({DrilldownLevel({{[Date].[Fiscal].[All Periods]}})})
DIMENSION PROPERTIES PARENT_UNIQUE_NAME ON ROWS
FROM [Adventure Works]
    CELL PROPERTIES VALUE, FORMAT_STRING, LANGUAGE, BACK_COLOR,
    FORE_COLOR, FONT_FLAGS
```

	Growth in Customer Base	Growth in Customer Base Goal	Growth in Customer Base Status	Growth in Customer Base Trend
All Periods	NA	NA	1	0
FY 2002	(null)	0.3	-1	0
FY 2003	0.460562103354488	0.3	1	1
FY 2004	4.40409683426443	0.3	1	1
FY 2005	-0.94653112795773	0.3	-1	-1
FY 2007	-1	0.3	-1	1

Figure 17-53

Named Sets

Excel 2007 also shows the named sets defined in the SSAS UDM in a folder called Sets under appropriate dimensions as shown in Figure 17-54. This helps the end user or the person creating pivot table reports include the named sets directly in the pivot table rather than doing additional filtering in Excel. We recommend that you experiment with including named sets within your pivot table.

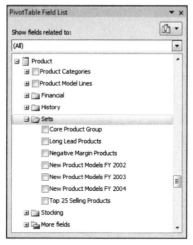

Figure 17-54

Sheet Data Reports

As you saw in the previous section pivot tables are really useful for analyzing data and to a certain extent also help in creating Excel reports against SSAS. However, pivot tables do not provide the flexibility to create Excel reports such as asymmetric reports, inserting blank columns or rows to make the report suit specific formatting requirements. Excel 2007 introduced new functions that can retrieve data from SSAS. Excel 2007 also supports converting your pivot table into a sheet data report so that you can make additional enhancements to your Excel report to be viewed by your end users. In this section you learn how to convert pivot tables to sheet data reports, learn about the new Excel functions to retrieve data from SSAS called cube functions, and learn about the benefits you gain from using sheet data reports.

To convert an existing pivot table into a sheet data report, follow these steps:

1. Create a new sheet in your Excel workbook.

2. Create a pivot table connecting to the AdventureWorks cube on your SSAS instance with Customer Geography in the Row Labels, [Internet Sales Amount] in the Values section, and Date.Fiscal in the Column Labels. This is the same as the first pivot table you created at the beginning of this chapter and should look like Figure 17-12.

3. Click the Options tab on the Ribbon.

4. Click the OLAP Tools in the Tools group and select Convert to Formulas as shown in Figure 17-55.

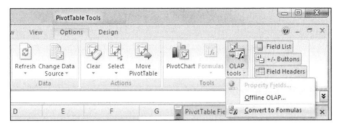

Figure 17-55

Excel now converts the pivot table into regular Excel spread sheet data with formulas rather than member names and numbers in the cells. If you click each cell you will see the formula used to retrieve the data in the Excel formula bar as shown in Figure 17-56. Each cell uses one of the cube functions available in Excel 2007. You will see members retrieved using the CUBEMEMBER function and you will see the numeric cell values retrieved using the CUBEVALUE function. Notice you cannot drill down on the members as you do in the pivot table. However, if you had drilled down in your pivot table and then converted to the formulas, you will see members at the various levels seen in the pivot table at the time you converted to formulas.

You can now insert columns into the report and change the background color of the inserted columns to make the report more presentable to the end users, as shown in Figure 17-56. You can rename the Row and Column Labels if needed. We recommend that you explore the enhancements to your Excel report. If you have page report filter conditions in your pivot table, those are also included when you convert to formulas. You will still have the option to select members from this filter. Each cell has a separate cube function so each cell in the spreadsheet can be queried separately from your SSAS instance. However, sending so many queries to SSAS would not be optimal. That's why Excel optimizes the number of queries being sent to an SSAS instance and whenever feasible it batches data being retrieved for multiple cells into a single query.

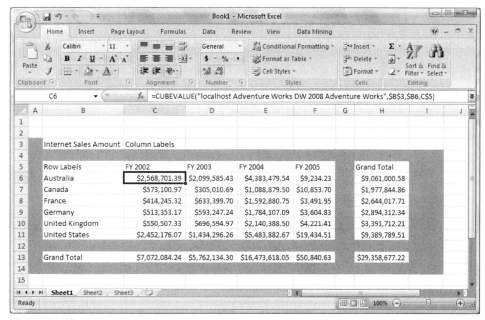

Figure 17-56

Perform the following steps to create a summary report for each country based on Internet Sales Amount with appropriate calculations. Here you create a table that shows the growth in sales from FY 2002 to FY 2003.

1. Select the six cells from members Australia down to United States and press Ctrl+C to copy the data to your clipboard.

2. Paste the cells below the entire table as shown in Figure 17-57.

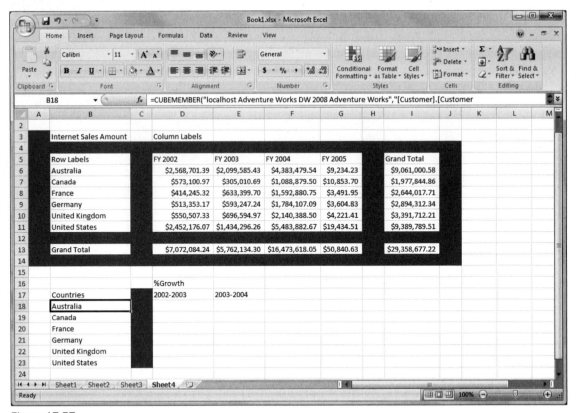

Figure 17-57

If you click each member you will notice the new cells have the same formula. You will now calculate the percentage growth/increase in [Internet Sales Amount] between the years 2002 & 2003 and 2003 & 2004 in your aggregated report.

3. Insert a column before column C in the spreadsheet and fill the cells with blue as shown in Figure 17-57.

4. Enter **Countries** as a heading above the country members you pasted in step 2. Enter **2002-2003** and **2003-2004** in columns D and E in the same row that you entered the Countries heading. Enter **%Growth** in the cell above **2002-2003** as shown in Figure 17-57.

5. For the cell corresponding to Australia and 2002-2003, cell number D18, enter the following formula:

```
= (E6-D6) / D6
```

6. Copy the formula from cell D18 to cells D19-D23. You can do this by clicking cell D18 and dragging the right bottom corner of the selection box down to the member United States. The mouse cursor will change to a plus sign when you are at the right place to do the drag. You will now see all the cells in the 2002-2003 column populated with data.

7. Copy and paste the formula from cell D18 to cell E18.

8. Similar to step 6, copy the formula from cell E18 to cells E19-E23.

9. Select all the cells between D18 and E23.

10. Click the "%" button in the Number section of the Home tab of the Ribbon as shown in Figure 17-58 to format the cells as percentages.

You will now see the summary report you have created shown in Figure 17-58. You have learned that you can refer to cells using cube functions that retrieve data from the SSAS instance and utilize the cells with formulas similar to regular cells in Excel spreadsheet reports such as copying, referencing other cells, and applying formatting. The cube functions therefore provide you with a higher flexibility and freedom to create custom reports than can be accomplished using pivot tables.

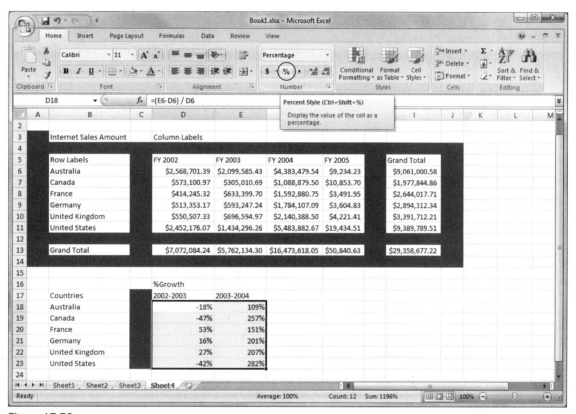

Figure 17-58

Cube Functions in Excel 2007

Most of the cube functions include the name of the connection to the cube as the first argument, and reference all the members used to obtain the values. The first member, Australia, is retrieved using the cube function CUBEMEMBER with the following expression:

```
=CUBEMEMBER("localhost Adventure Works DW 2008 Adventure
Works","[Customer].[Customer Geography].[Country].&[Australia]")
```

The first parameter is the connection information, and the second parameter is the name of the member to be retrieved. There is an optional caption parameter for the CUBEMEMBER function that is not utilized in this example.

The corresponding [Internet Sales Amount] for FY 2002 is referred to using the CUBEVALUE function and the following expression:

```
=CUBEVALUE("localhost Adventure Works DW 2008 Adventure Works",$B$3,$B6,D$5)
```

The first parameter is the connection information, the second parameter references the measure name, Internet Sales Amount, and the third and fourth parameters correspond to the members to be utilized while retrieving the data. The CUBEVALUE function accepts a series of member expressions after the connection parameter.

Excel 2007 supports auto completion for the cube functions to help you guide the parameters being passed. If you click a new cell and enter **=CUBEVALUE("** you will see the list of connections available, as shown in Figure 17-59. If you select one of connections using Tab and then type double quotes to start the second parameter you will see the list of dimensions available in the cube to be selected as shown in Figure 17-60. This feature helps you to enter the correct member expression in the formula and saves you from having to remember the full MDX expressions needed to retrieve the data.

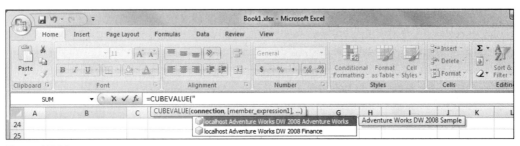

Figure 17-59

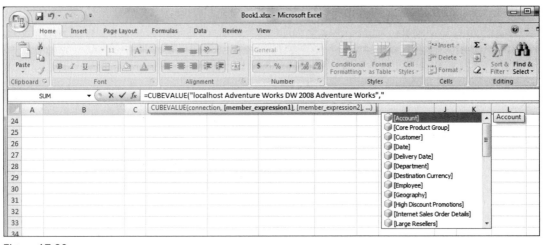

Figure 17-60

The following table lists the cube functions supported in Excel 2007 along with a brief description of each cube function:

Cube Function Name	Description
CUBEMEMBER (connection, member expression, caption)	Used to retrieve the member from a hierarchy.
CUBEVALUE (connection, member expression1, member expression2 , …)	Used to retrieve the value based on the member expressions passed as parameters.
CUBEKPIMEMBER(connection, kpi_name, kpi_property, caption)	Used to retrieve values from KPIs. You need to specify the KPI name and the property value you need to retrieve as parameters.
CUBESET(connection, set_expression, caption, [sort_order], [sort_by])	Used to return MDX sets of values based on the set expression. This function allows you to specify the sort order for the members in the set.
CUBESETCOUNT (set)	Used to count set items for the specified set.
CUBERANKEDMEMBER(connection,set_expression, rank, caption)	Used to retrieve the Nth member of a hierarchy in a cube.
CUBEMEMBERPROPERTY(connection, member_expression, member_property)	Used to retrieve the member property of a member of a hierarchy.

Pivot Charts

Pivot charts allow you to view pivot table data graphically. Creating pivot charts is fairly quick in Excel 2007 and allows the end user to understand and interpret the data more easily than viewing them in a pivot table. Excel has various chart types and styles that you can easily switch to from the Ribbon. You will be able to create the most efficient chart to analyze the data based on your business needs. The following steps show you how to create a pivot chart:

1. Create a new worksheet in your Excel workbook.

2. Create a pivot table with Customer Geography on the Row Labels, Internet Sales Amount in the Values section, and Date.Fiscal in the Column Labels.

3. On the Ribbon select the Insert tab.

4. In the Charts group select the Column option and select the first 2-D column chart as shown in Figure 17-61.

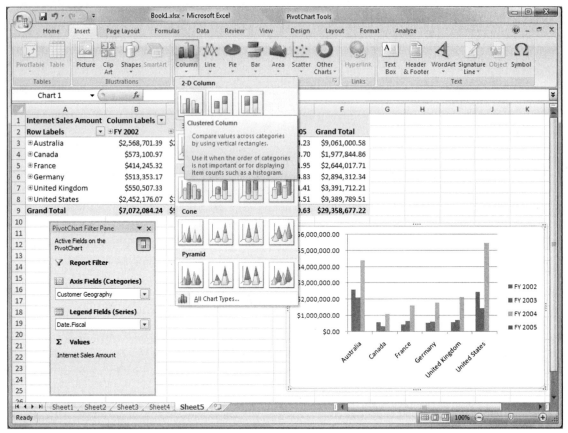

Figure 17-61

5. Once you select the chart, experiment with different chart types by going to the Ribbon in the Chart group section and choosing the different chart types as shown in Figure 17-62.

You can see that creating a pivot chart using the data in the pivot table was quite fast and provides you with better insight and the ability to interpret the data easily. The pivot chart has its own filtering pane where you can select a single member or multiple members in the pivot chart. The pivot chart and pivot tables are synchronized so if you select a specific member on an axis you will also see the corresponding data being updated in the pivot table. We recommend you explore the various options of the pivot chart.

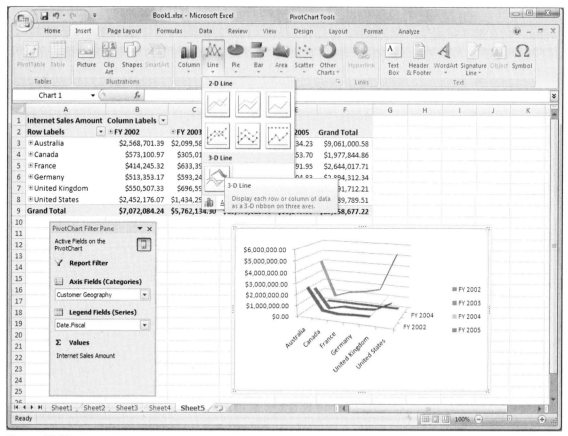

Figure 17-62

Local Cubes

Being busy executives, many consumers of business intelligence information want to be able to access their cubes from the most remote of locations, like from business class aboard a Boeing 747. Yes, some people actually find themselves with a laptop and no Internet connection. Once you stop shivering from the very thought of not being connected to the Internet, consider this alternative: you can create what are called local cubes for your customers. With these offline cubes you can distribute an analytic environment to someone sans a network connection. In other words, these customers do not need to have access to an Analysis Services instance to see the data. Local cubes can be created directly by sending the DDL of the database or using Excel. Typically, local cubes are small sections of a server cube that are distributed to the end users to analyze the data offline. Customers using local cubes can do almost all of the operations associated with online analysis. However, there are some restrictions that you need to be aware of while using local cubes.

The user creating a local cube from a server cube should have the ability to drill-through to the source data so that appropriate data can be retrieved from the server cube to form the local cube. Appropriate permission to see the source-level data is specified using a role that has specific access permissions to the cubes and dimensions in a database. Though local cubes behave similarly to a server cube in functionality, there are certain restrictions. Local cubes created from Analysis Services 2008 do not have the ability to execute stored procedures (.NET assemblies as well as COM DLLs). Hence, if the server cube has a stored procedure that is called while querying the cube, you would not be able to send such queries against the local cube. Because the local cube is often a section of the server cube, some of the calculations in the MDX scripts might not be able to access tuples because they are not available in the local cube. These are some things for you to consider during creation of local cubes that might be distributed to end users. To create a local (or "offline") cube, follow these steps:

1. Create a pivot table connected to the sample Analysis Services database Adventure Works DW 2008 that includes the hierarchies: Customer Geography in Row Labels, Date.Fiscal in Column Labels, Product Categories as a report filter, and the measure Internet Sales Amount in the Values area.

2. Select a cell in the pivot table to activate the Ribbon.

3. Select the Options tab and then select the OLAP Tools within the Tools group.

4. Select Offline OLAP as shown in Figure 17-63.

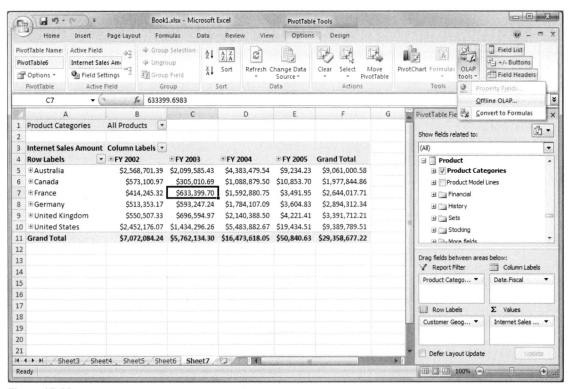

Figure 17-63

5. Select "Create offline data file" in the Offline OLAP Settings dialog as shown in Figure 17-64.

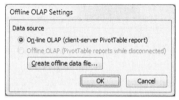

Figure 17-64

6. Click the Next button in the welcome screen of the Create Cube File Wizard. You will now be in the level selection page where you choose the list of dimension hierarchies and the levels you want to be included in the offline cube file, as shown in Figure 17-65. In this dialog Excel shows the hierarchies of all the dimensions. By default Excel selects the hierarchies that are included in the pivot table. You can alternatively add additional dimensions to your local cubes if you or the end users using the local cube would need them to analyze the data.

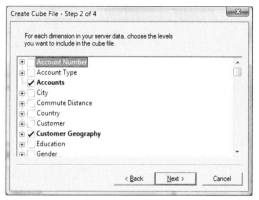

Figure 17-65

7. Traverse through the hierarchy selection, and only select the hierarchies: Customer Geography, Date Fiscal, and Product Categories. Click Next.

8. In the third page of the Create Cube File Wizard, you have the option of only including certain members, as shown in Figure 17-66. Review the hierarchy selections you made and click Next.

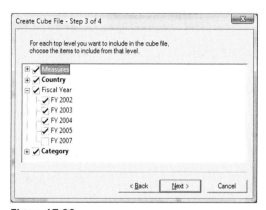

Figure 17-66

9. In page 4 of the Create Cube File Wizard, provide a storage location where you have access to write a local cube file and click Finish.

10. In the Offline OLAP Settings dialog (shown in Figure 17-67) select Offline OLAP and click OK.

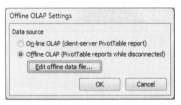

Figure 17-67

Following is the statement sent to the Analysis Services instance to create an offline cube with your selection of measures and hierarchy levels. This statement can also be executed from SQL Server Management Studio. SSAS sends a sequence of queries to retrieve data and then creates the local cube.

```
CREATE GLOBAL CUBE [Adventure Works 2008] STORAGE 'C:\Users\sivah\temp\Adventure
Works.cub' FROM [Adventure Works]
(
  MEASURE [Adventure Works].[Internet Sales Amount],

  DIMENSION [Adventure Works].[Customer].[Customer Geography]
  (
    LEVEL [(All)],
    LEVEL [Country],
    LEVEL [State-Province],
    LEVEL [City],
    LEVEL [Postal Code],
    LEVEL [Customer]
  ),
  DIMENSION [Adventure Works].[Date].[Fiscal]
  (
    LEVEL [(All)],
    LEVEL [Fiscal Year],
    LEVEL [Fiscal Semester],
    LEVEL [Fiscal Quarter],
    LEVEL [Month],
    LEVEL [Date]
  ),
  DIMENSION [Adventure Works].[Product].[Product Categories]
  (
    LEVEL [(All)],
    LEVEL [Category]
  )

)
```

The operations, including drill up and drill down, appropriate member selections, and so forth, all of which you did online, can also be performed offline. Once the offline cube (usually a subset of the server cube) is created, it can then be distributed to business decision-makers who do not need real-time access to the server cube. We recommend you experiment with performing drill down and drill up operations on the offline cube that you have created.

Excel Services

Excel Services is a hosted service within Microsoft Office SharePoint Server (MOSS) 2007, which is part of the Office 2007 release. Excel Services allows you to upload and share Excel workbooks via web access for multiple users. Excel Services serves as an alternative to Office Web Components (OWC). With Excel Services, users are able to share reports containing pivot tables, tables, and charts by simply publishing the reports on to their MOSS 2007. Once your report has been published on your MOSS 2007, you can use Excel Services to access them via the web, as shown in Figure 17-68, or you can open the workbook using your Excel application.

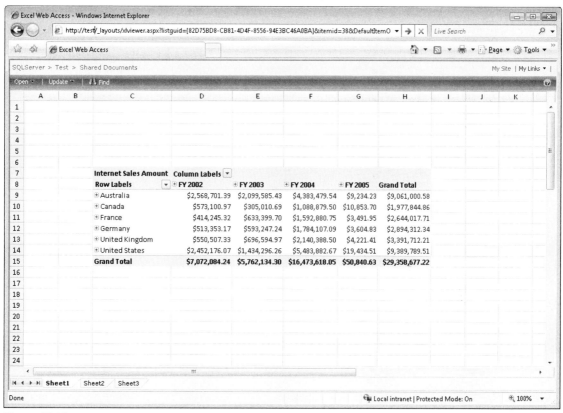

Figure 17-68

If you view the workbook using web access, you will have most of the functionality available such as drill down, drill up, and filtering members but you will not have the ability to add additional fields or filters, which are available only in an Excel application.

ProClarity

ProClarity, a suite of client tools and a server helps end users to analyze data from SSAS. ProClarity was recently acquired by Microsoft and integrated into the Microsoft product suite. It now forms the foundation for Microsoft Performance Point Server 2007.

ProClarity consists of several components: ProClarity Analytical Server, ProClarity Desktop client, and a Web component to integrate with Microsoft Office SharePoint Server. In addition, ProClarity also helps in expediting the creation of Microsoft Reporting Services reports. The ProClarity Analytical Server helps you to store your organization's business logic and metadata about an SSAS cube. Typically, you will want information such as custom calculations, named sets, and annotations that can all be stored on your ProClarity Analytical Server. Using your ProClarity desktop client you can connect to your SSAS cube using the ProClarity Analytical Server. The desktop client also helps in directly connecting to your cube and analyzing data. ProClarity provides you with several ways of analyzing the data so that you can interpret the data efficiently. In this section you learn to use the ProClarity desktop applications to connect to your SSAS cube and analyze your data.

The Chart and Grid Views

The following steps show you how to use ProClarity to analyze the AdventureWorks cube in the Chart and Grid views:

1. Launch the ProClarity desktop application from Start ⇨ All Programs ⇨ Proclarity ⇨ Proclarity Desktop Professional and on the File menu select Open Cube to connect to your Analysis Services instance.

2. Enter your Analysis Services instance name as shown in Figure 17-69 and click OK.

Figure 17-69

3. Select the Adventure Works cube from the Adventure Works DW database in the Open Cube dialog as shown in Figure 17-70 and select OK. The Open Cube dialog allows you to see all the databases on your Analysis Services instance. If you click a specific database, you can see the cubes and perspectives along with the last updated time.

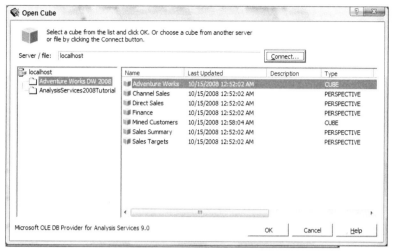

Figure 17-70

4. Select the Chart View visualization shown in Figure 17-71.

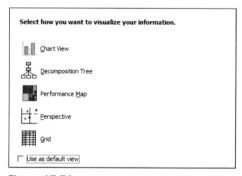

Figure 17-71

5. Click the Setup icon to view the Setup Panel that shows the hierarchies as well as what is viewed in the rows and columns of the chart as shown in Figure 17-72.

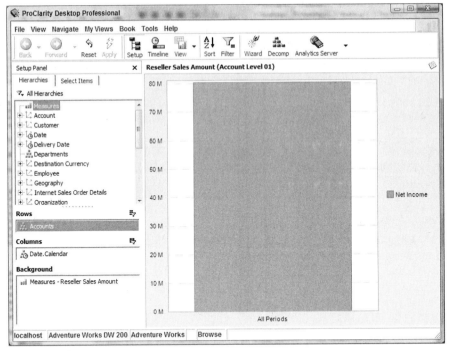

Figure 17-72

ProClarity sends a series of discover requests to the SSAS instance to retrieve the members of all the hierarchies. It retrieves the default measure and the default members on Accounts and Date dimensions and shows those values in the default chart view as shown in Figure 17-72. ProClarity sends the following MDX query to retrieve the data:

```
SELECT      { [Date].[Calendar].DEFAULTMEMBER }
            PROPERTIES PARENT_UNIQUE_NAME, MEMBER_TYPE ON COLUMNS ,
            { [Account].[Accounts].DEFAULTMEMBER } PROPERTIES
            PARENT_UNIQUE_NAME, MEMBER_TYPE ON ROWS
FROM        [Adventure Works]
WHERE       ( [Measures].[Reseller Sales Amount] )
```

6. In the Setup Panel, right-click Accounts and select Remove.

7. Drag and drop Customer ⇨ Customer Geography to Rows or right-click on Customer Geography and select Move to Rows.

8. Select the Date.Calendar in the Columns area in the Setup Panel and select Remove.

9. Select the Date.Fiscal hierarchy from the hierarchy selection area of the Setup Panel and select Move to Columns.

10. Double-click Measures and select the measure [Internet Sales Amount].

11. Click the Apply icon. You will now see the background changed to the measure [Internet Sales Amount] and also the chart is being updated with the new rows, columns, and data.

12. Double click the chart to see all the countries and double click the Date.Fiscal hierarchy member All Periods to see all the fiscal years.

13. Select the drop-down next to the View icon and select Grid ⇨ Bottom. You will now see the data corresponding to the chart shown below the chart in a tabular format as shown in Figure 17-73.

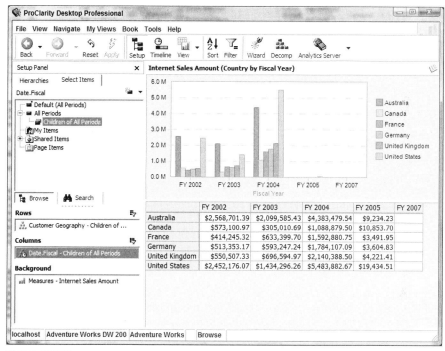

Figure 17-73

14. Select a specific member such as FY2003 in the chart and then drill down or drill up by right-clicking as shown in Figure 17-74. If you navigate further down to Drill Down you can see you can drill down based on various attributes.

Figure 17-74

15. You can expand or collapse items in the grid by clicking a specific item or holding the Shift key and then clicking the item, respectively. Click the member Australia, and then click the member FY 2002.

You will now see the chart has only the relevant data for Australia and FY 2002, as shown in Figure 17-75. You might have observed how easy it is for an end user to drill down or drill up and only view the relevant data in focus rather than all the data as you saw in the pivot table. This is a simple example of how ProClarity helps in efficient data analysis of the SSAS cube.

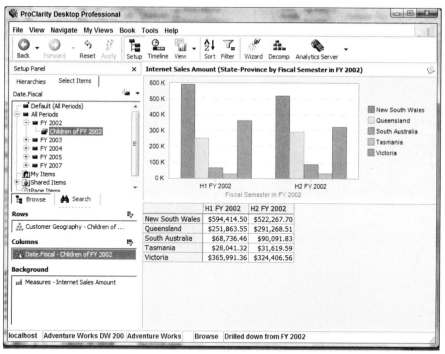

Figure 17-75

The Decomposition Tree

Having seen the power of analysis using the Chart and Grid views, this section looks at one of the important features of ProClarity, the Decomposition Tree, and how it helps you to analyze data efficiently. Follow these steps to analyze SSAS data using the Decomposition Tree:

1. Hold the Shift key and click in the grid to get back to All Customers on the Customer Geography hierarchy. Then do it again to get back to all Fiscal Years.

2. Click the Decomp icon to launch the Decomposition Tree Wizard.

3. Click Next in the Welcome screen.

4. In the Decomposition Tree Wizard, select [Internet Sales Amount] for breakdown and Customer Geography for "For items in" as shown in Figure 17-76 and click Finish.

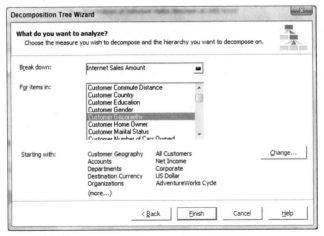

Figure 17-76

You will now see the top level of the tree with All Customers as shown in Figure 17-77.

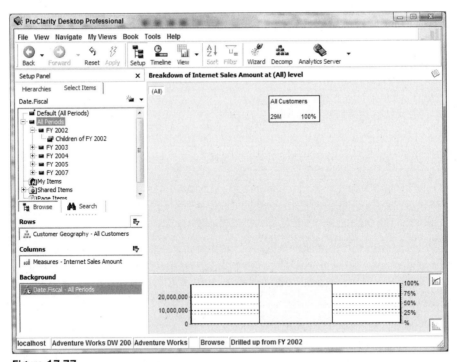

Figure 17-77

5. Click All Customers to see all the countries.

6. Click the member United States to see all the States.

You will now see the various members in the Decomposition Tree as shown in Figure 17-78. If you look at each member in the Decomposition Tree you will see how the customers in each country or state contribute toward its parent as a percentage. If you hover over a member you can see detailed data of the [Internet Sales Amount]. In the default view the Decomposition Tree rounds to the closest value to show the data in the same view. The Decomposition Tree helps you to visualize and interpret drill-down data efficiently along with percentage contribution.

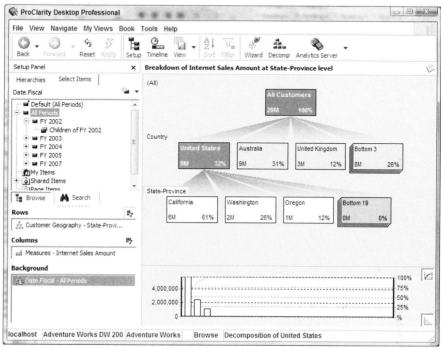

Figure 17-78

The Performance Map

ProClarity provides another view of the data called the Performance Map. In this section you get an overview to analyze the [Internet Sales Amount] for various Customers using the Performance Map:

1. In the Decomposition Tree, click All Customers.

2. Select the drop-down list next to the View icon and select Advanced Analysis Tools ⇨ Performance Map as shown in Figure 17-79.

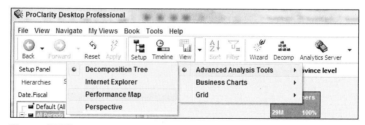

Figure 17-79

3. You will see the Performance Map for All Customers as shown in Figure 17-80. Similar to the Decomposition Tree you can drill down on the customers by clicking a pane. Double-click All Customers to get to the Country level.

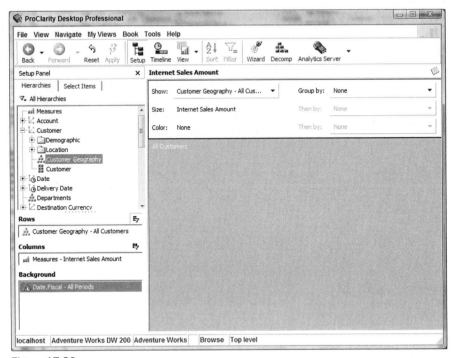

Figure 17-80

4. Click the Group By drop-down list and select Customer Education ⇨ Education.

You will now see the Performance Map based on Country of the customers as well Education in the same map as shown in Figure 17-81. You can see that the Performance Map helps you to analyze the [Internet Sales Amount] data on multiple hierarchies in a unique way where you can interpret the data effectively. You can see that Bachelors in Australia contribute to the maximum [Internet Sales Amount] of the products. If you need further analysis you can drill down to various states or have additional hierarchies added to the Performance Map for analysis.

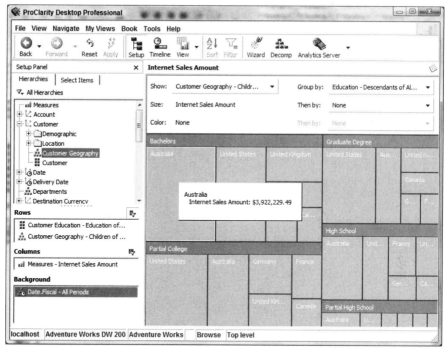

Figure 17-81

ProClarity sends the following MDX query for the preceding Performance Map. You can see that the MDX query is quite simply retrieving the Internet Sales Amount for Customers in various countries along with their education information. The education information for various countries is obtained by a crossjoin of the two hierarchies.

```
SELECT      { [Measures].[Internet Sales Amount] } PROPERTIES
            PARENT_UNIQUE_NAME, MEMBER_TYPE ON COLUMNS ,
            { { { DESCENDANTS( [Customer].[Education].[All Customers],
            [Customer].[Education].[Education] ) } *
            { [Customer].[Customer Geography].[All Customers].CHILDREN } } }
            PROPERTIES PARENT_UNIQUE_NAME, MEMBER_TYPE ON ROWS
FROM        [Adventure Works]
WHERE       ( [Date].[Fiscal].[All Periods] )
```

In this section you learned some of the key features of the ProClarity desktop application and how they help in analyzing the SSAS cube data effectively.

Microsoft Performance Point Server 2007

In the previous section you learned ProClarity is the foundation of the analytics for Performance Point Server 2007. Performance Point Server (PPS) provides you with tools to help your business users monitor, analyze, and plan your business requirements. Performance Point Server is a separate product and providing examples on PPS in this chapter is not in the scope of this book. However, we would like to point out that PPS leverages and builds on top of SSAS.

Using PPS users can create business dashboards or scorecards from their own or imported KPIs from SSAS using the Dashboard Designer to be later stored within PPS for future monitoring and taking actions based on the results. Users typically have access to SharePoint and the dashboards are typically integrated into your Microsoft Office SharePoint Server. Users have the ability to subscribe to the KPIs using SharePoint's web component. Figure 17-82 shows the PPS Dashboard Designer. You can see the Dashboard Designer allows you to connect to data sources, define KPIs, and then publish them on your PPS. Figure 17-83 shows the KPIs published on to a SharePoint server, which can then be accessed by the end users. The users can monitor these published KPIs and take appropriate actions based on their status. We recommend you get a more in-depth understanding of PPS from the tutorials and whitepapers available at `http://www.microsoft.com/bi/products/performancepoint-overview.aspx`

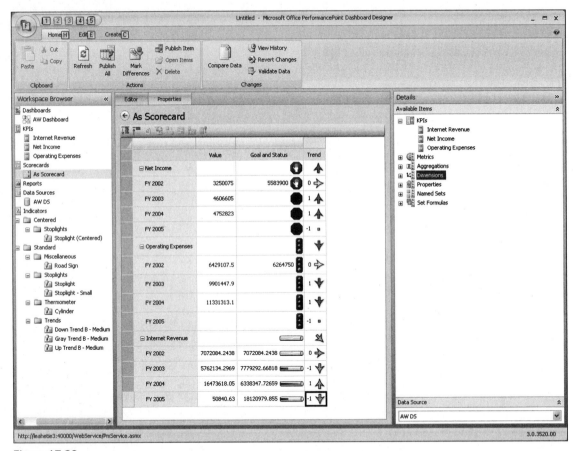

Figure 17-82

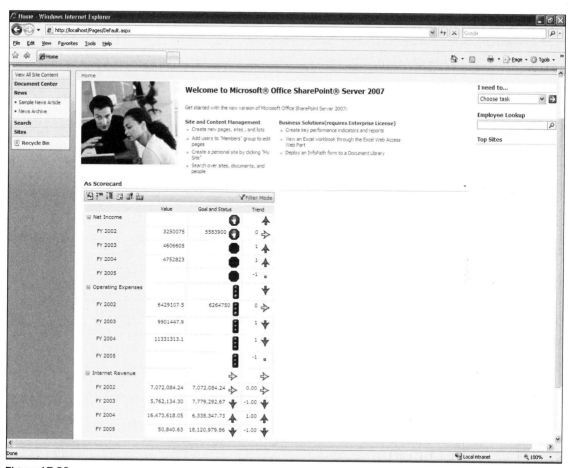

Figure 17-83

Summary

As a business intelligence application developer you will likely do your proof-of-concept browsing in BIDS, but in using the cubes you've built for them, your customers will actually do the slicing and dicing in Excel pivot tables or by using Excel Services or Office Web Components technology. In this chapter you learned how Excel 2007 efficiently allows end users to generate effective reports from SSAS either using pivot tables or using the new cube functions in sheet data reports. SQL Server Analysis Services, Excel, and Performance Point Server together make a formidable business intelligence platform and there is no reason not to take advantage of that. Furthermore, there are very few business professionals who don't know Excel; it really is a nearly ubiquitous application. Nonetheless, there are tools from other companies that provide connectivity to and leverage from SQL Server Analysis Services 2008, each with their own value-add proposition. You can obtain more information about other client tools from http://www.ssas-info.com and http://www.mosha.com.

Using Data Mining with Office 2007

In Chapter 16 you learned about data mining and how it is useful for analyzing data and helping you make decisions that will improve your business. Traditionally, data mining has been considered a specialized area and you need to have an in-depth understanding of the data mining algorithm to create and analyze data mining models and to recognize interesting patterns in the data set. We believe that you still need to understand data mining to effectively replicate the mining models using Business Intelligence Development Studio. SQL Server 2008, however, aims at making data mining available to end users in an intuitive way that helps them to analyze the data without having to understand data mining.

The Microsoft SQL Server 2008 Data Mining Add-ins for Office 2007 shipped with SQL Server 2008 help end users analyze data in Excel. There are three components that are part of this add-in: Table Analytics, Data Mining Client, and Visualization. Table Analytics and Data Mining Client are add-ins for Excel, and Visualization is a Visio template to effectively visualize and present data mining. In this chapter you learn how to analyze data using the Data Mining Add-ins for Excel 2007 and then learn how to effectively present data mining models using Visio 2007.

The Microsoft SQL Server 2008 Data Mining Add-ins for Office 2007 is a redistribution package available for download from www.microsoft.com as part of the SQL Server 2008 release. You first need to have Office 2007 installed on your machine. After installing Office 2007 we recommend you download and install the redist package. The add-ins by themselves will not be sufficient to perform the analysis. You also need SQL Server Analysis Services 2008 to perform the analysis of the data at the backend. You should install SQL Server Analysis Services (SSAS) 2008 on the same machine as the add-ins or make sure you have access to it to create session mining models. Once you have access to SSAS 2008 and have the add-ins installed you are ready to analyze data in an Excel spreadsheet. Without further delay, you next learn how the add-ins help in data analysis.

Configuring Your SSAS

Once you have installed the Microsoft SQL Server 2008 Data Mining Add-ins for Office 2007 you need to configure your SSAS instance to enable creation of temporary mining models. Perform the following steps to configure your SSAS:

1. Click Start and click the Server Configuration utility from All Programs ⇨ Microsoft SQL Server 2008 DM Add-ins.

2. Click Next on the welcome screen.

3. Enter your SSAS instance name in the Server box and click Next to view the Allow Creation of Temporary Mining Models page.

4. Please make sure the checkbox that enables session mining models is enabled (checked) and click Next.

5. On the Create Database for Add-in Users page you have the option of creating a new database or using an existing database that can be used by the data mining add-in users for creating temporary and permanent mining models. The wizard connects to your SSAS instance and retrieves the list of databases.

6. Select the default Create New Database with the database name DMAddinsDB. In the final page of the wizard you can add all the end users who would be using the Microsoft SQL Server 2008 Data Mining Add-ins for Office 2007, as shown in Figure 18-1. All these users would need to have full database permissions on the chosen database. By default the wizard adds the user running the wizard as database admin of the database.

7. Enter any users that need to use the Microsoft SQL Server 2008 Data Mining Add-ins for Office 2007 and click Finish.

Figure 18-1

Once you click the Finish button the wizard connects to the SSAS instance, configures the instance to enable the session mining model by changing the appropriate server property, creates the database DMAddinDB, and adds permissions to the users specified. You can see each action taken by the wizard along with the status on the confirmation page.

You have now made the necessary configuration to your SSAS instance that will allow you to use the Microsoft SQL Server 2008 Data Mining Add-ins for Office 2007. As we mentioned earlier, there are three components to the add-ins: Table Analytics, Data Mining Client, and the Visio template. In the next section you learn about Table Analytics.

Table Analytics

Table Analytics, one of the Microsoft SQL Server 2008 Data Mining Add-ins for Office 2007, helps you to analyze the tables within Excel spreadsheets. You will use the sample Excel spreadsheet DMAddins_SampleData.xlsx shipped with the Microsoft SQL Server 2008 Data Mining Add-ins for Office 2007 to learn about the Table Analytics component. To start using Table Analytics, follow these steps:

1. Open the sample spreadsheet DMAddins_SampleData.xlsx by clicking Start ⇨ All Programs ⇨ Microsoft SQL Server 2008 DM Add-ins ⇨ Sample Excel Data.

   You see the default page of the Excel Sample Data spreadsheet. The spreadsheet has nine sheets that contain sample data to highlight various features of the Microsoft SQL Server 2008 Data Mining Add-ins for Office 2007.

2. Click the sheet named Table Analytics Tools Sample.

3. In the sheet click one of the cells in the table. You see additional tabs in the Excel Ribbon called Analyze and Design.

4. Click the Analyze Ribbon. You see the various Table Analytics features from the Table Analytics Tools add-in as icons shown in Figure 18-2. Each icon is used to perform specific tasks on your table to provide results from which you can potentially take meaningful action. Each icon uses a data mining algorithm from SQL Server 2008 to create a mining model and perform predictions. For the end user who does not have knowledge of data mining, this is presented in simple form as easy-to-understand names that intuitively suggest the outcome of the icon. For example, the Analyze Key Influencers icon can be used to identify the key columns of the table in Excel that contribute to influencing the data. You first need to establish a connection to the SSAS instance to use the various options in the Analyze Ribbon.

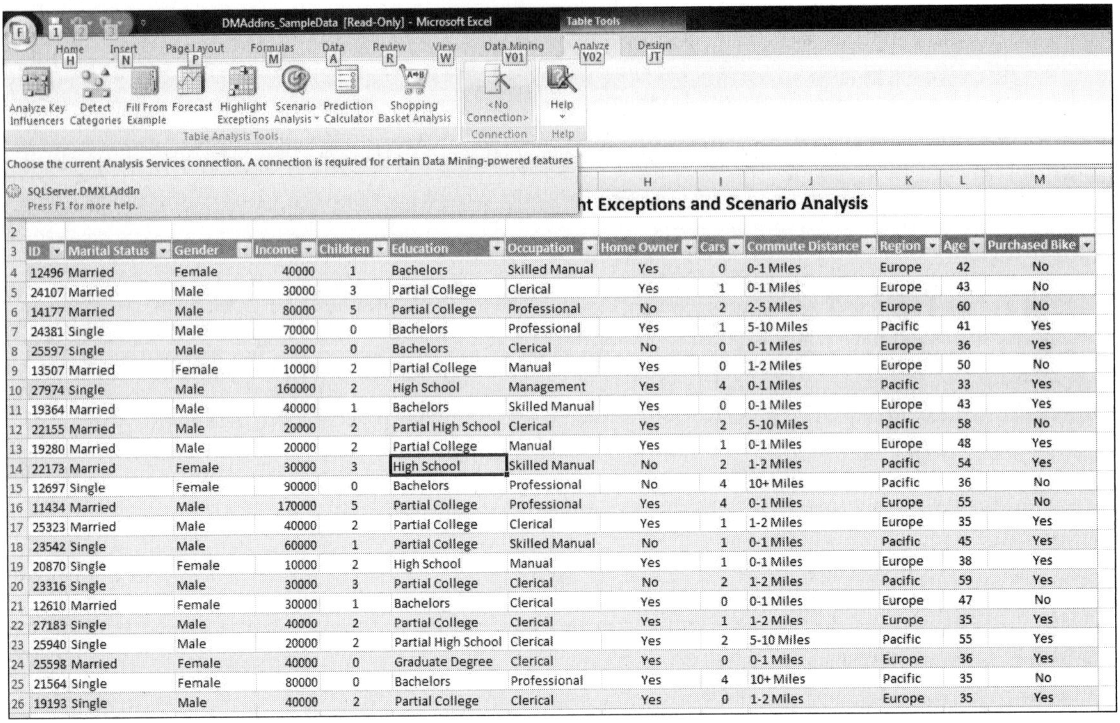

Figure 18-2

5. Click the Connection group.

6. In the Analysis Services Connections dialog that appears, click New.

7. In the Connect to Analysis Services dialog, enter your SSAS instance name and in the Catalog name field select the Analysis Services database DMAddinDB and click OK.

   The Connect to Analysis Services dialog combines the SSAS instance name and the database name to form a friendly name, which you have the option of changing. A new connection to your SSAS instance is created and shown under the Current Connection in the Analysis Services Connections dialog. The Analysis Services Connections allows you to manage connections to SSAS instances. When there are additional connections, they are shown under a separate group called Other Connections.

8. Click the Close button in the Analysis Services Connections dialog.

Now that you have established a connection to your Analysis Services database, you next look at the various table analytics features.

Analyze Key Influencers

Analyze Key Influencers helps to analyze data in a column that holds significant interest or business value to see what factors are important in indicating or differentiating values. For example, from the data in the Table Analysis Tools Sample sheet you can identify the factors (columns) that indicate whether a person is married or single. In this example you use Analyze Key Influencers to determine what factors indicate whether people purchased a bicycle:

1. After clicking a cell in the table, click the Analyze Key Influencers icon as shown in Figure 18-3.

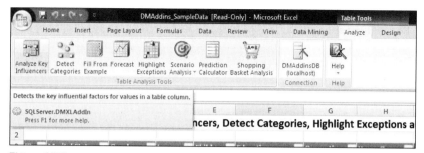

Figure 18-3

2. In the Analyze Key Influencers dialog, select the Purchased Bike column.

3. Click the link Choose Columns to Be Used for Analysis.

4. In the Advanced Columns Selection dialog select each column except ID as shown in Figure 18-4 and click OK.

Figure 18-4

5. Click Run to start the analysis.

The wizard will provide status on the operations being performed in a status window. The wizard first reads the table data, creates a data mining model on your SSAS instance, and then retrieves the results of the mining model and displays them in a new spreadsheet. In this example, the wizard creates a worksheet called Influencers for Purchased Bike to the show the key influencing columns that determines if a person buys a bike.

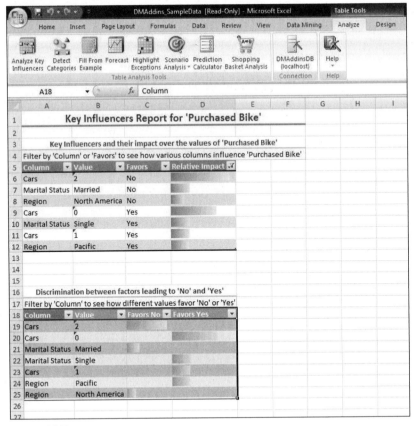

Figure 18-5

The column chosen to analyze key influencers can contain several values. A discrimination report is extremely valuable in this case because it indicates the various values of the columns and the influencing values of other columns and helps you to compare any two values. In this example the Purchase Bike column only has two values, Yes and No. The Analyze Key Influencers Wizard upon creating the new spreadsheet shows a dialog to add the discrimination report to your new spreadsheet.

6. In the Discrimination Based on Key Influencers dialog box, click Add Report, and then click Close.

You should see the discrimination report for the Yes and No values of the Purchased Bike column added to the Key Influencers for Purchased Bike spreadsheet as shown in Figure 18-5. Now let's analyze the results provided by the dialog.

The first report, the key influencer report, shows influencers for all values of the column Purchased Bike. In this case you can clearly see that people in the data set who are married, own two cars, and live in North America tend not to purchase bikes, whereas single people with zero or one car that live in the Pacific region do. The length of the bar in the Relative Impact column indicates the importance of this particular factor in indicating the specified value. In this case, you can see that not owning a car, for example, is much more important than marital status or region in indicating whether people have bought a bike.

You can filter for specific values in each column of your report to analyze specific data. This is especially useful when you have several rows in your report and you would like to analyze the effect of specific values on the column being analyzed.

The discrimination report is similar to a key influencer report except that it shows very clearly the distinction in factors that influence one value over another. The factors are ordered by their importance. This report is generally more useful when the column you are analyzing has more than two values, however, even with this example, you can see that being married is a stronger influencer of not being a bicycle purchaser in the data set than being from the Pacific influences being a purchaser.

Once your analysis is complete, you can share your results with any of your end users or SharePoint users via Excel Services by sharing or posting (Publish Option) your workbook.

You should note that because this is being done by end users the Table Analytics add-in does not use words specific to data mining. The Key Influencer Wizard uses the Naive Bayes data mining algorithm to predict the columns that are key influencers. If you know about data mining you would want to know what commands are sent to your SSAS instance. The Data Mining add-in, which you learn about in the next section, provides you with the functionality to view the sequence of commands sent by the Data Mining add-in to the SSAS instance. Click the Trace icon from the Connection section at the far right of the Data Mining tab on the Ribbon as shown in Figure 18-6.

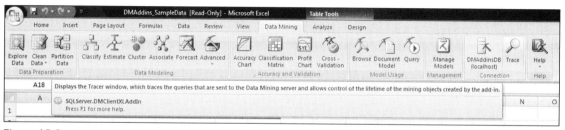

Figure 18-6

The Trace icon helps you view and analyze the sequence of commands sent by the Data Mining add-in to your SSAS instance. After clicking it, you see the SQL Server Data Mining Tracer dialog. If you browse through the dialog you will see the command to create the Naive Bayes algorithm. Now let's review the next icon, Detect Categories.

Detect Categories

Data is being gathered periodically for your personal or business needs. You can analyze the data based on individual columns or a combination of columns with ease. However, there are just too many combinations to analyze to take meaningful action. Categorization is a way to group similar entities. You can then analyze each category to understand and interpret the data, which is easier than analyzing based on combinations of columns and their values. The Categories icon helps you group the data in the spreadsheet using data mining, which then enables you to analyze your data efficiently. In this example you group people with similar characteristics using the data set in the Table Analytics Tools Sample spreadsheet. Categories help you to reduce paralysis by analysis.

Detect Categories analyzes your data to see which rows are similar to each other by examining all of the column values for each row. It then creates a report to assist you in understanding the categories that are found and labels each row as to which category it belongs. You also have the option of adding an additional column within the spreadsheet to indicate the category, which makes it easier to analyze a specific category.

1. Switch to the Table Analytics Tools Sample spreadsheet.

2. In the Analyze tab click the Detect Categories icon at the left end of the tab as shown in Figure 18-7.

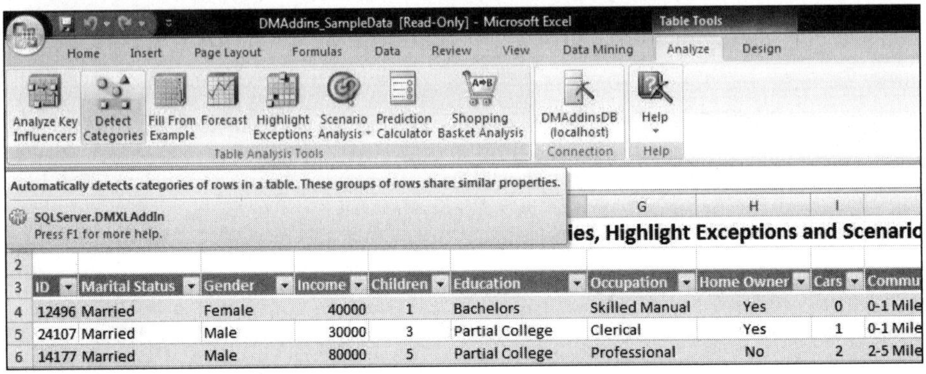

Figure 18-7

You will see the Detect Categories dialog where you can select the columns that you want to utilize to categorize the data set from the list. Columns that uniquely identify each row in the table, such as the ID column, are not useful for data categorization because these identifiers are normally used as a key to access the data and rarely have any categorical meaning to the outside world. Therefore, we recommend not including any column that can serve as unique identifiers such as IDs, phone numbers, and addresses. By default, the dialog identifies the identifier column ID and does not include the column in the selection. You have the option to create a specific number of categories and have the default option Auto-detect where SSAS is able to detect the right number of categories. You also have a checkbox to add a new column within the spreadsheet and add the category name so that you can utilize this column for further analyzing the data.

3. Choose the defaults in the Detect Categories dialog and click Run. Detect Categories takes the data and sends a request to SSAS to create a cluster session mining model. The dialog later queries information from the created cluster data mining model to create a new spreadsheet called Categories Report as shown in Figure 18-8. After the analysis is complete, Detect Categories will create a new sheet containing a report of its findings. This report has three parts: a category list showing the size of each category that can be used to re-label the categories, a table containing descriptions of the categories, and a pivot chart allowing you to analyze how column values are distributed among the categories. In addition to this the Detect Categories dialog adds a column to the original table indicating the category of each row as shown in Figure 18-9.

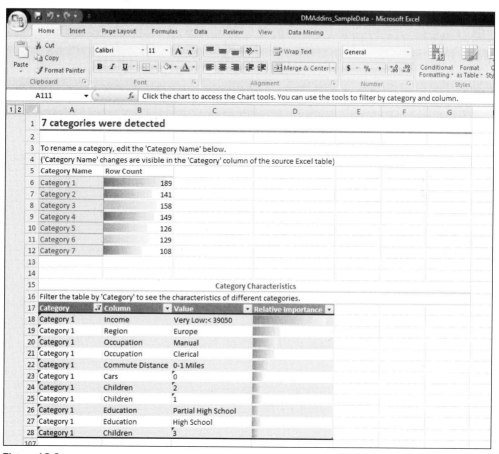

Figure 18-8

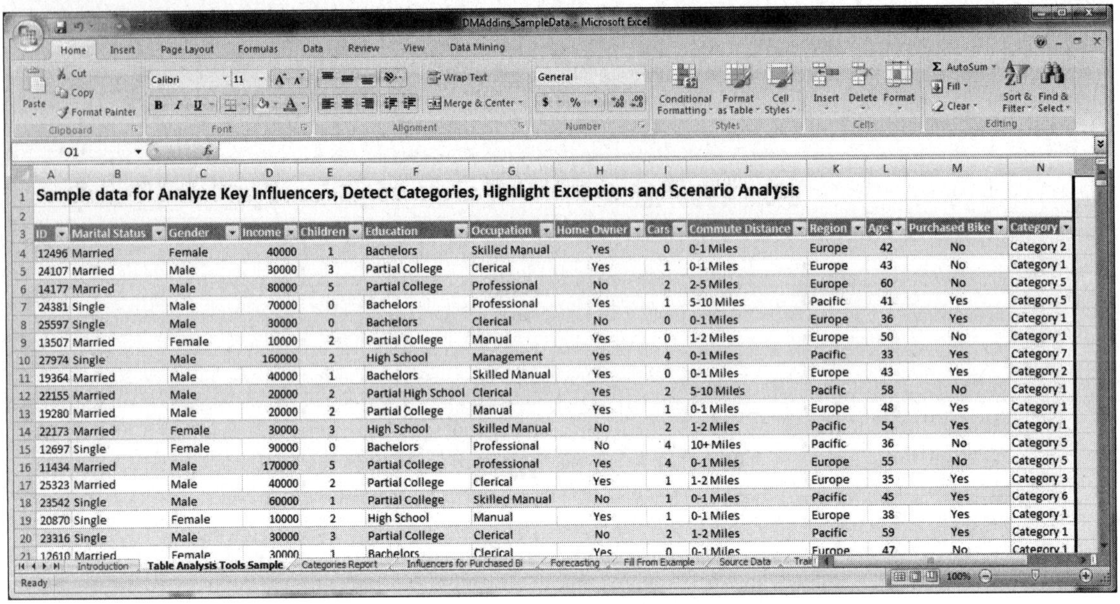

Sample data for Analyze Key Influencers, Detect Categories, Highlight Exceptions and Scenario Analysis

ID	Marital Status	Gender	Income	Children	Education	Occupation	Home Owner	Cars	Commute Distance	Region	Age	Purchased Bike	Category
12496	Married	Female	40000	1	Bachelors	Skilled Manual	Yes	0	0-1 Miles	Europe	42	No	Category 2
24107	Married	Male	30000	3	Partial College	Clerical	Yes	1	0-1 Miles	Europe	43	No	Category 1
14177	Married	Male	80000	5	Partial College	Professional	No	2	2-5 Miles	Europe	60	No	Category 5
24381	Single	Male	70000	0	Bachelors	Professional	Yes	1	5-10 Miles	Pacific	41	Yes	Category 5
25597	Single	Male	30000	0	Bachelors	Clerical	No	0	0-1 Miles	Europe	36	Yes	Category 1
13507	Married	Female	10000	2	Partial College	Manual	Yes	0	1-2 Miles	Europe	50	No	Category 1
27974	Single	Male	160000	2	High School	Management	Yes	4	0-1 Miles	Pacific	33	Yes	Category 7
19364	Married	Male	40000	1	Bachelors	Skilled Manual	Yes	0	0-1 Miles	Europe	43	Yes	Category 2
22155	Married	Male	20000	2	Partial High School	Clerical	Yes	2	5-10 Miles	Pacific	58	No	Category 1
19280	Married	Male	20000	2	Partial College	Manual	Yes	1	0-1 Miles	Europe	48	Yes	Category 1
22173	Married	Female	30000	3	High School	Skilled Manual	No	2	1-2 Miles	Pacific	54	Yes	Category 1
12697	Single	Female	90000	0	Bachelors	Professional	No	4	10+ Miles	Pacific	36	No	Category 5
11434	Married	Male	170000	5	Partial College	Professional	Yes	4	0-1 Miles	Europe	55	No	Category 5
25323	Married	Male	40000	2	Partial College	Clerical	Yes	1	1-2 Miles	Europe	35	Yes	Category 3
23542	Single	Male	60000	1	Partial College	Skilled Manual	No	1	0-1 Miles	Pacific	45	Yes	Category 6
20870	Single	Female	10000	2	High School	Manual	Yes	1	0-1 Miles	Europe	38	Yes	Category 1
23316	Single	Male	30000	3	Partial College	Clerical	No	2	1-2 Miles	Pacific	59	Yes	Category 1
12610	Married	Female	30000	1	Bachelors	Clerical	Yes	0	0-1 Miles	Europe	47	No	Category 1

Figure 18-9

In this example, you see that Detect Categories has identified seven distinct categories of people in the data set with the largest group having 189 members and the smallest having 108 members as shown in the category list report. You can switch to the Table Analytics Tools Sample sheet to see which row of data belongs to which category based on the Category column as shown in Figure 18-9. Because the column has been added as an auto-filter column you have the option of selecting rows specific to a single category by selecting a specific category in the drop-down list box under Category. You have the option of renaming a specific category in the Categories report after analyzing each category. The new name for a category is automatically reflected in the Category column in the Table Analytics Tools Sample sheet.

The Category Characteristics report shows factors that are important in describing each category. By default it only displays factors for the first category, Category 1, as shown in Figure 18-8. Analyzing Category 1 you can see the category is comprised of manual or clerical workers in Europe with very low incomes. Many other factors are also interesting to Category 1, but by looking at the relative importance bars, those factors are much less important. Now let's look at characteristics of Category 2.

1. Click the filter next to the Category column (shown in Figure 18-10).
2. Select Category 2, de-select Category 1, and click OK.

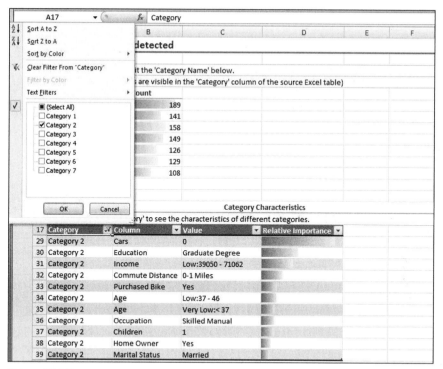

Figure 18-10

Analyzing people in Category 2, you see that it is comprised of people who do not have a car, but do have a bike. In addition these people have a graduate degree but earn less and live very close to their work, which is indicated by their commute distance. You can in fact rename Category 2 as LowIncomeGraduates by clicking the Category 2 cell in the Category Name report and typing in the new name.

You will notice that the category name has also changed in the Category Characteristics report. If you switch to the Table Analysis Tools Sample page you will see the new category name also reflected in the Category column.

The third part of the Categories report is the Category Profile report. This report shows the distribution of column values across all of the categories. The report utilizes a pivot chart to show the distribution. By default the report shows the first column ordered alphanumerically, in this case by age.

You can choose a different column to analyze values across all categories by doing the following:

1. Click the report to enable the pivot chart tools.

2. Click the filter next to the Column field, de-select Age, select the Income field as shown in Figure 18-11, and click OK.

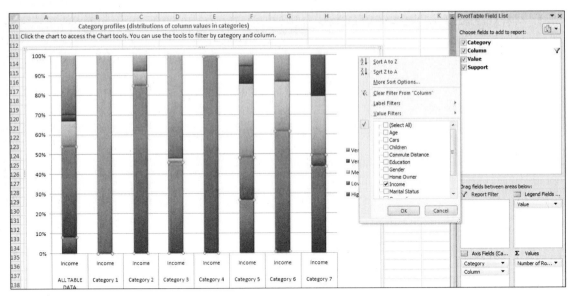

Figure 18-11

You will see the distribution of the Income field as shown in Figure 18-11. You can see that Category 1 has the maximum number of people with the lowest income, and Category 7 has the maximum number of people in the high income bracket. Because this is a standard pivot chart you can click the chart to change what is displayed. Because the pivot chart is used to show the category profiles, you can show more than one column distribution at a time. However, it can quickly become very confusing if you display too many at the same time, so we recommend you analyze the categories one column at a time. You can identify the people in categories who are more likely to purchase a bike by selecting the PurchaseBike column. You can see from the resulting distribution that people in Categories 3 and 4 are most inclined to purchase a bike compared to those in other categories.

Once your analysis is complete on the various categories you've identified, you can share the results with any other Excel or SharePoint users via Excel Services by sharing or posting your workbook. The Microsoft SQL Server 2008 Data Mining Add-ins for Office 2007and SSAS 2008 are required only to run the analysis and not for viewing or manipulating the results.

Fill From Example

Excel has always had this terrific feature of understanding patterns and extending them. For instance, after entering 2, 4, and 6 in adjacent cells in the same column, you can select the three cells, click and drag (or double-click the bottom right of the selection), and Excel will happily enter 8, 10, 12, and so on, on your behalf. Fill From Example takes a similar approach. Based on the entered values and implicated patterns, Fill From Example will predict and fill in values for all other unfilled rows in a specific column. For this example you use Fill From Example to identify if a person is a highly valued customer:

1. Switch to the Fill From Example sheet in the workbook as shown in Figure 18-12. You can see the column called High Value Customer, which shows a few rows that have the values Yes or No.

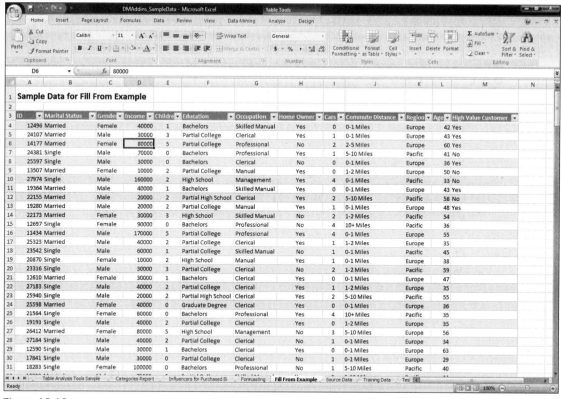

Figure 18-12

2. Click one of the cells in the table, and then click the Analyze tab to view the Table Analysis Tools Ribbon.

3. Click the Fill From Example icon. The Fill From Example Wizard displays a column that it detects as potentially needing to be filled. In this example the wizard has selected the High Value Customer column by default because it has detected that this column has only a few values and the remaining values are not filled in. You can select another list of columns that you want to be included for analysis by clicking the "Choose columns to be used for analysis" link.

4. Select the default values in this dialog and click Run.

The wizard now creates a mining structure with the columns, inserts the values into the mining structure, and then creates a logistic regression mining model. Once the mining model is created the wizard creates a new spreadsheet called Pattern Report for 'High Value Customer' as shown in Figure 18-13. In addition to that the wizard creates a new column called High Value Customer_Extended and fills in the predicted values for each row using the mining model. You can see the new column with the predicted values if you switch to the Fill From Example spreadsheet as shown in Figure 18-14.

In this example, from the High Value Customer Patterns spreadsheet shown in Figure 18-13, you can see how each column in the table influences if a customer is a highly valued customer (Favors column value is Yes). In addition to having the information on whether a column is impacting the value you also see to what extent the column is influencing the value by the length of the bar shown in the Relative Impact column.

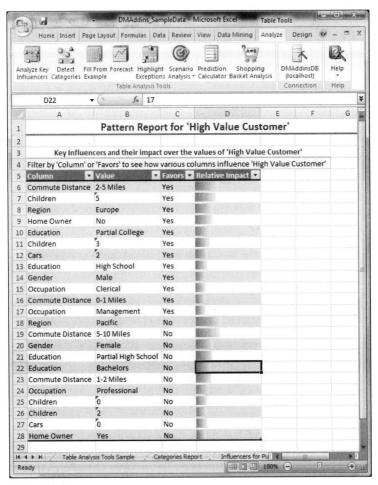

Figure 18-13

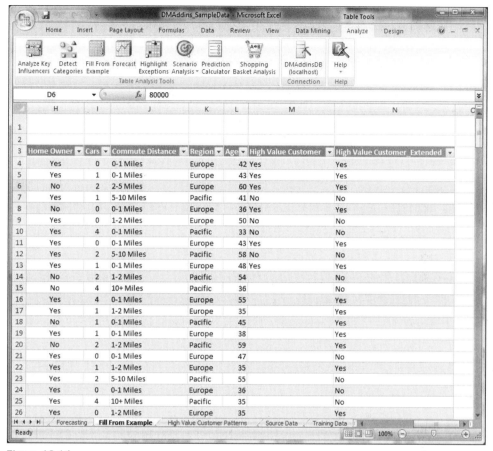

Figure 18-14

Fill From Example is useful in scenarios where you have some missing data for certain columns due to data entry errors or someone accidentally deleting it. Based on the other information in the table you would have a high probability of getting the right value using Fill From Example.

Forecast

The Forecast tool allows you to extend a series of data using the predictive power of SSAS. The data series must be in columns for the tool to work. If your data is in rows, you must first pivot the data before running the Forecast tool. You can pivot your data by copying it and selecting Paste Special and choosing the Transpose option.

Let's practice using the Forecast tool using the sample data in the spreadsheet provided in the DMAddins_SampleData:

1. Click the Forecasting worksheet and click one of the cells in the table.

2. Click the Analyze tab to see the Excel Ribbon, and then click the Forecast icon as shown in Figure 18-15.

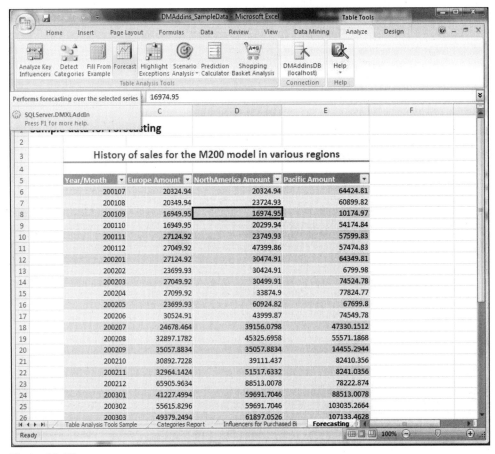

Figure 18-15

The Forecast dialog allows you to select the columns in the table for which you would like to forecast. The dialog has automatically detected that Year is a column that indicates time and has de-selected that column for prediction. You need to select the column that is to be used as a time slice. In addition to this you can indicate the number of time units to forecast for. Optionally, you can select the periodicity of the data if the data is available on a daily or hourly basis, which provides more information to the dialog and allows for better forecasting.

3. Select the Year_Month column for the time-stamp option.

4. Make sure the remaining default values are chosen for the number of time units and periodicity of the data as shown in Figure 18-16 and click Run.

Figure 18-16

The Forecast dialog gets all the inputs, and sends them to your SSAS 2008 instance to create a time series mining model using the data provided. After the analysis is complete, Forecast creates a new spreadsheet containing the original data with the forecasted results highlighted by dotted lines as shown in Figure 18-17. The original data set in the Forecast worksheet will have the forecasted values appended at the end as shown in Figure 18-18.

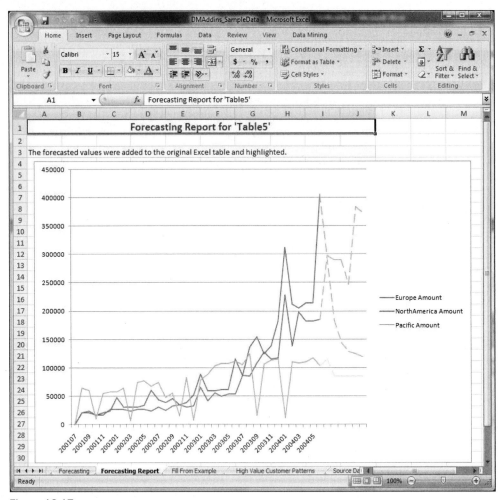

Figure 18-17

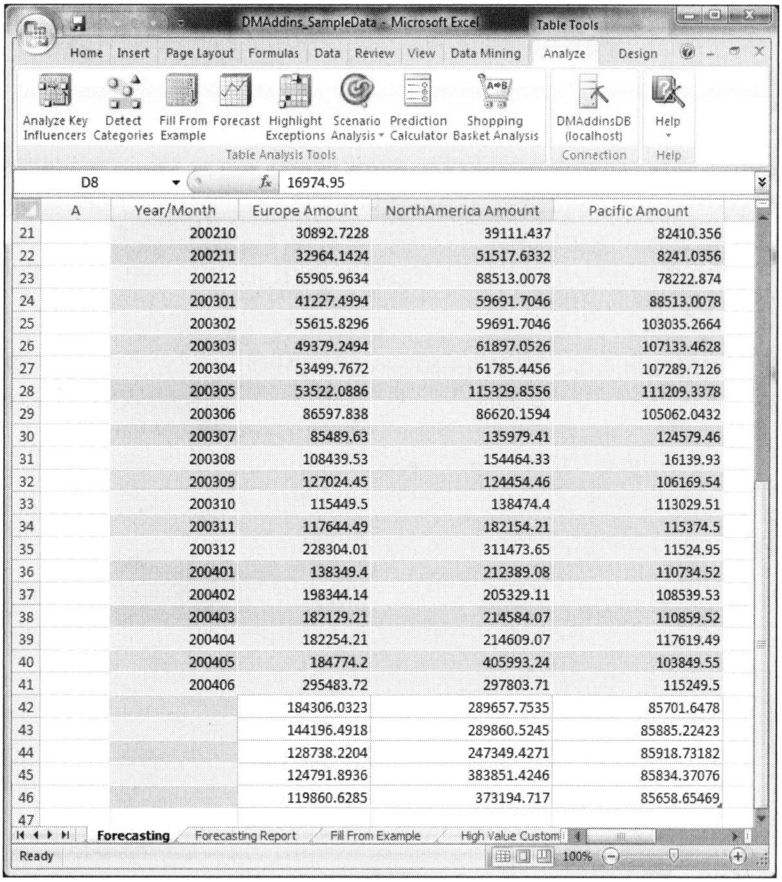

	A	Year/Month	Europe Amount	NorthAmerica Amount	Pacific Amount
21		200210	30892.7228	39111.437	82410.356
22		200211	32964.1424	51517.6332	8241.0356
23		200212	65905.9634	88513.0078	78222.874
24		200301	41227.4994	59691.7046	88513.0078
25		200302	55615.8296	59691.7046	103035.2664
26		200303	49379.2494	61897.0526	107133.4628
27		200304	53499.7672	61785.4456	107289.7126
28		200305	53522.0886	115329.8556	111209.3378
29		200306	86597.838	86620.1594	105062.0432
30		200307	85489.63	135979.41	124579.46
31		200308	108439.53	154464.33	16139.93
32		200309	127024.45	124454.46	106169.54
33		200310	115449.5	138474.4	113029.51
34		200311	117644.49	182154.21	115374.5
35		200312	228304.01	311473.65	11524.95
36		200401	138349.4	212389.08	110734.52
37		200402	198344.14	205329.11	108539.53
38		200403	182129.21	214584.07	110859.52
39		200404	182254.21	214609.07	117619.49
40		200405	184774.2	405993.24	103849.55
41		200406	295483.72	297803.71	115249.5
42			184306.0323	289657.7535	85701.6478
43			144196.4918	289860.5245	85885.22423
44			128738.2204	247349.4271	85918.73182
45			124791.8936	383851.4246	85834.37076
46			119860.6285	373194.717	85658.65469
47					

Figure 18-18

You can see from Figure 18-17 that the Forecast tool has predicted that the sales values for Pacific, North America, and Europe are expected to fluctuate. This information has been forecasted by the mining model based on the data for the previous year and months. In Figure 18-18 you can see that data has been forecasted for five new time periods as requested in the Forecast dialog. You should be aware that in some cases the Forecast tool will return fewer results than requested. This occurs when Analysis Services determines that it can no longer produce viable predictions and therefore stops. This behavior is entirely determined by the data itself and cannot be modified.

In SSAS 2008, the time series algorithm that is used for forecasting has been refined from the SSAS 2005 time series algorithm to give better quality predictions that are better suited for short- and long-term predictions, respectively. Once your analysis is complete, you can utilize the forecasting results to take appropriate business actions.

Highlight Exceptions

Assume you have data that you have received as an Excel spreadsheet that has been entered manually by several users. You may want to find out if there are exceptions or anomalies in the data entry. The

Highlight Exceptions tool will help you in such a scenario. In this example, assume the income of one of the customers was entered incorrectly to see if the tool can detect the exception:

1. Switch to the Table Analysis Tools Sample spreadsheet and click one of the cells in the table.

2. Click the Analyze tab to view the corresponding Excel Ribbon.

3. To simulate an incorrect data entry, change the Income for the ID number 27974 from 160000 to 1600 as shown in Figure 18-19.

4. Click the Highlight Exceptions icon as shown in Figure 18-19. The Highlight Exceptions dialog allows you to select the column you suspect might have exceptions. By default the dialog excludes a column that it detects as a unique identifier.

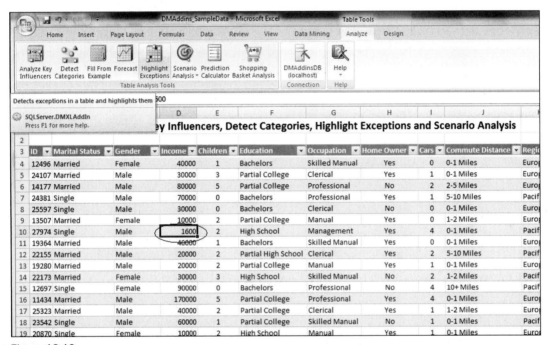

Figure 18-19

5. Accept the default selection suggested in the dialog and click Run. The Highlight Exceptions tool creates a clustering algorithm on the provided data set and then predicts the values to identify if there are exceptions. The dialog creates a new worksheet called Table2 Outliers. This worksheet shows the threshold for detecting exceptions. The default value chosen is 75 percent. In addition to that it shows each column and how many exceptions were identified for each column.

6. Increase the exception threshold from 75 percent to 95 percent. You now see that the Table2 Outliers worksheet shows only two exceptions, one in Income and one in Age, as shown in Figure 18-20.

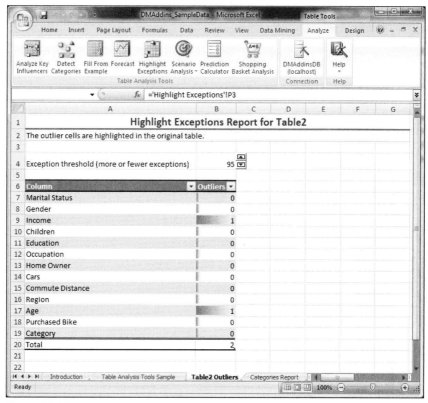

Figure 18-20

7. Switch to the Table Analysis Tools Sample worksheet. You will see that the row for customer ID 27974 where you changed the income from 160000 to 1600 in step 4 is highlighted in Figure 18-21.

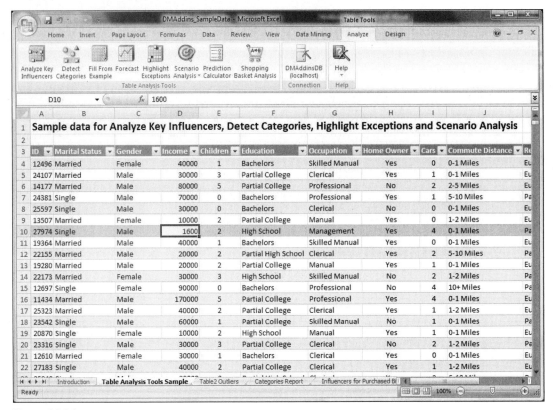

Figure 18-21

8. Change the income for the customer with ID 27974 to the original amount of 160000. You will now see that the Highlight Exceptions tool automatically detects that the value is within the range of what was expected based on the clusters that were created. Hence the background highlight for this row is now removed. If you switch to the Table2 Outliers worksheet, you see that the Income column is no longer considered to be an exception because the Outliers column is set to zero.

Shopping Basket Analysis

The Shopping Basket Analysis tool helps you to explore cross-selling opportunities. Assume you have a table with transaction data that contains the products sold within a transaction. The Shopping Basket Analysis tool helps you to identify the products that have been bought together. SSAS 2008 provides a separate data set that contains four columns: the transaction ID, and the category, name, and price of the product to help you understand Shopping Basket Analysis. The transaction ID column contains several entries for certain transactions because customers bought multiple products in the same transaction.

1. Click the worksheet Associate. You will see that the first two entries in the table have the same transaction ID SO61269.

2. Click one of the cells in the table.

3. Click the Analyze tab in Table Tools and then click the Shopping Basket Analysis icon seen in Figure 18-22.

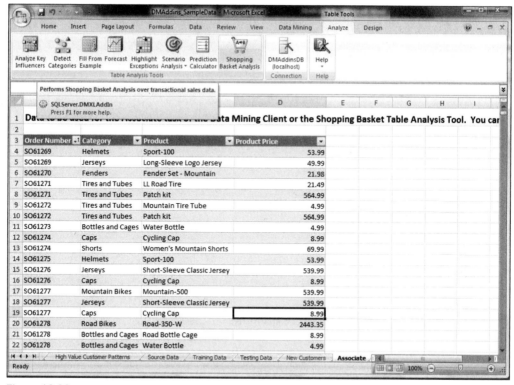

Figure 18-22

The Shopping Basket Analysis tool first analyzes the table to identify the likely column that indicates the transaction number. You can see in the Shopping Basket Analysis dialog shown in Figure 18-23 that the tool has identified the Order Number column as the transaction ID. It has identified the Category column as the Item and the Product Price column as the Item Value.

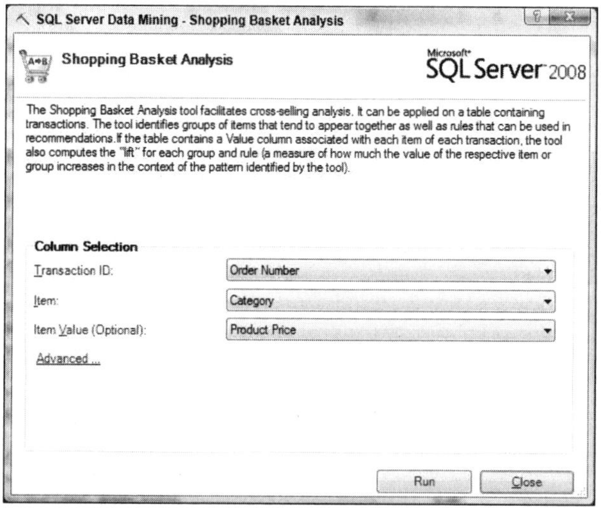

Figure 18-23

The Shopping Basket Analysis tool will use the Microsoft Association Algorithm to perform the analysis on the table. You can specify advanced settings for the association algorithm by clicking the Advanced link.

4. Select the defaults suggested by the dialog and click Run. The Shopping Basket Analysis dialog creates an Association mining model on your SSAS instance, analyzes the results, and then creates two spreadsheets called Shopping Basket Related Items and Shopping Basket Recommendations. The Shopping Basket Bundled Items sheet shown in Figure 18-24 provides you with an aggregate view of the number of products, the product names, the number of each type of bundled sale, along with the information on average sales per transaction and the overall value of the products.

In this example we chose the category column as the Item and therefore the overall value of the bundle is the aggregation of all the products in the categories selected. For example, you see that the overall value of the bundle of the products in Road Bikes and Helmets (first row in Figure 18-24) is quite large as compared to the average sales. You can format the sales amounts as currencies using Excel's Format Cells option to have better readability, which eventually aids you in your analysis. You can use this sheet to analyze the list of products that customers shop together. This will provide you with an indication of the items to bundle and promote to customers.

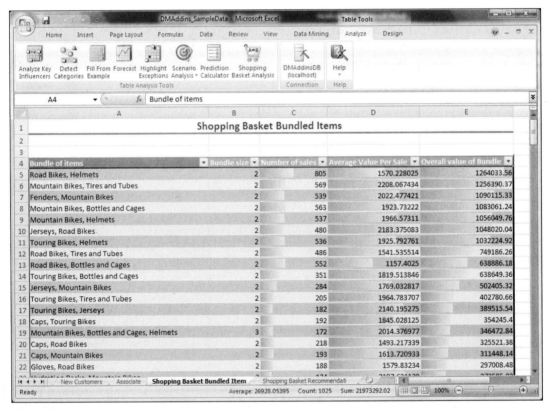

Figure 18-24

The Shopping Basket Recommendations spreadsheet provides you with suggestions of what items to recommend, the probability of customers buying the additional recommended items, and what your overall increase in sales would be due to these recommendations.

5. Switch to the Shopping Basket Recommendation worksheet.

6. Select the columns Average value of recommendation and Overall value of linked sales.

7. In the Home Ribbon, under Cells, select the drop-down Format menu.

8. In the Format Cells dialog, select Currency as the Category and click OK. You now see the columns Average Value of Recommendation and Overall value of linked sales formatted as currencies. See Figure 18-25. This worksheet helps you to understand the average gain you will have based on the recommendation. Assume you recommend Tires and Tubes for customers purchasing Bike Stands. Approximately 80 percent of the customers are likely to buy your recommendation as indicated by the "% of linked sales" column. The average value/ increase in revenue due to your recommendation is $243 as indicated by the Average Value of Recommendation column. This worksheet will help you to understand the percentage of customers that might buy certain products if you recommend them and what additional revenue you would make due to this recommendation.

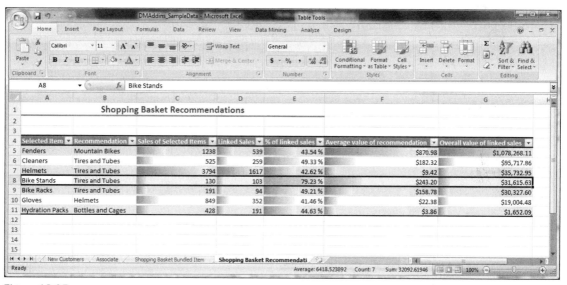

Figure 18-25

The Scenario Analysis tool allows you to understand what factors (columns) would help in influencing a change in specific columns. For example, if you want to convert a bike buyer from No to Yes, what should be their income? This tool helps in scenarios where there are multiple parameters you can change to achieve a desired goal. For example, you might want to increase your revenue by 10 percent for certain products. You can probably allocate a certain amount in promotions and you can decide whether to invest the promotions in television advertisements or advertisements in papers, online coupons, and so on, and decide what factor or combination of factors might provide you with the maximum benefit. The Prediction Calculator tool allows you to detect patterns in various columns of the table to predict a specific value in one of the columns. We recommend you explore these two tools.

In this section you learned about various tools available to you to analyze data in your Excel spreadsheets using the Microsoft SQL Server 2008 Data Mining Add-ins for Office 2007. For a more in-depth discussion of the Table Analytics tool, we recommend that you read *Data Mining with Microsoft SQL Server 2008* by Jamie MacLennan, ZhaoHui Tang, and Bogdan Crivat (Wiley, 2008).

Data Mining Tools

Table Analytics is aimed at end users who might not have knowledge of data mining. The Table Analytics tools do use the functionality of data mining but do not provide the full-fledged functionality of creating, refining, and viewing the models like you would have with Business Intelligence Development Studio. In addition, some end users might have in-depth knowledge of data mining and would like to create their own data mining models on the data in an Excel spreadsheet.

In this section you learn to create, refine, and view a data mining model on data in an Excel spreadsheet using the Data Mining Tools add-ins that are part of the Microsoft SQL Server 2008 Data Mining Add-ins for Office 2007. You learn to create a classification mining model using the sample data set that has been provided as part of the DMAddins_SampleData.xlsx document. You first need to select the Source Data worksheet and then select the Data Mining tab. You will then see the Data Mining Ribbon shown in Figure 18-26.

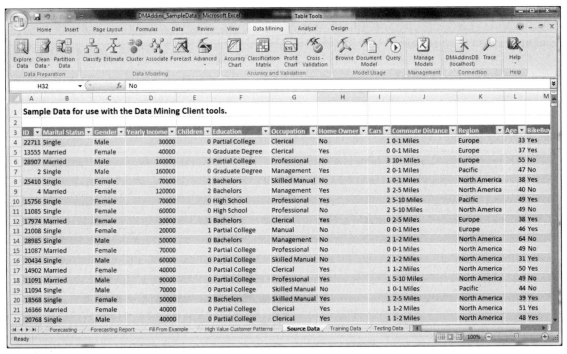

Figure 18-26

If you have used the Business Intelligence Development Studio (BIDS) for creating data mining models, you might think that the icons in the Data Mining Ribbon will be able to support the features you have seen in BIDS. You are correct. Most of the features supported in BIDS can be accomplished on the data within the worksheet. In this section you learn how to create one of the data mining models supported by the data mining add-in, Classify.

Similar to the Table Analytics Tools add-in you first need to connect to your SSAS instance. You can launch the connection manager tool by clicking the icon in the Connection group as shown in Figure 18-27. In this example you use the existing DMAddinDB database. The first step is to select the data set to analyze. The Data Mining tools provide you with the option of not only analyzing data within an Excel spreadsheet but also analyzing data from external data sources. You first learn various ways to select a data source for analysis.

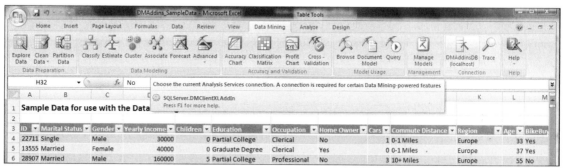

Figure 18-27

Click the Classify icon under the Data Modeling group of the Ribbon to launch the Classify tool. If you chose you can review the Getting Started page to understand more about the Classify tool and click Next to start the Classify Wizard. You will see a Select Source Data dialog box that provides you with three options for selecting data: from a table, from a range, or from an Analysis Services data source.

By default, the dialog selects the table in the current worksheet as the data source to be used. You can use the drop-down list to select a table from a different worksheet.

The second option is to select a data range, where you can either type the range descriptor in the text box or click the Range tool to make your selection. Note that when using data in a table or range with the Data Mining Client, with the exception of the data preparation tools, your Excel data is remoted to the Analysis Services instance where the data mining work is performed. The data preparation tools perform their work on the client and therefore do not remote the data.

The third option is the External Data Source. This option is provided for you to either choose existing external data sources such as a relational database within your connected Analysis Services database or create new ones for analyzing. This option allows you to perform mining operations on data sets that are much larger than what will fit inside your Excel workbook, or that you simply do not want to manage inside your workbook. To choose an external data source you need to click the button next to the data source name to launch the data source query editor. Similar to the data source query editor in BIDS you can create new data sources or select existing ones on your connected Analysis Services database.

Now that you have learned to connect to Analysis Services and understand ways of selecting various data sets from the Data Mining client tools, you are ready to start using the Data Mining Client for Excel. You should be aware that the Analysis Services Data Source option is not available for all tools, in which case it will not be presented as an option. Now let's go through the various steps you would need to take to analyze the data, build a model, and understand the results.

Explore Data

The first step to understanding any data set is to explore and identify statistical information in the data that can help you in further analysis. The Explore Data tool allows you to see histograms of numeric and non-numeric data in your worksheet, and to group numeric data into equal-sized buckets. First you need to load the data you want to explore into an Excel workbook. The Explore Data tool works only on data in Excel and not on external data sources.

1. Click the Explore Data icon in the Data Preparation section of the Data Mining tab as shown in Figure 18-28.

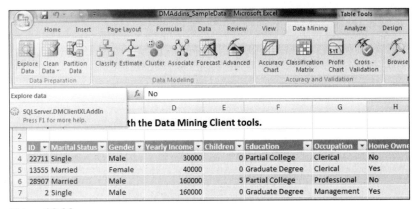

Figure 18-28

2. Review the content in the Getting Started page of Explore Data and click Next. In the Select Source Data dialog you can choose to explore data in either a table or an Excel Range. Explore Data does not work with data from an external data source. If you want to explore data from a database you first need to import the data into your Excel workbook. Because the data from an external data source can be really large you may have to get a sample data set to perform the exploration. The Partition Data tool provides the functionality to extract a sample of database data into Excel.

3. Select Source Data in the Source Data dialog box (the default provided by the dialog) and click Next.

    In the Select Column page the dialog shows the entire table within the dialog. You need to choose a specific column of interest to get the histograms. You can do this by either selecting the column in the drop-down list next to Select Column or selecting a specific column by choosing the header of the column. The column chosen is highlighted as shown in Figure 18-29.

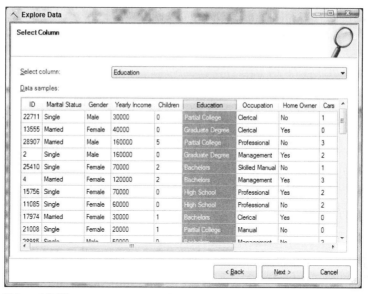

Figure 18-29

4. Choose the Education column, which has non-numeric and discrete values. You will see the histograms for the Education column in the Explore Data dialog. See Figure 18-30. The histogram shows the count of the distinct values in the entire table for the chosen column in descending order.

5. At this point, you can click Finish to exit the wizard, click Copy to copy a bitmap of the chart to the clipboard, or click Back to analyze another column. For this example, click Back to select a numeric column and explore the options available.

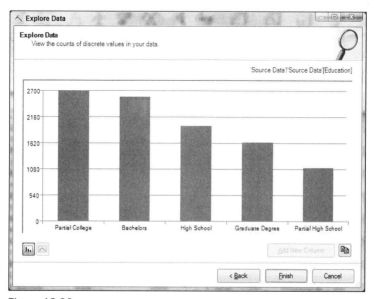

Figure 18-30

6. In the Select Column dialog select the Yearly Income column as shown in Figure 18-31 and click Next.

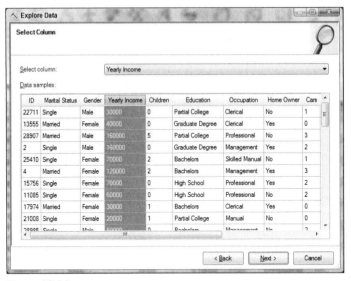

Figure 18-31

When viewing numeric data, the Explore Data Wizard shows the data grouped into buckets of equal ranges. In Figure 18-32 you can see the default bucket value is 8. By changing the value of the buckets, you can increase or decrease the number of buckets across the range. You can also toggle between the View as Discrete and View as Numeric buttons that are available at the lower-left corner to change how the data is viewed. These buttons are available whenever you are exploring a column with numeric or mixed numeric and non-numeric data. If you want to use the bucketed data as a column in the worksheet for further analysis, you can click the Add New Column button, which inserts a column with the appropriate ranges into your source data.

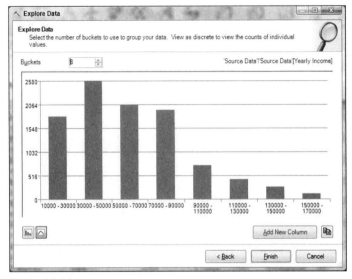

Figure 18-32

We recommend that you continue to use the Back button and the column selection screen to explore the other columns in your table.

7. Click Finish in the Explore Data dialog after you have explored all the columns.

The Explore Data Wizard provides a simple interface for viewing histograms of your non-numeric and numeric data. It also allows you to add bucketed columns and histogram views to your workbook. You can see the flexibility and options provided by the Explore Data tool to make your analysis more efficient.

Clean Data: Outliers and Re-Label

After you have done an initial analysis of your data the next step is to determine if the data is clean. Often the data you want to analyze might have unknown values that are represented in a specific way that might not add useful information, or there might be outliers you have identified in the data exploration part that you do not want to be considered for analysis. You would need to clean such data to get meaningful information. If not, you need to clean the data in order to create a good mining model. Data mining model creation typically requires that the data within a column be consistent. Each distinct value in a column has a unique meaning, and therefore each column should be checked to ensure that there aren't multiple values with the same connotation. For example, if you have a column indicating a person's marital status, and the column had a value "Married" and "Currently Married," a data mining algorithm would treat these values as different, even though you know them to be the same. The Re-label tool can be used to quickly correct such inconsistencies in a column. Another typical scenario is when there are many different values in a column that can be summarized into fewer values. For example, using the Marital Status example, the column could have the values "Single," "Married," "Divorced," and "Widowed," among others. For the problem you are trying to solve, you may only be interested in people that are currently married or not, or possibly that have never been married. Using the Re-label tool allows you to quickly consolidate many states into a smaller set.

The Clean Data tool provides two tools called Outliers and Re-label. The Outliers tool helps you to detect outlier values in a specific column and remove them, and the Re-label tool allows you to easily change values within a column of data to your desired value. In order to understand these tools, first make a few changes in the table you are using. To start, change the cells F4 and F13 to "Some College" in the Source Data worksheet.

There are several ways to eliminate states that are duplicate in meaning, but entered differently in the Excel worksheet. One method to determine if a column has such situations is to drop down the filter control on a column header in a table. Doing this on the Education column, you can see that you have the values "Partial College" and "Some College," which have the same meaning. You will now use the Clean Data ⇨ Re-label tool to quickly correct these issues.

1. Launch the Re-label tool by clicking Clean Data in the Data Mining Ribbon and selecting Re-label data as shown in Figure 18-33.

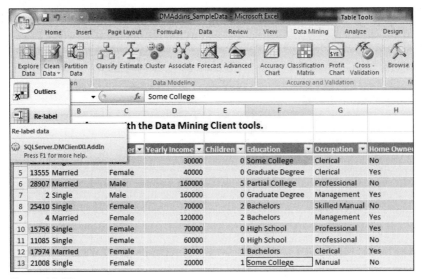

Figure 18-33

2. Read the Start page of the Re-label tool and click Next.

3. In the Select Source Data dialog use the default Source Data table selection and click Next.

   The Education column in the table has values "Some College" and "Partial College," which have the same meaning. You will be re-labeling them to a single value using the Re-label tool.

4. In the Select Column dialog, make sure the Education column is selected as shown in Figure 18-34 and click Next.

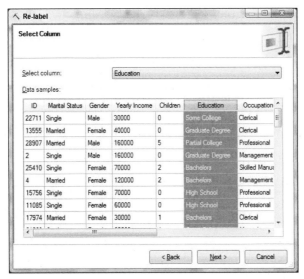

Figure 18-34

You will see the various values in the Education column along with the count of rows that has those values. You can provide the new labels to existing labels in this dialog.

5. In the Re-label dialog select Partial College as the new label for Some College as shown in Figure 18-35 and click Next.

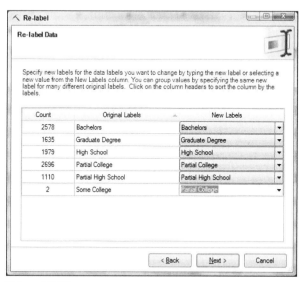

Figure 18-35

The Select Destination page provides you with three options for applying the new values chosen. The first option is to create a new column in the same worksheet, update all the values in the new column, and copy the remaining values. The second option is to create a new worksheet and apply the updates for the values. The third option is to update the data within the same worksheet. A key aspect to understand is that the actions performed by the Re-label tool cannot be reverted. This is extremely important for option three. Therefore we recommend you use option one or two to be safe, because they will allow you to delete the new sheet or the new column. For this example, however, choose option three.

6. Select the option to Change Data in Place and click Finish. You should see the tool has updated the values for cells F4 and F13 to Partial College as shown in Figure 18-36.

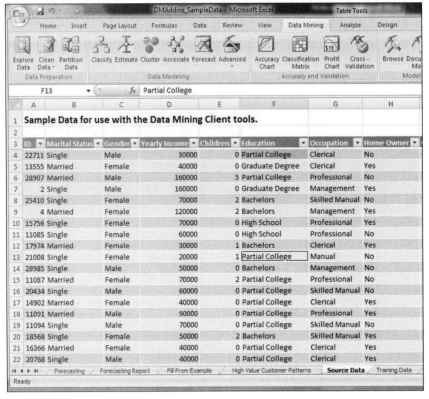

Figure 18-36

Now consolidate the various Education values to two values indicating if a customer has a college degree or not. You can do this using the Re-label tool.

7. Launch the Re-label tool again by clicking Clean Data in the Data Mining Ribbon and selecting Re-label.

8. Click Next in the Getting Started page.

9. Accept the default selection of Table Source Data in the Select Source Data page and click Next.

10. Select the Education column in the Select Column page and click Next.

11. On the Re-label Data page, change the New Labels to Has Bachelors and No Bachelors as shown in Figure 18-37 by clicking in the New Labels column for each row and typing the appropriate values. Click Next to proceed to the Select Destination page.

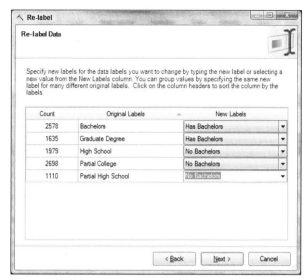

Figure 18-37

12. Select the option Add as a New Column to the Current Worksheet, and click Finish. The tool adds a new column called Education2 to the table and populates the value for each row based on the new labels.

13. Rename the Education2 column "Has College Education."

The Re-label Data Wizard provides a convenient interface for making comprehensive changes across the values of a column in your worksheet. It can be used to consolidate values, ensure consistency, or for many other purposes where you need to quickly view and modify all of the values in a column. Now that you have learned to clean the data before creating mining models, next you learn why you need to partition the data set and how you can do that within the Data Mining Client.

Sample Data

As you learned in Chapter 16 one of the key processes of building the data mining model is to split the input data set into training and testing data. The Sample Data Wizard allows you to do that. The wizard also helps to sample data from a larger data set in an Excel sheet or in an external database, and create samples that balance distributions of a target variable. By validating your models against a testing set, you can estimate how well your model will perform against new data. This is particularly important for Classification and Estimation tasks.

1. Click the Sample Data icon in the Data Preparation group in the Data Mining Ribbon, as shown in Figure 18-38, and read the information about the Partition Data Wizard in the Getting Started page. Click Next.

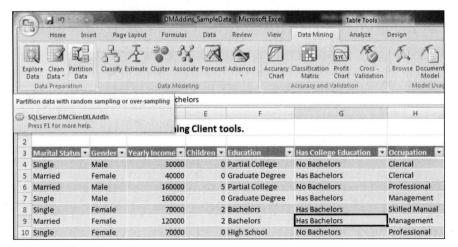

Figure 18-38

2.   In the Select Source Data page of the Sample Data Wizard dialog select the default selection Table as shown in Figure 18-39 and click Next.

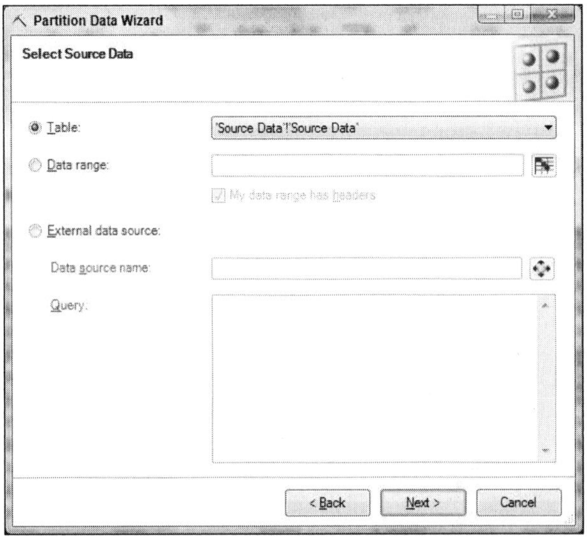

Figure 18-39

3. The sampling page provides you with two options for splitting the data set training and testing sets: Random Sampling or Oversample to Balance Data Distributions. The oversampling is needed when the distribution in the data set is not uniform. You would need the right distribution in the training set to make the model effective. Select the Random Sampling option under Sampling Method and click Next.

4. You can perform random sampling either as a percentage of the data set or by specifying a row count. On the Random Sampling Options dialog you can sample the data for training, and conversely, how much is left over for testing. The default split of 70 percent training and 30 percent testing is a good rule of thumb for most Excel-sized data sets, but you may want to split differently, based on the size of your data and the distribution of your target variable. In the Random Sampling Options dialog leave the default percentage selected and click Next.

5. The Finish page allows you to provide names to the new worksheets that will be created by the Sample Data tool. You have the option of creating a new sheet for unselected data. Specify the Selected set sheet name as **Training Data Sheet** and the unselected data to be moved to **Testing Data Sheet** as shown in Figure 18-40 and click Finish. The Sample Data Wizard now samples the data and creates two new sheets called Training Data Sheet and Testing Data Sheet as shown in Figure 18-41.

Figure 18-40

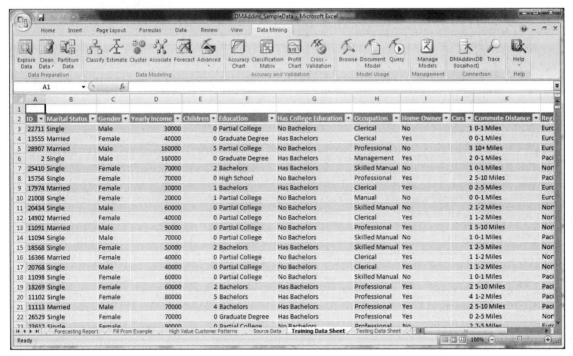

Figure 18-41

The Sample Data Wizard provides a convenient interface for the necessary data preparation step of splitting your data into two sets, one for training a mining model, and another for validating models that you have created.

Classification Model

After you have cleaned the data and partitioned it into training and testing data sets you are ready to start building the mining model. In this section you create a classification mining model. The Classify icon uses the decision tree data mining algorithm to create the appropriate nodes and splits. You can then predict values for new data sets based on the mining model created.

Model Creation

To create your classification model, follow these steps:

1. Switch to the Training Data Sheet that was created by the Sample Data tool. Click the Data Mining tab.

2. Click the Classify data mining algorithm in the Data Modeling group as shown in Figure 18-42.

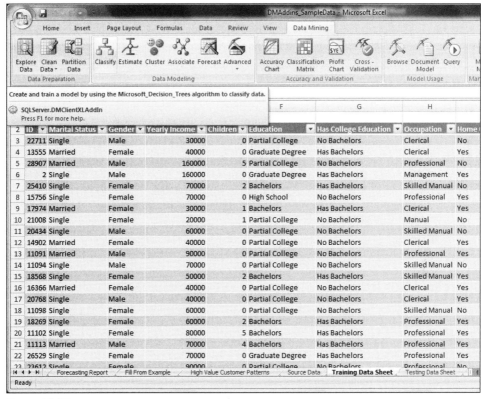

Figure 18-42

3. Review the information on the Getting Started page and click Next.

4. Select the default Table selection in the Select Source Data page as shown in Figure 18-43 and click Next.

   The Classification page (Figure 18-44) allows you to choose the column to analyze/predict and the input columns to find the influence of the input column(s) on the column to be analyzed. You can specify parameters for the decision tree algorithm, such as score method, split method, and support using the Parameters dialog that can be launched using the Parameters button.

Figure 18-43

5. Select BikeBuyer as the column to analyze.

6. Select all the remaining columns as input columns except the ID as shown in Figure 18-44 and click Next.

    The Split Data into Training and Testing Data dialog that appears allows you to specify a percentage or number of rows to split the data. You have already partitioned the original data set into training and testing data.

Figure 18-44

7. Specify the percentage of data for testing as 0 and click Next.

8. The Finish page of the Classify Wizard allows you to specify names for the mining structure, mining model, and add your description to the structure and model. In addition to that you have the options to create the model as a temporary model and enabling Drillthrough to the source data similar to the BIDS Decision Tree Wizard as you learned in Chapter 16. Select the defaults for the mining structure and mining model names but enable Drillthrough by enabling the checkbox as shown in Figure 18-45 and click Finish.

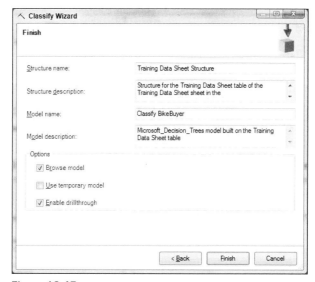

Figure 18-45

The Classify Wizard now creates the mining structure and the mining model based on options provided, and reads the data from the worksheet to train the model. Once the model has been trained you will see the mining model browser window.

Browse the Model

The Classify Wizard launches the mining model browser shown in Figure 18-46. You can also launch this browser from the Browse icon in the Model Usage group and select the model you want to browse from the connected SSAS database. The Decision Tree view shows all the nodes and splits of the mining model that was created from the table in the Training Data Sheet. You can click each node to see the percentage of customers with a specific characteristic who are likely to buy bikes. The decision tree indicates that the most important factor for customers who buy bikes is the customer's age. The mining model has split the customers into four nodes based on their age, which can be seen in Figure 18-46. The Mining Legend displays the percentage of customers in a specific node and the likelihood of them buying bikes. For example, when you click the node Age >= 33 and Age < 41, you see that 16.45 percent of customers in this group buy bikes. You can identify potential customers based on the information in the mining models and use that information to send out targeted mails to customers who are likely to buy bikes instead of sending the mail to all customers.

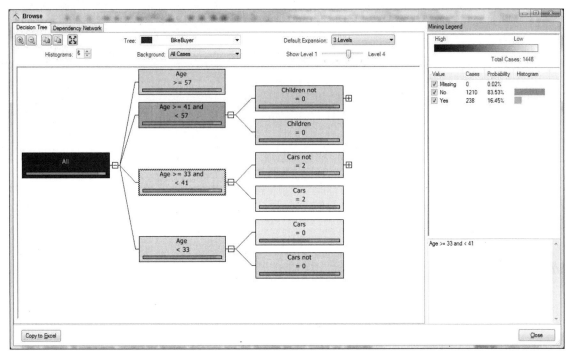

Figure 18-46

The Browse dialog has a Dependency Network tab. If you click the Dependency Network tab you will see the dependencies between various columns and the analyzed column Bike Buyer, as shown in Figure 18-47. The decision tree mining model has identified that the columns Cars, Age, Marital Status, and Children are the columns that influence the Bike Buyer column. By default the slider on the left is at All Links. If you move the slider down you will see that the strongest influencing column for bike buyers is Age, which you identified in the Decision Tree view.

You need to connect to your SSAS instance to retrieve the data and browse the model. If some of the end users with whom you want to share this data do not have access to your SSAS instance, you can share the graphs in model browsing. You can copy the dependency graph or the decision tree to a new sheet in the same Excel spreadsheet by clicking the Copy to Excel button so that you can share the details in the model Browse dialog with other end users who access the data.

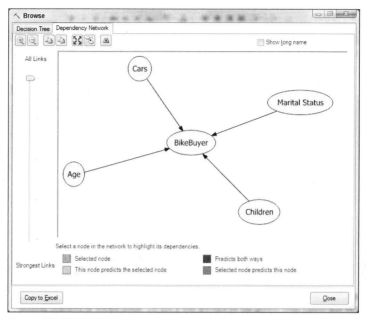

Figure 18-47

Model Accuracy

You have created a decision tree mining model using 70 percent of the table data from the Training Data Sheet and browsed the model to understand the results from the mining model. You need to identify how good the mining model is in predicting bike buyers using the 30 percent of the data that you originally partitioned in the Testing Data Sheet.

1. Click the Testing Data Sheet worksheet and click the Data Mining Tools tab.

2. Click the Accuracy Chart icon in the Accuracy and Validation group as shown in Figure 18-48.

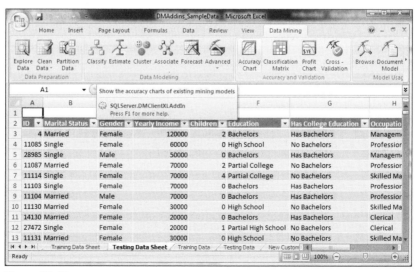

Figure 18-48

3. Review the Getting Started page of the Accuracy Chart Wizard and click Next.

4. In the SelectStructure or Model dialog, select the Classify Bike Buyer mining model as shown in Figure 18-49 and click Next.

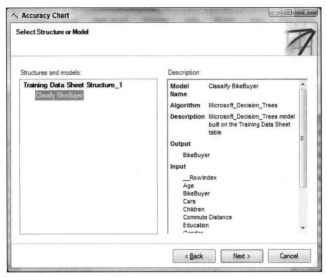

Figure 18-49

5. In the Specify Column to Predict and Value to Predict page, make sure you have BikeBuyer as the column to predict and Yes as the value to predict as shown in Figure 18-50, and click Next.

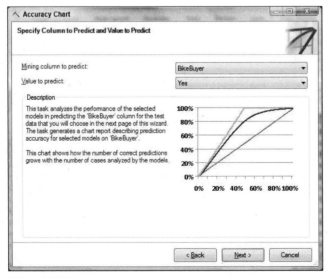

Figure 18-50

6. The Select Source Data page allows you to select test data held back while creating the model, a specific table, or a data range in the Excel spreadsheet or even an external data source. Select the Testing Data Sheet table from the drop-down menu and click Next.

7. In the Specify Relationship page, the relationship between the columns in the mining model and the columns in the Testing Data Sheet are shown by default. Accept the default as shown in Figure 18-51 and click Finish.

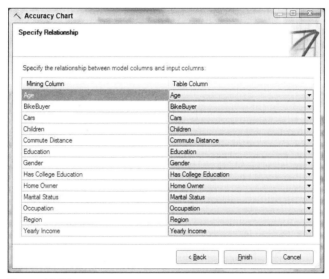

Figure 18-51

The Accuracy Chart Wizard predicts the rows in the Test Data Sheet that should contain the value Yes and compares the results to that of an ideal model. The result of the wizard is a new spreadsheet as shown in Figure 18-52. You can see graphical information comparing the decision tree mining model you have created to that of an ideal model where the predicted value for the BikeBuyer column is expected to be Yes. Below the graph the wizard populates a table that indicates the percentile of the population and the percentage of the correct predictions for an ideal model and the current model. We recommend you create another Accuracy Chart where the predicted BikeBuyer column value is No.

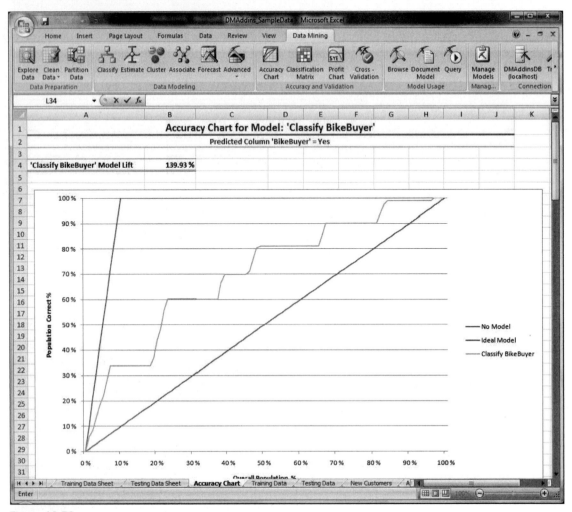

Figure 18-52

Classification Matrix

You might be interested in understanding the overall effectiveness of the matrix for the values Yes and No for the BikeBuyer column. As seen in Chapter 16, the Classification Matrix will help you compare the predicted values for all values of the BikeBuyer column with the original value.

1. Switch to the Testing Data Sheet and click the Data Mining Tools tab.

2. Click the Classification Matrix icon in the Accuracy and Validation group as shown in Figure 18-53.

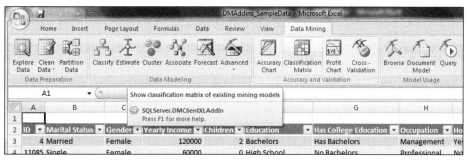

Figure 18-53

3. Review the Getting Started page and click Next.

4. Select the Classify Bike Buyer mining model as shown in Figure 18-54 and click Next.

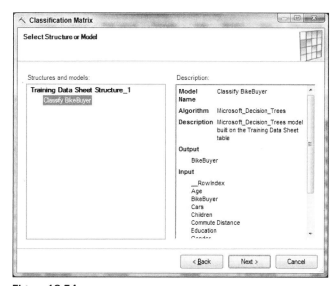

Figure 18-54

5. On the Specify Columns to Predict page, you have the option of providing the results as a percentage or as a count. It would be helpful to understand both options. Select the defaults as shown in Figure 18-55 and click Next.

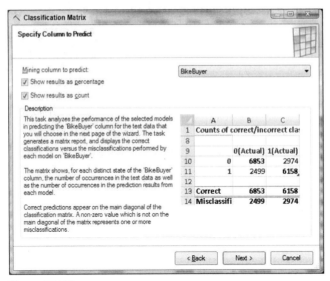

Figure 18-55

6. On the Select Source Data page, select the Testing Data Sheet table and click Next.

7. Because the Specify Relationship page has already mapped the columns from the mining model to the columns in the table (see Figure 18-56), accept the default selection and click Finish.

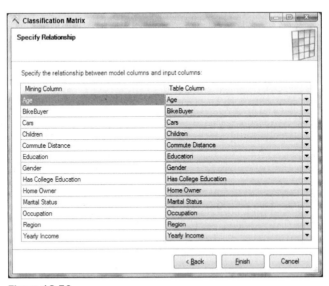

Figure 18-56

The wizard creates a Classification Matrix sheet that predicts the values for Yes and No and compares the values with the actual values as shown in Figure 18-57. This matrix gives you a good understanding of how effective the mining model is in predicting whether a customer will buy a bike.

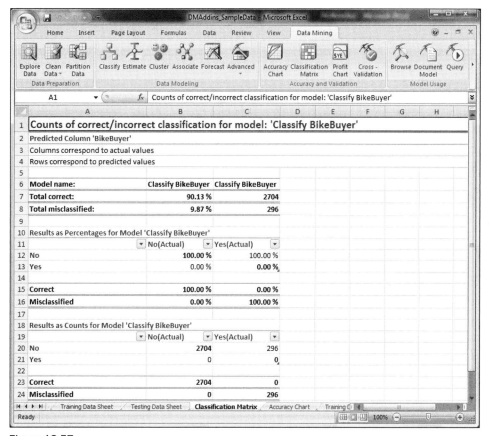

Figure 18-57

In this section you have learned the usefulness of the Data Mining Client add-ins. You learned to explore data within an Excel spreadsheet, clean the data, and partition the data. Then you created a classification mining model, analyzed the results by browsing the model, and determined if the mining model is predicting values effectively using the Classification Matrix and Accuracy Chart. Similar to the classification model you can create other mining models supported by the Data Mining Tools: Estimate, Cluster, Associate, and Forecast. We recommend you explore creating these models using the sample data. You also have a way to document mining model information using the Document Model tool. The Data Mining Client add-in gives a friendly interface to harness the full power of data mining features in SSAS 2008. To get an in-depth understanding of all the mining models and features supported by the tools, we recommend you read *Data Mining using SQL Server 2008* by Jamie MacLennan (Wiley, 2008).

Visio Add-In

You can create mining models using BIDS or using the Microsoft SQL Server 2008 Data Mining Add-ins for Office 2007. After you analyze the mining models and interpret the results, the next step is to make business decisions. Typically we expect the mining models to be created and analyzed by developers and present the information to decision-makers. BIDS and the Microsoft SQL Server 2008 Data Mining Add-ins for Office 2007 do not provide an effective way to present information to the decision-makers. Microsoft Visio, on the other hand, has been a great tool for presentations that rely on diagrams and figures. Therefore the Microsoft SQL Server 2008 Data Mining Add-ins for Office 2007provides you with an add-in for Visio to help you view, edit, and present information from mining models to the decision-makers. The add-in provides a Visio template that helps you to create data mining model representations as figures that you can edit and enhance.

To learn about Visio templates you will use the Adventure Works 2008 Analysis Services project sample that is available from http://www.codeplex.com. To launch the Visio template, download and deploy the Adventure Works 2008 Analysis Services project to your SSAS instance. Next, click Start ⇨ All Programs ⇨ Microsoft SQL Server 2008 DM Add-ins ⇨ Data Mining Visio template. You will see a new Visio document with the Data Mining Shapes template open showing three shapes: Dependency Network, Cluster, and Decision Tree. These objects help you to view all the mining models on your SSAS 2008 instance.

The Decision Tree Shape

The Decision Tree Shape helps you to view decision and regression tree mining models from your SSAS 2008 or SSAS 2005 instance. To use this shape, follow these steps:

1.   Drag and drop the Decision Tree Shape icon from the template onto the Visio document drawing surface to launch the Decision Tree Visio Shape Wizard. The Select a Data Source dialog that will appear allows you to choose a connection to SSAS instance. This is the connection dialog you used in the Microsoft SQL Server 2008 Data Mining Add-ins for Office 2007.

2.   In the Select Data Source dialog create a new connection to the Adventure Works 2008 database Adventure Works DW using the New button.

3.   In the Connect to Analysis Services dialog specify your SSAS instance name, select the Adventure Works 2008 sample database you have deployed, and click OK.

4.   In the Select a Data Source dialog select the Analysis Services connection and click Next. The wizard now requests for all the mining models on your SSAS instance, filters the one that can be viewed by the Decision Tree Shape Wizard, and shows them for your selection.

5.   On the Select a Mining Model page, select the TM_Decision_Tree model as shown in Figure 18-58 and click Next.

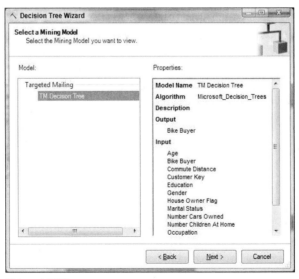

Figure 18-58

The wizard now requests you select a decision tree from the mining model that you would like to view within Visio along with the depth of the tree you would like to view as shown in Figure 18-59. The default number of levels is three, which may or may not be adequate for your analysis. Bear in mind that increasing this number may cause the resulting decision tree diagram to become more complex and harder to read and interpret in Visio. However, you have the flexibility to show sub-sections of the trees or move certain sections to a newer page. You have the option to change the values of the predicted values for display using the Select Decision Tree page as well as have the option to choose different colors.

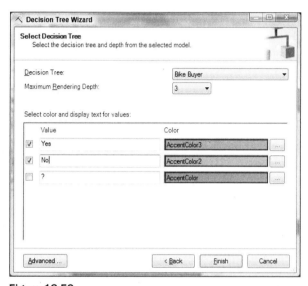

Figure 18-59

6.   Change the value of 1 to Yes and 0 to No as shown in Figure 18-59 and click Finish. The wizard now retrieves the decision tree mining model information and draws a decision tree diagram on the Visio page. The wizard shows the status page of all the operations performed.

7.   Click Close on the Confirmation of Decision Tree Rendering Wizard page.

You will see the entire decision tree with all the nodes along with the splits as shown in Figure 18-60. You can zoom in using Visio into a specific node such as the fifth node as shown in Figure 18-61. You can see the node is being split on the mining model column Region into three nodes with values North America, Pacific, and Europe. Each of the nodes shows the percentage of customers likely to buy bikes along with the values Yes or No. The decision tree diagram within Visio helps you view the mining model better as well as add any additional annotation using Visio for you to present the mining model information to the decision-makers.

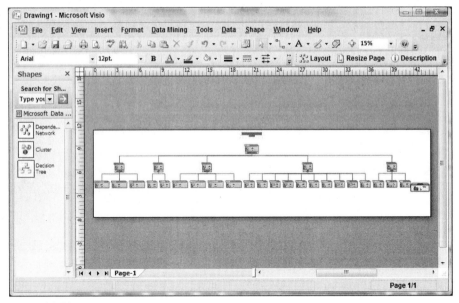

Figure 18-60

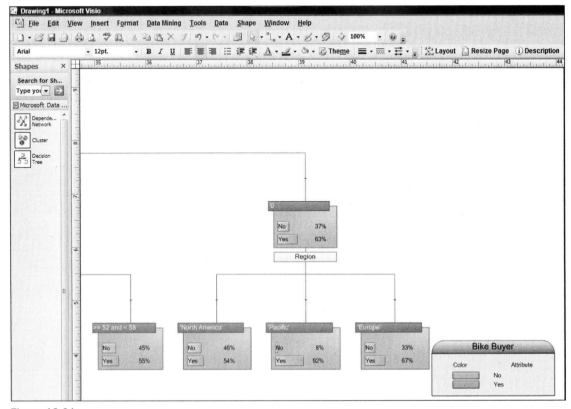

Figure 18-61

You will also see the Data Mining toolbar as shown in Figure 18-62 floating within the Visio diagram after you close the Decision Tree Rendering Wizard. You can move the Data Mining toolbar if needed. The Data Mining toolbar shows context-dependent icons based on the mining model being viewed and contains three icons named Layout, Resize Page, and Description for the decision tree mining models as shown in Figure 18-62.

Figure 18-62

The Layout icon helps in re-laying the nodes. This is useful if you have made a few changes to the nodes' location and want the layout to be restored. The Resize dialog helps you to resize the drawing page. The Description icon helps you to view more information about a specific node.

Note that the icons displayed on the Data Mining floating toolbar vary depending upon the data mining template you are using. If you don't like floating toolbars, you can dock the toolbar by clicking it and dragging it to the top menu strip. The menu will remain docked the next time you open Visio. You can also drag the floating toolbar beneath you diagram if you wish. In this case, a toolbar will be created for you if one does not already exist

1. Click the node that has a split on Region (the node shown in Figure 18-61).

2. Click the Description icon in the Data Mining toolbar.

You will see a more detailed description of the node as shown in Figure 18-63. The node can be identified by the description, which indicates that this is a node due to the split of Number of Cars Owned = 0 from the root node. If this is a node at the second level you will see an additional condition such as Number Cars Owned = 0 and Region = North America. You can see the support value shown in the dialog, which is the number of total customers who have 0 cars. Within these customers the people who buy bikes are shown with the State = Yes along with support and Probability information. This dialog helps you to understand a specific node better.

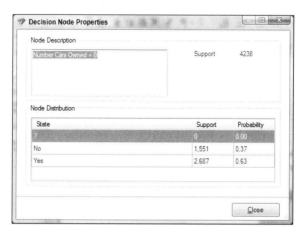

Figure 18-63

3. Click Close in the Decision Node Properties dialog. The decision tree shown in the Visio page can contain a lot of nodes that makes the analysis or viewing of the nodes a bit challenging. Hence the data mining template provides you with certain operations that help you to move sub-sections of a specific node efficiently.

4. Select the node where the value for Number Cars Owned is 1, right-click, and select Collapse Child Nodes as shown in Figure 18-64.

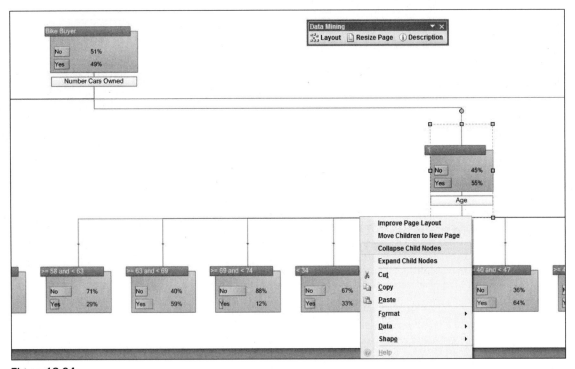

Figure 18-64

5. Repeat the previous step for the nodes with the value of Number Cars Owned equal to 0, 2, and 3.

6. Click the Layout icon in the Data Mining toolbar. You should now see all the collapsed nodes. The collapsed nodes are indicated with a shadow behind the actual node, as shown in Figure 18-65.

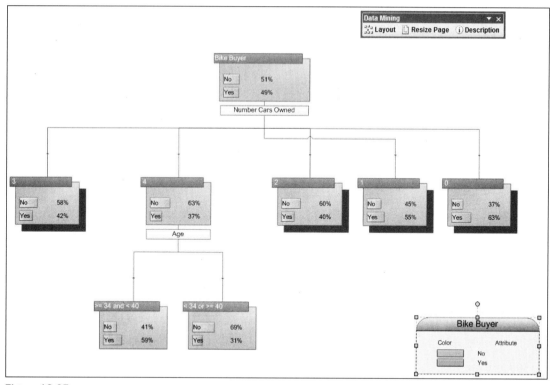

Figure 18-65

In addition to collapsing the nodes the decision tree shape also provides you with the ability to move the children of a specific node to a separate page. Instead of collapsing all the nodes that you are not interested in and then analyzing a specific node, this option isolates the specific node you are interested in to a separate page so you can analyze it better. A link from the original node is automatically added to the new Visio page you have created.

7. Right-click the node that has Number Cars Owned = 2 and select Move Children to New Page as shown in Figure 18-66. You will see a link created from the main page to a new page indicating that the child nodes are continued on Page 2 as shown in Figure 18-67.

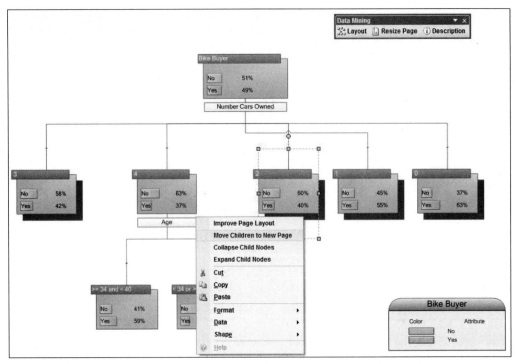

Figure 18-66

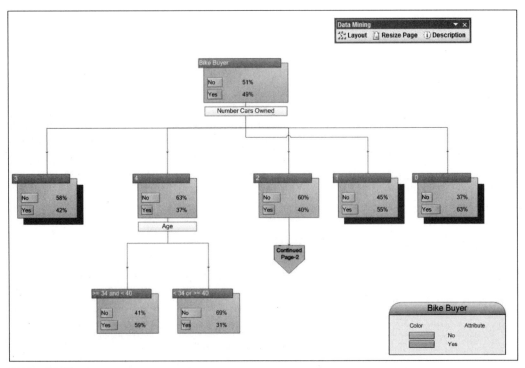

Figure 18-67

8.   Double-click the link Continued Page 2. You will now be taken to page 2, which has the children of the node Number Cars Owned = 2 as shown in Figure 18-68. You have the link back to Page 1 that enables you to move between pages 1 and 2 easily. In addition to that the legend is also included in page 2. You can now add appropriate annotation specific to customers having two cars and present the information.

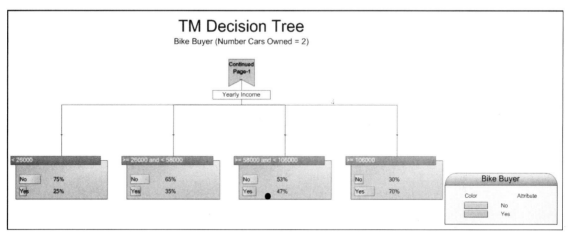

Figure 18-68

You can now save the Visio document with your annotations and send them to people interested in the results. The end users do not have to have the Microsoft SQL Server 2008 Data Mining Add-ins for Office 2007installed to view the results. Alternatively you can publish the Visio page as a web page with interactivity included so that you can publish the results on a web site for others to view it.

1.   Click the File menu and select Save as Web Page.

2.   In the Save As dialog enter DTModel.htm and click Publish.

3.   In the Save As Web Page dialog enter DTModel for the page title and click OK.

Visio saves the Visio pages as a web page and launches the web page within Internet Explorer. Based on your security settings you might be prompted to enable ActiveX controls. Right-click the warning and select Allow Block control to enable ActiveX controls. You will see the mining model published as a web page. You can navigate between the various Visio pages.

You have learned to view decision tree mining models within Visio using the Decision Tree Shape Wizard as well as options to efficiently view and present information in Visio and publish the pages as a web page. In the next two sections you learn about viewing additional mining models supported by SQL Server 2008 using the Cluster Shape Wizard and the Dependency Network Wizard.

The Cluster Shape Wizard

The Cluster Shape Wizard helps you to analyze and present the cluster mining models using Visio. The wizard allows you to customize the shape, size, and profiles of each cluster being shown in the Visio page.

1.   Click the Insert menu and select New Page.

2.   Drag and drop the Cluster Shape icon to the new page.

3.   Read the information in the Cluster Visio Shape Wizard introduction page and click Next.

4.   Select the Adventure Works connection in the Select a Data Source page and click Next.

     The Cluster Shape Wizard retrieves all the mining models from your chosen Adventure Works database, filters the cluster mining models, and shows them to you along with the details of the mining models such as name, algorithm, and input and output columns.

5.   Select the targeted mailing TM Clustering model and click Next.

     The Options for Cluster Diagram dialog provides you with three options: Show Cluster Shapes Only, Show Clusters with Characteristics Chart, and Show Clusters with Discrimination Chart. For this example choose the Show Cluster Shapes Only option, but take a look at how the cluster diagram would look if you chose each of these options:

     ❏   **Show Cluster Shapes Only:** This draws a simple cluster shape. The default shape is oval as shown in Figure 18-69. The relationships between clusters are shown by lines with no other details. This is useful in cases where there is a large number of clusters. Each cluster is shown as a single node.

Figure 18-69

     ❏   **Show Clusters with Characteristics Chart:** This option will show the list of characteristics with the percentage representing the likelihood that the characteristic will appear in the cluster as shown in Figure 18-70.

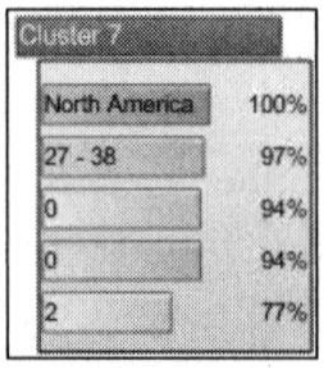

Figure 18-70

     ❏   **Show Clusters with Discrimination Chart:** This option allows you to compare attributes between clusters. The attributes are now displayed in order of their importance when discriminating between clusters as shown in Figure 18-71. The size of the bars shows how strongly the attributes favor the characteristic.

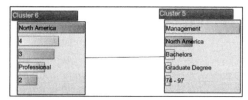

Figure 18-71

The number of rows in the chart helps you to specify the number of rows of attributes to show in the cluster diagram for options two and three. The default value of five displays the top five characteristics in each cluster.

The Advanced button allows you to choose additional options for Font, Fill, and Line colors as well as choosing various shapes to represent clusters. If you click the Advanced button you will see the Cluster Options dialog (Figure 18-72). You also have the option of previewing the cluster within this dialog.

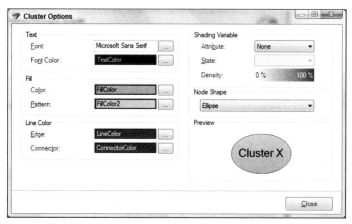

Figure 18-72

6. Select the Show Cluster Shapes Only option in the Options for Cluster Diagram dialog as mentioned in the previous step and click Finish. The Cluster Shape Wizard now retrieves the details of the mining model chosen and renders the diagram within the Visio page. The wizard also shows a dialog with various options taken during this rendering process.

7. Click Close as soon as the diagram has been rendered.

You will see the cluster diagram in the Visio page as shown in Figure 18-73. You can see the Data Mining toolbar has more options as compared to a Decision Tree dialog. The Layout, Resize Page, and Description have similar functionality as what you have seen earlier and we recommend you explore these for the cluster diagram.

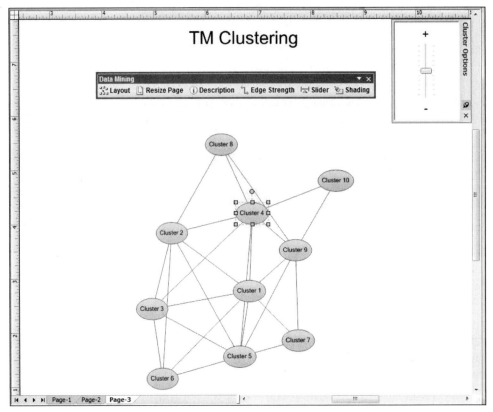

Figure 18-73

The Edge Strength helps you to show the strength of the relationship between any two clusters. If you click the Edge Strength you will see the cluster diagram is updated with the edge strength values as shown in Figure 18-74. The Edge Strength icon serves as a toggle icon, which means you can turn off the display of edge strength by clicking the icon again. The strength of the Edge is represented as a number between 0 and 100, where 0 indicates no relationship and 100 indicates the members of the clusters are closely related.

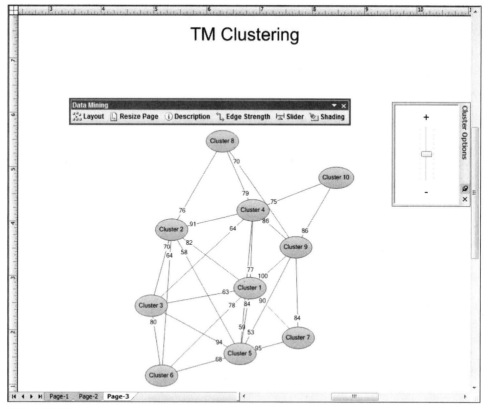

Figure 18-74

The Slider icon is used to enable the slider window (seen on the right of Figure 18-74) if it is closed. This is not a toggle switch. The slider window helps you to identify the strongest relationships between various clusters. By default the slider window is in the middle. If you move the slider toward the plus sign you will only be able to see the strongest link, and if you move the slider to the minus sign you will see all the links. For this example, move the slider close to the plus sign.

Now the edges with the strongest links are the only ones that are displayed, as shown in Figure 18-75. Now from the diagram you can identify that Clusters 1 and 9 have the strongest relationship. However, you do not know the characteristics of the clusters or what uniquely distinguishes them. Displaying the cluster characteristics or cluster discrimination information in the diagram will help you analyze the clusters better.

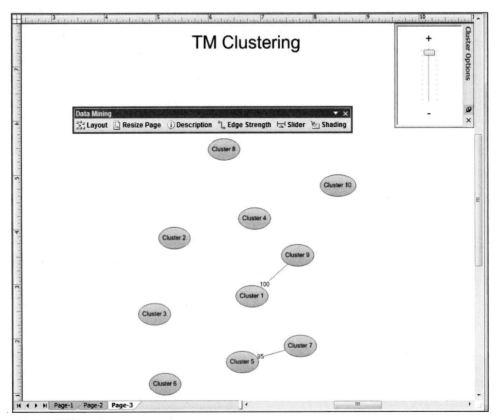

Figure 18-75

Select Cluster 1, right-click, and select Display Discrimination for all clusters as shown in Figure 18-76.

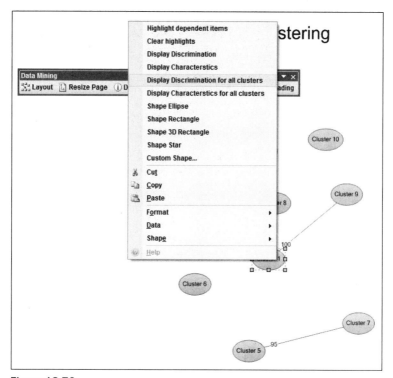

Figure 18-76

You will see that the cluster characteristics for all the clusters are displayed with five rows of attributes displayed as shown in Figure 18-77. You can see that Clusters 1 and 9 have the characteristics of members having Bachelors degrees and being between the ages 40 and 47. The legend for the attributes is shown separately as shown in Figure 18-77. The attribute values or states that are unique to a specific cluster along with the support values are indicated within the cluster characteristic.

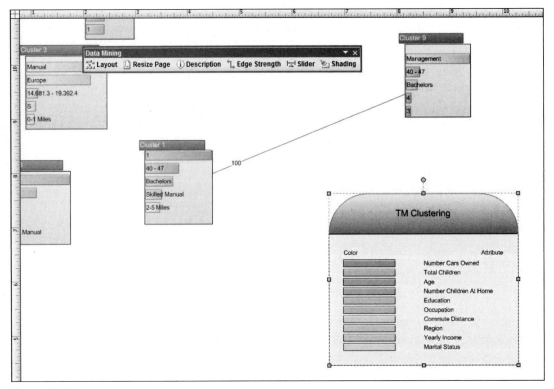

Figure 18-77

The Shading icon in the Data Mining toolbar is used only when you have the clusters represented as shapes without the cluster characteristics or discrimination information. When you click the Shading icon you see the shading window within the Visio page. The shading window is shown in Figure 18-78. You need to select the attribute name and a specific state and click Apply for the clusters to be shaded. The shading helps you to easily identify visually which clusters are favored by a specific attribute and state.

Figure 18-78

Figure 18-79 shows the cluster diagram with shading applied for the Education attribute with the state Graduate Degree. A darker shading indicates that there are large numbers of customers in a specific cluster. You can easily observe that Cluster 7 has the maximum number of graduates as compared to other clusters. We recommend you try various shading options.

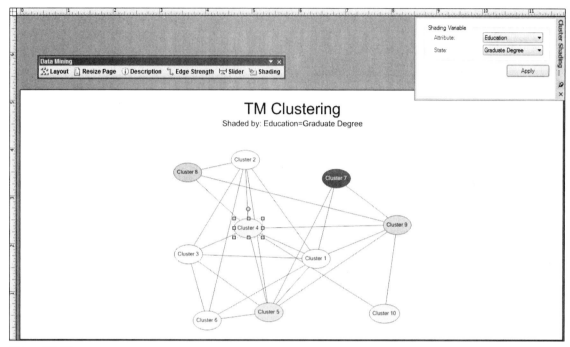

Figure 18-79

When you are using shapes for a cluster you have the option to select any image to display a cluster. For example, you can replace the shape for Cluster 7 with a diagram that has graduates indicating that this cluster has a lot of graduates. You can do this by right-clicking the cluster and selecting Custom Shape.

The Dependency Shape Wizard

The Dependency Shape Wizard helps you to visualize Naive Bayes, decision trees, and association rule mining models supported in SQL Server 2008. In this example you view an association mining model.

1. Drop down the Insert menu and select Insert New Page.

2. Accept the default page name and click OK.

3. Drag and drop the Dependency Network shape into the new page.

4. Read the description of the Dependency Network Visio Shape Wizard welcome page and click Next.

5. In the Select a Data Source dialog that appears, select the Adventure Works database as the current connection.

The wizard now retrieves all the mining models within the chosen database. It then filters the mining models that can be rendered by the Dependency Network Shape Wizard and shows them in the Select a Mining Model page as shown in Figure 18-80. The mining models are listed along with the mining structure. You can also get information on each mining model in the Properties pane of the dialog.

Figure 18-80

6. Select the Association mining model (Figure 18-80) and click Next. The Select Nodes to Render page helps you to choose a specific number of nodes to be rendered based on certain selection criteria. You can either choose a number of nodes to be fetched or optionally provide wild card searches based on the node names. For example, typing the word "Cage" into the text box would result in retrieval of nodes Mountain Bottle Cage and Road Bottle Cage in the chosen mining model.

7. Choose the default five nodes and click the green arrow button to retrieve the nodes. You will see five nodes retrieved and shown in the Query results pane. You have the option to specify which nodes you want to be rendered by the wizard on the Visio page by using the checkboxes.

    The Dependency Network Wizard also has an Advanced button to help you specify font, color, or shape for the nodes to be rendered using the Advanced dialog shown in Figure 18-81, which can be launched using the Advanced button of the Select Nodes to Render page. You have the option of choosing various Name styles for each node. The Advanced page of the Dependency Network Wizard also has a preview of the nodes based on the selections.

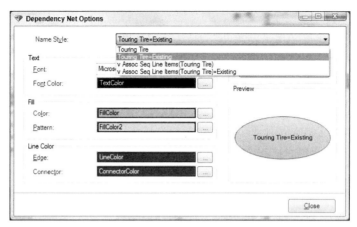

Figure 18-81

8. Click Finish in the Select Nodes to Render page with the five nodes that have been retrieved. The Dependency Network Wizard retrieves the nodes and their properties and renders the dependency network on the Visio page. The sequence of steps taken by the wizard is shown in the confirmation page.

9. Click Close in the Confirmation of Dependency Network Rendering Wizard page. You can see the dependency network with five nodes rendered in the Visio page as shown in Figure 18-82. The Data Mining toolbar's icons Layout, Re-size page, Edge Strength, and Slider have the same functionality as the ones you learned for the Cluster Shape Wizard. In the dependency network you see the slider by default is closer to the minus sign to show all dependency links.

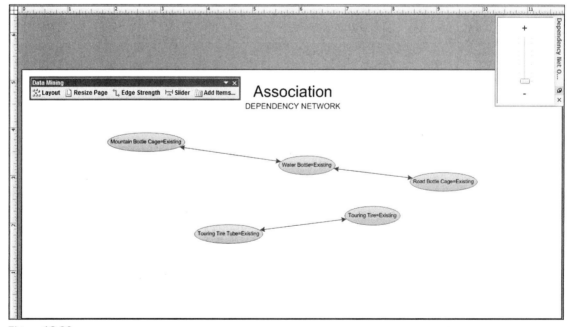

Figure 18-82

10. Click the Edge Strength to see the strengths between the nodes. The edges between the nodes have a bi-directional arrow unlike the cluster diagram, which didn't have any directions. The arrows indicate the strength of relationship from one node to another node. As soon as the edge strengths are enabled, you will see the values. The dependency network shows that someone buying Touring Tire Tubes are 100 percent likely to buy Touring Tires, whereas if they buy Touring Tires they will probably buy Touring Tire Tubes 50 percent of the time. Therefore the dependency network diagram allows you to visualize the association mining model information that identifies items that are purchased together so that you can utilize this information to cross-sell products to customers to increase your overall revenue.

To improve visualization of related nodes the dependency network shape provides you with several options that can be viewed when you select a specific node and right-click as shown in Figure 18-83. You can choose the option to highlight dependent items or highlight items that the current node depends on. You can also move certain nodes to a new page. In addition, you can add additional nodes to the Visio page by either selecting the Add Related Items in the right-click context menu or using the Add Items... icon in the Data Mining toolbar.

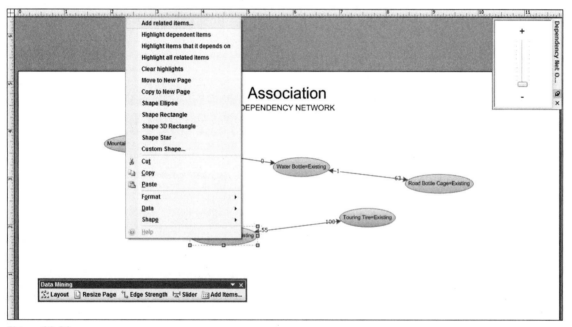

Figure 18-83

To add related items, select the node Touring Tire Tube = Existing, right-click, and select Add Related Items as shown in Figure 18-83.

In the Select Nodes to Render dialog click the green arrow to retrieve the nodes related to Touring Tire Tube. You will see two additional nodes retrieved as shown in Figure 18-84.

Figure 18-84

Click Finish to add the new nodes to the existing Visio page. You will see the new nodes along with existing nodes as shown in Figure 18-85. You can change the shape of a specific node, new nodes being added, or all nodes using the options provided by the dependency network shape or add annotation to your diagram to have appropriate recommendations. We recommend you explore these options.

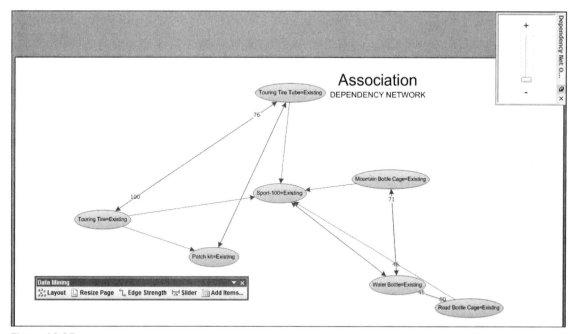

Figure 18-85

You have successfully learned to create Visio diagrams that represent the SQL Server 2008 mining.

Summary

In this chapter you learned about the Microsoft SQL Server 2008 Data Mining Add-ins for Office 2007. You first learned about the various features of Table Analytics tools that help you to analyze tabular data in your Excel spreadsheets. If you recall, the features in Table Analytics were more intuitive operations on your spreadsheet and didn't use any specific data mining terms. After the Table Analytics you learned the Data Mining tools that help you to create and visualize data mining models on tabular data in Excel or even from external data sources. Finally, you learned to visualize mining models using Visio 2007 and the ability to add annotation to your mining models so that you can present them efficiently to the business decision-makers. We believe this chapter has provided you the ability to use the Table Analytics and the Visio templates effectively along with an introduction to the Data Mining Tools add-in. For an in-depth understanding of Microsoft SQL Server 2008 Data Mining Add-ins for Office 2007 and all the algorithms in Data Mining Tools in SQL Server Analysis Services 2008, please refer to the book *Data Mining with Microsoft SQL Server 2008* by Jamie MacLennan, ZhaoHui Tang, and Bogdan Crivat (Wiley, 2008). In the next chapter you learn about SQL Server Integration Services 2008 (SSIS), its integration with SSAS 2008, and how the tasks and transforms in SSIS help you to perform certain SSAS operations effectively.

19

Integration Services

SQL Server Integration Services (SSIS, or Integration Services) 2008 is the improved version of SSIS 2005. It is similar to what used to be called Data Transformation Services (or DTS for short) in SQL Server 2000. Like the names suggest, this service is all about integrating data from disparate data sources to one or more destinations with the ability to apply transformations on the data based on business requirements. SQL Server Integration Services is a collection of utilities that helps you to Extract, Transform, and Load (ETL) data from heterogeneous data sources to one or more data destinations, apply transformations to clean the data before loading them to data destinations, bulk load data to OLTP and OLAP systems, perform predictive analytics with the Analysis Services Data Mining Services, and automate administrative tasks on relational and OLAP databases. Integration Services is not just about integrating data from and into databases; it helps you to perform operations on files ranging from simple file search operations on disk to transferring files using FTP. It also allows you to write managed code and execute it as a script, and define and automate your complex business processes as routine/scheduled tasks. Finally, the SSIS extensible object model allows you to build your own custom tasks and transform components that can be added to the SSIS platform.

An Enterprise Data Warehouse (EDW) is a data warehouse that serves an entire company rather than having individual data marts for each organization. Businesses use a single data warehouse to provide "one version of the truth" for many users. EDWs can be built in several ways. Because most companies generally have individual data marts, creating an EDW typically includes extracting data from multiple operational data sources of various kinds (database servers, FTP, files, Excel files), transforming them to match the warehouse schema, and loading them into tables. SQL Server Integration Services is designed to help in building the EDW and making the use of EDW more productive and reliable. The reason Integration Services is important to the Business Intelligence professional is simple; data is almost never clean or formatted quite the way you would like and the data almost always comes from heterogeneous data sources. It is imperative to get the data squared away and ready for processing, and Integration Services is one of the ways to accomplish that. It helps in presenting the right data in the right format. Although these things are important parts of the story, they are not the whole story. If there is one thing you have learned working through this book, it is that there are multiple ways to accomplish almost any given task. Integration Services adds a whole new dimension to that equation! It provides the functionality to do a specific operation via different methods and you can choose the one that is most convenient for you.

Integration Services is based on two fundamental principles, namely data flow and control flow. These are exposed as tasks and stored as packages. SSIS is used to move data from a source to a destination (including whatever transformations are appropriate). A simple scenario would be to extract data from one operational store, do a simple transformation, and load the data into a data warehouse. The Data Flow components of SSIS handle the extraction, transformation, and loading using true data pipeline architecture that makes efficient use of CPU pipelining and parallelism (CPU and I/O). Not all data movement scenarios are simple. Even simple scenarios need controls on exception handling, logging controls, and dependency management. The data flow pipeline and the process control components give you the basic workflow, which SSIS provides through the Control Flow components. Precedence constraints are what connect tasks in a control flow and define the criteria for progression through the package. Control flow elements take account of cases such as some tasks that fail should result in the termination of the whole package, whereas failure for another task might mean nothing more than a speed bump and the processing should continue. In this chapter you see examples of SQL Server Integration Services tasks and transforms that help you manage your SQL Server Analysis Services efficiently.

Creating an Integration Services Project

At this point, it may come as no surprise that a data source formulated for use in Integration Services isn't any different than a data source formulated for use with Analysis Services. Not only that, but Data Source Views play the same role across both Integration Services and Analysis Services. A great benefit of having a common data source is to share it across multiple SSIS packages. Perhaps you recall from earlier in this book that Data Source Views are similar to views in SQL Server. If you want to work with a limited set of tables, that is, a view in the relational world, you can emulate that using a Data Source View when creating SSIS packages. If you want to use the same table more than once for certain operations, you can create named queries, all of which utilize a shared data source connection in turn. You learn more about these capabilities when creating an SSIS package.

The Integration Services Task

In this chapter you learn specifically about Analysis Services–related tasks, but you should know that there are many control flow items (most of which are tasks) and several maintenance plan tasks. Examples of commonly used tasks are the Send Mail task, which is used to notify the administrator of job status; the Bulk Insert task, which is used to insert data from flat files into tables at high speed; and the Data Flow task, which contains a number of transforms internally — a container that helps to complete tasks like merging data and then sorting it, and so on. One capability of interest regarding the tasks is that the product allows you to have multiple tasks in the designer that can be executed in parallel — more on that later this chapter.

The Integration Services Transform

The process of populating data warehouses and data marts requires clean data. Getting to clean data requires the use of capabilities found in Data Flow Transformations. These transforms can be used, for example, to sort, merge, and transform data. Because there are many transforms under Data Flow Transformations, there is no lack of possibilities you can use to make your data conform to whatever format and design you wish it to take.

In Chapter 1 you saw an example that included various representations of Microsoft such as MSFT, MS, Microsoft, and MSoft. These different representations from various source systems might cause some difficulties; there could be a strong business need to have a standard format and merge the relevant data. SSIS fuzzy look-up transformations help you in achieving the transformation by means of comparing the various Microsoft strings and deriving a standardized output MSFT. You can use the lookup transforms and do conditional split transforms, or write your own code to perform this operation using the script transform. This example demonstrates a typical data cleansing operation with SSIS transforms and multiple ways of achieving the end goal.

Creating Integration Services Packages for Analysis Services Operations

Using Integration Services is convenient and improves administration productivity by executing administrative tasks on a periodic basis on Analysis Services. Integration Services provides several tasks and transforms that are specifically designed for integration with Analysis Services to help you in building packages in the Business Intelligence Development Studio (BIDS) you have been working with in Analysis Services 2008.

The Execute DDL Task

The Execute DDL task is used for sending a DDL script to Analysis Services. This task is typically used to accomplish administrative tasks like backup, restore, or sync operations that need to be performed on a periodic basis. You can also use this task to send process statements to Analysis Services for processing Analysis Services objects or include this task along with other Integration Services tasks to create a more generalized package; for example, dynamically creating a new partition in a cube by analyzing the fact data — and then processing that partition. To create a package that will backup your Analysis Services database on a periodic basis, do the following:

1. Open BIDS and load the AnalysisServices2008Tutorial project sample available for download on this book's web site at www.wrox.com.

2. Once you have loaded it, go ahead and deploy the project. This specific project has some additions to the ones you have created earlier, so make sure the full project is deployed.

3. While still in BIDS, create a new Integration Services project named IntegrationServicesTutorial by selecting File ⇨ New ⇨ Project and selecting the Integration Services Project template. You will now be in the Integration Services project shown in Figure 19-1.

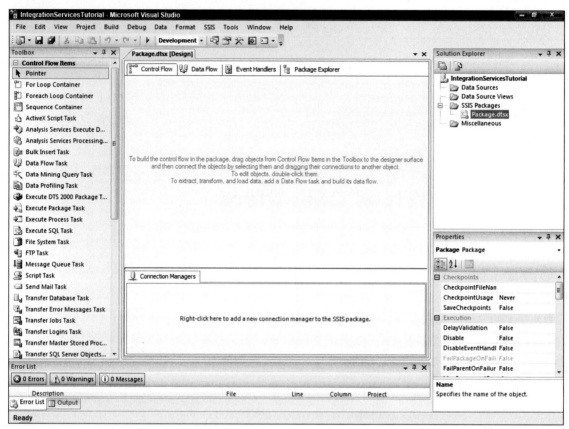

Figure 19-1

The Solution Explorer window shows four folders containing the following: Data Sources, Data Source Views (DSVs), SSIS Packages, and Miscellaneous as shown in Figure 19-1. As with Analysis Services you can create connections to data sources and add them to a data source object. The main purpose of data sources is to share connections between multiple SSIS packages within a single project. Again, as with an Analysis Services project, DSVs help you create a subset of tables, views, named queries, and named calculations that can be used by SSIS packages rather than creating equivalent views on your relational backend. If you are designing a single SSIS package that uses a database too small to merit a view, you might not use the Data Source Views. The Properties window helps you to define properties of various objects. The primary objective of SSIS is to retrieve data from a source, perform some operations to transform the data, and store the data at a destination. Therefore, we expect most of the SSIS projects will have some form of connection object. Familiarize yourself with the design surface and the various other windows in SSIS. All the connections used in your SSIS package will be shown in the Connection Managers window thereby providing a consolidated view. If you right-click in the Connection Managers window you can see the various types of connections that SSIS supports. The main window, which is a graphical designer, is used to create SSIS packages. The SSIS Design window has four views: Control Flow, Data Flow, Event Handlers, and Package Explorer. You explore the use of these views in this chapter.

All the tasks and transforms provided by SSIS are represented within the Toolbox window. To see the Toolbox window, click View ⇨ Toolbox in the drop-down menu. The Toolbox window can be docked by clicking the pin icon as shown in Figure 19-2.

4. Drag and drop the SQL Server Analysis Services Execute DDL task to the Control Flow tab. You will now see the task in the window as shown in Figure 19-2.

The SSIS designer in BIDS completes a validation on every task and transform in your package. Each task has a certain set of required properties and some optional properties. If the required properties are not specified, you will see a red "x" mark within the task. If the optional properties are not defined you will see a yellow "x" mark within the task. If any of the tasks or transforms within your package have a red "x" mark, that indicates that there is an error in your package and you will not be able to run the package without resolving the error. The Execute DDL task needs the connection details to Analysis Services and the DDL to execute. Because these properties have not been defined when you drag and drop the task in your editor, you will see a red "x" mark as shown in Figure 19-2.

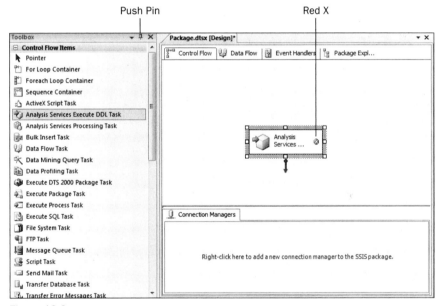

Figure 19-2

5. One of the properties for the Execute DDL task is to specify the connection details to an Analysis Services database. To create a connection to the AnalysisServices2008 Tutorial database, right-click the Connection Managers window. You can see all the various types of connections SSIS supports as shown in Figure 19-3. Select New Analysis Services Connection.

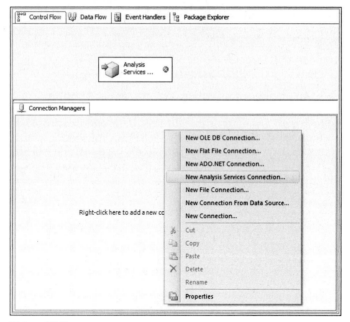

Figure 19-3

The Add Analysis Services Connection Manager dialog is launched as shown in Figure 19-4. You have the option of establishing a connection to an Analysis Server database or to an Analysis Services project within your solution. BIDS supports having multiple projects within the same solution. This means that you can have Analysis Services and Integration Services projects within the same solution. If you are building an SSIS package for the Analysis Services project within the same solution, you would choose the second option.

6. Select the first option as shown in Figure 19-4 and click Edit.

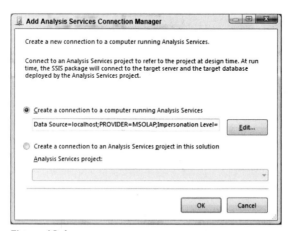

Figure 19-4

7. In the Connection Manager dialog you can specify the connection details to your Analysis Services database such as Server or file name and the Initial catalog as shown in Figure 19-5. After you have specified the connection details, click OK to complete both dialogs.

Figure 19-5

8. To specify properties needed by the Execute DDL task, double-click the Execute DDL task object within the designer. You will see the Execute DDL Task Editor as shown in Figure 19-6. Click the DDL option.

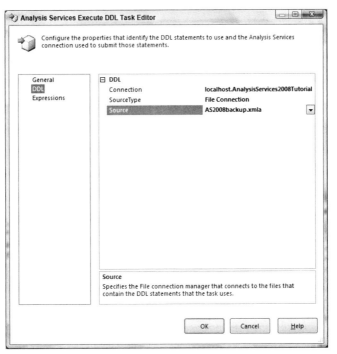

Figure 19-6

9. From the drop-down list for Connection you can either create a new connection or select an existing connection. Select the Analysis Services connection you established in step 7. There are three ways of specifying the DDL to be executed:

❑ **Enter the DDL in a text box:** Whenever you know that your DDL is static and will not change you can use this option.

❑ **Specify a connection to the file:** This option is used whenever you have a file containing the DDL. This file can be static or dynamic in the sense that the DDL contents can be changed by another operation, such as a different SSIS task or an external program.

❑ **Specify the DDL using a variable in the SSIS package where the value of the variable is the actual DDL:** This option is used whenever the results from one task need to be used as an input to another task. The variable can be initialized during package execution, or the task setting the value for the variable needs to be executed before the Execute DDL task in the control flow.

10. Select the source type as File Connection. Select the drop-down list under Source and select New Connection. In the File Connection Manager dialog, select the DDL file AS2008backup.xmla provided under the Chapter 19 directory of the downloaded sample from the web site. The following shows the contents of the DDL. This DDL will take a backup of the Analysis Services 2008 Tutorial database.

```
<Backup xmlns="http://schemas.microsoft.com/analysisservices/2003/engine">
  <Object>
    <DatabaseID>AnalysisServices2008Tutorial</DatabaseID>
  </Object>
  <File>AnalysisServices2008Tutorial.abf</File>
</Backup>
```

11. Once you have specified all the properties for the Execute DDL Task Editor as shown in Figure 19-6, click OK.

If you run the SSIS package you have created, a backup of the Analysis Services 2008 Tutorial database will be created in Program Files\Microsoft SQL Server\MSAS10.MSSQLSERVER\OLAP\Backup. Backup is usually an operation scheduled for when the load on Analysis Services is minimal. Many companies do backup operations on a nightly basis, but if you are a multinational company or have customers using the database across the globe, you would have to factor in your customers' needs and take the backup at an appropriate time.

Regardless of when the package is run, you want to know whether the operation succeeded or failed. Obviously you can check the logs on Analysis Services or the logs of the SSIS package, but as an administrator one of the easiest ways is to send an email about the results of the operation. To facilitate this operation, SSIS provides a task called the Send Mail task. By specifying appropriate parameters to this task you can send an email upon completion of a specific task or an entire SSIS package.

12. To add the Send Mail task to your SSIS package, drag and drop two instances of the Send Mail task to your designer.

You will use one task to send an email when the Execute DDL task succeeds and the other one to send mail when the Execute DDL task fails. Now that you have two Send Mail tasks in the Control Flow pane, it is time to connect the Execute DDL task to the Send Mail tasks.

13. You can connect tasks in a control flow by clicking the originating object (a downward facing green arrow will appear) and dragging the arrow end to the target object. Do that for the first Send Mail task.

14. For the second Send Mail task, just click the Execute DDL task again and you will see another green arrow appear as an output of the item. Drag the green arrow and connect it to the next Send Mail task. Your package should look like the one shown in Figure 19-7.

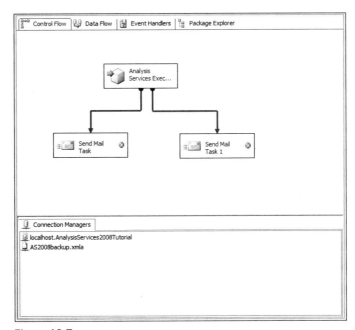

Figure 19-7

The connecting line represents precedence constraint functionality; in fact, if you double-click the green line, the Precedence Constraint Editor will appear. The green lines indicate success, and whenever the Execute DDL task completes successfully, execution continues with the task connected on the success line.

15. To configure the second mail task to send email on failure, double-click the connecting line.

You should see the Precedence Constraint Editor as shown in Figure 19-8. The connecting line between the two tasks has several properties that are evaluated after the completion of the source task. You can specify an expression and/or constraint that can be evaluated after the completion of the task. The value property of the connecting line helps you to choose the constraint and determines whether the control will be transferred to the next task. The three options for the value property are Success, Failure, and Completion. Change the value from Success to Failure. You can also configure the precedence control by right-clicking the connecting line between two tasks and selecting Success, Failure, or Completion.

16. Click OK after you have completed specifying the constraint value to Failure as shown in Figure 19-8.

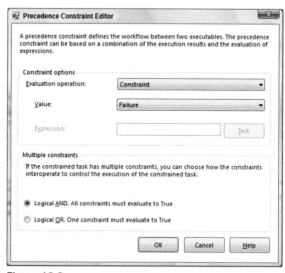

Figure 19-8

17. You need to specify the mail server and details of the mail content in the properties of the Send Mail task. Double-click the Send Mail task to configure the properties of the task. The Send Mail Task Editor is shown in Figure 19-9. Specify the details of the mail server by clicking the drop-down list of the SmtpConnection property. Your company should have an SMTP server. Contact your IT administrator to get details on the name of your SMTP server. Specify the email address from which you want this mail to be sent, the people who need to receive the status of this package execution, and the content of the mail, as shown in Figure 19-9. Based on the Send Mail task you have chosen, provide the appropriate subject and message source. Figure 19-9 shows the contents of the Send Mail task that will be executed on successful completion of the Execute DDL task created in a previous step.

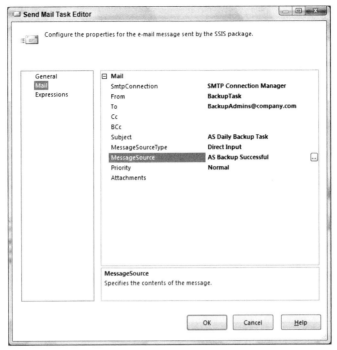

Figure 19-9

18. Make sure the second Send Mail task properties are appropriately changed to reflect the failure of the backup of the Analysis Services database.

19. Rename the Send Mail tasks as Send Mail Success and Send Mail Failure by changing the name of the tasks as shown Figure 19-10. Appropriate naming makes the SSIS package easily readable and can be interpreted immediately by another person working on this task.

Green Line   Red Line

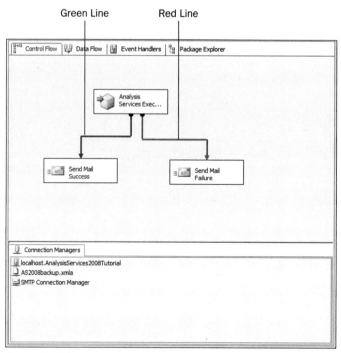

Figure 19-10

20. The SSIS package is now ready for execution. You can select Debug ⇨ Start, hit the F5 key, or right-click the package name and select Deploy.

The BIDS now starts the execution of the SSIS package. The BIDS will operate in the debugging environment, similar to debugging a program. You will first see the SQL Server Analysis Services Execute DDL task highlighted in yellow as shown in Figure 19-11, which indicates that the task is currently under execution. If the task completed successfully, the status of the task is shown in green, and if it failed the status is shown in red. You do have the ability to insert break points, and analyze variables used within tasks or transforms in the debug environment. Once the entire package is completed, status on each of the tasks is shown; that is, the two tasks are shown in green having completed successfully.

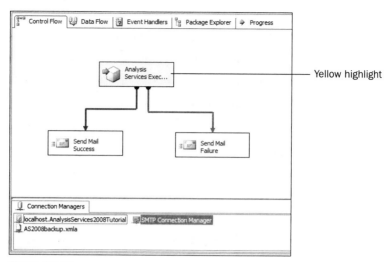

Figure 19-11

21. In the debug environment you can see detailed information for each task and the time taken by the task for completion in the Progress window. You can switch to the Progress window when the package is being executed. The Progress window gets updated when the control moves from one task to another. Figure 19-12 shows the progress report of the execution of the package. You can see that the DDL Execute task, which took a backup of an Analysis Services database, took 47 seconds to complete.

Figure 19-12

Processing an Analysis Services Object

SSIS provides a task for processing Analysis Services objects. You can process an entire Analysis Services database or choose a specific dimension, cube, or even partitions for processing using the SSIS task called the SQL Server Analysis Services Processing task. The Analysis Services Processing task is useful whenever you have changes in your relational data that need to get propagated to the cube. Often retail companies have new products added to their catalog every day, and the products table gets updated with the new products or changes in existing products as a daily batch process. Also, the daily sales data gets updated in the relational database as a nightly batch process. To propagate these changes to the cube for analysis, the dimensions and cubes need to be processed unless you have set the storage mode as ROLAP for dimensions and cubes. Several considerations are involved in determining frequency of processing. Should cubes be processed on a daily, weekly, or monthly basis? The decision to process the Analysis Services objects is typically based upon the size of the dimensions and cubes, how often data changes on the relational database, and the frequency with which business analysts analyze the cube data. In most cases there are additions to the products table rather than updates, and hence an incremental process of the products table might be sufficient. If your fact table gets updated with daily transactional data in the same table, you have the option of creating new partitions in the cube on a daily/weekly basis or doing a full process of the cube. The Microsoft operations guide for Analysis Services suggests you have a new partition for every 20 million records or when the partition file reaches 5GB — in this way you can achieve optimal performance. How you partition your data is based on decisions that relate to your business needs. To create an Integration Services package that processes an Analysis Services Sales partition, do the following:

1. Right-click the SSIS Packages folder and select New SSIS Package. Name the package PartitionProcessing.

2. Similar to what you did in the Backup package earlier in this chapter, create a connection to the AnalysisServices2008Tutorial database in the Connection Managers window.

3. Drag and drop the SQL Server Analysis Services Processing task and two Send Mail tasks into the SSIS designer

4. Configure one of the Send Mail tasks for success and another one for failure. Make the connections from the Analysis Services Processing task to Send Mail tasks similar to the Analysis Services Backup package you created in the previous example. Double-click the SQL Server Analysis Services Processing task. This launches the Analysis Services Processing Task Editor as shown in Figure 19-13. This dialog is similar to the Processing dialog of Analysis Services, which you learned about in previous chapters.

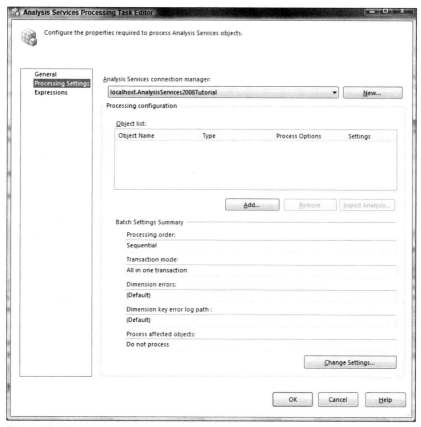

Figure 19-13

If you click the Change Settings button, the Change Settings dialog pops up as shown in Figure 19-14. The Change Settings dialog allows you to process the selected Analysis Services objects sequentially or in parallel. You can use the Dimension Key Errors tab to configure the processing options so that appropriate actions are taken when errors are encountered during the processing operation. The selected option will apply to all the Analysis Services objects chosen in the Analysis Services Processing Task Editor.

Figure 19-14

5. To add Analysis Services objects for processing, click the Add button on the Analysis Services Processing Task Editor (see Figure 19-13). The Add SQL Server Analysis Services Object allows you to choose the object you want to process. Select the Fact Internet Sales Partition as shown in Figure 19-15 and click OK. Click OK again to accept the modifications in the Analysis Services Processing Task Editor dialog.

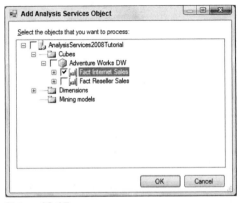

Figure 19-15

6. Press the F5 button on your keyboard to deploy the SSIS processing package and make sure it executes correctly. If everything has been specified correctly you will see successful completion of the SQL Server Analysis Services Processing task and the Send Mail Success tasks — also, these tasks will be highlighted in green indicating the successful execution. Of course you do need appropriate privileges on the Analysis Services instance to perform these operations.

Loading Data into an Analysis Services Partition

Typically, the data from the transactional source database (production system) is extracted, staged to some intermediate storage, and then undergoes transformations before being stored in a data warehouse (flat file or relational format). This data then needs to be propagated to the cube for analysis. Analysis Services has the ability to read data from various data sources from flat files to various relational databases. One way to add new fact data to the cube is to create new partitions that read data from the data sources. You can use SSIS's Script task to create a new DDL, execute the DDL using the Execute DDL task, and then process the partition using the Analysis Services Processing task. You can create a package that will integrate all these tasks. Even though you can utilize these tasks to load fact data, it is not easy to load new dimension data to an existing dimension table. Therefore, SSIS provides an easy way to load new fact and dimension data into your current cube using SSIS transforms. The two transforms that help in loading such data are the Partition Processing transform and the Dimension Processing transform.

Many large retail stores still use flat files to extract data from the transactional systems. Your company probably does the same. Often the columns in the flat files do not contain clean data. During the staging process you clean the data and format it with appropriate IDs that match your cube in order to load the data into your cube. SSIS provides transformations to do lookups, get the correct IDs, clean the data on the fly, and then load the data into your cube. In the following example you will be working with clean data that needs to be loaded from a flat file into one of the partitions of the AnalysisServices2008Tutorial cube:

1. Create a new SSIS package under the SSIS Packages folder and name it PipelineDataLoad.

2. The SSIS task that helps you to read data, perform transforms, and then push the data into a destination is called the Data Flow task. Drag and drop the Data Flow task into your SSIS editor as shown in Figure 19-16 and name it Data Flow Partition Load.

Figure 19-16

Double-click the Data Flow task. You will now be in the Data Flow view. The Toolbox window will show you the SSIS transforms available for use in the Data Flow view. The data flow transforms are categorized into three main areas, namely, data flow sources, data flow transformations, and data flow destinations. Data to be loaded into the partition of the Analysis Services 2008 Tutorial cube is provided as a flat file in the Chapter 19 samples folder named AdventureWorksPartition3Data.txt. To retrieve this data you need to use the Flat File Source transform. This data needs to be pushed to the partition in the Analysis Services2008Tutorial cube. Therefore, you need a Partition Processing transform.

3. Drag and drop the Flat File Source and Partition Processing transforms from the Toolbox to the Data Flow Editor and join them through the connector as shown in Figure 19-17.

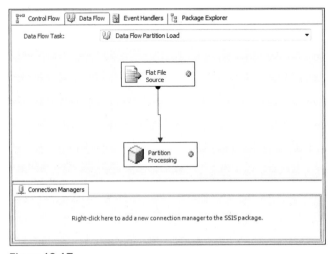

Figure 19-17

4. Double-click the Flat File Source transform to specify the connection to the flat file. You will now be in the Flat File Source Editor as shown in Figure 19-18. You need to specify the flat file using the Flat File Connection Manager. Click the New button.

Figure 19-18

5. The Flat File Connection Manager Editor dialog as shown in Figure 19-19 now pops up. Click the Browse button and select the flat file AdventureWorksPartition3Data.txt, which is available in the Chapter 19 samples that can be downloaded from the book web site. The dialog now parses the data in the flat file. You have the option to skip rows from the flat file if the first row or the first few rows indicate column headers. Click the Column Names in the First Data Row checkbox. You also need to specify the type of delimiter used in the flat file to separate the columns. Click Columns and set the delimiter as Tab as shown in Figure 19-20. To see if the dialog is able to read the data from the flat file correctly based on the delimiter, click the columns property.

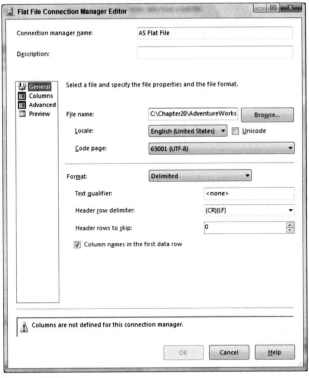

Figure 19-19

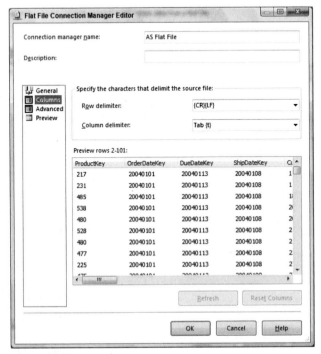

Figure 19-20

6. You will now see the data from the flat file organized as rows and columns as shown in Figure 19-20. After you have confirmed that the dialog is able to read the data in the flat file, click OK.

7. In the Flat File Source Editor dialog click Columns as shown in Figure 19-21. By default SSIS will use the column names to be the output column names. You can change the output column names in this dialog by editing the appropriate row. Leave the default names suggested by SSIS and click OK.

Figure 19-21

8. After configuring the flat file source, you need to specify the partition into which this data needs to be loaded. Double-click the Partition Processing transform in the Data Flow Editor. You can now see the Partition Processing Destination Editor as shown in Figure 19-22. Similar to the first two SSIS packages, you need to specify the connection to the database. Click the New button to specify the connection to the AnalysisServices2008Tutorial database. You will now see the cubes and partitions within the database.

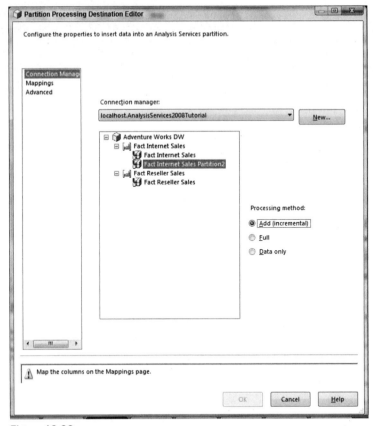

Figure 19-22

You now need to select the partition under which the data needs to be loaded and specify the processing method that needs to be applied. If the data is new you typically need to use the Add (Incremental) option that processes the partition incrementally. Processing the partition incrementally means that the new data will be incrementally added to the cube while the current data is available for querying. Once the new data has been processed, the data is committed and it is available for querying. The incremental processing method's primary functionality is to serve the customer's queries even when the new data is being added to the partition. In addition, you get the performance benefit of only adding the new rows to the partitions rather than re-processing the entire partition. Analysis Services is able to accomplish this by cloning the existing version of the partition and adding data to that. Once the entire data has been processed in the new version of the partition, and when the original partition is free from any query locks, Analysis Services switches the versions and the new version containing the entire data set is now available for querying.

9. Select Fact Internet Sales Partition2 as the partition to add the data and Add (incremental) as the processing method as shown in Figure 19-22.

A more typical package using the Partition Processing transform will contain several lookup transforms to map the incoming dimension columns to the right ID in the dimensions of the OLAP database. Once the correct ids for each dimension are obtained, retrieved dimension ID columns are mapped to the partition processing columns to load the data.

10. Click Mappings as shown in Figure 19-23 to specify the right mappings from the columns from the flat file to the columns in the partition. The columns in the flat file have been specified to be the same names as the ones in the cube. Hence you will find it easy to map each column directly as shown in Figure 19-23. Make sure you mark all the columns correctly in this page. You can ignore the Dim Geography.Dim Geography destination column because Dim Geography is a reference dimension and hence the key for this dimension does not exist in the fact table. Click OK after completing all the mappings in the Partition Processing Destination Editor.

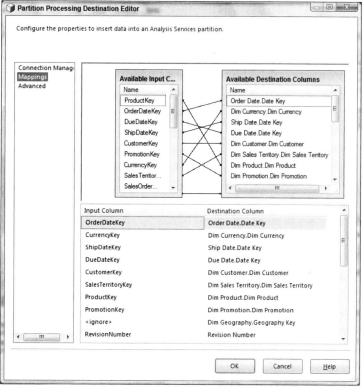

Figure 19-23

11. You have completed all the necessary settings in the SSIS package to load data into a partition. Hit the F5 key to test the execution of your SSIS package. You will see that the background colors of the two data flow transforms Flat File Source and Partition Processing are highlighted in yellow indicating that the SSIS package is being executed. Along the connector line between the two transforms Flat File Source and Partition Processing, you can notice the number of rows being processed as shown in Figure 19-24.

Figure 19-24 shows a snapshot of the SSIS package execution. After all the data has been loaded without errors, you will see the background color of the two transforms turn to green indicating successful completion of the package. During this SSIS operation that does incremental processing, Analysis Services creates a new temporary partition, loads the data from flat file, and then merges the partition to Internet Sales Partition 2. We believe there is a potential bug in Analysis Services 2008 that causes the partition processing to fail since the data source of the partition and the flat file are not the same. We plan to provide an update on the book's web site for this sample. In order to understand partition processing, we recommend you load the flat file data to a relational database, change the source from flat file source to OLE DB source, and retrieve the same data from the new table.

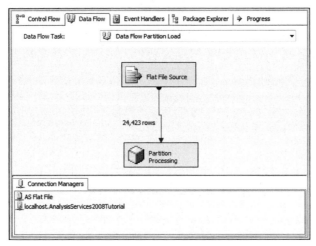

Figure 19-24

In the preceding data load example there was one-to-one mapping between the columns in the flat file and the measures and granularity attributes of the partitions, except for the reference dimension granularity attribute DimGeography. This was possible because all the measures in the partition directly mapped to the columns in the flat file. Assume you have a fact data column that was used twice in a measure group as two measures: one with Sum as the aggregation function and another as Count or Distinct Count as aggregation functions. Such a scenario is pretty common. In this scenario you will not be able to map the corresponding column from the flat file to the two measures because the SSIS Partition Processing transform disallows a column from the source (in this example, the flat file) to be mapped to multiple destination columns that are part of the partition. If you ignore mappings even for a single destination column that is part of the partition, your data load will fail. You would need to either have additional columns in the source so that you can map those to the corresponding columns in the partition or use the SSIS transform Copy Column to duplicate existing columns to serve as input to the Partition Processing transform. We recommend you modify the AdventureWorks2008Tutorial database to have a distinct count measure in Internet Sales partition and then create an SSIS package with the Copy Column transform between the Flat File Data Source and Partition Processing transforms to map the column from the flat file to the distinct count measure.

You have successfully learned to create SSIS packages for performing administrative tasks on Analysis Services such as backup and processing. Other administrative tasks such as synchronization, restore, and so on, can be performed using the tasks and transforms provided by SSIS. In addition to providing tasks and transforms for OLAP features, SSIS also provides tasks and transforms for data mining, which you learn about in the next section.

Integration Services Tasks for Data Mining

SSIS 2008 provides tasks and transforms specifically targeted for Data Mining objects in Analysis Services 2008. With the Data Mining Query task you can query mining models and store the results in a destination like a relational database. One of the common uses of such a task is to predict a list of customers for a targeted marketing campaign. If the company wants to offer promotional discounts to targeted customers every month, they would predict if a new customer is valuable based on the customer's attributes, calculate an appropriate discount, and mail them a coupon. The Data Mining Query transform is used when you want to manipulate the source data to the mining model or the output of the mining model in a better format. For examples and illustrations of Integration Services Tasks for Data Mining please refer to *Professional Microsoft SQL Server 2008 Integration Services* by Brian Knight, et al. (Wiley, 2008).

Automating Execution of SSIS Packages

Integration Services works on a slightly different model compared to Analysis Services. With Analysis Services, you deploy projects to the server; not so with Integration Services. There are three ways to make a package available to Integration Services; first through SQL Server, second through the file system, and finally through the SSIS Package Store (which is a variant of the file system solution). Here we'll look at the file system approach. Specifically, from BIDS, you save off a package in the form of an XML file (a .dtsx file). You might be wondering why the extension dtsx. As mentioned earlier, SSIS was originally called DTS in SQL Server 2000 and hence the file extension starts with dts. You can see the source for a .dtsx by right-clicking a package in Solution Explorer and selecting View Code. After you check that out, do the following:

1. In BIDS Solution Explorer, click one of your working packages and select File ⇨ Save <filename> As and give the file a descriptive name. In this way you save off an XML version of the package to the file system.

2. Next, open up SSMS and connect to Integration Services; open it in Object Explorer, and right-click Stored Packages. At this point you can select Import Package as shown in Figure 19-25.

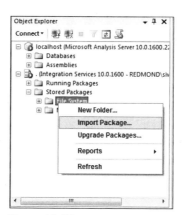

Figure 19-25

3. The Import Package dialog will appear and you should change Package Location from SQL Server to File System. Then click the button associated with Package Path to specify the dtsx file you want. If you just click the Package Name textbox, it will fill in the package name for you. At this point, the dialog should look something like Figure 19-26.

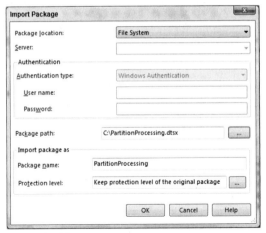

Figure 19-26

With the package in the Stored Packages area, you can easily run it by right-clicking the package name and selecting Run Package. What you really want to be able to do, however, is schedule to have your package run on a regular basis so you don't have to think about it. Scheduling SSIS packages to be run periodically can be accomplished by using the SQL Server Agent. The Agent is its own process, which you can access by opening a connection to the Database Engine as shown in Figure 19-27.

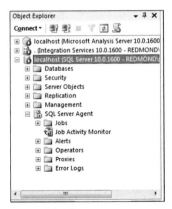

Figure 19-27

4.   To create a scheduled job, right-click the Jobs folder and select New Job. Give it an appropriate name and description as shown in Figure 19-28.

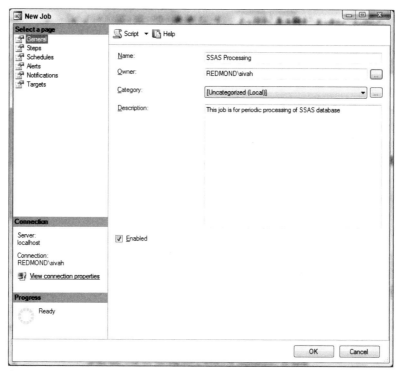

Figure 19-28

5. On the Select a Page pane at the top, click Steps. Click the New button that appears at the bottom of the dialog. On the New Job Step page, name your step SSAS Processing and under Type (type of operation) select SQL Server Integration Services Package as shown in Figure 19-29.

6. For the Package Source you need to select File System (because you will use the dtsx previously saved to the file system).

7. Click the ellipsis button for Package and select the package you saved before. At this time, your New Job Step dialog should look something like the one in Figure 19-29. Click OK to continue; when you are asked if the On Success action is intended, click Yes.

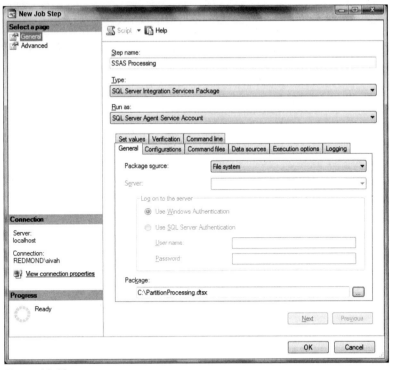

Figure 19-29

8. On the Select a Page pane at the top right, click Schedules and then the New button that appears at the bottom of the dialog. The dialog that comes up now is the New Job Schedule dialog; it is here that you can schedule your package to be run on a recurring basis. For illustrative purposes, select Schedule Type: One Time. Select today's date with a time of five minutes from now. After you have entered the details your job scheduler dialog should resemble Figure 19-30.

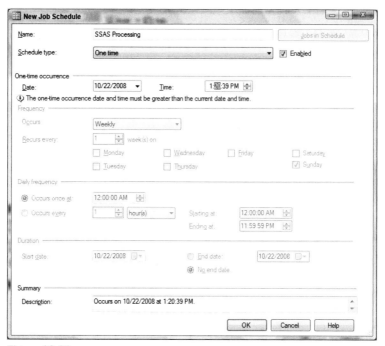

Figure 19-30

9. Click OK in the New Job Schedule dialog.

To see the job kicked off as scheduled, you only need to double-click the Job Activity Monitor icon, which is under the SQL Server Agent Folder in SSMS's Object Explorer. Once your job starts, you will see the Status change to Executing as shown in Figure 19-31.

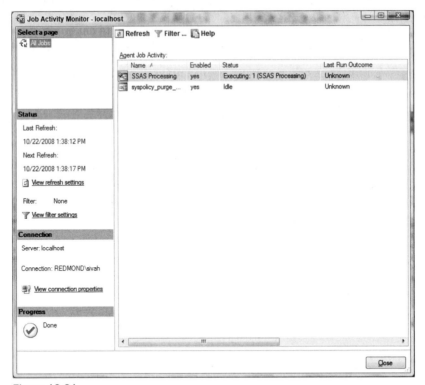

Figure 19-31

We're sure you can see the power of this approach — the ability to create packages chock full of administrative functions to manage your instance of Analysis Services, all scheduled to run on a recurring basis and send out emails based on success or failure. This is great stuff, especially for users who want to automate as much as possible and utilize their remaining time to learn and implement new things! We are confident you have gained sufficient knowledge of SSIS by now that you can create Analysis Services SSIS packages and schedule them. Make a habit of using SSIS when and where applicable for your business.

The SSIS tasks and transforms for SSAS 2008 were available in SQL Server 2005. There are enhancements made in SSIS such as data flow performance that can benefit your SSIS packages. In addition, SSIS 2008 supports Visual Studio Tools for Applications (VSTA) 2.0, which makes it easier to write reliable, robust, and secure scripts within SSIS packages. With VSTA you can write scripts using C# or other .NET programming languages, which helps you to create SSIS packages for SSAS 2008 using the Analysis Services Management Object (AMO). SSIS 2008 has made several enhancements to SSIS 2005 for better performance and scalability of tasks and transforms in addition to adding new tasks and transforms. For an in-depth understanding of SSIS 2008 features and enhancements, we recommend you read *Professional Microsoft SQL Server 2008 Integration Services* by Brian Knight, et al. (Wiley, 2008).

Summary

Integration Services provides the mechanism for automated tasks ranging from data cleansing, data split, to data merging. In this chapter you learned that a package must have a control flow and may also have data flows; the control flow is represented by tasks and containers, which are connected by precedence constraints. These precedence constraints determine the fate of a control flow after each step is completed. The precedence constraint can be an expression that leads to a success or failure condition, or the constraint can be set to "completion" without further consideration for continued control flow. Finally, you learned how to import packages into Integration Services using SSMS and create scheduled jobs of packages using SQL Server Agent.

In the previous chapter summary, you were promised a wonderful synergy between Integration Services and Analysis Services and from the section on "Creating Integration Services Packages for Analysis Services Operations" to "Automating Execution of SSIS Packages," you got it! The fun is not over, because in the next chapter, you learn about yet another profound and cool form of product synergy. Only this time it is about integrating Business Intelligence with Reporting Services. There is some amazing stuff in store, like designing static and ad-hoc reports on top of UDM. Don't miss it!

20

Reporting Services

Microsoft first introduced Reporting Services in January of 2004 under the product name SQL Server 2000 Reporting Services. SQL Server Reporting Services is a server-based report generation environment. It is used to deliver both interactive and printed reports. Since that time it has become an award-winning product (see the *Intelligent Enterprise* Reader's Choice award for Ad-Hoc Query & Reporting, 2004). Reporting Services 2005, in addition to providing several Reporting Services features, provided a tighter integration with Analysis Services with the ability to build reports easily using MDX and DMX query designers. Reporting Services servers 2000 and 2005 were hosted inside IIS. The Reporting Services 2008 server has been re-architected for scalability. Reporting Services 2008 is no longer hosted inside IIS. It is now based on components that provide high scalability for the database server. The Reporting Services service component is also streamlined so that rendering, Web Service enablement, and background processing (scheduling, subscriptions, delivery, and others) scale in proportion because they use a common memory management and application domain management substrate. More importantly, Reporting Services has become a critical part of many Business Intelligence solutions. Query, Reporting, and Analytics are the basis for classic Business Intelligence solutions. With SQL Server Reporting Services 2008, you can not only create tabular and matrix reports; you can add Gantt charts, Funnel, Pyramid, Histogram, Radar, and Pie Callout charts to regular tabular reports that show the results in a much more appealing and easy-to-understand fashion. Related to that is the ability to embed your own custom static graphics in your reports, like your company logo, for example. Microsoft ISVs and partners integrate seamlessly with Reporting Services to provide additional enhancements beyond those described here.

SQL Server Reporting Services is a free-form reporting environment. Not only can reports be built by dragging and dropping data objects onto a canvas with SQL subsequently generated behind the scenes, but you can also drag and drop Analysis Services–specific objects, like dimensions and calculated members, onto that same canvas with MDX subsequently generated behind the scenes. Using the Report Designer you can design reports from relational as well as multidimensional databases. Indeed, you get to use a highly integrated Business Intelligence reporting infrastructure that requires little more than drag-and-drop techniques to create reports.

Before you learn the techniques briefly mentioned here, you should understand the life cycle of reporting to deliver a key aspect of Business Intelligence functionality. The life cycle consists of 1) Report Authoring, 2) Report Management, and 3) Report Delivery. You learned about the basics of Business Intelligence tasks for organization in Chapter 1. Report Authoring is the process of designing the formats, identifying parameters that are needed, and creating the reports as needed by end users. Report Management deals with controlling who can view the reports and when to refresh the reports. Report Delivery deals with the techniques of how to alert or deliver reports to end users. You learn to do the following things in this chapter: how to create a report on top of a relational database, deploy that report to the reports server, and then browse it locally or over your corporate network or the Internet. You learn to create a report using an Analysis Services database from the Report Wizard, and further enhance your Analysis Services reporting skills by creating calculated members and using specific properties within a report. You also learn to create charts in reports for better representation of data, how to manage reports from the Reports Server front end, and finally, how to build ad-hoc reports from a UDM using the report builder capability.

Report Designer

Report Designer is used to design a report that includes the infrastructure and layout for a report. The infrastructure first requires specification of one or more data sources. Data sources supported include anything accessible through the list of Providers shown in the Data Link Properties dialog (what you're used to seeing when creating data sources for other purposes). For the extraction of specific data, you have query builders that facilitate the query building process. This is built into Business Intelligence Development Studio and hosts a similar look and feel to Analysis Services and Integration Services projects. These tools enable the creation of tabular and matrix-based reports using a common infrastructure called tablix data region. You learn about tabular and matrix reports through examples in this chapter. Tablix supports the needed features for tabular or matrix reports. It also enhances the Reporting Services 2005 matrix feature to provide parallel row/column support and dynamic nesting of column groups and parallel row groups for the Reporting Services 2005 tabular feature. In addition, charts types like Gantt, Funnel, Pyramid, Histogram, Radar, and Pie Callout are also supported in Reporting Services 2008. You can customize your report to span multiple pages based on conditionals and grouping; this capability supports readability as does the judicious use of fonts and colors. Note that less is often more when it comes to things like fonts and colors; the fewer variations displayed in a report, the more meaningful are those that are used. So, for best results, use the power of customization sparingly that includes parameterization and subreports. And the user can seamlessly navigate all these reports because you can provide clickable cells in the reports. Once you have defined your report, it can be previewed within the designer; only after you are pleased with the layout do you deploy the report to a Report Server.

Report Definition Language

Report Definition Language (RDL) is an XML-based language used to specify all the characteristics that make up a report; RDL is created in the Report Designer and manifests itself when a report is processed and viewed. When you create your report, all the definitions are in this form of XML. It is this definition that is deployed on to the server. If you are a reporting whiz, you might take to editing RDL files easily; all of the element definitions and appropriate XML Diagrams are described in Books On-Line. Beware that any malformed XML you feed the Report Server will likely have less than desirable consequences at runtime! The following table shows some sample report definition XML elements from Books On-Line:

Element	Parent	Description
Axis	CategoryAxis, ValueAxis	Defines properties for labels, titles, and gridlines on an axis.
DataCollectionName	Grouping	Contains the name of the data element of the collection containing all instances of the group in a report rendered using a data rendering extension, like the XML rendering extension.
Parameters	Drillthrough, Subreport	Contains a list of parameters to pass to the report or control.
Visible	Axis, DataLabel, Legend	Indicates whether the item is displayed in the chart.

Report Wizard

The Report Wizard provides time-saving functionality that simplifies the creation of the most basic reports; actually, you can get as sophisticated as you like in terms of query building because the Query Builder is covered in the wizard. Of course, you also have the option to create reports without use of the Report Wizard.

Report Server

As the name suggests; the Report Server "serves" reports to users. The manageability of the Report Server is provided through a web interface as well as through SSMS (SQL Server Management Studio). Some of the management tasks on Report Server include credentials definition, which is needed by Report Server to retrieve data from the data source, to provide appropriate access to the reports for end users, and to define a report execution schedule. You can cache the results of a report on Report Server, which really comes in handy when the report takes a long time to run (a batch SQL query is used to do this).

Creating a Report on a Relational Database

The Report Designer is used to design reports based on a relational database. The Report Designer provides the functionality to retrieve data from various data sources, design the actual report and, finally, deploy it. The Report Designer also allows you to preview the report before you deploy to the Report Server and provide subsequent access to various users. In this section you will be designing a report on Sales of products from the AdventureWorksDW2008 database. To design this report, perform the following steps:

1. Launch the BIDS and create a new Project.

2. In the Business Intelligence Projects Project Type, select Report Server Project and provide a new project name, as shown in Figure 20-1.

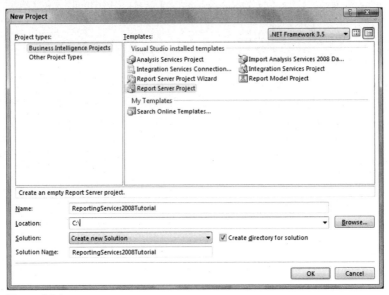

Figure 20-1

3. You will see two folders called Shared Data Sources and Reports in the Solution Explorer window. The Shared Data Sources folder is used to share data sources between multiple reports. Right-click the Reports folder and select Add New Report, as shown in Figure 20-2, to launch the Report Wizard.

Figure 20-2

4. If you get the Welcome page, dismiss it. The first real page of the Report Wizard allows you to specify the data source. The default data source type is Microsoft SQL Server, as shown in Figure 20-3. Click Edit to specify the data source connection detail.

Figure 20-3

5. In this example you will be creating a report based on the AdventureWorksDW2008 relational database. Specify the connection details in the Connection Properties dialog as shown in Figure 20-4. Click OK once you have tested the connection to the data source using the Test Connection button.

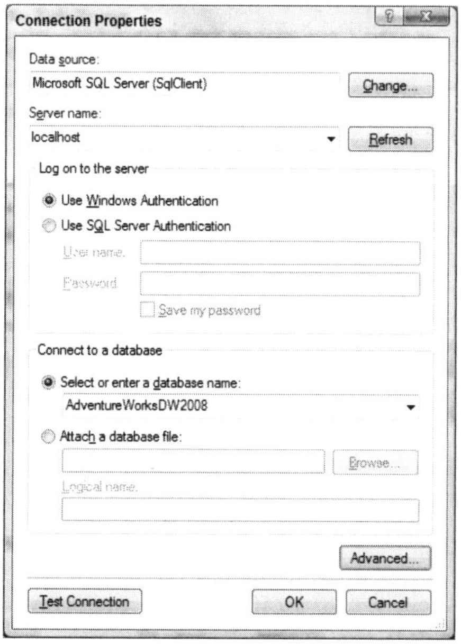

Figure 20-4

6. Click Next to see the Report Wizard's Design the Query page; here you will form the query to retrieve data from the relational data source using a query builder. Click Query Builder to launch the Query Builder page.

7. The default query builder page is a generic query builder that can be used against any relational data source. Click the leftmost icon on the query builder page to switch over to a graphical designer user interface. This query builder has four panes as shown in Figure 20-5.

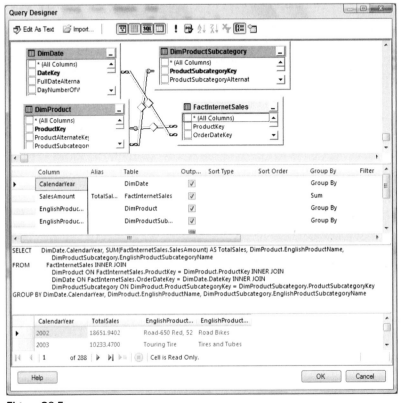

Figure 20-5

Initially, the Table Organizer pane is empty. Right-click within this pane and select Add Table. You will see the list of tables available within the AdventureWorksDW2008 database. Select the FactInternetSales, DimDate, DimProduct, and DimProductSubcategory tables and click Add. The query builder will retrieve the relationships between tables from the database and show them graphically in the Table Designer pane (see Figure 20-7). You can select the required columns from the Table Designer pane by clicking the checkboxes adjacent to the columns. The designer in the Query pane will create appropriate SQL queries. You can edit the selections in the Column Chooser pane or the query directly in the Query pane. The query used for retrieving the sales information in Figure 20-5 is shown here. Enter the SQL query in the query designer.

```
SELECT    DimDate.CalendarYear, SUM(FactInternetSales.SalesAmount) AS
             TotalSales,
       DimProduct.EnglishProductName,
       DimProductSubcategory.EnglishProductSubcategoryName
FROM     FactInternetSales INNER JOIN
       DimProduct ON FactInternetSales.ProductKey = DimProduct.ProductKey
       INNER JOIN
       DimDate ON FactInternetSales.OrderDateKey = DimDate.DateKey INNER JOIN
       DimProductSubcategory ON DimProduct.ProductSubcategoryKey =
       DimProductSubcategory.ProductSubcategoryKey
GROUP BY  DimDate.CalendarYear,
       DimProduct.EnglishProductName,
       DimProductSubcategory.EnglishProductSubcategoryName
```

If you already have a SQL query from which you want to create your report, you can type the query in the Query pane. The query designer will validate the query. If you click the exclamation (!) icon in the Query Builder page you can see the results of the query in the Result pane near the bottom of Figure 20-5. Click OK after you have completed the query and click Next in the Report Wizard.

8.   Next, you need to select the type of report to create as shown in Figure 20-6; the two forms of report available are the tabular report and the matrix report. In the tabular report, the report contains the values in the row column format similar to the relational tables. The columns have a header corresponding to the column and each row contains the values. In the matrix report there are headers for rows and columns and each cell in the report corresponds to a specific row and column. For example, you can have Time on rows and Cities on columns and the cells will indicate the sales amount of a product or a store for a given time and a city. Select the tabular report type and click Next.

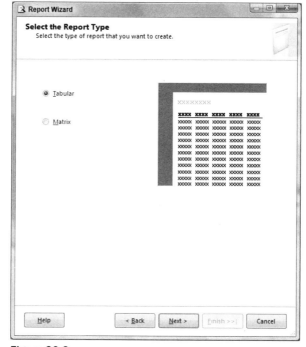

Figure 20-6

On the Design the Table page, you can choose the results from the data source to be shown in the report as well as how you want to show them. You can move the fields to one of the Page, Group, or Details panes. If you choose a specific field on the page, then for each value of that field a new page will be created that shows the fields in groups and details. A typical example would be to show the sales of products by each year or by each store. In this example you will be creating a report that creates a new page for the sales of products for each year.

9. Select the CalendarYear field and click the Page button. Rows can be grouped based on a specific field. For example, sales of various sizes of televisions in a store can be grouped under a category called TVs. In this example you will be grouping the sales of products based on the subcategory name. Grouping helps you to organize reports for enhanced readability. Select the EnglishProductSubCategoryName and click the Group button. Typically there is a one-to-many relationship between a field in the group and the fields in the details. The fields in the group are shown exactly once in the report. Select the fields for the detail level reporting. Select the TotalSales and EngineProductName fields and click the Details button. Your Design the Table page should look like Figure 20-7. Click Next.

10. On the Choose the Table Layout page you can choose the layout of the report, specify the visual layout, and include subtotals for groups. The Enable drilldown option, which allows you to drill down into the details of the report, can be enabled here too. Stepped and block report styles are quite similar; they only differ due to the values being housed in a block. If you click the options you can judge the visual impact of the final report. Select the desired options in the table layout page as shown in Figure 20-8 and click Next.

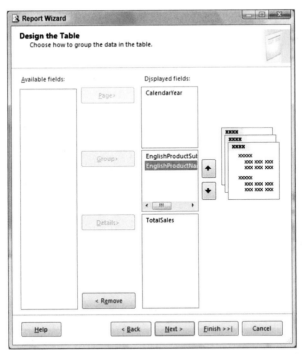

Figure 20-7

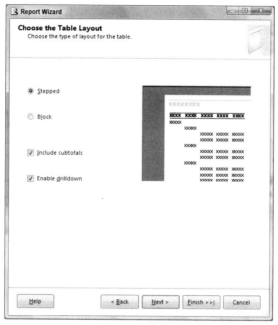

Figure 20-8

11. The next page of the Report Wizard provides you with the option to choose predefined report styles or templates. When you select the specific option you can see a preview of the style within the pane on the right side. The slate style is shown in Figure 20-9. Select the template of your choice and click Next.

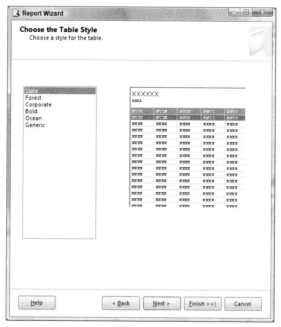

Figure 20-9

12. In the final page of the Report Wizard you can specify the name of your report. Enter the name **AdventureWorksDW2008SalesRelationalReport** and click Finish.

The Report Wizard creates the RDL for the report you designed, and you will now be in the Report Designer as shown in Figure 20-10. The Report Editor has two tabs: Design and Preview. The Design pane helps you create and edit data sources to modify your queries and design your report. The Preview pane helps you to preview the report within the Report Designer with your current credentials. The list of report items available to build your report is within the Toolbox window. If you do not have the Toolbox window showing, just select the menu item View and click Toolbox under that.

Now that you have created the report, you no doubt want to see a preview. Click the Preview tab to view the report you have created. Figure 20-11 shows the preview of the report you have created. This report spans multiple pages, one page for each Calendar Year. You have controls to move between various pages. Within each page you can see the product subcategories along with the sales information. Because the report is grouped and you selected the drilldown option, the default view of the report does not show all the details. You can click the + sign associated with a product subcategory to see the details of the total sales of that product category. You have now successfully created a simple report from a relational data source using Reporting Services 2008 and previewed the results of your report. You can design modifications to your report to change alignment, color, and other properties.

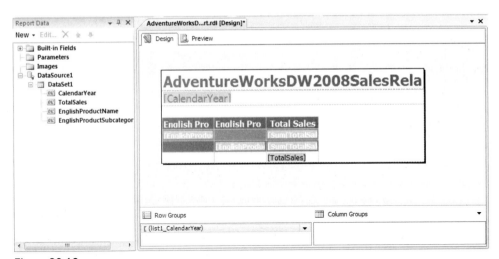

Figure 20-10

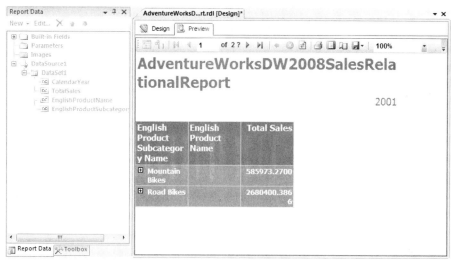

Figure 20-11

Creating Reports Based on a UDM

You have so far seen some capabilities provided by Reporting Services 2008 and how it can facilitate the creation of reports from a relational database. In Chapter 19 you learned the tight integration of Analysis Services with Integration Services that helps you load data into Analysis Services and perform administrative operations. By adding to those functions, Reporting Services 2008 provides you with the ability to create reports from the UDM by which Microsoft's SQL Server 2008 provides a truly end-to-end Business Intelligence solution to the market. Designing reports from Analysis Services 2008 databases is actually similar to designing reports from a relational database using Reporting Services 2008.

In the event you have experience with Reporting Services 2000 or 2005, you will be excited to know that Reporting Services 2008 contains both new features and extended capabilities associated with the original feature set. In Reporting Services 2000, specifying an MDX query and using the OLE DB provider for Analysis Services to integrate cube-based data into your reports was about the extent of the integration between the two products. There are significant improvements on that model; you will find much tighter integration existed between Reporting Services 2005 and Analysis Services 2005. There aren't major enhancements made with respect to integration between Report Services 2008 and Analysis Services 2008. However the enhancements made in Analysis Services 2008 should improve the query performance of your reports. In addition, the Reporting Services 2008 enhancements with respect to scalability of the Report Server and the new chart types can be leveraged within reports created from Analysis Services 2008. The MDX query designer in Report Designer enables you to retrieve data from any UDM through the technique of drag and drop, without you actually having to understand and write MDX queries. Assuming you have worked through this whole book, you already know some MDX. You have the option to write your own MDX query in the query designer, but your MDX query should only have two axes and be in a specific format of having measures on columns and dimension members in rows.

Some other points more than merit mention here. In the Reporting Services 2000 version, you could only pass a single parameter to Analysis Services from a report for dynamic report building. For example, you could send a single country name. Now, you can send a whole list of country names as parameters; this enhances what you can accomplish in terms of building dynamic reports. The ability to retrieve intrinsic properties for dimension members such as unique name, parent unique name, and so on, and cell properties such as background color, is intact with 2008, not to mention accessing member and extended properties. You are sure to love this next one — Reporting Services 2008 takes advantage of aggregated data provided by Analysis Services! This helps increase performance of report processing — especially when there is a large amount of source detail-level data (like sales per store) and the report includes aggregations based on that (like sales per region) but more importantly in the case where the aggregation of member values to their parent is semi-additive in nature such as Account dimension, which you learned in Chapter 8. There is much to like about the integration between Reporting Services and Analysis Services in this SQL Server 2008; report building directly off a UDM, for one, is awesome.

Designing Your Analysis Services Report

In this section you create a sales report from the UDM for the AdventureWorks2008Tutorial using the Report Wizard. You later refine the report based on certain requirements surprisingly imposed by your boss at the last moment. At the end of this section you will be familiar with creating specialized reports on a UDM. The following steps will help you to build reports from Analysis Services by establishing a connection to Analysis Services, building the MDX query, and previewing the report. Follow the steps to create your Analysis Services reports:

1. Open the AdventureWorks2008Tutorial under Chapter 20 from the book's site (www.wrox.com) and deploy it to your Analysis Services instance.

2. In the ReportingServices2008Tutorial project, right-click the Reports folder and select Add ⇨ New Item. Select the Report Wizard and click the Add button. If a Welcome to the Report Wizard page appears, click Next.

3. The first step in the Report Wizard is to provide the connection details to the data source. In the Data Source Wizard select the Microsoft SQL Server Analysis Services option for data source type, as shown in Figure 20-12.

4. Click the Edit button in the Select the Data Source page to launch the Connection Properties dialog. In the Connection Properties dialog enter the machine name of your Analysis Services instance, select the AdventureWorks2008Tutorial project as shown in Figure 20-13, and test your connection. Once your connection has been tested successfully, click OK.

Figure 20-12

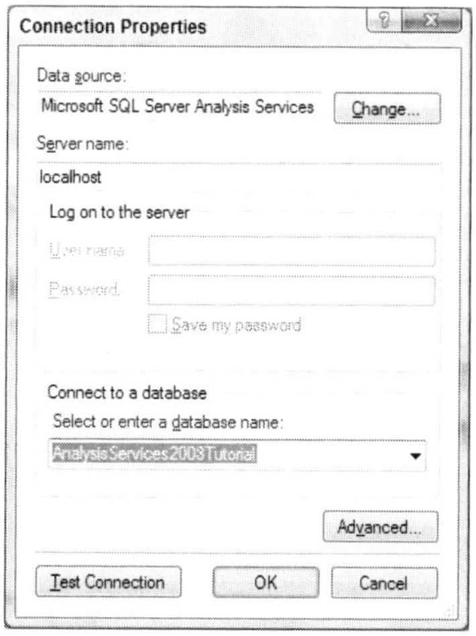

Figure 20-13

5. The next page of the Report Wizard is the Query Builder page. Click the Query Builder button to launch the MDX query builder shown in Figure 20-14. The MDX query builder contains a Metadata pane where you can select a specific cube from the database and see the measures and dimensions of the cube. There is a pane in which you can specify calculated members that will be within the scope of the query sent to your Analysis Services instance. There is a Filter pane to restrict data, and finally, there is a Data pane where you can drag and drop the dimensions and measures that you want to include in your report.

Figure 20-14

6. Drag and drop the measure Sales Amount in the Fact Internet Sales measure group from the Metadata pane to the Data pane. At this moment the MDX query builder creates the MDX query to retrieve the selected measure from the Analysis Services instance and shows the results in the Data pane. Using the Report Wizard you will create a report of Internet sales of products in the U.S. along with the customer's gender information. Drag and drop the gender attribute hierarchy from the customer's dimension and the State Province Name attribute hierarchy from the geography dimension, which indicates the customer's geographical location. You will now see results set in the Data pane. Because the UDM contains Internet sales information from various countries, you see the data for all the provinces of various countries.

7. To restrict the data to the provinces in the United States, drag and drop the English Country Region Name attribute from the Dim Geography dimension to the Filter pane. Similar to filtering data while browsing a UDM, set the filter expression equal to United States by selecting the United States member. You will see the Sales Amount for the Internet Sales measure group from various provinces within the United States along with the gender of the customer as shown in Figure 20-14. You can see the MDX query by switching from the graphical design view to the MDX query view by clicking the Design Query Mode icon shown in Figure 20-14.

❑ The MDX query generated by the query builder (which you can happily ignore if so inclined) is:

```
SELECT NON EMPTY { [Measures].[Sales Amount] } ON COLUMNS,
NON EMPTY { ([Dim Geography].[State Province Name].[State Province
Name].ALLMEMBERS
* [Dim Customer].[Gender].[Gender].ALLMEMBERS ) }
DIMENSION PROPERTIES MEMBER_CAPTION, MEMBER_UNIQUE_NAME ON ROWS
FROM (
  SELECT ( { [Dim Geography].[English Country Region Name].&[US] } ) ON COLUMNS
  FROM [Adventure Works DW])
  WHERE ( [Dim Geography].[English Country Region Name].&[US]
        )
CELL PROPERTIES VALUE, BACK_COLOR, FORE_COLOR, FORMATTED_VALUE, FORMAT_STRING,
FONT_NAME, FONT_SIZE, FONT_FLAGS
```

❑ The query generated by the MDX query builder within Report Designer is an MDX sub-select query. The preceding query contains two MDX select queries. The inner SELECT query restricts the cube space based on the member [Dim Geography].[English Country Region Name].&[US], and the outer SELECT query retrieves the data within the cube space provided by the inner SELECT query.

❑ One important thing you should be aware of in the MDX query builder is that if you switch from the design view to the MDX view and make changes, at that point you are at risk of losing the original configuration built in the design view if you then return to the design view. Therefore, we do not recommend that particular action — if you want to return to the design view. In the design view as you drag and drop fields, the automatically generated MDX query is executed immediately and displays the results. If you know that your query is going to retrieve a large result set, you can turn off the autoexecute query mode using the icon in the toolbar or by right-clicking in the Result pane and deselecting auto-execute mode. If you are an MDX expert, you might actually prefer to use the MDX view. In such a circumstance, switch to the MDX view, type in your MDX query, and then click Execute to ensure your query is correct and returns results expected by you. Click OK once you have selected the fields you need for the query.

8. The MDX query will now be shown in the Design the Query page, as shown in Figure 20-15. Click the Next button.

9. In the Select the Report Type page select the Tabular report, which is the default option, and click Next.

10. In the Design the Table page you will see the three fields you selected in the MDX query builder. In this report you will group the sales of customers based on the provinces. Therefore, select the State_Province_Name and click the Group button to move the field to the Group pane. Select the Gender and Sales_Amount fields and click the Details button to move the fields to the Details pane as shown in Figure 20-16.

Figure 20-15

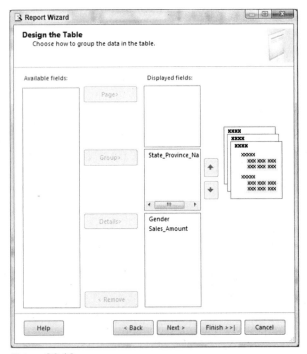

Figure 20-16

11. Similar to the relational report you created earlier, select Stepped layout in the next page. Select the option to have subtotals displayed as well as enable drilldown in this page as shown in Figure 20-17 and click the Finish button. In the final page of the wizard, name the report **AnalysisServicesSalesReport** and click the Finish button.

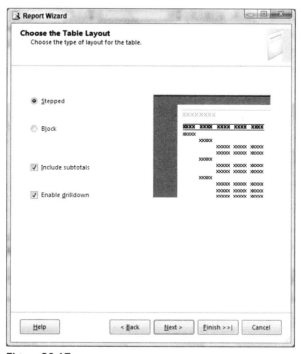

Figure 20-17

12. You will now be in the Design view of the Report Designer. Click the various items in the layout such as the table and the grouping row within the table based on the State Province, and look at their properties to have a brief overview of how the Report Wizard created your layout. Once you have created your report, you will want to see the behavior of the report before you deploy it on to your Report Server. To preview your report, click the Preview tab. You will now see a report as shown in Figure 20-18.

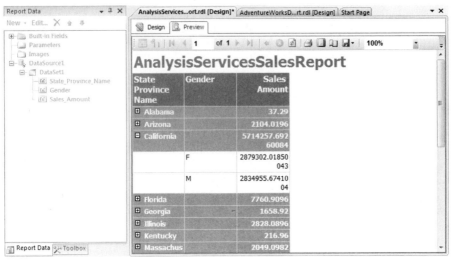

Figure 20-18

Enhancing Your Analysis Services Report

You have successfully created your first report on top of a UDM. This is a very basic report. The report you created in the previous section only includes the Sales Amount information for the states within the U.S. and the genders of various customers. In this section you enhance your report by including the countries, and instead of sales information you will be creating a report that shows sales profits of each state for various years.

First you need to change the query that retrieves the results from your Analysis Service instance. To change the MDX query, switch from the Preview pane to the Design pane. Because your new report needs to include the profit, you need to create a measure that will calculate the profit. The Adventure Works DW cube contains measures for Internet and Reseller sales along with the cost of the products sold over Internet and Reseller sales. You need to create calculated members in the cube to aggregate these data and then calculate the profit. Instead of creating these calculated measures within the cube, you know you can create calculated measures in an MDX query using the WITH MEMBER clause, which you learned about in Chapter 3. You can edit the dataset to launch the MDX query designer. The MDX query designer allows you to graphically specify these calculated members instead of writing the full MDX query. Creating the calculated members using the designer allows you to still work in the design mode. Follow the steps below to enhance your report:

1. Right-click the DataSet1 in the Report Data pane and select Query as shown in Figure 20-19. You will now be in the MDX Query Editor.

Figure 20-19

2. To create a calculated measure Total Sales, click the calculator icon or right-click in the Calculated Members pane (shown in Figure 20-14) and select New. The Calculated Member Builder dialog shown in Figure 20-20 will be launched.

3. Type **Total Sales Amount** in the Name text box for the calculated measure. Drag and drop the Sales Amounts from Fact Internet Sales and Fact Reseller Sales measure groups from the Metadata pane and add a plus (+) sign between these measures as shown in Figure 20-20. Click OK to create the calculated measure.

Figure 20-20

4. Create a calculated measure called Product Cost as the sum of the Total Product Cost measures from the Fact Internet Sales and Fact Reseller Sales measure groups.

5. Create a calculated measure called Total Profit, which is the difference between the numerical values in the calculated measures Total Sales Amount and Product Cost. You will now see the three calculated measures in the Calculated Members pane of the query builder as shown in Figure 20-21.

6. Remove the Internet Sales Amount measure from the Result pane by dragging and dropping the field from Result pane to the Metadata pane or by selecting the field, right-clicking, and selecting Remove.

7. Remove the field Gender from the Data pane.

8. Drag and drop the calculated member Total Profit from the Calculated Members pane to the Result pane. Add the attribute hierarchy English Country Region Name from the Geography dimension and Calendar Year hierarchy from the Order Date dimension to the data field as shown in Figure 20-21.

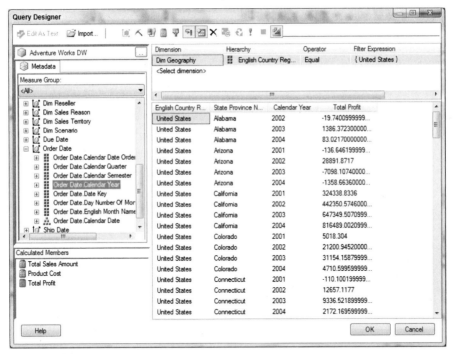

Figure 20-21

9. Click the filter English Country Region Name and drop down the Filter Expression list box. Select all the countries except Unknown from the list as shown in Figure 20-22.

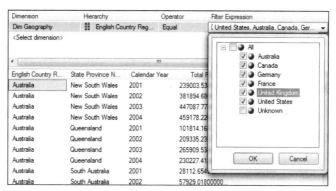

Figure 20-22

10. The Result pane now shows the Sales profit for various countries and provinces for all the years, as shown in Figure 20-23. Now you have all the data required for enhancing your report. Click OK in the Query Designer dialog. The Report pane now contains the fields State_Province_Name, English_Country_Region_Name, Calendar_Year, and Total_Profit as shown in Figure 20-24. You can now redesign the report using these fields.

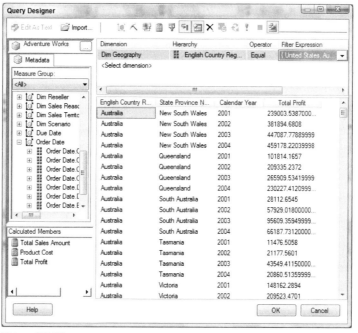

Figure 20-23

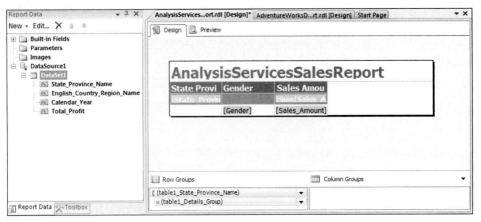

Figure 20-24

11. The Design pane contains an object that was used for the first report you created. This object, called table, includes the fields State Province Name, Gender, and Sales Amount as shown in Figure 20-24. A table report item is used whenever you have multiple rows of data to show. Select the existing table object, right-click, and select Delete to delete the table. Once you delete the table, you will notice that the grouping within the RowGroups is also removed.

12. In your report you need the profits of each country to be seen on different pages. In order to design such a report you need a report item called List in your Report Designer layout. Click the Toolbox window and drag and drop the report item List to your Report Designer layout below the title of the report as shown in Figure 20-25. If you cannot see the Toolbox window select Toolbox from the View menu item.

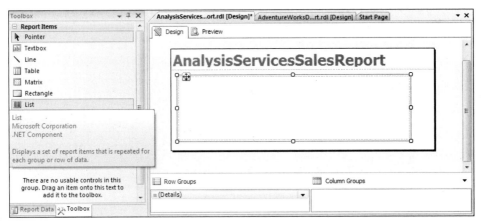

Figure 20-25

13. Drag and drop the English_Country_Region_Name into the list area and center it. You want to get a report so that the state-provinces are grouped within the same country and each country has its own page. To do this, right-click within the Row_Groups area and select Group Properties as shown in Figure 20-26.

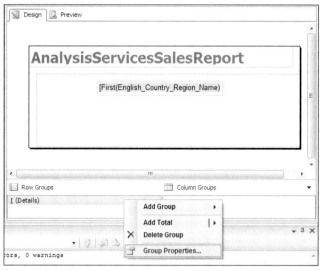

Figure 20-26

14. In the Group Properties dialog under the General tab, select English_Country_Region_Name as shown in Figure 20-27.

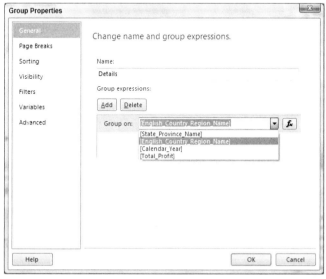

Figure 20-27

15. Select the Page Breaks tab and select the checkbox for "Between each instance of a group" as shown in Figure 20-28 and click OK.

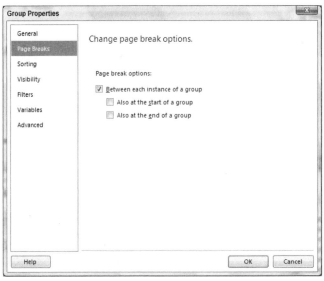

Figure 20-28

16. Drag and drop the Table report item from the Toolbox to within the List item.

17. You will see a table with three columns and two rows. Delete the left-most column in the table. Your table should now have two columns. Drag and drop the Calendar_Year field to the first column in the Data area. You will see the Header row is automatically populated with the name Calendar Year. Drag and drop the Total_Profit field to the data row of the second column. Your Design view should look like Figure 20-29.

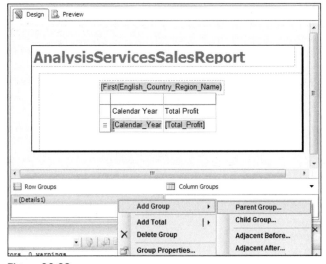

Figure 20-29

18. Select the table. Right-click the Row Groups area and select Add Group ⇨ Parent Group as shown in Figure 20-29.

19. In the Tablix Group dialog, select State_Province_Name in the field next to the Group By radio button as shown in Figure 20-30. Select the checkboxes for Add group header and Add group footer and click OK.

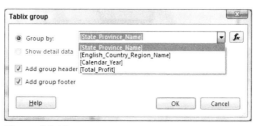

Figure 20-30

20. You will now see a new row and a new column added to the table. The new column has the field State_Province_Name included in the cell with a header named Group 1. Rename the header to "State_Province" as shown in Figure 20-31.

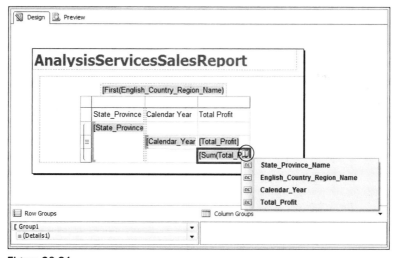

Figure 20-31

21. Click the last cell of the Total_Profit column. You will see a small table icon as shown in Figure 20-31. Click that table and select Total_Profit. The designer now adds Sum(Total_Profit) as the expression for the cell.

22. Click the Preview tab to see the initial version of the report you have designed. You should see a report as shown in Figure 20-32. The report shows the profit report for a specific country in a single page, which includes the states within the country along with profits for each year. The report also shows the aggregated profit for each state. You can switch to the profit report for the next country by selecting the next page or entering a specific page number as shown in Figure 20-32.

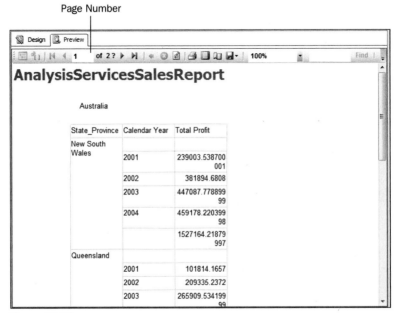

Figure 20-32

23. The report you just designed will not win any beauty contests, nor is it particularly well formatted. You can enhance the presentation of the report by making the headers bold, adding a background color, and so on. Switch to the Design view. Select all the cells within the table by holding down the Ctrl key and then selecting each cell in the table. In the Properties window change the Border ⇨ BorderColor to Solid; next change the Fill ⇨ BackgroundColor to Silver. Select the header row and in the Properties window change the Font property so that the Font ⇨ Font Size is 12 pt and Font ⇨ FontWeight is Bold. For the text box showing the Country, change the property such that the BackgroundColor is Silver, the FontColor is Dark Red, FontSize is 12 pt, and FontWeight is Bold. If you preview the report you will see a report similar to the one shown in Figure 20-33.

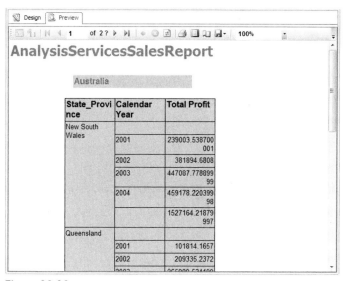

Figure 20-33

24. One of the key things in reports involving profit is the ability to easily distinguish the amount of profit. Typically, in ledgers positive amounts are shown in black and negative amounts are shown in red. In this report you will modify the profit to be shown in green or red depending upon the profit amount. To specify appropriate colors to be displayed for profit select the cell corresponding to the profit in the Design mode. In the Properties window set the property Color to be an expression. You will immediately see the Expression editor dialog. You can use VBA functions as part of the expressions. To check if the profit amount is positive or negative, use the VBA function IIF. Set the expression for Color to check if the value for profit is greater than zero. If yes, the function will return the color green, or else the color red. Once you specify the expression, your expression window should look like Figure 20-34. Click the OK button.

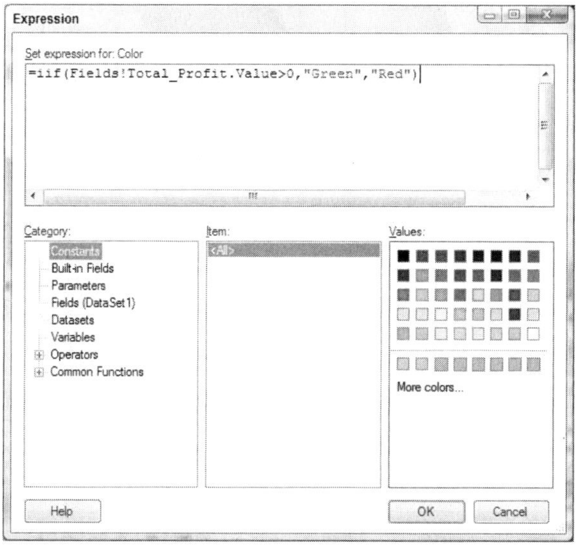

Figure 20-34

If you preview the report after setting the colors and go to the page to view the Total_Profit for United States you will see a report as shown in Figure 20-35. You have seen some of the enhancements that can be made to your UDM reports using the Report Designer. Next you look at some of the extensions in Reporting Services that have been specifically added to have a tighter integration with Analysis Services.

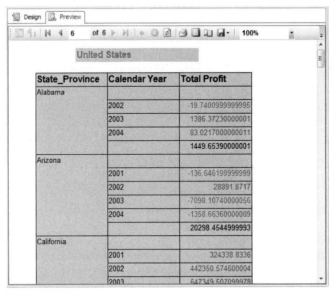

Figure 20-35

Enhancing Your Report Using Extended Properties

The dimension members and cells in Analysis Services have certain specific properties associated with them. These properties can be retrieved from the Analysis Server along with the query result. Certain properties from Analysis Services get mapped on to properties in Reporting Services. These are called *predefined properties* and are accessed within reports as Fields!FieldName.PropertyName. Predefined properties in Reporting Services are: Value, UniqueName, IsMissing, BackgroundColor, Color, FontFamily, FontSize, FontWeight, FontStyle, TextDecoration, FormattedValue, LevelNumber, and ParentUniqueName. Extended properties are additional properties that are returned from Analysis Services. Because these properties are not returned as fields, you cannot drag and drop from the field list to your report layout. Reporting Services provides functionality to access these values in a unique way and include them in the report. You can access the extended properties in one of the following formats:

❏ Fields!FieldName!PropertyName

❏ Fields!FieldName("PropertyName")

❏ Fields!FieldName.Properties("PropertyName")

To see an example of how extended properties can be used in your reports, you will now enhance the report in the previous section by using the extended property FormattedValue that is returned by Analysis Services for the measure Total Profit.

1. Switch to the Design mode in the Report Designer.

2. Select DataSet1, right click, and select Query to launch the MDX query designer.

3.   Select the calculated member Total Profit, right-click, and select Edit.

4.   Add the text **, FORMAT_STRING = "Currency"** as shown in Figure 20-36 in the Calculated Member Builder dialog and click OK. You might see a Parser error. We believe this is a bug. If you see an error, click the OK button for the error message. Switch to the MDX window mode in the Query editor and re-execute the MDX query. Click OK in the MDX Query Editor dialog.

Figure 20-36

5.   Select the Total_Profit cell as shown in Figure 20-37, right-click, and select Expression.

6.   In the Expression editor change the expression of the cell from using Value to FormattedValue as shown in Figure 20-38 and click OK.

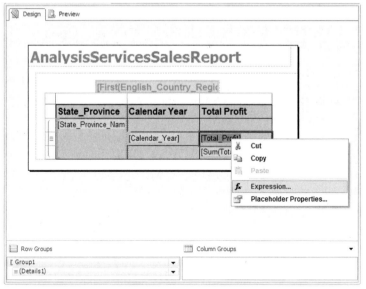

Figure 20-37

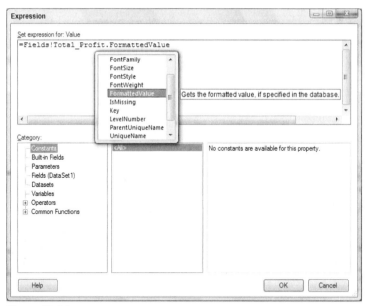

Figure 20-38

7. Save the report and switch to the Preview mode. You will see a report where the profit values are formatted based on the currency format and the values are retrieved from Analysis Services as shown in Figure 20-39. Using the extended properties you will be able to retrieve and use the member properties for dimension members and cell properties for cells that are not part of the predefined reporting services properties.

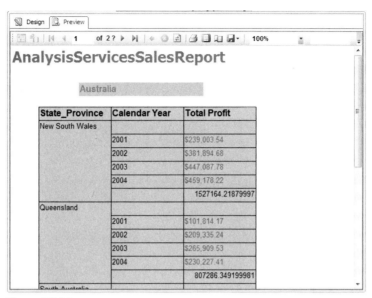

Figure 20-39

Custom Aggregates

When you create reports that contain groups, most likely you have subtotals for the group members. For example, if you have sales for various years and products, you might want to view the sales for each year. Therefore, each year will need to be aggregated. Reporting Services provides you with a set of aggregation functions such as sum, count, distinct count, and so on. For a detailed list of the aggregation functions supported by Reporting Services 2008 please refer to the product's documentation. In addition to these aggregate functions, it supports custom aggregates supported by data providers. If a data provider such as Analysis Services supports custom aggregates, Reporting Services has the ability to retrieve that data for the aggregate rows by the aggregate function called Aggregate. Custom aggregates are also referred to as server aggregates.

An example of a custom aggregate in Analysis Services 2008 is semi-additive measures. They use aggregate functions such as ByAccount, FirstNonEmpty, LastNonEmpty, FirstChild, LastChild, AverageofChildren, or None. Other examples of Analysis Services 2008 custom aggregates include cell values controlled by custom rollups or parent-child hierarchies, or custom aggregates specified in MDX scripts. Some of the custom aggregate functions supported by Analysis Services 2008 are also supported by Reporting Services 2008. However, we recommend you use custom aggregates for improved performance; in this way Reporting Services does not have to calculate the aggregate once again, because that was already done by Analysis Services. In this section you create a report that uses custom aggregate functions to retrieve semi-additive measures from Analysis Services 2008. Follow these steps to generate a custom aggregate report:

1. Add a new report item to the Reporting Services project you used in the last section called CustomAggregate.rdl.

2. In the Report Data pane, select the drop-down New and select Data Source.

3. Create a connection to the AnalysisServices2008Tutorial database.

4. Select the created DataSet1, right-click, and select Add Dataset.

5. In the Dataset Properties dialog, click the Query Designer button to launch the MDX query editor.

6. Select the measure Unit Price in the Fact Internet Sales measure of the cube Adventure Works DW, which is a semi-additive measure with the aggregate function FirstNonEmpty. Drag and drop this measure from the Metadata pane to the Result pane. Drag and drop the hierarchy Products from the Product dimension and Calendar Year hierarchy from the Order Date dimension. Your Result pane should now include columns: Calendar Year, the two levels of the Products hierarchy Model Name and Product Name, and the measure Unit Price as shown in Figure 20-40. Click OK in the Query Designer and the Dataset Properties dialog.

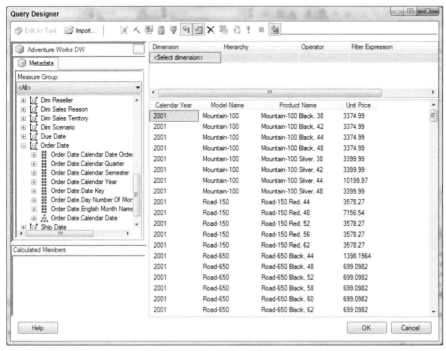

Figure 20-40

7. Add a List report item to the Report Designer. Drag and drop the Calendar_Year field to the List report item and then change the Grouping/Sorting option to be Calendar Year, similar to the report you designed in the previous section by right-clicking RowGroups and selecting Group properties.

8. Drag and drop a table item within the list item.

9. Drag and drop Product_Name and Unit_Price to two columns in the table.

10. Delete the third column in the table.

11. Right-click the Details in the Row Groups pane and select Add Group ⇨ Parent Group.

12. In the Tablix group dialog, select the Model Name field for the Group By radio button and enable the checkboxes for Add Group Header and Add Group Footer.

13. You will see a new column and row created. The column field has the expression for the field Model_Name with the header Group1. Change the header to Model_Name.

14. Change the Background Color property to Silver and FontWeight property to Bold for the header row, the Year field, and the cell corresponding to the aggregate as shown in Figure 20-41.

15. In the cell corresponding to the aggregate of the Unit_Price column, select the field Unit_Price. The Report Designer automatically adds the expression Sum(Unit_Price) as shown in Figure 20-41.

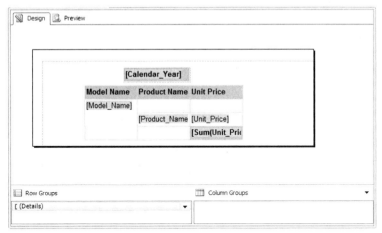

Figure 20-41

16. Select the cell having the aggregate value Sum(Unit_Price), right-click, and select Expression.

17. In the Expression dialog enter the following expression:

```
=Aggregate(Fields!Unit_Price.Value)
```

18. Save the report and select the Preview pane. You will now see the aggregate of Model Names is not a sum of all the Product Names as shown in Figure 20-42. The Unit_Price value is now being retrieved from Analysis Services rather than being calculated by Reporting Services.

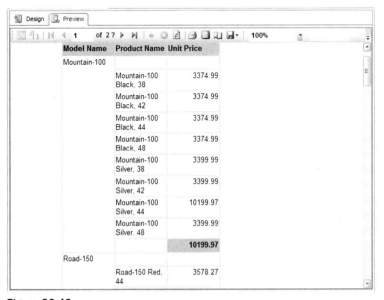

Figure 20-42

19. When you change the aggregation function from Sum to Aggregate, the Report Designer changes the MDX query to retrieve appropriate results from Analysis Services instance. You can see the results in the MDX query editor. Right-click the DataSet1 and select Query. Click Execute Query to see the results of the modified MDX query. You will see null values for various Model Names as shown in Figure 20-43. Reporting Services detects the rows with null values for Product Name as the aggregate rows and uses this information to render the report.

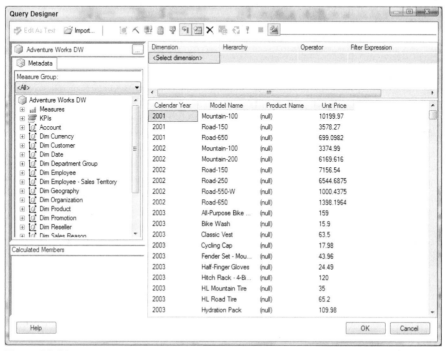

Figure 20-43

Custom aggregates, as mentioned earlier, are useful to create reports that need the aggregated data from Analysis Services. You definitely need to use custom aggregates when the aggregate function is not supported by Reporting Services. In addition to that we recommend you use custom aggregates whenever you need aggregated data from Analysis Services because you will see performance benefits, especially when the report retrieves a large set of members from Analysis Services.

Deploying Your Report

Using BIDS you have learned to design and preview the reports. However, when the reports need to be accessed by the end users, you need to deploy the reports to a centralized location. This centralized location contains the Report Server, which can render the reports to the end users. Access to the functionality of the Report Server is provided through the Report Server Web Service, which uses SOAP (Simple Object Access Protocol) over HTTP and exposes interfaces for report execution and report management. When you install Reporting Services, SQL Server 2008 setup sets up a web interface to the Report Server. You can access your reports and perform management operations through http:// <machinename>/reports. Reporting Services provides a configuration tool that enables you to configure Reporting Services to run on a specific port of choice. In addition to this interface you can perform management operations through SQL Server Management Studio. In this section you learn to configure your Reporting Services server and then deploy and access reports.

1. Open your web browser and connect to `http://localhost/reportserver`. If you encounter an error reaching your Report Server, launch Start ➪ All Programs ➪ SQL Server 2008 ➪ Configuration Tool ➪ Reporting Services Configuration Manager. When asked to run in administrator mode, click Continue.

2. In the Reporting Services Configuration Connection dialog (Figure 20-44), enter the instance of your Reporting Services server, click Find, and then click Connect.

Figure 20-44

3. Click the Web Service URL configuration, specify TCP Port 8080, and click the Apply button. You will now see the URL specified for your Report Server as shown in Figure 20-45.

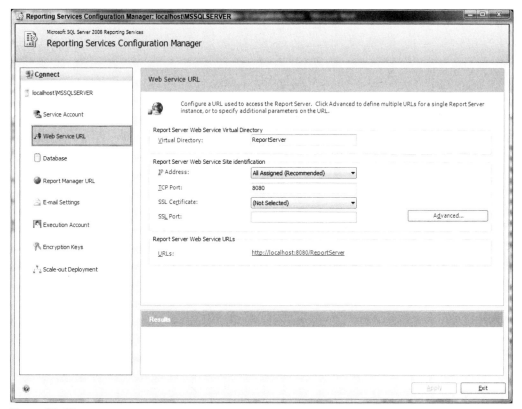

Figure 20-45

4. Click the Report Manager URL and then the Advanced button.

5. In the Advanced Multiple Web Site Configuration dialog (Figure 20-46), click the Add button and specify the TCP Port as 8080 in the Add Report Manager HTTP URL dialog. You should finally have an entry with TCP port 8080 as shown in Figure 20-46. Click OK. Click the Apply button to configure the Report Manager URL, and click Exit.

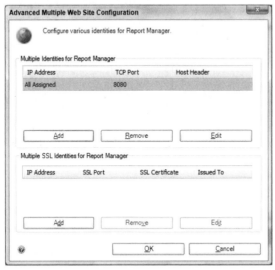

Figure 20-46

6. Open your web browser in administrator mode and connect to `http://localhost:8080/Reports`. You should see the Home page of your Reporting Services server as shown in Figure 20-47.

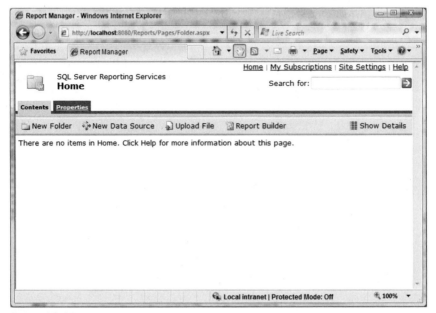

Figure 20-47

7. Click the Site Settings tab, select Security, create a new role, and add yourself as a System Administrator and System User using your username.

8. You are now ready to deploy your reports to your Reporting Services server. To deploy the reports you designed in the previous section you need to set the location of your Report Server. Right-click the solution Report Project Tutorial in the Solution Explorer and select Properties. You will see the Property dialog shown in Figure 20-48.

9. Specify `http://localhost:8080/reportserver` for TargetServerURL also shown in Figure 20-48.

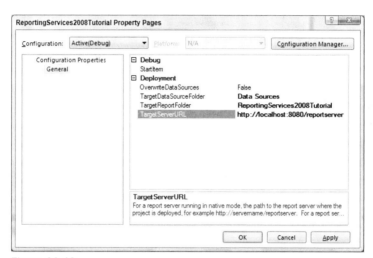

Figure 20-48

10. Deploy the reports by right-clicking the solution and selecting Deploy.

If there were any errors in deployment, you will see the errors in the BIDS Output window. To make sure your reports can be accessed, open Internet Explorer and go to the URL `http://localhost/reports`. You will see the reports under the folder ReportingServices2008Tutorial. When you select the AnalysisServicesSalesReport, the Report Server renders the report and you will see the report as shown in Figure 20-49. Reporting Services allows you to export the report in various formats. If you want to export this report, select the desired format such as PDF, CSV, Excel, etc., and then click Export.

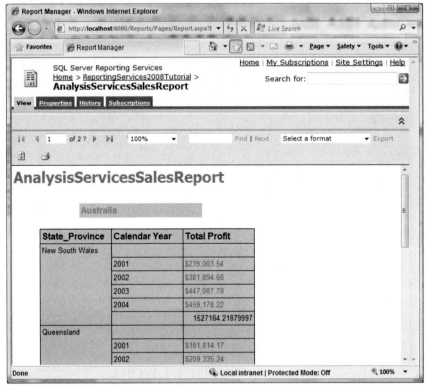

Figure 20-49

Once the reports are deployed to your Report Server, the next important task is to manage (group, setup security permissions, delivering options) the reports through the web interface or through SQL Server Management Studio, which you learn in the next section.

Managing Your Analysis Services Reports

Most likely you are the administrator on your machine and you are able to design, deploy, and view reports on your machines. However, you do not want to provide administrative privileges to all your users. If you are a Report Server administrator, you would need to provide the appropriate access to your report designers who build and deploy reports as compared to the end users who consume the reports. You can also provide certain administrative privileges to certain users on your Report Server machine. Managing your Report Server by itself could be a separate chapter because it is so vast and is not covered completely in this section. You can manage your Reporting Services server via the web interface. In addition you also have the option to connect to your Reporting Services server using SQL Server Management Studio (SSMS). However, in this section you learn a few basic operations of management including defining security permissions on how the reports have to be rendered, as well as creating permissions to end users to view reports that are specifically targeted toward reports built on top of Analysis Services databases. Finally, you learn to automate reports so that they can be delivered to end users on a periodic basis.

Security and Report Execution

First and foremost you need to define the right permissions under which Reporting Services should retrieve the data from Analysis Services. To define the permissions, click the Properties tab of a report as shown in Figure 20-50. You will see the options: General, Data Sources, Execution, History, and Security. The General tab provides information about the report, such as the user who creates the report along with the date and time when it was created or accessed. The Data Sources tab allows you to specify specific credentials under which Report Server should retrieve data from the data source. The AnalysisServicesSalesReport shown in Figure 20-50 has a custom data source connecting to the AnalysisServices2008Tutorial. When the report is deployed from BIDS the default setting for the Report Server connection to Analysis Services is Windows Integrated Security. You can modify this setting to one of the remaining three options. In general the users of the AnalysisServicesSalesReport need not have access to query data from the database AnalysisServices2008Tutorial. In such circumstances you would need to choose the option "Credentials stored securely in the report server" and provide a valid domain username and password that has access to query data from an Analysis Services instance. We recommend the use of this option compared to other options if you want to ensure that your users can view the report without appropriate permissions set on your Analysis Services database. If you want to provide access to users whose security is managed only through the Analysis Services instance, choose the option "Credentials supplied by the user running the report." Specify the right permissions and then click the Execution tab.

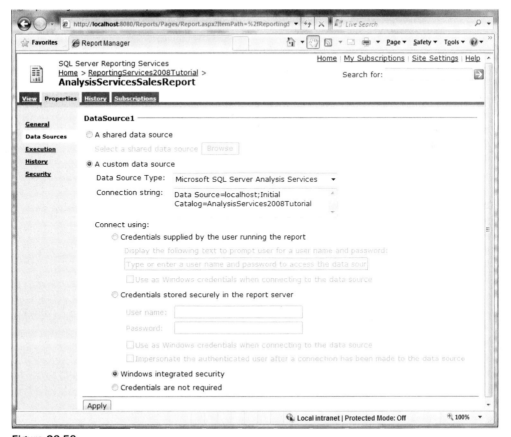

Figure 20-50

The Execution tab shows the various ways in which the report can be rendered on the Report Server (see Figure 20-51). You can have the report run at the time when users access the report or schedule the report to be run every 30 minutes or a specific time interval. In this way data is cached on your Report Server ensuring the reports are rendered immediately. If you do want the most recent data, you should not cache the report. The query to retrieve data from the data provider (in this example it is Analysis Services) can take a long time. You do have the option of specifying snapshots at which this specific report or additional reports get rendered and stored on the Report Server using the option "Render this report from a report execution snapshot." The Report Server provides you with certain options in report execution to limit the amount of time the Report Server should wait to retrieve the data. The last option under Report Execution Timeout is to define a specific timeout value. Use the default settings for report execution and then click the Security tab.

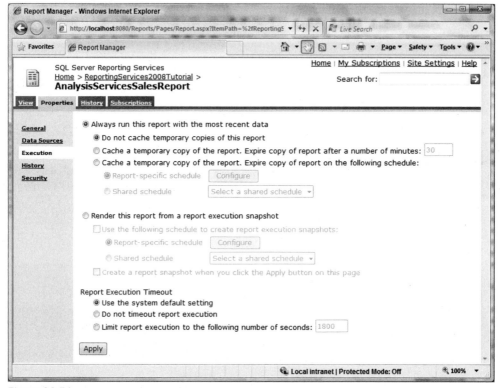

Figure 20-51

The Security tab provides you with the option of specifying security to the end users accessing the report. You can add new users and provide access to specific roles from the Content Manager who has administrative rights to just viewing reports. Figure 20-52 shows the default security settings for the reports.

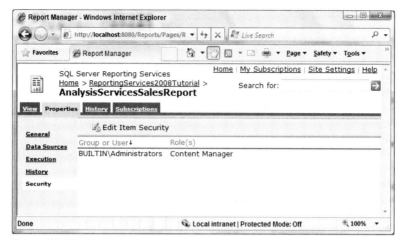

Figure 20-52

If you want to add a new user and provide specific permissions for the user, click Edit Item Security. When asked if you want to change the security items for this item to be different than the parent item, click OK. You will now see two buttons, New Role Assignment and Revert to Parent Security. Click the New Role Assignment button. You will now be in the New Role Assignment page as shown in Figure 20-53. Specify the domain username or a group next to Group or user name. You next need to select the predefined roles on your Report Server such as Browser, Content Manager, and so on. If you want to see what type of tasks a specific role can accomplish, click the role. You also have the ability to define new roles and select specific tasks by clicking the New Role button. Once you have chosen the roles for the user, click OK. You will now be in the default Security page, which lists all the users or groups who have specific access permissions for the report.

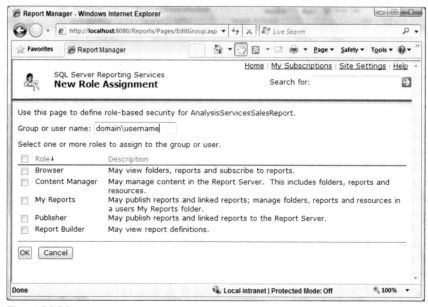

Figure 20-53

Part IV: Integration with Microsoft Products

You have successfully learned to specify credentials under which the Report Server needs to connect to your Analysis Services instance, report execution parameters, and finally provide access to your end users. You can perform all the management operations available through the web interface through SQL Server Management Studio by connecting to your Report Server.

Automating Your Reports

Your end users can access reports through the web interface. In addition to this, Reporting Services 2008 provides you with certain ways of delivering the reports to end users through a file server or email. To deliver reports at periodic intervals you need to set up report subscriptions:

1. Click the Properties tab for the AnalysisServicesSalesReport.

2. Click Data Sources, select the option "Credentials stored securely in the report server," and specify a domain username and password.

3. Enable the checkbox for the option "Use a Windows credentials when connecting to the data source" and click Apply.

4. Click the Subscriptions tab for the AnalysisServicesSalesReport.

5. Click the New Subscription button, and you will see the subscription page as shown in Figure 20-54.

Figure 20-54

The subscription page allows you to choose a specific subscription type. Reporting Services supports two types of subscription delivery — email and file share. You can build your own subscription delivery mechanisms through the extensions provided by the Reporting Services platform. In the subscription page select the Windows File Share delivery as shown in Figure 20-54. You now need to choose a format for the report (PDF, Excel, CSV, and so on), specify the path where the report needs to be delivered, and credentials to access the file share where the report needs to be delivered. Once you specify the options for report file share delivery you need to specify when the report needs to be delivered. The report can be delivered based on a schedule that you define in the subscription page of a shared schedule that was already defined. Once you specify the delivery options, click OK. The report is then scheduled to be run using SQL Agent and hence you need to have SQL Agent running on your machine. Reports will be delivered to the file share based on the defined schedule and the end users can access the reports from that file share.

The second delivery option is to deliver the reports via email. You need to set up your mail server configurations on your Report Server and enable the email delivery option. Refer to the Reporting Services 2008 product documentation on setting up the email delivery option on your Report Server. Once the email delivery option is enabled you can choose this option and specify the email addresses for the TO, CC, and BCC lines along with the delivery schedule.

Managing Your Reporting Services Server Using SSMS

You can manage your Reporting Services server using SSMS. You need to be an administrator on your Reporting Services server to manage your server. Using SSMS you can create and edit role definitions including System roles as well as manage schedules of reports. You can connect to your Reporting Services server using the Object Explorer and specifying your instance name. When you connect to your Reporting Services server, you can see the various folders as shown in Figure 20-55. We recommend that you explore the various management operations that can be performed via SSMS.

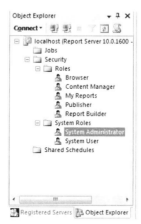

Figure 20-55

Ad-Hoc Reports Using Report Builder

You have so far learned to create reports using Report Designer from relational and multidimensional databases. However, these reports are pre-defined and often business users want to modify reports to better understand the data. Business users are most likely not used to understanding the underlying data sources and the query languages to retrieve data and design their reports. Most of them do understand entities and relationships between entities because they analyze data. Reporting Services

2008 provides Report Builder 2.0 as a feature pack that can be downloaded from www.microsoft.com. Report Builder is for the business users to explore the data in a timely way and to make effective decisions. Report Builder 2.0 exposes the business data through a model called the report model and translates users' actions into appropriate queries to retrieve the underlying data source.

Report Builder is a Winforms application that is accessed from the Report Server for centralized management. Users can create reports using Report Builder through simple drag and drop of entities that are exposed through the report model. The reports generated by Report Builder are published to Report Server using the Report Definition Language (RDL).

Report Model

A report model is a metadata description of data objects and the relationships between the data in the underlying data source. Report models expose the data objects and relationships from the data sources as entities and relationships logically grouped together. Also, note that the entities and relationships are easier to understand than the underlying data source objects for business users. A Report Designer or a Report Server administrator would typically create a report model using a report model project in BIDS and deploy it to the Report Server. These report models can then be accessed through the Report Builder application by business users.

You can create report models from relational and multidimensional databases. The report model consists of three objects — the semantic model, the physical model, and the mapping between the semantic model and physical model. The semantic model is the end users' view of the data, which is defined using the Semantic Model Description Language (SMDL). The physical model is the physical representation of the objects such as cubes, dimension, levels, measures, and so on. The mapping between the semantic model and physical model is used by Report Builder to translate users' actions into appropriate queries to the data source.

A Report Model project is created using BIDS when you need to create a report model from a relational data source. You need to create a data source, Data Source View, and then finally, using the Report Model Wizard, you create the report models. The generated model is then deployed to the Report Server. To create report models from an Analysis Services data source you create a data source on the Report Server using SSMS and then generate a report model.

In this section you create a report model from an Analysis Services UDM. Each UDM from Analysis Services is translated to a single report model. You will not be able to edit the report models generated from Analysis Services. Follow these steps to generate a report model from the Adventure Works DW cube in the AnalysisServices2008Tutorial multidimensional database:

1. Download the Report Builder 2.0 feature pack for SQL Server 2008 and install it on your SQL Server Reporting Services instance.

2. Open the management interface for Reporting Services by connecting to `http://localhost:8080/reports` from your web browser.

3. Click the Data Sources folder.

4. Click the New Data Source button.

5. Provide a name for the data source, select the Data Source Type as Microsoft SQL Server Analysis Services, and provide the connection string to the AnalysisServices2008Tutorial database as shown in Figure 20-56.

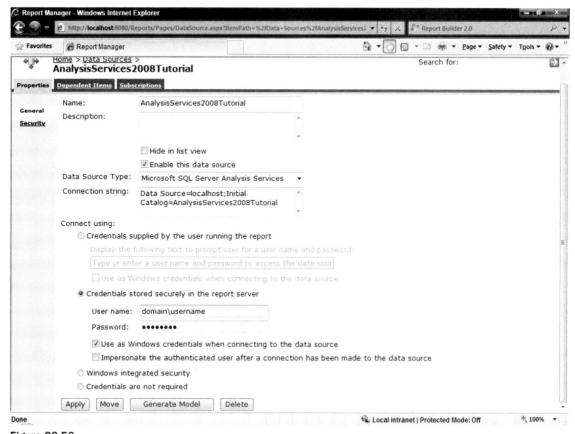

Figure 20-56

6. Select the option "Credentials stored securely in the report server" and enter your username and password credentials as shown in Figure 20-56 and click the Apply button.

7. A new data source to your Analysis Services database has been created. Now you need to generate the model that can then be used by Report Builder 2.0. Click the Generate Model button.

8. Specify AnalysisServices2008TutorialModel for the Name as shown in Figure 20-57 and click OK.

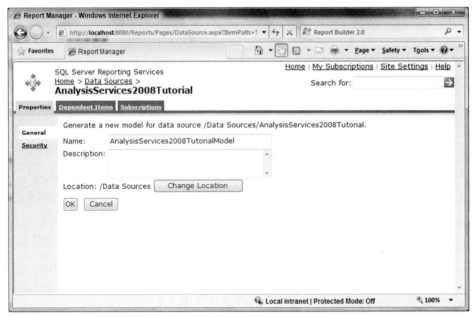

Figure 20-57

The report model AnalysisServices2008TutorialModel is now generated under the Data Sources folder. You have now successfully created a report model from the AnalysisServices2008Tutorial database. In the next section you learn to create reports using the Report Builder application.

Ad-Hoc Reports

Once the report models are available on the Report Server, users can create ad-hoc reports using the Report Builder application. Report Builder represents the report model as entities and relationships and makes it easy for business users to generate ad-hoc reports. You can use Report Builder 1.0 or Report Builder 2.0. Report Builder 1.0 is shipped along with SQL Server Reporting Services 2008 and can be launched from `http://localhost:8080/reports`. The following example uses Report Builder 2.0, which you installed in the previous section. Follow these steps to create a report using the Report Builder application:

1. Launch Report Builder 2.0 from Start ➪ All Programs ➪ Microsoft SQL Server Report Builder 2.0 ➪ Report Builder 2.0.

2. The Report Builder 2.0 application should have the windows as shown in Figure 20-58. Select the New drop-down under Report Data and select Data Source.

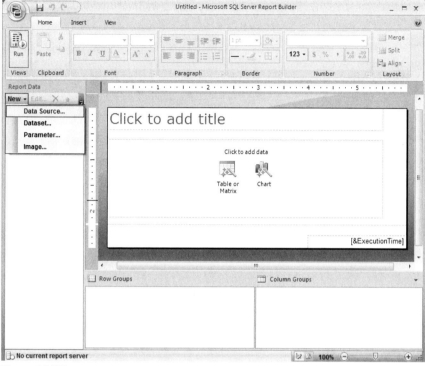

Figure 20-58

3. In the Data Source Properties window click Browse.

4. In the Select Data Source dialog, select the AnalysisServices2008TutorialModel report model under the Data Sources folder as shown in Figure 20-59 and click Open.

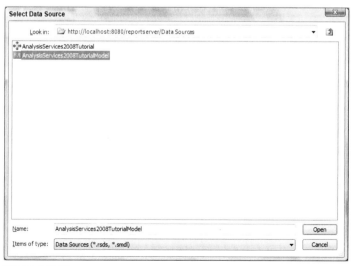

Figure 20-59

5. Specify the name AnalysisServicesModel in the Data Source Properties dialog, select the chosen report model, and click OK.

6. Click the Table or Matrix icon.

7. Select the data source connection AnalysisServices2008TutorialModel as shown in Figure 20-60 and click Next.

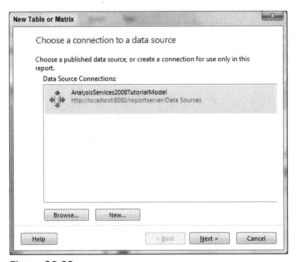

Figure 20-60

8. Select the AdventureWorksDW perspective in the Choose Perspective dialog and click OK.

9. In the Design a query window, you will see various entities as shown in Figure 20-61. Select the entity Dim Sales Territory. Drag and drop the Sales Territory Region into the column fields area in the design surface area as shown in Figure 20-61.

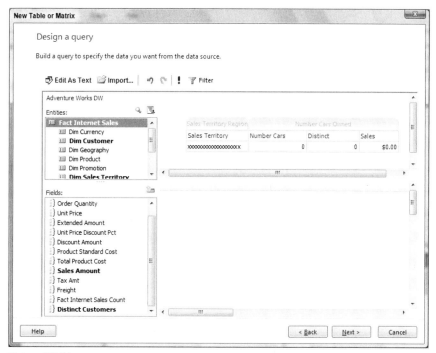

Figure 20-61

10. The entities related to Dim Sales Territory are shown in a hierarchical way in the Entities window. Select the entity Fact Internet Sales. You will now see the entities related to Fact Internet Sales. Select the entity Dim Customers. Drag and drop the field Number Cars Owned next to the Sales Territory field.

11. Now select the entity Fact Internet Sales under Dim Sales Territory. Drag and drop the fields Distinct Customers and Sales Amount to the design surface next to the Sales Territory field as shown in Figure 20-61.

12. Click the Next button.

13. Drag and drop the Sales Territory Region and Number Cars Owned fields to the Row group and the remaining fields to Values as shown in Figure 20-62 and click Next.

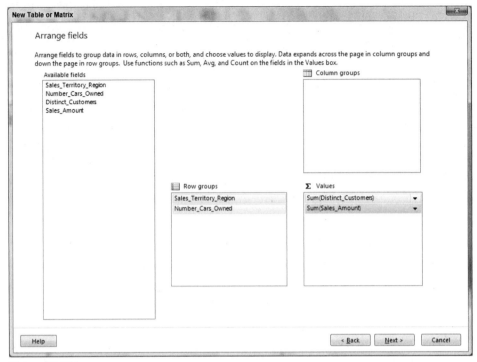

Figure 20-62

14. In the Choose the Layout page select the defaults and click Next.

15. Choose the default selection in the Choose the Style page and click Finish.

16. You will see the table inserted within the design surface along with the groupings you have specified. Add the title "Sales Territory and Cars Owned by Customers" as shown in Figure 20-63.

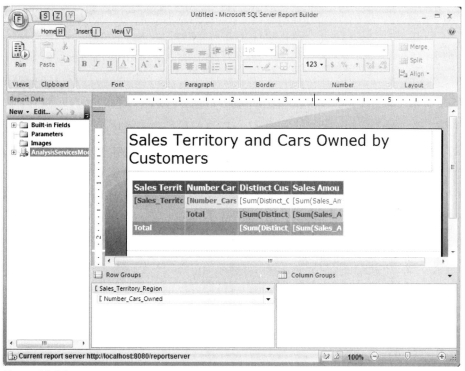

Figure 20-63

17. Click the Run icon to see the results of your report.

You have now successfully created an ad-hoc report using Report Builder 2.0 in a few minutes. When you look at the Report Builder 2.0 design interface, you can see that it is consistent with the Office 2007 theme with a Ribbon and icons that can easily help you to design your ad-hoc reports. You can see a preview of the report you have built as shown in Figure 20-64. To publish the report from your Reporting Services 2008 instance, click the large button (similar to the large Office button) at the top-left end of the Ribbon and select Save As. In the Save As Report dialog, choose a specific folder on your Report Server and specify an RDL name for the report. You can then view the published report from the Reporting Services web interface.

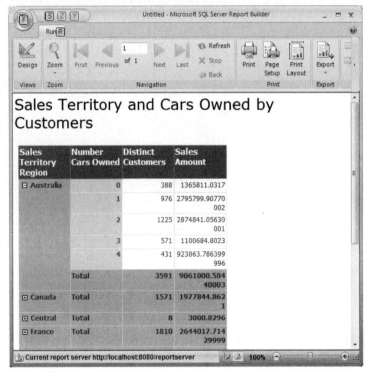

Figure 20-64

In this section you have learned about creating report models and later generating ad-hoc reports using the Report Builder. Several features in the Report Builder application help you to filter, sort, and group the data in the report, which were not covered in this section. We recommend you explore these features to refine your reports.

Summary

In this chapter you discovered that Reporting Services isn't the only stellar example of product feature integration for enterprise Business Intelligence software. Indeed, Microsoft's Reporting Services provides an awesome platform to round out the Business Intelligence lifecycle. Specifically, this chapter covered three scenarios: First, there was an introduction to Reporting Services by way of building a report on a relational database. Then, you created a report on top of a UDM, which showed some of the great integrated features of Reporting Services such as drag-and-drop-based query generation and retrieving dimension and cell properties for inclusion in a report. You learned some of the key enhancements in Reporting Services integration with Analysis Services such as custom aggregates, retrieving extended properties, and the ability to manage Report Servers and set up security for your reports. Finally, you learned to create a report model from the Analysis Services database and to generate ad-hoc reports using the Report Builder application. If you need an in-depth understanding of Reporting Services 2008, we recommend you read the book *Professional Microsoft SQL Server 2008 Reporting Services* by Paul Turley, et al. (Wrox, 2008).

Part V
Scenarios

21

Designing Real-Time Cubes

Are you ready to create real-time cubes? Or perhaps you would be if only you knew what real-time cubes were? We define real-time cubes as cubes that are configured for automatic data updates on a time scale that makes them appear to be working in real time. This can be profoundly useful for certain types of analytical applications. First, consider an application for which real-time cubes would not be useful: An application designed to create profit projections and economic analysis of harvesting an old growth forest (a renewable resource) — that would require updates, say, every five years or so to reflect macroeconomic trends. There is a much more exciting application that would exploit real-time techniques. Consider a case such that your cube is directly built against your transactional data that has several transactions per second, which need to be updated in your cube so that users can query the data real time. With the use of real-time streaming stock quotes of your company, results of a business analysis could be fed into a digital dashboard for viewing results. Okay, it is an unlikely example, but you get the idea. Such a dashboard might house multiple Key Performance Indicators (KPIs), clearly indicating the performance of target metrics with changes in color or graphics displays based on the data. Attaching the real-time stock quote stream to analyze the constantly changing cube and/or dimensions can be done through a .NET stored assembly. All this is possible in SQL Server Analysis Services (SSAS) 2008 due to the flexibility of the Unified Dimensional Model (UDM).

What does real-time mean to you or your business? Does it mean the ability to query the cube at any time? Does it mean you have the most up-to-date data in your cube? If you think of "most up-to-date data," what does that mean to you? Perhaps it means something like the previous quarter's data or previous month's data or perhaps it is weekly or daily data. There are cases where even seconds count, as with the stock-related example. The question of how soon the data needs to be available in the UDM is what you need to think about when you are designing a real-time cube. The daily transactional data in most retail companies arrives at the data warehouse nightly or on a weekly basis. Typically these companies have a nightly job that loads the new data into their cube through an incremental process.

If your company is multinational, the concept of a nightly job (which is typically considered a batch process) is not nightly at all — due to the many time zones involved. Assume your company had offices in the USA and you were loading new data during the night. If your company expanded to include data-generating offices in Asia and those employees needed to access the cubes, you would need to make sure the UDM was available for querying throughout the day and night while giving consistently correct data. Some companies can find the right sweet spot of time needed to upload the data while users do not access the cube; and do the data load then. What if your transactional data arrives at regular intervals during the day and the end users of the cube need access to the data instantaneously? Then you would have to design a special way to meet the needs of your users. SSAS 2008 allows you to address these very sorts of challenges. You simply need to choose the right method based on your requirements.

By now, you are very familiar with MOLAP, HOLAP, and ROLAP storage modes; they can be crossed with varying methods of data update for both fact and dimension data through a technique called *proactive caching*. With the proactive caching technique you can count on getting the real-time data with MOLAP performance through the use of cache technology. In addition, proactive caching provides you with the ability to manage any changes that occur to the source transactional data being propagated to the end user through the UDM (that is where the real-time part comes in). It is important to understand that proactive caching itself does not provide real-time capability; it is a feature that helps you manage your real-time business needs. This chapter provides you with some thoughts on which approach to take in which case and why. We have divided this chapter into three general scenarios to explain proactive caching and how it is useful for designing real-time cubes. They are: a long latency scenario for those times when quick updates are not required; an average latency scenario for those periodic, non–time-critical updates; and finally, a short latency scenario for the most demanding of users.

Proactive Caching

Traditionally, OLAP refers to fast access of aggregate or summarized data, with the source data retrieved from a relational data warehouse and stored in a storage format called MOLAP (Multidimensional OLAP). Relational databases are nonetheless really helpful for detail-level data and also helpful for reporting. You learned that MOLAP storage is optimal and provides the best performance, whereas ROLAP storage provides immediate access to the latest data but does not have the same performance as that of MOLAP storage. Proactive caching is an important feature in SSAS 2008 because it aids the UDM in delivering the best of relational and OLAP worlds, most importantly real-time data access with near MOLAP performance. Proactive caching helps UDM to achieve real-time data by providing controls that help in data propagation from the source data to the UDM, which is then available for users' queries. When appropriate proactive caching properties are set, Analysis Services starts building a new MOLAP cache when data in the underlying data source changes. While the cache is being built, Analysis Services serves users from the existing MOLAP cache. As soon as the new MOLAP cache is built, users are served from the new MOLAP cache and start seeing the new data. You will see this concept in action throughout this chapter.

As mentioned earlier, the UDM merges the relational and OLAP worlds. We consider proactive caching to be a management feature that helps the administrator or database designer specify certain settings that help to achieve real-time data access based on customer needs. Proactive caching can be applied to both partitions and dimensions. In Figures 21-1, 21-2, and 21-3, you can see details of how this feature works. Figure 21-1 shows a UDM that has proactive caching enabled. SSAS 2008 creates a MOLAP cache of the UDM on SSAS 2008 from which users query for information. When there are updates to the relational database that affect the UDM data, Analysis Services is notified as shown in Figure 21-2. If proactive caching has been enabled on the UDM, Analysis Services spawns a background thread, which we refer to as the Proactive Caching Management thread. This thread controls operations within Analysis Services that ensure the customers get the real-time data access requested as shown in Figure 21-3.

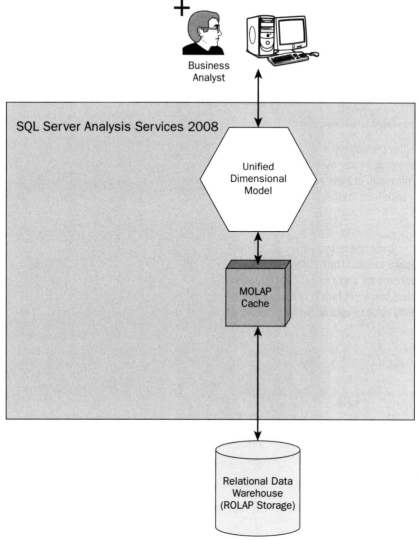

Business
Analyst

SQL Server Analysis Services 2008

Unified
Dimensional
Model

MOLAP
Cache

Relational Data
Warehouse
(ROLAP Storage)

Figure 21-1

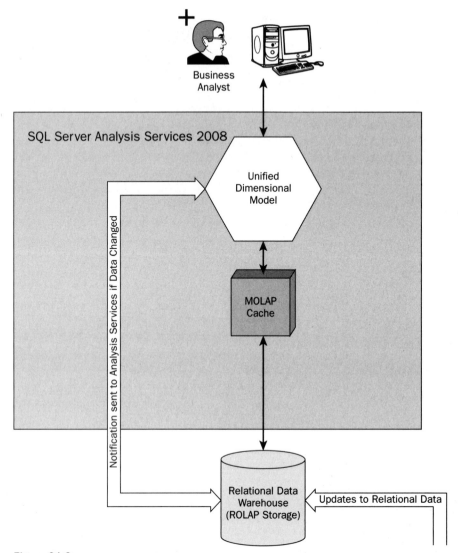

Figure 21-2

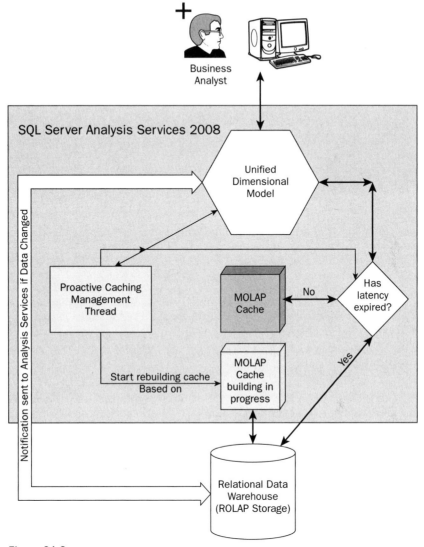

Figure 21-3

The typical configuration, shown in Figure 21-3, is to have MOLAP storage mode for the UDM with proactive caching enabled. If users send queries to your cube, data is retrieved from the existing MOLAP cache. In the background, the proactive caching management thread looks for changes to the relational data warehouse based on certain mechanisms, which you will see later in this chapter. As soon as the thread notices a change, it starts rebuilding a new MOLAP cache and, when the new cache is built, clears the existing MOLAP cache. Note that you can set properties that control the time at which the current MOLAP cache gets cleared and the time at which the new MOLAP cache is rebuilt.

Any query that comes to Analysis Services is first checked to see if it can be served with the existing MOLAP cache. If the current cache is valid based on proactive caching settings, results are retrieved from that. If the current cache is not valid, that means a new cache is being rebuilt. Because Analysis Services does not know how long it will take to rebuild the cache, it will then directly go to the relational data warehouse to retrieve the data. Analysis Services creates SQL queries to retrieve the correct data. The SQL queries generated by Analysis Services are optimized to efficiently retrieve data from the relational data warehouse. Any calculation that cannot be done in the relational data warehouse is then computed within Analysis Services after retrieving the data, and the results are returned to the user.

Keep in mind that there might be slight performance degradation during the time data is being retrieved from a relational data source; this is likely due to involvement of query translation as well as network activity — nonetheless, users get the real-time data. If the users do not mind getting the data from the existing cache and they only want to see the refreshed data with good performance, they can set a proactive caching property called *latency*, which is the time up to which the current MOLAP cache will be valid even after the notification of change in data in the relational data warehouse. Setting the latency (inactivity time interval) close to the rebuilding time helps in getting MOLAP-level performance — keep in mind that a slight delay in the real-time data to users is to be expected.

Fortunately for the users, MOLAP cache building is done on a background thread that is assigned a low priority. This means that if queries are submitted to Analysis Services databases, the queries will be given higher priority than the background proactive caching thread. If at any time during this rebuild process the user initiates a process that will change the data in the cube — for example, by reprocessing the cube or doing a writeback to the cube — the background proactive caching thread to rebuild the MOLAP cache will be cancelled. Similarly, if Analysis Services receives another notification of a data change, the MOLAP cache rebuilding process will be cancelled unless you have explicitly specified not to do so through a proactive caching property. It is important for you as an administrator or database designer to be aware of this behavior so that you can make sure the proactive caching properties are set with desired values based on your business requirements.

Proactive Caching at Work

To demonstrate how proactive caching works, this section uses the sample Adventure Works Analysis Services project that comes with the product. You need to download and install the SQL2008. Adventure Works DW BI v2008.x86.msi sample database from http://www.codeplex.com/MSFTDBProdSamples/Release/ProjectReleases.aspx?ReleaseId=16040. The sample should be installed in the directory within your SQL Server installation (%SystemDrive%\Program Files\Microsoft SQL Server\100\Tools\Samples\AdventureWorks 2008 Analysis Services Project\Enterprise). To understand proactive caching functionality, do the following:

1. Open the enterprise version of the sample Adventure WorksDW 2008 Analysis Services project. This Analysis Services project contains a cube called Adventure Works that has several measure groups and dimensions. The measure group ResellerSales retrieves the data from the relational table FactResellerSales. The data from the FactResellerSales table has been partitioned within Analysis Services so that the ResellerSales measure group has four partitions, one for each year. You will see the behavior of proactive caching by adding rows to the last partition of the FactResellerSales measure group.

2. Click the Partitions tab of the Adventure Works cube and expand the ResellerSales measure group. You will see the four partitions of the ResellerSales measure group as shown in Figure 21-4. If you click in the Source column for year 2004, you will be able to see the SQL query that restricts the data for that year (where OrderDateKey >= '20040101' and OrderDateKey <= '20041231').

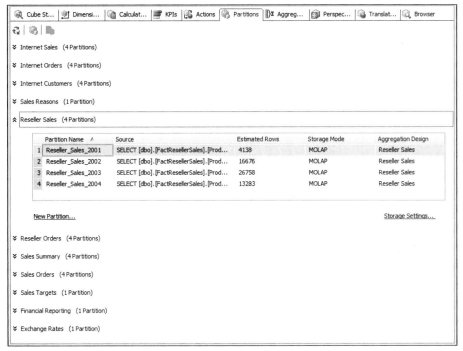

Figure 21-4

From here, you'll delete some rows from the ResellerSales table and do a bulk insert of these rows to see the behavior of proactive caching.

3. Open SQL Server Management Studio and execute the following query to your relational database AdventureWorksDW2008. You will see 3002 rows are retrieved. Select the entire results set and press Ctrl+C to copy it to the clipboard. Open notepad and paste the entire results within notepad and save the file as AdventureWorksFactResellerSales.txt.

```
SELECT *          FROM [dbo].[FactResellerSales]
WHERE OrderDateKey >= '20040601' AND OrderDateKey <= '20041231'
```

4. Execute the following SQL statement to delete the rows from the table:

```
DELETE   FROM [dbo].[FactResellerSales]
WHERE OrderDateKey >= '20040601' AND OrderDateKey <= '20041231'
```

5. Deploy the Adventure Works DW 2008 project to your Analysis Services instance. Connect to your Analysis Services instance using SQL Server Management Studio and execute the following MDX query. You will see the results as shown in Figure 21-5.

```
SELECT [Measures].[Reseller Sales Amount] ON 0,
NON EMPTY [Geography].[Country].MEMBERS ON 1
FROM [Adventure Works]
```

6. Now you need to set the proactive caching settings for the ResellerSales partition so that changes in source data are automatically detected by Analysis Services and you get real-time data while querying the UDM. Connect to the Analysis Services instance in the Object Explorer from SSMS. Navigate to the Reseller_Sales_2004 partition in the [Adventure Works] cube. Right-click the partition Reseller_Sales_2004 and select Properties.

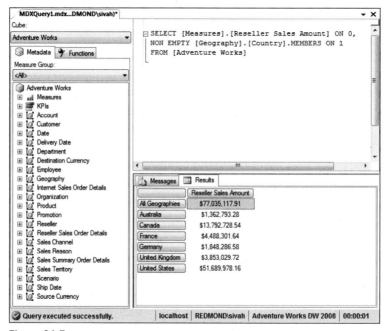

Figure 21-5

7. You will see the properties dialog for the partition. Select the Proactive Caching page as shown in Figure 21-6. You will see the various storage options for the partitions from Real-time ROLAP to MOLAP. In order to have this partition as MOLAP as well as enable proactive caching, you need Automatic MOLAP; also you need to set some additional proactive caching properties. Click the Custom setting radio button and then click on the Options button at the bottom right of the dialog.

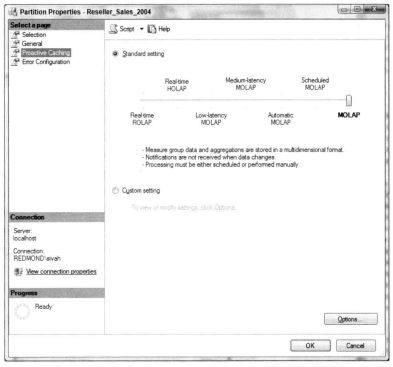

Figure 21-6

8. You will see the Storage Options dialog as shown in Figure 21-7. Enable proactive caching for the selected partition by clicking the checkbox next to Enable proactive caching. Select the Drop outdated cache checkbox and set the Latency to zero seconds. Finally, select the option Bring online immediately. This ensures that you do see the updated results immediately. By default, the silence interval and silence override interval are at 10 seconds and 10 minutes, respectively. This means that the MOLAP cache will start rebuilding 10 seconds after the notification of data change. Now you need to inform Analysis Services of the method of detecting change in the relational data source. Click the Notifications tab.

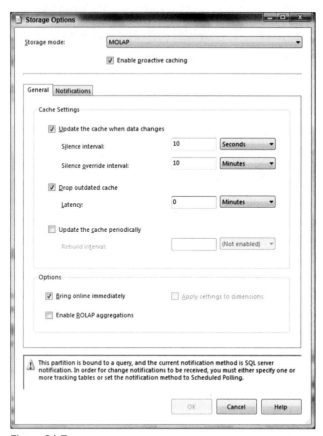

Figure 21-7

9. Select the SQL Server option and specify the tracking table as FactResellerSales as shown in Figure 21-8. This is a unique option specific to Microsoft SQL Server. The Analysis Services instance is able to detect changes in the data with the help of SQL Server notifications. This option is not available with other relational databases. In those cases, you would have to choose the second option of specifying a query that will result in a value that indicates the change in data. Click OK to accept changes made in the dialog.

Figure 21-8

10. You have now set up proactive caching successfully for the 2004 Reseller Sales partition. To see the results, you just have to load the rows you deleted from the FactResellerSales table in step 4. Execute the following bulk insert SQL query to your relational database. Make sure you use the correct path!

```
BULK INSERT dbo.FactResellerSales
FROM 'C:\Chapter21\AdventureWorksFactResellerSales.txt'
WITH
(
        FIELDTERMINATOR ='\t',
        ROWTERMINATOR = '\n',
        FIRE_TRIGGERS
)
```

11. The preceding statement adds 3002 rows to the FactResellerSales table. Now you need to verify if you are able to see the real-time data by querying the UDM AdventureWorksDW. Go to the MDX query editor and execute the MDX query from step 5. You will see that the Reseller Sales for all the countries are higher than their original value, as shown in Figure 21-9. This is due to the 3002 new rows added to the FactResellerSales table. At the moment the MDX query is executed, the new MOLAP cache is not rebuilt. Therefore, Analysis Services retrieves the data for the 2004 partition from the relational data source, aggregates the data along with the data from the remaining three MOLAP partitions, and provides you with the results.

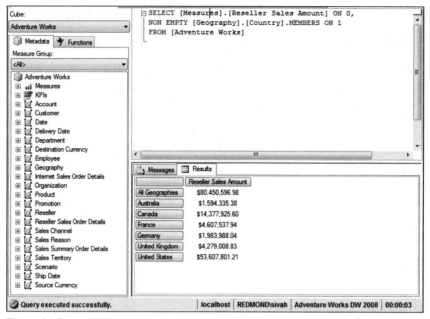

Figure 21-9

You have now successfully been able to set the proactive caching option for a partition using the SQL Server notifications option and are able to see real-time results. Similarly, you can manage other partitions and dimensions with proactive caching based on the real-time needs of your business users. Having learned about the basics of the proactive caching feature and how it works, now you can look at important scenarios where this feature would be useful for your business.

Long Latency Scenario

Assume you own a small company that is selling a key set of products that is essentially static in nature; the base list of products just doesn't change. New products may be added to the list, but the original set of products remains the same. In this scenario, several of your products are sold each day and the sales data arrives at your data warehouse sometime after normal business hours. Further, your company is headquartered in the United States. The business analysts on your team want to see sales data no later than the next working day following the actual sale. In this scenario, assume incremental processing of your cube takes a relatively small amount of time (just 1–2 hours), which can be completed before start of the next business day. Also, assume that data updates (information about new products added into the system) in your relational databases arrive within a reasonable time.

The traditional approach to solving the outlined scenario would be to have the dimension storage as MOLAP and do an incremental update of dimensions after the relational data update is completed. This approach is computation intensive and is a fairly costly operation. Following the dimension data update, an incremental process of the relevant measure groups is required and, once that completes, the consumers of the cube can browse the results. This approach has advantages. Indeed, this approach is good whenever your relational data updates occur regularly at a specific time interval and you have sufficient time to update the cubes. Several existing Analysis Services users in the retail space use this solution. Data typically arrives during the night and the cubes are processed nightly for use the next business day.

As with the traditional approach, you can do an incremental process of dimensions and measure groups. Or, for the sake of completeness and given the time, you could even do a full process of the entire cube. Again, these things typically take place during the night so time is not often a constraint. You could use SQL Server 2008 Integration Services to create a package to do this job as seen in Chapter 19. Alternatively, you can use the proactive caching feature. There are two basic methods (with multiple variations) within proactive caching that can be used to initiate data updates. They are the query-based method and the time-based method; the method you choose will depend on your needs.

One of the solutions for the long latency scenario is to use the proactive caching feature in Analysis Services 2008. In the proactive caching solution, you set proactive caching to kick in as soon as the data changes using the option Scheduled MOLAP. For the Scheduled MOLAP option you need to specify a query that is to be run at scheduled time intervals to determine if there has been a change to the source data. Here is how it works: The first time Analysis Services sends the specified query to the relational data source, it collects and stores the response. That stored response provides a baseline against which subsequent query results can be compared. When a subsequent query returns a result set that does not match the baseline, it is presumed there has been a data update and proactive caching will start the process of incremental update. Depending on the other proactive caching settings such as latency, the cache will be updated. The latency setting tells Analysis Services how long to wait between cache updates. This is what provides that real-time appearance to the end user.

Figure 21-10 shows the proactive caching option where you specify a polling query that will detect the change in source data. This could be as simple as a count of rows in the relational table or as complex as a hash value of the entire result set. For the long latency scenario you would need to click the Enable Incremental Updates option so that dimension and partitions are processed incrementally only with the data that has been added. If this option is enabled, Analysis Services processes the dimension or partition object by sending a Process Add statement. If you do not specify this option, Analysis Services will automatically send a Process Update statement to the dimension or the cube partitions. Process updates on dimensions could be expensive based on the size of the dimensions and the partitions and aggregations built for the partitions. For tradeoffs on which processing option (Process Update or Process Add) would be good for your cube, please refer to Chapter 14. After specifying the polling query, you need to specify the processing query that will retrieve appropriate data from the relational data source for processing.

> Here is a handy proactive caching technique that can be applied to dimensions which can optimize your incremental processing query. First, specify the polling query. The results of the polling query can then be used as parameters to the incremental processing query. For example, if you have SELECT max(product_id) from Products — let's say initially it returns 100 — then 50 products are added. When the polling query is subsequently run, you would get 150. These two parameters can then be used to create the incremental processing query as
>
> ```
> SELECT * from Products where product_id >COALESCE(?,0) And
> product_id <=COALESCE(?,-1)
> ```
>
> In this way, the processing query returns only those rows that were added since the last data change. This technique can be a real timesaver if your Products table is the size of, say, Wal-Mart's or Amazon's.

Figure 21-10

Proactive Caching Using Timed Updates

The second method of proactive caching is to update the dimension and partition data periodically. Though this approach could hardly be considered sophisticated, there is no doubt it gets the job done and doesn't take much in the way of setup. Here is how it works: You set proactive caching to update any new source data and itself (the cache) at a predetermined time. For example, if you want to set the update at "24 hours since last process," you set a proactive caching property that ensures the MOLAP cache is rebuilt every 24 hours. In the long latency scenario, you would typically not set the latency property because you want the new data to be available as soon as the MOLAP cache is rebuilt. You specify the option of when to rebuild the cache using the option Update the cache periodically as shown in Figure 21-11. This option ensures that the MOLAP cache is rebuilt every 24 hours. However, you should be aware that the cache update occurs 24 hours after the previous update. For example, on the first day if the processing started at 12 midnight and it took 30 minutes for the cache to be updated, then on the second day the cache update will start at 12:30am instead of 12 midnight. It would have been nice to have the update cache happen at the same time each day. Probably we will get this option in future releases. However, you can implement this functionality using SQL Server Integration Services as seen in Chapter 19. You might have to reset the proactive caching property periodically to keep it aligned with your business needs so that the most up-to-date data is available for your end users. The configuration you set up using for updating the cache periodically is also referred to as Scheduled MOLAP because the cache update is scheduled. If you click OK in the dialog shown in Figure 21-11 you will be in the partition's Partition Properties pane where you will see the Scheduled MOLAP option selected as shown in Figure 21-12.

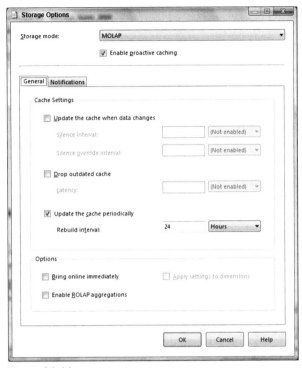

Figure 21-11

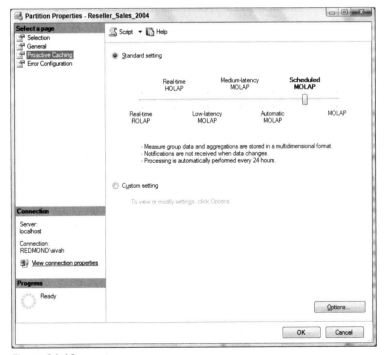

Figure 21-12

Average Latency Scenario

For the average latency scenario, assume you are running a large retail business intelligence implementation with several hundred product-related data changes being added overnight, every night. These additions come in the form of stocking and pricing changes. Actual sales information arrives in your data warehouse periodically and your users really want to see the data under reasonable real-time conditions. For this case, assume updates are available every two hours or so and your cube typically takes about an hour to process. However, your users are willing to see old data for up to four hours. Assume the data partition itself is not large (say, less than 5GB) for this scenario.

Proactive Caching with MOLAP Storage Option

Let's say you have built the cube, and its dimensions are updated nightly using incremental processing. Incremental processing is good whenever you want the current dimensions to be used by customers, because incremental processing can take place in the background and not prevent customers from querying the data.

The case for which it makes sense to use proactive caching with the MOLAP storage option is when you need to update the sales information (or other information) into the measure groups on a periodic basis so that users see near real-time data without any performance degradation. In this case, the data arrives in your data warehouse in the form of a bulk load from your relational transactional database. Further, let's say that incremental processing of your cube is faster than the time required for a bulk load to your data warehouse. You can set up proactive caching for the average latency scenario to be Medium-latency MOLAP as shown in Figure 21-13 so that as soon as a notification arrives, Analysis Services automatically starts building the new MOLAP cache. Because your users are willing to wait to get the new data for up to four hours, the proactive caching property called latency is set to 4 hours. If the new MOLAP cache is not built within 4 hours of the last data change, Analysis Services switches to ROLAP mode to retrieve data from the relational data source. As soon as the build of the new MOLAP cache is complete, Analysis Services will serve the users from the new MOLAP cache. Typically in this scenario you would want to specify the latency time interval to be much higher than the incremental processing time for the partitions. If the incremental processing takes much longer than the latency, you might experience occasional degradation in performance because the existing MOLAP cache in Analysis Services is outdated and Analysis Services needs to fetch the results from the relational data source.

Latency simply refers to the amount of time you want the system to wait before unceremoniously dumping an existing MOLAP cache that is used to serve users. The SilenceInterval property indicates that no less than the specified period must elapse before initiating the rebuilding of a MOLAP cache upon data change. The SilenceOverrideInterval property is a little trickier to get your head around, but by no means daunting. If SilenceInterval is reset time and again due to frequent data changes, the MOLAP cache never gets rebuilt fully and gets dumped often whenever data changes. There is some limit to our patience because users will always see performance degradation from the time Analysis Services switches to fetching the data from the relational data source after the specified latency time. To overcome this issue, the SilenceOverrideInterval property ensures that it stops resetting the silence interval for future data changes till the existing MOLAP cache is rebuilt fully.

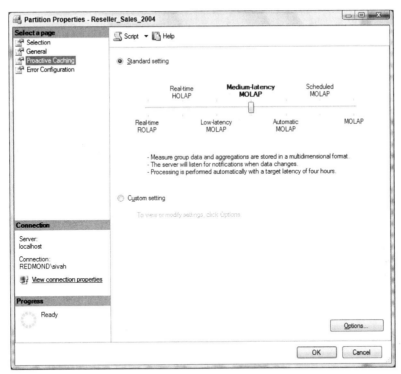

Figure 21-13

Normally you know how frequently updates are occurring to your relational data source. Based on that information you can specify the SilenceInterval. On certain occasions there might be frequent data changes that result in the Silence Interval timer being reset, and this can potentially lead to not rebuilding the MOLAP cache. That's when SilenceOverrideInterval comes in handy. Think of SilenceOverrideInterval as simply your way of saying, "I don't care if the update notifications keep coming, I want to do an update no longer than, say, every sixty seconds." So, even though SilenceInterval keeps on ticking away the seconds, SilenceOverrideInterval will override it if SilenceInterval overstays its welcome — and that is just what happens in Figure 21-14. You can see how SO (SilenceOverrideInterval) times out and a rebuild of the MOLAP cache is kicked off. Typically, if the SilenceInterval is specified in the order of seconds, your SilenceInterval override would be specified in minutes so that your MOLAP cache is not too long outdated. Figure 21-14 shows a graphical timeline representation of events occurring due to proactive caching being enabled, but is demonstrated using smaller time intervals for SilenceInterval and SilenceOverrideInterval rather than typical values. Once the cache is rebuilt, the normal process of proactive caching using the SilenceInterval during future notifications will be handled by Analysis Services.

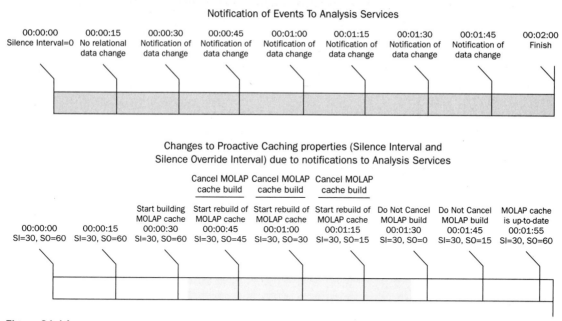

Figure 21-14

For the average latency scenario example explained here we recommend you customize the medium-latency MOLAP default settings so that you set the Silence interval, silence override interval, and Latency as shown in Figure 21-15. Silence interval is set to 10 seconds so that the MOLAP cache rebuilding starts 10 seconds after the data update. The processing of the partition takes approximately 2 hours. If there are multiple data updates within the first two hours, you want to make sure the Silence override interval kicks in and stops frequent cache update attempts and by the time of the 4-hour time limit (Latency) you have a new MOLAP cache ready for users to query. There might be some times where you have frequent data updates on the relational database and your MOLAP rebuilding has not completed yet but latency has expired. During that time all requests will be served by retrieving results from the relational data source. You need to ensure this time period is as small as possible so that users perceive the data is real-time and with very good performance (due to MOLAP cache).

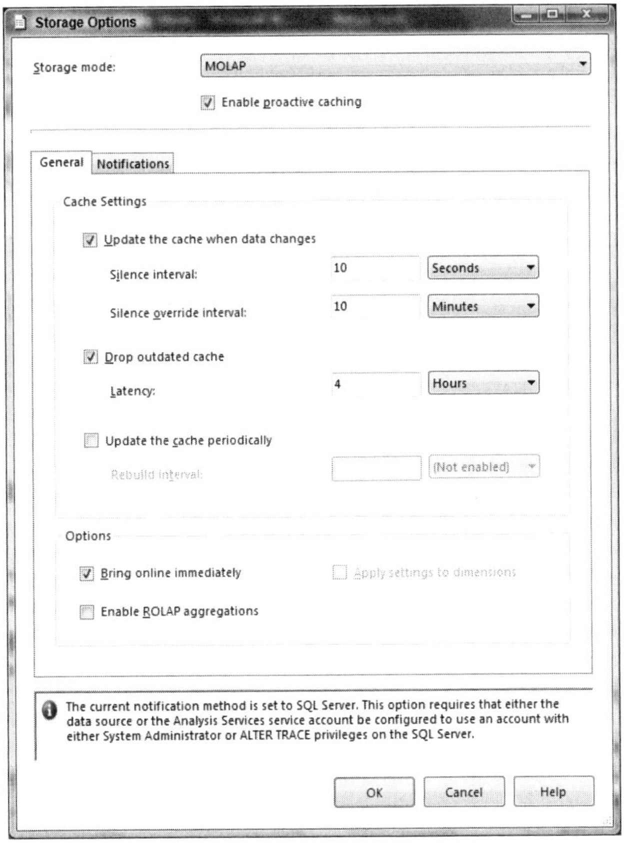

Figure 21-15

To recap, Analysis Services serves data to users with the help of a cache. If the data in the relational data warehouse changes, the cache needs to be updated (that is, rebuilt). It takes some amount of time to rebuild the cache. Latency is a proactive caching property that allows you to control serving your customers from an old MOLAP cache for a certain period of time, or to instantaneously serve the customers with the latest data. If your users are concerned about getting the most up-to-date data, you would set the property called Latency to zero. This informs Analysis Services that users are interested in the latest data and the existing MOLAP cache needs to be cleared. Because the new MOLAP cache might take some time to be rebuilt, you want to keep the results coming to the users. During the time the MOLAP cache is being rebuilt, Analysis Services fetches the data from the relational data warehouse to accomplish this. Even though you do get the most up-to-date data, you might see slight performance degradation because Analysis Services needs to retrieve the data from the relational data warehouse.

As soon as the MOLAP cache is rebuilt, Analysis Services starts serving the customers with the new MOLAP cache and you will start seeing your original query response times. If you want the users to continue using the existing cache while a new cache is generated based on new data, you can specify the time that it would take for rebuilding the MOLAP cache as latency. For example, if it takes 15 minutes to rebuild your MOLAP cache, you can specify the latency as 15 minutes. By specifying this, the current users would be receiving slightly old data for 15 minutes but at the MOLAP performance level. As soon as the MOLAP cache is rebuilt, Analysis Services starts serving all the customers using the new MOLAP cache and they would instantaneously see the new data. The trade-off here is how current the data is versus query performance. This is a key configuration that we expect many users to utilize if they want to see near real-time data but with MOLAP performance. In this scenario, customers need to be willing to wait for a certain period of time for data to be propagated through the UDM.

We do not recommend this solution for dimensions (changes to existing dimension members) because occasionally you might end up in a state where you would have to query the data from the relational data source. This is feasible, but when the dimension storage mode switches from MOLAP to ROLAP, it is considered a structural change by Analysis Services, which means that the partitions have to be rebuilt. This can potentially have a significant performance impact and clients might have to reconnect to query the UDM. However, if your business needs demand this and your users always establish a new connection to send queries, you can still use the settings for dimensions.

No Latency Scenario

In this short latency scenario you are in charge of an eCommerce site that provides customers' links to the most up-to-date products on the Web, which when sold, provide you with a commission. Your Internet affiliates are adding additional products to your catalog electronically, and at this point you are at 2.3 million product SKUs and the number is rising. Meanwhile, your partition data is changing frequently, and you have large numbers of members in the product dimensions. What does a BI application developer do?

Real-Time ROLAP Storage Option

The recommended solution here would be to set up the measure group and dimension data (which are frequently changing) to use ROLAP storage mode so that data is automatically retrieved from the relational data store as needed by the user. Working in this way does not come without a price. Indeed, although it is definitely a useful storage mode, the query performance of ROLAP mode is much slower than that of the MOLAP mode. In general we would always recommend a MOLAP solution for large dimensions, but if your dimension members are constantly changing and these changes need to be reflected immediately to end users, ROLAP would be a better option. This is because the data is being retrieved directly from your relational data source, which often requires over-the-net communication. Yes, you could go with HOLAP, but performance depends largely on your aggregated data and how frequently it is impacted due to changes in the data.

Just setting the storage mode to ROLAP is not sufficient. Analysis Services caches data and if there is a change in your relational data warehouse, this might need to be immediately reflected in your users' queries. If you definitely need real-time, as in zero latency updates, you need to specify Real-time ROLAP, which amounts to setting up proactive caching on ROLAP partitions or dimensions. Under this configuration, on a change in the source data, Analysis Services immediately drops the cache and gets the data from the relational data warehouse. Figure 21-16 shows the selection for Real-time ROLAP in the Proactive Caching dialog. If you click the Options button you can see the proactive caching properties set up so that latency is 0 and you bring the new data online immediately as shown in Figure 21-17.

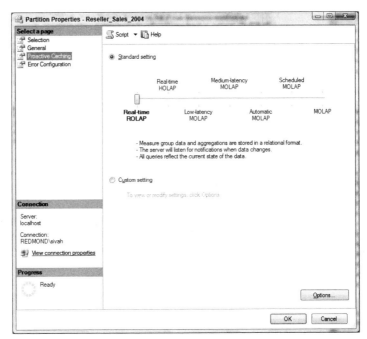

Figure 21-16

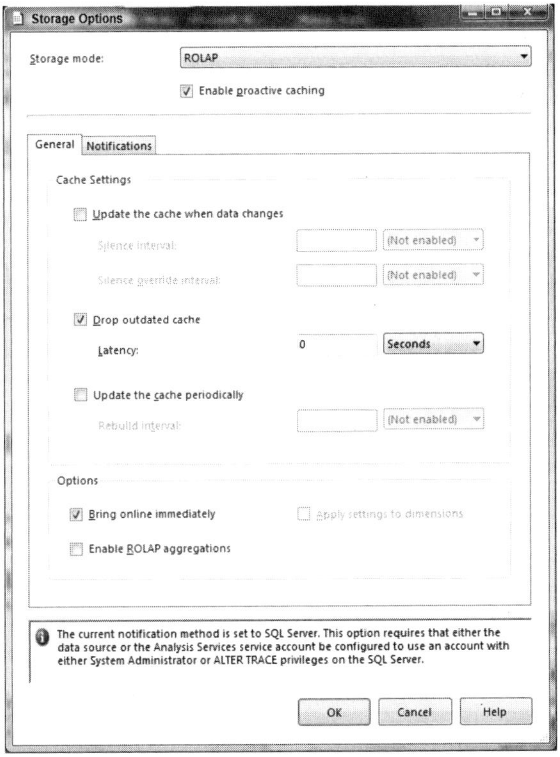

Figure 21-17

Billions and Billions of Records

The American astronomer Carl Sagan seemed fond of pondering the number of stars in a galaxy or cluster of galaxies. These days it is not a stretch to have similarly mind-boggling numbers of records in your transactional repositories. For reference, the Milky Way contains about 200 billion stars. Anyway, you don't have to ponder how to deal with them because we have a recommended solution for you right here. If you have a large number of fact data (on the order of billions of rows), ask yourself if the dimension data does not change much as compared to the fact data that changes regularly. If this is the case, building the cache might take a disproportionate amount of time because the dimension and fact data needs to be updated. Typically you will have the fact data split across hundreds of partitions. However, if the fact data is changing frequently, and if you do need real-time access of the data, the cache needs to be updated frequently and needs to be merged with existing partitions for the new fact data, and Analysis Services needs to aggregate the data from multiple partitions to the end users.

The way to approach this type of situation is to store historical data (data that does not change) using the MOLAP storage method and store current data (which can be defined as hours, days, or weeks) in ROLAP mode. Then set proactive caching to operate on the ROLAP partition only. In this way you will get fast access to fact data from the MOLAP store even when there are changes being processed on the ROLAP partition. We recommend this solution whenever you have a very large amount of fact data with new fact data arriving periodically and which you need to see in real-time.

> **Even if you have a MOLAP cube specified, if you still want real-time data you should use the connection string property "Real Time OLAP" and set it to True while connecting to Analysis Services. This will help provide you with the most up-to-date data from the relational data source**

Summary

Now you really are ready to go real-time with your cubes! To let you in on one of the arcane secrets of "real-time" anything, there is no such thing as real-time in computing, unless you plan to violate the cosmic speed limit (about 186,000 miles per second). There are varying degrees of latency. However, the shortest appear instantaneous to the user. Your job as an architect of Business Intelligence solutions is to design your application in such a way as to satisfy the needs of your users. That often means application of these techniques with particular attention paid to keeping the production system online and available during specified hours.

In this chapter you read about three real-world scenarios with one or more recommended solutions for each. These scenarios addressed solutions to long, average, and no latency requirements. A key takeaway here is that you should remain calm in the face of massive amounts of source data; there are ways to contend with it. If you get it right, your users will remain blissfully ignorant of the challenges you faced in keeping up the illusion of real-time data presentation. Indeed, your business decision makers using the system won't know (or care) how the system is implemented; they'll know, "...it just works and has amazingly up-to-date data." That is where you want to be.

22

Securing Your Data
in Analysis Services

Your data has value, and as with any item of value it must be protected from outside threats. Security is the set of techniques used to provide you with that protection. Indeed, security is an important consideration in the area of business intelligence. Think about it — the very keys to your company's profitability can be surfaced through your data and analytical applications. Just as you secure your personal belongings in a safe place, like a safe deposit box, you must secure your corporate data and applications. In the real word, a safe deposit box has a lock on it requiring a key for entry; only people to whom you give access (provide with the key) can actually open the secured object. These concepts map directly onto Analysis Services security. Analysis Services provides you with ways to protect your data so that you can restrict access to only those users who are authorized.

The environment within which you are working has a significant impact on the security precautions you should take. In general, if a server is running within the confines of a firewall it helps mitigate the external threats posed and provides increased protection. Disabling unused services/features that can potentially be exploited by hackers is yet another way to reduce risk. Running servers under least-privilege accounts like the network service account also helps ensure your system will not be compromised. Analysis Services provides you with the ability to enable or disable features such as stored procedures or ad-hoc queries, which thereby reduces the product areas that are likely to have security attacks and also run under least-privilege accounts on the system, as seen in Chapter 7. In addition to these techniques, you learned about additional core security features in Analysis Services that restrict access to unauthorized users in Chapter 9.

In this chapter you learn about the security features in Analysis Services that allow the administrator to define access permissions such as read or write to objects in Analysis Services, followed by restricting access to sensitive data only to those who are allowed to access the data. Restricting access to cube and dimension data is done by specifying MDX expressions that define if the member or cell can be viewed by the user. What better way to learn how to restrict the data than a real-world scenario? You learn the functionality of restricting dimension and cell data by means of scenarios targeted for these features.

Securing Your Source Data

You need to ensure your source data is not compromised through Analysis Services. Analysis Services 2008 provides you with several authentication mechanisms to ensure your source data is retrieved securely by Analysis Services. To retrieve data either at processing time or at query time, an Analysis Services instance needs to connect to data sources based on the storage options (MOLAP or ROLAP) specified for the dimensions and cubes within the database. In order to connect to the relational data source and retrieve the data, the Analysis Services instance needs appropriate credentials.

Analysis Services 2000 supported integrated security as the main authentication mechanism to the data source. The drawback with integrated security is that the Analysis Services 2000 instance used the credentials of the service startup account to connect to the data source. One of the main limitations of Analysis Services 2000 is that you need to provide access to the service startup account for each data source used within databases of an Analysis Services instance, and that can be a little tiresome. If the data source provided username and password options as with Microsoft's SQL Server or Oracle, you were able to specify those in connection strings to the data source. Analysis Services 2005 and Analysis Services 2008 overcome this deficiency by providing additional control and flexibility using Data Source Impersonation while connecting to the relational data sources, as seen in Chapters 2 and 4.

As with prior versions of Analysis Services, when you establish a connection to the data source, you can specify an authentication mechanism provided by the data source. For example, if you choose Microsoft's SQL Server you have the choice of either Windows authentication or SQL Server authentication, as shown in Figure 22-1. Instead of connecting to the data source as the service startup account as in Analysis Services 2000, Analysis Services 2008 provides four options to connect to data sources, as shown in Figure 22-2. Once a data source has been created, you can then specify the credentials under which you want the Analysis Services instance to retrieve data. The Impersonation Information tab in the Data Source Designer page shown in Figure 22-2 provides you with the flexibility to specify the impersonation option suited to your database. Whenever the Analysis Services 2008 instance connects to the data source, Analysis Services uses the impersonation information specified in the data source.

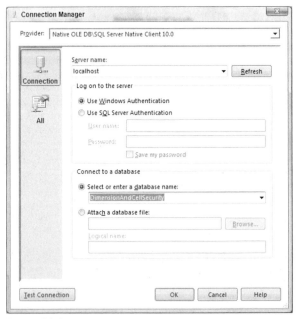

Figure 22-1

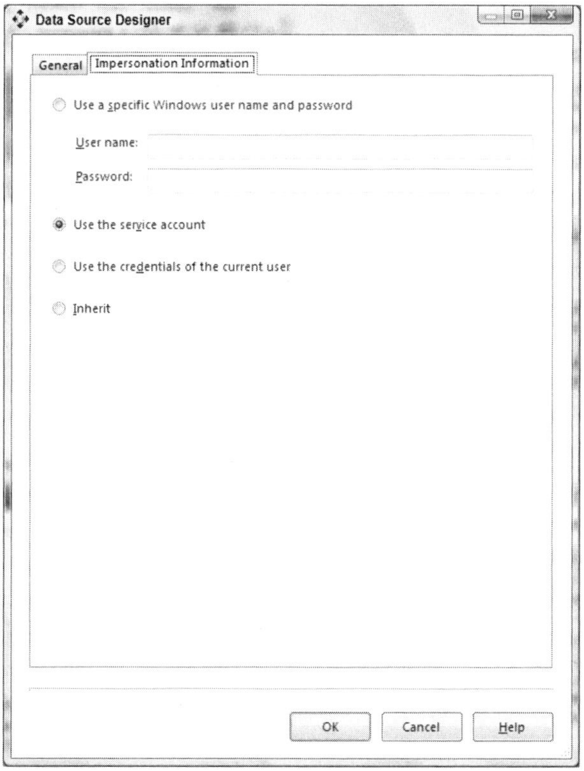

Figure 22-2

If the "Use the service account" option is chosen, Analysis Services 2008 impersonates the Windows account used as the services startup account for the Analysis Services instance to connect to the specified data source. When the option "Use a specific Windows username and password" is chosen, you need to specify a valid Windows credential account username and password. The Windows username is specified as <domainname>\<username>. With the "Use a specific Windows username and password" option, you can have different Windows accounts having access to various data sources within a single database or across Analysis Services databases. If a specific account has access in the data source, that account can just be specified in the Impersonation tab and you do not have to provide data source access to the service startup account of Analysis Services. We recommend that you configure the Analysis Services service startup account as a low-privilege account such as network service. This helps to reduce the attack surface on your system because the network service cannot have access to the majority of the system resources. In such circumstances the network service will typically not have access to your data sources. You can certainly provide data source access to Analysis Services by providing access to the network service account under which Analysis Services is running and choose the service account option for Impersonation Information. However, we recommend you use the "Use a specific Windows username and password" option with Analysis Services running under a low-privilege account to have a more secure environment. However, you do need to be aware that whenever the password of the Windows account expires you would need to update the passwords in data sources, which you can do via SQL Server Management Studio if you have permissions to administer the database, or through a custom AMO program if needed. The third option in the Impersonation Information page is "Use the credentials of the current user." This specific option is selected primarily for issuing open rowset queries, which are used during data mining querying and for processing objects that have out of line bindings (the object to be processed retrieves data through a query or a table dynamically at the time of processing through the process command). The last impersonation option is "Inherit." When the Inherit impersonation is selected, the impersonation information is obtained from the impersonation information specified for the entire database object that also has the same four options. If the impersonation information is Inherit even for the database object, the service startup account is used for impersonation while retrieving data for processing Analysis Services objects, server synchronization, and ROLAP queries and Use the credentials of the current user option for data mining open rowset queries and out of line binding data sources.

You have learned the various impersonation modes that can be set on data source objects in Analysis Services 2008 databases along with the recommended option to ensure that source data exposed through Analysis Services is secure. You next learn to secure your dimension and cube data appropriately for your end users.

Securing Your Dimension Data

Often in business you have to restrict data access from certain sets of users. You might have to restrict members and their children of a dimension or just cell values. Restricting access to members of a dimension from users is called dimension security. Restricting access to cell values from users is called cell security. You learn more about securing dimension members in this section, followed by restricting access to cell values in the following section with the help of a business scenario.

Dimension security helps you to restrict access to members of a dimension for your Analysis Services database users based on your business needs. For example, you can have a dimension named Account that could have members such as accounts payable, accounts receivable, and materials inventory for your company. You might want to restrict user access such that certain users can see only the account types that they are authorized to work with. For example, the personnel working in the accounts payable department should only be able to see the members under accounts payable and should not be able to see all the accounts under accounts receivable or materials inventory. Here is another example: If your company is selling products in various cities, you might want to restrict access for sales employees so that they can only see the data for which they are responsible on a city-by-city basis.

Analysis Services provides security restrictions on objects using an object called "role," as seen in Chapter 9. You can define roles in your database and then restrict permissions to certain dimension members or cells of the cube based on those roles. There are several techniques to model security based on the user, and you learn those techniques in this section. A user or a group of users is typically part of a specific role, and all the users in a role will have the same level of security. A user can be part of one or more roles. An Analysis Services instance identifies a user based on their Windows login credentials. When a user connects to an Analysis Services instance, the server iterates through various roles within the server to determine the roles the user is part of. Based on the list of roles a user belongs to, Analysis Services establishes appropriate security restrictions specified in those roles. If a user is part of multiple roles, Analysis Services provides access to a union of all the roles the user is part of. The important thing to know about this union is that if two roles give contradicting indications for user access of some object, access will be allowed.

If you have a group of users whose security constraints keep changing dynamically, you do have design alternatives by which you can specify security dynamically. That this is called dynamic security should come as no surprise. Analysis Services provides you with the capability to appropriately model and secure your data for your business needs. You learn the use of dimension security in the following business scenario; you also see the various approaches of securing dimensions that have been mentioned.

A Scenario Using Dimension Security

Business Problem definition: You are the data warehouse designer for the sales team in your company. You have sales representatives in certain states in the U.S. and each sales representative is responsible for sales within that state. The sales representatives report to regional managers who might also be responsible for sales in a state, and the regional managers report to the U.S. sales manager. The sales representatives can see the sales information of their state. The managers can see the sales information specific to them, as well as the data of the sales representatives reporting to them. You need to design a sales cube so that all the preceding security restrictions are applied to the users when they browse the cube.

We have generated data specifically for this scenario so that it will help you understand the various design techniques that can be applied. This data set contains a list of employees in a company along with several months' worth of sales data; there is also a geography table that contains a list of states. Follow these instructions to restore the relational database from which you will create a cube:

1. Copy the file `DimensionandCellSecurity.bak` to the backup folder (which for your SQL Server instance would be at <drive>:\Program Files\Microsoft SQL Server\ MSSQL10.<instancename>\MSSQL\Backup) of your Microsoft SQL Server 2008.

2. Connect to the relational SQL Server 2008 using SQL Server Management Studio. Right-click the Databases folder and select Restore. You will see the SQL Server Restore dialog as shown in Figure 22-3.

3. Select the "From device" option. Click on the ... button and specify the entire path to the relational database backup. You will now see the various databases within the backup file listed below "Select the backup sets to restore."

4. Select the database "DimensionandCellSecurity-Full Database Backup" to restore as shown in Figure 22-3.

5. Select the "To database" drop-down box and select DimensionAndCellSecurity as shown in Figure 22-3.

6. Click the Options page in the Restore Database dialog and make sure the paths for restoring the backup for the database and log files are specified correctly as shown in Figure 22-4. Once you have verified this, click the OK button. The database will be successfully restored on your machine.

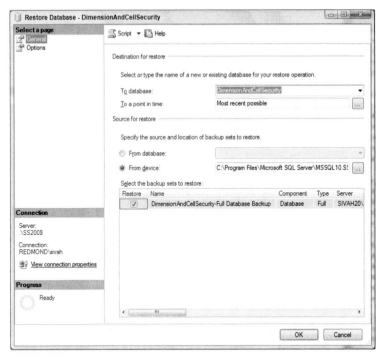

Figure 22-3

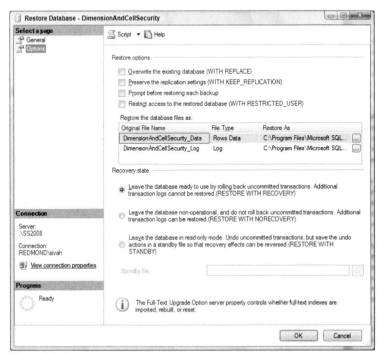

Figure 22-4

7. To demonstrate the dimension and cell security, you need users on a domain. To keep it simple you will create local users on your current machine. Run the batch file `adduserscript.bat` that is provided in the Chapter 22 download samples available at `www.wrox.com`. If you are using the Windows Vista or Windows Server 2008 operating system, you need to run this script as an administrator by right-clicking this script in Windows Explorer and selecting Run as Administrator, as shown in Figure 22-5. You can see that 15 users are added to your machine on your computer's computer management console, as shown in Figure 22-6.

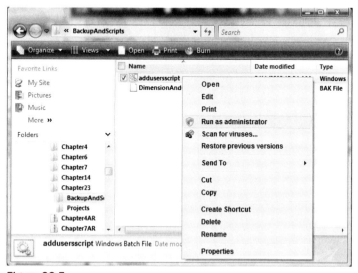

Figure 22-5

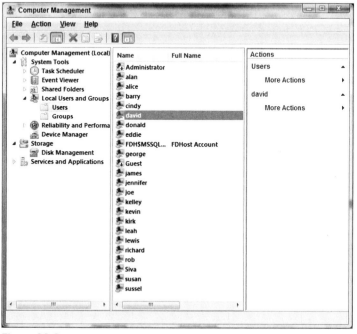

Figure 22-6

Some of the recommended solutions would need to detect the username along with domain name. The Employee table within the DimensionAndCellSecurity database has two columns called Employee Login and Manager Login. You have already created the login names for the users in the Employee table in step 5. You need to update the domain name in these columns to your machine name.

8. To get the machine name of your system, open a command prompt and type **hostname**.

9. Open the Employee table by right-clicking it in SQL Server Management Studio and selecting Open Table. You will now have all the rows of the Employee table, as shown in Figure 22-7.

10. Update the Login, Manager Login, and Access Rights columns by replacing domain with your machine name. (You can see that some of the logins and manager logins for a few rows are updated with domain name as sivah20.)

You are now ready to create a cube and restrict users to view sales information only for the states for which they are allowed to see the information.

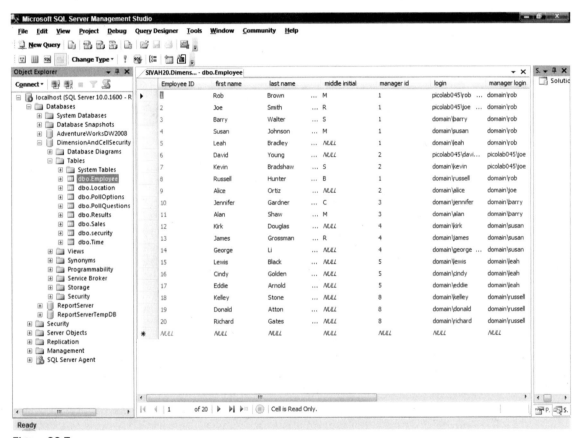

Figure 22-7

11. Create an Analysis Services project called DimensionAndCellSecurity-Scenario1.

12. Create a data source to the DimensionAndCellSecurity relational database you restored.

13. Create a Data Source View using the data source to the DimensionAndCellSecurity database and select the tables Employees, Location, Time, and Sales. Select the columns in each table as shown in Figure 22-7, right-click, and select "Select Logical Primary key." Create the relationships between the tables as shown in Figure 22-8.

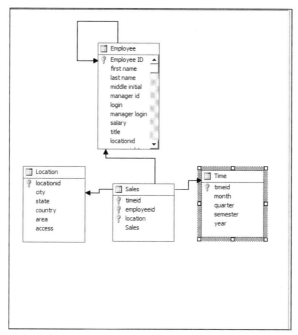

Figure 22-8

14. Right-click the Employee table and select "New Named Calculation."

15. Enter **Full Name** as the column Name.

16. Enter the following expression for the column "Full Name" under Expression:

[first name] + ' ' + [last name]

17. Create a UDM using the Cube Wizard by selecting the Sales table as Measure Group table and select the defaults in the other dialogs of the Cube Wizard. The Cube Wizard will create the three dimensions Location, Employee, and Time.

18. Open the Location dimension by double-clicking the Location.dim dimension object.

19. Add the columns Access, Area, City, Country, and State as attributes within the Location dimension by dragging and dropping the columns from the Dimension Designer's Data Source View pane to the Attributes pane.

20. Create a user hierarchy with levels Country, Area, State, and City as shown in Figure 22-9.

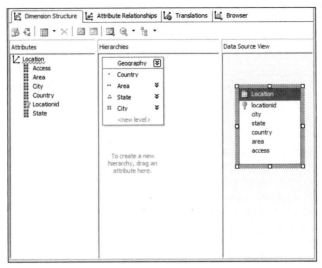

Figure 22-9

21. Create attribute relationships between the various attributes of the Location dimension as shown in Figure 22-10.

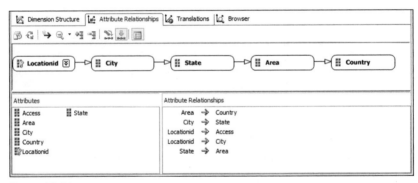

Figure 22-10

22. Open the Time dimension by double-clicking the `Time.dim` dimension.

23. Set the Dimension Property Type for the Time dimension to Time in the Properties window of BIDS.

24. Add the columns Month, Quarter, Semester, and Year as attributes by dragging and dropping the columns from the Dimension Editor's Data Source View pane to the Attributes pane.

25. Create a user hierarchy with levels Year, Semester, Quarter, and Month as shown in Figure 22-11.

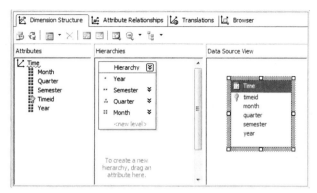

Figure 22-11

26.   Create the attribute relationship between the attributes of the Time dimension as shown in Figure 22-12.

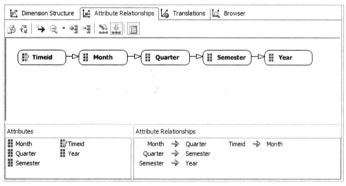

Figure 22-12

27.   Open the Employee dimension by double-clicking the `Employee.dim` object.

28.   Add the columns Full Name, LocationId, Login, Manager Login, Salary, and Title as attributes of the Employee dimension. From the Dimension Editor of the Employee dimension, you can observe that the dimension contains a parent-child hierarchy. The manager-employee relationship in the Employee dimension is modeled as a parent-child hierarchy.

29.   Select the key attribute "Employee ID." Change the Name Column Property for the key attribute to "Full Name." This step enables you to see the employee's name while browsing the parent-child hierarchy.

30.   Select the parent attribute Manager ID and rename the attribute to Employees.

31.   Deploy the cube to your Analysis Services instance.

Once you have created your UDM, the next step is to define security to restrict the data being seen from the users based on their location. The roles object in Analysis Services allows you to restrict data access based on the login of a user. The roles object contains a collection called membership, which you learned about in Chapter 9. You can add a user or a group of users to this membership collection. The security restrictions applied in this role will be applied to all the users in the membership collection. In this business problem you need to limit access to the sales representatives so that they can see only the sales information relevant to their state or their direct reports. You will learn several solutions to restrict the dimension member access along with their merits and de-merits.

Restricting a user to see only certain members of the dimension Location automatically restricts the user from seeing the sales information for that location. Location is a dimension and applying security or restrictions to users to certain members of a dimension is therefore called dimension security. If a user is part of more than one role, Analysis Services restricts the user to just a union of the roles the user is member of. For example, if a user is a member of Role1 where you have restricted the users to see the location New York, and the user is also a member of Role2 where you have restricted the users of Role2 to the location New Jersey, the user can see both these locations when he connects to Analysis Services. If Role1 had security restrictions for a user that did not allow you to see the dimension member New York but Role2 had security restrictions that allowed you to see the member New York, then Analysis Services would allow the user to access and retrieve the dimension member New York.

Now you will see the various design techniques concerning role definition and what the trade-offs are for those design techniques. Some of the techniques mentioned in the following sections are from the dynamic security presentations by Dave Wickert, Program Manager, Microsoft Corporation. These design techniques have been modified for Analysis Services 2008.

The User-Role Approach

One approach is to restrict location access by defining the list of locations a user can see. In order to do this you need to create a role for each user and define the restrictions so that user can have access only to members of specific states. In the following example you create roles for the users David and Robert. The following instructions show how to solve the problem of definition by creating roles for each user:

1. To create a new role for the Sales UDM, right-click the Roles folder and select New Role. A new role is created with the name Role and you will now see the Role Designer.

2. Right-click the Role.role in Solution Explorer and rename it **David.role**.

3. You will be prompted with a dialog box asking you if the object name needs to be changed. Click Yes. The Role Designer has several views, as shown in Figure 22-13. In the General view you can define administrative tasks on the cube, such as process permissions or permission to read definitions of the objects in the database. You can also give full control at the database level, which means the users have full control to edit objects within this database.

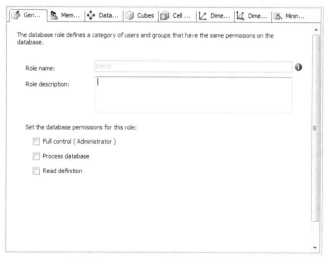

Figure 22-13

4. Click the Membership tab in the Role Designer.

5. Click the Add button to add a user to this role, and add the user David. You have already created a user account on your machine for David earlier in this section. David's login account will be <machinename>\David, where machinename is the name of the machine you are working on. When you click the Add button you will see a dialog where you can enter the domainname\loginname. Enter your machine name followed by **\David** in this dialog as shown in Figure 22-14 and click OK.

Figure 22-14

You will now see that the user David has been added to the role Role as shown in Figure 22-15.

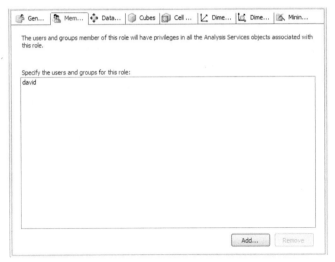

Figure 22-15

The next step is to provide access to the cubes and dimensions in the database.

6. Click the Cubes tab in the Role Designer. You will now see the list of cubes within the database, as shown in Figure 22-16. You can see your UDM Dimension and Cell Security.

7. From the drop-down list box under Access, select Read access to the UDM, as shown in Figure 22-16.

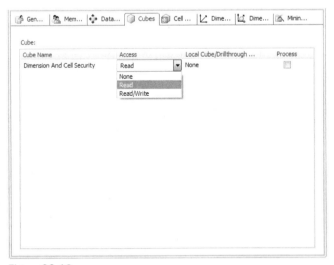

Figure 22-16

By selecting the access type Read, you allow users or groups with the role of David to read the data from the cube Dimension And Cell Security. In addition to providing access to the cube, you can also provide access to the users to drill-through to detail data or to process the cube in this pane. By default when you provide access to the cube for the users of the role, they do not get drill-through to fact data or the ability to process the cube unless these security permissions are explicitly enabled. Leave the Local Cube/Drillthrough Access option to None. After providing access to the cube, you can provide access to the database dimensions as well as the cube dimensions in the Dimensions View.

8. Click on the Dimensions tab of the Role Designer, and you will see the list of dimensions along with options to provide permissions to Access, Read Definition, and Process, as shown in Figure 22-17.

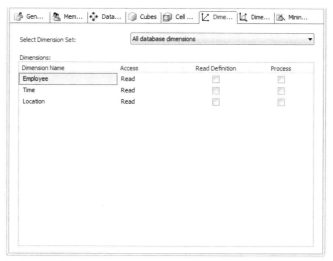

Figure 22-17

To provide permissions to a dimension in the database, you can select the Read or Read/Write option in the Access column in the Dimension tab of the Role Designer. By default access to the dimension is set to Read. If you select the Read Definition checkbox, users have the ability to send discover statements to see the metadata information associated with the dimension. You can provide permissions to processing a dimension by selecting the checkbox for the specific dimension.

9. You can provide access to specific dimension members of the database by using the Dimension Data tab in the Role Designer. Click the Dimension Data tab of the Role Designer.

10. Select the dimension Location from the Dimension drop-down list box.

11. Select City from the Attribute Hierarchy drop-down list box. The Dimension drop-down allows you to choose the database dimensions in the database. The default view shows the first dimension in the database. Once you select a specific dimension, the list of attribute hierarchies is shown as a drop-down list by Attribute Hierarchy as shown in Figure 22-18.

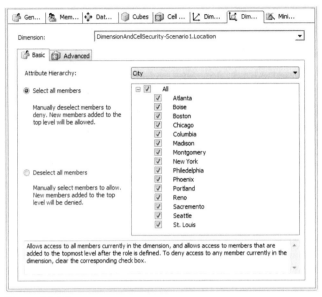

Figure 22-18

12. Click the Dimension Data tab to restrict the members that can be seen by the current role. In this example assume you are restricting access to the user David. Because David is responsible for New York City, he should only be able to see sales information pertaining to New York City. To specify this you need to select the dimension Location from the Dimension drop-down list, as shown in the next few steps.

13. Select the radio button "Select all members."

14. Select the attribute hierarchy City from the Attribute Hierarchy drop-down list.

15. Deselect all the members except New York, as shown in Figure 22-19. The selection of the city New York restricts the users of the role from seeing other cities when they access the dimension Location. If you have complex business logic concerning access to members of a hierarchy, you can implement your logic using MDX expressions in the Advanced tab.

Figure 22-19

If you click the Advanced tab, you will see three sections: Allowed member set, Denied member set, and Default member, as shown in Figure 22-20. You will see that the Denied member set shows all the members of the City hierarchy, except New York, that were not selected in the Basic tab. Analysis Services interprets all members not in the Denied member set (New York in this scenario) to automatically be included in the Allowed member set. That's the reason why you do not see the member New York in the Allowed member set. You can include your business logic to select the members that are to be allowed or denied for this specific role. The MDX expressions should result in a set of members of the current hierarchy in the Allowed member set and Denied member set. The result of the MDX expression specified in the Default member pane should be a single member from the current hierarchy.

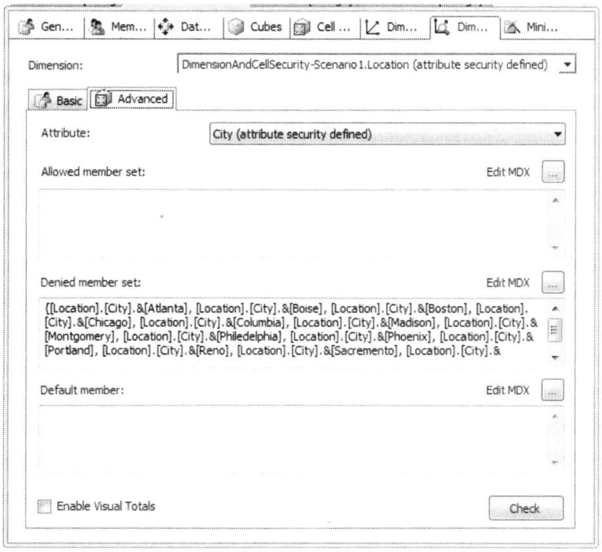

Figure 22-20

> An empty set for the Allowed member set (shown in Figure 22-20) indicates all the members of the current role have access to the members of the current hierarchy. An empty set in the Denied member set indicates there are no restrictions applied. {} is not the same as an empty set. Having {} in the Allowed member set simply disallows the role members to see any other member.

16. Similar to restricting access to New York City using the Basic tab in the Dimension data, you can restrict access for the attribute hierarchies Area, State, Country, and LocationId to the members East Area, New York State, USA, and 1 respectively so that the user David can only see members relevant to New York City.

Having defined the dimension security, you need to test the security you have defined for user David.

17. Deploy the entire project to your Analysis Services instance.

18. Open the Dimension Security cube and switch to the Browser pane.

By default, if you select Sales and the hierarchy Geography you will be able to see the sales information for all the cities.

19. Click the Change User icon as shown in Figure 22-21.

Figure 22-21

20. You will now have a dialog where you can select the role you have created. Select the role David as shown in Figure 22-22 and click OK.

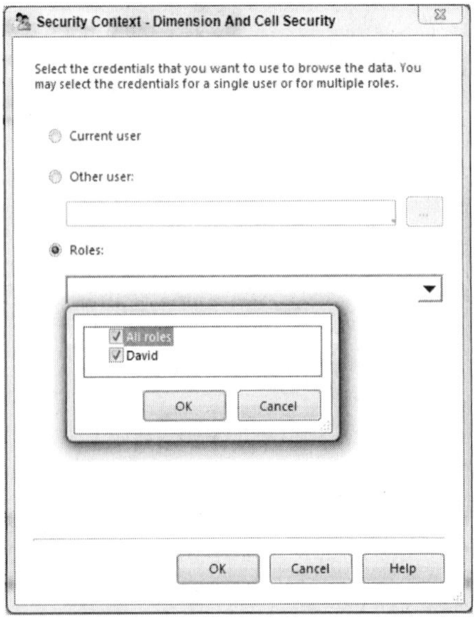

Figure 22-22

21. Drag and drop the sales measure and the Geography hierarchy of the Location dimension into the Cube Browser, as shown in Figure 22-23.

22. Drill down to the various levels of the Geography hierarchy.

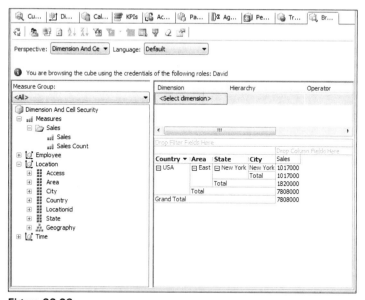

Figure 22-23

As you can see, the user David can only see results for the member New York; his access to the sales information is restricted to that and the totals. However, the Totals for the State, Area, and Country do not match the value for city New York. This is because sales for other cities are included in the totals.

You can define security permissions on roles so that the totals returned by Analysis Services are calculated for the visible members rather than all the members in the dimension.

23. Open the role David and switch to the Dimension Data tab.

24. Select the cube dimension Location and the attribute hierarchy Area.

25. Switch to the Advanced security definition tab and enable the checkbox Enable Visual Totals as shown in Figure 22-24.

26. Enable the checkbox for the attribute hierarchies City, Location, and State, and deploy the project to your Analysis Services instance so that new security definitions are updated on the server.

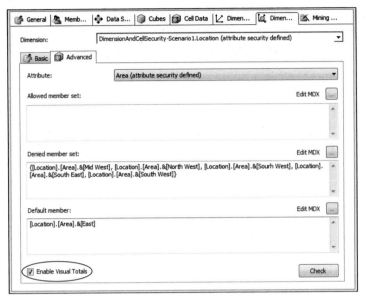

Figure 22-24

27. Switch back to the Cube Browser and reconnect to the SSAS instance.

28. Change the user and select the role David.

    You will see that user David can see the sales information for the city New York and all the totals now match the sales of the city New York as shown in Figure 22-25. By enabling visual totals in dimension security, you have ensured that the role David can only see aggregated data for cities that can be accessed by users of the role David.

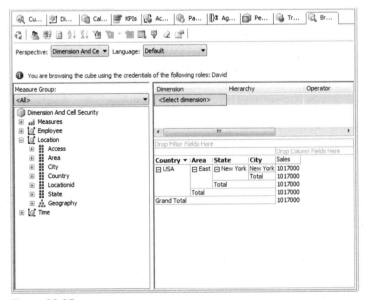

Figure 22-25

Similar to David, you would need to define appropriate security for all the users in the organization to be able to access data from the cube. The goal of defining dimension security in this scenario is to restrict the regional sales managers to be able to only see the results for all the cities of just their direct reports while the U.S. sales manager is able to see the entire set of cities. Just as you specified security on the Location dimension for the role David, we recommend you repeat the process to create a role for each user and provide access to the cities that can be accessed by the user. In this way you can restrict data access to users of the cube using the dimension security feature of Analysis Services.

29. To restrict the user David to only see sales data relevant to him, you can restrict him from seeing other employee members in the Employee dimension. The Employee dimension has a parent-child hierarchy called Employees. Switch to the Dimension Data tab.

30. Select the Employee database dimension and the attribute hierarchy Employees.

31. Select the member David Young and the members Joe Smith and Rob Brown (who are managers of David Young). Also, select All from the Employees hierarchy as shown in Figure 22-26. You have now restricted the user David to have appropriate permissions on the Employee dimension.

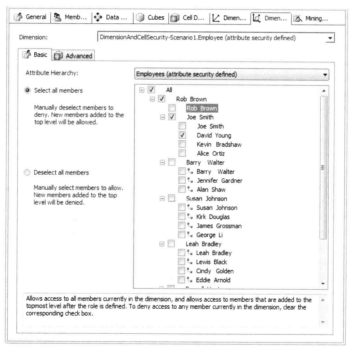

Figure 22-26

The members of role David can only see the dimension member David and its parents under the parent-child hierarchy Employees. In order to make sure David truly can see only data relevant to himself, verify it once again using the Cube Browser, as in the next few steps.

32. Save and deploy the project to your Analysis Services instance.

33. Switch to the Cube Browser.

34. Change the user to simulate David by selecting the role David.

35. Drag and drop the measure Sales amount in the Data area of the OWC in the Cube Browser.

36. Drag and drop the Location ⇨ Geography hierarchy from the metadata browser to the row area of the OWC in the Cube Browser.

37. Drag and drop the Employee ⇨ Employees hierarchy from the metadata browser to the column area of the OWC in the Cube Browser, as shown in Figure 22-27. You will now only see the user David. However, you can see that the users of role David can also see the totals of David's managers Joe Smith and Rob Brown, as shown in Figure 22-27. This is due to the security definition that is unique to parent-child hierarchies. In order to make sure David sees only the sales amount sold by him, you might be thinking you can enable visual totals for the Employees hierarchy. However, Analysis Services 2008 does not support enabling visual totals for parent-child hierarchies. Hence you would need to restrict access to the fact data of Joe Smith and Rob Brown using cell security, which you learn about later in this chapter, or change the hierarchy from parent-child to a multilevel hierarchy.

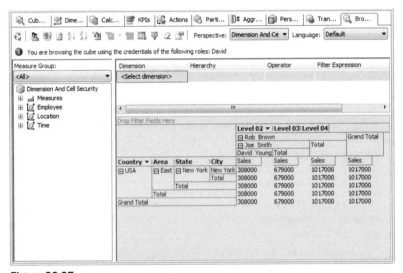

Figure 22-27

Each hierarchy has a default member that can be specified using the properties of the hierarchy or by using an MDX script. When you define dimension security, the default member of a hierarchy might be restricted to the users of a role. Hence the Role Designer allows you to specify the default member for hierarchies in a dimension for a specific role. To specify the default member for a hierarchy, you can either enter the member name in the Default Member pane or use the Edit MDX button. Follow the next steps to specify the default member.

38. Switch to the Role Designer for David.

39. In the Dimension Data tab of the Role Designer click the Advanced tab.

40. Select the Location database dimension and the State hierarchy.

41. Click the Edit MDX button for the Default member pane to launch the MDX Builder dialog, shown in Figure 22-28.

42. Double-click the member you want to set as the default member for the hierarchy chosen; New York for the hierarchy State in the Location dimension. You will see the unique name of the member in the Expression pane, as shown in Figure 22-28.

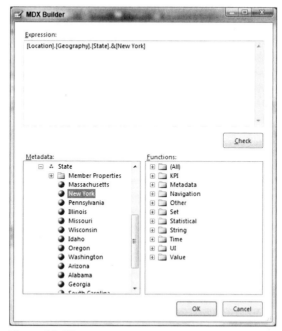

Figure 22-28

43. Click the Check button to make sure your chosen MDX expression is correct.

44. Click the OK button. You will see the default member expression is the Role Designer.

45. Specify the default member for the remaining hierarchies for which you have applied dimension security, New York for the City attribute, East for the Area attribute, 1 for LocationId, and David Young for the Employees attribute in the Employee dimension.

46. Specify default members for the cube dimension hierarchies State, City, and Area in the dimension Location and the Employees hierarchy in the dimension Employee.

47. Deploy the changes to your Analysis Services instance.

To verify your default member setting, you can run SQL Server Management Studio as a specific user who is part of the role you have created.

48. Open a command prompt on your machine.

49. Type **runas /user:<yourmachinename>\david ssms.exe** as shown in Figure 22-29.

Figure 22-29

50. When prompted for a password, enter the password for david: **divad*123!**.

You will now see the SQL Server Management Studio launched under the user david.

51. Open the MDX query editor in SQL Server Management Studio using the MDX icon or File ⇨ New ⇨ Analysis Services MDX Query.

52. Select the DimensionAndCellSecurity database.

53. Send the following MDX query by substituting for dimension, hierarchy, and cube name, and you should see the results for the default member, as shown in Figure 22-30.

```
SELECT <Dimension>.<Hierarchy>.Defaultmember on 0
From <CubeName>
```

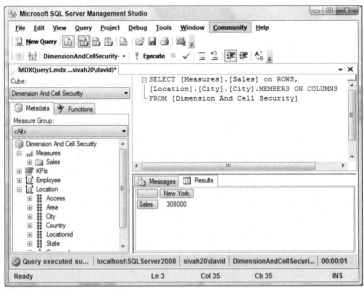

Figure 22-30

If a user belongs to more than one role, the default member for the first role in the roles collection is chosen as the default member for the hierarchy. The user-role approach is suited to business scenarios where you have a limited set of users and their security permissions do not change frequently. Typically, when the permissions for users are static, this approach will be sufficient to suit your business needs and is easy to implement and maintain.

The Access-Role Approach

In the user-role approach, you solved the business problem of restricting data access for certain employees in the company. You created a role for each employee in the company and provided appropriate restrictions. Under that design, if new employees are joining the company, the administrator of the cube needs to create a new role for every new salesperson and appropriately provide the restrictions. Similarly, if employees are leaving or changing roles, such as a salesperson promoted to sales manager, you would have to appropriately update the dimension security within the cube. There are two design alternatives from which you can choose to accommodate changes of this nature: to create a role for each city where employees get the permissions, or to create roles based on Windows users groups where the users get added or removed to the Windows groups.

You can create roles based on cities rather than the users. In this design alternative you add all the users who have the right to access specific cities to the role of a specific city. If your company had 100 employees selling into 10 different cities, you would create 10 roles and assign users to those roles — as opposed to creating 100 roles with cities assigned to each. This design leaves open the question of how to go about restricting the employee name in the Employee dimension. Assuming the employees have an account of the format <domain name>\<login name>, you can restrict employee access by using an MDX expression that uses the MDX function USERNAME as shown here:

```
FILTER(employee.[employees].MEMBERS,
INSTR(employee.[employees].CURRENTMEMBER.NAME,
RIGHT(USERNAME,len(USERNAME)- instr(USERNAME,"\"))))
```

In this dimension security scenario, the logins of each employee match the first name of the employee. The employees parent-child hierarchy in the Employee dimension has been modeled in a way that the employee's full name is the named column for the hierarchy. Therefore, while browsing the Employees hierarchy you see the full name of the users. If you check the name in the login and match it with the appropriate employee name, you will automatically get the employee member for the user who has logged in. The preceding MDX expression completes the operation of identifying the employee member for the corresponding login using the MDX function username. The username MDX function returns the <domainname>\<loginname>. Finally, the third line in the MDX expression extracts the loginname. This loginname is used in the condition of the Filter MDX function to iterate through all the members of the employees hierarchy and extract the member(s) where the employee name contains the login name.

To extract the login name from the employee name, the VBA function Instr is used. The result of the MDX expression is the correct employee member name. Most companies do not have login names that match exactly to the first name or last name of the employees. In such a case you would need to form a complex MDX expression that will return the correct employee member for the Allowed set. You will see an example of a complex MDX expression in this chapter under the "Securing Your Cube Data" section.

To test the preceding solution you can go to the Cube Browser and bring up the user of interest as shown in Figure 22-31. Analysis Services now impersonates the user account specified in the "Other user" option to access the cube data. Security restrictions are applied to the user based on the roles that user is part of. You can now browse the dimensions and cell values in the Cube Browser to ensure your security restrictions were applied correctly. You do need to be aware that the "Other user" option is supported by Analysis Services only on a valid domain account and not a local machine account.

Figure 22-31

If your business needs are such that data access restrictions for users are reasonably static but the number of users is large as compared to the data members in the dimension, the access-role approach might be best suited for your business problem. If your business needs are such that the security restrictions of users change due to modification of roles or location, you need a solution where you can dynamically add or remove users. We recommend the approach of creating Windows user groups and adding the users to those Windows groups. The Windows groups will actually be added to the membership of a role rather than the users themselves. For the current scenario, you would create a Windows group for each city. If the employees move from one location to another, they can easily be removed or added to the appropriate city group. In this way, you do not have to make changes to the roles in Analysis Services. This solution is feasible because Analysis Services leverages Windows authentication to authenticate users, and users' permissions keep changing through Windows security groups, and Analysis Services is able to handle the security restrictions dynamically. This solution is suited for an enterprise where multiple applications connecting to Analysis Services can utilize this. However, in this technique you still need to maintain a role for each Windows group. Therefore your Analysis Services database can potentially have several roles that are equivalent to the number of members in the dimension. If you only want to have one role that provides you with the ability to restrict data for all users dynamically, you have three different techniques, which are explained in subsequent sections. Restricting dimension data access using one role for several users whose data access permissions change periodically is called dynamic dimension security.

The Member Property Approach

One of the ways to provide access to locations for employees is to have a column in the relational data source that contains the list of employees who have access to that location. When you need to modify user access to a location, you can either restrict them or provide access by updating the list of users who have access in the relational column. You might be wondering how this translates into defining the security in Analysis Services dynamically — when a list in the relational data source must be maintained. Actually, it is quite simple with the help of an MDX expression.

First, you need to make sure the relational column in the dimension table is added as an attribute hierarchy in the dimension. You do not necessarily need to browse this attribute, but you need to make this attribute a member property for the Attribute hierarchies for which you need to apply dimension security.

1. Launch SQL Server Management Studio and connect to your relational database server.

2. Open the relational table called "Location" in the DimensionAndCellSecurity database from within SQL Server Management Studio.

3. Replace all instances of the name domain\<username> in the Access column to your local machine name\<username> and save the changes.

4. Open the Analysis Services project DimensionAndCellSecurity you created in this chapter.

5. Open the Location dimension.

6. Specify the Access attribute as a member property for the attribute City by dragging and dropping the City attribute onto the Access attribute in the Attribute Relationships tab of the Dimension Editor.

7. Your Attribute Relationships pane of the Dimension Editor for the Location dimension should look like Figure 22-32.

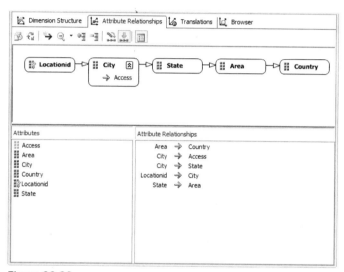

Figure 22-32

8. Next you need to create the MDX expression in a single role that will define dynamic security for all the users. Once again, you need the MDX function username. Start by creating a new role.

9. Add all the users who need access to the cube to the membership collection of the role.

10. Once you have provided read access to the cube and the dimensions, go to the Advanced tab of the Dimension Data pane. Select the dimension Location and hierarchy City. Enter the following MDX expression for the Allowed set:

```
Filter(Location.City.City.members,
Instr(Location.City.currentmember.properties('Access'),
USERNAME))
```

This expression filters the list of cities that can be accessed by the current user. Member property Access for each city is checked to see if the current user has access using the VBA function Instr. The expression Location.City.currentmember.properties('Access') returns a string that contains the login names of all the users who have access to the current city. The username function returns the string containing the login name of the current user. The Instr VBA function searches for the occurrence of the current user in the member property attribute

"Access" of the City attribute. If there is a match, the `Instr` function returns a positive number and the `Filter` expression uses that as an indication the condition is true, and therefore the current city can be accessed by the current user. Thus the `Filter` function is used to retrieve a set of cities that can be viewed by the current user.

You can have additional columns that contain the users who have access to State, Area, and Country. Similar to step 6 you can utilize these columns to create additional attributes to the dimension and make them as member properties to the corresponding attributes State, Area, and Country. If you use the same access column for more than one attribute, you can see redundant relationships in the Attribute Relationships designer along with the warnings, which you can ignore. By default the access attribute is a member property of the key attribute "LocationId." If you do not want your users to browse this attribute, you can disable the attribute hierarchy Access by changing its AttributeHierarchyEnabled property to false. You also need to specify the MDX expressions for the attributes State, Area, and Country respectively in the Location dimension in the Dimension Data tab to restrict the access to the right users. We recommend that you add appropriate columns in the relational database and set up the security restrictions for the attributes State, Area, and Country.

11. The Analysis Services project modeling the business problem using the member property approach is provided with the code download for Chapter 22 and is called DimensionAndCellSecurity-Scenario2. You can test the preceding expression by deploying the current role to the Analysis Services instance and then browsing the cube using a specific user as shown in Figure 22-31.

The member property approach is one of the three dynamic security approaches recommended in this chapter. This is easy to implement and the cost of maintenance (updates of permissions to users in the relational table) is typically low because only a few columns get updated for security changes. One of the advantages of the member property approach over the previous approaches is that you have a single role to maintain. However, the important trade-off in this approach is that whenever you change the security restrictions for the users, the dimension needs to be processed to reflect the changes in the database, thereby restricting the right dimension members. Based on your business requirements you can enable proactive caching on the dimension so that the dimension is processed automatically without intervention from an admin. If your dimension has a large number of members and if you need security changes to be in effect immediately, you might have performance implications because Analysis Services would have to use the dimension in ROLAP mode until the time the MOLAP cache gets updated. Based on the size of the dimension members and your business need, you can choose to implement this approach.

The Security Measure Group Approach

In this approach dimension security is modeled using a fact table. A relational table will hold the access permissions of users for the dimension members. If a user has permission for a specific location, that is indicated by a row containing the username, the location, and another column containing a value 1, which indicates the user has permissions to the location. A value of 0 indicates that the user does not have permissions. Ah, something simple! Now you really want to learn this approach, right?

The fact table containing the dimension security restrictions is added as a measure group to the existing cube. The relational column that contains the value of 0 or 1 is the measure that will be used for modeling dimension security. An MDX expression using the measure from the security measure group is used to restrict the dimension members to authorized users. Follow these steps to model the measure group approach for restricting access to users:

1. Use the Analysis Services project you used in any of the approaches discussed earlier and delete all existing roles.

2. In the DSV designer, right-click and select Add/Remove Tables. Select Table Security and click OK.

3. Mark the employeeid and locationid as key for the security table and make appropriate joins to the dimension and employee tables in the DSV as shown in Figure 22-33.

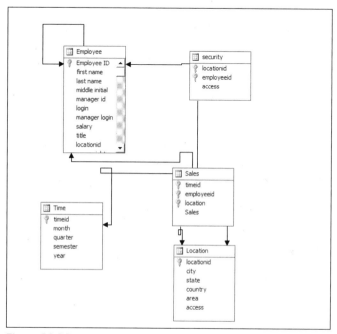

Figure 22-33

4. Open the cube DimensionAndCellSecurity and click the Cube Structure tab.

5. Right-click the cube name in the Measures pane and select New Measure Group.

6. Select the security table from the DSV. The Analysis Services cube designer automatically adds a new measure group called Security and creates two new measures, as shown in Figure 22-34. The Analysis Services tools automatically define the right relationships between the existing dimensions based on the joins specified in the DSV. If you click the Dimension Usage tab you will see the details of the dimension types and the granularity attributes. Deploy the new cube structure to your Analysis Services instance.

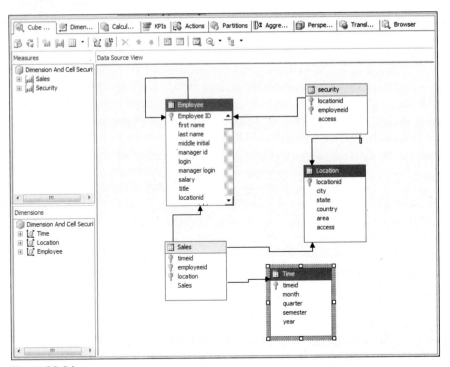

Figure 22-34

7. Create a new role, add all the users who need to access the Dimension Security cube, and provide read access to the cube and dimensions in the database.

8. Go to the Dimension Data tab in the Role Designer and select the Advanced option.

9. Select the dimension Location and hierarchy City. Enter the following MDX expression for the Allowed set:

```
FILTER(Location.city.city.MEMBERS,
(FILTER(Employee.Employees.MEMBERS,
instr(Employee.Employees.CURRENTMEMBER.NAME,
right(USERNAME,len(USERNAME)- instr(USERNAME,"\")))).ITEM(0),
measures.access)=1)
```

In this expression, the login of the current user is retrieved using the `username` MDX function. The inner filter expression iterates through all the members of the Employee dimension and retrieves the set of members who have the name same as the login name. Because there is a one-to-one relationship between users and logins, the inner filter condition results in a set with one member. The returned set cannot be used directly to form a tuple in the conditional expression. There are several ways of forming the condition expression using the outer filter function to retrieve the list of cities accessible by the current user. In the preceding MDX expression, you can retrieve a single tuple of the inner filter function using `.ITEM(0)`. You then have to check if the current user has access to the location. In order to do so, the outer filter function is used, which checks for a value of 1 for each tuple. The resulting set from the outer filter function is the set of cities for which the current user has access. Thus you form an MDX expression that secures the location for each user.

10. Similar to the MDX expression used in step 10, form an MDX expression with the remaining attribute hierarchies Area, Location, State, and Country in the Location dimension, and set the allowed member set for each hierarchy.

11. Restrict the access to members of the Employee dimension, using the following MDX expression, which uses the login of the user and restricts access to members in the Employees parent-child hierarchy in the Employee dimension.

```
FILTER(Employee.Employees.MEMBERS,
instr(Employee.Employees.CURRENTMEMBER.NAME,
right(USERNAME,len(USERNAME) - instr(USERNAME,"\"))))
```

12. Deploy the project to the Analysis Services instance.

The Analysis Services project modeling dimension security scenario using a fact table is provided under the Chapter 22 download samples and is called DimensionAndCellSecurity-Scenario3. Using the Cube Browser's change user option you can verify the dimension security restrictions you have applied in the measure group approach. However, as mentioned earlier in this chapter, you need to use a valid domain account rather than machine account.

The security measure group approach is an extension of the member property approach. Similar to the member property approach, you can implement this approach fairly quickly and maintenance is also fairly low cost. You do need to process the security measure group whenever there are security changes and you need the security permissions to take effect immediately. This approach has a lower performance impact as compared to the member property approach because only the specific measure group needs to be updated. For automatic updates you can set up proactive caching on the security measure group. If you have proactive caching set on this measure group, retrieving the data from this measure group would be fast even if you have a very large number of members in the dimension for which security has been updated. Once the security information is cached on Analysis Services, you do not have a dependency on the relational data source.

The External Function Approach

The member property approach and the secure measure group approach require appropriate dimensions and measure group processing to keep abreast of changes. You can certainly set up proactive caching on the dimension and measure group so that changes to security are immediately reflected. However, processing does involve some cost. The external function approach alleviates the problems of processing and ensures that only the most up-to-date security restrictions are applied to the users.

In the external function approach you write a UDF or a .NET stored procedure that will retrieve the list of locations the current user is authorized to access. For example, the stored procedure can return the list of cities or states or areas that a specific user can access as an MDX set. This set is then defined in the Allowed member set as the dimension security restrictions for the current user. Analysis Services exposes the security permissions for .NET stored procedures, which restricts the stored procedures access on specific resources such as accessing a network or creating a new file. The security permission provides an extra level of code security so that your Analysis Services is more reliable. There are no such security permissions that can be defined for COM UDFs and you need to trust that the programmer has written good quality code. In addition to that you have the option of using the ADOMD server object model in your .NET stored procedure to perform custom business logic, which is not available if you code a COM UDF. You still need to maintain a relational table that provides information on a user's access to locations via a column. In this example you use the security table that was used in the measure group approach. Because the security table only contains IDs of employees and location you will need to make joins to Employee and Location tables in the relational database to retrieve the right location members. However, you can create a new table that will have the list of locations for employees based on the login information. Such a table will probably have the columns Login Name, City, State, Country, location ID, and access where the column access has values 1 or 0 that indicate if the user has access or not to the specified location.

The .NET stored procedure either needs to return a string that contains the list of locations or an MDX set of locations. The string needs to contain the unique name of the locations separated by a comma so that you can be converted to a set using the StrtoSet MDX function. This function in a .NET stored procedure or a UDF allows you to get an MDX set of members that need to be allowed or denied for the users of the current role. Your .NET stored procedure alternatively can return an MDX set using the ADOMD server object model that can be directly used in the Allowed members or Denied member sets for dimension security restrictions. To create the set of members, your .NET stored procedure needs to identify the member(s) from Analysis Services based on the security restrictions defined in the relational database.

In this dimension security you will create a .NET stored procedure that returns a string containing the unique names of the locations accessible for the current user. The stored procedure will take two arguments, login and location, which are strings. For the login of the current user you can directly pass the MDX function username. The location argument will be the column name of the attribute hierarchy for which you need to retrieve the list of members accessible by the current user. What follows is the pseudo-code for translation into a function in your favorite .NET language:

```
Public string getAllowedSet(string login, string location)
{
        1. Connect to your relational data source database
        2. Form the SQL query using the login and location to retrieve
           the members that can be accessed by the users
        3. Iterate through the result set and form the output string so that the
           members are returned in the unique name format.
}
```

The stored procedure first needs to connect to the relational database and send the following query:

```
select <location>
from employee, location, [security]
where employee.[login]= '<login>' and
employee.[employee id] = [security].employeeid and
location.locationid = [security].locationid
```

The words within <> are the parameters passed to the stored procedure. There is a potential for SQL injection attacks with the following query. We recommend use of a parameterized SQL query, which will help you to prevent a breach of security. The stored procedure retrieves the results from the query and forms the output string, which needs to be in the following format:

```
{[Location].<location>.<location>.&[<resultvalue1>],
[Location].<location>.<location>.&[<resultvalue2>],
[Location].<location>.<location>.&[<resultvalue3>],...}
```

The unique name for a member is represented as [Dimension].<Hierarchy>.<Level>.&[MemberName]. For attribute hierarchies the Hierarchy name and Level name will be the same. If the key column and named column for an attribute hierarchy are the same, the member in an attribute hierarchy can be referenced as [Dimension].[AttributeHierarchyName][AttributeHierarchyName].&[MemberName]. Follow the same approach to build a string that will represent the set of members for the members of a hierarchy in the Location dimension. The values resultvalue1, resultvalue2, and so on are the results from the SQL query, which you need to iterate to form the output of the function. You need to add appropriate error handling to your stored procedure. Once you have compiled your stored procedure, add the stored procedure to the assembly collection of the database with the appropriate impersonation mode and permission set. This stored procedure will require an external access permission because it needs to access an external resource (the relational database).

Create a new role and add all the employees' logins to the membership collection. Then specify read access to the cube and dimensions. Assuming the name of the assembly that contains the getAllowedSet function is SecurityMemberSet, specify the following MDX expression for the Allowed member set:

```
StrtoSet(SecurityMemberSet.SecurityMemberSet.getAllowedSet(USERNAME, "City"))
```

Test the security restriction using the Cube Browser and change to one of the local users and verify the current user is only able to see the locations for which he has been given access.

The external function approach provides maximum flexibility in terms of design approaches. Also, you do not have the overhead of processing a measure group or dimension whenever there are changes to security restrictions. Security restrictions are always immediate because they are queried directly from the relational database each time; hence, you need to make sure the relational server is up and running all the time. Implementing this involves some amount of coding and proper error handling, but it should be worth spending the time up front to implement this type of solution.

Securing Your Cube Data

Restricting access to certain cell values of the cube for users is referred to as cell security. For example, in the case of confidential information like employee salaries, you can allow your employees to browse information about other employees such as number of years in the company, title, phone number, address, and login information, but restrict salary information. Because you want the information viewable by the person's manager, you need to control access at the cell value level rather than for whole dimension members.

Similar to dimension security, Analysis Services allows you to specify permission to cells using the roles. Access to cell values in a cube is restricted through an MDX expression that can be defined similar to dimension security. The MDX expression needs to evaluate to true or false. You can specify read and write permissions for cells in a cube. When a query is sent to the Analysis Services instance, the cells that are part of that query result are evaluated and returned. Whenever a cell is being evaluated, Analysis Services checks the permissions set for the cell. If the permission is set, it evaluates the condition to see if the user has access to the cell. If the user is allowed to view the cell, that cell value would be returned as part of the result. If the user does not have access to that specific cell, an appropriate message will be returned to the user.

Scenario Using Cell Security

Business Scenario definition: You are the director of the company and you want to take a satisfaction survey or poll of your employees. Employees can only view results of the survey they have filled in. However, managers can view the aggregated results of the poll if and only if they have more than two direct reports. Managers cannot see individual responses of their direct reports because this is a confidential survey. As an administrator you need to implement a UDM in Analysis Services 2008 so that you give appropriate security restrictions to the users to see the results.

You will use the same Dimension And Cell Security relational database. This database contains tables that have the questions of the poll and the results from the employees. The following steps show how to create the right UDM and then apply cell security restrictions for the employees:

1. Create a data source to the relational database Dimension And Cell Security relational data source.

2. Create a data source view that includes all the tables from the data source except the security table.

3. Create the joins between the tables as shown in Figure 22-35.

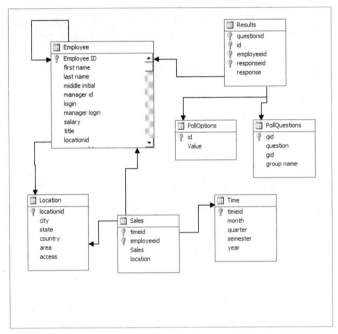

Figure 22-35

4. Create a calculated column in the Employee table called Full Name with the following expression:

```
[first name] + ' ' + [last name]
```

5. Browse the tables Poll Questions, Poll Options, and Results so that you get a good understanding of the scenario. You will notice there are 25 poll questions with responses from each employee stored in the Results table.

6. Create a UDM using the Cube Wizard by selecting the Sales and Results tables as Measure Group tables and select the defaults in the other dialogs of the Cube Wizard.

7. The Cube Wizard will create the dimensions Location, Employee, Time, Poll Questions, and Poll Options. You will now have the UDM as shown in Figure 22-36.

8. Open the Location dimension by double-clicking the Location.dim dimension object.

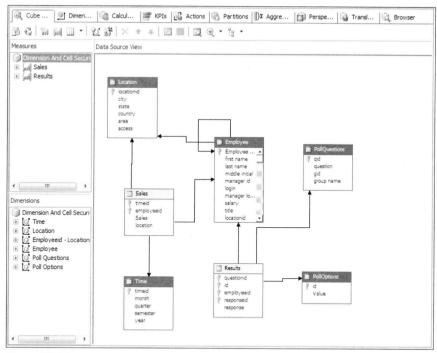

Figure 22-36

9.   Add the columns Area, City, Country, and State as attributes within the Location dimension by dragging and dropping the columns from the Dimension Designer's Data Source View pane to the Attributes pane.

10.   Create a user hierarchy with levels Country, Area, State, and City named Geography.

11.   Define attribute relationships between the attributes City, State, Area, and Country.

12.   Open the Employee dimension.

13.   Specify the name column for the Employee ID attribute to point to Full Name column.

14.   Rename the Manager ID attribute to Employees.

15.   Add the attributes Login, Manager Login, Salary, and Title to the Employee dimension.

16.   Open the Time dimension.

17.   Change the dimension type of the Time dimension from Regular to Time by changing the Type property.

18.   Add the attributes Year, Semester, Quarter, and Month.

19.   Create a user hierarchy called Time with the levels Year, Semester, Quarter, and Month.

20.   Define the attribute relationship between the attributes in the Time dimension.

21.   Open the Poll Questions dimension.

22.   Add Group Name, GID, and Question attributes to the dimension.

23.   Create a user hierarchy called Questions with the levels Group Name and Question.

24. Define the attribute relationship between the attribute Group Name and Question because there is a one-to-many relationship between these attributes.

25. Open the Poll Options dimension and add the Value attribute to the dimension.

26. Switch to the Dimension And Cell Security cube.

27. Delete the Sales Count and Results Count measures created by the Cube Wizard because they are not needed for analysis in this scenario.

28. The response measure contains a value corresponding to whether the employee agrees or disagrees to the question. Make the AggregationFunction (a property of the measure) for the response measure Count instead of Sum because we want to analyze how many users agreed or disagreed to the poll questions.

In this cell security scenario, managers are also involved in the survey. You need a way to distinguish the responses of the manager the responses of the aggregated results of her direct reports. To distinguish the results of a specific manager, change the property MembersWithDataCaption for the parent hierarchy, as shown in the following steps.

29. Open the Employee dimension.

30. Set the MembersWithDataCaption property of the parent attribute to " (* data)" as shown in Figure 22-37.

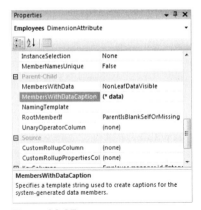

Figure 22-37

31. Having created the UDM, you now need to define security restrictions for the cells as per the business requirement. Similar to dimension security, create a new role in the database, add all the employees to the membership collection, and provide read access to the cube and the dimensions in the database.

32. Click the Cell Data tab. Click the drop-down list box for the Cube and select the cube Dimension And Cell Security as shown in Figure 22-38. The three panes shown in Figure 22-38 help you define the MDX expression for securing the cells. The MDX expression specified here needs to evaluate to either true or false, and this expression gets evaluated for each cell. You need to be careful in specifying the right MDX expression so that you secure the cell values correctly. You can define read permission, read-contingent permission, and read/write permission to the cells. The read and read/write permissions are intuitive as to what the behavior is. If the MDX expression evaluates to true, either read or read/write access for that specific cell is provided to the current user accessing the cell. If an expression is specified for read-contingent permission, the cells specified as viewable by the MDX expression are viewable under two conditions. If those cells are not derived from other cells, they are viewable based on the MDX expression. If those cells are derived from other cells in the cube, those cells are viewable only if that cell and all the cells from which it is derived are viewable.

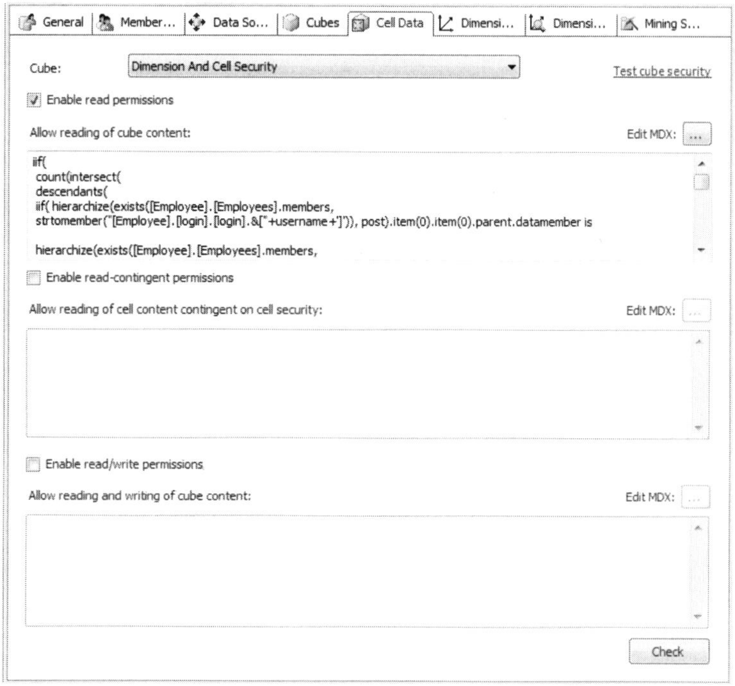

Figure 22-38

Following is the MDX expression that needs to be entered in the Enable read permissions pane to meet the business requirement of allowing employees to view their individual responses and managers to see the aggregated response of the poll questions if they have more than two direct reports. In the dimension security section, we mentioned that we will demonstrate a complex MDX expression to retrieve the employee name based on the login. The following MDX expression is a generic MDX expression and does not depend on the login name to be the user's name:

```
iif(
count(intersect(
descendants(
iif( hierarchize(exists([Employee].[Employees].members,
strtomember("[Employee].[login].[login].&["+username+"]")),
post).item(0).item(0).parent.datamember is

hierarchize(exists([Employee].[Employees].members,
strtomember("[Employee].[login].[login].&["+username+"]")), post).item(0).item(0),

hierarchize(exists([Employee].[Employees].members,
strtomember("[Employee].[login].[login].&["+username+"]")),
post).item(0).item(0).parent,

hierarchize(exists([Employee].[Employees].members,
strtomember("[Employee].[login].[login].&["+username+"]")), post).item(0).item(0))

).item(0)
, employee.employees.currentmember)) > 2   // Condition Check


(count(employee.employees.currentmember.children) > 2
and
count(intersect(
descendants(
iif( hierarchize(exists([Employee].[Employees].members,
strtomember("[Employee].[login].[login].&["+username+"]")),
post).item(0).item(0).parent.datamember is

hierarchize(exists([Employee].[Employees].members,
strtomember("[Employee].[login].[login].&["+username+"]")), post).item(0).item(0),

hierarchize(exists([Employee].[Employees].members,
strtomember("[Employee].[login].[login].&["+username+"]")),
post).item(0).item(0).parent,

hierarchize(exists([Employee].[Employees].members,
strtomember("[Employee].[login].[login].&["+username+"]")), post).item(0).item(0))

).item(0)
, employee.employees.currentmember))

    > 0 ) or  (strcomp(employee.employees.currentmember.properties("login"),
username) =0),
 // Value 1

( count(intersect(
descendants(
iif( hierarchize(exists([Employee].[Employees].members,
strtomember("[Employee].[login].[login].&["+username+"]")),
post).item(0).item(0).parent.datamember is

hierarchize(exists([Employee].[Employees].members,
```

```
    strtomember("[Employee].[login].[login].&["+username+"]")), post).item(0).item(0),

    hierarchize(exists([Employee].[Employees].members,
    strtomember("[Employee].[login].[login].&["+username+"]")),
post).item(0).item(0).parent,

    hierarchize(exists([Employee].[Employees].members,
    strtomember("[Employee].[login].[login].&["+username+"]")), post).item(0).item(0))

    ).item(0)
    , employee.employees.currentmember))

        > 0 ) or (strcomp(employee.employees.currentmember.properties("login"),
username) =0)
    ) // Value 2
```

33. Enter the preceding MDX expression to the "allow reading of cube content" pane in the Cell Security tab of the Roles editor.

Now, take a look at how this MDX expression helps in defining the intended cell security. The MDX expression can be broken up into three different parts for easier understanding. First, the MDX expression checks if the current user logged in is a manager. If the user is a manager with more than two direct reports, then value 1 expression is evaluated. If the user is a regular employee, then value 2 expression is evaluated. This is done using the IIF statement. The following MDX expression is used to identify if the current user is a manager with more than two direct reports:

```
count(intersect(
    descendants(
// Check if current employee is a manager
    iif( hierarchize(exists([Employee].[Employees].members,
    strtomember("[Employee].[login].[login].&["+username+"]")),
    post).item(0).item(0).parent.datamember is

    hierarchize(exists([Employee].[Employees].members,
    strtomember("[Employee].[login].[login].&["+username+"]")), post).item(0).item(0),
// End of check if current employee is manager

    hierarchize(exists([Employee].[Employees].members,
    strtomember("[Employee].[login].[login].&["+username+"]")),
post).item(0).item(0).parent,

    hierarchize(exists([Employee].[Employees].members,
    strtomember("[Employee].[login].[login].&["+username+"]")), post).item(0).item(0))
    ).item(0)
    , employee.employee.currentmember)) > 2
```

The username function is used to retrieve the current user's login. With the help of the StrToMember function and appropriate string concatenation the corresponding member in the Login hierarchy is identified. The MDX function Exists is used to identify the intersection of the Employee hierarchy with the member in the Login hierarchy for the current user. The result of the Exists function is a set that will contain the employee's name and all his parents. To retrieve the employee's name, we use the Hierarchize MDX function with the parameter Post so all the members in the set are ordered in a hierarchical order so that the employee name is the first item in the set. We then retrieve the first item of the set using .ITEM(0).ITEM(0) to retrieve the employee's name. In a parent-child hierarchy, if a member is a parent and also has data values (manager having sales quotas), the same employee name is used to represent the real member as the one that will have the aggregated values. However, these employee names will be at different levels in the parent-child hierarchy, which helps in distinguishing its own data value from the aggregated value for that member. This is shown in Figure 22-39 for the employee Rob Brown.

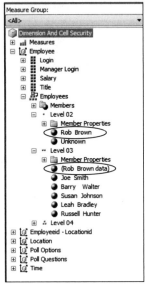

Figure 22-39

To check if the current member is a manager or not, we use the `.parent.datamember` function and compare it against another MDX expression that just gives the employee name. This MDX expression for evaluating if the current user is a manager is enclosed within comments in the preceding MDX expression. Based on the evaluation, the correct employee name is identified and we check if the employee has more than two direct reports using the MDX function `Descendants`.

Once a member has been identified as a manager having more than two direct reports, the `IIF` function chooses the following expression as the expression for evaluation:

```
(count(employee.employees.currentmember.children) > 2  // Check 1
and
count(intersect(
descendants(
iif( hierarchize(exists([Employee].[Employees].members,
strtomember("[Employee].[login].[login].&["+username+"]")),
post).item(0).item(0).parent.datamember is

hierarchize(exists([Employee].[Employees].members,
strtomember("[Employee].[login].[login].&["+username+"]")), post).item(0).item(0),

hierarchize(exists([Employee].[Employees].members,
strtomember("[Employee].[login].[login].&["+username+"]")),
post).item(0).item(0).parent,

hierarchize(exists([Employee].[Employees].members,
strtomember("[Employee].[login].[login].&["+username+"]")),
post).item(0).item(0))).item(0)
```

```
, employee.employees.currentmember))
    > 0 )  // Check 2
or
(strcomp(employee.employees.currentmember.properties("login"),username) =0)//
Check 3
```

In this expression two checks are performed to give access to the cells for the employee. The first conditional check (Check 1 AND Check 2) is for providing access to the aggregated cell for the managers, which involves checking if the employee corresponding to the current cell has more than two direct reports followed by the second condition (Check 3), which is an OR condition to allow access to the cells of the employee themselves. The second check (Check 3) is a simple check to match the employee with the login name because login is a member property for the employee attribute. The first condition has two conditional checks, Check 1 and Check 2, which are combined by a logical AND. By default parent members can see the cell values of their descendants (Check 2). To make sure individual cell values are not seen by managers, rather just the aggregated cell values can be seen, the additional conditional check (Check 1) is done in the preceding expression.

If the first argument of the IIF function evaluates to false, the result of the third argument of the IIF function will be the result of the function. The third argument is basically the MDX expression to allow regular employees or managers with less than or equal to two direct reports to see their individual responses of the poll.

You may have grasped the entire MDX cell security expression that solves the business problem by now. You can verify the results of your expression using the Cube Browser and choosing a specific user or by sending queries from SQL Server Management Studio as a specific user. Launch SQL Server Management Studio using the Run As command with the user Rob. Send the following query to an instance of Analysis Services:

```
SELECT [Measures].[Response] ON 0,
{DESCENDANTS([Employee].[Employees].[Level 02].&[1])}*
[Poll Options].[Value].MEMBERS ON 1
FROM [Dimension And Cell Security]
```

You will see results for the query with certain cell values showing #N/A, as you can see in Figure 22-40.

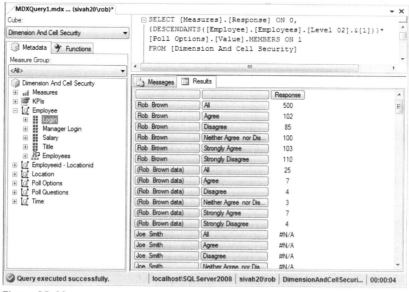

Figure 22-40

If you click the cell with #N/A you will see a message that the cell has been secured, as shown in Figure 22-41. You have now successfully solved the business problem of securing the poll results so that managers can only see the aggregated results if they have more than two direct reports.

Writing an MDX expression like the one shown in this example is not trivial. Even an expert MDX developer is bound to make some mistakes. We recommend you execute sections of your MDX expression as MDX queries or create MDX expressions as calculated members (especially in the cases where the MDX expression contains .currentmember), and then ensure the results of the MDX expressions are correct. Once you have validated your MDX expressions, you will be able to successfully define cell security and verify that cell security is applied correctly.

Figure 22-41

Summary

Just because you're paranoid doesn't mean they're not out to get you! That should be your mantra as you ponder the possibilities in the security space. In this chapter, you have seen many possible approaches to keeping your data secure. You learned about applying permissions to your relational data sources to help keep them secure, and about how you can restrict access to data in your Analysis Services databases using one of two types of restriction — dimension security and cell security. You learned the techniques of applying dimension security, like how to define roles and how to manage security in a dynamic business environment. Further, you learned about the relevant design choices and how they can be implemented in a real business scenario. Specifically, you learned five different approaches to secure dimension data using the user-role approach, the access-role approach, the member property approach, security measure group approach, and the external function approach. You learned how to apply cell security to restrict data at the cell level for certain defined roles at your company using the poll results scenario. That technique can prevent members of the targeted roles from seeing confidential information. With all that information and the samples demonstrated in this chapter, you should have a good grasp of the techniques and challenges associated with security in SQL Server Analysis Services 2008.

Inventory Scenarios

The goal of understanding your inventory is to keep enough stock in order to meet customer expectations and desired service level agreements (SLAs). Yet at the same time, you want to keep a minimum amount of stock on hand to reduce the overhead costs of keeping that stock or potentially wasting the stock. For example, big box retailers will want to keep winter sports clothing on hand during the winter months for sale to their customers. Yet, they want to keep minimal stock on hand to meet customer demand so when the spring months come, they do not have the overhead of storing winter clothing. This can also include the logistics and tracking of how many burgers a fast food restaurant has available every hour of the day. Because the burgers can go bad after some time period, it is important to know what typical customers demand every hour so you can have enough burgers on hand to meet the needs of your hungry customers yet not waste too many burgers when they expire.

Inventory scenarios involve understanding when to order products and how much to order, forecasting customer demand, and identifying the most effective supply source for your items. A comprehensive review of effective inventory management is beyond the scope of the book. For that, I suggest you review Jon Schreibfeder's Distribution Inventory Management White Paper Series www.microsoft.com/dynamics/industry/wholesale_distribution_whitepapers .mspx). But what is interesting about inventory scenarios is that they are applicable to many data warehousing scenarios. We focus on these scenarios in this chapter:

- ❑ Creating a simple orders report including calculated accumulated totals.
- ❑ Calculating rolling averages and weighted rolling averages.
- ❑ Calculating using snapshots and semi-additive measures.

Inventory Control and Orders

Understanding inventory control is not so much about understanding what you have in stock, but what is being ordered over some time period. Whether you're talking about fast food and tracking the number of burgers you need to have every hour or a retail big box store keeping its store shelves stocked, the key here is to understand the amount people are ordering so you can then understand what to keep in stock.

The following table provides an example of how to rank your inventory of stock. For supplies that are ordered more often, they will need to be kept in resupply at a faster rate. This translates to the product being ordered more often so you can ensure you have enough inventory available for your customers to purchase.

Rank of Product	Description	Days Resupply Required
A	Fast-moving products	7–14 days
B	Medium-moving products	30–60 days
C	Slow-moving products	Stock quantity
X	Surplus and storage	Stock quantity

* This table is based off of the Product Rank table in "The First Steps to Achieving Effective Inventory Control" (Schreibfeder, www.microsoft.com/dynamics/industry/ wholesale_distribution_whitepapers.mspx, 2004).

For slow-moving products or products that receive very few to no orders, you establish a threshold stock quantity and order only once you dip below that threshold. How does all this relate to your orders? You want to build some criteria for your product ranking based on the number of orders created instead of the amount of stock you will keep before you resupply your inventory. To do this, you want to build some threshold based on the preceding resupply requirements (see the following table):

Rank of Product	Percentage of Total Orders
A	> 20%
B	10–20%
C	<= 10%
X	0

* This table is based off of the Hits Percentage Table in "The First Steps to Achieving Effective Inventory Control" (Schreibfeder, www.microsoft.com/dynamics/ industry/wholesale_distribution_ whitepapers.mspx, 2004).

Simple Orders Report

To provide an easily accessible example, we will use the Adventure Works cube to execute our queries. If you do not have one available, you can go to www.codeplex.com/ and search for **SQL Samples**. Refer to the SQL Server Product samples and you should be able to find the Adventure Works relational data warehouse as well as the AS project so you can build your own cube.

Recall that to better understand and have control over your inventory, you first need to understand what has been ordered for the time period that you are concerned with. Because we're using the Adventure Works cube, an easy orders scenario is to understand the number of Internet clothing orders that had occurred in Fiscal Year 2004 as in the following report table:

Clothing Products	Orders	Orders Pct	Orders Rank
Jerseys	3179	36.69%	A
Caps	2095	24.18%	A
Gloves	1363	15.73%	B
Shorts	958	11.06%	B
Socks	543	6.27%	C
Vests	527	6.08%	C
Bib-Shorts	0	0.00%	X
Tights	0	0.00%	X

To produce this simple orders report, please refer to the following MDX statement:

```
with
member [Measures].[Orders] as
    iif([Measures].[Internet Order Count] = null,
        0,
        [Measures].[Internet Order Count])
set [OrderedProducts] as
    Order([Product].[Product Categories].[Clothing].children,
          [Measures].[Orders],
          DESC)
member [Measures].[Orders Total] as
    sum(Crossjoin([Measures].[Orders], {[OrderedProducts]}))
member [Measures].[Orders Pct] as
    [Measures].[Orders]/[Measures].[Orders Total], FORMAT_STRING='0.00%'
member [Measures].[Orders Rank] as
 iif([Measures].[Orders] = 0, 'X',
        iif([Measures].[Orders Pct] < 0.10, 'C',
            iif([Measures].[Orders Pct] < 0.20, 'B', 'A')
        )
 )
select {
 [Measures].[Orders],
 [Measures].[Orders Pct],
 [Measures].[Orders Rank]
} on columns, {
 [OrderedProducts]
} on rows
from [Adventure Works]
where ([Date].[Fiscal].[Fiscal Year].&[2004])
```

Let's examine the interesting components of this MDX statement:

```
member [Measures].[Orders] as
    iif([Measures].[Internet Order Count] = null,
        0,
        [Measures].[Internet Order Count])
```

For easier readability of the numbers, the preference is to show users that they had 0 orders instead of NULL orders. Therefore, we have applied an IIF statement to review any NULL values.

When reviewing the Adventure Works cube, notice that there is a many-to-many relationship between the [Sales Reason] dimension and the [Internet Orders] fact by way of the [Sales Reasons] fact-dimension table as indicated by the infinity sign (see Figure 23-1). To clarify, there could be more than one sales reason that could explain why an order had occurred. For example, if a person had ordered a bike reflector because of the advertising promotion and a product review, that is two different sales reasons for this one order.

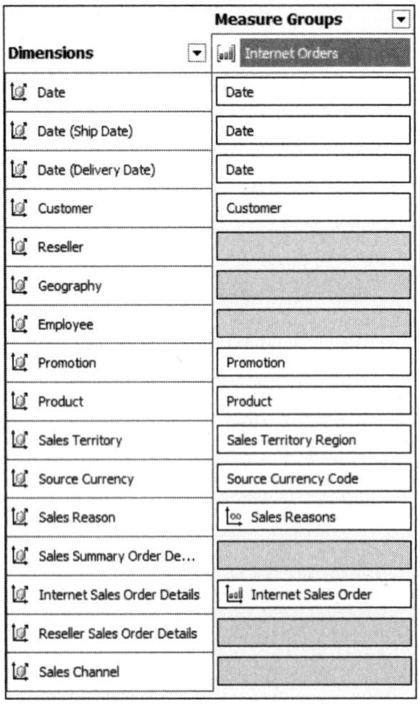

Figure 23-1

As well, the [Internet Order Count] measure is a *distinct count* measure if you review the properties of the measure. The reason for this is that a single order can contain references to multiple products. For example, if you were to run the following MDX statement:

```
with
member [Measures].[Orders] as
    iif([Measures].[Internet Order Count] = null,
        0,
        [Measures].[Internet Order Count])
member [Product].[Product Categories].[Total Clothing] as
```

```
          [Product].[Product Categories].[Clothing]
select {
  [Measures].[Orders]
} on columns, {
  [Product].[Product Categories].[Clothing].children,
  [Product].[Product Categories].[Total Clothing]
} on rows
from [Adventure Works]
where ([Date].[Fiscal].[Fiscal Year].&[2004]);
```

You would get the output in the following table:

Clothing Products	Orders
Bib-Shorts	0
Caps	2095
Gloves	1363
Jerseys	3179
Shorts	958
Socks	543
Tights	0
Vests	527
Total Clothing	**7110**

Yet, if you total all of the products together, you will not get the "Total Clothing" value of 7110 but a much larger value of 8665. As noted previously, there were multiple orders where more than one product was purchased, hence this observation.

For the purpose of inventory, the concern is not the number of orders that were made, but the need to observe that each distinct product ordered is a single order (another term used is that every single distinct product ordered is a *hit*). To get the total number of orders based on the summation of the orders for each clothing product, we have created the [OrderedProducts] set as noted in the following MDX statement. It is a CrossJoin of the Product Categories and Internet Order Count measure, using the `Order` function so we can sort by the number of Internet Order Counts.

```
set [OrderedProducts] as
    Order([Product].[Product Categories].[Clothing].children,
          [Measures].[Orders],
          DESC)
member [Measures].[Orders Total] as
    sum(Crossjoin([Measures].[Orders], {[OrderedProducts]}))
```

We can also use the [OrderedProducts] set in the on `rows` section of the MDX statement so we can view the products by the number of orders for easier readability.

Now that we will get a correct Orders Total summation, the next thing we want to do is to create the orders percentage measure and then based on that percentage value, apply the business logic from the second table in the section "Inventory Control and Orders" (reproduced here for your convenience) to get the product ranking.

Rank of Product	Percentage of Total Orders
A	> 20%
B	10–20%
C	<= 10%
X	0

```
member [Measures].[Orders Rank] as
   iif([Measures].[Orders] = 0, 'X',
          iif([Measures].[Orders Pct] < 0.10, 'C',
                iif([Measures].[Orders Pct] < 0.20, 'B', 'A')
          )
   )
```

Together, this MDX statement will provide you with the Clothing Internet Orders for Fiscal Year 2004.

Product Categories	Orders	Orders Pct	Orders Rank
Jerseys	3179	36.69%	A
Caps	2095	24.18%	A
Gloves	1363	15.73%	B
Shorts	958	11.06%	B
Socks	543	6.27%	C
Vests	527	6.08%	C
Bib-Shorts	0	0.00%	X
Tights	0	0.00%	X

Based on the preceding information, you can observe that the Bib-Shorts and Tights were never ordered (Product Rank = X) and Caps and Jerseys were the fastest-moving products.

Although this simple orders report is specific to an inventory scenario, it is very applicable to many other data warehousing scenarios such as categorization of top support issues, top sales calls, and so on.

Orders Report with Accumulated Totals

If you review "The First Steps to Achieving Effective Inventory Control" (Schreibfeder, www.microsoft .com/dynamics/industry/wholesale_distribution_whitepapers.mspx, 2004), you will notice the sample report is based on a calculation involving accumulated totals. This is a common occurrence within inventory scenarios where we want to review a report by the number of orders so that we can immediately understand what the most popular orders are. It is a form of Pareto analysis where you are trying to determine which set of items in your inventory have the most turnover so that you can keep them in stock. To do this, we have a slightly more complicated MDX statement to provide this information.

The Pareto principle states that 80 percent of effects come from 20 percent of causes. It is also known as the 80-20 rule. Loosely applied here, it would be considered that 80 percent of your orders are for 20 percent of the items in your inventory.

```
with
member [Measures].[Orders] as
    iif([Measures].[Internet Order Count] = null,
        0,
        [Measures].[Internet Order Count])
set [OrderedProducts] as
    Order([Product].[Product Categories].[Clothing].children,
        [Measures].[Orders],
        DESC)
member [Measures].[Ordered Products Ranked] as
    Rank([Product].[Product Categories].CurrentMember, OrderedProducts)
member [Measures].[Orders Running Total] as
    sum(
        head([OrderedProducts], [Measures].[Ordered Products Ranked]),
        [Measures].[Orders]
    )
member [Measures].[Orders Total] as
  sum(Crossjoin([Measures].[Orders], {[OrderedProducts]}))
member [Measures].[Orders Running Pct] as
  [Measures].[Orders Running Total]/[Measures].[Orders Total],
    FORMAT_STRING='0.00%'
member [Measures].[Product Rank] as
 iif([Measures].[Orders Running Pct] <= 0.70, 'A',
        iif([Measures].[Orders] = 0, 'X',
            iif([Measures].[Orders Running Pct] <= 0.90, 'B', 'C')
            )
        )
select {
  [Measures].[Ordered Products Ranked],
  [Measures].[Orders],
  [Measures].[Orders Running Total],
  [Measures].[Orders Running Pct],
  [Measures].[Product Rank]
} on columns, {
  [OrderedProducts]
} on rows
from [Adventure Works]
where ([Date].[Fiscal].[Fiscal Year].&[2004])
```

As with the previous full MDX statement, we start off with the [OrderedProducts] set, which orders the products by the number of [Orders]. We also want to know how the product ranked with all of the products; hence we created the [Ordered Products Ranked] measure:

```
member [Measures].[Ordered Products Ranked] as
    Rank([Product].[Product Categories].CurrentMember, OrderedProducts)
```

This measure makes use of the Rank function and compares the tuple expression with a set expression to determine the tuple member's numeric ranking. More specific to this scenario, the function compares the CurrentMember of the [Product].[Product Categories] hierarchy (which is specified in the on rows section) with the set of [OrderedProducts] to determine its numeric ranking. This is especially important within the context of the next measure, which involves calculating a running total or accumulated sum.

Within your inventory list, a running total (or accumulated sum) is a good way to see your inventory list grow as you add products over time. If your product has issues of various priorities, running totals will help determine where to focus (the higher the percentage, the more important it is to resolve). In this case, there is an [Orders Running Total] measure that calculates the aggregate (sum) of the current row of orders with all of the orders before it. In your typical date scenario or when referring to the product dimension directly, you can calculate a running total using the following MDX statement:

```
with
member [Measures].[Orders] as
    iif([Measures].[Internet Order Count] = null,
        0,
        [Measures].[Internet Order Count])

/*** Calculate Running Total Starts Here ***/
member [Measures].[Orders Running Total] as
    sum(
        {[Product].[Product Categories].[Clothing].children(0):
            [Product].[Product Categories].CurrentMember},
        [Measures].[Orders]   )
/*** Calculate Running Total Ends Here ***/

select {
    [Measures].[Orders],
    [Measures].[Orders Running Total]
} on columns, {
    [Product].[Product Categories].[Clothing].children
} on rows
from [Adventure Works]
where ([Date].[Fiscal].[Fiscal Year].&[2004])
```

The bold statement (between the two comments) is of interest because it is where you can get a running total of the Clothing product category by creating a range from the 0th ordinal of the [Clothing] hierarchy to the CurrentMember value. You can see the running total calculation in the following table:

Clothing Products	Orders	Orders Running Total
Bib-Shorts	0	0
Caps	2095	2095
Gloves	1363	3458
Jerseys	3179	6637

Clothing Products	Orders	Orders Running Total
Shorts	958	7595
Socks	543	8138
Tights	0	8138
Vests	527	8665

But notice that though we were able to perform this running total calculation, we were doing it following the natural order of the [Product] dimension. If you were to try to apply the same MDX logic for an ordered set, this would not work. This is because the ordinal positions as noted by using children(0) and CurrentMember are properties of the product dimension, not the output or set (for example, [OrderedProducts]) that you create.

To resolve this, the calculated measure [Orders Running Total] was calculated by using the Head function, which provides the first specified number of elements in a set (in this case, the [OrderedProducts] set):

```
member [Measures].[Orders Running Total] as
  sum(
        head([OrderedProducts], [Measures].[Ordered Products Ranked]),
        [Measures].[Orders]
  )
```

The remaining [Orders Total] and [Orders Running Pct] measures are the same as the first full MDX query. The [Product Rank] measure is slightly different than the original MDX statement because we wanted to calculate it based on [Orders Running Pct] instead of [Orders]. Instead of following the second table in the section "Inventory Control and Orders," the product ranking categorization is based on the definition in the table that follows:

Rank of Product	Percentage of Total Orders
A	The first 70%
B	The next 20%
C	The next 10%
X	No Orders

* This table is based on Running Totals from "The First Steps to Achieving Effective Inventory Control" (Schreibfeder, www.microsoft.com/dynamics/industry/ wholesale_distribution_whitepapers.mspx 2004)

Although the second table in the section "Inventory Control and Orders" and the preceding table have the same product ranking results and their product ranking definitions are similar, they are not the same. One is based on the percentage of total orders, and one is based on the percentage of the *running* total of orders. Based on the desired business logic, you will need to properly choose which business logic you want to apply as your inventory control mechanism.

The output of this running total MDX statement can be seen in the following table with the included product rank:

Clothing Products	Ordered Products Ranked	Orders	Orders Running Total	Orders Running Pct	Product Rank
Jerseys	1	3179	3179	36.69%	A
Caps	2	2095	5274	60.87%	A
Gloves	3	1363	6637	76.60%	B
Shorts	4	958	7595	87.65%	B
Socks	5	543	8138	93.92%	C
Vests	6	527	8665	100.00%	C
Bib-Shorts	7	0	8665	100.00%	X
Tights	8	0	8665	100.00%	X

Forecasting

Now that you have your orders (and accumulated orders) reports to understand the ranking of your products, the next thing you want to do is to expand on this to see if your past orders can help you understand what future demand will entail. Therefore, the following sections focus on some of the MDX calculations needed to provide trend analysis as well as rolling averages and weighted rolling averages. For more information specific to inventory forecasting, suggested reading includes the whitepaper `Improving the Accuracy of your Forecasts` (Schreibfeder, `www.microsoft.com/dynamics/industry/wholesale_distribution_whitepapers.mspx`, 2004).

> *A good reference for calculating rolling averages is Mosha Pasumansky's blog "post" Moving Averages in MDX* (`sqlblog.com/blogs/mosha/archive/2007/09/04/moving-averages-in-mdx.aspx`).

Trend Analysis

In many inventory and data warehousing scenarios, the first thing that needs to be done is to understand your trends over a time period. For example, to obtain a six-month trend of clothing products ordered on the internet from Adventure Works, you can run the following query:

```
with
member [Measures].[Orders] as
    iif([Measures].[Internet Order Count] = null,
        0,
        [Measures].[Internet Order Count])
select {
    Crossjoin(
        [Measures].[Orders],
```

```
        [Product].[Product Categories].[Clothing].children
    )
} on columns, {
    [Date].[Fiscal].[Month].[February 2004].Lag(5):
    [Date].[Fiscal].[Month].[February 2004]
} on rows
from [Adventure Works]
```

Converted to a graph, you can see some interesting trends such as the purchase of jerseys had a spike and dropped over time, whereas the orders of caps is in general increasing (see Figure 23-2).

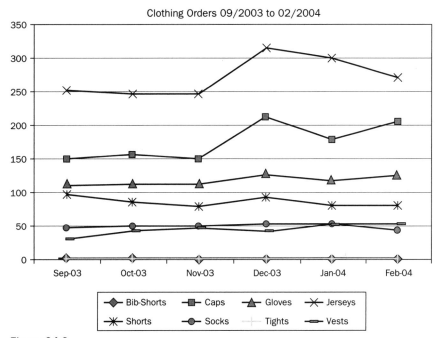

Figure 24-2

But do not forget to note that trend analysis is ever-changing and you should re-examine it based not only on each progressive month, but also different time ranges. To get a 12-month trend of clothing products for June 2004, change the on rows section to

```
[Date].[Fiscal].[Month].[June 2004].Lag(11):
[Date].[Fiscal].[Month].[June 2004]
```

You will notice a slightly different trend where in reality the purchase of jerseys has continued an upward trend (see Figure 23-3).

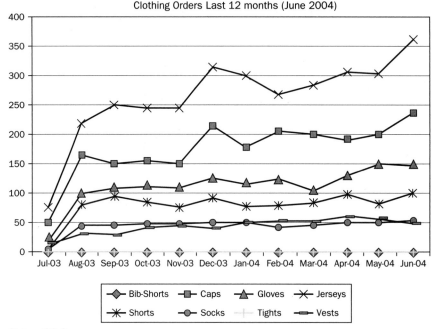

Figure 23-3

Rolling Average

A common method within inventory (and other data warehousing) scenarios to forecast future orders is to calculate the average orders of the past few months as a way to forecast what is needed for the next month. For example, let's review the last seven months from April 2004 for the internet order of caps:

```
with
member [Measures].[Orders] as
   iif([Measures].[Internet Order Count] = null,
       0,
       [Measures].[Internet Order Count])
select {
 [Measures].[Orders]
} on columns, {
   [Date].[Fiscal].[Month].[April 2004].Lag(6):
   [Date].[Fiscal].[Month].[April 2004]
} on rows
from [Adventure Works]
where ([Product].[Product Categories].[Clothing].[Caps])
```

This MDX statement generates the following table:

Month	Cap Orders
October 2003	156
November 2003	150

Month	Cap Orders
December 2003	212
January 2004	178
February 2004	205
March 2004	199
April 2004	190

If we were to calculate a rolling average for April based on the previous six months, we want to do an average based on the cap orders from October 2003 – March 2004, which can be done by the next MDX statement. Notice within the calculated measure [Measures].[RAvg Orders] that we have specified the end range for the rolling average to be the previous month (that is, March 2004) because we have specified April 2004 in the on rows section.

```
with
member [Measures].[Orders] as
    iif([Measures].[Internet Order Count] = null,
        0,
        [Measures].[Internet Order Count])
member [Measures].[RAvg Orders] as
    avg(
        {[Date].[Fiscal].CurrentMember.Lag(6) :
          [Date].[Fiscal].CurrentMember.Lag(1)},
          [Measures].[Orders]
    ), FORMAT_STRING='0.00'
select {
  [Measures].[Orders],
  [Measures].[RAvg Orders]
} on columns, {
 [Date].[Fiscal].[Month].[April 2004]
} on rows
from [Adventure Works]
where ([Product].[Product Categories].[Clothing].[Caps])
```

Based on this calculation, the rolling average orders for April (based on an average of the previous six months) is 183.33, which is reasonably close to the actual orders of caps (190). See the following table:

Month	Orders	Rolling Average Orders
April 2004	190	183.33

But although this scenario works out quite well, if you were to expand this to view all clothes for the entire fiscal year (of 2004) where the rolling average is based on the previous 12 months, the forecast falls short.

```
with
member [Measures].[Orders] as
   iif([Measures].[Internet Order Count] = null,
       0,
       [Measures].[Internet Order Count])
member [Measures].[RAvg Orders] as
         avg(
             {[Date].[Fiscal].Lag(12):
         [Date].[Fiscal].PrevMember},
         [Measures].[Orders]
   ), FORMAT_STRING='0.00'
select {
  [Measures].[Orders],
  [Measures].[RAvg Orders]
} on columns, {
  [Date].[Fiscal].[Month].[June 2004].Lag(11):
  [Date].[Fiscal].[Month].[June 2004]
} on rows
from [Adventure Works]
where ([Product].[Product Categories].[Clothing])
```

The results of this MDX statement can be seen in the following table as well as represented graphically with Figure 23-4:

Month	Orders	Rolling Average Orders
July 2003	153	0.00
August 2003	519	12.75
September 2003	541	56.00
October 2003	559	101.08
November 2003	554	147.67
December 2003	684	193.83
January 2004	643	250.83
February 2004	637	304.42
March 2004	650	357.50
April 2004	689	411.67
May 2004	703	469.08
June 2004	778	527.67

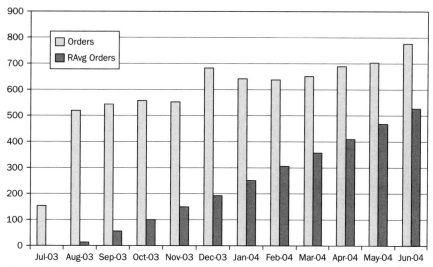

Figure 23-4

As you can see, the left bar represents the actual orders for each month, and the right bar represents the forecast for orders for each month based on an average of the previous 12 months. For June 2004, though there were actually 778 orders, the rolling average calculation was 528 (527.67 rounded up). If you had stocked simply on the rolling average, you would be off by 250 items.

Weighted Rolling Average

To help alleviate some of the discrepancies presented in the previous section, one approach is to weight the months. Instead of calculating based on a simple average in which each month has the same weight, we will put more weight on the more recent months. The following table shows the calculation for weighted calculations for June 2004 based on the previous 12 months.

Month	Orders	Weight	Weighted Orders
June 2003	0	1	0
July 2003	153	2	306
August 2003	519	3	1557
September 2003	541	4	2164
October 2003	559	5	2795
November 2003	554	6	3324
December 2003	684	7	4788
January 2004	643	8	5144
February 2004	637	9	5733

(continued)

(continued)

Month	Orders	Weight	Weighted Orders
March 2004	650	10	6500
April 2004	689	11	7579
May 2004	703	12	8436
Total		78	48236

Therefore, the weighted rolling average for June 2004 is 620 (round up 48236/78). Though this is still not the actual value of 778, it is much closer than the rolling average value of 528. Saying this, based on the trend analysis earlier in Figure 23-4, Internet orders had only started tracking in July 2003. It may make sense to base your weighted rolling average over the last three or six months instead of calculating it based on a full 12 months as noted in the following table:

Month	Actual Orders	Based on last 12 months	Based on last 6 months	Based on last 3 months
June 2004	778	620	674	690

As you can see from this table, the predicted weighted rolling average is closer to the actual orders based on using only the last three months. But instead of doing this manually or using Excel, you can also do this using MDX:

```
with
member [Measures].[Orders] as
    iif([Measures].[Internet Order Count] = null,
        0,
        [Measures].[Internet Order Count])
member [Measures].[Date Range Count] as
    Count([Date].[Fiscal].Lag(3):[Date].[Fiscal].PrevMember)
member [Measures].[WRAvg Orders] as
    Round(sum(
            ([Date].[Fiscal].Lag(3):[Date].[Fiscal].PrevMember) as
[Date Range],
            ([Date Range].CurrentOrdinal) * [Measures].[Orders]
    )/
    ([Date Range Count] * ([Date Range Count] + 1)/2))
select {
    [Measures].[Orders],
    [Measures].[WRAvg Orders]
} on columns, {
    [Date].[Fiscal].[Month].[June 2004].Lag(12):
    [Date].[Fiscal].[Month].[June 2004]
} on rows
from [Adventure Works]
where ([Product].[Product Categories].[Clothing])
```

The results of this MDX are shown in the following table:

Month	Orders	Weighted Rolling Average Orders
June 2003	0	0
July 2003	153	0
August 2003	519	76
September 2003	541	310
October 2003	559	469
November 2003	554	546
December 2003	684	554
January 2004	643	620
February 2004	637	642
March 2004	650	647
April 2004	689	644
May 2004	703	667
June 2004	778	690

As you can see from Figure 23-5, using a weighted rolling average based on only the last three months provides you with a closer prediction, that is, a closer forecast to the actual values.

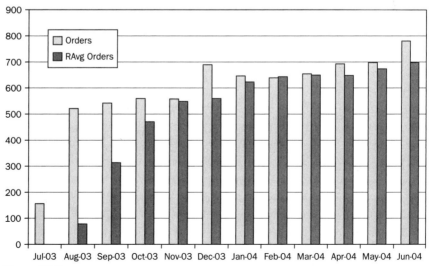

Figure 23-5

Recall that forecasting is an attempt to predict inventory based on your existing information. Although it is outside the scope of this chapter, you can also consider using Analysis Services data mining tools to help predict your inventory model as well. For more information, you can refer to the "Inventory Predictive Modeling via Microsoft SQL Server 2005 Analysis Services" white paper at www.microsoft .com/technet/prodtechnol/sql/2005/ipmvssas.mspx.

Understanding Inventory

We have reviewed the calculation of orders and accumulated totals (to understand Inventory Control) as well as un-weighted and weighted rolling averages, but we have yet to address inventory itself. In order to do this, we have modified the Adventure Works sample to include sample inventory data for the data warehouse and modifications for the Adventure Works cube to include this data. For the purpose of this chapter, we have sample generated clothing inventory data for June 2004. To run the tests yourself, you can execute the sample file FactSampleInventory.sql against the Adventure Works Data Warehouse SQL database while deploying the modified Adventure Works database.

Within inventory and many other data warehousing scenarios, you can look at the data from the standpoint of transactions and snapshots. We will now review these concepts.

Transactions

When reviewing the FactSampleInventory table, its structure is similar to the FactInternetSales table (within the Adventure Works DW SQL database) where each row represents some transaction that has occurred. For example, when executing the following SQL statement:

```
select f.InventoryID,
    t.FullDateAlternateKey as OrderDate,
    s.EnglishProductSubcategoryName,
    f.SalesOrderNumber,
    f.SalesOrderLineNumber,
    f.OrderQuantity
  from FactSampleInventory f
    inner join DimProduct p
      on p.ProductKey = f.ProductKey
    inner join DimProductSubCategory s
      on s.ProductSubCategoryKey = p.ProductSubCategoryKey
    inner join DimProductCategory c
      on c.ProductCategoryKey = s.ProductCategoryKey
    inner join DimCurrency u
      on u.CurrencyKey = f.CurrencyKey
    inner join DimDate t
      on t.DateKey = f.OrderDateKey
  where f.ProductKey = 463
    and f.CurrencyKey = 19
```

you will get the following output pertaining to the inventory of gloves in Canadian currency:

InventoryID	OrderDate	Subcategory	OrderNumber	OrderLineNumber	Quantity
21	2004-06-01	Gloves	P10674631019	1	6
65	2004-06-01	Gloves	SO71963	2	-1
193	2004-06-05	Gloves	SO72218	1	-1
226	2004-06-06	Gloves	SO72296	2	-1
318	2004-06-09	Gloves	SO72527	3	-1
392	2004-06-09	Gloves	P10754631019	1	3
447	2004-06-11	Gloves	SO72667	3	-1
488	2004-06-12	Gloves	SO72764	3	-1
554	2004-06-14	Gloves	SO72910	4	-1

As you can see from the table, on 6/1/2004 and 6/9/2004, inventory purchases were made of 6 and 3, respectively, to restock dwindling supplies. For the other days, these transactions correspond to purchases made, which are recorded in the FactInternetSales table.

But what is interesting about inventory scenarios is that though there is a row for each transaction, you have to sum up the entire date range in order to obtain the current inventory of an item. For example, if you were to simply query this glove inventory information on a specific date, e.g., 6/6/2004, you would get only:

InventoryID	OrderDate	Subcategory	OrderNumber	OrderLineNumber	Quantity
226	2004-06-06	Gloves	SO72296	2	-1

This would leave you with the false impression that on 6/6/2004, you had -1 gloves in stock. In reality, what you have in stock is 6 – 1 – 1 – 1 = 3 gloves in stock. But to do this, you need to do a running total from the beginning of your current inventory stock (which is 6/1/2004 in our sample).

When reviewing the modified Adventure Works cube, you will notice that it contains the [Inventory Quantity Sum] measure, which has a sum aggregation type on the Quantity column (Figure 23-6).

Figure 23-6

When executing the MDX statement, which is based on a sum aggregate type, you will notice the same discrepancy previously mentioned.

```
select {
  [Measures].[Inventory Quantity Sum]
} on columns, {
  [Date].[Fiscal].[Month].[June 2004].[June 1, 2004]:
  [Date].[Fiscal].[Month].[June 2004].[June 3, 2004],
  [Date].[Fiscal].[Month].[June 2004].[June 28, 2004]:
  [Date].[Fiscal].[Month].[June 2004].[June 30, 2004],
  [Date].[Fiscal].[Month].[June 2004]
} on rows
from [Adventure Works]
```

As noted in the following table, the June 1, 2004 quantity is correct because this is when inventory had started being tracked. Every date value after June 1, 2004 is a negative or incorrect value because it is a sum of the transactions for that day instead of a rolling total for all transactions.

Date	Inventory Quantity
June 1, 2004	455
June 2, 2004	-28
June 3, 2004	-33
June 28, 2004	-33
June 29, 2004	-30
June 30, 2004	-23
June 2004	208

Note that the June 2004 monthly query is correct, but only because the sample data only contained data for June, so its summation ended up being correct for this scenario.

Properly calculating inventory counts requires us to modify the MDX statement to include a rolling summation as noted in the following statement:

```
with
member [Measures].[R Inventory Quantity Sum] as
  sum(
        [Date].[Fiscal].[Date].members(0):
        ClosingPeriod([Date].[Fiscal].[Date]),
        [Measures].[Inventory Quantity Sum]
  )
select {
  [Measures].[Inventory Quantity Sum],
  [Measures].[R Inventory Quantity Sum]
} on columns, {
  [Date].[Fiscal].[Month].[June 2004].[June 1, 2004]:
  [Date].[Fiscal].[Month].[June 2004].[June 3, 2004],
```

```
    [Date].[Fiscal].[Month].[June 2004].[June 28, 2004]:
    [Date].[Fiscal].[Month].[June 2004].[June 30, 2004],
    [Date].[Fiscal].[Month].[June 2004]
} on rows
from [Adventure Works]
```

As you can see with the [Measures].[R Inventory Quantity Sum] measure, we are calculating a rolling summation from the beginning of time ([Date].[Fiscal].[Date].members(0)) to the current closing period. This is done by using the ClosingPeriod function, which intersects with the dates specified in the on rows section of the MDX statement. Following is the updated table to include the [Rolling Inventory Quantity] measure:

Date	Inventory Quantity	Rolling Inventory Quantity
June 1, 2004	455	455
June 2, 2004	-28	427
June 3, 2004	-33	394
June 28, 2004	-33	261
June 29, 2004	-30	231
June 30, 2004	-23	208
June 2004	208	208

As you can see, the [Rolling Inventory Quantity] is a summation of all inventory transactions up to the date specified and this can now be used to calculate your inventory transactions. For more information, including how to run a faster version of the preceding MDX statement, you can refer to Richard Tkachuk's Inventory Management Calculations in SQL Server Analysis Services 2005, which is available at www.sqlserveranalysisservices.com/OLAPPapers/InventoryManagement% 20in%20AS2005v2.htm.

Snapshots

As implied in the preceding section, calculating your inventory using a rolling total since the beginning of time (when you started keeping track of inventory) can become resource intensive over time. To have your ETL (Extract-Transform-Load) process handle more of these calculations, it may make sense for you to make use of snapshots, which provide you with a point-in-time view of your inventory for the time granularity desired. In many enterprise inventory solutions, often there is a combination of snapshots performed (for example, monthly) while transactions are kept for the incremental time periods (for example, daily). You would then use a combination of snapshot and transaction data to calculate what your current inventory counts are. Saying this, the focus in this section is to talk about snapshots.

In the FactSampleInventory.sql file, you will notice that the SQL script also created and populated the FactSampleInventoryDailySnapshot table. The modified Adventure Works cube also contains the Inventory Quantity Snapshot measure group, which uses the FactSampleInventoryDailySnapshot table as its source.

When querying for the inventory count for June 2004 gloves/Canadian currency, instead of referring to the Quantity column (used for rolling sum calculations), you can use the FactSampleInventoryDailySnapshot table, which already calculates the specified daily snapshot. For example, when running the following SQL query:

```
select t.FullDateAlternateKey as OrderDate,
    s.EnglishProductSubcategoryName,
    f.SnapshotQuantity
from FactSampleInventoryDailySnapshot f
    inner join DimProduct p
        on p.ProductKey = f.ProductKey
    inner join DimProductSubCategory s
        on s.ProductSubCategoryKey = p.ProductSubCategoryKey
    inner join DimProductCategory c
        on c.ProductCategoryKey = s.ProductCategoryKey
    inner join DimCurrency u
        on u.CurrencyKey = f.CurrencyKey
    inner join DimTime t
        on t.TimeKey = f.OrderDateKey
where f.ProductKey = 463
    and f.CurrencyKey = 19
    and f.OrderDateKey in (20040601, 20040605, 20040606,
                    20040609, 20040611, 20040612, 20040614)
```

you get the following table of snapshot values:

Snapshot Date	SubCategory	Inventory Snapshot Count
2004-06-01	Gloves	5
2004-06-05	Gloves	4
2004-06-06	Gloves	3
2004-06-09	Gloves	5
2004-06-11	Gloves	4
2004-06-12	Gloves	3
2004-06-14	Gloves	2

Though more ETL intensive (that is, it requires the relational database to perform this calculation), you no longer need to write a rolling total to calculate your inventory counts. When you review the modified Adventure Works cube, you'll notice that there is also the [Inventory Quantity Snapshot] measure group, which contains two inventory quantity snapshot measures (see Figure 23-7).

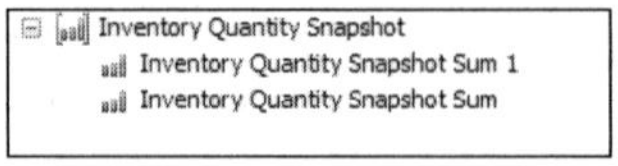

Figure 23-7

Let's start with the [Measures].[Inventory Quantity Snapshot Sum 1], which has an aggregation type of sum, which seems to make sense when applying it to a snapshot table. When running the following MDX query:

```
with
select {
  [Measures].[Inventory Quantity Snapshot Sum 1]
} on columns, {
  [Date].[Fiscal].[Month].[June 2004].[June 1, 2004]:
  [Date].[Fiscal].[Month].[June 2004].[June 3, 2004],
  [Date].[Fiscal].[Month].[June 2004].[June 28, 2004]:
  [Date].[Fiscal].[Month].[June 2004].[June 30, 2004],
  [Date].[Fiscal].[Month].[June 2004]
} on rows
from [Adventure Works]
```

you will get the values noted in the following table:

Date	Inventory Quantity Snapshot Sum 1
June 1, 2004	455
June 2, 2004	427
June 3, 2004	394
June 28, 2004	261
June 29, 2004	231
June 30, 2004	208
June 2004	11348

Looking at the individual days, the inventory snapshot counts match the rolling sums (calculated in the previous section) and do not require the use of a rolling sum. But notice June 2004: It has an inventory count of 11348! This occurred because a regular sum aggregation type will sum up all of the values from June 1, 2004 to June 30, 2004 for the monthly rollup. But the problem you can see here is that the June 2004 value isn't 11348, but it actually should be 208, which is the last value of the month (that is, the value for June 30, 2004).

Snapshots and Semi-Additive Measures

To solve the discrepancy presented in the previous section, we bring up the concept of semi-additive measures. These measures work the same as most other measures except that they do not rollup the values when working with the context of time. In inventory and many other data warehousing scenarios, it is common for you to create snapshot reports where you do not want to rollup the values for your time hierarchy (that is, sample on specific days). Instead, you may want to use:

- ❑ **Weekly Snapshot:** The value on Saturday.
- ❑ **Monthly Snapshot:** The value from the last day of the month.
- ❑ **Yearly Snapshot:** The value from the last day of the year.

There are other types of snapshot definitions; for example, some may want the monthly snapshot to be the value from the first day of the month instead. You can choose the type of semi-additive measure by choosing the appropriate aggregation type of FirstChild, LastChild, FirstNonEmpty, or LastNonEmpty (Figure 23-8).

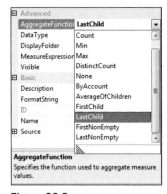

Figure 23-8

Therefore, when we created the [Inventory Quantity Snapshot Sum] measure, we specified the LastChild aggregation type. But as soon as we had done this, the Business Intelligence Development Studio provided an AMO warning noting that the Aggregation Usage should be set to Unrestricted because we had included a semi-additive measure.

By switching the Aggregation Usage type for the [Date] attribute to **Unrestricted**, the AMO warning was removed. (As shown in Figure 23-9, click the [Date] attribute in the Dimensions pane in the bottom left, then view the Properties pane on the right, and change the AggregationUsage property.) This AMO warning popped up because based on best practices from working with semi-additive measures (when it was first introduced in SQL Server 2005 Analysis Services), setting the aggregation usage to unrestricted would provide you with better overall performance. It does this by telling the Analysis Services engine to create as many aggregations as it sees fit (that is, unrestricted) so a query against this semi-additive measure can hit the aggregation instead of searching for the LastChild (in this scenario).

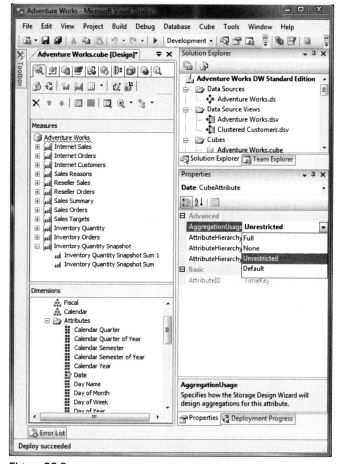

Figure 23-9

The following MDX statement has been modified to also query the semi-additive measure:

```
with
select {
 [Measures].[Inventory Quantity Snapshot Sum 1],
 [Measures].[Inventory Quantity Snapshot Sum]
} on columns, {
 [Date].[Fiscal].[Month].[June 2004].[June 1, 2004]:
 [Date].[Fiscal].[Month].[June 2004].[June 3, 2004],
 [Date].[Fiscal].[Month].[June 2004].[June 28, 2004]:
 [Date].[Fiscal].[Month].[June 2004].[June 30, 2004],
 [Date].[Fiscal].[Month].[June 2004]
} on rows
from [Adventure Works]
```

The output of this statement is shown in the following table:

Snapshot Date	Inventory Quantity Snapshot Sum 1	Inventory Quantity Snapshot Sum
June 1, 2004	455	455
June 2, 2004	427	427
June 3, 2004	394	394
June 28, 2004	261	261
June 29, 2004	231	231
June 30, 2004	208	208
June 2004	11348	208

As you can see, by using the semi-additive measure, your snapshot report will accurately represent your inventory by choosing the last day of the month as the value for the month.

Summary

This chapter has provided some basic inventory scenarios with some background information and resources to better understand inventory. But whether we are talking about ordering the data set for readability, tabulating running totals, un-weighted/weighted rolling averages, snapshots and/or semi-additive measures, these are fundamental in many data warehousing scenarios.

24

Financial Scenarios

The end point of many data warehousing scenarios is to produce actionable business intelligence from a financial aspect. Whether you are talking about inventory, Web Analytics, advertising, or healthcare, there is some financial component (cost of goods, money earned) that requires you to calculate the return on investment for spending money in the first place.

The purpose of this chapter is to go through various financial scenarios. An exhaustive review of all financial tools is beyond the scope of this chapter. But a review of some key financial scenarios from the standpoint of Analysis Services are reviewed, including:

- ❑ Presenting budget information including date comparative analysis, trend analysis, usage of KPI, and variance analysis.

- ❑ Reviewing currency conversion scenarios that involve the use of many-to-many dimensions.

- ❑ Reviewing precision considerations when working with Analysis Services.

- ❑ Reviewing employee parent/child dimension scenarios.

- ❑ Reviewing custom rollup scenarios including parent/child dimensions and unary operators and custom member formulas.

All of the examples in this chapter reference the Adventure Works Data Warehouse Enterprise sample, which you can download from www.codeplex.com/. You can search for **SQL Samples**. Refer to the SQL Server Product samples and you should be able to find the Adventure Works relational data warehouse as well as the AS project so you can build your own cube.

This chapter uses trend analysis and comparative analysis. Trend analysis is the process of collecting data and recognizing developing patterns in the information. Comparative analysis is the process of analyzing data from multiple sources and dealing with existing patterns in the information.

Presenting Budget Information

This section delves into the common analysis and reporting techniques to present budget information in an easily readable format. It is not just important for your Analysis Services users to understand the data, but to understand it correctly. Please note, in this section we define fiscal year from July to June; this may be different for your business.

A very readable resource on presenting budget information is Larry Melillo's help and how-to article "Summarize financial data for senior management" (http://office.microsoft.com/en-us/excel/HA011999971033.aspx). The article summarizes the various components that are important for reporting on budget information. Ultimately, that will be defined by your business requirements. But there are forms of analysis that are important so you can get a complete big picture of your financial situation.

Date Comparative Analysis

Although this is common for most if not all data warehousing scenarios, understanding what is happening by date is the most common and important aspect of financial reporting. Throughout this book, there are various MDX queries that will query a cube by date. Though that is relatively straightforward, let's review two common date functions: ParallelPeriod and PeriodsToDate. (ParallelPeriod is discussed further in Chapter 3.)

> *There are MDX functions like YTD, QTD, and MTD that are shortcuts to the PeriodsToDate function. For details on the respective functions, you can also review SQL Server Books Online.*

The MDX query is an example of one wanting to know the clothing sales by month for the entire fiscal year. In this case, we have specified the starting month of the fiscal year (July 2003) to the current month (May 2004):

```
with
member [Date].[Fiscal].[May 2004 YTD] as
 Aggregate(
         PeriodsToDate(
                 [Date].[Fiscal].[Fiscal Year],
                 [Date].[Fiscal].[Month].[May 2004]
          )
 )
member [Date].[Fiscal].[May 2004 PPQ] as
 ParallelPeriod(
      [Date].[Fiscal].[Fiscal Quarter],
       1,
      [Date].[Fiscal].[Month].[May 2004]
)
select {
 [Measures].[Internet Sales Amount]
} on columns, {
 [Date].[Fiscal].[Month].[July 2003]:[Date].[Fiscal].[Month].[May 2004],
 [Date].[Fiscal].[May 2004 YTD],
 [Date].[Fiscal].[May 2004 PPQ]
} on rows
from [Adventure Works]
where ([Product].[Product Categories].[Category].[Clothing]);
```

The output of this query for Internet Sales is shown in the following table:

Time Period	Internet Sales Amount
July 2003	$6,507.86
August 2003	$23,335.39
September 2003	$26,144.46
October 2003	$25,925.53
November 2003	$25,528.19
December 2003	$30,806.54
January 2004	$29,219.75
February 2004	$28,064.80
March 2004	$28,769.31
April 2004	$32,028.22
May 2004	$31,140.09
May 2004 YTD	$287,470.14
May 2004 PPQ	$28,064.80

If we had chosen the month of June 2004, to get the entire fiscal year of Internet Sales we could specify the fiscal year member:

```
[Date].[Fiscal].[Fiscal Year].[FY 2004]
```

But, because we specified May 2004, we need to perform a year-to-date calculation where we can aggregate all of the months from July 2003 to May 2004. This can be easily done by using the `PeriodsToDate` function:

```
member [Date].[Fiscal].[May 2004 YTD] as
  Aggregate(
        PeriodsToDate(
               [Date].[Fiscal].[Fiscal Year],
               [Date].[Fiscal].[Month].[May 2004]
        )
  )
```

This function allows us to specify all periods to the end point of May 2004 at the level of the fiscal year. If you were to tabulate all of the values from July 2003 to May 2004, you would get the same value as specified by the calculated member [May 2004 YTD].

As well, we also specified the [May 2004 PPQ] (parallel period quarter) calculated member, which specifies the parallel period at the level of the fiscal quarter:

```
member [Date].[Fiscal].[May 2004 PPQ] as
  ParallelPeriod(
       [Date].[Fiscal].[Fiscal Quarter],
       1,
       [Date].[Fiscal].[Month].[May 2004]
  )
```

That is, because our current month is May 2004 (which is the second month of the current quarter), the parallel period one quarter back would be the second month of the previous quarter, which is February 2004. Notice in the previous table that the [May 2004 PPQ] value is the same as the [February 2004] value.

These functions are handy when writing MDX statements for comparative analysis purposes; that is, when you are reviewing the current month of data, you would also like to know what your (for example) quarter-to-date values are as well as compare the sales of this month (2nd month of this quarter) to the sales of the parallel month of the previous quarter (2nd month of the previous quarter). Following is the MDX statement to perform this comparative analysis when looking at the Internet Sales and their sale reasons:

```
with
member [Measures].[Internet Sales Amount PPQ Month] as (
  [Measures].[Internet Sales Amount],
  ParallelPeriod(
          [Date].[Fiscal].[Fiscal Quarter],
          1,
          [Date].[Fiscal].CurrentMember
  )
), FORMAT_STRING='$0.00'
member [Measures].[Internet Sales Amount Prev Month] as (
  [Measures].[Internet Sales Amount],
  ParallelPeriod(
          [Date].[Fiscal].[Month],
          1,
          [Date].[Fiscal].CurrentMember
  )
), FORMAT_STRING='$0.00'
member [Measures].[Internet Sales Amount QTD] as
  sum(
          Crossjoin(
                  [Measures].[Internet Sales Amount],
                  {PeriodsToDate(
                          [Date].[Fiscal].[Fiscal Quarter],
                          [Date].[Fiscal].CurrentMember
                  )}
          )
), FORMAT_STRING='$0.00'
select {
  [Measures].[Internet Sales Amount],
  [Measures].[Internet Sales Amount PPQ Month],
  [Measures].[Internet Sales Amount Prev Month],
  [Measures].[Internet Sales Amount QTD]
} on columns, non empty {
  [Sales Reason].[Sales Reason].children
} on rows
from [Adventure Works]
where (
    [Product].[Product Categories].[Category].[Clothing],
    [Date].[Fiscal].[Month].[May 2004]
);
```

The output of this MDX query is shown in the following table:

	Internet Sales Amount	Internet Sales Amount PPQ Month	Internet Sales Amount Prev Month	Internet Sales Amount QTD
Manufacturer	$225.47	$161.97	$215.96	$441.43
On Promotion	$3,203.60	$2808.60	$3098.12	$6301.72
Other	$1,110.16	$731.80	$1044.18	$2154.34
Price	$24,129.62	$21838.67	$25610.69	$49740.31
Review	$2,343.64	$2267.66	$2919.06	$5262.70
Television Advertisement	$431.92	$863.84	$485.91	$917.83

Notice in this MDX statement that we have only specified the date once in the WHERE clause. This way, as each month progresses, instead of rewriting the MDX statement to indicate the starting and end dates, it is possible to simply change the WHERE clause component and the use of the ParallelPeriod and PeriodsToDate function will cover the rest.

If you refer to the [Measures].[Internet Sales Amount PPQ Month] calculated measure, you may notice that we are using the .CurrentMember function, which will become translated into "May 2004" once the WHERE clause is applied:

```
member [Measures].[Internet Sales Amount PPQ Month] as (
  [Measures].[Internet Sales Amount],
  ParallelPeriod(
        [Date].[Fiscal].[Fiscal Quarter],
        1,
        [Date].[Fiscal].CurrentMember
  )
), FORMAT_STRING='$0.00'
```

Once we know which month it is, the ParallelPeriod function will be able to choose the parallel month and provide the [Internet Sales Amount] for the appropriate time period (in this case, February 2004).

Meanwhile, you may want to understand the quarter-to-date sales as you are looking at the monthly sales figures:

```
member [Measures].[Internet Sales Amount QTD] as
  sum(
        Crossjoin(
                [Measures].[Internet Sales Amount],
                {PeriodsToDate(
                        [Date].[Fiscal].[Fiscal Quarter],
                        [Date].[Fiscal].CurrentMember)
                }}
        )
), FORMAT_STRING='$0.00'
```

To do this, we're using the `PeriodsToDate` function to provide all of the periods at the quarter level to the current member (May 2004). Summarizing the crossjoin of all of those months with the Internet Sales Amount provides the quarter-to-date Internet Sales (that is, Internet Sales Amount QTD). If you want to make sure, you can add the [Internet Sales Amount Prev Month] (which is April 2004) with the [Internet Sales Amount] (filtered to May 2004) and you will get the same value as the [Internet Sales Amount QTD].

In the end, many financial scenarios (and many data warehousing scenarios in general) need to perform some date comparative analysis. The use of these functions will allow you to create MDX calculated members and/or templates so you do not need to specify your date ranges.

Trend and Variance Analysis

Expanding on the Inventory Scenario Trend Analysis in Chapter 23, let's take a quick view of a trend and variance analysis report. Whereas trends review values over time, variance analysis focuses on the comparison metrics (for example, month-to-month). The following MDX query provides you with six months of clothing sales (end month of June 2004) within Adventure Works:

```
select {
  [Measures].[Sales Amount],
  [Measures].[Order Count],
  [Measures].[Gross Profit],
  [Measures].[Gross Profit Margin]
} on columns, {
  [Date].[Fiscal].[Month].&[2004]&[6].Lag(5):
  [Date].[Fiscal].[Month].&[2004]&[6]
} on rows
from [Adventure Works]
where [Product].[Product Categories].[Category].[Clothing]
```

The output of this query notes incrementally increasing sales ([Measures].[Sales Amount]) and orders ([Measures].[Order Count]) as shown in the following table:

	Sales Amount	Order Count	Gross Profit	Gross Profit Margin
January 2004	$73,793.40	707	$14,508.12	19.66%
February 2004	$80,756.03	747	$17,619.46	21.82%
March 2004	$83,496.75	753	$17,730.62	21.24%
April 2004	$97,359.62	748	$15,105.87	15.52%
May 2004	$116,187.05	817	$21,615.31	18.60%
June 2004	$118,848.97	889	$20,205.16	17.00%

Translating this data visually, you can see the trend line rather nicely in Figure 24-1.

Figure 24-1 was generated by using Excel 2007, as discussed earlier in this book.

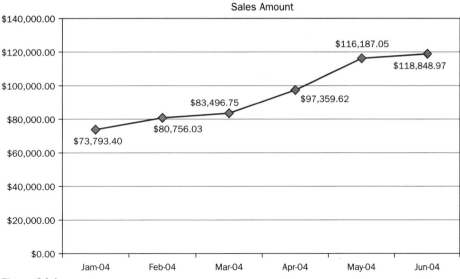

Figure 24-1

But don't forget that trend analysis is only as good as the data as you observe. While the sales amount has been increasing from January to June 2004, the gross profit has its shares of ups and downs, which can be seen in the Gross Profit and Gross Profit Margin. This is graphically observed in Figure 24-2.

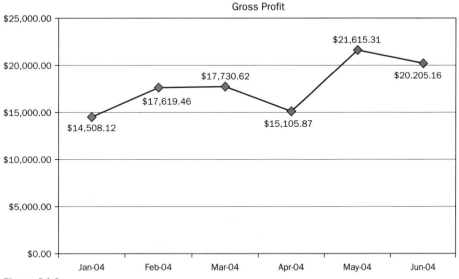

Figure 24-2

In this six-month period, you can see that the profit margin for June and April had dropped. But there are times in financial scenarios where you just want to look at one particular month (for example, June 2004) and be graphically told if your goals are being met and if the trend is going up (for example, profit went up in February, March, and May) or down (for example, the profit margin went down in April and June) when doing a month-by-month comparison.

Defining and Viewing KPIs

To define and view key performance indicators (KPIs), as noted in Chapter 9, SQL Server Analysis Services introduced the notion of KPIs in the server, which allows you to define a set of MDX statements to denote if your goals, status, and/or trends are increasing, decreasing, or have no change based on the parameters defined. For more details, you can review Chapter 9 of this book. Saying this, let's go through a financial scenario where we'd like to understand the goals, status, and trends associated with the Gross Profit Margin on a month-by-month basis.

To define and view KPIs, go to the Adventure Works cube in the Business Intelligence Development Studio, click the KPIs tab, and choose the [Product Gross Profit Margin] KPI as shown in Figure 24-3.

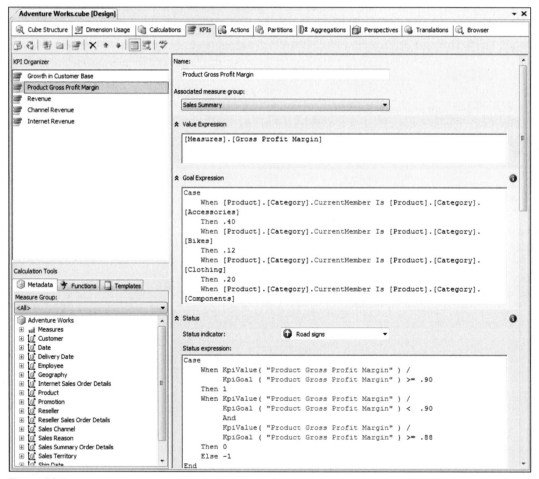

Figure 24-3

When evaluating each component of this KPI within Figure 24-3, you'll notice that it is associated with the [Sales Summary] measure group as defined by the Associated measure group. This makes sense because this KPI is based on the [Measures].[Gross Profit Margin] (as defined by the Value Expression). This is a calculation based on the [Measures].[Sales Amount] and [Measures].[Total Product Cost], both of which belong to the [Sales Summary] measure group (you can click the Calculations tab in BIDS to find the definition of the [Gross Profit Margin] if you like).

Goal Expression

Already provided in this KPI is a definition of what goals are to be associated with the gross profit margin. The goal expression is a hard-coded numeric value that one wants to achieve (that is, goal):

```
Case
    When [Product].[Category].CurrentMember Is
        [Product].[Category].[Accessories]
    Then .40
    When [Product].[Category].CurrentMember Is [Product].[Category].[Bikes]
    Then .12
    When [Product].[Category].CurrentMember Is [Product].[Category].[Clothing]
    Then .20
    When [Product].[Category].CurrentMember Is
        [Product].[Category].[Components]
    Then .10
    Else .12
End
```

The preceding MDX case statement notes the fact that when we choose the product category of clothing, the goal is to achieve a gross profit margin of 20 percent.

Status

As shown within Figure 24-3, the subsection after Goal Expression is Status, which defines whether the Gross Profit Margin actually had met the goal. In our scenario, this is whether the gross profit margin for clothing sales had met the goal of 20 percent. The Status section from the BIDS KPIs tab can be more clearly seen in Figure 24-4.

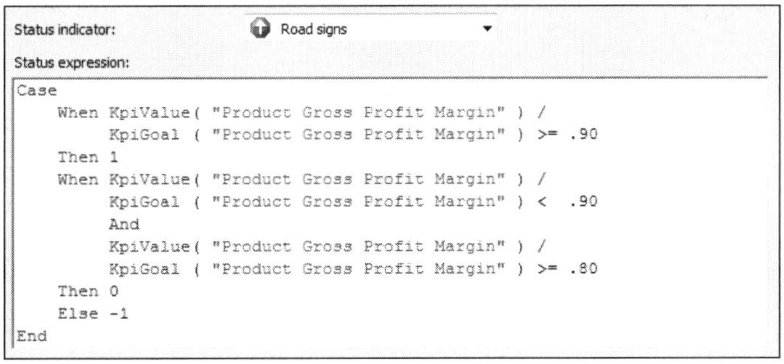

```
Status indicator:              Road signs              ▼
Status expression:
Case
    When KpiValue( "Product Gross Profit Margin" ) /
        KpiGoal ( "Product Gross Profit Margin" ) >= .90
    Then 1
    When KpiValue( "Product Gross Profit Margin" ) /
        KpiGoal ( "Product Gross Profit Margin" ) <  .90
        And
        KpiValue( "Product Gross Profit Margin" ) /
        KpiGoal ( "Product Gross Profit Margin" ) >= .80
    Then 0
    Else -1
End
```

Figure 24-4

The status is comprised of a status indicator (in our case, we had chosen Road Signs for easier readability) and the MDX case statement. As you can see from Figure 24-4, the business logic for this case statement is:

❑ If Gross Profit Margin/Goal is >= 90 percent, you have a value of 1 meaning you had achieved better than your expected goal.

❑ If 80 percent <= Gross Profit Margin/Goal < =90 percent, there was no change of status for your goal.

❑ Otherwise, you did not achieve your goal.

Trend

Continuing with the BIDS KPIs tab view, the bottommost section (beyond the border of Figure 24-3) contains the trend component to set the current trend of your KPI based on the MDX case statement provided. For the trend, we have chosen the Faces trend indicator for easier readability (see Figure 24-5).

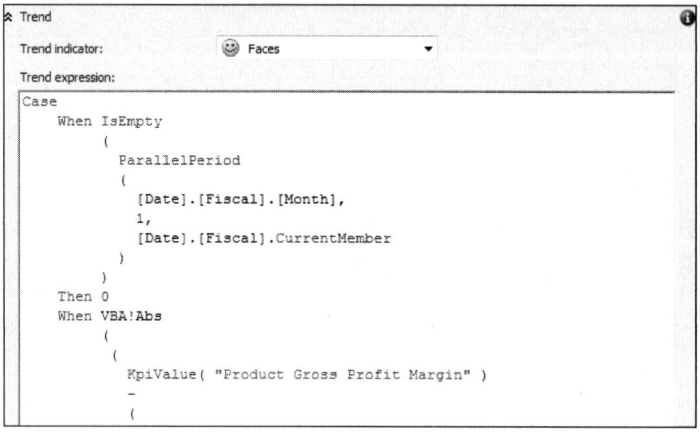

Figure 24-5

We have also modified the original MDX statement to provide a month-to-month view instead of year. Therefore, we need to change the MDX to work off of the [Date].[Fiscal].[Month] value as per the following Trends expression; to do this, modify the trend statement of the [Gross Profit Margin] within the KPIs tab of BIDS (as seen in Figure 24-3):

```
Case
    When IsEmpty
        (
            ParallelPeriod
            (
                [Date].[Fiscal].[Month],
                1,
                [Date].[Fiscal].CurrentMember
            )
        )
    Then 0
    When VBA!Abs
        (
            (
                KpiValue( "Product Gross Profit Margin" )
```

```
            -
            (
              KpiValue( "Product Gross Profit Margin" ),
              ParallelPeriod
              (
                [Date].[Fiscal].[Month],
                1,
                [Date].[Fiscal].CurrentMember
              )
            )
          )
          /
          (
            KpiValue( "Product Gross Profit Margin" ),
            ParallelPeriod
            (
              [Date].[Fiscal].[Month],
              1,
              [Date].[Fiscal].CurrentMember
            )
          )
        ) <=.02
    Then 0
    When (
          KpiValue( "Product Gross Profit Margin" )
          -
          (
            KpiValue( "Product Gross Profit Margin" ),
            ParallelPeriod
            (
              [Date].[Fiscal].[Month],
              1,
              [Date].[Fiscal].CurrentMember
            )
          )
        )
        /
        (
          KpiValue( "Product Gross Profit Margin" ),
          ParallelPeriod
          (
            [Date].[Fiscal].[Month],
            1,
            [Date].[Fiscal].CurrentMember
          )
        ) >.02
    Then 1
    Else -1
End
```

Similar to the preceding business logic, the gross profit margin will be compared to a parallel period of one month; the formula underneath this MDX case statement shown in Figure 24-6 is:

$$Trend\ Value = \frac{(GPM_{CurrentMonth} - GPM_{PreviousMonth})}{(GPM_{CurrentMonth})}$$

Figure 24-6

where if the *Trend Value*:

❑ Is empty or the absolute value of the trend value is <= 2 percent, there is no change;

❑ Is > 2 percent, the trend is positive;

❑ Is otherwise negative.

Once all of these changes have been completed, process and re-deploy your Adventure Works cube so the KPIs can be calculated for consumption.

Querying the KPIs

Now that your KPIs have been created, you do not need to necessarily have a UI to view this data. You can just re-write the previous MDX statement to include your KPI values:

```
with
member [Measures].[Percentage of Desired Goal] as
    '[Measures].[Gross Profit Margin]/KPIGoal("Product Gross Profit Margin")'
member [Measures].[Trend Value] as '
        (
            (
            KpiValue( "Product Gross Profit Margin" )
            -
            (
                KpiValue( "Product Gross Profit Margin" ),
                ParallelPeriod
                (
                    [Date].[Fiscal].[Month],
                    1,
                    [Date].[Fiscal].CurrentMember
                )
            )
            )
        /
        (
            KpiValue( "Product Gross Profit Margin" ),
            ParallelPeriod
            (
                [Date].[Fiscal].[Month],
                1,
                [Date].[Fiscal].CurrentMember
            )
        )
        )', FORMAT_STRING = '0.00%'
select {
 [Measures].[Gross Profit],
```

```
  KPIValue("Product Gross Profit Margin"),
  [Measures].[Percentage of Desired Goal],
  KPIGoal("Product Gross Profit Margin"),
  KPIStatus("Product Gross Profit Margin"),
  [Measures].[Trend Value],
  KPITrend("Product Gross Profit Margin")
} on columns, {
        [Date].[Fiscal].[Month].&[2004]&[6].Lag(5):
  [Date].[Fiscal].[Month].&[2004]&[6]
} on rows
from [Adventure Works]
where [Product].[Product Categories].[Category].[Clothing]
```

As you can see from this MDX statement, you can now view all four KPIs, which include:

❑   The actual product gross profit margin: KPIValue("Product Gross Profit Margin")

❑   The goal you desire: KPIGoal("Product Gross Profit Margin")

❑   The status you desire: KPIStatus("Product Gross Profit Margin")

❑   The trend you desire: KPITrend("Product Gross Profit Margin")

As well, we've added the [Measures].[Percentage of Desired Goal] so you can see the gross profit margin in relation to the goal (recall to achieve the goal, the Gross Profit Margin/Goal needs to be greater than or equal to 90 percent). The output of this is shown in the following table:

	Gross Profit	Gross Profit Margin	Percentage of Desired Goal	Product Gross Profit Margin Goal	Product Gross Profit Margin Status	Trend Value	Product Gross Profit Trend Status
January 2004	$14,508.12	19.66%	98.30%	0.2	1	0.26	1
February 2004	$17,619.46	21.82%	109.09%	0.2	1	0.11	1
March 2004	$17,730.62	21.24%	106.18%	0.2	1	−0.03	−1
April 2004	$15,105.87	15.52%	77.58%	0.2	−1	−0.27	−1
May 2004	$21,615.31	18.60%	93.02%	0.2	1	0.20	1
June 2004	$20,205.16	17.00%	85.00%	0.2	0	−0.09	−1

Recall that the Product Gross Profit Margin status is defined as shown in the following table:

Goal Status	Range	Status Value
Achieved	>= 90%	1
No Change	80% <= x < 90%	0
Not Achieved	<80%	−1

To better visualize this, we have also included the [Percentage of Desired Goal] calculated member, which is the basic MDX formula for this status. Based on these criteria, only April 2004 did not achieve the goal and June 2004 did not change. Recall the trend analysis is defined as shown in the following table:

Goal Status	Range	Status Value
Trend Up	>2%	1
No Change	Abs(x) <= 2%	0
Trend Down	Else	−1

To better visualize this, we have also included the [Trend Value] calculated member, which is the basic MDX formula for this trend. Based on these criteria, March, April, and June 2004 all had trending downward months.

Though this is very informative, let's go back to the original desire, which was for you to be able to graphically understand whether a goal was achieved and if the trend was up or down. You can do this from BIDS by clicking the Browser View button on the KPIs tab. From here, limit your dimension criteria to the Product category of clothing and we will now review the three months of April, May, and June 2004.

Recall that for this scenario for April 2004, we did not achieve our goal and the value was trending downward. In the Browser view, you can see the stop sign (see Figure 24-7) noting the unachieved goal and the unhappy face noting the downward trend.

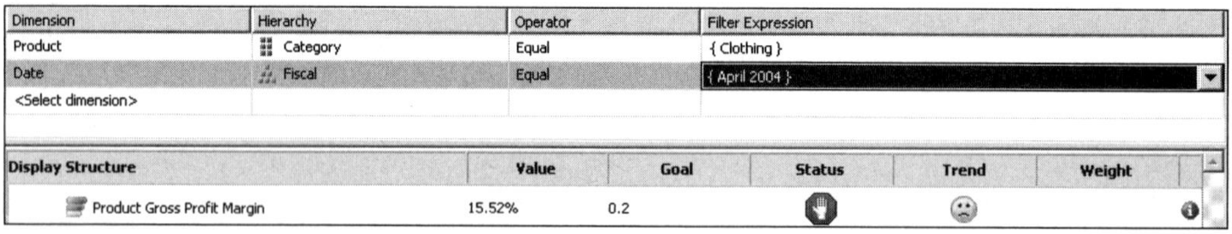

Dimension	Hierarchy	Operator	Filter Expression
Product	▦ Category	Equal	{ Clothing }
Date	⣴ Fiscal	Equal	{ April 2004 }
<Select dimension>			

Display Structure	Value	Goal	Status	Trend	Weight
▦ Product Gross Profit Margin	15.52%	0.2	✋	☹	ⓘ

Figure 24-7

Meanwhile, you'll notice the green status arrow noting the achieved goal and the happy face (Figure 24-8) for the upward trend for May 2004.

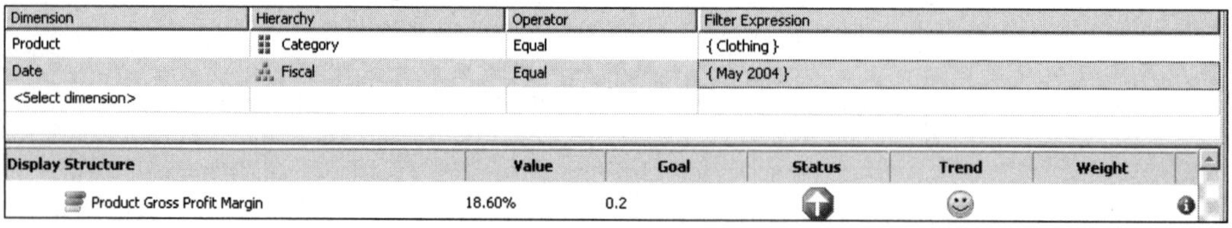

Dimension	Hierarchy	Operator	Filter Expression
Product	▦ Category	Equal	{ Clothing }
Date	⣴ Fiscal	Equal	{ May 2004 }
<Select dimension>			

Display Structure	Value	Goal	Status	Trend	Weight
▦ Product Gross Profit Margin	18.60%	0.2	⬆	☺	ⓘ

Figure 24-8

As well, you'll notice for June 2004 the warning sign (no change in goal) and the unhappy face (Figure 24-9) for the downward trend.

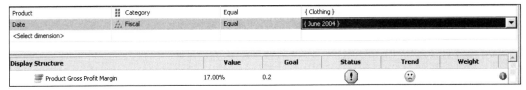

Product	:: Category	Equal	{ Clothing }
Date	.:. Fiscal	Equal	{ June 2004 } ▼
<Select dimension>			

Display Structure	Value	Goal	Status	Trend	Weight
⊒ Product Gross Profit Margin	17.00%	0.2	⊙	☹	ⓘ

Figure 24-9

By using KPIs, you can more quickly present key information using a visual context that will allow readers to more easily understand the important aspects of what you are reporting. For more information on tools that can easily view KPIs, please refer to:

❑ Viewing KPIs using KPIUtil.exe: `http://download.microsoft.com/download/7/b/c/7bc71039-af45-49de-84b7-5c02311d458c/ReadMe.htm`

❑ Using Office SharePoint 2007 to view KPIs: `http://office.microsoft.com/en-us/sharepointserver/HA100800271033.aspx`

❑ Using Performance Point Dashboard to view KPIs: `http://office.microsoft.com/en-us/performancepoint/HA102411051033.aspx`

Currency Conversion Scenario (m:n)

A good many-to-many dimension financial scenario is the currency conversion scenario. Here the goal is to provide you with the ability to look at your sales figures in the desired currency. Let's start by reviewing the [Internet Sales Amount] for June 2004:

```
select {
  [Measures].[Internet Sales Amount]
} on columns, non empty {
  [Destination Currency].[Destination Currency].[Euro],
  [Destination Currency].[Destination Currency].[US Dollar]
} on rows
from [Adventure Works]
where ([Date].[Fiscal].[Month].[June 2004]);
```

The output of this MDX statement provides you with the June 2004 Internet Sales Amount value in the US dollar and Euro currencies, as shown in the following table:

Currency	Internet Sales Amount	Average Rate
Euro	1,969,575.15	.99
US Dollar	$1,949,361.11	1.00

This conversion looks relatively simple but recall that the preceding query is for the month of June 2004 and exchange rates are calculated on a daily basis (and for that matter, intra-day rate). You actually calculate this by taking each day, applying the US Dollar Internet Sales Amount, dividing it by the average rate (which is that day's average exchange rate to the US dollar), and then summarizing the value:

```
with
set [My Currencies] as '{
    [Destination Currency].[Destination Currency].[Euro],
    [Destination Currency].[Destination Currency].[US Dollar]
}'
select {
  Crossjoin(
      [My Currencies],
      {[Measures].[Internet Sales Amount], [Measures].[Average Rate]}
  )
} on columns, non empty {
  [Date].[Fiscal].[Month].[June 2004].children
} on rows
from [Adventure Works]
```

The preceding MDX query breaks out those daily details as shown in the following table:

	Euro		US Dollar	
	Internet Sales Amount	Average Rate	Internet Sales Amount	Average Rate
June 1, 2004	€45,485.67	.98	$44,650.70	1.00
June 2, 2004	€36,177.55	.98	$35,496.03	1.00
June 3, 2004	€60,290.31	.97	$58,528.60	1.00
. . .	. . .	. . .	. . .	. . .
June 30, 2004	€48,051.22	1.01	$48,375.33	1.00

To do this, the Adventure Works cube uses a measure expression for the [Internet Sales Amount] measure so that it calculates the [Internet Sales Amount] measure not only by the [FactInternetSales]. [SalesAmount] SQL column, but also by dividing it by the [Average Rate]; that is, [Internet Sales Amount] = [Internet Sales Amount]/[Average Rate] (refer to Figure 24-10).

Measure expressions are available only in the enterprise edition of Adventure Works.

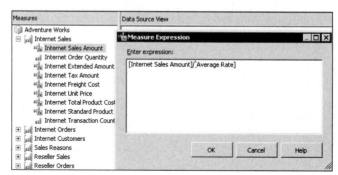

Figure 24-10

But that is only half the picture; the other half is to provide a many-to-many dimension relationship between the [Destination Currency] dimension to the [Internet Sales] measure group by using the intermediate fact table [Exchange Rates], as seen in Figure 24-11.

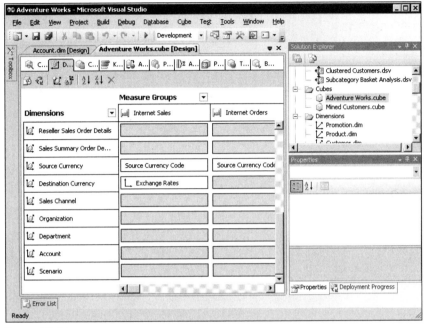

Figure 24-11

When defining the relationship between the [Destination Currency] dimension and [Internet Sales] fact, as noted in the Define Relationship dialog within Figure 24-12, you will notice that the relationship type is Many-to-Many.

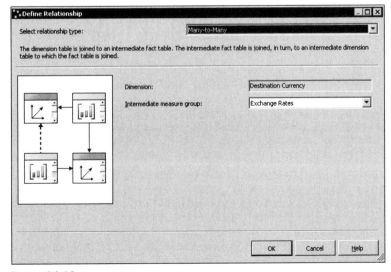

Figure 24-12

It is this many-to-many relationship that allows you to relate the many different currencies. The many-to-many relationship is analogous to the following SQL statement, which will provide you with the same results as the previous table:

```
select t.FullDateAlternateKey,
    cast(sum(f.SalesAmount/e.AverageRate) as decimal(8,2))
as EuroSalesAmount,
    MAX(e.AverageRate) as EuroAverageRate,
    cast(sum(f.SalesAmount/u.AverageRate) as decimal(8,2)) as USSalesAmount,
    MAX(u.AverageRate) as USAverageRate
  from FactInternetSales f
 inner join DimDate t
   on t.DateKey = f.OrderDateKey
 inner join FactCurrencyRate e
   on e.DateKey = f.OrderDateKey
  and e.CurrencyKey = 36 -- Euro
 inner join FactCurrencyRate u
   on u.DateKey = f.OrderDateKey
  and u.CurrencyKey = 100 -- USD
 where f.OrderDateKey >= 20040601 and f.OrderDateKey <= 20040630
 group by
     t.FullDateAlternateKey
 order by
     t.FullDateAlternateKey
```

Notice that whereas the Destination Currency has a many-to-many relationship (so we can convert the dollar value into multiple currencies), the Source Currency Code is not a many-to-many relationship (refer to Figure 24-11 where the relationship between the [Source Currency] dimension to the [Internet Sales] measure group is by the Source Currency Code. This is a regular relationship that implies that although there is a source currency code associated with each sale, the amount stored is in US Dollars (in this case) as opposed to the source currency.

This actually is a good idea from a manageability and performance standpoint.

The purpose of this section is to focus on the many-to-many dimension, not currency conversion. If you want to deal with converting currency, the Currency Conversion Wizard is an obvious choice. However, because the concept of currency conversion is easy to follow, it is used here to show the basic methodology of the many-to-many dimension. Armed with this knowledge, you can apply these techniques to a variety of scenarios.

Manageability

Using a single source currency makes things easier to manage because typically most businesses will accept payment in a single currency or through some credit card payment system that takes care of the currency conversions so that you need only worry about receiving payment in your currency of choice. Once you can deal with multiple source currencies in one system, the issue then becomes, When you reconcile all of your income and expenses, how do you do it? It would be far easier to have only one currency for the purpose of doing all of your business.

But for some enterprise financial systems, this may not be possible because they are receiving income and paying out expenses globally in multiple currencies. Typically in situations like these, two measures will be created — one for the source currency (for example, Euros, Yen, CDN, and so on) and one for the currency for which you typically perform your reconciliation (for example, USD). For these environments, it is often common to do intra-day currency conversions. Therefore, instead of trying to keep a separate dimension table for currency rate conversions, the fact transaction will contain the source currency, exchange rate, and destination currency for each and every transaction.

Performance

A key concern with the usage of many-to-many dimensions is that of performance degradation. That is, as your many-to-many dimension bridge table (the Exchange Rates table in the preceding scenario) becomes larger, your queries will become incrementally slower. So your query that may originally have taken seconds to complete may take tens of seconds or minutes (or longer) to solve.

Ultimately, even with all the data manipulation, the general rule is that once your intermediate fact table goes above 1,000,000 rows you will see performance degradation. The reason for this is because the vast majority of queries that involve many-to-many relationships will be done at query time. From the standpoint of the Adventure Works model, this is probably somewhat manageable because even if you're dealing with 180 currencies for each day of the year, this would result in 65,700 combinations per year; it would take 15 years to reach 1,000,000 rows.

A number of whitepapers and technical notes talk about query performance degradation when working with very large intermediate fact tables. A great starting point is Richard Tkachuk's "Many-to-Many Dimensions in Analysis Services 2005" whitepaper (`http://msdn.microsoft.com/en-us/library/ms345139.aspx`), which is also applicable to Analysis Services 2008. From there, I would suggest the technical note "Analysis Services: Should You Use Many-to-Many Dimensions?" (`http://sqlcat.com/technicalnotes/archive/2008/02/11/analysis-services-should-you-use-many-to-many-dimensions.aspx`) to make sure you have examined all of your options about whether you should be using many-to-many dimensions.

From here, a great paper to optimize many-to-many scenarios is "Analysis Services: Many-to-Many Dimensions: Query Performance Optimization Techniques" (`www.microsoft.com/downloads/details.aspx?FamilyID=3494E712-C90B-4A4E-AD45-01009C15C665&displaylang=en`). This paper provides details about how to use a matrix solution to reduce the overall size of your intermediate fact table by reducing all of the many-to-many relationships to the distinct existing many-to-many relationships. You can also refer to Eugene Asahara's "Compress Many-to-many C# Utility," which you can find at `http://sqlcat.com/toolbox/archive/2008/03/24/compress-many-to-many-c-utility.aspx`.

Precision Considerations

Going back to the previous table in the section "Currency Conversion Scenario (m:n)," you may recall that for June 1, 2004, you had conversions (see the following table):

	Euro		US Dollar	
	Internet Sales Amount	**Average Rate**	**Internet Sales Amount**	**Average Rate**
June 1, 2004	45,485.67	.98	$44,650.70	1.00

Recall that the Internet Sales Amount in Euros is calculated by taking the [Internet Sales Amount (US dollars)]/[Average Rate (Euro)]. If you were to do the math here, you'll notice that $44,650.70/0.98 = $45,561.94 and not the indicated value of $45,485.67 in the table.

The issue we have here is a case of precision; the [Average Rate] measure displayed its value with a FORMAT_STRING='#,#.00' which means it is showing data only to two decimal places. If you were to execute the SQL query from the "Currency Conversion Scenario (m:n)" section, it would reveal that the actual exchange rate for June 1, 2004 between the Euro and the US dollar is: 0.981643270835379. Now, if you were to do the [Internet Sales Amount (USD)]/[Average Rate (Euro)] you would get the same [Internet Sales Amount (Euro)].

There are two important things to note here — the first is that Analysis Services is performing the division calculation using the full precision of the average rate value even though it is only presenting the value to two decimal places.

The second point is that you need to be careful about the impact of precision in your calculations. Please refer to the "Precision Considerations for Analysis Services Users" whitepaper (`http://sqlcat.com/whitepapers/archive/2007/11/19/precision-considerations-for-analysis-services-users.aspx`) for more details on the potential impact of precision on your calculations. But as you can see, when aggregating a floating point number, there may be a loss of precision and no guarantee that the results will be consistent. Therefore, for your results you should format the values to a lower precision or scale by using the FORMAT_STRING property (as in the preceding table). As well, instead of using floating point data types use exact data types like Analysis Services currency and SQL Server money for all of your calculations to reduce precision issues.

The purpose of this section is to focus on the precision, not currency conversion. If you want to deal with converting currency, the Currency Conversion Wizard is an obvious choice. However, because the concept of currency conversion is easy to follow, it is used here to show the basic concepts of precision, which you can then apply to a variety of scenarios.

Employee Scenario (P/C)

The employee scenario is a great example of the need for a parent/child dimension because the hierarchies involved are both unbalanced and ragged. For example, as noted in Figure 24-13, employee Wanida M. Benshoof is two levels away from Ken J. Sánchez, and the employee Ashvini R. Sharma is three levels away from Ken J. Sánchez. Employee scenarios often involve this type of hierarchy where it is best represented by using a parent/child dimension. Note that we also go over some more details on parent/child dimensions in Chapter 25 (involving the Web Analytics scenario — path navigation hierarchy).

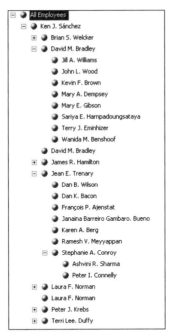

Figure 24-13

Let's focus for a moment on the hierarchy reporting to Amy E. Alberts (who reports to Brian S. Welcker) for the calendar year 2004 for the sales quota (see Figure 24-14).

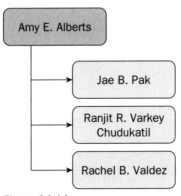

Figure 24-14

Ms. Alberts is the European Sales Manager with three people reporting to her. When we want to discover what her sales quota is, we can run the following MDX statement:

```
select {
  [Measures].[Sales Amount Quota]
} on columns, {
  [Employee].[Employees].[Amy E. Alberts].children,
  [Employee].[Employees].[Amy E. Alberts]
```

(continued)

(continued)

```
} on rows
from [Adventure Works]
where ([Date].[Calendar].[Calendar Year].[CY 2004])
```

This provides you with the output shown in the following table:

Employees	Sales Amount Quota
Jae B. Pak	$2,212,000.00
Rachel B. Valdez	$993,000.00
Ranjit R. Varkey Chudukatil	$1,615,000.00
Amy E. Alberts	$4,937,000.00

You may notice that in this parent/child dimension, you can see that Amy E. Alberts has a total of $4,937,000 as her sales quota, which is a combination of her own sales quota and her three directs. If you were to add up Ms. Alberts' directs it would total up to $4,820,000.

A common mistake when working with parent/child dimensions (whether dealing with employee or any other data warehousing scenario) is forgetting that when rolling up a parent/child dimension it includes both the children and the parent together. Creating your own member and/or using the .[datamember] function will allow you to identify and isolate the children and/or parent values respectively.

```
with
member [Employee].[Employees].[Amy E. Alberts Directs] as
  aggregate([Employee].[Employees].[Amy E. Alberts].children)
member [Employee].[Employees].[Amy E. Alberts Rollup] as
  [Employee].[Employees].[Amy E. Alberts]
select {
[Measures].[Sales Amount Quota]
} on columns, {
[Employee].[Employees].[Amy E. Alberts Directs],
[Employee].[Employees].[Amy E. Alberts].DataMember,
[Employee].[Employees].[Amy E. Alberts Rollup]
} on rows
from [Adventure Works]
where ([Date].[Calendar].[Calendar Year].[CY 2004])
```

As you can see from the MDX statement in the previous code and its output in the following table, we have created an aggregate of the Amy E. Alberts directs (children) to provide the [Amy E. Alberts Directs] member. As well, if you use the .DataMember function, you can see the sales amount quota assigned specifically to Amy E. Alberts herself as shown in the following table:

	Sales Amount Quota
Amy E. Alberts Directs	$4,820,000.00
Amy E. Alberts	$117,000.00
Amy E. Alberts Rollup	$4,937,000.00

Custom Rollup Scenarios

At times you will want to run a query but you want the information to be rolled up differently than the standard aggregation up the hierarchy. In this section, we review unary operators and custom member formulas. To apply custom member formulas and unary operators, Analysis Services has column bindings that allow you to add these operator metadata. Although there is extra effort to metadata within the relational database (instead of Analysis Services directly) this allows you to simplify the application of these custom rollups down to the lowest level of granularity desired.

Some would prefer rewriting these custom rollups in MDX as part of a calculated member, and depending on your comfort level with MDX, there are both advantages and disadvantages to this approach. For example, if you wanted to apply your custom rollup only to a few employees or to only a few accounts (for example, Income Expense), writing custom MDX to be included in a calculated member may be advantageous because it would be a relatively simple IIF statement within your calculated member. If the custom rollup is applicable to a lot of accounts, you will have performance degradation due to the Analysis Services formula engine traversing through all of the different IIF statements. You could improve performance by using a SCOPE statement instead of IIF but after a while, this may become a very complex MDX statement to write and manage.

But please do note that unary operators and custom member formulas are potential bottlenecks in terms of MDX query performance, so be diligent and careful about how and when you use these operators. You can find more information about these bottlenecks (and other MDX query performance bottlenecks) within the "Identifying and Resolving MDX Query Performance Bottlenecks in SQL Server 2005 Analysis Services" whitepaper (http://sqlcat.com/whitepapers/archive/2007/12/16/identifying-and-resolving-mdx-query-performance-bottlenecks-in-sql-server-2005-analysis-services.aspx).

Account Dimension and Unary Operators

The basic idea of a unary operator is that it is a custom rollup for parent/child dimensions. As you are rolling up and aggregating the children to a parent, you can choose to perform a custom operation that includes the parent or child (+), subtracts the parent or child value (−), multiplies it (*), divides it (/), or ignores it (~). You can find more details about unary operators within SQL Server Books Online (http://msdn.microsoft.com/en-us/library/ms175417.aspx). As well, unary operators allow you to apply weight (instead of the operator symbol) as noted in Mosha Pasumansky's Weighted "Aggregation in Analysis Services blog post" (www.sqljunkies.com/WebLog/mosha/archive/2005/03/27/9723.aspx).

A great Adventure Works example of unary operators in action is the Account dimension. To see this in action, let's first start by viewing the Account dimension within BIDS, as seen in Figure 24-15.

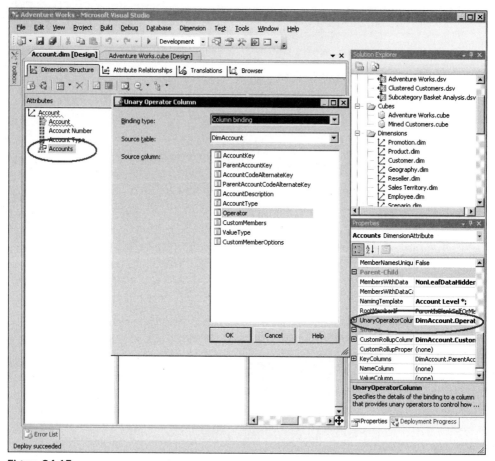

Figure 24-15

As you can see, the unary operator is applied to the [Account].[Accounts] attribute, which is the parent/child dimension attribute of the Account dimension. Accounts are also another good example of parent/child dimensions because of the unbalanced and ragged breakdown of income and expense attributes. Under the Properties section, you will also notice the UnaryOperatorColumn property. Clicking it brings up the Unary Operator Column dialog box, which points to the Operator SQL column. That is, for unary operators to be applied in this manner, you will need to place the operator information in a column of your SQL dimension table:

```
select AccountDescription, AccountType, Operator
   from DimAccount
 where AccountKey = 88 or ParentAccountKey = 88
```

The preceding SQL statement against the DimAccount table within the Adventure Works DW database reveals the unary operator operations in the table that follows. We've manually added some additional indenting to the table to denote that the [Other Income and Expense] is the parent of the [Internet Income], [Internet Expense], [Gain/Loss on Sales of Asset], [Other Income], and [Curr Xchg Gain/(Loss)] members.

Account Description	Account Type	Operator
Other Income and Expense	Revenue	+
Interest Income	Revenue	+
Interest Expense	Expenditures	−
Gain/Loss on Sales of Asset	Revenue	+
Other Income	Revenue	+
Curr Xchg Gain/(Loss)	Revenue	+

This means that when you aggregate all of the values under [Other Income and Expense], the unary operators are indicating that all members except for the [Interest Expense] should be aggregated (added) together and the [Interest Expense] value should be subtracted. To visualize this for this category for June 2004, you can execute the MDX statement in the following code:

```
select {
  [Measures].[Amount]
} on columns, {
  [Account].[Accounts].[Other Income and Expense],
  [Account].[Accounts].[Other Income and Expense] .children
} on rows
from [Adventure Works]
where ([Date].[Fiscal].[Month].[June 2004])
```

The output of this MDX statement is shown in the following table:

	Amount
Other Income and Expense	$6,747.10
Interest Income	$3,691.00
Interest Expense	$5,676.00
Gain/Loss on Sales of Asset	($4,541.00)
Other Income	($43,737.90)
Curr Xchg Gain/(Loss)	$57,011.00

The rollup value for [Other Income and Expense] is the first value in this table, which has a value of $6,747.10. But if unary operators had not been used, the aggregate value would be:

$3,691.00 + $5,676.00 + (−$4,541.00) + (−$43,737.90) + $57,011.00 = $18,099.10

But recall the unary operator for the [Internet Expense] member is (−), which results in a calculation of:

$3,691.00 + **(−$5,676.00)** + (−$4,541.00) + (−$43,737.90) + $57,011.00 = $6,747.10

Custom Member Formulas

Custom member formulas are similar to unary operators except that they use MDX expressions (instead of unary operators or weights) to determine rollups and/or member values. These are also applied to regular dimensions. Let's apply a custom member formula based on time (at the monthly level):

```
select {
 [Measures].[Order Count]
} on columns, {
 [Date].[Fiscal].[Q1 FY 2005],
 [Date].[Fiscal].[Q1 FY 2005].children
} on rows
from [Adventure Works]
```

For example, if you run the MDX query in the previous block of code, you'll notice that the month of August 2004 has no values associated with it (see the following table):

	Order Count
Q1 FY 2005	976
July 2004	976
August 2004	(null)

For the purposes of reporting, you know that the monthly order count for August was 1.25 times the value for July 2004. But instead of actually making changes to the underlying data source, you want to create a custom member formula that will change the August values. To do this, you need to create a custom member formula similar to how you had created a unary operator. Just like unary operators, you can create your own column within your dimension table to specify the custom MDX formula to be applied.

To do this scenario, connect to the Adventure Works DW database and add a new CustomRollupMDX column to the DimTime table:

```
alter table DimTime
 add CustomRollupMDX nvarchar(2048) null
```

Because you want to apply for just the month of August 2004 that its value is 1.25x the value from July 2004, apply the following SQL statement to populate the [DimTime].[CustomRollupMDX] SQL column:

```
update DimTime
    set CustomRollupMDX = '[Date].[Fiscal].[Month].[July 2004]*1.25'
 where FullDateAlternateKey >= '2004-08-01 00:00:00.000'
```

From here, now you can go to BIDS and open up the [Date] dimension. Make sure to go to the [Adventure Works.dsv] Data Source View and refresh it so the DSV takes into account the new CustomRollupMDX column that you've added.

Because we want to apply this custom rollup at the month level, notice in BIDS (see Figure 24-16) we have chosen the [Month Name] attribute. Then in the Properties dialog we've clicked the CustomRollupColumn property and chosen to bind the recently created CustomRollupMDX column in the DimTime table.

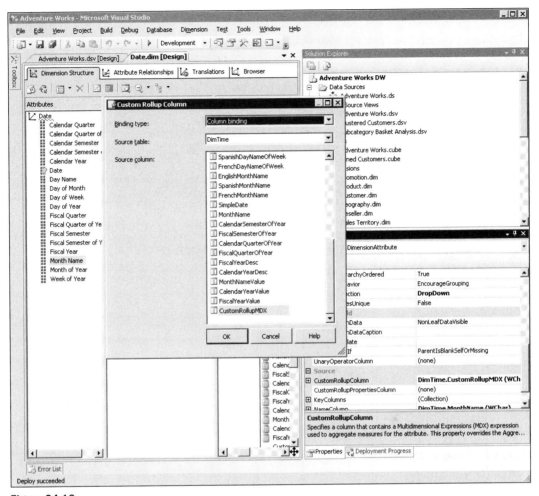

Figure 24-16

Now that you have completed this task, process the Adventure Works cube and then run the following MDX statement:

```
select {
 [Measures].[Order Count]
} on columns, {
 [Date].[Fiscal].[Q1 FY 2005],
 [Date].[Fiscal].[Q1 FY 2005].children,
 [Date].[Fiscal].[Date].[August 1, 2004]
} on rows
from [Adventure Works]
```

The output shown in the following table has some interesting observations because you had applied your custom member formula only to the month attribute:

	Order Count
Q1 FY 2005	976
July 2004	976
August 2004	1,220
August 1, 2004	(null)

You'll notice that the value of August 2004 is 1,220, which is the 1.25 x [July 2004] that was defined in the CustomRollupMDX column. But because we had applied the custom member formula only to the month, you'll notice the value of [August 1, 2004] remains null (recall, there is no order data for the entire month of August 2004) and that the rollup of fiscal year 2005 quarter 1 (which is July 2004 + August 2004 in this case) is still 976. This is a reminder that although custom member formulas can be pretty handy to provide you with the ability to customize your rollup, you need to be aware of the impact (or lack of) on other levels of the hierarchy and their rollups as well.

Summary

This chapter has provided some basic financial scenarios that are commonly applied. We have reviewed how to work with Analysis Services in the context of financial comparative, trend, variance analysis, and the use of KPIs. From the standpoint of many-to-many dimensions, we have reviewed the currency conversion scenario and noted that you should also be concerned about precision. We also reviewed parent/child dimension scenarios concerning employees and accounts and delved into the creation of unary operators and custom rollup scenarios. But as you can see, although these scenarios are specific to financial scenarios, they are also applicable to many other data warehousing scenarios.

25

Web Analytics

The goal of Web Analytics is to transform data from different sources to obtain meaningful intelligence about your web site. It involves the process of collecting, storing, filtering, and analyzing click-stream, commerce, and third-party data. These click-stream BI scenarios range from understanding navigation patterns to designing your web site better to understanding what users are searching in order to personalize recommendations. In this chapter, we take a closer look at the Web Analytics data and determine the type of reports and information it can provide (business intelligence). As we go through these ideas, you will understand why Web Analytics has become the latest trend in data warehousing.

In this chapter we look at:

❑   Understanding what Web Analytics is and the infrastructure it requires

❑   Understanding the business questions that can be answered by Web Analytics

❑   A step-by-step guide to create an OLAP cube from web log data

What Is Web Analytics?

Web Analytics is the analysis of web data. More specifically, it is business intelligence that allows analysts to gain insight into their web-based businesses (for example, e-commerce, customer support, and so on). Web Analytics allows you to understand customer behavior and identify common sales trends so you can personalize services for your customers and increase customer satisfaction. With it, you can understand how well your products, content, and online processes are working.

The difficulty of Web Analytics is that it requires you to combine different sources of data and correlate the data to resolve these issues. With the complexity of web sites, offerings, multiple locations, and promotions, it is difficult to answer even the most basic questions concerning these online businesses. For example, to answer the question "How well did our web promotion work?" you will need to:

- ❏ Transform web log data to determine the number of users who visited the site due to the promotion.

- ❏ Transform commerce data to determine the number of users who made purchases due to the promotion itself.

- ❏ Associate the commerce data to the web log data to include only purchases that were made due to those promotions.

- ❏ Transform banner ads and email marketing campaign data to determine the number of users who actually received the promotion.

- ❏ Correlate all this data.

To answer the previous question, you need to transform three completely different data sources (web log data, commerce data, third-party data), create the data warehouse to hold all of this information, transform the data so it is possible to correlate these different data sources, and finally deliver reports that can actually provide these answers.

Similar to any other business intelligence endeavor, Web Analytics requires the building of a data warehouse to store the detail web data (to understand individual events) so you can more easily understand aggregate events as well (for example, usage patterns). Though it is possible to simply build a report by processing the log data, many bits of information and usage patterns are not easily understood. By having this detail data, it provides you with the ability to find these patterns and validate your report calculations. This process of taking web data and building a data warehouse involves:

- ❏ **Collecting Data:** Obtaining data from web logs, commerce data, campaign advertising, and third-party data sources.

- ❏ **Transforming Data:** Transforming existing web log data into something meaningful and relating this data to your commerce, campaign advertising, and third-party data sources.

- ❏ **Reporting Data:** Storing and publishing this data in a meaningful manner so that analysts, directors, and VPs can understand what they are reading.

The purpose of creating a data warehouse is to store information so that it can be used to answer any number of business questions. But a well-designed OLAP solution or data mart depends on these questions being known and well-defined because they are built to answer specific business questions. Therefore, before proceeding with this process, it is important that you know the types of questions that can or cannot be answered. The next section, "Collecting Data," goes over the different types of data sources and what questions they can answer.

Collecting Data

In most Web Analytics endeavors, there are typically three types of data sources:

- ❏ Web log data
- ❏ Commerce data
- ❏ Campaign advertising data

Most of the data that you will be analyzing is actually based on the web log data, because it describes the actions and patterns of your web site visitors. The commerce data identifies what purchases were made, but the web log data allows you to identify the actions that customers made for those purchases. This allows you to possibly simplify the flow from viewing to buying. Banner ad data (one example of campaign advertising data) allows you to know which customers visited your web site, but the web log data allows you to determine how effective the banner ads were. Customers who click banner ads and see only the first page hardly indicate a successful banner ad campaign, whereas customers who click banner ads and make purchases (based on the clicked banner ads) reveal something that is being done right.

Web Log Data

The primary source for Web Analytics is the web server log files. Depending on how the web server is configured, each time it has been accessed, the web server records each instance to a log file. This information is also known as click-stream data, because each click of the mouse produces data. These log files contain valuable information including the visiting patterns, pages viewed, browser and operating system information, and the length of time your customers spent online.

Issues with click-stream data include the fact that web log data is asynchronous in nature. Each web click that your customers make gets recorded into these log files. Note that users click on web pages at different times and the information stored in the web log is organized by date time, not by the users and their clicks. So how do you know if the user actually stayed on this page or was redirected to another page? How do you identify which web instance or page view belongs to which customer?

Before transforming your web server log data, the first thing you will need to do is to understand what this data provides and what this data lacks. Following is a sample from a Microsoft Internet Information Services (IIS) 6.0 web server log in the World Wide Web Consortium (W3C) Extended Log File format; the W3C is an organization for setting standards for web-based technologies — you can find more information at www.w3c.org/. IIS logs can typically be found in the %WindowsDirectory%\System32\ LogFiles directory on your Windows Server.

```
#Software: Microsoft Internet Information Services 6.0
#Version: 1.0
#Date: 2007-12-17 00:00:27
#Fields: date time s-sitename s-ip cs-method cs-uri-stem cs-uri-query
        s-port cs-username c-ip cs(User-Agent) cs(Referer) sc-status
        sc-substatus sc-win32-status sc-bytes cs-bytes time-taken

2007-12-17 00:00:26 W3SVC145 72.15.199.197 GET /MainFeed.aspx  80
        24.9.185.182 Windows-RSS-Platform/1.0+
        (MSIE+7.0;+Windows+NT+5.1)   304 0 0 597 428 109

2007-12-17 00:01:14 W3SVC145 72.15.199.197 GET
        /technicalnotes/rss.aspx  80   213.199.128.149
        Mozilla/4.0+(compatible;+MSIE+7.0;+Windows+NT+6.0;
        +SLCC1;+.NET+CLR+2.0.50727;+.NET+CLR+3.0.04506;+InfoPath.2;
        +MS-RTC+LM+8;+MSOffice+12)   304 0 0 379 514 156

2007-12-17 00:04:21 W3SVC145 72.15.199.197 GET /top10lists/rss.aspx
        80   213.244.24.142 Mozilla/4.0+(compatible;+MSIE+7.0;
        +Windows+NT+5.1;+Maxthon;+SIMBAR={AAD55C1C-701C-488A-831E-
        2BCD732CA50C};+InfoPath.1;+.NET+CLR+2.0.50727;
        +.NET+CLR+1.1.4322;+.NET+CLR+3.0.04506.30;+InfoPath.2;
        +MS-RTC+LM+8;+MSOffice+12)   200 0 0 100527 499 1046
```

The following table shows that there is much information that can be extracted from your web logs. What type of analytics or business intelligence you obtain depends on how well you organize this data.

Field	Data Type	Description
date	timestamp	The date the activity occurred.
time	timestamp	The time the activity occurred.
s-sitename	string	The Internet service name and site instance number that served the request.
s-ip	string	The IP address of the server that generated the log file.
cs-method	string	The request action, for example, POST method.
cs-uri-stem	string	The target of the action, for example, a web page like default.aspx.
cs-uri-query	string	The query, in the form of parameter value pairs, the client was trying to perform (if at all).
s-port	integer	The server port number that received the request.
cs-username	string	The name of the authenticated user that made the request.
c-ip	string	The IP address of the client that made the request.
cs(User-Agent)	string	The client request User-Agent header.
cs(Cookie)	string	The client request Cookie header.
cs(Referrer)	string	The client request Referrer header.
sc-status	integer	The response HTTP status code.
sc-substatus	integer	The substatus error code.
sc-win32-status	integer	The Windows status code.
sc-bytes	integer	The number of bytes sent by the server.
cs-bytes	integer	The number of bytes sent by the client.
time-taken	integer	The elapsed time in milliseconds for the action to occur.

The fields for this web log file are specific to the IIS web server from which the log was obtained. Differences in server or web log configurations will have variations in what fields are included and what order they may be in. As you can see, web log data can provide you with a vast amount of information that will allow you to identify the behavior of your customers on your web site. The trick is to be able to decipher this information.

Page View Information

Page view information describes the page that has been viewed when a user performs the click of a mouse. The page view information that can be easily identified includes:

❑ Date/time information the customer accessed the web page (date/time).

❑ The web site/server the user is accessing (s-computername, s-sitename, s-ip, s-port).

❑ The web page the customer is accessing (cs-uri-stem).

❑ The time taken for the web page to process on the web server — this information is important to help you determine if a web page is too slow to render (`time-taken`).

❑ The previous web page (for example, search engine, other web sites, and so on) that linked to the current web page (`cs-referrer`).

❑ The bytes sent and received by the web server to the client (`cs-bytes`, `sc-bytes`).

❑ The query string the customer is accessing via this web page (`cs-uri-query`).

The query string is of particular importance in Web Analytics because of the additional information you can obtain from it. The following table contains example meanings, created by the authors, based on the following query string:

```
lid=20&evt=1000&cat=books
```

As you will see, the meanings of these query strings are in the form of parameter-value pairs, defined at the discretion of the web developers, and can mean anything they want.

Query String Components	Example Meaning
`cat=books`	Category Information, for example, what category and/or subcategories the customer is accessing. Using the example of an online store, the customer is currently accessing the store category of books.
`evt=1000`	Event Information, for example, what event has recently occurred on the web site. For example, this particular identifier could indicate that the user has added an item to his shopping basket.
`lid=20`	Local Identifier Information, for example, a particular subject or object that requires identification. For example, this particular local identifier could be describing a particular book (*Hiking in Western Washington*).

In the preceding example, the query string identifies that the customer added the book *Hiking in Western Washington* to his shopping cart when looking in the category books. This is a simple example of how web data can be organized so that its web logs can provide you with information concerning your customer browsing and shopping habits.

User-Agent Information

User-Agent information — the `cs(UserAgent)` field — allows you to identify information such as the browser and operating system the user is using to access your particular web sites. As well, it allows you to identify what search engines, RSS readers, robots, spiders, crawlers, and so on (programs that automatically fetch web pages in order to index a web site) that are keeping tabs on your web site as well.

Following the W3C Extended Format, you can take the following User-Agent string and obtain interesting information about whom or what is accessing your web site:

```
Mozilla/4.0 (compatible; MSIE 7.0; Windows NT 6.0; SLCC1; .NET CLR 2.0.50727;
    Media Center PC 5.0; .NET CLR 3.0.04506; Tablet PC 2.0; InfoPath.2; .NET
    CLR 3.5.21022; MS-RTC LM 8)

Feedfetcher-Google;+(+http://www.google.com/feedfetcher.html)
```

The first User-Agent string indicates that the person accessing this site is using Microsoft Internet Explorer 7.0 (Mozilla/4.0; compatible; MSIE 7.0) on a Windows Vista (Windows NT 6.0) computer. The second User-Agent string indicates that Google's feedfetcher has grabbed an RSS feed from your web site.

By knowing what browser and operating system information is accessing your web site, you can design your site for a particular browser or operating system configuration. For example, if you were to find out that many of your customers were Windows Mobile 6.0 users, it may make sense for you to design your web site to be better customized for mobile users. By knowing which search engines, robots, spiders, or crawlers are accessing your web site, you can determine if your search engine optimization campaign (to have your site ranked high in top search engine queries) was successful.

Web Site Visitor Information

Web Analytics on web site visitor information allows you to identify and personalize information for your customer. Though many would suggest that Web Analytics on customer information is for the purpose of spamming, the primary purpose of Web Analytics of customer information is in fact *personalization*. Each visitor has his or her own preferences and performing Web Analytics on these preferences allows you to design a service that caters to their needs. For example, if a user is viewing football information from a sports web site, knowing this allows you to tailor the site to the football preferences (instead of wrestling, badminton, or some other sport).

Saying this, the visitor information that you can obtain directly from the web logs does not provide you with the whole picture:

❑ The client IP (c-ip) can tell you an approximate geographical location of where the customer is logging in from. But this location information may not be reliable because this client IP may be the IP address of the Internet service provider, not the actual customer.

❑ The username (cs-username) for external-facing web sites are typically not populated. Most web sites will have an alternate form of authentication that does not populate this field.

❑ The cookie (cs(Cookie)) information is a bit of information that allows you to "unique-ify" a user who has viewed the web pages. We use the term "unique-ify" because a cookie by itself typically does not have the information to actually identify who that user is. This allows us to differentiate one web site visitor from another; this also allows us to perform page path analysis (what sequence of pages a web site visitor went through).

Depending on your web site design, you may require users to log in and provide some form of profile information (for example, personal preferences, geographic location, and so on), which can be associated with a cookie. By doing this, it's possible to associate visitor profile information with web traffic (for example, the number of people from Seattle who visit this web page).

Client-side JavaScript Tagging

A common method for Web Analytics providers (for example, WebTrends, Google Analytics, Omniture, and so on) to obtain data from your web site is in the form of a client-side JavaScript. On your web page, you insert a JavaScript that is executed every time your web page is requested. The JavaScript then makes a request for a small image file (typically a 1-pixel-by-1-pixel clear gif file that is not visible on the web page) from the Web Analytics provider web site. This request can also transmit to the Web Analytics provider web site parameter-value pair information such as the event, category, and local identifier information noted in the table in the section "Page View Information."

As you can see in Figure 25-1, the actions of client-side JavaScript tagging are:

1. A web site visitor visits a page on your web site by initiating a page request.

2. Your web server sends the requested web page with a JavaScript script.

3. From the web site visitor's browser, the JavaScript script requests a small clear gif file. Within that request, it will also contain parameter-value pairs within the `cs-uri-query` that is recorded within the web server log.

4. The tracking web site provides a clear gif to complete this request.

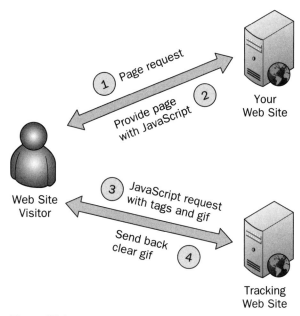

Figure 25-1

The advantage of this approach is that you can have the JavaScript perform the task of creating the cookie and transmitting it and the other parameter-value pair information to a separate web server (Tracking Web Site).

Both the parameter-value pair information and this cookie (used to unique-ify the user) will show up in the Tracking Web Site server log as part of the `cs-uri-query` *field.*

On your web server, the web server log records an entry for each request for the web page including images (for example, if your web page has six images, you will then have one entry for the page and six entries for each image). But with this approach, the Tracking Web Site server log will record only one entry for a page view, which will make transformation of the data for downstream analysis easier.

Commerce Data

Commerce data includes the products and transactions that have occurred on an e-commerce site. Typically you will have a separate commerce database to keep track and reconcile fiscal transactions. But, the joining of this commerce data with web server logs allows you to better understand the impact of your web site navigation and design in fiscal terms.

One way to associate commerce information with a web site visitor's activity is to put additional parameter-value pairs to the page query string thus being recorded in the `cs-uri-query` field of a web server log. For example, the parameter-value pairs

```
/hiking.aspx?lid=20&evt=1000&cat=books&cost=10.00
```

indicate that a shopping cart event (evt=1000) with a category of books (cat=book) had occurred on the web page about hiking (hiking.aspx). In this scenario, presuming this is a U.S. commerce site, we also note the monetary value of this book, which is $10.00 (cost=10.00).

Whether you are using the client-side JavaScript tagging or a web page generation to create these parameter-value pairs, the result is that web server log will have following information, which you can then decipher:

cs-uri-stem	cs-uri-query
hiking.aspx	lid=20&evt=1000&cat=books&cost=10.00

Campaign Advertising Data

Campaign advertising data ranges from text ads to email campaigns. The goal of these advertisements is to increase the visibility of your web site. But how do you track which ads are more effective than others and which ones provide you with a better return on investment?

Most commonly, when a user clicks a link in the advertisement, the link has additional parameter-value pairs on the URL. For example, a search engine text ad URL may be in the form of:

```
Mysite.com/hiking.aspx?ad1=202
```

In addition to going to the hiking section of your web site, there is an additional query string component of ad1=202 (for example, Microsoft AdCenter text advertisement on www.live.com). The exact format of the query string component is decided by the one creating the advertising campaign. Nevertheless, the concept is that there are cs-uri-query string components within the URL indicating where the advertising campaign had come from. From the standpoint of web analysis, you need to parse out the cs-uri-query for this advertising information (just like you will for the event, category, and sales information) to know which advertising campaign is directing more traffic to you.

By itself, associating campaign information with your web traffic is very interesting. You can learn fundamental things such as the purchase of a text ad increased your web site traffic by 25 percent or that web site visitors who visit your site through an email campaign spend more time on your site.

But even more interesting is to associate the commerce information with the campaign information to understand what your return on investment is for your advertising campaign. This idea is conceptually tricky because most users who click some advertising campaign to a web site do not immediately make a purchase. Here is a common scenario:

- ❑ User A clicks a text advertisement from live.com to your site on Day 1
- ❑ User A clicks another text advertisement from google.com to your site on Day 2
- ❑ User A clicks an email advertisement to your site on Day 3
- ❑ User A searches on live.com to your site on Day 5
- ❑ User A clicks a banner ad to your site on Day 7
- ❑ User A purchases an item on your site on Day 9

In the preceding scenario, which advertisements do you associate with your purchase to perform a ROI analysis? There are a number of approaches:

❑ **Last Advertisement Viewed:** This is a very common approach where you want to associate the purchase with the last advertisement the web site visitor has seen; in this case, it was the banner ad on Day 7.

❑ **First Advertisement Viewed:** Sometimes business analysts care about the first advertisement a user viewed and want to associate that advertisement with the final purchase; in this case this was the text ad from live.com on Day 1.

❑ **Second-to-Last Advertisement Viewed:** Some analysts believe that it is the second-to-last advertisement viewed that should be associated with the final purchase; in this case this was the email advertisement on Day 3.

❑ Note that, the second-to-last advertisement was not the live.com search on Day 5. The reason for this is because most analysts want to decipher the difference between a paid link compared to a search link. If a search engine is able to bring you all the necessary visibility, you probably do not want to pay for an advertising campaign. Therefore, analysts will often differentiate between a search and paid links in their analysis.

Typically, the window for applying this logic is a 30-day rolling window. That is, once a purchase has occurred, you go back up to 30 days to associate the appropriate campaign to that purchase. If the advertisement occurred beyond 30 days, you do not associate that purchase with an advertising campaign. Whether you choose one approach or all three approaches is outside the scope of this book — it is a decision that needs to be made by your business.

What Can I Do with This Data?

With this, now you have an end-to-end picture of your web site visitors from where they came from (for example, search engine, paid advertisement link), what they did (that is, page view, User Agent, and web site visitor), and what they ultimately did (for example, purchase). As you can see, web log information with commerce and campaign data associated to the web log as query string components can provide a rich data set for analytics.

Transforming Web Log Data

Many methods exist to transform the collected data into your SQL and OLAP data warehouse. Common methods include utilizing SQL Server Integration Services (SSIS), using Log Parser (www.logparser .com), or developing your own parsing process to go through the data. In general, the difficulty is not in transforming your transactional data, but in making sense of the web log data. In this section you learn about the issues involved in transforming the data rather than various parsing technologies.

Filtering

As noted in the previous section, web logs record every single request to the web page. What this implies is that there is a lot of data that needs to be filtered out, leaving the actual data that describes customer actions and patterns. Recall that when a user clicks a web page, there actually is more than one hit recorded in the web server log. This is not applicable in the case of using a Tracking Web Site with client-side JavaScript tagging. The instances recorded include images, style sheets, JavaScript, ASP include files, and other files that are called upon by the web page and are integral for the web site, but not for the purposes of analysis. For example, the table that follows specifically calls the URI stem and referrer:

URI stem	Referrer
/shop/WebPage.asp	—
/images/ico_A.gif	http://www.wrox.com/shop/WebPage.asp?lid=20&vID=1000 &cat=books
/doc/OLAP.asp	—
/images/ico_B.gif	http://www.wrox.com/shop/WebPage.asp?lid=20&vID=1000 &cat=books
/shop/WebPage2.asp	http://www.wrox.com/shop/WebPage.asp?lid=20&vID=1000 &cat=books

As you can see from this table, the only pieces of information that you really are interested in are that users clicked the /shop/WebPage.asp, /doc/OLAP.asp and /shop/WebPage2.asp pages.

In addition to filtering out these files, you may want to also filter out search engine, crawler, robot, or spider activity. As noted previously, these are programs that automatically fetch web pages to index your web site. It may be interesting to note the activities of these programs (hence recording this information), but they have nothing to do with customer activity. Determining whether to filter out this information or how to organize it is dependent on the questions you want to answer.

Page Views

Once your data is filtered, what remains is the data indicating the web pages that web site visitors have hit. However, determining the number of page views is not the only interesting information that can be derived. As noted in the "Page View Information" section earlier, you can decipher category and/or event information by assigning values to the query string. The parser application must then perform the task of going through each page view in order to determine which page, category, and/or event has occurred for that particular page view. From this information, it is also possible to determine the number of visits and decipher from this data the distinct number of users.

Sessions

There are many ways to determine what constitutes a session within page views. The simplest definition is that one session is a set of sequential page views to the particular web site where each page view is within 30 minutes of each other. The following is a table containing sample URI stem, date/time, and cookie data:

URI stem	Date/Time	Cookie
/shop/WebPage.asp	2008-03-31 06:50:47	58C673C195B84D249FE0FB9DCCF02E9E
/doc/OLAP.asp	2008-03-31 06:50:47	JKU198FB898D004758DE27FF9ED239C6
/shop/WebPage2.asp	2008-03-31 06:51:25	58C673C195B84D249FE0FB9DCCF02E9E

As you can see, the cookie allows you to identify a user and his or her sequential visits; one user visited `/shop/WebPage.asp` and then visited `/shop/WebPage2.asp` thirty-eight (38) seconds later, and another user visited `/doc/OLAP.asp` at 6:50:47 in the morning. However, as noted before, web log data is asynchronous in nature and has its own set of problems. For example, when does a visit start or end? If a user with the same cookie hits the web site throughout the day, when does one session end and another begin? A standard practice is if there is a time span of 30 minutes between user-clicks, then these are two different sessions. However, what if this particular page has a lot of content and it took more than 30 minutes for the person to read it? Do we now have two sessions? (Common practice is to report this as two sessions.)

What if a user visits a site at 2008-03-31 11:55 PM and continues to click until well after 2008-04-01 midnight? From the standpoint of reporting, here is how this session will be represented:

Reporting Period	Period Type	Sessions
3/31/2008	Day	1
4/1/2008	Day	1
3/30/2008 – 4/5/2008	Week	1
March, 2008	Month	1
April, 2008	Month	1

As you can see from the table, this single session started on 3/31/2008 and ended on 4/1/2008 counts as one session for each day. For the week, which includes both 3/31/2008 and 4/1/2008, you only have one session — that is, sessions are distinct and not necessarily additive.

How about if your site does not require users to register? If users do not register, they typically do not have any cookies associated with them. Then how do you identify users without using cookies? Do you use a combination of IP address and browser? If the user happens to be using a public library computer, the IP address and browser for that public computer would be the same for a large number of visits and users. How do you separate one visit from another?

You can use other methods such as cookies, IP address/browser combinations, user IDs within a web page form, utilizing session variables, or databases to help decipher web log data to determine visits. But, how you decide what constitutes a visit and which issues you tackle and which you abandon is purely a business function, rather than a technological one; web logs provide only so much information. Some information, such as browser and operating system information, is only beneficial for analysis from the visit level. After all, there is no point knowing the browser for every request, but it is important to know what browser each visitor is using to view your site.

Visitors

As implied in the previous section, there are two types of web site visitors for your web site: identifiable (users with cookies) and unidentifiable (users without cookies). It may be tempting just to count users who have cookies. However, plenty of users browse sites to read content, view products, and comparison-shop before making a purchase. If you were to force them to register before doing these simple tasks, you may risk irritating the customers you hope to attract.

Non-identifiable Visitors

Although certain visitors may not have registered, you still want to know their patterns and habits. This segment of your population makes up a large portion of your web traffic and failing to understand them will result in missed opportunities and poor customer service. After all, if the dominant browser for these non-identifiable visitors differs from your identifiable ones, you may want to optimize your site for the browser these non-identifiable visitors use as well. The time these non-identifiable visitors visit the site, what categories they peruse, and what events or actions they take are still important in understanding customer patterns and habits within your site. After all, by understanding these non-registered visitors, it may be possible for you to build incentives to make them into loyal registered visitors.

A common technique to "identify" non-identifiable users is to use the combination of their IP address and User-Agent string. An example scenario of the web page, client IP address, and User-Agent string data can be seen in the table that follows:

Page	Client IP	User-Agent String
/shop/WebPage.asp	192.168.0.1	Mozilla/4.0+(compatible;+MSIE+7.0;+Windows+NT+5.1)
/doc/OLAP.asp	204.148.170.161	Mozilla/4.0+(compatible;+MSIE+6.0;+Windows+98)
/shop/WebPage2.asp	192.168.0.1	Mozilla/4.0+(compatible;+MSIE+7.0;+Windows+NT+5.0)

As you can see, even without the cookie information, you are able to identify the fact that the same user has hit the /shop/WebPage.asp and the /shop/WebPage2.asp. This technique is not foolproof (due to issues with how ISPs often provide client IP addresses and issues with User-Agent strings) but it does allow you to estimate the count of non-identifiable visitors.

Identifiable Visitors

As noted in the previous section, you can identify visitors of the web site by utilizing the cookie, but how do you uniquely identify each visitor? Just because a visitor has a different cookie does not mean it is a different person — it simply means that there is a new visit. How do you identify who the visitor is? For that matter, why are you concerned about each visitor?

In most e-commerce environments, customers can make purchases after registering with the web site. The action of registering saves key customer properties (for example, age, geography, income, and so on) and allows you to create an association between a cookie and the specific user and store this in a database. Thus, it is possible to associate the page view actions within the web log to a single visitor. Though you may not be interested in analyzing the habits of a single visitor, being able to identify which transactions belong to which visitor will allow you to classify this data by customer properties (for example, which age group of visitors visited the site at 12 AM). Furthermore, this association allows you to associate web log data and all of its information to commerce and campaign data.

Visitor Identity Addendum

So far you have seen some standard examples to identify users (cookies for identifiable users; User-Agent and client IP for non-identifiable users), but these are not the only techniques. How you perform this task will depend on many factors ranging from how much control you have over the web site (adding query strings, session variables, cookies, and so on) to the type of environment. The questions that were raised show how the analysis process is iterative (for example, first classify users with cookies, then use session variables to identify non-cookie users, then use client IP and User-Agent strings, and so on). As you go through the data, you will have to redefine your identification scheme to classify more of the data. There may be a point when you will no longer be able to identify these users — for that matter, it may simply be not worth the effort. How much of this data you leave unidentified is more a business decision than a technological one.

Dimensions

In the process of building and organizing your fact information (for example, page views for your web log data, sales transactions for your commerce data, click-through for your banner ad data), you will need to remember to update your dimension tables as well. Examples of dimension data from the web logs include web page hierarchy, categories, events, browser, operating system, and crawler (if so desired) information. Recall that the advantage of OLAP is that it allows end users to quickly view the fact data by dimension data. For example, to get a count of page views correlated against browser information over a span of time, your OLAP cube would need to contain a fact table of page views and dimensions of browser and time. Neglecting to populate the dimension data will result in an important piece of information being missed or an error during processing.

Step-by-Step Guide

It is important to note here that many more complex concepts within Web Analytics are not covered in this chapter. Recall that the purpose of this section is to provide a step-by-step guide on how to build a *basic* Web Analytics cube on top of web log information. Therefore, in this section we review:

- Basic parsing of a web log file
- Simple web log transformation
- Transforming the page path
- Creating the fact table
- Identifying visitors and sessions
- Creating the Analysis Services cube (and its many steps)

This section uses files that you can download from www.wrox.com.

Reviewing the Log File

Let's start with the included log file ex20071217.log, which is an IIS 6.0 W3C format log file (see Figure 25-2). Please note that this is a test log file, not an actual log file, because we do not want to be sharing personal information.

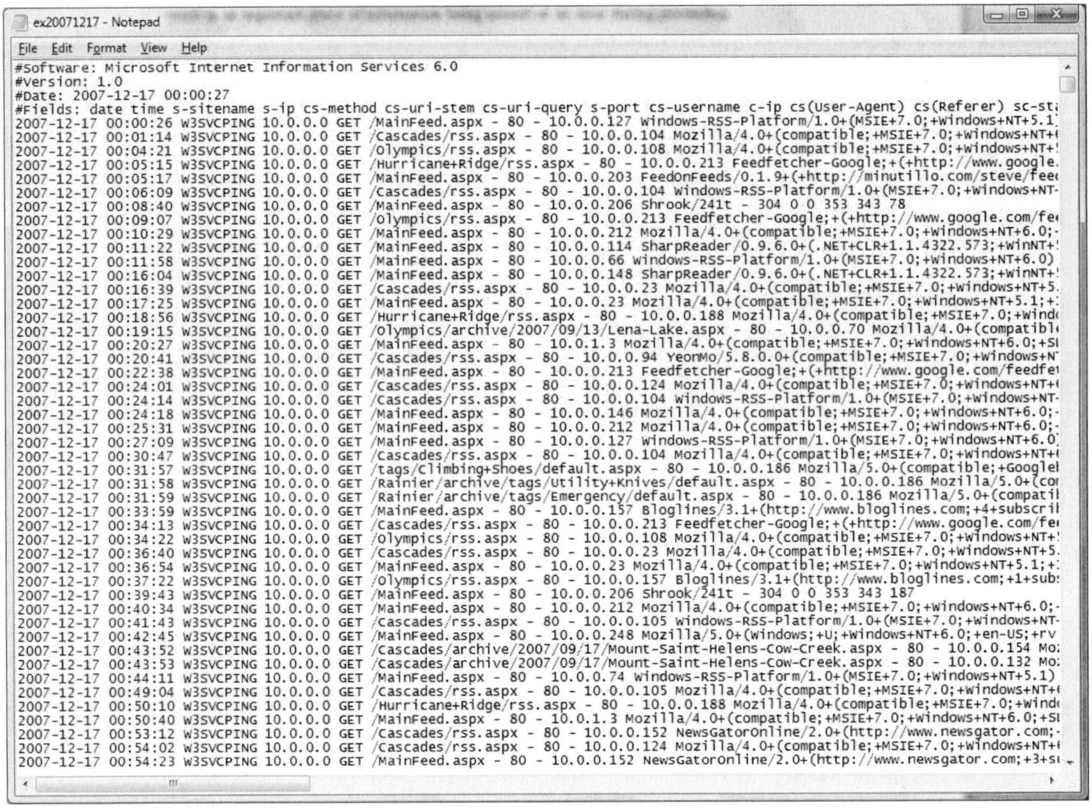

```
ex20071217 - Notepad
File Edit Format View Help
#Software: Microsoft Internet Information Services 6.0
#Version: 1.0
#Date: 2007-12-17 00:00:27
#Fields: date time s-sitename s-ip cs-method cs-uri-stem cs-uri-query s-port cs-username c-ip cs(User-Agent) cs(Referer) sc-st
2007-12-17 00:00:26 W3SVCPING 10.0.0.0 GET /MainFeed.aspx - 80 - 10.0.0.127 Windows-RSS-Platform/1.0+(MSIE+7.0;+Windows+NT+5.1
2007-12-17 00:01:14 W3SVCPING 10.0.0.0 GET /Cascades/rss.aspx - 80 - 10.0.0.104 Mozilla/4.0+(compatible;+MSIE+7.0;+Windows+NT+
2007-12-17 00:04:21 W3SVCPING 10.0.0.0 GET /Olympics/rss.aspx - 80 - 10.0.0.108 Mozilla/4.0+(compatible;+MSIE+7.0;+Windows+NT+
2007-12-17 00:05:15 W3SVCPING 10.0.0.0 GET /Hurricane+Ridge/rss.aspx - 80 - 10.0.0.213 Feedfetcher-Google;+(+http://www.google.
2007-12-17 00:05:17 W3SVCPING 10.0.0.0 GET /MainFeed.aspx - 80 - 10.0.0.203 FeedOnFeeds/0.1.9+(+http://minutillo.com/steve/fee
2007-12-17 00:06:09 W3SVCPING 10.0.0.0 GET /Cascades/rss.aspx - 80 - 10.0.0.104 Windows-RSS-Platform/1.0+(MSIE+7.0;+Windows+NT-
2007-12-17 00:08:40 W3SVCPING 10.0.0.0 GET /MainFeed.aspx - 80 - 10.0.0.206 Shrook/241t - 304 0 0 353 343 78
2007-12-17 00:09:07 W3SVCPING 10.0.0.0 GET /Olympics/rss.aspx - 80 - 10.0.0.213 Feedfetcher-Google;+(+http://www.google.com/fe
2007-12-17 00:10:29 W3SVCPING 10.0.0.0 GET /MainFeed.aspx - 80 - 10.0.0.212 Mozilla/4.0+(compatible;+MSIE+7.0;+Windows+NT+6.0;-
2007-12-17 00:11:22 W3SVCPING 10.0.0.0 GET /MainFeed.aspx - 80 - 10.0.0.114 SharpReader/0.9.6.0+(.NET+CLR+1.1.4322.573;+WinNT+
2007-12-17 00:11:58 W3SVCPING 10.0.0.0 GET /MainFeed.aspx - 80 - 10.0.0.66 Windows-RSS-Platform/1.0+(MSIE+7.0;+Windows+NT+6.0)
2007-12-17 00:16:04 W3SVCPING 10.0.0.0 GET /MainFeed.aspx - 80 - 10.0.0.148 SharpReader/0.9.6.0+(.NET+CLR+1.1.4322.573;+WinNT+
2007-12-17 00:16:39 W3SVCPING 10.0.0.0 GET /Cascades/rss.aspx - 80 - 10.0.0.23 Mozilla/4.0+(compatible;+MSIE+7.0;+Windows+NT+5.
2007-12-17 00:17:25 W3SVCPING 10.0.0.0 GET /MainFeed.aspx - 80 - 10.0.0.23 Mozilla/4.0+(compatible;+MSIE+7.0;+Windows+NT+5.1;+
2007-12-17 00:18:56 W3SVCPING 10.0.0.0 GET /Hurricane+Ridge/rss.aspx - 80 - 10.0.0.188 Mozilla/4.0+(compatible;+MSIE+7.0;+Wind
2007-12-17 00:19:15 W3SVCPING 10.0.0.0 GET /Olympics/archive/2007/09/13/Lena-Lake.aspx - 80 - 10.0.0.70 Mozilla/4.0+(compatibl
2007-12-17 00:20:27 W3SVCPING 10.0.0.0 GET /MainFeed.aspx - 80 - 10.0.1.3 Mozilla/4.0+(compatible;+MSIE+7.0;+Windows+NT+6.0;+S
2007-12-17 00:20:41 W3SVCPING 10.0.0.0 GET /Cascades/rss.aspx - 80 - 10.0.0.94 YeonMo/5.8.0.0+(compatible;+MSIE+7.0;+Windows+N
2007-12-17 00:22:38 W3SVCPING 10.0.0.0 GET /MainFeed.aspx - 80 - 10.0.0.213 Feedfetcher-Google;+(+http://www.google.com/feedfe
2007-12-17 00:24:01 W3SVCPING 10.0.0.0 GET /Cascades/rss.aspx - 80 - 10.0.0.124 Mozilla/4.0+(compatible;+MSIE+7.0;+Windows+NT+
2007-12-17 00:24:14 W3SVCPING 10.0.0.0 GET /Cascades/rss.aspx - 80 - 10.0.0.104 Windows-RSS-Platform/1.0+(MSIE+7.0;+Windows+NT-
2007-12-17 00:24:18 W3SVCPING 10.0.0.0 GET /MainFeed.aspx - 80 - 10.0.0.146 Mozilla/4.0+(compatible;+MSIE+7.0;+Windows+NT+6.0;-
2007-12-17 00:25:31 W3SVCPING 10.0.0.0 GET /MainFeed.aspx - 80 - 10.0.0.212 Mozilla/4.0+(compatible;+MSIE+7.0;+Windows+NT+6.0;-
2007-12-17 00:27:09 W3SVCPING 10.0.0.0 GET /MainFeed.aspx - 80 - 10.0.0.127 Windows-RSS-Platform/1.0+(MSIE+7.0;+Windows+NT+6.0
2007-12-17 00:30:47 W3SVCPING 10.0.0.0 GET /Cascades/rss.aspx - 80 - 10.0.0.104 Mozilla/4.0+(compatible;+MSIE+7.0;+Windows+NT+
2007-12-17 00:31:57 W3SVCPING 10.0.0.0 GET /tags/Climbing+Shoes/default.aspx - 80 - 10.0.0.186 Mozilla/5.0+(compatible;+Google
2007-12-17 00:31:58 W3SVCPING 10.0.0.0 GET /Rainier/archive/tags/Utility+Knives/default.aspx - 80 - 10.0.0.186 Mozilla/5.0+(co
2007-12-17 00:31:59 W3SVCPING 10.0.0.0 GET /Rainier/archive/tags/Emergency/default.aspx - 80 - 10.0.0.186 Mozilla/5.0+(compati
2007-12-17 00:33:59 W3SVCPING 10.0.0.0 GET /MainFeed.aspx - 80 - 10.0.0.157 Bloglines/3.1+(http://www.bloglines.com;+4+subscri
2007-12-17 00:34:13 W3SVCPING 10.0.0.0 GET /Cascades/rss.aspx - 80 - 10.0.0.213 Feedfetcher-Google;+(+http://www.google.com/fe
2007-12-17 00:34:22 W3SVCPING 10.0.0.0 GET /Olympics/rss.aspx - 80 - 10.0.0.108 Mozilla/4.0+(compatible;+MSIE+7.0;+Windows+NT+
2007-12-17 00:36:40 W3SVCPING 10.0.0.0 GET /Cascades/rss.aspx - 80 - 10.0.0.23 Mozilla/4.0+(compatible;+MSIE+7.0;+Windows+NT+5.
2007-12-17 00:36:54 W3SVCPING 10.0.0.0 GET /MainFeed.aspx - 80 - 10.0.0.23 Mozilla/4.0+(compatible;+MSIE+7.0;+Windows+NT+5.1;+
2007-12-17 00:37:22 W3SVCPING 10.0.0.0 GET /Olympics/rss.aspx - 80 - 10.0.0.157 Bloglines/3.1+(http://www.bloglines.com;+1+sub
2007-12-17 00:39:43 W3SVCPING 10.0.0.0 GET /MainFeed.aspx - 80 - 10.0.0.206 Shrook/241t - 304 0 0 353 343 187
2007-12-17 00:40:34 W3SVCPING 10.0.0.0 GET /MainFeed.aspx - 80 - 10.0.0.212 Mozilla/4.0+(compatible;+MSIE+7.0;+Windows+NT+6.0;-
2007-12-17 00:41:43 W3SVCPING 10.0.0.0 GET /Cascades/rss.aspx - 80 - 10.0.0.105 Windows-RSS-Platform/1.0+(MSIE+7.0;+Windows+NT-
2007-12-17 00:42:45 W3SVCPING 10.0.0.0 GET /MainFeed.aspx - 80 - 10.0.0.248 Mozilla/5.0+(Windows;+U;+Windows+NT+6.0;+en-US;+rv
2007-12-17 00:43:52 W3SVCPING 10.0.0.0 GET /Cascades/archive/2007/09/17/Mount-Saint-Helens-Cow-Creek.aspx - 80 - 10.0.0.154 Mo
2007-12-17 00:43:53 W3SVCPING 10.0.0.0 GET /Cascades/archive/2007/09/17/Mount-Saint-Helens-Cow-Creek.aspx - 80 - 10.0.0.132 Mo
2007-12-17 00:44:11 W3SVCPING 10.0.0.0 GET /MainFeed.aspx - 80 - 10.0.0.74 Windows-RSS-Platform/1.0+(MSIE+7.0;+Windows+NT+5.1)
2007-12-17 00:49:04 W3SVCPING 10.0.0.0 GET /Cascades/rss.aspx - 80 - 10.0.0.105 Mozilla/4.0+(compatible;+MSIE+7.0;+Windows+NT+
2007-12-17 00:50:10 W3SVCPING 10.0.0.0 GET /Hurricane+Ridge/rss.aspx - 80 - 10.0.0.188 Mozilla/4.0+(compatible;+MSIE+7.0;+Wind
2007-12-17 00:50:40 W3SVCPING 10.0.0.0 GET /MainFeed.aspx - 80 - 10.0.1.3 Mozilla/4.0+(compatible;+MSIE+7.0;+Windows+NT+6.0;+S
2007-12-17 00:53:12 W3SVCPING 10.0.0.0 GET /Cascades/rss.aspx - 80 - 10.0.0.152 NewsGatorOnline/2.0+(http://www.newsgator.com;-
2007-12-17 00:54:02 W3SVCPING 10.0.0.0 GET /Cascades/rss.aspx - 80 - 10.0.0.124 Mozilla/4.0+(compatible;+MSIE+7.0;+Windows+NT+
2007-12-17 00:54:23 W3SVCPING 10.0.0.0 GET /MainFeed.aspx - 80 - 10.0.0.152 NewsGatorOnline/2.0+(http://www.newsgator.com;+3+s
```

Figure 25-2

Parsing the Web Log

As you can see from the log file, there are a number of columns and parameter-value pairs that you need to parse through in order to extract the data that you need. Though there are many methods that can be used, a handy and straightforward tool to do this is the Log Parser tool that is available at `support.microsoft.com/kb/910447`. Download the logparser tool from the link provided and install it on your machine. For more information about the logparser, I would also recommend *Microsoft Log Parser Toolkit* (Giuseppini, 2005).

Ultimately, we want to load this log data into a database; the Log Parser tool allows you to parse log files using a "SQL-like" syntax to the benefit of database administrators. For example, the "SQL-like" code found within the included `IISLogQuery.sql` file is:

```
select
TO_TIMESTAMP(Date, Time) as CurrentDate,      -- Page View date/time
 c-ip,                                         -- Client IP Address
 Extract_Token(c-ip, 0, '.'),                  -- Oct1
 Extract_Token(c-ip, 1, '.'),                  -- Oct2
 Extract_Token(c-ip, 2, '.'),                  -- Oct3
 Extract_Token(c-ip, 3, '.'),                  -- Oct4
 cs-uri-stem,                                  -- Page Hierarchy
 cs-uri-query,                                 -- Parameter-Value Pairs
```

```
     cs(Cookie),                              -- User Cookie (Not Used Here)
     cs(User-Agent),                          -- User Agent: Browser, OS
     cs(Referer)                              -- Referrer
  from %InputFile%
  where
    cs-uri-stem like '%.aspx' and             -- Only Web Pages
    cs-uri-stem not like '/themes%'           -- Do not include: CSS / web
                                                 site themes
```

Although this looks like a SQL statement, you cannot run this within the SQL Server Management Studio. Instead this is a statement that Log Parser will execute (more on this in a bit). What is helpful here is that in Log Parser you can specify that the input file format — in this case a IIS log file in the W3C format — so that it will automatically recognize the columns within the log files. For example, you can type the command statement:

```
logparser -i:IISW3C -h
```

which provides you with the fields that exist within the log file. The fields we are interested in are noted in the following table translated from the preceding "SQL-like" statement:

IISLogQuery field	IIS Log fields	Description
CurrentDate	Date, Time	Use the Log Parser TO_TIMESTAMP function to concatenate together date and time fields of the log file into a datetime field. This will provide the date and time when the page was viewed.
ClientIP	C-IP	This is the Client IP address; note, the values within the log file are from 10.0.0.1 – 10.0.1.9 because we do not want to provide real users' IP addresses.
Oct1	C-IP	Recall that a user's IP address can identify a user's geographic location. To do this, it may be faster downstream in SQL processes to join together by the individual octets. Because the Log Parser is already going through C-IP column, there is negligible overhead to have it also parse out the Client IP into its individual octet values using the Log Parser EXTRACT_TOKEN function. Oct1 is the first octet of an IPv4 address.
Oct2	C-IP	Oct2 is the second octet of an IPv4 address.
Oct3	C-IP	Oct3 is the third octet of an IPv4 address.
Oct4	C-IP	Oct4 is the last octet of an IPv4 address.
cs-uri-stem	Cs-uri-stem	The target of the action, for example, a web page like default.aspx.
Cs-uri-query	Cs-uri-query	The query, in the form of parameter-value pairs, that the client was trying to perform (if at all). For the purpose of this book, we will not be extracting the values from this column. Note that there may be interesting information in this column, which can be extracted by the Log Parser function EXTRACT_VALUE.

(continued)

(continued)

IISLogQuery field	IIS Log fields	Description
cs(User-Agent)	string	The client request User-Agent header, which provides the OS and Browser information. As well, because we do not have cookie information, we will be using this value in combination with the ClientIP address to "unique-ify" the users.
cs(Cookie)	string	The client request Cookie header. For the purpose of this book our log files will not contain any cookies. But if they do, you can use this cookie to "unique-ify" your web site visitors instead of using the ClientIP address/User-Agent string combination.
cs(Referrer)	string	The client request Referrer header, which includes information such as which web site search engine had referred you to this page.

You will notice the SQL-like statement includes the WHERE clause:

```
cs-uri-stem like '%.aspx' and                    -- Only Web Pages
```

We include this WHERE clause because we only wanted to analyze what web pages users had queried instead of supporting files like CSS files, scripts, and images. Understanding files like CSS, scripts, and images and/or web log columns such as `time-taken` (elapsed time for the server to provide the content) and `sc-substatus` (any error codes) are interesting from an operational perspective. But recall that the purpose of Web Analytics is to understand what your users are viewing and doing on your web site.

Simple Web Log ETL

To execute this `IISLogQuery.sql` file, we created a simple batch command file called `ExtractFields.cmd`, which performs the basic functions of extracting the data from the web log file, transforming the data, and loading the data into a SQL database. Review the command below:

```
@echo off
REM Extract the fields from the log file
logparser -i:IISW3C -o:TSV file:IISLogQuery.sql?InputFile=ex20071217.log
       -headers:OFF -stats:OFF > ExtractedFields.tsv
```

This command tells the Log Parser that your input file is in IIS W3C format (`-i:IISW3C`) without an output file of tab-separated values (`-o:TSV`). You can use the `file:` parameter to indicate that you are using a SQL file to execute your statement and you can also enter your own parameter-value pairs to replace parameters within your SQL file. For example, you may notice within the `IISLogQuery.sql` file that the FROM statement is the from `%InputFile%`. The `%InputFile%` parameter can have its value replaced at execution time so that you can execute this on multiple log files without the need to change your SQL file.

As you can see, the preceding command statement instructs Log Parser to execute the IISLogQuery SQL file to create a new `ExtractedFields.tsv` tab-delimited file with the columns specified within the SQL file:

```
REM truncate table
sqlcmd -S. -d WebLogs -E -Q "TRUNCATE TABLE log_20071217"


REM Bulk insert data into database
bcp WebLogs.dbo.log_20071217 in ExtractedFields.tsv -c -S. -T -t\t
```

This is rather simplified, but the idea is that you will now load the data from the recently created `ExtractedFields.tsv` tab-delimited file into your database, appropriately named WebLogs into the table `log_20071217`. The schema of your initial database table is:

Field	DataType	Description
CurrentDate	Datetime	The date and time when the page was viewed.
ClientIP	Varchar(15)	IPV4 addresses are in the format of xxx.xxx.xxx.xxx with a maximum of 15 characters.
Oct1	Tinyint	Octet values of an IPv4 address are from 0 to 255 which is a tinyint.
Oct2	Tinyint	Octet values of an IPv4 address are from 0 to 255 which is a tinyint.
Oct3	Tinyint	Octet values of an IPv4 address are from 0 to 255 which is a tinyint.
Oct4	Tinyint	Octet values of an IPv4 address are from 0 to 255 which is a tinyint.
PagePath	Varchar(256)	This is the web page and folder it is in.
QueryString	Varchar(2048)	Originally the `cs-uri-query` column, this contains the parameter-value pairs. The reason this column is so large is because a query string URL can be up to 2k in length.
Cookie	Varchar(256)	The client request Cookie header, also known as `cs(Cookie)`.
UserAgent	Varchar(512)	This is the browser User-Agent string containing browser and OS information, also known as `cs(UserAgent)`.
Referrer	Varchar(1024)	The client request Referrer header, also known as the `cs(Referrer)` column.

Following is the command file that we used to execute the parsing of the log file and loading of the data into the SQL fact table:

```
REM Extract the Page Path from the log file
logparser -i:IISW3C -o:TSV file:IISLogPagePathQuery.sql?InputFile=
    ex20071217.log -headers:OFF -stats:OFF > ExtractedPagePath.tsv

REM truncate table
sqlcmd -S. -d WebLogs -E -Q "TRUNCATE TABLE stg_PagePath"

REM Bulk insert data into database
bcp WebLogs.dbo.stg_PagePath in ExtractedPagePath.tsv -c -S. -T -t\t
```

Transforming the Page Path

As noted previously, the cs-uri-stem column of our web log contains the web page path. For example, the first few web page paths from our web site logs are:

```
MainFeed.aspx
Olympics/rss.aspx
Olympics/archive/2007/09/13/Lena-Lake.aspx
```

The page is the name with the aspx suffix (for ASP.NET web pages), and the folder name is delimited by the forward slash character. For the file path Olympics/archive/2007/09/13/Lena-Lake.aspx, the hierarchy would be graphically represented within an OLAP dimension as shown in Figure 25-3.

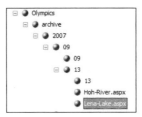

Figure 25-3

The goal is to create a parent/child dimension table so we can have a web page hierarchy within our OLAP cube. The following table shows the parent/child table translation for the preceding three page paths:

ParentID	ChildID	Value	Full Page Path
NULL	5	MainFeed.aspx	MainFeed.aspx
7	25	Archive	Olympics/archive
7	29	rss.aspx	Olympics/rss.aspx
25	66	2007	Olympics/archive/2007
66	125	09	Olympics/archive/2007/09
125	182	13	Olympics/archive/2007/09/13
182	239	Lena-Lake.aspx	Olympics/archive/2007/09/13/Lena-Lake.aspx

To perform this task, you'll note the ExtractedFields.cmd batch file executed the IISLogPagePathQuery.sql SQL file and loaded this data into the stg_PagePath table (as noted in Figure 25-4). A simple way to convert the forward slash delimited page path is to create separate columns for each level of the page hierarchy as noted in the stg_PagePath table.

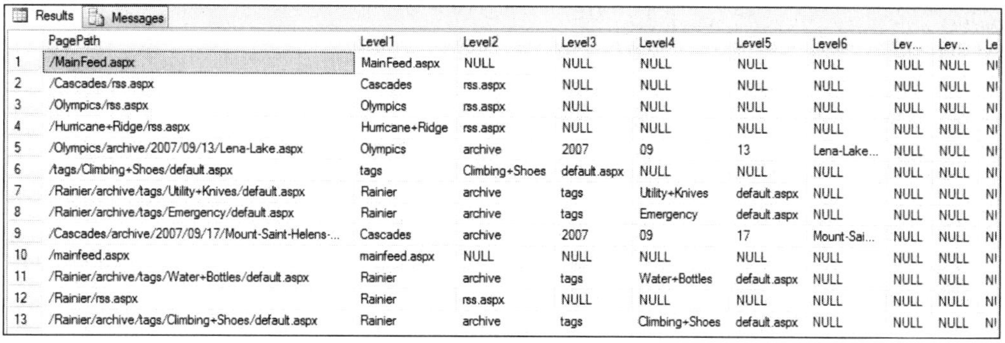

Results | Messages

	PagePath	Level1	Level2	Level3	Level4	Level5	Level6	Lev...	Lev...	Le
1	/MainFeed.aspx	MainFeed.aspx	NULL	NULL	NULL	NULL	NULL	NULL	NULL	N
2	/Cascades/rss.aspx	Cascades	rss.aspx	NULL	NULL	NULL	NULL	NULL	NULL	N
3	/Olympics/rss.aspx	Olympics	rss.aspx	NULL	NULL	NULL	NULL	NULL	NULL	N
4	/Hurricane+Ridge/rss.aspx	Hurricane+Ridge	rss.aspx	NULL	NULL	NULL	NULL	NULL	NULL	N
5	/Olympics/archive/2007/09/13/Lena-Lake.aspx	Olympics	archive	2007	09	13	Lena-Lake...	NULL	NULL	N
6	/tags/Climbing+Shoes/default.aspx	tags	Climbing+Shoes	default.aspx	NULL	NULL	NULL	NULL	NULL	N
7	/Rainier/archive/tags/Utility+Knives/default.aspx	Rainier	archive	tags	Utility+Knives	default.aspx	NULL	NULL	NULL	N
8	/Rainier/archive/tags/Emergency/default.aspx	Rainier	archive	tags	Emergency	default.aspx	NULL	NULL	NULL	N
9	/Cascades/archive/2007/09/17/Mount-Saint-Helens-...	Cascades	archive	2007	09	17	Mount-Sai...	NULL	NULL	N
10	/mainfeed.aspx	mainfeed.aspx	NULL	NULL	NULL	NULL	NULL	NULL	NULL	N
11	/Rainier/archive/tags/Water+Bottles/default.aspx	Rainier	archive	tags	Water+Bottles	default.aspx	NULL	NULL	NULL	N
12	/Rainier/rss.aspx	Rainier	rss.aspx	NULL	NULL	NULL	NULL	NULL	NULL	N
13	/Rainier/archive/tags/Climbing+Shoes/default.aspx	Rainier	archive	tags	Climbing+Shoes	default.aspx	NULL	NULL	NULL	N

Figure 25-4

To convert this information from column-based to a parent/child row-based table, you will need to pivot the data as noted in the included `PivotToPageHierarchy.sql` file. This file includes the PivotToPageHierarchy stored procedure and the supporting `ExtractToken` function. To transform the data within the stg_PagePath table into the parent/child dimension table PageHierarchy, you need only to execute

```
exec PivotToPageHierarchy
```

to perform the transformation as noted in Figure 25-5.

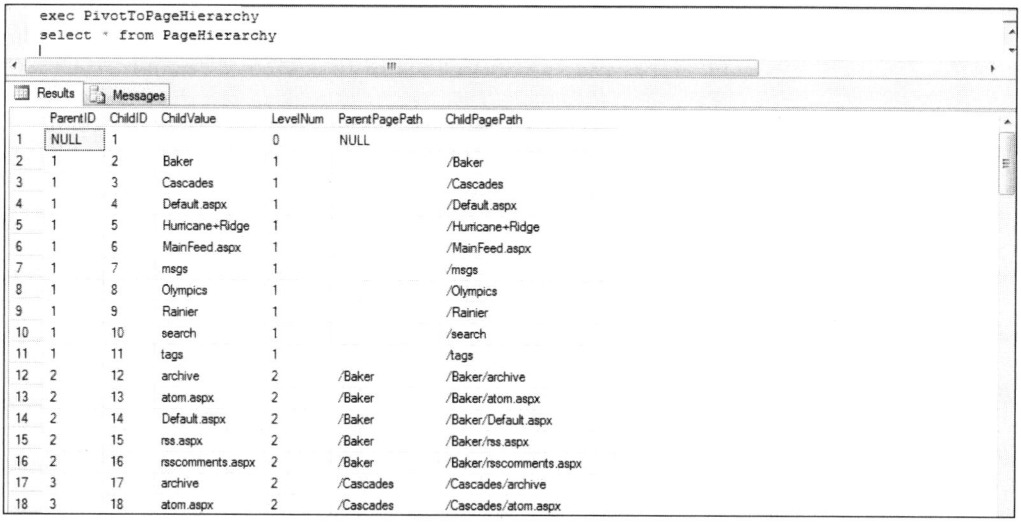

```
exec PivotToPageHierarchy
select * from PageHierarchy
```

Results | Messages

	ParentID	ChildID	ChildValue	LevelNum	ParentPagePath	ChildPagePath
1	NULL	1		0	NULL	
2	1	2	Baker	1		/Baker
3	1	3	Cascades	1		/Cascades
4	1	4	Default.aspx	1		/Default.aspx
5	1	5	Hurricane+Ridge	1		/Hurricane+Ridge
6	1	6	MainFeed.aspx	1		/MainFeed.aspx
7	1	7	msgs	1		/msgs
8	1	8	Olympics	1		/Olympics
9	1	9	Rainier	1		/Rainier
10	1	10	search	1		/search
11	1	11	tags	1		/tags
12	2	12	archive	2	/Baker	/Baker/archive
13	2	13	atom.aspx	2	/Baker	/Baker/atom.aspx
14	2	14	Default.aspx	2	/Baker	/Baker/Default.aspx
15	2	15	rss.aspx	2	/Baker	/Baker/rss.aspx
16	2	16	rsscomments.aspx	2	/Baker	/Baker/rsscomments.aspx
17	3	17	archive	2	/Cascades	/Cascades/archive
18	3	18	atom.aspx	2	/Cascades	/Cascades/atom.aspx

Figure 25-5

Recall in Figure 25-4 that the stg_PagePath table is a tabular translation of the web page hierarchy, which is forward slash delimited. In a tabular environment, we want to pivot this table to represent this as a parent/child hierarchy. To do this, we make use of the SQL PIVOT operator as noted in an excerpt of the following PivotToPageHierarchy code:

```
select cast(replace([Level], 'Level', '') as smallint) as [LevelNum],
        ChildValue, PagePath
    from (
          select PagePath, Level1, Level2, Level3, Level4, Level5, Level6,
                  Level7, Level8, Level9, Level10
            from stg_PagePath
        ) pvt
unpivot (
        ChildValue for [Level] in
                (Level1, Level2, Level3, Level4, Level5, Level6, Level7,
                  Level8, Level9, Level10)
    ) as unpvt;
```

The preceding statement does the operational task of transforming the column-based representation of this information vertically as noted in Figure 25-6.

	LevelNum	ChildValue	PagePath
1	1	MainFeed.aspx	/MainFeed.aspx
2	1	Cascades	/Cascades/rss.aspx
3	2	rss.aspx	/Cascades/rss.aspx
4	1	Olympics	/Olympics/rss.aspx
5	2	rss.aspx	/Olympics/rss.aspx
6	1	Hurricane+Ridge	/Hurricane+Ridge/rss.aspx
7	2	rss.aspx	/Hurricane+Ridge/rss.aspx
8	1	Olympics	/Olympics/archive/2007/09/13/Lena-Lake.aspx
9	2	archive	/Olympics/archive/2007/09/13/Lena-Lake.aspx
10	3	2007	/Olympics/archive/2007/09/13/Lena-Lake.aspx
11	4	09	/Olympics/archive/2007/09/13/Lena-Lake.aspx

Figure 25-6

The rest of the code performs the task of looping through the "vertical-ized" data, inserting it into the PageHierarchy table, and creating the appropriate parent/child hierarchy by associating the correct ParentID to the values:

```
-- Insert Level 1
insert into PageHierarchy (ParentID, ChildValue, LevelNum, ParentPagePath,
        ChildPagePath)
select 1, ChildValue, LevelNum, '', '/' + ChildValue
    from (
          select distinct ChildValue, LevelNum from @pivot where LevelNum = 1
        ) a;


-- Loop through Level 2 to max Level
declare @LevelNumMax smallint, @LevelNum smallint
set @LevelNum = 2
select @LevelNumMax = max(LevelNum) from @pivot

while @LevelNum <= @LevelNumMax
begin
        -- inset the data
        insert into PageHierarchy (ParentID, LevelNum, ChildValue,
                ChildPagePath, ParentPagePath)
        select distinct b.ChildID, a.LevelNum, a.ChildValue,
```

```
                    a.ParentPagePath + '/' + a.ChildValue, a.ParentPagePath
        from (
            select LevelNum, ChildValue, PagePath as ChildPagePath,
                dbo.ExtractToken(PagePath, LevelNum, '/') as
                ParentPagePath
            from @pivot where LevelNum = @LevelNum
        ) a
        inner join PageHierarchy b
            on b.LevelNum = @LevelNum - 1
            and b.ChildPagePath = a.ParentPagePath

        -- loop through
        set @LevelNum = @LevelNum + 1

    end
```

Please note that we used Log Parser and SQL as our method to create the parent/child table based on the page hierarchy to more easily show what type of transformation is needed. Saying this, from the standpoint of production code, you may want to build an SSIS package that performs the parsing (or uses Log Parser), takes the web page hierarchy information, performs the necessary pivots and transformations in memory, and have it create the PageHierarchy table. Nevertheless, regardless of which method you use, the point is for you to transform the page folder structure into a page hierarchy so your end users can better understand what is being navigated throughout your web site.

Creating the Fact Table

Now that the PageHierarchy table is populated, let's do the final transformation of the log data into a fact table ready for OLAP cube consumption. To create the fact_20071217 table, execute the script TransformFact.sql (included in the book's downloadable files from www.wrox.com). A code snippet of this script is included here:

```
select
    cast(Hashbytes('SHA1', IsNull(f.UserAgent, '') + f.ClientIP) as bigint)
        as VisitorID,
    f.UserAgent,
    f.ClientIP,
    cast(cast(f.CurrentDate as varchar(11)) as smalldatetime) as EventDate,
    datepart(hh, f.CurrentDate) as EventHour,
    g.GeoID,
    p.ChildID as PageID,
    case
        when f.UserAgent like '%MSIE+7.0%' then 1
        when f.UserAgent like '%MSIE+6.0%' then 2
        when f.UserAgent like '%MSIE+5.5%' then 3
        when f.UserAgent like '%Firefox/2.0%' then 4
        when f.UserAgent like '%Firefox/1.5%' then 5
        when f.UserAgent like 'Mozilla%' and f.UserAgent
            not like '%Firefox%' and f.UserAgent not like '%MSIE%' then 6
        else 0
    end as BrowserID,
```

(continued)

(continued)

```
    case
        when f.UserAgent like '%Windows+NT+5.0%' then 1
        when f.UserAgent like '%Windows+NT+5.1%' then 2
        when f.UserAgent like '%Windows+NT+5.2%' then 3
        when f.UserAgent like '%Windows+NT+6.0%' then 4
        when f.UserAgent like '%Linux%' then 5
        else 0
    end as OSID,
    case
        when Referer like '%google%' then 1
        when Referer like '%live%' then 2
        when Referer like '%yahoo%' then 3
        else 0
    end as SearchID
  from log_20071217 f
    left outer join dim_IPGeo g
      on g.Oct1 = f.Oct1
      and g.Oct2 = f.Oct2
      and g.Oct3 = f.Oct3
      and g.Oct4 = f.Oct4
    left outer join PageHierarchy p
      on p.ChildPagePath = f.PagePath
  order by
    f.CurrentDate
```

The following sections provide a quick breakdown of this script to view the type of transformations needed.

VisitorID Creation

As noted in previous sections, the VisitorID has been created so it is possible to "unique-ify" the web log transactions. If a cookie was available, we would normally choose this as our method for identification:

```
cast(Hashbytes('SHA1', IsNull(f.UserAgent, '') + f.ClientIP) as bigint)
    as VisitorID,
```

Because this was not available, another common method is to use a combination of the client IP address and the User-Agent string. In the script, we have concatenated the two fields together and used the SQL `HashBytes` function to convert this value into a big integer. The reason we want to convert this value into an integer value is because it is optimal for Analysis Services to perform distinct counts against an integer data source.

Identifying the Browser and Operating System

The browser is determined by parsing out the User-Agent string and obtaining the pertinent information. Note that the User-Agent string is often dirty and visitors can spoof their User-Agent strings with miscellaneous values. There are various .NET projects or Perl (HTTP::BrowserDetect) modules that can make it easier for you to perform the conversion. As well, there are third-party resources such as www.useragentstring.com/ that allow you to take a User-Agent string and determine the browser and OS (among others) components.

```
    case
        when f.UserAgent like '%MSIE+7.0%' then 1
        when f.UserAgent like '%MSIE+6.0%' then 2
        when f.UserAgent like '%MSIE+5.5%' then 3
        when f.UserAgent like '%Firefox/2.0%' then 4
        when f.UserAgent like '%Firefox/1.5%' then 5
```

```
         when f.UserAgent like 'Mozilla%' and f.UserAgent
             not like '%Firefox%' and f.UserAgent not like '%MSIE%' then 6
           else 0
      end as BrowserID,
      case
         when f.UserAgent like '%Windows+NT+5.0%' then 1
         when f.UserAgent like '%Windows+NT+5.1%' then 2
         when f.UserAgent like '%Windows+NT+5.2%' then 3
         when f.UserAgent like '%Windows+NT+6.0%' then 4
         when f.UserAgent like '%Linux%' then 5
         else 0
      end as OSID,
```

A simple conversion can be seen in the preceding code, which looks for very specific text patterns; for example *MSIE+7.0* is Internet Explorer 7.0 which is `BrowserID = 1` in the dim_Browser table that was pre-populated with browser values. We have also done the same thing with the operating system; for example, we're looking for any text pattern of *Linux*, which represents the Linux operating system, represented by `OSID = 5` pre-populated in the dim_OS table.

Although this conversion is simple and straightforward, it is not all encompassing. For more enterprise Web Analytics implementations, developers often create their own custom User-Agent parsers (or use third-party code or libraries) to quickly parse and identify the browser and OS components from the User-Agent string. So although this SQL script is straightforward, it is relatively simple representation.

Identifying the Referrer

Recall that the Referrer tells you which page and/or site a web site visitor came from to your site. This is very important from the standpoint of campaign information because it tells you what site is leading visitors to your site. From the standpoint of advertising campaigns, this first page on your site with a combination of query string parameters will often tell you which advertising campaign has brought visitors to your web site.

For the purpose of this basic Web Analytics cube, we will not be getting into the process of parsing out the parameter-value pairs of the query string to identify the advertising campaign. Also, the code required to resolve the logic assigning which campaign to a visitor (first visit, last visit, second-to-last visit, and so on) is out of scope for this book. What we concentrate on right now is identifying which of the three main search engines is responsible for directing traffic to your web site:

```
      case
         when Referer like '%google%' then 1
         when Referer like '%live%' then 2
         when Referer like '%yahoo%' then 3
         else 0
      end as SearchID
```

As you can see from this code snippet, we are looking within the Referrer string to do a simple pattern match of the three respective search engines. If we cannot find them, we simply denote a 0 value; these values correspond to the pre-populated dim_Search table within the WebLogs database:

```
http://www.google.fr/search?hl=fr&q=hikingclimbing++Chalk+issue&meta=
```

Please recall that the Referrer often has other interesting information even if it does not include parameter-value pairs from campaign information. Some of the information we know from the preceding query string include:

❑ The search came from Google France (google.fr)

❑ The default language chosen is French (hl=fr)

❑ The search terms that were used are hikingclimbing, chalk, and issue (the text after q=).

A quick way to extract out this information can be to use the EXTRACT_VALUE function within Log Parser. At the same time, you may also want to consider building your own custom code and/or using SSIS to perform the task of parsing out these parameter-value pairs and business logic.

Identifying Geographic Information

To ensure that we were not releasing privacy-revealing information, the IP addresses included in the original log file to the populated fact_20071217 table were all generated. Understanding geographic information based on IP address can be quite precise and very imprecise at the same time. The precision is based on the fact that third-party vendors have IP address information down to the zip code and connectivity type (dialup, broadband, and so on). This can be awfully precise as noted in a study that found that 87 percent of the U.S. population could be uniquely identified based on the three characteristics of 5-digit zip code, date of birth, and gender (Sweeney, 2002).

Because of the risk of revealing sensitive information, for the purpose of this book the logic used in the TransformFact.sql script was a straightforward join between the generated Client IP addresses with the dim_IPGeo table, which contains generated IP addresses with generated country and state locations.

But realistically, you will want to work with third-party vendors and/or generate your own mapping of IP address to geographic information. For example, you can ping the registries in the following table to obtain the databases of IP addresses to geographic mappings:

Registry Source	Information
www.arin.net	North America Registry
www.ripe.net	Europe, Middle East, and Central Asia
www.lacnic.net	Latin America and Caribbean Registry
www.apnic.net	Asia Pacific Network
www.afrinic.net	Africa

Whether you are working with the mapping databases from one of these Regional Internet Registries (RIR) or through third-party sources, you typically will have a mapping of IP address *ranges* to geographic location (in various formats). Because you will be working with IP address ranges, the processing of this data will be more resource-intensive.

Session Creation

As noted earlier, the concept of a web session is that a single web site visitor will click a web page within 30 minutes from the last time the same visitor had clicked a web page on your site (note that some may define a session to be an hour). To "sessionize" the fact data for this sample, execute the SessionizeFact.sql script (included in the book's downloadable files from www.wrox.com).

Before we dig into the details of this script, please note that this script is not entirely correct in that it only needs to sessionize one day of data. If there were multiple days of data, this script would count a single visitor that had crossed a day boundary (visited page 1 on Day 1 11:59 PM and visited page 2 on Day 2 00:10) as two different sessions. In real session implementations, this scenario should really be counted as one session, not two. Nevertheless, this implementation provides you with a simple example of how to sessionize your data.

When we sessionize the data, the goal is for the transformation process to generate a unique SessionID for each visitor's web page views (following the 30-minute logic).

One way to sessionize your data is to go through each row and compare it with the previous row to figure out if it fits within the 30-minute business logic. This is very effective when using custom code or using SSIS as your mechanism for sessionizing. Many enterprise Web Analytics applications follow this method.

Because we have created this fact table already in SQL, following is another method that does not rely on cursors (notoriously slow) to perform a similar feat.

To help with this process, the first part of this script is to insert the data into a temporary table (_Sessionize) that has its own identity value (lid). Notice from Figure 25-7 that the data is organized by the VisitorID and the CurrentDate.

	lid	VisitorID	CurrentDate	Fact...	SessionID
1	1	-9194024213840506970	2007-12-17 23:34:39.000	2138	NULL
2	2	-9136005506339901440	2007-12-17 18:07:36.000	1504	NULL
3	3	-9136005506339901440	2007-12-17 18:07:39.000	1505	NULL
4	4	-9136005506339901440	2007-12-17 18:08:28.000	1506	NULL
5	5	-9136005506339901440	2007-12-17 19:37:45.000	1712	NULL
6	6	-9109923581819936123	2007-12-17 16:27:32.000	1310	NULL
7	7	-9104333599989351281	2007-12-17 00:43:53.000	40	NULL
8	8	-9095705529166783528	2007-12-17 02:03:16.000	119	NULL
9	9	-9095705529166783528	2007-12-17 02:03:21.000	120	NULL
10	10	-9095705529166783528	2007-12-17 02:03:21.000	121	NULL
11	11	-9095705529166783528	2007-12-17 02:03:22.000	122	NULL
12	12	-9095705529166783528	2007-12-17 02:33:05.000	167	NULL
13	13	-9095705529166783528	2007-12-17 02:37:32.000	186	NULL
14	14	-9095705529166783528	2007-12-17 02:37:32.000	187	NULL
15	15	-9095705529166783528	2007-12-17 02:37:33.000	188	NULL
16	16	-9095705529166783528	2007-12-17 03:03:10.000	233	NULL

Figure 25-7

Though we want to resolve this session-izing by SQL, we do not want to use a cursor to loop through row-by-row to perform this task. A *set* based approach is to have the sessionize table join to itself by its VisitorID and an offset of 1 for the identity value. Because we have ordered the data by VisitorID and CurrentDate, we can now compare the previous row with the current row. If they have different VisitorIDs, then they will have different SessionIDs. If they have the same VisitorIDs and the *current row* [CurrentDate] – *previous row* [CurrentDate] is less than or equal to 30 minutes, they are in the same session with an assigned value of 0. If the time span is greater than 30 minutes, a new sessionID is assigned.

```
update a
  set a.SessionID =
  case
        when datediff(mi, b.Currentdate, a.CurrentDate) < 31 then 0
        else a.lid
  end
  from _Sessionize a
    left outer join _Sessionize b
      on b.lid = a.lid - 1
      and b.VisitorID = a.VisitorID
```

The first few rows of results can be seen in Figure 25-8.

Figure 25-8

Though all of the non-zero SessionIDs have been assigned with this one statement, there are quite a few rows where the SesssionIDs are 0. Let's focus on the first four rows in the _Sessionize table. Notice that the first two rows have a populated SessionID, whereas the third and fourth rows currently have a SessionID of 0. A quick examination of these four rows note that the third and fourth rows do belong to the same session as row 2 (that is, should have SessionID = 2).

lid	VisitorID	CurrentDate	FactID	SessionID
1	−9194024213840506970	2007-12-17 23:34:39.000	2138	1
2	−9136005506339901440	2007-12-17 18:07:36.000	1504	2
3	−9136005506339901440	2007-12-17 18:07:39.000	1505	0
4	−9136005506339901440	2007-12-17 18:08:28.000	1506	0

If we were to then execute the following update statement

```
update a
    set a.SessionID = b.SessionID
    from _Sessionize a
        left outer join _Sessionize b
            on b.lid = a.lid - 1
            and b.VisitorID = a.VisitorID
    where a.SessionID = 0
    and b.SessionID > 0
```

now the third row will be assigned with a SessionID = 2. But the fourth row will still have a SessionID = 0.

lid	VisitorID	CurrentDate	FactID	SessionID
1	−9194024213840506970	2007-12-17 23:34:39.000	2138	1
2	−9136005506339901440	2007-12-17 18:07:36.000	1504	2
3	−9136005506339901440	2007-12-17 18:07:39.000	1505	**2**
4	−9136005506339901440	2007-12-17 18:08:28.000	1506	0

You can also see this happen for other SessionID = 0 rows in Figure 25-9 when comparing it to Figure 25-8.

Figure 25-9

Therefore, the `SessionizeFact.sql` script executes the previous update statement in a WHILE loop where it will continue to loop through until there are no SessionID = 0 rows:

```
/* Loop through until there are no SessionID = 0 */
declare @SessionID0Cnt int
declare @LoopCnt int
select @SessionID0Cnt = count(*)
  from _Sessionize a
    left outer join _Sessionize b
      on b.lid = a.lid - 1
      and b.VisitorID = a.VisitorID
 where a.SessionID = 0
   and b.SessionID > 0
set @SessionID0Cnt = IsNull(@SessionID0Cnt, 0)
set @LoopCnt = 0

-- while loop
while @SessionID0Cnt > 0
begin
  -- Update SessionID values to the SessionID in the row above
  update a
```

(continued)

(continued)

```
      set a.SessionID = b.SessionID
   from _Sessionize a
          left outer join _Sessionize b
            on b.lid = a.lid - 1
            and b.VisitorID = a.VisitorID
  where a.SessionID = 0
    and b.SessionID > 0

  -- LoopCnt
  set @LoopCnt = @LoopCnt + 1

  -- Update
  select @SessionID0Cnt = count(*)
    from _Sessionize a
          left outer join _Sessionize b
            on b.lid = a.lid - 1
            and b.VisitorID = a.VisitorID
  where a.SessionID = 0
    and b.SessionID > 0
  set @SessionID0Cnt = IsNull(@SessionID0Cnt, 0)

  end
```

In the preceding SQL script, the WHILE statement will loop through 71 times to assign the non-zero SessionID values. Though this is a lot of iterations, it is far less than the 2234 iterations required from a CURSOR statement. Saying this, for your production environments, we recommend an ETL mechanism such as custom code or SSIS to perform this task.

The final step of this script is to assign the SessionIDs determined by this script (and stored in the _Sessionize table) back to the original fact table:

```
update f
   set f.SessionID = s.SessionID
   from fact_20071217 f
     inner join _Sessionize s
       on s.VisitorID = f.VisitorID
       and s.CurrentDate = f.CurrentDate
       and s.FactID = f.FactID
```

Now, we have a populated fact table that is ready for Analysis Services cube consumption.

Creating an Analysis Services Cube

The previous chapters in this book have covered how to initially create a data source, Data Source View (DSV), dimensions, and cubes. Therefore, this section covers the steps to specifically create the dimensions and cubes for your WebLogs cube. Please note that you can also refer directly to the WebLogs BIDS solution part of this chapter, which you can download from the companion web site.

Reviewing the Data Source View

Based on all of the transformations you have done, Figure 25-10 provides you with a graphical view of the DSV, which includes all the tables you just created with which you will populate your OLAP cube.

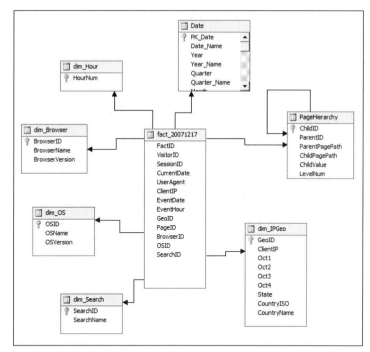

Figure 25-10

The following table provides you with the mapping of the dimension tables with the fact tables:

Fact Table Column	Dimension Table and Column
EventDate	[Date].[PK_Date]
EventHour	[Dim_Hour].[HourNum]
BrowserID	[Dim_Browser].[BrowserID]
OSID	[Dim_OS].[OSID]
SearchID	[Dim_Search].[SearchID]
GeoID	[Dim_IPGeo].[GeoID]
PageID	[dim_PageHierarchy].[ChildID]

Creating the Date Dimension

As noted in previous chapters, SQL Server 2008 Analysis Services includes the ability to generate time tables automatically. To take advantage of this option, within the Dimension Wizard (shown in Figure 25-11), we will choose to generate a time table in the data source.

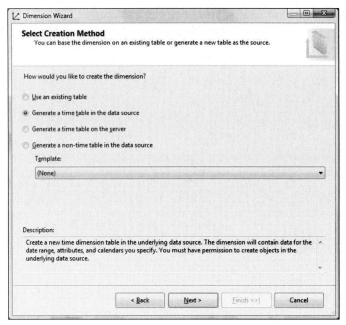

Figure 25-11

Though we only have one day of fact data, for the purpose of the cube creation, we will generate a time table for December 2007 (Figure 25-12). What is great about this feature is that you have the options to generate your time dimension specific for your OLAP cube; it will also generate the table in your relational data source if so desired.

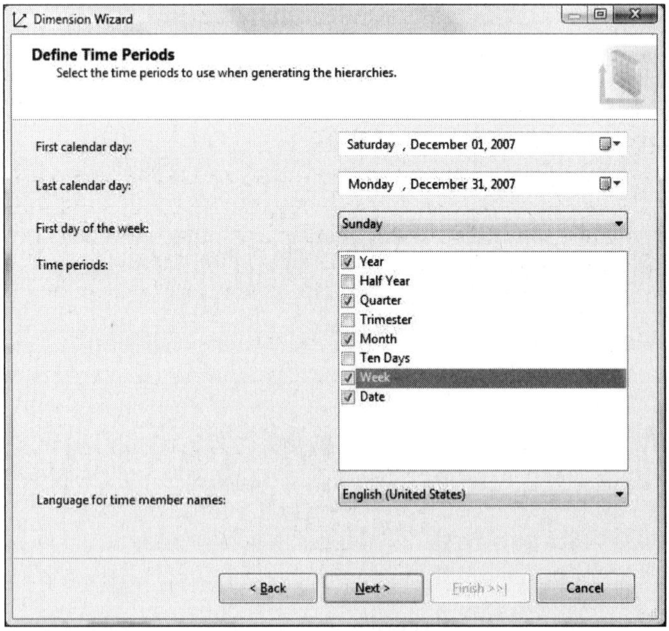

Figure 25-12

A quick review of the Date dimension shows that we have results in two different hierarchies, one for Year – Quarter – Month – Date (YQMD) and one for Year – Week – Date (YMD) as noted in Figure 25-13.

Figure 25-13

Figure 25-14 shows a BIDS Browser tab view of the Date dimension, YQMD hierarchy.

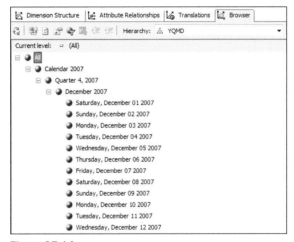

Figure 25-14

Creating the Page Hierarchy Dimension

Recall from the previous section that all of the work we had done to pivot the page information was to create a parent/child dimension table called Page Hierarchy so we could deal with the fact that navigation of a web page hierarchy on a web site is ragged (a member's parent is not at the same level as other members) and unbalanced (branches of the hierarchy descend to different levels). Therefore, it is important that you specify in the Data Source View the parent/child relationship between the ChildID and the ParentID (Figure 25-15).

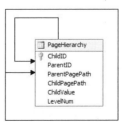

Figure 25-15

If you view the relationship, you will notice the source is the ParentID and the destination column is the ChildID (Figure 25-16).

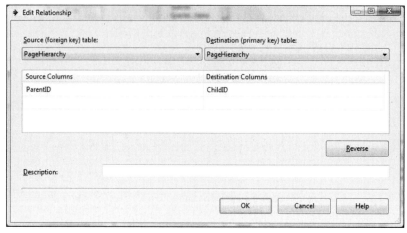

Figure 25-16

Because we have already specified the relationship within the DSV, the SQL Server 2008 Analysis Services Business Intelligence Development Studio (BIDS) will be able to automatically build a parent/child dimension. Do not forget to specify the following as you create this dimension.

In the first dialog of the Dimension Wizard (Figure 25-17), specify the Name Column as ChildValue.

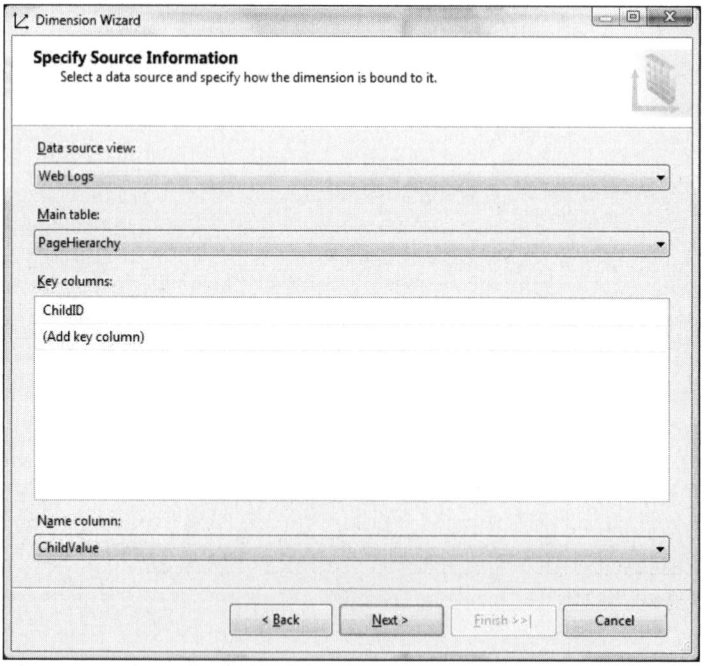

Figure 25-17

As well, do not forget to specify under the Properties tab for the ParentID member that the MembersWithData should be NonLeafDataHidden. With the way this particular parent/child dimension was built, we want to only show members where data was specified (Figure 25-18).

Figure 25-18

Notice the parent/child reference icon within the ParentID (Figure 25-19).

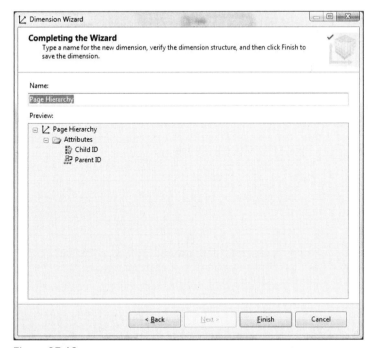

Figure 25-19

Figure 25-20 shows a BIDS Browser tab view of this new parent/child dimension.

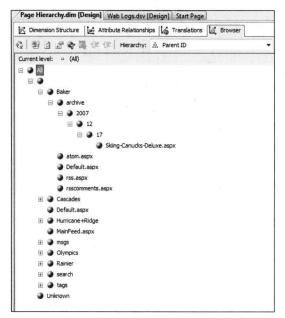

Figure 25-20

Creating the Other Dimensions

For this basic Web Analytics cube, the other dimensions are quite straightforward, involving either just one or two levels of hierarchy. The following table gives the breakdown of the dimensions:

Dimension Table	Dimension	Hierarchy
Dim_Hour	HourNum	[HourNum]
Dim_Browser	Browser	[Browser Name] > [Browser Version]
Dim_OS	OS	[OS Name] > [OS Version]
Dim_Search	Search	[Search Name]
Dim_IPGeo	Geography	[Country Name] > [State]

To review the dimensions and how they were created, please refer to the included WebLogs.sln BIDS solution file.

Creating the Page View Count Measure Group

Recall that we created the fact_20071217 fact table that was filtered to contain only *.aspx files, which are the pages viewed. Therefore, the first measure we will create is the Page View measure, which is an aggregate type of Count.

To do this, we will choose to create a measure on the FactID (Figure 25-21), which is the identity value created on this fact table. We could have also chosen to do a count on any of the other measures if so desired because this is a count measure.

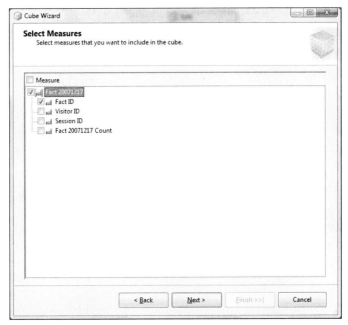

Figure 25-21

After including all of the dimensions we just created, we complete the Cube Wizard by creating the **Web Logs** cube (see Figure 25-22).

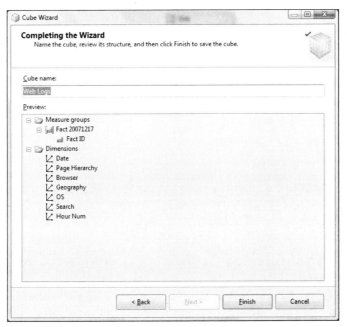

Figure 25-22

To create a cleaner view of the cube, it is a good idea to change the Measure name and Measure Group name to something more meaningful than [Fact ID] and [Fact 20071217], respectively. For the measure group, let's rename this as [**WL Page Views**] as shown in Figure 25-23.

Figure 25-23

As for the measure, let's rename this as [**Page Views**] and don't forget to change the Aggregate Function to **Count** (Figure 25-24).

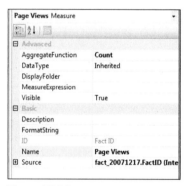

Figure 25-24

Now we have finished creating our measure group with regular (as opposed to distinct count) measures.

Creating the Distinct Count Measure Groups

Recall that through the SQL transformation processes, we had created distinct Visitor and distinct Session information. What this means is that we need to create distinct count measures for our Visitors and Session information. To do this, we will show this with the Visitor distinct count measure and you can then repeat this for the Session distinct count measure.

Distinct count measures and queries can be quite performance-intensive, especially when dealing with large amounts of data. For optimization techniques of distinct count measures, you can review the "Analysis Services Distinct Count Optimization" whitepaper at:
`sqlcat.com/whitepapers/archive/2008/04/17/analysis-services-`
`distinct-count-optimization.aspx.`

From BIDS, click New Measure, choose a usage of Distinct Count, and then choose the Source Column of VisitorID (for the Session distinct count measure, you will choose SessionID) as shown in Figure 25-25.

Figure 25-25

Similar to the Page Views measure group, rename your measure group and measures for your Visitor distinct count measure group to **WL Visitors** and **Visitors**, respectively. Notice within the Properties of the Visitors measure that the AggregateFunction is set to **DistinctCount** (see Figure 25-26).

Figure 25-26

Please repeat this task and create a new measure group for your Sessions distinct count measure. Note that BIDS will try to ensure that you create a distinct count measure within its own measure group. This is a best practice because for both distinct count processing and querying, it is optimal to have distinct count measures in their own measure groups. When you have created the Sessions measure, you will have three measure groups within your Web Logs cube (Figure 25-27).

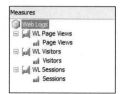

Figure 25-27

Reviewing Your Cube

With your [Web Logs] cube deployed, now you have a basic Web Analytics cube that will allow you to better understand who and what is navigating throughout your web site. To do a quick view of just the measures of your cube, you will notice that 346 web site visitors had 944 sessions — that is, 346 visitors viewed your web site 944 times. And within those 944 times, there were a total of 2234 pages viewed (refer to the Grand Total within Figure 25-28).

Drop Filter Fields Here

Level 02 ▼	Level 03	Level 04	Level 05	Level 06	Level 07	Level 08	Visitors	Sessions	Page Views
⊟ (Blank)	⊞ Baker						10	13	53
	⊞ Cascades						108	260	510
	⊞ Default.aspx						53	61	236
	⊞ Hurricane +Ridge						12	53	78
	⊞ MainFeed.aspx						79	400	779
	⊞ msgs						5	7	13
	⊟ Olympics	⊟ archive	⊟ 2007	⊞ 09			3	3	4
				⊟ 11	⊟ 21	⊞ Big-Quilcene-River.aspx	29	30	37
						⊞ Dosewallips-River.aspx	31	34	37
						⊞ Duckabush-River.aspx	38	40	44
						⊞ Elwha-River.aspx	25	27	27
						Total	100	111	145
					Total		100	111	145
				Total			103	114	149
			⊞ tags				3	3	3
			Total				105	117	152
		⊞ atom.aspx					3	3	3
		⊞ default.aspx					7	7	14
		⊞ pingback.aspx					3	3	3
		⊞ rss.aspx					33	102	188
		⊞ rsscomments.aspx					4	4	6
		Total					137	220	366
	⊞ Rainier						23	32	108
	⊞ search						6	6	10
	⊞ tags						33	49	81
	Total						346	944	2234
Grand Total							346	944	2234

Drop Column Fields Here

Figure 25-28

By drilling down the Page Hierarchy, you will also notice that 100 visitors were interested in finding out more information about the Olympics with visitors reading about the Big Quilcene River, Dosewallips River, Duckabush River, and Elwha River (Figure 25-29).

⊞ Big-Quilcene-River.aspx	29	30	37
⊞ Dosewallips-River.aspx	31	34	37
⊞ Duckabush-River.aspx	38	40	44
⊞ Elwha-River.aspx	25	27	27

Figure 25-29

If you were to further pivot and add the Geography dimension, you can see that although the majority of the web site visitors reading about these four rivers in the Olympics were from the United States, quite a few people from outside the United States were reading about these rivers as well. For example, there were three visitors from the United Kingdom also reading about these rivers (Figure 25-30).

Level 08	Country Name ▼											
	⊞ united kingdom			⊞ united states			⊞ Unknown			Grand Total		
	Visitors	Sessions	Page Views	Visitors	Sessions	Page Views	Visitors	Sessions	Page Views	Visitors	Sessions	Page Views
				6	6	29	4	7	24	10	13	53
	3	3	3	52	126	251	15	15	21	108	260	510
	1	1	4	35	42	187	8	9	18	53	61	236
				11	49	66				12	53	78
	1	1	1	37	182	314	9	47	147	79	400	779
	1	1	2	2	3	3	1	2	7	5	7	13
				1	1	2				3	3	4
⊞ Big-Quilcene-River.aspx	3	3	3	16	17	24	4	4	4	29	30	37
⊞ Dosewallips-River.aspx	1	1	1	16	18	19	5	5	6	31	34	37
⊞ Duckabush-River.aspx	4	4	4	15	16	16	3	3	3	38	40	44
⊞ Elwha-River.aspx	4	4	4	12	14	14	3	3	3	25	27	27
Total	9	9	12	44	53	73	13	13	16	100	111	145

Figure 25-30

At this point, it's all about analyzing the cube and asking/answering questions about the number of visitors, sessions, and page views that had occurred. To analyze this yourself, you can restore the included WebLogs.abf OLAP database and/or generate your own using the WebLogs.sln file to pivot and analyze these web site visitors.

Summary

This chapter has provided a high-level overview of understanding Web Analytics and the components it requires. Also, we have reviewed the many business questions and business logic complexities that can be derived out of a relatively simple web log. While we have reviewed issues ranging from visitor unique-ification to campaign logic, within scope for the purpose of this Analysis Services book we have provided the steps to create a basic Web Analytics cube. As you build a more complex Web Analytics cube and/or need to process much more data, the implied complexities of parsing out query string parameters to understanding campaign data will become more apparent, but it is well outside the scope of this book.

In addition, this cube created has not been optimized for performance because its purpose is to provide a step-by-step guide of a basic Web Analytics cube. You can refer to other chapters in this book as well as resources like http://sqlcat.com/ to find out more information on how to design and implement high-performance OLAP databases

Appendix A: MDX Functions

SQL Server Analysis Services 2008 supports several MDX functions that are used in MDX expressions and queries. You had an overview of the MDX functions in Chapter 3. Appendix A is a detailed reference to the functions and operators of standard MDX, and extensions as implemented in Microsoft's Analysis Services 2008. We thank Microsoft for providing the MDX Function and Operator reference content. The appendix lists the functions and operators in alphabetical order, along with any arguments and the result's data type. We have included a pair of indexes at the beginning to help you navigate the appendix. We have also provided examples to illustrate how the MDX functions can be used. Most of the examples provided use the sample Analysis Services project shipped with SQL Server 2008.

Appendix A is available for download from the companion web site of the *Professional SQL Server Analysis Services 2008 with MDX* book at www.wrox.com. Appendix A has been provided as a download rather than part of the book (as was the case in *Professional SQL Server Analysis Services 2005 with MDX*). We made this decision in the interest of providing more content relevant to SQL Server Analysis Services 2008 and additional scenarios that can help you understand Analysis Services. We hope you will find the downloadable appendix to be practical and convenient.

Index

SYMBOL

- operator (MDX), 84

* (asterisk) operator (MDX), 84

/3GB flag, SQL Server installation and, 478–479

: (colons) in MDX, 85

[ ] (brackets) in MDX, 71

{ } (curly braces) in MDX, 85

+ (plus) operator in MDX, 84

< operator in MDX, 84

<= operator in MDX, 84

<> operator in MDX, 84

= operator in MDX, 84

> operator in MDX, 84

>= operator in MDX, 84

, (comma) in MDX, 79, 85

80-20 rule, 903

A

access permissions (cubes), 358–361

access-role approach (dimension security), 879–880

Account dimension, 945–947

Account Intelligence, 267–272

accumulated totals, order reports with, 903–906

Accuracy Chart Wizard, 721

actions, 315–328

  action target types, 316–317

  defined, 315

  DRILLTHROUGH action, 324–328

  Report actions, 322–324

  types of, 316

  URL actions, browsing, 320–322

  URL actions, creating, 317–320

activities, monitoring (Analysis Services), 450–451

ad-hoc reports, creating with Report Builder, 821–830

ADOMD Server

  object model, 397

  stored procedure, 398–400

ADOMD.NET

  defined, 18

  KPIs, querying with, 313–315

  object model, 397

advanced MDX. *See* MDX, advanced

Adventure Works DW 2008, 23, 38

advertising data, campaign. *See* campaign advertising data

Aggregate Function property, 330

aggregate functions (cubes), 183, 987

aggregates, custom, 809–812

aggregations

  AggregationPrefix property (cubes), 182

  AggregationUsage property, 511

  applying design, 497–499

  assigning design to partitions, 498–499

  basics, 487–489

  building, 351–354

  creating, 489–497

  defined, 11, 351

  design options. See aggregation design options

  usage-based, 499–505

BI (Business intelligence)

as data analysis, 13–14

overview, 3

SQL Server 2008 and, 14–16

BIDS (Business Intelligence Development Studio)

creating Analysis Services database with, 38

creating partitions in, 215

creating project in, 35–36

defined, 17

online mode database connections with, 239–241

Output pane, 37

overview, 24

Properties pane, 37

query performance and, 538

Solution Explorer pane, 36–37

BIDS Wizard

Account Intelligence, 267–272

currency conversion and, 332–337

Dimension Intelligence, 275–277

enhancing cubes with, 329

Time Intelligence, 272–275

bottlenecks, resource, 486

browsers

Browser page, 169

Dimension Browser, 414, 423

identifying (Web Analytics), 972–973

mining model, 717–719

budgets

date comparative analysis, 924–928

KPIs, defining and viewing, 930–937

trend and variance analysis, 928–930

Builder, Report, 821–830

Building the Data Warehouse (Inmon), 4

built-in UDFs, 395–397

Bulk Insert task (SSIS), 748

Business intelligence (BI). See BI (Business intelligence)

Business Intelligence Development Studio (BIDS). See BIDS (Business Intelligence Development Studio)

C

caching, proactive. *See* **proactive caching**

calculated measures

cubes and, 188–191

defined, 187

querying, 191

calculated members

calculations and (MDX), 374–376

cubes and, 187–191

MDX queries, 79–82

calculations

adding to cubes, 297–305

Assignments, 521

basics of, 368

CALCULATE command, 520

Calculate statement (cubes), 298

CALCULATE statement (MDX scripts), 369–372

Calculation Tools pane (cubes), 187

Calculations view (Cube Designer), 187

dimension attribute calculations, 521

fundamentals, 368. *See also* scripts and calculations

MDX Script, 519–520

moving to DSV, 546

overview, 518–519

Scope and Assignment statements, 521

scripts and. *See* scripts and calculations

session and query calculations, 521–522

call center applications (data mining), 559

CALL statement, 406

campaign advertising data, 958–959

CAPTION property, 374, 375–376

CASE statements

cell calculations and, 380–381

vs. SCOPE statements, 545

categorization with data mining, 683–688

cell security scenario (cube data), 887–896

cell writeback

enabling, 427–430

example, 413

Performance Point 2007, Microsoft Office, 16

query. *See* query performance

performance design

aggregations, designing. *See* aggregation design

basics of, 457–459

scalability, 513–515

UDM and. *See* Unified Dimensional Model (UDM)

PeriodsToDate function, 928

permissions

access permissions (cubes), 358–361

assemblies and, 222–223

set options, 404

personalization of customer information, 956

perspectives

browsing, 194–196

creating, 192–193

defined, 162, 192

filtering data with, 643–644

pivot charts, 657–659

pivot tables (Excel)

analyzing data in, 608–613

conditional formatting feature, 642–643

converting into sheet data reports, 651–655

creating with Analysis Services data, 603–606

custom grouping in, 623–626

drilling down to detailed data, 618–621

filtering data, 635–641

filtering in, 613–618

highlighting exceptions, 629–631

KPIs, reviewing in, 648–651

multiple measures, analyzing, 621–623

named sets, 651

number formatting, 628–629

overview, 602–603

perspectives, 643–644

pivot charts and, 657–659

PivotTable Field List, 112, 613–614, 627–628

PivotToPageHierarchy stored procedure, 969

reports, 633

sorting data, 634–635

style and design of, 641–642

tool tips, 632–633

translations, 644–648

updating SSAS connection information, 606–608

viewing member properties, 631–642

plug-ins, Analysis Services 2008, 408–409

PowerShell, Analysis Services and, 449–450

PPS (Performance Point Server), Microsoft, 673–675

Precedence Constraint Editor (SSIS), 755–756

precision considerations (calculations), 941–942

predefined properties, 806

Predict Probability value, 576

primary keys

adding to Geography dimension, 119

defined, 8–9

specifying in DSV Designer, 103

proactive caching

applied, 838–845

basics, 834–838

with MOLAP storage option, 848–852

ProactiveCaching property (cubes), 181

using timed updates, 846–847

Process command (Analysis Services), 206–209

ProcessIncremental/ProcessAdd options, 480–482

processing

AMO databases, 441–446

cubes, 208–212

dimensions, 212–215

speed, partitions and, 478

processing performance (UDM)

aggregation design and, 480

Analysis Services installation and, 478–479

basics of, 476–477

data types and, 478

incremental processing, 480–482

parallelism and, 482–486

1009